THE GLADSTONE DIARIES

WITH
CABINET MINUTES
AND
PRIME-MINISTERIAL
CORRESPONDENCE

VOLUME XI
JULY 1883–DECEMBER 1886

Edited by

H. C. G. MATTHEW

D0709297

CLARENDON PRESS · OXFORD
1990

Oxford University Press, Walton Street, Oxford OX2 6DP

Oxford New York Toronto
Delhi Bombay Calcutta Madras Karachi
Petaling Jaya Singapore Hong Kong Tokyo
Nairobi Dar es Salaam Cape Town
Melbourne Auckland

and associated companies in
Berlin Ibadan

Oxford is a trade mark of Oxford University Press

Published in the United States
by Oxford University Press, New York

© Oxford University Press 1990
Introduction © H. C. G. Matthew

All rights reserved. No part of this publication may be reproduced,
stored in a retrieval system, or transmitted, in any form or by any means,
electronic, mechanical, photocopying, recording, or otherwise,
without the prior permission of Oxford University Press

British Library Cataloguing in Publication Data
Gladstone, W. E. (William Ewart, 1809–1898)
The Gladstone diaries: with Cabinet minutes and
prime-ministerial correspondence.
Vol. 11, July 1883–December 1886
1. Great Britain. Gladstone, W. E. (William Ewart)
1809–1898
I. Title   II. Matthew, H. C. G. (Henry Colin Gray)
941.081′092′4
ISBN 0–19–821138–4

Library of Congress Cataloging-in-Publication Data
(Revised for vol. 10–11)
Gladstone, W. E. (William Ewart), 1809–1898.
The Gladstone diaries.
Vols.   edited by H. C. G. Matthew.
Contents: v. 1. 1825–1832—[etc.]—
v. 10. January 1881–June 1883.—v. 11. July 1883–
December 1886.
1. Gladstone, W. E. (William Ewart), 1809–1898—
Diaries. 2. Prime ministers—Great Britain—Diaries.
3. Great Britain—Politics and government—1837–1901.
I. Foot, M. R. D. (Michael Richard Daniel), 1919-   .
II. Matthew, H. C. G. (Henry Colin Gray) III. Title.
DA 563.A34   942.081′092 [B]   68–59613
ISBN 0 19 821138 4

Typeset by Joshua Associates Limited, Oxford
Printed and bound in
Great Britain by Biddles Ltd
Guildford and King's Lynn

Gladstone in the mid-1880s

CONTENTS

LIST OF ILLUSTRATIONS

NOTE ON ABBREVIATIONS &c.

Lists of abbreviations used in this volume and an Introduction covering its years will be found at the start of Volume X.

Sunday July One 1883. [*The Durdans, Epsom*][1]

Church mg & aft. Read Johnson on Maryland Law[2]—Harrison's Charge[3]—Green on Engl. People[4]—Contemp. Rev. Manning—and Froude on Luther.[5] Also accounts of the Clergy in 'Sporting Anecdotes'.[6]

2 M. [*London*]

Wrote to Ld Granville—Sir W. Harcourt—Ld Spencer—Sir H. Ponsonby l.l.—Mr Saunders[7]—The Queen—Dr A. Clark—Mr Chamberlain—Mrs Th.—and minutes. Returned to D.St at 11 AM. Saw Mr H—Ld RG—Ld Granville *cum* Ld Hartington—Sir W. Harcourt—Ld Rosebery—Dr Nevins—Ld Halifax—Ld Wolverton. H of C. $4\frac{3}{4}$–$7\frac{3}{4}$ and $10\frac{1}{2}$–1.[8] Dined with the Halifaxes. Read Scoones Letters[9]—Lady Cowper's Diary.[10]

To J. CHAMBERLAIN, president of the board of trade,   Chamberlain MSS 5/34/19.
2 July 1883. '*Private*'.

I think that general opinion, which I accept for myself, is to the effect that your speech on Saturday[11] has substantially obviated any inconvenient results that might have been apprehended from the preceding speech at Birmingham,[12] or from the construction put upon it. And I thank you for the effort you have made.

On the other hand, I venture to anticipate your concurrence on two points. The first is, that though speech cannot universally be confined by a minister within the limits of action to which he has conformed, yet that declarations, tending to place him markedly in advance or in arrear of his colleagues on subjects of high politics, or otherwise delicate, should be made as rarely and reservedly, and if I may so say as reluctantly, as possible. If, for example, the Government were about proposing a County Suffrage Bill as the measure proper, in its province, to meet the wants of the country, it is evident how its dignity and weight would be lessened, and the prospects of the measure itself put in jeopardy, if the slowest 'boy in the class' were then to signify his apprehensions that it went too far, and the quickest his readiness to go a good deal farther.

---

[1] Rosebery's house by the race course.

[2] 'The foundation of Maryland and the origin of the Act concerning religion of April 21, 1649' (1883), sent by the author, Bradley Tyler Johnson, 1829-1903, lawyer and Confederate historian; Add MS 44482, f. 125.

[3] B. Harrison, 'A charge . . .' (1883).

[4] J. R. Green, see 19 Feb. 78.

[5] H. E. Manning, 'Without God, no commonwealth'; J. A. Froude, 'Luther', *C.R.*, xliv. 1, 19 (July 1883).

[6] [P. Egan], *Sporting anecdotes; original and select . . . by an Amateur Sportsman* (1807).

[7] Knighthood for his dentist, after consultation with Clark; Add MS 44482, f. 1.

[8] Declined for this session Broadhurst's request for a Royal Commission on housing; spoke on corrupt practices; *H* 281. 52, 131.

[9] See 7 Mar. 83n.   [10] See 26 June 83.

[11] To the Cobden Club; a defence of his independence, see Garvin, i. 397.

[12] Chamberlain's call for electoral reform and comments on the Tsar's coronation at the Bright jubilee, 13 June; for the Queen's, and Gladstone's, irritation and Gladstone's attempt to encourage an apology, see to Ponsonby, 22, 26 June 83 and Garvin, i. 396.

My second point is that, as Ministers, we are bound to recognise the balanced character of the system under which we live, and of which we are the official defenders. So that the rights of the Crown, guaranteed by the Constitution, and not less sacred in the eyes of the people than are their own liberties, and not these only but all that belongs to the person and family of the Sovereign, are specially in our charge, and are to be watched over by us with careful and even jealous respect. Of course I am not using words as a test or formula, but simply as expressive of a general spirit and mode of action which, so far as I know, have been loyally acknowledged by all Statesmen of Liberal opinions, and have left them abundant scope for the purposes of public duty.

3. Tu.

Wrote to Lady Salisbury—Ld Coleridge—Dr Pitman[1]—The Queen l.l.l.—and minutes. H of C. $2\frac{1}{2}$-7 and $10\frac{1}{2}$-$12\frac{3}{4}$.[2] Saw Harris [R]—Mrs Th. Saw Mr H—Ld RG—Chancr of Exr—Sir W. Harcourt—Lady Ponsonby—Sir H. Ponsonby. Twelve to dinner: evening party afterwards. Read Scoones, Letters—Lady Cowper's Diary.

4. Wed.

Wrote to Sir R. Cross—Sir H. Ponsonby—Mr Vickers—Mrs E. Talbot—The Queen—Watsons—and minutes. Dined at Lucy's. H of C. $12\frac{1}{4}$-2, $2\frac{1}{2}$-6.[3] Saw Mr H—Ld RG—Mr Godley—C. Lyttelton—Lady Reay—Chancr of Exr. Mrs Flower's concert. Pleased with Ld Bath's daughters, so fresh & gentle, with much of beauty.[4] Saw Scarsdale—Hume [R]. Read Bp Wordsworth's Article in Fortnightly[5]—Mercy d'Argenteau.[6]

5. Th.

Wrote to Sir E. Watkin—Chancr of Exr—The Queen—Mr Prescott Hewett—Ld Spencer—and minutes. H of C. $4\frac{3}{4}$-$8\frac{1}{2}$ & $9\frac{1}{4}$-12.[7] Read Fortnightly on Radicalism[8]—Lady Cowper's Diary. Saw Mr H—Ld RG—The Speaker—Mr Bright—Chancr of Exr—Sir D. Currie—Mr Bolitho[9]—Mr Birkbeck. Fifteen to breakfast: Mad. N. Neruda played afterwards, better than ever. At 12.30 to the Fisheries Exhibition which we surveyed with deep though bewildered interest: then a sumptuous luncheon.[10] What dissipation!

To H. C. E. CHILDERS, chancellor of the exchequer,   Add MS 44546, f. 134.
5 July 1883.

I hope that the very striking statements contained in Sir A. Clarke's report[11] will be carefully considered at the Admiralty. If verified, they would seem to me to point to a

---

[1] Knighthood for Henry Alfred *Pitman, 1808–1908; physician.
[2] Questions; corrupt practices; H 281. 186.   [3] Corrupt practices; H 281. 318.
[4] Bath's daughters, Alice, Katherine and Beatrice, were all unmarried at this time.
[5] F.R., xl. 50 (July 1883).   [6] See 23 Apr. 83.
[7] Questions: corrupt practices; H 281. 477.   [8] F.R., xl. 1 (July 1883).
[9] Thomas Simon Bolitho, 1808–87; Cornish banker and worthy.
[10] Large international exhibition at the Royal Pavilion.
[11] On defences of Alexandria, casting doubt on the 'utility of the monster ironclads which we have been constructing during the last 20 years'; Add MS 44130, f. 262.

review of our method of ship-building & to economy in the result; economy which has not I think yet been realised according to expectation fondly cherished, & the consideration of which becomes in certain points of view especially interesting as the Parliament begins to travel through the second moiety of its allotted time.

6. Fr.

Wrote to Messrs Watson—Ld Lymington—W.H.G.—The Queen—& minutes. H of C. 2¼–7 and 11½–1.[1] Saw Mr H—Ld RG—Ld Dufferin (who told me ἀρρητα[2] of a dinner at Houghton's)—Chancr of Exr—Ld Spencer. Read Lady Cowper's Diary—Mercy d'Argenteau.

7. Sat. [Berkhampstead]

Wrote to The Queen—Sir S. Northcote—The Speaker—and minutes. Cabinet 12–3¼. Saw Mr H—Ld RG—Herbert G—Chancr of Exr. Off to Lady S. Spencer's (Berkhampstead) at 3.50.[3] Much conversation & a pleasant evening with our incomparable hostess. Read Mercy d'Argenteau—Lang, The Library[4]—Knight, Printer & Modern Press.[5]

Cabinet. Sat. Jul. 7. 83. Noon.[6]

✓ 1. Cholera in Egypt. Send a Doctor with Indian experience.
✓ 2. Suez Canal. Childers authorised to hold out (agt. Chamberlain's view) the 'intermediate plan'.[7]
   3. Bradlaugh. Yes as proposed by WEG.
   4. Lord Mayor's dinner. Wed. Aug. 8.
   5. Business a) Grand Committees. Yes as proposed by WEG. b) Bills to be dropped.
   6. Dover Harbour. Recommendation of Committee of Cabinet accepted. Spend 1 ₥. & the convicts = 0. Time 16 y. income, interest on ½ ₥
   7. Patents query to run against the Crown. *No.* Chamberlain to resist amt. in Committee.
   8. Bills & business.
   9. Zululand. Cetewayo to be warned off the Reserve: for the protection of those who do not wish to be under him, & whom we engaged to provide a home for.

I. *To Go On.*[8] 1. Grand Committee Bills and Two Principal Bills (or three). 2. National Debt Bill; Medical Bill; Scotland—Local Govt.; Ireland: Registration, Poor Relief 3 R, Police reorganisation, Tramways, (Sunday Closing to go into Continuance Act).
II. *To drop*: Eight.

   [1] Questions, corrupt practices; *H* 281. 609.
   [2] 'not to be divulged'; Houghton had a large collection of pornography.
   [3] Spencer's sister (see 9 June 83), whom the Gladstones had met at Cannes (see to Spencer, 24 Jan. 83).
   [4] A. Lang, *The library* (1876).
   [5] C. Knight, *The old printer and the modern press* (1854).
   [6] Add MS 44644, f. 80.
   [7] Provisional Agreement with de Lesseps signed on 10 July for building a second canal with £8 million British loan at 3¼%; canal rates to be considerably reduced; see *H* 281. 1089 and *PP* 1883 lxxxiv. 309.
   [8] Add MS 44644, f. 82; Gladstone's marginal note: 'Small Bills omitted'.

III. *To Reserve.* 1. Welsh Educn.; 2. Criminal Law Amdt.; 3. Detention in Hospitals.
IV. *Private Members' Bills.*

8. 7 S. Trin.

Berkhampstead Ch mg & evg. Drive (malgré moi). Wrote to Ld Wolverton—Mr Trevelyan—Mr Hamilton. Read Renan Souvenirs[1]—Westcott Historic Faith[2]—Life of Rev. H. Elliot.[3]

9. M. [London]

Wrote to The Queen—Ly Goldsmid—and minutes. Back to town at [blank]. Saw Mr H—Ld RG—Chancr of Exr—Mr Knowles—Mr Trevelyan—Lady H. Forbes. Read Lady Cowper (finished)—Mercy d'Argenteau. Dined at Ld Granville's. Visited South Kensington Museum: to withdraw some objects from my show of Ivories.[4] H of C. $4\frac{1}{4}$-$7\frac{3}{4}$ and $10\frac{1}{2}$-1.[5]

10. Tu.

Wrote to Sir R.A. Cross—Ld Mayor—Mrs Vyner—Sir H. Ponsonby—The Queen—& minutes. $12\frac{3}{4}$-$5\frac{1}{4}$. To Windsor & back. Audience: pure form though over $\frac{1}{2}$ hour. Saw Mr H—Ld RG—Conclave on Cattle motion—Mad. Novikoff—C. Münster—Musurus—M. Damoys. H of C. $5\frac{1}{4}$-$7\frac{1}{2}$ & $11\frac{1}{4}$-2. We were beaten by 8, less than we had expected on a class question like this.[6] Read Blackie on Goethe, really a marvel[7]—Mercy d'Argenteau. Sixteen to dinner: evening party afterwards.

11. Wed. [Windsor Castle]

Wrote to Ld Derby—Ld Granville—Mr Borlase MP—and minutes. Saw Mr Hamn—Ld RG—Ld Granville *cum* Ld E. F[itzmaurice]—Sir H. Ponsonby—Sir J. Cowell—The Queen. Read Mercy d'Argenteau—Burke, 16th Cent Portraits.[8] Went off to Windsor at $4\frac{3}{4}$. The dinners there want enlivening & it is necessary to start subjects & not merely give replies. H. of C. $12\frac{1}{4}$-$2\frac{1}{2}$ & 3-$4\frac{3}{4}$.[9]

12. Th. [London]

Wrote to Ld Halifax—The Queen l.l.l.—Mr Justin—Ld Mount Temple—Prince L.L. Bonaparte—Mrs Vyner—and minutes. H of C. $4\frac{1}{2}$-$7\frac{3}{4}$ and 11-1. Back in D.St at 10 [a.m.] Saw Mr H—Ld R.G—Mr MacColl—Prof. Blackie—Mr C.E. Lloyd—

---

[1] See 1 May 83.
[2] B. F. Westcott, *The historic faith* (1883).
[3] J. Bateman, *The life of Henry Venn Elliott* (1868).
[4] Loan of eleven ivories for an exhibition; Victoria and Albert museum loan register.
[5] Questioned on H. J. Gladstone's speech on Irish land; corrupt practices; *H* 281. 794.
[6] Govt. defeat on Chaplin's resolution for restriction of imports of foreign cattle during foot-and-mouth outbreak; *H* 281. 1086.
[7] J. S. Blackie, *The wisdom of Goethe* (1883).
[8] Burke's last volume; see 15 Mar. 79.
[9] Suez canal agreement; *H* 281. 1089.

Mr Roundell—Conclave 3-4 Suez Canal.[1] Dined at Mr Barings: & showed the magnificent Vyner Tankard.[2] Saw Mr Candall. Read Mercy d'Argenteau.

13. Fr.

Wrote to Ld Granville—Mr Dawnay MP[3]—Dr Barry—The Queen l.l.l.—and minutes. Saw Mr H—Ld R.G—Dr Westcott—Mr Benjamin—Mr Hayward—Sir R. Peel!—Lady Goldsmid (5 oc[lock] Tea) H. of C. (and Cabinet) $2\frac{1}{4}$-5. H of C. also 11-1. Dined at Ld Tweeddale's. Read Mercy d'Argenteau—Mrs Oliphant's Beleaguered City.[4]

Cabinet. Friday July 13 83. $2\frac{1}{2}$ PM.[5]
Chaplin's question. (an. with Dodson and Mundella)[6]
Kimberley & Indian Expenditure: proposes Committee on Railways.
Irish Sunday Closing Bill.
Suez Canal. Qy. Lesseps to send some one over here to *observe.* Let this be done. Three courses. Persevere & take vote; committee to examine; to withdraw in anticipation.[7]

14. Sat. [Dollis Hill]

Wrote to Ld Granville—Sir H. Dashwood—Mr Childers—and minutes. Expedition to Hertford House about the Vyner Tankard. Saw Mr H—Ld RG—Ld Tweedmouth—Mr Agnew. Read Mercy D'Argenteau—H. Greville's Diary.[8]

15. S 8 Trin.

Willesden Ch. mg and H.C. Tent service (for the haymakers) afternoon. Much and interesting conversation with Dr Ginsberg.[9] Read Beleaguered City (finished)—Westcott Historic Faith—Warton Art. on Willesden.[10] C. came down—better but rather shaken.

16. M. [London]

Wrote to The Queen l.l.l.—Sir W. Harcourt—Dr Ginsberg—Prince L.L. Bonaparte—Abp of Canterbury—Rev. E. Wickham—Mr Campbell—Earl of Derby—& minutes. Read Scoones, Letters—Mercy d'Argenteau. Saw Mr H—Ld RG—Ld Granville—Mr Childers. Luncheon at 15 G.S. Dined at Sir T.G.s. H of C. $4\frac{1}{2}$-$7\frac{3}{4}$ & $10\frac{1}{2}$-$12\frac{3}{4}$.[11]

---

[1] Jottings at Add MS 44767, f. 62.
[2] Mrs Vyner's ivory tankard, judged worth at least £2000; Add MS 44546, f. 136.
[3] G. C. Dawnay; see 1 May 84.
[4] M. O. Oliphant, *A beleaguered city* (1880).
[5] Add MS 44644, f. 86.
[6] On foot and mouth disease; *H* 281. 1520.
[7] Initial reaction to the Agreement (see 7 July 83n.) was strongly hostile, leading to its withdrawal; see 19, 23 July 83.
[8] H. W. Greville, *Leaves from the diary of Henry Greville*, ed. Lady Enfield (4 series, 1883-1905); a later part reviewed by Gladstone in *E.H.R.*, ii. 281 (1887).
[9] Christian David Ginsburg, 1831-1914; Hebrew scholar and liberal.
[10] Not found.
[11] Questions on Suez Canal; supply; *H* 281. 1518, 1525.

To Sir W. V. HARCOURT, home secretary,   MS Harcourt dep. Adds 10.
16 July 1883.

Re Mr Pease's letter which I return, the question after all is what do you advise?[1]

We seem to lie between an unauthorised pledge of Trevelyan's (a very serious *fact* no doubt) and a pledge of the Cabinet—What is to be *done*? Will not any attempt of the Cabinet to recede worsen matters?

It is necessary also to bear in mind what the Irish Govt. through Spencer insists on. Our reduced list contains no less than *five* Irish subjects:— Poor Relief (*now* disposed of); Registration—for which we have already had value received, as I believe Trevelyan knows & says; Tramways—a subject introduced *since* Trevelyan's pledge and forced on by the Irish Govt.; Emigration—not named in Cabinet but as I understand *enacted* by the Irish Govt.; Police reorganisation—reserved by Trevelyan acc. to Mr. Pease. I think this is *pretty well* for amount.

17. Tu.

Wrote to Mr Anderson—Ld Tweedmouth—Mrs Vyner—Sir R. Lingen—Mary G. (niece)—The Queen—Ld Lothian—& minutes. H of C. 4-6, $6\frac{3}{4}$-7, $10\frac{1}{2}$-1. Saw Mr H—Ld RG—Mr & Mrs Bolton—Mrs B. Dined at Lady F.C.s. H of C. $4\frac{1}{2}$-$8\frac{3}{4}$ and $10\frac{1}{2}$-1.[2] Read Scoones, Letters—Mercy d'Argenteau.

18. Wed.

Wrote to Mr Childers—Ld Carlingford—and minutes. Read Mercy d'Argenteau—Greville's Diary. Saw Mr H—Lord RG—Madame Loyson—rather sanguine. H of C. $12\frac{1}{4}$-6.[3] Dined at [blank.]

19. Th.

Wrote to Mr Murray—Mr Stewart MP—The Queen l.l.—Ld Carlingford—and minutes. Saw Mr H—Ld R.G—H.J.G.—Ld Granville—Sir W. Harcourt—Chancr of Exr l.l. Cabinet 3-$4\frac{1}{2}$. Ten to dinner. H. of C. $4\frac{1}{2}$-8 and $9\frac{3}{4}$-$12\frac{3}{4}$. Made an answer to Northcote wh was difficult.[4] Read Soeur Cunégonde[5]—Scoones's Letters (finished)—Greville's Journal.

Cabinet. Thurs. 3 PM. July 19. 83.[6]
1. Channel Tunnel. Chamberlain. have considered Report & the state of the circs. wh. it discloses. Accept report. Cannot be parties to the further progress of the Bills.
2. Letter of introduction to Palestine channel plan. Follow the usage exactly.[7]
3. Suez Canal. Decision postponed. A[nswer] to Northcote agreed on. We discussed until

---

[1] No correspondence found; perhaps on the Irish Sunday Closing Bill (dropped in August); see 13 July 83.
[2] Agricultural holdings; *H* 281. 1683.
[3] Agricultural holdings; *H* 281. 1798.
[4] On negotiations before the agreement; *H* 281. 1910.
[5] Perhaps *Vita S. Cunegundis Imperatricis* (1865).
[6] Add MS 44644, f. 87.
[7] For the Palestine canal plan, see *T.T.*, 17 May 1883, 10d and D. A. Farnie, *East and West of Suez* (1969), 310.

the latest moment the terms in wh. I was to reply to Northcote's question. At last I got down the closing & more critical words as within.[1] We discussed partially the question of dropping or persevering.

20. Fr.

Wrote to Att. General—Bishop of Melbourne (per Governor) tel.[2]—Dr Ginsberg—Mrs Vyner—Ld Spencer—Dr Barry—The Queen—& minutes. Dined at Mr Tennant's. Saw Mr H—Ld RG—Chancr of Exr. H of C. $2\frac{1}{4}$-7 and 11-12.[3] Read Soeur Cunégonde—Greville's Journal. Worked on Suez Canal Agrt.[4]

21. Sat.

Wrote to Mr Firth—Ld Carlingford—Ld Rosebery—M. de Lesseps—Dean of St Paul's—and minutes. Dined at Mr Childers's. Saw Mr H.—Ld RG—Ld Granville—Col. Lyttelton & his bride[5]—Ld Granville with Chancr of Exr—Ld Kimberley—Sir R. Wilson[6]—Mrs Gascoigne X & another—D. of Cambridge—Musurus Pacha—Ld Napier M. Read Greville's Journal.

To LORD ROSEBERY, 21 July 1883.   N.L.S. 10022, f. 224.

Primâ facie there is a strong case for my going to Midlothian, but I should like to discuss the matter with you when we are clear of the Suez Canal business; rather pressing at this moment.

Lord Lyons is coming from Paris & dines with me on Wednesday: also I *hope* Waddington. Could you & would you come?

22. 9 S. Trin.

St Margaret's mg. when E. Wickham preached admirably on the assassination and evg when Dr Farrar preached. Wrote to Mr Childers. Read K. Little on the Passion—on the Temptation—The Little Pilgrim[7]—Renan, Souvenirs—New Studies in Theology.

23. M.

Wrote to Mr Ilbert—Sir L. Mallet—Mr Monk—M. de Lesseps[8]—Mr Hankey—The Queen l.l.—and minutes. Dined at Grillions. Drive with C. Saw Mr H—Ld RG—HJG—Ld Granville. H. of C. $4\frac{1}{4}$-$7\frac{3}{4}$ & 10-$12\frac{1}{2}$. Spoke on Suez Canal affair.[9] Cabinet 12-2 on the Suez business. Read Mercy d'Argenteau—Soeur Cunégonde—H. Greville's Journal.

[1] Add MS 44644, f. 90; see *H* 281. 1908: proposition to be submitted by the end of July.
[2] On episcopal vacancies; Add MS 44482, f. 158.
[3] Questions; statement on business; *H* 282. 40.
[4] Mem. for Granville sent next day: inclined to abandon the provisional agreement; Ramm II, ii. 65.
[5] N. G. Lyttelton m. Katharine Sarah, da. of J. A. Stuart Wortley. See 1 Oct. 83.
[6] Back from Paris, negotiating with de Lesseps; *PP* 1883 lxxxiv. 313.
[7] Sent by Julia Vyner; Add MS 44482, f. 196.
[8] Thanking him for acknowledgement that cabinet not bound to 'press the Agreement on Parliament'; *PP* 1883 lxxxiv. 315.
[9] Announcing decision not to proceed with the Provisional Agreement; *H* 282. 141.

Cabinet. Monday Jul. 23. 83. Noon.[1]
Suez Canal. a. What to do. Drop agreement. b. who to announce & in what terms.
　WEG. State Lesseps's intention as independent action.
Qy. announce Lesseps's intentions? Yes. Publish his letter—yes. Childers to hold his ground in answer to Gibson.

24. *Tu.*

Wrote to The Queen 1.—Ld Granville—Mrs Vyner—Abp of Canterbury—Mr Macarthur—& minutes. H of C. $4\frac{1}{2}$–$8\frac{1}{2}$ & $9\frac{1}{2}$–$12\frac{1}{2}$.[2] Saw Mr H—Ld R.G—Ld Spencer—Sir T. Acland—Ld Granville—& others. Read Soeur Cunégonde—H. Greville's Journals.

25. *Wed. St James, & our 44th wedding day:*

a cause for much thanksgiving. Wrote to the Queen—Ld Granville—& minutes. H of C. & Cabinet $12\frac{1}{4}$–6. Holland House party afr. Fourteen to dinner. Conversation with Ld Lyons—Mr Waddington—Mr Richard—Mr Mitford. Saw Mr H— Ld RG—Ld Granville—Att. General. Read Mercy d'Argenteau—Sœur Cunégonde.

Cabinet. Wed. July 25. 83. $3\frac{1}{2}$ PM.[3]
1. Suez Canal. Northcote's motion. Amendment framed. Announcement for tomorrow sketched generally in terms.
2. Spencer urged Emigration. Vote from Church Surplus 100m[ille].[4] Agreed to as being the *best*[?]—so far as a judgment can be formed.

26. *Th.*

Wrote to The Queen l.l.l.l.—Mr Buxton—Ld Effingham—Attorney General—Sir E. Watkin—& minutes. H. of C. $4\frac{3}{4}$–8 and 10–$10\frac{1}{2}$.[5] Read Mercy d'Argenteau— Sœur Cunégonde—Greville's Journal—Kegan Paul on Newman.[6] Saw Mr H—Ld RG—Mr Bryce—Ld Wolverton—Ld Advocate—Lady Holker.

To Sir E. W. WATKIN, 26 July 1883.　　　　　　　　Add MS 44546, f. 140.
　I have consulted with Mr. Chamberlain on your letter of the 21st.[7]
　We have thought it our duty to accept the decision of the Committee, in the manner which Mr. Chamberlain has publicly made known on our behalf: & I think that after having done this we are not in a condition to become parties to proceedings of the nature of those suggested in your letter with a view to the construction of a Tunnel under the Channel.

　　[1] Add MS 44644, f. 92.
　　[2] Questions, agricultural holdings; *H* 282. 200.
　　[3] Add MS 44644, f. 94.
　　[4] Spencer's mem. had been circulated in June, but not discussed; *Spencer*, i. 248.
　　[5] Ministerial statement on Northcote's canal motion: govt. in agreement, but deprecate the passing of such a motion; *H* 282. 562.
　　[6] In C. Kegan Paul, *Biographical sketches* (1883).
　　[7] Add MS 44337, f. 23, on importance of British govt. support for the channel tunnel, with Gladstone's docket asking Chamberlain's views.

27. Fr.

Wrote to Sir J. Pauncefoot—Mrs Scott Maxwell—Mr Carbutt[1]—Ld Carlingford—Ld Granville—Mad. Novikoff—Sir R. Wilson—Mr Childers—The Queen—and minutes. Read Soeur Cunégonde—Mercy d'Argenteau: and Ld Stratheden's Pamphlet.[2] Saw Mr H—Ld RG l.l.l.—Sir Spencer Wells—Sir A. Clark—Mr Fawcett—Ld Rosebery—Ld Hartington respecting him. H of C. 2¼–7 and 9–11¼ Spoke on Indian Charge for Egypt.[3]

To Mrs. M. M. MAXWELL SCOTT, 27 July 1883.   Abbotsford MSS.

I am very glad to hear that your dear Father's[4] memory will be preserved in a worthy record.

My answer to your letter must I fear be hasty.

1. As regards the letters, I have no power of consulting them at present as they are at Hawarden. I would advise that the proofsheets should be sent to me, & I could then see whether there were any passages which I ought to ask you to omit, a request I would only make for *cause*.[5]

2. As regards Manzoni. I can give no clew to his family, but I think after this lapse of time you might fairly publish his letter,[6] unless any specific objection occurs to you, without seeking for a permission. Of course I assume that there is nothing in it which could be disagreeable to his representatives if they exist.

I went to see him in his house some 6 or 8 miles from Milan in 1838[7] & I afterwards wrote a letter of introduction for him to your Father in bad Italian. He was a most interesting man, but was regarded as I found among the more fashionable Priests in Milan as a *bacchettone*.[8] In his own way he was I think a Liberal and a Nationalist, nor was the alliance of such politics with strong religious conviction uncommon among the more eminent Italians of those days.

28. Sat.

Wrote to Mr Morley—Lady Holker—Mr Fawcett—Ld Granville l.l.—Mr Hubbard—and minutes. Dined with Mr Sands. Saw Mr H—Ld RG l.l.—Sir W. Harcourt—Mr Waddington—Ld Granville—Mr West—Mr Hubbard—Mrs Gascoigne X. Tea party at Mad. Novikoff's. Calls. Read Mercy d'Argenteau.

To H. FAWCETT, postmaster-general, 28 July 1883.   Add MS 44546, f. 141.

I received your message through Lord R. Grosvenor yesterday, during the debate on

[1] Edward Homer Carbutt, b. 1838; liberal M.P. Monmouth 1880–6; on Indian railways, Add MS 44546, f. 141.

[2] W. F. Campbell, Lord Stratheden, 'The ministerial position and its dangers' (1883).

[3] Arguing that Onslow's amndt. (regretting charging India for Egypt) to Stanhope's motion was a motion of 'no confidence'; *H* 282. 802.

[4] i.e. J. Hope-Scott, whose memoirs were being prepared by R. Ornsby; Mrs. Maxwell-Scott (Hope-Scott's da.) sent details of the plans on 26 July, Add MS 44482, f. 228, asking permission to publish from Gladstone's letters, and asking for Manzoni's family's whereabouts.

[5] See 13 Oct., 24 Nov. 83.

[6] Of 1845; in Ornsby, *Hope-Scott*, ii. 52.

[7] See 21 Sept. 38.

[8] 'hypocrite' or 'sanctimonious fellow'.

Mr. Onslow's motion; & I regarded it as a significant sequel to the conversation we had previously held.[1]

I willingly excused myself from sending on the instant any reply, for I could not send one of an agreeable character, & I felt that, in a matter of delicacy & importance such as this, I should do well to take time.

The situation is this. A vote of censure on an Administration is moved by reason of its having laid a certain charge on India, & the Postmaster-General of that Administration, on the ground that he disapproves of the act of the Government, & is pledged to that disapproval, claims the right not to vote against a measure which if carried would move them, & him, from the offices they hold.

I consider that the Indian case has now entirely gone by; & I merely name it by way of illustration, to make more clear the principle which is at issue between us, & which I look upon only for prospective purposes.

Thus regarding it, & well pleased that the discussion should be prospective only, I must nevertheless say that the principle is in my judgment inadmissible, & cannot be reconciled with the first principles & necessities of cooperation among those who are engaged together in the arduous work of Government.

Abstention by particular persons, in cases where no issue was raised as to the life of the Administration, is doubtful & dangerous; & it has been carried rather far in some instances under the present Ministry. But to such an extension of it as is involved in the claim now before us, I could not on any future occasion (none such I hope being likely to occur) be a party.

I do not write with the intention or desire of raising any argument, but simply because I think it demanded by justice to you, as well as to all our colleagues, that I should thus place upon record the conclusion at which I have felt myself compelled to arrive.[2]

29. 10. S. Trin. [Dollis Hill]

Chapel Royal mg—Whitehall aft. Saw Ld Spencer—Mr Hamilton. Wrote to Ld Rosebery—French Ambassador Tel. Read Modern Review on Renan's Souvenirs[3]—Talmud (Dr Oort).[4] Finished Renan. Read Esprit de Vinet.[5] C.G. & I drove to Dollis Hill & dined with the Aberdeens.

To LORD ROSEBERY, 29 July 1883.   N.L.S. 10022, f. 225.

When you told me of the daring exploit which you contemplate,[6] all the ideas associated with it did not at once take their proper place in my mind, usually rather bewildered, & for the moment stunned by contemplating in imagination a circuit of this planet, a kind of operation which perhaps the astronomers of other planets, if only their telescopes be a thought better than ours, may be wont to note with interest.

But, if you thus go wandering through fields of earth air & sea, what is to become of

---

[1] 'Fawcett ... said, "If I speak on Onslow's resolution, I can carry the bulk of the Liberal party with me". Mr. G. replied ... "This is an observation which ought not to be made by you to me". Fawcett subsequently declined to vote'; Bahlman, *Hamilton*, ii. 464. See also Fawcett's letters of 27 and 30 July, offering to resign if required; Add MS 44156, f. 169.

[2] Fawcett abstained again on 15 March and 12 June 1884 (Egypt, women's suffrage); see 13 June 84.

[3] *Modern Review*, iv. 494 (July 1883).

[4] H. Oort, *Evangelie en Talmud* (1881).

[5] Perhaps F. L. F. Chavannes, *Alexandre Vinet* (1883).

[6] A tour round the world.

Scotch affairs & the movement to which you have been the point of effective departure, & which to all appearances is on the point of arriving successfully at its *terminus.*

In other words I think Fate marks you for the office which Parliament is evidently about to create. It is at your disposal; we hope you will accept it on its establishment (which Parliamentary experts anticipate with an undoubting confidence): will not Scotland kick if you decline, & cannot Australia wait awhile for some unencumbered interval of your life.[1]

30. M. [London]

Wrote to Att. General—Rev. W. Cadman—The Queen—Miss Magee Tel.—and minutes. Drive with C. Worked on Suez Canal Question. H. of C. $4\frac{3}{4}$–$8\frac{1}{2}$ and $9\frac{1}{2}$–$1\frac{1}{4}$. Spoke.[2] Saw Mr H—Mr S—Ld RG—Chancr of Exr. Read Greville's Journal—Mercy d'Argenteau finished II.

31. Tu.

Wrote to Ld Spencer l.l.—Mr MacColl—Ld Hartington—Ld Sudley—Sir F. Doyle—Mr Samuelson—The Queen—& minutes. Saw Mr H—Ld R.G—Cardinal Howard: who is gentlemanlike & pleasing[3]—Chancr of Exr—Ld Hartington—Ld Spencer. Visited R. Academy, and Bartolozzi Gallery.[4] H. of C. (& Conclave of Ministers) $4\frac{1}{2}$–9 and 10–$12\frac{3}{4}$.[5] Read Soeur Cunégonde—Mercy d'Argenteau—Greville's Journal.

To LORD SPENCER, Viceroy of Ireland,   Althorp MSS K6.
31 July 1883. '*Immediate*'.

I receive from R. Grosvenor and from my son Herbert a deplorable account of the case of the Irish Police Bill. You will doubtless hear from Trevelyan what he thinks of the prospect of passing it. They had but nine men, one fourth of their force on the ground and they kept the House till near five this morning on the *introduction* of the Bill.

I understand that Hartington Harcourt & Dilke were on the ground, the last until the close, and I should be very glad if you could before you leave town learn from them or some of them their impression. *Grosvenor's* belief is that the Bill would add a month to the Session—this is sad, and the alternative is not satisfactory—but there are limits I fear to what human strength can accomplish, although we may ever so much regret the addition of this to other sacrifices.[6]

Wed. Aug. One. 1883.

Wrote to Prince L.L. Bonaparte—Ld Granville—Ld Rosebery—Ld Dunraven—Sig. Suardi[7]—and minutes. Dined at Sir C. Forster's. H of C. $12\frac{1}{4}$–2 & $2\frac{1}{2}$–$5\frac{1}{2}$.[8] Radcliffe Trust Meeting 2 PM. Saw Mr H—Ld R.G—Mr Waddington—Dr

---

[1] Despite this, Rosebery declined the offer next day, leaving for Australia *via* America on 1 Sept.; Crewe, *Rosebery*, i. 172 and Add MS 44288, f. 175.

[2] On Northcote's motion on de Lesseps' monopoly; *H* 282. 987.

[3] Edward Henry Howard, 1829–92; cardinal priest 1877, cardinal bishop 1884.

[4] Probably Angelo Bartolotti, foreign importer.

[5] Misc. busines; *H* 282. 1109.

[6] Bill withdrawn on 6 August.   [7] Autograph hunter.

[8] Agricultural holdings; *H* 282. 1228.

Quain—Chancr of Exr—do *cum* Mr Chamberlain. Read Mercy d'Argenteau—
Soeur Cunégonde (finished)—Greville's Journal.

To LORD ROSEBERY, 1 August 1883.   N.L.S. 10022, f. 232.

I have received your letter[1] and it is so full and decided upon the point at issue that,
much as I regret the position of affairs, I cannot press you to recede from a decision so
positively announced. Nor will I trouble you with any argument in relation to the very
great advantage (as I have felt it) of abiding stiff discipline on the first steps of the ladder.
It would be little short of impertinent in me to press on you what you already know, and
have considered, and decided on. I have only then to thank you for the thoroughly kind
frank and cordial manner in which you have conveyed to me your intentions.

I am sure that my colleagues will join in these acknowledgments as well as in my
regrets.

Nothing more will be done in the matter of the Scotch appointment until the Bill. This
I trust will be at latest during the coming week.

2. *Th.*

Wrote to Sir C. Dilke—Mr Chamberlain—Ld Halifax—Ld Chancellor—Mr
Arnold—The Queen—& minutes. Ten to dinner. H of C. $4\frac{3}{4}$–8 and $9\frac{1}{2}$–$12\frac{3}{4}$.[2] Saw
Mr H—Ld R. Grnr—Chancr of Exr—Sir C. Dilke. Drive with C.—Luncheon at 15
G.S. Read Mercy d'Argenteau—Souvenirs d'une Cosaque[3]—Greville's Journal.

To J. CHAMBERLAIN, president of the board of trade,   Add MS 44546, f. 143.
2 August 1883. 'Early'.

In connection with the winding up of business you will probably be asked whether you
propose to extend the Bankruptcy Bill to Ireland.

I understand there are currents for and against. But it seems to me that there may be
much objection on *principle* to extending this Bill to Ireland on Report in the month of
August, unless by *general consent.*[4]

To Sir C. W. DILKE, president of the local government board,   Add MS 43875, f. 140.
2 August 1883. '*Immediate*'.

With reference to your Bill on Cholera I am not sure whether you have fully borne in
mind the decision of the Cabinet. I do not think any department can now introduce any
fresh contentious matter, unless it be of the most urgent character; & I am afraid some of
your Clauses would not stand this test. We shall get into great difficulties if we change
our ground.[5]

(See Cross's very reasonable question for today.)

---

[1] See 29 July 83n.

[2] Questions, supply; *H* 282. 1340.

[3] Not found.

[4] On 6 August A. M. Porter announced that the govt. would include Ireland in the Bill; *H*
282. 1646.

[5] Dilke agreed to avoid contentious clauses and the Diseases Prevention Bill passed; Add MS
43875, f. 141; see his letter of 27 July on danger of cholera in London; Add MS 44149, f. 146.

To LORD HALIFAX, 2 August 1883.   Halifax MSS A4/88.

Thanks for your note.[1] We were in a hole. Instead of leaving us there, & pelting us a little, they lifted us out, & enabled us to come off with flying colours. It seems to have been a question of the Leadership! which made it necessary for Northcote to move *something*, & he moved accordingly what he thought would do the *least* mischief.

3. Fr.

Wrote to Sir H. Ponsonby—Ld Granville—Ld Hartington—Ld R. Grosvenor—The Queen l.l.—Sir T. May—Ld Dufferin—and minutes. Read, same as yesterday. Dined with Mr Hutton: Dean of St P. Dr Liddon Mr M'Coll. Saw Mr H—Ld RG—Ld Granville. H of C. $2\frac{1}{4}$-7.[2]

To LORD DUFFERIN, 3 August 1883.   Add MS 44546, f. 144.

I should much have liked to see you for a few minutes before your leaving town, had it so happened: for we are to be more or less challenged next week about Egypt.

I think you may be able to set down in few words our degree of advancement as respects the most important particulars of preparation for leaving Egypt.

How far are the following (among other) points disposed of, or otherwise: 1. Army. 2. Police. 3. Judiciary. 4. Legislative machinery—when will it have had its first effective trial? A *very* slight outline on main points is all, I apprehend, that we ought to give to Parliament at present.[3]

To LORD R. GROSVENOR, chief whip, 3 August 1883.[4]   Add MS 44315, f. 124.

Let me point out in a few words how the [Irish] Emigration matter stands.

When it was discussed in the Land Act, there was a very stiff opposition. But when we reach the *blank* & put in the moderate sum of 250 m[ille] this appeared to give satisfaction to the opponents, & it excited vehement displeasure among the Tory Emigrationists.

No action has taken place under the Act: the grant to be proposed this year, in consequence of the very urgent demand of the Irish Govt. is proposed as a single & occasional act, carrying no pledge or expectation of *any* kind as to the future, & it does not bring up the total amount to what was I may say agreed to in the Land Act.

4. Sat. [Osborne House]

Wrote [blank] and minutes. Off to Osborne at 11. Dined with H.M: & conversation after. Much pleased with the Hesse Princesses. Saw Mr H—Sir H. Ponsonby—Read Souvenirs &c. finished—Quart Rev. on Swift.[5]

5. 11 S. Trin.

Morning service in the dining-room. Mr Burnaby's Ch. in evg: much pleased with him.[6] Wrote to Dr Coatcott Tel.[7] Read Divorce Satyrique[8]—Philosophy of

---

[1] Not found; on the Canal; see 25-6 July 83.

[2] Local Govt. Board (Scotland) Bill; *H* 282. 1487.

[3] Dufferin replied, 5 August, Add MS 44151, f. 234, reporting fair progress in these areas, election arrangements 'made & published'.

[4] Holograph. See to Spencer, 31 July 83.   [5] *Q.R.*, clvi. 1 (July 1883).

[6] Robert William Burnaby, vicar of Cowes.   [7] *Sic*; untraced.

[8] *Divorce satyrique, ou les amours de la Reine Marguerite de Valoys* (1663).

Christianity[1]—Reghellini, Examen[2]—Borthwick's Hymns.[3] Audience of the Queen: & dinner as yesterday. Saw Sir W. Jenner & Sir H.P.

6. M. [London]

Off at 10.30. Wrote to The Queen—Bp of Exeter—Ld Derby—& minutes. Saw Mr H—Ld R.G.—Ld R.G. *cum* Mr Trevelyan—Ld Granville. Read Philos. of Christianity—Quart. Political Article[4]—Greville's Journal. H of C. $4\frac{3}{4}$-$8\frac{1}{2}$ and $9\frac{1}{4}$-1. Much speaking, some contentious.[5]

7. Tu.

Wrote to Ld Kimberley—Ld Granville—Mr W. Smith—Ld Brougham—The Queen—and minutes. Read Mercy d'Argenteau—Philosophy of Xty—Greville (finished). Saw Mr H—Ld R.G. l.l.—Rev. Mr MacColl—Sir C. Dilke—Mr Chamberlain—Mr Bryce—Mr Rathbone—Scotts. H of C. $4\frac{1}{2}$-$8\frac{1}{4}$ and $9\frac{1}{2}$-1. Spoke another polemic speech: I love it not.[6]

8. Wed.

Wrote to Mr M. Arnold—Mad. Novikoff—Ly Enfield—Viceroy of Canada—& minutes. Cabinet & House 2-6. Ld Mayor's dinner 7-$10\frac{1}{2}$. (Spoke for 'Ministers').[7] Read Mercy d'Argenteau. Saw Mr H—Ld R.G—The Lady Mayoress N.B.—Sir W. Harcourt—Sir C. Dilke.

Cabinet. Wed. Aug. 8. 1883. 2 PM.[8]
1. Egypt. Discussion on the withdrawal of the force. C. of E. proposed to reduce in October to 5 m[ille]—with the intention of reducing to 2m. (evacuating Cairo) for Alexandria. Granville proposed general [withdrawal] now: adhere to pledges: with desire to accelerate rather than retard.
2. a) Nat. Debt Bill (Reprint?)
   b) [Irish] Tramways Bill. (50m migration?)
   c) Extension of Bankruptcy bill.
   a) Proceed & reprint—pro formâ Commee.—b) Settled 50 m[ille] for migration—c) Saty. after Rules & Orders.
3. Duke of Wellington Statue.[9]
   i) Shall the statue be melted down: Aye 7; No 5.
   ii) Shall another be put up at the West End?: Aye 5; No 7.
   iii) Shall the Stephens monument be completed: Aye 5; No 7.

---

[1] *Philosophy of the plan of salvation* (1883).
[2] M. Reghellini de Schio, *Examen du Mosaisme et du Christianisme*, 3v. (1834).
[3] J. Borthwick and S. Findlater, *Hymns from the land of Luther*, 4v. (1854–62).
[4] [L. J. Jennings], *Q.R.*, clvi. 270 (July 1883).
[5] On Transvaal and native protection; *H* 282. 1709; his comments regarded as 'very shabby' by Sir H. Robinson; see P. Lewsen, ed., *Correspondence of J. X. Merriman* (1960), 136.
[6] On questions, and national debt; *H* 282. 1878.
[7] *T.T.*, 9 August 1883, 6b.
[8] Add MS 44644, f. 95.
[9] Shaw Lefevre next day announced the competition for a new statue outside Apsley House; *H* 282. 2067.

iv) That the proposal of the Committee be adopted, designs being called for: Aye 11; No 1 (WEG).
4. ⟨Tigris⟩
5. Madagascar dispatches. Errors on both sides. Ld G. to communicate with Waddington, make known our new inform[ation] [?] & inquire as to theirs with a view to comparison.[1]
6. Time of Lord Mayor's Dinner.
7. Seizure of Porto Nuovo (African W. Coast). Ld G. & Ld D. to open communications with Waddington.
8. Coleridge,[2] threats against. Telegram of U.S. govt. undertaking to protect. Very satisfactory. Make the request: leave the measures to the U.S. Govt. Tell Ld C. that we see no cause to interfere with his journey by discouraging.
9. Question respecting subsidy to Ameer 'to strengthen his position for defence'.[3]

To Matthew ARNOLD, 8 August 1883.   Add MS 44546, f. 146.

I have the pleasure of proposing to you that you should accept a pension of two hundred and fifty pounds a year, as a public recognition of the high place you have taken in the poetry and literature of England.[4]

To Madame O. NOVIKOV, 8 August 1883.[5]   Add MS 44546, f. 146.

Conservative members may not be safe interpreters of ministerial utterances.[6] The leading feature of my declaration was that we had nothing to retract or alter in our former declarations. Eight or nine months ago we had near 35,000 men in Egypt. We have now I believe 6,000.
I do not know if you are acquainted with an Article of mine in the 19th Century,[7] 4 or 5 years ago, on Egypt. It would be hard for me to *eat* that article: even had I an appetite, I should have no digestion for it. This reminds me of a quotation of Lady Holland's from an Italian friend. 'Il mangiare, il mangiare, sì, quest' è facile: ma il digerire, il digerire, quest' è il principale.'[8]
The latent jingoism still cherished by a portion of the country without doubt desires us to keep Egypt—and feeds itself with idle hopes, the value of which I hope that in no long time they will be able to estimate more soundly than they can now do.
[P.S.] Let me offer you my share of thanks for the excellent tea you so kindly sent.

9. Th.

Wrote to The Queen 1 and minutes. H. of C. 4¾-8¼ and 9-1. Spoke on Egypt in ans. to Sir S.N.[9] Eleven to breakfast. Saw Mr H—Ld R.G—Ld Mount Temple—

---

[1] Gladstone included a calming passage on Madagascar in his speech this evening; see S. P. Oliver, *The true story of the French dispute in Madagascar* (1885), 140-1.
[2] J. D. Coleridge, see 18 Apr. 66, on a visit to the U.S.A.
[3] Already in June given subsidy of 12 lakhs *p.a.*; Gopal, *Ripon*, 40.
[4] No reply found, but the pension accepted.
[5] Version in Stead, *M.P. for Russia*, ii. 135.
[6] Novikov wrote, 7 August, Add MS 44168, f. 290, complaining at conservative rejoicing at 'the "indefinite postponement of impratible [*sic*] pledges"'.
[7] On Egypt, if occupied, as 'the almost certain egg of a North African Empire'; see 'Aggression on Egypt', *Nineteenth Century* (August 1877), 21 July 77 and above, ix. xlii.
[8] 'The eating, the eating, yes, that is easy; but the digesting, the digesting, that is the main thing'.
[9] Having not expected to speak; H 282. 2196.

Mr Knowles—Ld E. Fitzmaurice. Visited the Spencer Cliffords: saw Miniatures & Pictures.[1] Read Mercy Argenteau & divers pamphlets.

10. Fr.

Wrote to Mr Chamberlain—Ld Granville—The Queen l.l.—and minutes. Saw Mr H—Ld RG—Mr Chamberlain—Sir T. May—Chancr of Exr. Saw one [R]. H of C. $2\frac{1}{2}$-5 & $5\frac{1}{2}$-7; 9-$11\frac{3}{4}$.[2] Read Mercy Argenteau—Divers pamphlets—Philos. of Plan of Salvation (finished).

To J. CHAMBERLAIN, president of the board of trade,   Add MS 44546, f. 146.
10 August 1883. *'Immediate'*.

The passing of your Bankruptcy Bill is of the very highest importance in my view on its own account and on account of the Grand Committees.

I am becoming seriously alarmed lest the Lords should throw it out if its passing the Commons be seriously delayed. They will have a most plausible case for doing it in the lateness of the Session and a powerful secret motive in making the chief fruit of the Grand Committees fail. This failure it is a capital object with them to achieve.

It will be impossible to get a second day for an Irish fight on Bankruptcy within another week.

[P.S.] R. Grosvenor will call on you.

11. Sat.

Wrote to Dowr Countess Crawford—Mr G. Howard—Sir T. May—The Queen l.l.—& minutes. H of C. $12\frac{1}{4}$-2 and 6-$8\frac{3}{4}$.[3] Saw Mr H—Lord R.G—Mr Chamberlain *cum* Ld RG—Ld Portarlington—Ld Kimberley. Saw Gascoigne X. Read Mercy Argenteau—Divers Pamphlets—19th Cent. on Ital Policy.[4]

12. 12 S. Trin.

Marylebone Ch at 11—Much pleased with the Sermon & the reviving congregation. Went on to Dollis Hill: back late at night. Saw G.L. Gower (much conversation)—Arthur Gordon and G. Russell. Read Creevey's Letters[5]—19th Cent on 'After Death'[6]—Barrett on the Temptation.[7]

13. M.

Wrote to Ld Coleridge—Ld Granville l.l.—The Queen, & minutes. Read Mercy Argenteau—Italian Tract on R.C. Educn. Saw Mr H—Ld R.G—Ld Advocate—Ld Northbrook—Ld E. Fitzmaurice—Chancr of Exr—Ld Granville. H. of C. $4\frac{1}{2}$-$8\frac{1}{4}$ and 11-$1\frac{3}{4}$.[8] Visited B. Museum to see the very curious Shapira MSS.[9] Then to

---

[1] Sir Robert Cavendish Spencer Clifford, 1815-92; 3rd bart. 1882; Black Rod from 1859; lived in Rutland House.

[2] Questions, corrupt practices; *H* 283. 63.

[3] Bankruptcy Bill; Parnell prevented adjournment deb. on the Irish clause; *H* 283. 188.

[4] *N.C.*, xiv. 339 (August 1883).   [5] Sent by R. H. Hutton, see 16 Aug. 83.

[6] *N.C.*, xiv. 262 (August 1883).   [7] See 9 June 83.

[8] Questions, supply; *H* 283. 277.

[9] Ginsburg drew Gladstone's attention to the 'wonderful fragments of Deuteronomy . . . temporally deposited in the British Museum for me to decipher'; Add MS 44483, f. 13.

Westells. Dined with Ld Alcester. Saw Pr. of Wales—Sir J. Lacaita—Dr Russell; a very agreeable party.

14. Tu.

Wrote to Prince of Wales—The Queen l.l.l.—Sir F. Doyle—Sir T. Acland—Dr Acland—Ld Chancellor—Ld Stair—Ld Granville—Mr A. Arnold—and minutes. Eight to dinner. H of C. $4\frac{1}{2}$–8 and $10\frac{1}{4}$–$12\frac{1}{2}$.[1] Saw Mr H—Ld RG—Lady Mar—Mr A. Acton—Mr Warren—Chancr of Exr cum Ld RG. Read Argenteau—Finished Proposta per l'Educazione Superiore dei Catholici Inglesi.[2]

15. Wed.

Wrote to Mr Knowles—Ld Yarborough (& others)—Ld Chancellor—Mr M'Coll—Ld Garvagh—C. Lacaita—Sir H. Ponsonby—Mr Lefevre—and minutes. Dined at Ld Rosebery's. H. of C. $2\frac{1}{4}$–$4\frac{1}{2}$.[3] Drive with C. Saw Mr H—Ld R.G.—Sir J. Lacaita (with whom I spent another hour over Cowper's Hymn)[4]—Ld Rosebery—Mrs R. Milnes—Mr Ward—Mrs Warner—Mr Waddington. Read Mercy Argenteau.

16. Th.

Wrote to Mr Onslow—Mr Chamberlain—Lady Mar—Ld Kimberley—Mr Hutton—Mr Knowles—Ld Advocate—The Queen—Ld Granville—& minutes. H. of C. 5–$7\frac{3}{4}$ and $10\frac{1}{4}$–$12\frac{3}{4}$.[5] Dined with Mr Knowles. Saw E. Bell X. Saw Mr H—Ld R.G—Dr Schraker—Mr Knowles. Read Mercy Argenteau—Nineteenth Century. Worked with Sir J. Lacaita on the Hymn 11–12: which I hoped we *had* finished—but not quite.

To R. H. HUTTON, editor of *The Spectator*,   Add MS 44546, f. 149.
16 August 1883.

I have read the Letters of Mr. Creery which you were kind enough to send me.[6] The argumentative matter is of great interest & so are the statistics—for the relative decline, & the stagnation, of the Unitarian body appear to show that the movement of the day is not, in the main, against too great a quantity of dogma, but against dogma in itself, that is I suppose against what we mean by Divine Revelation.

I sincerely hope Mr. Creery may become an efficient labourer in more fertile fields.

17. Fr.

Wrote to Sir J. Lacaita—The Speaker—The Queen—Sir Thos Acland—C.G.—Mr Chamberlain—& minutes. H of C. $3\frac{1}{4}$–6 and 9–$12\frac{3}{4}$.[7] Sat to photographer. Saw

---

[1] Bankruptcy Bill 3°R; *H* 283. 522.
[2] Untraced.
[3] Scottish government; *H* 283. 588.
[4] See 23 July 82; sent this day to Knowles for *N.C.*, xiv. 357 (September 1883). See 31 Oct. 83.
[5] Questions, supply; *H* 283. 748.
[6] A. M. Creery, *Reasons for giving up the Unitarian ministry* (1883); sent on 4 August, Add MS 44215, f. 309.
[7] Questions, supply; *H* 283. 964.

Mr H—Ld RG—Sir Chas Dilke. Read Browne on Lambeth Pal.[1]—Mercy Argenteau.

18. Sat.

Wrote to Chancr of Exr—Sir J. Lacaita—Mr Collings—The Queen l.l.l.—C.G.—and minutes. Saw Mr H.—Ld RG—The Speaker—Mr Chamberlain—Mr Agnew—Mr Mundella—Sir W. Harcourt—Ld Granville—Sir J. Lacaita—Ld E. Fitzmaurice. H. of C. $12\frac{1}{4}$-$7\frac{3}{4}$ (with short intervals) and 11–1.[2] Dined at the Duke of Argyll's: he was as interesting & cordial as ever.

To H. C. E. CHILDERS, chancellor of the exchequer,   Add MS 44546, f. 149.
18 August 1883.

I am delighted to see from this letter[3] that Lesseps both approves & has actually launched the idea of formal communication with ship-owning interests. This is the idea, which I think it is our business to develop & encourage, & above all to *keep in the front.*

This method of action is the only way by which we can avoid altogether the risk of again getting involved in negotiations.

It is not our fault, but the fault of the original arrangement that it is almost impossible to effect a separation between the character of the Directors as Members of the Administration of a trading body & as representatives of interests which lie outside. I do not see my way to getting over this difficulty. Virtually we the Cabinet are part of the direction of the Suez Canal Company & the position is essentially a false one. I doubt if it be possible to supply the anticipatory instructions which are desired of us, without getting into the thickest of our difficulties, & almost the alpha and the omega of our policy for the present should I think be to bring M. Lesseps into close practical communication with our shipowning & trading interests. If these are properly represented I should leave it to him in the main to settle what to do as to the traders & shipowners of other countries.

I have seen Granville who is I think very much of the opinions which I have expressed.

19. 13 S. Trin.

Chapel Royal mg, Westmr Abbey aftn. Wrote to Lady Holker—Mrs Thistlethwayte. Read Wilson, Inspiration of HS[4]—Denton, Alexandrian Church[5]—Blunt Reformation Hist.[6]—Stubbs, Lectures to Secularists.[7] Saw Sir T. Acland—Ld Cork.

20. M.

Wrote to Lord Advocate—Mr Errington—Mr Chamberlain—The Queen l.l.—Ld Granville—& minutes. H of C. $4\frac{1}{4}$-8 and 11-$2\frac{1}{2}$. *Late* speech[8] and much fatigue. Worked on Parliament Street plans.[9] Saw Mr H—Ld R.G—Ld Granville—Mr

---

[1] J. C. Browne, *Lambeth Palace and its associations* (1883).
[2] Questions, supply; *H* 283. 1113.
[3] Childers sent a mem. by Rivers Wilson on relations with de Lesseps; Add MS 44130, f. 286.
[4] D. Wilson, 'The inspired scriptures' (1861).
[5] W. Denton, 'The ancient church of Egypt' (1883).
[6] The second volume of the 5th ed. of J. H. Blunt's history (1882); see 11 Mar. 83.
[7] C. W. Stubbs, *Christ and Free-thought* (1883).
[8] On the *Clyde* court martial; *H* 283. 1438.   [9] See 25 Oct. 83.

Weaver—Ld Rosebery—Mr Knowles. Dined at Ld Reay's: conversation with him on Ld R[osebery]. Read Mercy Argenteau.

21. Tu.

Wrote to The Queen l.l.—Ld Granville—Ld Derby—Ld R. Grosvenor—Mr Knowles—Ld Carlingford—and minutes. Saw Mr H.S.—Ld R.G.—Sir J. Lacaita. Cabinet 12-3. H of C. $4\frac{1}{4}-7\frac{1}{2}$ and $11-12\frac{1}{2}$. Long speech in answer to Northcote.[1] Dined at Ld Northbrook's. Finished the valuable Mercy Argenteau Correspondence.

Cabinet. Tues. Aug. 21. 83. Noon.[2]
1. Agricultural [Holdings] Bills. i. England.[3] 2. Scotch Bill. To follow when common ground.
2. Suez Canal Directions.[4]
3. South Africa. Cetewayo in the Reserve. Not to be allowed to take possession. We must hold the Reserve. Bulwer to go to Jamaica at once.[5]
4. [blank]

To LORD R. GROSVENOR, chief whip, 21 August 1883.[6]   Add MS 44315, f. 126.

With reference to the *Irish* Parl. Registration Bill, I think that the Lords in throwing it out have done an act of violence & injustice and I hope that unless this limited measure be involved in some larger one we may have our opportunity of pressing it upon them at the beginning of next session.

22. Wed.

Wrote to the Queen l.l.—Ld Brougham—Mrs Bolton—Ld Granville l.l.—& minutes. Dined at Ld Sydney's. Cabinet $12\frac{1}{4}-3\frac{3}{4}$. House before and after it.[7] Saw Mr H.S.—Ld RG. Visited Holland House & went over the domaine. Read Hotel de la Reine Marguerite.[8] Saw divers [R].

Cabinet. Wed. Aug. 22. 83. 12¼ PM.[9]
1. [Queen's] Speech.
2. Privy Seal. Home Sec. will ascertain what wd. be the effect as to precedence & what the legal course—Cabinet generally inclined to attach the Seal to the office of P.M. provided no practical difficulty arise as to precedence.[10]

[1] Review of the Session; *H* 283. 1527.
[2] Add MS 44644, f. 100. Note by Derby requesting 'a few minutes' for South Africa at the end of other business; ibid., f. 101.
[3] Notes on Lords amendment at ibid., f. 104.
[4] Technical advice supported a widened canal (rather than a second narrow channel); negotiations led to agreement between de Lesseps and the shipowners on 30 Nov.; Childers, ii. 154-5 and *PP* 1884 lxxxviii. 50.
[5] i.e. expediting a vacancy in Natal.   [6] Holograph.
[7] Questions, Indian budget; *H* 283. 1645.
[8] C. Duplomb, *L'hôtel de la Reine Marguerite* (1881).   [9] Add MS 44644, f. 107.
[10] Carlingford was both Lord President and Lord Privy Seal; Gladstone hoped effectively to abolish the latter by amalgamating it with the premiership, a course which Carlingford persistently resisted.

3. Troops in Egypt.
(4. Medical Bill *gone. yesterday was our last hope.*)
0 5. Answer from Lord G. to the Queen respecting Registration of Votes & Scotch Local
Govt. asking what Govt. mean to do.
4. Granville submitted a draft[1]—withheld & postponed.
5. Order for Withdrawal of one battalion to take effect as soon as Cholera & considerations connected with it *permit.* Cabinet probably in October will deal with evacuation
of Cairo if not previously effected by the act of Ld Gr. & Hartington wh the rest of the
Cabinet wd be ready to approve.

23. Th.

Wrote to The Speaker—Ld Carlingford—Sir T. May—Sir T. Acland—Mr Trevelyan—Prince L.L. Bonaparte—The Queen l.l.—& minutes. H. of C. 3–7¼. Good
bye![2] Saw Mr H—Ld RG (long)—Lady Stepney—Ld Granville—Mrs Leo Ellis[3]—
Mrs Craven—Herbert G. Read L'Un d'Eux on the duty of Sovereigns.[4] Dined at
Holland House. Saw Cook, Howard [R]. Worked on books.

To G. O. TREVELYAN, Irish secretary, 23 August 1883.   Add MS 44335, f. 126.
'*Private*'.

I cannot feel surprised that, with so arduous a work on your hands in the House of
Commons, you should desire to prosecute it with all the authority which belonged to
your predecessor as a member of the Cabinet, and should sometimes think the pressure
too great for you to bear.[5] It is however, let me say in passing, just those portions of our
political lives in which we feel ourselves *almost* overborne and overwhelmed, that really
constitute the most telling and most valuable parts of the political education we are all
continually undergoing.

Looking, however, at the point practically, it is plain that the constitution of the Irish
Government offers a great impediment to the accomplishment of your wish at the
present time.

It is dangerous to generalise in politics, but I think it is nearly if not absolutely true that
you cannot have a working Viceroy with the Chief Secretary in the Cabinet. Under very
peculiar circumstances we *tried to try* [*sic*] the experiment of having both Viceroy and
Secretary in the Cabinet; and we could not even get our [*sc.* one] man up to the scratch.

I cannot think, however, that your position offers you a single subject of regret. Without the practical advantage which Forster had you have faced your opponents not less
successfully. You stand well for consideration when the time or times for new official
manipulations may arise. The gallantry of your acceptance after the terrible 6th of May
has been rewarded by success; and, with a future as well assured as that of any other man,
you are behind none of them in your claims on the acknowledgement, I will say the gratitude of the Government for the services rendered in the past.[6]

[1] On Madagascar; CAB 41/17/20.
[2] Questions; *H* 283. 1758.
[3] Harriet, wife of Leopold G. F. A. Ellis (see 28 July 71).
[4] Not found.
[5] Trevelyan wrote on 20 August, Add MS 44335, f. 122, that after 15 months 'of this terrible
office', he had waited till the end of the session to say that 'the time has come when I ought to be in
the Cabinet'.
[6] Trevelyan replied, 24 August, ibid., f. 128: 'I understand that the subject is closed, and shall put
it out of my mind.'

24. Fr.

Wrote to Sir T. Acland—Mrs Leo Ellis—Sir J. Lacaita—Ld Selborne—Mr Lefevre—C.G.—and minutes. Saw Mr H—Mr H.S.—Ld R.G—Ld Rosebery—Mr Westell—Ld Granville *on the outlook.* He said C'est autant de gagné.[1] Lady Stepney dined. Worked hard on books. Saw Amos—Stafford [R].

To Mrs GLADSTONE, 24 August 1883.   Hawarden MSS.

The work ended but only at twelve last night. The Prorogation will be tomorrow. Please to send for us to Chester as we shall come by the 2.45 due *7.20* & if we are punctual, which we may well be now that the Parliamentary rush is over, we ought not to be very late for your dinner. If you send the waggonet and pair Zadok[2] and the luggage can come with us I hope. Otherwise he would wait and go to Broughton Hall.

The Session ends I think well for the Government.—

I find at this moment 1. You may be at Abergele till latish tomorrow 2. Zadok thinks he cannot come tomorrow. Mary sends to Helen directives about the carriage, and what precedes is *bosh.*

The paragraph in the P.M.G. today about Northcote's retirement[3] is *credible.* His health may have to do with it but I think the horrors of the position must be the main reason if he is really to retire.

I am sorry to say the difficulty about Scotland looms large: not the Queen only or chiefly, but Midlothian. Godley started this hare—Rosebery said the thing was serious but he would not give an opinion. Granville said it would not do as it would be interpreted into slight and disrespect. We shall have to concoct something else. In meantime I trust that Abergele will have done you much good and that the giddiness will depart.

Mary tells me the Lord Advocate strongly backs Granville's opinion.

We had an interesting party at Holland House yesterday evening: but Mrs Craven & Mrs Leo Ellis dislike one another.

The death of Chambord is a considerable event. He was really a bulwark of the Republic. The French Ministers are in a great pucker, a peck of troubles. Our affair at Madagascar will go well. Ever your afft. WEG

25. Sat. [Hawarden]

Wrote to Mrs Hampton—Superior of All Saints Sisterhood—Mrs Locke Tel.—Ld Chancr Tel. and l.—The Queen—and minutes. Saw Mr H.—Ld RG—Cav. de' Giovanni. Very busy in preparation. 2¼-8 To Hawarden. Read Dr Claudius.[4]

26. 14 S. Trin.

Hn Ch mg & evg: read the Lessons. Wrote to Dean of ChCh—Ld Chancellor—Zadok—& minutes. Read Einsiedelen[5]—Jerusalem Bishopric[6]—Esoteric Buddhism.[7]

---

[1] 'That much has been achieved.'
[2] His valet.
[3] Retirement expected on health grounds; *P.M.G.*, 24 August 1883, 8.
[4] By M. Crawford (1883).
[5] One of the various religious publications from the abbey at Einsiedeln.
[6] By W. H. Hechler (1883).
[7] By A. P. Sinnett (1883).

To H. G. LIDDELL, dean of Christ Church, 26 August 1883.   Add MS 44546, f. 152.
'*Private*'.

When the Deanery of Westminster was offered to you not on my motion but under my responsibility, I could not be surprised at your declining it,[1] but some words used by you conveyed to my mind that you did not consider yourself immovable.

I had long thought there was one Deanery which might be acceptable to you, & only one, the Deanery of Durham: not only on account of the attractions which it has for all men especially of strong academical sympathies, but by reason of the connection of your family with the North. I may be right or wrong, & perhaps in what I am now doing I may be a little misled by the deep impression which the place & all its incidents have made upon me, but I feel sure that even if I am wrong you will set down my mistakes to a desire to do you honour.

It happens in the strangest way that at this moment the Deanery of Durham is likely to be vacant. Dean Lake, who lived so long in Somersetshire, finds a mild southern climate *necessary* for his health, & at his own request I have submitted his name for Exeter.

If, as I cannot doubt, this recommendation takes effect, & if it be agreeable to you to go to Durham, I shall have sincere pleasure in making the requisite recommendation to Her Majesty.[2]

27. M.

Kept my bed with slight lumbago till luncheon. Drive in aftn. Wrote to Ld Granville—Ld Carlingford—WHG—Mr Love Parry MP—Sir S. Scott & Co.—& minutes. Drive with C: to see the fields in full harvest-tide. Read Dr Claudius.

28. Tu.

Ch. 8½ A.M.—A joy. Wrote to Ld Granville—Ld Stanley Ald.—The Queen—Mr Hickman—Sir W. Harcourt—& minutes. Worked on books—a great business. Much shifting will be needed. Read Siga Morella[3]—Dr Claudius finished— Esoteric Buddhism finished.

To Sir W. V. HARCOURT, home secretary,   MS Harcourt dep. 9, f. 55.
28 August 1883.

I have no knowledge such as would justify me in pronouncing an opinion on the propriety of issuing a Royal Commission on the care of the Blind[4] but Fawcett's letter and inclosures seem to offer strong presumptions in its favour.

It seems probable however that you may encounter discrimination if not resistance on the part of the Institutions which appear to be so defective, and in his view it is a great disadvantage that the principal witness is not producible.

Could some of the better Institutions be moved to recommend the inquiry, and could a greater array of personal authorities be exhibited? It is a great disadvantage that the subject has not been publicly discussed.

Miss Gilbert (sister to Mrs Childers) who was herself blind worked hard in this business. I am not sure whether she is now alive.

[1] See 23 July, 2 Aug. 81.
[2] Liddell declined on 28 August, Add MS 44236, f. 383.
[3] [E. Haywood], *The agreeable Caledonian: or, Memoirs of Signiora di Morella* (1728).
[4] Suggested in Harcourt's letter of 26 August; Add MS 44198, f. 107. No action was taken at this time; the Egerton Royal Commission (*PP* 1889 xix) was appt. July 1885.

29. Wed.

Ch. 8½ A.M. Wrote to Scotts—Mr Ward—& minutes. Saw W.H.G. on Mine business. Cutting hollies with Herbert. Worked on books. Read Signora Morella—Warton's Pope[1]—Cooke on Latin Verse—and [blank.]

30. Th.

Ch. 8½ A.M. Wrote to Sir D. Currie l. & Tel.—and minutes. Cutting an alder with HJG. My performances of this kind draw to their close. Worked on books. Read Warton on Pope—Plutarch on delayed Retribution[2]—Siga. di Morella (finished). Saw Carington & W.H.G. on mining affairs.

31. Fr.

Ch. 8½ A.M. Wrote to Lady Lyndhurst—Mr Barker MP—Mr S. Ward—Lady Derby—Dean of Ch.Ch.—and minutes. Worked on books. We finished the Alder tree. Read Wharton on Pope—Plutarch on Late retribution—Slater, Religious Opps. of Heathen.[3] Worked on the Homeric Vocative.

To LADY LYNDHURST, 31 August 1883.   Add MS 44546, f. 154.

I send you herewith nine letters.[4] I fear they are all that I possess. Assuming that you are sufficiently supplied with Lord Lyndhurst's handwriting, I will beg you to return them when you have made such a use of them as you care. The dating is imperfect but they are in chronological order. The last letter refers to an accident I had when riding in the Park about 1863. To my great annoyance it prevented my dining with you & him.

I will tell you, in answer to your inquiry, an anecdote which I think is well worth preserving.

It was at the time either of the Life Peerage given to Lord Wensleydale, or of the Conspiracy Bill, I cannot say which. I called on him wishing to get legal light upon the question. Either Brougham was there, or he came in soon. Lord Lyndhurst expounded the matter in the most luminous way from his point of view. Brougham went into raptures, & used these words 'I tell you what, Lyndhurst, I wish I could make an exchange with you. I would give you some of my walking power, & you should give me some of your brains.' I have often told the story with this brief commentary, that the compliment was the highest I have ever known to be paid by one human being to another.[5]

I have often compared him in my own mind with the five other Lord Chancellors who since his time have been my colleagues in Cabinet: much to the disadvantage in certain respects of some of them. Once I remember in the Peel Cabinet the conversation happened to touch some man (there are such!) who was too fond of making difficulties. Peel said to your husband 'That is not your way, Lyndhurst.' Of all the intellects I have ever known his I think worked with the least friction.

If there is any question you might like to put to me, taking your chance of a reply, pray do not scruple to do it.

---

[1] J. Warton, *An Essay on the genius and writings of Pope* (1756).
[2] Plutarch, *De sera numinis vindicta*; on the puzzle of the apparent prosperity of the wicked.
[3] T. E. Slater, *The philosophy of missions* (1882).
[4] See Lady Lyndhurst's request of 29 August, Add MS 44483, f. 99, for letters for the biography of her husband, Peel's lord chancellor (see 3 Oct. 31).
[5] This para. in T. Martin, *Life of Lyndhurst* (1883), 506. See 4 Dec. 83.

Sat. Sept One 1883.

Ch. 8¼ A.M. Wrote to Sir C. Anderson—Mr Hamilton—Ld Granville—Sir G. Prevost—Mr J. Parker—Rev. Dr Liddon—& minutes. Worked on books. Read Wharton—Plutarch—the Laird's Secret.[1] Worked on the Homeric Vocative.

2. 15 S. Trin.

Ch. 11 AM (H.C.)—and 6½ P.M. Wrote to Lord Derby l. & Tel:—Lady Holland—Ld Granville—Padre Tosti BP.—Dr Stubbs—Ld Wolverton—& minutes. Read Sayce on gods of Canaan[2]—Slater on heathen opportunities—and other works.

To LORD DERBY, colonial secretary, 2 September 1883.   Add MS 44546, f. 155.
'*Private*'.

I have had no difficulty in telegraphing to the Under-Secretary at the Colonial Office 'I agree to telegram sent me by Secretary of State' & I quite agree in your view of Bulwer's proposal.[3] What I do not feel at all sure of is our knowledge of Cetewayo's real motives & intentions. It does not appear to me certain that it would be a very bad thing if he & the Boers were, in the old phrase, to put up their horses together. To piece together *anything* in South Africa is an attractive prospect rather than otherwise.

3. M.

Ch. 8¼ A.M. Wrote to Ld Granville Tel—Mr Hamilton l. & Tel—Sir W. Harcourt—Watson & Smith—Dean of Durham & minutes. Worked on books. Forenoon mainly spent on making arrangements for taking over the Aston colliery & brickwork: Mr Townshend, Mr Mayhew, & Mr Carrington chiefly taking part. Read Warton on Pope—The Laird's Secret.

4. Tu.

Ch. 8¼ A.M. Wrote to Lady Lyndhurst—Ld Granville—The Queen—Sir D. Currie—Mr Carrington—& minutes. Read Life of Dr Monsey[4]—Plutarch on delayed Retribution—Warton on Pope—The Laird's Secret. Helped to cut an Oak: visited by the Chester Training School. Worked on books. Worked on the Homeric vocative.

5. Wed.

Ch. 8¼ A.M. Wrote to Marq. of Ailesbury—Mr Monk MP—Marq. of Ripon—Mr Hamilton—Sir D. Currie—Messrs Watson—Mr R. Ellis—Mr Monk MP. Woodcraft. Worked on books. Also on Homeric vocative. Read Plutarch as before—Warton on Pope. Ten to dinner. Conversation with Mr Johnson.

[1] J. H. Jamieson, *The laird's secret*, 2v. (1882).

[2] In *C.R.*, xliv. 385 (September 1883).

[3] Telegram from Bulwer: danger of Cetewayo combining forces with Transvaal; does H.M.G. sanction 'active measures'; troops sent up; Add MS 44141, f. 143. Derby sanctioned troop movements as yet for 'moral support' only; ibid., f. 144.

[4] M. Monsey, *A sketch of the life and character of the late Dr. Monsey* (1789).

6. Th.

Ch. 8½ A.M. Wrote to Rev. B.W. Savile—Rev. Sir G. Prevost—Mrs Th.—Rev. Mr M'Coll—Rev. A. Church—and minutes. Worked on books. Cut down a small oak with S.E.G. Worked on Homeric Vocative. Finished Plutarch de Serâ vindicta, a work of great moral and Christian interest. Read Wharton—The Laird's Secret—finished I.

7. Fr.

Ch. 8½ A.M. Wrote to Mr St Geo. Mivart—Watsons—Sir W. Harcourt—Mr Waters—Ld Granville—Sir A. Liddell—Sir H. Ponsonby—Chester Post Master— Sir D. Currie—& minutes. Read Parish Registers[1]—G. Hamilton on Scholarship[2]—Warton on Pope. Worked much on books. Worked on Hom. Vocatives.

To Sir W. V. HARCOURT, home secretary,   MS Harcourt dep. Adds 10.
7 September 1883.

I had written my small say about the Strome Ferry insurgents (whom by prison rule you have appropriately made into Roundheads) in reply to Sir A. Liddell, before I found the post had brought me a letter from you.[3] But I send this line in reply because I find we are going to be near one another as Sir D. Currie stands bound to have us at or *near* Oban on Monday in the 'Pembroke Castle'. Probably your sailing arrangements are all made, but I think he will try to catch you if he can & I have let him know your intentions by this post.

Could you not harness one of each of the four kinds of prisoner and drive them four in hand? It might be an useful discipline.

The weather looks rather inclined to turn us inside out.

To Sir A. F. O. LIDDELL, 7 September 1883.   Add MS 44546, f. 156.

I return with many thanks the papers which Sir W. Harcourt kindly directed to be sent to me.[4]

On principle I regard with disapproval all attempts of colleagues as such to bias the mind of the Home Secretary in regard to the prerogative of mercy, & I suppose it to be a grave question how far it is expedient to bring it into action except upon offences of the highest classes with the severest punishment.

Only as one of the public I observe that these men have already suffered the really severe part of the penalty adjudged to their offences; and that if Sir W. Harcourt feels himself to be in a condition to abridge the term of confinement even more than Lord Moncreiff suggests, I for one should heartily rejoice in it.

I do not quite understand in what way Lord Moncreiff, admirable man as he is, thinks that he gave effect to the mitigating recommendation of the Jury.

As regret was expressed before sentence on behalf of the prisoners by their counsel, I presume they will not be called on to repeat the sentiment.

[1] R. E. C. Waters, *Parish registers of England* (new ed. 1883).
[2] G. Hamilton, *Scottish and English scholarship* (1883).
[3] Press cutting on the riots; Add MS 44198, f. 117. See next letter.
[4] Sir Adolphus Frederick Octavius Liddell (1818–85; undersecretary at Home Office from 1867) sent papers on the 10 men imprisoned for 4 months for violently preventing transmission of fish on a Sunday at Strome Ferry, Ross and Cromarty.

8. Sat. [On the Pembroke Castle][1]

Wrote to Sir H. Ponsonby—Ld Granville—Mr Hamilton Tel.—and minutes.
Read Mad. De Sevigné, Introdn Memoirs &c.[2]

Off to Barrow at 9.20. Much popular feeling on the way. Met Tennyson at
Warrington, Sir D. Currie at Lancaster. Much conversation with the intelligent
Mayor of Barrow who got in. Saw the E. Cavendishes at Cark. Embarked in
rough water at Barrow, but passing from our tug to the magnificent Pembroke
Castle, we were as if on a rock. A very pleasant party, not more than about 15
today in all. Anchored in Ramsay Bay where the Man outlined showed right
well.

9. 16 S. Trin.

A. Lyttelton read the service mg, & part with hymn singing in evg.

We anchored for the night under the Lee of Islay. Much & free conversations
with Tennyson (especially), A. Gordon, West, A. Lyttelton & others: H. Tennyson included. Read the admirable Nicole,[3] & Miss Yonge's recollections of
Keble.[4]

10. M.

Wrote to Ld Granville by telegrams 1. Mada[gascar] 2. France & China
3. Egypt ...—Ld Derby—Mr Griffiths—Chancr of Exr—Rev. S.E.G.—and
minutes. Visited Oban and Dunstaffnage Castle. Took in Ld Dalhousie & other
company. Read Mad. de Sevigné & Aberdeen Correspondence. Anchored in
the Sound of Mull.

Both the company & the occasion much favour conversations, and I have
many. One long one with Tennyson on the state & prospects of belief, another
on Homer.

To H. C. E. CHILDERS, chancellor of the exchequer,   Add MS 44546, f. 157.
10 September 1883.

1. My answer to your letter of the 7th[5] must be full of reserves. For I can hardly say at
this moment whether I am to regard myself as part of the Government for the coming
year, & I must also take into view what, had I no shade of uncertainty on the point just
named, can be done by us as individual Ministers or must be reserved for the Cabinet.
Individually I see little chance of a London Bill next year though there ought to be a good
prospect (if any *paulo post futurum* prospect is good) for 1885. Courtney is much to be
commended in looking out for an expedient, & I should not think the transfer to the
charge as to Buildings at once to be dismissed. But as only the Cabinet can say whether

---

[1] One of Sir D. Currie's steamers, 4000 tons; Currie's invitation was for a week's cruise in the
West Highlands; Add MS 44483, f. 101.

[2] Unclear which ed.; perhaps that by P. E. de Coulanges (1820); see also 26 May 55.

[3] The prolific Pierre Nicole, seventeenth-century French theologian.

[4] C. M. Yonge, *Musings over the 'Christian Year' ... together with ... recollections of John Keble* (1871).

[5] Add MS 44130, f. 293: 1. demand for extra expenditure on metropolitan police courts and
magistrates; 2. what is to be done with local taxation next year?

there is to be a London Bill next year, may not the controversy with Harcourt have to stand over until that point is decided by the Cabinet when it meets for the autumn.

2. With regard to Local Government, again the Cabinet is wholly uncommitted. But I understood from Dilke, I think in July, that acting tentatively he had made considerable progress together with Thring in drawing up a scheme, & I hear it said that they have been doing very thorough & good work. At any rate I think the matter is clearly in a state in which without prejudice you might put yourself in communication with Dilke. When he spoke to me I rather encouraged him. Certainly it seems to me not only that there ought to be but also that there must be a Local Government Bill next year. I write in some haste to save this post.

11. Tu.

Wrote to Mr Hamilton Tel. Today we went up Loch Hourn and returned in the evening to the beautiful Harbour of Tobermory. Kind communication from the Municipality, as yesterday at beautiful Oban. Read the Aberdeen Corresp. and conversed on it with Arthur Gordon as to publication, biography, & otherwise.[1] Also read Mad. de Sevigné.

12. Wed.

Wrote to Ld Spencer—Ld Granville—Chancr of Exr—Mr Hamilton Tel. Today we came North to Gairloch: drove & walked over to Loch Maree: and saw at the Hotel how curiously the facilities of locomotion are piercing into the beautiful recesses of the country. Read Aberdeen Correspondence & Mr Waters's Parish Registers: also Report of Purity Society.[2] Tennyson who read us last night half of the Promise of May finished it this evening; & we discussed the plot among ourselves. Started anew after dusk: a rather heavy *roll* after emerging from the shelter of the Lewes.

To H. C. E. CHILDERS, chancellor of the exchequer,   Add MS 44546, f. 158.
12 September 1883.

I am very much pleased to hear that Lesseps is coming to England & likely to deal with the shipowners direct.[3] Nothing can be so likely to relieve us from the embarrassments of the false position in which we are placed from having a double character to bear as joint Directors of a Commercial Company & as representatives of a Country & of interests standing apart from & in some respects opposed to the interests of the Company.

13. Th. [*Off Kirkwall, Orkney*]

Wrote to Ld Granville—Mr Hamilton l. & Tel. Reached Kirkwall at 10.30. Landed amidst a concourse: saw the noble old Cathedral & other remains: then drove 10 m. to the Maes How, a most singular relic. The aspect of the people

---

[1] While he governed Ceylon (1883-98), Gordon completed the private printing of his father's correspondence on the governor's printing press; from this he wrote a short biography (1893), but the 13v. of correspondence were never published; there is a copy in the British Library.

[2] Perhaps a report of the Society for the Suppression of Vice.

[3] Childers sent Rivers Wilson's account of an interview with de Lesseps; Add MS 44130, f. 300.

bears testimony to their Scandinavian character. With us went the very intelligent Senior Baillie Mr Peace.[1] We had not time to [go] up to the Standing Stones but they were within view. At four we[2] received the Freedom of Kirkwall in the U.P. Kirk before a large assemblage of 1500 people—and I had to speak for Tennyson, by his desire, as well as myself.[3] We embarked soon after five but a fog forebade our starting & then the darkness. Tennyson read 'The Falcon'. Read Parish Registers.

14. Fr.

This day after emerging early from the fog we spent on the broad North Sea with a fine day & a cheery passage. Finished the curious & instructive Book of Parish Registers: & Mad. de Sevigné. In the evening, the Sailors gave us a singing entertainment: great humour & good execution.

15. Sat. [Off Norway]

Wrote to The Queen[4]—Chancellor of Exchequer—Mr Hamilton Tel. Read Ambrosius—with great admiration, in Miss Berry's translation[5]—and Mad. de Sevigné.

We sighted Norway early. The working of the pilot boats was wonderful—in such a sea. We reached Christiansand before luncheon, went through the town and drove to the Torrisdal Falls, returning by the steamer; splendid beauty, & a most courteous, & apparently happy, people. Re-embarked about seven & set off for Copenhagen.

To H. C. E. CHILDERS, chancellor of the exchequer,   Add MS 44546, f. 159.
15 September 1883.

There is a subject on which I ought to have spoken to you before we parted. It requires no immediate decision, but it calls for consideration from the Government & especially for much patient consideration from you. It is the question what we are to do in redemption of the pledge which we have substantially given to the House by accepting during the last session a general motion on behalf of reduction in the public expenditure.

One natural effect of such a motion will naturally have been to give encouragement to you & to Courtney in carrying on the standing & incessant work of resistance to augmentations & in looking for occasions of making those small savings on which so much in the aggregate depends.

I do not know how much may in this way have been accomplished but I suppose it to be evident that the motion will require more than mere Treasury administration, however efficient, can supply.

[1] Thomas Peace, 1832–92; *protégé* of D. McLaren; merchant and Senior Bailie; later Provost. Peace acted as host in the absence of the Provost.

[2] i.e. Gladstone and Tennyson.

[3] A graceful tribute: 'Mr Tennyson's exertions have been on a higher plane of human action than my own—he has worked upon a larger field, and he has in view a more durable inheritance'; *Orkney Herald*, 19 September, 7e.

[4] Apologising for not asking royal permission to visit a foreign country: the voyage beyond the Western Isles had not been originally envisaged; the Queen's rebuke was sharp; Guedalla, Q, ii. 242ff.

[5] C. K. F. Molbeck, *Ambrosius*, tr. from Danish by A. Berry (1879).

When this matter was before us during the session we leaned to the idea of working through Parliamentary Committees, & I do not know that that idea should be abandoned. But the definitive adoption of it would not absolve us from the duty of guiding the Committees (or Committee if only one) & selecting those branches of expenditure on which we may think the most profitable work could be done.

When the Cabinet assembles in London for its autumnal meetings you will I doubt not be fully prepared with your views on this subject.[1]

We are nearing Christiansand & we hope to be in Copenhagen tomorrow. My address will as usual be best found in Downing Street.

I was sorry to hear not the best account of your health some days ago but I hope you have now profited largely by the invigorating air of Deeside.

16. 17 S. Trin. [Copenhagen]

Service mg & part-service evg. Read Nicole—Bp Cotterill on Creation.[2] Wrote to Mr Hamn l. & Tel. More planning. Conversation with Mr Cowan—Sir A. Gordon. Reached Copenhagen about 6½: saw Mr Vivian[3]—Mr Hansen. The entering into the port was beautiful: great crowds to see the great ship. Tennyson & a large party landed to visit the Tivoli Gardens. Read Nicole—Bp Cotterill on the Creation.

17. M.

Tel. to Ld Granville. After breakfast we landed & saw the Museum of Northern objects—Thorwaldsen Museum—Thorw. Church and Rosenborg Castle: all very interesting. Returned on board to dress, & start from the quay at 3 PM to go by a railway (which competes successfully with the snails) to Fredensborg,[4] truly a peaceful retreat. Here we, a party of six dined in a party of seventy, including 12 to 15 adult royalties,[5] & nearly the whole of a circle of nineteen children. As a domestic scene it was of wonderful interest; there was no etiquette: the sovereign personages vied with one another in their simple & kindly manners, so that a distinction hardly could be drawn. No time can efface the recollection of the most interesting evening I ever passed among royalties, though my head is not strong enough, even on this solid ship—of which I may almost say she is firm as a rock and swift as an arrow—to give the description. We got back to the ship before half past ten. I must not omit to name the remarkable conversation of the Crown Princess, whom I took to dinner. The Emperor & King of D[enmark] both observed the old custom and drank wine with me.

---

[1] Childers replied, 19 September, Add MS 44130, f. 302, promising to write fully on redeeming the pledge on expenditure, but no such letter found.

[2] H. Cotterill, *Does science aid faith in regard to creation?* (1883).

[3] Hussey Crespigny Vivian, 1834–93; minister to Denmark 1881, to Belgium 1884; ambassador in Rome 1892; 3rd Baron Vivian 1886.

[4] Autumn residence, n. of Copenhagen, of Christian IX of Denmark.

[5] Including the King and Queen of Greece and the Emperor and Empress of Russia, who used the occasion to congratulate Gladstone on his Balkan policy; the possible diplomatic consequences of the meeting caused a storm.

18. Tu. [At sea]

We drove to the Deer park and Forest after breakfast through the long lines of suburban villas & got back before twelve, in time to receive the Imperial & Royal party, who were nearly forty strong (Sir D. C[urrie] has just told me 43) of these about 25 royalties. Nothing could go off better—the free & kindly manners of yesterday with the new incidents of a beautiful spectacle, & Tennyson's reading to them in the smoking-room. We sailed at 3.30, with the unusual accompaniment of bands playing & the rigging manned as we passed the great Russian Yacht & a Danish ship of war. So we went straight for England.

Read Madame de Sevigné and the Conservative Radical on a capital for the Empire in Palestine![1] Principal conversations today with Sir A. Gordon and Hallam Tennyson.[2] Tel. to Mr Hamilton.

19. Wed.

Movement in the earlier part of the day. We came straight from the Sc[agerrak] for England. Chief conversations: Sir A. Gordon—Mr Tennyson. Read Mad. de Sevigné and [blank]. Comic entertainment at night.

20. Th.

Wrote to The Queen l.l.[3]—Mr Hamilton Tel.—Princess of Wales Tel.

Tennyson read to us Elaine in the forenoon: & his wonderful Guinevere in the afternoon. Read Mad. de Sevigné.

With very rapid progress, we came near Gravesend (9 m off) at $6\frac{1}{2}$ in the evg: 670 knots in 51 hours: over 13 knots an hour. But the pilot would not go up to land us. Many arrangements had to be made for gifts & acknowledgements in ending our voyage of (I think) about 2000 miles.

21. Fr. [London]

Most friendly farewells and a rather triumphal landing at Gravesend with special train provided (*free*) to London. Arrived about one: with much cause for thankfulness to God. Saw Mr H.—N. Lyttelton—Sir H. Ponsonby—Mrs Gascoyne. X. Dined at Jane Wortleys. Wrote to The Queen—Ld Spencer—Ld Kinnaird—Mr Hamilton Tel.—Rev. Mr Kinnersley.

[22. Saturday [Hawarden]: no entry]

23. 18 S. Trin.

Ch. mg & evg. Wrote to Dean of St Paul's—Mr P. Salusbury—Mr Grimes[4]—

---

[1] 'The future capital of the British Empire. A possible solution of the Suez Canal and Eastern Question. By a Conservative-Radical' (1883).

[2] On an honour for Tennyson, Gordon suggesting a peerage; *The Gladstone Papers* (1930), 80 and Introduction above, vol. x.

[3] Requesting a barony for Tennyson; Guedalla, *Q*, ii. 245; see 25 Sept. 83.

[4] Thanking C. C. Grimes for a specially printed version of 'Senti, Senti'; Add MS 44546, f. 160.

Watson & Smith—and minutes. Read Brewster's 18th Cent.[1]—Nicole—Ben Hur[2]—and Drexelius, Heliotropium.[3]

24. M.

Ch. 8¼ A.M. Wrote to Mr Hamilton MP.—Mr Westell—Messrs Murray—Mr Hamilton Tel. l.l.l.—Mr Best—and minutes. Worked on books. Ld Granville came: much conversation. Read Mad. de Sevigné—Magazine of Amn History.

25. Tu.

Ch. 8½ A. M. Wrote to Mr Tennyson l.l.—Khedive of Egypt—Ld Kimberley—Mr Howell—Ld Derby—Mr Peace—Chancr of Exchr—and minutes. Forenoon, afternoon walk, & evening, gave me much conversation with Lord G. Worked on books. Read Mad. de Sevigné.

To H. C. E. CHILDERS, chancellor of the exchequer,   Add MS 44546, f. 161.
25 September 1883. '*Most Private*'.

The Queen has assented to a proposal of mine to bestow a Peerage upon Tennyson; but there will be a delay before it is actually given, so that it is to be kept quiet.

Although Tennyson's means are not so narrow as to exclude him from the honour, yet he is by no means a *rich* man; & I have examined the precedents to see whether he ought or ought not to be called upon to pay the fees (say £500)—I find that the charge has been remitted in four civil cases, three of which at least are by no means so strong as this, besides the military peerages where the remission seems to be very extended, embracing e.g. Lord Sandhurst. The four cases are Wensleydale & Elphinstone, with Canning on the step, & Brougham on the new patent (a very questionable case). I would therefore propose to let Tennyson off.

Macaulay appears to have paid; but he was a confirmed bachelor & there was no succession.

To LORD KIMBERLEY, Indian secretary, 25 September 1883.   Add MS 44546, f. 161.

I have received today your letters of 23rd and 24th[4] & have had the opportunity of showing them to Granville who is here for a couple of nights. We are both agreed in thinking that neither your sanction of the Bill, nor your finally assenting to the Bill which passed in India should be delayed for the meeting of Parliament.

Indeed I may add that I am not aware of any conclusive reasons which have led to the adoption of the amendments in the Bill, but this is not a practical point, as I would not propose to disturb them.[5]

[1] J. Brewster, *A secular essay* (1802); on the Hanoverian church.
[2] L. Wallace, *Ben-Hur: a tale of the Christ* (1880).
[3] Drexelius, *Heliotropium*, ed. R. N. Shutte (1881).
[4] Add MS 44228, ff. 105–111: proposes home govt. should allow the 'Ilbert' bill to proceed with amendments, leaving parliament to move a subsequent vote of censure, if it chooses; Viceroy's council agreed, save one. See 17 Apr. 83n.
[5] On 26 September, ibid., f. 113, Kimberley reported a letter from Ripon proposing postponement of the bill until after the Commons' vote next session; Gladstone wired Kimberley, 28 September, ibid., f. 116: 'I am strongly adverse to the request reported in yours of 26th. When ought it to be decided & do you think there should be a Cabinet upon it'. Northbrook and Hartington agreed in opposing postponement; ibid., f. 118.

To ALFRED TENNYSON, 25 September   Tennyson Research Centre, MS 3718.
1883.

[First letter:] I expect to receive tomorrow the Queen's answer to my submission respecting you.[1] I have no doubt whatever as to its favourable character. But it has occurred to me, since we parted, that it would be wise on your account, if some delay were interposed before any actual announcement is made, so as effectually to dissociate the peerage from the trip. As you know from various incidents of our conversation, I am not too ready in anticipating criticism. But in this case I am of opinion that some journals politically ill-natured would make use of the synchronism, and would intimate that something in the nature of a political service to the Government, by your lending lustre to the voyage, was at the bottom of a proposal, which it is desirable in a very high degree to cloud with no doubt as to its origin and purpose, which is to do honour first to you, and then to literature in your person. I think you will view favourably this suggestion, which of course does not import a single grain of uncertainty into the settlement of the matter.

Once for all, and in the fewest words, I wish to put on paper the expression of my intense satisfaction at my own share in this 'advancement': and to ask you to let Mrs. Tennyson know how entirely I have concurred with her view as to the terms on which you might properly part with your old and simple designation as a commoner.

The fully commented Dante of which I spoke to you is by Scartazzini, published by Brockhaus, of Leipzig, in three volumes. A less full but I think very good edition is Fraticelli's, in one volume of 700 pages, with a Rimario (Barbera, Florence). An edition at *one franc* with commentary is published by Camerini, (Milan, Sonzogno) dated 1879. Italy is still all alive about Dante: I have the commentary of De Marzo, quite recent, in two great quarto volumes.[2]

I have found the great passage of the 'darkness' cited in my poor article: but not the objection to which you referred. Could *your* memory have misled you?[3]

Tennyson Research Centre, MS 5964.

[Second letter:] I have not omitted to examine into the question of Fees in connection with your impending Peerage; and the result is such as to justify my communicating at the proper time[4] with the Chancellor of the Exchequer who I hope will raise no difficulty about allowing the charge to be borne by the Treasury.

26. Wed.

Ch. 8½ AM. Wrote to Mr Hamilton l. and tel.—Mr Lefevre—Lady Mar—D. of Devonshire—Ld Spencer—Prof. Worsaac—Mr H. Taylor—Rev. W. Goalen—Ld E. Clinton—Sir J. P. Hayward—Scotts—and minutes. Ld Granville went at 11.30 after a conversation which embraced my Ministerial prospects & the work of

[1] The barony, see 20 Sept. 83n.; for Gladstone's earlier attempts to honour Tennyson, see 28 Oct. 80.
[2] Editions of *La Divina Commedia* by G. A. Scartazzini, 4v. (Leipzig 1874–90); P. J. Fraticelli (Florence 1860); E. Camerini (Milan 1880); A. G. de Marzo, *Studi filosofici... su la Divina Commedia*, 3v. (1873–81).
[3] Tennyson's reply of 2 October, thanking Gladstone for being 'the first *thus* publicly to proclaim the position which Literature ought to hold in the world's work', concluded: 'I have truly forgotten what passage in Dante we were discussing'; Add MS 44483, f. 188.
[4] In fact this day.

next Session. Worked on books. Mr Costello[1] dined: very clever; without
ἀιδως.[2] Read Life of Ld Lawrence.[3] Drive with C.

27. Thurs.

Ch. 8½ A.M. Wrote to Ed. of Guardian—The Queen l.l.—Mr Cowan—Mr
Cameron—and minutes. Worked much on books. Conversation with Mr Cos-
tello mg: and *long* with Mr Scott Holland evg on the state & prospects of
Oxford. Read Millar on Robroy[4]—Life of Ld Lawrence.

To the Editor of *The Guardian*, 27 September 1883.   Add MS 44546, f. 162.
'*Private*'.

Mr. Gladstone presents his compliments to the Editor of the Guardian & having read
in yesterday's number the letter which couples his name with the Bishopric formed in
1841 at Jerusalem, is concerned to see that a quotation from a letter of his to Bishop Wilberforce, as it stands there, might be interpreted in a sense very disparaging to Archbishop Howley & Bishop Blomfield, for whose memories he entertains a deep & grateful
respect. The *full* sentence in the letter he thinks adequately explains the sense. It was discreditable to a Parliament to have passed the *two* Acts of 1841 and 1851: such at least is
his judgment.[5]
With respect to the Bishopric in question, Mr. Gladstone was requested by those
eminent Prelates to be a Trustee of the foundation. His extreme anxiety to act with them
at a critical time led him at first to comply. But as the proceedings developed themselves
he found them open to such grave objections that he was obliged to withdraw.
This letter is not intended for publicity, but there is no secret as to the contents.[6]

28. Fr.

Church 8½ A.M. Wrote to Ld Kimberley Tel.—Ld Granville—Watsons—Dean of
Durham—Ld Derby—Bp of Newcastle—Mr Dickson—Sir C. Dilke—Mr Bos-
worth Smith, & minutes. Worked on books. Further conversation with Mr
Holland. I want that some one should write the history of the singular & stupid
transformation of Oxford.[7] Read Life of Robroy—Life of Lawrence—Mad. de
Sevigné.

To LORD DERBY, colonial secretary, 28 September 1883.   Add MS 44546, f. 162.

I was under the impression, perhaps in error, that Bulwer had served his usual time, &
could be moved without scandal.[8]

[1] Perhaps Benjamin Francis Conn Costelloe, 1855–97; philosopher, and barrister and unsuccessful liberal candidate.
[2] 'a sense of modesty'.
[3] R. Bosworth Smith, *Life of Lord Lawrence*, 2 v. (1883).
[4] A. H. Millar, *The story of Rob Roy* (1883).
[5] 'Observer' in the *Guardian*, 26 September 1883, quoted Gladstone in 1861 in *Life of Wilberforce*,
iii. 40: 'I think there should be no recourse to that most discreditable Act of 1841', and quoted
extracts from Bunsen's *Memoirs*, i. 384, on Gladstone's reservations in 1840.
[6] No publication, or comment, found.
[7] i.e. the change in college statutes respecting the clergy; see, e.g. 24 Sept. 80.
[8] Derby reported, 26 September, Add MS 44141, f. 153, that Bulwer refused to go to Jamaica, and
to move him now would be to condemn his policy.

We shall I hope soon have the opportunity of talking over the matter. Meantime, like you, I do not feel that we have a case to condemn him. Perhaps in my own mind I am unconsciously unjust to him. What one desires is to have full confidence in one who represents & acts for us abroad in nice & difficult circumstances, & for whose proceedings we are absolutely responsible. To put the case at the worst, I was staggered at his change of opinion on the Zulu war; he strikes me as looking at every question through Natal spectacles; & I do not see in him that zealous desire to work in the spirit of those who instruct him, which I think there is a title to expect.

I wish I felt that we knew the real facts about Cetywayo.

What you say of the Reserve is I think indisputable:[1] & in the case of Grant everything depends on what the man is. I certainly should have thought it a strange course to give Blunt special facilities for communicating with Arabi.

I think Lady Derby may be interested in reading my report to Her Majesty, on our dealings with the Royalties (& Imperialities) at Copenhagen, & I send it accordingly. In writing to a less exalted personage I should have salted it a little.

It strikes me that on account of the old connection of your family with Hawarden, you may like to have a copy of a little Hand Book which has been drawn by my son.

To Sir C. W. DILKE, president of the local government board,   Add MS 43875, f. 143.
28 September 1883.

As the Cabinet is the many-sided buffer on which all the currents of will and opinion in the country spend themselves, so within the Cabinet the Prime Minister of the day is charged with the same passive function, & at the end of the session half his colleagues can usually make an excellent case against him for the chopping of Bills, which it has been their duty to press in vain.

Such is the law under which we live and such it will be, but I do incline to think that the catalogue of contemplated measures at the beginning of session 1883 was sanguine rather beyond the usual measure.

I am afraid however that the remedy is not so obvious as might at first sight appear. For in the very year in which the Cabinet included, we may say, too much in the Speech List, the House of Commons has outdone itself in forcing upon us abstract resolutions in favour of many other measures each of which amounts nearly to a declaration that we ought to have included more.

Still I hope that the list for next year will include your Ballot Act Bill,[2] & yet that it will be practicable to make it a very short list.

29. *Sat & St M.*

Ch. 8½ and Holy Commn. Wrote to Capt. Bigge Tel.[3]—Mr H. Mayhew—Scotts—Archdn Norris—Mr Jackson—Ly Tweeddale—Mr Hamn—Ld Hothfield—Mr Tennyson—& minutes. Worked on books. Saw Mr [blank] Parsee. Kibbling a beech. Read Only a Girl[4]—Bussy Rabutin, Hist. Am. des Gaules[5]—and [blank.]

---

[1] Cannot be given to Cetewayo: best hope that Bulwer will persuade him to return to his own country; ibid.

[2] Bill to extend hours of polling; passed in July 1884; see Gwynn, ii. 5.

[3] (Sir) Arthur John *Bigge, 1849–1931; Victoria's assistant secretary; secretary to prince of Wales 1901–10; cr. Lord Stamfordham 1911.

[4] C. Clayton, *Only a girl* (1883); Gladstone thought it 'beautiful' and sent it to Mrs Thistlethwayte.

[5] R. de Rabutin, Count de Bussy, *Histoire amoureuse des Gaules* (1666; many later eds.).

30. 19 S. Trin.

Ch. 11 AM 6½ PM. Wrote to Mrs Saunders—The Speaker—Rev. Mr Greig—and minutes. Read Mr Greig's MS & one Chapter[1]—Report of Free Italian Church—Allies, a Life's decision[2]—and 'Only a girl'.

Mond. Oct. One 1883.

Ch. 8½ A.M. Saw Bailey, for a little more bookcasing. Worked on books. Wrote to Ld Hartington—Mr Hamilton—Mr M'Coll—Dean of St Pauls—Mrs Bolton—Prof. Lankester[3]—& minutes. Read Hartington on Ilbert Bill[4]—Prof. Lankester's Lecture—Only a Girl—Mad. de Sevigné. C.G. came back from the Neville marriage[5]—God bless them.

2. Tu.

Ch. 8½ A.M. Wrote to Mr Trevelyan—Ld Spencer—Ld Derby—Lady Sydney—Chancr of Exchr—H. Irving[6]—Mr Escott—Mr Howell—and minutes. Worked on books. Eleven to dinner. Woodcraft with MG. Read Mad. de Sevigné—Only a Girl (finished)—Fortnightly R. on Balkans—French Col. Policy—and Biographies.[7]

To LORD DERBY, colonial secretary, 2 October 1883.   Add MS 44546, f. 165.

I cannot regret that the affair of the Florence[8] has had the effect of a reconsideration of the constitution under which Jamaica is now ruled.

And I read your letter and plan without stumbling, or even pause, so far as the argument & the merits are concerned, until I came to the last paragraph and the minority vote.

Here too I acknowledge that the peculiar circumstances of Jamaica fairly raise the question whether this plan of voting should not be adopted there.

But apart from the question of this paragraph I should have suggested to you whether an alteration of the existing state of things in Jamaica, *especially* if as I presume it requires legislation, should not be submitted to the Cabinet.[9] The introduction of the minority vote only serves to accentuate a little this idea.

[P.S.] I have the most perfect faith in your impartiality with respect to Bulwer; and I admit the weight of what you say. I was under the impression, as to the Zulu war, that, having originally objected, he came round to it.

---

[1] David Greig, d. 1903; rector of Addington from 1869; had sent the MS of a treatise on the Church; Gladstone successfully discouraged publication as Palmer still sufficient; Add MS 44546, f. 164.   [2] By T. W. Allies (1880).

[3] (Sir) Edwin Ray *Lankester (1847-1929; professor of zoology, London) had sent his 'Address to the biological section of the British Association' (1883).

[4] Hartington's 'admirable speech' on the Ilbert Bill, which Gladstone wished to send to the Queen; Add MS 44546, f. 164.   [5] See 21 July 83.

[6] Inviting the actor to Hawarden on his way to America; Add MS 44546, f. 165; see 9 Oct. 83.

[7] F.R., xl. 457, 521 (October 1883).

[8] Unofficial members of the Jamaican council had resigned following the vote on the costs of the 'Florence' affair, ship loaded with arms arrested 1877, a constitutional row ensuing; see PP 1882 xlvi. 125. Derby sent draft constitution, with representation of 'the minority' secured by cumulative votes or only two votes per elector; Derby commented: 'responsible government as in Canada and Australia is scarcely suited to a negro population'; Add MS 44141, f. 160.   [9] See 10 Nov. 83.

To LORD SPENCER, Viceroy of Ireland, 2 October 1883.					Althorp MSS K6.

1. Many thanks for your letter of the 30th.[1] I do not at all agree with the arguments used, as you report, by your magistrates and constabulary, and I am very glad they were resisted; but I think the prohibition you actually issued rested on a different ground and is fairly to be viewed as a measure for the preservation of the peace. 2. I do not know in what instance we yielded anything to Parnell in the House of Commons last year, except upon the merits. Does Mr. Dickson think that the desires of the 'Moderate Liberals' ought to be granted apart from a consideration of their merits? That is not a policy obviously safe or easy in a country where these moderate Liberals are reported to be so weak that we are threatened with their almost entire extinction at the next election. 3. Though the sharpest of the Irish crisis has gone by under your administration & the Land Law, I do not doubt, I wish I could, that the Government of Ireland in an honest way will still & probably long be a matter of continual anxiety to those who carry it on. 4. Your view of the question touching the Cabinet is a generous one. I am afraid I see more difficulties in it than you do. In the Irish Department, as such, it would not be easy to establish the superiority of the Peer resident in Ireland to his colleague who bears the Parliamentary pressure: and in the Cabinet have you considered how the absent man is to balance the present one? 5. We leave home on the 9th for some days: but I write to invite Trevelyan on the 13th by which day we shall return.

3. Wed.

Ch. 8½ A.M. Wrote to Attorney General—The Queen l.l.—Sir D. Currie—Ld Granville—Ld E. Clinton—Duke of Argyll—Mr Tennyson—Duke of Leinster— Watsons—Mr Seymour Tel.—and minutes. Read Roxana[2]—Lady Huntingdon's Hymns[3]—Conduct of the Duchess of Marlborough.[4] Woodcraft. Saw Mr Mayhew: & opened to Herbert the question whether he should take to the Aston brickwork. Worked on Books.

To the DUKE OF ARGYLL, 3 October 1883.					Add MS 44546, f. 166.

I hope you will entertain propitiously the proposal I now make to you, with the sanction of the Queen, that you should accept one of the two vacant Garters, cumulating it with your Order of the Thistle. That Order duly notes your general character and position. This I hope will acknowledge your long, loyal, and able services, and also your great distinctions outside the line of politics.

Looking back over the history of our relations in politics and in office, I have the most lively pleasure in conveying this offer, which will be stamped and sealed if and when you accept it.[5]

Remember me very kindly to the Duchess.

[P.S.] I see that in my retrospective sentence I have not mentioned, as I ought, personal relations: the truth is I was thinking of what was so very special in your case, your most generous efforts, in trying cases, to prolong the fulness of concord and cooperation.

---

[1] Add MS 44310, f. 155; difficulties of preventing National League meetings; Ulster M.P.s feel Parnell gets too much attention; Spencer will not stand in way of promotion of Trevelyan to the cabinet.

[2] D. Defoe, *Roxana, or the fortunate mistress* (1724).

[3] i.e. by Selina *Hastings, Lady Huntingdon, foundress of the Huntingdon connexion.

[4] [N. Hooke], *An account of the conduct of the dowager Duchess of Marlborough* (1742).

[5] He accepted; also offered this day to Leinster, who declined it.

To Sir H. JAMES, attorney general, 3 October 1883.   Add MS 44546, f. 166.

Though in the shape of a kind of gift of grouse we have had evidence of your activity, your latitude, and your benevolence, I know not your 'periodical time' nor where you may now be. But if you are moving or about to move southward, I venture to say how accept-able a visit from you would be.[1] On and after the 13th we hope to be at home. On that day I have some hope of Trevelyan.

There is a matter important though not very complex (as I hope) on which I want to consult you. I cannot think it unlikely that we shall try to deal with the County Suffrage next Session, and if so at the opening of it. If the Cabinet should decide to proceed with this measure for the three kingdoms, would it be practicable, as matter of drafting, to do it in one and the same Bill? There would obviously be very great Parliamentary advantage in such a course. It is conceivable that this might be done in either of two ways: either by an extension in each country of the town household suffrage to the country, or by a single enactment: but practically I suppose there may be insuperable difficulties of form attach-ing to this latter mode.

[P.S.] I hope that, after your time of relaxation, you are not the worse for your great labours during the Session.

To ALFRED TENNYSON, 3 October 1883.   Tennyson Research Centre, MS 5966.

It is only today that I am able to send you a conclusive and I hope satisfactory letter about the matter of the Peerage.[2]

I am sorry, especially considering *our* time of life, that there should be any delay. But I still more recoil from the idea of giving occasion to any silly scribe who might be tempted to associate the Peerage with the Pembroke Castle. The Queen suggested postponing until the time when the Session opens, say February 1. This seemed to me a little beyond the necessity of the case, and she agrees to its being before Christmas. Between Decem-ber and other date it is now for yourself to choose.

There is no public reason why Lionel should be excluded from this knowledge as with-out doubt he can keep the secret.

Also, having examined into the matter, I feel quite justified in saying that your Peerage will be accompanied with that remission of fees which has been very usual in the case of military Peerages, and which has been given in a few civil instances.

[P.S.] I have telegraphed in anticipation of this letter.

4. Th.

Harvest *Actio.* Ch. 8½ A.M. and part evg service. Wrote to Ld Kimberley Tel l.l.—Ld Granville l. & Tel.—Chancr of Exr—Mr Phillips—Archdn Watkins—The Speaker—Sir J. Lacaita—Mr Barry OBrien, & minutes. The André minstrels[3] came over & in the afternoon performed very nicely in the Library before a party. Worked on Books. Read Roxana—Duchess of Marlborough—Progress & Poverty.[4]

[1] See 19 Oct. 83.

[2] See 25 Sept. 83.

[3] Prof. André's Alpine Choir.

[4] By Henry George; perhaps Gladstone forgot his earlier reading, see 11 Nov. 79; see also to Bed-ford, 27 Dec. 83.

To R. BARRY O'BRIEN, 4 October 1883.   Add MS 44546, f. 168.

I have not forgotten your striking History of the Land Question for Ireland,[1] and I shall consequently read with much interest the work on the Half Century of Concessions[2] which you have been kind enough to send me, & for which I beg to return my best thanks.

5. Fr.

Ch. 8¼ A.M. Wrote to Ld Granville—Lady Derby—Mr Holt—Mr Irving—Rev. Mr Foxley—Lady Sydney—Mr Freeman—Mr Seymour—& minutes. Worked on books. Walk with S. & Mr [R.] Linklater. Read Roxana—Mad. de Sevigné—Duchess of Marlborough.

6. Sat.

Ch. 8¼ A.M. Wrote to Ld Granville—Mr Seymour—The Queen—Mrs Th.—& minutes. Read Moncure Conway on 'Gladstone'[3]—Conduct of Dss of M. (finished)—Roxana. Cut an oak with Herbert. Worked on papers.

7. 20 S. Trin.

Ch. 11 A.M. with H.C. and 6¼ P.M. Wrote to Ld Granville—& minutes. Read Allies Life's Decision—Green's Lay Sermons[4]—Divers Tracts—Bp Wordsworth's Charge.

8. M. [Knowsley Hall]

Ch. 8¼ A.M. Wrote to Mr Patterson (U.S.)[5]—Bp of Lincoln—Mr Beith[6]—Dean of Durham—The Queen—Mr Seymour—Dr Nevin—Mr Linklater—Rev. Mr Dunn—and minutes. In afternoon went to Knowsley; all courtesy & kindness there.[7] Much conversation with Lord D[erby]. Worked on papers. Read 'Marriage'[8]—Russell on Irving in F.R.[9]

9. Tu.

Wrote to Ld Granville—Ld Mayor Elect—and minutes. Mr Irving here 1½–6. We conversed freely on divers matters: he was treated with singular courtesy. Read Marriage—Barry OBrien's Hist Ireland[10]—Progress & Poverty. Large dinner party: conversation with Mr Holt: also with Mr Hale on the *old* Bootle, Sea-

---

[1] See 5 Nov. 80.

[2] See 9 Oct. 83.

[3] M. D. Conway, 'Gladstone', *N.A.R.*, cxxxvi. 223 (March 1883); an interesting radical critique of Gladstone's 'Right centre . . . embodiment'.

[4] T. H. Green, *Witness of God and faith: two lay sermons* (1883).

[5] C. B. Patterson.

[6] John Alexander Beith, Manchester merchant and liberal; on the disastrous by-election there; Add MS 44482, f. 213.

[7] For this visit, see below, Appendix I.   [8] S. E. Ferrier, *Marriage, a novel* (1818).

[9] *F.R.*, xl. 466 (October 1883).

[10] R. Barry O'Brien, 1st v. of *Fifty years of concessions to Ireland 1831–1881*, 2v. (1883–5).

forth, & shore. Went over the House again with Mr Irving. My memory for new visible objects is now sadly impaired.

10. Wed.

Wrote to The Queen—Ld Kimberley—Ld Granville—Ld Hartington—and minutes. Mr Latter[1] initiated me a little into the treasures of the splendid library. Long & interesting conversation with Lady D. on Lord B., H.M., D.s resignation, & other matters. We drove to Liverpool & had a great luncheon at Mr Holt's: a gathering of local liberal notabilities. Read Barry OBrien—Miss Ferrier's Marriage.

To LORD HARTINGTON, war secretary, 10 October 1883.   Add MS 44546, f. 170.

When Childers was Secretary for War, I looked into the question of employing Post Offices for recruiting [soldiers] and he appeared to me to be right.[2] I am willing if you like to write to Fawcett, but it would not I think produce any effect. The Treasury without doubt can override him: but I incline to believe that the most politic and most pacific course might be to let him come to the Cabinet and state his case & then settle the matter there by the highest which is also the greatest authority.
[P.S.] I told Granville to have no scruple about asking for a Cabinet in case of need, but I do not see that his matters are taking such a course as to make it likely that he will require one.

To LORD KIMBERLEY, Indian secretary, 10 October 1883.   Add MS 44546, f. 170.

I am very glad we all concur against postponing the Ilbert Bill.[3] Glad, but not surprised. The only thing that surprises me is the suggestion from over the water. Perhaps it would be kind if I write briefly to Ripon.
[P.S.] Derby has seen these papers and quite agrees with us. So now we have a strong *consensus* including three Indian Secretaries & a Governor General.

11. Th.

Wrote to Mr Bencke—Viceroy of India—Rev. Mr Greig—Ld R. Grosvenor—and minutes. At 10 we went off to see the Mersey Tunnel & walked to the close: conversation with the engineer & others. Then to the Exhibition of Pictures.[4] Conversation with Ld Gerard—Sir J. Lubbock—Lady D. Read as yesterday—and Symonds on Renaissance.[5] Large party. Conversation with Mr [blank] and Mr Lister;[6] both very able men.

[1] The librarian.
[2] Hartington had been working to remove Fawcett's objections to this, 'but without success'; Add MS 44146, f. 218. See cabinet, 13 Nov. 83.
[3] See 25 Sept. 83n. Kimberley, 12 October, Add MS 44228, f. 120, thought Ripon 'rather too anxious to shift the responsibility for the Bill off the Govt. of India'.
[4] i.e. the Walker art gallery.
[5] See 8 Nov. 77.
[6] Perhaps Edward Lister of Everton and Monmouthshire; D.L. and J.P.

To A. H. BENCKE, 11 October 1883.   Add MS 44546, f. 171.

I am very sensible of the importance of the subject of your letter.[1] But I feel some doubt and hesitation as to the extent of my own province in the matter. Lord Derby's having entered the Liberal Ministry may alter his position in regard to the S.W. Lancashire Election.[2] But I am not sure whether his having become my colleague alters my position with regard to him. Now my position in S.W. Lancashire is that of a voter qualified by an extremely small proprietary interest. I think the best course I can take is to refer to the political friend who may be called our central adviser on these matters which I need hardly say are not generally within my cognisance. I will therefore send your letter to Lord Richard Grosvenor and take his advice in regard to it.

To LORD RIPON, Viceroy of India, 11 October 1883.   Add MS 43515, f. 28.

A few words about your Ilbert Bill.[3] I hope you will not be surprised or vexed at our being strongly for the Bill as against postponement. I was quite ready to call the Cabinet: but as a preliminary opinions were taken from 6 ministers including 3 Secretaries for India & our ex Gov. General, & we were all agreed as I believe the rest of our colleagues would have been. I think it very likely that the object of your suggestion was to diminish pressure upon us, but we would rather meet the pressure whatever it may be. We could on no account take the initiative in submitting the Bill to the House of Commons for this would in our view be handing over our responsibility as an Executive to a branch of the Legislature. We do not believe your opponents would be conciliated by postponement. Quieter they might be till the time for resuming action came, but they would at once feel themselves stronger, & at the critical time would be fiercer, while native confidence would be shaken, and we should quiver under intimidation of no elevated order. So far I think we, I certainly, & deliberately, sanctioned counting out Ashmead Bartlett.[4]

1. Both sides wished it.
2. No direct issue *could* have been taken.
3. The numbers of the House were so thin, that no one could have called it a real Parliamentary judgement.
4. Ashmead would have discharged upon you a whole *main sewer* of filth with a thousand new & unheard of assertions which could not be submitted at once to confrontation by argument, & some of the dirt would have stuck.
5. The effect of the operation was judgment not for but in contempt.

I must close for the post with all good wishes.

12. Fr. [Hawarden]

Wrote to Ld Granville—Ld Wolverton—The Queen—Watsons—Archdn of Bristol—and minutes. Walk with Ld D: also long conversation. Read Marriage— Barry OBrien's Hist. and [blank.] Off to Hawarden at 3 after a visit made very genial by great kindness received. Saw Bp of Chester in Chester.

---

[1] Not found; Albert H. Bencke, liberal activist in Lancashire.

[2] The constituency where Gladstone was defeated in 1865; it was held by the tories until redistributed 1885.

[3] On 10 August, Add MS 44287, f. 7, Ripon argued for proceeding with the bill with some modifications; docketed by Gladstone: 'a. by Tel. S.5'; no later letter found. See 17 Apr. 83n., 26 Sept. 83n.

[4] On 3 August; Bartlett protested next day; nonetheless, he made a violent speech on the Ilbert Bill on 22 August; *H* 282. 1536, 283. 1670.

13. Sat.

Ch. 8½ A.M. Wrote to Mr Seymour Tel.—Ld Granville Tel. l.l. Ll. l.—Herbert J.G.—Mr W.T. Evans[1]—Mr E. Vincent—Mr Bright—Ld Wolverton—& minutes. Worked on books: I have new space for about 1700 volumes. Read Memoir of my dear friend J. Hope Scott in proof[2]—Marriage. The Trevelyans came. Conversation with him. Also Robert Gladstones. Eight to dinner.

To H. J. GLADSTONE, M.P., 13 October 1883.   Add MS 44546, f. 173.
'*Private*'.

I inclose a slip for the Postmaster General [Fawcett][3] and, referring to our conversation before parting, I add a few words upon it.

1. It will be a solecism and a mistake if the several constituencies of the country, or even the greatest and most intelligent among them—a class to which yours undoubtedly belongs—undertake to formulate the course of business in Parliament; for they cannot possibly have adequate information to guide their judgment in such a matter, which preeminently belongs to the Cabinet.

2. John Bright has got hold of the right end of the stick, and I advise you to work in the sense of recommending people, as far as you safely can, to *wait* for what he has to say, and to give weight to so experienced a judgment; nor would it be a bad thing if you could see Bright and tell him all you know of my lines on this matter which are I believe in conformity with his.

3. You can I think safely give an opinion that as far as you can judge taking the suffrage at once would not be likely to hurry the Dissolution.

4. And yet more would it be unlikely to hurry my retirement. I think I can, please God, face the suffrage question; I am by no means sure that I can remain in office for the two very large and complex measures relating to Local Government in the counties and to a London Municipality.

4. Let me know at what times during the next four weeks you are likely to be here. The Derbys come on the 1st November for two nights. We should like you to see them. Also we want to get the young Newcastle here.

14. 21 S. Trin.

Ch. mg & evg. Wrote to [blank] and minutes. Read (much) of the Proofs of my dear friend Jas Hope's noteworthy life. And the Durell Prayerbook.[4] Walk with the Gentlemen.

15. M.

Ch. 8½ A.M. Wrote to Mr Seymour Tel.—Ld Kimberley Tel.—Sir Thos G.—Ld Granville—Sir A. Gordon—Mr Ornsby[5]—Sir H.P.—& minutes. Worked on books. Further conversation with Trevelyan. Finished Proof Sheets. Read Marriage—Barry O'Brien's Hist. Tea at Mr Helberts & saw his 'improvement'.

---

[1] On 'Senti, Senti'; Add MS 44546, f. 173.

[2] Proofs of R. Ornsby's memoir.

[3] A strong protagonist of parliamentary reform, including proportional representation and women's suffrage.

[4] C. Marshall, *The Latin prayer book of Charles II* (1882).

[5] Comments on his proofs, in Lathbury, ii. 321.

16. Tu.

Ch. 8½ A.M. Wrote to Messrs Rivington—Ld Granville L. & 2 Tell.—Mrs Bolton—Sir W. James—Messrs Skeffington—Mr Stuart Reid—& minutes. Drive with C. to Park Farm. Woodcraft. Worked on books. Read Marriage (finished)—Barry O'Brien's Hist.—Life of J. Skinner.[1]

To S. J. REID, 16 October 1883.   Add MS 44546, f. 175.

I knew Mr. Sydney Smith for a good many years but I was not intimate with him.[2] I remember however one incident that may be told to the credit of his modesty. I was invited in 1833 to meet him at dinner in the House of Mr. Hallam the historian (the house made famous through *In Memoriam*). After dinner he spoke to me for some time very kindly. The conversation at one moment turned on the improvement which was then becoming visible in the character & conduct of the Clergy. He dwelt upon the rapid advance and wide scope of this improvement, and good humouredly added, in illustration of what he had said, 'Whenever you meet a man of *my* age, you may be sure he is a bad clergyman.'
[P.S.] I could not venture on such an estimate as you suggest.

17. Wed.

Ch. 8½ AM. Wrote to Ld Wolverton—Sir A. Gordon—Mr E. Arnold—Ld Granville L. & Tel.—Scott (Mr Hoare)—Archdeacon of Bristol—Mr Hayward—Mr Seymour Tel.—& minutes. Worked on books: what a (manual) job it is! Read Edinb. Rev. on Ld Aberdeen[3]—Defoe's Roxana—Q.R. on Provost Hawkins[4]—Barry O'Brien.

18. St Luke. Th.

Ch. 8½ A.M. and H.C. Wrote to Robn & Nicholson—Sir W. Harcourt—Mr Sturrock—Mr Seymour Tel—& minutes. Walk with C. Worked on books. I am now at last through the *rough* of it. Read Q.R. on Bugeaud[5]—Roxana, finished—Remarks on Duchess of Marlboroughs Tract.

To Sir W. V. HARCOURT, home secretary,   MS Harcourt dep. Adds 10.
18 October 1883.

We reckon that you and Lady Harcourt will about this time be setting your faces Southward, and we hope nothing need prevent your giving us the favour of a visit on your way.

As I was about to write this petition, a letter came in from Mr Rathbone expressing a desire that I should beg you to go a little further into North Wales and play the first part in a demonstration which is to serve as counterblast to the rather feeble affair of

___

[1] M. Trench, *James Skinner* (1883).
[2] Reid wrote asking for material for his work, published as *A sketch of the life and times of . . . Sydney Smith* (1884), and requesting 'an estimate of Sydney Smith's services to the state'; Add MS 44482, f. 245. This letter, the origin of this famous *mot* about the clergy, is printed on p. 368.
[3] H. Reeve, *E.R.*, clviii. 547 (October 1883); review of the 1850-3 privately printed vol. (see 11 Sept. 83); detailed observations at Add MS 44546, f. 176.
[4] *Q.R.*, clvi. 305 (October 1883).
[5] *Q.R.*, clvi. 452 (October 1883).

Northcote's visit. As there is to be a counterblast, it ought certainly to be a good one and [*sic*]: but I feel that I can only lay the case before you, both on account of my own abstention which makes it unseemly too much to press others, and on other grounds which may make you reluctant to undertake at this moment any public duties. But assuredly if you can brace yourself to the effort and are good enough to do it, the public advantage will be great.

I am just expecting the Attorney General and hoping for a full talk with him on the franchise question, without prejudice of course.

To MESSRS ROBERTSON AND NICHOLSON,   Add MS 44546, f. 177.
wine shippers, 18 October 1883.

Please to send to me, by good train, care of Hawarden carrier, Red Lion Inn, Chester, 3 dozen *dry* Port, same quality and price as you procured for me not long ago from a foreign gentleman or firm whose name I forget.

To J. F. STURROCK, 18 October 1883.   Add MS 44546, f. 177.

I need hardly assure you that all my wishes and hopes will be with Mr. Trevelyan in the coming election to the Rectorship of Edinburgh, and I feel that his election will supply an appropriate and most gratifying recognition of his excellent service to the Crown and the country in a very arduous office.

For my friend Professor Blackie I heartily desire every honour which a contest not political could confer on him. In this political contest, however, I fear that, while it may be impossible for him to win, his standing may have the effect of diverting votes from what you and I should call the good cause, and thus of impairing or worse than impairing the expression of the sense of the University which he so long adorned.[1]

19. Fr.

Ch. 8½ A.M. Wrote to Viceroy of Ireland—Bp of Manchester—Ld Granville—Mr Seymour Tel.—and minutes. Spent the forenoon with the A.G.[2] on Madagascar & (mainly) the franchise. Drive & walk with the party in aftn. Read Barry O'Brien. Duchess & Lady A. came over to tea.

To LORD SPENCER, Viceroy of Ireland, 19 October 1883.   Althorp MSS K6.
'*Private*'.

Since Trevelyan left us, a question has come up on which I should have been very glad to speak to him. I spent the whole forenoon today in preliminary conversation with the Attorney General, mainly on the subject of the Franchise. We got pretty well through England and Scotland, but where we have travelled into Ireland we found ourselves in a very deep quagmire. And I am very desirous to know whether you have anyone who could be sent over to England to give, to me in the first place, information on the subject—some one who knows thoroughly not only the statistics of your Parliamentary system but the composition temper and distribution of classes in Ireland, in effect the social state of the country.[3]

---

[1] Blackie declined to withdraw and Northcote was elected, the liberal vote being split. John F. Sturrock graduated in medicine from Edinburgh 1885; until 1886, many Edinburgh doctors were liberal.

[2] i.e. Henry James, summoned for the franchise, see 3 Oct. 83.

[3] Spencer suggested A. M. Porter, J. Naish (Irish law officers) and J. G. Greene, boundary surveyor; he informed Hartington of Gladstone's views; *Spencer*, i. 253.

It is impossible I think to touch the Franchise on this side the water without touching it on that; and I hold it also out of the question to offer Ireland an unreal[?] measure of extension. Beyond this I have not yet got, and I press my present petition with a view to future progress.

One grave point for consideration is whether the introduction of the labourers into the Constituencies would be a measure favourable or unfavourable to the interests of ultra-nationalism.[1]

[P.S.] Some chance of a Cabinet next week but I cannot yet say more. Please let this note be returned to me (in a day or two) it is written in haste to save the post.

Sat. 20.

Ch. 8½ AM. Read Barry OBrien—Defoe's Colonel Jack.[2] Mr Balfour[3] came: & Lucy. We sat late. Walk with the party in aft. Conversation renewed with A.G. who went off at 11. Wrote to Ld Granville l. & Tel.—Mr Childers—Mr Ornsby[4]—Mr Seymour Tel.—& minutes.

21. S. 22 Trin.

Ch. 11 A.M. and 6½ P.M. Wrote to Ld Kimberley—Mrs Th.—and minutes. Read Allies Decision of a Life—Life of Bp Rundle[5]—Brewster Ch. of 18th Cent.[6] We discussed the Cowper Hymn Translation. Walk with the party.

To LORD KIMBERLEY, Indian secretary, 21 October 1883.   Add MS 44546, f. 178.

My answer to your letter of the 18th[7] will be very short, first because as you know by this time we are to meet on Friday and secondly because I agree with the letter and adopt it *en bloc* while I understand and accept the reasons for reserved expression in your draft of Dispatch.

Ripon has got into an impenetrable mist. Hesitation on our part now would be a mistake of the worst kind, possibly with consequences of a very far reaching kind.

22. M.

Ch. 8½ A.M. Wrote to Mr Seymour Tel.—Ld Granville l. & Tel.—Sir H. Ponsonby—Sir J.K. James—Ld Bath—Rev. Mr Greig—Mr Wirz—Ld Hartington—Mrs Th.—& minutes. Walk with the party. Ten to dinner. Read Colonel Jack—Barry OBrien—Clare's Speech,[8] and Historic Tracts.

---

[1] Spencer replied, 20 October Add MS 44310, f. 159, that 'it is very formidable to be argued that if the Franchise is lowered, the Liberals will not be able to count on returning a single member in Ireland'—this the view of 'many men' and of the law officers; even so, objections to leaving Ireland out are even greater.

[2] D. Defoe, *Colonel Jack* (1723).

[3] i.e. A. J. Balfour; H.V.B.

[4] In Lathbury, ii. 323.

[5] Perhaps T. Rundle, bp. of Derry, *Memoirs* (1789).

[6] See 23 Sept. 83.

[7] *Sc.* 19th., Add MS 44228, f. 128, sending Ripon's letter, but still resolved against 'any symptom of wavering'. See 17 Apr. 83n.

[8] Probably 'Speech of the Earl of Clare on the subject of a legislating union between Great Britain and Ireland' (1800).

To LORD HARTINGTON, war secretary, 22 October 1883.   Add MS 44546, f. 179.
'*Private*'.

The immediate object of summoning the Cabinet is to dispose of the questions relating to Madagascar[1] and the evacuation of Cairo. But it may be convenient, as we move to assemble, that we should speak of some other things, and I think it is only due to my colleagues that I should say something of my own personal position. This connects itself with the business of the next session; and, though I do not wish to bind them in any way, I am ready to bind myself to a certain extent and on certain suppositions.

Your great kindness, & that of our colleagues in the House of Commons, allowed me to come through the last session, and might carry me through the next, if it were to be like the last. But I feel myself, in point of mental force, quite unequal to facing work such as that of 1881, or in fact any very grave and complex constructive measure.

The first and main question, then, arises, what do the public interests require the Government to undertake in the way of legislation for 1884. And here, at the outset, I entertain no doubt that the equalisation of the Suffrage is the question of questions for the time;[2] and that, as we all believe it is to be dealt with effectually by the present Parliament, it should be the first measure of the season.

I mean the equalisation of suffrage in town and country, apart from the much more complicated matter of redistribution: and such a question, so limited, I should not be afraid, according to any judgment I can now form, to face, if it is desired. Important as it would be, it need not occupy, perhaps, so much as half the Session; and it might thus leave room for a measure or measures of Local Government, comprehending England and Scotland, though hardly Ireland too. Such a programme would seem ample, as far as first class measures are concerned.

It would I think be impolitic and inequitable to exclude Ireland from both these great subjects: I believe too that the exclusion would ensure failure.

The Suffrage Bill, being single barrelled in respect to redistribution, would be fragmentary indeed if it dealt with England only and I apprehend it ought to deal with the three kingdoms.

It is an important question whether it should assimilate as between Counties & Boroughs in Ireland on the present Irish footing, unequal with Great Britain; or whether it should assimilate the franchise of all the three countries. On this I have not arrived at a conclusion: but I think the question, whether household suffrage might not be in Ireland more conservative than the £4 franchise, through the admission of the labourers to the vote, well deserves consideration.

This is, in brief, what I propose to lay out before the Cabinet, but there can be no occasion for pressing them to decide: indeed decision so long before action might entail inconvenience.

I write this as I do not expect to find you in London before the day of the Cabinet.[3]

To Sir H. PONSONBY, the Queen's secretary,   Add MS 45724, f. 148.
22 October 1883.

The Queen's observation upon the continuance of the agitation against the Ilbert Bill is, I fear, most just;[4] though I have looked inquisitively for arguments against the measure, & have not found them.

---

[1] Question of compensation for G. A. Shaw, British missionary arrested there by the French.
[2] i.e. the great N.L.F. conference on reform just held in Leeds; Jones, *1884*, 3.
[3] See 7 Nov. 83n.
[4] The Queen observed that the excitement had not abated; Guedalla, *Q*, ii. 249.

The objections to giving way are I conceive quite overwhelming. The Colonial & Indian policy of the last 50 years has not been regulated by the British minorities in India & the Colonies, & if it had been so its character would have been fundamentally different. What is still worse is that the postponement which is now demanded really means no more or less than handing over to the House of Commons the responsibility of the Executive, a course most injurious to the Crown & country, and in itself (I am afraid) when examined shabby to the last degree.

[P.S.] The few words I have used are an indication only.

I will acquaint Dean Lake.

I have summoned the Cabinet for Thursday: the occasion Madagascar, & also Cairo, on which we are now fully advised from Egypt.

23. Tu.

Ch. 8½ A.M. Wrote to Ld Derby l. & Tel.—Mr Seymour Tel.—Mrs Th.—Mr Milnes Gaskell[1]—Mrs B.—Mr Trevelyan—& minutes. Saw N. Lyttelton respecting Mr N. Grosvenor: Sir J. Lacaita respecting his son: Photographer respecting Castle: Mr Argyropulos & Mr Vitalis respecting the Statue for Greece.[2] Read the very interesting Vol. of C. Milnes Gaskell—Life of Rev. Mr Skinner.

To LORD DERBY, colonial secretary, 23 October 1883.   Add MS 44141, f. 169.

I hope that my telegram of this morning set your mind, which had naturally been discomforted,[3] at ease.

The direct objects of Thursday's Cabinet are two. 1 Cairo. To put members in a condition to 'submit' the evacuation with all the weight & authority we possess. 2. Madagascar. To accept the £1000 for Shaw—the rather restrained expression of regret for ourselves—& to decide on the exact method of proceeding as to Capt. Johnstone.[4]

I feel a strong assurance that the proceedings of the Cabinet on these points will be in harmony with your views.[5]

I intend on Thursday, or on Friday at a later time than 12, to enter on the subject of next Session's business by way rather of personal explanation, but not to ask for a decision.

I think it not unlikely that other questions may be raised but more probably on Friday than on Thursday. Bright is to meet you here on the 1st.

PS I go up to morrow by Irish mail.

To C. MILNES GASKELL, 23 October 1883.   Add MS 44546, f. 180.

The arrival of your book this morning has been, shall I say, an event in my life: at any rate I have been absorbed in it, and have read it with intense interest and delight from

---

[1] C. G. Milnes-Gaskell (see 5 Feb. 73) sent his privately printed ed. of J. Milnes Gaskell, *Records of an Eton schoolboy* (1883), which was published in a shorter form as *An Eton boy* (1939); it has much detail on Gladstone's schooldays.

[2] Statue for Athens; see 26 Oct. 83.

[3] Difficulty of attending cabinet; Add MS 44141, f. 166.

[4] Charles Johnstone, 1843-1929; rewarded for his part in the Madagascar affair by promotion to captain; later vice-admiral; see Ramm II, ii. 489.

[5] Derby replied, 24 October, Add MS 44142, f. 1: 'Your answer sets one quite at ease. I go with you entirely, as you know, on the Egyptian question. . . . As to Madagascar, assuming that Mr Shaw gets his £1000, and we an expression of regret, I think we may be glad to "close the incident". . . .'

beginning to end. It is a revived, almost a new image, of Arthur Hallam, a living exhibition of your father in his brightest light, a fountain of living comment & much interesting information from him on public affairs, and a renewal for a moment of boyhood and of youth in all their freshness.

And I can most sincerely congratulate you on the taste and ability with which you have executed the rather arduous task of presenting your subject to the world.

I believe that I have set apart your father's early letters to me as well as Arthur Hallam's; and I need hardly say that you would be most welcome to see them. If you would, with Lady Catherine, do us the favour to visit us here, it would afford an excellent opportunity: and I think that I could *vivâ voce* make some additions to the recollections supplied by the book.

I go to London tomorrow for one or two Cabinets: but I hope to return on Saturday night. Again in the week after next I shall be called southwards: but next week we should be free and happy to receive you: either on the 1st when Lord and Lady Derby come here, or earlier also, if you would excuse our fulfilling an engagement to a neighbour on Wednesday evening, when however a part of my family would be here to entertain you.[1]

One word more before closing. I cannot but deem it *possible* that this book may wholly or partially come before the public. I earnestly intreat that, if it does, the name of Wood may be struck out from the sad narrative of p.p. 8, 9. I have known the bearer of that name, who is concerned in the incident, for near sixty years, as one of the kindest, gentlest, and best of men.[2]

To G. O. TREVELYAN, Irish secretary, 23 October 1883.   Add MS 44546, f. 180.
'*Private*'.

It was just after you left us that the Attorney General came, and that I made some way with him at last into the outskirts of the Franchise question, so as to be prepared for all contingencies.

In our conversations we could not overlook Ireland. And in touching Ireland I felt the necessity of unusual care. Two courses offer themselves, assuming the establishment of a prospective uniform franchise throughout Great Britain. We might give Ireland the pure British franchise: or we might equalise the Irish franchise, as between Boroughs and Counties, but still keep it different from and less than the Irish [*sc.* British] franchise.

I am very anxious to be, in a preliminary way & without prejudice, supplied with information as to the respective merits of these two plans.

And among other matters I think it should not be at once assumed that the more limited franchise is the more conservative. I even would say, with plausibility if not more, that in so far as the Irish franchise is to be considered bad, its badness is such that it could not be aggravated. Other points may be raised, which go nearer the core of the question: was a forty shilling franchise more unmanageable than one of £8? taking each upon the experience of open voting, or experience and estimate as to the ballot. Is not the admission of another class, the labourer, by household suffrage, *quite* as likely to establish a dual current in the constituencies, as to increase the volume of that single force which now carries all before it?

I should be very glad if you would kindly open this matter with the Law Officers, and let me hear in due time from you, and also from them jointly or severally.[3]

---

[1] See 1 Nov. 83.

[2] Gaskell agreed to this, though the book was never published in its original form; Add MS 44483, f. 291. A. F. Ashley-Cooper d. 1825 after fighting C. A. Wood and drinking brandy.

[3] Trevelyan replied, 26 October, Add MS 44335, f. 130: 'we regard it as impossible to propose a different franchise for Ireland and Great Britain', especially if the Bill is to pass the Commons; 'the

I am due in London tomorrow to remain until Saturday afternoon; but I write from Hawarden.

24. Wed. [London]

Ch. 8½ A.M. Wrote to Mrs Hodgson—Ed. Guardian—& minutes. Off to London. 12¾-6¾. Saw S.E.G. respecting Dean Cowie—Mr Seymour—Lady Cork—Ld Granville respecting Madagascar. Dined with the Spencers. Read Collections of Epitaphs[1]—Pennants Tour in Scotl.[2]

25. Th.

Wrote to The Queen—The Speaker—Ld Derby—Mr Morley MP.—and minutes. Cabinet 12-4. Very good. Saw Mr Seymour—Lord R. Grosvenor. Dined at Mrs Th's—Col. H. Harrod's[3] remarkable recitations. Saw Percy X. Gascoigne [R]. Read Probyn's Poems.[4]+

Cabinet. Oct. 25. 1883 Noon.[5]
1. Madagascar. Ld Granville's draft considered & agreed to with amendments.[6]
2. Cairo. Baring's dispatch read and recomm[endatio]n for evacuation & reduction adopted.[7]
3. Parliament Street. Cabinet [Committee] appointed to consider the two plans.[8]
4. Minister of Commerce. Mentioned Monk's letter.[9]
5. Ilbert Bill. Ripon's proposal. Kimberley recited proceedings.[10]
6. Committee of Cabinet on West African territorial questions. Course approved—& draft wh is to be submitted to the Council.[11]
7. Suffrage conversation introduced by WEG.[12]

To LORD DERBY, colonial secretary. 25 October 1883.   Add MS 44546, f. 181.

The recommendation for evacuating Cairo, and a draft summing up the Madagascar case, have been agreed to and in a sense which I think you would generally approve. We had also a preliminary conversation on the Suffrage, the *tone* of which was I think rather favourable to dealing with the question.

introduction of all the classes in the nation would do good', reducing the influence of farmers and giving classes presently excluded 'some sense of political responsibility'.

[1] Perhaps W. Andrews, *Curious epitaphs* (1883).
[2] See 25 Sept. 37.
[3] Not further identified (not in the Army List); perhaps a member of the Norfolk family; or a *nom de guerre* for the Thistlethwayte *soirée?*
[4] M. Probyn, *A ballad of the road* (1883).
[5] Add MS 44644, f. 108.
[6] On reparation for G. A. Shaw (see 22 Oct. 83n.); see Ramm II, ii. 62n., 110–11.
[7] 3000 troops were retained at Alexandria.
[8] Development of Parliament Street, Add MS 44629, f. 68; 1884 bill not pressed; negotiations between govt. and Met. Board of Works; *H* 289. 1061.
[9] Not found.
[10] Its passing not to be further postponed; Bahlman, *Hamilton*, ii. 496. See 17 Apr. 83n.
[11] 'Derby, Northbrook, Kimberley, Chamberlayne [*sic*], Granville'; Add MS 44644, f. 109.
[12] Preliminary discussion; see 10, 13 Nov. 83.

But I write specially to say that Granville proposed a Committee of Cabinet on territorial questions relating to the West Coast of Africa. The Cabinet agreed that this Committee should be appointed subject to your approval. If you should not approve please to write to Lord Granville who with you has the chief or most direct interest.[1]

Cabinet meets again November 10th.

To J. MORLEY, M.P., 25 October 1883. '*Private*'. Morley MSS.

Mr. Schnadhorst has on behalf of a Deputation asked for an interview with me on the County Franchise on some day after Nov. 1. It would be entirely contrary to the usual practice to receive a political deputation of this kind at the present season of the year, and I do not think it prudent to introduce a change in this respect. If there is to be a deputation, it should I think be shortly before the opening of the session. I admit however that I am not very friendly to these demonstrative deputations. The proper object of a deputation is to inform. But any information on this subject would be far better received and considered if in writing. It may be said that sometimes it is a legitimate object to impose (I use the word in a good sense). But in this view nothing can be added by a deputation to the fact of the great gathering at Leeds; and its real and genuine significance. I expect to see Bright next week and will talk to him about this matter. I may say that Lord R. Grosvenor has seen this note and thoroughly agrees.[2]

26. *Frid*

Wrote to The Queen l.l.—Lord Mayor—Sir H. Parkes—Sir H. Ponsonby—Scotts Tel.—Speakers of Legisl. Houses New Zealand—Mr Tennant—C.G.—and minutes. Dined at Mr Godleys. Conversation with him. Saw Mrs Th. afr. Saw Mr Seymour—Ld Granville—M. Vitalis—Ld Spencer—Mr Knowles—Ld R. Grosvenor—Scotts—Mr Chamberlain. Read Love's Martyrdom.[3]

To Mrs GLADSTONE, 26 October 1883. Hawarden MSS.

I have been busy most of today with interviews, and have given another long quasi-sitting to Vitalis, who seems a very clever fellow, and went away perfectly satisfied. Also I think Granville Spencer & Chamberlayne [*sic*], all of whom I have seen, are well satisfied with the upshot of yesterday's Cabinet, when such objections as cropped up, with respect to the future, seemed at once to be lost in one smooth even forward current of opinion & feeling.

Among my employments of today have been 1. writing *by request* to recommend that Woolner should execute a statue of the Queen for New South Wales and 2. declining an invitation sent me by the Speakers of the two Legislative Chambers, on behalf of themselves and the Chambers, to visit New Zealand. In fact I should say matters general look tranquil and rather comfortable—is this a sign of *coming* storms?

Tomorrow between the Marriage and the breakfast I hope perhaps to call on Mrs Birks.

At two I am *probably* hooked in to attend a Play with R. Grosvenor & Seymour, whom I shall treat if we go there; we (R.G. and I) shall not leave till 6.30 & reach Chester 11.10 or

---

[1] Derby, 26 October, Add MS 44142, entirely agreed in the proposal.
[2] Morley replied next day that the deputation, once announced, must go forward, 'to impose by informing'. See 31 Jan. 84.
[3] J. Saunders, *Love's martyrdom: play and poem* (1882).

11.15 when I reckon on your kindly sending a light open trap to meet me: and well content even after this short absence shall I be to get back again.

I dine with Godley today. Wynne is very hospitable, and Stume (I have explained to her) in force. Ever your afft WEG

To the SPEAKERS OF THE LEGISLATIVE HOUSES OF   Add MS 44546, f. 182.
NEW ZEALAND, 26 October 1883.

I have the honour to acknowledge with sentiments of respect and gratitude the invitation to visit New Zealand which you have addressed to me on the part of the Legislative Houses of that advanced and important Colony, as well as on your own part.

It is unhappily impossible for me to comply with this invitation, on account of the constant pressure of my official duties which ill admit of my removal even to points much nearer this island and this metropolis.

It is not without much regret that I make this reply to your courteous proposal, for I am very sensible of the practical benefits produced by interchange of visits between the inhabitants of the different portions of the Empire, in closer sympathies as well as in enlarged information.

I have many reasons for wishing to see this interchange frequent and extended, besides the fact that nearly forty nine years ago I was first placed in official relations with the Colonies, and that the early impressions thus produced do not easily depart. But all general considerations which I feel to be applicable tell in the case of New Zealand with peculiar force. Besides the fact that one of my near relatives has a distinct interest in its prosperity, and has repeatedly visited its shores, and that one of my dearest friends was its first and illustrious Bishop, I took a warm interest in the proceedings connected with its earlier history, and I consider that in that history were worked out many of the soundest principles which now regulate the Colonial connection, and which promise to render it alike honourable, beneficial, and enduring.

To C. S. ROUNDELL, M.P., 26 October 1883.   Add MS 44546, f. 182.

Mr. Webb's[1] is certainly an interesting letter & there is a great advantage in communication at close quarters. He is somewhat loose in thought or information, e.g. in the parallel between Charles I & Lord Spencer, and seems to have a rough tongue, but I would not on that, or any account, deprecate the continuance of the correspondence. I suggest and even recommend your inducing him to be a little more particular on such points as these. Does he consider that Ireland was free before the Union. What are the fundamental differences (other than physical) between her relation to the United Kingdom, and that of Scotland, or that of Wales (and he should be a little cautious in what he says about Wales). Does he admit that in the last 50 or 55 years some inequalities have been removed, and if he admits this, why should he deny that others may be removed also. In repealing the Union is he satisfied to go back to an historical or does he demand an ideal standing-point. In what respects is his Irish Parliament to be subject to the Imperial Parliament & in what respects is the supremacy (as distinguished from the action) of the Imperial Parliament to be abated?

[1] Alfred Webb, secretary to the Irish National League; his letter to Roundell is at Add MS 44483, f. 281.

27. Sat. [Hawarden]

Wrote to Mr Rathbone—Mrs Th.—Mrs Bolton—Ld Wolverton—& minutes. Saw Lady Salisbury—Mr Seymour—Ld Chancellor—Mr Lefevre—Mr E. Talbot—D. of Norfolk—Ld R. Grosvenor. 4½–10¼. To Hawarden. Read Love's Martyrdom—and [blank]

28. 23 S. Trin. & SS. Simon & Jude.

Ch. 11 AM. 6½ P.M. Walk with Miss Grosvenor[1] and a party. Wrote to Mr Seymour Tel.—The Queen—Mr L. Morris—and minutes. Read Morris, Songs Unsung (and aloud at night)[2]—Higginbotham's Address[3]—Skinner's Life.

29. M.

Ch. 8½ A.M. Wrote to Mr Seymour Tel.—Ld Wolverton—The Queen—Messrs Watson—Dr Acland—Ld Granville—& minutes. Woodcraft with S. & H. Miss Grosvenor went: much regretted by us all. Worked on books. Read Skinner's Life (finished)—Prometheus & Pandora[4]—Love's Martyrdom (finished)—Acland's King's Coll. Address.

To Dr. H. W. ACLAND, 29 October 1883.   Acland MS d. 68, f. 66.

I thank you for your most interesting Lecture[5] which I have lost no time in perusing. Your notice of me, however indulgent, is acceptable; and as you quote me I inflict upon you herewith another translation made, under an impulse, not very long ago.[6]

Do you think any man can safely say that the individual human being is advancing? I have no doubt he advances in certain respects. But his gains in one direction may be balanced by his losses in another. And there is one cause in action over the whole field of knowledge, which has a powerful tendency to reduce his dimensions. I mean that we were all coming to be specialists. In your own great profession, I think they are not rated high: and so I believe it will be all along the line.

In a book just published by Mr. Morris, called Songs unsung, you will find a piece called A New Creed and another called Suffrages, which contain a wonderfully powerful statement of the use of Will and Spirit against Matter and force, and upon the whole perhaps of Belief against unbelief.

If your son[7] has written his ideas of Cetewayo, Grant, Colenso, and others, not excluding even Bulwer, Osborn, and Fynn, I shall be much pleased to know his ideas.

[1] Victoria Charlotte Grosvenor, 1832–1913; da. of Lord Ebury; H.V.B.
[2] Lewis Morris (see 22 Feb. 77) had sent his *Songs Unsung* (1883).
[3] Perhaps J. J. Higginbotham, *Men whom India has known* (1874).
[4] Sent by the author, G. K. Wlastoff; Add MS 44483, f. 284.
[5] 'Groundwork of culture. An address', sent on 24 October, Add MS 44091, f. 137: 'the paper gave me much trouble'; it refers to Gladstone as 'a chief force in modern progress', quoting his tr. 'Scis te lassum' (see 10 Oct. 75).
[6] See 15 Aug. 83.
[7] (Sir) William Alison Dyke Acland, 1847–1924; 2nd bart. 1900; travelled widely; F.R.G.S. No report found.

30. Tu.

Ch. 8½ A.M. Wrote to Ld Mayor of London—The Queen Tel.—Mr Seymour—
The Speaker—Watsons—Mr Armstrong—Mr L. Morris—Ld Shaftesbury—Sir H.
Ponsonby—Mrs Benson, & minutes. Woodcraft with W. & H. Worked on books.
12–1¼. Saw Mr Robertson & his party on his plans for the River Dee. C. & I
dined with Mr Johnson: the gentlemen discussed the River question. Read
Colonel Jack—Skinner's *Poems.*

31. Wed.

Ch. 8½ A.M. Wrote to Lady G. Fullerton—Mr Ridler—Mr Coleman—The
Queen—Mr Knowles—& minutes. Worked on books. Woodcraft as yesterday.
Read Colonel Jack—Proof-sheets Hope Scott's Life.[1] Saw [blank]

To J. R. KNOWLES, editor of the *Nineteenth Century*,   Add MS 44546, f. 184.
31 October 1883.

(1). The Review has duly arrived and I have transmitted it to the Queen with a suitable
commendation of it to her notice. If any notice of it arrives, you will be duly informed.

(2). Your criticism on Milnes Gaskell's book[2] is I think admirable. Pray be careful not to
mention the name of Wood in connection with the sad Ashley tragedy at Eton: he is
alive, and a most excellent man. About Milnes Gaskell the elder, it is a puzzle. When he
was a boy at Eton he had never been used to make the slightest effort to conquer a difficulty or do what he did not like. Hence I imagine came such a relaxation of fibre as was
fatal to all manly distinction.

(3). So you have cast another £20 into my insatiable maw.[3] Many thanks. I told you
that it swallowed easily all that was put into it.

(4). Thanks also for your judgment on my Parliament Street Nostrum.[4] Unless forbidden, I will send your sketch to Childers or Lefevre.

Novr One. All Saints 1883.

Ch. 8½ A.M. with H.C. Wrote to Mr Ornsby—Mr Seymour—Ld Devon—Miss G.
Ward—The Queen—& minutes. Walk with Bright the O[sborne] Morgans &
party. The Derbys & Milnes Gaskells came. Read Colonel Jack—Fortnightly on
Ireland—on Suez Canal—on Recent Poetry.[5] Eleven to dinner.

2. Frid.

Ch. 8½ A.M. Wrote to Mr Seymour Tel—Bp of Manchester—Dean of do—Dean
of Carlisle—Ld E. Fitzmaurice—& minutes. Morning chiefly with Ld D on many
matters. Then with the Piercy[6] Railway and River party. Saw C. Milnes Gaskell.

[1] See 13 Oct. 83; further comments at Add MS 44546, f. 184.
[2] See 23 Oct. 83. Knowles asked 'But why did that "marvellous boy" Milnes Gaskell not do more
as a man?'; 30 October, Add MS 44232, f. 11.
[3] For 'Senti, senti', in this number, see 15 Aug. 83.
[4] On the improvements (see 25 Oct. 83); Knowles was also an eminent architect.
[5] *F.R.*, xl. 713, 728, 737 (November 1883).
[6] Word scrawled.

Wood walk with the D.s & party. Read Colonel Jack—Nineteenth Cent on Jewish Trial.[1]

3. Sat.

Ch. 8½ A.M. Wrote to Sec. Ulster Convcn[2]—Ld Granville—The Queen—Sir Ch. Dilke—Mr Russell—Mr Seymour—Mr Childers—and minutes. Walk with the Derby's mg. Saw Mr Bright—Mr Redington—Mr West—Sir R. Welby. The Derbys went. They have been most cordial, kind, & easily pleased. Woodcraft with Herbert. We were all photographed by young Harcourt.[3] Read Colonel Jack—Outcast London.[4] Twelve to dinner.

4. 24 S. Trin.

Ch. 11 A.M. with H.C. & 6½ P.M. Wrote to Mr Seymour Tel.—Lady Dudley—Mr Strangeway—Sir H. Ponsonby—and minutes. Read Dr Driver's remarkable Sermon[5]—Mivart on Law & Nature[6]—Brewster, Ch. of 18th Cent. Walk with friends.

5. M.

Ch. 8½ A.M. Wrote to Dean of Carlisle l. & 2 Tell.—Bp Manchester Tel.—Dean of do Tel.—Sir W. Harcourt—Dr Liddon—Ld Granville l. and Tel.—Mr Guthrie—Attorney General—Mr Seymour—& minutes. Walk with Sir R. Welby. Morning with Mr West—Mr Milnes Gaskell—Sir R. Welby—successively. Read Brown's Kirké[7]—Colonel Jack (finished)—Aretino's Marescalco.[8]

To Sir W. V. HARCOURT, home secretary,   MS Harcourt dep. 9, f. 57.
5 November 1883.

Your son left us this morning for Nuneham to see his Uncle. He hoped, and we hope, that the summons has no ominous meaning. He had charmed every one; and we were very sorry to lose him.

I have your note of yesterday, and shall be happy to see you and Dilke before we touch any great legislative question in Cabinet—but this I think we cannot do on Saturday afternoon. Perhaps Monday would suit you.

To Sir H. JAMES, attorney general, 5 November 1883.   Add MS 44546, f. 186.

I think it might be well that you should now, without prejudice, and to see how the thing looks, have a Bill drawn on the lines of your paper about the Franchise.

---

[1] N.C., xiv. 753 (November 1883).
[2] W. M. Wylie, thanking him for a resolution; Add MS 44546, f. 185.
[3] Lewis ('Loulou') *Harcourt, 1863-1922, then acting as his father's secretary; a skilled amateur photographer. See 5 Nov. 83.
[4] [A. Mearns], 'The bitter cry of outcast London. An inquiry into the condition of the abject poor' (1883); an important stimulus to the rise of the housing question.
[5] Not found published.
[6] S. G. J. Mivart, Nature and thought (1882).
[7] R. Brown, The myth of Kirkê (1883).
[8] P. Aretino, Il Marescalco, comedia (1536).

I would observe that, in the drafting of the Bill, form is of the utmost political importance. And by form I mean brevity. The endeavour will be to beat us by and upon entangling details. The Cabinet were clear I think that, if we went on, there must be extension to
Ireland, and that upon the broader of the two bases. It would be a great thing if we could
extend for the three countries by reference to the existing English Act. Every needless
word inserted will be a new danger. Pray consider how far we can go in this sense. The
feeling of a draftsman as such, his natural feeling as an artist for presentation of form, will
be against us: but we should fasten our eyes on what is cardinal and primary. I understand
our principle to be (provisionally) one franchise, for the three kingdoms, in County and
Borough; by reciprocal extensions; abuses of property-rights being restrained by prohibition of subdivision & the like (except in certain cases), but without personal disfranchisement.
[P.S.] I am due in London on Thursday.

6. *Tu.*

Ch. 8½ A.M. Wrote to Mr Palmer Tel.—Mrs Th.—Mr W. Ridler—Watsons—Mr
Seymour—Sir A. Gordon—Mr S. Denison—Sir C. Dilke—Lady G. Fullerton—&
minutes. Lady Stepney & Sir R. Welby went: last of the 'company'. Woodcraft
with W. & H. Read Defoe on the Plague[1]—Cutts on the East[2]—Hardy on Dorset
Labourers[3]—Brown's Kirké—Aretino's Marescalco.

To Sir C. W. DILKE, president of the local government   Add MS 43875, f. 150.
board, 6 November 1883.

   I thank you for your note of the 3rd[4] & I think our best plan will be to make arrangements for a conversation early next week on the steps to be taken for obtaining such
information about the effect of any changes in the franchise as may be requisite.
[P.S.] I send a paper from Jenkyns.

7. *Wed.*

Ch. 8½ A.M. Wrote to Sir W. Harcourt—Mr L. Stanley—Mr Reader—Ld Wolverton—Ld Hartington—Mr Childers—Ld Granville—Dean Oakley Tel—Ld Mayor
Elect—Mr Seymour Tel—Bp of Manchester Tel.—Mrs Th. & minutes. Worked
much on books. Woodcraft with W. Saw Mr MacColl. Read Kirké—Il Marescalco finished—Laing on Connemara.[5]

To H. C. E. CHILDERS, chancellor of the exchequer,   Add MS 44546, f. 188.
7 November 1883.

   1. The Harcourts have also promised a visit towards the close of the year, & perhaps
you will communicate with him & make a joint proposal.
   2. I am so glad to hear that Lesseps & the Shipowners are to lash their vessels together,
& the strongest will I hope board the other & bring him to terms.
   3. If you approve, I think you should mention this, & the subject of Expenditure, on

---

   [1] See 4 July 38.
   [2] E. L. Cutts, *Christmas under the crescent in Asia* (1877).
   [3] Thomas Hardy, 'The Dorsetshire labourers', *Longman's Magazine*, ii. 252 (July 1883).
   [4] Add MS 44149, f. 150 on statistics on the franchise; see 9, 10 Nov. 83.
   [5] S. Laing in *F.R.*, xl. 674 (November 1883).

Saturday:[1] please also to consider whether it would not strengthen your hands if we arrange that the Departmental results shall go before one or more Committees. Clearly, I presume, the Defence Estimates cannot be excluded.

4. As to the one per cent on Guaranteed Turks for Sinking Fund, I am with you, if only on the ground of its being (as Welby showed me) a defensive measure, which Granville may not have taken into view. The proper course will be for you to compare notes with him before any intervention of mine. He *may* have considerations to allege which may not have entered into our view; though I hardly expect it.

To LORD HARTINGTON, war secretary, 7 November 1883.   Add MS 44146, f. 231. '*Private*'.

You are perfectly correct in your recollection,[2] and I think it will be convenient if on Saturday you, or any other member of the Cabinet, will put down *heads* of information which you wish to be obtained in respect to the Franchise. I have as you will remember *proposed* nothing to the Cabinet; but have merely stated hypothetically a course of main business, which would enable me in my 75th year—at least to begin the Session with my colleagues.

I am not at all anxious for an early decision as to business; for it seems sure to *leak.* Indeed there is a leakage even of what has not been decided; but this can in some degree be counteracted by contradiction. But our materials may be prepared and I have asked the A.G., for my own guidance, to try to put a Bill into shape, as one is also in preparation, 'without prejudice' in regard to local Govt. Certainly at present no one is committed. It is however a fact of weight and interest that—as I gather—Trevelyan and the Irish A.G. agree with Spencer in thinking that Irish & English suffrage must stand or fall together, & that there would be no advantage, were it open to us, in attempting to hold the £4 line.

8. *Th.* [*London*]

Ch. 8½ AM. Wrote to Bp of Manchester—Dean of Carlisle—Mr Laing—Chester P. Master Tel.—Mr R. Brown jun.—Ld Derby—and minutes. 11¾–5¾ To London by Oxford. Saw Mr Hamilton—Ld Granville—Mr Seymour. Saw Cooper [R]. Read Hope Scott proofsheets—Baur's Relig. Life in Germany[3]—Life of Mrs Fitzherbert[4]—Trollope's Autobiography.[5]

To LORD DERBY, colonial secretary, 8 November 1883.   Add MS 44546, f. 188.

I take it for granted that on Saturday you will have something (to say) to us on the Transvaal, as well as *possibly* on Cetewayo; and as that matter is I suppose urgent, I will keep the first place for you, unless the Foreign Office should happen to compete.

9. *Fr.*

Wrote to Ld Northbrook—Mr R. Ornsby—Ld Waveney—Mr King Parks—Queen Tel.—and minutes. B.M. Trustees Meeting 4.P.M. Read Mrs Fitzherbert's

[1] Childers agreed; Add MS 44130, f. 328.

[2] Of 6 November, Add MS 44146, f. 228, that the cabinet should have information on reform; see also Hartington's letter of 24 October, cautious about a franchise measure, alarmed about consequences in Ireland, and reluctant to separate suffrage and redistribution; in Holland, i. 395.

[3] W. Baur, *Religious life in Germany during the wars of independence*, 2v. (1870).

[4] See 25 Mar. 56.

[5] A. Trollope, *An autobiography* (1883).

Memoirs. Saw Sir C. Dilke—Do *cum* Sir W. Harcourt—Mr Seymour—Mr Hamilton—Ld Hartington. 6½-10½. To the Lord Mayor's dinner. Spoke for Ministers. *Intended* a hint to the Princelets of the Balkan.[1]

10. Sat.

Wrote to The Queen—and minutes. Cabinet 2-5. Conclave on the Speakership 12-2. Almost an *impasse.*[2] Saw Mr H—Mr S—The Speaker—Ld Spencer—Ld Granville. Made calls of ceremony. Worked on books. Read Mrs Fitzherbert (finished)—Amours d'Anne d'Autriche[3]—Gouvernement de Richelieu &c.[4]

Cabinet. Sat. Nov. 10. 83. 2 PM.[5]
1. ⟨Transvaal⟩ Cetewayo—case to be presented in writing.[6]
    3. Basutoland. Ld Derby to invite Basutoland to come in—on terms already agreed.
2. Suez Canal. Lesseps arrived [in England]—& arrangements going forward for his meeting the ship owners in the *Provinces*: London not come in.
⟨3⟩9. Expenditure Resolution. Childers proposes to appt. Departmental Committees to examine. Chamberlain to contact [?] Norwood if possible in aid of Lesseps.
4. Information respecting Franchise. Return to be expedited by Sir C. Dilke & the Irish Govt.
⟨5 The Speakership⟩
2. Cetewayo. Ld Derby detailed wants. C. has broken conditions of restoration: has been beaten. No step.
4. To try to ascertain Cape's views on Bechuana frontiers.
5. Jamaica Constitution. Outline stated—& approved.[7]
6. Spanish Treaty. a. *modus vivendi.* 30° in lieu of 28. Gibraltar grievance, remove if possible. b. negotiate further.[8]
7. Military occupation in Egypt. £4 per man per month with modified railway charges. C. of E. & Ld H. to examine the other claims.
(Spencer). Ireland. Pledged: Parl. Registration; Police reorganisation; Sunday Closing. Much desired: Union Rating.

11. S. 3 Preadv.

Chapel Royal mg and Whitehall aft. Saw Mr Hamilton. Read Palmer on the Church[9]—Heraud's Deluge[10]—[blank] on Prophecy—Anne d'Autriche finished: Poverina.[11] It must have been a beautiful soul—and divers other works.

[1] 'Smaller potentates' need to 'seek their strength' in the 'goodwill and affections of their people'; *T.T.*, 10 November 1883, 6f.
[2] First of a series of discussions, leading, eventually, *via* Herschell and Goschen, to nomination of A. W. Peel; see 3 Dec. 83.
[3] *Les amours d'Anne d'Autriche, Epouse de Louis XIII* (1693).
[4] Perhaps *L'histoire du ministère de . . . Richelieu*, 4v. (1649).
[5] Add MS 44644, f. 112. Headings written out in advance, but taken in different order; Gladstone's original order retained, with renumbering.
[6] i.e. the case to be put in writing by the Transvaal deputies; CAB 41/17/23.
[7] Derby's despatch of 1 December rejected most of the Jamaican petition of April 1883, but conceded a Royal Commission on a possible franchise; PP 1884 lv. 7.
[8] i.e. wine duties, and smuggling in Gibraltar; CAB 41/17/23.   [9] See 15 Aug. 38.
[10] J. A. Heraud, *The judgement of the flood* (1834).   [11] 'wretched woman'.

12. M.

Wrote to Sir H. Ponsonby—Mr Fitzgerald[1]—Sir H. Taylor—Mr Lefevre—Watsons—Granville & Hartn (minute)—Dowager Duchess of Roxburghe—Mr Ridler—& minutes. Dined with the Godleys.+ Tea at Mr MacColls—& conversation on Palmer. Saw Mr Hamilton—Mr Goalen. Read Recherche du Paganisme[2]— and Godwin's Life.[3] Worked on books.

To Sir H. PONSONBY, the Queen's secretary,   Add MS 45724, f. 152.
12 November 1883.

With relation to the interesting matter of the Luther commemoration,[4] pray read the article in the Standard today. It may not be perfect, but it is far above the usual newspaper level, and is written in a large and historic spirit. I feel myself to owe a deep debt of gratitude to Queen Elizabeth in connection with British religion and history. But I should think twice before recommending a Centenary for her (were it the time) on the ground that live controversies are bad enough without rekindling dead ones.
[P.S.] I think Her Majesty may like to see the inclosed Memoranda[5] from some Ministers to whom I made known H.M.s letter on Housing. The great case is London: and the great want, as I believe, is the want of a *motive power*, much more vigorous, authoritative, and raised above private interests, than the Parish Vestries.

To G. J. SHAW LEFEVRE, first commissioner of works,   Add MS 44546, f. 190.
12 November 1883.

I have no doubt that, when Distribution comes up, your varied qualifications for work will render you a most valuable ally in working it into shape. But I own myself to lean in the opposite direction from you with respect to the policy of combining the two questions of redistribution & franchise, were it *only* (and it is not *only*) on the ground that the coming redistribution ought not to be an instalment but a settlement. I am not for a very 'moderate' redistribution. But your statements are very interesting & I will circulate your letter among the members of the Cabinet.[6]

13. Tu.

Wrote to Mr Childers—Att. General—The Queen—& minutes. Dined at Lady Chesham's: conversation with Charles.[7] Saw Mr H—The Solicitor General[8]— Mrs Malcolm. Conclave (small) on Speakership at 12. Transvaal Deputn at one. Cabinet 2–5. Read Godwin's Life.

[1] J. E. Fitzgerald (see 20 Sept. 48), recommending W. Goalen, leaving for New Zealand, to his attention; Add MS 44546, f. 189.
[2] G. E. J. Guilhem de Clermont-Lodère, Baron de St. Croix, *Recherches . . . sur les mystères du Paganisme*, 3v. (1817).
[3] C. Kegan Paul, *William Godwin; his friends and contemporaries*, 2v. (1876); see 29 Nov. 83.
[4] Quatercentenary of Luther's birth.
[5] Not found, but Ponsonby's notes on them at Add MS 45724, f. 154.
[6] Long letter of 7 November, Add MS 44153: increase of population mainly in great cities 'and in the Counties immediately adjoining them'; need for 'moderate' redistribution at same time as franchise bill; letter docketed 'Circulate WEG N.12'.
[7] i.e. Lord Chesham; see 14 Nov. 77n.
[8] Offering Herschell the Speakership, which after reflection, he declined; Bahlman, *Hamilton*, ii. 505.

Cabinet. Tues. Nov. 13. 83. 2 PM.[1]

1. Speakership—better outside 1. Cabinet 2. Office. a) Herschell b) Goschen c) A. Peel.
2. Franchise. Circulate A.Gs paper? Let us be ready with Bills—(London Govt—County Govt. and the) Franchise.
3. Transvaal Deput[ation]. Recital by W.E.G. Paper to come in tomorrow.
4. Division of the Sees of Gloucester and Bristol. General approval, reserving consideration of circumstances as to legislation.
5. County Government Bill. Committee of Cabinet appointed.[2]
6. Employment of postmasters in [army] recruiting. P.M.G. introduced [to the Cabinet]— stated his views. W.O. circular to go out as proposed.
7. Westminster Improvements. Parliament Street. Agreed. See letter to H.M.[3]
8. Childers named Parlt. St. & that Metrop. R.R. Co. now stands in the place of Metrop. Board. Committee to act notwithstanding.[4]
9. Spencer stated his attitude in Ireland as to Ulster & other meetings.
10. Northbrook read proposed paragraphs of approval of Capt. Johnstone[5]—approved with amendment.

14. Wed.

Wrote to Rev. Dr Nevin—Attorney General—Mr Ornsby—Earl Granville—Mr Osborne Morgan—and minutes. 11 AM. Attended the Bath-Shaw Stewart marriage.[6] Saw Mr H—Herbert J.G. (respecting Serj. Simons)[7]—Sir J. Mowbray—Saw Stafford [R]. Dined at the Middle Temple: plenty of conversation. Read Godwin's Life—Hope Scott, Proofsheets.

15. Th.

Wrote to Ld Coleridge—Dr Schliemann—Ld Rosebery—The Speaker—Mr S. Ward[8]—Mr A. Denison—& minutes. Dined with the Wests. C. & I made our notes separately but alike on C.W.[9] Read Godwin's Life—Trollope's Autobiogr. Saw Mr Hamilton—Dr Farrar. Saw Gascoigne: with good hope [R].

To LORD ROSEBERY, 15 November 1883. '*Private*'.   N.L.S. 10022, f. 234.

I *will* reply to your kind letter[10] though I might find no better address for you than *orbis terrarum*, or for the benefit of postmasters, Planet Earth. I believe there is some notion of a real post office, at a certain spot, not over 15000 miles off.

[1] Add MS 44644, f. 115.
[2] Childers, Dodson, Dilke, Kimberley, Chamberlain, Carlingford, Derby (and Fitzmaurice not in Cabinet); ibid., f. 117.
[3] Railway station near George Street 'and a Railway under the Parks to Edgware Road'; CAB 41/17/24; never built, but roughly the line of the later Jubilee Line.
[4] See 25 Oct. 83.
[5] i.e. supporting the action of Capt. Charles Johnstone, 1843–1929, in safeguarding British property in Tamatave, Madagascar; see Ramm II, ii. 110 and CAB 37/11/53 and 55.
[6] (Sir) M. H. Shaw-Stewart (8th bart. 1903) m. Alice, da. of Lord Bath.
[7] Obscure.
[8] Samuel Ward, American author and friend of Rosebery, had sent his *Lyrical recreations* (1865, 1883); Add MS 44564, f. 193.
[9] Constance, Sir A. West's da.; being considered for one of the Gladstone boys?
[10] Of 19 October, from San Francisco; Add MS 44288, f. 183.

Many thanks, in the first place, for your recommendation of books. They will have to pass the ordeal of my daughter's judgment, that she may be a second sponsor, for I am very fastidious now about novels, from having gone astray, from having a taste formed upon Scott whom the world has for the moment thrust aside, & from having grown into an old curmudgeon, difficult to stir, & perhaps halfdead, though believed by his countrymen to be alive.

This brings me back to the arena of my liveliness such as it is. At the present moment, odd to say, our toughest difficulty is the choice of a Speaker: Whitbread, who would be perfect, being disabled by health. But this must be made to solve itself. The nut must crack, though the tooth may go. In the rear of it comes the Transvaal. There again we must squeeze our question into such dimensions that it can be handled. The Boers seem really strong in the point that the natives have multiplied enormously under them, & in great part by Immigration. So also by withdrawing from Cairo we have narrowed the scope of the Egyptian problem. But it remains a serious one; how to plant solidly western & beneficient institutions in the soil of a Mahomedan community? And if the planting be not solid, the result may be out tomorrow, in again the next day. The Balkan Peninsula is in danger, mainly so far as I can see owing to its having two *petit-maitres* installed as rulers, Milan in Servia & Alexander in Bulgaria: the latter gives some hope of being curable but not a great deal. We have I think ended the Madagascar business pretty well, & generally the Government has a kind of 'clean bill of health'. As to the Session, nothing is decided; but the odds are 3 to 2 (at least) in favour of a *Franchise* Bill for the three kingdoms, with a heap of Local Government behind it.

And now good bye & kind remembrances. I must reserve the 'Pembroke Castle' till your return. When that comes, you will be more agreeable than ever.

[P.S.] Mr. S. Ward is singularly kind to me.

16. Fr.

Wrote to Sir H. Ponsonby—Sir W. Harcourt—The Queen—Sir C. Dilke—Mr Dodds—Ld Portarlington—and minutes. Saw Mr Hamilton—Ld R.G.—The Solicitor General. Saw Martin—Grey (I hope rescued)—& another [R]. Read Godwin's Life—Drummond's Comm. Speeches.[1] Dined at Mrs Leo Ellis's. Conversation with Bp Vaughan—Lady Londonderry—Mr Ward—Mr Hutton.

Ld. Derby: can answers to the queries on this page be briefly given. W.E.G. N. 16. 83.[2]
1. What is the exact juridical relation of the Orange Free State to Great Britain? [Entire freedom. No control over external relations].
2. What are the reasons against taking that relation for the basis of our relation to the Transvaal? [None if you do not object to sweeping away the Convention of two years ago.]
3. Can the proposition be maintained that the Sand River Convention is utterly dead? [The Sand River Convention is utterly dead. If we return to any similar arrangement it should be an entirely new departure.]
4. Has the Deputation indicated in any way the nature of the connection with Great Britain which (8.2) they propose to maintain? [I know nothing as to this beyond what is in their statement. V. page 6, section 8, subsection 2.]

---

[1] H. Drummond, *Speeches in parliament*, 2v. (1860).
[2] Add MS 44644, ff. 121-2; Derby's replies in [   ]; in Schreuder, 391.

17. Sat [Stratton Park, Micheldever][1]

Wrote to The Queen—Mr Goschen—& minutes. Cabinet 12-2¾. Saw Mr Hamilton—Dean of Winchr. Read Life of Godwin. Off at 3.10 to Stratton Park: house full of treasures: large & pleasant party.

Cabinet. Sat. Nov. 17. 83. Noon.[2]

Transvaal. Discussed—Questions to be put to the delegates—Cabinet to consider further on Tuesday

1. Speakership. Sol. Gen. [Herschell] No.[3] Take Goschen.
2. West Africa. Treaties with Niger chiefs recommended against cession of Sovereignty & for free trade—within due limits.
3. *Modus vivendi* with Spain. Substitute 30° [?] for 26° & agree to *basis* of negotiation for Treaty.

[*Note to Lord Derby:*] 1. (8.2) What connection is it that you desire to uphold. 2. What boundary do they ask for. 3. What arrangements they contemplate for ⟨the⟩ order on the frontier. It may be intimated that if need arise that Sand River Convention is dead & the idea of a new Convention not rejected *in limine*.[4]

To G. J. GOSCHEN, M.P., 17 November 1883. '*Secret*'.   Add MS 44546, f. 193.

You are aware how serious a question the choice of a successor to Brand has become & how much the Cabinet are bound to look, not merely for what will or might satisfy, but for the best & strongest man who can & will undertake the charge. In these circumstances, I together with my colleagues have to express a most earnest hope that you will allow us to put you in nomination for the Chair.

I am aware of the grave nature of this proposal, but I hope you may accede to it, & I feel sure you will consider it maturely. It is needless to enumerate the qualifications which you possess for this elevated & arduous office, in which *now* not only good but splendid service is to be rendered to the country & the Crown.

I will only at this moment further observe that the future of political affairs seems to me at some points favourable to my opening this subject, & that I do not consider that your accepting the Chair at this time need in any way entail a permanent renunciation of your political career.

I have asked Hamilton to take this letter to you, for the sake of expedition & possibly convenience in other respects. I go down to Northbrook's this afternoon & I am to return to London on Tuesday morning.

[P.S.] I hope Mrs. Goschen's health is now completely re-established.

18. 26 S. Trin.

Micheldever Ch. mg. Ch in Park aftn. Hymn singing 6½-7½. Conclave Granville & Northbrook. Saw Mr Warburton. Read Drummond &c.—Anything possible to Will.[5]

---

[1] Northbrook's house.
[2] Add MS 44644, f. 120.
[3] i.e. he declined; see 13 Nov. 83.
[4] Add MS 44644, f. 123; see 16 Nov. 83.
[5] Not found.

19. M.

Winchester Cathedral 4 P.M. Excursion to Winchester $12\frac{1}{2}$–$5\frac{3}{4}$. Saw Cathedral —School—Deanery. Speeches to the Boys, Liberal Assocn and Municipal Corpn.[1] Cathedral service 4 P.M. Conclave on Egypt & *divers.* Read Godwin's Life. Wrote minutes.

20. Tu. [London]

Off at 10.30 from this kind house. Wrote to Bishop of Moray—The Queen—Rev. M. M'Coll—and minutes. Cabinet 2-5. Saw Mr Hamilton—Ld Granville—Ly Holker—Mr Goschen—Att. General. Dined at Horace Seymour's. Read Godwin's Life—Duke of Argyll's Lecture.[2]

Cabinet. Tues. Nov. 20. 83. 2 PM[3]

1. Transvaal. No answer yet recd. Questions discussed—Shall we reserve a *veto* over any engagements they may make with foreign countries. Cabinet inclined to make this demand. Freedom of trade. Treatment of subjects &c.[4]
2. Cetewayo.[5] Determine & telegraph against extension of the Reserve—against restoration of Cetewayo by us—prefer if possible to leave Zulus outside reserve to settle their own affairs. Can Useibebu hold his own?
3. Granville mentioned that in face of last telegrams & probable *issues* at once in China he had written to Waddington to express desire for a peaceable solution & readiness to recommend to *both* parties a reference to a Third Power (Europe or U.S.) if encouraged to do it by France.[6]
4. Baring on Soudan. Refuse English & Indian troops. Recommend abandoning part [? post].[7] Do not encourage British officers to serve ⟨Greatly doubt whether⟩ invitation to Turks might go but not through Egypt proper—on landing N. of Souakim[:] would not be for the interest of Egypt.
5. List of Bills considered.

21. Wed.

Wrote to Sir H. Ponsonby—Rev. Sir W. Palmer—Ld Chancr—Countess of Mar— Archdn Hessey—Mrs Gray—Dean of St Pauls—The Speaker Tel.—Dean Oakley Tel.—& minutes. Saw Mr Hamilton—The French Ambassador—Marquis of Lorne—Mr Reeve—Mr H. West—Lady Cork. Dined at Lady Cork's. Wrote Mem. on Franchise Redistribn.[8] Read Life of Godwin—Trollope, Autobiography. Saw Gray [R].

[1] *T.T.*, 20 November 1883, 6b.

[2] G. D. Campbell, duke of Argyll, 'Continuity and catastrophes in geology' (1883).

[3] Add MS 44644, f. 124.

[4] Control of foreign relations 'might with advantage be reserved . . . while on the other hand the great increase of Native population within the Transvaal and the immigration it receives from the surrounding districts appear to show that there is no occasion for retaining any power of interference within their frontier'; CAB 41/17/25.

[5] Correspondence and notes in CO 179/148, ff. 270–365.

[6] Affairs in Touquier 'hastening towards a rupture'; CAB 41/17/25.

[7] Rest of this entry uncertain; much alteration and deletion, but unclear which passages, if any, intended to stand.

[8] Sent to Hartington, 23 November, and apparently not returned; no copy found at Chatsworth.

To Rev. Sir W. PALMER, 21 November 1883.   Add MS 44546, f. 194.

I received your letter of the 19th[1] with deep concern, as it indicated some misunderstanding between yourself & Mr. MacColl, two persons in whose honour & character I have the most entire confidence.

I have however the satisfaction of being enabled to assure you in the most distinct terms that I have never given utterance to the disparaging opinion which you suppose me to have found. Not having seen your recast or revised work, I have not been in a condition to say any thing, & I at once relieve you so far as I am concerned, since you are good enough to request it, from any imputation whatever. It will I presume rest with Mr. Rivington in the position he has assumed, & with Mr. MacColl, to conduct any needful communications with you, & I trust they may be such as all must desire in consideration of the great & conspicuous service you have rendered to the Church by the work now as we hope to be still further fitted for new & more extended service. To promote the attainment of this object by the harmonious action of all concerned has been my sole desire.

22. Th.

Wrote to Watsons—Mr Ayrton—Mr S. Morley—The Queen—& minutes. Cabinet 2—5. Decided against uniting Franchise & Redistribution. But went over some rough ground. Saw Mr Hamilton—Attorney General—Mr Goschen—Ld Granville—Mr Knowles—Ld de Vesci—Mr Chamberlain. Read Godwin's Life—and Queen's Religion.

Cabinet. Thurs. Nov. 22. 1883. 2 PM.[2]
1. Reported Goschen's probable acceptance of nomination to Speakership.
2. Transvaal. No answer yet from Deputies. Ld D. will try to expedite[.] Door not shut against ratification of the S.W. Frontier if other arrangements be satisfactory. But arrangement for boundary outside wd be assumption by the Cape. Next a tripartite arrangement.[3]
3. Question from the Sultan. Cannot answer hypothetical questions. Sultan aware Germany has[?] most powerful military secrets, & has no ambitions against Turkey. We wish to maintain Treaty of Berlin. Advise Sultan to avoid entangling engagements[.] cannot encourage any proceedings wh tend to promote war between ⟨England⟩ Russia & Germany, allied countries.[4]
4. Hick's Army—destroyed. Adm. Hewett to ⟨protect⟩ maintain existing authorities in Suakim and Massowah. ⟨At the same time maintain as far as possible friendly relations with Abyssinians at Massowah.⟩ If Abyssinians found in possession[?] of Massowah refer home.
   Baring to consult as to any danger to Egypt proper? & to *tender* advice about retirement from Soudan.[5]

---

[1] Not found. For the planned republication of the *Treatise*, see 20 Mar. 81.
[2] Add MS 44644, f. 126.
[3] Schreuder, 394: awaiting answer to Derby's letter of 20 November to the Transvaal deputies.
[4] See Dufferin to Granville this day, FO 195/1432, no. 639: the Sultan is inclined to side with Russia in the Russo-German war he anticipates; how far would Britain in such circumstances be ready to protect Turkey?
[5] Defeat and death of Hicks and much of his Egyptian army at Kashgal, 3–5 November; start of the immediate Sudan crisis; see reports in F.O.C.P. 4917, 4932. Baring replied that the Egyptian govt. could not hold Khartoum; Cromer, i. 376.

5. Report from West African Committee of Cabinet—accepted.[1]
6. Redistribution—not to be united with franchise.[2]
7. Parlt. to meet Feb. 5.

23. Fr.

Wrote to Ld Granville—Sir C. Dilke—Att. General—Mr H. Reeve—Ld R. Grosvenor—Lady Cork—Sir W. Farquhar—Sir C. Wood—Dean of Carlisle—Ld Hartington—Mr Osborne—and minutes. Read Sainte Croix, Myst. du Paganisme—Life of Hope Scott, proofs—Life of Godwin. Saw Mr Hamilton—Sir J. Stokes[3]—M. Gladstone—Sir W. James *cum* Lucy Cavendish—Mrs Procter[4]—Ld Coleridge. Dined at Ld Coleridge's.

To LORD R. GROSVENOR, chief whip, 23 November   Add MS 44315, f. 131.
1883. '*Secret*'.[5]

I have heard something of you from De Vesci (whose fingers I rejoiced last night to see bending freely) & I fear you are not yet wholly relieved from anxiety, but yet I trust the happy moment may be near.

Meantime I write to inform you that the Cabinet yesterday decided that if they proceed with the Franchise next session it shall be with the franchise *alone*.

Also, Goschen has *all but* agreed to be nominated for the Chair. The only point remaining to be more thoroughly examined is that of sight; on which he is to see Bowman, now absent from Town. But he *expects* that there will be no barrier.

I have had a letter from Reeve following up a conversation on the Franchise. He is friendly to the extension, & has asked me for figures. He is to have an article on it in January, written by Sellar.[6] But here we come to the point. Has not Sellar been touched more or less with the Scotsman's crotched, or opinion?[7] Can you take care that if he writes he shall say nothing in prejudice of the decision which I have mentioned to you above?[8]

I go to Windsor tomorrow—Oxford Monday—Hawarden Wednesday.

To LORD HARTINGTON, war secretary, 23 November   Add MS 44546, f. 196.
1883.

My memorandum shall forthwith be written out fair, & sent to you.[9] The subject is no doubt very weighty and many sided, and though I regret that there should be any doubt on your mind, yet as it is there I freely admit nothing can be more proper than that the whole subject should be carefully and exactly weighed.

[1] See 25 Oct. 83; consul E. Hewett to annex ports in W. Africa to maintain 'unfettered trade'; see P. Gifford and W. R. Louis, *France and Britain in Africa* (1971), 223.

[2] A decision which Hartington was only very reluctantly brought to accept.

[3] Sir John *Stokes, 1825–1902; soldier and engineer; strongly opposed Channel tunnel; director of Suez Canal Council; supervised Egyptian expeditionary arrangements 1882, 1884–5.

[4] Not further identified, but see 29 Nov. 83.

[5] Holograph.

[6] [A. C. Sellar], 'Parliamentary reform', *Edinburgh Review*, clix. 264 (January 1884).

[7] *The Scotsman* opposed the inclusion of Ireland; Jones, *1884*, 75–6.

[8] Grosvenor replied, 25 November, Add MS 44315, f. 133, that the Cabinet 'never made a more sensible decision' than 'the Franchise *alone*', though he still preferred precedence for county government; he suggested Gladstone invite Sellar to Hawarden.

[9] Requested by Hartington (Add MS 44146, f. 233), who could 'not very well grasp all the considerations' on a single hearing; see 21, 22 Nov. 83.

The figures about the Irish Provinces are not included in it, but these also are at your command.

To Sir H. JAMES, attorney general, 23 November 1883.   Add MS 44546, f. 194.
'*Secret*'.

I send you the inclosed letter[1] on account of the point it raises:—
There is no great hurry about the matter and I have not knowledge enough to offer a suggestion but I suppose it will be desirable to find some means of access for the large class represented by the writer of this letter to the Register although they pay no rates and the public officer (I suppose) has no cognisance of them.
The Cabinet decided yesterday that *if* they proceed with the franchise it shall be dissociated from redistribution.
[P.S.] Do not reply.

24. Sat. [*Windsor Castle*]

Wrote to Mr Ornsby—Ld Granville—Mr Birkbeck MP—& minutes. Saw Mr Hamilton—Lord Granville—Ld Derby. Arrangements for departure. Tea at Mrs Haywood's. 5.10 tr. to Windsor. Saw Sir H. Ponsonby—Sir W. Jenner—Sir J. Cowell—The Queen—after dinner. Sat by Duchess of Edinburgh: frank, forthcoming, & kind as usual. The *third* Hesse Princess, very promising.[2] Read Dr Ince on Luther Commn[3]—Godwin's Life—Mackintosh, Civilisn in Scotl.[4]

To R. ORNSBY, 24 November 1883.   Add MS 44547, f. 1.

I return the proofs I have received from you;[5] and I add to my thanks for the copy of my letter of May 1845 my regret for your having had the trouble of transcribing, which it was far from my thought to impose upon you.
The fifth and sixth sheets of the volume carry us over the supreme crisis, and you will readily believe that the perusal of them revives in me a profoundly anxious past. I have indeed seriously considered whether I ought not to request you to drop out of the text my two letters at page 70 and page 88, not because I recede from anything contained in them but because they appeared to me to touch another biography,[6] and to be of such a character as to be hardly fit for publication during my life-time. But, having submitted these sheets to one or two persons on whose judgment as well as sympathy I can rely, I waive my own impressions. I admit that, if we consider the biography as a work of art, they appertain to its completeness; and, in a higher point of view, they belong to the full exhibition of his character and elucidation of his mental history.
I am a depreciator of the Parliamentary Bar, which I consider to be a machinery for grinding down great men into small ones. But your narrative of this part of his career is full of interest, & tends to raise even my appreciation of his great gifts & endowments; of which it is perhaps the capital achievement that they shed a lustre upon the sorry region in which he moved.

[1] Not found.   [2] Victoria, m. 1884 Prince Louis Alexander of Battenberg, later Mountbatten.
[3] W. Ince, 'The Luther commemoration of the Church of England' (1883).
[4] J. Mackintosh, *The history of civilization in Scotland*, 3v. (1878–83).
[5] This batch sent on 21 November, Add MS 44484, f. 111.
[6] i.e. Gladstone's own; p. 70 is a letter of 1845 on the 'engagement' (see also above, iii. xliv) in which the rescue work began; p. 88 is his 'epitaph' of their friendship in 1851 on Hope's conversion to Roman catholicism.

The hunting day, & the comparison of Liverpool of [*sic*;? with] Manchester, are wonderful; & the latter especially because I pretty well know it is the exact reverse of the truth.

In p. 128 is a reference to a change in his style of pleading during the latest years. Once, if not twice, I was myself cross-examined by him as counsel for the London & North-Western [Railway]. I know not whether it was old recollection, or *capites reverentia cani*, but I could not help feeling the extreme gentleness & even tenderness of his behaviour.

25. *Preadvent S.*

Chapel 10. & 12 (AM): St George's aft. Luncheon Sir H. Ponsonby's. Long audience of H.M: not much on public affairs. Wrote to Mr Hamilton 2 l. & Tel.—Mrs Ellice—Mr Mundella—Lord Derby—and minutes. Dined again with H.M. Pleasant conversation with Duchess of Albany. Read Macintosh—Engstrom on Evolution[1]—Revised Liturgy (my 25th?)—Johnson's Four Gospels.

26. *M.* [*Keble College, Oxford*]

Wrote to M. Grey—Mr Tennyson—Ly Holker—Ld Granville Tel.—C.G.—Mr Lockwood—& minutes. Went with Sir J. Cowell after Castle prayers to the new vaults & saw the *bowels* of the Terrace. Then the Kitchen. Off at 10.30 to Reading & the Coppice.[2] Staid 3½ hours with my dear old friend & had much conversation. Well pleased on the whole with his state of health. Disappointment about C.G. Reached Oxford, & Keble at 5.20. Evening with much interesting conversation. Read Bagehot on the Franchise.[3]

To ALFRED TENNYSON, 26 November 1883.   Add MS 44547, f. 3.

At Windsor where I have just been I had speech of the Queen about you. She inquired whether you had thought of a title yet. I replied that I had heard nothing from you on the subject. But I presume you will soon consider whether the announcement is to be before or after Xmas—a point in which the Queen leaves you perfectly free—& will make known to me your ideas as to title. It is usual to refer any proposed title to the Garter King at Arms, who makes observations on it if any point arise requiring consideration.

You are aware that in the matter of the John Brown Inscription the anonymous lines (that is to say I suppose your own) were preferred. But you sent others for choice, one of them from Byron & I found Her Majesty desirous to know where in Byron they are to be found. If you will supply me with chapter & verse I will report accordingly.

I presume Mr. Milnes Gaskell has sent you the little volume he has printed privately.[4] You may like to know that Knowles is charmed with the light which for him it throws on the revered character of Arthur Hallam. He has been at Hawarden & I gave him Arthur Hallam's letters to me for perusal. I cannot recollect enough to be a guide, but he says they are of more interest even than those to his Father, & I think he may wish to print some of them.[5]

[1] C. R. L. Engström, 'Christianity and evolution' (1883).
[2] Sir R. Phillimore's house near Henley.
[3] W. Bagehot, *Essays on parliamentary reform* (1883); a posthumous collection.
[4] See 23 Oct. 83.
[5] Tennyson replied, 2? December, Add MS 44484, f. 168: 'Don't let Knowles print A.H.Hs letters—at least let them be first submitted to me. I think that I of all living men should be allowed a voice in this matter. K. is a very clever man & a kindly—but he is ... Knowles of the 19th Century'.

Let me offer my best congratulations on Hallam's coming marriage. I do not doubt that he will be as good a husband as he has been a son, & better he cannot be.

27. Tu.

Keble Prayers 8 AM. Wrote to Sir Ed. Sullivan—Bishop Hellmuth[1]—H.G.—Ld R. Grosvenor—M.G.—Mr Ornsby—Ld Lorne—Mr Hamilton—& minutes. Saw new Buildings—Magd. Coll. Bridge[2]—Schools[3]—Balliol. Saw Dr Stubbs, Dr King, Bp of Oxford, Dean of Ch.Ch., Ld Weymouth, Mr Perceval, Mr Lock,[4] Dr Driver, & more than I can count. Read Hope Scott, another proof—Sayce's Preface[5]— Briefe, of Dss of Saxe-Coburg.[6]

To LORD R. GROSVENOR, chief whip, 27 November 1883.[7]   Add MS 44315, f. 136.

I am glad you were nearly, I trust you are wholly, out of the wood.

My asking Mr. Sellar[8] to Hawarden would be 'a measure' entailing many more for which I am too old, & I think it would make too much of the matter, & that the medium of communication would be less convenient & more committing than through you.

We went through the list of *remanets*[9] with some other Bills: perhaps I need not enter on these till we meet—perhaps at Hawarden, where the Duke is coming. There is an ample Bill of Fare. It is proposed to try the Scotch Bill again. I think there will be a fair allowance of *remanets* for 1885!

Late incidents & especially the Soudan disaster have very much ruffled the aspect of foreign affairs & Egypt again looks as if it might work out into a serious difficulty.

28. Wed.

Keble Chapel 8 AM. Wrote to Mr Hamilton l.l.—Ld Granville—Dr Acland—and minutes. Conversation with Lavinia [Lyttelton] on her brother Spencer. Breakfast in Keble Common Room. Read Briefe—Schliemann's Troja—K. Paul's Memoir of Mrs Woolstonecraft.[10] Visited Bodleian Library: the Librarian[11] was most kind. Held many conversations: & slept very sound.

29. Th.

New Coll Chapel 8 AM. Wrote to Mrs Burnett—Ld Granville l. & Tel.—Mr Hamilton Tel.—Mr Duckworth—Ld Derby—Mr Kegan Paul—Sir H. Verney—& minutes. Long conversation with the Vice Chancr (Dr Jowett). Cranbourne[12] &

---

[1] Isaac Hellmuth, formerly bp. of Huron.   [2] Then being widened and restored.
[3] The New Examination Schools, recently built in the High Street.
[4] Walter Lock, 1846–1933; sub-warden of Keble 1880–97.
[5] Preface by A. H. Sayce to H. Schliemann, *Troja: results of the latest researches* (1884).
[6] Not found.   [7] Holograph.
[8] See 23 Nov. 83.
[9] 'sum remaining as debts are being paid off'.
[10] Mary Wollstonecraft, *Letters to Imlay, with a prefatory memoir by C. Kegan Paul* (1879); see next day.
[11] Edward Williams Byron *Nicholson, 1849–1912; Bodley's librarian from 1882; modernised and expanded the library. For this visit, see E. W. B. Nicholson, 'Mr Gladstone and the Bodleian' (1898), 8.
[12] James Edward Hubert Gascoigne-Cecil (1861–1947; Lord Cranborne; 4th marquis of Salisbury 1903); then an undergraduate at University College (rather than Christ Church, his father's college).

G. Talbot[1] dined: an odd but pleasant trio. Saw Mr Price, Mr Merry, and divers persons. Visited the two Ladies' Halls.[2] Read Briefe (Duchess of Coburg) finished—Wollstonecraft Letters.

To LORD DERBY, colonial secretary, 29 November 1883.   Add MS 44547, f. 4.

I am sorry to share your impressions as to the Transvaal reply[3] but they correspond with my own. Indeed I assent to everything in your letter, & especially to your suggestion, accordant with that of Robinson that we should make the South West boundary & the frontier policy in that direction the preliminary stage & first condition of the whole discussion.

I hope to be in London tomorrow before 10, & I am going to see Granville about the Soudan. I should not wonder if it became necessary to call the Cabinet.

To C. KEGAN PAUL, 29 November 1883.   Add MS 44547, f. 4.

I thank you very much for sending me the volume of Mrs. Wollstonecraft's letters.[4] Mrs. Procter in no way misrepresented me, & it is to me, as it must be to many, of profound as well as mournful interest. It presents to me again Heloise, not to say Dido, with the freshness which nearness gives. She is one, I think, of the women of whom all should be known that can be known; a chapter of human nature in herself. I say this, with the feeling that, as far as I have yet read, her mental history is not fully told in the Imlay letters, & I should crave to know it all. Her early letters, given in your ably written & most interesting Life of Godwin,[5] command my unmixed admiration. How a woman so good & great could have fallen into so terrible an error is one of the many mysteries of this dispensation. I think that error modified her character, & I long to know both how far & how.

Nor am I able to make out what, *under the rules* of life which they adopted in common, was the precise outline of the offence which the wretched Imlay committed against her. For I understand that in their view marriage means the reciprocal attachment of the moment, & lapses *ipso facto* when that attachment dies. I hope you will take it as a special indication of my interest that I am sorely grieved whenever I come to any blanks or asterisks. I am grieved also not to have Imlay's letters, to integrate this strange & sorrowful record of humanity.

30. Sat. [London]

8¾-10¾. To D. St. Wrote to Duke of Westminster—Mr Goschen—Mr Putnam[6]—Duke of St Albans—The Queen—Bp of Carlisle—D. of Westminster—& minutes. Dined with Lucy Cavendish. Saw Mr Hamilton—Mr Bowman[7]—Ld Granville—Conclave on Span. Negotiations—Superior St Marg. Sisters—Mrs Th. Read

---

[1] (Sir) George John Talbot, 1861-1938; s. of J. G. Talbot; undergraduate at Christ Church.

[2] i.e. Somerville and Lady Margaret Hall.

[3] Derby's letter, 28 November, Add MS 44142, f. 10, pessimistic: 'They ask everything, and will concede nothing. They claim all those parts of Bechuanaland to which white freebooters have emigrated'; proposal for a boundary line being prepared.

[4] Sent on 27 November, on Paul's hearing of Gladstone's interest from Mrs. Procter; Add MS 44484, f. 146.

[5] See 12 Nov. 83.

[6] G. H. Putnam, American publisher; on including 'Kin beyond Sea' in a collection of essays; Add MS 44547, f. 5.

[7] On Goschen's eyesight; see 2 May 82.

Wollstonecraft Letters—Secret Hist. of Elisabeth & Essex.[1] And so ends the finest November I have ever known.

To G. J. GOSCHEN, M.P., 30 November 1883.   Add MS 44547, f. 5.

On receiving your letter of yesterday[2] I thought I had better see Bowman which I have done. Granville came in while he was here, & I have since had the opportunity of speaking to one or two other colleagues. We agree in thinking that the element of risk, to which you properly refer, is not such as would justify our foregoing the great advantages in other respects of having you in the Chair. Acting therefore on the liberty you give me I propose to regard the arrangement between us, which stood for further consideration, as final, although still, & until a time to be agreed on, confidential.

There is much in the Speakership which demands high powers of mind, apart from the ordinary duties of presiding over the daily sitting of the House: & I am very glad that such powers as yours are likely to be brought into contact with the subject as a whole.

I am certain that my colleagues will regard with much satisfaction the conclusion at which we have arrived.

Sat. Dec. One. 1883.

Wrote to Ld Granville—Mr Goschen l. & tel.—The Queen tel. & l.—Ld Monson—Mr A. Peel (Tel.)—& minutes. Dined at Mr Godley's. Saw Mr Hamilton—Mr Bowman—Sir A. Clark—Sir W. Harcourt—Mr Godley—Sir C. Dilke. Read Essex & Elisabeth (finished)—Wollstonecraft Letters (finished).

2 Advent Sunday.

Chapel Royal mg & evg. Saw Sir A. Clark—Mr Hamilton—Lady S. Spencer—(Gladys) Lady Lonsdale. Dined with Lucy Cavendish. Read Bp of Winchester on Anti-christ:[3] Rev. A. Moore on Science & Religion[4]—the first excellent, the last superficial. Read also Life of Godwin—Hesperas[5]—and divers. Catherine thank God advances rapidly: a galloping return of health.

To E. H. BROWNE, bishop of Winchester,   Add MS 44547, f. 6.
2 December 1883.[6]

When your sermon arrived, a day or two back, I told my private secretary we might dispense with the ordinary formal thanks. But I have read it to-day, and I must now send thanks more than formal. It seems to me to put into a practical and pastoral form the matter of a learned and careful dissertation. And this upon a subject so liable to what I will call wilful interpretations that in general the very name of it frightens me away.

It has, I think, much cleared my ideas, and I thank your lordship very much for such assistance, especially in regard to your exposition of 'he that letteth.' I understand this to be, in your view, the strong hand of law, embodied as well as represented in the Roman

---

[1] *The secret history of the earl of Essex and Queen Elizabeth. The happy slave and the double cuckold* (1699).
[2] Add MS 44161, f. 286; stronger glasses impossible; has doubts as to his shortsightedness but places himself in Gladstone's hands; further opinion from Bowman, ibid., f. 293.
[3] E. H. Browne, 'Antichrist. A sermon' (1883).
[4] A. L. Moore, *'Evolution and Christianity'* (1883).
[5] By E. M. Edmonds (1883).
[6] In Lathbury, i. 180. Browne replied, 3 December, Add MS 44115, f. 208, that Gladstone had exactly interpreted his thoughts.

Empire, on and after which was modelled the Roman State. And this State, not allowing free opinion, repressed licence as well as liberty, and prevented the profession and extension of atheism in its now multitudinous forms.

I have no doubt we have among us an idolatry of 'Church and State'; and the idolaters, or some of them, would not scruple to say that what is barbarously termed voluntaryism, which is making progress, though slow progress, in the world, was Antichrist. Yet I suppose it to be incredible that Apostles who were teaching Christianity as (in this sense) a private opinion, against or in fear of the State, could have *meant* to describe as Antichrist a full and free permission by the State to teach.

I suppose also that if communism or any of its kindred belong to Antichrist they belong to it consequentially; and that substantially, actually, and directly, it may mean the denial of God and setting up laws and rules of action self-chosen, and other than God.

It is not, I think, over forty-five years since Manning was the first to point out to me that the Church was passing back into the condition which it held before Constantine.

It all shows as a vast, overpowering, and bewildering Drama; but not without a key to its plan and meaning.

To A. W. PEEL, M.P., 2 December 1883. '*Secret*'.   Add MS 44547, f. 5.

It was after post time when I telegraphed to you yesterday: &, as I am not to see you until tomorrow, I think I had better put you in a position at once to weigh the subject I have to introduce, by acquainting you that I wish for your permission to have you proposed for the Chair of the House of Commons. I will not now enlarge upon the importance & dignity of this office, always great & of late enhanced. But, remembering that you felt called upon to relinquish your official position from considerations of health, I am not deterred by that recollection from my present proposal; & I will simply observe for the moment that I have never known a Speaker whose health gave way under the pressure of his duties, & I believe there has been no such case.

Few indeed are the offices which it is now so difficult to fill, & I very earnestly hope you will not withhold the aid we believe it is in your power to give from the Government & the House.[1]

3. *M.*

Wrote to The Speaker l.l.—The Queen l.l.—Ld Spencer—Ld Hartington—Ld Granville—Mr Chamberlain—Mr Linton—Mr Ornsby—Mr Milnes Gaskell—and minutes. Saw Mr Hamilton—Mr Lefevre—Mr A. Peel (our Speaker)—Mr Seymour. Read Life of Godwin—Imlay, Letters from U.S.[2]—M. Wollstonecraft, Reply to Burke[3]—and Letters from Sudan &c.[4]

To H. B. W. BRAND, the Speaker, 3 December 1883. '*Secret*'.[5]   Brand MSS 355.

This will be carried down to you by messenger who will be with you between four and five.

I have received your kind, considerate, and public-spirited offer, made in the hope of rescuing the Goschen proposal.

[1] Peel succeeded Brand as Speaker.
[2] G. Imlay, *A topographical description. . . in a series of letters to a friend in England* (1792); see 29 Nov. 83.
[3] M. Wollstonecraft, 'A vindication of the rights of men, in a letter to E. Burke' (1790).
[4] Perhaps J. Colborne, *With Hicks Pasha in the Sudan* (1883).
[5] Second letter, offering a Viscountcy, at Add MS 44547, f. 6.

I reluctantly abandoned hope in that quarter after the following incidents.

1. Bowman brought me on Saturday morning a dissuasive letter.

2. In forwarding as was my duty this letter to Goschen, I told him it did not alter my mind, while I admitted that it entitled him to claim his freedom from what, at that moment, had assumed the form of a settled arrangement.

3. He at once wrote back and claimed his freedom accordingly. This I thought conclusive (He had before referred to the contingency of your being willing to hold till Easter but this was *before* Bowman's dissuasive and my clinching the affair).

4. Time pressing I at once asked Arthur Peel to come up to town & last night I gave him notice that he might think the matter over.

5. He has *no* difficulty on the score of health; and with a due diffidence, but without hesitation, he accepts.

6. May he come down to see you tomorrow?+ Please reply by messenger.

7. And please again give me your opinion whether, after all that has been said in the papers, we shall attempt to maintain secrecy, and *for how long?*

+This has been altered as Peel himself will explain. So, since time does not press, I send no messenger, desiring not to attract attention.

To J. CHAMBERLAIN, president of the board of trade,   Chamberlain 5/34/20.
3 December 1883. '*Secret*'.

I see you are to speak tomorrow at Wolverhampton. Will you forgive my expressing the hope that you will do it with as much reserve on pending & proximate subjects as your conscience will allow. You will already have perceived that effects not intended or desired result from the opposite course. It is I know difficult and disagreeable to maintain these reserves, and rein in a strong conviction, a masculine understanding, and a great power of clear expression: but pray be as cruel as you can to your own gifts. I cannot now explain my reasons for writing, but you may divine them, and will I am sure excuse that act.[1]

[P.S.] Goschen finally deterred by the question of sight. A. Peel accepts.

To LORD HARTINGTON, war secretary, 3 December 1883.   Add MS 44146, f. 239.

The practical part of my reply to your weighty letter[2] need not at present be a long one; but I must introduce it with two explanations.

1. I have read Chamberlain's speech in a vilely printed Times, and I admit that it is provocative.[3] At a time when the Cabinet has carefully adjourned its decision, it has too much the air of a manifesto on the part of the Government, and he certainly should learn to speak, in office, with more reserve, or he will come at some time, and perhaps bring others to grief. I cannot wonder that it led you further than you would otherwise have thought it right to go. Opportunity may accordingly have been taken by some Journals to taunt and challenge you; but I hope you will not walk into the snare. For there the fact remains, that the Cabinet has decided nothing as to the measures it will proceed with except that *if* it proceed with the franchise, it will be the franchise alone. 2. I mentioned

---

[1] Chamberlain replied, 4 December, Add MS 44125, f. 209, promising to 'avoid any reference direct or indirect to Lord Hartington's speeches'; but he understood Gladstone to have agreed to public discussion of franchise provided no express commitments given.

[2] Of 2 December, alarmed about Chamberlain on franchise reform, on franchise reform in Ireland and need for safeguards for the north of Ireland; unable to be a party to a simple franchise bill; hinting at resignation; Holland, i. 396.

[3] Chamberlain's speech to N.L.F.: franchise including Ireland and separate from redistribution; *T.T.*, 27 November 1883, 7a; Jenkins, 185.

in the Cabinet a conversation which I held with Granville before the recess; when I told him that *if* perchance it should be the decision of the Cabinet to begin the proceedings of next Session with a Franchise Bill, I could undertake as I thought the charge of such a Bill, which would occupy the earlier portion of the Session. I had no idea in saying this that I was treading upon ground that could be difficult for you. Even in regard to Ireland I did not suppose any declaration you had made could bind you to withhold from that country some boon proposed at the time to be given to England and Scotland. As regarded re-distribution—bearing in mind your votes,[1] I did not dream of any embarrassment in this direction: though I might indeed have expected it, had I been urging that redistribution ought to be incorporated in a Franchise Bill. Granville must, like me, have been innocent of any apprehension, for he appeared to be pleased with what I said, and replied '*C'est autant de gagné*'.

Now I come to touch directly the subject matter of your letter, and especially the appeal to me, with which it closes. On the subject of your own declarations I am aware of nothing you have said which ought to fetter your liberty of action on the singularly important question whether you are to continue in connection with the Government. I take it for granted that you do not ask me with reference to any immediate act, for you would not think of acting on what the Cabinet may decide: and if Chamberlain, standing alone, has made declarations which would lead to the belief that it will decide in a par-ticular sense, this inconvenience is already neutralised by your own declarations, which again, if they stood alone, would foster a different expectation.

I hope, then, that in the interval which is before you, you will thoroughly sift a question which is, both politically and personally, deeper than the writers of newspaper articles suppose. I will only offer you a single suggestion, and append one or two queries in con-clusion. My suggestion is that you should consult Spencer, in whom I think you have much confidence, on the *pros* and *cons* (for doubtless there are both as to including Ire-land in any extension of the franchise). My queries are as follows. 1. Have you satisfied your own mind that there *is* any really available plan for the 'representation of the loyal minority' in the provinces, or in the northern province of Ireland? Besides not being satis-fied as to its utility, I greatly doubt whether such a plan can even get into the region of fact so as to be tried. 2. If a full expression of the voice of five millions in Ireland is to carry weight will there be no sufficient countervailing weight in the similarly full expression of the voice of thirty millions on this side of the water? 3. Will you fully consider whether, if prior declarations are to guide you, there is not great force in your own prior declarations by voice or vote from 1866 onwards in favour of sole dealing with the franchise? 4. Have you considered fully the effects to be produced by an action on your part which would have for its termination, as is most probable, your removal along with mine, and would leave the liberal party and the present Parliament able to count upon neither of us? No other man is in a position resembling that which you hold in the House of Commons, for you hold there your commission as Chief, although it is in temporary and accidental abeyance.

Pray consider these questions also as suggestions printed with a query, not as invita-tions to reply.[2]

To LORD SPENCER, Viceroy of Ireland, 3 December 1883. '*Secret*'.   Althorp MSS K6.

I send you herewith for perusal a copy of a letter I have had today from Hartington, & of my reply. You will see that in this reply I have recommended free communication with

[1] See to Hartington, 18 Dec. 83.
[2] Hartington replied, 5 December, promising no hasty action; Add MS 44146, f. 243.

you. Even our second conversation in Cabinet (& much less the first at which I think you were not present) did not give me the impression that his mind was in such serious disturbance.

Experience convinces me more & more from year to year that while Ireland has plenty of power to vex this great Empire, she has no power at all to wound it.

I hope you will make Lady Sarah visit us going or coming. I spoke of this, & she took it kindly.

[P.S.] I am truly glad that equal justice has been done upon Lord Rossmore.[1]

4. Tu. [*Hawarden*]

Wrote to . . . & minutes. Saw Mr Seymour—Scotts—Mrs Birks. Twelve o'clock train to Hawarden with C. & party: successful journey. Read Life of Lyndhurst[2]—Mrs Godwin on French Revolution[3]—Miss Thackeray on Tennyson.[4] Sorting papers &c.

5. Wed.

Ch. 8½ A.M. Wrote to Mr Seymour—Lord Devon—and minutes. Woodcraft with W. & H. How thankful should I be for the remarkable vigour with which Catherine has recovered. Unpacked books. Read Harcourt Papers[5]—Lyndhurst's Life—Mrs Godwin French Rev.

6. Th.

Ch. 8½ AM. Wrote to H. Tennyson Tel.—Ld Spencer l. & Tel.—Mr Seymour Tel.—Mr Goschen—Ld Carlingford—Mr Lefevre—Ld Hartington—The Queen l.l.—Mr Chamberlain—Abp of Canterbury—& minutes. Felled a tree with WHG. Read Lyndhurst's Life—[blank] on Deer Forests[6] &c.—Harcourt Papers—Mary Godwin on Fr. Revolution.

To J. CHAMBERLAIN, president of the board of trade,   Chamberlain MSS 5/34/21.
6 December 1883.

Your letter explains to me a passage in your speech,[7] which had seemed to me mysterious: that in which you implied that the decision of the Cabinet might change from intervening circumstances. This I now see you put in as a needful reserve. But unfortunately you proceeded upon a misapprehension such as will sometimes occur: the Cabinet only decided the one extremely important point that *if* we proceed with the subject of Representation it shall be with Franchise only.

I do not recognize the words which you write in inverted commas, and in particular the word 'expressly'. There was nothing I think to prevent members of the Government from stating considerations bearing in a particular direction, and it is in the manner of doing this that so much care is required: since all, whatever their leanings, may claim an equal

---

[1] Removed from the magistracy for inciting Orangemen to attack Home Rulers.
[2] See 31 Aug. 83.
[3] M. Wollstonecraft, *An historical and moral view of the origin . . . of the French revolution* (1794).
[4] Paper reprinted in Mrs. R. Thackeray, *Records of Tennyson, Ruskin, Browning* (1892).
[5] See 3 Sept. 81.
[6] Untraced.
[7] See 3 Dec. 83n.

liberty. In the present instance some difficulties have resulted which I shall of course do my best to overcome. If you speak again you will perhaps let it be seen that the field is still open & the Government unfettered as to its measures for 1884, however we may have endeavoured to appreciate the various considerations bearing upon them. I say 'let it be seen' in contradistinction to anything like a formal announcement.[1]

To LORD HARTINGTON, war secretary, 6 December 1883.   Add MS 44146, f. 247.

1. You will, I think, have seen that my *query* about representation of minorities means such a representation in Ireland only. This it is which I must admit I meant to point at as impossible either in a Franchise Bill or a Bill for re-distribution. The minority question is indeed most formidable. It is very closely allied with that of electoral districts, which I think it would entail. But there are two things about it which appear to me indisputable: 1. That it cannot be applied in one of the three countries without the other two: 2. That it belongs to the re-distribution branch of the subject.

In my own mind, I go a step further and would say that the difficulties of this point alone supply an adequate reason against mixing them with the necessary difficulties of the franchise. This I give only as an opinion, without presuming to say it is indisputable, though *I* cannot dispute it. 2. Reading your letter again I find words which I cannot but hope are due to a *lapsus* of the pen: those which imply that apart from the disclosure (which you, differing from me and others, suppose to have taken place) you do not think you could have been a party to a simple Franchise Bill for Great Britain. Such words would surely imply a recession from public acts (and declarations?) which I do not think we have been led to expect. 3. I wrote to Chamberlain a note of caution; and from his reply I find that he spoke under a misapprehension of what had taken place in the Cabinet. He thought we had decided to bring in a Franchise Bill, which most certainly is not the case.[2]

To LORD SPENCER, Viceroy of Ireland, 6 December 1883.[3]   Althorp MSS K6.

I thought it well to use the telegraph, on receiving your very acceptable letter, to the following effect. 'Thanks I am not at all dissatisfied with opinion stated near the close of your letter it may be the very thing required by the present circumstances I speak of it in this light only.'

My meaning of course is that if you can draw Hartington to your view that the minority question is a branch of redistribution, you will gain everything required for the present time, and very possibly everything required for the ulterior stage.

The minority question, you may remember, is one of those which I pointed out to the Cabinet as a most formidable addition to the difficulties of redistribution. (No, I am afraid you were not present, but I did it) and a reason for not now attempting to deal with it.

But I feel confident of your concurrence in the opinion I have conveyed (by query) to Hartington that we cannot have a minority plan *for Ireland only.*

Minority representation is a most unfortunate and annoying subject which may split the Liberal Party but why should we take it before its proper time. Men are not only divided upon it but vehemently divided. It is improbable that I shall personally have a share in its settlement; this perhaps abates my heat. It would be more suited to electoral districts than to units naturally defined like town and country. Now I have no fears

[1] Further exchange on this at Add MS 44125, ff. 213-7.
[2] No reply found.
[3] In *Spencer*, i. 258.

whatever of electoral districts: but I am inclined to prefer the old constitutional division. It is a very great hardship on very large constituencies to be *exclusively* subject to the minority clause, and thus to have their majorities made far less important in Parliament than the majorities in very many smaller boroughs. Electoral districts with three members each would perhaps give the best form of minority clause. But who would take this plan?

7. *Fr.*

Ch. 8½ A.M. Wrote to Ld Hartington—Ld Granville Tel—Lady Mar—Mr Seymour Tel.—May Talbot—Messrs Leeman—& minutes.—Bp of Gloucester—Sir H. Ponsonby. Woodcraft with WHG. Read Life of Lyndhurst—Schliemann's Troja—Godwin Fr. Revolution—Harcourt Papers.

To LORD HARTINGTON, war secretary, 7 December 1883.   Add MS 44146, f. 249.

I thank you for the assurance contained in your note [of 5 December] from Hardwick, which has crossed a letter from me. I was not aware of your sharing Chamberlain's impression that the Cabinet had reached a decision on the introduction of a Franchise Bill at the beginning of the Session. Yet I can confidently assure you that it is not so. You would I think find me supported in this by other colleagues. Moreover it is my very special duty to take notice of the exact scope of any material proceeding in the Cabinet for immediate report to the Queen; and had the decision been arrived at in this case as supposed, my error would have been a very gross one in sending to H.M. a different account of much narrower scope.

8. *Sat.*

Ch. 8½ A.M. Wrote to Ld Granville l.l. & Tel.—Mr Seymour l. & Tel.—Mr Mivart—Mr Ford—Mr Duckworth—Ld Derby—Viceroy of Ireland Tel—Sir C. Dilke—& minutes. Woodcraft with W. & S. Read Life of Lyndhurst—Harcourt Papers—Schliemann's Troy—Godwin French Rev.

To LORD DERBY, colonial secretary, 8 December 1883.   Add MS 44547, f. 10.

With the whole of the condemnatory part of your letter on the Resolutions of the Australian Convention[1] I need hardly say that I am in absolute sympathy. This is a little qualified when I come to the affirmative part, & the New Guinea protectorate.

Is it usual to constitute such a relation without either the concurrence of the protected state or peoples or else the intervention, as in the case of the Ionian Islands, of a higher authority? This is by the bye.

I feel many scruples about this Protectorate, but I should pay due deference to your opinion, & generally to those who have a longer base of politics before them than I have.

Apart however from the broader considerations, I should rather doubt the policy of raising the question of a Protectorate in New Guinea as part of an answer to the

---

[1] Intercolonial conference on annexation of New Guinea reconvened at Sydney on 6 December; Australian Federal Council formed 7 December. Derby told Gladstone, 7 December, Add MS 44142, f. 14: 'what can be said in favor of the Monroe doctrine laid down for the whole South Pacific? . . . This is mere raving . . . I have come to the conclusion that as regards New Guinea we cannot hold out against the demand for a protectorate.'

preposterous proposals of the Convention.[1] They have supplied the best possible ground for a negative answer; and may it not be argued that it would be best to leave them to raise if they think proper the narrower question, treating their scheme for the present as one.

Were we to suggest a Protectorate as an alternative, they would begin to hook on more to it, & our position would be a false one. So at least it appears to me at first sight.

To Sir C. W. DILKE, president of the local government board,   Add MS 43875, f. 154
8 December 1883. '*Private*'.

In the present circumstances, it is desirable to put together the list of former votes and declarations about the county franchise & its relation to Redistrn. I think you have almost done this and if so I would ask you to undertake or superintend the confidential work of getting it completed.

If you cannot do this, I will refer to R. Grosvenor but I think it would cost him much labour.[2]

9. 2 S. Adv.

Ch mg & evg. Wrote to The Speaker—Ld Derby—Mr Hitchman—The Queen—& minutes. Read Grammar of Assent[3]—Life of Princess Alice[4]—Whyte, Shorter Catechism[5]—N. Hall, Lord's Prayer[6]—Miller, Heavenly Bodies.[7]

To LORD DERBY, colonial secretary, 9 December 1883.   Add MS 44547, f. 11.

I am concerned to hear that the Dutchmen are obstinate as I had hoped that their idea of drawing the frontier line[8] according to the inclination of the chiefs would if workable prove a good one.

As to the trade route I am not well able to judge, but we could not give up Bechuana Land against the inclination of the chiefs. Nor can any very new or important resolution, I think, be taken without a reference to the Cabinet.

10. M.

Ch. 8½ A.M. Wrote to Mr Milnes Gaskell—Ld Granville l.l.—Ld Spencer—Sir H. Ponsonby—Dr Whyte—Mr Chamberlain—Mr Murray—Mr Goschen—& minutes. Woodcraft with WHG. Read Life of Lyndhurst (finished: too optimistic)—Hope Scott, proofs—Harcourt Papers—Godwin, French Revolution.

[1] Arthur Gordon, 8 December, misled Gladstone into underestimating Australian feeling on New Guinea, *T.A.P.S.*, n.s. li. 89, Thompson, *Australian imperialism*, 87.

[2] See 13 Dec. 83.

[3] By J. H. Newman; see 27 Mar. 70.

[4] *Alice, Grand Duchess of Hesse . . . biographical sketch and letters* (1884).

[5] A. Whyte, *Commentary on the shorter catechism* (1883).

[6] By C. N. Hall; various eds.

[7] By W. Miller (1883).

[8] Derby's letter, 8 December, Add MS 44142, f. 19: 'We have had an unsatisfactory answer . . . from the Transvaalers . . . we ought to consider whether we shall break off all rather than give them Bechuanaland, if they persist'; feeling in the Commons 'main element' in this decision.

To LORD SPENCER, Viceroy of Ireland, 10 December 1883.   Althorp MSS K7.
'*Secret*'.

If Hartington does not soon write to you, I would suggest your writing to him, on the ground of your knowledge that he means to consult with you, and of the prudence of an early solution.

Your ideas about the minority plan,[1] combined with its necessary postponement, seems more likely to build a bridge for him amidst his present embarrassments, than any other expedient. Of course it would be best of all if he would frankly abandon an untenable ground.[2]

11. Tu.

Ch. 8½ A.M. Wrote to Sir W. Harcourt—Mr C. Russell MP.—Rev. Dr Chase—Mr H. Tennyson—Lady Mar—Ld R. Grosvenor—Mr Moulton—Sir S. Northcote—Dr Nevin—Rev. Newman Hall—Mr Hitchman—and minutes. Read Cleveland[3]—Harcourt Papers finished VI—Godwin, French Revolution—Fettis foundation.[4] Woodcraft with W.

To Sir S. H. NORTHCOTE, M.P., 11 December 1883.   Add MS 50014, f. 270.

It had just been settled between the Speaker and me that a short time hence I was to write and appraise you of the intention of the Government as to the nomination of a successor, when I was taken by surprise on seeing this morning notifications in the newspapers that Mr. Peel had forestalled our little plan.

Doubtless some constituent has forced his hand and incidentally deprived me of the opportunity of paying you an attention which on every ground I should have wished to render.

The substance of the statement I need hardly say is correct and you will join in a regret, which I believe will be universal, for the retirement of an admirable public servant from the discharge of duties, always weighty, and now become more arduous.

12. Wed.

Ch. 8½ A.M. Wrote to Ld Granville l.l.l. & Tel.—Bp of Gloucester—Archdn Norris—Mr Kegan Paul—Mr Seymour Tel.—and minutes. Woodcraft with W.—Much to do after the storm. Read Cleveland—Harcourt Papers I.—Mrs Godwin Fr. Rev. finished and [blank.]

13. Th.

Ch. 8½ A.M. Wrote to Sir W. Harcourt l. & Tel.—Mr C. Russell—Mr H. West—Prince L.L. Bonaparte—Duchess of Edinburgh—Lord Granville Tel.—Sir C. Dilke—Mr Russell MP—Chairman of Statue Committee[5]—and minutes. Woodcraft with Willy. Company arriving. Conversation with E. Talbot. Worked upon books. Read Harcourt Papers—Progress & Poverty[6]—Cleveland: Sir R. Peel (l).

---

[1] Seen by Spencer as an aspect of redistribution; Jones, *1884*, 45 and 6 Dec. 83.
[2] Spencer replied that he had written to Hartington; Add MS 44310, f. 179.
[3] Mrs M. Gartshore, *Cleveland: a tale of the Catholic church* (1847) or see 22 Mar. 84.
[4] May read 'Fettis'; on the Edinburgh school?
[5] Unveiling this day of E. Onslow Ford's statue at the City Liberal Club, *T.T.*, 14 December 1883, 7c.
[6] By Henry George; see 11 Nov. 79, 4 Oct., 27 Dec. 83.

To Sir C. W. DILKE, president of the local government board,   Add MS 43875, f. 156.
13 December 1883.

I think it will be quite enough to trace from 1866[1] our committals on the Franchise—
and especially all that bears on its severance from re-distribution.

Many thanks, my wife has quite recovered.

14. Fr.

Ch. 8½ A.M. Wrote to Dowr Ly Queensberry—Ld Granville—The Queen—Ld
Leitrim—Ld Derby Tel.—Mr Hamilton l. & Tel.—and minutes. Walk & conver-
sation with F. Leveson [Gower]—Saw Mr A. Montgomery—E. Talbot—C.
Lacaita. Read Harcourt Papers—Progress and Poverty—History of Orkney[2]—
Cleveland.

15. Sat.

Ch. 8½ A.M. Wrote to Mr Trevelyan—Ld Granville l. & Tel.—Ld Ailesbury—Mr
Ornsby—Ld Northbrook—Ld Derby Tel.—and minutes. Conversation with
C. Lacaita—Mr Leveson—E. Talbot. Neuralgia in evg. Retired early to bed &
quinine. Read Harcourt Papers—Progress & Poverty—Cleveland.

To LORD NORTHBROOK, first lord of the admiralty,   Add MS 44547, f. 16.
15 December 1883.

I need hardly tell you that I have read Major Biddulph's letter[3] with much pain; but I
none the less thank you for sending it, as it is needful for us to know what is said, & the
worst of what is said. I suppose there cannot well be worse than what we have heard. It
leaves Parnell & even his friends (so far as I know) far behind, & it certainly shows the
crisis to be very serious indeed. It also makes me additionally thankful that we did not fall
into the trap by acceding to the unhappy proposal that the matter should be decided by
the House of Commons.

The letter says 'Gladstone's speeches have done an immense lot of harm because they
have made Englishmen believe' etc. . . . what they (Englishmen) say is this; & then follows
what purports apparently to be a description of my speeches. In this description I cannot
detect the slightest resemblance to anything I said. The violence of the passion is shown
by the violence of the caricature.

I did indeed, under a sad conviction of its necessity, say one very painful thing—I compared those loyal English (as they believe themselves) to those with whom I have been
familiar for 50 years.[4] The British party in all our colonies & in the Ionian Islands under
the old system of Downing Street Government, including the same party in the West
Indies. But these gentlemen, if Major Biddulph's account be correct, beat them all.

I wish I could learn from it any other lesson than the one you appear to draw.

---

[1] Dilke asked if he should start in 1859 or 1866; Add MS 44149, f. 194.

[2] Probably J. B. Craven, *History of the episcopal church in Orkney* (1883).

[3] John Biddulph, 1840–1921; on Northbrook's staff in India and still resident there. Biddulph's
letter not found; Northbrook commented: 'our English countrymen in India have gone quite wild . . .
I hope Ripon will be firm & go steadily on with the [Ilbert] Bill'; 14 December, Add MS 44267, f. 33.

[4] On 21 August; *H* 283. 1537.

16. 3 S. Adv.

Ch. mg & evg. Wrote to Mr Ornsby—Mr Tupper—& minutes. Read the closing proof sheets of dear Hope Scott's Life—Drummond, Natural Law[1]—Allies, a Life's decision[2]—Poletto, Libertà e Legge.[3]

17. M. [Soughton Hall]

Ch. 8½ A.M. Conversation with E. Talbot—Wrote to W.L. Gladstone—& minutes. Woodcraft: initiated Ld Aberdeen,[4] a very good workman. Worked on books. Read Harcourt Papers—Progress & Poverty—Mr Cleveland. Dined and slept at Soughton: large party & very hospitable house.[5] Got instruction about the Peak of Teneriffe & its shadow.

18. Tu. [Hawarden]

Wrote to The Queen—Ld Granville l.l.—Sir H. Thring—Ld Hartington—Att. General—Ld Chancellor—& minutes. Returned to Hawarden at noon: after inspecting Mr Bankes's House & Trees. Woodcraft with WHG. Read Mr Cleveland—Harcourt Papers.

To LORD HARTINGTON, war secretary, 18 December 1883.   Add MS 44146, f. 253.
'Secret'.

I am really sorry to have given you trouble[6] by referring to your votes and speeches on the junction of the two subjects of franchise and redistribution. It came about in this way. I recollected that as a member of the cabinet of 1866, you had shared in our resistance to the junction:[7] and I gathered from some observations of Dilke's in the Cabinet, to which I did not understand you to take exception at the time, that you had continued to be of the same opinion. I now understand that this was wrong, and that you had altered your mind, more or less positively, during the interval. You will forgive my mis-apprehension under the circumstances. But indeed I am not quite sure that I should have been right even had there been no error as to the facts, in mentioning the point, when there are so many other points, of deeper moment than the exterior consistency of any among us, to consider, in connection with the possible issues of our present deliberations. Through these I in vain endeavour, thus far, to see my way: I do not mean my own personal way, for that, thanks to the course of nature, is indeed the shortest and simplest portion of the subject.

19. Wed.

Ch. 8½ A.M. Wrote to Ld Derby l. & Tel.—Ld Granville l. & Tel.—Ld Hartington—Mr Childers—Sir F. Sandford—Mr Chamberlain—Mr Anstey—Mr Godley—Prince L.L. Bonaparte—W.L. Gladstone. Read Harcourt Papers—Mr Cleveland.

[1] H. Drummond, *Natural law in the spiritual world* (1883).
[2] See 30 Sept. 83.
[3] Not found.
[4] The 6th earl (see 12 Jan. 70), staying with his wife Isabel.
[5] Seat in Northrop of J. S. Bankes; see 28 May 57.
[6] Hartington wrote on 16 December, Add MS 44146, f. 250, denying he was committed to franchise separate from redistribution.
[7] Though Hartington was not in the Cabinet until February 1866, after the first cabinet vote had been taken; see 29 Jan. 66.

Woodcraft with WHG. More conversation with young Newcastle:[1] who has character and promise. Houghton, Harcourt, Childerses came: & Mr Stuart[2] with whom I had an academical conversation.

To J. CHAMBERLAIN, president of the board of trade,   Chamberlain MSS 5/34/23. 19 December 1883.

So far as I can judge you have managed skilfully your reference to the Throne in your speech of the 18th at Birmingham, and I hope it will give satisfaction. But I own my regret at the form of words, unexplained as it is, which you employed about the House of Lords, & which I fear may raise a new controversy. I think I understand your meaning, thus namely, that the Lords should not stop the progress of a franchise Bill; & in this I altogether concur. But those readers who are not predisposed to equitable construction will interpret this as a wider demand, & fresh objection may be founded upon it. Nothing could be easier than a word of explanation, should you have another opening by letter or otherwise.[3]

To LORD DERBY, colonial secretary, 19 December 1883.   Add MS 44142, f. 30.

I think you will agree with me that the course you suggest for consideration as to Zulu-land[4] would require that consideration from the Cabinet. I do not feel able to come to a final judgment about it, partly from what seems to me a confusion in the Bulwer telegram (of this I have asked by telegraph an explanation).

But I should if possible avoid this course, as a new departure, & especially on this ground that there is a want, I think, of definiteness in the aim. In Egypt we had at any rate a definite aim; but this would only be, as I understand it, something like waiting till rivers ceased to flow. But I can quite understand that we cannot keep Cetewayo in the Reserve and let him pull the wires from that sheltered place; nor do I suppose it possible for him to be prevented from putting [sc. pulling] the wires while he remains there. I am quite ready therefore, and I suppose it to be within the meaning of the past action of the Cabinet, to require his departure. He would have to choose, I presume, between taking his chance in his own country and his coming into ours for refuge.

Might he ask our friendly intervention for a settlement with Usibeba, & in this perhaps unlikely contingency need we refuse it? But if he went back to fight it out I am by no means convinced that this would be a greater evil than our territorial intervention.

20. Th.

Ch. 8½ A.M. Wrote to Ld Granville (2)—Ld E. Clinton—H. Tennyson—and minutes. Spent forenoon in conversation chiefly on the anxious subject raised by H[artingto]n's state of mind. 1-4¾. Visit to Eaton. It has certainly much of

[1] Henry Pelham Archibald Douglas Clinton, 1864-1928; 7th duke of Newcastle 1879; had 'a wooden leg and large head' (*Mary Gladstone*, 297). Though no longer a trustee, Gladstone maintained an interest in Newcastle estate matters.

[2] Of Cambridge; see 26 Oct. 78.

[3] Chamberlain refused, quoting Forster as a precedent; Garvin, i. 403; see 22 Dec. 83.

[4] Derby's letter, 18 December 1883, Add MS 44142, f. 25: Usibeba as sovereign impossible; Cetewayo only restorable 'under control'; but a British solution necessary; a provisional expedient would be occupation up to Usibeba's boundary until a solution devised: 'You will not like this notion, nor do I', but no alternative available.

grandeur; & of beauty. Read Mr Cleveland—Harcourt papers. Whist in evg. The Westminsters came to dine and sleep. About 16 to dinner.

21. Fr.

Wrote to Sir W. Harcourt Tel.—Sec. Eccl. Commn. Read Cleveland—Harcourt papers—Theosophic reply to Sinnett[1]—Mr R. Brown's Kirké.[2] Walk with Childers & Stuart. Conclave on H[artingto]n and the Franchise. Ch. $8\frac{1}{2}$ A.M. and H.C. Party reduced.

22. Sat.

Ch. $8\frac{1}{2}$ AM. Wrote to Sir H. Ponsonby—Mr Chamberlain—Sir D. Currie—Ld Granville—Rev. Dr Nevin—Sir J. Lambert—and minutes. The Derby Deputation came for presentation of the fine dessert service. Spoke half an hour or so.[3] Then luncheon, showing the Castle & Park, coffee, & all over before five. Read Cleveland—Brown's Kirkè. Saw Sir W. Harcourt.

To J. CHAMBERLAIN, president of the board of trade,   Chamberlain MSS 5/34/24.
22 December 1883.

My suggestion[4] did not, as I meant it, go to altering or qualifying, but only to making clear the sense of the words which appeared to me rather to risk misapprehension, or invite misapprehension.

You must be the judge in such a matter: you will forgive me for seeming officious, because my difficulties in keeping things together at this moment are very great and I do not well know what will be the end.

I am however the *less* anxious about this collateral matter, because I find that your observations about the Throne appear to have had a good effect.

It is my misfortune to have a very considerable degree of concurrence with your estimate of the legislative performances of the House of Lords, & it would not have a savoury effect, were I to speak out all I think on that matter. But not being prepared to take any steps I am loath, for myself, to use any language which might be misinterpreted.

You are perfectly correct in your reference to Forster. But his words made a general stir in the Cabinet, although he spoke upon the provocation of an outrageous proceeding actually taken.

In accepting a dessert-service from Derby today I have said a few words (not naming the Lords) intended to have a pacifying effect.

[P.S.] Since I wrote to you last, I have discovered a segment of the Cabinet who hold that at the last sitting *nothing* was decided!

---

[1] A. Kingsford and E. Maitland, 'A letter to the Fellows of . . . the Theosophical Society' (1883); attack on A. P. Sinnett's *Esoteric Buddhism* (1883).
[2] See 5 Nov. 83.
[3] *T.T.*, 24 December 1883, 8a.
[4] See 19 Dec. 83.

To Sir J. LAMBERT, 22 December 1883.   Add MS 44547, f. 19.
'*Private & Confidential*'.

It has given me great pleasure to receive your valuable paper.[1] It may be taken I hope as the confutation of a rumour which reached me that you were out of health, and which alone prevented me from asking some time back for your assistance in a specific form.

This being so, you will not be surprised if in making two or three remarks upon it I likewise include here and there a question.

(1). I will begin by putting aside for the present the question of redistribution, and saying that I think any plan of it which a Government may now propose will be expected to settle the question, and in this respect to vary very greatly from the redistribution carried in 1867 and even from that proposed in 1866.

(2). Occupation franchise. Here you aim at a complete identity. Would not the simplest form be to enact, together with the two extensions you propose from Borough to County, a third extension from County to Borough, viz. an extension of the £12 franchise combined with its reduction to £10 so as to supersede the £10 franchise in Boroughs.

(3). Ancient rights franchise. Can it be assumed that the first three of these are so insignificant that they might safely & conveniently be abolished, except as to persons already registered?

(4). Property franchise (though I incline to hold that franchises of industrial occupation belong to this category in principle). You speak at the head of page 3 of the difficulty which would attend the introduction of freehold & property voting, with the 7 miles limit, into Boroughs. But would not the condition of residence to which you refer farther down bear on this subject in a very important way? Would there be a great jealousy, supposing: (a) that the property vote could only be exercised on condition of residence or industrial occupation (b) that subdivision of hereditaments by rent charge or otherwise, were prohibited (with a reserve for industrial occupation). If something of this kind could be done, for Borough and County, it would be a great further step towards assimilation.

(5). Could it be provided that an occupation-voter in a Borough, having also a property qualification, might register *as now* in respect of it for the County?

(6). As to registration. Will it not be fair to provide (a) that rated inhabitancy and occupation votes be put on the register by a public authority, but (b) that lodger-voters, and property voters of all kinds, must come there by claim?

(7). If occupation voting (in which I now include lodgers) be assimilated as you propose, have you estimated the proportion which occupiers of all kinds will form of the total constituency? (Even if the freehold qualification be introduced into Boroughs it cannot be numerically large I presume).

23. *4 S. Adv.*

Ch. mg & evg. Wrote to Bishop of Lincoln—Ld Mayor of Dublin—Ld Granville Tel. l.l.—Sir W. Harcourt—The Queen—Mrs Bolton—& minutes. Read Drummond on Law—Allies, a Life's decision.

To Sir W. V. HARCOURT, home secretary, 23 December   MS Harcourt dep. 9, f. 68.
1883.

I had not time yesterday to speak to you of the sequel with Chamberlain. He held his

---

[1] Mem. on county franchise with tables, his proposals advancing 'as much as possible on the old lines'; Add MS 44235, f. 138. Lambert replied, 26 December, ibid., f. 141, after working with Arnold's returns, with a separate list of replies to Gladstone's questions.

ground firmly about the House of Lords.[1] I pointed out that I only ⟨begged him to⟩ suggested he might make it clearly understood that he meant to express a hope that the Lords would take no violent course about a Reform Bill. I told him his language about the Throne had done good. He writes with perfect temper but I do not think good would arise from any further application to him now. I have signified to him that there are rather heavy clouds in the sky.

To C. WORDSWORTH, bishop of Lincoln,   Wordsworth MS 2148, f. 93.
23 December 1883.

I have had the pleasure to receive your Lordship's letter touching the new See of Southwell:[2] but together with it has come one from Sir G. Pringle, in answer to an inquiry from me, which acquaints me that the substantial arrangements are not quite complete and that we cannot say when the certificate of the Ecclesiastical Commissioners is likely to issue.

This being so I can only thank your Lordship for the excellent list which you have given me of qualifications for the See, and tender in return the assurance that when the proper time arrives it will be my desire to proceed in this important matter with the utmost care and caution.

24. M.

Slightly unwell. Wrote to E. Hamilton l & tel.—Sir W. Harcourt—G. Leveson—Ld Granville—& minutes. Read Allies, Life's decision—Maryatt MP on Chamberlain[3]—Whitehead on Fruit Farming[4]—Campbell, the Land Question[5]—Cleveland. Worked on books. We are now a family party with only Lucy who is altogether one of us.

25. Xmas Day.

Ch 11 AM with H.C. and [blank.] Wrote to Dr Nevin—Ld Granville l. & Tel.—Sir H. Ponsonby—& minutes. Read Allies finished—S. Leathes on Xty[6]—Wiclif's Polemical Latin Works.[7] The usual Xmas Dinner above and below. Yesterday I read with ease at 4.30. At 4.50 the sky was splendid with rose colour all round (as far as I saw) & the glow was still strong at six. Today has been gloomy: yet at five o'clock the upper sky was faintly tinged with rose-colour.[8] Query have not November and December been about the two most delightful months of this year?

[1] See 19, 22 Dec. 83.

[2] Of 21 December, Add MS 44346, f. 433, with list of required qualities, e.g. 'accurate knowledge of the History, the Laws and the Doctrines of the Church Catholic'; letter of 24 January 1884, ibid., f. 438, urged speedy appt.

[3] W. T. Marriott, 'The liberal party and Mr Chamberlain' (1883).

[4] Sir C. Whitehead, *Profitable fruit farming* (1884).

[5] Perhaps G. Campbell, 'Impressions of the Irish Land bill', *F.R.*, xxxv. 552 (May 1881).

[6] S. Leathes, *Characteristics of Christianity* (1884).

[7] John Wiclif, *Memorial works in Latin*, ed. R. Buddensieg, 2v. (1883).

[8] Exceptional sunrises and sunsets said to be caused by dust from eruptions of Krakatoa in August.

26. *St Steph.*

Ch. 8½ AM. Wrote to E. Hamilton—Ld Granville l. & Tel l.l.—Ld Kimberley—E. Talbot—Sir W. Harcourt—Mr Giffen[1]—and minutes. Read E. Talbot on Pusey[2]—Giffen's (masterly) Address—Cleveland—Progress and Poverty.[3] Felled a tree with WHG: & inspected the Stable.

To Sir W. V. HARCOURT, home secretary,   MS Harcourt dep. 9, f. 69.
26 December 1883. '*Secret*'.

I wish I could with a good conscience *pocket* your liberal tribute to my better qualities.[4] All I can dare to say is that I think experience of life has taught me something; and I must hope to go on learning.

I think Chamberlain is now in his most conciliatory mood, and I am very glad you are to see Hartington.

It will be a blow to me if I have to mortgage another piece of my small residue of life: but I will not allow my personal consideration (except inability) to be a bar to a favourable agreement.

I think one of the phantoms which have been scaring Hartington's usually manly mind, is that of Electoral districts; and he probably suspects me of looking to a plan on this basis. Now, as my faith is in the nation, I cannot say it would be much shaken in whatever way the country may be district-ed. But I am against Electoral districts, so far as I can see my way into the subject, as I am against all changes which distract and disturb, and which are not called for by any motive of necessity.

There is one point on which I must reserve my freedom, and that is to press upon Hartington, (should I see cause,) if he absolutely refuse to concur in our policy, to assume the responsibility of trying his own, with all the support we can give him, rather than wreck the ship by going, or by letting others send us, to the country in two camps.

Heartily glad you have such good accounts of your son, and brimful of wishes for your Happy New Year.

To LORD KIMBERLEY, Indian secretary, 26 December 1883.   Add MS 44547, f. 20.

Like you, I do not greatly relish a second and enlarged edition of concessions[5] in a case where the opponents hardly affected to stand upon reasons and according to report out-did Parnell & co. in their disloyal violence. But of the concessions in themselves I am not a competent judge and in any case I think you had no choice under the circumstances though I feel perplexed at Ripon's mode of conducting the affair. Perhaps further light may be thrown upon the question from the native side.

I feel assured that postponement was the right course to take as to the address in London. It will have to be dealt with hereafter.

Many thanks for your good wishes combined with hearty returns all the way across the Island.

[1] Thanking him for 'The progress of the working classes in the last half century', *Journal of the Royal Statistical Society*, xlvi. 593 (1883): 'in form and in substance the best answer to George. And I hope it may be practicable to give it a wide circulation'; Add MS 44547, f. 21 (letter printed in *J.R. Stat. Soc.*, xlvii. 174 (1884)). See next day.
[2] By E. S. Talbot; not traced; perhaps privately printed.
[3] See 13 Dec. 83.
[4] On Gladstone's 'courteous kindness & indulgence'; 25 December, Add MS 44198, f. 166.
[5] Telegrams from Ripon proposing compromise on the Ilbert Bill; Add MS 44228, f. 133.

27. Th. St John.

Ch. 8½ A.M. Wrote to Abp of Canterbury—Ld Granville Tel.l.l.l.—Duke of Bedford—H. Tennyson—Professor Owen—Mr Hamilton—Mr Wratislaw—Ld Ailesbury—Duke of Leinster—Lady Mar—The Queen—& minutes. Read Progress & Poverty—Seeley, Extension of England—Palmer's Wrexham[1]—Rees, Welsh Nonconformity[2]—Cleveland. Felled a tree with WHG. Sir A. Wood came.

To the DUKE OF BEDFORD, 27 December 1883.   Add MS 44547, f. 21.

Knowing your mental as well as material interest in questions of the land, I assume that you have heard of, & probably may have read, the well-written but wild book of Mr. George on Progress & Poverty.

The object of this note is to recommend to your notice the masterly address of Mr. Giffen, of the Board of Trade, in the Statistical Society on the condition of the labouring classes in this country now and 40 or 50 years back.

It is I should think the best form of answer to Mr. George & I do not think the task could have been better executed.

You will probably have no difficulty in laying your hand on this address. But if it should be otherwise pray make use of me.[3]

To HALLAM TENNYSON, 27 December 1883.   Tennyson Research Centre, MS 5971.

I am very glad to learn that the title is fairly launched, and the Apotheosis accomplished.[4]

I think that by it we certainly succeed in decorating the House of Lords, and I think your Father will also be pleased with having given, as I believe, some real pleasure to the Queen in the grant of the honour.

I thank him very much for sending me Mr. Seeley's book.[5] Although I think a Professor gets upon rather slippery ground when he undertakes to deal with politics more practical than historical or scientific, yet it is certainly most desirable that English folk should consider well their position, present and prospective, in the world. It is fearful in moral responsibility, but magnificent in strength, in security, in magnitude, and in moral capabilities.

Have you heard of the pamphlet of Mr. Zincke, who shows, by fair probable argument, that the English-speaking peoples are likely by 1983 to be a thousand millions.[6]

At some time or other, but at the proper time, and if it is allowable, I want to ask for a copy of the Promise of May: there is so much delightful dialogue, that I wish not to be without record in my mind.

When I see you, I think I can satisfy you that Milnes Gaskell's not sending a copy to your Father was by no means due to any want of respect.

---

[1] A. N. Palmer, *The town . . . of Wrexham in the time of James I* (1884).

[2] T. Rees, see 27 Apr. 76.

[3] Bedford replied, 31 December, Add MS 44484, f. 349, that he had already read Giffen, but welcomed the suggestion; he feared 'disturbance may be at hand. . . . If anyone can steer us, it is yourself'.

[4] i.e. his father's title, eventually decided on as Baron Tennyson of Aldworth and Freshwater; see R. B. Martin, *Tennyson* (1980), 543–4.

[5] J. R. Seeley, *The expansion of England* (1883).

[6] See 6 May 83.

28. Fr. Innocents.

Ch. 8½ A.M. and H.C. Wrote to Ld Granville l.l.l.—Mr Hamilton—Lady Holker—W.H. Gladstone—Sir H. James—and minutes. Walk with Sir A. Wood. Read Cleveland (finished)—Progress and Poverty. Conversation with Lucy who reported her interview with Hartington.

To Sir H. JAMES, attorney general, 28 December 1883.   Add MS 44547, f. 22.

I thank you for your letter of Christmas Day, but I will not now enter on the subject of it further than to say I hope you will arrange so that no difficulty as to drafting for Scotland or Ireland may arise to bar our introducing our Bill *immediately* after the address & Speaker—even possibly Friday 8th.

As far as I have yet seen, the only important detail which hangs free is the introduction of the freehold into towns.

I have asked Lambert to compute how far we should tread on the road to uniformity if, without any freehold or property votes for Towns we (1) took occupation & lodger franchise into counties (2) required residence (3) prohibited subdivision & rent charges. (2) & (3) with the necessary reserves.

[P.S.] A happy New Year to you & many of them.

29. Sat.

Ch. 8½ A.M. Sir A. Wood accompanied me: & left at 11. The Westminister party most kindly came over to luncheon. A day of much pressure & confusion: over 200 I think of letters & telegrams, including one which would of itself have sufficed for many days.[1] Wrote to Sir W. Harcourt—Ld Hartington l. & Tel.—Ld Granville l.l.l. & Tel.—Mr Hamilton l. & Tel.l.l.—Prince of Wales—Mr Cowan—Dr Rowsell—Mr Coplestone—Hn PMaster l.l.—and minutes. I discoursed with my people on the strangely menacing situation created by Hartington's prepossessions (more than reasoning): and felt little doubt as to the steps I had to take.

It was indeed an unbirthdaylike birthday, for it was loaded with grave and difficult anxieties from one side, while from the other the masses of letters & crowd of telegrams & tokens of congratulation were fatal to recollection, of which I have such grievous need. It stands adjourned.

To J. COWAN, chairman, Midlothian Liberal Association,   Add MS 44547, f. 23.
29 December 1883.

When the resolutions passed at Penicuik[2] came to my hand, I did not fail to send a formal reply to them.

But I wish now to add, in my own person and with my own hand, a few words more. I have been, I know, as scanty in demonstration since the Election of 1880, as I was abundant before it. This was indeed due to nothing else than serious physical incapacity twelve months ago, when all the arrangements had been made for my rendering an account, which I am not less desirous than bounden to give. Time and events have marched on; and there has not since appeared in view an opportunity for the discharge of this important duty. But out of sight is not always out of mind: and though my daily

---

[1] Probably the Prince of Wales's greetings; Bahlman, *Hamilton*, ii. 534.
[2] Sent by Holmes Ivory, supporting a Scottish department, and franchise reform; Add MS 44484, f. 247.

duties keep pretty well up to the mark of my daily strength, I still contemplate with the utmost interest the time when I may be enabled to fulfil that which is still lacking in my duty to my generous constituents.

With regard to the resolutions passed at Penicuik, they one and all indicate that the fountain of that generosity remains unexhausted: and on my own part, as well as on that of my colleagues, I venture to say we shall still seek to deserve their confidence, and that the subjects which they name do not and will not cease to engage our thought and care.

To Sir W. V. HARCOURT, home secretary,   MS Harcourt dep. 9, f. 83.
29 December 1883. '*Secret*'.

It was probably well that you did not write at once, for your letter[1] is faintly illumined by a ray of light, whereas in the missives[?], which have arrived this morning from Hartington, I do not at present see any glimmering. I am very glad you were able to combat his immediate tendency with your whole force.

As regards the Crimes Act, Parnell, and the Irish people, no doubt you judged that a strong statement of a strong view—and yours *is* a strong view—would give you a hold upon his sympathies and might help in turning them to good.

I am glad the time has not come when new points of departure in Irish legislation have to be considered, and that good old Time, who carries me kindly upon his back, will probably plant me before that day comes outside 'the range of practical politics'.

I have telegraphed to Hartington at once to ask for his alternative. Meanwhile I will try to consider carefully & coolly how to make the best or not to make the worst of the existing rather sorry situation.

[P.S.] I may probably have to come up early next week.

To LORD HARTINGTON, war secretary, 29 December   Add MS 44146, f. 267.
1883. '*Secret*'.

I need hardly assure you that your letter & memorandum have had the best consideration I could give them.[2]

It occurred to me at once that that consideration must be imperfect until I should know what is the advice you would offer to your colleagues as an alternative to the plan of action which you deprecate. Accordingly I telegraphed in cypher to London, according to the date of your letter, to obtain it.[3] I find you had left town, & I telegraphed to ask that my enquiry might follow you. I hope to have your reply before this is in your hands.

Proceeding however as far as I can with the material in my hands, I will say first that which is of least importance; I regret that my willingness to consider whether I could remain in the Government to share the responsibilities of redistribution has not in any degree availed towards bringing about a solution of the difficulties before us.

The main points I think are these. I. As to redistribution generally, after reading what you say, I should enter without fear on a free conversation with you. While looking to a comparatively large arrangement, I am not friendly to Electoral districts, am ready to consider of some limitation on the representation of the largest town populations, & am

---

[1] Of 28 December, Add MS 44198, f. 170 and Gardiner, i. 497, at great length on Ireland.

[2] Mem. of 25, letter of 27 December, Add MS 44146, ff. 254–65, welcoming the understanding, *via* Harcourt, that Gladstone would stay on to deal with both franchise and redistribution, and reserving his position on Ireland; the mem. opposed breaking up constituencies and apportioning seats by population distribution.

[3] Add MS 44146, f. 266.

desirous to keep alive within fair limits the individuality of towns with moderate population. II. I do not admit that an enlarged franchise has the effect you describe on the urgency of redistribution, & I do not believe in the plot for postponement which you seem to apprehend, but in any case I am ready to use every effort for settling the question during the present Parliament. III. I do not think you could reasonably ask every member of the Cabinet to bind himself, publicly or otherwise, as to the main outlines of a measure to be proposed in 1885; but I take it for granted that this proposition of yours might be a subject of friendly discussion. IV. With respect to Ireland I hope that I do not apprehend you rightly: &, until I receive your reply to my telegram, I cannot speak positively. But I think that according to all the authorities you greatly overestimate the effect of an altered franchise in augmenting the power of Parnellism. And more especially I believe that to withhold franchises from Ireland while giving them to England & Scotland, & to proclaim the principle of an unequal Union, is the greatest blow that can be struck by any human power at the Act of Union & would be *the* way, if any way is possible, to make the Irish question a question of real danger to the Empire.

Time is running short. Had we not better compare our views in conversation? For this purpose I propose to go up on Monday, to be due at Euston 3.50 p.m., & to see you in Downing Street if you can make it convenient at 4.15.[1]

30. S. aft Xmas.

Ch 11 AM and evg. Wrote to Viceroy of Ireland—Ld Hartington Tel.—Mr Hamilton l. & Tel l.l.—Chester Station Master Tel.—Hn Postmaster—Transvaal Deputation[2]—Col. Carington—Ld Derby—The Queen l.l.—Mrs Th.—Hn Postmaster, & minutes. The fierce movement of yesterday not yet subsided: the 'swell' remained even on this day of peace. I read the remarkable Preface to Il Vaticano Regio:[3] and Wratislaw's Life of Huss.[4]

To LORD DERBY, colonial secretary, 30 December 1883.[5]   Add MS 44142, f. 33.
'*Secret*'.

I think I ought to let you know, in a brief & preliminary way that matters look ill with Hartington and the matter of Reform.

By what process I do not understand, but he seems to have been moving in the wrong direction, since we saw him in London.

He finds it conceivable that he might see his way as to the severance of redistribution were Great Britain alone concerned, but does not know how he can consent to any means which shall alter the franchise in Ireland, without some sweeping plan for the protection of minorities. He does not propose any plan as one [*sic*] alternative.

I have begged him to let me know what is his alternative, and have likewise requested him to meet me in Downing Street tomorrow at a quarter past three. To add to other mischief, he is at Kimbolton.[6] Of course I shall try my best with him, but I am not very

---

[1] See 31 Dec. 83; Hartington regretted his failure to state his views more forcibly in cabinet; Holland, i. 402.

[2] Thanks for its birthday greetings; Add MS 44547, f. 23.

[3] C. M. Curci, *Il Vaticano Regio* (1883); the preface describes Curci's difficulties with the Vatican encountered while writing the book.

[4] A. H. Wratislaw, *John Hus* (1878).

[5] Copy in Mrs Gladstone's hand.

[6] i.e. with his mistress, the duchess of Manchester, a tory.

sanguine. Under such circumstances you will not be greatly surprised if I should have to beg for your presence in town, however unwilling I must be to disturb you.[1]

31. M. [London]

Wrote to C.G.—Ld Granville Tel.—Mr Hamilton Tel.—and minutes. Off at 9.15. D. St at 3.5. Hartington came *punctually*—and staid till 5.45. He is unsettled and uncertain, & this is the best that can be said. Granville came later and staid one hour. He, ever so gentle & considerate as well as acute & cautious, is of immense value at these times. I dined with the Speaker & had conversation with him & Sir T. May on H. of C. affairs. Also The Speaker gave some sound opinions on the Franchise.

I found myself here in the first winter: a hard, caustic, nipping East wind. Saw three [R].

Hartington takes time: & so leaves it also to me. Let me look a little backward, & around. My position is a strange one.[2] A strong man in me wrestles for retirement: a stronger one stands at the gate of exit, and forbids. Forbids, I hope only for a time. There is a bar to the continuance of my political life fixed as I hope by the life of the present Parliament, and there is good hope that it may not last so long. But for this, I do not know how my poor flesh & blood, or my poor soul and spirit, could face the prolongations of cares & burdens so much beyond my strength at any age, and at this age so cruelly exclusive of the great work of penitential recollection, and lifting of the heart which has lingered so long. I may indeed say that my political or public life is the best part of my life: it is that part in which I am conscious of the greatest effort to do and to avoid as the Lord Christ would have me do and avoid, nay shall I say for this is the true rule as He would Himself in the like case have done. But although so far itself taken up out of the mire, it exhausts and dries up my other and more personal life, and so to speak reduces its tissue, which should be firm and healthy, to a kind of moral pulp. I want so much more of thought on Divine things, of the eye turned inwards & upwards & forwards, of study to know and discern, to expose and to renounce, my own secret sins. And how can this be done, or begun, or tried, or tasted, while the great stream of public cares is ever rushing on me, & covering my head with its floods of unsatisfied demand.

Yet it is a noble form of life which ministers by individual action to the wants of masses of Gods creatures. Man has one neck, not for the headsman, but for the inflow of good. So I abide, and as I trust obey, until He who knows shall find the way to signify to me that I am at length permitted to depart, whether it be from this world, or as I trust first from the storm and fierceness of it into the shade and coolness and calm where the soul may for a while work in freedom before going hence.

---

[1] Derby replied, 31 December, Add MS 44142, f. 35, unsurprised: 'There are many social influences at work to detach Hartington . . . the real trouble . . . does not arise out of the reform question, but that he dislikes the prospect of having to lead, with the assistance of colleagues with whom he is not wholly in agreement . . . the one [effective] assurance . . . would be the assurance that you do not contemplate that early retirement at which you have so often hinted'.

[2] Version of next four sentences in Hammond, 166.

Let me not close the year without acknowledging the great blessing of temporal health accorded me during its course. The visit to Cannes, required by necessity, lifted me to a higher level than theretofore, and this gain was not wholly exhausted by the Session, so that in many important respects I have been stronger than I was before the decline twelve months ago. May I not dishonour this mercy by my life.

Mem. in train to town. D.31.83.[1]

Alternatives.   Cabinet may postpone whole subject.[2]
1. Severance of redistribution.
2. Principles of it.
3. *Declaration* of them *now.* How as to minority clause?
4. Party. Not disruption but dissolution
   with Chamberlain rising *in the distance.*
5. Ireland. 1. Social. 2. Political difficulty. Party and Parliament. Extreme. 3. Danger is *none—except* a quarrel, *with Ireland in the right.*

[3]This day Hartington sat with me from 3.15 to 5.45.

I urged upon him first that the Cabinet had not decided on its course with respect to Parliamentary Reform generally—that the severance of the two branches had been decided on in ignorance of his real sentiments—and that he was bound if he objected to the *contemplated* plan now much expected by the world, to advise an alternative.

I urged principally a. the ruin to the party, immediately, or else in a short time hence, and the prospect of its re-forming hereafter under extreme auspices, b. the fearful evil of branding Ireland with political inequality—the only way which could make her really dangerous.

We discussed the particulars of redistribution—as soothingly as I could.

I contended

That to postpone the entire subject to 1885 seemed to be its absolute immolation as I could not see a chance of passing a 'complete measure' in the sixth & last session of a Parliament,

That a wide application of the minority principle in England & Scotland especially in a Franchise Bill and by a Liberal Government, was at the present time impossible—would break up all the support of the Bill without conciliating opponents. Such a measure would hardly reach a 2d Reading,

That there could be such[4] application of the principle in Ireland, unless it were also applied to England & Scotland.

[The back inside cover contains:—]

6 West Terrace Folkestone
Sim 7 Great Russell St: Axford, Marlb.
6 West Terrace Folkestone
Wade care of Mrs Sim Axford Marlborough

---

[1] Add MS 44767, f. 131; version in *Autobiographica*, iv. 64.
[2] This phrase added later.
[3] The rest an undated holograph; Add MS 44767, f. 131; in *Autobiographica*, iv. 64.
[4] Presumably 'no such' intended.

29 Poplar Grove W.K. Park
14 Westbourne Street Hyde Park
60 Marine St London   16 Qu St

Wr, To Mr C. Ap 19. 82. May 3

Saw 25. with S. & F.
    27. Sto go to I.[1]

---

[1] A note, once tipped in but now missing, read: 'Please send me a note of my letters of Sunday 0.16.'

[1 January 1884 to 7 September 1885]

[The inside front cover contains in pencil:—]

£1
£1 Olewood   Allns 2–7
                                                  Coll. 150

[In ink:—]

Private.

No 36.

Jan. 1. 84–Sept. 85.

ὄυπω

Τὰν Διὸς ἀϱμονίαν
Θνατῶν παϱεξίασι βουλάι.[2]
Prom. V. 548.

London. January 1884.

1. Tuesday.

Wrote to C.G.—W.H.G.—Mr Goschen—Ld Derby—and minutes. Saw Mr Hamilton—Miss Ponsonby—Mr Schlaaf—Ld Granville—Scotts—Mrs Birks, with whom I visited the Natural His. Museum S. Kensington. Dined with Mr & Mrs Th. at their 'Cottage'. Read Wallace's Egypt[3]—Horace Walpole & his World.[4] Long conversation with Mrs H[ampto]n.

To LORD DERBY, colonial secretary, 1 January 1884.   Add MS 44547, f. 24.
'*Secret*'.

Many thanks for your letter,[5] on which I need not comment by reason of my so much agreeing with what it contains. It is certainly impulse more than reasoning, which has moved Hartington in the wrong direction. However, I had a long talk with him yesterday; & he spent most of the rest of the evening with Granville. I have given him various assurances, which he admits to be not wholly without weight: one of them being that I am ready to waive my title—so to call it—to retire upon getting quit of the franchise Bill, &

---

[1] Lambeth MS 1450.
[2] Aeschylus, *Prometheus Vinctus*, 550: 'Never yet did the plans of mortal men bypass the ordering of affairs by Zeus'.
[3] D. M. Wallace, *Egypt and the Egyptian question* (1883).
[4] L. B. Seeley, ed., *Horace Walpole and his world* (1884); with correspondence.
[5] See 30 Dec. 83n.

(other things permitting) to remain in the ship with a view to a similar effort for redistribution; & none I hope being such as are likely to raise difficulty in other quarters. The impulse in the wrong direction will be considerably counteracted I think by an impulse in the right one, not to inflict upon his friends, the public, & the cause of good government, the grievous mischief that would follow from the step he has meditated. To speak in few words, the case is by no means without hope, yet the Irish knot is by no means yet cut, & there lies the danger.

My belief is that, if his brother Freddy had been alive, we should never have heard of the present trouble.

I think that, if he goes right, he will cling very much to the idea of dealing with redistribution during the present Parliament. He is haunted with the idea that Birmingham wishes to postpone it & do something very terrible.

He asked to have the Cabinet postponed to Thursday which so far as it goes is a good sign.

[P.S.] On Thursday I think the Cabinet will hope to hear from you the state of your proceedings on the South African question.

To Mrs GLADSTONE, 21 January 1884.[1]   Hawarden MSS.

Thanks for your delightful letter, even more than usually sustaining & consoling.

Granville's first view of the Hartington case was *one shade* less than mine: he had another interview later in the evening, which slightly improved[?] that shade. He desired more time which in itself is rather a good sign. The Cabinet therefore will not be held till Thursday. But if things go well I have every hope of clearing out by the end of the week, so that your birthday shall not pass, or shall not pass wholly, in my absence.

Hartington is gone to Sandringham: I am sorry to learn through Granville that *she*[2] is there.

Very good letter from Derby who is at Knowsley—and a good one also from Duke of Bedford 'the humble Abbot of Woburn' to whom I wrote last week.

I have been to luncheon with Mrs Birks & offered 'pompous' thanks. She gushed about you: gave me a drive on lift and we went to the Natural History Museum together.

I had a full half hour with Mrs Hampton this morning, and very good company she is. she had made up her mind to remain here through the week. The brother in law is but creaky. According to her account there was provided for good old Wynne an easy passage out of this troublous world. She ate her little supper at half past nine, and before eleven she was gone

I dined with Mr Speaker. Oh how Lady Brand 'lets down her leg'. They are packing in preparation for the move. She only wishes the Peels may be as happy in that House, as they have been. *He* was strong on the impossibility of omitting Ireland if any thing is done about the Franchise. Ever your afft WEG

[P.S.] I have looked to the Bishop's Resignations Act. It contains, as I believed a power to assign upon special grounds to the retiring Bishop any Episcopal residence he may have occupied. *Clearly* these special grounds would apply in the case of the Bishop of Chester. It snows somewhat this evening. Note for Willy William

To Sir H. JAMES, attorney general, 1 January 1884.   Add MS 44547, f. 23.

Either today or tomorrow I should like to compare notes with you on the formation of our Bill.

---

[1] Part in Bassett, 243.
[2] The duchess of Manchester, Hartington's mistress; see 30 Dec. 83.

As far as I can judge, it is not improbable that the Cabinet *may* decide upon keeping the freehold franchise for counties only, & so avoiding an innovation of doubtful and perhaps capricious working, & one of the reception of which by our own friends we are not quite sure.

My own impression is that if we proceed in other points as contemplated the occupation & lodger votes will form from 3/4 to 5/6 of the County Constituencies and if so the approximation to identity of suffrage will be such that no violent change will attach the future taking boroughs out of counties. On the other hand I hope we have *done with* the practice of throwing rural districts into boroughs.

Please to name your hour—by bearer if you can.

I have assumed you to be in town. Precipitating coming up, if you are away, may be inconvenient. If you cannot manage (today or) tomorrow, any early hour on Thursday would suffice.

2. *Wed.*

Wrote to Mrs Gascoyne—Mrs Bolton—Ld Kenmare—C.G.—...—and minutes. Saw Mr Hamilton—Ld R. Grosvenor—Ld Spencer—Sir J. Lambert—Mr West— Mrs Herbert. Saw Mrs Martin: pleased with the two books. Dined at Mr Wests. Read Wallace's Egypt.

To LORD COLERIDGE, lord chief justice, 2 January 1884.   Add MS 44547, f. 24.

A letter, this, of sincere thanks for your kindness. Yet it must begin with protest or dissent. There is no person in London, save one, who thinks that the Lord Chief Justice shines with a derivative light.

In other aspects I heartily accept your friendly wishes. Yet subject to this reservation that the most friendly wish of all is that I may be permitted soon to escape the strain & rid myself of the excess which inheres in the labours of my present office or in the attempt to pursue them at my time of life.

I read Lyndhurst's life at once; it was the life of a colleague in Sir Robert Peel's cabinet.[1] It seems to catch Campbell a good deal. Otherwise it is too eulogistic & at the same time too apologetic. It shows Lyndhurst in a delightful way as to the great point of domestic affection.[2]

A superior piece of workmanship to this is I think on the eve of appearing—the life of Hope Scott by Mr. Ornsby, himself a seceder. Unhappily my name appears in it much oftener & more seriously than I could have wished.

When you have written (active voice or *middle*, caused somebody to write) a great work on the social condition & movement of America, I have another subject to commend to you, for which I would like to see a real author forthcoming. It is, the transformation of Oxford during the last half century, & the manner in which the throes of that University have acted on England & the world.[3]

3. *Th.*

Wrote to Ld Hartington—Ld Granville—Ld Spencer—Mr Lefevre—C.G.—The Speaker—Mr Westell—Bp of Sydney—Messrs Murray—The Queen—& minutes.

[1] See 31 Aug., 4 Dec. 83.
[2] Coleridge had found *Lyndhurst* dull; Add MS 44138, f. 260.
[3] Coleridge replied, ibid. f. 263, that he hoped to write using his father's diary; he never published it.

Saw Mr Hamilton—Ld Granville—Mr Ponsonby—Do *cum* Ld Hartington—Ld R. Grosvenor—Mrs Bolton X. Gascoigne X. Cabinet 2-5¼. Dined at Miss Ponsonby's. It was very interesting. Today our little crisis was virtually over:[1] a great mercy, though in one sense I have to pay the piper by an extended engagement. Read Wallace's Egypt.

Cabinet. Thurs. Jan. 3. 84. 2 PM.[2]

1. Egypt. Ld G. read Baring's Tel. with proposal of Egn. Govt. to call in Turkish aid—if not got to rest[?] on to the Empire &c. & defend Khartoum which B. says they cannot do.[3]

   Reply. 1. ⟨Ministers in Egypt:[4] to conform to our advice. 2. Nubar: refuse condition of protectorate.⟩ See margin of Baring's Telegram for substance of Telegram to be sent.[5]
   Also the separate & secret [blank]

2. South Africa. Basutos (Proposal of General read by Hn.). Nothing at present.
   Zulu. Five alternatives of Bulwer. Wait his next dispatch.
   Transvaal. Bechuanaland. Apart from the question of boundary, which seems not hopeless, put forward the question of frontier police. In what way will they [blank][6]

Grand Committees. Heads of Depts to consider what Bills they will have.

⟨1. Send no troops.

Separate & secret ⟨2⟩ Baring to make himself obeyed—especially now.

3. We hold they cannot recover[?] & they shd. not spend money or men in operations.

1. ⟨4⟩ No objection to any proposal to surrender authority over Soudan to Sultan.

2. 5. Glad to see them bring the Turks in the Red Sea Ports.

3. Make every effort to withdraw the garrisons & authorise the withdrawal of the garrisons. Authorise the withdrawal from Khartoum.

4. Undertake no pecuniary obligation to the Porte.⟩[7]

⟨We offer no objection to the two paragraphs of Cherif's[8] communication respecting his proposed application to the Porte. We see no likelihood that Egypt can hold Khartoum & cannot be responsible for any consequences, whatever they may be, which may arise from ineffectual efforts to hold it.⟩[9]

To H. B. W. BRAND, the Speaker, 3 January 1884.   Add MS 44547, f. 25.

On every ground, I feel a great anxiety to prevent, or limit, the occurrence this year of the promiscuous & enormously prolonged dissension on the Address which discredited the opening of the last Session.

Of these grounds one has relation to yourself personally; at least, it occurs to me that

---

[1] i.e. Hartington agreed to continue.

[2] Add MS 44645, f. 2.

[3] Of 2 January; Add MS 44645, f. 7.

[4] Further phrase here smudged.

[5] Ibid., f. 7. Granville's instructions, and his secret order (hoping to avoid appointment of British officials to rule Egypt direct), in Cromer, i. 381-2.

[6] This offer made to the Transvaal deputies on 9 January; *PP* 1884 lvii. 49, Schreuder, 411.

[7] Whole page deleted, though the 'Separate & Secret' instruction only very lightly; Add MS 44645, f. 6.

[8] Chérif Pasha, 1819-88, Ottoman in the service of the Khedive, presently as chief minister; hostile to Egyptian surrender of Sudan; resigned on 7 January.

[9] Draft, deleted; Add MS 44645, f. 5.

the prolongation for a week or a fortnight of your occupancy of the Chair, with its actual close dependent on a division expected first on one day & then on another, would not be a satisfactory mode of arranging the last scene of a dignified career.

I understand that Mr. Chaplin means to move an amendment respecting the importation of cattle; but this might, with an understanding, be disposed of in a few hours if it were insisted on.

Can anything be done to confine the proceedings within moderate bounds?

There are three parties concerned in the answer to the questions.

Of course the Government will do all it can, & its friends I think will sympathise. With the Irish we cannot communicate on such a subject; they will be orderly or disorderly according to their own separate views & purposes. But Northcote also can do something, & I do believe he would do all he could if he at all concurred in my view of the effect of an irregular interminable debate on your closing appearance in the Chair. Whether he can & should be 'got at' is what I would beg you to consider. Pray do not take the trouble to answer this note, which I can only hope will stand excused by its patriotic motives.

To LORD HARTINGTON, war secretary, 3 January 1884.   Add MS 44147, f. 7.

Your letter[1] was a great relief and I thank you much for it.

I have been carefully considering how I can put into the form best in itself & most satisfactory to you that which you wish me to do. Of course this has been hasty and I will do my best, & you will hear further from me, I trust, before the day is out.

No franchise in Cabinet today: but appoint it for tomorrow.

4. *Fr.*

Wrote to Mr Hayward—Bp of Chester—The Speaker—Sir A. Hobhouse—The Queen—Atty General—C.G.—and minutes. Saw Mr Hamilton—Mr Chamberlain—Att. General—Ld Hartington: with whom, having previously made good the ground with Mr C. I arranged everything for the Cabinet. Cabinet 12–3½: very harmonious and satisfactory. Saw Ld Granville—Ld Spencer. Visited Hayward: with a good deal of consolation. Dined at Sir W. Harcourt's. Saw Harris X. Read Wallace's Egypt.

Cabinet. Friday Jan. 4. 1884. Noon.[2]
1. Franchise Bill adopted.[3] Principal particulars considered. See Mem. of this day.[4] Statement of WEG, of Hartington, of Spencer, of Chamberlain, accepts one qualification not absolutely final. Harcourt—Carlingford—Chancellor of Exchequer—Derby—Chancellor.
General satisfaction.
2. London Govt: County & Local Govt.: which first? London Bill first.

---

[1] Of 2 January 1884; Add MS 44147, f. 6.

[2] Add MS 44645, f. 8. [Gladstone:] 'In my innermost I utterly disbelieve in minority clauses, and believe we shall never have it'; [Granville:] 'I absolutely agree, but it is an admirable bridge, which been [*sic*] combined in a very fair manner; ibid., f. 9.

[3] No linkage between franchise and redistribution, but Cabinet 'think that the question of redistribution may conveniently be taken up by the present Parliament in the year following the settlement of the Franchise'; CAB 41/18/2. Dodson noted 'Redistribution. Gle. deprecates any conclusion'; Monk Bretton 62.

[4] Later sent to Hartington and perhaps not returned (see to Hartington, 1 Mar. 84); see also that dated 3 January: the case against a Franchise and Redistribution Bill; Add MS 44768, f. 2.

To Sir H. JAMES, attorney general, 4 January 1884.   Add MS 44547, f. 25.

(1). On No. 6. of the Memorandum of today[1] the Chancellor suggested & the Cabinet agreed that when there is neither residence nor occupation there shall be bona fide receipt of rents and profits.

(2). On No. 7. they understand your intention to be that as a *general* rule only one person shall vote in respect of one hereditament corporeal or incorporeal.

(3). Property franchises to remain as now & condition of residence not to be enforced.

(4). On your No. 9. the Cabinet would like to have (a fortnight hence) your proposal— but some doubts were expressed.

(5). Your No. 10: not accepted—you will of course be heard upon it, it may not have been fully understood.

(6). Every thing else stands as in the Memorandum of today.

Should *you* desire to see me, you will find me at 10.30 tomorrow.

[P.S.] Some question was raised about a freehold 40/- franchise for Ireland & Spencer is to consult his people. I do not think it will come to much.

5. *Sat.* [*Hawarden*]

Wrote to Mrs Bolton—Lady Phillimore—Ld Granville—& minutes. Read Life of Drake[2]—Walpole & his World. Packing & preparations. Journey to Hawarden 11½-5, the quickest I ever made: sent through to Broughton Hall, outrageous luxury ἐφ' ἁρμαμάξων μαλθάκων κατακείμενοι!³ Found all, including Lucy, well, & delighted at the good upshot.

6. *Epiph.*

Dearest C.s birthday. God blessed her & surely will bless.

Ch. 11 AM (with H.C. at which all [the family] except Harry were present) and 6½ evg. Wrote to Ld Chancellor. Read Il Vaticano Regio[4]—Woods Five Problems[5]—Harness on Christianity and Mankind.[6]

7. *M.*

Ch. 8½ A.M. Wrote to R.E.E. Warburton—Rev. Sir G. Prevost—Mr Ridler—Abp of Canterbury—Ld Granville—Mr Nightingale[7]—and minutes. 'Company' came: 14 to dinner. Conversation with Mr Bankes—Mr Parker. Read Nightingale, Chelsea China—Life of Drake (finished)—Scottish Church Review I[8]—Walk with Mr Bankes.

---

¹ No copy found; referred to in letter to James, 10 Jan. 84, as 'the memorandum you had on the 4th.'.

² Perhaps J. Barrow, *Life of Drake* (1843).

³ Aristophanes, *Acharnians*, 70: diplomatic envoys who complain at discomforts but travel at public expense 'stretched out in soft travelling-carriages'.

⁴ See 30 Dec. 83.

⁵ W. C. Wood, *Five problems of state and religion* (1877); American.

⁶ Perhaps untraced article by W. Harness.

⁷ Thanking James Edward Nightingale, d. 1892, antiquarian, for his *Contribution towards the history of early English porcelain* (1881); Add MS 44547, f. 27.

⁸ Published in Aberdeen; only two vols. (1884-5) appeared.

8. Tu.

Ch. 8½ AM. Wrote to Central Press Tel.—Manchr Exam. do—Avery & Sons—& minutes. Read 19th Cent. on Ireland (Duffy) Religion (Spencer)—Mormons—Ld Melbourne (Earl Cowper)[1]—Alice, Leben und Briefen[2]—H. Walpole & his world. Woodcraft with H. Saw Dean of Chester.

9. Wed.

Ch. 8½ AM. Wrote to Ld Granville Tel—Mr Seymour Tel & l.—P. of Wales—Mr Bemrose Tel.—Ld Coleridge—Ld Kimberley—Ld Stair—and minutes. Attended the Rent (*after*) dinner & spoke on Fruit Farming &c.[3] Woodcraft with H. Dinner party of 14. Read Walpole & his world—Nineteenth Cent. on Mediaeval Convent Life.[4]

10. Th.

Ch. 8½ A.M. Wrote to Sir W. Harcourt—Ld Granville Tel.—Att. General—Mr Norman Tel.—Mr Rowley Hill[5]—and minutes. Powerscourt & Mrs Cope came to luncheon & lionised. Read Pepys & his Times—Walpole & his World—Br. Quart. on Ulster.[6] Company went & came. Worked on arranging papers.

To Sir W. V. HARCOURT, home secretary, 10 January 1884. MS Harcourt dep. Adds 10.

Mr Illingworth certainly 'takes Time by the forelock.'[7] I have not yet read the Report to which he refers: but as High Church Low Church Nonconformists, with the great mass of the people, are all against it, I do not think he need be under immediate alarm, and I think he may in any case rest assured that he will have plenty of notice before the question grows, if it is indeed to grow, into a shape for legislative handling.

I admit that I am concerned when I see some gentlemen representative of Nonconformists indifferent or hostile to measures of practical reform in the Church of England such as the prevention of the sale of presentations, a rank and demoralising abuse; while I also admit that they have such justification for their course as can be afforded by the policy which the Clergy and Laity of the Church have too much pursued towards them.

To Sir H. JAMES, attorney general, 10 January 1884. Add MS 44219, f. 143.

I fear I must have failed to convey to you, when we met *chez* Harcourt, that the Cabinet had (I believe wisely) decided upon leaving the property franchises as they are. The difficulties of assimilation in the Three Kingdoms seem of themselves to constitute a sufficient reason for this decision.

The greater part therefore of this printed correspondence need not impose upon you any further trouble.

[1] *N.C.*, xv. 71 etc. (January 1884).
[2] C. Sell, *Alice, Grand Duchess of Hesse. A biographical sketch* (1884).
[3] *T.T.*, 10 January 1884, 7c.   [4] *N.C.*, xv. 100 (January 1884).
[5] 'Ulster and home rule' ('an impregnable barrier'), *B.Q.R.*, lxx. 101 (January 1884).
[6] Thanking Thomas Rowley Hill (1816–96; liberal M.P. Worcester 1874–85) for porcelain; Add MS 44547, f. 27.
[7] Harcourt sent papers from Illingworth on the Ecclesiastical Courts Commission; Add MS 44199, f. 1.

The memorandum you had on the 4th holds except that the condition of residence is not to be imposed. I should like some such title as the following—Bill to establish an Occupation Franchise for the United Kingdom of Great Britain and Ireland, and to amend the law with respect to other Franchises (and to Parliamentary Voting?)

11. Fr.

[Church] 8½ A.M. Wrote to Abp of Canterbury—Ld Granville l.l. & Tel.—Mr Seymour l. & Tel.—Mr Ayrton—and minutes. Woodcraft with H. Read Walpole &c. (finished)—Essay on Manchester Fruitmarket[1]—Defoe's Satire.[2]

To E. W. BENSON, archbishop of Canterbury, 11 January   Add MS 44547, f. 28.
1884.

In regard to the question which Your Grace has put to me in your letter of the 9th,[3] much would depend upon the prior question whether the Report of the Commission on Ecclesiastical Courts was generally accepted by the Church & out of doors. Such a Report is an element of real force in the settlement of any matter; but there are other elements.

In the cases of Clerical Subscription, of the new Lectionary, & of the new Shortened Services, the Government of the day not unwillingly took responsibility on itself, but in all those cases it had strong antecedent evidence of the concurrence of the authorities of the Church, & indeed of the Church & public generally. In the case of the Public Worship Act, although that had some relation to the Report of a Commission, & was introduced into the House of Lords with the highest episcopal authority (never unequivocally withdrawn) differences of opinion were pretty sharply developed, & the Government as a Government stood aloof. The course taken in the House of Commons was peculiar; but the votes of Ministers fully bear out what I say.

I believe the Cabinet would have the same disposition as that of former Cabinets to act in concert with the general feeling of the Church, & especially with the Episcopal body.

But I do not think it would be politic for me to submit any question to my colleagues at the present moment. I should be open to the reply that all the evidence is not yet before them, & that the judgment in favour of any proposed measure which would warrant their action would require to be a judgment given on its merits & not influenced by any prior intimation of the course which the Administration of the day desired to pursue in regard to it.

All that I have said would have been said by me 10 or 15 years ago in respect to any like measure. But I grieve to add that within these latest years the question has been greatly complicated by a new consideration, the block of business in the House of Commons, & the use which is frequently made of it by those, even if few in number, who may have special antipathies to any particular measure. To this evil, I may say this monster evil, we have laboured, & we shall labour, to apply a remedy. But our efforts have been encountered by formidable & most persistent opposition; &, though ground has been gained, the main part of the mischief remains, & constitutes a most formidable fact in estimating the prospects of any proposed legislation, especially if such is not to enter into the class of primary political questions.

---

[1] Possibly 'Shudehill markets mismanagement' (1875).

[2] i.e. *Moll Flanders*, see next day.

[3] Add MS 44109, f. 60: if the clergy with 'practical unanimity' accept the Ecclesiastical Courts Commissioners' report, would the govt. support the consequent bill?

12. Sat.

Ch. 8½ A.M. Wrote to Abp of Canterbury—Att. General—R. Grosvenor—Parl. Circular—Ld Granville Tel.—Mr Hamilton do.—& minutes. Worked on books. Read Duchess of Kingston's Life[1]—Defoe's Moll Flanders[2]—Hall on Irish Land.[3] Felled a tree with Herbert.

13. 1 S. Epiph.

Ch. mg & evg. Wrote to Mr Seymour 1. & Tel.—Miss Phillimore—Sir J. Lambert—Ld Hartington—The Queen l.l.l.l.—& minutes. Read Bp of Lincoln on Appeal Court[4]—Brewster on 18th Cent.[5]—Rees, Welsh Nonconformity[6]—Divers Tracts.

14. M.

Ch. 8½ A.M. Wrote to Chancr of Exr—Ld Granville—Ld Spencer—Dean of Chester—Mr Parker BP—and minutes. Worked on papers & accounts, which are in chaos and arrear. Read V. Stuart's Egypt[7]—Goldwin Smith's Art. on Peel[8]—Moll Flanders—Albany Christie on Luther.[9]

To H. C. E. CHILDERS, chancellor of the exchequer,   Add MS 44547, f. 29.
14 January 1884.

With regard to the Post Master General[10] he is I fear incapable of taking any other than a Departmental view but you will not find the Cabinet disposed to indulge him unduly.

As to the Army[11] I told you I think that both Granville & I had urged upon Hartington making use of the marines by which I understood the greater part of the difficulty could be rounded off.

Supposing we were to make a serious increase, & could not show that it was due to a sudden cause, the unpleasant question would be put 'why, when you agreed last year to a Resolution for retrenchment, did you conceal from the House that the Army Estimates were to be increased?'—I certainly had no inkling of such a necessity. You will probably have had the answer to your question as to the Cabinet.

To LORD SPENCER, Viceroy of Ireland, 14 January 1884.   Althorp MSS K7.

I thank you for your letter of the 12th[12] & I think we may now regard it as a settled matter that no change is to be proposed in the property franchises except what may be requisite to guard them against abuse.

[1] See 4 Aug. 72.
[2] First published 1722.
[3] W. H. B. Hall, *Gleanings in Ireland after the Land Acts* (1883).
[4] C. Wordsworth, 'On the proposed Court of Final Appeal' (1884).
[5] See 23 Sept. 83.
[6] T. Rees, *History of protestant nonconformity in Wales* (2nd ed. 1883); see 27 Apr. 76.
[7] H. W. V. Stuart, *Egypt after the war* (1883).
[8] Goldwin Smith, 'Peel', *Macmillan's Magazine*, xix. 97 (December 1868).
[9] A. J. Christie, *Luther's jubilee* (1883).
[10] Childers, 13 January, Add MS 44131, f. 7: 'the Post Office is also giving me anxiety'.
[11] Proposed increases 'alarming'; ibid.
[12] Add MS 44311, f. 2: Spencer and Trevelyan opposed to creation of 40/– freeholder in Ireland.

15.

Ch. 8½ A.M. Rose at 5 AM to send off stopping telegrams to Sir H. Ponsonby—Mr Seymour—Mr Forster: as I have been, I fear, hasty about Bp Moorhouse.[1] Telegraphed also to Rev. E. Talbot—Ld Granville—and Archbishop of Canty. Wrote to Archbishop of Canty—Ld Tavistock—Mr S. Smith—Dean of St Paul's—Mr Hamilton—Sir H. Ponsonby—Ld Spencer—and minutes. Woodcraft with sons. Walk with Mr Bryce. Worked on letters & accounts. Read Q.R. on The Session (84)[2]—Ch of Engl. in 18th Centy—Schliemann's Troja[3]—Borlase on Scilly Islands[4]—Moll Flanders.

To LORD TAVISTOCK, M.P., 15 January 1884.   Add MS 44547, f. 30.

I hope you will receive propitiously the request I have now to submit to you. It is, that you will kindly undertake to move the Address in answer to the Queen's Speech on the 5th of February.

I should not make this request if I believed that the Speech was likely to include matter unpalatable to you.

There will be no novel announcement I believe of policy; and in regard to legislation, if as is probable the Franchise and Local Government in one or more of its possible shapes should form the leading topics they will be touched, I feel certain, in a spirit of sobriety.

It is usual on these occasions to look to a large town as well as to a county and I am writing to Mr. Smith M.P. for Liverpool to beg of him to be seconder.

If, as I trust will be the case, you comply with the wish of the Government, I shall hope to have the advantage, some days at least before the meeting, to give you all needful information upon particulars.[5]

16. *Wed.*

Ch. 8½ A.M. Wrote to Ld Granville—Mr Hamilton—The Queen l.l.—Sir Thos Acland—and minutes. Walk with Mr Bryce & much conversation with this 'full man'. Saw Mr Mayhew—Conversation and reflection on Bp Moorhouse, & the Evang. party now so barren. Read Moll Flanders—Life of Erasmus.[6] Mr Yorke[7] acted in evg.

17. *Th.*

Ch. 8½ A.M. Wrote to Ld Granville Tel.—Mr Fitzwilliam—Mr Hamilton—Ld Coventry—Bp of Chester—Mr Childers—Mr Woolner—Sir W. Harcourt—Sir C. Dilke—Ld Aberdare—and minutes. Woodcraft with WHG. Read Moll Flanders (finished): the penitence is a poor affair & altogether the $\mathring{\eta}\theta o\varsigma$ low: below that

---

[1] Being considered for Southwell, but Gladstone was 'troubled with a report of his having allowed a Presbyterian to preach in his Cathedral' (to R. W. Church, 15 January, Add MS 44547, f. 28); G. Ridding was appt.

[2] *Q.R.*, clvii. 272 (January 1884).

[3] H. Schliemann, *Troja* (1884).

[4] W. Borlase, 'Observations on the ancient and present state of the islands of Scilly' (1756).

[5] He declined, A. R. D. Elliott moving, and S. Smith seconding the Address.

[6] A. P. Pennington, *The life and character of Erasmus* (1874).

[7] Alexander Yorke, guest at the Castle; H.V.B.

of Roxana I think. Read L. Tollemache on C[harles] Austin[1]—Pennington's
Erasmus. 8–10 P.M. Attended the entertainment in the Hn Schoolroom. Mr
Yorke was admirable.

18. Fr.

Ch. 8½ AM. Wrote to Ld R. Grosvenor—Mr Hamilton—Ld Ripon—Mr Trevelyan—Mr Firth—Messrs Watson—Mr Tupper—Abp of Canterbury—and
minutes. Wrote some sketch Paragraphs for Queen's Speech. Walk with
Stephy. Worked on books. Read Tollemache on Dean Stanley & others—The
Gudeman of Ballengeich.[2]

To LORD R. GROSVENOR, chief whip, 18 January 1884.   Add MS 44315, f. 144.
'*Most Private*'.[3]

I thank you very much for the report of Parnell's intentions & real opinion. Both correspond with what I had anticipated. I should be glad if you could find any *convenient* occasion of letting Hartington know in a quiet way what view Parnell takes of the effect of the
extended franchise on the interests of his party. All this is much in conformity with
Spencer's ideas. But do not let Hn. suppose you have been coquetting with these
worthies.

I have written to Tavistock & to Smith but no reply yet.

To LORD RIPON, Viceroy of India, 18 January 1884.   Add MS 43515, f. 30.

If I answer very briefly your interesting letter[4] on the winding up of the Ilbert controversy, it is not (true as that is) because I have grown old & weary, neither is it because I
have any differences to express, but because in truth I have only to congratulate you on
your escape from what must have been a very wearying as well as trying period.

Your position & knowledge have made you entire master of the question as to all that
was to be done in India, & there is no disposition, I am sure, in the Cabinet to raise doubts
about such concessions as you have found it prudent to make, as neither could there have
been any misgivings about supporting you had you deemed it proper to withhold them.

Your explanation of the concessions gives me much satisfaction. And altogether I cannot but rejoice that another great forward step has been made in the business of governing India; from which you will reap I trust an ample mead of honour.

I am reluctantly dragging my old limbs after me into the fight again: all the more
reluctantly because duty to my most kind & faithful colleagues has obliged me to entertain the idea of joining them in a subsequent effort at redistribution of seats if we now
succeed in settling the franchise.

The Egyptian business has been sadly entangled & is now the most perplexing of our
cases. Nor are we making much progress in South African affairs. But the tone of the
public mind is healthy & the Government shows no sign of decrepitude.

---

[1] L. A. Tollemache, *Safe studies* (1884), 211.
[2] J. Paterson, *James the Fifth; or the 'Gudeman of Ballengeich': his poetry and adventures*
(1861).
[3] Holograph. Grosvenor's report on Parnell untraced.
[4] Of 23 December, Add MS 44287, f. 14: bill passed after modification, without affecting the
principle, to exploit the 'opening' offered by the European community. See 17 Apr. 83n.

19. Sat

Ch. 8½ A.M. Wrote to Abp of Canterbury—D. of Newcastle—Mr Childers—Ld Granville—Sir H. Verney—Canon Venables—Ld Derby—D. of Grafton—The Queen—& minutes. Walk with S. & E. Wickham. Worked on books. Tea at Miss Coleman's. Read Villiers Stuart's Egypt—Baker, Records of Seasons[1]—Gudeman of Ballengeich. Wrote Testamentary Memoranda on my affairs.[2]

To H. C. E. CHILDERS, chancellor of the exchequer,   Add MS 44547, f. 32.
19 January 1884. 'Private'.

The demand of 1,400 m[ille] is fortuitous, beyond all apprehensions. I hope it may be found capable of large compression.[3]

It would probably lead to an indirect financial attack and a combination between Tories, Economists, and Irishmen.

This would introduce with force almost irresistible the inquiry I mentioned before— 'Why did you give no inkling of this coming demand when you led us to adopt last year a resolution in favour of economy?'

I write in ignorance of justifying particulars, & on the general aspect of the affair.

20. 2 S. Epiph.

Ch mg & [blank] Wrote to Rev. Mr Linklater[4]—Mr Hamilton—Helen G.—Mr Furnivall—& minutes. Read Harness, Results of Xty[5]—Miller on Heavenly bodies[6]—Henderson on Vaudois[7]—Wright Autobiography[8]—Rees, Nonconformity in Wales.

21. M.

Ch. 8½ A.M. Wrote to Mr Richardson MP—Mr Childers—Mr Ph. Smith—Mr Hamilton Tel.—and minutes. Saw Mr MacColl—Dr Liddon. Drive with C. Worked much on books. Read Grey Festival 1834[9]—Young Savage Girl[10]— Gudeman of Ballengeich—Princess Opportunity.[11]

To H. C. E. CHILDERS, chancellor of the exchequer,   Add MS 44547, f. 32.
21 January 1884. 'Private'.

In going through the army estimates, you will probably perform a double process, or proceed by a double standard—one will be to consider what you would yield out of deference to a colleague—the other to determine what, if you were War Minister you would *of yourself propose* on your own responsibility. You will do me a favour, & improve our

[1] T. H. Baker, *Records of seasons, prices of produce and phenomena* (1883).
[2] Hawn P.
[3] Childers had written, 16 January, Add MS 44131, f. 9, that army estimates 'need not exceed those of 1883-4', and on 18 January that Hartington requests an increase of £1,400,000.
[4] Robert Linklater, on repairs to his church in Plymouth; Add MS 44547, f. 32.
[5] One of W. Harness's many works.
[6] W. Miller, see 9 Dec. 83.
[7] E. Henderson, *The Vaudois: observations...* (1845).
[8] Perhaps J. H. Wright, *Confessions of an almsgiver* (1881).
[9] Obscure.
[10] Untraced.
[11] C. M. Phillimore, *Princess Opportunity* (1882).

materials of judgment, if you will kindly keep them distinct: or at least if you will take care to let me know the last-named of the two as exactly as you can.

I have thought a good deal on the matter, of course taking a view without specific knowledge, and it does not improve.

It seems to me so easy to draw, on our proposing anything like such an augmentation, a motion that would put us out.

22. Tu. [London]

Wrote to The Queen—and minutes. Arranging for departure: off at 9.20, reached D. St 3.25. Cabinet at once and until 6¾. Dined at Lady Chesham's. Saw Granville *cum* Childers on our grave position as to Estimates. Read Lady of the Lake:[1] how beautiful, how soothing.

Cabinet. Jan. 22. 84. 3 PM.[2]
1. Application [by Egyptian govt.] to Rothschild for loan of a million to Egypt for 6 mo. He asks what we say. General terms of answer agreed on.[3]
2. Gordon's mission—a mission to report. Instructions to him read placing him under Baring. His suggested proclamations read. Baring authorised to settle the terms & put them in operation if he thinks fit.[4]
3. Musurus had communicated wish of Sultan for a complete understanding with us as to Egypt. G[ranville] replied that if Sultan wd. communicate the basis he wd. make it known to his colleagues.[5]
4. Pr. Leopold proposed himself for Victoria.[6] Cabinet inclined to entertain & further consider it.
5. D. of Wellington Statue. Ld Hn. to get information as to the memorial at Aldershot.
6. Queen's intention.[7] Thank for communication.

Baring exercising his best judgment on the present necessities and means of Egypt, has approved of the application ⟨of the Egyptian Government⟩: and we approve of Baring's proceeding and shall be glad if he finds that he can come to terms with the Egyptian Govt.

23. Wed.

Wrote to Sir W. James—Abp of Canterbury—Mr Holmes—Dr W. Phillimore—Ld Granville—Rev. Mr Curteis—Rev. Mr Baxter—& minutes. Read Debate of

[1] Scott (1810).
[2] Add MS 44645, f. 8.
[3] i.e. support Baring in approving this; CAB 41/18/3.
[4] Gordon reached Cairo on 24 January; Baring's instructions to him read 'You will bear in mind that the main aim to be pursued is the evacuation of the Soudan. . . . I understand, also, that you entirely concur in the desirability of adopting this policy'; Gordon asked that the phrase that the policy 'should on no account be changed' be added; Cromer, i. 390–1, 444–51, *PP* 1884 lxxxviii. 348. He was appt. Governor-General of the Sudan by the Khedive on 26 January 'for the time necessary to accomplish the evacuation'.
[5] Musurus had also suggested that the Sultan might 'substitute Halim Pasha in the place of Tewfik Pasha as Khedive', a manoeuvre vetoed by H.M.G.; see Dufferin to Granville, 11 January, FO 78/3620.
[6] i.e. to be governor of Victoria; the Queen objected; he went instead to Cannes and d. this year.
[7] Of visiting Darmstadt; CAB 41/18/3.

Ap. 15. 83[1]—Life of Godwin.[2] Dined with Mrs Birks. Saw two X. Saw Childers on the very grave question of the year's finance: Conclave 3–5 on the particulars of the Reform Bill. Saw also Ld Kimberley—The Chancellor—Mr Chamberlain—Mr Seymour.

24. Th.

Wrote to The Speaker—Mrs Maxwell Scott—Lady Derby—Bp of Carlisle—Ld Granville—Ld Northbrook—The Queen—and minutes. A nervous morning. Cabinet 12–2½. All went well. Dined at Sir T. May's. Read Lady of the Lake—Life of Godwin—Life & Letters of Burns.[3] Saw Sir Thos May—Mrs A. Peel—Mr Pope—Mr Harrison—Mr Hamilton—Lady Derby. Visited Christie's.

Cabinet. Jan. 24. 1884. Thurs. Noon.[4]
Estimates & financial situation. Conversation & progress, as within.[5]
Standing Committees. Renew proposal of last year. List of Bills within.[6] No other Bill except with general concurrence. Refer to Sol. General on Copyholds Enfranchisement. Temperance. Sunday Closing. Qy. Combine England & Ireland. To be further considered. Ponsonby's letter to D. of Albany read.

To H. B. W. BRAND, the Speaker, 24 January 1884.   Add MS 44547, f. 34.

How kind of you to write,[7] though the intimation is unwelcome.

Today in Cabinet we worked into shape to a certain extent a scheme for a second Grand Committee which I will talk over with Sir Erskine May tonight, and further communicate with you upon, in due time.

We have suggested to Arthur Peel Sir Hussey Vivian as proposer and Dillwyn as seconder.

Gordon goes to Egypt in our sense and there is a reasonable hope I think of much good from his exertions.

To LORD NORTHBROOK, first lord of the admiralty,   Add MS 44547, f. 33.
24 January 1884.

Childers will state to the Cabinet when it meets today the figures of the financial account for the year as it stands on the basis of the demands made by the War Office, Admiralty & Post Office.

They create a situation of extreme gravity which I had not at all anticipated when at our former meetings I undertook serious personal engagements.

If you will kindly call at a quarter before 12 I shall be able to state to you in few words some part of the difficulty to which I refer. But I think the Cabinet ought not to be asked to come to any decision today.

25. Fr. Conv. St Paul.

Wrote to Sir John Mellor—Bp St Andrew's—Abp of Canterbury—Scotts—Sir H. Ponsonby—The Queen—Prince Leopold—Mrs Gascoyne—& minutes. Worked

[1] *Sic*; a Sunday; perhaps 13 April 1883 intended.   [2] See 12 Nov. 83.
[3] J. Currie, *The life of Robert Burns* (1826 ed.); with correspondence.   [4] Add MS 44645, f. 14.
[5] Jottings at ibid., f. 16.   [6] Not found.   [7] Not found.

on Egypt. Dined at Sir W. Harcourt's. Read Lady of the Lake—Life of Godwin—
Stewart's Report on the Soudan.[1] Saw Mr Hamilton—Sir W. Harcourt—Sir C.
Dilke. Saw Harris & two [R].

To H. C. E. CHILDERS, chancellor of the exchequer,   Add MS 44547, f. 34.
25 January 1884. '*Private & Confidential*'.

Now that the Admiralty demand has disappeared *en bloc*, you will not I presume consider the whole sum you named of 400 m[ille] to be available for the demands of the
sister-service.

The 'situation' though diminished in tension, is & must remain grave, whatever you
may be able to effect with your balance, so long as we shall be compelled to present an
augmentation of expenditure without being clearly able to refer the whole of it either to
causes unforeseen or to causes wholly beyond our control.

26. Sat.

Wrote to Mr Cross—Sir H. Ponsonby—The Queen—Sir John Hay—& minutes.
Cabinet 12-2¼. Saw Dean of St Paul's—Dr Liddon—Ld Sudeley. Visited Mr
A[dams] Acton's Studio with C: & we both *sat*.[2] Saw Walters X. Dined at Ld
Reay's. Read Poems by T.S.—Life of Godwin finished—Lady of the Lake.

Cabinet. Sat. Jan. 26. 84. Noon.[3]
1. Finance. C. of E. will proceed upon a balance of Income & Expenditure without
   increase of taxation. He gave the figures.
   To the bad: Army 300; Navy 50; India, 100.
   To the good: Civil Dim[inutio]n 100m; 6d. Tel. postponed, Parcels charge not to
   exceed Income (Suppl. Est. of this year 250).
   Present Est. 86436 m[ille] + Suppl. in all £86900. Next year £86,500.
   Increase of 2400 men in Army—with a very small increase of charge. Hn. represented
   cutting & paring to have been extreme. Much discussion: plan not adopted in deference to Hn. by WEG—general acquiescence.
2. Ceylon—reduction of military charge. *Not* included in the statement.
3. Liquor trade. Harcourt reported after consultation. Strike out Clause from London Bill
   & announce intention to support transfer to local authorities. By a separate & general
   measure after the Local Govt. Bills. Mention in Queen's Speech. WEG broached the
   idea of a naming[?] reference without promising a Bill.

27. 3 S. Epiph.

Chapel Royal mg & evg. Wrote to Mr Elliot MP—Mr MacColl. Saw Miss Hayward. Saw Rivers X. Read Toulmin's Socinus[4]—Reply to Laud's Fisher Conf.[5]—
L. Morris Ode of Life[6]—Bp Webb on Holy Spirit.[7]

---

[1] Report by Col. J. D. H. Stewart on the rising at Bahr Gazal and the general condition of the
Sudan; summarised with comments in FO 78/3685 together with report of Col. de Coetlôgon
recommending immediate withdrawal from Khartoum.
[2] Probably the marble head and plaster bust at Hawarden; see B. Keith-Lucas, *The Gladstone-
Glynne collection* (1934), 49.   [3] Add MS 44645, f. 20.
[4] J. Toulmin, *A series of letters to the Rev. J. Freeston* (1812); on Socinianism.
[5] See 27 Oct. 61.   [6] L. Morris, *The ode of life* (1880).
[7] A. B. Webb, *Notes of six addresses* (1879).

28. M.

Wrote to Pr. of Wales—Archbp of York—Ld Granville—Sir H. Ponsonby—The Queen—Mrs Bolton—Mr Kitson—Mrs Th.—W.H.G.—and minutes. Read the New Godiva[1]—Life of Burns. Saw Ld Granville—Ld Derby—Mr Hamilton—Mr M'Coll—(Rev) Mr Addis.[2] Saw Rivers X. Conclave on Reform Bill from 3 to 5.

29. Tu.

Kept my bed all day, deranged stomach. Read Lady of the Lake—Life of Burns (Currie). Saw Mr Cross.

30. Wed.

Wrote to Mr M'Coll—Lady Holker—Abp of Canterbury—and minutes. A *stretch* of work from 11 to past 7. Laboured hard on the Queen's Speech. Saw Mr Hamilton—Chancr of Exr—Ld Granville—Ld R. Grosvenor—The Speaker—Sir A. Clark. Read Poems by T.S.[3]—Poems by Geo. Heath[4]—Currie's Life of Burns. A more touching life is hard to find.

To Rev. M. MacCOLL, 30 January 1884.   Add MS 44547, f. 35.

I return Lord Bath's letter, reciprocating all his kind sentiments, and sympathising with the real difficulties of his position.[5] My own are limited by the nearness of my horizon.

One remark only I will offer. His son's opinions are, it appears, Conservative. What does this mean? Is it that they echo the current notions of our public schools and Universities, or is it that he has read and considered the recent history of his country, and that he regards Conservatism as that which has brought us through that history, safer than any other country, and stronger by far than we ever were before?

The same statement was made to me twenty years back by a Liberal Peer, who asked my advice about his eldest son. Knowing but one book which details the political story of the last half century, May's Parliamentary, or Constitutional History, I recommended the Father to advise its perusal. He used no other influence. The person so advised read the book and has ever since been one of the soberest but firmest Liberals.

Why do I thus seem to throw a fly? Simply because I fear that, in the absence of wise guidance for the House of Lords, conflicts dangerous to it may be, not indeed in my future, but in a future by no means distant.

[P.S.] Pray speak to the Dean of St. Paul's about Mr. Spence[6] mentioned in your letter.

31. Th.

Wrote to The Queen l.l.—Archbishop of Canterbury—Ld R. Grosvenor—and minutes. Dined with the A. Russells. Saw Mr Hamilton—Mr Adams (sitting)—

---

[1] *The new Godiva. A dialogue* (1883).

[2] William Edward Addis, a Roman Catholic priest, hence Gladstone's brackets; see to Acton, 3 Feb. 84.

[3] Possibly *A yoke for the Roman-Bulls; being a poem . . . by T.S.* (1666); on Jesuits.

[4] G. Heath, *Poems* (1880).

[5] Bath, described as a conservative in Dod's *Parliamentary Companion*, supported the liberals on the Eastern question; in 1896 his son was active in the Armenian crusade.

[6] 'A *protegé* & creature of the Bp. of Gloucester'; Add MS 44244, f. 221.

Four Deputations: & as many *oratiuncula*.[1] Worked again on Speech. Cabinet 2½–6¼ on the Speech. A stiff one. We got well through. Finished Lady of the Lake: a splendid poem especially in the earlier parts. Read Fawcett Reply to George.[2] Finished Currie's Burns.

Cabinet. Thurs. Jan. 31. 84. 2½ PM[3]
1. Queen's Speech. Considered & amended.
2. Secret Service money. C. of E. proposes 1. 1883-4 Add 10 m[ille]; 2. 1884-5. Add 10 m.; 3. Declarations to be made; 4. Audit Office Decl.

To LORD R. GROSVENOR, chief whip, 31 January 1884.[4]   Add MS 44315, f. 145.

The Cabinet considered with real care the proposal made by Dodson & approved (very naturally) by you for a Bill about Cattle. With their eyes open to what will probably happen on the Address, they determined *not* to entertain it & I am sorry to say I think they were right upon the whole. It is rather sad.

Frid. Feb. One 1884. [*Osborne House*]

Wrote to Mrs Wolffsohn[5]—Messrs Robn & Nichn—Mrs Th.—Mr Hamilton Tel.—and minutes. Saw Mr Hamilton—Mr Hemingway (and S. Lyttelton)—11-12 Mr Elliot & Mr Smith on the Speech. Off at 1.30 to Osborne. Saw Lady Ely—Sir H. Ponsonby—and H.M., who was exceedingly gracious, from 6¾ to 8. I put down over 20 subjects of this conversation. Read Burns's Letters—Dixon's Mano.[6]

To Sir W. V. HARCOURT, home secretary,   MS Harcourt dep Adds 10.
1 February 1884.

Mr Smith, who seconds the Address, may I think wish to talk to you about Liquor Laws.

He leans to the idea of a separate body which I do not understand to be your basis. But I have pointed out to him that while he is not in any way precluded from expressing a personal wish, it is most important to avoid any discussion of particulars of our forthcoming measures, in as much as all such discussions would give a handle to the enemy.

2. Sat. [*London*]

Wrote to Mr Bryce MP—The Queen l.l.l.l.—Abp of Canterbury—Lady Pembroke—& minutes. Read by permission about half of the Queen's new book, not yet published. It is innocence itself.[7] Read Burns's Letters—Dixon's Mano. Back to London at six. Dined with Ly Chesham. Saw H.M. Attended Council & 'read' Speech.

---

[1] 'little speeches'. Deputations on franchise from the Leeds Conference, the T.U.C. and various trade unions, the Conference of Metropolitan Liberal Associations; on success of liberal policy in India, from Indians resident in Britain; *T.T.*, 1 February 1884, 10a.
[2] H. Fawcett, 'State socialism and the nationalisation of the land' (1883).
[3] Add MS 44645, f. 24.   [4] Holograph.
[5] Permission to dedicate to him her book on animal plants; Add MS 44547, f. 36.
[6] R. W. Dixon, *Mano: a poet*, 4v. (1883).
[7] *More Leaves from the Journal of a Life in the Highlands* (1884); see Guedalla, *Q*, ii. 258.

3. *4 S. Epiph.*

Chapel Royal mg (with H.C.) & evg. Called at Mr Hayward's. Wrote to Ld Granville—Lord Acton. Read D. of Argyll[1]—Laveleye on Regulated Vice[2]—Calcraft's Defence of the Stage.[3] Dined with Alf. Lyttelton.

To LORD ACTON, 3 February 1884.   Cambridge University Library.

You will without doubt have in your hands, now or very speedily, the Life of Hope Scott,[4] & you will perhaps, think as I do, that I occupy a space in it greater than is either convenient or desirable.

The state of the case was this. Hope and I had been in such close relations for a number of critical years, that an exhibition of my personality, in a certain degree, was indispensable for the true and full presentation of his; and by withholding assent from the publication of my letters I should have seriously marred what was the purpose of the book. I considered the matter as well as I could, and took advice, but an unwillingness to maim the account of so remarkable a man prevailed over every other feeling.

It is probable that the work has been produced with more or less of a polemical aim, nor can one complain that the members of any religious communion should feel a desire to exhibit to the world so great a trophy. I place him as second only to Newman in the long list of remarkable or able men who left the Church of England, between 1840 and 1850 (or thereabouts), for the Church of Rome.

The book is written in a strongly Roman spirit, as was to be expected, but from that point of view it is not unfair, and I think it is not unfair, and I think in other respects it deserves great praise for completeness and conscientious care. Perhaps you know Mr. Ornsby: he took the same step, as Hope did.[5]

The memory of last year, and the combination of pleasures & of relief which Cannes gave me, has brought to me at this time many covetous yearnings; all the worse because Wolverton tells me you have no idea of repatriation but are again quietly ensconced at the Madeleine; where I pray you to diffuse around you our kindest remembrances.

I have made the acquaintance of Mr. Addis, R.C. priest, and am struck by him. I take him to be in much sympathy with you. Should an American named Hurlbutt drop among you at Cannes, you will find him very agreeable. He gives the most sanguine accounts of the Latin Church in his own country.

[P.S.] A stormy time is threatened us in Parliament.

4. *M.*

Wrote to Mr Hubbard—Mr Whitbread—D. of Argyll—Dean of Westminster— and minutes. Read Burns's Letters. and Cooke on G. Eliot.[6] Saw Mrs Bolton— Mr Bolton—Mr Hamilton—Mr Mundella—Ld R. Grosvenor. Conclave on Reform at 3—Conclave on Egypt 4-5.—Ld Gr. & C. of E. on Eg[yptian] Finance. Forty one came to the Speech dinner. Large evening party afterwards. Saw

---

[1] G. D. Campbell, duke of Argyll, *The unity of nature* (1884).

[2] E. de Laveleye, 'Regulated vice in relation to morality' (1884); opposing licensed brothels.

[3] J. W. Calcraft, *A defence of the stage* (1839).

[4] See 27 July, 24 Nov. 83.

[5] Acton replied, 9 February, Add MS 44093, f. 242: 'we seem to remember two different men. . . . I do not quite recognise a man capable of attracting and influencing you so deeply, in the indifferent, languid, selfcontained Hope that I knew from 1851 to 1864.'

[6] G. W. Cooke, *George Eliot* (1883).

Musurus, Carolyi, Münster. Retired at twelve: & wound up with sharp neuralgia.

5. Tu.

Wrote to Sir C. Dilke—The Queen—& minutes. Read Burns's letters. Saw Mr Hamilton—Ld R. Grosvenor—much—do *cum* Sir T. E. May. H. of C. 4½–11: except ½ hour.[1] Kept my bed until 11 AM.

6. Wed.

Wrote to Mr Hastings MP.—The Queen l.l.—W.H.G.—Ld Chancellor—H.M.G. (begun)—Rev. Dr Ridding—Rev. Dr Stubbs[2]—and minutes. H of C. 12¼–5¼.[3] Cabinet 11½ & at H. of C. Saw Mr Hamilton—Bp of Exeter—Lady Derby—Ld R. Grosvenor. Read Burns's Letters. Dined at Lady Chesham's. Attended the part-funeral service of Hayward[4] at St James's at 10.30. Saw Messrs Elkington.

Cabinet. Wed. Feb. 6. 84—11.30 A.M. D[owning] St & H. of C.[5]
1. Query introduce in H. of Lords? Limit to Foot & Mouth. Yes. Notice to be given. Bill (in Lords) to enlarge the ⟨discretion⟩ power of the Privy Council under the Contagious Diseases Animals Act with regard to the prohibition & regulation of the importation of Animals from Foreign Countries.
2. Reinforce Adm. Hewett[6] with marines.

7. Th.

Wrote to Prince Leopold—Ld Northbrook—Sir R. Owen—Mr Heneage—Mr Dodson—Ld Granville l.l.—Mr Godley—The Queen—& minutes. H of C. 4¼–8 & 8¾–12½.[7] Saw Mr Hamilton—Ld R. Grosvenor—Mrs Th.—Ld Hartington—Att. General—The Speaker—Sir C. Dilke. Read Burns's Letters—[blank] St Petersburgh.

8. Fr.

Wrote to Mr Whitbread—Mr Rathbone—Ld Spencer—The Queen l.l.—& minutes. Cabinet 3–4½: an anxious question was disposed of with tolerable safety. Saw Mr Hamilton—Ld R. Grosvenor—The Speaker—Ld Granville—Attorney General—Sir C. Dilke—Ld Carlingford. Dined at Sir C. Forster's. H of C. 4¾–8¼ & 10¼–12½.[8] An anxious & hardworking day.

[1] Gave notice of the Franchise Bill; Queen's Speech; *H* 284. 39.
[2] Offering him see of Chester; for the consequence, see to Freeman, 14 Feb. 84.
[3] Spoke on the Address; *H* 284. 105.
[4] i.e. A. Hayward, buried this day in Highgate.
[5] Add MS 44645, f. 25.
[6] Baker Pasha had been routed at El Teb on 4 February; Suakin was defended by Admiral Sir William Nathan Wrighte *Hewett, 1834–88, who from 10 Feb. acted as governor for the Khedive.
[7] Questions; Queen's Speech; *H* 284. 201.
[8] Questioned on *United Ireland's* articles on Sudan; *H* 284. 314.

Cabinet. 3 P.M. Friday Feb. 8. 84.[1]

Lord Hartington read letter from Gordon. Discussed. Telegram of last night to Gordon through Baring read.[2] Explanatory telegram agreed on.

While adhering to our general Soudan policy we desire to know whether in order to carry out the plan of evacuation entrusted to you you would wish any military demonstration at Suakim or Massowa.[3]

Form agreed on: Make it clear to Gordon that request for his suggestion is not confined to the single point of his proceeding to Khartoum but extends to any alternative for assisting the object.[4]

We wish General Gordon to understand by the last telegram that he is free to make whatever suggestions recent events may seem to him to require.

Take care that Gordon has perfect freedom to express his opinion.

To Baring: Let Gordon understand that he is free to give his view on whole case and to state alternatives which he may think open concluding words of last nights telegram are not limited to question raised in the first part.[5]

9. Sat.

Wrote to Ld Kimberley—Ld Granville—Mr Godley—The Queen—and minutes. Dined with Lucy Cavendish. Visited Royal Acad. Exhibn. Saw Mr H.—Mr S.—Ld R. Grosvenor—Madame Waddington—Lady Stanley—Calls. Bad account of Pembroke:[6] found the family setting out. Read Burns's Letters (finished)— Schuyler's Peter the Great.[7]

Lord H[artington]'s Circulation Box.[8] My belief that Gordon has a perfect freedom of advice under our two last telegrams is confirmed by a reference to his own Memorandum, which does not quite correspond with some recollections of it expressed in Cabinet yesterday.

The 'irrevocable decision' of which he speaks is, it will be found, not a decision under no conceivable circumstances to employ a soldier in the Soudan, but the decision 'to evacuate the territory' and 'not to incur the very onerous duty of securing to the peoples of the Soudan a just future government'.

This decision '*as far as possible*' involves the avoidance of any fighting and he will strive to effect the evacuation 'with avoidance as far as possible of all fighting'.

I much regret that we had not this expression of General Gordon's views on starting from Cairo before us yesterday. WEG Feb. 9. 84.

[1] Add MS 44645, f. 26. Royal Commission on Housing of the Working Classes also agreed to; see Gwynn, ii. 16.

[2] Gordon proposed to Baring he go S. of Khartoum, take the equatorial provinces and give them to the King of the Belgians; on Baring's advice, Gordon was instructed *via* Baring 'not to proceed at present south of Khartoum'; Cromer, i. 464 and Add MS 44629, f. 73.

[3] Draft in Childers' hand; Add MS 44645, f. 27.

[4] Note by Gladstone; ibid., f. 28.

[5] Add MS 44645, f. 29.

[6] Presumably 13th earl of Pembroke, though he lived until 1895.

[7] E. Schuyler, *Peter the Great*, 2v. (1884).

[8] Gladstone's holograph; Chatsworth MSS 340. 1413.

To J. A. GODLEY, 9 February 1884.   Add MS 44547, f. 39.

In framing our Bill about the franchise the elementary dictates of prudence have taught us *not* to attempt to bring all the franchises of the county into the best form within the compass of our measure;[1] and I shall probably make the strongest appeal in my power to our friends not to do the work of our enemies by deck-loading the ship.[2]

Of all franchises that of the University seems the fittest for separate dealing & the least entitled to clog a measure which is beset with covert dangers, none so great as the multiplication of the points.

[P.S.] I shall be glad to talk to you about the Hope Scott Memoir.

10. *Septa S.*

Ch. Royal mg & ev. Wrote to Ld Granville—Ld Northrbook—& minutes. Read Toulmin's Socinus—Johnson's Dies Irae[3]—Fun. Sermon on Sir G. Grey—Lilly on Xtn Revolution.[4] Walk with C. Saw Ld Granville—Ld Wolverton—Mr Seymour.

No. 2. Circulation Box.[5]

I agree with Lord Granville's memorandum of today.[6]

It appears to me absolutely undeniable that a man who says he will do a thing 'with avoidance as far as possible of all fighting' must know himself to be *at liberty* to say that he finds he cannot do it without some 'fighting' or that some fighting will aid his mission. I must add that Gordon's written words, at Cairo, on the 25th, when his plan was matured and he was on the point of setting out, are of higher authority than recollections of his unrecorded conversations in London eight or ten days before. W E G F.10.84.

To LORD NORTHBROOK, first lord of the admiralty,   Add MS 44267, f. 41.
10 February 1884.[7]

I presume we have now to look about from hour to hour for replies to the telegrams of Thursday night and Friday for the expression of Gordon's views: but I see no objection to keeping him (or trying to keep him for he moves sharply) at Berber until, with adequate information from Baring, he has given us his views.

I assume that he will make it one of the first objects of his friendly communications to obtain relief for Sincat & Tokar.

[P.S.] I send this through Granville.

---

[1] Godley, 6 February, Add MS 44223, f. 28, suggested giving the franchise to Oxford B.A.s (rather than M.A.s).

[2] Gladstone again used this phrase introducing the Reform Bill; *H* 285. 123.

[3] *Sic*, but no tr. found by Samuel or any other Johnson; perhaps further study of Shipley's papers; Gladstone's earlier comment linked Johnson with the poem; see to Shipley, 14 May 83.

[4] W. S. Lilly, *C.R.*, xlv. 241 (February 1884).

[5] Gladstone's holograph; Chatsworth MSS 340. 1416.

[6] Chatsworth MSS 340. 1415: if we thought that Wolseley's plan was good, then no harm in 'putting to him [Gordon] a leading question in favour of the plan', but as we mostly dislike the plan 'I do not think it right to place upon Gordon the responsibility of rejecting it'. Wolseley this day told Hartington, Chatsworth MSS 340. 1417: 'in my conversations with Gordon previous to your seeing him in the War Office, I told him most emphatically that the Cabinet would not consent to the use of British troops at Suakin ... the employment of an English Brigade will not enter into his Calculations as a *possible* operation'.

[7] Holograph draft.

11. M.

Wrote to Ld Granville—The Queen l.l.l.l.—Ld Northbrook—Ld Hartington & copy—and minutes. H. of C. $4\frac{1}{2}$-$10\frac{1}{2}$ except half an hour.[1] Cabinet 12-$2\frac{1}{2}$. The times are stiff & try the mettle of men. What shd *we* have done, with the Mutiny at the Nore? Saw Mr Hamilton—Ld Granville. Read Cooke on G. Elliot [*sic*]—Benson's Poems.[2]

Cabinet. Feb. 11 84. Noon. Monday.[3]
1. Bradlaugh: to be introduced today. We deprecate Ls moving. But vote.
2. Telegraphic message A. agreed to.[4]
3. Course of debate. To leave the Soudan question *so far* open as it has been left up to this time.
4. Ld Carlingford stated form of his Bill—to be positive & *directory.*[5]
5. Chancellor's Bill on restitution of conjugal rights: to abolish imprisonment for disobedience to orders.

To LORD NORTHBROOK, first lord of the admiralty,   Add MS 44547, f. 39.
11 February 1884.

Could you send me, today or early tomorrow, from any information you possess, a dotted outline of the Sudan, ever so rough, with the places & numbers (as far as we know anything about them) of the Egyptian forces?

12. Tu.

Wrote to Dean Church—The Queen l.l.l.—Abp of Canterbury Tel.—Bp of Lincoln—Bp of Lichfield—& minutes. Saw Mr Hamilton—Ld Granville—do *cum* Ld Hartington—Ld Northbrook *cum* Ld Kimberley. Cabinet 11-1. Worked on Egypt papers. H. of C. $4\frac{1}{2}$-$9\frac{1}{4}$. Speech of 1 h. 50 m, history & controversy.[6] Thank God it is off. This has been rather a sore time combining difficulties in Council constantly renewed with effort for & in the House. But God sent to me His words: 'when thou passest through the waters, I will be with thee; through the rivers, they shall not overthrow [*recte* overflow] thee'.[7] So I have been in His sight: praise be to His great Name.

Cabinet. 11 AM Feb. 12. 84. Tuesday.[8]
1. Agreed to collect a force at Suakim with the object if possible of relieving Tokar garrison if it can hold out: if not, of taking any means necessary for defence of ports.

[1] Spoke on Sudan, on Bradlaugh; *H* 284. 441, 450.
[2] Perhaps W. Benson's tr. of Virgil (1725).
[3] Add MS 44645, f. 30.
[4] 'It has been suggested by a military authority [i.e. Wolseley] that to assist the policy of withdrawal, to send a British force to Suakim, sufficient to operate if necessary in its vicinity. Would such a step injure or assist your mission'; not quite grammatical draft by Dodson with Gladstone's amendments; ibid., f. 35.
[5] Contagious Diseases (Animals) Bill, introduced in Lords, 14 February; *H* 284. 837.
[6] Vote of censure on govt.'s Sudan policy, moved by Northcote; *H* 284. 700.
[7] Isaiah, 43. 2.
[8] Add MS 44645, f. 38; telegram to Hewett announcing Graham's expedition of 3 battalions and cavalry, ibid., f. 40.

To LORD NORTHBROOK, first lord of the admiralty,   Add MS 44547, f. 40.
12 February 1884.

It occurs to me that you might well consider whether, as a sister message to the one you have directed Hewett to send if he can to the Tokar garrison, he should also if he can send one to the commander of the investing force (Osman Digna) to summon him to let the garrison depart, on pain of being otherwise compelled to do it by a British military force: that he might however have a dissension if he saw any serious military objection.

This opens a chance, if a remote one of an earlier release, as well as a release without blood.[1]

I need hardly say that the Gordon telegrams of last evening filled up for me the gap in the evidence which made my assent to the message into Tokar yesterday the last & most reluctant. But I cannot get over the sickening effect produced upon me by Hewett's contingent proposal of a vengeance raid upon men who are fighting to deliver their country from the stranger.

To C. WORDSWORTH, bishop of Lincoln, 12 February   Wordsworth MS 2148, f. 97.
1884.

I inclose a note from Dr. Ridding, Headmaster of Winchester, (was it not your old School?), from which you will perceive what I was anxious you should first learn from or through me, that he has agreed to be presented for Consecration, on the nomination of the Crown, for the Bishopric of Southwell. Canon Stubbs will at the same time be announced as the successor to Bishop Jacobson.

I have like inquired, and consulted, a good deal about Dr. Ridding, and I believe him to be one of those large minded men who will work on the one hand with great devotion and energy, on the other hand with a liberal and just regard to the various shades of sentiment and practice united in the communion of the Church. Your Lordship will I am sure observe with satisfaction his allusion to the (partially) resigning Bishops, who have so munificently promoted the new foundation.

Have the kindness to let his letter be returned to me.[2]

13. *Wed.*

Wrote to Dean of ChCh–Dr Stubbs Tel.–The Queen l.l.–Crown Princess of Denmark–Ld Northbrook–& minutes. Dined at Marlboro' House: home at midnight. Conversation with Princess, Archbp of Canterb., D. of Cambridge. Saw Mr Hamilton–Warden of Keble–Lord Acton. 12¼-6. H. of C. & work there, off and on.[3] Drive & walk with C. Read The Queen's 'More Leaves'.[4] The part about N. Macleod questionable here and there?

To H. G. LIDDELL, dean of Christ Church, 13 February   Add MS 44547, f. 40.
1884.

An article in today's Times reminds me that there is the Modern History Professorship to become vacant by the coming advancement of Dr. Stubbs.

[1] Northbrook next day sent telegrams to Hewett following Gladstone's suggestion; Add MS 44267, f. 44. Graham's force to relieve Tokar, negotiations having failed, was too late; Osman Digna led the revolt in the E. Sudan.
[2] Add MS 44485, f. 152. Wordsworth's reply, 13 February, Add MS 44346, hoped Gladstone's 'anticipations may be fully made real'.
[3] Spoke on standing cttees.; *H* 284. 792.   [4] See 2 Feb. 84.

You kindly helped me with information of value when Pusey died. This is less difficult, but I should be glad of your aid.

The first Oxford man by far in position is Freeman. Lord Derby may even be said to have passed him by;[1] but he is a strong Liberal.[2]

I fear he makes enemies & I am told he is little versed in manuscripts. On the other hand he seems to be by far first in position, & it is believed by excellent authorities (I do not mean his friend Dr. S[tubbs]) that he would give a powerful impulsion to historical study at Oxford.

Other good names are I suppose Gardiner & Revd. Creichton [*sc.* Creighton]. But Freeman's first.

What do you say? Do you know the income at all?[3]

14. Th.

Wrote to Ld Wolverton—Mr Hutton—Rev. Mr Rudd—Ld Tennyson—Mrs Wellesley—Dean of ChCh. (Tel.)—Chancr of Exchr—Mr E.A. Freeman—The Queen l.l.—and minutes.[4] Nine to dinner. Saw Mr Hamilton—Chancr of Exchr—Ld Granville—Canon Stubbs—Mr Addis—Ld R. Grosvenor—Herbert J.G.—Scotts—& minutes. Read The Queen More Leaves.

To E. A. FREEMAN, 14 February 1884.   Bodley MS Top. Oxon. d. 238, f. 86.

I received your letter[5] with pleasure. It anticipated my action only by a few hours. In my own mind I did not doubt; but thought it right to survey the field, and to consult a little.

I have now written to submit your name to Her Majesty. I cannot think there will be difficulty (all secret at present) and I anticipate with lively satisfaction the introduction into academical life of a fresh and solid piece of not less stout than healthy Liberalism, as well as the great impulse which your depth range and vigour will impart, in our loved Oxford, to a study so vital to all the best interests of man. I will also heartily wish you what in these times is more difficult, a peaceful reign, after the happy example of your admirable predecessor.

15. Fr.

Wrote to Rev. Mr Walford—The Queen l.l.—Musurus Pacha—and minutes. H. of C. 5-8¼, 9½-12: the debate went well.[6] Saw Mr H—Ld R.G—Rev. Dr Ridding—Chancr of Exr—Ld E. Fitzmaurice. Read More Leaves—Burns's Poems.

16. Sat.

Wrote to Sir T. May—Sir H. Ponsonby—Rev. S.E.G.—Ld Kilcoursie[7]—The Queen Tel.—Ld Northbrook l.l.—Ld Hartington—Ld Wolverton—& minutes.

---

[1] i.e. on Stubbs' appt. in 1866.   [2] See next day.

[3] No reply found; Liddell's letter of 23 February, Add MS 44236, f. 385, requested a pension for James Murray so as to assist the dictionary.

[4] And the Commons, speaking on Gordon; *H* 284. 912.

[5] Freeman proposed himself as successor to Stubbs as regius professor of modern history at Oxford; 13 February, Add MS 44485, f. 197: 'I believe my holding it for a few years might be useful to historical learning. Specially I believe . . . I could give more importance to the public lectures which Stubbs never liked having to do'.   [6] Sudan; *H* 284. 1025.

[7] Frederick Edward Gould Lambert, 1839–1905; Lord Kilcoursie; Liberal M.P. S. Somerset 1885–92; 9th earl of Cavan 1887.

Saw Mr H–Ld R.G–Baron A. de Rothschild–Sir C. Dilke–Mr Morley. Ten to dinner. Read Burns's Poems. Drove to Gunnersbury & saw Baroness Lionel [de Rothschild]: quite well.

To LORD HARTINGTON, war secretary, 16 February 1884.Chatsworth MSS 340. 1420.

On the question of the duty or no-duty of the Opposition to have a *policy*, I trouble you with my general recollections in a few words. Peel in 1840 or 41 said he would prescribe when he was called in. But this had reference to Legislation; and an Opposition objecting to the Bills of a Government cannot be expected to formulate its own plans, however the Govt. may try to turn its reticence to account.

But I think that in motions of Foreign Policy this has not been so and when a continuing course of action has been in question, I believe it is a somewhat new course to decline presenting an alternative. Do not take the trouble to reply.

17. Sexa S.

Chapel Royal mg and evg. Saw Mr Hamilton–Lady Dudley–Sir W. Gull–Ld Acton. Read Toulmin's Socinus–Newman on Inspiration[1]–Calcraft Defence of the Stage–Corona Catholica[2]–Medd's Bampton Lectures[3]–and Tracts.

18. M.

Wrote to Lord Mayor–Rev. Mr Scott Holland–Sir T. May–Abp of Canterbury–The Queen Tel. & L.l.l.–Ld Northbrook–Ld Granville–and minutes. Saw Mr H–Ld R.G–Ld Granville–Cabinet 2½-4. H of C. 5-8 and 10-12.[4] Dined at Sir W. Harcourt's. Read The Minister's Wooing[5]–Burns's Poems.

Cabinet. Feb. 18. 84. 2½ PM.[6]
1. Answer to Lyons–sketched & approved.[7]
2. Baring's demand for two more battalions in Egypt: 1 Battn. from Malta and 1 from Gib. to Malta & go on if need be.[8]
3. Berbera & Zeila (Summali country below Babelmandeb). Wait consul Hunter's report.[9] (300 can be spared from normal Aden garrisons).
4. Porte–will British Govt. ask Sultan's assent to sending troops to Suakim. Explain expe[ditio]n to S[uakim] conformable to our obligations & not derogatory to Sultan's rights. It will give us much satisfaction if he expresses his concurrence.[10]
4. [*sc* 5] [Onslow's] Question about Merv.[11]

[1] J. H. Newman, 'On the inspiration of scripture', *N.C.*, xv. 185 (February 1884).
[2] Untraced.   [3] P. G. Medd, *The one mediator* (1884).
[4] Onslow's question on Merv; *H* 284. 1201.
[5] H. Beecher Stowe, *The Minister's Wooing* (1859), sent by the author; letter of thanks, sending *Homeric Synchronism* in return, at Add MS 44547, f. 66.   [6] Add MS 44645, f. 41.
[7] Possibly permission for French police to have details of an English suicide; FO 27/2663.
[8] Baring's tel. on 'mutinous spirit' among Egyptian troops, Add MS 44645, f. 46.
[9] Frederick Mercer Hunter, British consul on the E. African coast.
[10] Conveyed in Granville to Dufferin, 19 February, FO 78/3620; later despatch to Dufferin, 29 February, regretted the Sultan's 'suspicion' and stressed the defensive nature of the Suakin operations, Granville adding to the despatch: 'they likewise tend to limit the area of disturbances which might otherwise have extended beyond the Red Sea'; ibid.
[11] On its annexation by Russia; answered by Gladstone; *H* 284. 1201.

19. Tues.

Wrote to The Queen l–Ld Granville–Mr Graham–& minutes. Saw Mr H–Ld R.G–Ld Northbrook–Ld Granville–Att. General. Read Gordon in the Soudan[1]–Minister's Wooing. H of C. 5-8$\frac{1}{2}$ and 9$\frac{3}{4}$-2$\frac{1}{2}$. Much attack, chiefly declamatory, outweighed by Hartington. Division (311:262) will do good.[2] Monday and tonight made reckonings of the Line of Prime Ministers as such since the H[ouse] of Hanover's accession. I have now touched 9 years & am the 7th of 31.

20. Wed.

Wrote to The Queen–Ld Granville–Sir S. Northcote–Ld Spencer–& minutes. H of C. 12$\frac{1}{4}$-4.[3] Saw Mr H–Ld RG–Att. General–Mr Murray–Bp of Ely–Lord Acton above all: divers conversations: I had to declare him the most wicked of men, for he would not even allow that the decline & end of this Parliament fixed a term for my labours, but insisted on one session of the next. Dined at Ld Reay's. Read Sybil[4]–Burns.

To LORD SPENCER, Viceroy of Ireland, 20 February 1884.   Althorp MSS K7.

I shall be extremely sorry if you cannot legally appoint an inquiry respecting the relation of some Orange Lodge to the brutal and loathsome murder of Maguire, as it gives a convenient handle to the ill-disposed, and may well bewilder an honest judgment insufficiently informed. But of course you will & must act legally.[5]

If nothing is done in the way of inquiry, it has occurred to me whether I (if you have no fund for the purpose) should do well to give the bereaved mother a sum out of Royal Bounty. If you approve & the occasion arise, please to let me know what sort of 'compensation' would probably have been awarded to her under the Act, and whether it should be given her in a lump sum, or by way of annuity.[6]

21. Th.

Wrote to The Speaker–Cardinal Manning–Mr Duckham–The Queen l.l.–Mr W.H. Smith–& minutes. Read Sybil–Burns's Poems. Saw Mr H–Ld R.G–Ld E. Clinton (weak, weak, weak)–Musurus–Mr Waddington–C. Mohrenheim–Mr Chamberlain–Ld Granville *cum* C. of E. Cabinet 2$\frac{1}{2}$-4$\frac{1}{4}$. H of C. 4$\frac{3}{4}$-8$\frac{1}{4}$ & 9$\frac{3}{4}$-1$\frac{1}{2}$.[7]

---

[1] *England, Gordon, and the Soudan, Pall Mall Gazette Extra*, N. 7 (2 February 1884).

[2] *H* 284. 1458.

[3] Queen's Speech; *H* 284. 1465.

[4] By Disraeli, 3v. (1845); Gladstone's first reading.

[5] Spencer, 19 February, Add MS 44311, f. 34, thought the case of Maguire no worse than '20 or 30 others brought before me under this question of compensation'.

[6] Spencer replied, 22 February, ibid., f. 39, declining an inquiry; Maguire was murdered 'by assailants returning from a meeting of the Salvation Army'; no evidence of direct Orange involvement.

[7] Queen's Speech; *H* 284. 1609.

Cabinet. Thurs. Feb. 21. 84. 2¾ PM.[1]

1. Sultan of Soudan—gravest objections to nomination by our authority.[2] Do not see necessity of going beyond mem of Jan 29 [*sc.* 23] a special provision for govt. of Soudan. Exclude Zebir.[3]

2. Forward movement to Assouan. As to Wood's troops: & British in support if found necessary for keeping order. Yes. but no change as to the (so called) permanent army establishment in Egypt.

3. *Reserve* to be recommended to Gordon. Answer to Wolff's question[4] agreed on.

4. Ld Derby's may conclude.[5]

To CARDINAL MANNING, 21 February 1884.[6]   Add MS 44250, f. 199.

I have examined your letter and inclosures[7] with interest, and have also looked back to answers given by me in Parliament on the 14th & 18th and reported in the papers of the following days respectively.

You will find from them that the question is not so much, at present, one of the merits, as of the *locus standi.* Now on this your letter does not bear neither I have found much aid in the inclosure.

We have promised any aid in the way of good offices for which an opening may present itself at Rome—can we do more?

In 1866 (I think this was the year) when I was in Italy & out of office I bestirred myself to the best of my ability on behalf of Monte Cassino,[8] and the Italian Government, who might have treated me as an impertinent, were extremely tolerant and kind. But I have lost the character in which I then acted, without acquiring any other similarly available.

Lady Herbert gave me a less flourishing account of you the other day than I would have wished to receive—I hope it was due to some cause purely fugitive.

22. Fr.

Wrote to Ld Granville—Archbp of York—Prince of Wales—The Queen—& minutes. H of C. 4¾-8¼ and 9½-1. The Speaker announced his retirement.[9] Drive with Mary. Saw Mr H.—Ld R.G—Rev. E. Talbot—Ld Wolverton (who dined). Conclave at F.O. on Merv.[10] Read Sybil—Burns.

23. Sat.

Wrote to The Queen—Mr Norwood MP—Earl of Fife—Mr M. Wilson—Ld Spencer—and minutes. Saw Mr H—Ld R.G—The Speaker—Mr Estcourt—Mr Maylen—Ld Granville—Lds Hartington & Northbrook. Seventeen to dinner: shell of an evening party afterwards. Read Sybil.

[1] Add MS 44645, f. 48.

[2] i.e. nomination of a successor to Gordon as governor-general of the Sudan; see Guedalla, ii. 262. Draft on this, marked 'cancelled', at Add MS 44645, f. 51.

[3] Gordon, supported by Baring, requested the nomination of Zobeir Pasha, a well-known slaver, as his successor; Cromer, i. 486.

[4] In fact put in by Gibson, on Egyptian slave trade; *H* 284. 1608.

[5] i.e. the negotiations for the London convention, signed on 27 February; Schreuder, 427, 498.

[6] Holograph.

[7] Not found; on the legal status of the Propaganda; see Manning's reply, 22 February, Add MS 44250, f. 201. See 30 Apr. 84.

[8] See above, v. lxxi.   [9] And Queen's Speech; *H* 284. 1734.

[10] 'delimitation of the Afghan frontier was . . . pretty much decided'; Gwynn, ii. 87.

24. Quinqua S.

Chapel Royal mg & aft. Read Toulmin's Socinus (finished)—Argyll on Unity of Nature Ch VI—Ed. Rev. on Spencer[1]—Memoirs of Marie Mancini[2]—Memoirs of Miss Jones.[3] Saw W.H.G.—Sir A. Clark.

25. M.

Wrote to The Queen l.l.l.l.—Ld Spencer Tel l.l.—Ld Kinnaird—& minutes. H of C. 5¼-9 and 10-12. The farewell scene with the Speaker.[4] Saw Mr H—Ld R.G—Mr Trevelyan—Ld Granville. Cabinet 3-4¼. Read Sybil.

Cabinet. Mon. Feb. 25. 84. 3 PM.[5]

1. Egypt. Answer to Salisbury's demand for policy. Summary refusal. Soudan's operations.[6] Reserve information. Protect 1. fugitives from Tokar 2. Suakim.
2. Ld H. to restrain [?] publication at Cairo of our messages by strong words.
3. Blunt demands admission into Egypt. Support refused.
4. Message to Osman Digna summoning to disperse & go to Khartoum—otherwise blood on his own head.[7]
5. A battalion to be 'put under arms for the Mediterranean'.

Orange Societies.[8]

26. Tu.

Wrote to Mrs Roundell—Sol. Gen. Ireland—Mr Luttrell—Chancr of Exr—Mr Healy MP.—The Queen—and minutes. Saw Mr H—Ld RG—Sir H. Brand—Dr Simeon—Lady Brand—Mrs Bolton—Mr Kingsworth. Conclave on Egyptian matters. Thirteen to dinner. Read Sybil—Escott's Article on Hayward[9]—Mrs Roundell on Cowdray.[10]

27. Ash Wedn.

St John's Ch 11 A.M. House at 2 & 5.45 carrying forward the operations of the Speakership.[11] Wrote to Ld Hartington—Ld Granville—The Queen—Mr Childers—Ld Spencer—and minutes. Saw Mr H—Lord RG—Ld & Lady Mar(cum Ld Adv.)—Sir Henry Thring. Worked much on the Franchise Bill & papers. Read Sybil.

[1] *E.R.*, clix. 41.
[2] Perhaps Marie T. B. M. Mancini, *Pensées diverses* (1870).
[3] *Memorials of Agnes Elizabeth Jones* (1871).
[4] Gladstone moved the Resolutions of thanks; *H* 284. 1879.
[5] Add MS 44645, f. 52.
[6] Salisbury was absent and his question went unasked; see *H* 285. 11.
[7] Graham defeated Osman Digna's troops at El Teb on 29 February, capturing Tokar on 3 March.
[8] Enquiry to be made into extent of Orange Society activities; Monk Bretton 62.
[9] T. H. S. Escott, *F.R.*, xli. 414 (March 1884).
[10] J. A. E. Roundell, *Cowdray: the story of a great English house* (1884).
[11] *H* 285. 238.

To LORD HARTINGTON, war secretary, 27 February 1884.   Add MS 44547, f. 45.

Would it be agreeable to you to have your name on the back of the Franchise Bill?[1] The others would be, with me, Trevelyan (Ireland) & Advocate (Scotland) and the Attorney General. There is no necessity, but, as you will see, plenty of room, & good company.

28. Th.

Wrote to The Queen—and minutes. Read Cowdray—Sybil. Dined at Sir T. May's. Saw Mr H—Ld RG—Attorney General $1\frac{1}{2}$ hour (cruel enough: he was full of gout). H. of C. $5\frac{1}{2}-8\frac{1}{2}$ and $10-12\frac{1}{2}$. After some menacing signs, introduced the Franchise Bill, in a speech of $1\frac{3}{4}$ hours, to a favourable House.[2] Worked much on subj. & notes.

29. Fr.

Wrote to The Speaker—Sir W. Harcourt—Mr Hutton—Sir H. Brand—Dr Stubbs— The Queen l.l.—& minutes. H. of C. 5–9 and 10–11.[3] Read Sybil—Burns's Poems. Saw Mr H—Ld R.G—Lord Granville—Chr of Exr—Cabinet $2\frac{1}{2}-4\frac{1}{4}$.

Cabinet. Frid. Feb. 29. 84. $2\frac{1}{2}$ PM[4]
1. Egypt. Baring's No (179?) See A within.[5]
   Turkish *Entente*. Two dispatches read—& agreed with.
   Gordon's proclamation about Brit. troops to Khartoum—have received no application to that effect & are not sending.
2. Procedure. a. Cattle Diseases. As planned. b. Egyptian Vote. Thurs. as contemplated.
   c. Parnell's Bill Wedy—oppose. Shall we as Spencer suggests bring in an amending Bill of small scope? *No.*
3. Dynamite outrages. Harcourt to supply material for a dispatch.
4. Empower civil authorities may send Engl. troops on to Assouan if necessary.

To Sir W. V. HARCOURT, home secretary,   MS Harcourt dep. 9, f. 103.
29 February 1884.

My leaning has been against silence in the face of the U.S. Govt. and I think it would be a great advantage if you would act on Granville's suggestion and supply materials for a dispatch on the dynamite outrages. I own that my idea is that the US Govt. ought not to escape responsibility of knowledge & of meeting such arguments as we can make: while in *this* country always sufficiently excitable about such matters I would avoid as far as may be giving them importance, on the ground that so doing would be the best advertisement O Donovan Rossa & the other villains could desire, & would raise the wind for him better than his own blustering professions.

[1] Hartington preferred not; Add MS 44147, f. 28; his name is not on the bill.
[2] 'It is ... if it is to be described by a single phrase, a Household Franchise Bill for the United Kingdom'; *H* 285. 106.
[3] Spoke on Egypt; *H* 285. 238.
[4] Add MS 56452, f. 14.
[5] Unclear which; note marked 'Baring 179' reads: 'Viewing Gordon's & your recommendation Cabinet ready to approve choice of Zebir as Governor but not to make appointment. This should be by Egyptian Governor & should not invade Sultan's sovereignty ...'; ibid., f. 28. Unclear if this was sent; see 5 Mar. 84.

Sat. Mch One 1884.

Wrote to Ld Hartington—Chr of Exr—Mr OShea MP.—and minutes. Saw Lady Chesham: an edifying sight.[1] Dined at Ld Carlingford's to make the list of Sheriffs. Saw Mr H.—Ld R.G—Mr Hutton—Ld Sydney—Duke of Argyll—& tea-party—Mr & Mrs Th.—Ld Carlingford. Read Sybil—Cowdray.

To LORD HARTINGTON, war secretary, 1 March 1884.   Add MS 44547, f. 46.

Here is the memorandum.[2] You will find the reference to Ireland in the last page but two. I think that I read the memorandum; I am sure that I omitted no point in it: my reference to the number of Irish members in the speech was somewhat more pointed in form. In substance, I had meant to convey the same thing in the memorandum.
[P.S.] There is no copy of this memorandum. But one can be made for you if you like it.

2. 1 S. Lent.

On account of a chill yesterday afternoon kept my bed & the House: service accordingly. Saw E. Lyttelton—E. Hamilton—Sir Thos G.—Read Life of Agnes Jones—Harrison, Ghost of Religion[3]—Liddon, Sermon on Pusey[4]—Budge on Nebuchadnezzar[5]—The Minister's Wooing.

3. M.

Wrote to Sir Jos. Pease—Ld Northbrook—The Queen—and minutes. H of C. $5\frac{1}{4}$-$8\frac{1}{4}$ & 9-$1\frac{1}{2}$. Brought in the Franchise Bill.[6] Read The Minister's Wooing—Cowdray. Saw Ld Granville—Ld Northbrook—Mr H—Lord R.G—Ld E. Fitzmaurice—Sir C. Dilke.

4. Tu.

Wrote to Ld Kimberley—The Queen—& minutes. Saw Mr H—Ld RG—Ld Granville—Mr Collings—Mr Gorst—Sir H. Ponsonby—Ld Carlingford—Mr Dodson—Ly Aberdeen. Conclave on procedure in evg. Ten to dinner. $12\frac{3}{4}$-$4\frac{3}{4}$. To Council at Windsor. Rather long audience of the Queen. Read Minister's Wooing.

Soudan.[7]

1. Sultan to recognise Gordon's mission.
2. The two Powers to concert as to a successor when the time comes.
3. Successor to be subsidised for a time on Baring's plan.
4. Turks to take over custody of Suakim & any other ports of Red Sea it may be deemed necessary to hold.

[1] Probably Henrietta Frances, widow of 2nd Baron Chesham; she d. May 1884.
[2] Apparently that read to cabinet on 4 January; Hartington did not recall maintenance of present number of Irish M.P.s; Add MS 44147, f. 30.
[3] F. Harrison, 'The ghost of religion', *N.C.*, xv. 494 (March 1884).
[4] H. P. Liddon, 'E. B. Pusey. A sermon' (1884).
[5] E. A. T. W. Budge, *Nebuchadnezzar, King of Babylon* (1884).
[6] And spoke on Sudan; Franchise Bill 1°R; *H* 285. 375, 466.
[7] Add MS 56452, f. 16.

5. The two Powers agree to prohibit slave trading therein & use force agst. it by land or sea.

Egypt.

1. Should it be found that the military system hitherto contemplated—viz. Egyptian force under British Officers—cannot be relied on, then might we perhaps entertain the idea of a convention with the Sultan for the maintenance of order & the Khedive's throne in Egypt?
2. Wood's army would then be disbanded in due course.
3. Sultan to be limited in numbers: 4000 or 5000?
4. and in time.
5. To receive a capitation—limited to a *maximum* of (say £150000?)
6. English to hold Alexandria: for the same time, or less, if they think they can remove without prejudice to public order.
7. (Charge to be borne out of Suez Canal profits.)
8. If this is done it would have to be done promptly.
9. To be jointly communicated to the Powers.
10. *The case arising*, should Baring be brought home to consult: all depending on the decision as to an Egyptian force.
11. Present basis cannot *long* be held.   WEG. Mch.4.84.

To LORD NORTHBROOK, first lord of the admiralty,   Add MS 44547, f. 46.
4 March 1884. '*Private*'.

I agree in what you say on this telegram & on the situation.[1] The position is getting too like a dance on the tight rope. A critical moment may come when we get to the bottom of the case respecting Wood's army. I have been speaking to Granville in this sense.

My son in Calcutta writing about the Ilbert Bill uses almost the very same words as Sir A. Lyall. He is convinced Ripon will come home before the year is out.

5. *Wed.*

Wrote to The Queen—& minutes. Saw Mr H—Ld R.G—Mr Chamberlain—Scotts. Dined at S. Lady Lyttelton's. H of C. 12¼–2 & at 5½.[2] Cabinet 2½–5¼. Rèad Cowdray—The Minister's Wooing.

Cabinet. Wed. Mch 5. 84. 2½ PM [3]
0. Merchant Shipping Bill. Query Select Ctte. on Clauses or Railway Bill first.
6. Members of Govt. & Proportional Voting. Nothing need be said to C[ourtney] & F[awcett] at present.[4]
1. Shall we alter procedure as to tomorrow? No.
2. Teleg. about Zobeir No. 192. Answer agreed on: Chanr. & W.E.G.[5]
3. Conversation on communications with Porte as to Soudan.
4. General Graham's Tel. of Mch 5 rcd. this day—authorise him to act accordingly—proclaim, & attack in case of need.

---

[1] Perhaps the note at Add MS 44267, f. 48 (?4 March): 'so far as India is concerned the Mahomedans look to the Sultan & not to the Mahdi'.
[2] Barry's bill to amend 1881 Land Act; *H* 285. 551.
[3] Add MS 56452, f. 18.
[4] i.e. to the proponents of proportional representation, on their votes.
[5] Draft at ibid., f. 20, reiterating 'negative' to Gordon's double demand for Zobeir.

5. Education Committee. Question of Chair to be colourless[?]
7. Quetta Railway. Communication with Ripon. No official step now.
8. New gun factory in Birmingham.
Telegram agreed to States. We have no information at present to justify changes of views as to Zobeir. Challenge him on three points. 1. complete evacuation 2. slave trade. 3. safety of Egypt. Enquire as to garrisons & notables.

Childers is of opinion that no assumption of sole guarantee would release us from dependence on the Powers. Under law of liquidation, Egypt has no *power to borrow* without consent of Caisse. Nor without consent of Sultan. WEG. Mch. 5, 1.15 P.M.[1]

6. *Th.*

Wrote to Mr Chamberlain—Ld Hartington—Ld Granville—Sir W. Harcourt—The Queen—and minutes. Read Doyle on Hope Scott[2]—Tomlinson on Stubbs[3]—Minister's Wooing. H. of C. 5-8 and 10¼-12½. Spoke 45 m. on Egypt—again![4] Saw Mr H—Ld RG—Ld Hartington *cum* C. of E.—Mr Trevelyan. Drive with C. Dined with Lucy.

To LORD HARTINGTON, war secretary, 6 March   Chatsworth MSS 340. 1425.
1884.

I admit that, probably owing to haste, my statement about reduction of the number of Irish members was more *direct* in the Speech than in the Memorandum,[5] but I am not able to see any difference in the substantial purport, for no one in my opinion can read the paragraph without saying 'plainly this means he will not reduce the Irish members'.

Subject, I allow, to one small qualification: when I wrote the paragraph I had it not before my mind that the Irish members under the Act of Union were 100, whereas they are now 103.

After what Goschen said, I shall have to touch the question again, & I will be very careful to speak of my own opinion only.

7. *Fr.*

Wrote to Mr Chamberlain—Bp of London—Mr Gorst—The Queen l.l.l.—& minutes. H of C. 4¾-8½ and after 12.[6] Saw Mr H—Ld RG—Ld Granville—Ld Kimberley—Mr Chamberlain. Cabinet (at H of C) 5¾-7. Read Tomlinson on Stubbs &c.—Cowdray (finished)—The Minister's Wooing.

Cabinet. at H. of C. Frid. Mch. 7. 84. 5½ PM.[7]
1. French claim to Obole. Say it has not been admitted by Egypt but we desire to know what are the geograph. limits of the French claim.
2. Ld G's conference with Musurus: 1. recognition of Gen G[ordon?]; 2. Confer as to successor; 3. Turk in Red Sea ports on terms; 4. Union as to Slave Trade. Make this offer

---

[1] Add MS 56450, f. 140; no year given; Granville's docket reads: 'This is Pauncefote's opinion. G.'
[2] Sir F. H. Doyle, 'James Hope-Scott', *Macmillan's Magazine*, xl. 321 (March 1884).
[3] J. T. Tomlinson, *The 'Legal History' of Canon Stubbs reviewed* (1884).
[4] During the army supply deb.; *H* 285. 699.
[5] Point made by Hartington in this day's letter; Add MS 44147, f. 34.
[6] Questioned on vote of credit; *H* 285. 873.
[7] Add MS 44645, f. 53.

to Turkey: the matter to be arranged by Firmans. If he does not accept, we must make other arrangements.
3. Abyssinians & Bogos. Qy. withdraw Egyptian garrison from Bogos & let Abyssinian walk in: does not touch the sea. It was Abyssinian till taken by Egypt. Massauah: to be free port for their *use*.

8. Sat.

Wrote to Mr Childers—Lord Reay—and minutes. Tea at Lady Stanley's: an interesting party. Saw Mr H.—Lord R.G—Lady Blennerhassett—Lady Aberdeen. Dined with the Hayters: & evg party. Read Minister's Wooing—and other books.

To H. C. E. CHILDERS, chancellor of the exchequer,   Add MS 44131, f. 49.
8 March 1884.

As at present advised, I am by no means prepared to go even your length in regard to a force of Englishmen in Egypt.[1] But I think the time has not come for considering the question. We have asked for, and are in early expectation of receiving, the full information about Wood's army, which we do not yet possess. Indifferently as the case looks at present, we could not give it up except with full knowledge & conviction. If and when we have to give it up, my eyes will not readily be turned to any measure for strengthening the military & governmental hold of England upon Egypt, in which I see no advantage whatever, & the seed of every possible future difficulty, though I admit that it might perhaps obtain for us a momentary peace by placing on our side the most powerful but most mischievous & least honest elements of Anglo-Egyptian opinion.
I will send your letter and my reply, for the present, to Granville only.

9. 3 S. Lent.

Ch. Royal mg, St Margaret's evg. Read Minister's Wooing (finished)—Memoirs of Marie Mancini—Memoirs of Miss Jones—N.A. Rev. on Theolog. Readjustment.[2] At night, *recognised* the fact of a cold & began to deal with it.[3]

10. M.

Kept my bed all day for strong perspiration. Saw Mr H—Ld R.G—Ld Gr. Wrote to Ld Granville—Mr Chamberlain—Ld Hartington. Political troubles came thick enough. Read Sybil—'Cathol Back'—Marie Mancini.

To LORD HARTINGTON, war secretary, 10 March 1884.   Add MS 44547, f. 47.

I hope we shall soon have a Cabinet more of the ordinary kind than some of our recent meetings.[4]

[1] Proposing, 7 March, Add MS 44131, f. 46, in the light of 'the future so far of the Egyptian Army under Sir Evelyn Wood', battalions in Egypt consisting 'entirely of English soldiers under the Egyptian Flag'.
[2] H. Ward Beecher, 'The revision of creeds', a series in *North American Review*, cxxxvi. 1 (January 1883).
[3] Extracts until 13 Mar. in Morley, iii. 159.
[4] Hartington requested discussion of colonial defences and salary of governor of Malta; Add MS 44147, f. 37.

The Maltese question will no doubt require decision; but is there anything really urgent in that of Colonial Defence?[1] and if not could there be a fairer case for letting it stand over than is now supplied by the unusual amount of our responsibilities, military and civil, abroad and at home.

11.

Bed as yesterday. The Cabinet sat, & Granville came to & fro with the communications,[2] Clark having prohibited my attendance. Saw Mr H—Ld RG—WHG—H.J.G.—Ld Granville—Sir A. Clark. Read Sybil—Australian Poems—Mancini (finished).

12. Wed.

Bed as yesterday. Wrote to Ld Granville—Mr Bouverie—all done by dictation only. C. went to Windsor alone. Saw Mr H—Ld RG—H.J.G.—Ld Gr—Sir A. Clark. Finished Sybil. Began Société de Berlin.[3]

13.

Got to my sittingroom in the evening. It has however taken longer this time to clear out the chest, and Clark reports the pulse still too high by ten. Wrote to Ld Granville—Mr Davies—Ld Lorne. Saw Mr H—Ld RG—H.J.G.—Ld Granville—Sir A. Clark. Conclave $7\frac{1}{2}$-$8\frac{1}{2}$ on tel. to Baring for Gordon.[4] I was not allowed to attend the Cabinet. Read Société de Berlin—Lady Grizel[5]—Tod on Woman Suffrage.[6]

14. Fr.

A bettermost day, but not yet out of the wood. Saw Mr H—Ld RG—Ld Rosebery—Ld Granville—Sir A. Clark. Read Lady Grizel—Société de Berlin.

15 Sat.

A day of backward movement. Saw Mr H—Ld RG—HJG—Ld Granville & Ld Hn before Cabinet—& after[7]—Chancr of Exr. Read Lady Grizel—Société de Berlin (finished).

1. Increase in danger and difficulty through cutting of the wires, and rising of tribes between Khartoum & Berber.
2. Impossible under these circs. to send peremptory order for retreat from Khartoum.
3. Have not our agents in Egypt now a right to enlarged discretion & to our support whichever way they may use it?

[1] The Carnarvon commission report; see 5 May 84.
[2] See this day's letter of suggestions to Granville on Sudan; Ramm II, ii. 163.
[3] Perhaps H. Blaze de Bury, *Les salons de Vienne et Berlin* (1861).
[4] In Cromer, i. 522: Zobeir unacceptable; Gordon, if settled govt. at Khartoum impossible, should withdraw at once.
[5] L. Wingfield, *Lady Grizel*, 3v. (1878); set in 1760s, on Bute, Pitt, Wilkes etc.
[6] Isabella M. S. Tod, 'Women and the franchise bill' (1884).
[7] i.e. Gladstone did not attend the Cabinet.

4. If they think it best to evacuate we should do all in our power to support the movement.

5. If Baring, with or without further support from Gordon, thinks it best to send Zobeir, and can make what he may think a proper arrangement with him, we will support him.

(I much regret that we have been so much frightened about Zobeir though the proposal was certainly not one to be hastily adopted or without testing the opinion entertained in Egypt. WEG. Mch. 15. 84).[1]

16. 3 S. Lent

Solitary prayers. Weather lovely. I drove with C: neutral as to effects. Saw Mr H—Sir A. Clark—Ld G. & Ld Hartington from the Cabinet, wh *has* I think gone wrong.[2] Wrote to Ld Granville. Finished Miss Jones's Memoir. Read Jackanapes[3]—Doyle on Catholic claims.[4]

17. M.

Wrote to Ld Northbrook—Mr Evan Morris[5]—Ld Spencer—Sir N. Rothschild—and minutes. The voice & larynx are now chiefly affected, and the mischief though not more formidable has been more persistent than on other occasions. Saw today only Mr H. besides Sir A. Clark twice. Read Lady Grizel—Lundsell's Siberia[6]—Statesman's Year Book.[7]

18. Tu.

Wrote to Mrs Goalen—Lady Dudley—& minutes. Saw Mr Hamilton—Sir A. Clark: reports me better today: persists in regimen of *silence*, inhalation, potash drafts, and lozenges. Read Lady Grizel—Lunsdell's Siberia—Saffi on Inferno XIX.[8]

19. Wed. [Coombe Warren, Kingston]

Wrote to The Queen—and minutes. Saw Mr H—Lord RG—Sir A. Clark. Went off at 3¼ to Mr Bertram Currie's[9] beautiful house at Coombe Warren: such kindness! Finished Lady Grizel: a book of much force, but: Pelion on Ossa &c.[10] Read Maurice's Life[11]—OHagan on O'Connell.[12]

[1] Notes for cabinet in pencil; Add MS 56452, f. 22; the cabinet divided 7:6 for sending Zobeir; ibid., f. 24; next day two votes changed and Gladstone gave way, see Morley, iii. 160.

[2] i.e. on Zobeir; see previous day's n.

[3] J. H. Ewing, *Jackanapes* (1883).

[4] See 20 Dec. 70.

[5] Regretting illness prevents him appearing before the select cttee. on the Chester and Conah's Quay Railway Bill; Add MS 44547, f. 48.

[6] See 25 Jan. 82.   [7] 1884 ed. just published.

[8] A. Saffi, *Sul Canto xxvi dell'Inferno* (1882).

[9] Bertram Wodehouse Currie, 1827–96; s. of Raikes Currie; banker and member of India Council 1880–95.

[10] i.e. upside-down (the Giants put Mount Ossa on top of Mount Pelion).

[11] J. F. Maurice, *The life of F. D. Maurice*, 2v. (1884), using much Gladstonian material.

[12] T. O'Hagan, *Occasional papers and addresses* (1884), 129.

To LORD HARTINGTON, war secretary, 19 March 1884.   Add MS 44547, f. 49.

1. Evidently Baber Pasha cannot at present be restored. Whether anything else can be done for him I have not knowledge enough to judge. You will see the memorandum herewith.[1]

2. I hope you will have no third victory. It would be probably for us a victory such as was known among the ancients by the names of Cadmean and Pyrrhian; a victory which will not bear repetition.

3. I presume the order of revocation sent to Hewett has been framed upon a knowledge of modern military usage & in conformity with it: if so it is doubtless all right.

[P.S.] I mentioned to R. Grosvenor today that it would be an excellent thing if the Law Grand Committee could possibly be got to write.

20. Th.

For the first time, perhaps, I felt really better, from the change of air. Wrote to Chancr of Exr—Ld R. Grosvenor—Ld Granville—& minutes. Read Maurice's Life—Gouraud, Grandeur de l'Angleterre[2]—The Mill on the Floss: it is wonderfully written.[3] Saw Mr Seymour—Sir A. Clark.

To H. C. E. CHILDERS, chancellor of the exchequer,   Add MS 44547, f. 50.
20 March 1884.

The case of Egyptian finance as you represent it[4] seems to require the immediate attention of Granville & the Cabinet. I suppose that every day's delay, in a case of this kind, means aggravation of the evil. You will have to frame some outline of a scheme with Granville's concurrence. I assume that it must touch the Law of Liquidation. And, that if it does touch that law, attempts will be made to cast upon us special responsibilities of a pecuniary kind. This may be in respect of the occupying force or otherwise.

Whatever we may have to pay, in order to procure the necessary adjustment, should I think be paid out of the accruing value of the Canal Shares. But it would be objectionable I think to treat them as *equivalents* if, as I take to be the case, there is in equity no claim upon us.

To LORD R. GROSVENOR, chief whip, 20 March 1884.   Add MS 44547, f. 49.

I think it would be premature & unsafe to fight on Monday for progress *de die in diem* with the Franchise Bill.

The obstruction offered has been immense; but it has been wholly indirect & veiled and it has been *assisted* by the Irish friends of the Bill, & by a small but active section or regiment of our own friends. It would be the subject of unbounded discussion & vast masses of Egyptian matter would be imported.

I would wait for the first clear development of direct obstruction—and *then*.

My removal has answered. I am stronger, cough open & under control, & I am very sanguine as to shaking it off.

---

[1] Perhaps Gladstone's docket for Hartington, warning of risk of 'taking in the tribes', on wire from Graham; Hartington had in fact already warned Graham; Add MS 44147, ff. 41–5.

[2] G. Gouraud, *Histoire des causes de la grandeur de l'Angleterre* (1856); up to 1763.

[3] By G. Eliot, 3v. (1860).

[4] Report of talk with Vincent: large deficits developing in Egyptian govt., and the 'system of financial control (in our sense) is deplorably bad'; Add MS 44131, f. 50.

21. Fr.

Wrote to Ld Granville—Ld Hartington l.l.—Duke of Bedford—& minutes. Saw Mr Seymour—Sir A. Clark, who reported favourably. Read F.D. Maurice's Life—Gouraud Grandeur &c.—The Mill on the Floss.

To LORD HARTINGTON, war secretary,   Add MS 44547, f. 50.
21 March 1884.[1]   Chatsworth MSS 340. 1426.

[First letter:]   I am but poorly enabled to help you, & I could by no means undertake to guide you or any one who had to speak upon the motion about Bishops in the House of Lords. There are two matters of *fact* which may be noted. This is one of a knot of political questions in which the innovating or reforming party have seemed to lose ground during the last forty-five or fifty years. The question of Short Parliaments and of abolishing capital punishment are other examples. When I began Parliamentary life, the motion against the Bishops was an annual one. For a long time it has only been made once in five or ten years.

A second fact is that the attendance of Bishops in the House of Lords, except upon Church and semi-Church questions, has immensely fallen off, and the political function is, properly upon the whole, sacrificed to diocesan duty. This, of course, cuts both ways; but it is *not*, I think, true that the Peerage as now worked interferes with Episcopal efficiency.

Looking at the case broadly, this proposal really cuts into the two great questions—(*a*) of National or Established Church, (*b*) of the constitution of the House of Lords.

Does the House think it wise to open either of these questions? As to the first, how are Bishops to be controlled and called to account for diocesan dealings? And is this last shadow of representation for the clergy, who are shut out from the House of Commons, to be swept away without any other legislation? As to the second, has not the hereditary principle strain enough laid on it already, and is it not a serious matter to cut out of the House of Lords a body of nearly thirty Peers, who are now (it may be said) habitually chosen by the Crown for their personal distinctions? But I find my time up. By hook or by crook I shall, of course, appear on Monday if possible in any way.

[Second letter:]   With reference to the debate of Monday, I should wish to open it with a short speech, by straining a point for the purpose, if straining a point will do.

There are but two topics that I should wish to urge; 1. briefly to show how we have endeavoured to divert the measure of a polemical character, 2. to round off a little my unauthoritative statement about redistribution and signify that the points of it rather hang one upon another. For example, I think that in moderation the questions of distance ought to be considered (a) as between London & the country generally (b) as between the three Kingdoms. If the House declined to admit any such rule, that might bear on what I have said as to relative representation.

You have plenty of speakers. I would add the Sol. General to those whom you name. I agree as to your holding back—and in a *minor degree* about the Att. General.

If I begin it might not be needful to reply straight upon J. Manners: but some one should I think speak later in the evening.

What I hope is that we shall avoid the trap opened for us (perhaps unconsciously) by Goschen when he expressed his hope that the rest of the Cabinet would follow my example & give respectively their heads of redistribution. You know how very far this is from the sense in which my proceeding was approved by the Cabinet. My duty will be to

---

[1] Partly printed in Lathbury, i. 181. Hartington, 20 March, Add MS 44147, f. 46, asked guidance on Willis' motion on bps. in the Lords (see 22 Mar. 84n.) and on distribution of speakers on the Franchise Bill.

state strongly that while I would not have submitted my sketch unless I had believed it to be generally & in the main agreeable to the views of my colleagues, I meant to speak of its general scope & not of every particular it contained. Some liberty as to particulars, as I have stated above, must be reserved even for me. This I hope will help to make their & your course easier.

I am most sorry let me assure you that my stupid & not quite manageable cold should cause such a serious addition to your personal labours.

22. Sat

Wrote to C. of E. l.l.—Ld Hartington l.l.—Ld Granville—Ld Wolverton—& minutes. Saw Mr Seymour—Sir A. Clark. Read same as yesterday, & Prevost's Cleveland.[1]

To LORD HARTINGTON, war secretary,   Add MS 44547, f. 51.
22 March 1884.

If Bright *likes* the suggestion about J. Manners, I think it is excellent. We must however take care not to drive him upon the dinner hour. It would seem also rather beyond the mark to have Bright and two Ministers one night and that the first of the debate. Perhaps I had better give up the notion of saying anything at the outset. If this is your judgment I am quite ready to act accordingly. I have however little hope of being able to make a considerable effort of voice *late at night* for some little time.

A *rumour* reached me yesterday that the Opposition are hugging the idea of an Egyptian debate for my return. If this be so it is an argument for my keeping away.

Clark's idea has been to *get me up* for the early hours of Monday in the House and that I should then drive down again to this house Coombe Warren & not finally quit it for some days later. He regards Monday as an experiment and possibly would be willing enough to postpone it.

[P.S.] You might mention Baker's case in the Cabinet. I would acquiesce in what they may decide.

To LORD WOLVERTON, 22 March 1884.[2]   Add MS 44547, f. 51.

You see that the Bishops had a *squeak* for it in the House of Commons last night.[3] Herbert was inclined to vote against them (though he is not ready for disestablishment) but he staid away in condescension to my infirmities.

Brighton & Cambridgeshire have not been agreeable but I believe the party is sound enough and by no means in the condition which it had reached in the 4th year of *your & my* Government.[4]

Egypt is worked relentlessly for purposes of mischief, and it pays, in a case of that kind, with a position essentially false; for even if we are right in the measures we take how can we know we are right, and every hour on this subject is so much obstruction to the Franchise Bill. On that subject men seem very sound; I cannot say much for Goschen, or his speech, except that it was an extremely clever one; he can I think desire nothing better than a clear field and a good stand up fight on that subject.

[P.S.] My wife is unlawfully laid up here but I hope only for a couple of days.

[1] A. F. Prévost d'Exiles, *Le philosophe anglois, ou Histoire de monsieur Cleveland*, 8v. (1744).

[2] Long section on health omitted.

[3] Willis's motion proposing removal of bishops' legislative powers defeated in 148:137; *H* 285. 547.

[4] Byelection defeats, Cambridgeshire being Brand's seat.

23. 4 S. Lent.

Church prayers with C. both being disabled. Wrote to Granville l.l.l.—Saw Mr S—WHG—H.J.G.—Sir A. Clark: much progress made. Read F.D. Maurice finished I.—Ld O'Hagan on Dr Russell &c.—Bouvier, Panthéisme.[1] Also saw Mr B. Currie our host & thanked for his unbounded kindness.

24. M.

Wrote to Ld Granville Tel. & l.—Sir W. Harcourt—The Speaker—The Queen— and minutes. Saw Mr Seymour—Mary G.—Ld Granville: half hour on Egypt. Read Maurice—Mill on the Floss—Gouraud finished—Bouvier, wretched stuff.

25. Tu. Annunciation.

Wrote to Ld Hartington—Mr Goschen—Chancr of Exr—Ld Derby—and minutes. Read Maurice—Mill on the Floss—Franchise Speeches—Bréolle, Principe Religieux (a poor affair).[2] Saw Mr S.—Sir A. Clark.

26. Wed.

Wrote to Sir A. Clark—Ld Hartington l.l.—Ld Northbrook—Ld Granville—Mr Goschen—Sir H. Ponsonby—& minutes. Read Maurice—Mill on the Floss— Gray's Poems[3]—Addison on the Jews[4]—Filon, Hist. Comparée[5]—Case of Mrs Rudd: now like *Rose*.[6] Saw Mr Seymour—Mrs Currie.

27. Th.

Wrote to Mr M. Arnold—Mr Chamberlain—Ld Aberdeen—Ld Hartington—Ld Granville—Mr Trevelyan—& minutes. Saw Mr Seymour—Ld Granville *cum* Ld Hartington—Ld Rosebery. Read Maurice—Mill on the Floss—Stanhope's Hist. Engl.[7]—D. of Buckingham, Private Diary.[8]

28. Fr.

Wrote to The Queen l & tel.—Sir H. Ponsonby l. & tel.—Sir W. Harcourt—Mr Grogan—Mr Burton—Mr Allport—and minutes. Saw Mr Hamilton—Sir A. Clark. The sad news of the Duke of Albany's death came from Windsor. He would have made his mark. Read Maurice: (too Maurician?)—Mill on the Floss—Stanhope's History.

---

[1] A. Bouvier, perhaps *Le Divin d'après les apôtres* (1882).
[2] *Sic*; untraced.
[3] See 13 April 65.
[4] L. Addison, *The present state of the Jews* (1675); notes on it at Add MS 44768, f. 19.
[5] C. A. D. Filon, *Histoire comparée de France et de l'Angleterre* (1832).
[6] D. Perreau, *An explicit account of the lives of . . . D. and R. Perreau . . . likewise the remarkable case of Mrs Rudd* (1776); perhaps an allusion to the Rose case, see above, v. lxvii.
[7] See 21 Mar. 70.
[8] Probably R. Grenville, duke of Buckingham, *Memoirs of the court of England during the Regency*, 2v. (1856).

29. Sat.

Wrote to The Queen l.l.—and minutes. Saw Mr Hamilton—Ld Granville—Sir W. Harcourt—Lucy Cavendish. Cabinet 3½–6. Read Maurice—Mill on the Floss (finished)—Stanhope's Hist.

Cabinet. 3.30 PM. Coombe Warren. Mch. 29. 84.[1]
1. Hartington's Telegram of today to Graham read. Chermside[2] to try with natives to negotiate & open Berber road. Grahams force to return to Egypt.
2. Answer to Labouchere considered.[3] We will not cross examine our commanding officers on anonymous authority.
3. Chermside to be Civil Governor but[?] to employ Egyptians for administration of the ordinary law.
   Private. C. to mix[?] as little as possible with slavery questions & other like matter.
4. Granville's draft on the Gordon mission considered & approved subject to comment in detail.[4]
5. Easter Holidays. Tuesday Ap 8 to Monday 21st if London Bill be introduced on Tuesday. But we must sit till London Bill is introduced.
6. Budget on 24th.
7. Sunday Closing Bill. Not to support 2 R.

30. 5 S. Lent.

Church still forbidden. Prayers with C. Read Maurice—Carneton, Poetry of the Pentateuch[5]—Les Trois Imposteurs[6]—Addison on the Jews—Radford on Ordinances.[7] Saw L.C.—W. & H. came—Mr Currie: & visited the Gardens. Saw Sir A. Clark. Wrote to Ld Rosebery.

31. M. [London]

Wrote to The Queen—Ld Hartington—and minutes. Read Maurice—The New Abelard.[8] After a walk, started for London at 12¾. Saw Mr H—Ld RG—Sir A. Clark—Lord Gr. *cum* Ld Hartington. H of C. 5–8. Proposed Address of Condolence.[9]

Tues Ap. One. 1884.

Wrote to Chancr of Exr—Lord Spencer—The Queen—and minutes. Drive with C. Saw Mr H—Lord R.G.—Sir A. Clark. Conclave of Ministers 3.30–4.30. H of C.

[1] Add MS 44645, f. 55.
[2] (Sir) Herbert Charles Chermside, 1850–1929; soldier in Egypt and Sudan; governor general of Red Sea coast Oct. 1884–6.
[3] Question on slavery; *H* 286. 1161.
[4] Probably Granville's two long letters to Baring, dated 28 March, on Zobeir and the Gordon mission generally; *PP* lxxxix. 5–11.
[5] Name apparently *sic*; untraced.
[6] *Les trois imposteurs ou les fausses conspirations* (1700?).
[7] D. Radford, 'The theology of Christian Ordinances' (1884).
[8] R. Buchanan, *The new Abelard* (1884).
[9] On d. of Prince Leopold; *H* 286. 1175.

$4\frac{3}{4}$–$8\frac{1}{2}$.[1] Read the New Abelard—Life of Maurice—Herbert Spencer in 19th Cent.[2]

2. Wed. [Coombe Warren]

Wrote to Mr Childers—Ex. Mayor of Dover[3]—Sir H. Ponsonby—Mr Pell MP.— and minutes. Saw Mr H—Ld R.G—Lord Granville—Cabinet 2–$5\frac{1}{4}$. Then returned to Coombe Warren: an indifferent evening. Read The New Abelard— finished the Life of Maurice: 'A spiritual splendour: an intellectual riddle'.

Cabinet. 2 Ap. 84. 2 PM.[4]
1. Statement on Egypt in H. of C. Tomorrow.
2. Berber. There will be negotiation if possible to open & keep the road.
3. Suakim: conditionally agreed to recommend sending Wood's battalion.
4. Tel. authorising Gordon's removal: cons[ideratio]n postponed till answer had been recd. to Tel. of 28th.
5. Buxton's question. Time not come to reply. Gordon has not been put under orders to remain: has full discretion. (Harcourt absent).[5]
6. Egyptian finance. See last Par. of my letter to the Queen.[6]

3. Th.

Much pain & wakefulness in the night. Back to London at 3.45. Saw Mr Seymour—Ld R.G—Ld Hartington—Sir A. Clark—and above all dearest Harry who returned this evening to our arms and loving welcome. H of C. $5\frac{1}{2}$–$7\frac{3}{4}$. Then returned to Coombe Warren: we took Harry & had much conversation. Plenty of H. of C. work in the two hours. Answered Northcote on Egypt and put on all the steam I could.[7] Let me say thankfully, I was weak, but strength was given me. Wrote to Ld Dunraven—The Queen—Mrs Th.—and minutes. Read Tod's Preface to Wiclif[8]—Milner on Gibbon[9]—The New Abelard.

4. Fr.

A good day: pain on occasionally. Wrote to Princess Louise—Sir S. Northcote— Mr Dodson—Mr Hamilton l. and Tel.—and minutes. Walk with C. We had a visit from that vision of glorious beauty, little Elspeth Campbell.[10] Harry & M. came in evg: much more talk. Read The New Abelard (finished)—Mounier, Un Guet-apens[11]—Ld Byron[12]—Bennett's Ballads[13]—Sollen die Juden Christen Werden.[14]

[1] Moved motion of precedence for the Franchise Bill; *H* 286. 1288.
[2] In pencil; in fact H. Spencer, 'The coming slavery', *C.R*, xlv. 461 (April 1884).
[3] Business untraced.   [4] Add MS 56452, f. 31.
[5] Gladstone and Hartington both replied in these terms; *H* 286. 1510.
[6] Conference of relevant powers to be proposed, £8 million needed for Egypt but unobtainable without altering Law of Liquidation; CAB 41/18/17. See also Ramm II, ii. 175.
[7] *H* 286. 1510.   [8] J. H. Tod, ed. Wycliffe's *The last age of the Church* (1840).
[9] J. Milner, *Gibbon's account of Christianity considered* (1781).
[10] Elspeth Angela, da. of Lord Archibald Campbell, 2d. s. of 8th duke of Argyll.
[11] Apparently *sic*, but name and title uncertain.   [12] See 21 Dec. 26.
[13] W. C. Bennett, *Narrative poems and ballads* (1875).
[14] Perhaps *Sollen sich die Christen beschneiden oder die Juden taufen lassen?* (1800).

To J. G. DODSON, chancellor of the duchy of Lancaster,   Monk Bretton 41.
4 April 1884.

Please to consider (as I might not have an opportunity before the recess) whether it would be well for you and the Attorney General (with the Speaker's approval,) to ask an interview with Northcote and submit for his consideration the Resolution which has been drawn with regard to a supply for the Chair in the event of the double disability.[1]

5. *Sat.*

A good night. A very sharp bout about 10 AM. Not over 15 min. Wrote to Sir W. Harcourt—Ld Granville—Mr Courtney—and minutes. Saw Mr Hamilton—The Dalhousies, luncheon—Ld Rosebery, dinner. Began Silas Marner.[2] Read Byron, English Bards etc. Drive with C.

To Sir W. V. HARCOURT, home secretary,   MS Harcourt dep. Adds 10.
5 April 1884.

I see no reason for objecting to the proposal to reduce the Manx Rectory of St Andrews under the circumstances stated.[3] My only reason for delay was a desire to suggest whether the whole case of the Manx Church arrangements does not require some consideration. My impression is that since the Bishopric ceased to be the paternal sort of office which it was under Bishop Wilson it has gradually, without any reproach to the Prelates personally been approximating more or less to a Sinecure? How this is to be corrected I do not quite know: but I think it would not be a bad measure to consult the Archbishop of York on the subject, Man being in his province. This is in some degree you will say my affair: but I should like to move in conjunction with you.

6. *Palm S.*

Got to Church deplorably late (by erroneous directions), just so as to receive the H.C. Saw Harry & M. from London—Mr Bertram Currie—Ld A. Campbell & *the* child—Sir A. Clark: who was well pleased. Wrote to M.G. Read Milners Ans. to Gibbon—Quinet Genie des Religions[4]—Youart on Establishment.[5]

7. *M.* [*London*]

Wrote to Chancr of Exr—The Queen l.l.—Mr Blair—Murrays—Scotts—Archbp of York—and minutes. Read Silas Marner. Reached D. St before luncheon. Saw Mr H—Ld R.G.—Sir A. Clark—Ld Hartington—Mr Leveson Gower. H of C. 5–8½ and 10¼–1¾. Spoke 1 h on Franchise Bill and voted in 340:210 for 2 R. A great & fruitful division.[6]

---

[1] Undated draft by Gladstone, providing for the appointment of a former Deputy Speaker, in Monk Bretton 41.
[2] See 11 May 61.
[3] Harcourt to Gladstone, 3 April, Add MS 44199, f. 31, requested his advice on reducing the stipend.
[4] E. Quinet, *Du génie des religions* (1842).
[5] H. G. Youart, *'Disestablishment' viewed in the light of history* (1877).
[6] *H* 286. 1826.

8. *Tu.* [*The Durdans*]

St Margaret's 11 AM. Wrote to Ld Hartington—D. of Argyll—Ld Spencer—Sir H. Ponsonby—The Queen—Ld Granville Tel.—and minutes. Cabinet and H. of C. 2-6.[1] Then off to the Durdans. Saw Mr H—Ld RG—Ld Granville *cum* Ch. of Exr—Ld Rosebery—Mr Millais. Read Eugene Aram.[2]

Cabinet. Tues. Ap. 8. 84. 2 PM. H of C.[3]
1. Is Clifford Lloyd to be supported? Telegram framed—accomm[odatio]n most desirable if impossible full authority given to drop Clifford Lloyd.[4]
2. Draft on Egyptian finance proposing a Conference. (Münster's representation. This proposal agreed to.
3. Propose Baring, Nubar & Vincent as a Commission of Finance at Cairo to establish equilibrium in prospective expenditure.
4. Bill enabling R.C. to hold the Viceroyalty.

To LORD SPENCER, Viceroy of Ireland, 8 April 1884.[5]   Althorp MSS K7.

I cannot doubt that we ought to *vote* for the Bill[6] authorising the appointment of a Roman Catholic as Lord Lieutenant of Ireland, though we cannot I think undertake to find time for its several stages.

I have spoken to Childers about the time for your coming over as he is the person most directly concerned as to fitting in the time for the Irish financial proposal with that for the Budget and what I may almost call his Egyptian Budget: as I understand your visit had better be after the 24th but he will write himself in order to settle what may be most convenient.

I am happy to report myself today, after a longer affair than usual, off the sick list.
[P.S.] The division yesterday, or this morning rather, was of very great importance. Goschen's speech was a most unfortunate incident, most of all for *himself.*[7]

9. *Wed.*

Parish Ch. 11 AM. Wrote to Sir W. Harcourt—Lord Hampden—The Queen—Ld Granville—& minutes. Most lovely drive with Ld R. And much & varied conversation. Read Eugene Aram—Marie Antoinette[8]—The Red Manor.[9]

10. *Th.*

Ch.Ch. & H.C. 11-12½ A. M. Wrote to Mr Hamilton—Capt. Pryse[10]—The Queen—Ld Granville Tel.—Mr Ornsby—& minutes. Walk with C—& with

[1] Questions; London Govt. Bill; *H* 287. 33.
[2] E. Bulwer Lytton, *Eugene Aram* (1832).
[3] Add MS 56452, f. 34.
[4] From his post as undersecretary in Egypt; see 7 May 84.
[5] Letter appears mutilated, but is in fact complete bar the signature; see Add MS 44547, f. 56.
[6] Proposed by M. Brooks, W. Shaw, etc.; see Althorp MSS K7.
[7] Goschen announced his vote against the bill, fearful of the swamping of minorities; *H* 286. 1867.
[8] S. Tytler, *Marie Antoinette* (1883).
[9] Elizabeth, Lady Balfour, *The red manor* (1883).
[10] Capt. Robert Davies Pryse of Welshpool.

Rosebery. Read Sollen die Juden &c.—Carlyle's Letters to Mrs Montagu[1]—Taine Ancien Regime[2]—Prudence Palfrey.[3]

11. Good Friday.

Ch.Ch. service 11–1½. Walk with C—& with Rosebery. Wrote to Mr Hamilton l. & Tel.—Ld Granville—Ld Hampden—Mr E. Ashley—The Queen—Mr Millar—& minutes. Read Creighton's Memoir of Sir Geo. Grey[4]—Palmer's Narrative of Events conn. with the Tracts[5]—Sollen die Juden Christen Werden.

To LORD HAMPDEN, 11 April 1884.   Add MS 44547, f. 57.

Hamilton did me a favour in asking for the loan of the memoir of G. Grey, & you a still greater favour in granting it. I have read it with not only interest but delight. Twice his colleague, I can confirm every word of praise that is bestowed on him in his ministerial & political capacity. The personal portraiture here drawn is of a yet higher beauty, and is one which even those who are unable to imitate should admire.

The book has been in active circulation here.

Has a copy been sent to the Queen? I venture to put the question because I think she would like, and value it.

Mr. Creighton's task has been I think singularly well performed.

12. E. Eve.

A slight disturbance kept me at home. Wrote to Bp of St Andrews—Mr Hamilton Tel l.l.—and minutes. Read Palmer's Narrative—Prudence Palfrey (finished)—Sollen die Juden &c.—Mad. de Pompadour.[6] Prayers at home.

13. Easter Day.

And I was also unable to go to Church. More castor oil at night. Prayers at home: also used The Breviary. Wrote to Sir H. Ponsonby—Ld Hartington—and others—and minutes. Finished Palmer's Narrative—Also Sollen die Juden &c. Read Ground on Spencer—Mad. de Pompadour.

To LORD HARTINGTON, war secretary, 13 April   Chatsworth MSS 340. 1448.
1884.[7]

I have never heard mention in the Cabinet or otherwise of sending English troops to Khartoum, unless in the last and sad necessity of its being the only available means of rescuing him.

---

[1] T. Carlyle, *Letters addressed to Mrs Basil Montagu and B. W. Proctor* (1881).

[2] H. A. Taine, vol. i of *Les origines de la France contemporaine* (1876).

[3] T. B. Aldrich, serialised version of *Prudence Palfrey* (1886).

[4] M. Creighton, *Memoir of Sir George Grey, bart.* (1884).

[5] Sir W. Palmer, *Narrative of events connected with the publication of Tracts for the Times* (1843, new ed. 1883); see 13 Oct. 43.

[6] Perhaps H. Bonhomme, *Madame de Pompadour* (1880).

[7] In Holland, i. 440, replying to Hartington's of 11 April, ibid., i. 438: need to send troops to Gordon, either British or Turkish: Wolseley has drawn up a 'rough sketch' of a Nile expedition; Sir C. Wilson thinks Wolseley underrates the difficulties of the Nile route and prefers the Suakin-Berber route; see *Sudan campaign*, i. 26.

The dispatch of Turkish soldiers is of course a different matter but a serious one not yet accepted in Egypt or by us.

As far as I see the sending English troops to Khartoum, except as above, would be the most vital and radical change that could be made in our policy.

What I do think we ought to set about is sending a set of carefully prepared questions to Gordon about his future condition and plans; all the more so because it appears to me that in his telegrams he takes very little notice indeed of any general questions we put to him.

I *hope* to see Granville to-morrow at Holmbury, and I will show him your letter.

14. Easter M.

Much better, but not out. Saw Sir A. Clark. Wrote to Ld Granville—The Queen l.l.—Scotts—and minutes. Mr James the novelist[1] came & in evg I saw him. Read Daisy Miller[2]—The Treasure Island.[3]

15. Tu. [Holmbury]

Wrote to Sir C. Dilke—Lady Ely Tel.—and minutes. Read Daisy Miller finished—Khedives and Pachas[4]—Macmillan (Morley) on Colonies.[5] Saw Mr James—Ld Granville. At 3 we drove over to Holmbury: charming place competes with charming people.

To Sir C. W. DILKE, president of the local   Add MS 43875, f. 164.
government board, 15 April 1884.

I thank you very much for your note.[6] The question it refers to is one of much delicacy & importance which the Cabinet will have to consider.

But I think we shall examine it with much greater advantage when we get nearer the point. There is little chance of our being in Committee for a fortnight yet at soonest, & I should be for waiting until within 2 or 3 days of the time, or something like that, if possible.

16. Wed.

Wrote to The Queen—Sir W. Harcourt Tel.—Mr Hamilton l. & Tel.—and minutes. Drive & walk with the party. Whist in evg. Read The New Arabian Nights[7]—Pensées d'Une Reine.[8]

---

[1] See 28 Mar. 77 for their previous meeting. The Gladstone party was left by Rosebery 'in my [i.e. James's] care'; Gladstone discussed bookbinding, 'the vulgarity of the son of a Tory Duke', the bible and the Hebrew chair; James felt 'nervous about dinner this evening and should like to read up beforehand'; James to Rosebery this day, L. Edel, *Henry James Letters* (1980), iii. 38.

[2] By Henry James (1883).

[3] By R. L. Stevenson (1883); perhaps recommended by James, a friend of Stevenson.

[4] *Khedives and pashas. Sketches of contemporary Egyptian rulers . . . by one who knows them well* (1884).

[5] *Macmillan's Magazine*, xl. 471 (April 1884).

[6] Of 12 April, Add MS 44149, f. 211, *re* woman's suffrage: Dilke would feel 'no difficulty in voting against the amendment on the ground of tactics' provided Fawcett and Courtney did also, but he could not vote if they abstain. See 13 May 84.

[7] By R. L. Stevenson (1882).

[8] Elizabeth of Roumania, *Les pensées d'une reine* (1882).

17 Th.

Wrote to Abp of Canterbury—Bp of Cape Town—Ld Hampden—Sir H. Ponsonby—Lady Reay—Mr Bickersteth—and minutes. Whist in evg. Today D.G., I consider myself off the sick list. Much conversation with Ld Gr. on Egyptian mess. Read Eugene Aram—Farrer's Tour in Greece[1]—New Arab. nights finished (& bid goodbye): also *very* much official MS.

18. Fr.

Wrote to Sir R. Blennerhassett—and minutes. Wrote Queries on Egypt. Whist in evg. Read Walpole's Letters[2]—L. Stephen Thought of 18th Century[3]—Eugene Aram. Beautiful drive & walk with my kind host. Conversation with Granville: Egypt mainly.

19. Sat.

Wrote to Ld R. Grosvenor—Ld Spencer—and minutes. Walk with George L.G. Drive with Sir G. Dasent and much conversation about Oxford. Read Eugene Aram—Blennerhassett on Peasant Proprietary[4]—L. Stephen on opinion—Q.R. on Royal Vatican.[5]

20. Low S.

Ch. mg & H.C. Evg prayers with C. Walk with F.L. Conversation with Granville: Egypt again. Wrote to Abp of C: & minutes. Read Q.R. on Hope Scott—Do on Bossuet[6]—L. Stephen on Opinion in 18th C.—Ground on H. Spencer.[7]

To E. W. BENSON, archbishop of Canterbury, 20 April   Add MS 44547, f. 59.
1884.

I am much obliged for Your Grace's careful & valuable letter.[8] It prompts, however, a wish that I might, if Your Grace is coming on any early day to London, have an opportunity of calling on you at Lambeth, to talk the matter over, for it is many sided as well as important. I have no foregone conclusion to submit the name of a 'Low Churchman' (like Your Grace I use these names under protest) but only a wish to do it *ceteris paribus.* Yorkshire requires I should think what may be called a robust man. I had the idea that Mr. Spence might prove such & I am sorry that he breaks down.[9] I am also sorry that Mr. Cadman is too old but I recognise at once the fact that this see would be too much for him. I am doubtful about Mr. Boyd Carpenter's *physique.*[10] Outside the Low I am rather

[1] R. R. Farrer, *A tour in Greece, 1880* (1882).
[2] See 1 Jan. 84.
[3] L. Stephen, *History of English thought in the eighteenth century*, 2v. (1876).
[4] Sir R. Blennerhassett, 'Peasant proprietors in Ireland' (1884).
[5] *Q.R.*, clvii. 387 (April 1884).
[6] *Q.R.*, clvii. 289, 473 (April 1884).
[7] W. D. Ground, *An examination of the structural principles of H. Spencer's philosophy* (1883).
[8] Of 18 April, Add MS 44109, f. 89: candidates for Ripon, which 'must have an Evangelical Pastor'. W. Boyd Carpenter was appt.
[9] Henry Donald Maurice Spence, 1836–1917; scholar and vicar of St. Pancras 1877–86, dean of Gloucester 1886.
[10] Cadman and Carpenter were earlier considered for Westminster; see 17 Aug. 81.

inclined to make inquiries about Mr. Barker whom I got out of the Isle of Wight into the great Church at Marylebone.[1] There is an able man in the north, Mr. Creighton, author of an important historical work.[2] I imagine him rather young. Is your Mr. Mason too young? I should like to speak about Dr. Gott & L. Talbot.

21. M. [London]

Wrote to Mr Smith MP.—Dean of Wells—The Queen—Sir H. Ponsonby Tel.— and minutes. Cabinet 2-4¼. Off to London at 9.30. Saw Mr S.—Ld RG—Ld Granville—Chr of Exr—Mr Chamberlain—Do *cum* Sol. General. H of C. 4½-8½ and 10-12¾.[3] Read Eugene Aram.

Cabinet. 2 PM. Ap. 21. 84.[4]
1. French Flag cut down (Gold Coast)—Porto Nuovo. French demand reestablishment of *status quo.* Chancr., Ld G., Ld K., & Ld D. to consult this evening.[5]
2. Egyptian Telegrams. Inquiry as to means for helping Berber. Tel. agreed on.[6] Decisive[?] question as to Gordon postponed.

22. Tu.

Wrote to Lady Grey—Ld Rosebery—The Queen l.l.—and minutes. H of C. & Cabinet 2¼-5¼ & 5¾-7¼.[7] Evg at home. Saw Mr H.—Ld R.G—H.J.G.—Ld Granville—Do *cum* Ld E. Fitzmaurice. Read Eugene Aram—Walker's London to Melbourne.[8]

Cabinet. H of C. Ap. 22. 84. 3 PM.[9]
1. Wellington Statue. Committee may be appointed if Mr Lefevre can arrange with P. of W.
2. Budget. 1884-5. Est. surplus ¼ ℳ less 22 m[ille].
          1883-4 + 206m.
   outside Tax Bill. 1. Set straight the gold coinage ½ sov. = 9/-. 2. Reduction of 3%s: by option: giving £102 max 2¾ for £100 at £3.[10]
3. Conversation on Khartoum & Berber. To wait the expected reply from Egypt as to Berber. Much discussion on eventual necessity of relieving Gordon.

23. Wed.

Wrote to The Queen l.l.—R. S. Gladstone—Mrs Bolton—Mr Knollys—Sir W. Harcourt—Ld R. Grosvenor—& minutes. Saw Mr H—Ld RG—Ld Granville—do

[1] William Barker, 1838-1917; vicar of Cowes 1873-82; rector of Marylebone 1882-1908; dean of Carlisle.
[2] See 14 May 78(?), 11 Apr. 84.
[3] Questioned on Sudan; *H* 287. 138.
[4] Add MS 44645, f. 61.
[5] Britain argued the French flag had been mistakenly flown within the British protectorate, and could not be replaced; F.O.C.P. 4994, f. 77.
[6] Draft at Add MS 44645, f. 62.
[7] Questioned on Sudan; *H* 287. 289.
[8] R. Walker, *The two threes: 33,333 miles by land and sea. Holiday notes* (1883).
[9] Add MS 44645, f. 63.
[10] Childers' scheme for debt conversion.

cum Ld Hartington. Cabinet 3–7$\frac{1}{2}$. Read Eugene Aram (finished)—Silas Marner—Walker's Holiday Notes. Evelyn Garth[1] came to our family dinner. We were delighted with her. There was no ice to break.

Cabinet. Wed. Ap. 23. 84. 3 P.M.[2]
1. Cattle Diseases Bill. Dodson engaged with Heneage in considering amendment. Conversation on course to be taken in the event of rejection. Opinion leaned to the idea of letting the friends of the Bill carry it forward. Fix Tuesday 2 PM.
2. Telegram from Egypt 323 & 324. Discussion thereon. Hartington urges telling Governor of Berber we will help him if he can hold out till British troops can arrive. Telegram drafted by Kimberley: agreed to, Hartington dissentient.
3. Instruction to Gordon also agreed to.[3]

24. Th.

Wrote to The Queen—Sir H. Ponsonby—Rev. S.E.G.—Ld Northbrook—Ld E. Fitzmaurice—and minutes. Saw Mr H.—Ld R.G—Ld Granville—Mr Dodson—do *cum* Ld E. Fitzmaurice—Ld Spencer—Mr Grogan—Mr Anderson—Sir Thos G. H of C. 4$\frac{3}{4}$–8$\frac{1}{4}$ and 9$\frac{3}{4}$–11$\frac{3}{4}$.[4] Read Rose's Three Sheikhs[5]—Walkers Holiday Notes—Silas Marner, finished—noble, though with spots.

To LORD E. G. FITZMAURICE, foreign undersecretary,   Add MS 44547, f. 60.
24 April 1884.

Though agreeing that the principle of selection[6] cannot, as a rule, be applied to Gordon's telegrams there may be exceptions, & one I should think would be that in which he says that if the Mahdi sends his Krupt [*sic*] guns to Khartoum, they, i.e. he & his, are done for—or words to that effect.

To LORD NORTHBROOK, first lord of the admiralty,   Add MS 44547, f. 60.
24 April 1884.

I have little doubt that you have not let drop the question of the Nile Navigation at high flood, which was opened yesterday in the Cabinet, & on which our 'intelligence' department seems to be woefully behind hand.

It seems proper that besides ascertaining what the river will do & carry, we should in anticipation of such intelligence as may (though I hope it will not) come from Gordon inquire carefully what sorts and what number of vessels can be made available to put upon it, how far the country will itself yield a supply, or if it falls short to what quarter we should turn. My own hope is that a very limited supply is all that would be actually required but we ought to extend our inquiries beyond a minimum.

Although this may not properly be Admiralty business, it is I suppose still less within the view of the War Office, & I hope you will consider what agents would be best adapted to the task. It is possible that some intelligent man of business in Egypt itself might be

---

[1] Engaged to H. N. Gladstone; but see 25 Apr. 84.
[2] Add MS 56452, f. 45.
[3] Gordon to be told he 'cannot have troops for military operation in the Soudan, as at variance with the scope of his pacific mission'; CAB 41/18/21.
[4] Childers's budget; *H* 287. 499.
[5] H. Rose, *Three sheiks: an Oriental narration in verse* (1884).
[6] i.e. for printing in the Blue Book.

able to take the main part or else assist materially. Baring's early arrival will I hope be useful in considering this matter.[1]

25. Fr.

Wrote to Ld Granville l.l.—Abp of Canterbury—Ld Rosebery—The Queen l.l.l. & tel.—and minutes. Saw Mr H—Ld R.G—C of E—Trustees of Nat. Gallery[2]—Attorney General cum Ld RG—Mr Palmer MP.—Ly Derby. H of C. 4-7 and 9-12. Spoke on motion respecting Income Tax.[3] A day of distress as to Harry's marriage wh. is not to go on. Read Walker's Holiday Notes—Salmon at the Antipodes.[4]

26. Sat.

Wrote to Mr Duckham—Mr Chamberlain—The Queen Tel.—Messrs Rivington—& minutes. Drive with C. Visited Watercolour Exhn. Saw Mr Karl Haug. Saw Mr H.—Ld RG—Ld Granville. Read Holiday Notes—Valeria: Marriage Law Opinions.[5] More communications on the distressing matter.

27. Sun. 2 Easter.

Chapel Royal mg & aft. Wrote to Ld Granville. Saw Bp of London—Sir Thos G. The sad communications in Harry's matter were brought to a touching close. Read Ryder on Purity[6]—Gordon Reflections in Paleste.[7]—Aungervyle Papers[8]—Browne's Charge[9]—Wright on Divinity School[10]—Vaughan's Sermons[11]—Comm. on Genesis.

28. M.

Wrote to Ld Rosebery—Chancr of Exr—The Queen l.l.l.—and minutes. H. of C. $4\frac{3}{4}$-$8\frac{3}{4}$ & $9\frac{1}{2}$-$1\frac{1}{4}$ (Franchise Bill).[12] Saw Mr H.—Ld RG—Att. General—Ld Spencer. Cabinet 2-$4\frac{1}{2}$. Read Valeria—Hist. of Peter the Great.[13]

Cabinet. Monday Ap. 28. 2 PM.[14]
(2) Amt. to Franchise Bill. Att. General's proposal.[15] NO.
(1) Queen's Telegram. Duke of Albany. See WEG's letter.[16]

[1] Northbrook replied next day that the Admiralty had this in hand, expecting a reply shortly; Add MS 44267, f. 57.   [2] On the Blenheim pictures, see 7 May, 21 June 84.
[3] On Hubbard's motion on inequalities in income tax; *H* 287. 675.
[4] A. Nicols, *Acclimatisation of the Salmonidae at the antipodes* (1882).
[5] Untraced article by 'Valeria' [Eleanor Lloyd].   [6] Tract by A. R. Ryder.
[7] C. G. Gordon, *Reflections in Palestine 1883* (1884).
[8] *Aungervyle Society Reprints*, ed. E. M. Goldsmid, 4 series (1881-7).
[9] By E. H. Browne (1884).
[10] C. H. H. Wright, *The divinity school of Trinity College, Dublin* (1884).
[11] C. J. Vaughan, *Authorised or revised sermons* (1882).
[12] Replies to Raikes on redistribution; *H* 287. 766.
[13] See 9 Feb. 84.   [14] Add MS 44645, f. 64.
[15] Proposing to delay registration of new voters until January 1886 with next dissolution on present franchise; see Jones, *1884*, 132. Dodson noted, Monk Bretton 62: 'Gladstone is for James's proposal, to save time on Franchise Bill'.
[16] Increased grant for the duchess of Albany.

5. Tuesdays & Fridays (evening): ask for.
4. Answers & questions in H of C. Berber. Balfour.[1]
Volunteer expedn.[2]
3. Ireland Purchase Clauses. Plans explained.
Committee of Cabinet appointed.[3]
6. Answer on Merchant Shipping Bill agreed to.[4]

29. Tu.

Wrote to Sir R. Peel—E. Lyttelton—The Queen—Ld Granville—& minutes.
Read Valeria—Walker's Holiday Notes. Saw Mr H—Ld R.G—Archbp of Canterbury—Sir E. Baring—Sir C. Dilke—Ld Hartington—Chancr of Exr. Dined with
Northbrook: further long conversation on Egypt, Baring taking part. H. of C.
$2\frac{1}{4}$-7.[5]

30. Wed.

Wrote to Card. Manning—& minutes. Saw Mr H—Ld RG—Mr E. Lyttelton—E.
Wickham—Ld Granville—Mr Knowles—Mrs Th. Drive with C. Luncheon at 15
G.S. [Royal] Court Theatre evg: 'My Milliner's Bill' admirable.[6] Read Brewer's
Henry VIII[7]—Valeria.

To CARDINAL MANNING, 30 April 1884.   Add MS 44547, f. 62.

I have received your letter[8] & have consulted with Lord Granville.
The words used by me in the House of Commons when replying to Mr. Moore on February 18th were intended to express our interest in the subject. The request however
which you have transmitted to me refers I apprehend to the expression of an interest at
Rome. On this head I have to say that our ambassador at Rome has been authorised to
join with the representation of any other Powers in expressing such interest; & likewise
that the Episcopal memorial, which furnishes argument in support of such a friendly representative, will be forwarded to him.

Thurs. May One 1884.

Wrote to Duke of Roxburgh—Ld Granville—Ld Fife—Sir W. James—The Queen
l.l.—Sir H. Ponsonby Tel.—and minutes. Saw Mr H—Ld RG—Ld Derby—Mr
Goschen. Cabinet $2\frac{1}{2}$-$4\frac{1}{2}$. H of C. 5-$8\frac{1}{2}$ and $9\frac{3}{4}$-1. Spoke on Franchise Bill.[9] Read
Valeria. Finished Holiday Notes.

---

[1] Bartlett and Balfour's questions this day; *H* 287. 749, 751.
[2] Dawnay's scheme; see 1 May 84.
[3] Lefevre, Trevelyan, Childers, Chamberlain, Kimberley, Derby; Add MS 44645, f. 65
[4] Given by Chamberlain; *H* 287. 1041.
[5] Contagious Diseases (Animals) Bill; *H* 287. 901.
[6] He went again, see 17 May 84.
[7] J. S. Brewer, *The reign of Henry VIII*, 2v. (1884).
[8] Of 26 April, with a signed appeal from English Roman catholic bps. for help to safeguard the
Propaganda in Rome; Add MS 44250, f. 205.
[9] Now in cttee.; *H* 287. 1080.

Cabinet. Thurs. My 1. 1884. 2½ PM.[1]
4. Morning sittings. Tues. & Frid. to end of June.
1. Birthday dinner—none.
2. Wellington Statue. Vote to be proposed.
3. Scotch Govt. Bill. To be introduced in the H. of Lords.
5. Shall there be a vote of thanks to Graham? No.
6. Question on the Conference. Agreed on.[2]
7. Vacant Lordship in Waiting.[3] To telegraph to Ponsonby & stop proceedings. Gr. to write to see[?] then we shall represent. Not to mention Cabinet.
8. Answer respecting O'Kelly agreed on.[4] We concurred entirely in the proceeding of the Egyptian Govt.
9. Answer to Willis—recited.[5]
10. Dawnay's offer.[6] Thank but are unwilling that his personal safety should be brought into question.
11. Conversation on Egypt. Baring wishes to understand us on 1. Suakim; 2. Army; 3. Finance; 4. Native Govt.
12. Promote evacuation of Harrah.[7]
13. WEG read MS A:[8] 1. To hasten as much as possible the formation of some small & trustworthy army, probably black, to take the place of the Fellah army, found untrustworthy. 2. To consider further the question of the Turks *quoad* the Red Sea Ports.

2. Fr.

Wrote to B. Quaritch—Abp of Canterbury—Ld Portman—Ld Fitzwilliam—The Queen l.l.—and minutes. Visited Royal Academy. Saw Mr H—Ld R.G—Sir S. Northcote—Sir W. James—Sir G. Dasent—Mr Seymour—Mr Dodson—Dean Church—Mr MacColl. H of C. 4¾–7¾ and 11–1½. A good night: we have now the whip hand as to time.[9] Read Valeria—Kama Sutra.[10]

3. Sat.

Wrote to H.N.G.—Ld Granville—and minutes. Royal Academy 2¼–4. The least interesting exhibition I remember. Breakfast at Grillion's. Saw Mr H—Ld R.G—Ld Granville—Mr Forster—Archbishop of York—Ld Houghton. Carl Rosa Opera in evening, Carmen. Read Valeria—Gov. Hutchinson Letters &c.[11]—Kama Sutra—OBrien on the Round Towers.[12]

[1] Add MS 44645, f. 71.
[2] Announcing the Conference 'on certain Egyptian affairs'; *H* 287. 1055.
[3] Replacement for Torrington; Victoria, without consultation, asked Bridport; Bahlman, *Hamilton*, ii. 608.
[4] J. O'Kelly, M.P., acting as a reporter in Sudan, had been prevented from visiting the Mahdi; *H* 287. 1039.
[5] Willis's question on ending the Gordon mission; *H* 287. 1059.
[6] Guy Cuthbert Dawnay, 1848–89; tory M.P. N. Yorkshire 1882–5; offered to mount volunteer expedition to restore links with Gordon; killed by buffalo.
[7] Achieved by Hunter early 1885; Cromer, ii. 51.
[8] On a separate sheet; Add MS 44645, f. 74.
[9] Extra debating time voted; *H* 287. 1196.
[10] *The Kama Sutra of Vātsyāyana*, ed. Sir R. F. Burton and F. F. Arbuthnot (1883).
[11] P. O. Hutchinson, *The diary and letters of T. Hutchinson*, 2v. (1883–6).
[12] H. O'Brien, *The round towers of Ireland* (1834).

4. 3 S.E.

Off at 10.15 to Mr Boyd Carpenter's Church. His Sermon was admirable.[1] Wrote to The Queen l.l.l.—Sir W. Harcourt. Read Hutton on Newman[2]—Shorthouse on Maurice[3]—Reclus on Anarchy[4]—Fothergill on Pain.[5]—[blank] on Eccl. Courts. Chapel Royal aft.

To Sir W. V. HARCOURT, home secretary, 4 May 1884.   MS Harcourt dep. Adds 10.

Granville wished for a Cabinet yesterday to submit to it the French proposals about Egypt: but it was put off on our finding that you & Northbrook were away.

They now stand for tomorrow and they are of great importance: to me they on the whole look as if they might come to much good with regard to the evacuation of Egypt. I cannot but think you would be sorry to miss this Cabinet—& surely it would justify your excusing yourself at Derby.

5. M.

Wrote to Ld Hartington—The Queen Tel. & l.l.l.—and minutes. Saw Mr H—Ld RG—Ch. of Exr with R.G. Read Keay on India[6]—Brewer's Hist. H. VIII—O'Brien on Round Towers—Bluebook on Egypt.[7] H. of C. 5–8½ and 10–12.[8]

Cabinet. Monday May 5. 84. 2 P.M[9]
1. Duchess of Albany. On the Duchess's [*sc.* Duke's] death, a provision shd. be made.
2. Vote of censure. Monday to be given, & Tues. morning if necessary.
3. Granville's ans. to Salisbury. decline further information respecting Gordon.[10]
4. Vote of thanks [to Graham and Hewett]: none to be proposed. Hartington's answer approved with amt.[11]
5. French proposals respecting Egypt. Memoranda read.[12] Proposals well received—express satisfaction & ask a. is the new controul to operate before our withdrawal; b. are the arrangements likely to be acceptable to the Powers; c. what will be the nature of the controul—will it minimise the responsibility of the Govts?
6. Raouf Pasha: shall the Egyptian Govt. appoint him as inspector?[13] Not to interfere.
7. Colonial Fortification. Hartn. to speak if necessary in term of his draft.[14]

[1] At Christ Church, Lancaster Gate; Gladstone had previously found him inaudible, see to Wellesley, 17 August 1881; see also G. P. Gooch, *Under Six Reigns* (1958), 5–6.
[2] R. H. Hutton, 'Cardinal Newman', *C.R.*, xlv. 642 (May 1884).
[3] *N.C.*, xv. 849 (May 1884).
[4] E. Reclus, 'Évolution et Révolution' (1880).
[5] One of J. M. Fothergill's many medical articles.
[6] *N.C.*, xv. 721 (May 1884).
[7] On Egyptian finances and affairs published 6, 8 May; *PP* lxxxix. 35, 43.
[8] Army estimates; *H* 287. 1332.
[9] Add MS 44645, f. 75.
[10] *H* 287. 1268.
[11] *H* 287. 1313.
[12] Memoranda by Gladstone and Granville (Ramm II, ii. 185) on French proposal to make Egypt a European concern *via* a Conference in London.
[13] i.e. wanted by the Khedive in Harrar prior to evacuation; see 1 May 84; he was 'a bad specimen of a bad class', Cromer, ii. 52.
[14] On the confidential Royal Commission (see 12 June 80n.); Carnarvon raised the W.O.'s hostility to the treasury on 13 November; *H* 293. 1534.

6. Tu.

Wrote to Ld Kinnaird—Mr Cropper—The Queen—and minutes. Saw Mr H—Ld RG—Sir T. May—Sir W. Harcourt—Ld Granville—Sir C. Dilke—Scotch Deputation. Read Egyptn Blue Book—OBrien on Round Towers. H of C. 2-7 on Franchise and $10-12\frac{3}{4}$.[1]

7.

Wrote to Sir W.W. Wynn—Miss Scott—Ld Granville l.l.—Mrs Th.—The Queen l.l.—and minutes. Thirteen to dinner. Conversation with Musurus—Gen. Graham. Speaker's Levee afterwards. Cabinet $2\frac{1}{2}-5\frac{1}{4}$. Drive with C. Saw Mr H—Ld R.G.—and others. Read O'Brien—Egyptn papers.

Cabinet. Wed. May 7. 84. 2.30 PM.[2]
1. Nubar's coming to England. Not approved.
2. Clifford Lloyd—conversation as to the means of giving him another appointment.[3]
3. Account of interview with French Ambassador—read by Ld G.[4] 1. New Controul shd. not begin till our occupation ends—limit international controul or reserve it—admit in principle that a period may be found. Fix day for anr. to Waddington.
4. F.O. may open the question of the Red Sea Ports with Turkey making stipulations as to slave trade. Fair arrangements for Massowah.
5. Childers asked is our credit to be used in raising the loan for Egypt. Disposition to hold that the bondholders should bear their share.
6. Blenheim Pictures.[5] Altho' not indisposed to consider the manner of acquiring pictures of great importance the scale of price is so excessive that we are altogether unable to entertain.

8. Th.

Wrote to The Queen l.l.—Ld Kimberley—Ld Granville—& minutes. Thirteen to breakfast. Saw Mr H—Ld R.G—Mr Millais—Mr Knowles—Miss O. Hill[6]—Ld Granville—Do *cum* Sir H. Ponsonby—Sir W. Harcourt. Dined at Sir C. Forster's. Attended the opening of the Health Exhibition—A warm reception, strangely falsified by the newspapers.[7] H of C. 5-8 and $10-12\frac{1}{2}$.[8] Read O'Brien—Egyptian papers—Life of Lady Warner.[9]

---

[1] Franchise Bill in cttee.; *H* 287. 1484.   [2] Add MS 44645, f. 89.

[3] Charles Dalton Clifford Lloyd, 1844-91; as magistrate in Limerick controversially suppressed the Land League 1881-3; superintended internal reforms in Egypt 1883; undersecretary Egyptian dept. of the interior Jan. 1884; advocated English President of the Council; resigned late May 1884; back in Ireland, then governed Mauritius. See Cromer, ii. 482-8.

[4] In Granville to Lyons, 6 May, PRO FO 27/2660.   [5] See 21 June 84.

[6] Octavia *Hill, 1838-1912; philanthropist; active on housing; a founder of the National Trust; had just given evidence to the Royal Commission on housing.

[7] Health exhibition in S. Kensington; 'the entrance of Mr Gladstone ... was heralded by an unusual but quite unmistakable manifestation of popular disfavour, which could only be attributed to the intensity of public feeling among all classes with regard to the fate of General Gordon'; *T.T.*, 9 May 1884, 4d, 9b.

[8] Questions; navy estimates; *H* 287. 1690.

[9] [E. Scarisbrike], *The life of Lady Warner* (2d ed. 1692); notes on it at Add MS 44768, f. 41.

To LORD KIMBERLEY, Indian secretary, 8 May 1884.   Add MS 44547, f. 63.

Pray be kind enough to run to ground for me the passage you read from Gordon against sending any British soldiers to Khartoum. The bit cut out of Times will be a clew [*sic*].[1]

9. Frid.

Wrote to Mr Renton—Sir B. Leighton—The Queen—and minutes. Dined at Ld Reay's. H of C. 2½ and off & on to 7½.[2] Saw Mr H—Ld R.G—Mr Chamberlain— Ch of Exr—Mr Morley—M. de Laveleye—Sir C. Dilke—Mr Chamberlain—Sir W. Harcourt. Saw Tait X.[3] Worked on Egyptian papers. Read Lady Warner's Life— OBrien on Round Towers.

Ld. R. Grosvenor recommends strongly that he be authorised by the Cabinet freely to acquaint our friends that, if the vote for women's suffrage be carried, the Franchise Bill will be dropped, which of course entails the resignation of the Government.

This does not imply any judgment on the merits of the proposal, but only on its introduction into this Bill.

I am myself not strongly opposed to every form & degree of the proposal, but I think that if put into this Bill it would give the House of Lords a case for 'postponing' it and I know not how to incur such a risk.

I am therefore ready for my part to give Ld R.G. the authority he desires. His opinion is that if this step be taken we shall be safe. WEG May 9/84.[4]

P.S. Granville & Hartington agree.

10. Sat.

Wrote to The Queen—Ld Granville—Mr Heneage—Abp Boniface—Mr Anderson—and minutes. 12-2. To Walham Green: no one at home.[5] Drive with C. Dined with Argyll.[6] Worked[7] on Egyptian papers. Saw Mr H—Ld R.G—Duke of Argyll. Read O'Brien—Castle of Otranto.[8]

11. 4 S.E.

Chapel Royal mg & evg. Drive with C. Dined with Sir W. James. Read U. Presbn Magazine—Lady Warner's Life (finished)—Fuller's Sermons[9]—Wordsworth on N.T.[10]

[1] Kimberley next day forwarded a cutting from *T.T.* of an interview with Gordon at Khartoum; 'I am dead against the sending of any British expedition to reconquer the Soudan. It is unnecessary.'
[2] Questions; Municipal Elections Bill; *H* 287. 1853.
[3] Mrs A. Tait, a rescue case; see 4 Dec. 84n.
[4] Holograph for circulation; Add MS 44768, f. 37; note by Hamilton, ibid., f. 38: 'All agreed, save Sir C. Dilke, who asks instructions as to his course.'
[5] Evidently house of Mrs Tait, a rescue case; see 21 May 84.
[6] Gladstone spoke 'almost bitterly *against* any military measures ... although he admitted the *personal claim* of Gordon. I said to him: "When you speak on Monday, I hope you won't say what you have now said to me"'; Argyll to Selborne, 25 February 1885, Argyll, ii. 390.
[7] Facsimile in Masterman, 304, starts here.
[8] By Horace Walpole (1791).
[9] M. Fuller, *The Lord's Day* (1883).
[10] C. Wordsworth, *The New Testament* (1859).

12. M.

Wrote to Mr W. Fowler—Ld Lothian—Bp of Gloucester—Abp of Canterbury—
The Queen—& minutes. Read O'Brien—Castle of Otranto. Saw Mr H—Ld RG—
Ld Granville—Ld Hartn. Worked on Egyptian papers. Drive with C.

H of C. 5–8¼ and 10–11¾. Spoke for one hour on the Gordon question: the
best I could, though far from good: but I declare, in the eye of God, with an
active & absolute desire to speak according to truth & justice, & as I shall
answer to Him for it in the great day.[1]

To E. W. BENSON, archbishop of Canterbury,   Add MS 44547, f. 63.
12 May 1884. '*Private*'.

I thank Your Grace for making known to me the suggestions you had received that
public prayer should be offered up for Gordon by name.[2]

It seems ungracious to discourage any kind of prayer for any person in any circumstances; and all the more when the circumstances are difficult.

But the issuing of a public prayer for a particular person would be judged by comparison. There was no prayer for the army of Wolseley or Graham, when they were running
into considerable danger. But Gordon according to his own (I believe true) account is not
(what is called) in danger. His own words on April 9th were that for 2 months (one of
which has passed) he was as safe as at Cairo. I think therefore that the prayer would be
entirely misunderstood; & on that ground especially, I could not advise it.

13. Tu.

Wrote to Sir R. Peel—Sir C. Dilke—Sir F. Leighton—Ld Spencer—The Queen—
Ld Hartington—Ld Granville—& minutes. Read Castle of Otranto—O'Brien on
Round Towers. Saw Mr H—Ld RG—HJG—Tigroun Pacha[3]—Sir R. Welby.
H of C. 2¼–7 and 10–2. Voted in 303 agt 275 on the Vote of Censure.[4] Hartington spoke admirably, Goschen like a gentleman. On the failure of the conspiracy, revealed by the numbers, the Liberal cheering was perhaps the most
prolonged I have ever known.

To Sir C. W. DILKE, president of the local government   Add MS 43875, f. 165.
board, 13 May 1884.

The question as to the Votes of members of the Govt. on Woman Suffrage[5] is beyond
me & I have always intended to ask the Cabinet, and (like the Gordon rescue) at the
proper time. The distinction appears to me as clear as possible between supporting a
thing in its right place and thrusting it into its wrong place. To nail on to the Extension of
the Franchise, founded on principles already known & in use, a vast social question,
which is surely entitled to be considered as such, appears to me in principle very doubtful.
When to this is added the admirable patent, nay the fair argument, it would give to the
House of Lords for 'putting off' the Bill, I cannot see the ground for hesitation.

[1] On Hicks-Beach's motion of censure; *H* 288. 52.
[2] Benson's letter untraced.
[3] Tigrane Pasha, d. 1904; an Armenian who was Nubar Pasha's s.-in-law; Egyptian foreign-
undersecretary; 'a prey to intellectual over-subtlety' (Cromer, ii. 224).
[4] *H* 288. 302.
[5] See 9, 24 May, 13 June 84n.

But I quite understand what (I believe) is your view that there should be one rule for all the members of the Government.

To LORD HARTINGTON, war secretary, 13 May 1884.   Chatsworth MSS 340. 1459.

I have read Lord Wolseley's interesting memorandum.[1]

The first question that arises is whether in referring to preparations he means preparations for an expedition up the Nile, or preparations for an advance from Suakim to Berber. These respective routes would I apprehend require very different measures, & also different times.

The paper circulated the other day for the Cabinet left on my mind the impression that the conditions of the River at the different cataracts made it impossible for a large force such as Lord Wolseley had contemplated.

To LORD SPENCER, Viceroy of Ireland, 13 May 1884.   Althorp MSS K7.

I have circulated your note & letter on the [land] Purchase Plan.[2]

It can I think be considered in the Cabinet on Saturday. Can you come over? The matter is not less important than difficult.

I am inclined to *prefer* 4/4 with an effective guarantee to 3/4 with nobody between the Consolidated Fund & the debtor: & I doubt if Ireland can give any guarantee better than the one which has been devised. On the other hand it certainly seems to me that the annual payment by the debtor, together with the additional rates for which he would be liable, ought on every ground, not to fall short of, but somewhat to exceed, the rent for which he is now liable to the landlord. Any limit of amount in the Bill ought I should think to be annual, with a maximum absolute: not more than £ [blank] in any one year nor than £ [blank] in all.

These are very first impressions. The whole subject is one which I regard with misgiving, when once we get beyond the idea of facilitating a real purchase by select cultivators.

14. Wed.

Wrote to Ld Granville—Rev. Mr Boyd Carpenter—Ld Spencer Tel.—The Queen l.l.—Mr Goschen—and minutes. Saw Mr H—Ld R.G—Archdn Norris—Bp of Ely. Cabinet 2-6. Did much. Dined at Bp of Ely's. Read OBrien—Castle of Otranto (finished).

Cabinet. H of C. Wed. May 14. 84. 2 PM.[3]
1. Whitsun Holidays 27th Tues. to the Thursday week.
2. Zululand. Decline annexation & only defend the Reserve: acc. to Robinson's Telegram.
3. The affair Clifford Lloyd. He is to come home. He & Egerton[4] to arrange the mode. Inspectors qy. appoint two to look after Mudier[?]—Nubar suggesting.
   E. Baring came in at 4 P.M.[5]

[1] Of 9 May, Chatsworth MSS 340, 1458: small expedition 'silly' unless followed up; need 'at once' to make preparation for relief of Khartoum; no route mentioned.
[2] Letter of 12 May with copy of letter to Childers, Add MS 44311, f. 114, opposing Childers' purchase proposals; if Gladstone satisfied 'that Childers proposals can safely be accepted, I shall acquiesce ... very unwillingly'.   [3] Add MS 44645, f. 91.
[4] (Sir) Edwin Henry Egerton, 1841-1916; *locum tenens* for Baring; see Cromer, i. 432.
[5] Baring was in Britain from late April-September. At this Cabinet he recommended the return

4. Communications with Waddington: a. the controul cannot be while we remain in occupation; b. we are not unwilling, at the expiration of a time, to refer the matter to the Powers; c. the limits of the controul to be fixed by the Powers?
The discussion passed into a wider field: finally a memorandum was drawn. Herewith.[1]
Much conversation with Baring on the bifurcation of the policies of withdrawal & retention.
5. Childers submitted his plan founded on 1. Preponderance[?]; 2. Deduction from Dividend; 3. Our raising the loan; 4. Retrieve army charge.[2]
Baring—wd. let in international controul with defined functions.

15. Th.

Wrote to Ld Hartington—The Queen—& minutes. Read O'Brien. Nine to breakfast. Dined with the Rosebery's. Saw Mr H—Ld RG—Ld Rosebery—Sir C. Dilke—Ld Granville—Mr Chamberlain. H of C. 5-8 and 10-12$\frac{1}{2}$.[3]

16. Fr.

Wrote to Ld Hartington—The Queen—& minutes. *Drafted* an important Telegram to Gordon authorising use of money.[4] Saw Mr H—Ld RG l.l.l.—Ld Spencer—Chancr of Exr—H. of C. 2-7 (Franchise Bill) and 9-10$\frac{3}{4}$.[5] Read O'Brien.

To LORD HARTINGTON, war secretary, 16 May 1884.[6]   Chatsworth MSS 340. 1461.

I received & read yesterday General Stephenson's report.[7] It appeared to me to be an honest & able paper: conclusive; together with other arguments, against the idea of any large operations by the River, but most alarming in regard to English treasure and life, & giving occasion for much reflection & deliberation.

Granville tells me you think of proposing a Committee of Cabinet but will not the *first* thing be for the War Office to go to work and frame its estimates? taking care I make no doubt to frame them as was done in the case of the China Vote of Credit (1860) and of the Ashantee [*sc.* Abyssinian] War (1866) [*sc.* 1867] so as to bring out the full charge.

Also ought there not to be a medical report on the degree of risk to life which will have to be encountered.

17. Sat.

Wrote to The Queen—Ld Maclaren—Sir G. Dasent—and minutes. Cabinet 12-3$\frac{1}{2}$. Read O'Brien—Tract on Servia.[8] Court Theatre 8-11$\frac{1}{4}$.[9] Visited Argyll Lodge.

of Lloyd, requested strict financial control, preferred 'international to dual, or even single Control', and advised presence of Turks at the Red Sea ports; Monk Bretton 62.

[1] Much deleted; Add MS 44645, f. 93.
[2] i.e. Childers's plan for Egyptian finance, later in conflict with Northbrook's.
[3] Questions; spoke on finance; *H* 288. 512.
[4] Drafts at Add MS 44768, f. 43.
[5] *H* 288. 607.
[6] In Holland, i. 460.
[7] Of 4 May, from Cairo; Chatsworth MSS 340. 1457; *Sudan campaign*, i. 31.
[8] Perhaps *Servia: her aim and story* (1884).
[9] 'Devotion' and 'My Milliner's Bill'.

Cabinet. Sat. May 17. 84. Noon.[1]
1. Communication with H.M. stated by Ld Granville.[2]
2. Communication with France: to be made known by binding engagement. Answer Monday discussed & agreed on in substance.[3]
3. Tel. of last night respecting S. Africa.[4] Stand on former telegram: to defend Reserve only. Tel. read.
4. Purchase Clauses Plan considered.[5]

18. 5 S.E.

Chapel Royal mg & aft. Saw Sir M. Wilson. Wrote to Sir H. Ponsonby *bis*, on Egypt: cancelling the first—also to Mrs Tait. Read Dr S. on Xtn Religion—Taylor Morality &c of Plants[6]—Dr Brewer, Articles[7]—Mr Ottley, Sermon[8]—S.P.G. Report.

19. M.

Wrote to Sir D. Currie—Dr Acland—Rev. E. Capel Cure—Mr Mowatt—Mr Ponsonby Fane[9]—The Queen—& minutes. H of C. 5-8½ and 10-11¾.[10] 11¾-3¼. To Windsor, Council. Saw Ld Sydney—Mr Peel—Sir H. Ponsonby—& had a satisfactory audience of the Queen. Quasi Cabinet 3½ (Purchase) & Conclave at H of C (Egypt). Read Oldtown Folks[11]—OBrien on Round Towers (finished).

20. Tu.

Wrote to Ld Seafield—Ld Chancellor—Mrs Th—Mrs Beecher-Stowe[12]—Prof. Villari—Ld Canterbury—The Queen—and minutes. H of C. 2½-7. (Franchise).[13] Tea with Mrs Peel. Saw Mr H—Ld R.G—Mr Dillwyn MP.—Mrs Bolton. Twelve to dinner. Read Oldtown Folks.

21. Wed.

Wrote to The Queen—Ld Morley—Mr West—and minutes. Second trip manqué to W[alham] Green. Called for Tait: removed [R]. Saw Mr H—Count Carolyi—

[1] Add MS 44645, f. 94.
[2] Her objections to a fixed limit of 5 years for occupation of Egypt; *L.Q.V.*, 2nd series, iii. 500.
[3] To Barttelot, emphasising limitation of Conference to law of liquidation; *H* 288. 670; Hamilton's note of liberal as well as tory anxieties, at Add MS 44645, f. 98.
[4] Derby's note, Add MS 44645, f. 99: 'Bad news from South Africa. May I read the telegram when this is over?'
[5] 'Admit advance of the whole [purchase money]: *Aye*: Childers, Chamberlain, Harcourt, Kimberley, Derby, Gladstone; *No*: Carlingford, Northbrook, Spencer, Dilke, Selborne, Hartington, Dodson'; Add MS 44645, f. 95 with notes on the plan.
[6] J. E. Taylor, *The sagacity and morality of plants* (1884).
[7] See 30 Apr. 84.
[8] H. Ottley, 'The challenge of the Church' (1882).
[9] G.C.B. for Spencer Cecil Brabazon Ponsonby-Fane, 1824-1915, comptroller of royal accounts.
[10] Questions; Merchant Shipping Bill; *H* 288. 680.
[11] H. Beecher Stowe, *Oldtown folks*, 3v. (1869).
[12] Letter of thanks, see 18 Feb. 84n and 19 May 84.
[13] Franchise Bill cttee; *H* 288. 853.

Ld Granville—H.J.G. Dined at Ld Tweedmouth's. Read D'Heylli's curious volume.[1] Visited Mr Joy's Studio. Saw Mrs Heywood—Mr Quaritch.

22. Th. Ascension Day.

Seven to breakfast. Conversation with [Lord] Morley on the Provostship [of Eton]. Attended Holy Commn at St Paul's afterwards. Wrote to Ld Granville—The Queen—& minutes. Mr H—Ld R.G—Mr Heneage—Mr Kitson—Sir H. Locke—Col. Kingscote—Chr of Exchr—Sir C. Dilke—Mr West. Dined at Mr West's. Read 'Le Parlement la cour et la Ville'[2]—In the slums.[3] H of C. 5-8 and $10\frac{1}{2}$-12.[4]

23. Fr.

Wrote to Ld Granville l.l.—Sir W. Harcourt—Mr Childers—Ld Portarlington—The Queen—and minutes. Saw Mr H—Ld RG—Ld Granville. H of C. 2-7 (Franchise) & 9-11.[5] Read the curious work on the Damiens Trial[6] and [blank.]

24. Sat.

Wrote to The Queen. Saw Mr H—Ld R.G—Mr Burnand—Mr Tenniel—Mr Agnew. Dined at Mr Agnew's. Visited Nat Hist. Museum. Cabinet $12-4\frac{1}{2}$. Finished Damiens. Read Rochford Tracts[7] &c.

Cabinet. May 24. 1884. 2 PM.[8]
1. Woman franchise. To be treated as vital to the Bill.[9]
2. Insertion of date in Franchise Bill (Nov. 1. 85 or Jan. 1. 86). Left to our discretion according to tactics.[10]
3. Neutralisation of Egypt. Derby[?]:[11] for equal rights under a general guarantee. Remain on ground already taken—reserving right & defining it a little.
4. Draft of conversation with Waddington read. We are to ask their opinion on finance as necessary. Englishman shall be President of the Caisse [de la Dette Publique]. Inspection by Caisse admitted. Five years: (H. dissenting) point to be reserved to see whether we agree on other points. General interference of Caisse with Budget disapproved.
5. Statement on Turks & Suakim. Not to be precipitated.

[1] G. d'Heylli [i.e. A. E. Poinsot], perhaps *Delaunay-Sociétaire de la Comédie Française* (1883).
[2] Not found; many with approximately this title.
[3] D. Rice-Jones, *In the slums* (1884).
[4] Row with de Worms on Egypt; *H* 288. 1025.
[5] *H* 288. 1194.
[6] Of R. F. Damiens; perhaps W. H. Dilworth, see 19 Sept. 81.
[7] Possibly *The velvet coffee-woman, or, the life, gallantries and amours of the late famous Mrs A. Rochford* (1728).
[8] Add MS 44645, f. 100.
[9] i.e. too time consuming and divisive to be allowed to endanger the Bill. See 9, 13 May 84. None the less, Dilke, Fawcett and Courtney abstained on Woodall's amndt. on 12 June; see 12 June 84n.
[10] 'Fixing a date has this advantage—that the Government thereby give a distinct earnest of their intention not to dissolve without making an attempt to carry a measure of Redistribution'; Bahlman, *Hamilton*, ii. 623.
[11] Word smudged.

6. Morocco. Statement of Ld G. Italian alarms & French assurances. Will tell Italy he is in friendly communication with France about Ortega.[1]
7. Hartington gave particulars as to expedition.[2] Berber Suakim R[ail] R[oad] might be made in 130 days for $1\frac{1}{4}$ ⋒. (For £310 m[ille] might make 50 m[iles] say middle of Octr.) Expedition to cost another ⋒. 6000 or 7000 men. Admiralty charges not excluded.

25. S. aft Asc.

Chapel Royal mg and aft. Wrote sketch of answer on Egypt. Dined with Mrs Heywood. Read Crossleigh on Xty[3]—Rochester Funeral Sermons[4]—Sermon on Clergy—Statham on Free & True Thought[5]—and M'Kenzies Cape Mission.[6]

26. M.

Wrote to Mr Smith—Mr Westell—The Queen—and minutes. Arr. & sent off books for binder. Third search for Tait: again failed. Saw Mr H—Ld RG—Ld Hartington—Mr Childers—Ld Granville. H of C. 5–$8\frac{1}{4}$ and 9–$12\frac{1}{4}$. Franchise Bill.[7] Luncheon at 15 G. Square.

27. Tu. [Hawarden]

Wrote to Mr Isaac—The Queen—& minutes. Cabinet $12\frac{1}{2}$–$2\frac{1}{4}$. H of C. $2\frac{1}{2}$–$4\frac{1}{4}$.[8] Read Brewer's Henry VIII[9]—Latin verses of Pope Leo: (not equal to the English standard)[10]—Dryden's Epistles.[11] Saw Mr H—Ld R.G—Ld Granville—Mr Isaac— Sir W. Harcourt—Sir C. Dilke. $4\frac{1}{2}$–$10\frac{1}{2}$. To Hawarden with C.

Cabinet. Tues. May 27. 1884. 12.30 P.M. (afternoon).[12]
1. Agreed to promise the results of the communications préalable to Parlt. before the Conference.
2. France to understand clearly as per A.[13]
3. Certain preparations to be made for preparing to meet the chance of a Gordon Operation. Proposed. Nothing to be done now beyond preliminary proceedings.
4. Granville detailed last communication with Waddington: a. new powers of the Caisse; b. Englishman President; c. Length of *term*: to give in at the last moment.

[1] French consul in Morocco.
[2] Costs prepared in response to Gladstone's request and Wolseley's urgings; Holland, i. 459–61.
[3] C. Croslegh, *Christianity judged by its fruits* (1884).
[4] Untraced.
[5] F. R. Statham, *Free-thought and true-thought* (1884).
[6] *In Zululand, the story of the Mackenzie memorial mission* (1872).
[7] Spoke against restriction of household suffrage; *H* 288. 1357.
[8] Questioned on Egypt; *H* 288. 1482.
[9] See 30 Apr. 84.
[10] *Poesie Latine di Sua Santità Papa Leone XIII.*
[11] Unclear what is meant here; perhaps those of Dryden's poems written as letters.
[12] Add MS 44645, f. 106.
[13] 'A. Tell France 1. That we shall stand or fall by the arrangements; 2. Subject only to the conclusion of a financial arrangement'; ibid., f. 108.

¹1. Present circumstances do not warrant the expect[atio]n of an expedition to Khartoum.

2. We ought not to be in *any degree* committed.

3. If there² wd. be serious delay in the *event* of an expedition unless we do *something* now I am willing to do something but let it be as small as possible. £312 m[ille].

28. Wed.

Ch. 8½ A.M. Wrote to Ld Northbrook—Ld Granville—Sir C. Dilke—Mary G.— Mr Bright—The Queen—& minutes. Read Herodotus B. III—Virgil—& Bades Transln³—Ann. Register for 1840—Kildrostan⁴—Dryden's Poems. Went to Aston with W. & H. and made a survey.

To John BRIGHT, M.P., 28 May 1884. '*Secret*'.   Add MS 43385, f. 330.

I have not seen so much in the papers as I could have wished, about your recovery; & I should greatly like to be assured that it is well advanced, & advancing. Then again I go back upon the days when I used (with much tolerance on your part) to lecture you about your health & about the wonderfully skilful care which the best London doctors take of us as we descend the hill of life, teaching us to avoid the besetting dangers of our declining years, & to husband the resources that remain. I do hope that you are taking the best care of your valuable health & life.

Had you remained in London I would have called on you again to talk, in the full confidence which prevails between us, on the state of public affairs. I would give much to have you in the Cabinet at this moment; & I feel sure that, if you were there, you would not regret being there. The situation is intensely interesting, for it is fraught with very grave results. It is summed up in these words: the Franchise; Egypt; & the race between them. The two subjects are so disparate, that it seems ludicrous to associate them. But in the first is involved the question of liberty at home; in the second the interests of peace & civilisation for Christendom will probably be brought to an issue in the sharpest form before six weeks (say) are over. I am quite *certain* that your heart & mind would go fully with what we are doing. But is there a rift in the Liberal Party? Has Forsterism got among us? Read the speech of Rylands yesterday: the more so because he is a good & honest fellow. He says (if I understand him) 'I denounced your entrance into Egypt as a crime: but *I* tell you evil will befall you if you compromise the advantages which by that crime you have acquired'. *If* we conclude the arrangements we are about (& I hope we shall) we shall have a regular battle of Armageddon upon it.⁵

To LORD NORTHBROOK, first lord of the admiralty,   Add MS 44547, f. 67.
28 May 1884.⁶

I have received & read this morning Sir Cooper Key's very interesting paper on an expedition to Khartoum.⁷ I write however to suggest that it would be a great advantage if two suggestions it contains were to be fully examined & developed.

---

¹ Undated holograph, Add MS 44645, f. 107.

² Word smudged.

³ Perhaps one of the various works of Josse Bade.

⁴ W. C. Smith, *Kildrostan; a dramatic poem* (1884).

⁵ No reply found.

⁶ This letter also send to Dilke, Add MS 43875, f. 164.

⁷ Key favoured a compromise: railway to the hills, camels to Berber, then up the Nile; P. H. Colomb, *Memoirs of . . . Cooper Key* (1898), 468-9.

1. The *small* river expedition which he thinks practicable.

2. The *small* desert expedition from Korosk to which he also adverts as an auxiliary method.

The second is a military matter, but, on the first of these, should not both Sir Cooper Key, & Lord John Hay, who I think has the same idea, set out the particulars of what they think might be done? Pray consider this.

Clear as is the case for the Railway from Suakim as against a large expedition by the Nile, in every other view it is attended with the most formidable difficulties of a moral & political kind, assuming the merely physical difficulties to be easily surmountable. It is I think very doubtful whether, from a practical point of view, the 'turning of the first sod' of a Soudan Railway will not be the substitution for an Egyptian domination there of an English domination over the whole or a part, more immaterial, more costly, more destructive, & altogether without foundation in public right. It would be an immense advantage that the expedition (should one be needed) should be one occupying little time, & leaving no trace behind it.[1]

29. *Th.*

Wrote to Ld Morley—Bp of London—Miss Santley[2]—Reeves & Turner—E. Hamilton—& minutes. Saw Mr Mayhew. Conversation with H. on his affairs. Walk with W. & H. in the beautiful woods. Read Kildrostan—Guthrie on H. Spencer[3]—Bade, L'Art Grec—Mulhall, Dict. of Statistics.[4] Ch. 8½ A.M.

30. *Fr.*

Ch. 8½ A.M. Wrote to E. Hamilton l. & Tel.—Sir C. Dilke—Mr Childers, & minutes. Woodcraft, with three sons. Read Bade—Brugsch, Hist. of Egypt[5]—Kildrostan—Seeley, Expansion of Engl.[6]

To H. C. E. CHILDERS, chancellor of the exchequer,   Add MS 44547, f. 69.
30 May 1884.

I am not sure that I understand Sir John Adye's letter[7]—what is tramway, according to his meaning? And what is the force he contemplates? Any contraction he could effect of War Office ideas would be a good [*sic*], but this letter is too sketchy I fear to be made use of. It will indeed be provoking if, when we have great aims in view by our Egyptian plan, Gordon is again to be trailed across the scent, & the finance of the year to be overset in preparing for a possible need which there is very fair reason to hope may never arise.

---

[1] Northbrook replied, 30 May, Add MS 44267, f. 62, that he expected, but looked to, an expedition 'with thorough repugnance', that the desert expedition was too risky unless Kitchener reported the Mahdi's power on the wane, that the Admiralty was ready: 'the steamers now on the Nile would be sufficient', but that the Nile route was unsatisfactory; that the railway need not go as far as Berber; Northbrook sent Baggally's report, 'about the only man who has been up the Nile to Khartoum'.

[2] Edith Santley, 1860–1926, singer and mystic, m. R. H. Lyttelton, 14 July 84.

[3] M. Guthrie, *On Mr. Spencer's unification of knowledge* (1882).

[4] M. G. Mulhall, *Dictionary of statistics* (1883).

[5] See 3 Jan. 79.

[6] See 27 Dec. 83.

[7] Not found—nor the letter from Childers.

To Sir C. W. DILKE, president of the local government   Add MS 43875, f. 171.
board, 30 May1884.

I have not seen the plan of Colonel Sartorius,[1] & I do not know where to find it. Nor do
I know what may be the weight of his judgment. But undoubtedly if he be a capable man,
& can develop a plan, it ought to be examined at the War Office (not Admiralty) where
you may remember Lord Wolseley contemplated something of the kind for the relief of
Berber. If I had had the paper I would have sent it to Hartington at once; it will save
time if you do it; this note may accompany it if you like.

Suakim & Berber route has utterly beaten Nile route for a larger expedition, & Railway
has also fairly beaten canals. But the question of a small expedition has hardly yet been
touched, while some believe Gordon is or will be free, & there need be no expedition at
all.[2]

31. Sat.

Ch. 8½ A.M. Wrote to Attorney General—Ld Granville—Mary G.—Mr Seymour—Watsons—Mr A.E. West—and minutes. Drove to Halkin: saw the
Church, & walked on the hill. Read Brugsch, Hist. Egypt—Kildrostan (finished)—Extension of England.

To Sir H. JAMES, attorney general, 31 May 1884. '*Private*'.   Add MS 44547, f. 69.

The Cabinet has left it in our hands to accede, if we find it prudent, to the insertion of a
date in the Franchise Bill.[3] Is it the fact that if the Bill were to pass before (a) the end,
(b) the middle of July, the *bulk* of the new voters might come upon the Register? Though
with much confusion and trouble to the operating functionaries.

Please let me know your answer to this. We ought to see, as clearly as we can, how far
the argument for a date is only sustainable as tending to mitigate opposition & avert conflict with the Lords, or how far we can show that it is required by practical convenience
for the making of the measure itself.

There is also the question between November 1st 1885 and January 1st 1886 to consider.

Whits. June One. 1884.

Ch. 8 A.M. (H.C.) 11 A.M. and 6 P.M. Wrote to Mr H. Seymour l. & Tel.—Rev.
Mr Howell—The Queen—Mary G.—& minutes. Read Mary's article: extremely
well done[4]—Paul Bert on the French Church[5]—Fairbairn on Religion[6]—Con-
greg. Jubilee Lectures.[7] Clerical conversation.

---

[1] Plan for a fast expedition of riflemen (see Dilke's docket on this letter) sent by Col. George Sartorius, 1840–1912, who was, with his wife, at Suakin as Baker's principal staff officer.
[2] Dilke sent this letter on to Hartington and Northbrook; Gladstone's docket of 6 June encouraged development of the plan, but nothing further on it found.
[3] The bill originally had the date of royal assent as the date of effect, i.e. before a seats bill could
have passed. On 17 June H. H. Fowler successfully moved 1 January 1885 as the commencement
date (i.e. voters would come onto the new register on 1 January 1886); *H* 289. 627.
[4] Mary Gladstone, 'The Princess Alice's letters', *C.R.*, xlv. 857 (June 1884).
[5] P. Bert in *F.R.*, xli. 781 (June 1884).
[6] A. M. Fairbairn in *C.R.*, xlv. 354 (March 1884).
[7] Perhaps *The jubilee memorial of the Scottish congregational churches* (1849).

2. M.

Ch (H.C.) 9 A.M. Wrote to Ld Granville l.l.—Mr Childers—Ld Morley—Rev. Mr Pennington—Duchess of Sutherland—Ld Northbrook & minutes. Read Brugsch Egypt—Colburn Poems[1]—Miss Macpherson Tr. +[2]—Pennington's Wiclif[3]—Extension of England. Visited the new station. Walk with S. Saw Mr MacColl.

To LORD NORTHBROOK, first lord of the admiralty,   Add MS 44547, f. 70.
2 June 1884. 'Private'.

There are two points in your interesting letter[4] on which I would say a word. I quite agree that we should be most careful to avoid in any case a military reverse, and the military authorities accordingly for the most part (not all) recommend a large force. But they do this not knowing with whom, if at all, they will have to fight: and it is to be remembered that we have referred to Gordon for information and advice, and that he may and probably does know infinitely better than they, and may report to the effect that a small and not a large force ought to be sent.

I earnestly hope that there may be no force at all; but, for the reason I have given, it seems to me that any mode suggested by well-informed & competent persons of acting by a small force ought to be fully examined & considered.

You also say that if Gordon cannot *or will not* come away we shall have to do our best to relieve him. I do not feel certain that I am making more than a verbal criticism on these words when I demur to them for I suppose you would hardly say that if he is able to come & will not come we are to send a force with the certain loss of many lives either to attend his bidding there or even to bring him away by force.

[P.S.] Sir John Adye recommends 'an English Regiment & a few guns', & say 1000 troops from India to guard the line if necessary.

I return Captain Baggallay.[5]

3. Tu.

Ch. 8½ A.M. Wrote to Ld Granville l. & tel.—Acting Editor of the Times[6]—Bishop of St Asaph—Mr J.M. Sing—H. Seymour Tel.—and minutes. Read Ilaria +—Brugsch Hist. of Egypt—Pindar, Nemeans[7]—Curzon on Oxford politics[8]—Expansion of England. We brought down an oak.

4. Wed.

Ch. 8½ A.M. Wrote to Ld Northbrook—Ld Granville—Mr Seymour—Sir H. Wrendfordsley—The Queen and minutes. Read Contemp. on Gordon—Brugsch Hist. Egypt—Humours of Oxford[9]—Thibaut on Musical Art.[10] Woodcraft.

---

[1] *Sic*; untraced.

[2] F. Macpherson, *Poetry of modern Greece* (1884).

[3] A. R. Pennington, *John Wyclif* (1884); letter of thanks at Add MS 44547, f. 70.

[4] Not found.

[5] See 28 May 84n.

[6] On his 1870 article on the war; Add MS 44547, f. 70; apology from Buckle 'for the serious error' in Add MS 44486, f. 231.

[7] i.e. Pindar's Nemean odes.

[8] G. N. Curzon, 'The conservatism of Young Oxford', *Nat. Rev.*, iii. 515 (June 1884).

[9] J. Miller, *The humours of Oxford. A comedy* (1730).

[10] A. F. T. Thibaut, *On purity of musical art*, tr. W. H. Gladstone (1877).

Circulate. I hope my colleagues will not fail to read the Conversation on Gordon in the Contemp. Review for June. The querist is dual. Mr. Bunting, Editor of the Review, and Mr Chesson, well known in Slavery & peace matters. The [anonymous] respondent is Sir H. Gordon: and the paper illustrates the *whole* Gordon question, especially the mind with which Gordon is, voluntarily according to Sir H. G., remaining at Khartoum. WEG. Ju. 4. 84.[1]

To LORD NORTHBROOK, first lord of the admiralty,   Add MS 44547, f. 70.
4 June 1884.

I return Sir Cooper Key's letter with thanks: and I am glad to see that according to him 15 miles of Rail would suffice.[2]

I have grave doubts whether we shall arrive at a state of facts which will warrant an expedition: and if, as may or may not be right, there is to be preparation for the contingency, it must be in a great degree speculative. It seems pretty clear that it would be a misfortune to upset the finance of the year by an effort of this kind, and this the smaller mileage might avoid.

As regards impression, which in the eyes of many is the chief advantage, all mileages are alike.

5. *Th.*

Ch. 8½ A.M. Wrote to J. Watson & Smith—Mr Seymour Tel.—Reeves & Turner—Ld Granville—& minutes. Read Morley on The Month[3]—Pindar, Nemean Odes—Expansion of England—Thibaut on Musical Art. Egyptian correspondence still troubled, especially *within* the Cabinet. But the path of right was never clearer, if we can only hold off collateral & cross questions. Woodcraft with W. & H.

6. *Fr.*

Ch. 8½ A.M. Wrote to Mr Seymour Tel. & l.—Att. General—Ch. of Exchr—Rev. Mr Jones Tel.—Dr Schliemann—Ld Granville—& minutes. We brought down a fine Spanish chestnut. Conversation with Harry on property arrangements. And on his recent matters. Sat to Mayall, Photographer. Read Expansion of England—Schliemann's Orchomenos[4]—Thibaut on Musical Art.

To H. C. E. CHILDERS, chancellor of the exchequer,   Add MS 44547, f. 71.
6 June 1884.

I am not sure that I clearly understand the inclosed note by Seymour of what he supposes you to have said on the 15 miles suggested for the inception of a Railway. Does it mean that *any bit of Railway large or small means & involves an expedition?* If it does, then there is, in my opinion, no case for such a measure. *If* it can be defended as a mere

---

[1] Add MS 56452, f. 48. 'The position of General Gordon: a conversation', *C.R.*, xlv. 866 (June 1884); see also Ramm II, ii. 217.

[2] Key's comment on copy of Northbrook's letter (see 28 May 84n.), Add MS 44267, f. 68.

[3] J. Morley in *Macmillan's Magazine*, 1. 147 (June 1884).

[4] By H. Schliemann (1881).

preparation for a contingency, then surely it becomes most important that any vote to be asked at once should be only of such an amount as not to break up the year's finance.[1]

7. Sat.

Ch. 8½ A.M. Wrote to Ld Granville l.l.l. and Tel.—the Queen l. & Tel l.l.—Mr J. Wilson—Ld Morley—Mr Hamilton Tel.—and minutes. Read Pindar Nem. (rather too hard for my somewhat wearied brain)—Expansion of England— Newman's Poems.[2] Sat to Mayall. Drive with Edith & much family conversation. A heavy day of business.

8. Trin. S.

Ch. 8 A.M. for H.C. 11 AM. 6½ PM. Wrote to The Queen Tel.—Ld Granville do—Ld R. Grosvenor do—Mr Childers—Ld Grey—and minutes. Conversation with H. and H. on Egypt: a holy subject. Conversation with Mr M'Coll on Palmer. Read Fairbairn—Drummond—Kirkman on the Kingdom of God[3]—& [blank.]

To H. C. E. CHILDERS, chancellor of the exchequer,　　　　Add MS 44547, f. 72.
8 June 1884.

Do you consider that (in round numbers) 300 m[ille] can be taken without disturbing your finance & creating a call for taxation?[4] Do you think it visionary to hold that a preparation for a contingency may be made, & yet the conditions defining the arrival of the contingency may be resolutely held by? And to what practical course do you incline with regard to this awkward & slippery subject of an experimental link? As to a real case for an expedition, I think the odds are seriously against its occurring, though no doubt it may occur.
[P.S.] In a *month* more we ought to hear *per Zebehr* from Gordon: & one would say any preparations now ordered ought at any rate to be limited to what would fill that month.

To 3rd EARL GREY, 8 June 1884.　　　　　　　　　　Add MS 44547, f. 72.

Your recollection of Cabinet practice goes further back than that of any other living man, & on this account I take the liberty of asking whether your memory serves you as to any particulars connected with the form of what is termed a Minute of Cabinet? In particular, is it signed by the Ministers individually?
This form of document has gone very much out of use, but it appears to have some recommendations for exceptional cases & thinking so I take the chance of being enabled by your courtesy to make up the deficiencies of my own recollection by an appeal to yours.[5]

---

[1] Childers replied, 7 June, Add MS 44131, f. 82: any expenditure on a railway from Suakin was 'a new service' requiring parlt. sanction and thus open to debate.
[2] See 16 Jan. 48.　　　　　　　　　　　　　　[3] One of T. P. Kirkman's many papers.
[4] Childers replied, 9 June, Add MS 44131, f. 84: 'we might add £300,000 to the Estimates without fresh taxation; but not more'; he had not seen 'fair proof of the reasonableness of the preparation'; if he had, he would ask for 'much more'.
[5] Grey replied, 10 June, Add MS 44486, f. 242, that until the regency 'it was the practice invariably to record all the important decisions of the Cabinet in minutes which were submitted to the King', that his father revived this practice, minutes being written 'in the Cabinet room by my father himself & read over by him to his colleagues before they separated'; Melbourne dropped minuting. Grey's reply in full, misdated as 1892, in *The Gladstone Papers* (1930), 105. See 11 June 84.

9. M. [London]

Ch. 8½ A.M. It was crowded: & most touching. Preparations: & off at 10.15 AM. D. St. 3.10 P.M. Cabinet to 4.30 P.M. H of C. 5–12¾ (½ h for dinner). Franchise Bill.[1] Read Backhouse on French Protestants[2]—M. Wallace on Egypt.[3] Saw Mr H–Ld R.G—Mr M'Coll—Mr Rathbone. Wrote to The Queen l.l.—and minutes.

Cabinet. Monday June 9. 84. 3 PM.[4]
1. WEGs answer to Bourke today agreed on.[5]
2. What reply shall be made about proposals[.] No proposal to send Turks into the Soudan. Some further correspondence has taken place on the matter already mentioned in the Blue Book with regard to certain of the Red Sea ports but it has not made any progress.
3. Formulation of the proceedings with France. Ld Gr. read Waddington's dispatch.

10. Tu.

Wrote to The Queen l.l.l.—Mr Woodall—Sir J. Hay—Mr Firth—and minutes. H of C. 2–7 (Cabinet intermixed). Franchise Bill: much speaking.[6] Saw Mr H—Ld R.G—Ld Granville—Sir W. Harcourt—Sir C. Dilke—Ld Hartington—Mrs Bolton. Dined with Lady F.C. Read Old Town Folks.[7]

[Cabinet] Tues. June 10. 84. 4 PM. H of C.[8]
1. Communication from Caine[9] & respecting Woman suffrage. Apart from Bill, it will of course be open.
2. RR. from Suakim. Hartington now uncertain whether RR can be completed within the winter.
   Suggested certain preparatory measures to be on the basis of a paper from Sir A. Clark[10]—wh do not imply an expedition but wd save time in case one should be found necessary.
   Cabinet will place on record the view with which they adopt these measures.
3. Cabinet (WEG absent in House) received Ld Gr's last operation with M. Waddington.

To W. WOODALL, M.P., 10 June 1884.   Add MS 44547, f. 72.

In acknowledging the receipt of your letter,[11] let me say that I am very sensible of the kindness of its tone, of the singleness of your motives, of your thorough attachment to the Franchise Bill, of the weight due to the signatures you have placed before me, and of the just title which your subject possesses to full consideration at the proper time.

[1] And questions; *H* 288. 1787.
[2] J. Backhouse, 'A lecture on French protestantism' (1884).
[3] Sir D. Mackenzie Wallace, *Egypt and the Egyptian question* (1883).
[4] Add MS 44645, f. 109; draft of it at Add MS 56452, f. 50.
[5] On the Conference; *H* 288. 1787; draft answer at Add MS 44645, f. 111.
[6] Including opposing as inexpedient Woodall's amndt. for women's suffrage; *H* 288. 1957.
[7] See 19 May 84.
[8] Add MS 44645, f. 112.
[9] Presumably W. S. Caine, M.P., but letter untraced.
[10] Mem. of 19 May by Sir A. Clarke, inspector general of fortifications; see J. Symons, *England's pride* (1965), 68–9. Instructions for preparations for Suakin-Berber railway given on 14 June; *Relief of Gordon*, xxx.
[11] With a memorial; on women's suffrage amndt., Add MS 44486, f. 238.

But the question with what subjects, viewing the actual state of business and of parties, we can afford to deal in and by the Franchise Bill, is a question in regard to which the undivided responsibility rests with the Government, and cannot be devolved by them on any section, however respected, of the House of Commons.

They have introduced into the Bill as much as in their opinion it can safely carry. The introduction of what it cannot safely carry endangers a measure which the heart and mind of the country alike desire. Assent to such introduction would therefore on our part be a breach of duty to the Bill and to the nation.

11. Wed. St Barnabas

Wrote to Ld Derby—Lord Grey—Mr Wilson—and minutes. Saw Mr H—Ld RG—Herbert G—Lady Holken—Rivingtons. Thirteen to dinner: & large evening party. Saw Musurus Pacha—Madame Novikoff—Mr Buckle—Lady L. Egerton—and others. Read Bithell on Agnosticism[1]—Plerling's [sic] Un Nonce du Pape[2]—Tudor on Orkneys[3] &c.

To LORD DERBY, colonial secretary, 11 June 1884.   Add MS 44547, f. 72.

I cannot help being much struck with Bulwer's letter of May 6th. By these three matters in particular so frankly stated—1. The leaders of the Asutus have thrown themselves into the hands of the Boers. 2. No way of action visible except an arrangement with the Boers. 3. It is not for the Empire, nor for humanity, that we have a concern in Zululand beyond the reserve but because it affords a solution for the native question in Natal. I also observe 4. The Free State is indicated as in the same boat with the Transvaal *quoad* this question. Does not this seem like an opportunity for settling our Zululand difficulties by a friendly arrangement with the Dutch element, much easier I should hope if we have to deal with the Free State also, than if we had to deal with the Transvaal alone. Is it unreasonable to think that as the Dutch have Africa for their country, as they went out from the Cape greatly to our relief, as they have solved the native question within their own borders, they are perhaps better qualified to solve the Zulu question outside the Reserve, than we can in dealing with it from Downing Street? If Natal were a real self governing colony it would be another matter.[4]

To 3rd EARL GREY, 11 June 1884.   Add MS 44486, f. 246.

Your interesting letter[5] claims my cordial thanks. On one point only would I trouble you further. Do you know whether, *or ever*, Minutes of Cabinet were signed by members of the Cabinet?

The present practice does not of necessity exclude minutes of Cabinet, but is in itself very inferior to that which formerly prevailed, and which, I must with regret believe, has now become impossible through the great increase, during the last half century, of the volume of public business.

When I first became Prime Minister, the Queen apprised me that she would expect to hear from me after every Cabinet; and this practice which I presume to have been established for some time, is the only formal substitute for the old & more satisfactory one.

---

[1] R. Bithell, *The creed of a modern agnostic* (1883).
[2] P. Perling, *Un nonce du pape [A. Possevino] en Muscovie préliminaires de la trève de 1582* (1884).
[3] J. R. Tudor, *The Orkneys and Shetland* (1883).
[4] No reply found.
[5] See 8 June 84n.

I have myself added to it what I had never before seen, namely the hasty noting down, scratching rather than writing, on paper the heads of business as it goes on, so that I may not have to rely solely on my memory. Also I do not think that in any case my report to the Queen has been delayed for as much as twelve hours after a Cabinet Council.

But the word 'slipshod' is I fear the best description of the manner (not the method) which comes more & more to prevail in the transaction of some parts of the public business.[1]

12. Th.

Wrote to Mad. Novikoff—Musurus Pacha—Watsons—The Queen l.l.—Sir H. Ponsonby, & minutes. Luncheon at Mad. Novikoff's: saw Count Beust. Visited Christie's. Saw Mr H—Lord R.G—Mr Davis—Sir W. James. Determined to republish Egyptian article of 1877: & wrote preface to it.[2] H of C. $4\frac{1}{4}$-$8\frac{1}{4}$ and $9\frac{1}{2}$-$11\frac{3}{4}$.[3] Read Old Town Folks—Plerling Un Nonce du Pape.

13. Fr.

Wrote to Ld Hartington l.l.—Bp of London—The Queen l.l.—Mr Waddington—Ld Coleridge—and minutes.[4] H of C. $2\frac{1}{4}$-7 Franchise Bill &c.[5] Saw Mr H—Ld RG—Abp of Canterbury—Conclave on Provostship of Eton—Ld Hartington—Mr Goschen—Sir W. Harcourt—Sir C. Dilke. H of C. $2\frac{1}{4}$-7 and $10\frac{3}{4}$-$12\frac{1}{2}$. Dined at Stafford House. Read Plerling—Old town folks.

14. Sat. [The Deanery, Windsor]

Wrote to Ld Granville—The Queen—& minutes. Cabinet 2-$4\frac{1}{2}$. Saw Mr H—Ld RG—Herbert & Harry Saw M. Waddington at noon. Off to the Deanery at Windsor by 5.10 train. Walk & much conversation with the Dean,[6] who opens upon me at every step. Dinner party. Saw Sir H. Ponsonby: Miss P. Read The Entailed Hat[7]—Plerling. Saw Mr H—Lord RG—Herbert J.G. (Egypt)—M.G. respecting G. Russell.

Cabinet. 18 Carlton H. Terrace. Sat. Jun. 14 1884. 2 PM[8]
1. M. Waddington's communication to W.E.G. at noon today, & his coming[?] repetition to Ld G. 1. Shall we insist? 2. Shall we accept the suggestion to carry it to the Powers? 3. Shall we give in (on the casting vote [on the Caisse])
Granville went to Waddington—will ask Ferry to reconsider 1. because of our sacrifices 2. to secure the course of business 3. For Parliamentary security for our plan.

[1] Grey replied, 12 June, Add MS 44486, f. 259: 'Cabinet minutes were never signed'.
[2] 'Aggression on Egypt', see 21 July 77 and above ix. xxxix-xl; republished, with a preface, by the National Press Agency (1884).
[3] Reform Bill cttee.; Woodall amndt. on female suffrage defeated (see 24 May 84n.); H 289. 92.
[4] Cabinet circularised: resignation not to be required of Dilke, Fawcett and Courtney (abstainers on female suffrage, see 24 May 84n.): 'crisis on a question of Foreign affairs ... [involving] possibly even the peace of Europe' made resignations inapposite; Add MS 44768, f. 51.
[5] And questioned on Sudan; H 289. 246.
[6] i.e. now R. T. Davidson.
[7] G. A. Townsend, The entailed hat (1884).
[8] Add MS 44645, f. 114.

Granville asks whether we will agree to let the matter go to the Powers with an understanding that France will support it. Waddington will refer to his Govt.[1]

2. Hartington proposes to restore Baker to the list (not for active service) but to make his commission saleable.[2] Discussion thereon.

3. Angra Pekueha [*sc.* Pequeña]—discussion as to assurance to Germany.[3]

15. 1 S. Trin.

St Georges 11 AM. with H.C. & 5 P.M. Walk & further conversation with the Dean. Saw Mr Parrot. Read Oxenham, Studies[4]—Lilly on Ancient Religion & Modern Thought.[5]

16. M. [London]

Wrote to Chancr of Exr—Mr Courtney—Mr Fawcett—Ld Granville ll—Sir R. Peel—Sir F. Leighton—Sir J. Hay—The Queen—and minutes. Back to London by 10.30. Saw Mr H—Ld RG—Ld Granville—Mr Childers—Sir H. Ponsonby—Miss Ponsonby—Mr Chamberlain—Ld Wolverton—Mr Stephenson. H. of C. 5-8 and 10-12½.[6] Wolverton, R. Lyttelton, Miss Santley dined. It looks happy. Read Lilly—Old Town Folks.

To H. C. E. CHILDERS, chancellor of the exchequer,   Add MS 44547, f. 73.
16 June 1884. '*Secret*'.

The account in the Daily News, which I have only just seen, has such an appearance of good authority on the side of France that it opens to me a new view as to your 8⋔ proposal.[7] I think it most difficult to change that proposal seriously, after all that has passed with France, *in invitam* (sic), but if they take the view, as they justly may, that the large sum may help to keep us in Egypt, & consequently are not unwilling that our direct pecuniary liability should be reduced, then indeed a door is open to you for what would, as it seems pretty plainly, be a great Parliamentary improvement.[8]

17. Tu.

Wrote to The Queen—Marchesa Bianchi—Miss Lambert—& minutes. H of C. 2-7 (Franchise) and at 9½ on Mr Stephenson.[9] Saw Mr H—Ld R. Grosvenor—Chancr of Exr—Ld Halifax. Thirteen to dinner. Read Old Town Folks.

---

[1] *Résumé* of the conversation in *PP* lxxxix. 118-20.

[2] i.e. 'shall he be restored to the retired list which carries with it repaying him the value of his Commission?'; Monk Bretton 62.

[3] 'G. to see Herbert Bismark & ask him what it is German Govt. want'; ibid. Exchange this day between H. Bismarck and Granville in F.O.C.P. 5060, ff. 44-6.

[4] H. N. Oxenham, *Short studies in ecclesiastical history and biography* (1884).

[5] W. S. Lilly, *Ancient religion and modern thought* (1884).

[6] Supply; *H* 289. 427.

[7] *D.N.*, 16 June 1884, 5f: correspondent understands that Ferry uneasy about a British guaranteed loan, as offering an excuse for staying in Egypt.

[8] Childers preferred a loan of £5 million to the Khedive and the payment of ¾ of the indemnity, to a loan of £8 million; Add MS 44131, f. 88.

[9] Spoke on J. C. Stevenson's motion on private member's bill; *H* 289. 661.

18. Wed.

Wrote to Mr A. Bartlett—The Duke of Bedford—Scotts—Rev. Mr Spurgeon—
The Queen—and minutes. Tea with E. H[amilton] at 5 (Miss Terry).[1] Worked
on papers & accounts. Saw Mr H—Ld R.G—C. of E.—and in evg Musurus,
Münster, Carolyi—Count Cantacuzene.[2] Visited Ld Albemarle, 85 today. Large
evg party $10\frac{1}{4}$-$12\frac{1}{4}$. Exhausting enough. Dined with Lucy. Read P. Smyth on
Pyramid[3]—Old Town Folks.

To the DUKE OF BEDFORD, 18 June 1884. '*Private*'.   Add MS 44547, f. 74.

I understand that some question has arisen whether George Russell should stand at
the next election for the county of Bedford.

You will not suspect me of the impertinence of seeking to interfere in a matter with
which you have a legitimate & principal concern, and I have no title or *locus standi* whatever. All that I seek to do by means of these few lines is to convey to you, as the head of
your historic house, my testimony on the only point connected with the case, in respect
to which your means of judgment are not very far superior to mine.

I refer of course to his performances and prospects in the House of Commons. He was
appointed to his office entirely for his merits, and not for his birth, and, young as he was,
he was within an ace of receiving a still earlier offer. I will say nothing of his general
character, culture, and capacity, because these important points come under the description where I have promised silence. But he has shown a faculty of speech, which is not
only beyond the common run, but is in my judgment altogether remarkable. I should
place him first among men of his age in the House of Commons. I think he promises to
do high honour even to your family, and to be the Steward & continuation of its fame.
Having now deposited my evidence in your keeping, I beg you not to take the trouble of
answering this letter.[4]

19. Th.

Wrote to The Queen—Ld Hartington—Sir R. Peel—Abp of Canterb.—Ld Gran-
ville—and minutes. Ten to dinner. H of C. 5-$8\frac{1}{2}$ & $9\frac{1}{2}$-$12\frac{1}{2}$.[5] Thirteen to breakfast.
Saw Mr H—Ld RG—Ld Hampden—Mr Godley—Sir F. Leighton—Ld Gran-
ville—Dean of Windsor. At 11 PM attended the curious Thought-reading of Mr
Cumberland at H. of C. To call it imposture is, as it seems to me, nonsense. I
was myself operated upon.[6] Read Old Town Folks—Martin on Cremation.[7]

---

[1] See Bahlman, *Hamilton*, ii. 639.
[2] Prince G. Cantacuzene, counsellor of Russian embassy in London 1884-5.
[3] C. P. Smyth, *Our inheritance in the Great Pyramid* (4th ed. 1880).
[4] Bedford replied next day, Add MS 44486, f. 281, that he could not support G. Russell; he 'is an
ultra radical politician and I am a Whig'. Russell unsuccessfully contested Fulham in 1885 and 1886,
but sat for N. Beds. from 1892.
[5] Questioned on Sudan; *H* 289. 827.
[6] Demonstration to about 50 M.P.s; Gladstone's number (366) was correctly guessed, as was
Stanhope's (41,049); *T.T.*, 20 June 1884, 8c.
[7] F. Martin, *Cimetières et crémation; étude historique et critique* (1881).

20. Fr.

Wrote to Mr Biddell MP—Rev. Mr MacColl—Ld Granville—The Queen—and minutes. Saw Mr H—Ld RG—Ld Granville—Mr Childers. H of C. 6¼ and 9.[1] Worked on Egyptian papers. Luncheon at 16 G. Square. Read Old Town Folks—Brewers Hist. H. VIII.—Opening of Brooklyn Bridge.[2]—Scots Families in Scandinavia[3]—& Tracts. Saw Tait [R].

21. Sat. [Combe Wood, Kingston-on-Thames]

Wrote to The Queen—& minutes. Read Colomba—F. Cenci e la sua famiglia.[4] Cabinet 12-3¼. Important. Saw Mr H—Ld R.G—C. of E.—Ld Granville. Went at 4 to (Combe Wood) Wolverton's charming villa. Conversation with him: making *confidences.*

Cabinet. Sat. June 21. 1884. Noon.[5]
1. Blenheim Pictures. Offer to be made for the Raphael—70m[ille] or for the three 100m. Childers writes—WEG signs.[6]
2. Childers on Eg. Finance. Committee (Baring, Blum P[asha],[7] [J.M.] Carmichael, R. Wilson, Welby) have reported.[8] Abstract read. 9,086m & gross. 8836 Nett Revenue. 9192 expenditure. Deficit 356m £. (Doubts on the deduction of 250m)[9]
3. Angra Pequeña.[10]

[11]*Egyptian Finance* 1. Charge ½ per cent on Privileged. 2. ½ *vice* 1½ to be charged on Suez Canal Bond interest. 3. Find the whole 8₥ by guarantee.[12] 4. Increase[?] Sinking Fund on 8₥ if possible.

22. 2 S. Trin.

Kingston Ch mg, Combe Ch evg. Saw Sir R. Welby—Mr Leadam. Read Vicar of Newton—Oxenham's Studies.

---

[1] Misc. business; *H* 289. 976.
[2] *The Brooklyn Bridge. A history ... with an account of the opening* (1883).
[3] Not found.
[4] A. Bertolotti, *Francesco Cenci e la sua famiglia* (1879).
[5] Add MS 44645, f. 117.
[6] Marlborough wanted 550,000 guineas for 11 pictures; the National Gallery trustees were particularly interested in Raphael's *Madonna degli Ansidei*, Van Dyck's *Charles I* and two Rubens. G. Howard expected Marlborough to settle for 300,000 guineas; Agnew's estimate was 250,000 (Add MS 44486, 256). This day's Cabinet decided for £70,000 for the Raphael or £100,000 for the Raphael, the Van Dyck and one Rubens; on 30 June Howard urged £140,000 for the Raphael and the Van Dyck; Gladstone docketed the letter 'Yes. Jul 1'; ibid., f. 321. The National Gallery paid £70,000 for the Raphael and £15,000 for the Van Dyck.
[7] An Austrian who was Egyptian financial secretary until 1889; Cromer, ii. 291.
[8] Reports in F.O.C.P. 4990.
[9] Jottings of figure omitted.
[10] 'No objection could be taken to the claim, or intention, of the German Government to provide means of protection for German subjects'; CAB 41/18/33 and F.O.C.P. 5060, f. 46.
[11] Add MS 44645, f. 119.
[12] i.e. the loan to be merely guaranteed, not advanced by Britain.

23. M. [London]

Wrote to The Queen l.l.—Earl Spencer—Mr Pease—and minutes. Read Francesco Cenci &c. Came up from Combe Wood at 11.30. Saw Mr H—Ld RG—Ld Granville. H of C. $4\frac{3}{4}$-$8\frac{1}{4}$ & 9-$1\frac{1}{4}$. I was much oppressed beforehand with the responsibility of my statement upon Egypt: but pleased with the reception of it & the subsequent course of the debate.[1] God is good: & I feel strong in the belief that we have the interests of justice, peace, & freedom in our hands. Worked on Egyptian papers.

24. Tu. St Joh Bapt

Wrote to The Queen l.l.l.l.—Ld Granville—and minutes. H of C. Cabinet 2–7. Dined at the French Embassy. Saw Mr H—Ld R.G—Lord Granville—The French Ambassador—Count D'Aubigny. Lady Cowper's party in evg. Read Francesco Cenci.

Cabinet. H. of C. Tues. June 24. 1884. 3 PM[2]
1. Egyptian Finance. Domains Loan[3] & General Balance 174m? Deduction of $\frac{1}{2}$% from Domains Loan as well as the other considered: & mentioned in plan sent to powers. Sir E. Baring attended. Interruption by H of Lords business.

25. Wed.

Wrote to Mr A. Denison—Mr Boyd Carpenter—& minutes. Attended the marriage of Hallam Tennyson in the Abbey[4] & saw the party afterwards at Lady S. Spencers. Visited Tait: with some hope of good [R]. Saw Mr H—Ld R.G. Dined at Ld Carrington's & went to see the Rivals: Mr Pinero rather below the mark.[5] Read Old Town Folks.

To Sir F. LEIGHTON, president of the Royal Academy, 25 June 1884.   RAC 5/26.

I thank you for your letter,[6] and my advice, tendered as you know in no unfriendly spirit, will I hope not be unacceptable to you. It would be to the effect that you should if possible give anew all that has been given before, but give it by way of voluntary communication, in whatever terms you think fit, addressed to me or to the Home Secretary as you may prefer.

The fact is, as far [as] I know, that there is no ill feeling, no misgiving, in the House, about the Royal Academy; but that the real interest felt by it, & by the public, in your proceedings would make an offering of information to the country through the Crown, by your own spontaneous act, a graceful & also an useful proceeding.

[P.S.] If you agree with this, I will write to Sir R. Peel accordingly.

[1] Gladstone's statement on the proposed Conference on Egyptian finance; *H* 289. 1104, 1142.
[2] Add MS 44645, f. 121.
[3] Loan of £8.5 million secured on the Domains negotiated with Rothschild 1878; Cromer, ii. 314.
[4] He m. Audrey Boyle.
[5] (Sir) Arthur Wing *Pinero, 1855-1934; actor and dramatist.
[6] Of 24 June, RAC 5/25; on Sir R. Peel's complaints about the Academy's returns; Gladstone defended the Academy on 29 July, though without the full information; *H* 291. 871. See also *H* 289. 1689.

26. Th.

Wrote to Mr G. Howard—Messrs Watson—Mrs Th.—Ld Walsingham—The
Queen l.l.—Ld R. Grosvenor Tel. & minutes. Thirteen to breakfast. Attended
Council at Windsor. Had audience of H.M. Saw Sir W. Harcourt—Ld Carling-
ford—Mr H.—Sir H. Ponsonby—Ld R.G. Back at $4\frac{3}{4}$ to infinite questioning.
Spoke on 3rd reading of Franchise Bill: under a deep sense of necessity. H of C.
$5-8\frac{1}{2}$ & $9\frac{3}{4}-11$.[1] Read Old Town Folks—M. Ferry's Speech.[2]

27. Fr.

Wrote to Mr Arnold MP—The Queen l.l.—& minutes. H of C. 2-5 and $9-12\frac{1}{2}$
(Cropless).[3] Cabinet 12-2. Tried as others did to draw amendments: but all
failed. Saw Mr H—Ld R.G (l.l.l)—Rev. Mr Cartwright—Mr Mundella—Sir W.
Harcourt. Drive with C. Read Francesco Cenci—Hamilton Clerke on Public
Speaking.[4]

Cabinet. Jun. 27. 1884. Noon.[5]
1. Vote of Censure—how to meet? By direct negative.[6]
2. Shall the Finance assume Egypt in or out of the Red Sea Ports? *Out.*
3. And on a prior Egyptian army—or one partly mercenary wh costs more. Take the
larger estimate.
4. Australia. Fresh alarm about New Guinea from Bismarck's announcement.[7] Postponement.

To Sir W. V. HARCOURT, home secretary,   MS Harcourt dep. Adds 10.
27 June 1884.

I have got your second communication.[8]
The authority of the Secretary of State is without doubt great in Scotch affairs, & you
may be sure this will be felt. But I think the matter can only be settled by the Cabinet if
two of its members do not agree. This can hardly be done tomorrow & I take it for
granted Carlingford will put off the Bill till we pass or are drowned in the Red Sea.

28. Sat. [Combe Hurst, Kingston Hill]

Wrote to Ld Granville l.l.—Sir W. Harcourt—Rev. A. Cartwright—Ld Carlingford—Ld Hartington—and minutes. Saw Mr H—Ld RG—Sir Thos G.—Ld Wol-
verton. Off at $12\frac{3}{4}$ to Vyner's: feeling more like a stone than a man. Drove in

[1] *H* 289. 1432: a quarrel with the Lords would be 'the most serious prospect' since the Corn
Laws.
[2] On an Egyptian settlement: France would not insist on dual control and would not occupy
Egypt if Britain withdrew; *D.T.*, 24 June 1884, 5d.
[3] i.e. no achievement: House counted out; *H* 289. 1639.
[4] Name scrawled; untraced.
[5] Add MS 44645, f. 125.
[6] Various draft amendments, preferred by Gladstone to direct negative, ibid., ff. 127–36; further
note on the procedure at Add MS 56452, f. 61.
[7] i.e. on Angra Pequeña which 'has excited Australians. If we swallow New Guinea we must give
French their head as to New Hebrides, provided that they do not send convicts there'; Dodson's
note, Monk Bretton 62.
[8] Not found. See next day.

Richmond Park with Mrs V. Small dinner party. Read Francesco Cenci—Dissolving Views. Memories of my dear Sister.[1] Requiescat in Domino.

To Sir W. V. HARCOURT, home secretary,   MS Harcourt dep. Adds 10.
28 June 1884.

I have received your Memorandum[2] & under the circs. have thought the best thing I could do was to write as within to Carlingford.

On the one hand I had not been aware of your having given any pledge. On the other I can assure you that a bill's having been circulated without objection in no degree commits the Cabinet.

This I learned 41 years ago from my colleagues in the Cabinet of Sir R. Peel.

To LORD HARTINGTON, war secretary, 28 June 1884.   Add MS 44547, f. 76.

I need not trouble you with a long reply.[3]

1. We ought not I think to press you to speak on this occasion, after all the good service you have done before.

2. Without derogating from this idea, I think I can remove any difficulty arising from the declaration you suppose me to have made.

I never said M. Ferry's description of the agreement was full & true, knowing as I do that on a point of very great importance we are ostensibly, perhaps really, at issue.

I said his account of the Caisse was full & true. From your remarks I almost doubt whether you have read it *in extenso*. He laid down strongly its essential difference from the control. What I said of the passage you refer to was that it contained no error of fact, & this is strictly accurate.

3. I do not think the approval of the police telegram had proceeded quite so far as you imagine.

4. As to our stay in Egypt, the formidable change which the defeat of Hicks brought about in its probable duration made it quite necessary, I think, to recognise that the territorial occupation of Egypt cannot be severed from the action of international law established in 1856 & 1878.

5. If you ask me now about our *condominium*, my reply is that I think it can only stand upon condonation.[4]

29. St Peter.

Ch. St Matthias Richmond mg: & the near Church evg. Saw Ld Granville—The Goldsmids—Conversation with Mrs Vyner. Saw Miss Chamberlain: *naïve* to a degree. Read Oxenham on O.T.—Power on Elijah[5]—SPCK on Prayerbook.

[1] [A. Gauntlett], *Dissolving views. A novel* (1849); the fate of a convert to Roman catholicism, like his sister Helen.

[2] On the Scottish Ministers Bill; Add MS 44199, f. 48; copy of note to Carlingford asking him to suspend circulation of his note until Egypt dealt with; MS Harcourt dep. Adds 8.

[3] No letter found; clearly a criticism of Gladstone's statement on 23 June 84.

[4] Hartington asked for a short cabinet as 'I really do not feel that I know the mind or intention of the Govt. in respect of the relief of Gen. Gordon'; 1 July, Add MS 44147, f. 82.

[5] Probably one of P. B. Power's many tracts.

30. M. [London]

Back in D St at 11. Wrote to Mr Samuelson MP.—Chancr of Exr—The Queen ll—Ld Granville—and minutes. Saw Mr H—Ld R.G—Conclave at H. of C.—Sir W. Harcourt—Sir C. Dilke—Ld Granville—Mr Goschen. H of C. $4\frac{3}{4}$–$8\frac{1}{4}$ and $9\frac{1}{4}$–11. Voted in 138 against 190, the majority right, but I was bound.[1] Very glad but much tired without any justification except a little lumbago.[2] Read Francesco Cenci.

Tues. Jul 1. 1884.

Wrote to Sir W. Harcourt—Mr Childers—Mrs Vyner—Ld Carlingford—Prof. Roscoe[3]—Provost [Okes] of Kings—Mr Firth—and minutes. Fifteen to dinner: large & exhausting evening party, tho' c. tenderly sent me off at 11.40. Saw Mr H—Ld RG—Mr Curzon—Ld Granville—Ld Normanby—do *cum* Ld Northbrook. Read Francesco Cenci—Defence of Lay Patronage[4]—Old Town folks. Went to see Louey. In the body she is indeed a mournful spectacle: but surely her soul is anchored fast.[5]

To LORD CARLINGFORD, lord president and lord   Carlingford MSS CP1/226.
privy seal, 1 July 1884. '*Private*'.

I regret extremely the difference of opinion which arose between you & Harcourt as to Scotch Education,[6] & I did & said, as you would have learned in due course, all that I could to avert any collision.

I do not know what may hereafter happen, as I have not heard from Harcourt since your division last night, but I think as matters now stand you have the more solid share in the division of the spoil.

2. Wed.

Wrote to Mr M'Coll—Ld Hartington—Ld Granville—Archbp of Canterbury (& dft) l.l.—Bishops of London (ChCh Padd.), Winchester, Chichester, Manchester, Salisbury, Bath & Wells, Carlisle, Ely, Oxford, Bangor, Durham, Exeter, St Asaph—and minutes. Saw Mr H—Ld R.G—Chancr of Exr—Mr L. Morris—Sir Farrar. Dined at Miss Swanwicks.[7] Read Sir S. Baker on Soudan[8]—Dicey on Egypt[9]—Sir L. Griffin on America[10]—Francesco Cenci.

---

[1] *H* 289. 1698 gives 148:190 as the vote on the motion for an immediate censure debate.
[2] 'P.M. in such spirits, he sang "My heart is true to Poll" all thro' dinner'; *Mary Gladstone*, 321.
[3] Knighthood for (Sir) Henry Enfield *Roscoe, 1833–1915; chemistry professor at Owen's College 1857–87; liberal M.P. S. Manchester 1885–95.
[4] Untraced tract.
[5] Louisa, da. of Sir T. Gladstone; she d. 12 January 1885.
[6] On future control of Scottish education; see to Harcourt, 29 June, Add MS 44547, f. 76.
[7] Anna *Swanwick, 1813–99; educationalist and author.
[8] S. W. Baker, 'The Soudan and its future', *C.R.*, xlv. 65 (January 1884).
[9] E. Dicey, 'The surrender of Egypt', *N.C.*, xvi. 156 (July 1884).
[10] L. H. Griffin, *The Great Republic* (1884).

To E. W. BENSON, archbishop of Canterbury,   Add MSS 44109, f. 97, 44547, f. 77.
2 July 1884. '*Private and Confidential*'.

[*First letter*:]   I should have felt repugnance and scruple about addressing your Grace at any time on any subject of a political nature, if it were confined within the ordinary limits of such subjects. But it seems impossible to refuse credit to the accounts which assure us that the Peers of the Opposition, under Lord Salisbury and his coadjutors, are determined to use all their strength and influence for the purpose of throwing out the Franchise Bill in the House of Lords; and thus entering upon a conflict with the House of Commons, from which at each step in the proceeding it may probably become more & more difficult to retire, & which if left to its natural course will probably develop itself into a constitutional crisis of such an order as has not occurred since 1832.

It is undoubtedly true that the House of Lords has a perfect competence, and in that sense a perfect right, in the exercise of an independent judgment, to throw out this, and likewise, if it see fit, to throw out *every* other Bill. But want of wisdom and moderation in the use of a civil or political right may bring into question the right itself.

Mindful of our duty to do all in our power for the purpose of arresting collision, we have presented a Bill large indeed but studiously moderate[1] which in Great Britain enfranchises classes in the counties that have already been beneficially enfranchised in the towns, and only adds, by what is called the servant franchise, a class which of all others is most likely to be swayed by the influence of property. Of Ireland I say nothing, because the assailants in the Lords do not venture to say that she could be excluded from the Bill.

When in 1832 the House of Lords by an indirect motion endeavoured to defeat the Reform Bill it had to undergo the painful process of submitting to pass the measure under the threat of an overwhelming creation of Peers. Again an indirect method is adopted and the poor plea is set up that Redistribution of seats, which would have made any Bill impossible, is not included in the Bill. Is it to be conceived that the Peers of the Opposition who failed in 1832 before a constituency of a few hundred thousand are to conquer half a century later in the face of voters already three millions & about to be increased to five. And we hoped that this moderation together with the remembrance of the disasters suffered in former conflicts would have enabled us to attain our end.

Forces beyond our controul have ruled it otherwise. And I must earnestly request Your Grace to consider if the danger of courting a conflict, which, if ever, in some very remote stage, it be referred for settlement to the nation will involve in its issue not only what is to be the constituency of the House of Commons, but what is to be the future of the House of Lords.

[*Second letter*:]   With reference to my principal letter of this day I have to add a few notes. I have felt that this is a question of which we ought not to aim at casting the whole responsibility on the head of the Episcopal body. Consequently I am sending copies of my letter to a number of other Bishops, selecting those whom I could least unbecomingly approach. I send them to the Bishops of Winchester, Durham, Salisbury, Oxford, Exeter, Carlisle, Bath & Wells, Manchester, Ely, Chichester, St. Asaph & Bangor.

I wish I could fully convey my sense of the pressure of that obligation, under which alone I write. The House of Lords has never come out of these conflicts except docked of some privilege, or shadowed with some indignity. We have run risks with our followers to put temptation out of their way. But all in vain.

I feel that it is, between this time & Tuesday, a great trial for the Heads of the Church;

---

[1] Subsequent deleted passage taken from holograph draft, Add MS 44109, f. 96.

and, having done my humble part, I have only to desire & pray that they may arrive at a right judgment.[1]

[P.S.] I think Lord Granville will write to Archbishop of York & Bishop of London.[2] Pray observe the leading article in the Times of today. The leanings of that paper are well known to be towards property & the dominant class, but pray notice the tone. It is I believe absolutely spontaneous.

To LORD HARTINGTON, war secretary, 2 July 1884.   Chatsworth MSS 340. 1471.

I will certainly ask the Cabinet if you desire it after reading this but what I would advise is that I should *circulate* your letter today,[3] & on seeing the answers you could judge whether to ask for one tomorrow.

I think the request for labourers could very well be disposed of without another meeting today, if as I understand it is wholly or mainly within the scope of what is already authorised, or at any rate involves no more than is expressed in the terms of it.

Our Cabinets this year have been (of necessity) beyond all precedent in frequency, & this makes me desire to avoid meeting where this can be done without inconvenience.

To LORD A. C. HERVEY, bishop of Bath and Wells,   Add MS 44547, f. 78.
2 July 1884. '*Private*'.

Our meetings though too rare have been tranquil. I now write to bring before you a subject full of menace & of mischief; & I cannot do it better than by begging you to peruse the inclosed copy of a letter which I have just addressed to the Primate.

Since you took your seat on the Bench I have never (as I hope) or hardly ever troubled you on a matter of politics; and I only thus far crave your attention now because I am sure that the issue before us is exceedingly grave and deeply involves what you would yourself consider as very weighty interests of Church and State.[4]

To Rev. M. MacCOLL, 2 July 1884.   Add MS 44547, f. 77.

There seems to be no doubt that the Ripon Canonry is, at this moment, with the Crown. Please, therefore, to consider as promptly as convenience will allow, the matter placed before you in conversation last night.

I wish it were one of less restricted emolument, though you think so little of such matters. Unfortunately the uncertainties of political affairs are now so marked, that I should only mislead you by referring to other & better chances which might, but also obviously which might not arise, & respecting which it is hardly possible to form judgments in anticipation.[5]

---

[1] All these, and those listed above, voted with Benson against Cairns' amndt. (see 8 July 84), except London, Salisbury, and Bangor.

[2] Benson replied next day, Add MS 44109, f. 99, that he had already seen almost all those named, who 'are quite alive to the gravity of the situation'. See 9 July 84.

[3] Hartington's letter of 1 July (see 28 June 84n.), requesting 'a short Cabinet' on military preparations for the Sudan, circulated with a note from Gladstone; Holland, ii. 464, Chatsworth MSS 340. 1472.

[4] Hervey was Gladstone's appt. to the see in 1869. He promised to vote, expecting only 3 or 4 bps. to vote against the bill; Add MS 44207, f. 299.

[5] After havering, MacColl accepted; see *MacColl*, 75.

To F. TEMPLE,[1] bishop of Exeter, 2 July 1884. '*Private*'.   Add MS 44547, f. 78.

I think we shall have your sympathy in every first effort to avert the constitutional crisis with which we are threatened by Lord Salisbury and his friends, and of which the first Act is to be presented in your House on Tuesday night.

To trouble you on a merely political matter would not be accordant with my feelings or my practice, but the issues here involved are so grave and far-reaching that I earnestly beg you to read the inclosed copy of a letter which I have just addressed to the Primate.

3. Th.

Wrote to Chancr of Exr—Mr L. Tennyson—The Queen—Ld Granville—and minutes. H. of C. 4-8¼ and 9¾-12.[2] Saw Mr H—Ld R.G—The Russian Ambassador—Sir Thos May—Mr Trevelyan—Conclave of Commons Ministers at H. of C. —Mr MacColl. Twelve to dinner. Read Old Town Folks—Francesco Cenci.

To Lionel TENNYSON, 3 July 1884.[3]   Add MS 44547, f. 79.

We should be very sorry to make any unnecessary demand on your Father, but the motion of Lord Salisbury on Monday raises issues of the utmost importance to the country & to the Order, & I make no doubt that we may count upon his being in his place on Tuesday for the Division.[4]

To LORD A. C. HERVEY, bishop of Bath and Wells,   Add MS 44547, f. 79.
3 July 1884.

Your kind note made me very desirous to see you. I thought I might venture to say to you as an old friend what I could hardly say to any other Bishop, & what even to you I hardly like to write. It was that as it appeared to me this most rash proceeding in the House of Lords offered an opening for the Bishops in particular to commend themselves afresh to the esteem & confidence of the country.

4. Fr.

Wrote to Ld Granville l.l.—Bp of Lincoln—Mr Childers—Ld Carlingford—Sir W. Harcourt—and minutes. Prevented by lumbago from attending the House. Saw Mr H—Ld RG—Sir A. Clark (for my lumbago)—Ld Acton. Read Lepel Griffin on U.S.—Francesco Cenci &c.—Old Town Folks. This day I reach the term of Lord Palmerston's Premierships.

5. Sat. [*Dollis Hill*]

Wrote to Ld Hampden—The Queen l.l.l.—and minutes. Cabinet 2-5½. Saw Mr H—Ld RG—GLG—Sir A. Clark—H.N.G.—Count Karolyi—Lady D. Neville. Dined with the Breadalbanes. Drove to Dollis Hill after. Read Sir L. Griffin—Francesco Cenci. Lumbago rather bad.

---

[1] Gladstone's appt. to the see in 1869. Temple replied, 3 July, Add MS 44487, that he had changed an appt. to be present.
[2] *Nisero* incident raised by S. Storey; London Govt. Bill; *H* 289. 1924.   [3] In *Tennyson*, ii. 305.
[4] Lord Tennyson replied, 4 July, Add MS 44487, f. 42: 'I cannot vote with you & I will not vote *against* you'; Gladstone's docket reads: 'Ld Granville Jul. 5!!!' See 6-9 July 84.

Cabinet. Sat. Jul. 5. 84. 2 PM.[1]

1. Conversation on our course of the coming debate, and on the *after*.
2. Nisero.[2] Pauncefoot's proposal to encourage[?] Dutch into cooperation. Send messages to Rajah that unless men are delivered to Pegasus in – days, we will join Dutch in punishing them.
3. New Guinea. Much discussion, & scruples of Chancellor [Selborne], Harcourt, & W.E.G. Subject postponed.[3]
4. Egyptian Army, Hartington read a Mem. Shall F.O. communicate with Sultan to obtain leave for recruiting Turks? Not yet.
5. Conversation on Exp. to Khartoum & conditions of it. Much difficulty felt.
6. Royal Commission on Shipping. (Cabinet dwindled to seven). Yes.[4]

6. 4 S. Trin.

Willesden Ch. (H.C.) 11 A.M. Saw Ld Tweedmouth—Mr Russell. Wrote to Ld Tennyson—Lady Tennyson—Mr Seymour—& minutes. Read Oxenham, Studies —S.P.C.K. Comm. on Prayerbook—Lisle on Ancient Religion[5] &c.

To LORD TENNYSON, 6 July 1884. '*Private*'.   Add MS 44547, f. 81.

I received your note[6] yesterday in London in the midst of bustle and baddish lumbago, for which I was scuttling off to the country. But upon consideration I cannot help writing a line, for I must hope you will reconsider your intention.

The best mode in which I can support a suggestion seemingly so audacious is by informing you

That all sober-minded Conservative Peers are in great dismay at this wild proceeding of Lord Salisbury's.

That the ultra-Radicals and Parnellites on the other hand are in a state of glee as they believe, and with good reason, that the battle, once begun, will end in some great humiliation to the House of Lords, or some important changes in its composition.

That (to my knowledge) various Bishops of Conservative leanings are on this account going to vote with the Government—as may be the case with lay Peers also.

That you are the *only* Peer, so far as I know, associated with Liberal ideas or the Liberal party, who hesitates to vote against Lord Salisbury.

And I earnestly hope that you too will come out, if without any great care for the extension of the franchise yet to prevent an act on the part of the Lords which is essentially suicidal.[7]

---

[1] Add MS 44645, f. 138.
[2] Crew of the wreck *Nisero*, imprisoned by Sultan of Tenom August 1883; see *PP* 1884 lxxxvii. 255-465 and *H* 289. 1891.
[3] See 6 Aug. 84.
[4] The Aberdeen Royal Commission on loss of life at sea; *PP* 1884-5 xxxv, xliii.
[5] Perhaps one of the many articles by L. V. De Lisle.
[6] See 3 July 84n.
[7] Tennyson replied, 7 July, Add MS 44487, f. 52: 'the extension of the Franchise I hold to be matter of justice;—the proper time of bringing forward the question, matter of opinion'; will vote for the bill, despite gout, if 'you solemnly pledge yourself that the Extension bill shall not become Law before Redistribution has been satisfactorily settled'. See 8 July 84n.

To LADY TENNYSON, 6 July 1884.   Add MS 44547, f. 81.

I was so sorry to miss you at the marriage, and so pleased to receive any message from you. But it almost provoked me to send you a couple of tracts on the franchise, published six or eight years ago. This however would be too vindictive.

It is most true as Mr. Burke says that the right to govern lies in wisdom and virtue. It is not less true that irresponsible power is a dangerous thing unless curbed by wisdom and virtue which often find this curbing difficult.

The House of Lords is the only irresponsible, absolutely irresponsible power, known to our Constitution. It is madness for Lord Salisbury to raise the question whether 250 gentlemen sitting by birth & responsible to nobody shall override and overrule this nation. If he will not correct such follies, the House of Lords should refuse his leading—as I yet hope it may.

That House may yet live a long time, if it uses its vast powers with some moderation. But not if it plays pranks such as are now impending, and are actually filling with joy the hearts of Ultra-Radicals and Parnellites.

I rely on your coming to the conservative view of this question, & even on your believing that the men of the counties are as capable & as trustworthy as those of the towns.

7. M. [*London*]

Wrote to Mr Firth—Mad. Novikoff—Sir W. Dunbar—The Queen l.l.—& minutes. H of C. 5-8¼.[1] Evg at home. Sat to Millais 11¼ AM.[2] Back to D. St. 12½. Saw Mr H—Ld RG—Ld Granville l.l.l.l.—Mr Childers—Sir C. Dilke—Sir A. Clark. Read Franc. Cenci—MacColl on Princess Alice[3]—19th Cent on Manifestations.[4]

8. Tu.

Wrote to Mr Courtney—The Queen—& minutes—Lord Tennyson (Tel.) Much occupied about getting Tennyson's vote. Saw Mr Knowles (l.l.) & Mr L. Tennyson with this view.[5] Saw Mr H—Ld RG—Ld Granville l.l.l.—Ld Acton. Got up the London case a little & spoke in the debate.[6] H of C. 4¾-8½ & 9¾-1½. Went to H. of L. late. What a suicidal act of the Lords![7] Read Lepel Griffin (finished).

9. Wed.

Wrote to Ld Norton—Abp of Canterbury—Ld Hampden—Ld Rosebery—Ld Granville Tel.—The Queen—and minutes. Dined with the P. Stanhopes. Considered the points of a Manifesto Speech. Cabinet 2¼-5½. Saw Mr H—Ld R.G Read Francesco Cenci &c.

---

[1] Supply; merchant shipping; *H* 290. 233, 348.

[2] Millais' second portrait, commissioned by Christ Church, Oxford, but obtained by Rosebery; see Introduction above and 15 June 85.

[3] *F.R.*, xlii. 126 (July 1884).

[4] *N.C.*, xvi. 68 (July 1884).

[5] Tennyson voted with the govt. for the Franchise Bill.

[6] *H* 290. 540.

[7] 2°R of the Franchise Bill negatived in 205:146; Cairns' amndt. (no franchise reform without redistribution in 'an entire scheme') then passed; *H* 290. 477. At 4.15 p.m. Granville offered the compromise of joint Resolutions on franchise and redistribution; see *H* 290. 833, Jones, *1884*, 153 and Ramm II, ii. 211.

Cabinet. Wed. Jul. 9. 84. 2. 15 PM.[1]
1. Course. Autumn Session.[2]
2. Announcement. Tomorrow [party] meeting at F.O.
3. Bills. Sacrifice 10 of 12 on list.
4. Conference. Expedite.
5. Blenheim Pictures. Offer 85. .90 m for R[aphael] M[adonna].[3]
6. Treasury to consider on W.O. & Adm. Report whether supple[mentary] Est[imate] is requisite.
7. Royal Commission for Indian & Colonial Health Exhibition. Cost £8000. Decline.

To E. W. BENSON, archbishop of Canterbury, 9 July 1884.   Add MS 44547, f. 82.

One word of hearty thanks to yourself, and to your Episcopal Brethren on whose behalf you joined in the debates not for an important vote only, but for a speech[4] the spirit of which, coming from your Grace, constitutes an historical event & almost marks an epoch, the might of which will be felt through the country, & the effect of which will I trust be felt in future times. I am entirely convinced that Your Grace & your Brethren have rarely rendered a more signal service to the Church.

To LORD ROSEBERY, 9 July 1884.   N.L.S. 10023, f. 17.

You will readily believe that this is with me a day of pressure, but I have read your speech[5] with care (I was doing penance on the London Government Bill while it was made), and I add one to the shower of compliments, not you will believe without sincerity & warmth.

What I admired most was your strong practical grasp of the vital question as to re-distribution, and the whole closing appeal to the House for the House's sake, which could not be surpassed I think either in skill or in elevation.

[P.S.] What you said of my Conservative *base* was true though they may have laughed.[6]

10. Th.

Wrote to Ld Rosebery—Ld Granville l l—Ld Spencer—The Queen—Mrs B.—and minutes. Saw Mr H—Ld RG—H.J.G.—Milham[7] *cum* Sir C. Dilke—Lord Wolverton—Dean of Durh. Expelled from my notes all dangerous ideas. Attended

---

[1] Add MS 44645, f. 144. Note from Hamilton at 5 p.m.: 'Sir H. Ponsonby is free'; Gladstone: 'I may tell him we are very sensible of H.M.'s kindness. We desired the plan of yesterday to give all possible solemnity to our pledge. *We do not see what first claim there is to move.* If H.M. asks why they are not satisfied with yesterday's plan, they will say it adds nothing to our pledge'; ibid., f. 146.

[2] Dodson's note: '*Gladstone*[:] To allow Lords to force a dissolution would be precedent against liberty worse than anything since beginning of reign of Geo. III'; Monk Bretton, 62.

[3] See Childers, 164 and 21 June 84; the Raphael and the Van Dyck were both bought by the National Gallery.

[4] On 8 July; *H* 290. 441.

[5] On 8 July in the Lords on the Franchise Bill; *H* 290. 412.

[6] 'There is no one who has the privilege and honour of Mr. Gladstone's acquaintance who does not know the essentially Conservative bases on which Mr. Gladstone's political opinions rest—[*Laughter*]—noble Lords may laugh; but, perhaps, they have not had the same opportunities of knowing that I have . . .'; ibid.

[7] Illegible name here; may read 'Victain'; no corresponding entry in Dilke's diary.

[party] meeting at F.O. $2\frac{1}{2}$-$3\frac{1}{2}$ and delivered my sense, which was well received by Goschen, Bright, & the meeting.[1] H. of C. $4\frac{1}{2}$-$7\frac{3}{4}$ & 10-$12\frac{3}{4}$. Announced our intentions simply.[2] Dined at Sir C. Forster's. Read F. Cenci.

To Sir W. V. HARCOURT, home secretary,   MS Harcourt dep. Adds 10.
10 July 1884.

I fear that I am without authority to recede from the decision of the Cabinet yesterday.

I suppose the best mode of statement will be to say that 1. We do not propose to put forward in the Commons any new Bill from the Lords of the class with which we deal today, i.e. important & likely to take time. This would include the Scotch Bill, without its being (spontaneously) named by you. 2. To accept Grand Committee Bills. 3. To slay nine Bills there & then. 4. If questioned on Medical Bill to reply as agreed. 5. To ask for Wednesdays.

11. Fr.

Wrote to Sir B. Leighton—Sir W. Harcourt—Ld Granville—The Queen—& minutes. Read Francesco Cenci. Saw Mr H—Ld RG—C. of E. H. of C. $4\frac{1}{2}$-8. Storm there which ended in revising our pacific plan.[3] Dined with the 80 Club: spoke another quasi-manifesto.[4]

To LORD ROSEBERY, 11 July 1884. '*Private*'.   N.L.S. 10023, f. 19.

Please to turn over in your mind the question whether there should be a County Meeting in Midlothian.

It would imply my attendance: and if it takes place it should follow in the wake of others as the Cabinet do not wish themselves to blow the trumpet.

Therefore I do not ask for an immediate answer. It is certainly desirable that opinion should be expressed as far as possible in the ancient & regular form of town & county meetings.

12. Sat. [Combe Wood, Kingston]

Wrote to The Queen—Ld Granville—Rev. Mr Ridgway—Ld Rosebery—Mr Childers—Ld Winmarleigh[5]—Lady Garvagh—& minutes. Rosebery came in with a plan which I encouraged for setting the Bill on its legs again.[6] Saw Mr H—Sir W. Harcourt—Ld Granville—Ld Wolverton—Sir R. Welby on Egypt (finance). Went to

[1] Report in *T.T.*, 11 July 1884, 10a.

[2] Autumn session 'for the purpose of again considering the Franchise Bill' and a Redistribution Bill which would be 'the principal object of the next Session', meaning the next normal Session, a point which Churchill, reasonably enough, misunderstood from Gladstone's statement; *H* 290. 693, 702.

[3] Row about confidentiality or otherwise of the compromise proposed by Granville (see 8 July 84n.); Gladstone accused Churchill of 'foul language'; eventually there were mutual apologies; *H* 290. 845.

[4] *T.T.*, 12 July 1884, 12d.

[5] Asking him to assist 'an accommodation, & avert a conflict'; he replied demanding redistribution also; Add MS 44487, f. 74.

[6] Joint address for autumn session to include discussion of a Redistribution Bill; see Bahlman, *Hamilton*, ii. 652.

Wolverton's house at Coombe: arr. 2 PM. Read G. Gemünder[1]—Francesco Cenci finished—The Apostle's Creed.

13. 5 S. Trin.

Kingston Ch mg and the small Church evg. Wrote to Mr MacColl—Ld Halifax—The Queen—and minutes. Saw Sir W. Harcourt—Ld Granville. The 'crisis' looked more hopeful today: for the moment only.[2] Read Oxenham—Prayerbook Commentary.

14. M. [London]

Wrote to The Queen l.l.—Duke of Argyll—and minutes. St Margaret's Ch. 11.30 for R. Lyttelton's marriage.[3] 2d sitting to Mr Millais. Marriage breakfast at Mr Santleys. Levee at 2 PM. H of C. $4\frac{1}{2}$–8 and 10–11$\frac{1}{2}$.[4] Dined at Grillion's. Saw Mr H—Ld RG—Ld Norton—Ld Granville—Sir C. Dilke.[5] Read G. Gemünder.

Cabinet. Monday Jul. 14. 2$\frac{1}{2}$ PM.[6]
1. Ld Wemyss's motion. Amt. proposed. With this amt. we support it.[7]
2. Westr. Hall West side. Lay plans (Pearson) before Parlt. If there be a consent[?] take Vote: if not a joint Committee of both Houses.

15. Tu.

Wrote to The Queen l.l.—Sir H. Ponsonby—Mr Millais—Chancr of Exr—& minutes. Saw Mr H—Ld RG—Mr Whitbread—Ld Rosebery—Sir Ch. Dilke—C. of E.—Mr Trevelyan—Mr Roundell—Mr M. Brooks *cum* Mr Findlater—Mad. Novikoff. Wrote Mem. on Eg. Finance.[8] Dined at Ld Dysart's. H of C. $4\frac{1}{2}$–7$\frac{3}{4}$ and 11–12?[9] Finished G. Gemünder.

16. Wed.

Wrote to The Queen—Ld Granville—and minutes. Saw Mr H—Ld R.G.—Ld Granville—Abp of Canterbury. Luncheon at 15 G.S. Dined at Dollis Hill. (A difficult & dangerous) Cabinet at $3\frac{1}{2}$ to $6\frac{1}{4}$. Read Old Town Folks—White's Architecture[10] &c.

---

[1] Perhaps G. P. von Gemünder, *Die Weltgeschichte chronologischsynchronistisch dargestellt* (1806).

[2] Temperate letter from Salisbury to MacColl, shown to Gladstone, Bahlman, *Hamilton*, ii. 652.

[3] R. H. Lyttelton (see 1 Feb. 54) m. Edith Santley.

[4] Questions; supply; *H* 290. 930.

[5] Dilke's diary this day, Add MS 43926: 'In the evening Mr G. broached . . . his views about redistribution, in order that I might begin to prepare the Bill. He is in favour of single member districts.' Dilke later recalled: 'we practically hatched the Bill'; Gwynn, ii. 64.

[6] Add MS 44645, f. 148.

[7] Motion for autumn sitting on Redistribution Bill; defeated on 17 July; *H* 290. 1377. See Jones, *1884*, 158-60.

[8] Not found.

[9] Navy estimates; *H* 290. 1137.

[10] W. H. White, *Architecture and public building in Paris and London* (1884).

Cabinet. Wed July 16. 3 PM. H of C.[1]

Egypt. Conference propositions. Conversation—against giving in to the French claims.[2] Great urgency.

Egypt. Baring's proposition on police. Discussed. General views favourable.

Egypt. Expedition to Soudan—much discussed. Opinions differ except as to showing front[?] at Assouan & Wadi Halfa.

Egypt Dongola. No troops to be sent but not to urge Mudir to abandon it. English officer may encourage arrangement for its being held by a peaceful tribe.

I was disappointed with the Cabinet of today in regard to an expedition for or towards Khartoum. Those who leaned to it were Hartington, The Chancellor (headlong), and with them Dodson, Carlingford, Northbrook, and even Granville a little.

17. Th.

Wrote to Lady Holker—Ld Granville l l l—Sir W. James—Mrs Jacobson—The Queen—Ld Winmarleigh—Mr Hutton—Ld Tollemache—& minutes. Saw Mr H—Ld R.G—Ld Hartington—Scotts—Sir W. Harcourt—Sir C. Dilke. Dined at Lady Stanley's. H of C. 5–7¾ and 10¾–12¼.[3] Read Morley on H. of Lords[4]— White's Architecture &c.

18. Fr.

Wrote to Sir H. Ponsonby—The Lord Mayor—Sir T.E. May—Mrs Jacobson— The Queen l.l.—Mr Roundell MP—& minutes. H. of C. 4¼–5¼ and 8–12¼.[5] Cabinet 2–4¼. Saw Mr H—Ld RG—Ld Spencer—D. of Argyll[6]—Ld Granville *cum* C. of E. in evg on the very menacing state of things as to the Conference. Lumbago followed in the night. Read Dissolving Views[7]—finished White's Architecture.

Cabinet. Frid. Jul. 18. 84. 2 PM.[8]

1. Lord Mayor's dinner—declined[9]
2. Aberystwith may have 4m[ille] for 3 years instead of £2500 for five.
3. Procession on Monday. Keep Parlt. open.
4. Conference Plans. Childers reported proceedings of commissioners & of Waddington. He was authorised to negotiate on bases A.[10]

[1] Add MS 44645, f. 150.

[2] Dodson's note: '*Gladstone*: "Our guarantee of £8,000,000 saves Egypt, & ∴ benefits its bondholders, 4 per 100 = £320,000 a year. We must take a stiff position in conference & say we decline (on the authority of our men in Egypt) to raise or estimate for more revenue than we have named"'; Monk Bretton 62.

[3] Questions; education estimates; *H* 290. 1421.

[4] J. Morley in *Macmillan's Magazine*, 1. 230 (July 1884).

[5] Questions; Indian medical service; *H* 290. 1609.

[6] At the request of the Queen, though not mentioning this, Argyll tried to persuade Gladstone to settle redistribution himself; *L.Q.V.*, 2nd series, iii. 521.

[7] See 28 June 84.

[8] Add MS 44645, f. 154.

[9] After circulation of Cabinet; list of excuses, ibid., f. 153.

[10] Details, ibid., ff. 155–8.

5. Hartington & the Lancashire meeting.[1] He will not attend if they insist on accepting Resolutions of organic change in the H. of Lords.
6. Tel. ordering 3 more steamers on the Nile for space between Assouan & Wadi Halfa.

19. Sat. [Wellington College, Wokingham]

Wrote to Mr Hutton—Ld Granville—Mr MacColl—and minutes. Saw Mr H—Ld R.G—Ld Granville *cum* Mr Childers and Duke of Argyll. Off at 12 to Wellington for Sunday. The children are delightful. We had a Racine recitation, very good. Walk with E. W[ickham]. Read Col. Rous's Glanki[2]—The Battles of Newbury.[3]

20 6. S. Trin.

Chapel 9 A.M., Noon, & 8 PM. Saw Mr Penny[4] & other masters, also boys. Walk with E.W., C.G., & W.W. Wrote to The Speaker—Mr Hamilton Tel. Read Mr Weldon's Sermon[5]—Oxenham's (remarkable) Vol. of Short Essays[6]—Power of the Church—Cowper's Letters.[7]

21. M. [London]

Wrote to The Queen—W. Phillimore—& minutes. Returned from Wellington at one. Saw Mr Seymour—Ld RG—Ld Granville—Ld Rosebery—Conclave on Egypt. Touched the meeting, really a wonderful one, at outside points. H of C. $4\frac{3}{4}$–$7\frac{1}{2}$ & 8–$12\frac{1}{4}$.[8] Read Battles of Newbury—Dissolving Views.

22. Tu.

Wrote to Ld Rosebery—Ld Granville—Mr Corbet MP[9]—The Queen—and minutes. Saw Mr S.—Ld RG—Mr Bute—Ld Granville—Sir H. Gordon—Ld Rosebery—Mr Childers—Sir C. Dilke—Mr Buckle—Mr Williamson—& others. H of C. $4\frac{1}{2}$–$7\frac{3}{4}$ and 10–$11\frac{1}{2}$.[10] Read Q.R. on Redistribution[11]—Dissolving Views.

To W. J. CORBET, M.P., 22 July 1884.   Add MS 44547, f. 87.

I thank you for your pamphlet,[12] which I shall peruse, or reperuse, with interest.
My opinion is worth little but I am sanguine enough to believe that the feelings of the Irish people towards England cannot have assumed a character of increased estrangement during the last five years.
The offices which fall to the share of the Irish Government are not always agreeable;

[1] The meeting proposed to move a formal protest against the Lords' activities; CAB 41/18/40.
[2] W. J. Rous, *Glanké* (1883).
[3] W. Money, *The first and second battles of Newbury* (1884).
[4] Rev. Charles William Penny, mathematics master.
[5] G. W. Weldon, 'A farewell sermon' (1882).
[6] See 15 June 84.
[7] Probably the ed. by W. Benham (1884).
[8] Questions; estimates; *H* 290. 1757.
[9] William Joseph Corbet, 1825–1909; home rule M.P. Wicklow 1880–92, 1895–1900.
[10] Estimates; *H* 291. 47.   [11] *Q.R.*, clviii. 229 (July 1884).
[12] Probably W. J. Corbet, 'What is Home Rule?'; no copy found; mentioned in *Dod's Parliamentary Companion* (1882) *et seq.*

but I sometimes ask myself whether their efforts to mitigate old mischiefs, when undeniably made, are always frankly acknowledged, and whether the function of the peace maker is not in this as in most other matters the best. In this sentiment I feel confident you will concur.

And you will forgive my adding the expression of my conviction that Mr. Trevelyan is most loyal to the interests of Ireland (as he does his best to understand them), but he has much to dishearten him and from more than one quarter.

To LORD ROSEBERY, 22 July 1884.   N.L.S. 10023, f. 20.

I am not sure whether I have mentioned to you an idea and a wish that dwell steadily in my mind about the meetings and discussions of the next three months. It is that they should be, as far as possible, meetings convened in the old and regular forms of town and county meetings, founded on a requisition in each case to the convening officer. This was I think largely the case at the time of the first Reform Bill, and it gives far more dignity and weight to popular assemblages. Of course it is free to opponents to present themselves; but this is the case, I suppose, with all really public gatherings.

I hope it may be possible to arrange this in Midlothian? At any rate I am sure that the weight of the proceedings generally depends in some not inconsiderable degree upon our walking in the 'old paths'.

We are writing to Col. F[arquharson] today to inform him of our altered date.[1]

23. Wed.

Wrote to Sir H. Gordon—The Queen l.l.—Ld Selborne—Ed. Lpool D Post—D. of Argyll—and minutes. H. of C. $2\frac{1}{2}$-$5\frac{1}{4}$. Spoke on Mr Bolton's case.[2] Saw Mr H—Ld RG—D. of Argyll—Ld Granville—Ld Gr. cum Chancr of Exr—Ld Hartington—Mrs Earle—Mr Bryce. Dined at Mr B. Curries (Combe). Read Dissolving Views.

To E. R. RUSSELL, editor, *Liverpool Daily Post*, 23 July 1884.   Add MS 44547, f. 88.

Have you an opinion, & if so would you kindly give it to me, as to the way in which the Municipal division of Liverpool into wards has worked. My recollection is that, when the Municipal Act passed, this mode of division was intended by the Conservative Opposition, or was at all events regarded as a powerful protection to their party. Has it so worked, & generally what are its merits or demerits?

Among the multitude of points to be considered in connection with the distribution of seats, this will of course come up.[3]

24. Th.

Wrote to Ld Col. Rous—Ld Kimberley—Ld Granville—Ld E. Fitzmaurice—The Khedive of Egypt—Mr Childers—The Queen 111—and minutes. H. of C. 5-$7\frac{3}{4}$ and $10\frac{3}{4}$-$12\frac{1}{4}$.[4] Dined with Mr & Mrs Sandys.[5] Saw Mr H—Mr S—Ld RG—Ld Granville—Mr Scharf—Ld Spencer—Mr MacColl—Ld Granville *cum* C. of E. Read Q.R. on Foreign Policy[6]—Corbet on Home Rule[7]—Dissolving Views.

---

[1] See 3 Sept. 84.
[2] Home Rulers' attack on George Bolton, Crown Solicitor for Tipperary; *H* 291. 257.
[3] No reply found.   [4] Questions; estimates; *H* 291. 340.
[5] Probably Richard Sandys of Clarence Gate.
[6] *Q.R.*, clviii. 229 (July 1884).
[7] See 22 July 84.

To the KHEDIVE OF EGYPT, 24 July 1884.   Add MS 44547, f. 88.

Your Highness will readily understand that I have been led to postpone my reply to the letter I have had the honour to receive from Your Highness,[1] by the very unusual complications, at the present moment, of the Egyptian question. As, however, these complications are not yet at an end, & as I feel that longer silence would scarcely be respectful, I offer the brief reply which alone circumstances will warrant.

Your Highness will not have failed to observe that, whatever rumours may have crept into local circulation, the language & proceedings of the British Government have from first to last assumed, & has been based upon, Your Highness's single-mindedness & good faith. And I may be permitted to add that on no other basis could we proceed with hope or satisfaction, & that our internal belief is in entire accord with our official language.

Anxiously awaiting the decisions of the Conference now assembled, I feel that I cannot go wrong in offering one further remark.

It will very greatly strengthen, not only the hands of the administration, but the Egyptian cause in this country, if we are enabled to show by the evidence both of words & acts, that the Government of Your Highness is steadily & consistently set upon preventing the recurrence of those abuses, whether in prisons, in the collection of the revenue, or in other forms, which have prevailed in other times. I know it to be the earnest desire of Your Highness to govern the Egyptian people with justice, equity & humanity. In this holy work we respectfully desire to render all the aid we can: & our aid will be both easy & effective if, especially after the recent withdrawal of Mr. Clifford Lloyd, we are enabled to point with confidence to a system of administration from which all these great & serious evils shall have disappeared. Entire reformations are not indeed always to be effected at a single stroke, but the firm intentions of the Government are certain to be traceable in an improved state of things.

To LORD KIMBERLEY, Indian secretary, 24 July 1884.   Add MS 44547, f. 88.

I quite understand your argument about the time of changing the Viceroy and I think it supplies you with a fair case.[2] The appointment ought not to be made (precedent notwithstanding) by a Government in its last agony, and if that contingency is within the bounds of reasonable calculation this may fairly weigh in the choice of the moment.

Perhaps we might be able to speak of this when the Cabinet breaks up tomorrow.

[P.S.] I have a private letter from Ripon by the same mail as yours and to the same effect.

25. Fr. St James.

My brother's birthday & our marriage day. Went to luncheon with him. Wrote to Ld Carlingford—Ld Spencer—The Queen 1 1 1—and minutes. Cabinet 2–4¼. Saw Mr H—Ld R.G—Sir W. Harcourt—Sir C. Dilke—The Russian Ambassador—Mr [R.H.] Hutton's very interesting conclave—after dining at Mr Jerningham's.[3] Read Dissolving Views—Delaydor on House of Lords.[4] H of C. 4¼–7¾ & 11½–12¾.[5]

---

[1] Add MS 44486, f. 298.

[2] Kimberley, 23 July, Add MS 44228, f. 144: if parliament dissolved following the autumn session, it would be difficult to appoint Ripon's successor, which ought to be done in November.

[3] (Sir) Hubert Edward Henry Jerningham, 1842–1914; diplomat, author and liberal M.P. Berwick 1881–5; governed Mauritius 1893–7; kt. 1893.

[4] Author's name scrawled; untraced.

[5] Questions; spoke on public business; *H* 291. 523.

Cabinet. Frid. Jul. 25. 1884. 2 PM.[1]
1. [Egyptian] Conference. Report of yesterday's meeting made. French plan, 10 years plan, Childers plan: all submitted.
2. Supplementary Army Estimate now or postponed. Now; unless unforeseen expenses should come.
If Childers basis is accepted may G[ranville] & C. admit a. any guarantee: *No.* b. *fix* the charge of Govt. which is to have precedence: *Yes, if necessary.* c. 40m Suez Canal may be treated as Sinking Fund? *Yes if necessary.* d. accept 3 years if necessary. e. Casting Vote [on the Caisse]—may be limited to period of the occupation? *Yes.*

26. Sat. [Eton College]

Wrote to The Queen l.l.—Sir Jas Watson—Sir Thos May—Ld Granville—Mr Griffith—Mr Chamberlain—and minutes. Off to Eton at 5.10: E. Lyttelton & Mr Donaldson our hosts. Saw Mr H—Ld RG—Ld Kimberley—D. of Argyll—Dean of Windsor—Prof. Stewart. Read Miss Colenso's Zululand[2]—A Tale of the Christ.[3] Dear Eton: what a delight to revisit it. And it is a *better* Eton.

To J. CHAMBERLAIN, president of the board of trade,   Chamberlain MSS 5/34/28.
26 July 1884. '*Private*'.[4]

Upon examining your speech with my best spectacles, I find a single passage which I should like to refer to you, as there are a few words in it, those about the 'future prospects' of the House of Lords, which I rather think may have been spoken inadvertently.[5]

I understood you most kindly & frankly to say that you accepted my statement at the Foreign Office as fairly indicating the range of discussion within which we should, at the present stage of the controversy, endeavour to confine ourselves. But certainly a main part of my purpose in that statement was to shut out the point of future prospects. And I hope that when we meet on Monday you may give me a word to assure me that I was not misunderstood.

27. 7 S. Trin.

Eton Chapel mg with H.C. & afternoon. Wrote to Ld Granville—Mr Trevelyan. Walk with Edward & a party to and over all the Salthill ground, which I have not visited (I think) for scores of years.[6] Read Mr Lisle on Religions—Lias on the Atonement[7]—Meyrick on Baptism.[8] Conclave of young masters in evg to converse on the Atonement.

28. M. [London]

Wrote to Mrs Vyner—Ld Granville—Mrs Th.—Mr Redington—The Queen—and minutes. Sat to Millais.[9] Saw Mr H——Ld R.G—Ld Granville *cum* Mr Childers—

---

[1] Add MS 44645, f. 159.   [2] F. E. Colenso, *The ruin of Zululand*, 2v. (1884-5).
[3] i.e. Wallace, *Ben-Hur* resumed, see 23 Sept. 83.
[4] In Garvin, i. 469, with Chamberlain's unmalleable reply.
[5] On 23 July at the Devonshire Club.   [6] See Matthew, *Gladstone*, 16.
[7] By J. J. Lias (1884).   [8] F. Meyrick, *Baptism; regeneration; conversion* (1884).
[9] Where he was photographed for the portrait by Rupert Potter, 1832-1914, barrister, fa. of Beatrix; see J. Taylor, *Beatrix Potter* (1986), 22, and illustrations in this volume.

do *cum* Ld Kimberley—Ld Hartington. Returned from Eton by the 10.30. Read Dissolving Views—Innocenzo X[1]—Ruin of Zulu Land.

29. Tu.

Wrote to Mr Millais—Sir W. Harcourt—The Queen—Mr Dillwyn MP—Canon Venables—& minutes. Dined with the Miss Monks. Saw Mr H—Ld RG—Mr Browning—Mr Villiers—Miss Monk (M. di S. Sisto)[2]—Ld Granville *cum* Chr of Exr l.l.—Mr Dillwyn MP. H of C. $4\frac{1}{2}$–8 and 11–$12\frac{1}{4}$.[3] Luncheon at 15 G.S. Finished 'Dissolving Views'.

30. Wed.

Wrote to The Queen l.l.—Ld Chancellor l.l.—Col. Ellis—Duke of Argyll—& minutes. H of C. 3–6. Spoke on Zululand.[4] Eleven to dinner at home. Saw Mr H—Ld RG—Ld Granville *cum* Mr Childers—Mr Russell—Mr Rylands. Luncheon at German Embassy to meet Crown Prince & Princess: both most courteous. Talked to Münster & the Delegate on the Bankruptcy.[5] Read Old Town Folks.

To the DUKE OF ARGYLL, 30 July 1884.   Add MS 44547, f. 90.

I have heard Chamberlain express the opinion that any just redistribution will be favourable to the Liberal Party.[6]

To quote supposed sentiments of Ministers on the principles of 'Russian Scandal' can only darken & embroil matters.

It is half a century's experience of the House of Commons which makes me know that the verbal adhesion by the Lords to the principle of the Franchise affords no hope or aid whatever towards the carrying, in present circumstances, of a Bill for Redistribution.

We have made I think a dozen steps towards unity. Let them make one.

We have undertaken obligations as to redistribution. Let them show wherein these are deficient.

I hope you have had a good journey & will have a kind sea.

[P.S.] No doubt representation under the Franchise Bill will not be 'fair'; that is entirely fair. But it will be fairer than it is now, for the counties with the same seats but more voters will have increasing weight.

To LORD SELBORNE, lord chancellor,   Selborne MS 1868, f. 275.
30 July 1884.

To begin with the closing part of your Memorandum,[7] I agree that we ought to spare no effort to ascertain & employ all available means for reopening communications with

---

[1] I. Ciampi, *Innocenzo X* (1878).

[2] The Misses Monk lived at 4 Cadogan Square.

[3] Questions; estimates; *H* 291. 869.   [4] *H* 291. 1119.

[5] On 24 July, Münster told Granville that there was a large amount of Egyptian bonds in German hands; see W. O. Aydelotte, *Bismarck and British colonial policy* (1937), 114.

[6] Responding to Argyll, 29 July, Add MS 44105, f. 187, on negotiations on redistribution with Salisbury who mentions Chamberlain's view that redistribution will be 'destructive ... on the permanent possibilities of the tories'.

[7] Long mem. of 29 July on Sudan, demanding action; Selborne MS 1868, f. 271 and Selborne II, ii. 141.

Gordon, and thus converting speculation into certainty. (Several of them are now in action). Thus only can we put ourselves in a condition to judge of the proposition about Zebehr. which Sir H. Gordon on one day eagerly pressed, and on the next precipitately abandoned, after seeing Forster.

With regard to the general argument of your memorandum, I have to note the following qualifications of it.

1. Our pledge with respect to Gordon contemplates his being in danger, not absolutely, but while fulfilling the mission he received from us.

2. It is true we do not *know* he has received our messages: but we have considerable reason to presume it.

3. So it is true we have not received an answer, but we have every reason to believe an answer is on the way from Dongola, and should very shortly be here. In this answer he appears to *inquire* about a relieving force; I do not know on what ground you can as yet say he expects one.

4. We have no knowledge that his supplies will not 'last beyond October'. The account just published, with great appearance of truth from a Greek merchant under date 11th, describes him as in need of money, but as having then abundance of supplies, without any limit of time named.

5. I do not understand why a massacre at Khartoum is to be expected more than at Berber. The massacre of the population generally at that place appears in a high degree improbable.

More generally

The Memorandum does not treat Gordon's position as one of present danger. I am very sensitive of the insufficient and unsatisfactory nature of the evidence before us. But we can only judge upon the probabilities of the case, & by weighing the difficulties & dangers on each side. The memorandum states only the reasons in favour of an expedition: but does not appear to take notice of any arguments against it. Of these I mention some.

1. There are many testimonies, none in itself conclusive, but deriving as a whole under force from their concurrence, that Gordon is master of the situation; that he acts frequently, perhaps habitually, on the offensive; that the tribes have for a long time either fled or been worsted; that he is free to leave Khartoum without probable danger; but that he will not go.

2. This determination not to go, which appears almost certain, appears also to be founded on a determination not to leave Khartoum till he can leave it with a settled Government. This at the very least, for it is more than doubtful that he would leave it without extending a similar consideration to the other places included in his telegram about 'indelible disgrace'.

It is not a question of condemning him for adopting this policy: but are we to adopt it and to be responsible for it, and its consequences? It is an entire change.

I put aside, as wholly out of the question, the idea of bringing him away by force.

Our pledges whatever they may be, have all been founded on the supposition 1. of his need to go, 2. of his willingness to go, neither of which do reason and probability at present allow us to assume.

There is no reason to suppose that he wants population *removed*: he wants it as far as we can judge, left where it is, with a settled government.

If he can effect his object without a British force, he will render great service. But the intervention of a British force (deprecated by Sir H. Gordon & utterly condemned by Mr Stanley) would wholly alter the character of the situation, involving us as is probable in a religious war, and nearly certain to end in a permanent establishment in, and responsibility for the Soudan.

Nor can I, in the present state of the evidence, put out of view the heavy & serious loss of British life which must in all likelihood attend the expedition.

I will not lengthen this by dwelling on two other points. 1. As to the question of route, we have gone backwards rather than forwards. 2. It is probable that a proposition now made by us in Parliament would have for its result, not our fall merely, but a long delay, and a far worse position for the adoption of any active measure than that which now exists.

31. Th.

Wrote to Ld Spencer 2 l. & tel.—The Queen—and minutes. Dined at Ld Dalhousies. H of C. 5–7¾ & 10¾–12¼.[1] Sat to Millais. Saw Mr H—Ld RG—Ld Granville—Mr Childers l.l.—Ld Hartington: ominously anxious for a Soudan Cabinet. Sat to Millais 4th. Read Old Town Folks—Fortnightly Review.[2]

I confess it to be my strong conviction that to send an expedition either to Dongola or Khartoum at the present time would be to act in the teeth of the evidence as to Gordon, which however imperfect is far from being trivial, and would be a grave and dangerous error. WEG Jul. 31. 84.[3]

Frid. Aug. One 1884.

Wrote to Ld Granville l.l.l.l.—Sir W. Harcourt—Ld Spencer—W.H.G.—The Queen—& minutes. I began to work on the Gordon telegrams but was alarmed by a letter from H. to G.[4]—very far from being the first he has written since Ap. 1880. I immediately set to work upon possible accommodation without the expedition to Dongola. Saw Sir W. Harcourt—Childers—Northbrook: the latter brought the excellent suggestion of a vote of credit. The day passed in these communications: a pleasant alternation from the twin troubles of the Conference. Saw Mr H—Ld R.G.—Sir C. Dilke—Dean of St Paul's. Drive with C. H of C. 4¾–7¾ & 10¾–12½.[5] Read Contemp. Rev.—Old Town Folks.

2. Sat.

Wrote to Mr Childers—Ld Spencer—W.H.G.—The Queen l & tel. & minutes. H of C. 5½–7½.[6] Saw Mr H—Ld RG—Ld Granville *cum* Mr Childers l.l.l.—Ld Spencer—Sir A. Clark. Cabinet 2½–4½. Wrote out heads for statement, under correction of G. & C[hilders]—then gave the statement to Parliament.[7] This day for the first time in my recollection there were three *crises* for us all running high tide at once: Egypt, Gordon, & franchise. Drive with M. Walk in evg. C.

[1] Questions on Egypt; estimates; *H* 291. 1184.

[2] The August number, sent with a note by Escott, drawing attention to comments on Salisbury in his 'Home and foreign affairs'; Add MS 44487, f. 119; Gladstone's docket: 'Very able. But I do not believe Ld S. to be governed by personal ambition.'

[3] Holograph in Chatsworth MSS 340. 1483; for cabinet circulation, with note from Chamberlain largely agreeing with Gladstone. Copy at Add MS 44147, f. 95 is headed: 'On Lord Hartington's Mem. of 29th July 1884 on despatch of Brigade to Dongola'; for Hartington's mem., see Holland, i. 472.

[4] i.e. Hartington to Granville, threatening resignation if no preparations for a Sudan expedition are made; Holland, i. 476.

[5] Supply; *H* 291. 1367.   [6] Supply; *H* 291. 1438.

[7] Failure of the Egyptian Conference; *H* 291. 1438, 1519.

too was unwell today. Evening chiefly at home. Read 19th Cent on Franchise: various authors.[1]

Cabinet. Sat. Aug. 2. 84. 2½ Pm.[2]
1. Results of Conference: course to be taken in Egypt discussed, nothing decided. Sir E. Baring called in. Proposal to Ld Northbrook previously made.[3]
2. Agreed to propose Vote of Credit for 300m[ille] for Gordon expedition if necessary, & for certain preparations.

To W. H. GLADSTONE, M.P., 2 August 1884.　　　　Add MS 44547, f. 91.

I think you are only performing your plain duty in declining avoidable expenditure till Hawarden affairs have rallied from the double depression of agriculture and mines.

On the other hand, I should be sorry to throw over the Worcestershire people in the event of a snap dissolution, to which alone this correspondence refers.[4]

I therefore, relying on Charles' statements and taking the risk of them, will cheerfully undertake that you shall hear *nothing* of the question of charge for an election under the circumstances anticipated.

3. 8 S. Trin.

Chapel Royal with H.C. mg: and again in aftn. Wrote to Ld Spencer—The Queen—Ld Granville. Saw Sir A. Clark—Mr H—Mr Welldon—Sir Thos G.—Ld Normanton. Read Mivart on Evolution[5]—Lilly on Religions[6]—Science without Religion—Stuart, Lecture on Science[7]—and [blank.]

4. M.

Wrote to Ld Northbrook—Ld Kimberley—Sir W. Harcourt—Ld Houghton— The Queen l. & two Tell.—& minutes. H. of C. 4¾-8½ & 9¼-11¼. Speaking in C. of Supply.[8] Saw Mr H—Ld R.G—Conclave at Ld G.s before luncheon on the Northbrook mission, and in D. St afterwards. All happily arranged. Sat to Millais 5%[9] & last: 3½ hours in all. Read Old Town Folks—Fellaheen & Ismail Pacha.[10]

To Sir W. V. HARCOURT, home secretary,　　　　MS Harcourt dep. Adds 10.
4 August 1884.

In substance, I think my lucubrations have led me to the same conclusion with you.[11] I hope the Northbrook Mission will come off & will render silence as to ulterior matters feasible.

---

[1] A. J. Balfour, G. Howell and others, *N.C.*, xvi. 169 (August 1884).

[2] Add MS 44645, f. 161.

[3] 'Northbrook [Granville]'; 'Excellent. I thought of him [Gladstone]'; 'May I start it [Granville]'; ibid., f. 162. To go to Egypt as special commissioner to report; see 15 Nov. 84.

[4] On 1 August, Gladstone had offered to pay his son £250 out of the £500 needed if there was a snap dissolution; Hawn P.

[5] In *N.C.*, xvi. 263 (August 1884).　　　　[6] See 15 June 84.

[7] J. Stuart, *Chapter of science* (1883).　　[8] And announcement of Vote of Credit; *H* 291. 1585.

[9] Variation of '5°', i.e. 5th.　　[10] Possibly B. Jerrold, *Egypt under Ishmail Pacha* (1879).

[11] Harcourt to Gladstone, 4 August, Add MS 44199, f. 83: the 'only safe thing is to maintain a resolute silence as to the future'.

To LORD NORTHBROOK, first lord of the admiralty,   Add MS 44547, f. 92.
4 August 1884.

I very earnestly hope you may find yourself able to entertain in principle the request made to you on Saturday by your colleagues;[1] a request which I feel certain would have received a much more copious verbal support, but for the feeling in the minds of all on the one hand that you would give full weight to *all* the considerations in favour of your accepting the mission, on the other that it was not fair to take you, or try to take you by storm. There are two things mainly to be considered: the purpose and the person. The first seems to me so essential, that I cannot see my way to getting on without it. Nor as regards the second am I able to perceive any choice comparable to that which has been suggested. I should perhaps have called on you this morning but for an engagement to sit to Millais, after which I expect to be at Granville's soon after one.

5. *Tu.*

Wrote to Lady Mar—Sir S. Northcote l.l.—The Queen l.l.—& minutes. H of C. $4\frac{3}{4}$-$8\frac{1}{4}$ and 9-$11\frac{1}{2}$.[2] Worked on Gordon Telegrams and pledges. Saw Mr H—Ld R.G—Mr Escott[3]—Ld Northbrook. Cabinet 2-$4\frac{1}{4}$. Read Old Town Folks.

Cabinet. Tues. Aug. 5. 1884. 2 PM.[4]
1. Northbrook Mission. Acceptance announced. His paper read[5]—partially discussed.
2. Hartington raised a question as to reserve or militia—adjourned.
3. Rothschild's communication[6]—early answer promised.
4. Terms of announcement about N[orthbrook] read.[7]
5. Vote of credit. Not to specify preparations.

6. *Wed.*

Wrote to The Queen—and minutes. Worked on Paragraphs for a Queen's Speech. Saw Mr H—Lord R.G.—Ld Northbrook. Cabinet $2\frac{1}{2}$-$4\frac{1}{2}$. Conclave on Viceroyalty of India. Went off at 5 to Woodford: was delighted with all I saw. I made a short address to the people.[8] Then we dined with the Courtenay Warners at Higham Hall, & drove back late. Read Old Town Folks.

Cabinet. Wed. Aug. 6. 1884. 2 PM. H. of C.[9]
1. Northbrook:[10] Harcourt's view & his paper: may be reconciled—without final pledge. Communication with Turkey discussed.
   Tel. agreed on communicating Northbrook as Commissioner to Cairo appointment to inquire & advise Br. Govt. but will not supersede Sir E. Baring. Express desire for

---

[1] To go to Egypt; see 2 Aug. 84.
[2] Moved the Vote of Credit, not exceeding £300,000: voted in 174:14; *H* 291. 1795.
[3] Interview on prorogation; see Add MS 44476, f. 119.
[4] Add MS 44645, f. 164.
[5] Perhaps his note on his relationship with Baring; ibid., f. 166.
[6] Dodson's note: 'Rothschild tells Granville he will renew his bill but what will Govt. do to help to secure his debt'; Monk Bretton, 62.
[7] Draft at Add MS 56452, f. 68.
[8] No report found.
[9] Add MS 44645, f. 167.
[10] Who had to leave the cabinet through illness; ibid., f. 171.

cooperation, encouraged by support received in Conference: adhere to former assurances. Also assure Khedive, in making the communication through Egerton, we are sure of his approval in steps intended to strengthen his Govt.[1]

2. Answer to Rothschild: agreed to lose[?] the last words. See A (to be returned by Granville)[2]
3. Hartington's draft—to be considered on Friday if necessary.[3]
4. Ld Derby introduced the question of a New Guinea Protectorate.[4]
Protectorate v. Annexation discussed. Chancellor for P. with recognition of Native Titles. By agreement with such as you could get at. Agreed to on the basis of Sir R. Herbert's memorandum dated (July 9 & 18) marked A.[5]
All native rights to be recognised & respect[ed] & native chiefs communicated with where practicable.

[*New Guinea:*] As to Confederation of Colonies with England. Extent of Coast. Request of Natives Protectorate. Proposes to protect natives against foreign settlements & against landowners on the coast only.[6]

To Sir W. V. HARCOURT, home secretary,   MS Harcourt dep. Adds 10
6 August 1884.

Be so kind as to send down to me a copy of the closing passage (or passages) of the paper you read yesterday, describing the basis of our *provisional* stay in Egypt.[7]

7. Th.

Wrote to The Queen l.l.—Sir H. Ponsonby—Ld Kimberley—and minutes. Shopping. H of C. 4¾-8 and 10-12¾.[8] Saw Mr H—Ld Kensington—Ld Northbrook—Chancr of Exr—Chancr of E. *cum* Sir W. Harcourt—Ld Hartington—Scotts—All Saints Sister—Ld Sherbrook—Sir C. Forster. Dined at Sir C. Forsters. Read O.T. Folks.

To LORD KIMBERLEY, Indian secretary, 7 August 1884.   Add MS 44547, f. 92.

I cannot but accede to your proposal[9] that you should, under the circumstances as they now stand, offer to Dufferin the Viceroyalty of India. I hope he will have in view Ellenborough and Lytton as lights to warn him off the rocks.
[P.S.] On inquiry I find that I submit the name chosen by us. But in this case I think I ought to make a submission to the Queen before you say anything to Dufferin: and all the more so because he is pretty sure to go.

[1] Telegram this day to E. H. Egerton, FO 78/3684.
[2] Not found; on renewal of Rothschild's loan; 'the answer expresses an interest in the matter and an opinion that the money can and will be repaid without any guarantee'; CAB 41/18/44.
[3] Hartington to Stephenson, 8 August: preparation of a Nile expedition; *Sudan campaign*, i. 45.
[4] And reported the decision for a Protectorate over non-Dutch New Guinea to the Queen, *L.Q.V.*, 2nd series, iii. 524. Granville's conversation with Münster on 8 August referred to British/colonial discussions 'nearer a conclusion than is yet known to the public'; Granville to Ampthill, 9 August, F.O.C.P. 5065, f. 58.
[5] For this mem. see L. Trainor, 'Policymaking at the Colonial Office . . . 1884-5', *Journal of Imperial and Commonwealth history*, vi. 119 (1978).   [6] Add MS 44645, f. 172; see Morrell, 254.
[7] Not found.   [8] Questions; supply; *H* 292. 116.
[9] Of 6 August, Add MS 44228, f. 150, rather curtly suggesting Dufferin; Kimberley wrote on 12 August, ibid., f. 154: 'Dufferin accepts'.

8. Fr.

Wrote to Ld Granville—Ld Huntley—Ld Spencer—Sir C. Dilke—Ld North-brook—The Queen—& minutes. Dined with Mr Knowles. Drive with C.G. Saw Mr H—Ld RG—H.J.G.—Prof. Huxley & Mr Knowles—Dr Jessop—Ld North-brook—Chanc. of Exr. Read Old Town Folks—H. of C. $4\frac{3}{4}$-$7\frac{3}{4}$ and $10\frac{1}{4}$-$11\frac{3}{4}$.[1]

What do you think of appointing a small Committee on Redistribution? Kimberley, Hibbert, Childers?, Sir C. Dilke, Lefevre (and Hartington if he liked) to prepare schemes or materials of schemes, & give directions for obtaining information as to Boundaries. W.E.G. Aug. 8 84.[2]

To Sir C. W. DILKE, president of the local government   Add MS 43875, f. 176. board, 8 August 1884.

I thank you for your very considerate note,[3] but I am glad you had a turn of repose, and I do not think there will be the least umbrage given in any quarter.
[P.S.] What do you think of appointing a small committee on Redistribution? Kimberley, Childers, Sir C. Dilke, Lefevre (& Hartington if he likes). To prepare schemes or materials of schemes, & give directions for obtaining information as to Boundaries.[4]

9. Sat.

Wrote to The Queen l.l.l.l.—Capt. Bigge Tel.—Mr Briscoe—Ld Granville—Archdeacon of Bristol—and minutes. H of C. $12\frac{1}{4}$-$1\frac{1}{2}$. Bpric Br. Bill.[5] Cabinet 4-$6\frac{1}{2}$. Saw Mr H—Ld RG—Ld Granville—Ld Northbrook—Chancr of Exr. Dined with Lucy. Finished Old Town Folks—Read Queen of the Humber.[6]

Cabinet. Sat. Aug. 9. 84. 4 P.M. at H. of C[7]
1. Queen's speech: read & settled.
2. New Guinea. Proposal to limit the Protectorate to the S. Coast of N. Guinea—with wide meaning of the phrase: leave N. Coast alone. From Dutch line on W. including S.E. Peninsula (Münster's communication with Granville reported by Northbrook).[8] C.O. to examine boundary carefully. Terms of communication to Münster arranged.
3. New Session probably 21st or 23rd. Prorogue till a day in Septr—about 13th or 15th.
4. Govt. Committee to prepare materials for Redistribution and give directions as to Boundaries.[9]

[1] Questions; supply; *H* 292. 277.
[2] Add MS 44645, f. 175.
[3] Of regret at absence for division on vote for Albany's funeral; Add MS 44149, f. 221.
[4] Dilke preferred no cttee.; if one appt., then suggests Kimberley, Lefevre, Hartington, Fitzmaurice, Cotes; the cttee. was set up; Add MS 44149, ff. 223-5.
[5] Bishopric of Bristol Bill; *H* 292. 358.
[6] S. Woodhouse, *The queen of the Humber; or legends . . . relating to Kingston-on-Hull* (1884).
[7] Add MS 44645, f. 173.
[8] Conversation on 8 August (see 6 Aug. 84n.), content later disputed by Münster; Granville told Münster this day that the Protectorate was for the 'part of the island which specially interests the Australian colonies'; Morrell, 256-7.
[9] Members: Kimberley, Hartington, Childers, Dilke, Chamberlain, Lefevre, plus Hibbert, Cotes; Add MS 44645, f. 174: Derby and James later added, Jones *1884*, 181.

10. 9 S. Trin.

Chapel Royal mg (Dr Wace preached) & aft. Saw Ld Sydney—Mr Hamilton—Sir Thos G. Dined at Lucy's. Read Hillocks[1]—Carter's Mem. of Mrs Monsell.[2] Wrote to Mr Hamilton—Mrs Tait.

11. M.

Wrote to The Queen l.l.—Ld Granville Tel.—Ld Kinnaird—Sir E. Grey—Ld Spencer—& minutes. Saw Mr S—Ld R.G. Shopping, packing books, & preparation for departure. Read Carter's Monsell. Dined at Lucy's. H of C. $4\frac{1}{2}$–8. Spoke once more! on Egypt.[3] Wrote a sort of will for Mrs Stume.

12. Tu. [Hawarden]

Wrote to The Queen—Ld Northbrook—& minutes. 2.20–7.45 Luxurious journey to Hawarden. Drew Mrs Stume's Will! Last preparations for departure. Read Carter's Monsell—Short Parliaments[4]—Ebers's Uarda.[5] The most *golden* harvest I have seen for many years.

To LORD NORTHBROOK, first lord of the admiralty,   Add MS 44547, f. 93.
12 August 1884.

I am much taken with the idea, I believe your's or Granville's, that the Mudir of Dongola might serve to play the part so unhappily projected by Gordon for Zebehr.

Could not you and he put in motion at once, to *try* whether any thing can be made of it.

Some Egyptian money would be well and cheaply bestowed on it if it can be made to work. You have Kitchener on the spot: and, were you yourself in Cairo, you would have to work through him by the telegraph.[6]

It is of such immense importance to solve the Gordon problem at once, and though this is only a chance, yet no chance should be neglected.

13. Wed.

Ch. $8\frac{1}{2}$ A.M. Wrote to Reeves & Turner—Mr Seymour Tel.—Ld Granville—Z. Outram—& minutes. Began the settling down. Read Sellon on Phallos worship[7]—Broca on hybridity[8]—Paul on Short Parliaments (finished). Wrote a serious & difficult Memorandum on the political situation.[9]

---

[1] J. I. Hillocks, *Hard battles for life and usefulness* (1884).
[2] T. T. Carter, *Harriet Monsell. A memoir* (1884); warden of the rescue house at Clewer, see above v. lxi; no mention of diarist's activities.
[3] Questions; spoke on Northbrook's mission in a spirited conclusion to the Session; *H* 292. 465.
[4] A. Paul, *Short parliaments. A history of the national demand for frequent general elections* (1883).
[5] G. Ebers, *Uarda* (1877).
[6] Northbrook agreed but commented: 'I think Kitchener has as yet hardly had time to master the situation.' Horatio Herbert *Kitchener, 1850–1916; with Wolseley in Egypt 1882, Sudan 1884–5; sirdar of Egyptian army 1892; conquered Sudan 1898; later field marshal etc.
[7] E. Sellon, *Annotations on the sacred writings of the Hindus . . . illustrating their priapic rites and phallic principles* (n.d., 2 ed. 1902).
[8] P. P. Broca, *On the phenomenon of hybridity*, ed. C. Blake (1864).
[9] See 19 Aug. 84.

14. Th.

Wrote to Mr J. Godley—Ld Northbrook—Sir H. Ponsonby—Ld Brougham—Bp of Liverpool—Sir S. Scott & Co.—Mrs Hawkins—and minutes. Finished Latin Epitaph on Dean G. Wellesley. Hawarden flower show in the grounds. Spoke to the people for C.G.[1] Saw Mr Johnson—Mr Applin—Mr Balfour of Liverpool.[2] Read Green, Stubbs, Ranke, English histories, thro' the morning.[3]—Ebers, Uarda—History of Reform.[4] Ch. 8½ A.M.

To LORD NORTHBROOK, first lord of the admiralty,   Add MS 44546, f. 93.
14 August 1884.

1. I send you by this post Egyptian letters,[5] one from a certain Sabinjie, unknown to me personally, who testifies to the dislike of the English in Egypt. I daresay you saw lately in the P.M. Gazette a more telling testimony of the same kind. The subject is serious.

2. Dufferin's telegrams of the 12th and 13th reached me today. The first expresses suspicions which I fully share, but the second seems to open a door of hope.

3. Every day increases the wonder of hearing nothing from Gordon, when in so many odd ways we have heard so much about him. His question to the Mudir of Dongola about a relieving force is in all likelihood a repetition of the *ruse* he tried soon after his arrival when he announced that English soldiers would almost immediately be at Khartoum. I find that Egerton has for himself arrived at the conclusion that Gordon *will* not correspond with us. All this makes it most perplexing to consider what is to happen if your expedition goes, & leads me more & more to hope that the matter may end with the preparations.
[P.S.] This needs no reply.

15. Fr.

Ch. 8½ A.M. Wrote to Mrs Glanville—Mr J. R. Hughes tel.—Ld Spencer—Ld Strafford—Mr Childers—Mr Callaway—W.H.G.—& minutes. Draft of a covering letter to the Queen[6] for my Memm. Walk with Canon Holland. Read Glanville's Essays[7]—Social Life under Anne[8]—Lay Argument on Butler's Analogy[9]—Hist. Reform Question.

To Sir C. W. DILKE, president of the local government   Add MS 44547, f. 95.
board, 15 August 1884.

I was on the point of writing to you as 'Convenor' (*Scoticè*) of the Committee on materials of Redistribution, to express my contrition for a *gross* act of forgetfulness in forgetting to name the Attorney General as a member of it.

He had long ago offered himself, but apart from this the offer to him was plainly due, &

[1] *T.T.*, 15 August 1884, 8b.
[2] Perhaps Alexander Balfour, Liverpool merchant.
[3] i.e. J. R. Green (see 19 Feb. 78), W. Stubbs (see 22 Nov. 75) and L. von Ranke, *A history of England principally in the seventeenth century*, 6v. (1875).
[4] A. Paul, *The history of reform* (1884).
[5] Returned on 18 April but untraced; Add MS 44267, f. 75.
[6] See 19 Aug. 84.
[7] Volume of essays sent by widow of a colonial, probably privately printed as not traced; note of thanks at Add MS 44547, f. 94.
[8] J. Ashton, *Social life in the reign of Queen Anne* (1882).   [9] Untraced.

I feel so sure the Cabinet would have jumped at it that I think we ought to treat it as a correction of an oversight, and I would ask you to write and invite him accordingly.

Since, your note reached me.[1] I hope local inquiries will not be stinted. They should not I think be restricted to Boroughs: but should show how, outside of Boroughs, the Counties, & especially the populous Counties, could best be divided into single-member districts. This would be a material element in considering the question whether we shall or shall not proceed upon the basis of such a division. It will be a great advantage if your researches bring into view the respective merits of several modes of proceeding: I am extremely glad to hear of such proofs of improvement in Sir J. Lambert's health; but I do not see why you or he should be burdened by writing to me at intermediate stages of the work, except when there is any special point on which you may think that I could usefully give an opinion. The judgment on the collected materials will of course have to be reserved for the Cabinet.

16. Sat.

Ch. 8½ A.M. Wrote to Mr Seymour Tel.—Ld Granville l.l.—Ld Rosebery—Rev. J.L. Ross—Mr Dodson—Sir J. Pauncefote—& minutes. Unpacking books. Walk with Harry, for family matters. Read Ch. Quart. Rev.—other papers of Glanville (inferior)—History of Reform—Beard Hibbert Lectures.[2]

To LORD ROSEBERY, 16 August 1884.   N.L.S. 10023, f. 22.

I am truly sorry that the overflow of my troubles should so frequently wash down on you.

I should think that either the first or the second free day, Thursday or Friday, would be better for the deputation[3] than one of the speaking days, on which it would be prudent for me to keep myself quiet till the time comes, for my *physique* as it is called is not now at all what it was during the campaign of 1879–80: I judge by the last three months in particular, & those things cannot mend.

If you settle that I should see the Depn. in Edinburgh Mr Macgregor (who has written to me) would I have no doubt be glad to receive them & me at his hotel. But in my opinion whatever is quietest is at present best, with reference to the question of Disestablishment.

The general situation is beyond any thing complicated, & there will be plenty to talk about.

I spoke to you about County Meetings & you blocked my ball effectively. But I suppose there ought to be *towns*meetings all over Scotland.

17. 10 S. Trin.

Ch. 11 A.M. and 6½ P.M. Wrote to Mr W. Rathbone—Ld Derby—Mr Applin—Ld Spencer—Mrs Th—The Queen—& minutes. Conversation with Mr Holland. Finished Carter's Mem. Monsell—Mr Beard, Hibbert Lectures—Christian Confession.

---

[1] Of 14 August, Add MS 44149, f. 225: 'we have not found much difference of opinion at the committee'.
[2] C. Beard, *The Reformation* (1883); Hibbert lectures.
[3] On disestablishment, led by Hutton; Add MS 44288, f. 199. See 29 Aug. 84.

18. M.

Ch. 8¼ A.M. Wrote to Sir H. Ponsonby—Ld Granville—Sir W. Dunbar—Ld Dufferin—Rev. Mr Palmer—Sol. Gen. for Ireland—Mr Seymour, & minutes. Worked on materials for Midlothian. Conversation with Canon Holland, who left us. Read Beard's Lectures—History of Reform—Tracts: Church Quart. Review. Drive with C.

19. Tu.

Ch. 8¼ A.M. Wrote to Ld Hartington—Ld Granville—Mr Seymour—Sir H. Ponsonby—The Queen—The D. of Westminster—Lord Rosebery—& minutes. Drive with C. Reviewed carefully my Memorandum and covering letter and sent them to the Queen. Also an anxious letter from & reply to Hartington. Finished History of Reform—Read Beard's Lectures.

To LORD HARTINGTON, war secretary,   Chatsworth MSS 340. 1498.
19 August 1884.[1]

I am not very well to-day, but I will answer your letter to the best of my ability.

A movement of British troops to Dongola (with or without Egyptian) would be a step of great political importance, and clearly could not be decided on without reference to the members of the Cabinet. It might depend upon the answers whether they need be called together, which would be on more grounds than one inconvenient.

Next I should like to know *at what date* this forward movement from Wadi Halfa *could* commence supposing it agreed on? While I entirely sympathise with your anxiety that we should not mar any operation which may be proper by delay, I think you would admit that, unless there is a necessity of time, the moment is more unfortunate than not for a decision, inasmuch as the lapse of time, and Gordon's renewed communication with the Mudir, while nothing is sent to us, seem to strengthen the presumption that he purposely refrains from communicating with us. I nearly, though not quite, adopt words received to-day from Granville, 'It is clear, I think, that Gordon has our messages, and does not choose to answer them.'[2]

If the time has come when a decision must be taken whether we go to Dongola or not, then I think the Cabinet should know what force you propose to send there, and most of all, for what purpose it is to go. These two questions are to a certain extent connected with one another.

May we reasonably believe that Gordon, if he thinks fit, can make his way to Dongola? This I can believe probable. But will he do it?

By much the best idea before us at this time is, I think, that of Northbrook that we ought to make the Mudir of Dongola play the part of Zebehr, and take over Khartoum, so putting an end to this most perplexing and distressing affair.

I think it possible that this may be your view too.

For one, I should not be unwilling to stretch a point for the purpose of forwarding this plan: though I should have thought it better forwarded by money, and perhaps material, than by a *British* force; with which I associate the very serious danger of stirring a religious war. Surely it is singular to note that our force, gallant as it was, could not get rid of

---

[1] In Holland, i. 480; Hartington on 18 August, Add MS 44147, f. 99, asked authorization of advance of a small force to Dongola.

[2] Ramm II, ii. 230; in fact Granville's words exactly.

Osman Digna, and that matters now look as if he might be more easily dealt with since the withdrawal.

You refer, I believe correctly, to Northbrook's opinion; but do not appear to have had full communication with him.

If I might make a recommendation it would be that you should bring your views into full comparison with his, and endeavour to frame a plan in concert with him, which he may endeavour to work out in Egypt.

Would it be quite fair to the Cabinet, or to certain members of it, to ask them to take a *step* in advance, without a plan, that they might know what they were about, and be assured that they were not about to become unawares the slaves of Gordon's (probably) rebellious ideas.

[P.S.] I am to see Northbrook at Dalmeny on Wed. or Thursday of next week.

To The QUEEN, 19 August 1884.   RA C49/71.

Mr Gladstone most humbly submits to Your Majesty's gracious consideration the accompanying *Memorandum* on the political situation in connection with the Franchise Bill.

He has never hesitated to lay before Your Majesty, if public duty seemed to call for it, any of the opinions, classed as popular, which he might sincerely hold.

The Memorandum has been drawn from him by a sentiment of a distinct character. That sentiment, closely allied with his convictions is an unwillingness to see political power further dissociated from the hereditary principle.

With this impression is associated the further belief that the hereditary principle, as it is embodied in the House of Lords, cannot afford to enter into a direct conflict with the representative power; and that the controversy on the Franchise Bill now represents the beginning of such a conflict, the further development of which it is, in the highest degree, for the interest of the State to avert.

The gravity of the considerations thus suggested will, as Mr Gladstone humbly hopes, suffice to excuse him for laying before Your Majesty a paper which goes beyond the ordinary limits of his official submissions.

Secret.   *The Franchise Bill and The present Situation*[1]

1. In this Memorandum an endeavour will be made to distinguish broadly all such propositions as are disputed between opposite parties from such as are, or seem to be, beyond dispute.

2. For example; it is contested between Tories and Liberals whether the Government or the Opposition are responsible for having brought about the present conflict between the majority of the House of Commons and the majority of the House of Lords: whether the mass of the nation are really with the Government and the Franchise Bill, or with the Opposition: and whether, in the event of a Dissolution of Parliament after the October session, and a second rejection of the Franchise Bill by the House of Lords, the present constituency would return a Liberal or a Tory Parliament. On these three questions the Liberals say one thing, and the Tories are believed to say another.

3. But there is no dispute upon the proposition that there is at the present juncture a very serious conflict between the majority in the Commons, and the majority in the Lords; and that this conflict will have some serious issue.

4. Again, it is indisputable that the Liberal party, and the great open, & open-air,

---

[1] Final version of the mem., copied by the secretary, initialled and dated by Gladstone, 19 August 1884; RA C49/71. Holograph draft at Add MS 44768, f. 93. See 25 Aug. 84.

meetings which it has promoted, have very generally, in consequence of the virtual rejection of the Franchise Bill, demanded organic change in the House of Lords.

5. Some persons think that this demand is so deeply rooted in feeling and conviction, that it has assumed a permanent form; and that the party as a whole will continue to press for organic change in the House of Lords, even if the Franchise Bill should be passed by that House in the October Session.

6. My judgment may be biassed by my wishes; but, such as it is, it does not lead me to adopt this opinion. What is termed 'tall talk' on the one side, necessarily begets the same on the other side. Undoubtedly, like most of those with whom I communicate, I had not anticipated so loud and general a demand, from Liberal and popular quarters, for this great organic change. Still I have a confident, a very confident hope, that if the Franchise Bill be passed when next presented, this cry, which will certainly receive no countenance from the Government as a whole, will die away.

7. From this point of view, the matter is comparatively simple, and no new feature of a fundamental character will be introduced into the political situation.

8. But the general expectation is that the Bill will be again rejected.

9. There can be no doubt that this will give additional intensity to the conflict.

10. Admirable as has been the conduct of the people in the present controversy, it may be doubtful whether in some few portions of the country, where the desire and demand for the franchise are the keenest, that 'violent pressure', of which Lord Salisbury has asserted the absence, may not be supplied by infractions of the law. But, setting aside this painful supposition, it may be taken as certain that a second rejection, not followed, as it was in 1832, by the almost immediate succumbing of the majority in the House of Lords, will produce an extreme exasperation of feeling in all those who are friendly to the Franchise Bill.

11. From that time forward, it may be no longer possible for the Government to maintain its present attitude. The question will be conclusively raised whether the hereditary or the representative majority is to prevail; and it will be thought impossible to avoid inquiring what provision should be made for saving the country, in future times, from the risk of being torn by the recurrence of similar crises.

11A. This result should be looked fully in the face; and one portion of the case on which the anticipation is founded, appears to be open to little dispute.

12. The safest way of considering this question is to assume, for the sake of argument, that the Tories are right, and the Liberals wrong, on the disputable matters which were named at the beginning of this paper; or at least on the one which the Tories regard as essential, namely this, that upon a Dissolution (whether following a resignation or not) they would come into power.

13. It is believed on all hands that the so-called National party in Ireland will on a Dissolution be increased. It is supposed that the increase will be from a little over forty to near eighty; that the principal part of this increase would be obtained by taking (say) twenty-five seats from the Liberal party; and that, if the Liberal Ministry were then still in power, these eighty votes, added to the votes of the Tories, would promptly displace it.

15. It is not necessary to inquire how far the position thus attained by the Tory party would be a stable one; and, so far as the main purpose of the present paper is concerned, it may for argument's sake be supposed, or assumed, that they would be strong enough to keep down not only the Liberal Opposition, but any of that united action between the regular Opposition and the Irish Nationalists, which has been so common in the present Parliament, and to which they would probably have owed their obtaining the reins of government.

16. If indeed the Tories are *wrong* in their expectations, their position will be most disastrous. Circumstances may be supposed under which it might in the House of Commons more or less resemble that, to which they had fallen in 1833 after the first Reform Act, with this addition that the whole Liberal party might have become finally committed to some proposal of organic change in the House of Peers. But the purpose of this paper

is to examine what will be the condition and prospects of the Constitution if all goes in favour of the Tory party, and as they would themselves desire and appoint it.

17. We have then before us, as conditions of the problem, the Tories, triumphantly installed in power; the Liberals in opposition, a disappointed and incensed minority.

18. I take it to be among things indisputable that in these circumstances, when the defeat of their Franchise Bill had been crowned by their own defeat, organic change in the House of Lords would become a prime and fundamental article in the Liberal creed, certain to be professed in every Liberal constituency.

19. The next question is, whether this will or will not, be a serious fact. It will not be a serious fact, if either (1). Organic change in the House of Lords is a light matter, or (2). The adoption of it into the Liberal creed is a light matter, as not being likely to lead to a practical result.

20. On the first of these questions, my reply would be without any hesitation, that organic change in the House of Lords is not a light but a very serious, matter.

21. The House of Lords has for a long period been the habitual and vigilant enemy of every Liberal Government. It might be difficult to cite a single occasion by way of exception, except that on which they supported the Government of Lord Palmerston in the matter of the Lorcha, or Bowring, War with China. At times, too, they have been more, and at times less, forbearing. But as a rule they have opposed and crippled, as far as they could, Liberal legislation, and have constituted a strong, permanent, impregnable fortress of the Tory party.

22. It cannot be supposed that to any Liberal this is a satisfactory subject of contemplation.

23. Nevertheless some Liberals, of whom I am one, would rather choose to bear all this for the future as it had been borne in the past, than raise the question of an organic reform in the House of Lords. The interest of the party seems to be in favour of such an alteration: but it should in my judgment, give way to a higher interest, which is national and imperial: the interest of preserving the hereditary power as it is, if only it will be content to act in such a manner as will render that preservation endurable.

24. I do not speak of this question as one, in which I can have a personal interest or share. Age, and political aversion, alike forbid it. Nevertheless, if the Lords continue to reject the Franchise Bill, it will come.

25. Perhaps after having asserted that the legislative action of the House of Lords is generally mischievous, I ought to say how and why it is that I wish it to continue.

26. I wish it to continue, for the avoidance of greater evils. These evils are not only long and acrimonious controversy, difficulty in devising any satisfactory mode of reform, and delay in the general business of the country, but other and more permanent mischiefs. I desire the hereditary principle, notwithstanding its defects, to be maintained, for I think it in certain respects an element of good, a barrier against mischief. But it is not strong enough for direct conflict with the representative power, and it will only come out of the conflict sorely bruised and maimed. Further; organic change of this kind in the House of Lords may strip and lay bare, and in laying bare may weaken, the foundations even of the Throne.

27. My first question then is answered by the conclusion, that organic change in the House of Lords is not then, a light matter in itself. I pass to the second.

28. Is it, then, a light matter that this article of organic change in the House of Lords should be incorporated in the creed of the Liberal party as a party?

29. The answer is, no: for such incorporation means that the thing will be accomplished.

30. At least such appears to be the lesson taught by history: and it is history, rather than inclination or imagination, which must in such a matter be our guide.

31. During the last half-century, the whole course of our legislation in great matters, has been directed by the Liberal party; though, in some cases, the work has not finally been finished in its hands. But every great question, once adopted into its creed, has marched

onwards, with real and effectual if not always uniform progress, to a triumphant consummation.

32. It may suffice to name Repeal of the Test Act, Roman Catholic Emancipation, Parliamentary Reform, Repeal of the Corn Law, Repeal of the Navigation Law, Reform of the Tariff, the Abolition of Church Rate, the Reform of the Universities, the abolition of Tests in them and elsewhere, the Disestablishment of the Irish Church, Municipal Reform, important changes in the Land Laws, Secret Voting, and National Education.

33. It seems difficult in reviewing this list, which might be greatly extended, to deny that we seem to have hold of something like a political axiom when we say that the adoption of a legislative project into the Creed of the Liberal party at large is the sure prelude to its accomplishment.

34. It appears to follow that it is now a great object of duty and policy to prevent the adoption by the Liberal party into its political creed of this great new Article, Organic Change in the House of Lords.

35. It has seemed plain that this cannot be prevented by the displacement of the present Government, or by the return of a Parliament hostile to it; but only by the passing of the Franchise Bill, which the Liberal party, having confined it within the limits of the strictest moderation, has definitively adopted as its own to stand or fall by.

36. It seems indeed, that the Franchise Bill would of itself, in one sense, be the death-warrant of the existing Government: for, followed in all likelihood by immediate redistribution and next by Dissolution, the Irish party and the Tory Opposition would (it is almost certain) then at once put an end to it; even supposing, which is most improbable, that an earlier opportunity could not in the present Parliament be found for the purpose. But whereas the disappearance of the present Administration *after* the passing of the Franchise Bill would be an affair of small moment, further rejection, or rejections, of the Franchise Bill would probably prove to be a very different affair: and, entirely apart from, perhaps even against the wishes of many or most of the present Ministers, would, through the agency of the party that supports them, although it might be in the moment of their defeat and discomfiture, inflict a mortal wound upon the present legislative constitution of the country.

37. The sum of this memorandum as a whole may be briefly thus presented. It goes to show that, whoever is right, and whoever is wrong as to the separation of Franchise from Redistribution, and as to the present action of the House of Lords, the way to keep the country quiet, and the present legislative constitution undisturbed, is to be found nowhere unless in the speedy passing of the Franchise Bill.

38. To present this proposition for consideration, which the importance of the subject-matter seems to claim for it, is the exclusive purpose of the present memorandum, which has not been written, at least not consciously written, in the spirit of controversy. To proceed further would be alike beyond its province, and my own.

39. Yet I may say in conclusion that there is no personal act, if it be compatible with personal honour, and likely to conduce to an aim which I hold very dear, that I would not gladly do for the purpose of helping to close the present controversy, and in closing it to prevent the growth of one probably more complex and more formidable. WEG. Hawarden Aug. 19. 1884.

20. *Wed.*

Ch. 8¼ A.M. Wrote to Sir H. Ponsonby Tel.—Ld Strafford Tel.—Ld Spencer—Ld Hartington—The Queen l.l.—Dr Hoffmeister[1]—Rev. Mr Mackey[2]—Sir H.

---

[1] Knighthood for (Sir) William Carter Hoffmeister, 1817–90; surgeon apothecary to the Queen.
[2] Donald John Mackey, antiquarian and episcopal incumbent in Perth, had sent a tract; Add MS 44547, f. 98.

Havelock [Allan]—and minutes. The whole 'family', 18 in number, sat to Webster Photographer: all assembled, & thank God all well. Drive with C. Worked on arranging the year's supply of books. Read Beard—Ingelow's Mopsa[1]—MacEwan on Caird.[2]

To LORD HARTINGTON, war secretary, 20 August 1884.   Add MS 44547, f. 98.

Doubtless you have seen Cowper's letter.[3]

I understand it to say that when our redistribution Bill is *introduced*, the Lords ought then, & not before, to *pass* the Franchise Bill.[4]

Is it conceivable that the Tories would come into such an arrangement? It would be most difficult for us to have a Bill ready for introduction early in November.

But perhaps you would say we ought to face that difficulty, *if* the Tories, or any considerable number of them, were willing to come into the arrangement.

That is also my opinion.

I can hardly look upon the matter as practical. But if men want a bridge for retreat in argument, they are not always fastidious as to logic.

I am inclined to think that, to prevent mischief from any appearance of obstinacy, I might say a word in Midlothian to the effect of this note.

21. Th.

Ch. 8½ A.M. Wrote to Sir H. Ponsonby—Mr Seymour Tel. l.l.l.—Ld Hartington—Mr? Stilkie[5]—Bp of Chester—Dean of Llandaff—& minutes. Saw W.H.G. on Estate matters. Worked much on books. Finished my draft of Epitaph for Dean Wellesley: consulting Willy and Edward. Read Beard—Ingelow's Mopsa. Thirteen to dinner. Conversation with Mr Mayhew—Mr Johnson.

To LORD HARTINGTON, war secretary,   Chatsworth MSS 340. 1504.
21 August 1884. '*Private*'.

With reference to the first paragraph of your letter,[6] I do not doubt that correspondence on Gordon & the Soudan is to all of us a matter of extreme anxiety. I know of no way of alleviating the case except much forbearance and giving eventual credit for the best and most considerate intentions.

The greatness of the difficulties already surmounted by these means encourages me to hope that we may also overcome what remains: I mean among ourselves, for whether we can survive the Egyptian business in Parliament is indeed very doubtful.

I shall probably receive from you to-morrow the information for which I asked: and in the meantime I would say a word on two points which I hope will create no difficulty.

1. I can take upon me to assure you that you are mistaken about Harcourt. He *consented* to the Vote of Credit, and the preparations under it. He certainly so consented out of

[1] J. Ingelow, *Mopsa the fairy* (1869).

[2] C. M. MacEwan, 'Dangerous Divinity' (1882); on a lecture by Caird.

[3] In *T.T.*, 18 August 1884, 8d, proposing compromise *via* a Seats Bill in the autumn session.

[4] Hartington agreed with this interpretation: unlikely the tories would undertake beforehand to pass the Franchise bill, 'but I think that, very probably, without any previous pledge they will actually do it'; 21 August, Add MS 44147, f. 115.

[5] *Sic*; unidentified.

[6] Of 20 August, Add MS 44147, f. 105: 'I have received your letter of the 19th, which has caused me considerable anxiety and does not diminish the difficulties with which I have to deal.'

deference to you, and in this he was not alone: but you would be the last person to say his claims to know what was going on were thereby diminished. I find he is at Oban and I would have written or telegraphed to him to-day to name the subject to him but that I do not like to interfere with you.

A special reason, I think, for letting him know anything you contemplate is that if my memory be correct nothing was proposed definitively about going beyond Wadi Halfa in the Cabinet of the *9th*. Perhaps my recollection is wrong: I cannot now rely upon it as well as formerly.

2. You say that you are making preparations of such a character as would make it appear almost absurd not to send the expedition; but, if these are the preparations stated by you to the Cabinet, we must take the risk. I am sure you would not put them in such a position without their consent.

I agree in the force of your argument from the silence of Stewart and Power: it has however much to meet.

22. *Fr.*

Ch. 8½ A.M. Wrote to Ld Hartington Tel. l.l.—Sir W. Harcourt Tel.—Mr Potter—Mr Seymour Tel.—D. of Argyll—Ld Rosebery Tel.—Wms & Norgate—and minutes. Worked on sorting & arranging drawers. Read Bp Stubbs's Lecture[1]— Mr Savile on the Situation—Beard's Lectures—Ingelow's Mopsa. Worked on my drawers.

To the DUKE OF ARGYLL, 22 August 1884. '*Private*'.   Add MS 44547, f. 100.

What do you think of Cowper's letter?[2]

It was foolish to write it, unless he has reason to believe that the Tories are willing to accept the form of proceeding he proposes. I understand that form to be that if the Lords introduce their measure of redistribution in the Commons the Lords are then to pass the Franchise Bill. That is they are to take the introduction as a satisfying indication of the views of the Government.

It would be absurd for us to do this unless they, that is to say a sufficient number of them, are ready to close with this method of arrangement. Have you any hope that they would do this? Certainly if they would, I would not hesitate to *propose* it to the Cabinet.

To T. B. POTTER, M.P., 22 August 1884.   Add MS 44547, f. 100.

You may depend upon it that nothing will induce me, or I believe the Government, to commit the fatal mistake of simultaneous treatment of the two subjects of Franchise and Redistribution.[3]

If I understand Lord Cowper's letter, this is not what he proposes. But is there any sign that the Tories would accept his proposal? To go on making first one offer and then another seems a little like a man who bids against his own bid at an auction.

You are eminently a true-hearted man, and as I believe the majority in the House of Commons is true-hearted also. The allegations of the other side remind me that just the same stories were told, and believed, among the Tories in the days of the first Reform Bill.

---

[1] W. Stubbs, 'An address . . . by way of a last statutory lecture [at Oxford]' (1884).

[2] Argyll, at Oban, only knew of Cowper's views by rumour, but wrote on 29 August agreeing with his proposal that Gladstone should introduce a seats bill in the autumn session, such a bill being '*virtually* assented to by all parties'; Add MS 44105, f. 192.

[3] Potter's letter of 20 August, Add MS 44282, f. 175, on Cowper's letter (see 20 Aug. 84n.).

23. Sat.

Ch. 8½ AM. Wrote to Ld Hartington—Mr Seymour l. & Tel.—Ld Rosebery—Mr Ivory Tel.—Mr Nicoll—Rev. C. Beard[1]—W.H.G.—and minutes. Finished Ingelow's Mopsa. Worked on materials for Midlothian. Drive with Lady Grosvenor.

To LORD HARTINGTON, war secretary,   Chatsworth MSS 340. 1506.
23 August 1884. '*Immediate*'.

I entirely appreciate the motives which lead you to substitute Wolseley for Stephenson.[2]

Clearly S.'s idea of this preliminary expedition has been a different one from yours & has approximated in some measure to a final one.

It occurs to me that in announcing Wolseley, while giving him much credit for accepting, you might perhaps refer to his achievement on the Red River [in 1870] as furnishing him with an experience which no one else possesses, & thereby fitting him for the peculiar work you have now in hand. It seems I think almost necessary to give a careful notice of the appointment.

We go to Dalmeny on Wednesday.

To LORD ROSEBERY, 23 August 1884.   N.L.S. 10023, f. 24.

I have just received the inclosed telegram from Mr Ivory;[3] and I send substance of my reply. I thought that after writing to you I was *functus officio*, and I was afraid of confusion if I corresponded in two channels; hence my lamentation that you should be so much troubled, but I knew your capacity for taking trouble to be equal to your inclination.

There is but one difficulty. For the last three or four months I have found a considerable diminuation in my power of lungs and voice. I feel quite uncertain how I should get on with any very large audience: but certain that I could not now undertake as in 1879-80 successive speeches to great audiences on the same day. No wonder if in this respect the wine of life is a little on the lees. In all other respects I am as heretofore at the command of the 'local authority'.

Wolseley is going to take command in Egypt. This does not mean any extension of plans, but indeed a contraction as compared with what Stephenson, now commanding, desires. Wolseley made a great exploit on a small scale at the Red River and will probably now do the same for Dongola.

24. 10 S. Trin.

Ch. 8 AM (H.C.) 11 A M & 6½ P.M. Wrote to Ld Hartington—Ld Rosebery—Sir H. Ponsonby—Mr Russell—Ld Granville—& minutes. Read Sephtons's Sermon[4]—Account of French RC Wars.[5] Finished Beard's Lectures. Conversation with E. Wickham on Future Punishment &c.

---

[1] Charles Beard, 1827-88; unitarian, journalist and historian; see 16 Aug. 84 and Lathbury, ii. 325.

[2] At this late stage, Wolseley superseded Frederick Charles Arthur Stephenson, 1821-1911, for the expedition, though the latter retained command of the army in Egypt until 1888; copy of Hartington to Granville, spelling out reasons, sent on 22 August; Add MS 44147, f. 128. See *Relief of Gordon*, 5, 7 and *Sudan campaign*, i. 51. Stephenson (rightly) thought Wolseley's use of rowing boats and Canadian voyageurs on the Nile impractical; F. C. A. Stephenson, *At home and on the battlefield* (1915), 325.   [3] Not found.

[4] J. Sephton, 'The Lenten element in life' (1884).

[5] Perhaps J. Michelet, *Guerres de religion 1547-72* (various eds.).

25. M.

Ch 8½ AM. Wrote to Sir H. Ponsonby—Dean of Llandaff—Mr Seymour l. & Tel.—Ld Rosebery Tel. l.l.l.—Ld Hartington Tel.—and minutes. Wrote abstract of the 'Secret' Memorandum. Worked on papers—& preparations. Saw Mr Jowett. Drive with the W.s. Read Russian Pamphlet—Uarda[1]—and [blank.]

To Sir H. PONSONBY, the Queen's secretary, 25 August 1884.   RA C49/75.

I send the queries and propositions, longer than I could wish, but still less than a fourth of the original 'Secret' paper.[2]

I have left out everything that relates in any manner to myself personally.

As to any touches beyond the limits of the paper now inclosed, Her Majesty's discretion will be a perfect guide.

I may be biassed, but it seems to me clear, almost glaring, that the further stoppage of the Franchise Bill involves a great constitutional hazard; with regard to which loyalty, patriotism, and selfishness, alike make me desire to clear my conscience.

To your question, why not join Franchise with Redistribution, my reply will be best given in Midlothian.

Confidential.

1. It is expedient to consider the present Parliamentary conflict from the point of view of the Opposition.

2. They are understood to desire, and expect, a second rejection, or effectual stoppage, of the Franchise Bill, in the Autumnal Session.

3. And to anticipate the support of the Country, or at all events of the existing constituency, in such a degree as must bring to an end the present Administration.

4. Let it be assumed, for the sake of argument, that their expectations on both points are well founded.

5. Such, then, is the position as they define it. Is it satisfactory from a Conservative point of view?

6. To answer this question, it becomes necessary to look one step farther.

7. Although the House of Lords is an institution opposed to Liberalism and to Liberal legislation, the Liberal party as a whole has cheerfully acquiesced in all the consequences of its action, until the vote of last July; since which there has already been a serious change.

8. It is assumed to be beyond doubt that, after a *second* rejection of the Franchise Bill by the House of Lords, a demand for organic change in the Constitution of that House will become an inseparable part of the policy, not of this or that individual, but of the Liberal party as a whole.

9. This result will be unimportant if either a. Organic change in the House of Lords is a light matter, or b. The adoption of it into the Liberal Creed is a light matter, and not likely to lead to practical consequences.

10. As to the first, is it or is it not the fact that fundamental change in the hereditary principle, the present basis (in the main) of the House of Lords, will be the deepest question raised in this country during the century, and that then *indeed* the 'balance of power' will be involved?

11. Separable as the subject of the Monarch may be in argument from that of the

---

[1] See 12 Aug. 84.

[2] See 19 Aug. 84. The Queen told Ponsonby to read this shorter version to Goschen; *L.Q.V.*, 2nd series, iii. 531.

Peerage, it is a momentous practical inquiry whether the Monarchy isolated and laid bare will have the same securities, as the Monarchy, associated with a gradation of kindred institutions, has hitherto enjoyed?

12. As to the second point, every great legislative change since 1828 has been conformable to the creed of the Liberal party, and due to its action, though in certain cases not effected by its hands?

13. Of the twelve Parliaments since the Reform Act, the last is the only one, which has not been marked by such legislative changes?

14. Nor is there any case in which such a change, having been taken up by the Liberal party as a whole has failed to take effect?

15. If the foregoing queries can only be answered in one way, it only remains to ask whether there is any method of saving the present Legislative constitution of the country from a vital wound, and the balance of power from hazard, other than the speedy passing of the Franchise Bill? WEG. Hn. Aug. 25. 1884.

26. Tu.

Ch. 8½ AM. Wrote to Mr Seymour l. & Tel l.l.—Mr Morris Tel.—Sir J. Ogilvy—Mr Green Tel.—Mr Budge—Ld Rosebery Tel.—The Queen—Dr Schliemann—Mr T.G. Law. French play well acted by the children at 5 PM. Saw Dr Waters. Spent a real two hours on papers about my affairs: a very rare event. Read Mr Law on the Elisabethan Seminaries—The Lady of the Rock.[1]

To Sir W. V. HARCOURT, home secretary,   MS Harcourt dep. Adds 10.
26 August 1884.

I quite approve of your plan of following Parnell[2]—unless, which is unlikely, anything in his speech should render a change advisable. We cannot I think be too firm in *refusal*: but I thought Trevelyan was wise in adopting a tone not uncivil to the Irish (Nationalist) members.

27. Wed. [Dalmeny, Edinburgh]

Off at 8.20. Edinb. at 4.45. Many at the stations. Said to none more than a few words.[3] Wrote to Sir H. Ponsonby—Ld Strathmore—Ld Granville—& minutes. We drove at once to Dalmeny and found a large party. Saw Mr Agnew MP—Ld Rosebery—Lady Hopetoun—Ld Northbrook: with whom I had a long & late conversation. Read Macintosh Civiln in Scotland Vol. III[4]—Cotton on the Soudan.[5]

28. Th.

Wrote to Ld Granville l. & Tel.—Chancr of Exr—Ld Spencer—Sir J. Pauncefote Tel—and minutes. Saw Barnbougle which I like much.[6] Visited the great bridge

---

[1] *The Lady of the rock; a rhyme* (1884).
[2] Not found.
[3] These speeches, and those in Scotland this visit, in *Political speeches, 1884*.
[4] See 24 Nov. 83.
[5] Untraced article, perhaps by H. J. S. Cotton.
[6] Medieval castle on the shore of the Forth, restored by Rosebery as his retreat.

in course of construction.[1] Forenoon chiefly with Ld Northbrook on Egypt and the Franchise chiefly. Saw Ld Rosebery—Mr Cooper—Mr Godley. Party larger still. Sat to Photographer. Read Macintosh—Guinness on Obstruction[2]—R. Churchill on Crisis[3]—Campbell, Promise & performance[4]—Letter to Ld Aberdeen.[5]

29. Fr.

Wrote to Ld Granville—The Queen l. & Tel.—Ld Dartmouth—Dean of Llandaff—Ld Northbrook—and minutes. 3–4¼ Deputn on Disestablishment.[6] Then to the Forestry Exhibition at Edinburgh: great crowds but we saw objects of much interest. Then to the Liberal Club. Large dinner party. Saw Mr Lang and other gentlemen: incl. Ex Prof. Blackie. Read Macintosh. Worked on the redundant material before me for the operation which begins tomorrow.

30. Sat.

Wrote to D. of Bedford—Mr Seymour Tel. l.l.—and minutes. At 3½ we drove a great cavalcade into Edinburgh; the rain kindly passing off to favour us. First, I received an Address from the Municipality & made a brief reply. Then I went to the most difficult part of my business here, and set forth the case of this crisis especially as to the H. of Lords, at the Corn Exchange, to an audience of 5000 or more, in a speech timed at 1 h. 37 m.[7] They were as good as possible. Returned to Dalmeny soon after 8. Very large party: but retired about 11. Read Macintosh.

31. 11 S. Trin.

On account of an inkling of cold, & in view of Monday kept my bed until 1.30. Read the prayers &c. Wrote to Duke of Argyll—Ld Acton—& minutes. Read The New Theology[8]—Scottish Review on Abp Sharp[9]—Newman's Retractatio.[10]

To LORD ACTON, 31 August 1884.[11]   Add MS 44093, f. 248.

Your letter[12] touches me in a tender place, for to have a visible & audible knowledge of Bishop Strossmayer is one of my great unfulfilled yearnings, and, though I now begin to

---

[1] The Forth Bridge, at Queensferry, 2 miles along the coast from Dalmeny, opened 1890, the chief glory of British industrial architecture. On 2 Sept. the workmen presented him with an axe, and on return to Hawarden he sent them 'entertaining and improving' volumes; Add MS 44547, f. 123; *D.N.*, 3 September 1884, 5g.

[2] J. Guinness Rogers, *N.C.*, xvi. 396 (September 1884).

[3] Lord R. Churchill, 'An antidote to agitation', *F.R.*, xlii. 285 (September 1884).

[4] Not found.

[5] Perhaps his own in *Gleanings*, iv.

[6] The dpn. deferred since 1881 (see Rainy, 29 Nov. 81); *verbatim* report in Add MS 44629, f. 103.

[7] *T.T.*, 1 September 1884, 7a; his 'declaration of personal adherence to the principle of a hereditary House was received in silence, broken only by a few murmurs of dissent'.

[8] J. B. Heard, *Old and new theology* (1884).   [9] *Scottish Review*, iv. 1 (July 1884).

[10] J. H. Newman's 'Postscript', with preface, to his article on inspiration of scripture; see *Newman*, xxx. 354ff.

[11] Holograph; secretary's copy at Add MS 44547, f. 103.

[12] Of 24 August, Add MS 44093, f. 246, on a meeting with Strossmayer.

feel most averse to journeys, I sometimes wonder whether you would take me, when my neck is fairly out of the yoke, to see him. In the meantime, the prospect you hold out of his coming to England is delightful, but the address which you have given him[1] is, not to be depended on. I am under no bond to finish the Egyptian question, or that of redistribution: my only bonds are a bond to carry the franchise Bill or end my official life in the attempt, & a bond in the event of carrying the Franchise Bill to make a serious effort to introduce & carry a measure of redistribution.

Is not this enough? And on what possible ground of equity can you maintain that while in other professions, even in the Government of the Church, there is a desire for an interval between the theatre & the grave, those who follow the profession of all others the most contentious, and 'the most immersed' as Bacon truly says 'in matter', are to be denied this breathing time, this space for the exercise, in their case more necessary than in any other, for recollection & detachment? You have never explained this to me & I am disposed to challenge you.

In the innermost cell of my soul I am inclined to believe that the prolongation of my official life (or my parliamentary life) is of very little consequence to this self-governing country, & that if any where it is of more value to the Slavs of the Balkan peninsula & their neighbours north & south than to anyone else. But they have now tasted freedom, & like other freemen must defend it.

At this moment I am engaged in the serious but interesting task of setting forth the character of the present crisis to a people whose loyalty [to] the Liberal cause is equalled by their singular intelligence & the practical turn of their understanding. They are no whit below the mark of 1879–80: indeed I think they are even more sensitive & keen.

To the DUKE OF ARGYLL, 31 August 1884.   Add MS 44547, f. 103.

I ought to say what I thought you had understood,[2] that after all the ineffectual bids we have already made for fair play from the Opposition without the smallest good result in mollifying them, our position is absolutely immovable, & we can make no more bids without some reasonable expectation of their being accepted, I do not say by the leaders who are I fear beyond hope, but by some considerable portion of the party, which might serve to modify the suicidal action of the House of Lords.

You remember what redistribution was in 1866. It is now used for the same purpose with yet more of concealment, & with an ulterior aim that of forcing a Dissolution.

I thought I was offering or saying a good deal in my letter of the 22nd. You do not seem to view it in that light. In these difficult circumstances the best thing we can do perhaps is to make large allowances for one another.

I am straining every nerve to keep back & to avert the organic reform of the House of Lords: & my greatest opponents are the flabby weakness of Northcote & the unrestrained character of Salisbury.[3]

Dalmeny Mon. Sept. 1. 1884.

Wrote minutes. Worked much on digesting & constructing subjects. Off to Edinburgh at 5: & a speech of 1 h. 50 m.[4] for which my voice, aided by egg-flip,

[1] i.e. Gladstone's address, 10 Downing Street.
[2] See 22 Aug. 84n.
[3] Argyll replied, ill in the Hebrides, 6 September, Add MS 44105, f. 195, accusing Gladstone of becoming suspicious; Argyll defended the Lords' action as not 'so monstrous as you represent it', though 'the balance of argument is against their course as a whole'.
[4] T.T., 2 September 1884, 10a.

lasted beyond expectation. Again an admirable audience. Finished Newman's
Preface. Read B. Doddington's Diary.[1] Saw Mr Law—Mr Stewart—Prof. Calder-
wood—Mr H. Cowper.

2. Tu.

Wrote to Mr Childers—Sir H. Ponsonby—Ld Granville l.l.l.—& minutes. Read
Dodington's Diary—and [blank.] Received Provost of Leith—[Forth] Bridge
Workmen's Depn.[2] Walk with Rosebery. Showed him my private Mem.[3] $6\frac{1}{4}$–$9\frac{1}{4}$.
Once more to Edinb. & spoke or rather bellowed in the Waverley Hall. A small
gang of the enemy at one end resolutely talked against me, with no great effect.[4]
Preparations for departure.

3. Wed. [Invercauld House, Braemar][5]

Wrote to Mr Baillie. Off at 8.15, Invercauld at $6\frac{3}{4}$: most kindly received. The
people gathered more or less at every station: in great crowds at some. I had to
deliver a few sentences to some of these bodies, in answer mostly to Addresses.
A large party. Conversation with Baron Hengenmüller:[6] & with Harcourt. Read
19th Cent on Lords—on Highland Crofters—Federation[7]—Contemp. Rev. on
Lords & on D. of Wellington.[8]

4. Th.

Wrote to Ld Granville—Mr Childers—Mr Hyam[9]—& minutes. We went before
one to the games.[10] Conversation there with the Prince of Wales who desires
the passing of the Franchise Bill. Saw likewise the other Royalties—Lady C.
Hamilton and others: especially Att. General. Conversation with Sir W. Harcourt—Mr Gerard—and others. The Games are of greater interest but still
apparently professional. We returned about five: most lively cheering on departure. Large party again. Read Madame de Sevigné (III)[11]—Bp of Carlisle on
Apparitions[12]—Wordsworth's Poems.

5. Fr.

Wrote to Mr Thomson—Ld Granville l.l. & Tel.—Mr Seymour l. & Tel. l.l.l.—Ld
R. Grosvenor Tel.—Mr Childers—Mr Muir—and minutes. Call of duty at Balmoral & walked back from the Gelder 7 m to try whether walking is for me a
thing wholly of the past. Spent time in reading the Analysis of the Report on
Highland Crofters: a very formidable subject.[13] Read Madame de Sevigné.

[1] *The diary of . . . Bubb Dodington*, ed. H. P. Wyndham (1784).   [2] See 28 Aug. 84n.
[3] See 19, 25 Aug. 84.   [4] *T.T.*, 3 September 1884, 10b.
[5] Seat of James Ross Farquharson, 1835–88; soldier and friend of Prince of Wales; see 30 Aug. 73.
[6] Austrian *chargé*; see 4 Oct. 80.   [7] *N.C.*, xvi. 451, 460 (September 1884).
[8] *C.R.*, xlvi. 313, 414 (September 1884).
[9] His tailor, to send court dress to Balmoral; Add MS 44547, f. 105.
[10] i.e. the Highland Games at Braemar.
[11] Probably the 3v. ed. of her *Lettres choisies* (1810).
[12] H. Goodwin, *C.R.*, xlvi. 423 (September 1884).
[13] Report of Napier's Royal Commission on crofters, *P.P.* 1884 xxxii.

6. Sat.

Wrote minutes. R. Grosvenor came over & we had two or three hours on the situation: of which he now takes a favourable and sanguine view. Also conversation with Sir W. Harcourt. Expedition to Loch Bullaig & back by another route. Walked about ten miles. *Stiff*, but the fine air keeps one fresh. The weather was perfect & the views so fine even for my rather poor eyes. Read Mad. de Sevigné.

7. 15 S. Trin.

Braemar wooden Church[1] 11 A.M. & Holy Communion. Church congregation music & *ensemble* all very good. Wrote to Ld Carlingford—Mr T.E. Rogers—and minutes. Read Nicole[2]—Life of Eliza Fletcher[3]—Ld Adv. on Crofter's Report.[4] Tea at the Fishing Lodge: a party arrived from Mar Lodge. Conversation with the Att. General.

To LORD CARLINGFORD, lord president and   Carlingford MSS CP1/227.
lord privy seal, 7 September 1884. '*Most Private*'.

Granville has made known to me that you are not disposed to take either of the vacant Embassies: I will say the Embassy at Constantinople, because I do not doubt that it is the one which, of the two, you would prefer. I know that I am now about to draw largely on your kindness and indulgence; but I am sure you will appreciate my motives, and the exigencies of the position, when I take upon me to express the hope that you may not decline further to consider this question. I need not dwell on the ability and tact, the thorough knowledge of British feeling & of the opinions of the Government, with which you would discharge the duties of this most important post, especially on the Egyptian, which is the most difficult, side of them; for on these points, taken alone, I have no title to impugn your decision, or raise prolonged argument upon it.

But two other motives urge me powerfully to plead for the request I have already made. The Government is definitively engaged in a crisis, the most grave since 1831–2. We must try to overcome the majority in the House of Lords, but we can only do it by our strength in the nation. To increase that strength by every means in our power becomes, under the circumstances, an urgent duty. In surveying the situation, regard must be had to the several parts of the United Kingdom. Scotland has felt, if not a little resented, the lack of any one in the Cabinet who could be at all addicted to her special interests, since the Duke of Argyll quitted it: and it is of real importance, with reference to the possibilities, I might say the likelihood, of a somewhat early dissolution, that we should take every means of keeping our phalanx complete, and, if we can, of enlarging it. There is no doubt that we should improve the position here, without worsening it elsewhere, by bringing some Scotchman, whom Scotchmen know and love into the Cabinet. This must evidently be a Peer; there is no Commoner with the requisite conditions. I think it quite clear that this cannot wisely be done by enlarging the Cabinet through the revival of a nominal office. Nor could we seek to remove any one of the Peer Ministers who hold the heavier administrative offices. Unfortunately, yours is the only office that does not fall under this description. If you could agree to take the Embassy at Constantinople, it would

---

[1] i.e. the episcopalian church, St Margaret's Braemar Mission.
[2] See 9 Sept. 83.
[3] E. Fletcher, *Autobiography of Mrs Fletcher of Edinburgh* (1874).
[4] Presumably a letter or mem.; not in Add MS 44483.

besides making an admirable provision for a weighty place, enable us to gain the required addition of strength in Scotland. I add my hope that it might secure to the country a larger continuance of your official services, than is promised by the *many* contingencies overhanging, and menacing, the existence of the present Cabinet.

Further. Much to my dissatisfaction, and a little to my surprise, I gathered from Childers, a short time ago, that there is to be a strong and practically an unanimous report from his Committee in favour of the appointment of a Minister of Education;[1] with the intention I apprehend that he shall be a member of the House of Commons. This being so, while the moment of the change may be a little uncertain, the principle of it must be regarded as established, and it seems a necessity that there should be a President of the Council either stripped of, or ready at a moment's notice to drop, his functions with regard to Education. I cannot conceal from myself that this would be a grave and heavy deduction from the dignity and weight of your office, as those functions are the most substantial which it possesses. They might more easily be dropped by a politician of short standing and experience, taking the office in full anticipation of the change, than by one who like yourself has been long before the public, and has been engaged in actual discharge of these very responsible duties.

As to the effect of this change in the office, I have given my opinion; which, if you share it, may exercise an influence on your mind in the direction of which my first and principal representation points. But as to the change itself, that, I apprehend, has to be viewed, prospectively, as a fact.

I have now, I think, laid before you the whole case as it presents itself to my mind: with many regrets on various grounds, but with full confidence you will justly and generously recognise, according to your character, the strength of the considerations which have not permitted me to refrain.[2]

[P.S.] It is probably hardly necessary to assure you that I cannot conceive the origin of the two paragraphs founded on 'Truth' which I have seen in the P.M. Gazette, unless they were bold speculations of the writer & nothing else.

8. M. [*Balmoral*]

Wrote to Mr Seymour—Ld Granville l. & tel.—Dean of Wells—& minutes. Mounted the hill behind in forenoon, also surveying this charming house. At one the party broke up & we went to Balmoral. Saw H.M. after luncheon: see reports. Again in evg. Also Crown Princess whose conversation was most interesting. Drive 3½ h. to Abergeldie, Birk Hall and the Muick. Conversation with Mr Peel—Sir H. Ponsonby. Read Mad. de Sevigné.

9. Tu.

Wrote to Ld Aberdeen—Ld Granville—C.G.—Watson & Smith—Mr Giblin—and minutes. Audience at 2.30. Dined with H.M. Walk with Sir H.P. in forenoon & much conversation on the situation. Read Giblin's Speech—Uarda[3]—Mad. de

---

[1] See to Carlingford, 16 Sept. 84.

[2] Carlingford replied, 11 September, Add MS 44123, f. 226, declining: 'I am not prepared to go abroad, and, in justice to myself, I must add that I cannot think ... that I ought to be expected to accept employment of that class, however important, as at all an equivalent for my Cabinet office ... it was as holder of that nominal office [lord privy seal], as a minister "without portfolio", that you invited me to join your Government, & take charge of Irish business in the H. of Lords.' See 8 Apr. 81.

[3] See 12 Aug. 84.

Sevigné. Council at 3 PM. I had to play Ld President. Conversation with Mr Peel.

To W. R. GIBLIN, prime minister of Tasmania,   Add MS 44547, f. 107.
9 September 1884.

I have this day had the honour to receive your kind and courteous letter and the copy of the speech delivered by you on moving Resolutions relating to the Southern Pacific and to a federal council for Australia.[1]

I shall peruse it with very great interest. Twice in my earlier political life, once so long as over forty nine years ago, I have held office in the Colonial Department of our Government. I have shared actively in all the legislation relating to the Colonies, and I rejoiced in the wise just and most necessary removal of the fetters which, at the beginning of my life, restrained their action. I view with warm satisfaction their remarkable growth, the durable nature of the ties by which they are associated with this country, and the large part which they are evidently destined to play in fulfilling the great designs of Providence for our ever expanding care.

10. Wed. [Mar Lodge]

Wrote to Miss Leeman[2]—Duke of Argyll—Ld Granville—H. Seymour l. & Tel—& minutes. Went with Sir H.P. at 10 to the Churchyard to see the Brown tombstones (and alack! *six* obelisks).[3] Then drive with Ld Fife to Mar Lodge. Much interested in his conversation. Drive to the Derry in afternoon & walk. Whist in evg. Certainly a most pleasant house with an admirable host. Read Mad. de Sevigné. Conversation with Lady Courdale[4] but not at close quarters.

To the DUKE OF ARGYLL, 10 September 1884.   Add MS 44547, f. 108.

I am sorry to hear of the interruption to your yachting[5] but I trust you are again well & free.

The inference I drew from your preceding letter was founded on negative evidence, on what you did not then happen to say, but now have said—I am glad to find myself mistaken, for I have it much at heart to avoid the too improbably impending controversy about the House of Lords & organic change in it.

My inference was untrue but I assure you there was no suspicion.

When you impugn me about the House of Lords I will defend or apologise as the case may be—meantime, I may observe that I should, alas, have said more & more sharply, but for my desire to avoid stimulating the desire for organic change in that body. To my mind, its legislative career has, during the last half century, on the whole been bad.

Of course I am in a great difficulty. On the one hand it seems requisite to show to the adverse majority that the path is a path of danger & that they had better not tread it. On the other hand by making the case strong I stimulate what I want to allay.

As you have mentioned this matter of the House of Lords I would ask you to peruse

[1] Add MS 44487, f. 103. William Robert Giblin, 1840–87; Tasmanian prime minister 1878, 1879–84; represented Tasmania at the Australasian Convention 1883.
[2] Declining request of Miss B. Leeman (of the York family) for an appt. for her lover; Add MS 44547, f. 107.
[3] The grave of John Brown, 1826–83, in Crathie churchyard.
[4] Apparently *sic*, but none of this name.
[5] See to Argyll, 31 Aug. 84n.

carefully the propositions set out in the paper which I inclose. They contain a view of the case which is quite distinct from that usually taken, & which seems to me important. Please do not use the paper as mine, but I take no objection to having the views set forth in it ascribed to me. I sincerely hold them, after much reflection.[1]

11. Th.

Wrote to Mr Seymour Tel.—and minutes. Off at $10\frac{1}{2}$ to the Derry, driving. Then a large party to the top of Beinna Muick Dhu.[2] I went on foot & made out the 20 miles with some effort. $11\frac{1}{2}$ to 7.10. We had no distant view. Four or five walked: Helen among the very best. Read Fitzgerald on the Times of William IV.[3] Whist in evg. Ten hours in the open air. What a change from H of Commons life!

To the DUKE OF ARGYLL, 11 September 1884.   Add MS 44547, f. 108.

There is a very material misapprehension of my language in your letter of the 6th[4] which I omitted to set right in replying to it. You think I have 'wished all parties to be under the halter on this subject that they may all the more readily agree to my terms'. No!

My propositions are these 1. The majority in the House of Commons is as to comprehensive & complex measures the servant of the minority, to this extent that they cannot be passed except with the minority's good pleasure. 2. The minority have no motive for giving us this good pleasure, as long as they know that by stopping redistribution they stop franchise (which nine-tenths of them hate, but dare not say so). 3. But as they hate most of all franchise without redistribution they will, when franchise has passed, have a motive for refraining from the use of their obstructive powers, in order that they may mitigate the franchise by redistribution, the majority (not the Government) will then have fair play. This is my statement: you will see how different.[5]
[P.S.] You would find it very instructive to read now some of the histories of the proceedings on the old Reform Bill between Oct. 31 and May 32.

To LORD CARLINGFORD, lord president and lord   Carlingford MSS CP1/229.
privy seal, 11 September 1884.

I do not question that my letter[6], considered in conjunction with your views & feelings placed you in a very painful position, and you will readily believe that I placed myself in a like position when I wrote it. But I had a public object in view which it was my duty to compass by the best means in my power. I would have contented myself at the present moment, just as your letter has arrived, with an acknowledgement, were it not that I am

[1] Argyll replied, 18 September, Add MS 44105, f. 201, that Gladstone's Edinburgh defence of a separate bill was 'quite good and sufficient' but that having gained his point he should now introduce a seats bill.
[2] i.e. he climbed Ben Macdhui, the highest point (4296 feet) in the Cairngorms, from the road to Derry Lodge. See 9 Sept. 36.
[3] P. H. Fitzgerald, *The life and times of William IV*, 2v. (1884).
[4] See 31 Aug. 84n.
[5] Argyll replied, 19 September, Add MS 44105, f. 205, questioning 'the right of any Government to *insist* on this kind of pressure being placed on a large section of the House of Commons'; Gladstone had gained his point; franchise reform was virtually certain; thus everyone should be 'reasonable on Redistribution'.
[6] See 7 Sept. 84.

not absolutely sure of the meaning of your reference to a seat without portfolio, as that originally offered you. Am I to understand that, with present circumstances, your letter does not exclude the alternative of your holding a seat in the Cabinet without specific office? You will I am sure understand my anxiety to know exactly the meaning of what at first sight I do not feel certain that I comprehend.

[P.S.] My address is Downing Street. You will see that I am at first sight attracted by an idea which if found eligible might enable more purposes than one to be gained.[1]

12. Fr.

Wrote to D. of Argyll—Mr Childers—Messrs Watson—Mr G. Harris—Messrs Parr—Ld Carlingford—and minutes. Mr Farquhar explained to me the whole Scott and Fife case.[2] Saw Mrs Clark. Beautiful drive to The Beinn, the Linn [of Dee], & the Quoich. Whist in evg. Read Fitzgerald.

13. Sat.

Wrote to Ch. of Exr—Ld Granville l.l. & Tel.—Mr Seymour—Scotts—Ld Hartington—Watsons—and minutes. Drive & walk in the Alt-more. Conversation with Mr Duff sen.—Mr R. Duff—Ld Dalhousie. Read Fitzgerald—Mad. de Sevigné. Torch dance of Highlanders at night: a most striking picture. I had to make a little speech.[3]

To LORD HARTINGTON, war secretary,   Chatsworth MSS 340. 1520.
13 September 1884.

Wolseley's telegram of the 11th.[4] We have reached a point at which I cannot dispute the propriety of putting Wolseley in a condition to proceed if necessary and this telegram I consider as only indicating the military means, of which you & he, aided too by Northbrook, are the proper judges. I therefore can make no difficulty and I rely fully on what you lately wrote to me about Wolseley's desire to avoid if it be possible, the advance for which nevertheless he requires to have the means at his command.

14. 14 S. Trin.

Chapel 11½ A.M. Madame Albani[5] sang. Wrote to Mr Gibson Craig[6]—Rev. A. Salmond—W.H.G.—and minutes. Finished Eliza Fletcher—read Scots Ch Magazine—Freedom of Faith—Nicole. Conversation with Madame Albani: & five o'clock tea at her house. Also with Lady Lonsdale: who greatly admires Sister Dora.[7]

To W. H. GLADSTONE, M.P., 14 September 1884. '*Private*'.   Add MS 44547, f. 109.

Thanks for the message received through Mamma about the Crofters.
The report of the Commissioners does not appear to be either wise or acceptable. I

---

[1] Carlingford replied, 15 September, Add MS 44123, f. 230, that he had not meant to imply that he would resign the presidency and remain in cabinet.
[2] Fife was a partner in S. Scott's, Gladstone's bankers; *G.E.C.*, v. 379.
[3] *T.T.*, 15 September 1884, 9f.   [4] Circulated to cabinet; Chatsworth 340. 1519.
[5] (Dame) Emma *Albani, 1852–1930; opera singer.
[6] Henry Vivian Gibson-Craig, b. 1847; gentleman; business untraced.
[7] See 15 Feb. 80.

think it will be important to consider whether something in the nature of the compensation for disturbance, introduced by the first Irish Land Act, could be introduced with advantage into Parishes of this class.

Mad. Albani, who is living at *Old Mar Lodge, Braemar N.B.*, has been singing in the Chapel here today, a singularly gracious act. Will you kindly order a copy of your Thibaut,[1] about which I have spoken to her, to be sent to the address above given.

We move about for ten more days before reaching Hawarden. We have had most delightful hospitality accorded to us. On Thursday I managed Bein-na-muich Dhu from Lord Fife's shooting lodge, 20 miles there & back—half of what I used to do in years gone by.

15. [*Haddo House*]

Wrote to Lord Granville—Sir H. Ponsonby—. . . Tel. & minutes. Off at 10½ from this charming abode. Saw Sir H. Ponsonby on the way: full conversation. Then The Princess of Wales at Abergeldie: & next the Duchess of Edinburgh at Birk Hall. Also conversation with Pr. Cantacuzene. Left Ballater at 3.5. All along the road there were concourses of people, enthusiastic demonstrations, & many short speeches wrung from me in spite of my intention till we arrived at Haddo & I spent the remains of my voice on the Tenants demonstration before the House.[2] Lord A[berdeen] had made admirable arrangements & I was greatly struck both by these & the careful organisation of his house (wh he has greatly improved yet but slightly *altered*) in all particulars. Thirty six to dinner.[3] Interesting conversations with Mr Matthew[4] and others. Read Mad. de Sevigné.

16.

Prayers in the beautiful Chapel at 9.15 and 7. P.M. Wrote to Ld Granville tel.— Mr Seymour tel. & l.—Mr Geddis[5]—Mr Hay—Mr John Rae (Tels)—Prov. of Montrose Tel.—and minutes. Drive to Formartine: & inspection of Institutions at Methlick. 36 to dinner. Saw Mr Bain—Lady Tavistock—Prof. Meiklejohn—Mr Stewart—and others. Read Macintosh III—Mad. de Sevigné.

To LORD CARLINGFORD, lord president and lord   Carlingford MSS CP1/231.
privy seal, 16 September 1884.

I have received your letter of yesterday,[6] and it will be well I think that I should enter on the subject of it which is important. I may however say that I think you took the Privy Seal on the old & regular footing. The salary of it could not now be revived. If asked by us, it wd I think be referred by the House of Commons; & no young Minister would I think be introduced without portfolio.

[P.S.]I inclose, as you may not have seen it, the Report of Childers's Committee,[7] which appears to portend considerable change. Please return it to Downing Street.

---

[1] W. H. Gladstone's tr. of A. F. J. Thibaut, *On purity in musical art* (1877).

[2] Demonstration of tenant farmers for the Franchise Bill; *T.T.*, 16 September 1884, 6a.

[3] The occasion for the group portrait by Emslie now in the National Portrait Gallery.

[4] A N.E. Scottish name; probably William Matthew of Meldrum, tenant farmer (the editor's great-grand-uncle), or Mr Matthews, then lord provost of Aberdeen.

[5] Thanking J. W. J. Geddis for a sonnet; Add MS 44547, f. 110.   [6] See 11 Sept. 84n.

[7] Childers' select cttee. recommended end of dual control in education; Gladstone announced govt. action but nothing was done; see G. Sutherland, *Policy-making in elementary education 1870-95* (1973), 30 and *PP* 1884 xiii.

17. Wed. [Brechin Castle, Brechin][1]

Wrote to Mr Peel—Sir W. Harcourt—Ld Strathmore—Ld Selborne—Mr Seymour Tel.—Ld Spencer, & minutes. Walk with Aberdeen about the policies, once well known. Planted a tree. Off at 1.30. The whole journey was a tempest of demonstrations, addresses, and replies. I think 60000 at *least* came out at Aberdeen & I found a meeting which approached 10 m[ille] in little Brechin.[2] I had five speeches to make, and was hoarse. Most kindly received by the Dalhousies. Conversation with Mr Barclay—Ld Southesk (who *did* a little spirit writing).[3] Read Mad de Sevigné—Macintosh. Prayers 9.15 AM.

To Sir W. V. HARCOURT, home secretary,   MS Harcourt dep. 9, f. 109.
17 September 1884.

I reserve details for the present but nothing except absolute & hard negations have been obtained from the receiver of the letter which you saw at Invercauld.[4] I have postponed the matter for further consideration, but have not dropped it. This is the footing on which it stands between us.
PS Granville does not take quite the same view of the title to resist as you & I do.

To LORD SPENCER, Viceroy of Ireland, 17 September 1884.   Althorp MSS K7.

1. I must be content with thanking you very briefly for your interesting letter,[5] adding only a word of comment on a single point. For I am myself much against my will involved in an almost incessant political activity attended with a good deal of fatigue. My resolution to receive no addresses, & to speak only in Midlothian, has given way under moral compulsion, & the immense enthusiasm of Scotland which I consider to be distinctly beyond what it was in 79–80.

2. You may readily believe that I share your concern at the mischief done by persistent calumny & violence, for I hear very much of it with my own ears, & certainly it makes the heart sink. But the most remarkable Irish speech of last session was perhaps that of Shaw, in which this really (as I believe & hope) constitutional man expressed his belief that the agitation would go on, & his desire that it should go on, until the Irish question was settled. This is hardly a question for me but it is sure to be one for you.

3. A word about Trevelyan. It seems to me on the whole desirable that he should keep his office & that a seat in the Cabinet should be offered him. The effect of his giving way to the Irish members would be nearly fatal to a successor especially to one taking it without special credit. He would answer with much greater authority, and it often occurs to me that he answers questions which would naturally fall to our Law Officers. I am thinking all this over: it is not the only point which now weighs upon my mind with reference to office & the strength of the Government. The case of Scotland presents almost a necessity for action.

---

[1] Seat of Lord Dalhousie.
[2] Number confirmed by *T.T.*, 18 September 1884, 7c.
[3] James *Carnegie, 1827–1905; 9th earl of Southesk; poet, antiquarian; sold Glendye estate to Sir T. Gladstone; at this time a liberal (see 27 Oct. 85).
[4] On Carlingford's position; see Add MS 44199, f. 89.
[5] Of 15 September, Add MS 44311, f. 196: state of Ireland in general adequate, but govt. suffers from persistent calumny, 'men like Shaw and other anti-Parnellites have not the moral courage to speak their minds'; why do no ministers speak in Ireland?

18. *Th.*

Wrote to Mr Seymour & minutes. Off to Fasque & Glendye at $10\frac{3}{4}$. Walked most of the hill. Glendye is now beautiful. Tea at Fasque.[1] J. very kind. Speeches (& addresses) at Fettercairn and Edzell. Home before eight. Read Mad de Sevigné. Ruminated on Gordon's wild telegram.[2]

19. *Fr.*

Wrote to Mr O'Shea—Ld Granville l.l. & Tel.—Mr Seymour Tel. Telegrams to: Ld Rosebery—Ld Provost Perth—Mr Michell—Mr Miller. 11-$6\frac{3}{4}$. Expedition to Panmuir—marred by fog. Conversation with Mr Shield & saw noteworthy employés. Much interesting conversation with Ld D. Also mg & evg with Lady D. Read Mad. de Sevigné—Ld Southesk's Poems.[3] More wild stuff from Gordon.

20. *Sat.* [*Glamis Castle*][4]

Wrote to Mr Childers—Mr Seymour L. & tel. l.l.—Ld Granville l.l.—Ld Prov. Perth Tel.—Ld Rosebery Tel.—Cowper Tel.—and minutes. Drive in forenoon with Lady D. Saw Ld Southesk. Visited the garden & park, with its cedars & copper beeches. Planted trees. Conversation with Mr [G.W.] Smalley on the English tongue. Off at $4\frac{3}{4}$ to Glamis Castle. Several speeches on the way. A great crowd at Brechin simply to witness departure. Read Mad. de Sevigné—Macintosh.

21. *S. Matt & 15 S. Trin.*

Wrote to Ld Chancellor—D. of Argyll—Miss Tennant[5]—Ld Granville—& minutes. Saw Mr Beal—Mr M'Coll—Lady Airlie. Chapel services $8\frac{1}{2}$ AM H.C. $11\frac{1}{2}$ AM and $5\frac{1}{2}$ P.M. Read Nicole—Bain on J. Mills character[6]—and [blank.] Went to the basement of this most remarkable house. There cannot be a kinder host or greater gentleman than Lord Strathmore.

22. *M.* [*St. Martin's, Perthshire*][7]

Chapel 9.15 AM. Wrote to Duke of Argyll—Mr Seymour—Ld Kinnaird—Ld Rosebery l. & Tel.—Ld Provost Perth—and minutes. Good conversation with Ld Strathmore. Visited the Garden—the Mortuary Chapel—the great stone, & kirkyard. Photographed. Read Mad. de Sevigné—Anticlimax in Midlothian.[8] Off at

[1] Seat of his br., Sir T. Gladstone, near Fettercairn.

[2] Gordon instructed Stewart to go to Berber, hold it for a fortnight, then burn it; one of several wires from Baring forwarding Gordon's; FO 78/3678, Ramm II, ii. 260. Wolseley commented: 'this will cause Mr. Gladstone to believe no expedition to *Khartoum* is necessary—why send troops to Gordon if he can come out when he likes?'; *Relief of Gordon*, 17. Baring countermanded Gordon's order *via* Kitchener.

[3] J. Carnegie, Lord Southesk, *The burial of Isis, and other poems* (1884).

[4] Seat of Claude Bowes-Lyon, 1824–1904; 13th earl of Strathmore 1865; a tory (but see to Grosvenor, 27 Sept. 84).

[5] Regretfully declining invitation of Laura Tennant (see 28 Feb. 81) to visit The Glen.

[6] A. Bain, *James Mill* (1882).

[7] Seat of Sir A. Clark, his physician, 5 miles N.E. of Perth.

[8] 'The Anti-Climax in Midlothian: a review of Mr Gladstone's Campaign in 1884, by an eyewitness' (Blackwood's, 1884); copy in N.Y. Public Library.

2½ to (St Martin's) Sir A. Clarks. Remarkable manifestations all along the road. Speeches at Cupar & St Martin's.[1] Dinner party. Conversation with Sir J. Kinloch & others.

23. Tu.

Prayers at 9¾. Wrote to Ld Granville—Mr Childers—The Queen Tel.—Rev. Munro Tel.—Mr Watson (Newcastle) Tel.—Postmaster Perth—Mr Seymour Tel.—& minutes. Read Mad. de Sevigné—Memorials of Scone.[2] Dinner party. 2¾–6¼ To Rossie Priory, where we saw the Kinnairds, and much to admire. Planted a tree there. Saw Sir D. Currie (Northcote &c. conversation)—Mr Bannerman—Mr Lyon—Mr [blank.]

To H. C. E. CHILDERS, chancellor of the exchequer,   Add MS 44547, f. 113.
23 September 1884.

As respects your letter of yesterday,[3] I have no power to authorise any military measure in advance of the decisions of the Cabinet, but after a correspondence with Hartington which entered into much detail I agreed personally to his sending forward a small body of men to Dongola. He did not state the precise number finally but I gathered that it was to be in hundreds, was broadly distinct from the 'expedition', was safe as a military measure, and was very likely to stand in stead of the expedition, through the action of the Mudir.

I left it to Hartington to apply for the consent of colleagues when necessary, and among these I have no doubt I assumed that the minister of Finance would be consulted. I thought Harcourt likely perhaps to dissent, and therefore I made it a point that his judgment should be obtained, which was done. I should certainly say it was an error, and it surprises me, if no communication was made to you, as expense would be involved, but perhaps he regarded it as not increasing total expense, and believed, on his responsibility, you would agree. I rather think he wrote to me that he had no doubt except as to Harcourt—I would refer you to the correspondence but that I think it, or part of it, is at Hawarden.

I think you interpret rightly the mission of Wolseley to which I fully assented, Hartington assuring me that Wolseley was most averse to our 'expedition' unless quite unavoidable, and being unable to work through Stephenson on account of difference of opinion.

24. Wed. [Dalmeny]

Prayers 9¾. Wrote to Mr Seymour Tel.—Ld Granville L.l.l. & Tel.—Messrs Scott—Kendall Tel.—Farnworth Tel.—Mr Muirhead—and minutes. Read Mad. de Sevigné. Long interview with Sir A. Clark chiefly on his affairs, which are of much interest. Off at one. Remarkable demonstrations, most of all at Scone. To Kinfauns[4] for luncheon: admired the lovely place & rather fine house with interesting pictures. Much kindness. To Perth at 3. Addresses, & speech in the suffocating City Hall (excellent if ventilated). Then away by rail. More addresses demonstrations & little speeches.[5] The feeling is nothing less than wonderful.

[1] In *Political speeches, 1884*.
[2] Perhaps the *Liber ecclesiae* of Scone published by the Maitland Club (1843).
[3] Add MS 44131, f. 146: what is authorised for an expedition beyond Wady Halfa?
[4] Gothic revival castle by Perth, seat of Edmund Archibald Stuart-Gray, 1840–1901; 15th earl of Moray 1895; antiquarian.   [5] *T.T.*, 25 September 1884, 10a.

Dalmeny at 7. Grieved to find Ld R. really suffering.[1] We are out of place but not suffered to go. Conversation with Mr Fraser.

25. Th.

Ld R. no better. Saw Mr Keith. Wrote to Sir H. Ponsonby l.l.—Ld Granville tel. & l.—Ld Hartington tel. & l.—Sir W. Harcourt—Mr Childers—Sir T. P. Hennessy—Kendall & Wigan Tel. Walk with the gentlemen: & much conversation with Mr Fraser,[2] who greatly instructed me in the history of my family, & gave me papers to read. Rosebery suffering much: yet we were relieved in the main on seeing him for a few minutes. Read Dodington's Diary—Sermoneta's Tre Chiose.[3]

To Sir W. V. HARCOURT, home secretary,   MS Harcourt dep. 9, f. 111.
25 September 1884. '*Private*'.

You have set forth with your usual lucid force, the argument against official freeholds.[4] In this case, the tenure has not been asserted in terms, but my proposal has been in every form most rigidly refused, so that it will only remain to consider what if any thing can be done *in invitum*. I am very jealous of the doctrine that we are all colleagues; and I push my own claim no further than this that for a great public object, and without circumstances of disparagement, it may be the duty of a Prime Minister in rare circumstances to suggest to a colleague the propriety of his withdrawal. I have never before done it: but I have insisted upon a change of Cabinet office, which is nearly as strong a measure.

I am sorry the clouds do not open in the Crofters' affair.

Granville told me you have written a letter looking towards resignation ere many months are over. I am not wholly averse. The demonstrations of feeling in Scotland have been really wonderful. I began by declining addresses and speeches—but this resolution broke like a wreath of snow. It is more than in 1880.

I am going to circulate letters between Sir H.P. (for H.M.) & me on the Franchise.

Rosebery has had a heavy fall suffers a good deal & is I grieve to say though not alarmingly yet seriously ill. We go to Hawarden tomorrow.

26. Fr. [Hawarden]

Wrote to Ld Granville—Lady Dalhousie—Lord Fife—& minutes. Off at nine to Edinburgh. Manifestations all along the way, & speaking at divers places. Preston vilely managed as usual. But Carlile [*sic*] admirably. Spoke 25 m to (I think) 10000 but could not trust my voice to reach them all.[5] Home at 5.40. Searched out our old exploit on Ben na Muick Dhu, in Sept. 1836. A change![6] Read Mad. de Sevigné—Mivart Conversion of England.[7] And so has ended a tour of the utmost interest: which grew into an importance far beyond anything I had dreamt of.

---

[1] A fall from his horse.
[2] Keeper of the records in Edinburgh; see 3 Nov. 57, 6 Dec. 79.
[3] M. Caetani, duke of Sermoneta, *Tre chiose* (1876).
[4] Harcourt to Gladstone, 22 September, Add MS 44199, f. 89 and Gardiner, i. 508; on the Carlingford affair, and crofters.
[5] *Political speeches, 1884*, 136.
[6] See 9 Sept. 36: 'We were not much tired.'
[7] St. G. Mivart in *Dublin Review*, xii. 65 (July 1884).

27. Sat.

Ch. 8½ A.M. Wrote to Ld R. Grosvenor—Ld Granville—Watsons—Robn & Nichn—Scotts—Mr Beaumont—Mr Murray—Messrs Murray—& minutes. Read Mad. de Sevigné—Law Review on Eccl. Courts—Law's admirable Preface to Hamilton:[1] with Collier, Dixon, &c., also Braemar. Went to see Willy's new house, which he had already made a comfortable interior.[2]

To LORD R. GROSVENOR, chief whip, 27 September 1884.   Add MS 44547, f. 115.

1. I regret on every ground public & private the sad affliction which has befallen Lord Leigh.[3] Pray assure him if you have an opportunity of my cordial sympathy.

2. But the cruel wheel of affairs still goes round, & rough enough is its movement at the present juncture. I send you the inclosed letters for perusal. You will see that nothing could be more unsatisfactory than my correspondence with Carlingford. I do not understand the tenacity of a man who finds it is thought that his room is better than his company; & I did not expect it of him. I think of gathering a few, you among them, to consider the matter. I have in no way closed the question with him. It might be possible to have Trevelyan *vice* Dodson, Lefevre *vice* Trevelyan, Rosebery Privy Seal with salary temporarily revived until Scotch Minister passes. But it has not been voted for this year, & could only come in upon a supplementary estimate. In various ways it would be a very awkward arrangement; and it would include stripping Carlingford of his only important duties, in consequence of the Report of the Committee.

3. The enthusiasm, *since* I saw you, has even exceeded what it was before.

4. In every place I have gone just as far for the Lords as I could without provoking hostile demonstration.

5. Doubtless you know Duff's opinion about a Dissolution under Salisbury. Harcourt's is the same.

6. Please to consider whether it is well to have a County meeting here. It would be almost ridiculous if the only one.

7. Also whether it would be well to make Breadalbane Marquis, W. James (Senior) a Peer and one or two Scotch or Irish.[4]

8. I understood from Lord Strathmore that he would vote with us.

9. The arrangements at Carlisle & generally for the crowds on my journey were admirable. At Preston (for the third time) scandalous. An engine was kept hissing half the time (10 or 12 minutes I think in all) which effectually silenced me; when I had spoken five minutes a man came & motioned me to leave off for the train with a dense crowd between him & me, which he made no attempt to open. It was really indecent.[5]

---

[1] Proof of T. G. Law, *The catechism of John Hamilton . . . 1552*, published (1884) with a preface by Gladstone dated 'October 1884'; notes at Add MS 44768, f. 132.

[2] The Red House (also Hawarden House), across the park from the Castle; built for W. H. Gladstone 1883, occupied by him and his family from 1884, rather than the Castle, which he technically owned.

[3] Death of his s., G. H. C. Leigh, liberal M.P. S. Warwickshire. The liberals lost the by-election heavily.

[4] Grosvenor supported for the Lords: James, Arran, Herries, de Vesci, and a marquisate for Breadalbane; Add MS 44315, ff. 150-3.

[5] Grosvenor replied, 3 October, ibid.: 'I am very sorry that Preston sinned again, the wicked hissing Engine must have been a Tory. . . . Remember that Preston is a Tory stronghold.' Gladstone's necessarily truncated remarks on woman's suffrage led to complaint; see *H* 293. 158.

28. 16 S. Trin.

Ch. 11 A.M. & 6½ P.M. Wrote to Mr Hamilton—Ld Granville Tel.—Duke of Argyll—& minutes. Read Murray on 'Abide in me'[1]—Dillon's Our Lady of Counsel[2]—Bp Lightfoot's Charge[3]—Bain on James Mill.[4]

To the DUKE OF ARGYLL, 28 September 1884.   Add MS 44547, f. 116.

The offer, to which you gave a generous & confiding reception in July, & which was never regarded by me as in any way private, is still I conceive available.[5]

Nor have I ever declined to produce our redistribution Bill before the Franchise Bill passes the Lords.

At Edinburgh I treated the question of producing it as one which I could only appreciate on it being proposed by the Tories, or in knowing what they thought in its favour.

Notwithstanding appearances in your letter, I think you & I are at the moment in the same lines. That is to say we both think (as far as I see) that the legitimate anxiety of the Opposition is to be assured on what principles redistribution is to be settled.

I made a step in this direction at the very outset. It drew no response. They ought to say what other steps are required.

With you, I believe I could well enough settle this point.

So far from wishing to swamp the rural by the urban element I am desirous to sever them by every reasonable means, & to adjust areas with this view.

In 1835 the Tories introduced into the Municipal Reform Bill the principle of Wards with a view to severing classes.

This at any rate showed a disposition to arrive at a conclusion. Why do they not attempt something of the same kind? I write offhand & without communication.

As to other matters, I can assure you that in speaking *for* the House of Lords I have sailed very near the wind with all the audiences I have addressed.

And as to future Liberalism, you will not have to differ from me, for I shall be out of this troubled sea.

But let us have a good heart. The country is after all strong & sound, though I do not think the men for the next fifty years will have a comfortable time of it.

29. M. St Michael &c.

Ch. 8½ A.M. Wrote to Sir H. Ponsonby—Ld Granville l. & tel.—Sir C. Dilke—Mr Hamilton—Mrs Th—Mr MacColl—Rev. B. Price—and minutes. Spent the morning chiefly on the Redistribution papers & plan, which generally I like. Read Mad. de Sevigné—Salisbury on Redistribution.[6] Conversation with W. & Harry.

---

[1] Perhaps Charlotte Murray, *Abiding in thee* (1st published 1887).

[2] G. E. Dillon, *The virgin mother of good counsel* (1884).

[3] J. B. Lightfoot, 'Primary charge. Two addresses' (1884).

[4] See 21 Sept. 84.

[5] Argyll wrote on 25 July, Add MS 44105, f. 211, on a private offer to him *via* Granville of proceeding by Resolution in the Lords; he regarded Gladstone's control of redistribution as important 'but on *every other* ground I think the Conservatives have a good case ... Liberalism is becoming daily less liberal'.

[6] Lord Salisbury, 'The value of redistribution', *National Review*, iv. 145 (October 1884).

To Sir C. W. DILKE, president of the local government   Add MS 43875, f. 177.
board, 29 September 1884.

What with journies, large parties, addresses, speeches & foreign telegrams & correspondence, I found it impossible to read with proper attention, until after my return here,
any of the interesting papers on Redistribution.[1]

Generally speaking I am well pleased with the plan; but I may add that as I do not at
present look forward to my handling the Bill in the House of Commons—a task for which
I doubt my sufficiency—I have every disposition to defer much to the opinion of my
colleagues.

I offer the following remarks:

1. In Wales, I am inclined to treat the representation of its small counties as we treat
Sutherland & Rutland and (by the plan) medium Boroughs, that is to respect individuality. Further, putting Wales & Ireland together I desire on the whole to maintain the
status quo. But I do not think you can do this conjointly with taking members from England. I therefore incline to what I think you at first meditated: 12 new members for Scotland, & the other three as they are.

2. I am satisfied with 10 m[ille] & 40 m. as the limits for our Schedules A & B; and I am
bound to respect individuality in some degree. I do not say it would have been my duty
utterly to resist a raising of these figures. But I really think we disfranchise as many as the
first Reform Act did if you cast out what were not towns at all from the Sch. A. of 1832.

3. My tenderness for individuality of communities in boroughs & counties does not
extend to *districts* of boroughs, where the union is purely conventional, and a different
limit might be adopted if it be for any reason desirable.

4. On these points I should not be disinclined to go a little further, if we could thereby
effectually promote peace & get the Franchise Bill passed. a. To extend the number of
single-membered constituencies, b. To reduce the limit of 40 m. as the condition of creating a new borough, *provided* there be local or municipal life. c. To carry Parliamentary
beyond municipal boundaries.

5. I think your plan of private conversation about Boundaries very judicious.

6. You have made wonderful progress, thus far, with the minority difficulty.

But the vision of the subject as now mapped out before my eyes shows with every
increasing force how completely, or how largely, we are at the mercy of a minority disposed, & able with impunity, to obstruct.[2]

To LORD SELBORNE, lord chancellor, 29 September 1884.   Selborne MS 1868, f. 294.

I think I can answer briefly & intelligibly the practical question put to me in your
letter.[3] The last passage in my letter to Ponsonby was intended by me simply as a forecast
of what would happen without any reference to the view & intention of my colleagues

---

[1] Printed mem. by Dilke sent on 20 September, Add MS 44149, f. 233: 'unanimous rejection of
single-member districts'; single-member counties 'will contain most of the largest of the unrepre-
sented boroughs'; 'our scheme almost exactly reverses the present proportion of borough to county
Members' (proposed 360 county, 289 boroughs, 56 boroughs disfranchised, 30 to lose one member).
Dilke was struck by the timidity of the English borough scheme: 'I do not see how it is to stand the
revolutionary criticism of Lord Salisbury'; he favoured a line for merger 'far above the 10,000 line'.

[2] Dilke replied, 1 October, ibid., f. 245, that to meet Gladstone's view he would split Lanarkshire
into single-member districts, and in England give 5 seats to boroughs, 5 to counties, with further
division into single-member districts.

[3] Of 28 September, Add MS 44298, f. 136, opposed to implication that a dissolution would imply
intention of 'organic change' of the Lords.

(whom I had no authority to commit), or even to my own, which I have carefully kept back.

Whether the thing will be, whether it ought to be, whether I shall engage in it, are three entirely distinct questions, and I have (knowingly) touched none but the first.

I am afraid I could not accept your view, if I understand it right, of a Dissolution, but this is a large & remote question, & there is room for doubt whether it will arise.
[P.S.] Nothing could be so grievous as a severance among ourselves, but at present, though the sky is full of clouds, I see no cause to apprehend it.

30. Tu.

Ch. 8½ A.M. Wrote to Ld Northbrook—Ld Rosebery—Lady Rosebery—Ld Granville—Mr Macdonald—Reporter of Chester Chronicle[1]—& others. Worked on unpacking books papers & addresses. Walk with E. Talbot: a model of dispassionate uprightness. Read Mad. de Sevigné—Mr St John's Hayti.[2]

To LORD ROSEBERY, 30 September 1884.   N.L.S. 10023, f. 30.

I need hardly say with what lively pleasure & thankfulness we have received the altered accounts of you,[3] which inspire us with the belief that only some moderate draft upon your patience yet remains to be met before you will have a full quittance from the effects of your ugly accident. At the same time I do not know when the time will have arrived for franking letters to you, & I therefore send this under cover to Lady Rosebery.

1. I inclose part of a letter from Northbrook, which deals with your suggestion about Dalhousie. Few things would give me greater pleasure than to see that admirable man worthily employed, but I think there are some difficulties in this case, nor am I sure that Stead's astounding proceedings as to the navy do not tend to increase them. I sincerely hope that no *long* time may lapse before the opportunity shall arrive. (But see lower down).

2. I think you may read not without interest, *if* you are so disposed, the inclosed memoranda from Mr. Mitford of the Office of Works, about St. Margaret's Chapel on the Castle Hill.[4] You may ask why should I have obtained them? It had occurred to me that, if St. Margaret's were a proper case for structural repairs, I might do them & leave them as a small memorial of the political association with Midlothian. But I am afraid from Mr. M.s language that it is doubtful whether anything should be done.

3. I am very very sore at having missed the chance of full conversation with you on a variety of matters in which you would have taken interest. The general upshot indeed would not have been to present to you at the moment any clear results. Upon the whole I think the air is thick & the sky cloudy though there can be no reason as yet for abandoning the hope that the majority may be reversed, or so much diminished as to leave room for the progress of the Bill. If however the division shall go decidedly wrong, I think the chances are that we may be out before Christmas. Nothing private of a promising kind has yet proceeded from the leaders of the Opposition. I do not however wholly dislike Salisbury's article in the National Review where there is a passage at page 157 seeming to

---

[1] Statement on desire for maintenance of the Lords; *Chester Chronicle*, 4 October 1884, 2a.

[2] S. St. John, *Hayti. The black republic* (1884).

[3] Recovering from 'a stupid fall'; Add MS 44288, f. 205. See 24 Sept. 84.

[4] At the summit of the Castle rock in Edinburgh. Gladstone instead restored the Mercat Cross in the High Street. See 23 Nov. 85.

describe what he desires in redistribution.[1] The paper is wonderfully pessimistic. If I see my way in any thing a short time hence I will write to you again.
[P.S.] I have written all this but I hope you will be extremely prudent, & docile in the highest degree until you are completely re-established.

Wedn. Oct. 1. 1884.

Ch. 8¼ A.M. Wrote to Ld Granville 1. & tel. 1.1.—Ld Hartington—Watsons—Ld Derby 1. & tel.—Mr Heneage—Mr Hamilton 1. & Tel—Mr Stevenson—& minutes. Walk with Harry & much talk on his position & prospects, and on financial history of the family here. Read 19th Cent on Monastery—Irish Emigration—Ld Beaconsfield's Irish Policy[2]—St John's Hayti—Mad. de Sevigné.

To LORD HARTINGTON, war secretary,   Chatsworth MSS 340. 1540A.
1 October 1884.

In the present embryonic state of negotiations, I need do little more than say in answer to your letter[3] that I hold myself quite open on the question whether we could wreck the Bill on the postponing clause if it were put in by the Lords. But my present opinion is (although I think James thinks otherwise) that a prior acceptance of the Clause would probably break up the party. This the Queen thought was a party argument in a national matter. But the party is the team that draws the coach.

What I feel most strongly is the extremely damaging nature of any debate on the *merits* of such a clause, & the utter lack, to my mind, of pleas in its favour.

2. Th.

Ch. 8½ A.M. Wrote to Ld Granville 1.1.1.—Mr Childers—Sir C. Dilke—Parl. Circular—The Queen—Hon S. Lyttelton Tel.—Mrs Bolton—& minutes. Read St John's Hayti—Swinburne on C. Reade[4]—Madame de Sevigné. Woodcraft with Harry.

To H. C. E. CHILDERS, chancellor of the exchequer,   Add MS 44547, f. 118.
2 October 1884.

Your letter[5] is not a surprise to me, more than rain would be after the fine weather we have been having.

With regard to supply, though I should be too glad to restrict business entirely to the Representation of the People, I am under the impression that with so large an expenditure we must go to Parliament & must therefore set up supply. Do you see your way to avoiding it?

If it is to be set up, need this be done at once? If it must, the inconvenience will be seriously aggravated.

As to Ways & Means, I cannot conceive how you can manage in a tolerable way to raise them during [the year]. But you may find modes of doing it. If you do not, what would you

---

[1] Salisbury, 'The value of redistribution', *National Review*, iv. 157 (October 1884): supports 'recourse, when it is needed, to Mr Cobden's principle of single-member constituencies'.

[2] *N.C.*, xvi. 530, 663 (October 1884).

[3] Of 29 September, Add MS 44147, f. 149: better to agree now on postponement to 1 January 1886 than to have to accept it later from the Lords.

[4] A. C. Swinburne, 'Charles Reade', *N.C.*, xvi. 550 (October 1884).

[5] Of 1 October, Add MS 44131, f. 171: 'revenue not in a very hopeful state . . . [but not] worse than sluggish'.

say to meeting the charge in the January quarter, by Consol. Fund Bills to throw it over into April and then providing fresh resources by an early Budget in February?

These are loose & little digested ideas.

3. Fr.

Ch. 8½ A.M. Wrote to Mr Hamilton Tel.—Ld Granville l.l.—Watsons—Ld Kimberley—Mr Childers—Lady Russell—& minutes. Arranged some private papers and examined my transactions in securities. I seem to have made one heavy mistake in buying largely into the District R. before it was in a paying condition.[1] Woodcraft with Harry. Read St John's Hayti—Mad. de Sevigné.

To H. C. E. CHILDERS, chancellor of the exchequer,			Add MS 44547, f. 119.
3 October 1884.

Please to think over before we meet the ultimate shape of the measures for giving effect to the report of the Committee on Ministry of Education.[2] I think it *may* be desirable to give them immediate effect.

To LORD KIMBERLEY, Indian secretary, 3 October 1884.		Add MS 44547, f. 120.

To work down the majority & work *up* the minority in the House of Lords seems to be our clearest & probably most fruitful duty at this time—and I hope you will be able to postpone Dufferin's departure so as to give him a chance of voting on it.[3] I cannot gather from Ripon's letter (though I am sorry anything should interfere with his arrangements) any idea tending to show that a postponement for two or three weeks of the Rent Bill can be comparable in importance to a vote in the Lords on the Franchise Bill at a period so critical as this.

I may say I have been suggesting that Lansdowne should if possible be brought from Canada.

4. Sat.

Ch. 8½ A.M. Wrote to Mr Hamilton Tel. l.l.—Ld Spencer Tel. l.l.—Mr Mitford—Ld Derby Tel.—Mr Edwards—Mr Jerningham—Mr Smalley l.l.—& minutes. A little more work on private papers. Drive with C. Finished St John's Hayti. Finished Mad. de Sevigné. Vol. IV.

To G. W. SMALLEY, London agent of the *New York Tribune*,	Add MS 44547, f. 121.
4 October 1884.

I have at length found time to answer your letter.[4] What a Tartar[5] you have caught! Pray think again, once twice & thrice, before you press any request for publication.

---

[1] For his losses on M.D.R. Stock (perhaps 50% on £50,000) see above, vii. cix and Matthew, *Gladstone*, 244.

[2] See to Carlingford, 16 Sept. 84.

[3] Kimberley, 5 October, Add MS 44228, f. 158, refused: Indian affairs too pressing.

[4] Of 29 September, Add MS 44487, f. 238, on Gladstone's views on G. Washington; ibid., f. 258 is a copy of a Gladstonian long eulogy on Washington sent this day, 'profoundly impressed by the moral elevation and greatness of his character'; if required to name 'the fittest occupant' for a pedestal of public purity, 'I think my choice, at any time during the last 45 years, would have lighted, and would now light, upon Washington'; printed in *T.T.*, 13 February 1885, 7d.

[5] To catch a Tartar: to find the victim more formidable than expected.

[P.S.] I think the best way will probably be, if agreeable to you, that you should in such words and as publicly as you please, state my opinions to be strongly on both points as you have described them in your letter.

5. [17] S. Trin.

Ch. 11 A.M.—with H.C. and 6½ P.M. Wrote to Sir S. St John[1]—Mrs Bolton—Chester Pmaster—Mr Suffield—and minutes. Read chiefly in the Modern Review:[2] on Quakerism, Converts to Rome, argument from Design, Prof. Newman, &c.

To Rev. R. R. SUFFIELD, 5 October 1884.   Add MS 44547, f. 122.

I thank you for the Modern Review, & I have at once read your too concise but very interesting paper on the Roman Converts.

I cannot but concur in your criticisms on the detail of Mr. Gorman's book & I was surprised to see that suggestions of mine were responsible for the arrangement that provoked them.

Why should you not take up the subject on a large scale?[3] These secessions from our great limb of the Tractarian movement, & all the parts of it, measured by their effects upon mankind, deserve to have their history written.

One most curious question is why, having come in with such force, these secessions have ceased so completely, as far as persons of weight & authority are concerned.

It would be most interesting to have an account of those with whom the step was not final. And the subject might be further illuminated by exhibiting the heavy losses which the Roman Church has suffered during the century, especially on the Continent where most of the powerful intellects, whom she had ranged in her service have either left her altogether or were thrown completely out of harmony with her ruling system.

6. M. [London]

Wrote to The Queen—Mr Chamberlain—and minutes. 9.15–3.15. To Downing Street. Cabinet 3–6½. Much conversation with Herbert. Dined with Godley & much conversation. Saw Sir C. Dilke. Read Freeman on H. of Lords[4]—Cadorna, Ricoltati[5]—Malmesbury's Autobiogr.[6]—English Pilgrimages (Erasmus).[7] Wrote *en route* paragraphs for a Queen's Speech.

Cabinet. Monday Oct. 6. 84. 3 PM[8]
1. Ld Granville has stated to Waddington we were always ready to be useful about China, never intrusive—were willing if France approved to propose to China[9]—

[1] Thanking Sir Spenser St. John (1825-1910; diplomat; in Haiti in 1860s, see 29 May 77) for his *Hayti*: 'I am afraid the inferences to be drawn are by no means hopeful'; Add MS 44547, f. 121.
[2] *Modern Review*, v. 617–762 (October 1884), its last number; see to Suffield this day.
[3] Suffield, a unitarian (see 31 Dec. 74), replied, 7 October, Add MS 444318, f. 338, that he had insufficient qualifications to refute W. J. G. Gorman, *Converts to Rome* (1884); details of 3000 former Protestants.   [4] E. A. Freeman on Lords reform, *C.R.*, xlvi. 465 (October 1884).
[5] C. Cadorna, perhaps *Il potere temporale dei papi* (1884).
[6] J. H. Harris, Lord Malmesbury, *Memoirs of an Ex-Minister*, 2v. (1884).
[7] D. Erasmus, ed. J. G. Nichols, *Pilgrimages to St. Mary of Walsingham and St. Thomas of Canterbury* (1849).
[8] Add MS 44645, f. 179.   [9] This phrase inserted.

ready to recommend to France 40m̊ fr—retention of mat. guarantees till paid—agree with Ld G.[1]

2. Massowah—we cannot hand to the Italians. Ask N[orthbrook] whether there is sufficient danger to make some step desirable.[2]

3. Northbrook not to initiate proposal for Gordon's going to the Equator.[3]

4. New Guinea. Protectorate to be declared, along the whole S. Coast, forthwith. To be communicated to the German Govt. in the act of being done. Without prejudice to any territorial question beyond this limit. That we have done the thing she [Germany] approved.[4]

5. Bechuana Land. See WEGs. MS.[5]

6. General conversation on Franchise. To be resumed.

To J. CHAMBERLAIN, president of the board   Chamberlain MSS 5/34/29.
of trade, 6 October 1884.[6]

I am extremely sorry to have missed seeing you in London; viewing the immense interests that are suspended upon the right course of the Franchise Bill & question.

I see that Salisbury by his declaration in the Times of Saturday, that the Lords are to contend for the simultaneous passing of the two Bills, has given you an excellent subject for denunciation, & you may safely denounce him to your heart's content.[7]

But I earnestly hope that you will leave us all elbow room on other questions which *may* arise. If you have seen my letters (virtually) to the Queen, I do not think you will have found reason for alarm in them. I am sorry that Hartington the other day used the *word* compromise, a word which has never passed my lips, though I believe he meant nothing wrong. If we could find anything which, though surrendering nothing substantial, would build a bridge for honourable & moderate men to retreat by I am sure you would not object to it.

But I have a much stronger plea for your reserve than any request of my own. It is this that the Cabinet has postponed discussing the matter until Wednesday simply in order that you may be present & take your share. They meet at twelve. I shall venture to count on your doing nothing to narrow the ground left open to us, which is indeed but a stinted one.

7. *Tu.*

Wrote to D. of Marlborough—Ld Kimberley—Mr Allen MP—Mr W. Fraser—Mrs Th.—D. of Sutherland—Mrs Bolton—C.G.—and minutes. Saw Mr Childers. Revised Queen's Speech. Saw the T.G. daughters, including Louey: it is deeply touching.[8] Dined at Brooks's. Conversation with Spencer—Sir W. Harcourt—Mr

---

[1] Seeking 80 million francs indemnity following a naval defeat earlier in the year, France destroyed much of the Chinese fleet at the battle of Ma-wei, Foochow, on 23 August. On 4 October Granville had suggested a settlement of 40 million francs; F.O.C.P. 5045, f. 321.

[2] Northbrook favoured letting Italy occupy Massowah; Ramm II, ii. 272.

[3] Suggestion of an attempt to rescue Gordon from the south.

[4] The C.O. had wanted to take some of the north of the island; on 30 September Germany objected to the projected extension of the British Protectorate in N. New Guinea; but the Australians wanted no delay; this decision maintained flexibility *re* the N. coast.

[5] Message to Robinson, on receiving Cape agreement, to call on Transvaal to disallow recent extension of jurisdiction in Montsioa, as a breach of the 1884 convention; Add MS 44645, ff. 180–1. See Schreuder, 451.

[6] Part in Garvin, i. 472.

[7] As Chamberlain did at Hanley on 7 October, with consequential royal rebukes; Garvin, i. 472.

[8] See 1 July 84.

Buckle. Saw Mr Hamn. Conclave on official arrangements 12–2¾.[1] Stiff enough. Read Pilgrimages &c.

8. *Wed.*

Wrote to Ld Granville—Mr Chamberlain—The Queen—Mr Maskelyne—C.G.— Sir R. Wallace—Count Cadorna—Musurus Pacha—Mr Ridler—Lady Rosebery—& minutes. Read 'Pilgrimages' &c. Cabinet 12–3½. Conclave on Offices 4–5½. Saw Chancr of Exr—Ld Granville—Mr Hamilton Dined at Mrs Th's. Walk afr.

Cabinet. 8 Oct. 1884. Wedy. Noon.[2]
1. Communication from Germany of a conference on colonising Africa & application of principles of Treaty of Vienna to Congo & Niger.
Committee.[3]
2. WEG asked for guidance as to question of arrangements on the Franchise Bill. 1. Govt. make no bids. 2. Date proposed—to be rejected as a basis of prior accommodation. 3. Nothing to be done by us under any circs. to put[?] Franchise Bill.
3. Provisional discussion of paragraphs of Speech: WEG to hold any needful communication.
4. Instructions to Wolseley approved with amendments.
5. Ld Spencer stated: Maamtrasna Case—inquiry utterly to be refused.
Bolton—denies the allegations & is believed.[4] Support him.
Conversation on Limerick police. Chancellor to be consulted. Bolton suspicion.

To J. CHAMBERLAIN, president of the board   Chamberlain MSS 5/34/30.
of trade, 8 October 1884.[5]

Having troubled you on Monday with a note of requests I must now write a line to *thank* you for the skill & moderation with which, according to the Report in the Times, you handled yesterday towards the close of your very able speech the subject of so-called compromise.

To Mrs GLADSTONE, 8 October 1884.   Hawarden MSS.

After three days of tolerably stiff work, I hope to come down tomorrow by the 2.45, and I make no doubt of being able to tell you in good time tomorrow whether they will or will not run me on to Broughton Hall.

I shall therefore reserve all public talk until I see you except to say that while Hartington's speech of Saturday caused some dismay and confusion Chamberlain made a rattling one yesterday which on the vital point was guarded & moderate, I mean the point about compromise.

We fear Col. Stewart has been massacred.[6]

[1] Attempts to ease out Carlingford and bring Rosebery and Trevelyan into the cabinet; Add MS 44768, f. 119.   [2] Add MS 44645, f. 182.
[3] Granville was formally told of German plans this day, and replied this day accepting in principle a Conference at Berlin; F.O.C.P. 5023, f. 9.
[4] Irish civil servant suspended under treasury minute; 'law officers say he is clearly entitled to removal of suspension'; Monk Bretton 62.
[5] Part in Garvin, i. 472.
[6] Gordon sent Stewart, his last British companion, down the Nile from Khartoum with his journal and the cipher books; Stewart and his party were killed, the steamer having run aground.

Yesterday I went to Eaton Square but it was all I could do to get back in time for my work so that even if I had had your monition about Aunt Coke[?] I would not have managed it.

I saw all the girls & we sat I should think twenty minutes in Louey's room.[1] She has now got a good first floor at her command. She had had a far better night than usual & this I suppose was the cause that she seemed to me better than when I saw her two months ago; less languid, rather stronger apparently & with less of the look which admonishes of approaching death. However I fear there is no substantial improvement. The doctor had shortly before felt her pulse and said it was 140—without fever. She was interested about Fasque. Tom and Louisa were both out the whole time, though I staid near an hour. Louisa does not like Tom's going down to Fasque without her: & she cannot move.

I have sent a good lot of books down to the Forth Bridge workmen.

I could not give Herbert any messages as I was in Cabinet 12-3½. Ever your W E Gladstone

9. Th. [Hawarden]

Wrote to Ld Spencer—Mr Howard MP—Mrs Th.—Mr Summers MP[2]—The Queen—and minutes. Saw Mr Hamilton—Mr Lefevre—do *cum* Chancr of Exr—do *cum* Lord Spencer—Mr Moon. 2.20-7.50 To Hn. Read Reid's Life of S. Smith[3]—Bitter Cry from Glasgow.[4] Found a family party.

10. Fr.

Ch. 8¼ A.M. Wrote to Mr Hamilton l. & tel.—Ld Rosebery—Mr Lefevre—Ld Hartington Tel.—Mr J. Grant—& minutes. Walk with Alfred Lyttelton. Read Souvenirs d'un Pianiste[5]—Reid's Sydney Smith—Wright on the Hittite Empire.[6] The first is an almost incredible book.

To LORD ROSEBERY, 10 October 1884. '*Most Private*'.   N.L.S. 10023, f. 34.

I have to trouble you with a letter which concerns you, but which I hope will not be found to impose upon you any burden. It is not the letter I had hoped to write to you, yet it may, from one point of view at least, give you satisfaction.

Many weeks ago, my mind was made up that the time was come when I ought to make an effort to bring you into the Cabinet, both in justice to the public service you have done, and with reference to the exigencies of the present crisis. I also judged that the proper office to clear for you was the Presidentship of the Council (from which, I may say in passing, its educational functions are likely very soon to be severed). I took advice on the subject from colleagues who agreed with me.

The embassies of Berlin & Constantinople were open and Granville placed them both at Carlingford's disposal, who declined them. I however wrote very strongly to him

[1] See 1 July 84.

[2] Asking William Summers (1853–93; liberal M.P. Stalybridge 1880–5, Huddersfield 1886–93) to second the Address.

[3] S. J. Reid, *A sketch of the life and times ... of Sydney Smith* (1884), with Gladstone's letter, see 16 Oct. 83.

[4] *City echoes: or bitter cries from Glasgow* (1884).

[5] R. Franz [pseud. of Olga Janina], *Souvenirs d'un Pianiste* (1874).

[6] W. Wright, *Empire of Hittites* (1884).

urging that he should reconsider the question and opening, as a principal reason, my desire to be in a condition to deal with his office. He again entirely declined, and appeared to think that his proposed successor might come into the Cabinet without office, to which there are two fatal objections. It is a mode of first entrance totally unknown: and it would make an addition to our number of Peers, already overlarge, which it would not bear. In replying to Carlingford's negative, I reserved my liberty of action.

On our assembling in town, and fully discussing the matter, Granville and Spencer kindly undertook to see Carlingford, and I have reason to believe they gave him the best advice in the plainest terms. To their astonishment and mine, he remained immoveable. And he is ready to submit to the stripping off of the weightiest of the functions now in his hands.

In this state of facts, there remained no alternative but that of eviction. There is an understood right to fall back upon this extreme measure. But I think that during the last halfcentury it has only been once exercised, namely by Beaconsfield in the case of Lord Chelmsford. It is a measure of the severest character to be taken against a man who has done good service. And the time, eminently suited for your introduction, is not favourable to an ejectment.

The upshot is that the matter stands over: at the same time there has now been an intimation to him that it may revive after a time.

It is a strange business and causes me much regret for the non-execution, at the present moment, of my purpose. But I regret also, & much, in the interest (as I think) of the person who is the obstacle.

I will trouble you no further, except with my best wishes for your speedy recovery. [P.S.] Pray construe the words at the head of this letter in the strictest sense.[1]

To J. G. SHAW-LEFEVRE, commissioner of works,   Add MS 44153, f. 191.
10 October 1884. '*Private*'.

I learn by a succinct Telegram (of course duly veiled) to my great disappointment & concern, that difficulties have occurred about the execution of the plan wh. yesterday appeared to be on the point of accomplishment: and that these difficulties, as I gather, are on your side & not on the side of the Lord Lieutenant.[2]

If this be a simple retraction of the answer which yesterday you appeared inclined to give, I have nothing to say. But if it is not a change of mind as to the offer, & means that you are repelled by fears of difference of opinion, I wish, before the door is finally closed, to beg of you that you will consider the matter a little further.

I have little doubt that if tomorrow the members of the Cabinet were to write in letters of iron their present views as to the renewal of the Coercion or Crimes Bill, and to act upon these views, the Cabinet wd. go to pieces. I have as little doubt that if they wait until the proper time for action comes, with the evidence ripe & full, & results in clear view, union is likely to prevail.

I do venture to assure you, at the end of a long life, that even decision too late is not in politics a more subtle or dangerous mischief than decision too soon.

We have immediately before us a crisis of the nicest, the most complex, the most diversified, the most vital character, quite unconnected with the Crimes Act. It is so highly

---

[1] Rosebery replied, 12 October, Add MS 44288, f. 210: 'nothing would be more distasteful to me than to enter upon an office which had been compulsorily or even voluntarily vacated'.

[2] See Lefevre's letter this day, Add MS 44153, f. 190: too much disagreement with Spencer on the Crimes Act to accept the Irish secretaryship.

probable, as to be almost a moral certainty, that the incidents of that crisis will give to all of us the means of shaping our future course in forms we cannot now define. Had the Viceroy made the difficulty I should perhaps have thought him fastidious; but your position is far clearer, you are covered more than amply, and I cannot but say to you, if experience teaches me anything that your holding back under the circumstances would be an error in judgment, and would be the refusal of a real public service.

I am not without the hope of hearing from you direct by telegraph. But if you cannot manage this, I would not ask you to enter into any argument for you are clearly master and entitled to do what you please.[1]

11. Sat.

Ch. 8½ A.M. Wrote to Ld Hartington Tel.—Mr Hamilton Tel l.l.l.—The Queen—Rev. Dr. Wright—Mr Hubbard—Watsons—Mr Aitken—and minutes. The Dean of Windsor with Mrs D[avidson] and Mr Murray,[2] came. Much conversation with the Dean. Read Memoirs of K. Bauer.[3] Wrote to [sc. an] Introd: Notice.[4]

12. 18 S. Trin.

Ch. mg 11 AM and evg 6½ PM. Wrote to Mr Hamilton l. & Tel.—Bp of Chester—Dr Lyons MP—Sir J.E. Wilmot—Mr Lawson—and minutes. Conversations & arrangements with Ld Spencer about the Irish Sec. ship.[5] Walk with guests. Read D'Alviella, Evolution Religieuse.[6]

To E. L. LAWSON, editor of the *Daily Telegraph*,   Add MS 44547, f. 124.
12 October 1884.

In the interests of all Governments, of Government as such, & even of something more & higher, I beg to offer you my thanks for your refusal to receive & divulge the paper on Redistribution of seats which has recently been published in the Standard.[7]

To comment on it as you propose is now the right of all—each of course at his own risk.[8]

13. M.

Ch. 8½ A.M. Wrote to Ld Hartington—Ld Granville—Ld Spencer—Mr G. Russell—Mr Lefevre—Mr Hamilton l. & tel.—Ld Winmarleigh—The Queen—&

---

[1] Lefevre replied next day, ibid., f. 192, still declining, adding in 'domestic difficulties'. See 12 Oct. 84.

[2] John Murray, the publisher; H.V.B.

[3] C. Bauer, *Posthumous memoirs*, 4v. (1884–5); Gladstone's short review, unpublished, is at Add MS 44768, f. 125.

[4] i.e. his preface to Law, see 27 Sept. 84n.

[5] Campbell-Bannerman appt. *vice* Trevelyan on 15 Oct.; Shaw-Lefevre made Postmaster with the Cabinet on 8 Nov.

[6] Count E. F. A. Goblet D'Alviella, *L'évolution religieuse contemporaine chez les Anglais, les Américains et les Hindous* (1844).

[7] Publication in *The Standard*, 9 October 1884, 5 (Lawson having declined the scoop) of the Lambert/Dilke mem. on redistribution, CAB 37/13/39; see Jones, *1884*, 179–80 and 22 Oct. 84.

[8] Lawson replied, 14 October 1884, Add MS 44487, f. 292, grateful; the *D.T.* 'during nearly thirty years, made some mistakes: but . . . it never could have made such a mistake as to obtain the draft scheme by the means which were offered'.

minutes. Further conversation with the Dean, who went away. Also Mr Haz-zopulo. Mr Murray went. Walk with Mr Millais. Read K. Bauer—Count D'Alviella. Dinner party.

To LORD HARTINGTON, war secretary,   Chatsworth MSS 340. 1556.
13 October 1884.

I agree in your recital of what passed in the Cabinet.[1] I think the conversation there did not exclude the Cowper suggestion as interpreted by me i.e. that the simple production of the Seats Bill was to secure the passing of the Franchise Bill (which would admit no doubt of prior communication on the contents). But this, which was never very likely, is utterly excluded by Salisbury's speech at Kelso which indeed seems to exclude *everything*.

It is just possible that, when he comes nearer the point, he may find cause to be more tractable.

The most discouraging sign of all is that Salisbury denounces the paper surreptitiously obtained by the Standard as drawn with purposed unfairness. He does not want an accommodation for he does not as Lady S. told Lady Spencer care for the House of Lords & wd. like to be in the H. of Commons better.

If the reason of the case were to prevail they ought to propose a framework of Resolutions, for us to accept or decline, & then be governed by the result.

My only hope is in the followers, against the leaders.

Negotiation with Lefevre has also failed—on a matter altogether extraneous. He has behaved very well.

Spencer is to see C. Bannerman today. Hamilton started the idea of the Att. General. But could he be had.

[P.S.] Winmarleigh writes to recommend the re-enfranchisement of Lancaster: they claim 40,000 in their Registration District. Is it possible?

To G. W. E. RUSSELL, M.P., 13 October 1884.   Add MS 44547, f. 125.

I receive with an unmixed thankfulness your most kind & valuable gift;[2] but behind this sense of gratitude, & in no way impairing it, are some stings of conscience, due to the reflection that in this case I have made a large profit out of my ignorance.

However, I turn from these troublesome reflections to say how glad (not surprised) I am that Burke has a place in your admiration, & on most subjects as I conjecture in your confidence. Yet I remember a young Tory saying at Oxford he could not wish to be more Tory than Burke.

He was perhaps the maker of the Revolutionary war: & our going into that war perhaps made the Reign of Terror; &, without any perhaps, almost unmade the liberties, the constitution & prosperity of our country. Yet I venerate & almost worship him, though I can conceive its being argued that all he did for freedom, justice, religion, purity of government in other respects & other quarters were less than the mischief which flowed out from the Reflections. I would he were now alive.

[P.S.] Mr. Lowell's note is delightful. I will examine carefully your reference. I hope Lord Charles is well.

---

[1] Letter of 11 October in Add MS 44147, f. 154: 'the next step of any kind must come from the other side'.
[2] Untraced; Russell was under consideration for the Irish secretaryship; Bahlman, *Hamilton*, ii. 704.

To LORD WINMARLEIGH, 13 October 1884.   Add MS 44487, f. 290.

I will take my best pains to examine the Lancaster case. Is the Registration District in any sense the town?[1] I have written to Hartington about it.

Our last correspondence[2] hardly left me with any warrant to write to you again. I should like to know the inside of your mind. I have no title to ask it. But I see no reason why I should not show you a piece of the inside of mine.

1. It is my opinion that Salisbury (who naturally rules the roost), does not want an accommodation, & does not care if the House of Lords is thrown into the cauldron along with our other materials.

2. It is my conviction that another rejection (or call it what you please) will effectually raise the question of the organic structure of the House of Lords.

3. And that that question, once raised, will & can only be settled by a great change, which it is my heart's desire if possible to avert.

But all this is no reason why you, a Wirral proprietor, should not come to the cutting of the sod for the new Railway on Thursday, & sleep at Hawarden before & after?[3] Only come & we will keep our politics in our pockets.

14. Tu.

Ch. 8½ A.M. Wrote to Att. Gen. Tel.—Mr Hamilton Tel.—Mr Dodson—Ld Spencer—Mr J. Morley—& minutes—Bp of Chester—Mr Millais. Dinner party. Read K. Bauer—Life of S. Smith.

15. Wed.

Ch. 8½ AM. Wrote to Mr Hamilton l. & T. 111—Mr Campbell Bannerman Tel.—Rev. B. Price—Mr Law[4]—Mr Dodson—Mrs Th.—Ld Spencer Tel.—& minutes. Read Reid's S. Smith—K. Bauer's Memoirs. Walk with Mr Millais: a *little* woodcraft: my sons felled an oak.

To J. G. DODSON, chancellor of the duchy of Lancaster,   Monk Bretton 37.
15 October 1884. '*Secret*'.

I have desired, and until a few days back I had expected, to postpone the day of acting on your request for a Peerage, and still to enjoy the benefit of your aid as a colleague. But circumstances beyond my controul have placed this out of my power: and I therefore propose at once to submit to the Queen a request that you may now receive an honour which you have, in my judgment, thoroughly deserved.

It will be with regret that I shall miss you on the bench and in the Cabinet, during the short period for which I may continue to frequent them. Trevelyan will I think be your successor: and I am sure he may count upon your good will.

16. Th.

Ch. 8½ A.M. Wrote to The Queen l.l.l.—Mr Downing—Ld Spencer—Mr Trevelyan—Mr H. Tracy—Mr C. Bannerman—Ld Derby—Mr Hamilton. 1-5¾. To

[1] The 1885 Act created Lancaster division, effectively a borough but technically a county seat.
[2] See 12 July 84.
[3] Winmarleigh unable to come; '*honestly* in favour of the Bill & am all for an accommodation', but Lords right to act; Add MS 44487, f. 320.
[4] In Lathbury, ii. 326; sending his preface, see 27 Sept., 11 Oct. 84n.

Birkenhead for Railway function. Two speeches: great enthusiasm.¹ 100,000 people out: or nearly. Read Caroline Bauer—Reid's Sydney Smith.

17. Fr.

Ch. 8½ A.M. Wrote to Bp of St Asaph—The Queen l.l.—Watsons—Ld Granville—Ld Spencer—Ld Winmarleigh—Mr Hamilton—& minutes. Our friends went. We began to cut the obnoxious tall Elm by the keep. Commenced a long letter to Bp of St Asaph.² Read Karoline Bauer and Reid's Life of S. Smith.

18. Sat. St Luke.

Agnes's birthday. Ch. 8½ AM & H.C. Wrote to Ld Granville Tel. l.l.—Mr Childers Tel.—Att. General—Messrs Robertson—Sir E. Watkin—Mr Hamilton Tel.—Ld Spencer Tel.—and minutes. Began l. to Bp of St A. Read Life of Sydney Smith. Finished the astonishing Memoirs of Karoline Bauer. A party of 40 or 50 came to tea: & we had the fall of a great Elm by the keep for them.

19. 19 S. Trin.

Ch. 11 A.M. and [blank] P.M. Wrote to Mr Hamilton l & tel—The Queen l. & Tel.—Ld Granville—Ld Kimberley—Lady Mar—Sir T.E. May—Bp of St Asaph—and minutes. Worked on letter to Bp of St A. Read Mozley's Letters³—'Alike and perfect'. Conversation with Lucy.

20. M.

Ch. 8½ A.M. Wrote to Bp of St Asaph l.l.—Mr Hamilton Tel.—Ld R. Grosvenor Tel.—The Queen Tel.—Ld Acton—Messrs Barker & Hignett—Mr W. Fraser—Rev. Dr Nevin—Mr H.A.J. Munro⁴—and minutes. Busy kibbling Elm with HNG. Read Sydney Smith. Dined at WHGs. They have made much comfort in little time. Unpacking books &c.

21. Tu. [London]

Ch. 8½ A.M. and farewells. Wrote to the Queen l.l.—Lord Derby—Mr Dodson—Mrs Howard—Mr Hamilton Tel.—and minutes. 10.50-4. Hn to D. St. My quickest journey. Saw Sir C. Dilke—Ld Spencer *cum* Ld R.G.—Mr Hamilton—Ld Granville—Do cum Mover & Seconder + Ld Belper. Read Life of Tennyson.⁵ Saw Howard [R].

---

¹ Cutting sod to inaugurate construction of railway link from Wales to Liverpool *via* Mersey tunnel; *T.T.*, 17 October 1884, 8a.
² Huge letter, over a column of *T.T.*, on disestablishment, dated 19 October and read to the St. Asaph Diocesan Conference; *T.T.*, 23 October 1884, 12a.
³ J. B. Mozley, *Letters*, ed. A. Mozley (1884).
⁴ Hugh Andrew Johnstone Munro, 1819-85, had sent his translations; Add MS 44547, f. 127.
⁵ H. J. Jennings, *Lord Tennyson, a biographical sketch* (1884).

22. Wed.

Wrote to Mr Millais[1]—The Queen l. & tel.—Ld Northbrook Tel.—Sir W. James—Mrs Th—Ld Hartington—Ld Arran—Ld De Vesci—Ld Herries—and minutes. Finished Jennings's Life of Tennyson. Read Froude's Carlyle.[2] Cabinet 2–4$\frac{1}{2}$. Saw Chancr of Exr—The Speaker—Ld Hartington *cum* Sir W.H.—Sir H. Ponsonby (on Carnarvon's offer &c)[3]—Mr Hamilton.

Cabinet. Wed. Oct. 22 84. 2 PM.[4]
1. China mediation.[5]
2. Reply to [W.H.] Smith agreed on[6]—subject to Northbrook's assent.
3. Notice of Franchise Bill for Friday—no speech beyond a very few sentences—endeavour to obtain a vote.
4. Mentioned change of a word in the Speech.
5. 'Standard Disclosure'[7] Question and examination whether proceedings can be taken against Master-Foreman. Shall the confidential printing be taken away from Queen's printers? Treasury will decide.

23. Th.

Wrote to The Queen Tel &—Mr Jennings[8]—Ld Chancr—Ld Northbrook Tel.—Ld Derby & minutes. Conclave on Offices at 1. Saw Mr H—Ld RG—Ld Granville—Ld Wolverton. H of C. 4$\frac{1}{2}$–8$\frac{1}{4}$ & 9$\frac{1}{2}$–11$\frac{3}{4}$. Spoke at some length on the Address as carefully as I could.[9] Read Froude's Carlyle.

To LORD DERBY, colonial secretary, 23 October 1884.   Add MS 44547, f. 128.

Clearly we cannot bring an Australian Confederation Bill into the House of Commons at this moment, nor can we engage to do it during the autumn.[10]

If however you think the Bill important at the present moment, as probably it is, & if you see your way as to the contents, could you introduce it in the House of Lords, with full & explicit notice that it could not, so far as Ministers are concerned, be allowed to delay or entangle in any way, & in either House, the movement of the Franchise Bill. I do not see any objection to such a course. Childers who happened to be with me on the arrival of your note approves it.

[1] Presenting him with a stick; Add MS 44547, f. 128.
[2] J. A. Froude, *Thomas Carlyle. A history of his life in London 1834–81*, 2v. (1884).
[3] Proposal for an inter-party group of 'men of weight', including Carnarvon, May and Norton, to attempt a solution; see Jones, *1884*, 177–9. See to Norton 24 Oct. 84.
[4] Add MS 44645, f. 186.
[5] War between France and China thought imminent (never in fact declared); France withdrew 'indemnity' claim, settling for 40 million francs, Granville's suggestion; Cabinet agreed further to promote mediation on French claim; CAB 41/18/47; see 6 Oct. 84.
[6] On state of navy: statement to follow; *H* 293. 58.
[7] See 12 Oct. 84; the leak was thought to have come from one of Eyre & Spottiswoode's printers.
[8] Thanking him for his *Tennyson* (see 21 Oct. 84) and disputing his claim that Disraeli offered Tennyson a baronetcy in 1868; Add MS 44547, f. 128.
[9] *H* 293. 83.
[10] Derby had been asked by Carnarvon whether such a bill was possible; 23 October, Add MS 44142, f. 93. Various explanations for delay were given; *H* 294. 1012. See 16 Feb. 85.

24. Fr.

Wrote to D. of Argyll—Prince of Wales—Ld Norton—Mr C. Bannerman (Tel)—
The Queen—and minutes. Saw Mr H—Ld R.G & others. Ld Dalhousie—Mr
Hamilton—Sir H. Ponsonby. Luncheon at 15 G.S. H of C. $4\frac{1}{4}$-$8\frac{1}{4}$ & 9-$12\frac{3}{4}$.[1] Read
Froude's Carlyle—Q.R. on Croker.[2]

To LORD NORTON, 24 October 1884.[3] *'Private'.*   Add MS 44547, f. 129.

You will have observed, I think with regret, that last night the terms demanded from a
large majority of the House of Commons were the unconditional acceptance of the views
of the minority who likewise represent the majority of the House of Lords. We on the
other hand say, we cannot do that: you must know we cannot do it: ask us something that
we can do. This they persistently decline.

When I saw you, you said your desire was that the separation of rural and urban interest should be aimed at by the Redistribution Bill. I consider your anxiety to be just. I think
that, within the limits of reason and convenience, which will not allow the matter to be
pursued into every detail, that separation should be studied & effected. I believe there is
nothing in reason which you could ask that would not be readily granted.

Perhaps you noted Carnarvon's recent suggestion; that three or four men on whom
much reliance could be placed by both parties, should meet together & consider the outlines of redistribution. Some good might I believe come of such a plan. He said he feared
it would not act; because of the perverse prejudice of his opponents, I have been doing
what I could to put onward his suggestion. I have not yet heard that any of his friends
have done the same; or are doing anything similar. But I still hope from the followers, if
not the leaders.[4]

25. Sat.

Wrote to Mr E. Clarke—The Queen—& minutes. Twelve to dinner. Saw Mr
H—Ld R.G.—Sir W. Harcourt—Mr Hill (D[aily] N[ews])[5]—Dean of St Pauls.
Read Croker Papers[6]—Q.R. on do (finished)—Froude's Carlyle.

26. 20 S. Trin.

Chapel Royal mg and evg. Wrote to Sir C. Dilke. Saw Mr Hamilton—Ld
Norton[7]—Ld Granville—Sir J. Lacaita. Dined reluctantly, at Marlborough
House. Conversation with the Prince on the situation. Read Fiske on Darwin-
ism[8]—Bp of Liverpool's Charge[9]—Nares's Burghley[10]—Q.R. on Massillon[11]—
Churton on Apocrypha.[12]

---

[1] Questions; Queen's Speech; *H* 293. 156.

[2] *Q.R.*, clviii. 518 (October 1884).

[3] Copy sent to Argyll. No reply found.

[4] Gladstone was thus the initiator, at least in part, of the compromise attempts of the 'men of
weight'; see Jones, *1884*, 178. He had worked with Norton (formerly Adderley) on colonial affairs in
the early 1850s; see above, iii. xxxvi.

[5] The *D.N.* editorial of 27 October 1884, 4f, protested at tory blocking of the Franchise Bill 2°R.

[6] L. J. Jennings, *The Croker Papers. The correspondence and diaries of the late . . . J. W. Croker*, 3v. (1884).

[7] Political discussion begun in the Chapel Royal; Jones, *1884*, 178.

[8] J. Fiske, *Darwinism and other essays* (1879).   [9] J. C. Ryle, 'A charge' (1884).

[10] E. Nares, *Memoirs of . . . Cecil, Lord Burghley* (1828).   [11] *Q.R.*, clviii. 495 (October 1884).

[12] W. R. Churton, *The uncanonical and apocryphal scriptures* (1884).

To Sir C. W. DILKE, president of the local   Add MS 43875, f. 186.
government board, 26 October 1884.

My own feeling is that 10 m[ille] give a better limit than 15 m. because many of the towns have municipal life & the character of a town in full, & are unsuitable elements for County Constituencies.[1] At the same time if it proves that the Cabinet generally (as is probable) leans in the same direction as the Committee, I certainly shall not set up my own opinion adversely. I should like however to know what you say to the point I have put.

Under the circumstances I suppose you will frame a scheme with the 15 m. limit.[2]

27. M.

Wrote to Ld Hartington l.l.—Ld Granville—Ld Derby—Sir H. Ponsonby—The Queen—Sir W. Harcourt—Sir H. Robinson l.l.—and minutes. Walk and shopping. Saw Mr H—Lord RG—Ld Hartington and . . .? Read Froude's Carlyle—Croker Papers. H of C. $4\frac{1}{2}$–$8\frac{1}{4}$–9–$11\frac{1}{2}$.[3]

To LORD DERBY, colonial secretary, 27 October 1884.   Add MS 44547, f. 129.

I was a little startled by the closing sentences of Sir H. Robinson's last telegram in which he appeared to recommend that, after having agreed to the mission of the Cape Ministers, we should import some new limitation and thus open a door to parting company with them.

I was surprised at this because on the one hand they are pledged to vindicating British authority and to the Convention of 1884 (as I understand) and on the other hand there could not be a more serious step taken than to break our partnership with them, lose our hold on the Colonial and Dutch population, & have to devise separate modes of action.

Granville whom I saw accidentally seemed to concur in this view, which I think it worth while just to mention but I feel sure you have carefully considered the point.[4]

28. Tu.

Wrote to The Queen l.l.—Mr Chamberlain—Sir C. Dilke—Sol. Gen. Ireland—Mr Ashley—and minutes. Read Froude's Carlyle. Saw Mr H—Ld R.G—Ld Herries—Sir Thos May—Mr Childers—Att. General. Worked on the Maamtrasna case; & spoke at some length. H of C. $4\frac{1}{2}$–$8\frac{1}{4}$ & $9\frac{1}{2}$–$12\frac{3}{4}$.[5]

---

[1] Dilke reported a meeting of the redistribution cttee. on 25 October, Add MS 44149, f. 251, 'unanimous in asking you to raise the 10,000 limit of merger to 15,000', and by a majority to extend single member districts to counties.

[2] Dilke sent details next day of the 16 boroughs between 10 and 15,000; ibid., f. 253.

[3] Questions; Queen's Speech; *H* 293. 258.

[4] Derby replied, 27 October, 4 p.m., Add MS 44142, f. 95, agreeing Robinson's language 'more peremptory than seems necessary or desirable'.

[5] *H* 293. 361; frequently interrupted by Irish members.

To J. CHAMBERLAIN, president of the board of trade,   Add MS 44547, f. 130.
28 October 1884.

Will you kindly answer MacIver's question today. And will you also be prepared to take part in any debate on the Transvaal & Bechuanaland, when you know so much of the case.[1]

29. Wed.

Wrote to Mr Childers—Duke of Argyll—Ld Chancellor—Atty General—Ld Spencer—Ld Hartington—The Queen—and minutes. Saw Mr H—Ld RG—Sir C. Dilke. H. of C. $2\frac{3}{4}$-6.[2] Dined at Mrs Hartmanns.[3] Mr Elkington [*sic*] came in evg. For the first time I was present at his operations of spiritism: quite inexplicable: not the smallest sign of imposture. I took down the particulars.[4] Read Froude's Carlyle—D'Alviella—Belgian Lib party.[5]

To LORD HARTINGTON, war secretary,   Chatsworth MSS 340. 1562.
29 October 1884.

Thanks for your important, full, and clear paper.[6]
I do not think it on the whole unhopeful either as to enactments or as to procedure: but the little you said seems to me thoroughly reasonable & judicious.
The largeness of the plan does not stagger me, if that is really the likeliest basis of an accord.
In my own mind, I feel a conservative objection to the very small recognition of communities (apart from mere populations) and of the traditional privileges of cities and boroughs now represented as compared with new communities. I do not say now it must be requisite to push this objection to extremes. I am glad the scheme leans so considerably to the one member principle. And that it does not broadly raise the question of proportional representation. The most serious difficulty is as to Ireland. Probably the best

[1] Chamberlain did not speak on S. Africa in the Queen's speech debs.; he answered MacIver on shipping depression; *H* 293. 353.
[2] Queen's Speech; *H* 293. 444.
[3] Emma Hartmann, living at 34 Grosvenor Square (see Add MS 44488, f. 44 and next n.).
[4] See notes at Add MS 44768, f. 128. The medium wisely declined to tip for the Cesarewitch (presumably next year's: the race had been run on 4 October). Notepaper headed '34 Grosvenor Square' (Lord Lothian's house); thus a probable Thistlethwayte link. The medium, William Eglinton, was well-known for 'slate writing'; he was controversially exposed as a 'clever conjuror' by Mrs. Sidgwick in June 1886 (see *Journal of the Society for Psychical Research*, ii. 449 (June 1886)). Eglinton gave a detailed account of this day's proceedings in *Light*, 8 November 1884, 466 and to the *Morning Post*, 7 November 1884, 3f, which gave details of the slate writing and reported Eglinton quoting Gladstone as saying 'that there were subtle forces with which "our puny minds" could not deal, and which he could not comprehend; he held the attitude, therefore, not of a scoffer, but of a student . . . his recent experiences of thought-reading were sufficient to show that there were forces in nature which were not generally recognised . . . he spoke at length of his own observations many years ago in the domains of clairvoyance and electro-biology . . .'. See to Mrs. Hartmann, 7 Nov. 84; see also 22 Aug. 85. For a discussion of Gladstone's brief involvement in the spiritualist movement, see above, Introduction in vol. X, section ix.
[5] Untraced.
[6] Notes made this day of his conversation with Sir M. Hicks Beach on franchise and redistribution; Holland, ii. 55. Copy at Add MS 44147, f. 158; note of his second conversation, on 4 November, ibid., f. 169.

practical means of handling it may be to isolate & postpone it: let it stand till the rest has in principle been dealt with.

I am more than doubtful as to exceptional provisions for Ireland; but then there is the suggestion of the one-member plan, which may meet the case.

I am very reluctant to entertain the idea of reducing the 103 members for Ireland. Among other difficulties it would entail reduction for Wales: and this would I suppose entail county amalgamation; and this would run into Scotland: how could you keep Sutherland alive.

May you not make further use of your paper? beginning perhaps with Childers. I should like a copy.

30. Th.

Wrote to Count Münster—Lady Sydney—Mr Chamberlain—The Queen l.l.—& minutes. Read Froude's Carlyle. Dined at Sir C. Forster's. Saw Mr H—Ld RG— Ld Granville—Ld Dufferin—Mr Chamberlain—Ld Hartington. H. of C. $4\frac{1}{2}$-$8\frac{3}{4}$ and 10-$1\frac{1}{2}$. Spoke for Chamberlain, who had made an impression by his most powerful speech: but the division from several causes was bad, 214:178.[1]

31. Fr.

Wrote to The Queen l.l.—Mr Chamberlain l.l. & Tel.—Sir W. Harcourt—Mr Hamilton—& minutes. H of C. $4\frac{1}{2}$-6 and 9-11.[2] Cabinet 2-$4\frac{1}{4}$. Saw Mr H—Ld RG l.l.—Mr Trevelyan—Mr Cowen—Ld Granville. Read Froude's Carlyle—Jessop's Hist. Diocese of Norwich.[3]

Cabinet. Oct. 31. 84. 2 PM.[4]

1. Merchant Shipping Commission. Dft. of answer prepared.
2. South Africa. Military preparations.[5] Cavalry regiments from India to be sent to Cape & Battalion from W-I[ndies] to be intercepted at Gibraltar for further orders.
3. Packets for the Royal Family. Postponed for a month.
4. Candidature of civil servants for Parliament. To be prohibited—by a minute of Treasury in the name of the Govt.
5. U. Sec. has lost Cabinet key. Committee of Cabinet to consider of an alternative to the present key.
6. Trevelyan[6] reported Queen's aversion to a Dissolution. W.E.G. reported generally. Hartington reported conversation with Sir M. H. Beach.[7] Idea of Resolutions broached not unfavourably.
7. Ponsonby's letter of 30 Oct. Plan inadmissible.[8]

[1] Churchill's amdt. to the Speech, censuring Chamberlain for justifying riot and disorder; *H* 293. 635.   [2] Queen's Speech; *H* 293. 668.
[3] A. Jessop, *Norwich* (1880).   [4] Add MS 44645, f. 190.
[5] i.e. the mission of (Sir) Charles *Warren, 1840-1927, to Bechuanaland, though not yet fully formulated; see 8, 11 Nov. 84.
[6] Who had been at Balmoral.
[7] See Hartington's mem. of 29 October, Holland, ii. 55: Beach's ambitious plan for single-member constituencies. See to Hartington, 29 Oct. 84.
[8] See Guedalla, ii. 309-11 for Ponsonby's letter suggesting the Lords 'read the Franchise Bill a second time then wait till the Redistribution Bill reaches them' and Gladstone's reply that 'the offer to concede the second Reading of the Franchise Bill alone would make no substantial difference in the situation'.

To J. CHAMBERLAIN, president of the board   Chamberlain MSS 5/34/31.
of trade, 31 October 1884.

I think that it would be very desirable that you should suspend the announcement to the public of the Commission[1] until you have made the names known to the Cabinet.

For as you truly hold the shipowners are keen and probably in their dominant feeling selfish, and amidst the many difficulties surrounding us they will have opportunities of making the question more than a Departmental one.

Indeed so far as I know the usage is in nominating Commissions of importance not to treat that work as simply departmental.

To Sir W. V. HARCOURT, home secretary,   MS Harcourt dep. Adds 10.
31 October 1884. '*Early*'.

Healy puts to me today a fivefold question which is subtle and embarrassing.[2] He is often courteous to me, and I do not wish to give him gratuitous offence. I am not however a proper person to answer this question, though personally I have no unwillingness to do it.

I send you Spencers note because he has considered the points. I understand him to mean that I should say I have not seen the declarations, that it was the exclusive office of the Viceroy to deal with them and that no particulars can be furnished about them, as we cannot bring the prerogative of mercy under review.

Please to advise me on this delicate matter, and I should be extremely glad if you could obtain the views of the Attorney General, as I know he has much & specially considered this part of the business.[3]

Sat. All S. Nov. 1. 1884 [*Cliveden*]

Wrote to Ld Hartington—Sir John Hay—Mr M'Coll—Mr Dodson—Mr Jerningham—Ld Coleridge—The Queen l. & Tel.—D. of Argyll—Mr V. Stuart MP—Watsons—& minutes. Sat to Mendelsohn.[4] Saw Mr H—Ld RG—Mrs Bastable—Sir C. Dilke. To Cliveden at 3.45. Read F. Newman Xtn Commonw.[5]—Jerningham on Norham Castle[6]—Jessop's Diocese of Norwich. A pleasant domestic party. Much conversation about the dear Duchess H.[7]

To the DUKE OF ARGYLL, 1 November 1884.   Add MS 44547, f. 133.

I write as you see from within the well known walls, where the air is thick with recollections, all as fresh as on the day when they took their birth.

I had intended not to be out of the way, even for hours, at a moment when every kind of rumour & movement connected with the Franchise Bill is so rife that there is no time of day at which something new may not arise. But Cliveden was not to be resisted, to say nothing of its hosts, who are of no small attraction.

[1] On loss of life at sea; *PP* 1884–5 xxxv.
[2] On depositions of the two men executed for the Maamtrasna murders with M. Joyce, exonerating him; Add MS 44199, f. 106.
[3] Harcourt entirely agreed with Spencer; ibid., f. 107.
[4] For photographs; Add MS 44547, f. 140.
[5] F. W. Newman, *A Christian Commonwealth* (1883).
[6] H. E. H. Jerningham, *Norham Castle* (1883).
[7] i.e. Harriet, duchess of Sutherland; see Matthew, *Gladstone*, 130, 150.

I had not time before leaving London to answer your kind letter[1] & I only gave a direction about it. But I have now full time to fill the void, and though I have little to say I take up my pen lest I should appear insensible either to your patriotism or your kindness.

I will not fail to act in the sense you permit, if I have opportunity. But I am doubtful whether I am likely to be able to release you from whatever responsibility may belong at this juncture to the initiative of independent Peers. It is from the spontaneous interaction of such persons that I principally cherish hopes. I have never known a time when a great political controversy was brought to a pacific issue by the initiative of leaders. Anything of that kind that may offer I shall not discourage, but promote. Yet without relying upon it greatly. I think it is, so to speak, from below, in the House of Lords, that most probably good is to be done. I beg therefore that, without reference to place, you will not let your activity depend upon the expectation of hearing from me. When I went after you last Saturday & failed, I felt I might justly speak to you on the spot, but my case was not definite enough to ask you to traverse the 500 (more or less) miles from Inveraray, nor is it likely to be. I have only dared & sought to put men in motion, not to employ them, and I believe that if I attempted more I should place myself & them in a false position, & should impede the end which I so heartily desire to see attained.

2. 21 S. Trin.

Hedsor Ch mg. Remarkable. Prevented by rain in evg. Drove & walked: Burnham Beeches: the colours splendid. Wrote to Ld Northbrook—Mr Hamilton. Read Bonet Maury, Christianisme l'unitaire[2]—Heath's Via Dolorosa[3]—Ficht, Destiny of Man (finished)[4]—The great Problem.[5]

3. M. [London]

Wrote to Ld Northbrook—Sir D. Currie—Mrs Hartmann—The Queen—& minutes. H of C. $4\frac{3}{4}$-$8\frac{1}{2}$ and 11-$2\frac{3}{4}$.[6] Conclave on offices at 2.30. Saw Mr H—Ld RG—H.J.G.—Ld Hartington—Sir C. Dilke—Sir W. Harcourt—Chancr of Exr—Ld Granville. Read Fortnightly Rev. on W.E.G.[7]—Bonet Maury—Contemp. Rev. Laveleye—Seeley—and Reed (Navy) Articles.[8]

4. Tu.

Wrote to Ld Hartington—Lady Sandhurst (Dowager)[9]—The Queen—Mrs Th.—and minutes. Dined at Lucy's. Saw Mr S.—Ld RG. H of C. $4\frac{1}{2}$-$8\frac{1}{4}$ and $9\frac{3}{4}$-$11\frac{1}{4}$.[10]

---

[1] On 27 October, Argyll sent 18 Propositions on the situation, concluding that the govt. should offer a suspensory clause and agree on outlines of redistribution.

[2] See 19 Aug. 81.

[3] R. Heath, The English Via Dolorosa (1884); on agricultural labourers.

[4] J. G. Fichte, The destination of man (1846).

[5] The great problem of Christianity (1881).

[6] Spoke on Queen's Speech; H 293. 858.

[7] T. H. S. Escott, F.R., xlii. 557 (November 1884).

[8] C.R., xlvi. 635, 617, 488 (November, October 1884).

[9] See 25 Sept. 63n.; in the 1880s she was an active liberal, prominent in the Women's Liberal Federation and elected 1889 to the L.C.C. (unseated as ineligible). Gladstone declined her invitation to attend her séance as for the time imprudent; Add MS 44547, f. 133. But see 18 Nov. 84.

[10] Discussion of the Speech completed; H 293. 988.

Read Froude's Carlyle—Contemp. Barrett on Church—Bryce on H. of Lords.[1] Westminster party to luncheon. 2–3¾. National Liberal Club function. Had to speak ½ hour. *The* incident was the Address from 550 workmen on the Metropole with about 12 exceptions.[2]

5. *Wed.*

Wrote to Sir T. Brassey—Ld Northbrook—Mr Fowler—Ld Sherbrook—Ed. Times[3]—The Queen l.l. & Tel.—and minutes. H of C. 12¼–1½ & 3¾–6.[4] Dined at the Speaker's. Saw Mr H—Ld R.G.—Ld Hartington—Sir C. Dilke—Mr Goschen—Sir T. May—Lady Jersey—Scotts—Sir A. Clark MD. Read Carlyle's Froude [*sic!*].

Points on which we may move in the direction of Hicks Beach?[5]
1. Extensive readjustment of electoral areas with reference to population and pursuits. 2. Smallest class of towns to merge in the Counties (say towns up to 10000?) or in any cases where they can ⟨be attached⟩ with special convenience. 3. Populations of 10000 and upwards, bearing the character and concentration of a town to be taken out of the Counties and enfranchised or grouped for enfranchisement. 4. Boundaries of Parliamentary boroughs to be reconsidered where the population has increased but with a due regard to local circs. 5. The principal of one member districts is to be generally applied, ⟨especially where the population though dense cannot be ranged in towns.⟩
Points of serious difficulty. The cumulative vote and minority vote are inadmissible. There can be no exceptional provisions against Ireland. We are reluctant to admit county grouping?

6. *Th.*

Wrote to Mrs Hartmann—Ld Northbrook—Mr Caine MP.—Ld Carlingford—The Queen l.l.l.—Mr Childers—Miss Stewart—Mrs Fawcett—and minutes. Read Froude's Carlyle. Saw Mr H—Ld R.G.—Ld Mayor Elect—Mr Bright—Mr H. Seymour. H of C. 4½–8½ & 9¾–12 Moved 2 R of Franchise Bill in a speech mainly about Redistribution.[6]

7. *Frid.*

Wrote to The Queen l.l.—Mrs Hartmann—Mr Childers—& minutes. Cabinet 2–4¼. Saw Mr H—Ld RG—Ld Granville. H. of C. 4½–8¼ & 9¾–1. Excellent division 372:232.[7] And debate very favourable. Read Froude's Carlyle.

---

[1] *C.R.*, xlvi. 673, 718 (November 1884).
[2] Workmen from the Hotel Metropole next the club, led by Broadhurst, entered the meeting to present a congratulatory memorial; *D.N.*, 5 November 1884, 2f.
[3] Which next day stated the cabinet had not discussed Chamberlain's dispute with the shipowners; *T.T.*, 6 November 1884, 9f.
[4] Secured precedence for Franchise Bill; *H* 293. 916.
[5] Undated holographs (dated 5 November 1884 by secretary), sent to Dilke; Add MS 43875, f. 192.
[6] *H* 293. 1121.
[7] Franchise Bill 2°R; spoke on d. of Fawcett; *H* 293. 1222, 1328.

Cabinet. Friday. N. 7. 1884. 2 PM.[1]
Redistribution. Recital of proceedings of Ld H.
Limerick Corporation: payment for Constabulary.[2] Matter to stand for legislation.

1. As to communication between leaders. H. nominates Dilke—invites Beach to do the same & press for more specific statements on both sides.[3]
2. Dilke recited views of Cabinet Committee on the points raised by Tories. General conversation indicative of lines. Grouping not to be welcomed for old boroughs but not to argue too high against it.

To LORD DERBY, colonial secretary, 7 November 1884.   Add MS 44547, f. 135.
'*Secret*'.

If I can get to your door before six today I will call & ask for Lady Derby.[4] But it is uncertain.

The Cabinet will probably deal with the Limerick case, & a very ugly one it is.

But the main subject is Redistribution, & the first & probably greatest question is whether we are or are not prepared, with proper assurances, & with a view to an early settlement, to accept the Salisbury-Beach radical scheme, which so far as I can comprehend adopts absolutely the principle of population, with a saving for present Boroughs of 25000 & upwards & with the very large reserve that town & country are to be ripped asunder everywhere & to the uttermost.

Bright does not at all like the idea of it.

The Northbrook report is too large a subject for this hasty note, & scarcely yet ripe. It oppresses me extremely.

To Mrs. HARTMANN, 7 November 1884.   Add MS 44547, f. 134.

I am sorry to find an article in the Morning Post[5] of today. The facts are I think pretty accurately stated, not so the conversation, though I have no doubt that the account is truthfully intended. But the serious matter is that the reporting it at all is a breach of trust & confidence; which Mr. Eglinton has properly respected in the case of yourself & the other ladies. This breach of trust I look upon as a serious matter; & I shall be obliged by Mr. Eglinton's *not* sending me the books which he was so good as to promise, & which under present circumstances I could not retain.

8. Sat. [*The Durdans*]

Wrote to Mr Arnold—Dr Döllinger—Dean of Wells—Mr Lefevre—Mr Childers l.l.—Prince of Wales—& minutes. To the Durdans—at midnight. Conclave 12–1½

---

[1] Add MS 44645, f. 196.

[2] Limerick refused to levy a rate to pay for extra constabulary; legislation to be introduced to avoid imprisoning the corporation; CAB 41/18/49.

[3] Gladstone told Victoria: 'The essence of the Tory plan seems to be to give almost unlimited scope to the principle of distribution by population, but to qualify this rule by the most minute and careful severance of rural and urban or quasi-urban pursuits. This latter provision is extremely repugnant, when carried to great lengths, to the ideas generally prevalent on the Liberal side'; CAB 41/18/49.

[4] Derby this day, Add MS 44142, f. 96, unable to attend cabinet: he supported Spencer on the Limerick magistrates, and first felt *re* Northbrook's 'large and bold' Egyptian scheme, '"this will never do"', but 'on second thoughts I am less hostile'.

[5] i.e. on the séance; see 29 Oct. 84. She replied that Eglinton was not to blame, and that attempts to find the culprit 'by writing' produced 'Herbert' and 'Chambermaid', messages from the other world; Add MS 44488, f. 4.

on offices &c. Saw Mr Childers—Mr Seymour—Ld R.G.—Ld Granville—Ld Dunraven—Mrs Hartmann. Saw Miss Anderson[1] in Romeo & Juliet. Great beauty and careful study. Read Malmesbury—Romeo & Juliet.

To H. C. E. CHILDERS, chancellor of the exchequer,   Add MS 44547, f. 135.
8 November 1884.

I think it quite plain that the charge for Bechuanaland requires the sanction of the Cabinet.[2] There is a broad distinction drawn in the Telegrams between preparations which are to go on, and operations, which are suspended. The 700 [mille] *can* I apprehend refer to the latter only and an important question will here arise as to the proper *time* for asking the sanction of Parliament.

9. 22 S Trin.

Ch. mg & evg. Read Bonet Maury—Feis on Shakespeare[3]—Greene on Exodus—Jones on Spiritism.[4] Saw Belgian Minr (Bauer). Walk & conversation with Rosebery. Made my proposal.[5] We had pretty full explanations. He takes time: puzzled about Egypt.

10. M. [London]

Wrote to Ld Coleridge—Ld Northbrook—Mr Lefevre—The Queen tel. & L.l.l.—The U.S. Minister—Ld Granville—& minutes. H of C. $4\frac{3}{4}$-$8\frac{3}{4}$. Wonderful.[6] 11-12. Back to Downing St. Saw Mr Seymour—Ld R.G.—Ld Northbrook—Sir W. Harcourt—Sir C. Dilke—Mr Childers. We went forwards *fast* with the Bill, but backwards from the changed attitude of the Tory party. Read Feis on Shakespeare—The Croker papers.[7]

11. Tu.

Wrote to The Queen l.l.l.l.l.—Mr V. Stuart MP.—Mr Richard MP—and minutes. Dined at Sir E. May's. Read Dowden on Scots Office[8]—Croker papers. Cabinet 2-$4\frac{1}{4}$. Saw Mr H—Ld RG—Mr Childers—Ld Northbrook—Ld Hartington. H of C. $4\frac{1}{4}$-$8\frac{1}{4}$. Spoke on 3 R. Franchise Bill. A bad prospect for lovers of peace.[9]

Cabinet. Tues. Nov. 11. 2 PM.[10]
1. Votes to be proposed in Supply Thursday, *and in Ways & Means.* Precedence for them. Postpone notice.

[1] Mary Anderson, 1858-1940; American actress, made her name as Juliet.
[2] Childers reported this day he had learnt of arrangements being made for a Bechuanaland expedition; Add MS 44131, f. 203. See 11 Nov. 84.
[3] J. Feis, *Shakespeare and Montaigne* (1884).
[4] J. Jones, *The natural and supernatural; man, physical, apparitional and spiritual* (1861); Christian spiritualism.
[5] Commissionership of Works with the Cabinet; see 12 Nov. 84.
[6] Report stage completed; *H* 293. 1436.   [7] See 25 Oct. 84.
[8] J. Dowden, *The annotated Scottish communion office* (1884).
[9] Also spoke on Egypt; regretted the 'change of tone' on the opposition benches, exemplified by Manners, to whom he replied; *H* 293. 1458, 1476.
[10] Add MS 44645, f. 198.

2. Franchise & Redistribution. Plan of debate tonight. Hartington to hold Beach as long as he can. If that fails WEG to offer H.M. to see Salisbury + some one.[1]
3. Northcote's question. Supply & Ways & M[eans] *de die in diem.*
   Northbrook's Report.
   Votes in Supply on Thursday. Separate Soudan from Bechuanaland[2] and Army and Navy.

	300m[ille]
War Office (+ 300m)	1$\widehat{m}$
Navy	324
Bechuana Land	675
Navy	50m
	2351?
Add Fortifn. Commee.	64
W.O.	160
	2575m[ille][3]
Egyptian deficits possible	600m
W. & M. Death Duty Arrears: balances in hand	500m
1d. Income Tax	2000m

12. Wed.

Wrote to The Queen—Ld Lymington—Ld Selborne—Ld Northbrook—Ld Rosebery—Watsons—& minutes. Dined with Dean Church. Saw Mr H—Ld RG—Ld Granville—Do *cum* Ld Hartington—Lady Derby. Drive with C. Read Croker papers.

To LORD NORTHBROOK, first lord of the admiralty,   Add MS 44547, f. 136.
12 November 1884.

So far as the House of Commons is concerned, I should be disposed to answer Mr. Smith to the effect that we should be prepared to take a day for a Naval statement immediately after the Financial votes.[4] This would not be at the present moment quite definite, and I agree with you that it is material that if there are two statements they should be on the same day. On the whole I advise you to consult with Childers and whatever you may agree upon I will accept. Perhaps it might come after Supply and before Ways and Means. Certainly I think the Lords affair ought not to precede that in the Commons.

To LORD ROSEBERY, 12 November 1884.   N.L.S. 10023, f. 48.

Having only just received your letter,[5] I should like to consider a little whether I can or cannot take upon me to say any thing upon the main proposition it involves.

---

[1] Gladstone's separate notes read: 'We are willing to adopt the basis of single-member districts if it can be made the ⟨general⟩ basis of general accord'; 'We have our own proposals[.] But are willing to modify[.] We cannot know how to modify till we know the direction of your views'; ibid., ff. 200–2.
[2] Discussed more than this reference suggests; see Schreuder, 452.
[3] Figures *sic*, though several corrected by Gladstone.
[4] Northbrook wrote this day that no statement should be made until after consultation and perhaps a cabinet; Add MS 44267, f. 111.
[5] Declining the First Commissionership of Works with the Cabinet, chiefly because of Egyptian policy; Crewe, *Rosebery*, i. 212 and Add MS 44288, f. 214.

But I think I ought to notice a passage in which you appear to convey that I have been made aware of serious differences between your views & those of the Government in regard to Egyptian policy.

So far as my memory and knowledge go, that subject was first opened between us when I made my proposal to you on Sunday last.

In September I went through a correspondence which had relation to you, without suspecting this impediment to the accomplishment of my wishes: & when I made known to you the nature and purpose of this correspondence, in a letter which you acknowledged most kindly (now unfortunately at Hawarden), I do not remember that there was any allusion to the subject on your part.

I was aware of some public expressions of yours about General Gordon which appeared to go beyond our views at the time; but any & every shade of such difference has I apprehend been disposed of by the tide of events which has brought us up to this point that you had sooner reached.

13. Th.

Wrote to The Queen Tel. & L.l.l.–Duke of Argyll–Sir T. Acland–Sir H. Vivian–Sir C. Dilke–Sir S. Northcote–& minutes. Read the Croker papers. Dined with the Wests. Saw Mr H–Ld R.G–The Servian Minister–Mr Childers–Ld Granville l l l. H of C. 4½–8.[1] But my time was much occupied with business about the 'situation': and I spent 11–12 at West's house in an interview with Northcote. See the minutes of today.

Will the Cabinet give me authority to promise the introduction of the Redistribution Bill before the Committee in the House of Lords provided I have full reason to believe that this can be done without ⟨putting in jeopa⟩ endangering or retarding the passing of the Franchise Bill? W.E.G. Nov. 13. 1884.[2]

Secret. No 1. Copy of Query placed in the hands of Sir S. Northcote at a private conversation on the night of Nov. 13. 1884, which he proposed to communicate to Lord Salisbury.

What assurances will you require about the character of our Redistribution Bill, as a condition of engaging that, if we produce it before the Franchise Bill reaches the Committee in the Lords, and make it a vital question, the Franchise Bill shall then be put forward without difficulty or delay? WEG. N.13/84[3]

Ld Granville, Ld. Hartington:

In consequence of a communication from Mr Northcote to Mr West, Sir Stafford Northcote and I met late last night at Mr Wests.

We agreed that the conversation should be *secret*, and I assured him that within those four walls I should speak to him with the freedom of entire confidence.

The sum of our conversation was I think as follows.

1. I placed in his hands the query which is written within having copied it for the purpose.[4]

[1] Questioned on navy; *H* 293. 1585.

[2] Circulated to the Cabinet; initialled in agreement by Granville, Selborne, Carlingford, Northbrook, and note of Hartington's agreement; Add MS 44645, f. 203; further circulars this day at Add MS 44768, ff. 139–145.

[3] Add MS 44768, f. 137.

[4] See above.

2. I told him that I saw no advantage in exchange of views except in order to procure the passing of the Franchise Bill peacefully and forthwith.
3. I did not see any objection to our making known our views *in extenso*, and even if requisite in the form of a draft Bill; nor in our engaging to make the Bill, especially as to any enactments which might be the basis of any understanding, a vital question.
4. On the question of procedure, he saw difficulties in my Query and evidently leaned to delay, which I shut out, but said we should not object to proceed with a Redistribution Bill before Christmas.
5. On the subject matter of Redistribution he was more satisfactory: he made no sine quâ non: was moderate on severance of rural and urban elements: admitted the great objections to grouping in important classes of cases: was not averse to one-member districts: and did not much cling to the minority vote.
6. He will answer me, first seeing Salisbury. WEG. N 13-14. 1884. 1 am.[1]
[P.S.] A Cabinet today would probably be premature?
[Granville's note:] It is sad to say, but if you had one you could not rely on secrecy. G.

To Sir T. D. ACLAND, M.P., 13 November 1884.   Bodley MS Eng. lett. d. 89, f. 52.

I thank you for your letter,[2] and I may mention in acknowledging it that we have never said a word against producing our Redistribution Bill provided that on that production the Franchise Bill is to be allowed to go forward.

To Sir C. W. DILKE, president of the local government board,   Add MS 43875, f. 195. 13 November 1884.

[First letter:]   Hartington made known to me yesterday the contents of your note;[3] and I should think your efforts would now be most beneficially directed towards getting the more moderate scheme of redistribution into a state for presentation as a Bill at the *earliest possible* moment, that we may be ready for the contingency. If this should not be your view, perhaps you will kindly speak to me.[4]

[Second letter:]   Many thanks. Would it be quite inadmissible to carry 15 m[ille] down to 12 m. (or 10 m.) & take compensation by letting no town under 50 m. have more than one member? No hurry.[5]

14. Sat.

Wrote to Sir C. Dilke—The Queen tel. l.l.—Ld Granville—Mr Childers—Ld Northbrook—and minutes. A day of hard constant work on the *two* problems. Wrote Mem. on Egyptian finance.[6] Saw Mr H—Ld R.G—Ld Granville l.l.—Scotts—Mr Childers. Nine to dinner. Read The Croker papers.

[1] Add MS 44768, 146; version in *Autobiographica*, iv. 66.
[2] Not found; precisely similar letter sent to Hussey Vivian this day; Vivian MS C 2453.
[3] Sent by Hartington but not found; Add MS 44147, f. 180. Dilke's letter to Hartington this day: Lefevre '*very* strong against *our* proposing a Beach scheme as *ours*'; Add MS 44149, f. 267.
[4] Dilke replied this day that he was preparing a bill, also sending notes anticipating 'formal conversation with the other side'; another note this day favoured meeting Salisbury; Add MS 44149, ff. 262-72.
[5] A further note—the ninth—from Dilke this day refused to reopen this question without Cabinet discussion, though personally willing to raise 40m. to 50m.; ibid., f. 276.
[6] See Ramm II, ii. 283.

To LORD NORTHBROOK, first lord of the admiralty,   Add MS 44547, f. 137.
14 November 1884.

1. I have written, with Mr. [W. S.] Caine's assent, to recommend his name to Her Majesty.[1]

2. The Cabinet tomorrow will have for its first duty to consider the question of communications bearing upon the Franchise & Seats Bill. I do not doubt that if you wish to speak of your report there will be time for the purpose. This might perhaps take place without a general discussion which I fear might develop sharp differences. I have thought much whether there is any course which might be taken at the present juncture without compromising your freedom or that of any of our colleagues as to eventual decisions. A conversation with Childers this evening has led him & me to the conclusion that the coming profits of the Suez Canal shares might supply us with the necessary means.

To Sir S. H. NORTHCOTE, M.P., 14 November 1884.   Add MS 50014, f. 274.
'Secret'.[2]

I understand your note[3] as written on behalf, at least, of Lord Salisbury and yourself.

While thanking you for the conversation of last night, I regret that your reply to my inquiry declines communications which should have as their 'objective point' the passing of the Franchise Bill without delay, and substitutes a new basis according to which the Lords would not pass the Franchise Bill until the Seats Bill was before them.

It is not in my power to enter into any negotiation or interchange of views, except to secure the passing of the Franchise Bill without delay. If that were secured I know not of any other demand, likely to be made, which need meet with refusal.

This being so, and there being no material for our further communications, I shall observe strictly the secrecy of our conversation: only desiring to make known to the Queen (not the Cabinet) my query, your reply, and this note in answer.

Of course it is open to me to consider whether, without any allusion whatever to what has passed between us, I shall state publicly on behalf of the Government the basis on which we are prepared to proceed.

[P.S.] My best thanks for your inclosure.[4]

15. Sat.

Wrote to Mr Childers—The Queen L.l.l. & tel.—Ld Durham—Sir J. Macdonald[5]—Ld Braye[6]—Ld Tennyson—and minutes. Cabinet 12–2½. Drew a declaration for Monday & announcement for the newspapers. Dined at Ld Aberdeens. Saw Mr H—Mr Seymour—Ld R.G.—Mr H. Fowler. Read Ld Malmesbury's Recollections.[7]

[1] As civil lord of the admiralty; earlier note from Gladstone this day, Add MS 44267, f. 122: 'What do you say to Caine? whom R. Grosvenor recommends. *He* also recommends Duff.'

[2] In *L.Q.V.*, 2nd series, iii. 572. Date altered from 13 November.

[3] This day, Add MS 44217, f. 229: Lords will not pass Franchise Bill until the Seats Bill is before them.

[4] Another note this day, ibid., f. 232, on complaints 'of the confidences which pass between Sir C. Dilke and Lord R. Churchill'.

[5] The Bath; letter in J. Pope, *Memoirs of Sir J. A. Macdonald* (1894), ii. 209.

[6] On diplomatic relations with the Pope; Add MS 44547, f. 138.

[7] See 6 Oct. 84; comments on its account of 1855 at Add MS 44488, f. 158.

Cabinet. Sat. Nov. 15 1884. Noon.[1]
1. Report from W.E.G. Decision for simultaneous public declaration by Lord G. Paper A.[2] agreed on.
2. Northbrook gave explanations on his Report.[3] Discussion postponed. Harcourt gave his opinion. Granville asked that alternatives shd. be considered. Some other indications. Hartington on army of occupation. Cannot give an opinion.

I report to Cabinet that in pursuance of the authority given on Monday I have used my best endeavours & come to no result. I do not propose to renew them.
Query make a public declaration a. by letter—to whom? b. by speech—in the two Houses—on Monday? c. our basis: 1. Passing of Franchise Bill without delay. 2. No other condition refused. Party meeting—No. Shall we give *private notice?* No. Intimate in Times & Daily News.

16. 23 S. Trin.

Chapel Royal mg and evg. Saw Ld Sherbrook, poor fellow, very susceptible of kindness: the T.G.s & Louey: Mr West. Wrote to C.G. Read Bonet Maury—Renouf, Hibbert Lectures[4]—Lang, Myth of Kronos[5]—Plumptre, Spirits Departed.[6]

17. M.

Wrote to Ld Granville—Mr Childers—Ld Derby—The Queen l.l. Further pondered & slightly modified the Declaration.[7] Quiet evg. H. of C. $4\frac{1}{4}$-$8\frac{1}{2}$. Made Decl. and spoke on Finance &c.[8] Saw Mr H—Duke of Argyll *cum* Ld Gr.—Ld Granville—Mr Childers—Sir W. Harcourt—Mr Heneage—Ld Hartington. Read Malmesbury—Feis on Shakespeare.

[1] Add MS 44645, f. 205.
[2] Notes used as basis for his ministerial statement on 17 November: 'Our object is to secure the passing of the Franchise Bill without delay . . . that is to say during the present autumnal sitting. If we are adequately assured as to the attainment of that object, I am not aware of any demand likely to be made in relation to the other measure to which we should not be able to accede'; ibid., f. 207 (fair copy to Victoria, CAB 41/18/52) and *H* 293. 1820.
[3] Gladstone's undated note reads: 'N's language to me before the Cabinet was—with a certain reserve of final conclusion—"My report and my report now—or nothing"'; note to Granville reads: '*I hope we shall not have a general discussion on this today*, for fear of creating difficulties? We should try to adjust among a few of us, N. of course included, some basis of possible present action. I rather think *today* I have something you would not disapprove'; Add MS 44645, ff. 212-13. See 19 Nov. 84. For Northbrook's report, in fact a long letter to Granville dated 24 Oct., printed for cabinet 6 Nov. (MS Harcourt dep. 313), concluded 'the effect . . . will undoubtedly be to substitute the financial control of England for the international control . . . proposed at the Conference'. Revised on Gladstone's insistance, 20 November; F.O.C.P. 5056, f. 127.
[4] P. Le P. Renouf, *Lectures on the origin and growth of religion* (1880).
[5] A. Lang, *Custom and myth* (1884).
[6] E. H. Plumptre, *The spirits in prison and other studies on the life after death* (1884); includes essay on Butler on life after death.
[7] Adding 1 January 1886 as effective start of the Franchise Bill; see Ramm II, ii. 284.
[8] *H* 293. 1820, 1883.

To LORD DERBY, colonial secretary, 17 November 1884.   Add MS 44547, f. 138.
'*Private*'.

It would be premature to draw any conclusion from the letter you inclose:[1] but were I to say anything it would be that such a letter makes me as much afraid, at least, of Sir C. Warren as of the Germans.

I hope you will keep a steadfast eye upon him. And I entirely agree with your remarks.

18. Tu.

Wrote to The Queen tel.—Ld Hartington l.l.—Ld Granville—Sir E. Malet—Dowager Lady Sandhurst—Bp of St Andrew's—Mr Caine. Saw Mr H—Ld RG.—Mr Childers—Do *cum* Ld Granville—Dowager Lady Stanley. (Tea).

I went at 3½ to Lady Sandhurst's:[2] where she introduced Mrs Duncan. In a little time she appeared and we had a very short interval before she fell into a sleep or trance. I had already stated my intention to be passive; and I declined all along for reasons which I gave to ask any questions. But Lady S. had told me that the "spirits" were wholly unconnected with me: one a most famous surgeon, one I think a doctor, one RC Priest. Lady S. had also explained to me the spirit & purpose, wholly Christian & biblical, of her proceedings in this matter.

After a few minutes, Mrs Duncan fell into a sleep or trance & presently a low voice from her began to address me, calling me my son, & not always easy to hear.

Incited me to rely on my own judgment rather than on others.

Promised me repeatedly help: & said I had been helped. Especially by my sister (no doubt Helen) who was now quite happy & was aware that she needed not to have made her religious change.

Exhorted me much to humility

And to prayer, again & again.

Spoke warmly of the Bible. Said obedience was the needful thing, & not what religion one was of. Said I was becoming more given to prayer & more religious but exhorted to an increase, & to more retirement

Bid me exhort my son 'who was in Parliament' (app[arent]ly meaning Herbert) to greater self-control, & to pray much

Spoke of great questions and great decisions immediately impending and promised help *to me* in them.

Commended reception of the "Blessed Sacrament" but *rather as an act of obedience* than from any mystical virtue

Ended by giving me certain medical prescriptions: said I had relaxation about the throat, but that my chest was all sound: and that 'these earthly doctors' were not always perfectly careful. Also advised me to have a person to read to me, with sufficient force. Invited me to put questions & ask for information (which for reasons I distinctly & repeatedly declined). Lady Sandhurst wrote down the medical recommendations.

---

[1] Add MS 44142, f. 100: letter from Sir C. Warren (not found) on danger of German interference in Transvaal.

[2] 20 North Audley Street, offered by Lady Sandhurst on 7 November as more private; Add MS 44488, f. 48. For Lady Sandhurst, see 4 Nov. 84. See also Introduction above, Vol. x, section ix.

These were the chief points of this singular communication in which I declined all active part hearing & noting it *ad referendum*. To mix myself in these things would baffle & perplex: but good advice is to be remembered come how it may.[1]

We went to the well-acted play 'Young Mrs Winthrop'[2] in the evening. Read Malmesbury—Feis on Shakespeare.

To LORD HARTINGTON, war secretary,   Chatsworth MSS 340. 1581.
18 November 1884. '*Immed[iate]*'.

I am rather ashamed to follow my note[3] with a second, simply about that answer of mine to Lawson. I cannot quite see whether I went too far or not. Clearly the Tories are entitled to expect of us every effort to pass the Seats Bill through the House of Lords, and if it failed there I do not well see that we could continue in office. The only question is whether it is a conceivable case that the Tories should use their majority in the Lords to stop the Bill improperly for the sake of getting a Dissolution on the old Franchise through our resignation. This seems hardly within the verge of likelihood and if it is not the matter stands well enough. But I should like to know, either by note or voice, what you think.[4]

To Sir E. B. MALET, ambassador to Germany,   Add MS 44547, f. 139.
18 November 1884.

I have read your interesting letter of November 15 to Lord Granville. I am a little surprised at the inaccuracy of Prince Bismarck's statement to you.

No reference was made by me to Germany in connection with the plans imputed to Austria by those who professed to be his friends in this country.[5]

My reference to Austria was as far as possible from being uncalled for, and had the effect of obtaining from the highest authority assurances which enabled me wholly to withdraw the remarks founded on those plans. But here matter of opinions is introduced and I do not seek to revive the discussion.[6]

[P.S.] I think that if the Chancellor had been asked what he referred to when speaking of my attack on Germany, he would have been rather at a loss to reply.

19. Wed.

Wrote to The Queen—Ld Hartington—Ld Granville—& minutes. Cabinet 12-3½. Meeting of Gr. & myself with Opposition Leaders (or Leader?) 4-5, all was courteous & free, & *rather* hopeful.[7] Saw Mr H—Ld RG—Ld Northbrook—

---

[1] Mrs Duncan sent a further exhortation, 'the Navy ought to be looked after', *via* Lady Sandhurst, 27 November, Add MS 44488, f. 154.   [2] Norreys, Marion Terry, at the Court theatre.

[3] This day, Chatsworth MSS 340. 1589, on publication of letters on the crisis; also: in error 'in my answer to Lawson about the House of Lords. It would not be bound to treat a defeat in the Lords like a defeat in the Commons'.

[4] Hartington thought the likelihood of the Lords rejecting a Redistribution Bill passed in the Commons 'so unlikely that it need not have been taken into consideration'; Add MS 44147, f. 183.

[5] The row about Balkan expansionism in 1880; see to Karolyi, 4 May 80.

[6] Malet replied from Berlin, 26 November, Add MS 44488, f. 143, that he had not dared interrupt Bismarck, and that he has represented Gladstone as the 'real conservative bulwark against democracy'; Gladstone's docket: 'Thank. I am quite satisfied. N. 28.'

[7] The preliminary meeting, Gladstone and Granville for the govt., Northcote and Salisbury for the tories, leaders in their respective houses; jottings at Add MS 44768, f. 157.

Ld Spencer—Ld Granville—M. Waddington: an interesting conversation on *entente*. Dined at Sir C. Forsters. Much conversation with Lady M. Beaumont. Read Malmesbury. A *severe* day.

Cabinet. Wedn. Noon. Nov. 19. 84.[1]
1. As to vitality of the Bill. And proceedings today.
2. Northbrook's report.[2] Northbrook—Childers:—Dilke proposes to write to the Powers—making known financial results & reporting our proposals—with or without variation. Derby wd. like to fix a short term for going out [of Egypt]. Kimberley—saw difficulties. Chamberlain against D[erby]—against N[orthbrook]. Long discussion.

To LORD HARTINGTON, war secretary,   Chatsworth MSS 340. 1582.
19 November 1884. '*Secret*'.

Granville and I thought our meeting tolerably satisfactory, he I think a shade rosier than I. I am sorry to say he is threatened with some internal disturbance. We meet again on Saturday at 12, when you and he are asked to be present.

Pray consider whether you can try anything to relieve the tension on the Egyptian question. I say this freely because I am not behind you in the importance I attach to Northbrook's report as to fact. In my opinion, if we cannot devise a fair intermediate proposal, it will be fatal to us, *whether* we accept or decline it. This, so far as I can now see. Were I prepared to accept it, I should still say the transition from the attitude in which we broke up the Conference is so vast, that I should seek to try first an intermediate proposal *to get us gently off the old ground* before making such a leap. I would put *something between* our dismissal of the Conference, & the entire reversal of our plans.

Surely it would be hard lines, considering all the *inception* of his mission, to put the pistol to the head of the Cabinet and say 'my report whole, & my report now, and no deviation or intermediate step permissible'.

The genuine reforms which he proposes, and which I much like, are I believe all compatible with the intermediate scheme. Which after all may come to be *non avenu* and may restore to every one his freedom.

20. Th.

Wrote to Mr Childers—The Queen L.l.l.l.—Ld Northbrook—Mr Courtney—and minutes. Read Malmesbury. Cabinet 2-3½. H of C. 4½-6. Statement on Franchise & Egypt.[3] Saw Mr H—Ld RG—Mr Childers—Mr Forster. Seven to dinner.

---

[1] Add MS 44645, f. 217.
[2] See 15 Nov. 84n. Northbrook's note (in Barings' archive, transcribed by Mr. D. Hyland) reads: '... after we had assembled Mr Gladstone called me out into the little side room to the left and told me that he could not propose my scheme now although it was not impossible we might come to it. This was the first intimation I received from him.... Excepting very light and casual talk, he constantly avoided up to then and has continued to do so any personal communication with me on the report.' Northbrook felt he had been shown less confidence than was being shown to Salisbury, as Childers' alternative scheme was produced for the cabinet without notice to him; see mem. in Mallet, *Northbrook*, 194—5 (in fact *re* this day).
[3] Answering Labouchere on redistribution, emphasising the 'every-day intercourse' of the talks; on Egypt: specific proposals soon, no *interim* papers; also, postponed ministerial statement on navy (see 2 Dec. 84); *H* 294. 65, 69.

Cabinet. Thurs. Nov. 20. 1884. 2 PM.[1]

1. Recital of proceedings at interview yesterday with Lord S. and Sir S. N.
2. Egypt. Statement to be made by WEG agreed to. Committee of Cabinet appointed to digest particulars of plan.
3. Ld Gr. to try to have the judgment in Egypt postponed—from the 25th.
4. Agree in principle with Bismarck that area of Congo in Africa may be neutralised—or at least the parties to the Conference shd. not make war *inter se* within those limits? ⟨Postponed for Ld⟩ Northbrook to inquire: ans. as above if no.
5. Postpone Navy Statement.

To L. H. COURTNEY, financial secretary, 20 November	Add MS 44547, f. 139.
1884.[2]

The full & able exposition of your views on proportional representation with which you have favoured me, has been brought *in extenso* under the notice of my colleagues in the Cabinet, who are well aware of your title to have your views carefully weighed. I am sure you will feel that in the peculiar circumstances of the moment I am not able to go beyond this assurance.

To LORD NORTHBROOK, first lord of the admiralty,	Add MS 44267, f. 139.
20 November 1884.

I should feel dismay about our Egyptian difficulties, but for the consciousness that what we have in hand, through no fault of our own, is really a business beyond ordinary human capacities, so that we cannot be surprised if opinions sometimes fall asunder, and can only seek to arrange for the best.

Acting in this spirit, I try to place myself in the position of one who thinks your recommendation could ultimately be adopted *by us*, and proposed to Parliament. Examining the question in this sense, I have still to consider our position as it was in the face of Europe, when we broke up the Conference because it wd. not consent to dock the dividends.

Please to consider the words which follow 1. Is it possible to execute such a sudden & entire *volte-face* before the Powers, without at least using first an effort which might re-establish negotiations, and might from your point of view serve as a stepping stone. 2. Even the *presentation* of a three years or other temporary plan would serve this purpose. 3. If rejected, as Hartington thought it sure to be, it would become *non-avenu* & we should be as we were, but a step nearer your plan. 4. If entertained & adopted it wd. in no way preclude the early consideration of a scheme of larger scope and greater endurance— i.e. of yours—while it will obviate the disturbing pressure under which we now move.

In conclusion, I do not differ from Hartington as to the great importance & weight on every ground *for us* of your report, in any event; but I hope you will consider a little, in equity, how wide its recommendations are of what we expected (I will not say had reason to expect but) expected [*sic*].

Your letter & Memorandum have just come in.[3] I feel confident that you are not going to insist on 'all or nothing' & this *now*. And I see no reason why I shd not send on what I have written, only observing, by way of approximation to you. a. I have not founded myself on the proposition you ascribe to me about Dividends, but only, I assure you, on

---

[1] Add MS 44645, f. 222.

[2] In G. P. Gooch, *Life of Lord Courtney* (1920), 201-5, with Courtney's long letter of 8 November; Courtney resigned, see 1 Dec. 84.

[3] Of 19 November, Add MS 44267, ff. 130-8, opposing Childers' view that the previous proposals be reiterated, and again objecting to multiple control and a limited three year period.

this 'we cannot *now* propose to make them good at the charge of England (in cash or credit)'. b. Under the plan which Childers after consultation with me proposed, & which Granville was desirous to accept, your reduction of the land revenue wd. take effect. c. I quite agree that there can be no multiple controul, and I wd. abandon the plan rather than accede to it.

I send this without consulting Granville, because the anxieties of this week have (or last evening *had*) laid him on his back, & I am fearful of worsening him.

21. Fr.

Wrote to Mr Bright—The Queen—Sir C. Dilke—Sir J. Lubbock—& minutes. Saw Mr H—Ld R.G—Mr Courtney—Sir C. Dilke—Mad. Neillson[1]—Mr Childers. H of C. 4½-8. Dined with Mr Hutton at the Devonshire Club: sat till 12. Read Ld Malmesbury. Spoke in reply to Labouchere. Difficult ground: a rather significant minority.[2]

22. Sat. [*Seacox Heath, Hawkhurst*]

Wrote to The Queen l.l.—Mr Rathbone MP—and minutes. Cabinet at 11.30. Second Salisbury Conference 12–2. Somewhat promising. Off 2.30–5.30 to Goschen's pretty but rather distant place. Saw Mr H—Ld RG—Ld Acton.

Cabinet. Sat. 22 Nov. 1884. 11½ AM.[3]
1. Cabinet gives considerable discretion in the Conference on Redistribution to those who are to meet Ld S. and Sir S.N., viz WEG, Ld Hn., Sir C.D.
2. Egyptian scheme for submission to the Powers: see over.[4] Mr Childers the *redacteur*.

[Notes for the Conference:] 1. Single-member districts. May be extended. 2. Minority representation. Not envisaged. 3. Grouping of old Boroughs. not required. 4. Schedule B extended up to 50 m[ille]. Schedule A remains. 5. Alteration of borough boundaries: to be extended in numerous cases. 7. Scotland: grouping of boroughs to be left very open. 8. Numbers of the House. change not to be encouraged.[5]

23. Preadv. S.

Ch mg & aft. Walk & conversation with Goschen. Wrote to Sir C. Dilke. Much conversation with Ld Acton. Read Bonet Maury—Teaching of the Apostles[6]—Renouf, Hibbert Lecture.

---

[1] Christine Nilsson, 1843–1921; Swedish opera singer, m. to Auguste Rouzeaud and friend of Sir A. Sullivan.
[2] Labouchere's resolution (defeated in 145:71) for 'alterations in the relations of the two Houses' in view of the Lords' obstructiveness; *H* 294. 157.
[3] Add MS 44645, f. 224.
[4] Jottings at ibid., f. 225, summarised by Hamilton, Bahlman, *Hamilton*, ii. 737, an overturning of the Northbrook Report.
[5] Holograph note, dated 22 November; Add MS 44768, f. 158. See Jones, *1884*, 208–9.
[6] See F. W. Farrar, *C.R*, xv. 618 (May 1884).

To Sir C. W. DILKE, president of the local government board,   Add MS 43875, f. 205.
23 November 1884. '*Secret*'.

1. I take it for granted that we shall tomorrow move the adjournment of the House for a week.

2. I find that the act of giving *notice* of a Bill will be an important & rather binding one, and if it is done, which seems rather needful, it would be desirable that we should do it with as much as possible of incitement from Salisbury: otherwise it may tend to fetter us more than him. What do you think of my writing a note to him tomorrow with the view of drawing from him this encouragement.[1] I think we have much less remaining to tell him, than he has to tell us, so that in fact he is the best judge of the likelihood of an arrangement.

But silence tomorrow would be very awkward, if I am right in supposing that great jealousies will arise on one or both sides if there be any appearance of prolongation without progress.

When you see him tomorrow evening I hope you will be able perhaps to add a point or two to the results already obtained.

I am due in Downing Street about a quarter to twelve.

24. M. [London]

Wrote to Ld Salisbury—Ld Hartington l.l.—The Queen—Mr Mendelsohn—Sir D. Currie—Sir E. Colebrooke—Mr Elliot—and minutes. H of C. $5\frac{1}{4}$-$8\frac{1}{4}$: all going smoothly there.[2] The objections do not take hold. Read Croker papers—Malmesbury. Saw Mr H—Ld RG.—Sir Thos G.—Ld Granville—Ld Acton. $9\frac{1}{2}$-12. Return from Seacox.

25. Tu. [Windsor Castle]

Wrote to Lady Russell—Lord Emly—Mr Fawcett—Ld Granville—Mrs Th—Mr Bright—& minutes. Read Malmesbury (Vol II). Off to Windsor 3.20. Saw Mr H—Ld RG—Sothebys—Sir J. Cowell—Sir H. Ponsonby—Sir J. Macdonald.[3] Sat an hour with the Queen who is in exuberant good humour over the Franchise question & has been very useful. Saw Princess Louise on Ld Lorne & Parlt.[4] Dined with H.M. Ld Derby very sprightly.

To John BRIGHT, M.P., 25 November 1884. '*Most private*'.[5]   Add MS 43385, f. 333.

I have looked again & again for you during these last nights in the House of Commons, but you have not happened to attend.

I therefore write you a line, not because I think there is need of it, but because it is due to you, & is a pleasure to me.

I wish to give you the assurance that in the private communications, which are now

[1] Dilke replied next day that Salisbury's absence meant there was no time for an exchange; Add MS 43875, f. 208.
[2] Gave notice of a Redistribution Bill, though not 'absolutely certain' he could introduce it; *H* 294. 282.
[3] Sir John Alexander Macdonald, 1815-91; prime minister of Canada 1867-73; see J. Pope, *Memoirs of Sir J. A. Macdonald* (1894), ii. 210.
[4] Princess Louise suggested his returning to the Commons; Gladstone smartly appt. him to govern N.S. Wales.
[5] Part in Morley, iii. 158.

going on, Liberal principles, such as we should conceive & term them, are in no danger. Those with whom we confer are thinking without doubt of party interests, as affected by this or that arrangement, but these are a distinct matter, and I am not so good of them [*sic*] as some others; but the general proposition which I have stated is I think one which I can pronounce with some confidence.

As far as I know your opinions on the question immediately before us, I think you have a great repugnance to two forms of provision in favour with many. My hope is that when our work is accomplished, if accomplished it is to be, you will find nothing to condemn on either ground.

The whole operation is essentially delicate & slippery, and I can hardly conceive any other circumstance in which it would be justified; but in the present very peculiar case I think it is not only warranted but called for.[1]

26. *Wed.* [*London*]

Wrote to Ld Hampden—Mad. Nilsson—The Queen l. & Tel.—Provost of Brechin—& minutes. Returned from Windsor 11.40. Read Ld Malmesbury. Saw Mr H.—Ld RG—Lord Emly—and minutes. 4–6½. Further Conference, the third. Considerable progress, and various eliminations. We dined at Ld Mount [*sic*] Brettons. Saw divers [R].

Demands. Nov. 26. 84:[2] 1. One member districts—universal in counties—with exceptions in towns, but to be the prevailing practice. 2. Boundaries. 3. Grouping Midland s. of Mersey Humber line.

[Gladstone:] There are 284 in all—98 one member already by this scheme: 186. Can we undertake to give them the *86*, retaining in all *100 double seats as a maximum?*
[Hartington:] Certainly; but I am afraid there is no chance of their accepting it.
[Gladstone:] Or give them ⅔ of the Borough seats.[3]

To Sir C. W. DILKE, president of the local government   Add MS 43875, f. 211.
board, 26 November 1884. '*Secret*'.

I send you herewith for your consideration a first sketch which I have made of a possible communication tomorrow after the Cabinet from us to the Legates of the opposite party.[4]

I think that if the Cabinet made it an *ultimatum* we should be safe with it.

There was a careful abstention today on their side from any language beyond pressing this or that: and [*sc.* at] the outset they spoke of the one member system for boroughs 'with exceptions' as what they desired.

It is proposed to frame the Bill by compact on the following points.[5]
1. Proportion of members between the three countries Scotland to be increased. If aggregate remain, the Irish member [*sic*] may be diminished to 100. We propose an

---

[1] Bright advised: 'stand on the Act of Union for the 100 [Irish] members', and preferred two-member seats though 'there seems to me no special *Party* interest in it either way'; Add MS 44113, f. 208.
[2] Add MS 44768, f. 161.   [3] Add MS 44768, f. 159; undated.
[4] Dilke agreed this day 'to make the whole Metropolis except the city single member seats' but reserved his position on central districts for discussion with Chamberlain; Add MS 44149, f. 287.
[5] Holograph placed with this letter; Add MS 43875, f. 211.

increase of the aggregate by 12, & do our best to carry it for practical reasons. 2. Minorities—not to be directly represented. 3. Boundaries—wards to be agreed on with Sir C. Dilke. 4. Grouping, as such, abandoned. 5. Schedule A to go to 20000. See Mem. A. 6. One member districts everywhere in Counties & Boroughs except City of London 2 and Class of Boroughs in Mem. B. 7. On the other side our proposal is that the Franchise Bill pass forthwith, without material change, that is to say without the introduction of new contentious matter. 8. No. 1 is to a certain extent open—the rest not so.

[1] *Secret.* 1. It is impossible to present our plans with the City of London and the three Universities of Oxford Cambridge and Dublin as they are, if the method for one member districts were to be applied to all the Boroughs. 2. We think it necessary in the presented Bill to save from compulsory division (with one or more exceptions) those urban constituencies (not Metropolitan) which, now possessing dual representation, are to be neither increased nor diminished. 3. We also think it necessary to propose in the Bill that the Cities and towns, not metropolitan, which are to receive four members and upwards, (ten in number), should have one central or principal area set apart with dual representation. In this proposal we have special regard to the cases of Edinburgh and Dublin. 4. The total number of Borough seats, as proposed, being 284, the *maximum* number affected by these two propositions would be about one fourth. 5. But, while we could agree not to *increase* this number of dual constituencies beyond the point thus indicated, we should leave it an open question whether in the passing of the Bill through its stages in the House of Commons it might be diminished should such be the pleasure of the House: and while we give this covenant on the subject, we ask none in return. 6. Under this proposal, one eighth of the House of Commons at the outside.[2]

27. Th.

Wrote to Ld Salisbury l.l.—The Queen l.l. & tel.—Sir C. Dilke—Mr Childers—Ld R. Grosvenor tel.—& minutes. Cabinet 12–1$\frac{3}{4}$. Saw Mr H—Ld R.G.—Ld H. *cum* Ld G. & Sir C.D. on the Conferences—Mr Childers—Mr Chamberlain. Fourth? Conference 2$\frac{1}{4}$–4$\frac{1}{2}$.[3] Apparently all was concluded. But a later letter from Salisbury raised a hitch on account of the Universities. Meanwhile we had drafted a Memorandum of Agreement, & sent it.[4] Read Ld Malmesbury—19th Cent. on the Lords and on Egypt. Dined with Mr Knowles: & commented on 19th Cent politics.

Cabinet. Thurs. 28 [sc. 27] *Nov. 1884. Noon.*[5]
1. Franchise & Seats Negotiations. WEG and Dilke stated the general course of the negotiations and the proposal (1) herewith.[6] Proposal agreed respecting single member districts. No change in Franchise Bill with 'contentious matter'.
2. The Turkish proposal to send a Commission. Not to send but ask for the basis.
3. China. Ld G. not to forward a wholly inadmissible proposition to France.
4. Meeting of the party at F.O. on Monday.
5. Ld H. Thynne's calumny on Chamberlain. To speak to the Law Officers.

[1] Secretary's copy placed with copy of the letter; Add MS 44149, f. 285.
[2] Holograph draft at Add MS 44645, f. 229, which is initialled and dated this day.
[3] In Salisbury's house in Arlington Street.   [4] Final version next day.
[5] Add MS 44645, f. 228.
[6] i.e. the mem. at 26 Nov. 84. See also Gwynn, ii. 76 and next day. Hamilton noted the Cabinet, except Childers, agreed to disfranchise up to 20,000; Bahlman, *Hamilton,* ii. 742.

To LORD SALISBURY, 27 November 1884, 7.30 p.m.   Add MS 44547, f. 141.

I will try to put Dilke in a condition to speak to you tomorrow morning, when I believe you meet, about the point you have raised.[1] Should you still require a meeting he will be empowered to appoint one. I hope, however, that you may not then think it necessary.

28. Fr.

Wrote to The Queen tel. l.l.—Sir S. Northcote—Mr Baillie—Col. Lindsay—Ld Granville—Ld Malmesbury—Ld Salisbury—& minutes. An anxious day, upon new points raised, much too late I think, by the leaders on the other side. Saw Mr H—Sir C. Dilke—Ld Hartington—Mr Agnew—Mr Childers—Mr Morley—Sir N. Rothschild. Finished Malmesbury. Read Croker. Twelve to dinner.

Franchise and Seats Bill: The substance is settled. The 15000 replaced.[2] Memorandum to be retained in duplicate, has been drafted, and sent to Lord Salisbury for review. WEG. Nov. 28. 7PM.
Amendments in Lords to be opposed.
7.10PM. Salisbury has made a hitch about Universities but I think we shall settle it.[3]

MEMORANDUM. Secret.[4]

It has been agreed on the part of Mr Gladstone with the other ministers deputed by the Cabinet on the one side, and by Lord Salisbury and Sir S. Northcote on the other, as follows:
1. The Government to propose to obtain the necessary increase of members for Scotland by an increase of the House; but in the event of the House declining to make an addition to its numbers, the necessary increase for Scotland to be provided partly by a reduction of three in the number returned by Irish Counties and Boroughs, thus reducing the Irish representation to the number of one hundred fixed by the Act of Union, and partly from the six vacant seats and a reduction of the numbers allotted to Counties and Boroughs in the rest of Great Britain.
2. Minorities not to be directly represented, but to be indirectly represented as proposed in Paragraph 7.
3. Boundaries to be settled by a Commission consisting of Sir John Lambert KCB, Sir Francis Sandford KCB, Mr Henley, one of the Inspectors of the Local Government Board, the Hon. T. [H. W.] Pelham, Col. Owen Jones, R.E., Head of the Boundary Department of the Ordnance Survey, and Major Hector Tulloch, R.E. The Commissioners to have regard in dividing Boroughs to the pursuits of the population, and in dividing counties to the following considerations: the population of the several divisions to be equalised as far as practicable; care to be taken in all those cases where there are populous localities of an urban character to include them in one and the same division, unless this cannot be done without producing grave inconvenience and involving boundaries of a very irregular and objectionable character. Subject to this important rule, each division

[1] Salisbury's letter this day, Add MS 44488, f. 150: 'What was said this evening about Universities came upon me like a knock-down blow'; clearly contrary to the agreed document, which Salisbury quoted.
[2] i.e. restored.   [3] Add MS 44768, f. 184.
[4] Add MS 43875, f. 218; copy by Hamilton, dated 28 November 1884; initialled and headed by Gladstone; 'The original' added to the heading by Dilke. This day's letter to Salisbury agrees to add as 'a large concession' a passage on university seats; Salisbury's letter next day accepted the whole, Add MS 44488, f. 164.

to be as compact as possible with respect to geographical position and to be based upon well known existing areas, such as Petty Sessional divisions. No alteration to be made during the passage of the Bill in the settled boundaries without Sir S. Northcote's consent.

4. Grouping as such to be abandoned as impracticable in England and Ireland, (the case of the Monmouth Boroughs excepted); but this principle not to prevent the uniting of contiguous localities.

5. Boroughs and groups below 15,000 population[1] to be generally merged in County Divisions, excepting in one or two possible cases which have been named, where they are to be brought above the 15,000 line. (This exception may disappear on reconsideration). Boroughs and groups between 15,000 and 50,000, having more than one member, to lose one. Similar Counties to lose one. The City of London to have 2 members. No diminution to take place in the number of members now allotted to existing constituencies other than those diminutions here mentioned.

6. No diminution to take place in the total number of members allotted to Counties in the Government scheme.

7. All counties in the United Kingdom to be in single-member districts. All Boroughs to be in single-member districts, except the City of London and those Boroughs (with a population of between 50,000 and 150,000) which having two members at the present moment are not to receive more than two. This proposal is subject to the reservation that nobody is to be precluded from supporting a proposal for creating a two-member nucleus in the large cities.

8. The Government will resist as a vital question (unless by common consent) the insertion in the Bill of any provisions inconsistent with those recited above. With regard to any other new and great matter proposed for insertion, they will consult with the Leader of the Opposition and will be prepared to deal with it in the same spirit by which they have been animated in the recent communications. Regarding this Bill as a Bill for the determination of electoral areas, they will use their best exertions to prevent the introduction into it of irrelevant and extraneous matter.

9. The Franchise Bill to pass forthwith without material change, that is to say without the introduction of new contentious matter.   28th Nov: 1884. WEG.

To Sir C. W. DILKE, president of the local   Add MS 43875, f. 217.
government board, 28 November 1884. '*Secret*'.

From the inclosed[2] you will see that Salisbury stands upon our printed statement as to Universities. This touches only the number and distribution of nine seats in the three kingdoms. And further it was only our first proposal which was spoken of, and not adherence to every detail.

However, I think it may be argued that the question whether Universities should be represented is a question of franchise not of distribution.

I am quite willing either a. that the Government should bind itself to maintain the *nine* University Seats in this Bill, & their distribution among the three countries. Or to assure Salisbury that I personally will *bind* myself out & out to this proposition. If you can settle the matter within these terms tomorrow when you meet him early (as I understand), well and good, if not, appoint such hours as you like in the afternoon.

[1] Hamilton notes: 'Lord Salisbury gave in about the 20,000 limit'; Bahlman, *Hamilton*, ii. 742.
[2] See 27 Nov. 84n.

29. Sat.

Wrote to Mr Knowles—The Queen Tel.—and minutes. Dined at Lucy's & saw 'Diplomacy': then we went *behind*.[1] Saw Mr H—Ld Chancellor—Col. Lindsay—The two together—Ld Granville—Ld Kenmare—Princess Louise—Sir C. Dilke. Read 19th Cent. on [blank]—Croker papers. Meditated on the 'situation'.

To Sir S. H. NORTHCOTE, M.P., 29 November 1884.   Add MS 44547, f. 141.

I am sorry that this question of the Universities has come up this late as a surprise to us all, but we may endeavour to deal with it in a sober spirit.

Lord Salisbury has written, but he does not say what he wishes.

He proposes another meeting, which must be had if necessary but is it necessary?

I entertain no apprehension whatever of any successful movement against the University representation in the Seats Bill. I shall do my best to keep their nine members secure to them so far at least as the present situation & the two Bills are concerned; and I do not doubt about carrying a large portion at any rate of the Liberal party with me. Can you ask more?

Dilke will see Lord Salisbury this morning I believe at their commission & I have written to prepare him. I need not say that this note is also for me.

30. Adv. Sunday.

Chapel Royal mg (with H.C.) & evg. Saw H.J.G.—WHG—& explained to them in anticipation. Read Bonet Maury—Renouf Hibbert Lectures—Cobbe's Faithless World,[2] profoundly interesting—Monsig. Servanesi's *Risposta*[3]—Dean of Wells on Curci.[4]

Mon. Dec. One. 1884.

Wrote to The Queen l. & tel.—Ld Granville—Ld Salisbury—Mr Courtney—and minutes. Saw Mr H—Ld R.G—Ld Granville—Mr Childers—Mr Bright. Meeting at F.O. of the Party, at 3. I explained the situation & some heads of the Seats' Bill. Very tranquil.[5] H of C. 5–7½. Introduced the Seats Bill to a calm but favouring House.[6] All prospects rosy. Dined at Sir C. Forster's. A quaint incident afterwards [?R]. Read Croker Papers.

To L. H. COURTNEY, financial secretary, 1 December 1884.[7]   Add MS 44547, f. 143.

If you unhappily quit the Government, the Queen & the country will lose a most able public servant, who has done in a short time much admirable work. To this conviction I shall add great & sincere personal concern.

Yet I feel we have no right to shun you, in a matter which you have I know considered seriously & with much pain.

I cannot help, however, pleading my grey hairs as an apology for stating to you that the step, even if at the last unavoidable, is as I think premature.

---

[1] With the Bancrofts, at the Theatre Royal, Haymarket.
[2] F. P. Cobbe, *C.R.*, xlvi. 795 (December 1884).   [3] Untraced.
[4] *Vaticanism as seen from the banks of the Tiber ... with a preface by E. H. Plumptre* (1884).
[5] Meeting of 216 liberals; *D.N.*, 2 December 1884, 3b.
[6] *H* 294. 372.
[7] In G. P. Gooch, *Life of Lord Courtney* (1920), 208.

It is in my opinion, & according to my experience, a fixed rule of English administration, that an official member of Parliament not yet in the Cabinet, only becomes responsible for any proceeding of the Government, outside his Department, when as a member of Parliament he has to take his line in regard to it.

This you will not do until the question of proportional representation shall be raised upon the Bill.

It is most important on general grounds that this rule should not be further lightened.

I hope then you will consider the decision as suspended.

But I go a step further. I believe that judges of great weight deem our proposal of one-member districts well adapted to the condition of Ireland, which I also believe has much to do with the resolution you announce. Would you not hear Lord Spencer on this subject? & if so allow me to arrange for your calling upon him.

Pray do not deem this a worrying letter.[1]

To LORD SALISBURY, 1 December 1884.					Add MS 44547, f. 142.

I thank you very much for your note:[2] and I think it will promote our purpose, if I trouble you with a few more lines.

We have a (Commons) meeting at 3 today, without Reporters. I wish to thank our friends for their confidence & describe the satisfactory tone of the procedures without pointing to repetitions of them, and state a few heads of the Bill on their merits.

The fact of an understanding will be implied & taken for granted; but I shall say nothing to fasten the idea upon any particulars. I am strongly impressed with the belief, in a common not a separate interest, that any deviation from this basis would be a serious error. I hope you may take the same view. It is absolutely required from me by the proposition I have already stated in public, that our responsibility for each & every part of the Bill, I mean the responsibility of the Government, is in no way impaired or altered by the conferences of the last 10 days.

2. Tu.

Wrote to The Queen l.l.–Ld Spencer–& minutes. Dined at Lady M. Alford's. *Such* a Walter Scott story. Saw Mr H–Ld R.G.–Ld Granville–Mr Childers[3]– Ld Spencer–Ld Brownlow. Cabinet 12-2½. H of C. 4-7¾ and 11-12.[4] Read Croker Papers.

Cabinet. Tues. Dec. 2. 1884. Noon.[5]
1. Egyptian Finance. Malet's telegram.[6] B[ismarck] recommends conversation between Ambassadors. Malet to summon his colleagues (but not to be a *Conference*) in concert

---

[1] Letter of resignation this day, Add MS 44488, f. 170. Courtney nonetheless resigned, J. T. Hibbert succeeding him after J. K. Cross declined.

[2] Perhaps that of 29 November, Add MS 44488, f. 164; university formula now satisfactory; 'of course, I shall feel myself similarly bound as to the women's case in the House of Lords: but I do not anticipate any difficulty'. No evidence has been found for the account in Cecil, iii. 124 that Lady Salisbury visited Gladstone to persuade him on the University seats question.

[3] Arranging that in Cabinet Childers would support Gladstone in reducing the navy increase to £6 million, but 'when the time came he [Childers] was dumb'; Bahlman, *Hamilton*, ii. 746.

[4] Statement on the navy by Brassey; *H* 294. 448.

[5] Add MS 44645, f. 234.

[6] Of 1 December on international recognition, circulated for cabinet's opinions; PRO 30/29/144.

with Bismarck (Carmichael to go at once) and supposing it to be agreeable to all the Powers.
2. Plan of extended Naval & Military expenditure stated by Northbrook [and] Childers. We now spend 1900m[ille] on Shipbuilding against French 1500.

83-4. Armourclad   1240   French   1130
      Nonarmour   694   against French   430

Harcourt discriminates a. Fighting Navy b. Police Navy. French much overstate their progress in building.
U.S. attaché considers us as powerful as any *two* not as any three.
In 20 we had not one breech loading gun.
4m̃ for works &c.
Agreed to spend as A [below]—and there are certain questions reserved: arming forts—defence of harbours. When these are thrashed out, the figures may be subject to *some* increase. Hartington will press the proposals hereafter and thinks the present plan unsatisfactory.

[1]£10,725 m[ille].
1. Now, or in the Estimates, 1885-6, something must be done. 2. Whatever the Govt. propose will have to pass under the view of the Finance Committee to be appointed after the Xmas Vacation. To be borne on the Estimates. 3. As one resolved on retirement when the 'situation' is cleared, I do not feel justified in using pressure with reference to a prospective plan reaching over a term of years, although it has not my sympathy.

[Plan] A:[2]   3,100,000 [shipbuilding]
               1,600,000 [naval guns]
                 825,000 [coaling stations]
              £5,525,000

3. *Wed.*

Wrote to Ld Spencer—Ld Hartington—Lady Russell—Lady Salisbury—Mr Villiers—Bp of Rochester—& minutes. Dined at Ld Corks. Read Croker: also Blackwood on Wiclif, Croker, the Crisis.[3] Saw Mr H—Ld RG—M. Waddington. A round of visits: Mrs Th. Ld De Tabley, the T.G.s and other calls. Tea with Lady S[alisbury]—Conversation with Ld S. on course of coming procedure.

4. *Th.*

Wrote to The Queen—Mr Anderson—Mr Heneage—Sir W. Harcourt—Mr Gaskell—Ld Northbrook—Mr Cross—Superior All s[aints] Sisterhood[4]—Dowager Lady Sandhurst—Mrs Tait—Sir S. Northcote—and minutes. Saw Mr H—Ld RG—Ld Portarlington—Ld Kenmare—Mr Childers—Sir C. Dilke—Sir W.

---

[1] Undated holograph; Add MS 44645, f. 237; this statement led several cabinet members to reduce their enthusiasm for increased naval expenditure; see Bahlman, *Hamilton*, ii. 746.

[2] 'A' noted in margin of Childers' cabinet paper on additional defence expenditure, which asked for an extra £10,725,000; the full amount asked for shipbuilding and gunnery was granted, with substantial reductions on coastal defences etc.; Add MS 44645, f. 238. Gladstone felt Childers had failed to resist the larger expenditure plan; see to Childers, 16 Dec. 84.

[3] *Blackwood's*, cxxxvi. 737, 817 (December 1884).

[4] A misunderstanding about the rescue case Mrs Tait; he will pay £10 'for any aid which on inquiry the Sisters might think it desirable to extend to Mrs Tait'; Add MS 44547, f. 144.

Harcourt—M. Arnold. Dined at Mr B. Currie's. Read Burke Fr. Rev.[1]—A. Grey, Proportional Repr.[2] Saw Clifton [R]. H of C. $4\frac{3}{4}$-8 and $10\frac{3}{4}$-1.[3]

5. Fr.

Wrote to Sir S. Northcote—Ld Salisbury—Ld Aberdeen—Sir W. Harcourt—Mr Childers—Hon. A. Gordon. Dined with Lucy. Finished Bonet Maury. Read Croker. Saw Mr H—Mr S—Ld RG.—Mr Hibbert—Mr E. Arnold—Ld Granville. Saw M.A. Jones (Clifton) & Mrs Armitage [R].

To Sir W. V. HARCOURT, home secretary,   MS Harcourt dep. 9, f. 113.
5 December 1884. '*Secret*'.

Hibbert comes to the Treasury and if you like to appoint Fowler to be your Under Secretary I see no objection. If otherwise, or if he declines, what would you say to considering the case of Geo. Russell, or of Duff who might be useful perhaps as a Scotchman. Should you approve the first suggestion pray write to or send for him if you think fit, mentioning my concurrence, and enjoining secrecy until I have communicated with the Queen. Time somewhat presses.

To LORD SALISBURY, 5 December 1884.   Add MS 44488, f. 215.
'*Private & Confidential*'.

A note about supposed leakage, from Northcote, alarmed me yesterday evening: but I have sent him explanations which appear to me satisfactory. I have also told him that with the exception of a point or two, which it was necessary to refer to the Cabinet, we have been *even* more reserved than you. Upon the whole I feel very well satisfied with the secrecy maintained: but doubtless, in the progress of the measure, we shall be subjected to further trials. And occasions of reference may arise which will be new trials of secrecy. As it is very desirable that these unusual proceedings shall not, when Parlt. reassembles, be gratuitously prolonged, I should be glad if you & Sir S. Northcote would consider whether, supposing we ask for additional time (beyond our two Government nights) for the Comee. on the Seats Bill, you would deem it right, on public grounds, to favour the proposal.

Allow me, in what is for the present at any rate a concluding note, to reciprocate very cordially some kind expressions of yours. Had we met in a captious spirit, we must have broken down. For myself I may truly say, I could not have desired any thing more in the way of equity & candour. In all respects those conversations will supply me with a most agreeable recollection.[4]

6. Sat. [Hawarden]

Wrote to Mr Childers—Ld Granville—Miss M.A. Jones—Ld Aberdeen—Mr R. Williams—and minutes. Book packing & preparations. Saw Mr H.—Ld RG—Ld E. Fitzmaurice—Sir C. Dilke—Sir W. Harcourt. Went to H. of C. & H of L. to see the Assent given: a stage onward in my now descending Life.[5] $2\frac{1}{4}$-$7\frac{3}{4}$. To Hawarden. Read Croker.

---

[1] See 1 June 31.   [2] In *N.C.*, xvi. 935 (December 1884).
[3] Replied to Courtney on proportional representation; *H* 294. 680.
[4] Salisbury replied, promising further confidentiality; Add MS 44488, f. 215.
[5] i.e. Royal assent to the Franchise Bill; *H* 294. 843.

7. 2 S Adv.

Ch mg (with H.C.) and evg. Wrote to Ld Granville. Read Mozley's Letters[1]—
Foreign Church Chronicle—Dr Rigg on Dr Pusey[2]—Evans 'St Paul the Author
of the Acts'.[3]

8. M.

Wrote to The Queen l.l.—E. Hamilton—Mr R. Fowler—Mr Buchanan—and
minutes. Worked on letters, & books. Read Croker (finished 2.)—De Tocqueville, Remains.[4] Ch. $8\frac{1}{2}$ A.M.

9. Tu.

Ch. $8\frac{1}{2}$ A.M. Wrote to Dowager Lady Sandhurst—Sir H. Ponsonby—Mr Hutton—Sir C. Dilke—Ld Granville—Mr Quaritch—& minutes. Worked on books.
Drive & walk with C. Read Quaritch Catalogue—Croker Papers—De Tocqueville—Reuss, Geschichte des alten Testament.[5]

10. Wed.

Ch. $8\frac{1}{2}$ A.M. Wrote to Mr Bayley Potter—E. Hamilton—The Queen—Mr
MacColl—& minutes. Worked on books. Woodcraft with WHG. Read Reuss—
Croker—Tennyson's Becket[6]—De Tocqueville Remains.

11. Th.

Ch. $8\frac{1}{2}$ AM. Wrote to Ld Granville—Mr Dawson MP—and minutes. Worked on
books. Drive & walk with C. On her advice I am going to spend the night at the
Rectory to try for better sleep. Read Croker—Reuss—Corresp. of Ward & D[7]—
De Tocqueville—Dryden.

12.

Ch. $8\frac{1}{2}$ A.M. The night was most successful. Wrote to Sir W. Harcourt—Ld
Granville—The Queen—Mr Max Muller—Mrs Sands—& minutes. Worked on
books. Woodcraft with W.H.G. Read Croker—Reuss, Geschichte &c.—De
Tocqueville—Egglestone's Stanhope.[8]

To Sir W. V. HARCOURT, home secretary,   MS Harcourt dep. Adds 10.
12 December 1884.

It is perhaps owing in some degree to the failing sight of old age but I do not yet see my
way about the matter of Playfairs letter.[9] However one difficulty in this odd world of ours

---

[1] See 19 Oct. 84.
[2] J. H. Rigg, *The character and life-work of Dr. Pusey* (1883); see to Rigg, 31 Dec. 84.
[3] H. H. Evans, *St Paul the author of the Acts* (1884).
[4] *Memoir, letters and remains of Alexis de Tocqueville*, 2v. (1861).
[5] E. W. E. Reuss, *Die Geschichte der Heiligen Schriften Alten Testament* (1881).   [6] Just published.
[7] Untraced.   [8] W. M. Egglestone, *Stanhope and its neighbourhood* (1882).
[9] Harcourt supported and Playfair opposed including education in the authority to be given to
the Scottish minister; Add MS 44199, f. 121.

oftentimes shuts out another: and, not to mention Egypt, I suppose your question of the Crofters is now the most urgent of those hailing (in two senses) from beyond the Tweed.

13. Sat.

Ch. 8½ A.M. (with Holy Communion). Wrote to Ld Granville l. & tel.—Manager Chester Theatre Tel—Mr Seymour Tel—Duke of Bedford—Mr Burt MP.—Mr MacColl—& minutes. Worked on books. Woodcraft with W. & H. Read Croker—Max Muller's Bunsen[1]—Stanhope Memorials.[2] Still sleeping at Rectory with advantage. A revelation about the Rector.[3]

To the DUKE OF BEDFORD, 13 December 1884.   Add MS 44547, f. 148.

I have not seen any report of G. Russell's speech,[4] but I have heard of it, & I understand that he adopts the doctrine of a second chamber but is adverse in the last resort to the hereditary principle for its construction.

I am, I must own, at a loss to understand your asking whether a recommendation to abolish the House of Lords has been made with the sanction of the Government, & therefore inclusively with mine; when I have many times & within the last two or three weeks, declared myself to be unfriendly to parting either with the House of Lords or with the hereditary principle in its construction.

Of course there can be no investigation beforehand of the opinions of persons admitted into office, nor would such an investigation if it had taken place have been of any avail; as the question of the hereditary principle in the House of Lords has only been raised, in a serious manner, since, & because of, the unfortunate vote of the House of Lords in July.

I am much concerned to see to what an extent that vote has brought the principle itself into question at any rate for the time; but I do not think that the opinion adverse to it can be treated penally. There are many who believe it to be the opinion of Lord Salisbury.

Speaking from memory, I think the object of my letter,[5] to which you refer, was to bear a testimony, warranted in my experience, to George Russell's parliamentary talent, success and prospects. I do not recollect to have spoken of his opinions, which must be better known to members of his family than to me; although the terms of your reference would lead me to suppose my memory must deceive me in these particulars.

You will I am sure forgive my writing with such frankness.

14. 3 S. Adv.

Ch. 11 AM and 6½. Wrote to Lady Russell—Mr Seymour Tel.—Sir C. Dilke—& minutes. Read Reusch, Bibel & Natur[6]—Hatch, Edinb. Lecture[7]—Smyth on Drummond[8]—Renouf on Egypt (finished)—Fairbairn on the function of Italy in the world.[9] Conversation with Stephy on the new prospect. It kept us both long awake.

[1] F. Max Müller, *Biographical essays* (1884), 311.
[2] W. M. Egglestone, *Stanhope memorials of Bishop Butler* (1878).   [3] See 20 Dec. 84.
[4] On 12 December, Add MS 44488, f. 254, Bedford asked if G. W. E. Russell's speech at Aylesbury advocating the abolition of the Lords was 'made with the sanction of H.M. Government?'
[5] See 18 June 84.   [6] F. H. Reusch, *Bibel und Natur* (1862).
[7] E. Hatch, 'Progress in theology', address given on 14 November 1884 (1885).
[8] W. W. Smyth, 'An examination of Mr Henry Drummond's work, *Natural Law* ...' (1884?).
[9] Untraced tract or article, probably by A. M. Fairbairn.

To Sir C. W. DILKE, president of the local government   Add MS 44547, f. 148.
board, 14 December 1884.[1]

I thank you for your information about the Chancellor, & hope you may be able to
arrange as you desire.

I hope also we may be able to make a plan for getting you here in January.

Terribly have I been puzzled & perplexed on finding a group of the soberest men
among us to have concocted a scheme such as that touching the mountain country
behind Zanzibar with an unrememberable name.[2] There *must* somewhere or other be
reasons for it, which have not come before me. I have asked Granville whether it may not
stand over for a while.

15. M.

Ch. 8¼ A.M. Wrote to Crown Princess—Ld Granville—Mr Murray—Mr Max
Müller—and minutes. Worked much on papers and on books. In the afternoon
we measured some thirty of the largest trees: running from 18.4. downwards.
Read Croker—De Tocqueville.

16. Tu.

Ch. 8½ A.M. Wrote to Ld Granville Tel.—The Queen—Mr Childers—Mr
Cameron Bookseller—Dean of Windsor—Mr Blackie—Mr Sexton MP.—&
minutes. Mr [R.H.] Hutton came: much conversation. Worked on books. Walk
with Ld Aberdeen. Read Croker—Tennyson's Becket.

To H. C. E. CHILDERS, chancellor of the exchequer,   Add MS 44547, f. 149.
16 December 1884.

A brief reply will suffice for me to a statement the great bulk of which relates to proceedings of yours never impugned by me in word or thought.[3]

My observation in the House of Commons had no reference whatever to anything
done by you in your office, or in communication with other Ministers or Departments, as
to military or naval expenditure. I thought that you had effected much, & was not prepared to say that you could have affected more. The Estimates are not such as I, or you,
or probably Northbrook, likes, but we cannot help ourselves. It may be that we are giving
the Tories such an opportunity as you will remember they gave us in 1868: if so it will be
all the better for the country. But this is a conjecture rather than a judgment, & if a judgment one that hits me as much as you.

What I spoke of was exclusively what passed in Cabinet.[4] You and I had fully talked
over the matter beforehand, & I thought it had been arranged between us that, you
having done all you could out of Cabinet, you were in Cabinet to accept the smaller
scheme, the one finally accepted, but to demur pointedly to the larger. When the time
came, I understood you to indicate the difference between the two, but not oppose the

---

[1] In Gwynn, ii. 83, from which italics are taken (holograph untraced).

[2] i.e. the Kilimanjaro region; C. Hill's mem. of 29 November on means of controlling the area
short of annexation (e.g. by buying Mombasa harbour) was circulated for cabinet opinions; many
recorded, but not Gladstone's (see Ramm II, ii. 294); PRO 30/29/144 and *Africa and the Victorians*,
189ff.

[3] Childers' long letter of 14 December, Add MS 44131, f. 233: 'I understood you to blame me for
not having more rigorously resisted Northbrook's & Hartington's proposed expenditures', and item-
ising his attempts at retrenchment. See *H* 294. 683.   [4] i.e. on 2 Dec. 84.

larger one. Consequently I had to break ground on the subject: & I remember that one at least of our colleagues, speaking after me, said that he had acquiesced in the full expenditure, on the ground either wholly or partially that it seemed to have been unanimously accepted.

Such does not appear to be your recollection of the facts, & in general I am slow to challenge any recollection of yours. But at any rate the case as I have given it is the case of which I spoke. My remark may have been right or wrong, but it had this limited scope only, & did not in the least imply abated confidence or dissatisfaction with your general procedure.

I cannot wonder at your feeling pained; you have most invidious duties to perform & their pressure ought not to be aggravated by inconsiderate criticism.

17. Wed.

Ch. 8½ A.M. Wrote to Duke of Bedford—Ld Northbrook—Mr J. Howard—Duke of Sutherland—Ld Granville—& minutes. Forenoon chiefly with Mr Hutton: on Butler, Palmer, & other matters. Also saw Ld Aberdeen—Mr Tomkinson. Walk with party. Read Croker—De Tocqueville—Bp Butler.

18. Th.

Wrote to Sir W. Harcourt—Ld R. Grosvenor—& minutes. Forenoon with Mr Max Müller on Egypt, Homer, and other matters. Walk with party. The Aberdeens went: leaving a good name. Granville came: conversation on Egypt.[1] Whist in evg. Read Croker—De Tocqueville—Homerische Vorschule. Ch. 8½ A.M.

To Sir W. V. HARCOURT, home secretary,   MS Harcourt dep. 9, f. 115.
18 December 1884.

The promised round of beef will be perfect if you & Lady Harcourt will come here to eat it. I believe it is among the many virtues of such rounds that they keep a good while so I will not despair of a favourable answer, in the meantime offering my cordial thanks.

The waters of Redistribution are at present marvellously smooth[2] but Courtney, young & sanguine, sends me with exultation, a letter from the O'Connor Don, which he thinks must settle the controversy in his favour.

I am afraid that in landing from our Egyptian trip we shall find heavy surf upon the beach. The effect on my mind is to impress sed contra audentior ito.[3] There are two things we must now do—must not oppress the people of Egypt—must not lay an intolerable burden on the neck of England. It now seems that if only the rich in Egypt were equitably taxed in relation to i.e. in comparison with the poor there would be enough to pay the bond-holders & every body else. But an internal act of justice like this is beyond our power, in our present lamentably weak position.

[P.S.] I receive with much pleasure your account of Col. Harcourt. Pray remember me kindly to him.

---

[1] Granville went to report on discussions in London on Egyptian finance and Sir J. Carmichael's mission to Paris; Northbrook deplored as impractical taxing the richer classes of Egypt (Carmichael's solution supported by Childers and Granville); Northbrook's notes in Barings' archives, transcribed by Mr. D. Hyland.

[2] Harcourt, 17 December, Add MS 44199, f. 131 and Gardiner, i. 510: 'Redistribution seems to be marching merrily and Proportional Representation to be nowhere.'

[3] Virgil, *Aeneid*, 6. 95: '[Do not give in to your ills], but go forward and face them all the more boldly.'

19. Fr.

Ch. 8½ A.M. Wrote to Ld Northbrook—Mr Courtney—Sec. Antislavery Society[1]—Mr Seymour l.l. & Tel l.l.—and minutes. Further conversation with Granville on Egypt—Duke of Bedford—& *alia*. Drive with C. Read Croker—De Tocqueville.

To LORD NORTHBROOK, first lord of the admiralty,   Add MS 44267, f. 163.
19 December 1884.

I received together with your last communication on Egyptian finance, on I believe or the next following day, a Memorandum from Childers which I now forward.[2]

Granville came here yesterday for a night. We have talked over & through the general subject of Carmichael's project[3] pretty fully. He is very desirous that this question shd. be considered, & concluded on, without waiting for other contingencies; whether a good plan for the equitable adjustment of taxation in Egypt can be framed, as he deems it possible that such a plan may be found, in the event of the failure of our present proposals, to afford the best solution of the problem. And I have undertaken to state to you & Childers the upshot of our conversation. We are agreed in thinking that a plan of this kind, viewed in itself, wd. be more equitable than either the taxation of the Bondholders or than placing the burden (either in cash or credit) on the shoulders of the British people. He states this, without any derogation from his original willingness to accept your recommendations. Next we agree with what appears to be the opinion of Childers, that we are not strong enough, in practice, to carry any such plan into execution in Egypt, while the Powers stand in a hostile, a jealous, or even a neutral attitude; but we think that it might be effected by the decided & united use of the moral influence of all the Powers.

We are entirely with you in the desire that the Egyptian Govt. should be armed with power amply sufficient to carry through this important & difficult measure, as it may affect either foreigners or natives, & we are inclined to suppose that the purpose in view, namely the restoration of financial equilibrium & credit, wd. throw the Powers into the same attitude. At the same time we do not differ from Childers that we should hold fast by our present proposals. But to bring our ideas into shape on Carmichael's proposition would as it seems (if we find it feasible) have a good effect either way. a. If our present proposals are rejected, we might be able to take a new departure with this scheme. b. If on the contrary they are accepted, which wd. secure the immediate future of Egyptian finance, being at length on common ground with the Powers, we might then say that there was a mode which, through united action, might so greatly improve the financial case as almost immediately to put an end to the necessity of making any deduction from the dividends of the bondholders. The fact that the scheme is wholly beyond our unaided force, while it might be carried by united action, seems to afford us a justification for not having put it forward originally by reason of our isolated position & the jealousies with which, especially in Egypt itself, it is beset. Granville appears to think that he could have no difficulty in sounding the French upon it when the time arrived.

I send copies of this letter to him & to Childers, & perhaps you will communicate with them, especially with Childers, with a view to arriving at a joint result.

---

[1] Subject untraced.
[2] Add MS 44267, f. 161; printed for the cabinet.
[3] Plan by Sir J. M. Carmichael for the proper taxation of Egypt; see ibid., f. 157 with Northbrook's criticisms.

Does Carmichael offer us the elements of a plan sound in principle, & next, what ought to be its shape; these are the points to which I should like to draw your joint attention.[1]

20 Sat.

Ch. 8¼ A.M. with H.C. Wrote to Ld Tennyson—The Queen l.l.l.—Mrs Th.—Superior Bridlington Convent—Mrs K. Hollins[2]—Mr C. Gore—Canon Venables—Dean of Windsor Tel—Rev G. Preston Tel.—& minutes. Drive with C. Read Croker—De Tocqueville—Life of Queen of Roumania.[3] In the forenoon Stephen came down to the Castle & conversed with his mother & me dutifully desiring our consent to his marriage with Miss A. Wilson.[4] We had only to commend reflection & express unbounded confidence in him. I promised to make up for him £10000 at once & recommended a considerable insurance.

21. 4 S. Adv. St Thomas.

Ch. 11 AM and 6¼ P.M. Wrote to Ld Granville Tel.—Bp of Ely—Mr Seymour l. & Tel.—Ld Derby—Mr Childers—Ld Stair—Mr Hutton—Mr H. Young—& minutes. Read Natur & Bibel—Pember Earths Earliest Ages[5]—Luccock on St Mark[6]—Dumaresq on Johnson[7]—and other Tracts. Good reading light at 4.10 and for better eyes at 4.30.

To H. C. E. CHILDERS, chancellor of the exchequer,   Childers MS 5/163
21 December 1884.

I should advise distinctly *not* to press for an early production of the Defence Estimates. I regarded it as an incidental advantage of our very long adjournment that we might be relieved by it, before fixing the Estimates for 1885-6 from circumstances of uncertainty in Egypt which I apprehend will be as we now stand the most forcible arguments for high expenditure. I cannot but think, & hope, you will concur in this view. I own that I fail to see why the apprehension of opposition from others should be a reason against your making arguments in the Cabinet which you believe to be sound, & to be material. A voice is a force, even if overruled or out-voted.

Without doubt you hold the most invidious office in the Cabinet and one of the most difficult. I have reason to know it from experience, for in 1859-65 the Estimates were ordinarily settled at the sword's point; and the anti-economic host was led on by the Prime Minister.

[P.S.] Is there any reason why you should not, for the regulation of your own course, converse occasionally with colleagues whom you may regard as more or less sympathetic. *I* have very nearly reached the point at which my title to press points of this kind becomes a vanishing quantity. A happy Christmas & New Year to you & Mrs. Childers.

[1] Northbrook replied, 21 December, with a mem. for the cabinet, printed 22 December, that Carmichael 'overestimates the result of the taxes' which may be put on the richer classes in Egypt, and proposing that Lyons negotiate with the French; Add MS 44267, f. 165.

[2] Rescue case at Convent of Good Shepherd, congratulating her on 'a happy change'; Add MS 44547, f. 151.

[3] *Carmen Sylva, or, Elizabeth Queen of Roumania* (1885).

[4] Annie Crosthwaite, d. of Charles Bowman Wilson, Liverpool physician; see 29 Jan. 85.

[5] G. H. Pember, *Earth's earliest ages and their connection with spiritualism* (1884).

[6] H. M. Luccock, *Footprints of the son of man* (1884).

[7] Not found published; perhaps a privately printed work by his Liverpudlian relative.

To LORD DERBY, colonial secretary, 21 December 1884.   Add MS 44547, f. 152.
'*Private*'.

Meade's paper, forwarded to Busch, appears to me alike able, ingenious, & interesting.[1]
But there is I think a speck in it. In the last line of the second page.[2] We have I think in
Parliament disclaimed charging the Transvaal Government with breach of faith in regard
to Bechuanaland. It seems to me inconvenient that a charge of this kind should be in the
hands of the German Foreign Office. Probably the passage might even now be amended,
& divested of this remnant of 'colonial simplicity' [*sic*].

I find in page 3 past the middle that Zululand is under our influence *& protection*.[3] No
doubt this is true of the Reserve; & influence can in such a case hardly be separated from
neighbourhood. But I am not aware of our having any rights in Zululand people. And for
my part I should be extremely glad to see the Germans become our neighbours in South
Africa, or even the neighbours of the Transvaal. We have to remember Chatham's conquest of Canada, so infinitely lauded, which killed dead as mutton our best security for
keeping the British Provinces.[4]
[P.S.] A Happy Xmas & New Year.

22. M.

Ch. 8¼ A.M. Wrote to Duke of Bedford—Ld Northbrook—Mr Childers—Prof.
Max Müller—and minutes. Read Topinard, Anthropol.[5]—Dicky Sam on Lpool
Slave Tr.[6]—Croker—Life of Queen of Roumania. Drive & walk with C.

23. Tu.

Ch. 8½ A.M. Wrote to Ld Granville Tel.—Mr A. Grey MP—Ld Castleton—Sir C.
Dilke—Mr Childers—Mr Seymour Tel.—and minutes. We felled a dead sycamore. Read Croker—The Empire—De Tocqueville. Worked on books.

24. Wed. Xm Eve

Ch. 8¼ AM. Wrote to Ld Spencer l. & tel.—Ld Hartington—Ld Granville tel—Mr
Seymour tel.—Mr Childers tel.—Mr M. Wood tel.—Ld Derby—Mr Murray—Ld
Northbrook—Mr Hamilton—and minutes. Read Croker (finished)—'The Chris-
tian Religion'—De Tocqueville (a man of real note. finished II.)—Carmen Sylva.[7]

To LORD DERBY, colonial secretary, 24 December 1884.   Derby MSS.

Many thanks for yours of yesterday. On reading Meade's letters to Granville of 18th
and 20th, which have reached me this morning, I have sent the inclosed telegram to

---

[1] Meade at the Berlin conference; mem. of 7 December (printed for cabinet, Add MS 44629, f.
148) of a talk with Dr. Busch, German foreign undersecretary: Britain had 'no jealousy whatever' of
recent German colonial enterprises.
[2] ibid.; Transvaal govt. had not obeyed the 1884 Treaty *re* Bechuanaland.
[3] 'Zululand was especially under our influence and protection'.
[4] Derby replied, 23 December, Add MS 44142, f. 106, agreeing with Gladstone's criticism of
Meade's paper.
[5] P. Topinard, *L'Anthropologie* (1876).
[6] *Liverpool and slavery. An historical account of the Liverpool-African slave trade by a genuine 'Dicky Sam'*
(1884).
[7] See 20 Dec. 84.

Granville,[1] which I do not think you will disapprove when you read the letters. No doubt we must be most cautious here as to Colonial alarmism: but any language at Berlin appearing to convey sympathy with it might at this moment do extraordinary mischief to us at our one really vulnerable point, Egypt.

To LORD NORTHBROOK, first lord of the admiralty,					Add MS 44267, f. 179.
24 December 1884.

I reserved my acknowledgement of your last letter[2] until I should have an opportunity of reading your memorandum[3] which arrived today.

The difficulties with the Egyptian question are such, & so entirely beyond the common range, that nothing, probably, except the excellent temper that has prevailed could have prevented them at various points from becoming the cause of irreconcilable differences.

The same trials may come back upon us, and may even come back soon. But I can hardly think it possible for the Cabinet to alter proposals framed with much care and difficulty, unanimously assented to, and formally presented by the Powers, before we have from them a word of answer in whatever sense, either entire or partial. The anticipation of Lyons may be gloomy, but can we run away before the trumpet sounds? Would it not exhibit a weakness which would expose us to be mercilessly ridden over. In 'holding fast' to our proposals I understood Childers only to mean that which seems almost a matter of course, that the matter should continue on the footing laid down by the Cabinet, (namely of our proposal with certain possible relaxations), until it should come to issue. If it does not succeed, then I apprehend we should all assume our liberty of action: and what you might recommend would I am sure be carefully considered.

I hope you have seen or will see a curious series of telegrams sent from Constantinople, which tend, in a direction quite different from Carmichael's account and go to show that assent or veto does not depend on the merits of our proposals but on extraneous considerations.

To LORD SPENCER, Viceroy of Ireland, 24 December 1884.					Althorp MSS K7.

You will have received my telegram.[4] This matter of the boundaries was during the conferences principally in Dilke's hands, & afterwards wholly. I think we cannot safely take a step without him. He said as far as I recollect that he would be back by Jan. 2.

On Salisbury's recital I have two observations to make. 1. We did not think as he seems to have done that in composing the [Boundary] Commission we were pitting so many Conservatives against so many Liberals. For my own part I had never heard of the politics of any one (I believe) of the Commissioners, till Lord S. proposed Sandford as a counterpoise to Lambert. Certainly special experience & general fitness were in our minds the guiding considerations. 2. Salisbury says we had agreed to place Ireland under the Commission as then projected. This I think is inaccurate. I do not *remember* that either Ireland or Scotland were mentioned. No doubt then he thought we were fixing a Commission for the three kingdoms.

Further, it is clear that, as he says, he is powerless, & I must do him the justice to say that he has performed his contract with regard to the Franchise Bill so fully, that I should be loath to quarrel with him on any doubtful point if it can possibly be avoided.

---

[1] Not in Ramm II, ii. 299.
[2] Of 22 December, Add MS 44267, f. 170, threatening resignation on Egyptian finance.
[3] See 19 Dec. 84n.
[4] Unable to act without Dilke; replying to Spencer's letter of 23 December enclosing Salisbury's letter (in *Spencer*, i. 283) attacking govt. handling of the Irish boundary commission; Althorp MSS K7, Add MS 44311, f. 257.

The only point which appears open to me to doubt is whether Lord S. should have been consulted in any degree upon the names.

I entirely agree with you that the principle of composition should be the same in Ireland as in England, that is to say general fitness & avoidance of marked party politics. Also so far as my knowledge goes the suggestion of C. J. Morris[1] is by no means a happy one. I have now I think said all that I have to say at present.[2]

P.S. Your telegram received. I think that you should have the opportunity of reviewing your letter to Salisbury, so I return the box.

25. Th. Xm Day.

Ch 11 AM and H.C.—7 P.M. Wrote to Rev. Mr Chappel[3]—Mr Bond—Ld Granville—Mr Scharf—Mr Stair Agnew—Mr H. Murray—Mr Brodie—Mr Seymour Tel. & minutes. We were all except Agnes & her husband at the Altar: God be praised. Read Pember, Spiritism—Bp Temple Bampton Lectures[4]—Happiness of Dead Clergyman[5]—Maurice Indian Antiquities[6]—The Gospel in Gr. Britain.[7]

26. St Stephen.

Ch 8½ A.M. Wrote to Rev. Mr Bickersteth—Ld Granville—Mr Clifford Lloyd—Ld Spencer—Sir Thos Acland—Sir Thos G.—Miss D. Beale[8]—& minutes. Made known to S. my views & intentions as to money provision on his marriage. Read Carmen Sylva—De Tocqueville Vol I—Blackie on the Highlanders[9]—Noel on Rabelais.[10] Sleep much broken these two nights.

27. Sat. St John.

Rose after 9. Wrote to Ld Hartington tel. l.l.—Ld Derby tel.—Ld Spencer—Mr Childers—Mr Lefevre—and minutes. Read Volkmann on Wolf and the Homeric question[11]—Blackwell on Homer—on Nine Abbeys[12]—Life of Carmen Sylva—Life of Ellen Watson:[13] what a grand soul. Went to sleep in the delightful room at the Rectory: but without good effect. Drive with C, walk with party.

28. S. aft Xmas.

Ch. 11 AM and 6½ PM. The Lesson in evg from Baruch was like a voice of divine assurance: much needed.[14] Wrote to Earl Granville l.l.—Lord Hartley—Ld

---

[1] Proposed by Salisbury; *Spencer*, i. 284.
[2] On 31 December Spencer reported 'Salisbury . . . caves in'; ibid.
[3] Rev. W. P. Chappel; Add MS 44547, f. 155.
[4] F. Temple, *The relations between religion and science* (1884).
[5] [W. Thom], *The happiness of dead clergymen, provided they die in the Lord* (1769).
[6] T. Maurice, *Indian antiquities*, 7v. (1793–1800).
[7] S. Macnaughten, *The gospel in Great Britain* (1884).
[8] Thanking Dorothea *Beale (1831–1906, principal of Cheltenham Ladies' College) for articles and asking if 'the Indian lady' needed funds for her course; Add MS 44547, f. 156.
[9] J. S. Blackie, *The Scottish Highlanders and the land laws* (1885); strongly historicist; see 15 Jan. 85.
[10] E. Noel, *Rabelais* (1850).
[11] R. Volkmann, *Geschichte und Kritik der Wolfschen Prolegomena zu Homer* (1874).
[12] Probably *sc.* Blackwood, but no relevant number found.
[13] A. Buckland, *A record of Ellen Watson* (1884).
[14] i.e. from the Book of Baruch in the *Apocrypha*.

Nelson—and minutes. Read Pellissier[1]—Le Normant[2]—Ward's Will to believe[3]—and Ellen Watson Life, most edifying. A much improved night followed.

29. M.

Ch 8½ AM. Wrote to Mr Seymour l & tel—Ld Granville l.l.—Ld Spencer l & tel. l.l.—Prince of Wales tel—Mr C. Acland MP. tel—Mr Walker—and minutes. Read Ellen Watson—Lenormant—Bellet on Paul Bert.[4] A little woodcraft, & various devices for helping sleep. Wrote Mem. on Egyptian Finances, which I hope may help to clear my brain and nerves.[5]

The flood of kind congratulations from every quarter, utterly beyond my sole power even to note, & hard to cope with even when aided by the regular staff in London and an excellent volunteer staff here, forbids the calm and recollection which the day demands of me. I had much to say on it, as I believe: but I seem to be in a mist, and to have seen nothing except the wonderful grace and favour by which I have been & am upheld, and that great army of prayers ever mounting to heaven and returning on me in benediction, despite all my unworthiness.

30. Tu.

Ch. 8½ A.M. Wrote to Mr Seymour Tel. l.l.—The Queen l. & tel.—Mrs Vyner—Herr Fleischer[6]—Ld Spencer—Cav. Cadorna—Ld Derby—Mr Hillson—Mr Murray—Mr Jerningham—and minutes. Read Deutsche Revue (a remarkable article on Bismarck and continental questions)[7]—Bellet on Bert & Ferry—Johnson Life & Aphorisms.[8] Last night good.

To LORD DERBY, colonial secretary, 30 December 1884.   Add MS 44142, f. 113.

An excellent map has reached me this morning from the Colonial office, and it will enable me to express clearly my meaning, in giving an answer to your letter[9] about the extension of British authority along the South African coast.

I heartily concur in the expediency of filling up the gap in the coast line to Natal. When this is done we shall as I understand it have all the coast line of the territory for which we are virtually or directly responsible. Why should we go further?

---

[1] Probably P. A. Pellissier, *Les grands leçons de l'antiquité* (1880).
[2] F. Lenormant, probably *Les origines de l'histoire*, 2v. (1880-4).
[3] W. Ward, *Wish to believe* (1884).
[4] C. F. Bellet, *Le Manuel de M. Paul Bert* (1882).
[5] Add MS 44768, f. 199, sent to Granville this day; see Ramm II, ii. 308.
[6] Thanking R. Fleischer for the *Deutsche Revue*, with comments; Add MS 44547, f. 157.
[7] K. Braun-Wiesbaden, 'Unterhaltungen mit dem fürsten Bismarck', or 'Bismarck und Arnim' (letters of 1873), both in *Deutsche Revue*, x. 1 (January 1885).
[8] R. Napier, *Johnsoniana. Anecdotes newly collected* (1884).
[9] Of 27 December, Add MS 44142, f. 110: 'I would claim the whole S. African coast, from the mouth of the Orange river on the west, to the beginning of the Portuguese territory on the south east. . . . The more I reflect on what Bismarck has done, and his way of doing it, the more I am convinced that it is meant as a deliberate expression, not perhaps of actual hostility, but of ill will to England. The reason is less clear: probably because we do not choose to take any step in regard to Egypt that will embroil us with France—the result for which he has been working ever since 1877.' See also Ramm II, ii. 304 and 3 Jan. 85n.

Is there any reason to suppose the Germans contemplate any assumption on the East coast of Africa?

Is it dignified, or is it required by any real interest, to make extensions of British authority without any view of occupying but simply to keep them out?

Is it not open to a strong positive objection in regard to the coast now in question between St Lucia Bay and Delagoa Bay? Namely that it tends powerfully to entail a responsibility for the country lying inland, which we think it impolitic to assume. And which in the case of Zululand we have publicly & expressly renounced?

Even were we for fear of the Germans (a most idle fear) to go to Delagoa Bay, how can we be sure that the Germans will not negotiate the Portuguese out of that settlement and so be our neighbours whether we will or no? These are at present my old fashioned notes upon the matter.

31. Wed.

In bed till breakfast, to make up sleep. Wrote to Ld Granville—Ld Carlingford—Mr Childers—Mr Seymour l. & tel 1 l 1 l—Mrs Th.—Rev. Dr Rigg—Messrs Blackwood—and minutes. Finished Bellet—read Johnson—Br Quarterly on Hope Scott—and on Pr. Bismarck.[1] Drive with C. & walk.

But the year closed with a bad night only $1\frac{1}{2}$ hour sleep—which will hardly do to work upon.

There is much more that I should like to have recorded. Honour received and not deserved: mercy poured out upon me in floods and not acknowledged in a life for the glory of God. But the pressure on me is too great for the requisite recollection. It is indeed a time of *sturm und drang*. What with the confusion of affairs and the disturbance of my daily life by the altered character of my nights, I cannot think in calm, but can only trust & pray to Him who heareth the prayer.

To Messrs. BLACKWOOD, publishers, 31 December 1884.   NLS 4456, f. 216.

It had been my intention to follow up what I thought the extraordinary case of the Almanack with which you have thought fit to connect my name.[2]

But an event trivial in itself, the recurrence of my birthday, has been made the occasion of indulgent and generous judgments, and of tributes far beyond any merit or claim of mine, from Conservative as well as Liberal organs, which have shown me that I should not do well to deal with this isolated case.

But I think I may justly refer it to your serious consideration, whether it is consistent with your position, or well in any other respect, to continue responsible for such a production, and to regard it as a legitimate article of trade.

---

[1] *Recte: London Quarterly Review*, 'The late Mr. Hope Scott and Mr. Gladstone' and 'Prince Bismarck', n.s. iii. 197, 240 (January 1885).

[2] *The Gladstone Almanack 1885*, a scurrilous, best-selling pamphlet, with mock-Tenniel cartoons, ending at 31 December 1885: "DESOLATION." Total eclipse. The G.O.M. disestablishes himself, 1885.' A sharp exchange between Hamilton and Blackwood's already published, *T.T.*, 20, 22 December 1884, 6c, 6e. Blackwood's replied, 3 January, Add MS 44489, f. 18 that no personal attack was intended, agreeing to 'have such passages as are especially offensive to you revised or deleted', the 'compilers' also apologising for 'personal annoyance'. Hamilton kept the correspondence back, doubting the wisdom of an 'expurgated edition'; Gladstone's docket: 'ask on my behalf & say it was a suggestion that I offered & not a desire. I propose to leave the matter in their hands. . . . Ja. 13.'

To H. C. E. CHILDERS, chancellor of the exchequer,   Add MS 44547, f. 158.
31 December 1884.

I have received the papers on the proposed 'Postal' Contract between Natal, Mauritius & Madagascar. I have initialled your minute & I concur in the view taken by you as well as by Mr. Courtney.

The Contract as it appears to me is not postal but political & has mainly to do with Naval Service on the Coast of Madagascar.

Whether some such service ought to be performed by the Navy I will not undertake to say: but it is not I think a legitimate use of public revenue to establish services called Postal where there is nothing (in substance not in name) to carry; the practice is unjust to our Postal system & tends to relax & disorganise the administration of a great revenue, & has also a tendency to hoodwink Parliament.

To Rev. J. H. RIGG, 31 December 1884.   Add MS 44547, f. 158.

I thank you for the London Quarterly and I shall read the article on Hope Scott with great interest & much confidence in its fairness.

These words describe my perusal of your Tract on Dr. Pusey.[1]

One observation in it appeared to me to be open to counter-observation. Why should a subscription to Dr. Pusey's Memorial imply a recognition of him as a perfect or model Churchman? Dr. Pusey was my kind friend from 1828 when I went to Oxford, where he was considered to smell of rationalism, and where he was simply very kind to me. I think he was a great servant of God and of the Church of England, but there are points and aspects of his teaching which I cannot accept. This has been my case with many memorials, but the case of Dr. Pusey had this recommendation that the points and aspects I refer to are such as will I think be effectually qualified by the spirit of the age, the country, and the Church.[2]

---

[1] See 7 Dec. 84.

[2] Rigg replied on 2 January 1885, Add MS 44489, f. 13, that Pusey 'has done vastly more than any other man to introduce into the Church of England some of the worst and most fundamentally evil superstitions'.

Thursday. Jan 1. 1885. Circumcision. [London]

Wrote to the Khedive—The Queen—P. master Chester tel.—Mr Seymour tel.—and minutes. Off at 12.40. D St. at 7. Saw Sir A. Clark. Dined at Mr Th.s. Read Ellen Watson finished—Boswell's Letters, and Introduction.[1] Was blessed with a good night.

2. Fr.

Wrote to D. of Argyll—Mr Macmillan—C.G.—Ld Northbrook—Mrs Th.—The Queen—and minutes. Improved night D.G. Cabinet 4-7. Saw Mr H.—Sir A. Clark l.l.—Lord Granville—do *cum* Mr Childers—Ld Northbrook—Ly Wolseley. Dined at Ld Reay's. Smart attack of Lumbago: a diversion I think.[2] Read Boswell's Letters.

Cabinet. Friday Jan. 2. 85. 4 PM.[3]

1. Representation of Germany & Russia on the Cairo Commission. Ld Granville's draft read out, arguing in principle to the change on the promise of facilitating the financial arrangements—not otherwise. G. to proceed with Münster on this basis.[4]
2. Intimation to France founded on announcement that there will be no answer before 15th & then a counter proposal. Draft agreed to.[5]

To Mrs GLADSTONE, 2 January 1885.   Hawarden MSS.

Incomparable Clark came last night & this morning and comes again this evening. Last night after a 'composing draught'—(which all but made me sick, & which he says I was only to take in case of need, but I took without waiting to see) I did very well—whether it was the bad night before, the draught, a walk home of half an hour, or a passage in the Psalms, or all combined, or whatever else; I slept from say 11¼ to 1¾: then lay awake, & partly read, until 4 when I had a grand sleep till 8¾. Clark however is preaching *rest*, and I know not what it will come to—Cannes is already, (in a degree) in the air.[6]

I am meantime swimming the best I can with all my arms and legs in the business of

[1] *Letters of James Boswell . . . to the Rev. W. J. Temple* [ed. Sir P. Francis] (1857),

[2] i.e. from insomnia.

[3] Add MS 44646, f. 2. Holograph note reads: Bismarck cannot be *absolutely* hostile viewing Heligoland?'

[4] See Add MS 44769, f. 1. Gladstone saw Northbrook before the cabinet to read him his mem. on Egyptian finance (see 29 Dec. 84); he also read it at the cabinet. Northbrook agreed with part of it but refused to agree to any concessions to France; he noted: 'There was in the Cabinet a general disposition to come to an agreement with France. Granville said that M. Ferry had expressed, unofficially, his dissatisfaction with our proposals. . . . There was a good deal of discussion as to the proposal in the memo: that delay would be taken as a refusal & that we must then take matters into our own hands. Harcourt objected to the ultimatum & the general opinion was against it. . . . I suggested that Ld Lyons might have latitude as to the payment of the whole of the Coupon . . . Mr. Gladstone at once answered very decisively, taking the responsibility entirely upon himself & saying he could not propose it—"present Govt cannot propose it"'; Northbrook decided to resign if next day's cabinet accepted Gladstone's mem. (Northbrook's notes, Barings' archives, transcribed by Mr. D. Hyland.)

[5] See Granville to Lyons, 3 January, *PP* 1884–5 lxxxviii. 723.

[6] i.e. another stay at Cannes to remedy insomnia. See 18 Jan. 83.

the day (which I shortened by not getting up till eleven). Probably there will be no time for me to write to you after the Cabinet. I think there is hope of our arriving at a joint decision which will govern our proceedings for some little time to come.

Meanwhile Clark much desires my going away tomorrow (without prejudice to ulterior questions) and I have good hope of it. Of course you will be duly informed. If I stay I am invited to dine with Mr & Mrs Sands. Today with the Reays. Clark approves.

Pray say to Annie how sorry I am not to have been on the ground to offer her an affectionate and hearty welcome. Ever your afft WEG.

You did not I think give me any pills.[1] A certain department seems rather to require them. In some way I am rheumatic today. But these things are such jests in comparison with the other.

3. Sat. [Hawarden]

Wrote to the Queen—Saw Mr H.—Ld Wolverton—Sir A. Clark. Cabinet 12–2¼. Reached Hawarden 7.45. Read Boswell. Better sleep; & lumbago, with stoppage. Clark hopes Hawarden & *rest* for a while may suffice without any more serious measure. This day Stephen made known [to] his mother & me, with much filial piety, his mind touching Miss A. Wilson. God bless them both.[2]

Cabinet. Saturday Jan. 3. 85. Noon.[3]
General conversation on the question of yesterday—Northbrook's remarks of a hostile character. Drafts of dispatches to be cons[idered] by the Cabinet: WEG satisfied to leave them in the hands of the Cabinet.[4]
2. New Guinea. German Declaration of Dec. 15 bisects them[5] & has been disregarded. Our case to be set out. Invite their explanations. Inform Colonies no understanding with Germany.[6]

4. 1 S. Epiph.

Ch. mg only, with H.C. Wrote to Ld Granville. Read Trevor[7]—Lenormant—Bp Temple Bampton Lecture—and [blank.]

[1] For constipation.
[2] His engagement; see 29 Jan. 85.
[3] Add MS 44646, f. 6; cabinet also agreed to annex part of coast between Natal and the Cape; *L.Q.V.*, 2nd series, iii. 592; see also to Derby, 30 Dec. 84.
[4] i.e. because of his early departure; see Ramm II, ii. 310. Northbrook noted: 'Gladstone rather seemed to suppose that the substance of his memo: was agreed to and that only the form remained to be settled. But I asked that the Drafts should be read. They had not yet arrived, so I said I could not agree in the course proposed. The proposals must either be accepted or refused. If refused, we had not decided how we should carry out our threat to take our own course. If accepted, we must agree to a multiple control which was contrary to everything I had contended for. Mr. Gladstone at once declared that he was against a multiple control & said he did not think it was involved in his plan. There was a good deal of desultory discussion. . . . Gladstone left in the middle of the Cabinet & we went through the drafts . . . the joint guarantee was subject to the proviso: "if this can be arranged without increasing international control". My objections therefore were removed. Mr. Gladstone at once approved the drafts when they were sent to him' (Northbrook's notes, Barings' archives, transcribed by Mr. D. Hyland).
[5] Reading of phrase uncertain.
[6] Germany annexed parts of New Guinea and neighbouring islands on 3 November 1884, Morrell, 257.
[7] G. Trevor, *On the ecclesiastical courts* (1882).

5. M.

Good night, but alas no Church. Rose at 10.30. Wrote to the Queen l.l.—and minutes. Read Boswell's Letters (the most singular of books)—Parkman's Montcalm[1]—Shorthouse's Mark (finished)[2]—Memoir of Roumanian Queen.[3] Drive & walk with C.

6. Tu. Epiph.

C.G.s birthday. Still a lazy morning when there were so many reasons for going solemnly before God. Trouble came from London by telegrams respecting Egypt. Wrote to Mr Hamilton Tel. & l.—Ld Hartington—Ld Northbrook—Ld Granville l.l.—Rev. Mr Fisher—and minutes. Bid farewell to Lucy. Drive with C., and walk. Read Boswell's Letters—Memoir of Q. of Roumania—Parkman's Montcalm.

To LORD HARTINGTON, war secretary,   Chatsworth MSS 340. 1615A.
6 January 1885.

On the unwelcome suggestion from Baring of an expedition to Suakim, I would gladly have heard the observations which a meeting in Cabinet will draw forth; but as matters stand I will at once state my own impressions, which are drawn from considerations clear & simple in themselves.

I have only before me telegrams to Baring No 4 & Baring No. 9 (or 7) with his ciphered telegram. I do not know what had preceded No. 4 to Baring.

As the papers before me read, they appear to indicate not the spontaneous demand of Wolseley for something required for the success of his expedition, but his acceptance of a suggestion made to him which he says may be acted on with great advantage and which 1. would pacify Eastern Soudan and 2. admit of using the return route if desirable.

Wolseley's *reasons* appear to me unsatisfactory. We have already performed once, of course with loss, & with frightful slaughter of most gallant Arabs in two bloody battles, this operation of 'pacifying' the Eastern Soudan, & I am very loath to have another such pacification, & quite unable to see how it is to be better or more effective. The second reason, good as far as it goes, does not appear adequate, & is purely contingent.

But what I think we ought really to know is *whether Wolseley upon his own responsibility deems a new expedition through Suakim against Osman Digna requisite for the efficiency & success of his own expedition against Khartoum.* If he does, I am not ready to refuse it: if he does not (i.e. if *his answer falls short of this*) & is merely accepting a collateral suggestion, I do not think we should be justified in granting it. A day will suffice to learn from him how this matter stands.[4]

I hope I have made this matter clear.

I think people were a good deal shocked at the two former battles, not without some reason.

[1] F. Parkman, *Montcalm and Wolfe*, 2v. (1884).
[2] J. H. Shorthouse, *The little schoolmaster Mark* (1883).
[3] See 20 Dec. 84.
[4] Wolseley replied that he wanted the fleet at Suakin as a demonstration but did not need men there; *Relief of Gordon*, 109.

To LORD NORTHBROOK, first lord of the admiralty,   Add MS 44547, f. 160.
6 January 1885.

I thank you very much for your letter[1] and am sorry you should have been troubled to give explanations on account of a frivolous alarm. As to myself I am thankful to say that my sleep has now been going well for some nights, and the other bodily derangements I have had are of a more bearable kind. The Egyptian flood comes on us again and again, like the sea on the host of Pharaoh, which had just as much business to pursue the Israelites as we have had to meddle in Egypt. I have written to Hartington, and to Granville, on the two questions; which you will have to consider tomorrow.

7. Wed.

Lazy again, under orders, after a good night. Wrote to Mr Hamilton l & tel.—Ld Granville—Ld Chancellor—Prince Albert Victor[2]—Mr Dobson—and minutes. Read Queen Elis of Roum.—Boswell's Letters (finished)—Parkman's Montcalm. Drive with C. & walk.

8. Th.

Again a good report, but again 12 h. in bed. Wrote to Ld Granville l. & tel.—Mr Hamilton l. & tel. l.l.—and minutes. Read Queen of Roumania—Parkman's Montcalm & Wolfe—Fitzgerald on Boswell—and Croker.[3] Walk with E. Wickham.

9. Fr.

Not a good night. 3 h. Wrote to Ld Hartington—Archbishop of Canterbury—Mr Childers—& minutes. Read Parkman—Fitzgerald on Boswell—Aus Carmen Sylva's Leben (i.e. Qu of Roumania). Walk with [blank.]

To E. W. BENSON, Archbishop of Canterbury,   Benson MS 3/6/32.
9 January 1885. 'Private'.

Mr. Hamilton has received from the Dean of St. Paul's the inclosed very clear and explicit letter on which I shall be glad to be favoured with Your Grace's full judgment.[4]

I do not know whether the Dean was aware of the statement that Dr. L. had declined to work with the late Archbishop nor had I previously to this occasion heard any thing of the kind. I could have understood it 20 years ago for at *that* time I think Archbishop Tait would have declined to work with Dr. Liddon. I should myself much wish to know, if it is known to Your Grace, the exact scope and bearing of the statement, as well as whether it is to be taken as fact, for I am at a loss not only to justify but even to understand it.

[1] Of 5 January, Add MS 44267: 'the stupid & mischievous article in the Times as to the alleged orders to the Channel Squadron'. *T.T.* reported channel fleet ordered to prepare for sea, 5 January 1885, 6a; admiralty denial and correspondent's reaffirmation on 6 January 1885, 5d.

[2] Letter of congratulation on attaining his majority; *T.T.*, 13 January 1885, 8a.

[3] P. H. Fitzgerald, *Croker's Boswell, and Boswell: studies in the 'Life of Johnson'* (1880).

[4] R. W. Church to Hamilton, 8 January 1885, Benson MS 3/6/31 (responding to a note from Hamilton), on Liddon's strengths and weaknesses—chiefly the former. Benson replied next day, Add MS 44109, f. 106, having written for information, and feeling Liddon perhaps too divisive for a bishopric, despite the dangers of 'exclusion'. For Liddon, tractarian, preacher and Pusey's biographer, see 5 June 57. Church was right *re* Lincoln (C. Wordsworth resigning); Gladstone was considering Liddon for Exeter (Temple translated to London in February); he appt. Bickersteth to Exeter and King, a greater ritualist than Liddon, to Lincoln, Liddon refusing. See to Acton, 27 Jan. 85.

The Church of England has suffered heavily within my recollection from the unnatural suppression of men who were in themselves great powers. I cannot but feel that that definition (of a great power not of suppression) strictly applies to Dr. Liddon. He has been nearly the first to associate a great thinking force with the masteries of a first rate preacher. To hear him is I [*sc.* to] apprehend the advice would be given to, or the course which would be spontaneously taken by, an inquiring unbeliever. May he not perhaps be called the first champion of belief. It is in this light that he appears to me so strong as to be entitled to have his claims *considered* carefully.

Should Your Grace's judgment be favourable I should think it well to learn if possible privately what his own inclinations are.

With regard to the See of Lincoln, I have not had any intimation that it is likely to be vacant for anything like immediate consideration.

To H. C. E. CHILDERS, chancellor of the exchequer,   Add MS 44547, f. 161.
9 January 1885. '*Private*'.

Many thanks for your interesting letter.[1] I think you were quite right not to let the question of charge drop out of view. You recollect how, during the Government of 1866–8, we used to say *they* were playing our game by increasing the expenditure. I am not sure that the day may not be near when they, if they have a little courage, may have a chance of returning the compliment.

Hartington's telegram to Lord Wolseley does not seem to me to give well balanced expression to the wish of the Cabinet stated to me by Granville 'to what was clearly desired by Lord Wolseley' for the assistance of his operation, and the facilitating [of] the retirement of his troops.

[P.S.] Have I not been waiting a good while for you to suggest a successor to Gore.

To LORD HARTINGTON, war secretary, 9 January   Chatsworth MSS 340. 1620.
1885.

A telegram dated 6th to you is mentioned by Baring which I do not remember to have seen. I have today yours of the 7th; it does not, I think, quite express the idea on which I wished to dwell, but rather seems to suggest to Wolseley a Suakim expedition. I admit however that the purposes are carefully guarded. His of the 8th to Granville appears to make it quite clear that the opening of the road for withdrawal is the only practical question open; and if he understands that it is a question of his asking something and not ours I feel confident of his making a just & sensible reply.[2]

10. Sat.

Right again D.G. Wrote to Ld Hartington—Mr Childers—Mr Hamilton—P. of Wales Tel.—and minutes. Read as yesterday. Walk with Mr Weldon—& with E. Wickham.

---

[1] Of 7 January, Add MS 44132, f. 19, on his urging of proper costing at the cabinet, attacked as wanting 'cheap & nasty' expenditure.

[2] See Wolseley's wire from Korti to Hartington, 8 January, Add MS 44147, f. 218: 'I am strong enough to relieve Khartoum, and believe in being able to send a force when returning by way of Berber and Suakin to open road and crush Osman Digna'; Berber railway irrelevant; Nile route with whalers the solution; 'please send me 2.000 strong thick white umbrellas at once'.

To LORD HARTINGTON, war secretary, 10 January   Chatsworth MSS 340. 1621.
1885.

I have your letter of yesterday,[1] & mine to you of the same date may be considered as
non avenu.

I own to being greatly relieved.[2] Though fully convinced of the necessity of supporting
Wolseley, & not disposed to be squeamish as to anything demanded by him, it would
have been with much pain that I should have seen the Osman Digna episode acted over
again, with the escape of that worthy for its probable if not certain end.

But what course do you propose to take about sending ships? Does it not seem rather
difficult to refuse him altogether what he asks. You & Northbrook will I conclude settle
this.[3]

Granville has favourable reports of Ferry's plan. If they be verified, it will become an
inextricable mystery why he kept it back so long.

11. 1 S. Epiph.

Ch. 11 AM. & 6½ P.M. Notable sermons. Walk with Mr Gore.[4] Wrote to Ld
Granville l.l.—Ld Hartington—Mr Forster—& minutes. Read Pembers *awful*
account of the facts of Spiritism (& Theosophy)[5]—Mozley's Letters.[6]

12. M.

Wrote to Ld Hartington—Abp of Canterbury—Dean of St Paul's—& minutes.
Read Parkman (Vol II)—'Carmen Sylva'—Blackie on Land Laws[7]—Heart of Midlothian. Ch. 8½ A.M. Another walk with Mr Gore, a person of very great
promise.

To R. W. CHURCH, dean of St. Paul's, 12 January 1885.   Add MS 44127, f. 368.

I was greatly obliged to you for your letter of the 8th[8] and I think I cannot do wrong in
sending you very privately a letter from the Archbishop written after seeing it. The Archbishop evidently feels the weight of the case. It is one in which my powers are limited:
and I also feel there are two sides to it, but the strength of it on one side seems to me to
be that in this age of unparalleled conflict between belief and negation, Dr Liddon is the
greatest personal power in the country on the side of belief.

You are aware, my dear Dean, what is the appointment I should *most* like to recommend. I do not worry you with solicitations but if from circumstances of climate (as to
Exeter) or any other cause your mind has changed I rely on your letting me know. For
greater clearness I add my own letter which drew forth that of the Archbishop.

---

[1] Add MS 44147, f. 207.

[2] Though the chief point of Hartington's letter was to regret the absence of an expedition.

[3] Hartington replied, 13 January, Add MS 44147, f. 212, that extra ships unnecessary, Wolseley
not knowing the number already at Suakin; but a battalion may be sent there to relieve the marines.

[4] Charles *Gore, 1853–1932; librarian of Pusey House, Oxford 1884–93; canon of Westminster
1894–1902; later bp.; anglo-catholic theologian; (H.V.B.).

[5] See 21 Dec. 84.

[6] See 19 Oct. 84.

[7] See 26 Dec. 84.

[8] Add MS 44127, f. 362; on Liddon's temper: spasmodic but on the whole controlled. See
9 Jan. 85.

13. *Tu.*

Ch. 8¼ A.M. Wrote to Sir A. Clark—Mr Hamilton Tel. l.l. and L.—Ld Granville l.l.l.—Sir C. Dilke—Ld Derby—Lady Brassey—Mrs Sands—and minutes. Read Parkman—Rae on Lassalle[1]—Heart of Midlothian. Conversation with Stephy. Walk & much conversation with F.L. Gower: a *rare* politician. 13 to dinner.

To Sir C. W. DILKE, president of the local government   Add MS 43875, f. 225.
board, 13 January 1885.

1. Many thanks for your interesting letter of yesterday.[2] I shall of course be happy to see Baxter, alone or with you, if I can be of use.

2. The difficulty, as I see it about communication with Northcote is that he seems to have little weight or influence, and to be afraid or unwilling to assume any responsibility. I have usually found him reasonable in his own views but obliged to reserve his judgment until after consulting his friends, which consultations I have found always to end badly. On the other hand, it is of course necessary to pay him due respect. What may prove to be best under these circs. is a. not to be bound always to consult *him*. b. to consult him freely on the easier & smaller matters, but c. in a stiff question, such as the number of the House may prove to be, to get at Salisbury if possible, under whose wing Northcote will I think mostly be content to walk. d. or if Salisbury cannot be got at alone, then Northcote & Salisbury would be far preferable to Northcote alone.

14. *Wed.*

Ch. 8½ A.M. Wrote to Ld Hartington—Mr Childers—Mr Hamilton—Archb of Canterbury—Ld R. Grosvenor—Sir Thos G.—and minutes. Long walk with F.L.G. Read Parkman—Carmen Sylva—H. of Midlothian—Life of K. Marx (Incredibly dull).[3]

To LORD HARTINGTON, war secretary, 14 January   Chatsworth MSS 340. 1627.
1885.

If Wolseley desires a demonstration to be made at Suakim by a battalion, I for one certainly should not hesitate to accede to his wish. If however he prefers the ships I should much regret to see him over-ruled.[4]

Of all the proposals made during this weary & interminable Egyptian affair, there is none that I have accepted with a better heart than your proposal to send Wolseley to the Soudan: & I look upon accession to his deliberate wishes, in a matter strictly military, as almost a necessary consequence.

Another *dictum* of his, about keeping Suakim for some years, I do not place in the same category: and I hope that if a battalion goes to that place it will be so sent as in no way to fetter the Cabinet with reference to ulterior occupation.

---

[1] J. Rae, 'Lassalle and German socialism', *C.R.*, xxxix. 912 (June 1881).

[2] Add MS 44149, f. 313: Dilke has frightened Baxter about his motion against the increase of the House; this increase, Dilke thought, 'the only really serious difficulty', and hopes to get Northcote's help in carrying it against Beach and Baxter.

[3] Probably G. Gross, *Karl Marx. Eine Studie* (1885).

[4] Hartington replied, 15 January, Add MS 44147, f. 214, that Wolseley 'ceases to press his suggestion'; *Relief of Gordon*, 117.

15. Th.

Ch. 8½ AM. Wrote to Lucy Cavendish—Ld Granville Tel.—Sir W. Harcourt—Ld Wolverton—& minutes. Read Parkman (finished)—Carmen Sylva—Blackie on Land Laws—Heart of Midlothian. Long walk with E. Talbot.

To Sir W. V. HARCOURT, home secretary,　　　　　　　MS Harcourt dep. Adds 10.
15 January 1885.

I have read with lively interest and great satisfaction your letter to the Chancellor,[1] and I thank you for sending it.

My sleep is mostly right again and I am only troubled with disturbances of less consequence, for which I may probably try change of air if I find the French proposals now immediately expected do not require us to meet again in London very soon. Prolonged reflection upon the alternatives *other* than agreement with France does not improve their aspect.

I am reading Blackie on the Crofters, thus far wholly without advantage.[2]

16. Fr.

Ch. 8½ A.M. Wrote to Ld Granville Tel & l.—Ld Stair—Mr Childers—Mayor of Liverpool—Mr Hamilton tel.—and minutes. Read Carmen Sylva (finished)—Heart of Midlothian—Blackie on L. Laws (finished)—Books of Poetry. Walk with E. Talbot.

17. Sat.

Ch. 8½ A.M. Wrote to Ld Granville tel.—E. Hamilton Tel. l.l.l.—Ld R. Grosvenor—and minutes. Walk with Herbert. Worked on books. Read Heart of Midlothian—Ld Selkirk on the Highlands[3]—Burton's Hist. last chapter[4]—Case for Disestablishment.[5]

18. 2 S. Epiph.[6]

Ch. 11 A.M. and 6½ P.M. Wrote to Ld Granville—Archbp of Canterbury—Mr S.C. Hall[7]—Sir Thos G.—E. Hamilton—and minutes. Read Rev. N. Loraine[8]—The Use of Spiritualism—Fragm. Liturgica & Reliquiae—Unigers Glory of the Bible.[9] Walk with M. & WHG.

---

[1] On 'the remarkable diminution of crime'; Add MS 44199, ff. 146-53.
[2] Harcourt replied, 17 January, Add MS 44199, f. 154: Blackie 'is a commentator whom too little learning has made mad', and sent further materials on the crofters.
[3] T. Douglas, Lord Selkirk, *Observations on the present state of the Highlands of Scotland* (1805).
[4] J. H. Burton, *History of Scotland*, 2v. (1853), ch. 24 on cultural decline.
[5] Not found.
[6] Chamberlain, *Political memoir*, 141, notes seeing Gladstone this day to report his talks with O'Shea on the central board; but Chamberlain was not at Hawarden.
[7] Samuel Carter Hall, 1801-89; journalist; had sent his *The use of spiritualism* (1884), read this day; Add MS 44547, f. 165.
[8] Nevison Loraine, vicar of Chiswick and controversialist; had sent his *The sceptic's creed* (1885).
[9] Author's name scrawled; untraced.

19. M.

Ch. 8½ A.M. Wrote to Bp of Lincoln—E.W. Hamilton L. & tel. l.l.—Ld Granville—M.G.—Sir A. Clark—Sir W. Harcourt l.l.—and minutes. Worked on books. Woodcraft with H.J.G. Finished Ld Selkirk on the Highlands—Read Heart of Midlothian—and [blank.]

To Sir W. V. HARCOURT, home secretary,   MS Harcourt dep. 9, ff. 120-31.
19 January 1885.

[First letter:] Certainly you have been most liberal, by the last two posts,[1] in supplying me with diet much less digestible than the round of Derby Beef (which has entered largely into the composition of my outer man.)

My first impulse would be to join the two subjects and say, let the Crofters behave with Temperance, and let the Temperance men have more elbow room.

Seriously: Childers is most anxious that Local Government should be the *pièce de resistance* this year, and if so I presume some temperance provision will come in. (I do not recollect that the Govt. had *supported* the Resolution for Local Option—did not Hartington & I hold off?)[2]

The other question is stiff indeed: so stiff that I will not touch it in a note with a preamble of nonsense. My declining powers of eyesight make it very difficult for me to read MS or small type in these unusually dark days, but those powers could not be better spent than in this case, and I have read with care & painful interest the Lord Advocate's lucid & able letter, and your own in which you supply the most emphatic illustration of the difficulties of the subject when after applying to it all the powers of your mind you still find yourself confronted by difficulties you have not yet been able to solve.

[Second letter:] Let me administer one drop of comfort by reminding you that there is no Queen's Speech in prospect, and that our first weeks of business are under mortgage to Redistribution; which again is flanked or backed by the Plagues of Egypt, and questions raised by the *rabies* for more land oversea. There is therefore, I think, no urgency as to days. Nevertheless, I also believe with you that no time is to be lost, and I answer your closing question by saying that I think the first step to be taken, & at once, is to print and circulate the papers which you have sent me, and which I now return.

You and the Lord Advocate have made very considerable advances in proposing (as I understand) the substantial application of the Irish Land Acts to the Highland parishes. On this application I will only observe that there seems to be a difficulty in limiting it to the case of compulsory leases, while it is admitted that they are inapplicable to the smallest holdings, and that these holdings constitute the great majority. Might it be worth considering whether there might be an option to grant a lease in holdings above some low figure, and that, apart from this option, there should be a fixity or stability of tenure, like that in the Irish Land Act, both above and below that line, for all lettings within the Act.

I will address the chief part of what I have to say to the two unsolved difficulties, though I may too probably leave them as I found them.

First, while it appears that there is happily at this moment an opening for giving 'more

---

[1] See 15 Jan. 85n and, on temperance, Add MS 44199, f. 174, supporting govt. action on local option.
[2] No: he had, unusually and in a change from 1880 and 1881, accepted Lawson's 'abstract resolution' in 1883; *H* 278. 1364.

land' in very many cases, the doubt is raised whether the tenants could stock it, whether the landlords could help them, and whether the State could assist the operation by means of advances, in view of the serious difficulty that liens upon livestock cannot be practically enforced for the benefit of the creditor, by reason of the ignorance of the officers of the Law, where grazings are held in common, which are the animals liable, and of the unwillingness of competent witnesses to inform them.

Is this difficulty quite insurmountable? I can readily perceive that some *primâ facie* available expedients, such as marking, might not meet the case. I also feel that if those, who are to enjoy the grazings, were a promiscuous body, it would be dangerous and harsh to introduce anything like the rule of common responsibility. But they are a people united by tradition, by neighbourhood, often by blood; by agitation, as it may now be added, and always by common interest and by the fact that every one of them would be in the enjoyment of privilege under an exceptional law. Further, the common responsibility would be one from which, if I am right, they might wholly escape by the simple expedient of giving information which they must needs possess. What I point at is, to give the creditor his lien against all, or rather any, of the livestock on the particular pastures, which he might seize, *after* having first applied to the parties to make known to him (either directly or by severing their own) *which* were the animals belonging to the person in default. Viewing the difficulties of the case, I commend this notion for examination. If it will hold water, Parliament might fairly advance on the stock a safe proportion of its value.

Now as to the still more serious difficulty, your prospect of a Land Bill extending beyond the Highland parishes to all Scotland, and, if to all Scotland, then in my judgment to England also.

Now, in my view, a Land Bill for the Crofter Parishes is just as well as politic; but I doubt whether it is just that the need of such a Bill in such Parishes should be made, or allowed to become, the cause of altering the land-system for the rest of the country; where the matter ought to be judged on its own merits, and not to be prejudged by the adoption of certain provisions to meet a case not only actually but historically exceptional. The Highland proprietors of these parishes were the Chiefs of the clans, and the produce which they sought to raise from their lands was not rent but men. From time immemorial these men had been upon the ground with them, recognised in general as kinsmen, and fed from the yield of the land as they were, and in a manner not very different. I do not know what or how old are the earliest documents of title to land in the Highland parishes, or how far back it can be alleged that there was a definite legal proprietorship, and that it was in the chief and in him only; but, in point of moral title to live upon the land, enjoyed uniformly *ab antiquo* I scarcely know how to distinguish between the Chief and his followers. It was might, and not right, which was on his side when, during the halfcentury or more which followed the '45, he gradually found that the rearing of men paid him in a coin no longer current, and took to the rearing of rent instead; backed by the law, which took no cognisance of any right but his. This was but four or five score years ago, and I cannot think that we have here a sufficient prescription against the Legislature to bar it from redressing wrong. Many excellent people may be among those who have bought out the vanished Chiefs, and they may suffer hardship from not having adverted to the specialties of the case, but I take it to be clear that they have acquired the land with its engagements. A vast mass of money-values has been created, in lieu of the flesh and blood values which were formerly in vogue; and the representatives of the old flesh and blood, still largely on the ground, cannot I think be ousted from their title to some legislative consideration.

In passing I may mention one instance of the growth of these values: a Highland property was offered to my Father, within my own recollection, for £10000, the hill part of which has recently let as a deer-forest for £2500 a year.

Now as the form, in which the great grievance was inflicted, was the withdrawal of the common grazings, to convert them into sheep-farms, the question arises whether it may not be possible here to find a test by which to separate broadly, if somewhat roughly, between the Crofter-parishes and the rest of the country.

Some criterion there must evidently be for no one intends to change at this moment the Land Law in general for the sake of the Crofter parishes. It seems on every ground important to find one which will rest on something in the nature of a principle, and not upon a purely conventional line, which it would be hard to draw, and harder to maintain.

It seems to me worth considering whether it might be enacted that the new law should take effect in Parishes where it should have been proved to the satisfaction of some proper judicial authority (specially appointed or otherwise) that within the last hundred years the hill lands of the parish, or some considerable part of them had been held and used in common pasturage? For it is, after all, this historical fact that constitutes the Crofters' title to demand the interference of Parliament. It is not because they are poor, or because there are too many of them, or because they want more land to support their families; but because those whom they represent had rights of which they have been surreptitiously deprived to the injury of the community.

I do not suppose that the *maximum* period of 100 years is too long to allow of credible, though it might be rarely first hand, evidence; and I presume that the Statistical account of Scotland, published early in the period, would afford much aid.

One word on Parliamentary grants, as distinguished from advances. I entirely agree with your objections, so far as Emigration is concerned. As to Telegraphs, if they are really of great importance in connection with the development of Fisheries, I do not think that the administration of a vast spending Department ought to be demoralised by the practice of unprofitable extensions charged upon its ordinary expenditure, and thus unfelt and unwatched by Parliament; but some small sum might be voted experimentally in the ordinary Estimates for Scotland, and entrusted to the Post Office to spend in the best cases, under regulations approved by the Treasury. With regard to fisheries, there might perhaps be grants in aid, with advances rapidly repayable for the remainder of the cost: for, as the improvement of fishing stations would improve rents in the neighbourhood, it seems equitable that the estates of the proprietors should come under a charge.

20. Tu. [London]

9.20–3.10 to Downing Street: Cabinet until 7.15. Wrote to Ld Hartington—Sir W. Harcourt—The Queen—Mrs Th.—C.G.—and minutes. Read Q.R. on Redistribution[1]—Heart of Midlothian. Saw Mr Hamilton—Sir A. Clark—Ld Granville l.l.—Sir W. Harcourt. An anxious evening.

Cabinet. Tues. Jany. 20. 85. 3 PM.[2]
1. Baring may assure the Khedive that we adhere to our pledges to him as heretofore.
2. As to definition of Protectorates, & its obligations.[3] Chancellor proposed that in Africa we sh[ould] undertake to secure ⟨see justice done⟩ having some Govt. in the country, other Powers engaging the same: but not absolutely, reserving a choice to let them exercise reprisals. General conversation. Agreed that we ought in Protectorates to do

[1] [P. Greg], *Q.R.*, clix. 220 (January 1885).
[2] Add MS 44646, f. 10.
[3] Discussion consequent to Selborne's mem. of 3 January, FO 84/1819, on judicial distinction between annexation and protectorate; see F.O.C.P. 5080 and P. Gifford and W. R. Louis, *France and Britain in Africa* (1971), 209ff.

for Foreigners what we do for our own subjects & to be empowered by Parlt. necy[?]. Chancellor to endeavour to draw words. Meantime ask meaning of formula proposed at Berlin.[1]
3. Dissention on the French proposals. See Mem. A marked Secret.

A Secret.[2] That the French proposals form a reasonable basis for friendly communications with a view to a settlement of Egyptian finances. [Yes:] Granville, Derby, Kimberley, Harcourt, WEG., Chancellor, Dilke, Trevelyan; [No:] Hartington, Northbrook, Childers, Carlingford.[3]
1. Recommend that the Commission should be *ad hoc* for inquiry not Govt. or administration.
2. Turkey & Egypt to be represented with the Six Great Powers.
3. We think it wd. undertake its inquiries with greater advantage, if they were not to begin until some time after Egypt had been administered with the benefits derived from the settlement in principle of the financial question.
4. As the Expenditure of Egypt was generally agreed upon in the discussions of the Conference, we assume that the principal object of the proposed inquiry is the present and prospective revenue of that country.
    Under Revenue as meaning the province of the Enquête, we understand that the receipts of Daira Domain & Railways and likewise their administrations be included. (Important savings might probably be effected).
    1. Joint Guarantee of interest recommended on Sinking Fund. Preference loan.
    2. Agreed to on the understanding that it is not to involve interference with the administration of the country.
So far as sacrifices of Bondholders are temporary and conditional, those of England to be placed on a similar footing.
    Canal. We adhere to our proposal & agree with France that it should be promptly agreed to & embodied in a Treaty.

To Sir W. V. HARCOURT, home secretary,   MS Harcourt dep. Adds 10.
20 January 1885. '*Private*'.

I have seen Granville. His idea is that it is best to press Hn 1. to consider & communicate fully before deciding. 2. to state his alternative. He will work through Northbrook.

To LORD HARTINGTON, war secretary,   Chatsworth MSS 340. 1633.
20 January 1885. '*Private*'.

I need not say that I have received your note[4] with much pain. But I am in some degree relieved by observing that you speak not of a conclusion now fully formed but of what is possible or probable. I earnestly hope that amidst the immense difficulties of this case you will consider the matter very fully, will allow me the advantage of talking it over with you, & will let me understand, what was not made clear in the Cabinet today by any counter-proposition, what was the alternative course of action which you would propose.[5]

---

[1] France and Germany argued that 'protectorate' implied jurisdiction; see Gifford and Louis, 209.
[2] Add MS 44646, ff. 14–20.
[3] See Bahlman, *Hamilton*, ii. 776; Chamberlain absent.
[4] Sent this day, Add MS 44147, f. 221; unable to 'accept the decision of the Cabinet' on Egypt.
[5] Hartington replied, 21 January, ibid., f. 224, 'very grateful to you and to the majority of the Cabinet for the concession you have made'.

21. Wed.

Wrote to The Queen—Ld Hartington—C.G.—Mrs Hayward—& minutes. Cabinet 12–2¼. Saw Mr H—Mr S. (adieu)—Ld Granville l.l.—H.N.G.—Sir Thos and Lady G.—Ld R. Grosvenor—Mr Godley. Dined at Mr B. Curries. Read Ed. Rev. on Napoleon's Depredations—Heart of Midlothian. Worked on books.

Cabinet. Wed. Jan. 21. 85. Noon.[1]
1. Promise of jurisdiction in New Guinea Protectorate sufficient to protect Natives against British & Foreigners. Given last August. Sovereignty to be declared in New Guinea within the limits of the British Protectorate. Agreed.
2. Words proposed at Berlin for Africa to be agreed to if preferable words drawn by Ld Chancellor.[2]
3. Niger Company. Query Charter?[3] More information wanted.
4. The Turkish Envoy Hassam?Fehmi.[4] Several topics raised. France has always sought to serve[?] Egypt. Suakim &c.—Turkish occupation for. Honourable ties to Tewfik. Maintenance of Firman. Absence of selfish views and policy of Evacuation.[5]
5. Enquête. Lyons to do what he can *by argument* of the *enquête* but not to threaten.

22. Th. [Hawarden]

Wrote to Ld Granville l.l.—Sir H. Ponsonby—and minutes. 1.10–6.30 back to Hawarden. Saw Mr H.—Sir A. Clark—Mr Childers—Archbishop of Canterbury—Dean of St Paul's—Ld Hartington—Ld Granville. Read Heart of Midlothian.

23. Fr.

Ch. 8½ A.M. Wrote to The Queen l.l.l. . . . and minutes. Woodcraft by the brook. Read H. of Midlothian—Marie Antoinette[6]—Wallace Vaccination Statistics[7]—A Great Delusion.[8]

24.

Ch. 8½ A.M. Wrote to Abp of Canterbury—Dean of St Pauls—Miss Brooks—Mr Trevelyan—E. Hamilton—Bp of Lincoln—and minutes. Worked on books. Walk

[1] Add MS 44646, f. 23. Granville's note: 'Shall I reopen question, or will you?'; Gladstone: 'I incline to think you should first take N. out of the room—& if he agrees get him to speak to H.—before opening it here. I have spoken to Harcourt'; ibid., f. 24.
[2] Selborne's suggestions in F.O.C.P. 5080.
[3] Formal request for a Niger Charter made by Aberdare on 12 February, finally granted on 25 June; *Africa and the Victorians*, 180–3.
[4] Hassan Fehmi in London to negotiate on Turkey's behalf over Egypt; his mission largely unsuccessful; see F.O. summary of it in F.O.C.P. 5126.
[5] Cabinet's views conveyed to Fehmi Pacha by Granville on 26 Jan., emphasising British desire to maintain Egypt's links with the Ottoman Empire; Granville to Wyndham, 26 January 1885, F.O.C.P. 5106, f. 60.
[6] R. C. S. L. Gower, *Last days of Marie Antoinette* (1885).
[7] A. R. Wallace, *Forty years of registration statistics, proving vaccination to be both useless and dangerous* (1885).
[8] Not found; possibly a comment on Wallace.

with C. & woodcraft. Read Lander on Popery[1]—Diderot's Bijoux,[2] an evil book—
Heart of Midlothian.

25. 2 S. Epiph.

Ch mg & evg. Wrote to Mr Trevelyan—Mr Hamilton Tel. l.l.—Archbishop of
Canterbury—Dean of St Pauls—Bp of Lincoln—& minutes. Saw S.E.G. Read
Geo. Cassander[3]—Loraine on Scepticism—and [blank.]

To LORD ROSEBERY, 25 January 1885. '*Most private*'.   N.L.S. 10023, f. 59.

Even now the time has not arrived when I can state to you the Egyptian case as a
matter absolutely out of the way in regard to the proposal I have made to you: owing
entirely to the astonishing delays of the French in *opening* the matter.

Still, it is so far cleared in essential particulars that I deem it possible you may be able to
approach the question at least in order to consider whether there is any other difficulty
besides the Egyptian.

Your Egyptian difficulty had reference I understand to the political not the financial
question, & I certainly expected that France would make some effort to combine the two.
But I can now say that she makes no such attempt & that the two questions stand entirely
apart. Also, a first 'exchange of ideas' has taken place on the finance, & although one can
never be certain where a hitch may be found, according to all appearances the matter will
be amicably settled, as they really have done much towards meeting us, &, especially,
seem to have quite abandoned the idea of international controul, to which we are now as
always opposed.

You will be able to judge how far what I have now said opens the way for your definitive judgment. I hope it may be of use in that respect.[4]

26. M.

Ch. 8½ A.M. Wrote to Ld Granville—Mr Childers—Mr Lefevre—E. Hamilton—
Mrs Heywood—and minutes. Long walk with H. and conversation on family
arrangements. Read 'Merit & Virtue'[5]—Biogr. Articles on Diderot—Chronicle of
the Cid[6]—Clayden on Redistribution[7]—Heart of Midlothian. Saw S.E.G.

27. Tu.

Ch. 8½ A.M. It was at last decided that Annie's[8] death on Sat. should not put off
the marriage from Thursday: such was *their* wish. C. & W. went to London for
the funeral. Wrote to Bp of Exeter—Abp of Canterbury—Rev. Mr Bickersteth l.
& tel.[9]—Ld Acton—Mrs Buckland—Sir R. Lingen—Mr Hamilton tel.—Sir T.G.

[1] G. Lander, *The anatomie of the Romaine clergie* (1623).
[2] D. Diderot, *Les bijoux indiscrets* (new ed., 2v. 1881); see 22 Aug. 66.
[3] Unclear which of his many works.
[4] After consultation with Hartington, Rosebery again declined; but on 8 February, in the face of
the Khartoum crisis, he accepted, becoming lord privy seal and first commissioner of works; Crewe,
Rosebery, i. 216.
[5] Untraced.   [6] Probably the 1883 ed. by H. Morley.
[7] Untraced article by P. W. Clayden, or his *The proposed electoral divisions of London* (1884).
[8] His niece, Sir T. Gladstone's da., died of blood poisoning; see 30 Sept. 50.
[9] Offer to Temple of bishopric of London, to Bickersteth of Lincoln; both accepted; Add MS
44547, f. 170. See 9 Jan. 85.

tel.—and minutes. Read Chronicle of the Cid—Stories of the Temple (a pure libel?)[1]—Heart of Midlothian.

To LORD ACTON, 27 January 1885.[2]   Add MS 44093, f. 254.

We must have not one only, but two new Bishops, for Lincolniensis resigns at once: and, as the name of Dr. Liddon will not appear for either of the sees I am desirous that you should know from me the cause. It is solely due to his own very strong unwillingness, amounting to negation, that I have not submitted his name to the Queen, backed by *high* ecclesiastical authority. So that he has really received a great recognition, and this is an important matter.

In his place I have recommended, & the Queen accepts Dr. King, an admirable man, who has been for 12 or 14 years Professor of Pastoral Theology in Oxford, and one of the mainstays of devout life in the University.

I understand that, in that much loved place (I am an old idolater of Oxford) there is a current rather steadily setting in the direction of the highest religious interests. Of the five open fellowships last taken by a wide competition, four are filled by men who seek holy orders.

Mr. Gore, head of the Pusey Institute, a man of very high promise, has already a society of twenty Tutors formed for Theological study under or with him.

I really doubt (but this may be extravagant) whether there is any single place in Christendom which might—if any single place could be so honoured—be more truly termed its heart, than Oxford.

Do you despise me if I say that (having read a limited portion) I am much disappointed in Reuss's *Geschichte*.[3] I always thought Pusey on Daniel the worst written book I knew, till I tried to read this. But I think it wordy, oracular, dogmatic to a degree, and searching for his *arguments* amidst the ocean of words is the old way of seeking a needle in a bundle of hay.

In despair I turned to Reusch, *Bibel und Natur*,[4] and that, so far as I have gone, I like extremely. The wife of one of my Lyttelton nephews has almost finished a translation of it.

I have just written to Bishop Temple, proposing to him the See of London.

There is every likelihood of a satisfactory arrangement, so far as France is concerned, as to Egyptian finance.

Wolseley is not at present anxious as to the Stewart column; and we have much faith in him.

Moderate measures, change of air, and partial remission of business, have much mended me, thank God, and I may now hope to go on until the early date when—you and I are to quarrel!

To Sir R. R. W. LINGEN, permanent secretary to the   Add MS 44546, f. 170.
treasury, 27 January 1885.

The plan[5] you have sent me through Hamilton for an alteration in our administrative arrangements in relation to Education, is indeed one of great interest and importance,

---

[1] Perhaps C. Foster, *The story of the bible* (1885).

[2] Holograph; in Figgis and Laurence, i. 196 with Acton's reply from Cannes on Oxford, theology and the importance of Gladstone's retaining office to fight the next election. See 11 Feb. 85.

[3] By E. W. Reuss (1881).

[4] By F. H. Reusch (1862), tr. in 2v. (1886) by K. Lyttelton (Gladstone's relative).

[5] Letter and printed mem., 'Public education and local government', 19 January, Add MS 44489, f. 81. Lingen proposed a block grant administered through county boards; for his mem. and Gladstone's replies see G. Sutherland, *Policy-making in elementary education 1870–1895* (1973), 243–5.

and I hardly feel competent at this stage to pass a positive judgment upon it. I am strongly prepossessed however in favour of its decentralising character. There are indeed some other changes, which I cannot help desiring, in the same direction.

A formidable question arises, whether these local bodies would command the confidence of voluntary school managers, to whom they would stand in a somewhat stepmother like relation.

My own leaning is in favour of a greater reliance on *results*, and therewith of a discharge from part, perhaps from a great part, of the responsibility now assumed for the means and instruments of attaining them. Of course if this could be done it would so far tend to diminish the jealousy of the *voluntarians.*

As regards union of the central function with those of the Local Government Board, it certainly has some great recommendation, and would uplift by a natural means the dignity of the central office, which there is now a very strong disposition to uplift *quocunque modo.*

As regards this part of the case, and the relation of your plan to the report of the recent Committee,[1] I presume you will take an early opportunity of obtaining the opinion of Mr. Childers.

[P.S.] It would not be right in me to omit saying that I see in this paper another strong proof of your and of Sir R. Welby's unsleeping vigilance for the public interests.

28. Wed. [Norris Green]

Ch. 8½ A.M. Wrote to Chester Pmaster Tel.—Bp of Gloucester—Mr Carlisle[2]—Dean of St Paul's—Ld Derby—Mr Hamilton—Rev. Dr. King[3]—Sir H. Ponsonby. Cutting down alders. Read Carnegies (bold) Address[4]—H. of Midlothian (finished)—Chronicle of the Cid. Worked on books & papers. Off at 3.20 to Norris Green.[5]

To LORD DERBY, colonial secretary, 28 January 1885.   Add MS 44547, f. 171.

I return Mr. Froude's interesting letter[6] with many thanks. It certainly causes me misgivings when my (our) countrymen, who are much too apt to lump all grievances together, affect to make light of the Dutch element at the Cape & of the tenacity of its resisting power. I cannot but wish that they had experience of Dutch blood & fibre in the House of Commons: such as it has been or is, even when diluted, in G. Bentinck, Bishop Bentinck, & Beresford Hope.

I reported to Childers, in view of the estimates, the only very satisfactory point namely that concurrence in the opinion that Warren may get through without fighting.

29. Th.

Wrote to Mr Hamilton Tel. l.l.—Mr Chamberlain Tel.—Sir Thos G. l. & tel.—Mr Toole—Mr Childers—Ld Granville—Ld Spencer—Rev. Mr B. (Tel)—and

---

[1] Childers' cttee.; see to Carlingford, 16 Sept. 84.

[2] Henry E. Carlisle, ed., with much fuss, *A selection from the correspondence of A. Hayward* (1886); this letter, on the volume, Add MS 44489, f. 103.

[3] Offer of bishopric of Lincoln; accepted; Add MS 44547, f. 171.

[4] One of A. Carnegie's many addresses to college students.

[5] J. P. Heywood's house near Liverpool.

[6] Froude was briefly in Cape Town in December 1884; see W. H. Dunn, *J. A. Froude* (1963), ii. 518. This letter not found, forwarded by Derby on 25 January, Add MS 44142, f. 119: 'He [Froude] was always a friend to the Boers, but what he says is interesting.'

minutes. At Croxteth. Walk with Ld Sefton. At 11¼ we drove in to the marriage,[1] then to Abercromby Square where we saw the very pleasing family and the presents. It was a cheerful & happy scene, in touching contrast with the funeral in London yesterday.

To H. C. E. CHILDERS, chancellor of the exchequer,   Add MS 44547, f. 171.
29 January 1885.

What I thought was that if Navy Estimates were accepted on 13th & circulated on 20th no inconvenience would arise from having the Army a day or two later. The figure for that Department[2] is indeed startling but (among other things) it does not seem unreasonable to hope that a shorter time than 6 months after April 1 may probably suffice to bring the troops home from the Soudan.

Your Uncle has most courteously declined [the living of] Rendlesham.

To LORD SPENCER, Viceroy of Ireland, 29 January 1885.[3]   Althorp MSS K8.

I have read your interesting and important letter,[4] but for the moment my reply to it will be brief. For I do not think the time has come when it or its subjects rather can be with advantage submitted to the Cabinet. At the same time I would strongly advise that you should digest your plan of Local Government for Ireland, and even prepare the Bill.

Our position is peculiar. Our obligations with regard to the Redistribution Bill are of an order far higher than those which usually attach even to legislative measures of very great importance. It is *almost* a certainty that the bare six weeks which have to elapse between the 19th inst. and the Easter holidays will be occupied with business of an unavoidable character, as to which we shall have no option, under the following heads
1. Redistribution
2. Egyptian Finance and Egypt
3. Estimates.
These subjects may indeed take us beyond Easter.

30. Fr. [*Holker Hall*]

Wrote to Abp of York—Mr Hamilton l. & Tel.—Sir R.R. Lingen—Sir H. Ponsonby—and minutes. Read Chronicle of the Cid—(Began) Tales of a Grandfather[5]—Mozley's Letters. Saw Sir J. Lumsden—Ld Hartington. 1¼-5. To Holker.[6] Found the Duke wonderfully well: kind as ever.

To Sir R. R. W. LINGEN, permanent secretary to the   Add MS 44547, f. 172.
treasury, 30 January 1885.[7]

If in one point the Prime Minister is the Atlas (whom agreeing with your criticism on the common mode of representation, I am used to consider as the 'Pole'), in another, as I

---

[1] Of his son Stephen to Annie Wilson; see 20 Dec. 84.
[2] £19,355,000 as opposed to original estimate of £15,930,000; Add MS 44132, f. 34.
[3] In *Spencer*, i. 293.
[4] Of 26 January, Add MS 44312, f. 1, on prospective Irish legislation: need to renew 1882 Crimes Act; local govt. reform 'essential'; success might satisfy 'moderate Home Rulers', failure would create 'immense difficulty in resisting a cry for something like Repeal of the Union'.
[5] By Scott (1827-9); Scottish history.
[6] The Duke of Devonshire's house by Cartmel, Lancashire.
[7] See 27 Jan. 85.

well know, he is the 'odd man' of the Government. But even as Atlas he would not be strong enough to start a scheme like yours effectually, except by concert & consultation. I like the report of the Education Committee no better than you do. One of the considerations which would incline me to your plan is that it would qualify, I think, the mischievous tendencies of that Report, which, evil as it is, is a rather commanding fact. As Chairman of that Committee, Mr. Childers would speak with a good deal of authority, and as C[hancellor] of E[xchequer] he would I think have favourable predisposition. I fear however that this year would afford no room for dealing with a great contentious question of Educational machinery & that any such question would have to stand on the unmeasured list of arrears till the House of Commons shall be pleased to adopt some practical method of self-adjustment to enable it to cope with its enormous business. You do not as I understand you think the time has come for sending your paper to C. of E. I shall *inact* accordingly.

Sat. 31.

Wrote to Ld Granville l.l.l.—Mr Chamberlain l.l.—Mr Hamilton—and minutes. Drive & walk with Lucy. Read Chronicle (finished)—Mozley, and Tales. Conversation with Hartington.

To J. CHAMBERLAIN, president of the board of   Chamberlain MSS 5/34/33.
trade, 31 January 1885.

I send you herewith a letter received by R. Grosvenor from Foljambe[1] when you were ill, on which I made a minute of reply. It referred to a then recent speech of yours[2] and inquired if you had expounded the sentiments of the Cabinet. Foljambe, I believe, is thought by some to be 'weak-kneed'; but I am bound to say that similar representations have reached me from Liberals who have never been subjected to that imputation.

You were absent during the last Cabinets from a painful cause now, I am glad to know, no longer existing; or it would perhaps have been convenient to have had some conversation on this subject.

It rarely happens, even in less anxious and busy times, that members of the Cabinet find themselves tempted to go so far afield into political questions not proximate, as your abundant store of energy and vigorous period of life have enabled and induced you to do.

You would not be insensible to the risk that other members of the Cabinet, exercising an abstract right in an opposite direction, might feel that silence would be interpreted as consent, and might deliver some opinions contradictory to yours: or again that, as will probably occur, there should be comment in Parliament on the subject, such as to require notice. The consequence of such divarications [*sic*] is discredit *pro tanto* to the Government, & the weakness which ought to wait upon discredit.

I would have sent you this sooner, had I been aware that the Birmingham meeting was at hand. Many thanks for your reference to Parnell.[3]

Copy of Minute of Mr Gladstone on Mr Foljambe's letter of 15 Jan. 1885:[4] 'They (Mr Chamberlain's statements) are statements made on individual responsibility on matters entirely

---

[1] See 21 June 72; described himself in *Dod* as 'attached to the old Whig principles'.
[2] Chamberlain opened his series of radical campaign speeches on 5 January; see Garvin, i. 548–58.
[3] Chamberlain replied, after consulting Dilke, hinting at resignation; Garvin, i. 559.
[4] In E. W. Hamilton's hand.

outside the actions of the Govt., and having no relation to any matter which it has in hand or in view.

'Mr Foljambe knows well the spirit and language which has marked all declarations made on behalf of the Government, and in these there is no sort of change.

'Rather severe illness of Mr Chamberlain has I think prevented communication with his colleagues since the speech, which might otherwise have taken place.

'All this for Lord R.G. to use at his discretion.' Jan. 23.

Feb. One. 85. Septa S.

Cartmel Ch 10½ AM. & H.C. A noble fabric: & full church. Flukeborough [*sc.* Flookburgh] Ch. aft. Wrote to Mr Hamilton Tel.—and W.H. Gladstone Tel. Walk & conversation with the Duke. Read Bibel und Natur[1]—Contemp. Rev. on Apologetic and on Autom. Writing[2]—Pascal Pensées (1830 Ed).

Th[eology]. The complaint of Mr Fairbairn is[3] that Newman placed himself in sheer antagonism to the spirit of the age, conceived by him under the name and form of Liberalism, and evoked in order to resist and repel it the idea of a Church 'divine and infallible' which was to join battle with it, and in celestial strength to put it down. This Church was in the first stage of his action the Anglican, afterwards the Roman, but the essential conception was the same, and it had the same work to do.

Substantially I suppose this to be a true conception and if it be so the presentation of it may help to show how widely different from Newman's is the work and aim[?] of many, who have so many points of material contact with him that they may seem to be engaged in one & the same undertaking. He sees before him a monster of all-Evil, and he thinks there exists only waiting to be evoked & set in action a Power of all good. In thus bringing the Church into the fight, he reformed as he went along the religion of his country, regenerating its worship, transforming its clergy, and filling up many a gap which time and conflict had wrought in its current and popular theology. But these are objects perfectly different from what he is made out to have had in view. They do not presuppose a combat of life and death with Liberalism, or a Church which is to assume a supreme rule over the minds and lives of men, and to hem their mental and moral liberty into a corner of the space wherein they walk. The re-establishment of the historical Church as a working conception apart from insularity and State-machinery undoubtedly supplies a powerful factor in life and its works, but it introduces a tempered not a despotic authority, & while anchoring in all the ages is essentially in harmony with the[4] liberty which has been the strength & glory of this land.[5]

2. *M. Purification.*

Wrote to Rev. Mr Bickersteth—Mr Hamilton Tel. 1.1.—Mr Childers 1.1.—Sir R. Lingen—Rev. E. Talbot—Dean of Ch.Ch.—Ld R. Grosvenor—Ld Crewe—Watson & Smith—and minutes. Drive, & walk with Lucy. Long *sederunt* with

---

[1] See 27 Jan. 85.

[2] A. M. Fairbairn, 'Catholicism and apologetics', F. W. H. Myers, 'Automatic writing', *C.R.*, xlvii. 164, 233 (February 1885).

[3] Gladstone's note: 'Contemp. Rev. Feb. 1885 pp. 182-4'; see this day's entry. For the congregationalist A. M. Fairbairn, see 16 Dec. 79.

[4] Adjective here illegible.

[5] Holograph dated 1 February 1885; Add MS 44769, f. 13.

Hartington. Read Tales of Grandfather—Nineteenth Cent. on Federation[1]—&
on [blank.]—Contemp. on Crofter Problem.[2] Drive. Walk with Lucy.

To H. C. E. CHILDERS, chancellor of the   Add MSS 44132, f. 50, 44547, f. 173.
exchequer, 2 February 1885.

[First letter:]   The two figures you have sent me for the services are somewhat appal-
ling,[3] and they suggest to me the question whether even after some docking they would
not require in the Ways & Means for 1885-6 indirect as well as direct taxation to be
touched. Such a proceeding, esp. in the last year of a Parlt., would raise a political question of the first order.

As far as you can see, is this so or not?

If it is, it drives me upon saying why should we not proceed first & at once with our
work on Supplemental Estimates, & *postpone for a time fixing the Estimates for the coming year.*

We should thus probably get more light as to the war demands in Soudan & S. Africa.

If matters went well, the strain on you would be relaxed—if they went ill, the case in
Parlt. for high estimates would at any rate be improved. Pray consider this & give me all
the light you can upon it. Meantime I will do nothing about Cabinet for 9th.

[Second letter:]   I think the proposal in your letter[4] on Egyptian Finance involves a deep
question of policy with which only the Cabinet is competent to deal. It establishes a
single controul in a very stringent form: and I should suppose that the announcement of
it at this moment would blow up the accord with France. Neither do I agree in the charge
of vacillation & evasion against our policy: and I believe nothing but the support of the
Powers, especially of France, would make it possible to bring about the adjustments of
taxation which you & I both desire. I am all for strengthening the Treasury Department in
the Egyptian Government. Beyond that, a very large question would arise. Perhaps you
would make your arrangement temporary & limited, & I can conceive that possibly this
might be agreed to or not resented abroad, but at every step 'incedis per ignes Suppositos
cineri doloso'.[5]

3. *Tu.*

Wrote to The Queen—Prince of Wales—Dean of St Pauls—Sir C. Dilke—Sir H
Ponsonby—Ld Granville l. & tel.—Ld R. Grosvenor—Mr Childers—Mr Hamilton—& minutes. Drove to Mr Hibbert's[6] & saw him. Conferences with Ld H. & a
heavy bag. Whist in evg—as for some nights past. Conversation with Ld H.
Read Brown's Grypha[7]—Tales of a Grandfather.

[1] *N.C.*, xvii. 201 (February 1885).
[2] *C.R.*, xlvii. 185 (February 1885).
[3] For army, see 29 Jan. 85n.; Childers reported an increase of £1,750,000 over the original navy
estimates; Add MS 44132, f. 38.
[4] Of 30 January, again proposing 'an English Minister of Finance' in Cairo, in *Childers*, ii. 213;
Childers responded to Gladstone on 3 February that the Minister would be for the occupation only.
[5] Horace, *Odes* 2. 1. 7-8: you are walking on treacherous ashes below which the fires still burn.
[6] J. T. Hibbert, then secretary to the treasury; at Hampsfield, Grange-over-Sands.
[7] By R. Brown, see 23 Oct. 81; Gladstone was interested in the unicorn to be restored on the
Mercat Cross in Edinburgh; see R. Brown, *Mr Gladstone as I knew him* (1902), 28.

4. Wed.

Wrote to Ld Spencer—Archbishop of York—Ld Granville Tel.—Mr Childers—Ld Granville l.—Rev. Dr. King—Rev. Dr. Butler—Sir C Dilke—Ld Rosebery—E. Hamilton l. & tel. l.l.l.—and minutes. Read Tales of a Grandfather—Bryce on Theodora—J. MacCarthy on Dublin Castle[1]—Mozley's Letters. Walk with the Duke. Whist in evg.

To LORD ROSEBERY, 4 February 1885.   N.L.S. 10023, f. 63.

The decision which you virtually announce in your letter of the 1st[2] is I am sure matter of sincere & deep regret on both sides. I think it easy to show that a guarantee of loan does not entail a right of controul: I do not know a single instance of it, and in the case of Turkey the guarantee of 1855 was followed by a solemn disclaimer of the right of interference in the Treaty of 1856. Further as to the financial situation I can only say that we *seem* very near a settlement whereas in November we were obviously very far from it. But I cannot deny that the political situation is unchanged: and that while the Cabinet is *free*, it has never abandoned the policy of withdrawal. Its 'constructive work' is I think accomplished, except as to defensive provisions to take the place of the occupying army. But your view of our position & our 'supremacy' in Egypt is one of which I admit (so far as I understand it) that you could not rely on its adoption by the Cabinet. And unfortunately, as the office of works has now been kept long open, & the time has arrived for deciding on its plans for the year, I ought at once to take measures for filling it up.

Political life is full of these sad occasions on which duty & feeling come into apparent conflict. I am sure however that on this occasion there will be not only a reciprocal confidence in motives of action but likewise the firmest confidence that our personal relations cannot be shaken but will remain free & warm as heretofore.

5. Th. [*London*]

Wrote to The Queen—Mr Hamilton Tel. l.l.l.—Mr Chamberlain—Walter Phillimore Tel.—and minutes.

[3]After 11 AM I heard the sad news of the fall or betrayal of Khartoum:[4] H. & I, with C. went off by the first train & reached D. St soon after 8.15. The circumstances are sad & trying: it is one of the least points about them, that they may put an end to this Govt.

Saw Ld Granville. Read Tales of a Grandfather—Mozley's Letters. Found myself compelled to write a long letter to the Queen.[5]

---

[1] Both in *C.R.*, xlvii. 153, 266 (February 1885).

[2] See 25 Jan. 85n.

[3] Facsimile starts here, until 9 Feb., in Masterman, 305.

[4] On 26 January; Wolseley heard on 4 February; for his wire see 6 Feb. 85n.; it was not immediately clear that Gordon was dead; Wolseley noted in his diary: 'I earnestly pray he [Gordon] may have been killed.... If anything can kill old Gladstone this news ought to ...' (*Relief of Gordon*, 134-6).

[5] On the Queen's rebuke, telegraphed '*en clair*', and quickly made public, Guedalla, *Q*, ii. 326; she also wired Hartington and Granville '*en clair*' (*L.Q.V.*, 2nd series, iii. 597).

To J. CHAMBERLAIN, president of the board of   Chamberlain MSS 5/34/34.
trade, 5 February 1885.

I think that after all which has passed a conversation in the Cabinet, when an opportunity offers, will be the best means of enabling you to estimate your personal situation:
the matter being one of common interest to all our colleagues. But that need not prevent
me individually from stating what occurs to me upon it, and my first duty is to thank you
for the kind and friendly terms towards myself, in which you write.

I understand you to hold that as your opinions and those of Dilke are but partially
represented, and sometimes even contravened, by the action of the Government, you
conceive that you may properly seek some compensation for sacrifices thus made, or
defend yourself against misapprehension thus brought about, by giving your own unrestrained opinions on questions of the future.

I do not go so far as to meet this proposition, or rather this opinion (which I have
endeavoured to put in general terms only) by an absolute assertion of its opposite but I
think it cannot safely be admitted as a practical guide.

Every Liberal Government from & since that of Lord Aberdeen has had one or more
Radical members on it, who have sat as representative men. But these gentlemen, Molesworth, Gibson, Bright, Stansfield [*sic*], have not found it necessary to sustain their
character as ministers, as a general rule (and the exceptions have I think been very rare),
by drawing on the future and opening up questions not in immediate reach with a view to
sustaining faith out of doors in the integrity of their principles.

Further, a liberty of this kind cannot be confined to any particular Minister or section.
And if there is a title for those who wish to pass beyond the line of action marked by the
Government to deliver strong popular enunciations of these extraneous matters, those,
on the other hand, who have strained themselves to keep up with the Government must
be equally free to seek a similar compensation. There would thus be opened a wide field
of contradictions, required by no practical purpose, and tending to trouble overburdened
men with endless controversies, and to estrange from them that confidence without
which they cannot carry on their work. It is certainly true that from time to time a
minister may on some question lying nearer hand embarrass his colleagues by some
premature or one-sided declaration of opinion. More or less of inconvenience always
follows. But the discussion of these proximate questions cannot always be avoided, and
an occasional mistake in the manner of doing it is not quite the same thing as the opening
of new chapters of contested matter with regard to which no practical issue is depending.

These are general considerations to which I am sure you will allow such weight as
they deserve. With respect to the present case, I feel individually a great anxiety that
nothing should be done to disturb in any way our united action at the present moment,
for reasons over and above those which would always prompt and warrant such a feeling. We have placed ourselves in a very peculiar position in respect to the Seats Bill,
and our covenant to try our best towards passing it imposes on us peculiar obligations,
now that its provisions have been made the subject of an honourable accord. Differences may at any time be forced upon the members of a Cabinet, but I should be
deeply grieved if anything like a self-sought cause of difference were now to cause any
difficulties among us. It is a very high duty at the moment to complete that important
work of domestic [reform] in which we have advanced far and prosperously, and to
which, by moderation and by loyal adhesion I am bound to add that you and Dilke
have so largely contributed.[1]

---

[1] Chamberlain replied, 7 February, Add MS 44126, f. 65 and Garvin, i. 563, retreating but
lengthily reaffirming the radical position.

6. Fr.

Wrote to Ld Spencer—Lady Phillimore—The Queen—Mr Baxter—W.H.G.—and minutes. Cabinet 11–2. Our discussions were difficult but harmonious. Saw Sir H. Ponsonby—Mr H—Mr Childers with whom I discussed the whole finance—Ld Granville. Walk with C. Read Mozley's Letters—Tales of a Grandfather.

Cabinet. Friday Feb. 6. 1885. 11 AM.[1]
1. Wolseley's telegram announcing fall of Khartoum.[2] Ld H[artington] submitted draft telegram adopted with some modifications (WEG & Gr wished it to indicate[?] negotiation but it was thought that W[olseley] would do this himself).[3]
2. Paragraph considered for public announcement: also for the Khedive.
3. Conversation on Fehmi's mission.

7. Sat.

Wrote to Ld Hartington—The Queen—Ld Spencer Tel.—and minutes. Cabinet 12–3½. Saw Ld Granville—Mr H.—Ld Dalhousie—and Lady Holker who spoke to me of her testamentary dispositons & of Mr D.[4] Read Mozley's Letters—Tales of a Grandfather. Dined at Ld Dalhousie's.

Cabinet. Sat. Feb. 7. 1885. Noon.[5]
1. Proposal of Trustees of [British] Museum to open Nat. Hist. [Museum] on Sunday Est. £300.[6]
2. Wolseley's answer considered and telegraph in reply agreed to.[7]
3. Visit of Prince of Wales to Ireland. Paragraph agreed to.[8]
4. Warings proposal to deal with the Egyptian Bondholders. Cabinet not disposed to take any initiative in the matter.[9]
5. Conversation on Indian Troops [for the Sudan]. Cabinet disinclined.
6. German Land Claims in Fiji. Premature letter stating Cabinet had decided to fix any charge arising upon the Consolidated Fund. Statement to be withdrawn.[10]

[1] Add MS 44646, f. 28.
[2] Wolseley to Hartington, from Korti, 4 February, 9.10 P.M.: 'News in this moment from Gubat: Khartoum is reported to have fallen but commanding officer there gives no details.... Nothing is known of Gordon's fate; most probably a prisoner. Correspondent says place was delivered to Mahdi by treachery'; F.O.C.P. 5106, f. 101; further wire, Wolseley to Baring, 5 Feb., confirming fall of Khartoum; fate of Gordon still uncertain; in *T.T.* 6 February 1885, 5e.
[3] Final version in *L.Q.V.*, 2nd series, iii. 602: objectives: safety of Gordon if still alive; check advance of Mahdi in undisturbed districts. For 'negotiation' see 7 Feb. 85n.
[4] Mary Lucia, widow of Sir J. Holker, one of Disraeli's law officers.
[5] Add MS 44646, f. 29.
[6] No govt. contribution until the new Parliament; CAB 41/19/6.
[7] Wolseley to inform cabinet immediately of any 'proposals' from the Mahdi; Add MS 44646, f. 46; also 'Your military policy is to be based on the necessity ... that the power of the Mahdi at Khartoum must be overthrown'; Wolseley given discretion over 'military matters' needed and as to advance this season or next; asked if further troops needed and whether Osman Digna to be attacked immediately (Hartington to Wolseley, 7 Feb., F.O.C.P. 5106, f. 114).
[8] On his protection there *via* secret service grant. Add MS 44646, f. 30.
[9] Waring Bros. proposed to administer Egyptian railways etc. if backed by a £26 millions British govt. loan; Childers was interested, Northbrook opposed; Northbrook MSS 6. 1, f. 329 and 13. 20.
[10] Colonial office to treasury, 5 Nov. 1884, and other papers in PRO FO 64/1109.

To LORD HARTINGTON, war secretary, 7 February　　　Chatsworth MSS 340. 1655.
1885.

I do not feel quite sure that in the Telegram of yesterday we have given a sufficiently marked place to the safety of Gordon as the one object with which at the present moment hardly any other can stand on a footing of equality.

It seems little probable that he can be holding out, as one rumour goes, in some portion of Khartoum, for the time of rejoicing could then scarcely have arrived. But *if* he were it might weigh greatly upon the question whether Wolseley ought to make an advance.

Please to turn this over in your mind.

18. [sc. *8*] *Sexa S.*

Ch. Royal noon. Westmr Abbey (2½ h) aft. Wrote to Ld Rosebery—Rev. Dr. King. Saw Mr H.—Archbishop of Canterbury—Dean of Westminster—Mr B. Currie. We dined with Mr B.C. Read Mozley's Letters—Xmas at Greycastle[1]— Acct of Marylebone Church—Fremantle's B. Lectures.[2]

To LORD ROSEBERY, 8 February 1885.　　　　　　　N.L.S. 10023, f. 65.

I have just received your letter[3] and I highly appreciate the patriotic spirit in which it is written.

I believe that the resolutions at which the Cabinet has arrived under the painful circumstances recently made known are such as you would thoroughly approve.

When I said that our constructive work in Egypt was so advanced, I did not mean that I thought the time was close at hand when the question of evacuation would come up.

The present juncture overshadows all the future: and you would certainly form your own ultimate conclusions on our position in Egypt proper with much greater advantage from within the Cabinet than from beyond its precinct.

I therefore from my point of view do not see reason for throwing any difficulty in your way, and as the office is happily still open (which tomorrow in all likelihood it would have ceased to be) I will with your permission submit your name to the Queen.

I presume that the secondary arrangement for the discharge of business in the House of Commons will hold good, as you expressed I think a favourable opinion of it on its merits. Unless you telegraph to me to hold my hand I will proceed not later than tomorrow morning.

9. M.

Wrote to W.H.G.—Herbert J.G. Tel.—The Queen l.l.l.—& minutes. Cabinet 12–3½. We dined with Mrs Birks. Saw Mr H.—Ld RG—Ld Granville—Mr Childers. Directed a rather curt answer to Sir H.P. = Queen on the Telegram *en clair.*[4] Read Mozley's Letters—Tales of a Grandfather—F. Paget on [blank.]

This day my dear loyal excellent friend Sir R. Phillimore was laid in his grave at Shiplake. It was to my great grief that I did not faithfully perform for him, who was ever faithful, the last office of accompanying him.

---

[1] Untraced.

[2] W. H. Fremantle, *The world as the subject of redemption* (1885).

[3] Offering himself for office as a result 'less of policy than of patriotism', though still with reservations about Egypt; Add MS 44288, f. 221.

[4] Hamilton's sharp note to Ponsonby, 8 February, *L.Q.V.*, 2nd series, iii. 605. See 5 Feb. 85n.

Cabinet. Monday Feb. 9. 85. 2 PM[1]

1. Ld Rosebery to be recommended for Cabinet, Works, & P. Seal. Lefevre for Cabinet.
✔ 2. On the acceptance of Italian aid. Disapproved as tending to impair moral effect & exhibit weakness. Must bear[?] on our own shoulders alone satisfaction to any military exigencies arising out of Fall of Khartoum. Case of Canada Volunteers (if,) different.
✔ 3. Guarantee of Egyptian Loan. Opinion appeared to be that a tripartite Guarantee by Engl. France & Italy wd. be admissible. Conversation on communication.
✔ 4. Indian Troops: say 3000 as asked by Wolseley. Agree. Great Britain to pay any additional charge entailed on India by sending it.
✔ 5. Hartington stated the British force to be sent to Suakim. To make up a total of 6900 from home: 3 Batt. Guards, 2 Line, 4 Squadrons Cavalry.
✔ 6. Gen. Greaves to command? Ask whether W[olseley] prefers him or Alison.[2]
✔ 7. Naval & Military Estimates. Estimates for actual loan. Expenditure now contemplated to be made at once & presented.
   Increase 1½ₘ Navy, 1¼ₘ Army.
✔ 8. Part of the reserves to be called out.

10. Tu.

Wrote to Ld Rosebery—Ld Hartington l.l.—Mr Lefevre—& minutes. 12–1. Saw Fehmi and Musurus Pachas. 1–1.45. ditto Hobart Pacha.[3] A singular specimen of the 'British Tar'. Saw Mr H.—Mrs Bolton at Dr Simons. Short sitting to Millais. Read Mozley—Life of Geo. Elliot.[4] We dined with the Dalhousies, & I accompanied them to see 'The Candidate':[5] capitally acted.

Note for conversation with Musurus & Fehmi Pachas.[6]

Original policy: evacuation of the Soudan by Egypt, and its restoration to freedom. Approved by Khedive & Egyptian Govt. Has undergone no change. But events have occurred to prevent its immediate execution.

Up to Feby. 3, sanguine hope that the military problem was near its solution and that little wd. remain to be done.

News of Feb. 4 entailed new duties & decisions. The nature of the military object was changed. The recent decisions are military decisions.

A. It became necessary for General to know whether he was or was not to proceed on intention of ours to overthrow the Mahdi's power at Khartoum—by an expedition in the next cold season—or not—as his movements must be governed by this knowledge.

B. We decided in the affirmative. *Consequences*, required by the General from us 1. Action agst. Osman Digna, required to open the road to Berber. 2. Decision to commence construction of a railway. 3. Intention, on the present state of the facts, to

[1] Add MS 44646, f. 31.
[2] Wolseley thought 'Graham & Greaves would be best'; *Relief of Gordon*, 141.
[3] Acting in London for the Sultan; see F.O.C.P. 5106, f. 116.
[4] *George Eliot's life as related in her letters and journals*, ed. J. W. Cross, 3v. (1885).
[5] This visit to the Criterion theatre caused much offence, newspapers next day confirming, though without definite proof, Gordon's death.
[6] Holograph dated 10 February 1885; Add MS 44769, f. 18. Further note in French at ibid., f. 15.

overthrow the power of the Mahdi at Khartoum. If this could not be done now of which he must judge then after the hot season. Our impression is that Lord Wolseley may postpone it. All of which will of course be matter for the consideration of Parlt.

Accommodation with the Mahdi. 1. Public & authentic information has been conveyed to him. 2. The present situation does not allow of our making overtures with prospect of advantage. 3. Instruction given that any communication from him is to be sent home immediately for consideration.

11. Wed.

Wrote to The Queen—Ld Hartington—Ld Granville—Watson & Smith—Ld Acton—Archbishop of Canterbury—and minutes. Cabinet 11-12½. Saw Mr H.— Mr Lefevre—Ld Granville—Mr Childers—Ld R. Grosvenor—Att. General. Dined with the Att. General at Brooks's.[1] Read Life of G. Eliot—Tales of a Grandfather—Mozley's Letters.

Cabinet. Wed. Feb. 11. 1885. 11 AM.[2]

Command of Suakim expedition. Telegrams. Graham[3] & Greaves adopted.

    For further consulting Wolseley: Gladstone, Granville, Derby, Childers.

    Against: Hartington, + Harcourt, ≠ Kimberley, Northbrook, Dilke.

    + in deference to Hartington. ≠ rather than delay 12 hours.

WEG said I think we are departing from a general principle of importance, but I am overruled and the matter is settled.

To LORD ACTON, 11 February 1885.[4]   Add MS 44093, f. 259.

Since I received your kind letter,[5] a heavy blow has fallen upon us in the capture of Khartoum, apparently by betrayal from within. The further announcement of the death of Gordon, in papers of today, has not up to this time been officially confirmed. The calamity is, in any case, great. As in the case of Hicks our pacific policy was wholly thwarted, so now our confident hope of summary & conclusive action followed by prompt withdrawal has been dashed, and one of those crises created in which, whatever a Cabinet does, it can hardly be sure of doing right.

Now I turn to the polemical part of your letter. Your argument against letting the outworn hack go to grass depends wholly on a certain proposition, namely this that there is about to be a crisis in the history of the Constitution, growing out of the extension of the franchise, and that it is my duty to do what I can in aiding to steer the ship through the boiling waters of this crisis. My answer is simple. There is no crisis at all in view. There is a process of slow modification and development mainly in directions which I view with misgiving. 'Tory democracy' the favourite idea on that side is no more like the Conservative party in which I was bred, than it is like Liberalism. In fact less. It is demagoguism, only a demagoguism not ennobled by love and appreciation of liberty, ⟨which ennobles it⟩; but applied in the worst way, to put down the pacific, law-respecting, economic elements which ennobled the old Conservatism; living upon the fomentation of angry passions, and still in secret as obstinately attached as ever to the evil principle of class-

---

[1] See Bahlman, *Hamilton*, ii. 794.
[2] Add MS 44646, f. 35.
[3] To the chief command of the Suakim expedition, with Greaves as chief of staff.
[4] Holograph copy.
[5] See 27 Jan. 85.

interest. The Liberalism of today is better in what I have described as ennobling the old conservatism; nay much better, yet far from being good. Its pet idea is what they call construction, that is to say taking into the hands of the State the business of the individual man. Both the one and the other have much to estrange me, and have had for many many years. But, with all this, there is no crisis. I have even the hope that while the coming change may give undue encouragement to 'Construction' it will be favourable to the economic, pacific, law-regarding elements; and the sense of justice which abides tenaciously in the masses will more knowingly join hands with the Fiend of jingoism. On the whole I do not abandon the hope that it may mitigate the chronic distemper, and have not the smallest fear of its bringing about an acute or convulsive action.

You leave[1] me therefore rooted in my evil mind.

I have begun Mr Cross, whom, I see, you generously helped.[2] His work seems to have been executed with great care. I am as wrath as ever with Mary,[3] & with you, for lifting her above Walter Scott (even this I think your Titanic audacity has attempted), *or* putting her on his level, yet I freely own she was a great woman. I have not yet got to the bottom of her ethical history.

I am exceedingly soothed and gratified by the praises from all sides of Dr King as Bishop. He is I believe a saint, like Hamilton,[4] & is they say much beside; not however a great man of business, so the rumour runs.

12. Th.

Wrote to H.N.G.—Archbp of Canterbury—Ld Hartington—The Queen—and minutes. I remained in bed: the disturbance, wh has had so many forms, having at last taken the form of overaction of the bowels. Read Tales of a Grandfather—Fremantle, Bampton Lecture—Mozley's Letters (finished)—and examined various works.

To LORD HARTINGTON, war secretary,   Chatsworth MSS 340. 1658.
12 February 1885.[5]

I have read your & Childers' letters.[6]

I suppose that in one form or another Wolseley's demand must be acceded to.

While I lean towards your view of execution by contractors, I suggest that the records of the railway construction under Peto in the Crimean War should be consulted, as the experience then acquired may supply very useful suggestions as to the instrumentality which it may be best to use. I hope the question of the narrow gauge Indian system will not be overlooked.

The committee of Cabinet had better consist I should think of yourself, Childers, Chamberlain & Kimberley or Northbrook or such others as you may think fit to associate with yourself. I do not quite see the force of Childers' objection about contracting for the entire line over a great distance. Why should this be necessary at the outset?

---

[1] Could read 'have'.
[2] Thanks Acton in the preface, x.
[3] i.e. Mary Gladstone on George Eliot.
[4] W. K. Hamilton, late bp. of Salisbury.
[5] In Hamilton's hand, save the signature.
[6] On arrangements for staffing Wolseley's army; Add MS 44147, f. 241.

13. Fr.

Rose at 11; all right. Wrote minutes. Calls. Conclave on Egypt at $2\frac{1}{2}$. Saw Mr H—Lady Derby—Ld Granville—Mr Childers—E. Wickham. Read Tales of a Grandfather—Life of Miss Evans. Worked on papers.

14. Sat.

Rose at 11. Wrote to H.N.G.—Mr Mitford[1]—Mr R. Brown jun.—Sir C. Dilke—Ld Granville—Sir W. Harcourt. Visited the 'Ancient Masters' with C. Unexpectedly saw R. Spencer after his awful illness: and sat a very long time. Saw Ld Granville. Dined with Dowager Duchess of Montrose. Conversation with Mr Lythbunrey,[2] and Lady Sykes.[3] Read Tales of a Grandfather—Life of Geo. Eliot (much).

To Sir W. V. HARCOURT, home secretary,   MS Harcourt dep. Adds 10.
14 February 1885.

I think we may take the Crofters' Bill at the *next* Cabinet now fixed for Monday. I am prepared for a preliminary conversation, but only in case you think it will be useful. The Cabinet may not make up its mind on Monday.[4]

15. Quinqa S.

Chapel Royal noon and afternoon. Wrote to Abp of Canterbury—Bp of Gloucester—Dean Church—Dowager Lady Sandhurst—Mrs Bolton—Rev. Mr Paget—& minutes. Saw Dr Butler. Read Life of G. Eliot—Fremantle B. Lectures—Greswell's Evolution[5]—and examined Aitken, Knox Little, & other books of religion.

16. M.

Wrote to Sir C. Dilke—Mr Childers l.l.l.—The Queen—Lady Phillimore—Col. Kingscote—Ld Hartington—Sir Thos G.—and minutes. C. went to Hawarden—I dined with Mrs L. Ellis. Saw Mr H—Ld R.G. Saw Mrs Langtry: probably for the last time. Saw Sir C. Dilke. Read Life of G. Eliot. Cabinet $2-5\frac{1}{2}$.

Cabinet. Monday Feb. 16. 85. 2 PM.[6]
1. Russian proposal to guarantee $\frac{1}{6}$ only of the Loan.
2. Crofter Legislation. Harcourt expanded his scheme. Legislation needful. Cannot follow report. Cannot advise taking lands from A to let to B. Recited main heads. (The crofter wd. in England by adverse possession become a freeholder. Pay no rent but are removable. Hartington objected to plan as too much, Chamberlain as too little. Conversation especially on the 5 years & fixity of tenure. Discussion postponed: promise to be renewed.[7]
3. Discussion upon language to be held in Parliament. Reserve tomorrow.

[1] Arranging restoration of the Mercat Cross; Add MS 44489, f. 219.
[2] Unidentified.
[3] Caroline, wife of Sir F. H. Sykes, 5th bart., s. of Disraeli's mistress.
[4] Letter 'topped and tailed' by Gladstone, the rest in Hamilton's hand.
[5] Article by G. Gresswell, author of *Evolution* (1888).
[6] Add MS 44646, f. 38.
[7] See 27 Mar. 85; Bill introduced in May, lost with govt.; passed in 1886.

4. Ld. Hn. stated military measures. Army 65000 beyond normal Estimate. No compulsory calling out of Reserves but volunteering.
5. Chairman of the Finance Committees. Stansfeld (Military) & Courtney (Civil).
6. Scotch Minister Bill. Shall he have education? Postponed.[1]
7. Bills to be introduced into H of Lords, & *announced.*
   a. Australian Federal Council. b. Lunacy Law Amt. Bill. c. Extradition Bill. d. Scotch Minister Bill (Sec. for Scotland) To be announced.

To H. C. E. CHILDERS, chancellor of the exchequer,   Add MS 44547, f. 179.
16 February 1885.

What do you say to this view. The disadvantage to us of producing at once the Vote of Credit is enormous, for much of it relates to an operation of next winter in which Parliament has a right to reserve its judgment until the time is near at hand. *We* cannot say absolutely that an expedition to Khartoum is to take place, but only that we contemplate it, & that we make every preparation for it. Query whether the vote should be taken for a period less than the whole year. Just think this over.

To LORD HARTINGTON, war secretary, 16 February   Chatsworth MSS 340. 1661.
1885.

I had some conversation on Saturday with Granville about a matter, which may already have been present to your mind: if not, I hope you will give it consideration.

You remember the unfortunate proclamation which offered a reward for bringing in Osman Digna alive or dead. It could not be defended, and with its withdrawal the whole subject of his personal position has passed out of view.

But ought it not to be carefully weighed whether it may be possible in connection with any military operations from Suakim, to get hold of him? Perhaps I ought to go further and say, in case of failure to get hold of him, to take his life? A measure which if possible would in all likelihood be the saving of so many lives.

For, however we may reckon on the skill, gallantry, and success, of our force, I suppose we cannot after past experience put out of view the likelihood that they may all once more be frustrated by his retirement to the hills.

It is not for me to suggest whether an idea of this kind should be prosecuted by the use of British or of native instruments, by detailing men to act during an engagement, or by a surprise: these points will I hope be dealt with by more competent persons.

Similar considerations would apply to the Mahdi, were we at once about to have him in the field against us.

17. Tu.

Wrote to Mr Childers—Dowager Lady Sandhurst—C.G. l.l.—The Queen—& minutes. Cabinet 2½-5. Saw Mr H.—Ld Granville—The T.G.s. Dined at Mr Hankey's.[2] The father was born in 1730! My visit to Eaton Square was all I could hope. Read Life of G. Eliot. Examined documents & framed statement on the position in Egypt.

---

[1] See 28 Apr. 85.
[2] General Henry Aitchison Hankey (of Eaton Square), 1805-86.

Cabinet. Tues. Feb. 17. 85 2½ PM.[1]

1. Shall the Exchequer contribute any thing towards the New Guinea civil expenditure? Telegram agreed to inquiring as to cost.
2. WEG read sketch of language in which our position may be stated. Approved: item struck out as to 'friendly tribes'.
3. Statement to be made accordingly in presenting the papers: 'by leave of the House[']: notice to Speaker: & to Northcote. Dilke will do this tomorrow. Statement will grow out of the fact that military papers, on account of their nature [blank.]
4. Vote of credit. Childers stated 1. necessity of Suppl. Estimates for residue of this year. 2. Treasury recommendation as to dividing Vote of Credit 85–6 from Suppl. Estimate with the earlier part of the charge.
   Decided to lump the whole 85–6 charge in one Vote of Credit. *Times* of laying Vote of Credit need not be very early: can be discussed hereafter.
5. Canada not to be absolutely refused.

To Mrs GLADSTONE, 17 February 1885.   Hawarden MSS.

At present every day only opens more and more to view the extraordinary difficulties of the situation. We know nothing yet of the intentions of the Opposition: very likely they do not know themselves: I am not sure that their difficulties are less than ours.

Learning yesterday that there was to be no compulsory service of the reserves, but only volunteering, I sent for Mrs Smith but found that she knew this already. So that I hope the pressure is off her already.

I inclose a sad letter from Dowr. Lady Sandhurst. I have answered in terms of sympathy but with little hope of being able to do any thing especially not this time—I do not know why Lady S.s persuasion about herself should require intercourse with her to be barred.

I write before the Cabinet as I may have to go (I hope) to Tom after it. All hail for your return. Your afft   WEG

5. PM I am off to Toms. Cabinet has been less prolix than usual.

18. Ash Wed.

Chapel Royal 11 A.M. Wrote to Sir S. Northcote—The Queen—& minutes. Saw Mr H—Lord R.G—Sir C. Dilke—Ld Spencer—Mrs Godley (5 PM Tea). Worked on books. Read Life of Geo. Eliot. A moderate retrenchment of food made me weak in walking today: and the irritation of the hands returned at night.

19. Th.

Wrote to Sir Jas Paget—The Queen—and minutes. Further pondered my words about the Soudan & spoke them: the reception could not be warm. H of C. 4½–7½.[2] Worked on books. Saw Mr H.—Lord R.G.—Sir C. Dilke—Herbert J.G. Evening at home. Read Life of Geo. Eliot—Q.R. on Chatterton[3]—Tales of a Grandfather.

20. Fr.

Wrote to Ld Dalhousie—Lady Salisbury—Sir W. Harcourt—Mrs Bolton BP.— Superior All Saints Sisterhood—Ld Granville—The Queen l.l.—and minutes. Read

[1] Add MS 44646, f. 44.
[2] *H* 294. 873; Redistribution Bill then entered cttee.
[3] *Q.R*, clix. 147.

Geo. Eliot finished II—Tales of a Grandfather—Gomme on Gent. Magazine.[1] H of C. 4½–8 and 10½–12.[2] Saw Mr H—Ld R.G.—Ld Spencer—Ld Acton. Cabinet 2–4.

Cabinet. Friday Feb. 20. 85. 2 PM.[3]
1. Suez Canal Commission: will probably be given up in the form proposed. We are ready to declare adhesion to principles of freedom from Canal; Commission of experts to draft the terms.
2. Northcote's motion ⎫ negative both.
   Morley's amendment ⎭
   Course of the debate. Mr Morley if willing to follow Northcote. Then WEG. Day for the motion—papers will be distributed on Monday—offer Monday to Northcote.
3. Answer to Forster continued.[4]

21. Sat.

Wrote to Mr Woodall—Ld Granville—Ld Spencer—and minutes. Worked on books. Saw Mr H—Ld R.G.—Lady Wolverton—Mr West—Lady Ripon—Mrs Th. Drive with C. Dined with the Wests. Read Tales of a Gr. (finished)—Life of Geo. Eliot. Worked on Egypt.

To LORD SPENCER, Viceroy of Ireland, 21 February 1885.   Althorp MSS K8.

Perhaps the question between Committee & Commission on Industrial resources of Ireland may stand over till the pressure of the present moment is a little abated.[5]

There are various points which may have to be considered, & one which occurs to me is this, whether the Crown will be as *free* in dealing with the report of a Commission which it, or which the Viceroy, has appointed, as it would be in treating the Report of a Committee appointed on independent suggestion. Is there not also this, that you might find it difficult, in framing a Commission, either to appoint Nationalists or to pass them by. In a Committee Irishmen would not be a majority, but in a Commission could you avoid it? I am much pleased & relieved to hear the improved account of your brother this morning.

22. 1 S. Lent.

Chapel Royal noon (Bp of Ripon) & aftn. Saw Mr H.—Ld Spencer. Mr Tennant came to Luncheon with the very happy fiancés.[6] Wrote to Sir H. Gordon l.l.—Ld Kimberley—Ld Hartington. Read Oxenham's Papers—Statham on Free Thought[7]—Jenkins's Tract[8]—and other books.

---

[1] G. L. Gomme, ed., *The Gentleman's magazine library* (1883).
[2] Moved timetable for Redistribution Bill; *H* 294. 933.
[3] Add MS 44646, f. 48.
[4] On military support from the colonies; *H* 294. 923. Notes for answer at Add MS 44646, f. 47.
[5] Spencer, 20 February, Add MS 44312, f. 24, supported a Commission as a response to Sir E. Wilmot's proposal for inquiry into Ireland's industrial resources.
[6] Laura Tennant and Alfred Lyttelton; see 21 May 85.
[7] See 25 May 84.
[8] R. C. Jenkins, 'The last gleaning of a Christian life' (1885).

To Sir H. W. GORDON, 22 February 1885.   Add MS 44547, f. 181.

As long as a hope could in any way be entertained that your distinguished & excellent brother had survived the betrayal of Khartoum, I was unwilling to forgo the slender consolation it might afford; and I have also been delayed in writing this note for two or three days by an enquiry on a kindred subject.

But I cannot longer forbear from addressing to you my humble tribute to his memory, insignificant as that tribute must be when rendered to one, whose fame has not only become a national possession, but gone forth throughout the world.

Though I had not the privilege of his personal acquaintance, yet his was a character of which I think many features could be plainly read even from a distance. The judgment of mankind has pronounced him a hero; and the application of that lofty name is specially marked in his case by the fact that it applies not only to his public acts but to the man; to the spirit of self sacrifice such as distinguished martyrs & apostles, to a simplicity of character not less remarkable than his profound enthusiasm & his boundless courage. I cannot but add, though it is perhaps presumptuous, my admiration of his astonishing command, under circumstances so difficult of military resource, & of that inexhaustible strength of will which formed the crown of his powers.

It is difficult to wish any of his virtues had been in any respect restrained, yet I reflect with pain, now that the catastrophe has come, how ill his generous confidence was requited by some of those for whose welfare though they were of a foreign race it was his desire to live or die.

I congratulate you on your close & intimate association with General Gordon, & I trust that among us there are & will be many who will strive to learn lessons, in their several places, from this noble example of Christian heroism.[1]

23. M.

Wrote to The Queen—Ld Hartington—and minutes. Spent the morning on Egyptian papers with Hamilton's help to make sure of my ground. I cannot now get up Blue Books as of old. Drive with C. Read Life of G. Eliot. Saw Mr H—Ld R.G—Ld Hartington. H of C. 4½-9. Spoke 1¼ h. in defence of Govt.[2] The Almighty bore me through amidst all my weakness.

24. Tu. St Matthias.

Wrote to Ld Carlingford—Sir C. Dilke—Ld Rosebery—Mr Salkeld—Sir W. Harcourt—The Queen—and minutes. H. of C. 4¾-8 and 10-12½.[3] Saw Mr H—Ld R.G—Mr Chamberlain—Sir H. Gordon. Read Life of Geo. Eliot. Dined at Sir T.E. May's: conversation respecting Lewes & G. E[liot]. Serious conversation with the Speaker on the possible resignation.

---

[1] A further note this day hinted at civil list pensions for Gordon's sisters; Add MS 44547, f. 181.
[2] Answering Northcote's motion of censure and Morley's amndt. regretting use of British forces; *H* 294. 1079.
[3] Questions; row with Irish on procedure (W. O'Brien suspended); Sudan; *H* 294. 1174.

To Sir W. V. HARCOURT, home secretary,   MS Harcourt dep. Adds 10.
24 February 1885.

I meant more than a jest in my random shot at you in the last Cabinet and I very much hope you will speak in this debate, I presume you would take Thursday. And your intervention will give freshness as well as force to the discussion.[1]

25. Wed.

Wrote to Ld Rosebery—Sir H. Gordon—Mr Chamberlain—and minutes. Dined with Mr Millais. Worked on books. Saw Mr H.—Ld R.G.—Ld Granville—Sir C. Dilke—Mr . . .—Prince of Wales (nullity)—Sir F. Leighton—Mr Holl[2]—Ld Rosebery. Read Life of G. Eliot—Revue Contemp. on J. Ferry.[3] Conclave at Granvilles on Wolseley's Proclamation [as Governor General of the Sudan] &c. H. of C. 5–6.[4]

To J. CHAMBERLAIN, president of the board of trade,   Add MS 44547, f. 182.
25 February 1885.

The exigencies of debate require an increase in the number of Minister Speakers, so I have to beg of you to give your aid in the debate. Further, I would recommend your settling times & seasons with Harcourt. Evidently one of you should follow Forster if he speaks on Thursday, as it is from him that we are sure to hear the worst that can be said of us.[5]

26. Th.

Wrote to The Queen—Ld Granville l.l.—Mrs Th.—Ld Northbrook—and minutes. My letter of this night to the Queen was special.[6] Saw Mr H.—Ld R.G.—Ld Hartington—Sir C. Dilke—Sir W. Harcourt—S. Lyttelton sen.—Ld Acton. H. of C. 4¾–8 and 10–12½.[7] Read Norman's Tonquin[8]—Life of Geo. Eliot.

27. Fr.

Wrote to the Queen—Ld Hartington l.l. and minutes. Read Life of G. Eliot. Saw Mr H—Ld RG—Ld Ripon—Ld Granville—Lady Gladstone. H. of Commons 4¾–8¼ & 9½–2½. Saw Bright, Goschen,[9] & others, in the lobbies. The final division in my mind turned the scale, so nicely was it balanced.[10]

[1] Harcourt on 26 February belligerently defended Gladstone and the govt.; H 294. 1438.
[2] Francis Montague Holl, 1845–88; portrait painter.
[3] First number of new Revue Contemporaine, which soon failed.
[4] Misc. business; H 294. 1264.
[5] Chamberlain 'begged off': death of his relative; Add MS 44126, f. 70.
[6] RA A61/2: the 'aspect of the House is dubious and equivocal'; combination of Irish, tories, Forster, Goschen and some whigs may produce 'a majority too small to enable the Government to carry on' its duties; the 'next change of Government may possibly form the introduction to a period presenting some new features, and may mean more than what is usually implied in the transfer of power from one party to another'.
[7] Sudan deb.; H 294. 1425.
[8] C. B. Norman, Tonkin; or France in the far east (1885).
[9] Goschen and Forster (and many Home Rulers) voted with the Tories, Bright with the govt.
[10] After a strong conclusion by Hartington, the govt. had a majority of 14 on Northcote's motion, and of 343 on Morley's amndt.; H 294. 1719. Whips' notes at Add MS 56452, f. 131.

To LORD HARTINGTON, war secretary, 27 February   Chatsworth MSS 340. 1673.
1885.

None of us could follow Hampden.[1] I do not understand Trevelyan's minute, & his language is not safe. But I thought Dilke last night very happy in his treatment of the Railway, speaking hopefully of its utility. I mean to refer to him this afternoon in answering MacCoan: & Granville who has just come in joins with me in approving Dilke's as a safe good & conciliatory line.

28. Sat.

Wrote to Mr Bright—Mr Childers—The Queen—and minutes. Cabinet 2-7—long discussion on resign or not resign. Saw Mr H—Ld R.G—Ld Sydney—Ld Carlingford—Ld Spencer. Dined at Ld Carlingford's (Sheriffs). Read G. Eliot.

Cabinet. Sat. Feb. 28. 1885. 2 PM.[2]
    1. Retention of Office.
0   2. Grant to Gordon's family.
    3. Report of Daily Chronicle's correspondent.[3]
    Railway—language considered & agreed on.
    Draft in answer to Bismarck's insolent threat. Agreed on.
    New Guinea. Granville had professed readiness to consider rectification.
    Mentioned Pauncefoot's [*sic*] plan. Authorised to say that we will consider[?] it if likely to be acceptable.
    Afghan frontier. Lumsden not to advise fighting without reporting home.
    Wolseley—Gov. Generalship. Stands over.
    A. Chermside the Flag of Truce—Wolseley to report all the facts.

Conservatism so-called, in its daily practice, now depends largely on inflaming public passion, and thereby has lost the main element which made it really Conservative, and qualified it to resist excessive & dangerous innovation. This is my conviction, but no doubt it would be ascribed by many to my prejudice and partiality. W.E.G. F. 28. 85.[4]

To S. WHITBREAD, M.P., 28 February 1885.   Add MS 44547, f. 182.

It is supposed that the Parnellites may get 40 men on Tuesday to support an Adjournment for the purpose of discussing the conduct of the Speaker in the matter of Mr. O'Brien.[5]

It is in itself nothing less than monstrous that the Speaker's proceedings should thus be debated without the possibility of either motion or amendment.

It is not even 'urgent' for if it were why is a week allowed to elapse? (The real reason I suppose is to have O'Brien on the ground.)

It is a gross violation of the spirit of our rules, but I wish I could see or say that it is not within the letter.

   [1] Hartington's note not found.
   [2] Add MS 56452, f. 134.
   [3] Extract from *Daily Chronicle*, 28 February 1885, report of use of white flag to attract Buller's attention to note of Mahdi's offer to parley.
   [4] Add MS 44769, f. 35; docketed 'Suggestion for Hamilton (to Ponsonby) in expl. of my letter of Feb. 27-8. 85.'
   [5] See 24 Feb. 85n.; on 3 March the Speaker was challenged, but the adjournment was not moved.

Pray turn the subject over in your mind. I have not had an opportunity of speaking to May. Possibly you or he or both might find a little day light.
[P.S.] Perhaps if convenient you would come in *from the House* on Monday & dine when we might speak of this.

Mch One 1885

2 S. Lent.

Chapel Royal noon & H.C. Saw Sir A. Clark who advised bed &c. for a slight cold. Wrote to Mr Cameron—Chancr of Exr. Read Carson's Works[1]—Lilly on Islam Saints[2]—Memoir of Henry Smith[3]—Oxenham's Essays.[4]

2. M.

Kept my bed all day. Wrote to Ld Hartington—Ld E. Fitzmaurice—The Queen—Sir H. Gordon—& minutes. Wrote Mem. on Wolseley's demand.[5] Saw Mr H. l.l.—Ld R. Grosvenor l.l.—H.N.G.—H.J.G.—Mr Bright—Sir A. Clark. Read G. Eliot's Life Finished—Acton on do—Hutton on do[6]—Temple on Khartoum.[7]

3. Tu.

Wrote to The Queen l.l.l.—Sir W. Harcourt—Watsons—Ld Granville l.l.—and minutes. Saw Mr H—Ld R.G. l.l.—Ld Hartington—Sir A. Clark l.l.—Conclave on Speaker's case—Sir C. Dilke. Rose at 4 & went to H. of C., wonderfully better. Remained until $8\frac{1}{4}$.[8] Read Contemp. R. on Himalaya Faiths—on Drummond's book(+)[9]—Charles Dayrell.[10]

4. Wed.

Rose at eleven. Wrote to Ld Kimberley—Ld Granville l.l.—Mr Childers—Sir W. Harcourt—The Queen—and minutes. H of C. 4-5.[11] Drive with C. Saw Mr H—Ld RG—Ld Granville—Ld Rosebery—The Speaker—Ld E. Fitzmaurice. Dined at The Speaker's. Read C. Dayrell.

To LORD KIMBERLEY, Indian secretary, 4 March 1885.　　　Add MS 44547, f. 183.

I return Dufferin's letter. Your description of it seems in no way exaggerated.[12]
I presume that when we come to actual negotiation on the frontier & where the

---

[1] J. C. L. Carson, *Miscellaneous papers* (1883).
[2] *C.R.*, xliv. 203 (August 1883).
[3] H. Smith, *Sermons... with a memoir by Thomas Fuller*, 2v. (1866).
[4] See 15 June 84.
[5] Opposing Wolseley's demand to be made Governor General of Sudan; Add MS 56452, f. 146. See 12 Mar. 85.
[6] Acton's review in *N.C.*, xvii. 464 (March 1885), Hutton's in *C.R.*, xlvii. 372 (March 1885).
[7] R. Temple in *C.R.*, xlvii. 305 (March 1885).
[8] Redistribution Bill in cttee.; *H* 294. 1957.
[9] *C.R.*, xlvii. 392 (March 1885).　　　[10] H. Solly, *Charles Dayrell: a modern Bacchanal* (1883).
[11] Redistribution Bill; *H* 295. 2.
[12] Neither found; on the Afghan frontier boundary commission.

historic basis is insufficient, we ought to be liberal where the roads to India are not concerned, & stiff where they are. So far as any general rule can seem applicable to a case of
this kind.[1]

5. Th.

Regular. Wrote to Ld Hartington—Ld Derby—Ld Kimberley—Watsons Tel.—
The Queen—Ld Granville—& minutes. Dined at Rosebery's: long general con-
versation on Colonies & then long confidential conversation *a part* with Her-
bert Bismarck.[2] Saw Ld Granville l.l.—Mr H.—Ld R.G.—Russian Ambassador—
Ld Kimberley—Mr Childers. H of C. 5-7¾ and 11¼-1.[3] Read Patterson's Imam
Mahdi.[4]

To LORD HARTINGTON, war secretary, 5 March 1885.   Add MS 44147, f. 254.

I rather think, & a conversation with Kimberley confirms me, that you & some others
of us have different impressions as to Wolseley's meaning on a point of importance, viz.
whether the Berber-Suakim route is alike needful to be opened on the more forward & on
the more contracted of the two military policies.

I understand you think that it is only the plan of going to Khartoum which requires it
absolutely, & that Wolseley might in the case of necessity retire with his army by the Nile
route.

If there is a doubt on this question would you not do well to clear it up by telegraph?[5]

6. Fr.

Wrote to Ld Granville—Ld Spencer Tel.—The Queen—and minutes. H of C. 5-
8¼ and 9½-12¾.[6] Read Ch. Dayrell. Hands continue troublesome. Saw Mr H—Ld
R.G.—Ld Granville—Ld Acton—Fehmi Pacha. His visit was an extreme case of
the irony of Fortune. He came in pursuance of a telegram from the Sultan
expressly to congratulate the Govt. & me personally on the defeat of the Opposition & on our continuance in office.

7. Sat.

Wrote to Watsons—The Queen l.l.—& minutes. Cabinet 2-5. Dined with *Mrs*
Childers. Read C. Dayrell & other works. Conclave to visit & examine Dover
House. I am against renting it for Prime Ministers. Saw Mr H.—Ld R.G.—Ld
Rosebery—Mr Childers—Ld Kimberley.

[1] Kimberley this day reported his fear of 'an intolerable dilemma—on the one side a great war, on
the other, the certain estrangement of the Amir'; Add MS 44228, f. 170.
[2] Bismarck *père* had complained in the Reichstag at Granville's comments taken to refer to Germany's colonial ambitions; Granville explained his remarks on 6 March; *H* 295. 227.
[3] Questioned on Afghan frontier; *H* 295. 127.
[4] H. S. Patterson, *Imâm Mahdi, or the Moslem millenium* (1884).
[5] Hartington replied, 5 March, Add MS 44147, f. 256: 'As to the enquiry you propose I am afraid I
do not quite understand its meaning and object. There were a month ago two or perhaps three possible military policies; but I understood that the forward one had been adopted, and I am afraid that
to address questions to Wolseley about a more contracted policy or about retiring his army by the
Nile route would hopelessly confuse him as to our intentions.'
[6] Questioned on public business; Redistribution Bill; *H* 295. 294.

Cabinet. Sat. Mch. 7. 1885. 2 PM.[1]
1. Ld Wemyss Address of Thanks. House to be left free—if no fear of scandal.
2. Supplemental Military Estimate. (Fowler [?]anti-Suakim-Berber). Agree to his [Wolseley's] demands for Nile Route. Inquiry framed whether this being done, he considers prosecution of SB line[2] will assist him in *autumn* campaign.
3. (Egyptian finance). Ld Granville reported Waddington's telling him all was settled as he conceived[?] except wording as to Commission.
   H. Bismarck said Russian Govt. wd only get full text today. His Father had not been willing to sign while tension existed. Farther recital.
   Cons[ideration] today of everything as if as good as settled: N. Guinea; St Lucia; Cameroons; The Pole; Claims in Cameroons against G. (Bota may be given up).
4. Fehmi Pacha asks whether he is to recommend Sultan to send troops to Suakim. See Report as to Ld G's reply.[3]
5. Ld Granville to move Turkey to agree to the plan for Egyptian Finance.
6. Kimberley stated the effect of the recent telegrams & the situation on the Afghan frontier.[4]
7.

8. 3 S. Lent.

Chapel Royal mg (Bp of Truro) & evg. Wrote to Ld Granville—Mrs Bolton. Read Ffoulkes on Eucharist[5]—Dr Wyld's curious pamphlets[6]—Statham on Free-thinking—and divers tracts. Saw Mr Hamilton.

9. M.

Wrote to Sir S. Northcote—The Queen l.l.—Principal Librarian B.M.—and minutes. Saw Mr H.—Ld R.G.—Sir H. Ponsonby—Lady Reay P.P.C.—Chancr of Exr—Mr Trevelyan. H. of C. 5–8¾ and 10¼–12½.[7] Eight to dinner. Read Ch. Dayrell. Hitchman's 'Runnymede L'.[8]

10. Tu.

Wrote to Messrs Watson—Ld E. Fitzmaurice—Mr Meade—Mr Temple Leader—The Queen—& minutes. Dined at Mr B. Currie's. Conversation with him & Ld W[olverton]. H of C. 5–9 and 10–12¼.[9] Saw Mr H.—Ld RG—Sir H. Ponsonby. Read C. Dayrell—Hitchman's Runnymede Letters.

11. Wed. [*Windsor Castle*]

Wrote to Scott's—and minutes. Read Runnymede—Rucellai[10]—and Walpole's Letters.[11] Saw Mr H—Ld RG—Sir H. Ponsonby—Ld Granville—Sir J. Cowell.

---

[1] Add MS 44646, f. 51.   [2] i.e. Suakin–Berber railway line.
[3] To suggest a different point than Suakin, and encourage with respect to neutralisation; CAB 41/19/13.
[4] Russia reinforcing Yuletan and Pul-i-Khisti; 10 regiments anticipated; F.O.C.P. 5107, ff. 113–16.
[5] E. S. Ffoulkes, *Primitive consecration of the Eucharist Oblation* (1885).
[6] G. Wyld wrote widely on clairvoyance, hypnotism, etc.   [7] Sudan costs; *H* 295. 453.
[8] B. Disraeli, *The 'Runnymede Letters'*, ed. F. Hitchman (1885).
[9] Spoke on army estimates; *H* 295. 502.
[10] G. F. Rucellai, *Diario ... pubblicato da G. Temple-Leader e G. Mariotti* (1884).   [11] Many eds.

H of C. $2\frac{3}{4}$-$4\frac{1}{2}$.[1] Then to Windsor. Audience of H.M. not ungenial but somewhat reserved on her part. Conversation with Lady Ponsonby—Lady Kenmare.

12. Th. [London]

Wrote to The Queen l.l.l.—and minutes. Read Pattison Mem.[2]—Runnymede Letters (finished). Cabinet 12-$2\frac{1}{2}$. Saw Mr H—Ld R.G—Dean of Windsor. Saw the Angeli picture of H.M. and the Böhme monuments of D. of Albany and dear Dean Wellesley. To London by 10.30. H of C. $5\frac{1}{4}$-$8\frac{1}{4}$ & $9\frac{1}{4}$-12. Took an opp. of speaking on German Colonisation.[3]

Cabinet. Thurs. Mch 12. Noon.[4]
1. Arrest of Zebehr:[5] agreed to & telegram sent. Papers to be seized. He will be kept on board a man of war until his destination is decided. Strong reasons against Cyprus. Orders given to Admiral.
2. Dover House.[6] Discussed. Varieties of opinion as to letting or retaining. Cabinet Minister will visit it.
3. Declaration of emancipation of Slaves in Soudan has been suggested. Unavailable.
4. Wolseley—Gov. Generalship, Proclamation.[7]

Conversation on Afghan frontier. Try to get Cabuli regiments out of Herat so as to keep it open for British Escort[?] in case of need. Agreed.[8]
Agreement already established against any further advances.
Wolseley to restrict his promises of protection to those to whom he has come under obligation. To make known to him the possible danger wh may cause a change of military plans in connection with the Afghan frontier—in these circs. we are unwilling to take any step in the nature of a further general declaration of policy.

13. Fr.

Wrote to Mr Winthrop—Count H. Bismarck—The Queen l.l.—Ld Granville—& minutes. H of C. $4\frac{3}{4}$-$8\frac{1}{2}$ and $9\frac{1}{2}$-$12\frac{1}{4}$.[9] Cabinet $5\frac{1}{2}$-$7\frac{1}{2}$. Read Walpole, Memoirs. Saw Mr H—Ld RG—Mr Childers—Sir C. Dilke—Sir S. Northcote—Ld Northbrook.

Cabinet. (in WEG's room H of C). Friday Mch 14 [sc. *13*] *85. 5$\frac{1}{2}$PM.*[10]
1. Münster's communication from Bismarck: *entr'ouvrait*[11] a proposal either to omit Art. 26[12] or to provide by protocol for replacement of the sum withholden from the Sinking Fund.

---

[1] Redistribution Bill; *H* 295. 752.
[2] M. Pattison, *Memoirs* (1885); notes at Add MS 44792, f. 53.
[3] 'If Germany becomes a Colonizing Power, all I can say is "God speed her"'; *H* 295. 979.
[4] Add MS 44646, f. 55.
[5] Requested by Wolseley to prevent him liaising with the Mahdi; he was imprisoned in Gibraltar.
[6] See 7 Mar. 85. It became the London branch of the Scottish Office.
[7] Proclamation of Wolseley as governor-general of the Sudan drafted (F.O.C.P. 1506, f. 245) but never promulgated.
[8] Kimberley to Viceroy, 12 March: every possible step to insure willing acceptance of our help at Herat; if Cabuli regiments an obstacle, Ameer might employ them elsewhere; F.O.C.P. 5107, f. 123.
[9] Questioned on Afghan frontier; Redistribution Bill; *H* 295. 1083.
[10] Add MS 44646, f. 56.   [11] 'half-opened'.
[12] Of the draft 'Convention on Egyptian Finance', signed on 18 March.

He also after seeing the Ambassador proposed a protocol on declaration of verbal reserve. Granville went off
to take no notice of the nonproposed proposal,
to learn from Münster whether his form is a proposal—& whether it is a last word to be followed if accepted by signature—if it be, it will have our cons[ideratio]n.
Answer M[ünster] back.
Conversations today cancelled. M. will inform B. that he & the Ambassador have framed hopeful proposal, & will ask whether he may propose it to England as final.[1]
2. Mem. & covering letter as answer to Russian proposal read & settled.[2]

14. Sat.

Wrote to The Queen l.l.—Ld Kimberley—Ld Derby—Sir H. Ponsonby—Robn & Nichn—& minutes. Seven to dinner. Attended Levee at 2 PM. Saw Mr H—Ld RG—D. of Argyll—M. Waddington—Mr Rathbone. Read Croker on Ireland[3]—Walpole's Geo. I and Geo. II.[4] Tea & much conversation with Mrs Sands.[5] Drive with C.

To LORD DERBY, colonial secretary, 14 March 1885.   Add MS 44547, f. 186.

Dilke spoke to me after Cabinet last night in the House about Sir H. Robinson's important Telegram of yesterday which seems to require very early action. Dilke was for giving Robinson unequivocal support & maintaining his authority & responsibility.

This is my own strong impression. (Indeed I should have been very glad if Robinson had been Commissioner for the Natal quarter also—but this is past praying for.) Though I do not feel certain, I cannot but think it likely you would be safe in collecting the opinion of the Cabinet in a circulation box by an aye or no on Robinson's first alternative.

You may consider Dilke's aye (I think) and mine as given.

15. 4 S. Lent.

Chapel Royal mg & aft. Wrote to Sir H. Ponsonby Tel.—and minutes. Saw Mr H—Mr Primrose. Read The great problem[6]—Fremantle B. Lectures—Statham—Curteis on Difficulties.[7]

16. M.

Wrote to Ld Kimberley—Archbishop of Canterbury—Mrs Sands—Ld Granville—The Queen—Sir S. Northcote—& minutes. Read Morley on G. Eliot.[8] Saw

---

[1] For the 'Declaration on Egyptian Finance', signed on 17 March; see Ramm II, ii. 347.

[2] H.M.G. 'unable to give their adhesion to any understanding by which Penjdeh or other districts claimed as Afghan shall, without inquiry on the spot, be excluded from Afghanistan'; mem. sent by Granville this day; F.O.C.P. 5107, f. 125.

[3] J. W. Croker, *A sketch of the state of Ireland, past and present* (1808, republished 1885).

[4] H. Walpole, *Memoirs of the last ten years of the reign of George II*, 2v. (1822) and *Memoirs of the reign of King George III*, 4v. (1845).

[5] Mary, spouse of Mahlon Sands; described by Hamilton as 'the American beauty' (Bahlman, *Hamilton*, ii. 409).

[6] E. Carellis, *The great problem solved* (1885).

[7] G. H. Curteis, *Dealing with difficulties of belief* (1884).

[8] *Macmillan's Magazine*, li. 241 (February 1885).

Mr H—Ld R.G.—Ld Granville—Mr Childers l.l.—Ld Kimberley *cum* Mr Currie—
Mr Chamberlain (Ireland)—Sir W. Harcourt—Ld Hartington—Miss [blank].
Dined at Sir C. Forster's. H. of C. $4\frac{3}{4}$-8 and $10\frac{1}{2}$-2.[1] The pressure of affairs,
especially Soudan, Egypt, & Afghan, is now from day to day extreme.

To LORD KIMBERLEY, Indian secretary, 16 March 1885.   Add MS 44547, f. 186.

There is no difficulty about the word agreement.[2] The words of my statement carefully
avoided it.

I am sorry to say however that as I read them the telegrams do not quite come up to
the point as I stated it in the passage within brackets—which I inclose for convenience of
reference. I spoke of further advances—the telegrams seem to speak only of advances
beyond the line claimed by Russia. What am I to say on this? Is it literally the fact that 'the
outposts are facing one another' so that 'an advance will involve attack'? If it is perhaps
the matter in substance stands well enough.

17. Tu.

Wrote to Ld Spencer—Ld Granville—Mr Childers—The Queen—Mrs Bolton—
and minutes. Read Harrison on G. Eliot[3]—Vignettes of Travel.[4] Saw Mr H—Mr
Primrose—Ld Granville—Ld R.G.—Ld G. cum Mr Childers—Sir J.P. on the
Fin[ancial] Agreement.[5] H. of C. $4\frac{3}{4}$-8 & $8\frac{1}{4}$-$10\frac{1}{4}$.[6] Went to the Bedford party: saw
Musurus, Münster, and others. Saw MacLachlan [R].

18. Wed.

Wrote to Mr Childers—Sir S. Northcote—The Queen—Ld Provost of Edinb.
(draft)[7]—and minutes. H of C. 3-5 and $5\frac{1}{2}$-6.[8] Dined at Ld Aberdeen's. Saw Mr
H—Ld R.G—Col. Swain[9]—Mr Childers—Ld Granville—Sir W. Harcourt—Abp of
Canterbury. Read Walpole—Pattison's Memoirs.

To LORD SPENCER, Viceroy of Ireland, 18 March 1885.   Althorp MSS K8.

I send you copy of a memorandum[10] which I circulate today.

I hope we shall resolve on an Irish Local Government Bill, & in *announcing* our intentions we should I presume mention a Crimes Bill with modifications: of course declining
all statement of particulars.

19. Th.

Wrote to Sir W. Harcourt—Sir H. Ponsonby—Ld Enfield—The Queen—Sir Thos
G.—Count Munster—and minutes. Dined with the Roseberys, we four: much

---

[1] Questioned on Afghan frontier; *H* 295. 1245.
[2] Kimberley, 15 March, Add MS 44228, f. 176, reported: 'Your words have been taken to mean a
formal agreement, which cannot be said to exist.'
[3] *F.R.*, xliii. 309 (March 1885).   [4] By W. W. Nevin (1881).
[5] Signed this day.   [6] Questioned on Afghan frontier; *H* 295. 1439.
[7] Offering to restore the Mercat Cross in Edinburgh; sent on 21 March; *T.T.*, 25 March 1885, 7f.
See 23 Nov. 85.
[8] Redistribution Bill; *H* 295. 1589.
[9] Leopold Victor Swaine, F.R.G.S.; military secretary in Egypt 1884.
[10] On timetable of the Seats Bill; Althorp MSS K8.

conversation. H of C. 5–7¾ and 11–12½.[1] Saw Mr H—Ld RG—Mr Knowles—Bp of Ripon—Chancr of Exchr (on Budget). Read Pattison's Memoirs. 4–5. Attended the Bedford marriage, & *witnessed*.[2]

20. Fr.

Wrote to Mr Collings—The Queen l.l.l.—and minutes. Cabinet 2–4½. H of C. 4½–5½, 6½–8¼, & 9¾–12¾.[3] Finished Pattison's Memoirs. Drive with C. Dined at Ld Northbourne's. Saw Mr H—Ld RG—Attorney General (Gordon Journals).

Cabinet. Frid. Mch. 20. 1885. 2 PM.[4]

✔ 1. Egyptian Finance. Day for debate. Adhere to Thursday for Resolution. Thurs. *or* Monday for definitive vote. Parlt. may sit till Thursday.
✔ 2. Robinson & Warren.[5] *Via media* telegram framed. R. not to go up Mpersela[?].
  3. Gordon's Journal.[6]
✔ 4. Lubbock's motion on the cumulative vote. Agree.[7]
✔ 5. Advance of troops to Quetta 25m. K[imberley] proposes to approve Viceroy. Chamberlain agrees.
  Will it give any *fair* pretext to Russia for great military movements? No.
  WEG's suggestions: a. Herat: adopted as to defence in a general sense. (Place d'armes not desirable). b. that he [i.e. the Amir] is to place himself in our hands. c. question of the N.E. frontier: query to get there, & give on the N.W. Also removal[?] of veto upon Ameer taking two districts Sirah (?) and. . . .
  6. Granville introduced union with Turkey. Mentioned conversation with Fehmi. Requires[?] proposal for proclaiming Ottoman law to be law of Egypt. Entertained this: an Irade, confirming the law as it is, & renewing Khedive's power to legislate at large—also confirming Tewfik.
  7. Childers mentioned the Vote of Credit. Budget to be on Thursday 16th. Vote of Credit to be laid on the 9th. Prob. 7½ .
  8. Zebehr—ask for report on the papers. We remain [blank]
  9. Wolseley's telegram—as to divulging.[8] (Anything conspicuous wd. be undesirable). No result.

To Sir H. W. GORDON, 20 March 1885.   Add MS 44547, f. 188.

The pressure of public affairs kept me until last night in ignorance of some particulars as to General Gordon's Journal,[9] which I find it will be necessary for the Government to consider.

---

[1] Questioned on Egyptian finance; *H* 295. 1705.
[2] Ermyntrude, da. of 9th duke of Bedford, m. Sir E. B. Malet.
[3] Questioned on New Guinea, Egypt; redistribution; *H* 296. 57.   [4] Add MS 44646, f. 62.
[5] Dispute between Robinson and Warren *re* demarcation of authority; series of consequent wires and memoranda in CO 417/4, f. 288 etc.
[6] Note reads: 'Sir H. Gordon has brought to me his wrath about the Journal. Is there any advantage in mentioning the subject here today?'; Hartington replied: 'Yes. I think so if there is time'; Add MS 44646, f. 64.
[7] Select cttee. on school board elections agreed to; *H* 296. 517.
[8] Wolseley requested publication of his strictures on Wilson; see *Relief of Gordon*, 170.
[9] Published in July 1885 'in a very nearly entire state, only some six or seven pages being omitted' as *The journals of. . . Gordon at Khartoum*, ed. A. E. Hake. Cromer recalled that 'a good deal of violent and very foolish abuse of Lord Granville—and, if I remember correctly, of others—was omitted. It is . . . to be regretted that this was done'; Cromer, i. 432.

I am truly sorry that you should have seen reason to complain of any matter in connection with it, as, on all occasions of communication with you during a most painful and trying season, I have had occasion to observe your thoroughly kind and equitable spirit in treating of subjects which have deeply touched your feelings.

To LORD KIMBERLEY, Indian secretary, 20 March 1885.   Add MS 44228, f. 178.

I have now seen Chamberlain's box, and I send you within short notes on what appear to me to be, for the moment, the salient points of the situation in regard to the Afghan frontier, and the main matters on which Dufferin ought at this juncture clearly to know our views. Apart from these there are two observations that occur to me. 1. It is difficult to anticipate satisfaction if the territory ranged over by any given tribe of nomads is divided between two Powers. 2. I suppose that Russia will be far better able to maintain some sort of order among any Turcoman tribes than the Amir. I do not mean that this consideration can be applied without limit.

Notes sent to Lord Kimberley: 1. That the Viceroy of India should at the coming conference with the Ameer use his utmost endeavours not only to obtain all the information on the frontier question which the Ameer can give but to ascertain in the most distinct manner possible up to what point the Ameer is prepared to proceed in confidential relations with us, and in execution of the agreement which bound us as we stated in Aug 1880 to give him conditional support, and which wholly excluded Afghanistan from the sphere of Russian influence.
2. And particularly on certain definite points of which the first is—will he undertake to defend Herat to the utmost of his power & to make it defensible, receiving from us all necessary aid.
3. And further will he in regard to the settlement of a frontier by negotiation or otherwise (in this otherwise including the idea of arbitration should it seem expedient) *to place himself in our hands*, subject to the covenant already made with him, & to our engaging to act for him as we would act for ourselves, were we the claimants of the territory. For nothing could be so bad as that we should proceed to serious steps upon an equivocal and half explained understanding with him, the consequence of which might be his placing himself in the hands of Russia when we were already inconveniently committed.[1]

21. Sat.

Wrote to Ld Lyons—Ld Granville—Ld Hartington—& minutes. Dined at Ld Ripon's: much conversation with Lady A. Russell: pleased with her as to Geo. Eliot & Lewes. Saw Mr H.—Ld RG—Lady Goldsmid (tea). Saw Harris [R]. Read Gordon's Journal—l'Abbé Tigrane.[2] Worked on books & papers.

To LORD HARTINGTON, war secretary, 21 March   Chatsworth MSS 340. 1688.
1885.

The upshot of my thoughts about the Gordon Journals is this—(I have only seen VI).
1. It seems required in obedience to the injunction of Gordon that they should be pruned, if published. 2. Publication will probably be found inevitable. 3. We the Govt. are

---

[1] Copy, dated 20 March 1885; Add MS 44228, f. 181; Kimberley replied next day, ibid., f. 184: 'I have embodied your suggestions in the "secret" telegram'; on 22 March he reported embodying the formulae with modification in the official telegram.
[2] F. Fabre, *L'Abbé Tigrane, candidat à la papauté* (1877).

absolutely disabled by interest from taking any part in the business of pruning. 4. It seems difficult, perhaps impossible for us to select a pruner. 5. To give them over to the Executor would be the best course were his judgment as sound as his intention would be honest. 6. Notwithstanding the drawbacks I do not see anything better than giving them over to the Executor so far at any rate as *national* interests political or military are not compromised; but perhaps some better method of proceeding may occur to you before you have exhausted the legal question.

22. 5 S.L.

Chapel Royal mg (a powerful Sermon from Bp of Derry) & aft. Also at Marylebone Ch. (part) evening service. Wrote to Ld Kimberley—Ld Hartington l.l. Saw Mr Hamilton. Read L'Abbé Tigrane—Statham's Free Thought—The great Problem—Bp of Albany's Charge. I was granted this day two great & unmerited pleasures. At 8 North Bank I learned that 'Mrs Clifton' had gone home: & at Marybone Ch. lately a desert I saw a devout congregation of 1000 to 1200 under Mr Barker.[1]

To LORD HARTINGTON, war secretary, 22 March   Chatsworth MSS 340. 1689.
1885.

Please see my suggestions in pencil on your proposed letter.[2]

The only substantial change I desire is that we should not undertake the pruning office.

General Gordon, not content with charging mere error on us, which he might have done fairly enough from his point of view, insinuates against us (so I read him) the most abominable charges, & conveys plainly enough that we waited for & counted upon his ruin as the desired means of extricating ourselves from embarrassment.

How much more of this poisoned stuff the other five Fascicles contain I know not. But looking at No. VI alone I am strongly of opinion that we cannot in any way take upon ourselves the office of deciding whether the passages of accusation & insinuation against ourselves are or are not to be published.

23. M.

Wrote to Watsons—The Queen l.l. and Tel.—Ld Hartington—Ld Granville l.l.l. Saw Mr H—Ld RG l.l.—Sir W Harcourt—Sir C. Dilke—Chancr of Exr—Sir R. Cunliffe—Sir C. Forster—Mr Bright—Ld Hartington. Dined at Sir C. Forster's. Read L'Abbé Tigrane. H of C. $4\frac{3}{4}$-8 and 10-12.[3] Wrote out extracts &c. from Mark Pattison.[4]

24. Tu.

Wrote to Sir C. Dilke—The Queen l.l.l.l.l.—Sir S. Northcote—Mr Goschen—Sir H. Taylor—& minutes. Cabinet $5\frac{1}{2}$-$7\frac{1}{4}$: on *most* critical subjects all the way through. H of C. $4\frac{3}{4}$-8 and 10-12$\frac{1}{4}$.[5] Saw Mr H—Ld RG l.l.l.—Ld Granville—Sir

---

[1] William Barker, 1838-1917; rector of Marylebone 1882-1908.
[2] To Sir H. Gordon on the journals; Add MS 44147, f. 265.
[3] Spoke on Egyptian finance; *H* 296. 239.
[4] See 12 Mar. 85n.
[5] Redistribution Bill; *H* 296. 394.

W. Harcourt. Dined at Lucy's. Saw Mrs Godley. Read L'Abbé Tigrane. Began Taylor's Autobiography.

Cabinet. Tues. March 24. 85. 5½ PM.[1]
1. Turk has not signed the Convention & Declaration on Egyptian Finance. Unless the signature is firm tomorrow 1. Relations are suspended at once—passports given him & asked at Constantinople. 2. Basis of our future policy—severance of Egypt from Turkey. 3. No difficulty about his arranging about the Caisse in either of the forms he has proposed. He having acted contrary to his pledge last week *to us & to Europe.*[2]
2. Ld Kimberley: a. Ameer to place himself in our hands.
   b. Herat. If Russians invade undisputed Afghan territory with the object of seizing Herat we shall support the Ameer with the forces of H.M. & concert with him the best means of giving the support. (reserve choice of time[,] place & circs. for *our* direct intervention in fight.)
   c. Acquaint Russia in substance—her going against Herat will be a *casus belli.*
   d. Shall we send a force to Herat (it is admitted we are to supply Ameer with means.)
   e. Kimberley read his private telegram—amended & approved.[3]
3. Granville went. Supposed to have asked Cabinet to decide what we shall say to Russia. I urged that the form be left to him. but with all possible consn. as to the form.[4]

To Sir H. TAYLOR, 24 March 1885.   Add MS 44547, f. 190.

I did grudge parting with the old Autobiography,[5] and I thank you all the more heartily for the new one.

I am glad to see it has grown in bulk being well aware that I shall find no decline in quality. It gives me much pleasure to hear of Longman's offer which shows that 'out of sight' is not in your case 'out of mind'.

Certainly the surface of life in England is much troubled. It strikes me that we are at this moment more subject to thrills of panic & more hungry for excitement than any other people, more also than England was when you & I were young. At this moment we have impending in the House of Commons a motion on Thursday [in fact Friday] which if carried would kill us, but the chance of carrying which none view with so much dread as its promoters and concoctors.

I wish we could meet but what is the use of wishing. Except to wish you all good be it what it may.

25. *Wed.*

Wrote to Ld Hartington—Ld Granville l.l.—Archbp of Canterbury—and minutes. Saw Mr H—Ld RG—Mr Chamberlain—Sir C. Dilke—Ld Granville—do cum Ld Hartington—Lady Derby (Tea). Fourteen to dinner; including the two Turkish Ambassadors![6] Conversation with Musurus—Waddington—Harcourt—

---

[1] Add MS 44646, f. 66.
[2] Musurus signed for Turkey on 30 March.
[3] Gladstone's note: 'I am afraid the reproach of "too late" is just what would apply were we now to organise for a march on Herat. So according to the evidence before us—at least [blank]'; Add MS 44646, f. 69.
[4] This phrase written disjoint at bottom of page; appears to refer to this item.
[5] Privately printed (1877); see 15 May 83. Taylor had sent the published version in 2v.; Add MS 44490, f. 99.
[6] i.e. Musurus and Fehmi Pasha.

Granville. Attended the Speaker's Levee. Read Belinda[1]—L'Abbé Tigrane. H. of C. 2¼-4.[2]

26. Th.

Wrote to The Queen—Ld Granville—Scotts—& minutes. An anxious day with Granville, Childers, & otherwise on the Sultan's *rifiuto*[3] covered at last by falsehood (to all appearance). Drive for a while. H of C. 5-8. Spoke 1 h on moving agreement for Egyptian Finance.[4] Dined with Mrs Sands. Read Belinda. Saw Mr H—Ld R.G. Worked on Egyptian papers. Hoarse as a raven.

27. Fr.

Wrote to The Queen—Lord Hartington l.l.—Ld Derby—Sir W. Harcourt—and minutes. Poor little Christian[5] came up sadly deaf; but I hope, to be relieved. Saw Mr H—Lord R.G—Ld Derby. Cabinet 2-4½. H. of C. 4¾-5¼ & 9-2. Sham division: majority 48. Good for the world: no real strength shown.[6] Read Alg. Sidney's Life[7]—Belinda, finished Vol I.

Cabinet. Friday. Mch 27. 1885. 2 PM.[8]
4. Crofters Bill. Improving loans to be left out. Perpetual judicial rents.
5. Conversation on the Osman Digna situation—& possibility of withdrawal. Robinson & Warren. WEG had conversation with Derby & saw telegrams.
1. Telegram to Thornton respecting communication to Russia to make known our views as to Herat.[9]
2. Dufferin instructed to sound Amir as to mutual withdrawal from zone.
3. Queen's message[10]—consideration to be put off until after the recess. Manner of presentation not yet determined.

To LORD DERBY, colonial secretary, 27 March 1885.   Add MS 44547, f. 190.

I conclude you will have some proposals to make to the Cabinet today on Sir H. Robinson's last telegrams. They seem to contemplate total severance & irresponsibility which I hope you would not approve.[11]

---

[1] R. Broughton, *Belinda*, 3v. (1882-4).
[2] Redistribution Bill; *H* 296. 538.
[3] 'refusal'.
[4] Proposing loan of £315,000 (British share of international guarantee); Queen's Message read, enabling embodiment of Reserves and Militia; *H* 296. 681.
[5] Unidentified.
[6] Opposition amndt. abandoning the loan; *H* 296. 953.
[7] A. C. Ewald, *Life and times of the hon. Algernon Sydney* (1873).
[8] Add MS 44646, f. 71.
[9] Sent by Granville this day: any aggression on Ameer's territory 'a hostile act': but work to diffuse tension and promote honourable settlement; F.O.C.P. 5107, f. 179.
[10] Embodying the militia; read to Parliament on 26 March, considered on 13 April; *H* 296. 648, 1478.
[11] Derby replied, 1 April, Add MS 44142, f. 122, trying to 'keep the peace' between Robinson and Warren, but 'not sanguine'; he also proposed a compromise, a limited annexation of part of Bechuanaland to be soon transferred to the Cape; Schreuder, 458.

To Sir W. V. HARCOURT, home secretary, 27 March   MS Harcourt dep. Adds 10.
1885.

I have looked at your Crofters' Bill. Within, I put down one or two remarks on details.[1]

There is I think a larger question worth consideration both on the merits and to bring
the Cabinet to one mind, namely whether this local and exceptional law should be a
permanent one, or should be enacted (unless with regard to compensation for improvements) for the time you have chosen for the lease viz. 30 years. I give this as a suggestion
rather than a final opinion.

28. Sat. [*The Durdans, Epsom*]

Wrote to Rev. S.E.G.—Ld Hartington l.l.l.—Ld Granville—Mrs Christy (parcel)—
and minutes. Saw Mr H—Ld RG—Ld Granville—Ld Rosebery—Sir W. Harcourt—Sir Thos G. 4-7. Visited the T.Gs at Wimbledon. Dined with Sir W.
Harcourt. Then off to the Durdans, midnight train. Finished Mr Statham's Free
Thought & True Thought.

To LORD HARTINGTON, war secretary, 28 March   Chatsworth MSS 340. 1700.
1885.

I send you letters from Mr. Smith M.P. for Liverpool, and a certain Mr. Miller, not for
any immediate purpose but as indicative of what is brewing & what we shall have to
reckon with shortly.[2]

But I have a present suggestion to offer for your consideration—that you should desire
Wolseley to telegraph to you, now & from time to time, so far as he feels able, his views
on the course of military affairs in the region of Suakim.

I have seen nothing from him for some time on this subject. Not only, however, is he
Commander in Chief, but the whole expedition, except in the one particular of Graham's
appointment, is his affair, not ours: we are of course responsible but he is the father of the
whole thing which was adopted by many of us I think with extreme reluctance.

[P.S.] If as we hope things reach a turning point in that region, it would be most important to be in possession of his views.

29. Palm S.

Church mg with H.C. & Parish Church aft. Much conversation with Prof. [J.R.]
Seeley on Geo. Elliot; also Pattison. Read The Great Problem—Curteis on Difficulties. Escape from London at once sensibly improves my bodily condition.

30. M. [*Lion Mansions, Brighton*]

Wrote to Ld Granville—Ld E. Fitzmaurice—Ld Spencer—Mr Childers—Rev.
S.E.G.—and minutes. Drive with Lady R. Saw Ld Hartington—do *cum* Ld
Rosebery. Conversation with Rosebery at much length on the Egyptian situation. Off to Brighton at 4.30: Lion Mansions,[3] most comfortable. Read Catherine II Memoirs[4]—Taylor's Autobiography.

---

[1] Notes on details omitted. This year's bill lost, reintroduced and passed 1886.
[2] Not found.
[3] Apartment taken in this building, later the Adelphi Court Hotel.
[4] See 10 Aug. 69.

To Sir W. V. HARCOURT, home secretary, 30 March   MS Harcourt dep. 9, f. 132.
1885.

On reading the St Petersburgh telegram this morning I represented its character to
Hartington (who had not attached importance to it) and I also wrote to E. Fitzmaurice to
suggest to him that in answering Stanhope today he might cite Thornton's report about
the mischief done by the Questions in the H of C. but without hitting Stanhope whose
injury seems fair enough.[1]

I am afraid my re-appearance *ad hoc* after having been known to have left town, would
produce rather an exciting than a tranquillising effect, & would be a sort of justification
for a debate which we want wholly to exclude.

Hartington undertook in answering his questions on the preparations to say that they
were not caused by any evil prospect in the negotiations.

I will send some letters on the Osman Digna business for you to glance at—they are
important from the character of the writers.

To LORD SPENCER, Viceroy of Ireland, 30 March 1885.   Althorp MSS K8.

I have read your papers,[2] evidently the product of much reflection & entitled to great
weight. The four measures (1 + 3) are evidently, I fear, beyond our power as a whole.

The Seats Bill drags on, not from obstruction proper, but from its character & a talka-
tive age: it cannot leave the House of Commons much if at all before Whitsuntide, the
wretched Egyptian question cropping up as you see again & again.

I do not think that you will lose anything by not 'circulating' *now*: but I would suggest
your communicating with Childers on Land Purchase, & *also* with Chamberlain on the
Crimes' Bill. He has detailed to me his views on this Bill & on Local Government, & I do
not think that on either he is *very* far apart from you. I think he has probably the power &
certainly the will to be of use on both measures.

The idea of incorporating part at any rate of the new provisions in the general law
seems to deserve at any rate thorough probing.

P.S. It was with *great* pleasure that I received from Gull at the last levée sanguine assurances about your brother: *for* I have noticed his sagacity in such predictions before. He
spoke to me very boldly. I told Lady Spencer.

31. Tu.

St Martin's Ch 11 AM. Wrote to Ld Granville—E. Hamilton l. & tel.—The
Queen—Ld Hampden—Ld Derby—Ld Hartington—& minutes. Read Mivart on
Organic Nature[3]—Rawlinson, Afghan Frontier[4]—Taylor Autobiography. Divers
walks: much quiet.

Wed. Ap. One. 1885.

St Paul's 11 A.M. Wrote to Abp of Canterbury—Sir H. Ponsonby—Scotts—Sir
Jos Pease—Ld Granville l.l.—Ld Hartington—Mr Hamilton Tel—and minutes.

[1] Stanhope asked for the date and place of the start of the Afghan commission's work; Fitzmaurice was noncommittal, deprecating 'irritating' language, but without referring to Thornton; *H*
296. 994.

[2] Printed for Cabinet: 1. renewal of part of Crimes Act; 2. local and 3. central Irish govt. reform;
and, 4. land purchase; Add MS 44312, ff. 38–43.

[3] *F.R.*, xliii. 323 (March 1885).

[4] H. C. Rawlinson, 'The Russian advance in Central Asia', *N.C.*, xvii. 557 (April 1885).

Saw Ld Monson—Ld Hampden—W.H.G. Read Taylor Autobiogr.—Goldsmid on Afghan frontier—Arnold on Christmas X.[1]

To LORD HARTINGTON, war secretary, 1 April 1885.   Add MS 44148, f. 3.

In preparation for coming events, notably the Vote of Credit and the Budget, will it not be desirable to obtain from Wolseley on (if not before) his arrival at Cairo a full statement of the military means he will require for the contemplated though only contingent expedition to Khartoum.

After all that has happened we ought in connection with the Vote of Credit to present a liberal Estimate both as to men and money, so that the House may be able to regard it as final &, humanly speaking, as certainly sufficient. I have heard *rumours* of military opinions which may or may not be well founded, but which seem to contemplate a very large operation. Whatever it is to be, we ought to present an Estimate which is fully up to the mark, or we should be open to the reproach (not wholly *un*like Ferry) of having concealed, if not our mis-carriages, yet difficulties which we knew to be in prospect.

2. Th.

St Paul's 11 AM. Wrote to Ld Hartington—Mr Hamilton l. & tel. l.l.l.—Ld Granville tel.— . . . —Ld Aberdeen—& minutes. Saw Mr West—Archd. [J.] Hannah—Sir C. Forster—Mr Heathfield—Sir B. Phillips. Saw the Mayor with Mr . . . and visited the Pavilion, plans of Brighton &c. Visited the Aquarium: & especially delighted with 1. The coral, 2. The anemones, 3. The winged fish, 4. The hermit crab in the whelkshell. Read Taylor's Autobiography.

To LORD HARTINGTON, war secretary, 2 April 1885.   Chatsworth MSS 340. 1706.

Wolseley's letter[2] is indeed an extraordinary one but coming from him, who has thus far commanded every military measure since Feb. 3, it constitutes a very important element of the situation. Surely it was strange to make his first communication to Brett. He now desires us to view the advance to Khartoum, which in February he declared right and wise without any intimation of extraordinary demands, as the most serious affair since Waterloo. He hopes all the Cabinet comprehend its proportions. But he has never before the date of this letter given us the smallest idea of them.

I have telegraphed to you to know whether we should have a Cabinet upon these extraordinary communications. It will be well probably *before* we have it to hear from Wolseley *all* his mind.

When on the 19th February I announced that we had told Wolseley to take his measures on the supposition of our going to Khartoum, I pointed out that an opposite decision might have seriously compromised us on some important points which might call for reasonable effort.

One perhaps the chief was duty to Gordon's friends in Khartoum—that *population* to whom he held us pledged, and for whose sake (as G. could go at any time) we sent Wolseley up the Nile. But since that time all evidence has been to the effect that there was no such population. In fact I am under the impression that most or all of these

---

[1] Both in *C.R.*, xlvii. 457, 517 (April 1885).

[2] Gloomy letter on his difficulties sent to R. B. Brett who circulated it just as he was resigning as Hartington's secretary; the letter strengthened the case for withdrawal; Holland, ii. 28.

grounds are now untenable. There was that great though indeterminate idea of civilisation v. barbarous Mahometanism—but it is very difficult to prosecute it when nature offers such formidable barriers.

The whole situation requires careful review, and deliberation in common when we are ready for it.[1]

3. Good Friday:

holiday, flags flying in the streets! St Paul's matins 10¼ and Passion Service 12–2¾. Wrote to Ld Granville Tel—Mr Hamilton Tel—Mr Leverson Tel—and minutes. Read Taylor Autobiogr. finished I.—Dowden Shakespeare's Women—Fowler on Prices[2]—The Great Problem.[3]

4. Easter Eve. [Holmbury]

No day demands quiet so much as this: but I was torn away to London & Cabinet. Off at 9.30. Cabinet 12–3.30. Reached Holmbury soon after six. Wrote to S.E.G. & H.N.G.—The Queen l.l.—and minutes. Saw Mr H.—Ld RG.—Ld Rosebery—Mr Chamberlain—Ld Granville—Ld Derby—Sir W. Harcourt. Read Rucellai Journal[4]—Taylor's Autobiogr.—Life of Emerson.[5]

Cabinet. Sat. Ap. 4. 85. Noon.[6]
1. Dispatch of de Griers considered. (Harcourt advised acceptance of Russian zone as basis). Determined to negative the proposal of adopting Russian line as basis *pur et simple*. Granville drew evidence (& went off to see Staal at 2) W.E.G. contributing what is within.
2. War & Indian Sec. authorised to proceed with preparations demanded by Indian Govt.

De Griers of Mch. 15. 85. You the Russians appear virtually to exclude by disparagement your own zone, while by direct words you refuse ours. *If so*, there remains only the proposal of an inquiry upon a line prescribed by one of the parties, with the rejection *in limine* of that proposed by the other. This appears to proceed upon the principle that when the two powers are about to undertake a joint inquiry, it appertains to one of them alone to dictate the terms. It is impossible for the British Government to proceed on a basis which substantially denies the equal footing of the two Powers. W.E.G. Ap. 4. 85.[7]

5. Easter Day.

St Mary's Ch mg (with HC) and evg. Wrote to Mr Childers—and minutes. Saw Ld Granville—Sir R. Welby. Conversation on Pattison. Read The Great Problem—Hechler Jerus. Bishopric.[8]

[1] Hartington replied, 3 April, Add MS 44148, f. 7, that he had already asked Wolseley for 'the full extent of his requirements for the autumn expedition'; a cabinet was thus unnecessary.
[2] Both in *C.R.*, xlvii. 517, 536 (April 1885).
[3] See 15 Mar. 85..
[4] See 11 Mar. 85.
[5] Perhaps W. Hague, 'R. W. Emerson: life and philosophy' (1884).   [6] Add MS 44646, f. 72.
[7] ibid., f. 74; Griers' despatch of 15 March was communicated on 1 April; it refused Britain's proposals of 13 March for a frontier settlement, insisting on a Russian definition; FO 65/1238; Ramm II, ii. 355.
[8] See 26 Aug. 83.

To H. C. E. CHILDERS, chancellor of the exchequer,   Childers MS 5/165.
5 April 1885. '*Secret*'.

At the Cabinet yesterday[1] we found the Russian reply wholly unsatisfactory: it was that their line should be taken as a basis, & that the Commission should examine the details. No lightening of the sky yet in that quarter. Meantime Wolseley writes that he will want 12 more battalions of infantry to go to Khartoum; with other arms in due number. Further he writes to Hartington that we shall have on hand 'the most serious affair *since 1815*' and that though the people of England do not understand this, he hopes all the members of the Cabinet do.

On the Suakin side, Graham, rationally enough, appears to abandon all idea of getting at Osman Digna in the mountains.

These are great facts, pregnant perhaps with other matter. I thought it well to give you an intimation of them. It would not surprise me if your Budget had to be put off for a week.

Wolseley also names two years & some months as in his opinion the minimum time for the Railway. Future events will show whether he can take from the Suakin side any part of the force he wants.

As his telegrams have all been (& no wonder) a series expanding in demand & contracting in promise, I do not feel sure that we have even now before us the maximum of his wants.

This will be confided to your Private Secretary to be forwarded with all due respect to your incognito.

6. *Easter Monday.*

St Mary's Ch. at 11¼ A.M. Wrote to Watson & Smith—Rev. S.E.G.—Mr Hamilton—Rev. Mr Smithwick—and minutes. Drive & walk in afternoon. Saw Mr Sheehan.[2] Read Macmillan (Morley) on Pattison[3]—Hechler on Jerus. Bishopric—Taylor's Autobiogr. Ruminated much on the Soudan: also the Afghan frontier. Whist in evg.

7. *E. Tues.*

Ch. 11¼ AM. C.G. went off to Hawarden on her mission of mercy. Wrote to Sir H. Ponsonby—and minutes. Serious conversation with Granville on the *whole* outlook in the Soudan. Also, partially, with F. Leveson. Read Muir on the Eucharist as evidence.[4] Drove to Mrs Broadwood's. Read Card. de Bernio[5]—Taylor's Autobiography. Whist in evg.

8. *Wed.*

Wrote to Mr Childers—Sir C. Dilke—The Queen—Ld Hartington—& minutes. Wrote paper on the Soudan.[6] Read Power's Letters[7]—Taylor's Autobiography.

---

[1] Childers was in Paris, returning from convalescence in southern France.
[2] Perhaps Francis Sheehan, Roman catholic priest at St. George's, London.
[3] *Macmillan's Magazine*, li. 446 (April 1885).
[4] W. Muir, *The Lord's Supper* (1882).   [5] Not traced; name scrawled.
[6] Finished next day; very long paper, circulated to the cabinet on 11 April, 'The military position in the Sudan', Add MS 56452, f. 149, part in Morley, iii. 555; it concludes: 'it seems probable that Gordon . . . altered the character of his mission and worked in a considerable degree against our intentions & instructions. There does not seem to be any question now of the security of the army:

[*See opposite page for n. 6 cont. and n. 7*]

Late walk with the kindest of hosts. Whist in evg. But it was a very anxious day on account of the telegrams on the battle of Penjdeh (late).[1]

To Mrs GLADSTONE, 8 April 1885.[2]   Hawarden MSS.

I ought to have written to you by an early messenger, as you have no second post at Hawarden. But this has been, I am concerned to say, a troubled and painful day of successive telegrams each one more grave than its predecessor. The upshot at present is that— as we are officially informed by our own people—the Russians have impudently and perfidiously attacked the Afghans in Penjdeh the main point they occupied and slaughtered two companies of them in their entrenchments. Of course we have sharply demanded explanations, and the Russian account may give a different colour to the proceeding, but at present it looks *very bad*. The Cabinet meets tomorrow. I have been busy all day: Vita[3] has just come up to offer tea, reminding me of the hour, and at post time I am going out.

Well you had a hard day yesterday but your mission is one of gentleness and peace and I feel assured it will prosper in your hands. Ever your afft   WEG

To LORD HARTINGTON, war secretary, 8 April 1885.   Chatsworth MSS 340. 1711.

1. You will have been shocked, as Granville and I have been, by the news of the attack on Penjdeh and slaughter of Afghans there in their intrenchments. It is deplorable as apparently an act of perfidy, and further as tending to mix together the two questions of a just frontier and of the collision of advanced parties.

I am very far from giving up the notion of arbitration but as the contingency of war cannot be wholly shut out of view, and as the best military advice will be wanted I write to ask whether you will think of bringing Wolseley home from Cairo, & whether if you do it would not be well worth while also to summon Adye from Gibraltar. I only name these things for consideration—the time has not yet come.

2. I also started yesterday to Granville the notion of sending some secret agent into the Black Sea, and getting confidential reports on the condition as to defences & forces of the most important points such as (I suppose) Batoum, Kertch, Sebastopol, Odessa. I mention the last, because if Russia were (as some think she will) to levy fines upon our Colonies, Odessa would be open to retaliation.

9. *Th.* [*London*]

Wrote to Ld Selborne—The Queen l.l. and Tel.—Ld Granville—C.G.—and minutes. Return to town $10\frac{3}{4}$-$1\frac{1}{4}$. Cabinet 2-$4\frac{1}{4}$. H of C. $4\frac{3}{4}$-$8\frac{1}{4}$ & 9-$12\frac{3}{4}$.[4] Saw Mr H—Ld RG—Sir W. Harcourt—Mr Childers—Ld E. Fitzmaurice—Ld Granville. Read Taylor's Autobiogr.

but a most grave question whether we can demonstrate a necessity ... for making war upon a people who are struggling against a foreign and armed yoke. . . . The discontinuance of these military operations would I presume take the form of a suspension *sine die*, leaving the future open. . . . I do not enter on the question whether the adoption of such a policy ought to carry with it a tender of resignation. . . .'

[7] F. Power, *Letters from Khartoum* (1885).

[1] News at 5 P.M. of 'battle', at 6 P.M. from Thornton that Russia will not insist on holding Penjdeh; PRO FO 65/1239 ff. 156-205.

[2] Part in Bassett, 245.

[3] Lady Victoria Alberta, Granville's da.

[4] Answered Northcote on Penjdeh; *H* 296. 1159.

Cabinet. Ap. 9. 85. 2 PM.[1]
1. Russian attack on the Afghans[.] Statement for H of C. today discussed & agreed on.
2. Also communication to Stanhope.[2]
3. Budget to be on 23rd.

10. Fr.

Wrote to Mr Richards—K. of Belgians Tel.—Ld Granville—Ld Hartington—The Queen—& minutes. Saw Mr H—Ld R.G—Mr & Mrs Th. & Sir G. Armitage—Sir W. Harcourt—Mr Childers—Sir C. Dilke—Ld Hartington. H of C. $4\frac{1}{2}$-8 and 9-$11\frac{3}{4}$.[3] Read Taylor's Autobiogr.—Thomas Verax on the Chastity of the French Clergy.[4]

To LORD HARTINGTON, war secretary, 10 April   Chatsworth MSS 340. 1715. 1885. *'Immediate'*.

The confusion of affairs I am afraid may have found its way more or less into my brain. But a question has arisen in my mind whether we are *sure* of being ready to discuss the Queen's Message on Monday, & whether if we are not it would not be wiser to put it off tonight on general grounds in some such terms as I inclose, rather than to run the chance of putting it off on Monday without notice & so perhaps creating much alarm.
I look at the matter thus:
1. The military position generally, & especially in India & in the Soudan, must be considered with care in the Cabinet with a view to adequate explanations when the Message is considered in the House of Commons.
2. This consideration might lead to a necessity either for a further Cabinet on Monday or for communication with the Queen, or both.
3. There would not be time for all this between the Cabinet and Monday.
Unfortunately this did not occur to me until a few minutes after you had left the House. Of course nothing can be done now until later. I shall be here until past 8, and after 9.

11. Sat.

Wrote to The Queen—W.H.G.—C.G.—and minutes. Dined with Sybella Lyttelton: tea Lady Stanleys 5 P.M. Both interesting. Cabinet 12-$3\frac{1}{2}$. Weighty. Saw Mr H—Ld RG—Ld Granville. Read Taylor Autob. (finished)—Ninon et sa Cour[5]—Causes Celèbres Ecclesiastiques.[6]

Cabinet. Sat. Ap. 11 85. Noon.[7]
1. Answer to Smith on Rothschild advances[8]—agreed to.
2. Arrangement of business agreed to as in A.[9] Vote of Credit to be for a) Soudan b) military *preparations*. Will be occasion of unfolding policy.

---

[1] Add MS 44646, f. 75.
[2] E. Stanhope, tory M.P. and frequent questioner on Central Asia. See to Harcourt, 30 Mar. 85.
[3] Questions on Sudan, Afghanistan; *H* 296. 1305.
[4] Abbé Thomas 'Verax', *La verité, toute la verité, rien que la verité sur la chasteté et l'incontinence dans le clergé catholique* (1881).
[5] One of the various collections of the letters of Ninon de Lenclos (Mme. 'Libertine').
[6] T. D. Lewis, *Causes célèbres d'Angleterre* (1883).
[7] Add MS 44646, f. 77.   [8] To the Egyptian govt.; *H* 296. 1458.
[9] 'Monday 13th—message—very limited statement by Secy. of State—Thurs 16th. Egyptian Convention—Rest of the week, finish Committee seats. Monday 20th—lay Vote of Credit. Thurs 23rd—Budget. Rest of week—Report Seats'; Add MS 44646, f. 83.

3. Conversation at large on the question of the expedition to Khartoum and of military operations (offensive) in the Soudan.

4. Port Hamilton—pre-emption or refusal to be sought from China & Japan.[1]

5. Telegram to Lumsden[2] on his movements.

6. Viceroy's telegrams read.[3]

Secret. Cancelled.

Is there anything to prevent the prompt withdrawal of the Nile army by the River to Wadi Halfa if the Cabinet determines on the necessity in the present condition of the Empire of abandoning the offensive operations in the Soudan? The Railway was adopted as a military measure and as a military measure it has been abandoned.[4]

On account of the state of foreign affairs & the actual & possible demands on the resources of the Empire the abandonment of offensive operations in the Soudan and the evacuation of the country subject to some consideration of detail and opportunity [blank][5]

Secret. This paper stands quite apart from the conversation in the Cabinet of today, and contains the *broader* grounds of policy and justice which I conceive to be applicable to the present military position in the Soudan. I circulate it for the perusal of any of my colleagues who may think it worth their while. WEG. Ap. 11. 1885.[6]

Since the Cabinet deliberated in the beginning of February on the consequences of the betrayal of Khartoum, and arrived at the decisions announced to the House of Commons, much has happened, in and out of the Soudan, to throw light upon this very weighty matter.

Many victories have been gained without a single failure, & great honour has been done to the British arms.

But new and formidable evidence has been supplied as to the nature of the enterprise which has been kept in view, and the many demands it would make on the resources of the country. 1. It was assumed that Osman Digna would by a vigorous effort be readily crushed. All the fighting has been successful but he has gone into the mountains, and Gen. Graham tells us he cannot be followed thither. 2. It was assumed that a light infantry railway could be laid from Suakin to or on the road to Berber in such time as essentially to serve the advance on Khartoum in the Autumn. We now know from Lord Wolseley that his expedition to Khartoum can receive no such aid at that time. 3. It was assumed and intended that Berber could be taken before the hot season & a date was indicated in the middle of March. But this has also been found impossible. 4. It was assumed that Lord Wolseley would be able to proceed to Khartoum at first with the force now under his command and (when we decided) with an immediate addition to it. But he already states, that he will require twelve more battalions of infantry, with a proportion of other arms: and who can feel assured that as the enterprise approaches there may not be a call for still larger resources.

---

[1] In Korea; occupied by the British with a view to annexation in case of war; Gladstone felt the foreign office acted beyond the cabinet decision; see Ramm II, ii. 363.

[2] Sir Peter Stark Lumsden, 1829–1918; on Council of India 1883–93; British Commissioner for N.W. frontier demarcation 1884–5. Gladstone complained at his inadequate reports; Ramm II, ii. 356.

[3] Gladstone told the Queen that Kimberley's information that the 'Amir is dreadfully suffering from disease of the kidneys' had not been revealed to the cabinet; CAB 41/19/24.

[4] Undated holograph; Add MS 44646, f. 78. [5] ibid., f. 79.

[6] Holograph; Add MS 56452, f. 179.

I do not here enter upon the moral and political aspects of the question, but only attempt to present it in a limited view, for the chance that this limited view may commend itself to some who would hesitate to adopt wider grounds for a change of course in the Soudan, and that one & the same end might be attained with greater unanimity.

To proceed—While we have had this admirable conduct of the army, and these important military lessons, in Egypt, it is most of all to be noted that events have occurred elsewhere which bring into view the possibility of a war such as to require, if unhappily it came about, the whole resources of the Empire.

A most grave question then arises whether these military resources can with prudence be divided, and a large and increasing proportion of them can be, so to speak, sucked into the Soudan, at a time which so eminently demands that they should be consolidated and kept well in hand.

Apart from the defence of Egypt, which no one would propose to abandon, does there appear to be any obligation of honour, or any inducement of policy, (for myself I should add, is there any moral warrant,) which should induce us, in the present state of the demands on the Empire, to waste a large portion of our army in fighting against Nature, and I fear also fighting against liberty (such liberty as the case admits,) in the Soudan?

The Parliamentary arrangements of the Session at home, the state of our relations with Russia, and the commencement of the hot season in the Soudan, combine to mark out the present time as the proper time for dealing with the question.   WEG Ap.10.85.[1]

12. 1 S.E.

Ch. Royal mg & aft. Walk with Helen. Saw Mr Hamilton—Russian question all alive. Read The great Problem—Le Riche Possessions[2]—Le Fault Traité on Paillardise[3]—De Fonvielle, Miracles.[4]

13. M.

Wrote to Ld Chancellor—The Queen l.l. and Tel.—& minutes. Cabinet 12–4¼. Very stiff. H of C. 4¾–8 and at 10.[5] Wrote Mem. on Staal proposal.[6] Saw Mr H— Ld R.G—Sir W. Harcourt. Dined at Grillion's: alone![7] Read Le Riche, Possessions. Met C.G. at Paddington. Saw Tait: a moment: referred her to Margt Street [R].

Cabinet. Monday Ap. 13. 85. Noon.[8]

---

[1] Holograph; Add MS 56452, f. 173. A further and more generalised version of the mem. begun on 8 April; see 8 Apr. 85n. That mem. was probably circulated before this day's Cabinet.

[2] Abbé Leriche, *Études sur les possessions en général at sur celle de London en particulier* (1859).

[3] G. Lefault, *Petite traicte contre l'abominable vice de paillardise et adultère* (1868).

[4] W. de Fonvielle, *Les miracles devant la science* (1880).

[5] Discussion of Queen's Message enabling embodiment of Reserves; *H* 296. 148.

[6] Ramm II, ii. 357.

[7] Drank a bottle of champagne; see *The chronicle of Grillion's club* (1914), 96; letter of apology from Norton for the club, Add MS 44490, f. 141. See Introduction above, X, section viii.

[8] Add MS 44646, f. 86; rest of sheet blank; Egypt, Afghanistan and 'the actual and possible demands on the military resources of the Empire' were the topics mentioned to the Queen; CAB 41/19/25. Hartington this day announced probable need for 'a considerable portion of the Reserves'.

Secret. Mr. Brett's letter & the memorandum of Ap. 12. 85.[1]

We have *three* points to settle with Russia. 1) The retrospective question as to the affair of Pulikisti. 2) The military occupation of the debated territory. 3) The Frontier.

We agreed that we could not separate 3) from 1) and 2). But it is a different matter to separate 1) from 2) and 3). *They* call for an early solution: but 1) at present gets more & more involved by equivocal and partial statements, and will take time, in all likelihood, to clear up.

That Russia should (apparently) be ready to evacuate the debated land, and to accept Lumsden's line are if verified facts of immense importance. If she undertakes, as she readily may, to give full effect retrospectively, as far as circs. now admit, to the engagement of March 17, surely we may proceed for the benefit of both countries to consider the other points.

Lord Kimberley proposes to dispense with the inquiry on the spot. This I presume, if desired by us under present circs., would be taken by Russia as rather a concession than a demand. The military preparations would of course continue without any relaxation until a Settlement on the proposals of M. de Staal was arrived at.

I have assumed[2] that he could not have hazarded such a proposal without some suggestion or encouragement from his Government. W.E.G. Ap. 13.[3]

To LORD SELBORNE, lord chancellor, 13 April 1885.   Selborne MS 1869, f. 27.
'*Secret*'.

It pains me to write to you at such a moment on matters of business. I can only prevail on myself to do it by my consciousness that you would suffer a greater wrong if I refrained.

You will see my report of today's Cabinet to the Queen. I do not doubt that tomorrow they will submit a substantive recommendation, to the effect which I have generally described.

I hope however that you will find it to be in near conformity with the conditions you lay down. It will not be founded on the Soudanese reasons which some of us feel, & which I for one feel, but will proceed on grounds owned at least by some who deem the Soudanese reasons (so to call them) insufficient. Russia, named or not named, (she is as we believe making large preparations) will be the prominent consideration in the mind of the Cabinet & in all minds. I do not think she will stand alone. We have today received from M. de Freycinet through Lord Lyons a demand, shall I say a command, to procure the quashing of the proceeding on the Egyptian Government against the 'Bosphore':[4] he says unless he has full & immediate satisfaction he must proceed to all extremities. (He has, says Granville, 50,000 men ready for China, who will not now be wanted.) It seems there is none so poor who may not scoff at us, so long as we shall not have shaken ourselves free of our present unnatural entanglements.

We have tried to ward off any debate today, but men could not resist the temptation to use the Queen's message as an opportunity for assailing the War in the Soudan.

14. Tu.

Wrote to Ld Granville—Miss Hayward—Ld Kimberley—Sir S.Northcote—The Queen l.l.—Scotts—and minutes. Dined at Sir C. Forster's. Dr Liddon, Mr [H.?]

---

[1] Russian proposals forwarded *via* R. B. Brett; see Add MS 44490, f. 117. See also Gladstone's mem. of 13 April in Ramm II, ii. 357.

[2] Gladstone's marginal note reads: 'Perhaps this ought not to be *assumed*.'

[3] Add MS 44646, f. 89.   [4] See 25 Apr. 85.

W. Lucy. Saw Mr H—Ld RG—Sir W. Harcourt—Ld Hartington at great length, and stiff. Another anxious day. Cabinet 2¼–3¼. Read Le Riche, Possessions.

Cabinet. Tues. Ap. 14. 1885. 2 PM.[1]
1. Ld Granville recited his conversation with M. Staal yesterday & today on the Mem. & the frontier. Also there was a conversation in which Kimberley & Lessar took place [*sc.* part?].[2]
2. Russian reinforcement telegram. Express regret at any movement which is likely to add to present difficulties.
3. Soudan decision postponed.

To Sir W. V. HARCOURT, home secretary, 14 April   MS Harcourt dep. 9, f. 36.
1885. '*Secret*'.

I thought him [Hartington] a little stiffer this evening apparently not satisfied with my little Memorandum though without definite changes to propose, hankering after a possible resumption of the Khartoum expedition this autumn, and disposed to ask that all the railway work should go on with a view to it at Suakin as well as on the Nile, though speaking variably on the subject.

I cannot think it possible to ask Parliament for funds great or small which mean any advance on Khartoum & resumption of warlike operations.

[P.S.] I left the Memm. with him to consider whether & how to amend it. I do not quite see my way at present.

15. Wed.

Wrote to Mrs Bolton—The Queen tel. and l.—Ld Hartington—Sir W. Harcourt—& minutes. Completed, with the two H.s, the Mem. of policy. Saw Mr H—Ld RG—Mr P—H.J.G.—Chancr of Exr—Sir J. Carmichael—Mr Dickson MP—Sir W. Harcourt. Fourteen to dinner. Read Leriche—Lehec's Catalogue: charged as is so common in Paris with foul matter.[3] Drive with M. & walk.

Cabinet. Wed. Ap. 15. 1885. 2.30 PM.[4]
1. Soudan. WEG read the accord made which was approved.[5] Ld Hartington explained outline of preparation: & Wolseley's statement as to *mode*.
   Wolseley's long telegrams in favour of retaining Nile position. His plan for the defence of Egypt in tel Ap. 14 adopted. Concentrate other troops.
2. Bosphore.[6] Telegrams read from Baring & Lyons. Question of legality has gone to the Law Officers. Improved tone of Freycinet.
3. Suez Canal, superintendence & defence. Baring to develop his plan further.
4. Answer to Graham[7] about friendly tribe that we cannot enter into indefinite engagements & we desire to know how far it is that we propose to carry any assurances.

---

[1] Add MS 56452, f. 180.
[2] See Ramm II, ii. 359; Lessar was the Russian adviser in London on the frontier.
[3] Author's name uncertain; perhaps H. Lehec, *Généalogie des Bourbons de France, d'Espagne, de Naples et de Parme* (1880), with various tables etc.
[4] Add MS 56452, f. 182.
[5] Basis for statement on 21 April; Add MS 44769, f. 69.
[6] The Cairo newspaper; see 25 Apr. 85.
[7] Add MS 56452, f. 188.

To Sir W. V. HARCOURT, home secretary, 15 April   MS Harcourt dep. 9, f. 134.
1885. '*Secret*'.

Please to look at Hartington's note received *this morning* and inclosures herewith, and
at my reply: and send on the reply unless you see cause to write to or (better) see me
upon it. I also send a note which I wrote last night to you[1]—It has no practical meaning (I
hope) now but I send it to you as ⟨to make the⟩ *history*. If you think it well to carry my
reply to Hartington instead of sending it, pray do so. I think it *might work well*.

16. *Th.*

Wrote to Ld Spencer—The Queen tel & l.—Ld Hartington—Mr Chamberlain—
Sir W. Harcourt—and minutes. Dined at Lucy's. H of C. 4¾-8 and 10-11½.[2] Saw
Mr H—Ld RG—Mr Childers & Ld E. Fitzmaurice. Read Leriche. Wrote Mem.
on Palmer.[3] Shopping.

To Sir W. V. HARCOURT, home secretary, 16 April   MS Harcourt dep. 9, f. 135.
1885.

You are the best judge of the question who should introduce the Crofters' Bill, and I do
not dissent from your view. It will of course remain under your special responsibility & no
doubt your name will be on the back.

I think you can probably raise your point about aid to Crofters Emigration at any
Cabinet after the Budget Cabinet on Monday. (Till then after the recent unusual series I
hope there will be a rest.)

17.

Wrote to The Queen tel. & l.—Ld Spencer—Ld Derby—Att. General—Ld Granville—and minutes. H of C. 4¾-8½ and 10-12¼.[4] Saw Mr H—Ld RG—Ld Granville—Mr Childers—Ld G. *cum* Ld Kimberley. Finished Le Riche—began Story
of an African Farm.[5]

18. *Sat.*

Wrote to The Queen Tel.—Chancr of Exr—Ld E. Fitzmaurice—Ld Hartington—
and minutes. Dined at Argyll Lodge. Saw Lambert—Burdell—M'Lachlan [R]. Saw
Mr H—Chancr of Exr—Sir R Welby—Duke of Argyll. Read Fonvielle, Miracles
hors de l'Eglise—South African Farm—Conversion [*sic*] of Ld Lyndhurst.[6]

19. *2 S. Easter.*

Chapel Royal mg & aft. Wrote to Ld Hartington—The Queen tel.—and [blank.]
Saw Ld Granville—Mr Primrose—S. Lyttelton. Read The Great Problem (finished)—Lynch's Remains[7]—Fonvielle—Curteis on Difficulties.[8]

[1] Hartington's note, presumably on Sudan, untraced. See 14 Apr. 85.
[2] Questions on Penjdeh; statement on Egyptian finance; *H* 296. 1865, 1874.
[3] On W. Palmer's *Treatise*; Add MS 44769, f. 77.   [4] Redistribution Bill; *H* 297. 35.
[5] Ralph Iron [i.e. Olive Schreiner], *The story of an African farm*, 2v. (1883); notes on it at Add MS
44767, f. 140.
[6] *Sc.* conversation?
[7] T. T. Lynch, *Gatherings from notes of discourses*, 1st series (1885).   [8] See 15 Mar. 85.

20. M.

Wrote to Ld Granville 1.1.–Ld Hartington 1.1.–The Queen tel. and 1.1.1.–Mr Childers–and minutes. Saw Mr H–Ld RG–Ld Granville–Ld Hartington–Sir W. Harcourt. Cabinet 2–4¼. H. of C. 4¾–7¼ and 9–11½.[1] Read S. African Farm.

I have never known (I think) political anxieties or more crowded, or more complicated. I feel as if I could never have strength for the day. But 'when thou goest through the waters'. And our rule is plain: in each and all to strive to do what the Lord Christ would have done: though at an immeasurable & awful distance.

Cabinet. Monday Ap. 20. 85. 2 PM.[2]
1. Vote of Credit. Detail explained. 11m̄ sanctioned.
2. Budget. New provision required on ordinary Estimates say 4m̄.

Death Duties +	350m
Spirit Duties up 2/-	1000m
Beer ⅓ penny per gallon	650
Income tax 1d at 6d	2000
	4000 m 4 m̄ thus =

To meet the 11m̄. 1d I.T. for 3 years making 7d: 5700m.

Stands over.[3]

21. Tu.

Wrote to Ld Granville 1.1.–Mr Childers–Sir C. Dilke–Mr Hibbert–The Queen 1.1.–Abp of Canterbury–and minutes. Cabinet 2–4¼. Saw Mr H–Ld RG–HJG–Ld Granville–Mr B. Currie–Do & Conclave at H. of L. Dined at Mr B. Currie's. H of C. 4½–7¾ and after dinner. Delivered my statement on the 11m̄: a great relief.[4] Read South African Farm.

Cabinet. Tuesday Ap. 21. 1885. 2 PM.[5]
1. Vote of Credit–two or one? To be taken on Monday.
2. Budget–to be 30th of April. Settlement of disputed question postponed till Saturday. Childers agreed to 3 years limit.
3. Communication with Russia. Much conversation on reply received today.
4. Lumsden's Telegraph of today. Lay forthwith.[6]
   Two questions to decide. 1. Postponement of Budget a week in order to *take Vote of Credit on Monday*. (No change of sitn. special prepn.) 2. 1d. I.T. or Beer & Spirit Duty. Difficulty of 5¾m̄ direct & no Indirect. Death Duties. Any approx[imatio]n possible.

---

[1] Spoke on business of House; *H* 297. 169.

[2] Add MS 44646, f. 95.

[3] Gladstone's note: 'Would it be expedient to let this stand over till tomorrow?'; Granville: 'Might it not be decided at once–But we must settle the answers to questions . . .'; ibid., f. 96.

[4] Statement introducing resolution for Vote of Credit of £11 million for a) Egypt and Sudan, b) 'special naval and military preparations'; exposition of govt. policy avoided; *H* 297. 317.

[5] Add MS 44646, f. 97.

[6] Of 17 April, received this day, arguing Komarov's version of events at Penjdeh erroneous, as Russia had 'advanced to attack Afghan position'; P.P. 1884–5 lxxxvii. 22.

Ap. 21. 85. Russian reply on the three points.[1]

1. Point 1) Although Russia declines any covenant or understanding as to the further & full examination of our complaint respecting the attack on the Afghans & their expulsion from Penjdeh, it remains, quite apart from any misunderstanding the right and duty of any Government to lay before any other Government any complaint which it deems just and grave, and it is supposed on grounds of principle to be the duty of the Government receiving such complaint to see full justice done in the matter and the language of the Russian reply leaves the door open accordingly.

2. Point 2. Considering the quarter from which the suggestion of withdrawal from the debated land proceeded, the answer of the Russian Govt. causes surprise as well as regret. The execution of that suggestion would have had an admirable healing effect at a moment of serious & just irritation. We consider the refusal as a reasonable ground of complaint, and as casting upon Russia herself a very grave responsibility.

3. Notwithstanding this, we do not decline the proposal to prosecute at once the communications respecting the frontier and the delimitation of it on the spot as it may be agreed on by the two Governments.

[For viewing the nature of the replies on the preceding points, it is upon this course of action that we now found chiefly our hopes of an honourable & amicable settlement.][2]

To Sir C. W. DILKE, president of the local government   Add MS 43875, f. 243.
board, 21 April 1885. '*Secret*'.

I hope you will further consider what it would be for anyone to retire from the Government at such a moment as this on account of a proposal of taxation not essentially unjust.[3]

While I take upon me to say this, and while I feel it deeply for myself, and am prepared to give it much scope (as I have already done) in my own action, I shall also use every effort in my power towards a reasonable approximation if one can be found.[4]

22. Wed.

Wrote to Ld Granville—Ld Kimberley—Ld Chancellor—Ld Rosebery—Scotts— and minutes. Dined with the Godleys. Drive with C. Saw Mr H—Ld RG—Bp of London—Scotts. Saw Lambert [R]. Read South African Farm—Causes Célèbres Ecclesiastiques—QR. on Progress.[5]

23. Th.

Wrote to Sir C. Dilke—Ld Hartington—The Queen—Mr Chamberlain—and minutes. H of C. $4\frac{3}{4}$-7 and $11\frac{1}{4}$-$12\frac{1}{4}$.[6] Fifteen to a large breakfast for Miss Anderson.[7] We liked her extremely. Saw Mr H—Ld RG—Ld Granville—Sir W. Harcourt—Mr Chamberlain (on the financial difficulties)—Conclave for framing the answer to Russia. We went to the Lyceum & were delighted with Miss A.

[1] Add MS 44646, f. 100; for the 'points', see 13 Apr. 85.

[2] Gladstone's [ ].

[3] Dilke to Gladstone, 20 April, Add MS 44149, f. 336: 'I meant what I said, & I could not agree to the additional tax on beer under the present circumstances.'

[4] Dilke replied this day, ibid., f. 338 that he and others had made their position plain all along; 'I do not see a half way house'.

[5] [H. S. Maine] in *Q.R.*, clix. 267 (April 1885).

[6] Questioned on Vote of Credit; *H* 297. 485.   [7] i.e. Mary Anderson; see 8 Nov. 84.

acting in Pygmalion, & also in the Comedy & Tragedy.[1] Read South African Farm. Gave evidence for Wirral RR.

24. Fr.

Wrote to The Queen—Ld Granville—The Speaker—Sir C. Dilke—and minutes. H of C. $4\frac{3}{4}$-$8\frac{1}{4}$ and $11\frac{1}{4}$-$12\frac{3}{4}$.[2] Dined with Mr Knowles. Saw Mr H—Ld R.G—Mr Bright—Ld Granville—Mrs Grogan—Mr Childers—Conclave on dispatches to Russia. Read Fonvielle—South African Farm. The birthday of the Govt.

To Sir C. W. DILKE, president of the local government   Add MS 43875, f. 246.
board, 24 April 1885. 'Secret'.

1. Many thanks for the interesting memorandum you have sent me.[3] Chamberlain told me of it, & I said my say in return, purposely without waiting to see it.

2. I also had a long & interesting conversation with Chamberlain on the financial *knot*. I represented to him strongly what I feel more & more strongly as I reflect more, & as we come nearer to decision: that is, the very great importance of the proposal to establish equality in principle between realty and personalty as to the death duties. This must in all likelihood lead to a very serious struggle with the Tories for it strikes at the very heart of class-preference, which is the central point of what I call the lower & what is the now prevalent, Toryism.

I have a lively hope that you & he will feel a strong obligation as well as desire to join in the struggle which will require all our strength.

25. Sat.

Wrote to The Queen—Lord Spencer tel. & l.l.—Ld Hartington—and minutes. Dined with the Duke of Cambridge & had much conversation with him on P of W. in Ireland, on Gen Gordon, religious belief. Cabinet 12-$3\frac{1}{2}$. Saw Mr H—Ld RG—Ld Granville l.l. Drive to see the T.Gs at Wimbledon. He was a shade older.[4] Saw Maclachlan, who will leave, & gave me a test of it [R]. Such a case opens the most extraordinary questions. Read South African Farm.

Cabinet. Sat. Ap. 25. 85. Noon.[5]
     1. Finance. WEG stated Dilke & Chamberlain's expression[?] of the point of their objection[6] & thanked.
     2. A. O'Connor: division of Vote of Credit. Oppose: acting however for the best.
0   3. Russian answer.[7]
     4. Bosphore.[8] Law Officers summoned. Granville stated case & interview with Waddington. See A.

---

[1] Double bill: 'Pygmalion and Galatea', and 'Comedy and Tragedy'.
[2] Question on Afghanistan, Egypt; *H* 297. 658.
[3] Not found. On Manning's offer: Irish clergy would denounce separation and home rule if the central board scheme was passed; Gwynn, ii. 129-30.
[4] Death of two of his daughters this year.   [5] Add MS 44646, f. 102.
[6] To the rise in indirect taxation (beer and spirit duties).
[7] Granville saw de Staal after the cabinet, who said only the German Emperor would be acceptable as arbitrator, and that he would refuse; F.O.C.P. 5140, f. 88.
[8] Suppression of the *Bosphore Egyptien* on Baring's advice: an anti-British newspaper in Cairo; *PP* 1884-5 lxxxix. 665.

On the Vote of credit WEG proposes Soudan.

1. to state the exclusive character of the ground already stated for the concentration of the forces & the aims of the Vote. *Agreed*.
2. To review, without any special authority from the Cabinet the reasons urged by me on Feb. 19 for the resolution arrived at in the beginning of the month.
⟨3⟩5 As to 'special preparations'—what am I to state as the ground of our demand for the Vote? Stand simply on the known & public facts *or* virtually answer Northcote's inquiry.

A. *Substance copied out for Granville.*
1. Record our understanding that the French do not raise any question upon the suppression of the newspaper. 2. As to the manner, we are advised upon a consideration of all the facts that the closure of the printing office was not warranted in law. 3. As it appears that the conduct of the head of the police was in all respects under orders & without blame so far as he was concerned, we feel sure that the French Govt. will agree that the responsibility for the removal of the Consul does not rest with him. 4. As the Govt. have already stated that they do not disclaim responsibility for the decision to suppress the paper, they have no hesitation in associating themselves with the regret which they have advised the Govt. of the Khedive to express as to the incidents which attended the suppression.

To Sir W. V. HARCOURT, home secretary, 25 April   MS Harcourt dep. 9, f. 136.
1885.[1]

I have received your letter about the Scotch Secretary Bill.[2] I am settling with Spencer on what day next week to determine our Bills for the session in Cabinet so that he may come over. I hope the Lord Advocate is *ready* with the Crofters' Bill.

26. 3 S.E.

Chapel Royal mg and aft. Wrote to Ld Granville—Abp of Canterbury. Saw Mr H. l.l. (Russian & other matter). Drive with C. and walk. Finished S. African Farm. A most remarkable, painful, book. Read Wilberforce's Poems[3]—Causes Célèbres Eccles.—and [blank.]

27. M.

Wrote to Pr. of Wales—Sec. District Co.—Ld Chancr—Subdean Ch. Royal—The Queen l.l.—Lady Phillimore—Abp of Canterbury—Sir H. Ponsonby—& minutes. Saw Mr H—Ld RG—Ld Granville 11¾-1¼. Drive with C. Dined at Sir C. Forster's. H of C. 4¾-8½. We began with much contention. Spoke over an hour for Vote of Credit. Carried in a most effective manner.[4]

[1] 'Topped and tailed' by Gladstone, the rest in Hamilton's hand.
[2] Of 23 April, Add MS 44199, f. 203: Rosebery ('essential in order to commend it to the *chauvinists*') ready to introduce the bill, if education included.
[3] S. Wilberforce, *Poems*, ed. R. G. Wilberforce (1884).
[4] Successfully opposed dividing the Vote (i.e. avoided separate discussion of Sudan), and carried the Vote in cttee. without division; stung by Churchill, he made intemperate remarks on the 1878 Vote, for which he apologised on 30 April; *H* 297. 825, 847.

To Sir W. V. HARCOURT, home secretary,   MS Harcourt dep. 9, f. 137.
27 April 1885.[1]

To revert to the Scotch Secretary Bill.[2] I assume that you will in concert with Rosebery raise the question of the transfer of Education to the Cabinet. I think you would do best to raise it after the question of a Local Government Bill for Ireland has been considered tomorrow.

28. Tu.

Wrote to The Queen l.l.—Ld Hartington—Ld Granville—Sir H. Ponsonby l l— and minutes. Dined at Lucy's. Edith sang. H of C. $4\frac{1}{2}$-6, 7-$8\frac{1}{4}$ & after dinner.[3] Cabinet 2-$4\frac{1}{4}$. Saw Mr H—Ld RG—Mr Chamberlain—Ld Spencer—Mr Lefevre—& minutes. Read Society in London[4]—Causes Celebres Eccles.

Cabinet. Tuesday Ap. 28. 85. 2 PM[5]
1. Legislation of the year. Declaration cannot be Friday. Seats Bill occupies to Friday. Order of Registration Bills to be determined. See A. Bills considered—as within.
2. Ld Granville related his conversation with Waddington on the Bosphore.
3. Also Staal's new explications from [General] Komaroff. Thank & express satisfaction that Russia continues help in elucidation.[6]
4. Gordon [Journals]. As far as we have a desire it is for the publication of the whole, but we ⟨leave the matter absolutely to⟩ do not attempt to interfere with his [i.e. Sir H. Gordon's] discretion.

A.[7] Committee to prepare for consideration a modified Crimes Bill: Spencer, Harcourt, Trevelyan, Chamberlain, ⟨Carlingford or Rosebery,⟩ C. Bannerman. N.B. to consider question whether any provisions should apply to U.K.
Query also on Local Govt. Bill—modifying its [i.e. the Committee's] own composition—and Land Purchase—bringing in Childers, Lefevre.
1. Princess Beatrice. Inquiry.[8] 2. Crofters. 3, 3a, 3b: Irish: modified Crimes Bill. Local Government.
Scotch: Secretary for Scotland to have Education.
        Universities. no tie on this. Wales: Intermediate Education—to try.
1. First after Seats & Registration announce Inquiry[8] into present mode of making these provisions at an early period: say after the election if present ministers continue.
2. Crofters Bill.

29. Wed.

Wrote to Mr Trevelyan—Ld Hartington l.l.—and minutes. 11-$1\frac{1}{4}$. Ld Spencer & Mr Chamberlain on Irish matters: very grave. $2\frac{1}{2}$-$3\frac{3}{4}$. Ld Granville on do and on

---

[1] 'Topped and tailed' by Gladstone, the rest in Hamilton's hand.
[2] See 25 Apr. 85n.
[3] Questions; Redistribution Bill; *H* 297. 972.
[4] *Society in London. By a foreign resident* (1885).
[5] Add MS 44646, f. 107.
[6] See Granville to Thornton this day, F.O.C.P. 5140, f. 121.
[7] Add MS 44646, ff. 108-10.
[8] i.e. into the Civil List; 'the Queen would prefer that the inquiry should be held now, as she feels safe in Mr. G.'s hands'; Bahlman, *Hamilton*, ii. 857.

Russia. Saw Mr H—Ld R.G—Cav. Nigra[1]—Scotts—Sir N. Rothschild. 4½-7¼. A very interesting conversation with the Prince of Wales on his return.[2] He said 'I should not mind knowing Mr Parnell'. Dined at Sir N. Rothschilds. Lady N. & Mrs Flower, my neighbours, both of them very intelligent & well-informed. Read Causes Celèbres Eccl. Saw Maclachlan once more [R].

To LORD HARTINGTON, war secretary, 29 April   Chatsworth MSS 340. 1756.
1885.

1. I think your arrangement for communication with Northbrook & Kimberley on the directions to Wolseley is a good one.[3]

2. About Osman Digna, you will of course bear in mind what has been announced to Parliament about offensive operations which is taken to mean their cessation. All I can at this moment contribute to the solution of the difficulty is this.

(1) I take it for granted you see no chance of getting hold of him personally by some *ruse* or surprise not likely to entail serious bloodshed—as this would be a very good way out of the matter if practicable.

(2) But if this cannot be done, why should we not, as he is defeated & driven off the ground, invite or summon him through some appropriate channel to come in & confer with us on an understanding for the future, assuring him of liberty & honourable treatment?

(3) If this is refused by him it would clear the ground & give some more liberty of action. If it is accepted I can conceive no reason why it might not solve the question.

30. Th.

Wrote to Watsons—The Queen l.l.l.l.—Ld Hartington—Ld Shaftesbury—& minutes. H. of C. 4¾-8 and 10-12¼. Made my apology.[4] Drive with C.—& walk. Saw Mr H—Ld RG. 1 l.—Ld Granville (Mirabilia!)—Ld Derby—Ld Spencer. Eight to dinner. Finished Causes Celèbres Eccles.

To LORD HARTINGTON, war secretary, 30 April   Chatsworth MSS 340. 1758.
1885.

1. You will doubtless prepare yourself for such debate as may arise tonight on the military situation and policy in the Soudan: and I think it is far from improbable that the course of it may improve our means of judgement with reference to various points affecting both Suakim and the Railway.

2. I am, I think, the only min[is]ter who has yet spoken on the situation and policy in the Soudan as they now stand, and it is I think very desirable that you, and others, should now come out.

3. I wish to take as little part tonight as propriety will allow. I am told however that the Opposition means to complain of my having attacked the proceedings of 1878 on Monday. The fact is that I sincerely regret having allowed myself to be drawn off my proper path into the revival of an old controversy, without any premeditation. And

---

[1] See 3 Dec. 55; now Italian ambassador in London.

[2] From a tour of Ireland.

[3] See Add MS 44148, f. 36; Suakin operation 'ought *not* to be stopped' while chance of dispersing Osman's forces remains.

[4] *H* 297. 1127 (see 27 Apr. 85n.); Childers' budget followed.

considering that the Opposition behaved so well about the vote, I am even considering *whether I should not do well to express this regret at the commencement of business today.* It would be an unusual proceeding, but perhaps justified by the time & case. There is much to be said for as well as against it. You would do me a kindness if you would turn it over in your mind, and advise me before the House meets.

4. I will say no more about Suakim until tomorrow, except this, that the gigantic dimensions and menacing aspect of the Russian question seem to me to dwarf everything else, and that I hope you with Kimberley and Northbrook will give the whole force of your minds to considering how, and where, we can best apply in the case of need such resources as we possess against a big bullying adversary.

Fr. May One. SS. Phil. & J.

C. went off to Hawarden. Much reflection, even in bed & against rule, respecting what may happen in this really wonderful, yet it may be happy, crisis. H. of C. $4\frac{3}{4}$–$8\frac{1}{4}$ & 9–1.[1] Wrote to Sir S. Northcote–C.G.–The Queen–& minutes. Saw Mr H.–Ld RG l.l.–Mr Chamberlain–Ld Spencer–Sir C. Dilke. Read Society in London–Temple Bar on G. Sand and G. Eliot[2]–Abbé Thomas Verax.

2. Sat.

Wrote to Mr Bright–Ld Rosebery–The Queen–H.N.G.–C.G.–and minutes. Saw the American Maxey(?)[3] Gun at 25 George St: most curious & interesting.[4] Saw Mr H–Ld RG–HJG–Ld Granville l.l. He brought at the Academy the glad tidings of the Russian answer, which humanly speaking means peace. God be praised for His merciful and gracious work. $2\frac{1}{4}$–$3\frac{1}{2}$ At the Academy: saw Mr Agnew there. It seemed to me *good*. Cabinet at 5, suddenly called together. We framed our reply. Dined at Miss Monk's.

Cabinet. Sat. May 2. 1885. 5 PM.[5]
(Absent: Ld Spencer, Mr Chamberlain, Sir W. Harcourt, ⟨Mr Trevelyan, Mr Lefevre⟩ Ld Carlingford, ⟨Ld Rosebery⟩.
Russian answer[6] & Viceroy's telegram. Ans. agreed on as within [i.e.]: It has never been our desire to see gallant officers on either side put upon their trial but when circs. of so painful & grave a character had occurred we have deemed it essential to know that a deliberate covenant between two great States had been duly interpreted and applied as the honour of those countries required. We have the satisfaction of believing on the receipt of the dispatch of the [blank] from St Petersburg that it embraces all which is needed for this essential purpose. And we are willing accordingly to adopt it as the text of future proceedings and to settle at once the principal points for the delimitation of the frontier.[7]

---

[1] Spoke on Irish Registration Bill; *H* 297. 1324.

[2] *Temple Bar*, lxxiii. 480, 512 (April 1885).   [3] Gladstone's question-mark.

[4] Demonstration of the Maxim gun at the Institute of Civil Engineers; see Bahlman, *Hamilton*, ii. 854.

[5] Add MS 44646, f. 112.

[6] Proposing neutralization of Penjdeh district until frontier agreed on; *PP* 1884–5 lxxxvii. 378.

[7] Another draft at Add MS 44646, f. 116. Final version given to de Staal on 4 May; F.O.C.P. 5140, f. 133 and *PP* 1884–5 lxxxvii. 379.

To Mrs GLADSTONE, 2 May 1885.[1]   Hawarden MSS.

What was a ray of light yesterday, is a flood today, and the great Russian question is, according to all human probability amicably settled; as far as the present stage, and the point of threatening difficulty, are concerned.

Say this very quietly at Hawarden and in less flaming terms. It will be made known in Parliament on Monday. Probably the papers of that day will have got hold of it in one way or the other. I am told that the favourable announcement in today's Daily News raised the Russian funds five or six per Cent.

How is it possible to be sufficiently thankful.

> Praise to the Highest in the Height
> And in the depth be praised
> In all His works how wonderful
> How just in all his ways[2]

This great event—for such it is—will not solve the difficulties of the Govt. connected with Ireland—on the contrary it may even increase them. But I see my own way with tolerable clearness. Many weeks ago I told you that what then looked so dark was of such a character that it might become very bright. There are now reasonable likelihoods of a general winding up of this Parliament & Government such as to be beyond all my most sanguine anticipation.

The answer came from Petersburgh this afternoon—the Cabinet was summoned at a moment's notice, & all were agreed in framing a reply which may be called one of simple acceptance. Praise to the Most High.

A delightful day of showers. Very interesting academy. I dine with Harry at Paddington. Ever your afft   WEG

3. 4 S.E.

Chapel Royal mg (with H.C.) and evg. Wrote to Ld Granville—Mrs Bolton—C.G. Saw Mr H. Dined at Marlborough House. They were most kind & pleasant. But it is so unSundaylike & unrestful. I am much fatigued in mind & body. Yet very happy. Read Death in 19th Cent.[3]—Mrs Macdonald's Buddhism[4]—Gregoire, Xme et les Femmes[5]—De Rastignac on Divorce[6]—and other works.

4. M.

Wrote to Ld Granville—Lady Rothschild—Ld Herries—Lady Phillimore—Mr Mills—Canon Westcott—The Queen—Ld Fitzgerald—Ld Spencer—and minutes. Drive with Mary. Saw Mr H—Ld RG—Ld Spencer—Mr Chamberlain—Sir C. Dilke—Ld Granville—Ld Gr. and conclave. H of C. $4\frac{3}{4}$-$8\frac{1}{2}$ & $9\frac{1}{2}$-$2\frac{1}{2}$. Spoke on Russian question.[7] A heavy day: much knocked up. My head is blocked and choked: but the heart comparatively light. Read Fortn. Rev. articles on Conservatives.[8]

[1] Part in Bassett, 247.
[2] A curious rendering of Newman's hymn.
[3] N.C., xvii. 827 (May 1885).   [4] In F.R., xliii. 703 (May 1885).
[5] Entry in L. Grégoire's Dictionnaire, many eds.
[6] A. Sicaire de Chapt de Rastignac, Accord de la révélation et de la raison, contre le divorce (1790).
[7] Deb. on Vote of Credit; H 297. 1570.
[8] Three articles, 'Conservatives on themselves', F.R., xliii. 611 (May 1885).

Shown to Mr Chamberlain Monday evg. May 4. 1885. without naming an author. Coercion Bill for one year. Promise of a large measure of local Govt. in Ireland next year. Abolition of the Vice Royalty.[1]

5. Tu.

Wrote to Sir W. Harcourt—Ld Hartington l.l.—Ld Spencer—Ld Kimberley—Sir J. Lambert—The Queen—& minutes. H of C. 4¾-[blank].[2] Saw Mr H—Ld RG 1 l—Ld Granville—Sir C. Dilke—Mr Chamberlain—Ld Spencer—Ld Hartington. Drive with C. Read Roman d'une Russe.[3] Another anxious, very anxious day, and no clearing of the sky as yet. But after all that has come, what may not come?

Secret. Mr Chamberlain's idea is
1. That the two subjects of the Crimes Act and a large measure of Local Government for Ireland are at this time vitally connected.
2. That only two courses are open for choice: a. Both a Crimes Act and a large Local Government Act. b. Neither a Crimes Act nor a Local Government Act.
3. These propositions are subject to the following comments. That if there be a large local Government Bill, the Crimes Bill would not, if at all moderate, require to be very jealously restrained, though a sweeping reduction from the present measure is anticipated. That any Local Government Bill not embodying the principle of a Central Board would be unavailing for the purpose in view. That it might not be necessary to pass the Local Govt. Bill during the present year, provided it were introduced & distinctly stamped as the policy of the Govt. That the alternative of 'neither' need not prevent an amendment of the Jury Law to allow of Special Juries, *nor* an identity of Law as to boycotting and intimidation provided that a power of appeal to a special jury is allowed by the person arraigned. W.E.G. May 5. 85.[4]

To Sir W. V. HARCOURT, home secretary, 5 May 1885.   MS Harcourt dep. 9, f. 138.

From what you say,[5] I need not trouble you on the Burials' Bill you are preparing. Its comparative claims to be pressed will of course remain for consideration hereafter.

I propose to have a Cabinet on Thursday, mainly, as seems probable, on Soudanese affairs. I agree with you as to Wolseley's dispatch, which seems to me a piece of matchless impudence.[6] I do not see that we have any course before us but to adhere fully to our public declaration of Ap. 20 which was the result of such full deliberation.

6. Wed.

Wrote to Ld Kimberley—Mr Chamberlain—Ld Granville—Mr Childers—& minutes. Saw Mr H—Ld RG—Ld Granville[7]—Ld Spencer—Sir H. Ponsonby—Sir W. Harcourt. Dined at Mr Tennant's. Sat by Laura. Mr Woodall's party afterwards: Verbeck, & Bertram, conjurors, marvellous. The phrase sleight of hand

[1] Add MS 44769, f. 102.   [2] Questions; Registration Bill; *H* 297. 1647.
[3] Fanny Lear, *Le Roman d'une Americaine en Russie* (1875).
[4] Add MS 44769, f. 103; further notes on 6 May added at ibid., f. 105.
[5] Letter of 5 May, Add MS 44199, f. 205 on need for (a) a Burials Bill, (b) expediting of withdrawal from Sudan.
[6] See 7 May 85n.
[7] See mem. in Ramm II, ii. 366.

surely does not meet the case. H of C. at 5.30.[1] Drive with C. Read Roman &c.—
Amn Review on W.E.G.[2]

To J. CHAMBERLAIN, president of the board of   Chamberlain MSS 5/34/35.
trade, 6 May 1885.[3] '*Secret*'.

I think that to my conversations with you on the merits of the case as regards Crimes
Bill & Local Government Bill for Ireland I ought to add a word on my personal position,
which is peculiar at this moment.

I consider that my interposition in these questions is that of an *amicus curiae*. My
covenant with my colleagues about Redistribution is substantially fulfilled, & our foreign
difficulties are as I conceive (if the Financial Convention for Egypt can now be regarded
as safe in France) effectually relieved. Such at least are the appearances & probabilities of
the case: the result is that I am a free man, & am entitled to claim my release without
either rendering or having a reason, except that my work is done.

My opinions about Local Self Government in Ireland have I think long been well
known; but I have preserved an entire liberty of action as to the time & circumstances of
their application. Still I shall be most happy if in the smallest degree I can aid those who
are less free than myself towards the solution of a problem soon to come fully into view.

What I hope & am endeavouring to promote is that my colleagues shall communicate
freely among themselves, & shall also tender to one another whatever suggestions may
occur to them, during the days that have yet to pass before they come to any decision on
the course that they may have to pursue. Many difficulties have been solved during these
five years by time & thought, & this may yet yield to them like the rest.

7. *Th.*

Wrote to The Queen l.l.—Ly de Rothschild—Mr Childers l.l.—Ly Coleridge—Ld
Granville—& minutes. Cabinet 12-4. Saw Mr H—Ld RG—Ld Granville—Ld
Rosebery—Sir C. Dilke. Evg mostly at home. H of C. $4\frac{3}{4}$-7 and $10\frac{1}{4}$-$11\frac{1}{4}$.[4] Read
Roman d'une Americaine.

Cabinet. Thurs. May 6 [*sc. 7*] *1885. Noon.*[5]
R. Grosvenor attended.
Soudan. Plan of holding the Nile to Merawi. Hartington's anticipations & accounts of the
state of the army.[6] 'Original orders hold good & province of Dongola to be evacuated
with full consideration of all our military exigencies.'[7]

[1] Spoke on business of the House; *H* 297. 1810.

[2] Perhaps Conway's article in *North American Review*, cxxxvi. 223 (1883).

[3] In Garvin, i. 602, with Chamberlain's reply that the government had 'a chance—probably a final
chance—of settling the Irish difficulty . . .'.

[4] Questions; army estimates; *H* 297. 1857.

[5] Add MS 44646, f. 117; note from Chamberlain: 'I have to receive a very important deputation at
3 P.M. Dilke holds the same view as I do as to the necessity for carrying out retirement'; ibid., f. 119.

[6] Wolseley's long letter to Hartington of 16 April, received 2 May, putting forward options sup-
posedly evenhandedly, but in fact advocating the breaking of 'Mahdism' (supplemented by his
unequivocal telegram this day); Buller's report likewise, fowarded by Baring, received 3 May;
F.O.C.P. 5148, ff. 100, 102; Hartington's wire to Wolseley of 8 May, 11.55 p.m.: 'adhere to decision to
adopt proposal for defence of Egyptian frontier at Wady Halfa . . . I understand you to abandon plan
of concentration at Dongola', but decision not to be publicised; ibid., f. 133.

[7] Phrase scrawled; thus, in letter to the Queen.

Situation. Resolved to take (by previous agreement if possible) tomorrow for Seats—Monday for Regist. Charges with a view to serious issue. Postpone Budget.

Afghan frontier. Postpone until after Stevens[1] comes? We have the Ameer and Indian Council for the proposed arrangements. Why wait? Proceed at once. (Penjdeh the whole question).

Emperor of Germany: ask him to be Referee? Yes: (Conditional inquiry already sent). If he refuses shall we accept Denmark? Yes.[2] Question to Pauncefoot as to Commission on Suez Canal—information not received.

To H. C. E. CHILDERS, chancellor of the exchequer,   Add MS 44548, f. 13.
7 May 1885.

I forgot to announce today that the Budget could not come on next Thursday but it will do as well I think tomorrow.

Is it quite impossible to get out of the Spanish business? For really the embarrassment threatens to be very serious. It is a blot in the Budget beyond our power to cover that we do not touch wine. But if wine cannot be touched on account of Spain, & spirits & beer cannot be touched on account of wine, it follows that on account of the wretched Spanish concern we are shut out from the fairest field of extra taxation we possess, after the Income Tax.

Could this difficulty be got over I can imagine a possible though not very clear modification of the plan.[3]

8. Fr.

Wrote to Sir H. Ponsonby—Ld Granville—Ld Spencer—Mr Childers—The Queen—Sir W. Harcourt—& minutes. H. of C. $4\frac{3}{4}$-$7\frac{3}{4}$.[4] Saw Mr H—Ld RG—Fehmi Pacha—Ld Granville—Ld Hartington *cum* Sir W.H.—do *cum* Mr Chamberlain—Ld Rosebery *cum* Mr Chambn. Dined at Ld Rosebery's. Read Fanny Lear—Ly Bellairs on the Transvaal.[5]

To Sir W. V. HARCOURT, home secretary, 8 May 1885.   MS Harcourt dep. 9, f. 139.

I hope that in the conversation which you prosecuted with so much vigour this evening on the Bench you were not under the impression that some degree of secession from within the Cabinet would as matter of course have the same effect on our position as defeat in the House of Commons. It would be a deplorable, an ominous, perhaps a fatal event: but I for one do not think it would in itself have any of the absolving force which would belong to a vote of the House. I do not know who would or would not take a like view with myself.

9. Sat.

Wrote to The Queen—Ld Northbrook. Cabinet 2-5. Saw Mr H—Ld RG—Sir W. Harcourt—Ld Acton—Do *cum* Sir C. Dilke. Family wedding dinner for

---

[1] (Sir) Alexander Condie *Stephen (1850-1908; Lumsden's assistant on the Afghan border commission) returning to London to report.

[2] F.O. mem. of 18 June 1885 summarised developments: Bismarck objected, fearing Russian ill-feeling; 'it was agreed that, supposing the Emperor declined the proposal, it was to be treated as *non avenu*, and the conversation with Prince Bismarck as secret'; F.O.C.P. 5126.

[3] Childers replied, 8 May, Add MS 44132, f. 128, that 'we may be able to get out of the bargain'.

[4] Questions; Redistribution Bill; *H* 298. 33.

[5] Lady Bellairs, *The Transvaal war 1880-1881* (1885).

A. Lyttelton:[1] all seemed very happy. Tea at Argyll Lodge. Read Flabile's Arbor[2]—Fanny Lear.

Cabinet. Saturday May 9. 1885. 2 PM.[3]
1. German Emperor. Cabinet think it desirable to adhere to former advice—(Queen suggests King of Saxony).
2. G. Hamilton's motion & the Soudan. Ld Hartington stated substance of his intended address for Monday. Decisions practicably in [*sc* is] to be abandonment of the Khartoum expedition.
   Suakin. Northbrook's plan. a. Egyptians to renounce. b. Turkey to have a time allowed.[4]
Committee on provision for Royalties. Cabinet adhere.[5]
3. Kimberley recited progress in fixing points of Afghan frontier. Progress made. Question of line from Murirghab to Khoja Saleh. Proceed by Protocol. Proposed Article VI—not approved.
4. Postpone Budget until after Whitsuntide.
5. Wine duties. End the Spanish negotiation. Raise the duties. retain 26%.
6. Irish Legislation. Must be declared by next Friday at latest. Query Monday? Chamberlain stated the anti-Spencer view.
   Chamberlain's statement of his view of Irish policy as to a Central Board.[6]

To LORD SPENCER, Viceroy of Ireland, 9 May 1885.   Althorp MSS K8.

I am not going to bore you with doses of persuasion about a Central Board in Ireland. That subject is dead as mutton for the present, though as I believe for the present only. It will quickly rise again & as I think perhaps in larger dimensions.

But how as to the immediate future? Some members of the Cabinet, I do not know how many, will resign rather than demand from Parliament (without a Central Board Bill) the scheme of penal or repressive provisions which you desire. In what way, after such resignation, are such provisions to be carried through Parliament in what remains of the session.

I believe that if we all had the same point of view, and that point yours, we might *perhaps* by sacrificing all other legislation, fight the measure through. But there is some legislation which hardly can be sacrificed: and some among us will be no parties to the proposal, but will join the resistance to it.

You may ask me where I shall be. I shall be neither with the enacting nor with the resisting party, but shall avail myself, before the tempest bursts, of my title to retire on the simple ground that my engagements are fulfilled. No one has a right to ask me my opinion on a question which has not actually arisen, though it may be about to arise. Policy often determines duty: and it is my present impression that there will be no call of just policy on me to take part in the fray which I desire and seem entitled to avoid.

But the computation I make assumes my absence; and when I ask myself how is the Crimes Act you desire to be obtained? I am compelled to answer that I do not know.

[1] i.e. for Alfred Lyttelton and Laura Tennant.
[2] Untraced.
[3] Add MS 44646, f. 120. Holograph note: 'To discuss Crimes Act *now* is an unmixed mischief'; ibid., f. 122.
[4] Written on a separate sheet, ibid., f. 121v.
[5] Gladstone's mem., ibid., ff. 123–6.
[6] Dilke noted: 'Chamberlain's scheme received the support of all the Commoners except Hartington, and was opposed by all the peers except Lord Granville ...'; Gwynn, ii. 132.

In the rear of this arises another question. Is it not better to start with an insufficient Crimes Act (I am speaking for those who think it such) which could be raised to sufficiency upon practical proof of its not being enough, than to run the heavier risks presented by the picture I have drawn?[1]

10. 5 S.E.

Chapel Royal mg & aft. Saw Ld Wolverton—Mr H. 111. Dined at Mrs Heywood's. Wrote to Ld Chancellor—Ld Hartington l.l.—Ld Spencer.[2] Read Wilson on the Bible[3]—reperused Q.R.—Fairbairn on Card Newman & Protestantism[4]—Vaughan Ep. to Philippians.[5]

11. M.

Wrote to Mr Guinness—Ld Granville—Mr Martin—The Queen l.l.l.—Atty General—Ld Spencer l.l.—C. Lacaita—and minutes. Saw Sir W. Harcourt—Mr Chamberlain—Mr H—Ld RG—H.J.G.—Mr Ch. *cum* Sir C. Dilke—Ld Granville—Ld Hartington—Ambassadors of Russia, Germany, France, Italy, at the Levée. Dined at Grillion's: conversation Haute Politique. H of C. $4\frac{1}{2}$-$7\frac{3}{4}$ and 10-$2\frac{1}{2}$. Spoke on Russia & Soudan.[6] Read Fanny Lear.

To LORDS HARTINGTON and NORTHBROOK,   Add MS 44148, f. 58.
war secretary and first lord of the Admiralty, 11 May 1885.

Is the House to be told today how much of the 11⋒[7] is spent or pledged?
7⋒was mentioned in the Cabinet? Is any of this *moveable* and if so how much?

To LORD SPENCER, Viceroy of Ireland, 11 May 1885.   Althorp MSS K8.

I have seen Harcourt, & also Chamberlain, & I am glad to find that matters are in a fair way of adjustment.

It seems to me that they have reached a point at which it is time to throw the proposals into form & I would suggest that you should arrange a meeting with Harcourt & Chamberlain, having also C. Bannerman, the Attorney General, the Irish Solicitor, perhaps Trevelyan? & anyone else whom you may think proper, & should then dispose both of the final form of the proposals, & of the question how far they or any of them can be embodied in the permanent & general law.[8]

I fully recognise the considerate manner in which you have acted.

[1] Spencer thought this unacceptable, but argued against Gladstone's retiring; Add MS 44312, f. 97.
[2] Never sent; see Hammond, 371n.
[3] Perhaps D. Wilson, 'Holy Scripture the only infallible guide' (1835).
[4] *C.R.*, xlvii. 652 (May 1885); see also 1 Feb. 85.
[5] C. J. Vaughan, *St Paul's Epistle to the Philippians* (1883).
[6] *H* 298. 166.
[7] Of the vote of credit.
[8] Meeting next day appeared to reach a compromise on basis of no coercion or land purchase or central board until after the dissolution; Chamberlain, *Political memoir*, 149. But Spencer thought Chamberlain accepted a further year's coercion; Spencer, i. 302.

12. *Tu.*

Wrote to Chancr of Exr—Ld Rosebery—Mr Carnegie—Ld Spencer—Ld R.G.—
The Queen—& minutes. Dined with Sybella [Lyttelton], *family*. Saw Mr H—Ld
RG—Ld Granville—Sir C. Dilke—Conclave on Lopez motion. Drive with C.
H. of C. 4¾–7¾ & 11½–2½. Spoke against Lopez.[1] The Division (280:258) highly
advantageous to Govt. Read Fanny Lear.

13. *Wed.*

Wrote to Sir C. Dilke—Sir H. Ponsonby l l l—Ld Derby—Mr Chamberlain—Sir F.
Sandford—Ld Spencer l l—Ld Granville—Mr Buchanan N.S.W.—and minutes.
Dined at Lambeth Palace. H of C. 12¼–1½ and 3–4.[2] Saw Mr H—Ld R.G—
G.L.G.—Mr Chamberlain—Sir C. Dilke—Sir W. Harcourt—Bp of London—Mr C.
Bannerman—Abp of Canterbury. Drive with C. Finished Fanny Lear—read
Layard on Turkey[3]—'For the term of his Natural Life'.[4]

To LORD SPENCER, Viceroy of Ireland, 13 May 1885.   Althorp MSS K8.

I asked Hamilton to tell you that I hoped I had made some impression upon Chamberlain as to the one year plan. I have also seen Harcourt: & I am to hear from Chamberlain
early tomorrow.[5] On Friday we must have a Cabinet, & what I would press upon you is
that if you are very anxious for a Land Purchase Bill you should at once endeavour to
arrange the terms of it with Childers, as to the leading points. I will carefully follow up the
other subject to the best of my power.

14. *Ascension Day.*

Holy Commn in Lambeth Palace Chapel at 8.30. Wrote to Lord Hartington—
Ld Spencer—The Queen l.l.—Ld Hartington—Sir Thos G.—and minutes.
H. of C. 4¾–8½ and 10¼–12.[6] Audience of HM. 3–3¾. Saw Mr H—Ld RG—Mr
Chamberlain—Ld Spencer—Sir W. Harcourt—Mr Childers & others. Read His
Natural Life. Most of the day was spent in anxious interviews and endeavours to
bring or keep the members of the Cabinet together.

To H. C. E. CHILDERS, chancellor of the exchequer,   Add MS 44548, f. 17.
14 May 1885.

I am sorry for what I have to say because I know it will disappoint you, but since our
conversation I have entered further into the question of the Budget with several
members of the Cabinet, & I find it to be quite clear that any attempt to settle the final

---

[1] Lopez' resolution to recommit the Registration Bill so as to exclude election charges from local
rates; *H* 298. 371.
[2] Registration Bill; *H* 298. 441.
[3] Layard in *C.R.*, xlvii. 609 (May 1885).
[4] Untraced.
[5] See Gladstone's note to Spencer, 14 May, Althorp MSS K8: 'Chamberlain . . . apprehends Parliamentary defeat if the Bill to be substituted for the Crimes Act is to last more than one year'. On 15
May, ibid., Spencer withdrew objections to the modified Bill, but required it for two years.
[6] Spoke successfully for Princess Beatrice's annuity; *H* 298. 492.

form of the financial proposals now would result in *disaster*. You will I think have to run the risk of anticipated deliveries of wine when the rupture of negotiations with Spain is announced, & I think there is ground for believing it will not be very formidable.

I should think probably the best course will be to have the fresh Committee of Ways & Means fixed, after Whitsuntide, for the Monday which you have taken for the second reading of your Bill, or for the preceding Friday, & so to get the Wine Resolution before the Committee on the Bill. This is on the favourable supposition that a pacific arrangement may then be made, which at present would too plainly be impossible.[1]

To LORD HARTINGTON, war secretary, 14 May 1885. Chatsworth MSS 340. 1772.

It is not easy to convey a full answer to your letter[2] on paper in a hurried way, but as I understand the question for us all has been whether it was desirable for us to make efforts to avert a rupture in the Liberal party at the present time. C[hamberlain] and D[ilke] are those members of the Cabinet who prefer resignation and their answer to you would be that they have no desire to press Spencer and that if they are allowed to take their own course it will relieve him. My duty has been to try to bring them within reach of him as to their opinions and I have some *hope* that this has been effected.

15. Fr.

Wrote to Watsons—The Queen l.l.—& minutes. Cabinet 2-4½. Again stiff. But I must not lose heart. Saw Mr H—Ld RG—Mr Childers—Ld Rosebery—Ld Granville. Dined with Mr Hutton. Read His Natural Life. Spoke on Forestry. H. of C. 4¾-7.[3]

Cabinet. May 15 1885.[4]
    1. Statement for tonight. Considered & fixed.
0   2. Postponement of any change in Budget. (Order of business). *Tomorrow.*
    3. Provisions of substituted Crimes Act—recited & settled.
    4. K. Stated condition of the negotiation.[5]
      Local Govt. in Ireland.
      Land Purchase.[6]
      Govt. acknowledge duties in regard to both. Regret that the circs. of the year prevent any effectual attempt to deal with
      Chancellor protested against dropping the Public Meetings Clause of the Crimes Act.

      OMIT: Lords Bills (for England). Bills already before the House. *Condition of the Session. A serious work already done.* Have to add several Bills—not for England—but

[1] Childers' reply, 15 May, Add MS 44132, made 'a final appeal' against this course of action: 'it seems to me impossible to defer the decision as to the Taxes to be raised', and the Spanish negotiations too serious for suspension; his position untenable if the 'agitation' allowed to continue much more.
[2] Of this day, Add MS 44148, f. 62, objecting to the pressure 'to which Spencer is being subjected in regard to the . . . Crimes Act'.
[3] And on business of the House, announcing a new Crimes Bill and no time for Irish local govt. or land purchase this session; *H* 298. 626, 641.   [4] Add MS 44646, f. 127.
[5] Further sentence illegible; perhaps: 'Favourable to decentralising measures'.
[6] Gladstone told the Queen, in addition to these, 'Abolition of the Viceroyalty' though it was agreed not to proceed with this; CAB 41/19/37. See 16, 20-1 May 85 for the storm over land purchase.

SCOTLAND: Crofters: already named; Scottish Secretary (Lords)—WALES: Intermediate Education: *very early day*. IRELAND Crimes Act: *early day* after Wh[it]—Local Government—Land Purchase.[1]

SCOTLAND: Crofters Bill. Besides Lords Bills: Scottish Secretary. WALES: Intermediate Education on a very early day. IRELAND: land Purchase Bill which will extend & alter in important respects the provisions now embodied in the Law; Crimes Act: we shall embody various provisions of the Act, wh appear to us to be valuable and equitable, in a Bill to be presented during the present Session. Seek to find an early day after Whitsuntide for introducing it.

16. Sat

Wrote to Ld Spencer—Ld Hartington—The Queen—Ld E. Fitzmaurice—and minutes. Cabinet 12-2½. Meeting of B.M. Trustees 11¾. Saw Mr H—Ld R.G.—Mr Chamberlain—Sir C. Dilke—Ld Granville—Sir R. Peel. Drive with C. Dined at Lady Ashburnham's.

Cabinet. Saturday May 16. 1885. Noon.[2]
1. Budget. *Childers proposes as follows*: a. not to diminish proposed amount of taxation; b. wine. To raise 1/- to 1/3, 2/6 to 3/-, bottled wine 3/- + 300m; c. Spirits to be 1/- *vice* 2/-; d. Beer to be only till June 86; e. to set up Ways & Means forthwith for b. 'previous question' carried.
2. Kimberley's recital.
3. Queen's.
Childers' point:[3] 1. Chaos in Revenue Dept.; [2.] He will lay the storm; 3. which otherwise will increase.
Argument for time; 1. It is premature to *say on Thursday* we have got peace; 2. most desirable to carry on over the recess to complete the settlement of great questions; 3. There *was* an agreement—circs. have changed—we cannot yet say how much they are changed. Deficit 12m̂—whereof for the year only 8m̂—difference 4m̂. Taxation 7½m̂—whereof for the quasipermanent 4m̂: Residue 3½m̂ tax (against 8m̂). 4½m̂ Sinking Fund.

Very fair Cabinet today—only three resignations.[4]

Members of the Cabinet who within the last month have on one ground or other appeared to consider resignation: Lord Chancellor, Lord Northbrook, Lord Hartington, Mr Chamberlain, Sir C. Dilke, Mr Lefevre, Lord Spencer, Sir W. Harcourt, Chancellor of Exchequer. A majority.[5]

To LORD SPENCER, Viceroy of Ireland, 16 May 1885.   Althorp MSS K8.
'*Private*'.

    Some communications are going on among us about Land Purchase, and inquiry will be made to see whether a measure such as we sketched yesterday could probably be disposed of in a short time. If these proceedings should lead to a substantive result I need hardly say how much pleasure it will give me to inform you.

---

[1] This and following note at Add MS 44646, ff. 129-30.   [2] Add MS 44646, f. 132.
[3] Childers wanted to modify the Budget although the difficulties for which the Vote of Credit and increased taxation were raised had not yet been resolved.
[4] Add MS 44646, f. 134.   [5] Undated holograph; Add MS 44646, f. 133.

17. S. aft. Ascn.

Chapel Royal mg. Whitehall aft. Wrote to Ld Lyttelton. Read De Rastignac, Divorce[1]—Curteis on Difficulties[2]—Edersheim on O.T. criticism[3]—and [blank].

18. M.

Wrote to Scotts—Ld Granville—The Queen—Mr Childers—Mr P. Stanhope—and minutes. Wrote minute on Budget.[4] Saw Mr H—Ld R.G—Sir R. Welby—Mr C. Bannerman—Mr West l.l.—Sir W. Harcourt. H. of C. $4\frac{3}{4}$-$8\frac{3}{4}$ and $11\frac{1}{4}$-$12\frac{1}{4}$. Spoke on Central Asia.[5] Dined at Mr West's. Read 'His Natural Life'.

19. Tu. [Windsor Castle]

Wrote to Ld J. Manners—Ld Granville—Mr Acland MP—and minutes. Went to Windsor. Saw Mr H—Ld R.G—Ld Granville l.l.l.—Mr Phelps. Audience of H.M. Attended Council. Saw Pr. Henry of Battenberg. Saw Sir H. Ponsonby. Walk to the playing fields [of Eton]. Read His Natural Life—Femmes Abyssiniennes[6]—Lorne on Imperial Federation.[7]

20. [London]

Back in D.S. 11.40. H of C. $12\frac{1}{2}$-4.[8] Fourteen to dinner and evening party. Read His Natural Life—Femmes Abyssiniennes. Wrote to Sister Eliza[9]—Mr Chamberlain—Sir C. Dilke—Mr Macgregor—Mr Villiers—Mrs Nottage[10]—Sir A. Otway—Mr Childers—& minutes. Saw Mr H—Mr P—Ld RG—Sir W. Harcourt—Sir C. Dilke—Sir H. Ponsonby—Ld Granville l.l. Quasi Cabinet on Russian matters: a prompt reply sent. Tea with Miss Tennant & Mrs Myers.

To J. CHAMBERLAIN, president of the board of trade,   Add MS 43875, f. 255.
20 May 1885.

I have never been in greater surprise than at the fresh truth developed this afternoon.[11] I believed myself to be acting entirely within the lines of your & Dilke's concurrence—and surely I am right in thinking that you could not have supposed that the *notice* of our intention to bring in a Bill offered the occasion on which to refer to the distinct though allied subject of Local Government?

[1] See 3 May 85.
[2] See 15 Mar. 85.
[3] A. Edersheim, *Prophecy and history* (1885).
[4] Not found.
[5] And questions; *H* 298. 716, 743.
[6] *Les Abyssiniennes et les femmes du Soudan* (1876).
[7] J. D. S. Campbell, Lord Lorne, *Imperial federation* (1885).
[8] Announced an Irish Land Purchase Bill to be introduced after the recess; *H* 298. 971. See Garvin, i. 608ff.
[9] Of All Saints' rescue home, on case of Mrs Tait; Add MS 44548, f. 18.
[10] Widow of the Lord Mayor; giving her right to use title of wife of a knight; ibid.
[11] Chamberlain's letter this p.m. offering resignation on hearing of announcement of a Land Purchase bill; Add MS 44126, f. 79. His reply, ibid., f. 84, regretted the serious misapprehensions and felt the differences should be made public. See also Gwynn, ii. 135, Garvin, i. 611ff.

What I understand to be your and Dilke's proceeding was to agree to a Land Purchase Bill with a provision for funds for one year, which would leave the whole measure stranded next session, and dependent on a fresh judgment which might be associated with Local Govt. as its condition.

It seems to me to be a matter which we may perfectly well consider, and hope to arrange, in what terms reference shall be made to Local Govt. when the Bill is brought in. Will not that be the time to part, if part we must, which I do not believe.

I send a copy of this to Dilke & will only add, to the expression of my surprise, my deep concern.

To H. C. E. CHILDERS, chancellor of the exchequer,   Add MS 44547, f. 18.
20 May 1885.

I thank you very much for your letter[1] & I am convinced in every sense of the wisdom of your decision.

Learning that West was with Hamilton & also having had indifferent accounts (for the moment only, I hope) of your health, I thought I might encourage West to convey to the leading Brewers his opinion of what the Government will *at most* do concerning them, but with this reservation that the Government can say or do nothing to alter its financial position until they can assume as a fact the favourable issue of negotiations with Russia. [P.S.] We are very sorry to lose your company on Wednesday.

21. Th.

Wrote to Canon Butler—Bp of London—Sir C. Dilke—The Queen l.l.—Mrs Th.—and minutes. Saw Mr H—Ld R.G—Ld Rosebery—Mr Grogan—Sir W. Harcourt—Ld Granville. Attended the Lyttelton-Tennant[2] marriage at 11.30 and the breakfast at one: when I had to speak for the occasion. Houghton said 'Thanks for your poem'. A praise[3] of much beauty, if it had been deserved. 3-4. Conversation with Mr Chamberlain & Sir C. Dilke. H of C. $4\frac{3}{4}$-$8\frac{1}{2}$ & $9\frac{1}{4}$-$12\frac{1}{4}$. Spoke on Adjt.[4] Read His Natural Life.

At the request of Sir Charles Dilke and Mr Chamberlain, to which I readily agree, I send this Minute in circulation to explain to my Colleagues that a misapprehension has unfortunately arisen between them and myself with respect to the conditions under which they were willing to agree that a Land Puchase Bill for Ireland should be introduced.

It will be remembered that on Friday last the introduction of such a Bill (on the basis of an advance of the whole price with the reservation of one fourth of it until certain conditions should have been fulfilled) was very earnestly pressed by Lord Spencer. It appeared to me that the Cabinet in general were favourable to it, and that Mr Childers who like myself did not much desire it on the merits was, again like myself, willing to agree to it under the circumstances. But Sir C. Dilke and Mr Chamberlain took strong objection to it, and Sir W. Harcourt observing that they declared themselves taken by surprise, urged

---

[1] Of 18 May, Add MS 44132, f. 146: defeat of his proposal at Cabinet to 'soften' the Budget by a moderate addition to the wine duties, and a reduction of the increase on spirit duties and the extra beer tax temporary, 'a terrible blow' to the Budget, but will not 'insist on immediate resignation' so as to help the govt.

[2] Of Alfred Lyttelton and Laura Tennant.

[3] Phrase scrawled.   [4] *H* 298. 1092.

strongly that on that ground it should not be pressed upon them. Lord Kimberley also I think said it was a surprise to him.

Under these circumstances it was determined to forego the idea of introducing a Land Purchase Bill during the present Session.

Lord Spencer deeply lamented the decision, and used language which showed that it might even affect his tenure of office, though he eventually acquiesced with much reluctance on the ground of political consequences in Ireland.

Also the Irish friends of the Administration in Parliament were, as well as the Tories, sorely disappointed.

It was therefore with great satisfaction that I learned that my two colleagues might be disposed to waive their objections. I at once communicated with them on Saturday and gathered from my conversations, one before and one *after* the Cabinet of that day, that their main anxiety sprang from a fear lest the future handling of Local Government on their large scale in Ireland should be prejudiced by premature disposal of the question of Land Purchase, that they desired the connections of the two subjects to be recognised, but that in the main they thought the question of Local Government would not be prejudiced if the Bill to be introduced contained no provision of Funds beyond a single year.

Under this impression, and with an undoubting belief that the negative decision of the Cabinet had been a simple act of just deference to the strong objections they entertained, I thought I was giving effect to the real desire of my colleagues in general to meet the views of Lord Spencer, when I prosecuted inquiries as to the probable fate of such a Bill, and on finding the prospects somewhat favourable, & communicating further with the Viceroy, I proceeded on Wednesday to give notice of it. There was no Cabinet after I had (as I believed) ascertained the facts, and I saw no occasion to call one.

After giving this notice I learned with much pain that my estimate of the views of my two colleagues was fundamentally erroneous, that they intended to make, and believed they had made, much larger reservations as to the conditions on which they could alone assent to a Land Purchase Bill.

It is not necessary for me to attempt an exact description of their views, but manifestly they can in no way be held bound by my supposition of what they were; I will not for a moment presume to insist upon my own accuracy, and I am most deeply concerned if by any unintentional error I have in any way committed or embarrassed them.

I understand them to be quite willing that the matter should stand over until after the Recess when they will be better able to consider how far and in what way they will employ the liberty which they claim in regard to the Land Purchase Bill. WEG May 21. 1885.[1]

To Sir C. W. DILKE, president of the local government				Add MS 43875, f. 257.
board, 21 May 1885. '*Immediate*'.

I understand from Hamilton that Chamberlain is quite willing that his letter should stand as *non avenu* until after the recess: i.e. that (as I understand it) we should before the Bill is introduced consider in what terms the subject of Local Government should be referred to when the Bill is introduced.[2] I am not now trying to bind you to this understanding: but if you and he will come here at three we will try to get to the bottom of the matter.[3]

[1] Holograph, marked 'Circulate'; Add MS 44769, f. 118.
[2] See Dilke's letter of 20 May resigning; Add MS 44149, f. 347.
[3] Dilke demanded explanation to the cabinet before his resignation could be withdrawn; Add MS 43875, f. 258.

22. Fr. [Hawarden]

Wrote to Sir A. Clark—Bishop of London—Mr Chamberlain—Mr Childers—Mr Blackie—Ld Granville—The Queen—and minutes. H of C. 2¼-3.[1] Luncheon 15 G.S. Saw Mr H—Ld RG—Mr Villiers—Ld Granville—Do *cum* Sol. General—Ld Rosebery—Mr Grogan. Off to Hn 4.20. Arr. 10.30. Read Harper's Mag. on Washington Houses[2]—Tales of a Grandfather—Walpole's Geo. III.[3]

To J. CHAMBERLAIN, president of the board of trade,   Add MS 44548, f. 19.
22 May 1885.

The inclosed extract from the Birmingham Post[4] has been sent to me this morning. Statements of this nature form a heavy addition to other cases. I am at a loss to conceive how anything of this kind can have oozed out. But on account of the local origin, I refer it to you.

Sat. 23.

Church 8½ AM. Wrote to Ld Derby—The Queen bis: one very long & grave on Ireland & the Cabinet.[5] Read Lechler's Wiclif[6]—Harcourt Papers VIII[7]—Conrad on German Univv.[8]

24. Whits.

Ch 8½ & H.C. 11 A.M. and 6½ P.M. Wrote to The Queen l. & tel.—Mr P. Currie Tel.—Ld Granville Tel.—Mr Hamilton Tel.—and minutes. Read Cooper's Atonement[9]—Life of Thos Cooke[10]—Miss D. Tennant on the Ragamuffin.[11] Walk with C.

25. Whitm.

Ch. 8½ A.M. Wrote to Miss D. Tennant—Mr Hamilton l. & tel.—Ld E. Fitzmaurice—Mr E. Lever—Ld Granville—The Queen. Bands & festivities pleased and disturbed me. Walk with S.E.G.—Spoke of my retirement & its grounds. Spent most of the morning in examining Mr Lever's noteworthy gift, the

---

[1] Questions; not staying for Criminal Law Amndt. Bill; *H* 298. 1151.

[2] *Harper's Magazine*, lxx. 520 (March 1885).

[3] See 14 Mar. 85.

[4] Add MS 44126, f. 88, describing the cabinet row; Chamberlain replied, ibid., f. 90, that the *Post* went no further than the *P.M.G.* The article was written by [H. Lucy], see Garvin, i. 613.

[5] General review of Irish options, particularly of the central board proposal, and of cabinet differences about it; Guedalla, *Q*, ii. 354.

[6] G. V. Lechler, *Johan von Wiclif* (1873, English tr. 1884).

[7] See 5 Dec. 83.

[8] J. Conrad, *The German universities for the last fifty years* (1885).

[9] Perhaps A. Cooper, 'The Eucharist not a true sacrifice' (1875).

[10] *The life of Thomas Cooke, late of Pentonville, a miser* (1814).

[11] Article in the *Illustrated Magazine* with extra drawings, sent by Dorothy Tennant, painter and illustrator (da. of C. Tennant of Glamorgan), who m. 1890 H. M. *Stanley; Add MSS 44548, f. 19, 44490, ff. 238, 258.

Memorials of Liverpool.[1] Also read Skinner's Life & Poems[2]—Huxley, Physiography[3]—Machyn's Diary[4]—and [blank].

26. *Whit Tu.*

Ch. 8½ A.M. and H.C. Wrote to Ld Granville l.l.—Mr Hamilton tel.—Bp of London—Mr Grogan—Reeves and Turner—Memoranda and minutes. Read Zoroaster[5]—Old Liverpool—Neanderthal Skull[6]—and Machyn's Diary. Visited Rev. Mr Jones and walk with S.

27. *Wed.*

Ch. 8½ AM. Wrote to Ld E. Fitzmaurice—Rev. Mr Savile—Mr Carlisle—Mr Primrose tel.—and minutes. Attended the funeral service of the dear Nurse, now with God. Read Machyn's Diary—Zoroaster—Neanderthal Skull—His Natural Life.

To Rev. B. W. SAVILE, 27 May 1885.   Add MS 44548, f. 21.

I thank you very much for your book[7] which I am reading with interest.

I have no pretensions to follow the scientists on their own ground. But I am often surprised at their language and method when they get upon the ground of ordinary reasoning. And I am quite unable to understand why, even if the assumption about intermixture had been proved, evolution is less in harmony with theistic or Christian ideas than the special creation which some are so nervously anxious to get rid of.

I have to thank you also for your kind words & I am much gratified by your reference to the new Bishop of Exeter.

28. *Th.*

Ch. 8½ A.M. pleasant little dinner party: all so well done. Conversation with Mr Johnson—Mr Hurlbutt—Mr Mallock[8]—A. Bankes. Wrote to Ld Granville—Ld Spencer—& minutes. Cut down a holly, which impeded view. One of my last falls? Worked on books. Read His Natural Life—Cutts, Church History[9]—Neanderthal Skull.

29. *Fr.*

Ch. 8½ A.M. Wrote to Sir H. Ponsonby—Mr Primrose Tel.—Mrs Bolton—Bp of London—Mr C. Acland—Bp of St Asaph—Mr Martyn—Rev. Mr Sheepshanks[10]

---

[1] Ellis Lever, manufacturer, Bowdon, Cheshire, sent E. Howell's edition of Sir J. Picton's *Memorials of Liverpool* in 8 v. (1883); Hawn P.

[2] J. Skinner, *Songs and poems* (1859).   [3] T. H. Huxley, *Physiography* (1877).

[4] *The diary of Henry Machyn, citizen . . . of London* (1840).

[5] F. M. Crawford, *Zoroaster* (1885); see *Later gleanings*, 50.

[6] See next day's n.

[7] *The Neanderthal skull on evolution, in an address supposed to be delivered in A.D. 2085* (1885?), sent on 25 May, Add MS 44490, f. 263.

[8] John Jervis Mallock, curate of Sealand 1883–8.

[9] E. L. Cutts, *Turning points of English church history* (1874).

[10] Probably John Sheepshanks, curate in Anfield.

Studio photograph, 28 July 1884, taken for Millais by
Rupert Potter

Millais' second portrait of Gladstone, 1884–5

10. Downing Street. Whitehall

Facsimile of 30 August–2 September 1884

Gladstone's plan of Cabinet seating, June 1885, revised 1886
(encircled names were not in the 1886 Cabinet)

SERIOUS ANNOUNCEMENT.

Mr. Gladstone's Collars are worn out.
No more after to-day. Last appearance!

A Unionist chamber pot

(*left*) Harry Furniss' cartoon in *Punch*, pasted into the diary

'One of the People: Gladstone in an omnibus' by Alfred Morgan, 1885

Electioneering at Warrington, 28 November 1885
'Crowds at the stations . . . Some little speeches: chiefly to Reporters'

The house party at Haddo House, 15 September 1884,
Lord Aberdeen sitting between the Gladstones

—and minutes. Woodcraft with S. Read Hodgson on the Press &c.[1]—T.P. OConnor on W.E.G.[2]—Lechler on Wiclif—His Natural Life (finished). Ld Wolverton came.

To C. T. D. ACLAND, M.P., 29 May 1885.   Add MS 44548, f. 22.

I inclose a letter from the Bishop of St. Asaph on the Welsh Clause of your Bill.[3] I
should think Raikes a most unsafe guide on that clause. I have heard of one case where
the case has been pressed *too* far in favour of the Welsh. But I believe the Bishop is right
in the main, & I strongly concur with him, as to this Diocese in thinking that the prejudices of the average Welsh clergyman are likely to lean over much in the direction of his
English rather than of his Welsh parishioners.

To Sir H. PONSONBY, the Queen's secretary, 29 May 1885.   Add MS 44548, f. 21.

As to the Irish matter, it is indeed very large, but pray understand, & I hope Her
Majesty understands that it is not a 'proposal.'[4] It is rather, if I may so speak without
impropriety, a posthumous bequest. Nothing is to be decided or done upon [it], so far as
my knowledge or intention goes, & I do not expect anything to be raised upon it after this
recess. Lord Granville has seen it and it will probably go to Lord Hartington.

30. Sat.

Ch. 8½ AM. Wrote to Sir H. Ponsonby—Ld Hartington (on the situation)—Ld
Granville 1 & tel.—Mr Childers—Mr C. Bannerman—Mr Primrose tel.—&
minutes. Worked on papers. Drive & walk with Wolverton: much conversation:
& we opened rather a new view as to my retirement.[5] Read Anecdotes de Mad.
du Barri[6]—Lechler on Wiclif—Zoroaster.

To H. CAMPBELL-BANNERMAN, Irish secretary,   Add MS 41215, f. 7.
30 May 1885.

You will I hope have the draft of a Bill with a very judiciously chosen title, to succeed
the Crimes Act (or rather to displace it) when we meet next week. It will I trust be a very
short Bill.[7]

It may perhaps be found expedient to lose no time in bringing it in.

Will you kindly have prepared for me a summary statement showing the comparative
state of agrarian crime (1) and of evictions (2) now, & immediately before the enactment
of the Crimes Act.

[1] Untraced.

[2] One of T. P. O'Connor's many articles on the 1880-5 parliament, collected in his *Gladstone's
House of Commons* (1885).

[3] The Pluralities Bill; H. C. Raikes (see 30 Nov. 41n.), M.P. for Cambridge University, was a strong
establishmentarian.

[4] See 23 May 85.

[5] For reference to these conversations and the qualified resignation circular which were their
eventual upshot, see 16–17 June 85.

[6] See 9 Oct. 48.

[7] Two bills—one long, one short—were already in preparation; see *Bannerman*, i. 78.

To LORD HARTINGTON, war secretary, 30 May 1885.   Chatsworth MSS 340. 1785. *'Private'*.[1]

I am sorry but not surprised that your rather remarkable strength should have given way under the pressure of labour or anxiety or both.[2] Almost the whole period of this Ministry, particularly the year and a half since the defeat of Hicks, and most particularly of all the four months since the morning when you deciphered the Khartoum telegraph at Holker, have been without example in my experience, as to the gravity and diversity of difficulties which they have presented. What I hope is that they will not discourage you, or any of our colleagues, in your anticipations of the future. It appears to me that there is not one of them, viewed in the gross, which has been due to our own action. By viewing in the gross I mean, taking the Egyptian question as one. When we subdivide between Egypt proper & the Soudan, I find what seem to me two grave errors in our management of the Soudan business: the first our *landing* at Suakim, the second the mission of Gordon, or rather the choice of Gordon for that mission. But it sometimes happens that the errors gravest in their consequences are also the most pardonable. And these errors were surely pardonable enough in themselves: without relying on the fact that they were approved by the public opinion of the day and by the Opposition. Plenty of other and worse errors have been urged upon us, which we have refused or avoided. I do not remember a single good measure recommended by opponents, which we have declined to adopt, (nor indeed any good measure which they have recommended at all). We certainly have worked hard. I believe that according to the measure of human infirmity, we have done fairly well: but the duties we have had to discharge have been duties, I mean in Egypt and the Soudan, which it was impossible to discharge with the ordinary measure of credit and satisfaction, which were beyond human strength, and which it was very unwise of our predecessors to saddle upon the country.

At this moment we have but two great *desiderata*: the Egyptian Convention and the Afghan settlement (the evacuation of the Soudan being in principle a thing done). Were these accomplished, we should have attained for the Empire, at home and abroad, a position in most respects unusually satisfactory: & both of them *ought* to be near accomplishment. With the Egyptian Convention fairly at work, I should consider the Egyptian *question* as within a few comparatively easy stages of satisfactory solution.

Now as regards the immediate subject. What if Chamberlain & Dilke, as you seem to anticipate, raise the question of a prospective declaration about local Government in Ireland as a condition of their remaining in the Cabinet?

I consider that question as disposed of for the present (much against my will); and I do not *see* that any of us, having accepted the decision, can attempt to disturb it. Moreover their ground will be very weak and narrow, for their actual reason of going, if they go, will be the really small question arising upon the Land Purchase Bill.

I think they will commit a great error, if they take this course. It will be straining at the gnat. No doubt it will weaken the party at the Election; but I entertain no fear of the immediate effect. Their error will however in my view go beyond this. Forgive me if I now speak with great frankness on a matter, one of few, in which I agree with them, and not with you. I am firmly convinced that on the Local Government for Ireland they hold a winning position; which by resignation now they will greatly compromise. You will all I am convinced have to give what they recommend; at the least what they recommend.

There are two differences between them & me on this subject. First as to the matter; I go rather further than they do; for I could undoubtedly make a *beginning* with the Irish

---

[1] In Morley, iii. 196.

[2] Letter of 29 May from Dublin on his health, on cabinet leakages and on various suggestions of resignation; Add MS 44148, f. 75.

Police. Secondly as to the *ground*: here I differ seriously. I do not reckon with any confidence upon Manning or Parnell: I have never looked much in Irish matters at negociation or the conciliation of leaders. I look at the question itself, and I am deeply convinced that the measure in itself will (*especially* if accompanied with similar measures elsewhere, e.g. in Scotland) be good for the country and the Empire; I do not say unmixedly good, but with advantages enormously outweighing any drawbacks.

Apart from these differences, and taking their point of view, I think they ought to endeavour to fight the Election with you; and, in the *new state of affairs* which will be presented after the Dissolution, try and see what effect may be produced on your mind, & on other minds, when you have to look at the matter *cominus* [*sic*] & not *eminus*, as actual and not as hypothetical.

I gave Chamberlain a brief hint of these speculations, when endeavouring to work upon him: otherwise I have not mentioned them to any one.

About the leakage I entirely agree with you. About the one year, with you and Goschen. Beyond this we must see what happens when the Cabinet meets. The *first* business however must I suppose be the Budget. The present course of business seems to favour the acceptance of Childers's modified propositions or something near them.

I am sorry to trouble you with this long letter, but I do it in view of a future when I may not have the same opportunities of communication.

31. Trin. S.

H.C. 8 A.M. & Ch mg 11 AM & evg 6½ PM. Walk with Wolverton. Wrote to Ld Granville—Mr Childers—and minutes. Read Hatch on Liddon[1]—M'Dougall on The Ascension &c.[2]—Steps unto Heaven[3]—Thickness on Self Help[4]—Ryle agt Ritualism[5]—& various Tracts—also Lechler.

To H. C. E. CHILDERS, chancellor of the exchequer,   Add MS 44548, f. 23.
31 May 1885.

Your letter of 29th[6] (anticipated by my last) does not state the course you recommend. How can you inform Beach as to the Budget on Thursday & take the Resolution Friday? The two things must be done on the same day? How can the Tories object to taking Ways & Means *late* when the Resolution is *pro forma*? The reason I named Friday was twofold. 1. That viewing the slow measurement of the Russian negotiations it was desirable to take the latest day before deciding as to the Budget. 2. That you & other Ministers would have to meet on the Vote of Credit before it.

One point of difficulty occurs to me which you have doubtless considered: by what authority are you at once to reduce two shillings on spirits to one shilling?

There is also the question of repayment, which I should think you may find it not easy to avoid, although without doubt it has been paid by the consumer on most or all, perhaps on more than all, the delivered spirit.

[P.S.] I do not quite understand the 'great misfortune' if you have all the needful authority for levying your taxes?

[1] *C.R*, xlvii. 860 (June 1885).
[2] J. MacDougall, *The ascension of Christ* (1884).
[3] Perhaps *Steps towards heaven... twelve tracts* (1862).
[4] F. H. Thicknesse, *Self-help the help of all* (1885).
[5] J. C. Ryle, *What is ritualism? and why ought it to be opposed?* (1866).
[6] Add MS 44132, f. 153: asks advice on procedure for 'the Budget Bill'.

Mond. June One 1885.

Ch. 8½ AM. Wrote to Ld Granville—Mr Primrose tel.—The Queen tel.—Ld Hamilton—Mr Fraser—Major Walter—Mr Forsley—Dr Eade[1]—Mr Hamilton Tel.—Ld Spencer—& minutes. Worked on books. Read Zoroaster—Mrs Browning's Letters[2]—Monteagle on Crimes Act.[3] Settled the 10 m[ille] for Stephen with Harry. Conversation with Wolverton on the situation. Saw Dean of Chester.

To John BRIGHT, M.P., 1 June 1885.   Add MS 43385, f. 337.

I have written to Mr. Fry,[4] & I thank you for your note.

Since you left office, alas now three years ago, you have been not only mild & equitable, but most generous to us.

It is this, & the free terms on which I hope we shall always stand to one another, that encourage me to notice what I thought an occasional & accidental deviation in a letter of yours printed the other day.[5]

It is too true that we have done many acts of force. But there has not been one of them done by us except under the belief of an honourable necessity arising out of previous engagements inherited by us.

On the other hand we have done some pretty strong things in the sense of peace.

And we are now as I hope in the act of committing what the Jingo party consider an unpardonable offence.

I inclose for your amusement one of the indications which reach me by post.

I am sorry for the cause of your detention at Llandudno but I hope it may allow me the pleasure of your company on Saturday.

To LORD SPENCER, Viceroy of Ireland, 1 June 1885.   Althorp MSS K8.

I have just received your letter[6] & have read it with great interest.

I ought to have sent you two or three days ago the inclosed letters for perusal. They will I think sufficiently explain my reasons for writing them. The long statement addressed to the Queen has been seen by Granville & Hartington, & by them only.

The division of opinion in the Cabinet on the subject of Local Government with a Central Board for Ireland was so marked, & if I may use the expression, so diametrical, that I dismissed the subject from my mind & sorrowfully accepted the negative of what was either a majority or a moiety of the entire Cabinet.

This being so I am not in a condition to promote or encourage any change in the arrangements we now contemplate, whether it verge in the one direction or the other. Had it been otherwise, I could on no account recommend or favour the reduction to one year. Neither do I think that D[ilke] & C[hamberlain] have a case for demanding any change in point of prospective declarations, in consequence of *malentendu* about the Land Purchase Bill. On the other hand I should regard the introduction of Arms Act provisions

---

[1] Knighthoods for (Sir) Edward Walter, 1823–1904, soldier; (Sir) Peter Eade, 1825–1915, mayor of Norwich; C.B. for C. B. Forsey of the B.I.R.

[2] E. Barrett Browning, *Letters addressed to R. H. Horne*, ed. S. R. T. Mayer, 2v. (1877).

[3] *N.C.*, xvii. 1072 (June 1885).

[4] Joseph Storrs Fry of Bristol, on a Friends' memorial on foreign policy, forwarded by Bright; Add MS 44113, f. 215.

[5] *T.T.*, 20 May 1885, 10d: tory and liberal govts. 'are about equally at fault'.

[6] Of 31 May, Add MS 44312, f. 116: need to proceed with land purchase urged in a talk with Dilke; objects to Lefevre's proposal that bill be brought into operation by Order in Council.

into one *vice* Crimes Act Bill as a serious matter & as raising again the whole subject of Local Government.

A word on Lefevre's second suggestion. I should have thought your objection might as to the main point have been met by a provision that the Act should only be brought into operation by the Queen in Council. The responsibility would then surely be with the entire Government, as it ought to do [*sic*] if not accepted directly by Parliament.

Please consider this. But I regard the existing intentions as a compact with you.

2. *Tu.*

Ch. 8¼ A.M. Wrote to Sir H. Ponsonby—The Queen—Ld Granville—Mr Godley—E. Hamilton—Ld Kimberley. Worked on books. Read Lechler on Grosstête[1]—Matrimonial Brokerage[2]—Zoroaster (finished)—Cutts, Church History.

To LORD KIMBERLEY, Indian secretary, 2 June 1885.   Add MS 44548, f. 24.

1. I have read the Secret Despatch to the Viceroy about the Amir & Rawal Pindi with satisfaction. One point of phraseology strikes me as worth notice; you & your office will easily be able to dispose of it. The business of supplying Afghanistan with pecuniary & military aid has hitherto fallen upon India & is I presume so to continue. But the language of this dispatch, taken alone, seems to me as if it might be construed to make this an English matter. If it is diction sufficiently explained by habitual practice, well & good. If not please to provide that the language be so toned as not to be open to misconstruction.

2. If Lumsden is to have an honour I presume it will be the Star of India. Granville seemed to think he ought. Nothing can be more gross than his incapacity of expression, & he is a most rude and disagreeable subordinate. Still if the substance of his duty has been at once important, difficult, & disagreeable, & he has honestly & wisely advised the Afghans, I should think Granville is right. If so should you not recommend at once so as to be ready for Lumsden's arrival.

To Sir H. PONSONBY, the Queen's secretary, 2 June 1885.   Add MS 45724, f. 181.

With reference to your note of the 31st, my letter to the Queen on the Irish situation[3] was simply a preparation for the future, & contemplated no movement during the present Session; not even any declaration going beyond the most vague & general terms was in my mind. Should the Cabinet as a whole modify its view I will be careful to report.

3. *Wed.*

Ch. 8¼ AM. Wrote to Mr Hamilton tel & l.—Ld Granville l.l. & tel. l.l.l.—Stationmaster Broughton Hall—Mr Macdougall—and minutes. Drive with C. Worked on books & papers. Read Mrs Browning's Corresp.—Churchman & Scottish Church Review—Arnold Mahabharata.[4]

---

[1] G. V. Lechler, *John Wiclif and his English predecessors* (1878), i. 27.
[2] Untraced tract.
[3] On cabinet opinions on Ireland, 23 May, Guedalla, ii. 354.
[4] Sir E. Arnold, *The Song Celestial* (1885); from the Mahabharata.

4. Th. [London]

Ch. 8½ A.M. Wrote to The Queen—Ld Spencer—& minutes. Departure at 10.45: reached D. St 10.55 [*sic*!]. One of my quickest journies. H of C. 4½-8¾ and 10¼-11¾.[1] Read Louisiana[2]—Arnold, Mahabharata. Saw Chancr. of Exr.—Att. General—Sir Ch. Dilke.

5. Fr.

Wrote to Ld Spencer—The Queen & minutes. H of C. 4½-7½.[3] Dined at Sir A. Bass. Cabinet 11-2½. Saw Mr H.—Ld R.G.—Mr Childers—Ld Rosebery—Sir W. Harcourt—Ly E. Cavendish—Ld Kimberley—Sir A. Bass—Mr Grey.[4] Read Arnold.

Cabinet. Friday. June 5. 11 AM.[5]
1. Budget. Probable saving on Vote of Credit if all go well 2𝖒 (perhaps a little more): leave situation in the main unaltered.
2. Arrangements for business: Budget, Crofters, Irish Bill. Order agreed on. Irish legislation largely talked over. WEG to write.
Dilke said he had in Ireland[6] talked over these suggestions: 1. one year; 2. Act to operate by proclamation; 3. Fuller declaration upon Local Govt. Reports Spencer to be for a. Provincial Govt.; b. Central Boards for Legislation c. Ditto for Private Bill Legislation.[7]

6. Sat.

Wrote to The Queen l.l.—Mr Meiklejohn—Ld Spencer—Abp of Canterbury—Mr Arnold—Ld Selborne—and minutes. Company came in forenoon to see the Parade. Drive with C. Saw Mr H—Ld RG—Mr Childers—Dr Wilson. Worked on books &c to get the room free for the Childers party. Finished Arnold. Read Amiel Journal Intime.[8] [Queen's] Birthday dinner, 39; went very well. Much conversation with the Prince who was handy and pleasant even beyond his wont. Also had some speech of his son who was on my left. Saw Ld Fife & others.

7. 1 S. Trin.

Chapel Royal at noon (with H.C.) and 5.30. Wrote to Ld Granville—Ld Spencer tel. l.l.—Ld Tweeddale—Sir H. Ponsonby—and minutes. Saw Ld Granville—Do *cum* Ld Kimberley—Duchess of Sutherland—Mr Hamilton. Read Amiel Journal—Edersheim on O.T.

[1] Questions; dispute with Churchill on British govt's responsibility to Maoris; *H* 298. 1259.
[2] C. Gayarré, *Louisiana* (1851, new ed. in 4v. 1885).
[3] Questioned on Penjdeh; Childers' revised budget; *H* 298. 1189.
[4] In fact encouraging to enter Parliament Sir Edward *Grey, 1862-1933; liberal M.P. Berwick-on-Tweed 1885-1916; foreign undersecretary 1892-5, secretary 1905-16. See G. M. Trevelyan, *Grey of Fallodon* (1937), 30.
[5] Add MS 44646, f. 139.
[6] Gladstone had suggested to Dilke, visiting Ireland for the housing royal commission, that he negotiate further with Spencer on land purchase and local govt.; see Gwynn, ii. 135ff.
[7] Note from Dilke: 'I'm very sorry. I fear this looks like a break up'; ibid., f. 140.
[8] H. F. Amiel, *Journal intime*, tr. Mrs. Humphry Ward, 2v. (1885).

Commons Ministers except Childers: Several colleagues took much interest in determining final form of Budget proposal. Will they kindly be ready to help him in the debate tomorrow. He wishes to follow Beach. W.E.G. June 7. 85.[1]

Cabinet is summoned for tomorrow at two (as there is a *Levée* on Tuesday). I circulate this note by Spencer's desire.

I also send a letter which has come from Sir H. Vivian (Preceded by one from Heneage). I consider him a representative man. He told Hamilton last night that he knew he spoke for the opinion of many. He is *not* given to putting forward his individual opinion.

Upon the whole, unless the Executive act (in one form or another) is to be a precondition, a formidable division in the *party* (quite apart from the Cabinet) is to be anticipated; and such a division can only end in one way. W.E.G. June 7. 85.[2]

8. M.

Wrote to Ld Granville—Ld Rosebery—Ld Spencer—The Queen tel. l.l. & L.l.l.l.—and minutes. Pitiless rain. Cabinet 2–3¾. Saw Mr H—Ld R.G—Sir W. Harcourt—Ld Granville—Ld Rosebery. H of C. 4½–8½ & 9½–1¾. Spoke on Budget. Beaten by 264:252. Adjourned the House. This is a considerable event.[3]

Cabinet. Monday June 8. 85. 2 PM.[4]

1. Irish Bill *vice* Crimes Act. Ld Spencer stated his views. Though objecting, will agree to making operation of Act dependent on Proclamation, *except as to intimidation*—wh is increasing—and is hardly now coped with.
   WEG recommended acceptances—acknowledged generosity of S[pencer]. S. said he wd. at once *proclaim* a large part of Ireland. WEG said he cd. not accept the declaration. A proclamation must depend on the state of facts at the time. S. understood to agree—but it was what he expected. Chamberlain objected—reclaimed his original liberty. Lefevre & Dilke partially in the same sense. Trevelyan *ditto—against reserving intimidation*. Divers opinions. Postponed.
2. Granville stated the Russian answer. G[ladstone] G[ranville] & K[imberley] thought it equivocal as to Zulficar pass—also Staal's recent statement & his letter of yesterday in reply.[5]

9. Tu.

Wrote to Mr G Howard—Rev. Mr Creighton—Att. General—The Queen L.l.l. & tel. l.l.—Sir H. Parkes—Bp of London—and minutes. Cabinet 12–1. H of C.

---

[1] Add MS 44769, f. 123; notes by Dilke (willing but hoping Chamberlain will do it) and Chamberlain ('Dilke is the highest authority' on Death Duties, and 'the success of Beach's amendment would lead to what I believe to be just') at ibid., f. 124. Dilke answered Beach.

[2] Add MS 44646, f. 141. Vivian's letter of 6 June reluctantly willing to support coercion with 2 years Crimes Bill subject to Order in Council; Add MS 44481, ff. 20, 50.

[3] He wound up for the govt. on Beach's amndt. to the Customs and Inland Revenue Bill, concluding: 'It is a matter of life and death. As such we accept it . . .'; *H* 298. 1511. Lucy believed 'no one anticipated that the Ministry and the country were on the eve of a great political crisis . . . that it [the govt.'s majority] would be at least twenty nobody expressed a doubt'; Lucy, 476–7. But see Gladstone's warning to the cabinet in this day's note.

[4] Add MS 44646, f. 147. 'Mr. G. opened by saying that there was some chance of our being beaten on budget tonight'; Rosebery's diary this day, Dalmeny MSS.

[5] Russian proposals then accepted subject to Afghan control of the pass; F.O.C.P. 5140, f. 238–9.

4-4¾.[1] Saw Mr H—Mr P—Ld RG—Chancr of Exr—M. de Staal—Sir H. Ponsonby l.l.—M. Waddington. A quiet evening. Prince's Levee 2-2½. Worked on books & papers.

Cabinet. Tues. June 9. 1885. Noon.[2]
1. W.E.G. refers to Irish (intended) Bill. No result.
2. Agreed WEG to telegraph [to the Queen] announcing letter of resignation.[3]
3. To move Adjournment of H. of C. See A.[4]
4. Query to consider Princess B's jointure.
5. Ld G. writes to Ld Salisbury to mention a. we shall tender resignation; b. adj. H. of C. till Thursday & settle whether Lords shall proceed with Redistribution Bill. If they do, H. of C. will also consider Lords Amendments.
6. Levy of duties on Spirits & Beer.

10. Wed.

Wrote to Sir W. Harcourt—The Queen—Mrs Heywood—Ld Hartington—and minutes. Drive with C. & conversation on future residence.[5] Conclave on honours 12-2½. Saw Mr H—Ld RG—HJG—Sir H. Ponsonby—Mr Grogan—Ld Acton—Mr F Leveson—Ld Hartington—Do *cum* Ld Granville—Ld Wolverton— Lady Hayter. Dined at Sir A. Hayter's. Mr Capper exhibited 'thought-reading', disclaimed strongly the supernatural in the matter. Saw Thorne [R]. Read Amiel. Worked on books & papers.

To LORD HARTINGTON, war secretary, 10 June 1885.   Add MS 44548, f. 27.

Since you left me another plan has occurred to me which possibly might be used at Balmoral against an application to the Tories; viz that which is supplied by the composition of the majority. The main elements of it were 1. The Irish who are opposed to indirect taxation generally: 2. The Tories who are even more friendly to it than we are. It is not a case where party B. being in a minority wins by drawing off casually some votes from Party A the majority; but where party A is overcome mainly by the combination of two parties between whom it is a buffer.

I suppose it is some answer to say 1. That this was foreseen to be the only means by which the Tories could carry their motion. 2. And not only so but that they have habitually acted on the plan of endeavouring to defeat the Government by a combination with the Irish.

Ergo that such combination cannot relieve them from the responsibility of victory or from the duty of enquiry whether they will take the Government into their hands.

11. Th. St Barnabas.

Wrote to The Queen tel. l.l. & L.l.—Ld Granville—Att. General—Ld Kimberley— Mr Childers—Mr Love Parry—Ld Eversley—Ld Sherbrook. Saw Mr H.—Ld

[1] Announced 'the Cabinet have thought it their duty, through me, to submit a dutiful communication to Her Majesty'; House adjourned until 12 June; *H* 298. 1517. The Queen was at Balmoral.   [2] Add MS 44646, f. 149.
[3] Guedalla, ii. 361. Undated note reads '1. We shall carry on Govt. this Session by Tory support 2. Bismarck's & Russia's hostility. 3. Seats Bill—cannot pass rapidly'; Add MS 56452, f. 190.
[4] Notes on precedents of 1866 and 1873; Add MS 44646, f. 150.
[5] See 24 June 85 and n.

R.G.—Sir H. Ponsonby—Mr MacColl—Ld Cork—Conclave (on honours & on Afghan frontier)—Ld Kimberley—Ld Rosebery—Sir W. Harcourt. Dined at Roseberys. Drive with C. Worked on books & papers.

12. Fr.

Wrote to Sir A. Clark—The Queen l.—Watsons—Sir S. Northcote—Ld Granville—Mother Superior All Saints—and minutes. H of C. 4½–5¼.[1] Saw Mr H—Ld R.G—Sir H. Ponsonby—Sir W. Harcourt—Sir C. Dilke—Ld Granville—Mr Phelps—Mr . . .—Ld Wolverton. Worked on books & papers. Luncheon at Ld Dalhousie's & then, as supernumerary godfather attended the Baptism of the twins[2] & kissed them. Dined with Mr Sands. Saw Palmer. Read Peel's Sp. 1841 & Corn Law Memoir[3]—Amiel, Journal Intime. Prepared a sketch on Irish Contingency.[4]

To Sir S. H. NORTHCOTE, M.P., 12 June 1885.   Add MS 44548, f. 28.

1. Have you any suggestion to make as to the further adjournment which I presume ought to be made today. If not, I think of Monday, by which day Lord Salisbury would probably be able to express his wishes.

2. I understand him to desire that we should go forward with the Seats Bill at once. If you concur, I am disposed to do it. And if it is done, I think it will be best to do it today? If the proceedings in the Lords permit this course, of which I do not despair.[5]

13. Sat. [Coombe Hurst][6]

Wrote to Ly Dalhousie—The Queen L.l.l. & tel. l.—Ld Granville l.l.—Mrs Maxwell Scott—Ld Hartington—Sir W. Harcourt—Mr Hamilton. And, at Coombe Hurst, I vented 1½ hour on Ld Ripon. Saw Mr H—Ld RG l.l.—Mr Mitford *cum* Mr Mitchell—Ld Granville—Ld Acton. Off to Coombe Hurst at 4½. Worked on books & papers. Read Société de Londres.[7]

To Sir W. V. HARCOURT, home secretary, 13 June 1885.   MS Harcourt dep. 9, f. 142.

Now that Salisbury has gone to work, and Northcote by sending for Welby has shown that he is to be C. of E., ergo that we are in earnest, I write personally to beg you to

[1] Statement on resignation, caused by defeat on Beach's amndt. and 'founded on that reason alone'; Salisbury now at Balmoral; procedure for Redistribution Bill; *H* 298. 1528.

[2] Ronald Edward Maule and Charles Fox Maule, twins of 13th earl of Dalhousie.

[3] Probably Peel's speech moving motion of want of confidence, 27 May 41, and his mem. of 2 December 1845 with correspondence with Russell etc. in Lord Stanhope and E. Cardwell, *Memoirs by Sir Robert Peel* (1856), ii. 214ff. See 16 June 85.

[4] This phrase written sideways, next to this day, on right hand side of page. Mem. untraced; probably on liberal Irish policy should Salisbury decline office.

[5] Northcote thought 'the simple course will be to move the adjournment' but with Salisbury at Balmoral he could not speak for the Lords; Add MS 44217, f. 253.

[6] Mrs. Vyner's house in Kingston.

[7] Paul Vasili [i.e. Juliette Adam], *La Société de Londres* (1885, also tr. this year); harsh portrait of Gladstone's 'theory of pure opportunism', 'fatal in foreign affairs'. For his meeting with her, see 18 Oct. 79.

detach from my old hulk the barnacles that adhere to it (barnacles I admit of the very first water) in the shape of Police Officers.[1]

I have known for months that others have recovered their freedom and I hope you give me credit for having curbed my impatience, partly in recollection of your kind & watchful interest, partly because I did not like to seem to affront people who have tended me with every possible intelligence, attention, and consideration.

Receiving an intention to say good bye to them I beg you now to release them & me. I really believe my successor will have *more* need of their protection.

Salisbury, having undertaken the Govt. & left Balmoral at two today, *may* still start upon us some demand for support in regard to an Irish Bill, but he has certainly missed his proper and regular opportunity, and the event has become less probable.
[P.S.] A thousand thanks for Vol. VII.[2]

To Mrs. MAXWELL SCOTT, 13 June 1885.   Add MS 44548, f. 28.

I have this morning been engaged in settling the Plans of the Mercat Cross, now about to be re-erected in Edinburgh, with the history of which you are acquainted.[3]

I believe that out of eight stone medallion squares, which formed a portion, not of the original cross, but of the cross of the 17th century, five are embedded in a garden wall at Abbotsford.

Mr. Mitchell tells me he gathered from your words that you did not feel a special interest in them.

There can, I think, be no doubt that, if they were to take their places in the new erection, they would be regarded with a very special interest indeed by the people of Edinburgh and by the Scotch public at large, firstly by reason of their relation to the cross of other days, and secondly on account of the interesting and touching relation, established by the verses of Sir Walter, between the Mercat Cross and the illustrious name you bear.

Should you kindly permit me to instruct Mr. Mitchell to make arrangements for the removal and restoration of the stones, I shall feel much obliged, and every care will be taken to effect the operation in the most safe and convenient manner.

14. 2 S. Trin.

Ch. mg & [blank.] Wrote to The Queen l. & tel.[4]—Mr Hamilton l. & tel.—Ld Granville—Mr M'Coll—Sir S. Northcote—& minutes. Read Société de Londres (on W.E.G.)—Amiel—Bibel und Natur.[5]

15. M. [*London*]

Wrote to Ld Spr (cancelled)—Sir S. Northcote—The Queen (honours) in full—& minutes. Left Coombe Hurst 10.30. Sat to Millais 11.30–12¾.[6] Saw Mr H

---

[1] Harcourt declined, 16 June, Add MS 44199, f. 227: 'It will never do for Nelson to leave the command before Trafalgar'.   [2] i.e. of *The Harcourt Papers*.

[3] Hamilton had written in March about stones from the cross thought to be at Abbotsford; she had 'no clear recollection' of them: but they might be 'on the garden walls', irremovable; Add MS 44490, f. 23. See 23 Nov. 85.

[4] Declining the earldom offered on 13 June; Guedalla, *Q*, ii. 368; see to Sir T. Gladstone, 19 June 85.

[5] See 1 Feb. 85.

[6] A second version of the portrait painted in 1884 (see 7 July 84n), the first having been obtained by Rosebery; this second version is that now in Christ Church, Oxford, whose Governing Body Minute Book Index contains the following undated pencil note: 'Millais undertook to paint Mr

—Mr P—Ld R.G. l.l.l.—Prince of Wales—Ld Granville—Mr Godley—Sir F. Leighton. H of C. 4½-8¾: and a strange scene.[1] Read Société de Londres—Kings & Queens of an Hour.[2]

To Sir W. V. HARCOURT, home secretary, 15 June 1885.   MS Harcourt dep. 9, f. 144.

As to assurances. Granville is much in favour of the principle—not however as principle properly so called, but as policy.

I agree with you that they have no claim: not the shadow of a rag of a tatter of a claim.

I think I see my way to one thing. There can be no confidences. Anything said or done must be in the face of the day.

Again: I cannot deal for the ex-Cabinet as such. If any thing is said it should be from me & for my own sphere. But whether any thing & what should be said even within these conditions is a grave question, to be maturely considered if the case arise.[3]

To Sir S. H. NORTHCOTE, M.P., 15 June 1885.   Add MS 44548, f. 29.

I am under the impression that the adjournment should be moved by those who occupy the Front Bench. Otherwise ought not *you* to move also the Annuity Bill? Your note reached me 3.45 & the pressure of time is too great for thorough search. But my impression is that your party takes over these formal duties when the leading men have vacated their seats. Brand did it in 59. If your knowledge is more full & to an opposite effect I give way. In 1866 I made the motion several times.[4]

16. Tu.

Wrote to The Queen l.l.—Sir W. Harcourt—Ld Granville—Mr Childers—Mes. Grogan—Ld Granville—& minutes—incl. a Minute for circulation on my retirement. Saw Mr H—Ld RG—Sir H. Ponsonby—Mr A. Balfour. Conclave of 11 of the (late) Cabinet to consider the matters opened by Balfour 3-4¾. Dined at Sir C. Forster's: saw Childers, Att. General, Houghton. Packing books. Read Fitzgerald's Kings and Queens.

Mr. Balfour called, on the part of his uncle, soon after one. He wished to know 1. whether I should be prepared to support Lord Salisbury's government in giving preference to Supply, & to Ways and Means, on all days when they might be put down as first order. 2. whether if the Govt. made financial proposals & I disapproved them, I would support raising the money by Exchequer Bills.

I said the questions were very pointed & peculiar, & not such as I could have anticipated.

Gladstone's Portrait for Ch. Ch. This portrait Millais sold off to Lord Rosebery for (on dit) 1000£, & was then going to send us a Replica; but Mr Gladstone sat again, & the result is the Portrait now in Hall.' See 7 July 84, Introduction above Vol. X, section viii, and illustrations in this volume.

[1] Statement on the situation; House adjourned until 19 June, but cttees. sat; *H* 298. 1536.

[2] P. H. Fitzgerald, *Kings and queens of an hour*, 2v. (1883).

[3] Harcourt replied, 16 June, MS Harcourt dep. 9, f. 146: 'Pray do not entertain the notion that you can say anything *personally* which does not commit and bind the party. *You are the Party* and your acts are its acts. It will never consent nor will the Nation consent to regard you as an individual. . . . In such a situation the present timidity of Granville is formidable.'

[4] Northcote replied he would move the annuity bill for Princess Beatrice this evening and an adjournment until Friday; Add MS 44217, f. 254.

I referred to the communications of December 1845 between Lord J. Russell & Sir R. Peel—and gave him the 'Memoir'[1] for reference.

I told him

1. that I was not prepared to depart from the mode then pursued as to the initiative which I conceived to have lain with the Queen: that such inquiries would have to be presented in writing

2. that if there were any question of an understanding or covenant, I conceived (especially after the recent confidential & peculiar arrangement) that it must be made public

3. that if the questions he had reported were put to me, it would be necessary for me to consult with others upon them.

He asked if he might send me the questions unofficially and as from himself that I might have them before me.

I told him that this might economise time, and I had no objection.

He went away.   WEG Jun. 16. 85.[2]

Secret. To avoid misapprehension at this juncture, I circulate a few words among my colleagues.

I propose, when the new Government shall have been formed, to take my seat in the usual manner on the front Opposition Bench.

With the desire to restore my throat and voice to something like a natural condition, I hope to use the first proper opportunity (should one be found) of absenting myself from actual attendance. But this would be a bodily not a moral absence.

My place would remain unaltered for the rest of the Session.

I do not perceive, or confidently anticipate, any state of facts, which ought to alter my long cherished, and I believe wellknown, desire and purpose to withdraw, with the expiration of this Parliament, from active participation in politics. W.E.G. June 26 [*sc.* 16]. 1885.[3]

17. Wed.

Wrote to Harrison—Ld R. Grosvenor—Mr Mitford—Sir F. Leighton—The Queen—Ld Wolverton—& minutes. Worked on books & papers. Saw Mr H—Ld R.G. l.l.l.—Sir W. Harcourt—Sir R. Lingen—Lady Clark. Dined with Mrs Heywood. Drive with C. Read Amiel—Fitzgerald.

To LORD WOLVERTON, 17 June 1885.   Add MS 44548, f. 29.

I send you for perusal a secret memorandum which I have circulated among my (ex)Colleagues. You will find it, I think, in complete conformity with the tenour of the conversations between us two.[4]

[1] See 12 June 85.
[2] Add MS 44769, f. 129; in *Autobiographica*, iv. 67.
[3] Add MS 44769, f. 152; circulated next day, see Bahlman, *Hamilton*, ii. 887, which confirms the date. Harcourt docketed his copy: 'I saw Mr Gladstone on this before the Dissolution and with difficulty persuaded him to remain as leader. WVH'; Harcourt dep. 9, f. 158. See also Ramm II, ii. 387.
[4] Wolverton's reply next day, Add MS 44349, f. 182 and Jenkins, 241, hoped that 'your proposed Irish policy should produce the "state of facts" which would at least give you some grounds for the further consideration, before the close of the Parliament, of the position . . .'.

To LORD R. GROSVENOR, chief whip, 17 June 1885.   MS Harcourt dep. 9, f. 148.

I hope you will not fail at once (with leave) to reprint Harcourt's admirable speech,[1] although it contains sentences about me to which I cannot subscribe. The references to Randolph's speeches should be added. A month ago it would have been wrong to give him such prominence but not now, when he is the second, if not more than the second person in the new combination, and is dancing upon poor and ill-used Northcote's prostrate body.

18. Th.

Wrote to Ld Granville tel.—and minutes. Ex Cabinet gathered at [just] after 12.30 when I submitted the important communications of last night:[2] about eleven or twelve present. We were quite clear. Off to Windsor 1.50. Saw Sir J. Cowell—Sir H. Ponsonby from & for the Queen—and H.M. for over $\frac{3}{4}$ hour. I circulated a short Mem.[3] She was most gracious & I thought most reasonable. Drive with C. Worked on books. Read Amiel—Fitzgerald. Saw Mr H—Ld RG—Ld Rosebery. It is anxious work, even though I have seen my way clearly enough.

19. Fr.

Wrote to Att. General—Ld Spencer Tel l.l.l.—Mr Childers—Ld Carlingford—Sir Thos G.—Ld Salisbury—The Queen—and minutes. A clearance with Westell. Saw Mr H—Ld RG—Sir W. Harcourt—Ld Granville *cum* do—Mr Childers *cum* Mr Chamberlain—Mrs Bolton—Mr Stuart. Pleasant dinner with Mr Bryce. Struck by Mr Edmonds (U.S.)[4] Wrote minutes for a letter to D. News about Northcote.[5]

To Sir T. GLADSTONE, 19 June 1885.   Hawarden MSS.

Your most kind note instead of requiring apology demands my warm thanks. The difficulty of the position arises out of the political consequences which attach to the assumption of title.[6] The removal to the House of Lords in the case of Lord Beaconsfield was perfectly natural and proper: he had ceased to be physically strong enough for any considerable attendance in the H. of Commons, and the demands of the other House were mild. But my case is entirely different. My profound desire is retirement, and nothing has prevented or will prevent my giving effect to that desire, unless there should appear to be something in which there may be a prospect of my doing what could not be as well done without me. But going into the House of Lords would keep me until my dying day chained to the oar in a life of conflict & contention of which I have had more than enough, and more I believe, taken all together, than any other man. I do not doubt the force of what you say as to others but I think they are satisfied that the grounds on which

[1] On 16 June in St. James's Hall; see Gardiner, i. 529-30.
[2] Correspondence with Salisbury on possibility and timing of a dissolution, read to the Commons on 24 June.
[3] *Autobiographica*, iv. 69.
[4] George Franklin Edmunds, 1828-1919; republican senator and anti-bimetallist.
[5] Not published; *D.N.* leader and gossip column, 20 June 1885, 4g, 5c reported Gladstone's dislike of Northcote's holding the First Lordship dissociated from the Premiership, and his likely opposition to the salary; technically there was no 'First Lord'.
[6] See 14 June 85n.

I act are strong while there may perhaps be found other means of opening some door through which they may be able to carry some mark of lien to a very old public servant.

One consideration with me has also been that though we are in possession of a charming place for which we ought to be very thankful our fortune is not such as befits the kind of title usually carried by one who has been Prime Minister.

I am glad to hear of your thus far prosperous journey.

To LORD SALISBURY, 19 June 1885.   Add MS 44548, f. 30.

I have received your note[1] announcing your intention to propose an adjournment until Tuesday in the Lords, & I will take care to do the like in the Commons.

20. Sat. [Dollis Hill]

Wrote to Ld Granville—Sir W. Harcourt—The Queen—Mrs Th . . . & minutes. At 4.30 we went to Dollis Hill, and had a quiet evening with the Aberdeens. Prepared Mem. for H.M. which was suspended. Quasi Cabinet 11–12¼. Agreed on answer to (H.M. for) Salisbury. My letter approved.[2] Saw Mr H—Ld RG—Sir H. Ponsonby l.l.—Ld Granville—do *cum* Ld Hartington. Read Amiel—Société de Londres.

Quasi-Cabinet. June 20 (11 AM) 1885.[3]
I submitted letters on the situation.
Absent: Spencer, Rosebery, Hartington.

To Sir W. V. HARCOURT, home secretary, 20 June 1885.   MS Harcourt dep. 9, f. 154.

Rely upon my thinking over most carefully the duties & necessities of the coming days—& in the meantime a thousand thanks for your most kind letter.[4]

21. 3 S. Trin.

Willesden Ch mg with H.C. and Chapel Royal evg. Wrote to Mr Hamilton—The Queen draft & letter—Ld Spencer. 3–7. Went to London & met such colleagues as I could gather at 4.30 with the A.G. They agree to my draft:[5] we also discussed the difficulty as to Dissolution. Read Amiel—Ruskin, Praeterita[6]— Philips Brooks Serm. I. II.[7]

To LORD SPENCER, Viceroy of Ireland, 21 June 1885.   Althorp MSS K5.

I am sorry that you should be knocked about while going backwards & forwards but undoubtedly your presence here is absolutely indispensable in a certain contingency, namely that of *our* retaining or resuming office, for the gravest matter (as you will have

[1] This day, Add MS 44491, f. 153.
[2] Read to the Commons on 24 June.
[3] Add MS 44646, f. 153.
[4] Of 20 June, MS Harcourt dep. 9, f. 152: if Salisbury fails, Gladstone bound to resume office and his colleagues to support him.
[5] Read to the Commons on 24 June.
[6] First v. of J. Ruskin, *Praeterita*, 3v. (1885–1900).
[7] P. Brooks, *Sermons preached in English churches* (1883).

judged from the public journals) we should then have to consider would be that connected with the Crimes Act, on which you are of course a necessity.

It is impossible to estimate the chances & the Queen will I think make a decided effort to induce Salisbury to persevere (as it is quite right she should): but I cannot say the *odds* lie on that side.

22. M. [*London*]

Wrote to Sec. Gr. Trunk Co.—Ld Spencer Tel. l.l.—and minutes. Dined at Grillion's: saw Derby, and [blank]. Saw two [R]. 10.50–11½ A.M. Drive up. Conferences with Ld Granville l.l.—Sir C. Dilke—then Sir W. Harcourt l.l. Also with Sir H. Ponsonby l.l.l.l.l.l.[1] Saw Mr H. ever in & out. A day of much stir & vicissitude till 7 P.M. Read Amiel—Société de Londres.

23. Tu.

Wrote to Mrs Bolton—Sir R. Welby—The Queen—and minutes. H of C. 4½–5½.[2] A chaotic day: saw Granville who was much moved. Worked on books & papers. 11–2. My room peopled with visits & returns: Hamilton, Granville, Sir H. Ponsonby, Ld R. Grosvenor, Spencer. We insist on publishing a series after mine of 21st, IF the Queen's is published. Saw Sir R. Welby—Sir Thos May. Read Amiel: and had last night in D. St.

To Sir R. E. WELBY, 23 June 1885.   Add MS 44548, f. 30.

Lingen has resigned.[3] Will you consent to succeed him. Justice would not permit any other appointment and this I am sure the new First Lord will feel, for services & consummate public accomplishment like yours cannot be passed over.

I tried to see you but as you are out, & the hour glass keeps running I send this note.

24. Wed.

Wrote to Ld Northampton—Ld Breadalbane—Mr Brocklebank—Mr J.E. Millais—Mr Tennant—Ld Powerscourt—Sir R Collier—Sir N Rothschild—Mr Stephenson—Mr H. Edwards—Ld Sefton—Mr Philips—Mr Vernon—Mr Watts[4]—Mr Jardine—Ld Fife—Ld Henley—Ld Baring—Mr Morley—and minutes. These were all of them honour letters.[5] Worked on amending (in form) Sir H. Ponsonby's Memorial. Saw Mr Hamilton—R. Grosvenor—Harcourt—Granville. Wrote Mem. for HM respecting the Salisbury communications. He has been ill to deal with, requiring incessant watching. 12.30–4.20. To Windsor. Audience of H.M. & kissed hands, in farewell after half an hour of kindly conversation. Saw Sir H. Ponsonby & the honours were settled. Conversation with Prince of Wales: who asked my opinion of the new arrangements. I spoke only of Northcote and Holland. Saw Sir H. Verney—Mr Otway—Sir Thos

---

[1] Notes on these in *Autobiographica*, iv. 71.
[2] Announced Salisbury's definite acceptance of office, and adjourned the House; *H* 298. 1618.
[3] As permanent secretary to the treasury; Welby accepted, holding the office until 1894.
[4] Offer of baronetcy; declined; Add MS 44548, f. 30. See Introduction above, X, section viii.
[5] Reading of sentence uncertain.

May—Mr A. Myers—Miss Tennant—Lord Spencer—Mr Waddington. Went to H of C. & read the correspondence.[1] The effect was good. Dined with Miss Tennant. Slept at No 1. Richmond Terrace [Whitehall][2] for the first time. Much tired: as I well might be. Got to the 3 P.M. service at St George's Windsor.

To J. E. MILLAIS, 24 June 1885.[3]   Add MS 44548, f. 30.

It is with a very lively satisfaction, both personal & public, that I write with the sanction of Her Majesty (and lawfully, though at the last gasp) to ask you to accept the honour of hereditary title, & take your place among the Baronets of the United Kingdom.
[P.S.] Unless I hear to the contrary I hope to come & sit at 12 tomorrow.

To Sir N. M. ROTHSCHILD, 24 June 1885.   Add MS 44548, f. 31.

I have very sincere pleasure in proposing to you with the sanction of Her Majesty that you should accept the honour of a Peerage.
I hope on every ground that you may be disposed to undergo this translation, which alike on personal & on public grounds, will I am convinced be universally approved.[4]

25. Th.

We shall readily fall into our displacement. Went backwards & forwards today. At 11.45 cleared out of my official room & had a moment to fall down and give thanks for the labours done & the strength vouchsafed me there: and to pray for the Christlike mind. So I bade good-bye: still holding to the domestic rooms.
    Wrote to Watson & Smith—Ld Salisbury—Scotts—Sir S. Northcote—and minutes. Sat to Millais say 65 min. Saw Gertie. Luncheon at Mr Th.s. Conclave at Granville's. 3.30 (for the H. of Lords). Evening at the (Currie) home. Read Nationalités Slaves[5]—Swinburne's Marino Faliero[6]—Société de Londres. Saw Mr H—Ld Northbrook—& others.

To Sir S. H. NORTHCOTE, first lord of the treasury,   Add MS 44548, f. 32.
25 June 1885.

The date which I have written by your favour indicates the purpose of my letter, which is to thank you for the more than liberal allowance of time you have kindly offered me & to say that on Saturday as I hope my servants & household stuff of all kinds will be out of your way as far as all resort & official purposes are concerned.
I have however begged the favour of a room in which to deposit many of the books & other objects belonging to me until I am able to look about me & settle my domestic arrangements which are at present totally unfixed. A similar license has been obtained for me by the kindness of the Chancellor of the Exchequer to continue in the occupation of a

[1] Read from correspondence between himself, Salisbury and the Queen, 17–21 June; H 298. 1623.
[2] Loaned to the Gladstones by B. W. Currie (see 19 Mar. 84).
[3] Version in J. G. Millais, Life and letters of Sir J. E. Millais (1899), ii. 177.
[4] Rothschild's letter next day accepted; Add MS 44491, f. 189.
[5] Les nationalités slaves: lettres au R. P. Gagarin, par X. K-Branicki (1879).
[6] A. C. Swinburne, Marino Faliero. A tragedy (1885), sent by Mrs. Thistlethwayte. Gladstone commented to her, 1 July 1885: 'It is I think a work of great power: dramatic power, power of thought, and wonderful mastery over the English language, not to mention the hymnody in Latin which is memorable.'

basement room under the great dining room where I have been, in the shape of my effects, during the last five years: & I fear the packing of them for a removal to a regular depository would take some little time & cause inconvenience.

Should you at once come into this house, the room now holding my things might probably be wanted: but if in that case you would allow my Housekeeper to have them moved downstairs, there is a room on the ground floor which I do not think you would use, & the operation would be easy.

26. Fr.

Wrote to Sir S. Northcote—Ld Salisbury—Ld Coleridge—Mr B. W. Currie—Robn & Nichn—and minutes. Final arrangements & *Deo* Gratias in the old home, which I left just before twelve. Saw Mr H—Mr Primrose—Sir H. Thring—Mr Lennox Peel—The Speaker. 1-6¼. To the Crystal Palace for the Israel in Egypt wh was grand, & delightful. Arranging my effects in the new nest. Evg at home. Read Société de Londres—Life of Ld Salisbury.[1]

27. Sat. [*Dollis Hill*]

Wrote to Mr Cowan[2]—Ld Spencer—Sir E. Henderson[3]—Ld Rosebery—Sir C. Dilke—Mr Lefevre—& minutes. Off to Dollis Hill: a delightful children's party there. Saw Mr H—Mr MacColl—Sir W. Harcourt (on the situation)—Mr Currie—Ld Northbourn—Mr Westall—M. Waddington—Ld Aberdeen—Lady Somers—Mr Browning—Lady Malmesbury—Lady Airlie—Mr Drummond. Read Life of Brummell[4]—Société de Londres.

To LORD ROSEBERY, 27 June 1885.   N.L.S. 10023, f. 82.

I am in possession of a hint you gave to Hamilton about my answer to Mr. Cowan in which I might say that Midlothian has the first claim upon me.

Nothing can be more certain than that I shall never sit for any other constituency. But after studying & studying I have been quite unable to devise a method of touching this subject which would be safe, & would not set men's minds agog.

I hope you will think the tone of my letter satisfactory as towards Midlothian.[5] When you come southwards (I suppose in a few days) I shall hope for an opportunity of explaining my exact position.

To LORD SPENCER, 27 June 1885. '*Private*'.[6]   Althorp MSS K8.

I suppose you to be in possession of a paper said to contain Parnell's views on Local Government for Ireland, which was privately forwarded to me several months ago, &

[1] F. S. Pulling, *The life and speeches of the marquis of Salisbury* (1885).
[2] Keeping his options open as to standing again for Midlothian; read by Cowan at a meeting in Edinburgh; *T.T.*, 30 June 1885, 6a.
[3] Sending £25 for the police who guard 'the crossings and near the H. of C.'; Add MS 44548, f. 33.
[4] See 24 May 44.
[5] Rosebery's reply noted 'full satisfaction'; Add MS 44288, f. 235.
[6] In Hammond, 420.

which (if my memory serves me right) I sent on to you. Will you kindly let me have it, or a copy of it, that I may (for the first time) peruse it.[1]

28. 4 S. Trin.

Parish Ch mg. In afternoon there was prayer & sermon (Mr D.) with the hay-makers. How difficult for one in ease to preach to them. No bores or meeting today but a kind of dawn upon me. Saw Ly Tweedmouth & Ld T.—Miss Morgan—Sir A. Clark—Ly Tavistock—Ld Aberdeen—W.H.G. All garden conversations. Read Amiel—Trent documents[2]—Serm on Spirits—Bucklands Notes[3]—Drummond on Chastity.[4] The touch hardly delicate enough. Wrote to Mr Hamilton—Mr M'Coll.

29. M. (St Peter).

Wrote to Mr Carlisle—Mr Hamilton—Mr Millais—Sir H. Ponsonby—Watson & Smith—and minutes. Saw Mr H—Mr GLG—Mr Childers—Scotts. Drive to London—at the temporary home. Read Brummell's Life—Hosack's Queen of Scots[5]—Société de Londres, finished. What a book! not uniformly ill natured but with 1000 untruths, & catchpenny.

To Sir H. PONSONBY, the Queen's secretary, 29 June 1885.   Add MS 44548, f. 33.

Two things have happened unexpectedly.[6] 1. Watts declines his Baronetcy—which I had, indirectly, every reason to suppose he would accept. 2. Browning tells me that Leighton is hurt, and Leighton's family much hurt, and they do not find a plaster in my doctrine that the official headship of the profession is higher than any Baronetcy. With these I combine the fact that the Queen was *I think* inclined to prefer Leighton's claim to either of the others.

I may also notice that I referred to including Leighton, but feared that Her Majesty would (*justly*) think the number too large.

I am out of court and have no title to say a word—but if you think it desirable that these facts should as facts be made known to the Queen I hope you will place them before her.

30. Tu.

Wrote to Ld Spencer—S. Lyttelton—E. Hamilton—Mr Errington—Sir C. Dilke—and minutes. Much thought on the situation, actual & prospective. A short time to London: narrowly escaped a snare and I was but half hearted. I cut out from PMG. note of the extraordinary scene in Edgware Road yesterday afternoon.

[1] Sent by Spencer on 2 July, Add MS 44312, f. 171; this version untraced. See to Mrs O'Shea, 4 Aug. 85. Probably the paper given by O'Shea to Chamberlain on 18 January 1885, printed in *T.T.*, 13 August 1888, 8d; see also Chamberlain, *Political memoir*, 140.
[2] Perhaps *Canons and decrees of the... Council of Trent*, tr. J. Waterworth (1848); and see 1 Mar. 46.
[3] F. T. Buckland, *Notes and jottings from animal life* (1882).
[4] Untraced; perhaps in one of Henry Drummond's works.
[5] J. Hosack, *Mary Queen of Scots and her accusers* (1869).
[6] Only two baronetcies being deemed available, Leighton had been omitted; for the upshot, see to Browning, 2 July 85.

POPULARITY OF MR GLADSTONE.

Mr Gladstone and Mrs Gladstone are at present staying at Lord Aberdeen's villa at Dollis Hill. Mr Gladstone drove into London on business yesterday afternoon, and on his way back to Dollis Hill called at a bookseller's shop in the Edgware-road, where he had arranged to meet Mrs. Gladstone, who was also in town. His entrance into the shop being observed, in a short time a crowd assembled outside, and when Mr. Gladstone attempted to leave the thoroughfare had become blocked, some 3,000 persons being present. A gentleman at hand volunteered to fetch his own conveyance to enable Mr Gladstone to leave. The offer was accepted, and in a few moments a passage was cleared for the right hon. gentleman to enter the vehicle. His appearance was hailed with great enthusiasm and loud cheering. Mr Gladstone after riding a short distance met his own carriage, and proceeded with Mrs Gladstone to Dollis Hill.

Read Goldw. Smith on Ireland—Mrs Oliphant on Victor Hugo[1]—Swinburne, Marino Faliero—Life of Dean Stanley.[2]

To E. W. HAMILTON, 30 June 1885.   Add MS 48607A, f. 120.

Since you have in substance (and in form?) received the appointment,[3] I am unmuzzled, and may now express the unbounded pleasure which it gives me, together with my strong sense (not disparaging any one else) of your desert.

The modesty of your letter is as remarkable as its other qualities, and does you the highest honour.

I can accept no tribute from you, or from any one, with regard to the office of Private Secretary under me except this, that it has always been made by me a strict and severe office, and that this is really the only favour I have ever done you, or any of your colleagues, to whom in their several places and measures I am similarly obliged.

As to your services to me they have been simply indescribable.

No one I think could dream until by experience he knew, to what an extent in these close personal relations devolution can be carried, and how it strengthens the feeble knees and thus also sustains the fainting heart.

I am afraid that all is over and that I am now no longer to write on addresses the familiar name which for nearly sixty years has been dear to me.

God bless you.

To LORD SPENCER, 30 June 1885. '*Private*'.   Althorp MSS K8.

The debt you have laid upon me and on all your late colleagues is far heavier than any reciprocal obligation, if such obligation exist at all, which I can hardly think, for who could, if he reflected, be insensible to your unbounded claims?

You have had to stand the storm from East and West, to be smitten on the right cheek and on the left. You went to Ireland under all the odium and suspicion (in contrast with the preceding Irish Government or rather its main agent) of complicity with disorder. You have left it, the butt of all the sharpest arrows of Nationalism and disaffection, and you have borne both with a calm and even spirit.

[1] Both in *C.R.*, xlviii. 1, 10 (July 1885).
[2] G. A. Ellis, *Arthur Penrhyn Stanley* (1885).
[3] Succeeding Welby as head of the financial division of the treasury. Hamilton noted of this letter: 'It is a real heir-loom'; Bahlman, *Hamilton*, ii. 902.

It was certainly an important turning in your life, when (Decr./68) you with so much modesty accepted the Viceroyalty: for it was the opening of a great chapter of the discipline which searches, strengthens and expands a man. And you have left a name in Ireland proportional to that discipline, and to the unexampled calls which the situation of the country made upon you.

I rejoice that we were able to work together to the last.

The question with me now is whether I am to work any more or not.

I can neither meddle with a party which is simply a party, nor with a party which is in schism against itself.

Not that I undervalue the interests which are involved in the regular and standing contention between Liberalism and Toryism, especially the Toryism of the present day and the miserable imposture termed Tory Democracy. But the life of tension and contention which I have been living is an awful life, eminently unsuited to old age; and hence it is that I hand the strife of party to my successors who have not yet served out their time.

Nothing can withold or suspend my retirement except the presentation of some great and critical problem in the national life, and the hope, *if* such a hope shall be, of making some special contribution towards a solution of it.[1]

No one I think can doubt that, according to all present appearances, the greatest incident of the coming election is to be the Parnell or Nationalist majority. And such a majority is a very great fact indeed. It will at once shift the centre of gravity in the relations between the two countries.

How is it and how are its probable proposals, to be met?

If the heads of the Liberal party shall be prepared to unite in rendering an *adequate* answer to this question, and if they unitedly desire me to keep my present place for the purpose of giving to that answer legislative effect, such a state of things may impose upon me a formidable obligation for the time of the crisis. I cannot conceive any other form in which my resolution could be unsettled.

Your letter, your most kind letter,[2] reached me in London yesterday; & I reserved my reply for the quiet of this place.

[P.S.] I have not considered the question what will the Tories do with Ireland. But they may solve all these questions for me, & for us all, if it be true that they are really to grant Parnell's motion for an inquiry into the actual trial of the Maamtrasna case, not merely the conduct of the political authorities in regard to it.[3]

Wed. July One. 1885.

Wrote to Mad. Novikoff—Mr Arnold MP—Mrs Th.—and minutes. A rural day: imperfectly recorded. Read Swinburne (finished)—Life of Dean Stanley—Amiel. Ld Acton came in aft & dined. 2 to 3 hours of conversation wh. included Ireland & the situation.

To Madame O. NOVIKOV, 1 July 1885.[4]   Add MS 44548, f. 34.

Difficult as I should find it to write to you at this time on politics, I must not omit to thank you for your kindness in sending me the too favourable & indulgent article from

---

[1] Thus far in *Spencer*, i. 311, the rest partly in Hammond, 390.

[2] Complimentary letter of 28 June, Add MS 44312, f. 165.

[3] The Maamtrasna deb. on 17 July was notable for ministers' comments on Spencer's handling of the affair, it being normally held that the viceroy like the Crown could do no wrong; there was no inquiry; *H* 299. 1064.

[4] In Stead, *M.P. for Russia*, ii. 223.

the Journal de S. Petersbourg;[1] & also for your proposal to send me a work of which I had not heard, but which I shall gladly accept from you.

I left office happy in many respects as to the condition of affairs; but I should have been happier if the correspondence on the Afghan frontier had then reached the conclusion which shortly before there seemed to be reason & title to expect.

My countrymen are just now overlooking in me many defects, as they are commonly given to compassion for the fall. Prominent among them is the daily growing defect of age which is asserting itself from day to day in ways better known to me than to my over-partial judges.

2. Th.

Wrote to Mr Browning—Mr Ingram—and minutes. 10¾–5½ Visit to London. Saw Mr H—S.G.L.—H.J.G.—Ld Granville—Mr Carlisle—Deputn from Stroud Green Ch.[2]—Ld R. Grosvenor—who also came down for the evening. Read Brummell's Life—Amiel—Stanley's Life.

To ROBERT BROWNING, 2 July 1885.   Add MS 44548, f. 34.

Your conversation of Saturday evening was not lost upon me, and thinking that an opportunity had arrived, I made the *best* use of it I could with reference to Sir F. Leighton, who has behaved so admirably in this matter. Whether there will be any eventual result, it is, as matters now stand, beyond my power to say.[3]

3. Fr. [Keble College, Oxford]

Wrote to Mr Linklater—Sir W. Harcourt—Mr Bowron[4]—& minutes. Arrived in R.T. at noon: off to Oxford at 4. P.M. Saw Mr H—Mr P—SGL—Ld Hartington and Ld Wolverton on the situation. Saw the Warden[5] twice: he conversed freely on grave matters: his appearance, after *such* an illness, pleased me. Read Amiel—Brummell's Memoirs.

To Sir W. V. HARCOURT, 3 July 1885.   MS Harcourt dep. 9, f. 159.

I do not accept, far from it, your general estimate of the Archbishop: but I cannot defend his speech.[6]

I bear in mind that he is not a practised speaker and may well fail to express his true ideas in a slippery and complex matter: also that he headed a large body of Bishops last year in the best political act they have ever done, and the boldest. But a violent or at least extravagant idea of State Establishment was the pest of the late Archbishop, and may be so of the present. As to the common ruck of the Clergy, I incline to believe that an Estab-lished Clergy will always be a tory Corps d'Armée. In Scotland they are worse than here. Happily ⟨many⟩ a number of the younger and more stirring spirits are on the other side.

---

[1] Sent from Russia, 26 June, Add MS 44168, f. 312 with request that she might send Le Play, *La réforme sociale* (see 29 July 85).

[2] A row about ritualism; see letters to R. Linklater in Add MS 44491.

[3] Leighton was baroneted in February 1886, and cr. baron in 1896. See L. and R. Ormond, *Lord Leighton* (1975), 79 and to Ponsonby, 29 June 85.

[4] William Bowron, who gave him the lift on 29 June (see 30 June 85); Add MS 44548, f. 35.

[5] i.e. E. S. Talbot, warden of Keble.

[6] Benson's speech to the Canterbury diocesan conference, implying support for the tories; Add MS 44199, f. 235.

4. Sat.

Wrote to E. Hamilton (for the Speaker)—Sir E. Saunders—Mr Alden[1] & [blank].
Magd. Chapel 6 P.M. Saw Mr Paget—Mr Medd—Dean Church—Sir H. Acland—
Prof. Creichton [*sc.* Creighton]—Dr Bullen—& much with the Warden. Went
over the ground at Headington & elsewhere: but was not allowed to visit Mr
Gray the man of houses.[2] Read 19th Cent on Egypt—Victor Hugo (Swin-
burne)[3]—Amiel—Pater's Marius[4]—Brummell's Life.

5. 5 S. Trin.

Private celebration 8 A.M. Ch.Ch 10 A.M. New Coll. 5 P.M. Visited the Lay
Readers. Visited the 'Puseum' so called: disappointed: in the House and Lib-
rary.[5] Saw Sir H. Acland—Sir J. Paget—Mr Gore—Mr Pater[6]—and the Warden,
much: he is well reported of in the consultation. Read Amiel—Statham on
Incarnation[7]—Mivart on Liberty of R.C.s[8]—Theol. Examn papers. Wrote to. . . .
Drive with Sir H.A.

6. M. [*London*]

Wrote to Ld R. Grosvenor—Mr Godley—Mr Stead—Mr . . .—& minutes. Mr
Teale[9] endeavoured to make an inspection of my (interior) throat: but could not
effect it more than partially. Saw the Warden *bis*: and off at 11.45. In R.T. at
2.20. Conclave at 3 on Parl. business. Also saw S.G.L.—Ld R.G—Sir C. Dilke—Ld
Kimberley—Sir T. Acland—Ld Kensington—Count Münster. H of C. $4\frac{1}{2}$-$7\frac{3}{4}$.[10]
Dined at Count Münster's. Drive afterwards. Read Marius—Memoirs of
Brummell.

To LORD R. GROSVENOR, chief whip, 6 July 1885.[11]   Add MS 44316, f. 5.

You will remember that early in the present year Mrs O'Shea was good enough to send
me a paper which as she informed me contained the views of Mr Parnell on Local
Government.[12] The great question of the Representation of the people at that time
occupied my mind and the time of Parliament, so that I could do no more than put the
paper into the proper way of being carefully considered. That question is now happily
disposed of and the field is open for the consideration of future measures.

As this communication to me was spontaneous, and as the accompanying declaration

---

[1] E. Wenham Alden, Oxford surgeon.

[2] (Sir) Walter Gray, 1848-1918; former steward of Keble; developed N. Oxford; the 'founder of
Oxford conservatism', whose revival led to the city's disfranchisement 1881; see C. Fenby, *The other
Oxford* (1970).

[3] *N.C.*, xviii. 1, 14 (July 1885).

[4] W. H. Pater, *Marius the Epicurean*, 2v. (1885).

[5] i.e. the first Pusey House in St. Giles, later rebuilt; now part of St. Cross college.

[6] Walter Horatio *Pater, 1839-94; aesthete and fellow of Brasenose, Oxford; see 4 July 85.

[7] W. M. Statham, *The abiding Christ and other sermons* (1885).

[8] *N.C.*, xviii. 30 (July 1885).

[9] Thomas Pridgin Teale, B.M., of Brasenose, though no longer resident.

[10] Spoke on business of the House; *H* 298. 1710.

[11] Holograph.

[12] Obtained from Spencer, see 27 June 85.

has not since been withdrawn or qualified, I ought perhaps to assume at once that it stands good as when it was written. But as some time has elapsed, I wish you would kindly learn for me whether it is so, since it was to you that I handed the paper when I received it.[1]

7. Tu.

Wrote to Mary G.—Sir H. Ponsonby—Mr M'Coll—Mr Linklater—Mr Lefevre—& minutes. H. of C. $4\frac{1}{2}$-$7\frac{3}{4}$. Spoke nearly an hour on the new situation & outlook.[2] Saw Sir E. Saunders (12-$12\frac{1}{2}$)[3]—SGL.—Ld R.G—Mr Chamberlain—Sir W. Harcourt. Dined with Ld Northbourne: drive afterwards & another visit to H. of C. Read Amiel—Brummell's Memoirs.

8. Wed.

Wrote to Mr Hutt—Sir W. Farquhar—Mr West—and minutes. Dined at Argyll Lodge. Wrote Minute on Private Secretariat.[4] Saw S.G.L.—Ld R.G.—Mr Hamilton—H.J.G.—Duke of Argyll—Lady Derby—Mr Harrison. Calls. Drive with C. at night. Read Amiel—B.I.R. new Report[5]—Brummell's Memoirs.

9. Th.

Wrote to Mr Linklater—Rev. B.W. Savile—Watsons—Mr Acland MP—Ld Spencer—and minutes. Twelve to breakfast. Saw Sir E. Saunders—S.G.L.—Ld R.G.—Mr Godley (re Stead)[6]—Mr Knowles—Ld Granville—Sir H. Acland—Mr Childers—Ld Northbourne. Lord N. & E.H. dined. Drive afterwards. H of C. $4\frac{1}{4}$-$5\frac{3}{4}$.[7] Read Amiel—Prom. Vinctus[8]—Brummell's Memoirs.

10. Fr.

Wrote to Watsons—Sir J. Millais—and minutes. 7-11. Dined at Dollis Hill. Saw S.G.L.—G.L.G.—Ld R. Grosvenor l.l.—Ld Rosebery—Ld Wolverton. Indisposition kept me from the House. Read Prom. Vinctus—Amiel—Brummell's Memoirs.

11. Sat. [Combe Wood, Kingston]

Wrote to Mr Bellairs—Mr Goschen—Dr Stainer—and minutes. Went to Wolverton's villa. Another visit to Sir E. Saunders at 11. Saw S.G.L.—G.L.G.—Ld R. Grosvenor—Mr M'Coll—Ld Granville—Ld Spencer—Mr Currie. Attack of diarrhoea at night. Read Fortnightly on Ireland—on Oxford Professorship[9]—read Amiel—Memoirs of G.A. Bellamy.[10]

[1] No reply found. See to Mrs. O'Shea, 4 Aug. 85.
[2] *H* 298. 1845.   [3] His dentist.   [4] Add MS 44769, f. 181.
[5] 28th *Report* of the Board of Inland Revenue; comments on it at Add MS 44548, f. 36.
[6] The 'Maiden Tribute'; see 15 July 85.
[7] Ways and means cttee.; *H* 299. 127.
[8] Aeschylus, ed. H. M. Stephenson, *Prometheus Vinctus* (1885).
[9] *F.R*, xliv. 1, 102 (July 1885); the radical programme's National Councils proposal; see Appendix I.
[10] *Memoirs of G. A. Bellamy, including all her intrigues. By a gentleman of Covent Garden theatre* (1785).

To G. J. GOSCHEN, M.P., 11 July 1885.   Add MS 44161, f. 317.

The position from which I have not at this moment retired, entirely warrants the letter you have addressed to me.[1] But I am not sure if you are aware of the prospective independence, which is the hardly-earned prize now within my reach. Most justly do you refer to the closing words of my letter to the Midlothian Association.[2] They supply the key to my present conduct. They certainly had in view some (then) recent utterances. I hope, though I have no right either to demand or to expect, that others, who may be in various degrees centres of influence, may be disposed to act upon them.

Though I have thus referred to recent utterances, I am not at all sure that I know, as you appear to know, what is the 'programme of Mr. Chamberlain' as a whole; or that I should feel it necessary, if there be such a programme, to pronounce on all the points of it. The coming election offers grave enough matter for consideration, without going far into the future. My indisposition to travel beyond the bounds of need is not due to reserve; but is founded on the fact that my fifty three years of service, and the (for me) fortunate circumstances of the moment, absolve me from future cares, unless it should chance that with an emergency in near view, there should be a likelihood that I could seriously contribute to meeting it with effect.

I think, as perhaps you do, that there *is* an emergency at hand; and that it is a prime duty of all Liberal Statesmen to consider how they can best meet it. My starting point would be what I have now described; it would be affirmative and constructive. I should much desire fully to learn what are your views, what you can contribute to the common purpose. Will you for this purpose dine here quietly on Tuesday at 8? There shall be no one here except one or two friends, *such* as will not I think be impediments. I have spoken of a mode of approaching the subject which would be affirmative and constructive, because I think the mode of saying aye or no on a particular proposition has rather a negative look: and because, if any one has proposed 'separate National Councils' truly deserving the name, I am not yet aware of it.

12. 6 S. Trin.

Prayers at house mg & aft. Wrote to D. of Argyll. Saw Mr Harvey—Ld Acton. Read Revised Prayerbook—Amiel—Dulaure Div Generatrices.[3]

13. M. [London]

Wrote to Watsons—Sir T. Acland—Sir C. Forster—& minutes. Attended the Prince's Levée. Dined with Sir T. May. H of C. $4\frac{1}{2}$–$6\frac{1}{2}$ & $10\frac{3}{4}$–$1\frac{1}{4}$.[4] Last sitting to Millais. Saw S.G.L—Ld Cork *cum* Mr Foy—Mrs Meynell Ingram—Mr Chamberlain *cum* Sir C. Dilke—Ld R. Grosvenor—Sir W. Harcourt. Read Prom. Vinctus—Brummell's Memoirs—Amiel.

14. Tu.

Wrote to Duke of Argyll—Mr MacColl—Ld R. Grosvenor—Sir S. Scott & Co— Mr A. Carnegie—Sir E. Saunders—Mr Linklater—Mr Westell—Mr Dillwyn

[1] On 10 July, Add MS 44161, f. 313; on 'the policy with regard to the establishment of separate *central* national councils for the different parts of the United Kingdom, which have been distinctly foreshadowed by Mr Chamberlain'.

[2] Gladstone's 'efforts to prevent anything that can mar the unity and efficiency' of the party; *T.T.*, 30 June 1885, 6a.

[3] J. A. Dulaure, *Des divinités génératrices, ou du culte du phallus* (new ed. 1885).

[4] Questioned on his relations with Rome; *H* 299. 432.

MP—& minutes. Read Prom. V. (finished)—Brummell—Amiel (finished). 11.30 went to 40 B. Square & saw the splendid boy[1] born to Willy this morning. All was as well as could be. God be praised. Then to Sir E. Saunders—Scotts—Mrs Birks—and finally Dr Semon's[2] with Sir A. Clark. A thorough examination of the throat was made: and silence rather rigidly enjoined a condition of fairly probable recovery. *No* House of Commons. We then went to the Grosvenor Gallery. Saw S.G.L.—Ld R.G. Eight to dinner. I had to speak more than was desirable: the occasion was important; it was the coming Irish question.[3] Conversation with Acland, Goschen, & general. Saw Scotts—Mrs Birks—Mr Westell. Drive with C.

15. Wed.

Wrote to Mrs Th.—Sir H. Ponsonby—Mr Dillwyn—and minutes. Tea party in garden at 5. Read at Mrs M.I.s[4] request the first of the too famous P.M.G.s.[5] Am not well satisfied with the mode in which this mass of horrors has been collected, or as to the moral effect of its general dispersion by sale in the streets. Saw S.G.L.—Ld Granville—Mr Phelps—Ld R. Grosvenor l.l.—Mr ?MacClell. S.—Sir A. Clark—Ld Prov. Edinburgh—Sir James Paget. Dined at Sir A. Sassoon's. Read Heraclides[6]—Bellamy's Life—Irish Papers. Began Munro's Lucretius.[7]

16.

Wrote to Mr Linklater—Mr Childers l.l.—The Speaker—Mr J.K. Cross—& minutes. Saw S.G.L.—Mr West—Lord R. Grosvenor l.l.l.—Sir A. Clark: immediate 'treatment' of the throat decided on. Read Heraclides—Lucretius—Bellamy's Life—Memoirs! of Mrs Billington.[8]

To H. C. E. CHILDERS, M.P., 16 July 1885.   *The Times*, 17 July 1885, 10b.

The financial experience of the present session is so full of importance and of warning to parties too eager in opposition that, although I am prevented from taking part in the debate of this evening, I wish to say a few words upon the subject.

Although I consider that our indirect taxation still has, all circumstances considered, a rather unduly large proportion of our taxes upon property, it is an essential element in our system, and it seems most unwise for Parliament to weaken its hold upon that instrument.

In the debate of June 8 we warned the Opposition, but in vain, that the motion aimed

[1] William Glynne Charles, W. H. Gladstone's 1st s., heir to the Hawarden estates; liberal M.P. Kilmarnock 1911-15; killed in action 1915.

[2] (Sir) Felix *Semon, 1849-1921; German-trained throat specialist, settled in London in late 1870s; specialised in cancer of larynx; kt. 1897. See Introduction above, X, section ix.

[3] Present were Acton, Grosvenor, Goschen, Sir C. Forster, Sir T. D. Acland; Add MS 44788, f. 35. For Acland's notes on the dinner, see below, Appendix I.

[4] i.e. Mrs. Meynell Ingram.

[5] 'The Maiden Tribute of Modern Babylon', *P.M.G.*, 6 July 1885, W. T. Stead's *exposé* of child prostitution for which he was jailed, having bought a 13 year old girl for £5 to prove his case.

[6] Reading on this and next three days uncertain; if *sic*, then the works of the 4th century Greek philosopher.

[7] H. A. J. Munro's ed. of Lucretius, *De rerum natura* (1860 and later eds.).

[8] E. Billington, *Memoirs* (1792).

at by us would strike a blow at indirect taxation. This result has been accomplished without delay; the whole of the new taxation proposed by the Tory Government is to be supplied by property, and the future force of this precedent supplied by a Tory Government will not be inconsiderable.

Further, my apprehension is that the effect must be very greatly aggravated by the gratuitous declaration of the Chancellor of the Exchequer on Monday that the extreme limit of indirect taxation has been reached upon all great articles already taxed. He excepted tea, but such an exception in my view rather adds to than diminishes the mischief. I sincerely hope he may reconsider an opinion perhaps due to the haste and pressure consequent on accession to office.

I make no doubt you will also express regret that the Budget will make an addition to the National Debt under circumstances which hardly warrant it.[1]

17. Fr.

Wrote to Ld Derby—Ld Hartington—Sir C. Hobhouse—& minutes. Drive with C. Saw S.G.L.—E.H.—Lord R.G—Sir A. Clark. Read P.O. Report—Report on Trade abroad[2]—Mrs Bellamy's Life, and the *three* Volumes of Mrs Gooch's worthless Life.[3] Attended Dr Semon & had my first 'treatment'.

To LORD DERBY, 17 July 1885.[4]   Derby MSS.

I had hoped that the prospect we have now for the moment lost of full and free conversation with you would enable me to put you in full possession of what has taken place so far as I am concerned with respect to future legislation for Ireland during the last few & important weeks.

But a severe prudence has somewhat late imposed upon me a law of abstention from not only all public speaking but all serious exertion of the voice such as is apt to happen in prolonged conversation.

Under these circumstances I send you three letters, which have been seen by three or four of our colleagues and which I shall be glad if you will read, & return to me. They explain I think pretty fully my view, and the facts, of the situation as it was two or three weeks ago. Within that time it has undergone important changes. I am not fully informed but what I know looks as if the Irish party, so-called, in Parliament, excited by the high biddings of Lord Randolph, had changed what was undoubtedly Parnell's ground until within a very short time back. It is now said that a Central Board will not suffice, and that there must be a Parliament. This I suppose may mean the repeal of the Act of Union or may mean an Austro-Hungarian scheme or may mean that Ireland is to be like a great Colony such as Canada. Of all or any of these schemes I will only now say that of course they constitute an entirely new point of departure and raise questions of an order totally different to any that are involved in a Central Board appointed for local purposes.[5]

[1] Childers twice referred to Gladstone's concurrence in his attack on the budget; *H* 299. 928.
[2] Perhaps Giffen's report on foreign trade; *PP* 1881 lxxxiii. 149.
[3] E. S. Gooch, *The life of Mrs Gooch written by herself*, 3v. (1792).
[4] Part in Morley, iii. 215.
[5] Derby, 19 July, Add MS 44142, f. 138, reserved Gladstone's letter 'for reflection', felt the central board scheme 'either goes too far, or not far enough'; he wrote again on 25 July, ibid., f. 140, unwilling to offer a final opinion on undiscussed points, but preferring four separate local govt. centres to a central board; the Canadian precedent possible, but 'the English democracy' not inclined to 'large concessions to Irish sentiment'.

18. Sat. [Combe Wood, Kingston]

Wrote to Sir W. Dunbar—Ld Hartington—Ld Portarlington—and minutes. N.P. Gallery Trust meeting at 2½—Visited the Gallery afterwards. To Dr Semon at noon. Treatment No 2. Saw G.L.G—Lord R.G.—E.H.—Sir A. Clark. Drove to Ld Wolverton's: only the Harcourts there. Read Bellamy—Heraclides (finished).

To LORD HARTINGTON, M.P., 18 July 1885.   Chatsworth MSS 340. 1794.

I write a few lines on two important subjects, instead of calling, to spare my voice.

1. On Monday I saw Dilke and Chamberlain and told them in plain terms, which they appeared to understand, that they were absolutely responsible for the acts of Spencer in his Viceroyalty.

2. I have read all the material part of the important debate of last night.[2] As I understand the reports the Government laid down most formidable doctrines, subject only to a certain degree of ambiguity from shades of variance in the statements of its members.

It seems to me well to deserve consideration whether questions should not be put to clear up this ambiguity.

Perhaps you would consult with others such as Spencer, Harcourt, Selborne.

I am going down to Coombe but I return on Monday morning and can keep any appointment after one on that day.

I have put down some forms of query, to bring out the points.

[1](1) Do Her Majesty's Government, in declaring that they do not take upon themselves any responsibility for the Acts of the late Irish Administration, mean to extend this declaration to the judicial action of the Viceroy in regard to the prerogative of mercy?

(2) In declaring that 'every person in Ireland has the right of appealing to the Lord Lieutenant for the remission or reconsideration of his sentence', is it intended by them that on every change of Government in Ireland each prisoner has a right to demand from the incoming Lord Lieutenant such reconsideration, irrespective of investigations previously made, and without any new facts in the case, or is this an action limited to cases where such new facts are alleged?

(3) Has such a reinvestigation been promised in the Maamtrasna case, and is it on the ground of new facts, or irrespective of them?

19. 7 S. Trin.

Ch. mg & evg. Dr S. came. Treatment No 3. Saw Ld Wolverton (HNG)—Sir W. Harcourt (Irish affairs). Read Smyth on Old Faiths[3]—Reville Hist. Religions[4]—Dulaure Div. Generatr.—Wakeman on Religion in Engl.[5]

20. M. [London]

Wrote to Mr Caldwell—and minutes. Dined at Lansdowne House. Dr Semon at 11.30. Treatment No 4. Improvement reported. The malady is 'chronic laryngeal catarrh'. Saw S.L.G.—Ld R. Grosvenor—Ld Rosebery[6]—Ld Hartington—Ld

---

[1] Rest no longer attached to the letter; copy at Add MS 44548, f. 38.

[2] On the Maamtrasna affair and Spencer; *H* 299. 1064.

[3] N. Smyth, *Old faiths in new light* (1879).

[4] A. Réville, *Prolégomènes de l'Histoire des religions* (1883); see 6 Oct. 85.

[5] H. O. Wakeman, *The history of religion in England* (1884).

[6] 'Mr. G. took me aside to have a talk. He considers Central Board as done with: thinks of setting before country services of party in connection with Franchise, redistribution &c.'; Rosebery's diary this day, Dalmeny MSS.

Granville—Sir W. Harcourt—Sir E. Malet—Count W. Bismarck.[1] Read Lucretius—Bellamy's Life finished Vol II.

21. Tu. [*Dollis Hill*]

Wrote to Sir W. Harcourt—Mr Murray—Mrs Th.—Ld Granville—Mrs Bolton—Sir C. Dilke—Ld Northbourne—and minutes. Dined at Sir C. Forster's. Drove down to Dollis at night. Saw S.G.L.—Ld R. Grosvenor—Sir A. Clark—Dr Semon (Treatment No 5)—Mr E. Arnold & Miss Tennant—Sir C. Forster. Read Lucretius (began II)—Life of Baddeley I.—Q.R. on the Society Books.[2]

To Sir C. W. DILKE, M.P., 21 July 1885.[3]   Add MS 43875, f. 266.

I cannot forbear writing to express the hope that you and Chamberlain may be able to say or do something to remove the appearance now presented to the world of a disposition on your parts to sever yourselves from the executive, and especially from the judicial administration of Ireland as it was carried on by Spencer under the late Government.

You may question my title to attempt interference with your free action by the expression of such a hope, and I am not careful to assure you in this matter or certain that I can make good such a title in argument.

But we have been for five years in the same boat, on most troubled waters, without having during the worst three years of the five a single man of the company thrown overboard. I have *never* in my life known the bonds of union so strained by the pure stress of circumstances: a good intent on all sides has enabled them to hold. Is there any reason why at this moment they should part?

A rupture may come on questions of future policy; I am not sure that it will. But if it is to arrive, let it come in the course of nature as events develop themselves. At the present moment there appears to be set up an idea of difference about matters which lie in the past, and for which we are all plenarily responsible. The position is settled in all its elements, and cannot be altered.

The frightful discredit with which the new Government has covered itself by its treatment of Spencer has drawn attention away from the signs of at least passive discord among us, signs which might otherwise have drawn upon us pretty sharp criticism. It appears to me that hesitation on the part of any of us as to our own responsibility for Spencer's acts can only be mischievous to the party and the late Cabinet, but will and must be far more mischievous to any who may betray such disinclination. Even with the Irish party it can, I imagine, do nothing to atone for past offences, inasmuch as it is but a negative proceeding, while from Randolph, Hicks Beach, and Gorst, positive support is to be had in what I cannot but consider a foolish as well as guilty crusade against the administration of criminal justice in Ireland; which may possibly be defective, but, with all its defects, whatever they may be, is, I apprehend, the only defence of the life and property of the poor.

It will be the legislation of the future, and not this most unjust attack upon Spencer, which will have to determine hereafter your relations with Ireland, and the 'national' party. I may be wrong, but it seems to me easy, and in some ways advantageous, to say 'my mind is open to consider at large any proposals acceptable to Ireland for the develop-

---

[1] Wilhelm (Bill) Otto Albrecht von Bismarck, 1852–1901; one of the chancellor's sons; sec. to the Berlin conference.

[2] 'English society, and its historians', *Q.R.*, clxi. 142 (July 1885).

[3] In Gwynn, ii. 158.

ment and security of her liberties, but I will not sap the foundations of order and of public right by unsettling the rules, common to all parties, under which criminal justice has been continuously administered, and dragging for the first time the prerogative of mercy within the *vortex* of party conflict.' I dare say I may have said too much in the way of argument on a matter which seems to me hardly to call for argument, but a naked suggestion would have appeared even less considerate than the letter which I have written, prompted by strong feeling and clear conviction.[1]

To Sir W. V. HARCOURT, M.P., 21 July 1885.   MS Harcourt dep. Adds 10.

My *leanings* in the Crim. Law Court Bill are expressed on Clauses 4 & 5 of the copy herewith.[2] I am however open to correction. After what you said, I do not attempt to introduce specially the case of seduction.

22. Wed.

Wrote to Mr Grant MP—Hallam Tennyson—Mr Cope Whitehouse[3]—and minutes. Ret. to London at 12. Sixth treatment by Dr Semon before Sir A.C. Saw S.G.L—Lord R.G.—H.N.G. Read Munro's Lucretius—Mrs Baddeley's Life— Dulaure's Div. Gen. Back to Dollis Hill for evg.

23. Th.

Wrote to Ld Granville—Mr E.L. Stanley—Ld R.G.—Mr Childers—Mr J. Collings & minutes. Read Mrs Baddeley—Landor, H. VIII & A. Boleyn[4]—Munro's Lucretius—Perrot's 'Homère' in Rev. 2 M.[5]—Dulaure Divin. Gen. Saw S.G.L.—Ld R.G—Dr F. Semon & Sir A. Clark 7th treatment. Slept at Dollis.

To H. C. E. CHILDERS, M.P., 23 July 1885.   Add MS 44548, f. 40.

I think that by your original Budget you divided 15ɱ almost equally, providing half by new taxes, and, virtually or actually, finding the other half by stopping the repayment of Debt which in a normal state of things would be some 7ɱ. By how much is this worsened now?[6] By how much will the estimated charge exceed the new taxation & the sum obtainable by stopping altogether the repayment of debt? In other words what will be the effective addition to the National Debt during the financial year?

(2). I am sorry not to have been able to learn what counsel you have given in the matter of the Land Purchase Bill, and to hear that you are going off this evening for good. Am I to understand this as meaning that in your opinion the measure ought to be accepted?[7]

---

[1] See 13 July 85 and to Hartington, 18 July 85 for Chamberlain, Dilke and Maamtrasna.

[2] Not found. See to Stuart, 31 July 85.

[3] Frederick Cope Whitehouse, archaeologist, had sent tracts on Lake Moeris; Add MS 44548, f. 40.

[4] In W. S. Landor, *Imaginary conversations*, ii. 275 (1824).

[5] *Revue des deux mondes*, lxx. 275 (August 1885).

[6] Childers reported that govt. has added £1 million to the deficit; this, with reduction of additional taxation and other factors, gives a shortfall of about £4 million; Add MS 44132, f. 176.

[7] Will not actually oppose it, 'but were I to formulate amendments, I should be supposed to oppose the principle, and this would lead to misunderstanding'; ibid., f. 177.

24. *Fr.*

Wrote to Mrs Th.—Miss Tennant—Mr R. Brown jun.—& minutes. Saw G.L.G—
Ld R.G.—Dr Simon & Sir A.C. *8th* time. Read Mrs Baddeley—Dulaure Div.
Gen.—Smith, Chaldean Account[1]—Munro's Lucretius. Dined with Mr Hutton,
Father Whitty,[2] Mr De Vere, Dean of St Pauls.

25. *Sat. St James* [*London*]

Wedding [anniversary] & T.G.s birthday. Wrote to Mr Childers—Sir Thos G.—
Scotts—and minutes. Went to the Talbots at 4.30. Saw G.L.G.—H.N.G—Ld R.
Grosvenor—E.W.H.—Ld Spencer. Read Munro's Lucretius—Smith's Chaldean
History—Baddeley's Memoirs (finished) a painful & instructive book.—Dulaure
Div. Gen. Conversation with the invalid, who is like his wife wonderfully borne
up. They [the Talbots] give a most edifying spectacle.

To H. C. E. CHILDERS, M.P., 25 July 1885.   Add MS 44548, f. 40.

I am very much obliged to you for the statement of figures you have kindly sent me;[3]
but I hope you will consider further the course you are to take on the Land Purchase Bill.
Spencer thinks, and as it appears to me most justly, that in its present shape it is open
to the gravest objections and, as I understand him, ought not to pass.
What I understand to be your position is this. From a variety of motives, we strained
economical principles to a degree which you & I among others disliked. But now the new
Government have strained them a great deal more. How then can the fact that you
thought we went somewhat too far be a reason for refraining from objection to a measure
which gives greatly enhanced reasons for objecting?
Anything like discussion is strictly forbidden me but I cannot refuse to contribute to
the common counsels on this Bill.
I really do not see how as the person principally representing the finance of the late
Government, and still in the active prosecution of public life, you can avoid giving your
political friends the benefit of your counsels on this important subject.
I recommended Spencer to summon a meeting about it.[4]

26. *8 S. Trin.*

Ch. mg & evg. Great heat. Read Reville— Salmon, Introductory Lecture[5]—
Dulaure (finished): a sad but necessary book: the author is not to be approved—
Smith's Chaldean Hist. Conversation with E. Talbot.

27. *M.* [*Dollis Hill*]

Wrote to Mrs Meynell Ingram—and minutes. Meeting at Granville's 12.30 on
Land Purchase. Financial faith is very low! Dr Semon's at one. Tenth treatment.
Saw Sir A.C. Off to Dollis Hill at 4.30 for another visit. Read G.A. Bellamy Vol V
(skipping III and IV)—Munro's Lucretius—Hart's Memorials[6]—O'Grady's Cucu-

---

[1] See 4 Dec. 76.
[2] Robert Whitty, 1817-95; Jesuit priest.   [3] See 23 July 85n.
[4] Childers unable to attend it; Add MS 44132, f. 179.
[5] G. Salmon, *A historical introduction to the study of the ... New Testament*, 2v. (1885-6).
[6] S. A. Hart, *Reminiscences* (1882).

lain¹—Chaldean History. Saw E. Talbot—Mr Sankey—S.G.L.—Ld R. Grosvenor—Sir W. Harcourt—Ld Granville.

28. *Tu.*

Wrote to Dr Hutton—and minutes. Eight to dinner, including Lucy, and our hosts. Saw S.G.L.—Herbert & Harry on the projected voyage²—the Firm[?]—& Irish affairs—Dr Semon & Sir A. Clark 11th treatment.—Mr Murray—Ld Granville—Mr [blank] Smith (Aberdeen Sculptor)³ at Dollis. Read Munro's Lucretius—Smith's Chaldean Genesis—Life of G.A. Bellamy—Reminiscences of Hart R.A.

To Rev. Dr. G. C. HUTTON, 28 July 1885.   Add MS 44548, f. 41.

I much regret the accident which caused a delay in answering your letter.⁴

The letter written by my direction to Mr. Graham⁵ does not seem to be in itself ambiguous, but much allowance is to be made for varieties of construction where strong convictions and feelings are enlisted.

The basis of my own position in relation to the Established Church of Scotland remains precisely that which was laid down by Lord Hartington I think about seven years ago. It is a Scotch question and ought to be decided by the people of Scotland, i.e. Parliament ought to accept their sense. To lay down beforehand the mode in which that sense ought to be declared might be mischievous in excluding other modes, which might be as authentic as the one specified and yet might be shut out by the specification. Clearly it ought not (as I think) to be required by anticipation that an Election should be held upon the question.

29. *Wed.*

Wrote to Mr Mackey—and minutes. 12th Visit to Dr Semon & Sir A. Clark. Saw S.G.L.—G.L.G—H.J.G.—Ld R. Grosvenor—H.N.G.—Ld Granville—Dr Mackay—Mr Smith who again studied my head. Saw the Mikado.⁶ Back to D[ollis Hill] at midnight. Finished Chaldean Genesis. Finished Lucretius III—he is a powerful and splendid poet—G.A. Bellamy finished Vol. V.—began Le Play.⁷ Shopping.

30. *Th.* [*London*]

Wrote to Lady Aberdeen—& minutes. Return to London 11¼. Dr Semon & Sir A. Clark: 13th Treatment. Saw S.G.L.—Ld R. Grosvenor—Sir W. Harcourt. Read

¹ S. O'Grady, *Early bardic literature* (1879).

² See 8 Aug. 85.

³ Possibly Thomas Reynold Smith, 1839–?1910, miniaturist sculptor in ivory.

⁴ From the United Presbyterian minister (see 29 Nov. 81), of 2 July, Add MS 44491, f. 241, sending resolutions on disestablishment from the U.P. synods, and arguing that neutrality is untenable on this issue.

⁵ In June 1884 (ibid.), but not traced.

⁶ Gilbert and Sullivan, at the Savoy.

⁷ Sent by Novikov: P. G. F. Le Play, *La réforme sociale en France*, 2v. (1864). See 1 July 85.

Le Play—V. Lee's Countess of Albany[1]—Hart's Reminiscences (finished)—'Did F. Bacon write Shakespeare?' I.[2]

31. Frid.

Wrote to Mr Stuart MP—Mrs M. Ingram—Mr Smalley—Mad. Novikoff—Mrs Th.—Author of 'did F. Bacon write Shakespeare?' H of C. $5\frac{3}{4}$-7 and $10\frac{1}{2}$-$12\frac{1}{4}$.[3] Dr S. & Sir A.C. 14th treatment. Saw S.G.L.—E.W.H.—Ld R. Grosvenor l.l.—Ld Granville—E. Wickham (Mr L.)—Sir W. Harcourt. Read Le Play—Countess of Albany.

To J. STUART, M.P., 31 July 1885.   Add MS 44548, f. 41.

I find that Mr. Morley has inquired whether I object to its being known that in my opinion the protected age might properly be advanced beyond 16 in the Criminal Law Amendment Bill.[4]

I cannot consider that much weight is due to my judgment in this important matter, as compared with that of others. But I have considered it as well as I could, & I personally should have been glad if the Government had found it consistent with their views to name 18, rather than 16, as the protected age.

Sat Aug One 1885. [Waddesdon, Aylesbury]

Wrote to Mr Chamberlain—Sir E. Saunders—Ld Granville—& minutes. Dr Semon, 15th treatment. Quasi-sitting to Mr Ledward.[5] Saw G.L.G.—Lord RG— Mr Ledward (a man of promise)—Dr Cuyler.[6] Read Contemp. on Gold—Scotch Disestabl.[7]—Hamlet—Le Play Réforme sociale—Countess of Albany. Three hours journey to Waddesdon:[8] a remarkable construction, no commonplace host. Miss A. Rothschild a striking person in conversation.

To J. CHAMBERLAIN, M.P., 1 August 1885.   Chamberlain MSS 5/34/37.

Those of the late Government whom I have seen were reluctant, on political grounds, to take any step which would seem adverse to the Land Purchase Bill; and Childers, to my extreme disappointment & surprise absented himself from London & refused to return. Spencer read a letter from you, which leads me to write this note in order that you may not decide in the dark. I am sorry to say I understand that under this Bill public money is to be lent at *under three per cent* on a 49 years loan, which is a real subsidy to the Irish landlords. This point, which Spencer mentioned, evidently was not before you, when you wrote your note to him.

[1] V. Lee [i.e. V. Paget], *The countess of Albany* (1883).
[2] [Mrs H. Potts], *Did Francis Bacon write 'Shakespeare'? Thirty-two reasons for thinking that he did* (1885?). Cautiously sceptical reply to the anon. author, Add MS 44548, f. 41.
[3] Criminal Law Amndt. Bill, dealing with child prostitution; *H* 300. 687.
[4] The bill, twice lost during the Gladstone govt., was pressed through in the wake of the 'maiden tribute' campaign; see 15 July 85.
[5] Richard Arthur Ledward, 1857-1890; sculptor. Bust untraced.
[6] Theodore Ledyard Cuyler, American presbyterian minister.
[7] *C.R.*, xlviii. 188, 249 (August 1885).
[8] Presumably by coach. Imitation French chateau (1883) near Aylesbury, housing the huge art and china collection of Ferdinand James de Rothschild (1839-98, liberal (unionist) M.P. Aylesbury from 1885; friend of Rosebery and Hamilton) and his sister Alice.

There is some idea that—no thanks to us—the Bill will not be passed.

Pray remember me to Dilke if he is with you.

We remain here until the end of next week: & shall you wish to see me I am quite open to you but with limited powers of speech.

As yet I have entirely failed to extract any independent information on the question whether the Central Board scheme is dead or not.

2. 9 S. Trin.

Ch mg (with H.C.) & evg. Quiet Sunday owing in part to gumboil. The Church was satisfactory. Wrote to Rev. Mr Case. Read Reville—Le Play—19th Cent. on Reforming Jesuit & other articles.[1] Conversation with Mr Baron—Mrs White.

3. M. [Dollis Hill]

Three hours back to London. Wrote to Ld E. Clinton—Mrs Th.—& minutes. Quasi-sitting to Mr Ledward. Saw the fairy domain of Ethrope.[2] Political function in wh I was passive. Herbert spoke for me.[3] Dr Semon, 16th treatment. Saw S.G.L.—Ld Granville—Mr Chamberlain. Read Le Play—Countess of Albany (finished)—Did Bacon write Shakesp? (finished)—Accounts of Ramabai.[4] Came to Dollis for the Girls Home Festival: saw Mr Kinnaird.

4. Tu.

Wrote to Mr Stanley MP—Mrs O'Shea—and minutes. Read Le Play—Fitzgerald Vol II.[5]—and [blank.] Saw S.G.L.—Lord R.G—Herbert J.G. conversation on Ireland—Mr Ledward (quasi-sitting). Six to dinner at Dollis: Mr Godley, Mr Russell. Attended the Grant service[6] at Westminster Abbey. Farrar's Address eloquent but overdone & very long. Dr Semon, 17th treatment.

To Mrs. O'SHEA, 4 August 1885. Add MS 56446, f. 76.

Lord Richard Grosvenor has at my request addressed to you several letters, the last of them I think about a week ago, the purpose of which has been to learn whether the important paper forwarded by you to me early in the year[7] on the subject of Local Govt. in Ireland, as an exposition of the views & desires of Mr. Parnell, was still to be regarded as in any manner bearing that character.

The replies you have been good enough to make have not purported to be final & you will readily understand that after having received a spontaneous communication of that nature & importance (on which I at once took the steps which it seemed for the moment

[1] Including J. L. Field, 'The burden of Ireland' (see to Knowles, 5 Aug. 85), N.C., xviii. 249 (August 1885).

[2] Alice de Rothschild's bijou pavilion at Eythrope, the neighbouring estate.

[3] Aylesbury by-election consequent on Sir N. Rothschild's peerage; F. J. de Rothschild held the seat for the liberals.

[4] Perhaps Ramabai Sarasvati, The high-caste Hindu woman (n.d., 2nd ed. 1887).

[5] P. H. Fitzgerald, A new history of the English stage, 2v. (1882).

[6] Memorial service for President Grant; T.T., 5 August 1885, 5d.

[7] On the central board (see Hammond, 419) but no copy found (see to Spencer, 27 June 85). On 4 October Grosvenor reported, Add MS 44316, f. 42: 'no sign of any document from the lady'. See 24 Oct. 85.

to require) I feel it my absolute duty to learn, if I am able, whether it still exists for any practical purpose.

In one of four notes[1] you spoke of substituting for it my son Herbert's proposition. But from him I learn that he has made *no* proposition in substitution for that plan but has only indicated his opinion (of which I had not previously been aware) that it might under certain circs. if insufficient admit of addition or development.

As some weeks have now elapsed since Ld. R. Grosvenor addressed his question to you, & as I leave England before the close of the week, I am sure you will excuse my asking your early attention to this letter.[2]

To E. L. STANLEY, M.P., 4 August 1885.   Add MS 44548, f. 42.

I have not I think had any communication with Sir W. Harcourt on the question of Prison Sites.

Undoubtedly the more I think of the proposal in the Bill the more it wears to me the aspect of one of the very worst pieces of Socialism that has yet come into our view.[3]

5. Wed.

Wrote to Mr Knowles—Mr Croxden Powell[4]—Sir Thos G.—Lady S. Opedebeck—and minutes. Read Le Play—Fitzgerald Vol II—Mr Bull's Lecture on Soho.[5] Saw S.G.L.—Lord R.G—Dr Semon 18th treatment. Back to Dollis in afternoon.

To J. R. KNOWLES, editor of the *Nineteenth Century*,   Add MS 44548, f. 42.
5 August 1885. '*Private & confidential*'.

I read (among others) the Article in *Nineteenth Century* on Ireland.[6] I cannot say it seemed to me equal to the subject, but it was interesting as a sign of the times and as tending to *prog* the public mind. It is rather daring to offer a suggestion to you. But, were I in your place, I would have a series of articles, & considerable articles too, on the Irish question, with a view to the new Parliament. The chapter of grievance, properly so called, is pretty well closed. The chapter of material aid, eleemosynary aid, cannot close too

---

[1] Replies untraced, save that of 21 July (to Grosvenor), Add MS 44316, f. 18: 'I believe that nothing less than a scheme based on the lines of Mr. Herbert Gladstone's last speech at Leeds would be acceptable, or considered to settle the Irish question. This is however only my own idea. . . .'

[2] She replied, 5 August, Add MS 56446, f. 78, that 'those most interested are now quite agreed that it would be putting the cart before the horse to commence the reform of Irish Government by establishing County Councils and building upon that foundation . . . it is now felt that leaders of English opinion may fairly be asked to consider the question of granting to Ireland a Constitution of a similar nature to that of one of the larger Colonies with such modifications as may be necessary to secure practically certain guarantees for the Crown, for landowners, and for freedom of conscience and fair treatment of the minority'; 'Mr Parnell would like me to send you a draft of detailed propositions'.

[3] Stanley inquired, 3 August, Add MS 44492, f. 9, 'whether you still hold the views on the question raised in the bill for housing the Working Classes on which I wrote to you [on 22 July]', which included discounted sale of prison sites.

[4] G. H. Croxden Powell, secretary of the S.W. Lancs. Liberal Association; sent a fascinating report on prospects; Hawn P.

[5] C. Bull, *Soho in the olden time . . . a lecture* (1849).

[6] See 2 Aug. 85n.

soon. The chapter of competent administrative development is the one which remains to be treated. I can only indicate two sections of the question: a searching and impartial article on the history of the Union; and a careful account of the novel and critical Austro-Hungarian experiment, its terms and its actual working. You will ask me for authors—I cannot find them. You might try Mr. Bryce, M.P. There was also an O'Brien, I think a Barry O'Brien, who wrote an excellent book on the Parliamentary History of Irish Land.[1]

As to plans, I can say nothing. I take it to be very doubtful whether the Nationalist party at this moment know their own plan, or are in any way of one mind. But it strikes me that to collect and present to the world solid and relevant *materials* of judgment on what may be, three or four months hence, a most important & most urgent question, would be a *point* for your review. It is in that view, & not with any particular affection of my own, that I write this note.

6. *Th.*

Wrote to Ld Granville—Sir W. Harcourt—and minutes. Saw GLG—Scotts—HNG—Ld Spencer—Mr Knowles. Dr Semon 19th treatment. A castor oil day. Read Fitzgerald—Le Play finished Vol I—Paradise of Birds[2]—Tract on Ireland: nought.

7. *Fr.* [*London*]

Wrote to Lady Aberdeen—Mr Griffiths Tel.—Mr M'Coll—Mr White U.S.[3]—Sir W. Gregory—Ld R. Grosvenor—Mrs Bolton—Ld Granville—Mr Joseph—and minutes. Saw G.L.G[ower]—Ld Hartington 2-3—Ld R. Grosvenor (O'Shea correspondence &c.)—Scotts—Dr Semon 20th treatment—Sir J. Lacaita. Visited Gerty & the Baby. Read Paradise of Birds finished—Arnold on Future Life.[4] Goodbye to Dollis—with regrets.

Memorandum. Aug. 7. 85—read to Ld Hartington.[5]

Domestic

1. Procedure; 2. Local Govt (Liquor Laws); 3. Land; 4. Registration: for all.
5. Economy; 6. Reform of Lords; 7. Established Church: For such as please: & *as* they please.

Abroad

8. Egypt; 9. Afghanistan; 10 South Africa.
11. Ireland. An epoch: possibly a crisis. Grievance in the main gone, but administrative development remains. Considerable changes may be desired; & may be desirable if effected with a due regard to the unity of the Empire. I cannot treat the people of Ireland as foes or aliens, or advise that less shd be done for them than wd. in like circumstances be done for the inhabitants of any other portion of the U.K. Those are my opinions. What to say publicly must be most carefully considered on my return.

Had party been agreed, & other circumstances favourable, on the Central Board

---

[1] Knowles acted on this, O'Brien writing the article in consultation with Gavan Duffy; see 1 Nov. 85 and O'Brien, *Parnell*, ii. 101ff.
[2] By W. J. Courthope (1870).
[3] Henry White, 1850-1927; secretary in U.S. London embassy; later an ambassador.
[4] *F.R.*, xliv. 218 (August 1885).
[5] Add MS 44769, f. 217. Part in Hammond, 404. See to Grosvenor, 22 Aug. 85.

scheme, I shd. have been ready to offer myself at the Dissolution on that basis. (N.B. Granville & Derby view). But of this little chance.

If so no ground remains for me *unless it be* on the verdict of the country in the recent change in the Representation of the people & on those who have made it.

In my case, if I should stand again, I must make it clear that my age does not permit me to overlook the difference, for me, between 1880 & 1886; or to expect in the coming Parlt. the work of the last one. Aug. 6.

8. Sat. [*Voyage on* Sunbeam]

Wrote to Mr Currie—Russian Ambassador—Sir S. Scott & Co—Editor of The Times—& minutes. Dr Semon: 21st treatment. Saw H.N.G.—Mr MacColl—Mr Westell—Ld R. Grosvenor—Mr Chamberlain. Much work for our *flit* from 1 R[ichmond] T[errace] yesterday & today. Off at $3\frac{1}{4}$ to Greenhithe: & from thence in the Sunbeam between 6 & 7, steaming: wind favourable. Read Le Play Vol. II—Under Aurora Borealis.[2]

To Mrs. O'SHEA, 8 August 1885. '*Private*'.[3]   Add MS 44269, f. 225.

I have to thank you for a very interesting letter.[4] Too interesting, almost, to be addressed to a person of my age and to weakened sight, since it substitutes for a limited prospect a field almost without bounds. You do not explain the nature of the changes which have occurred since you sent me a spontaneous proposal, which is now, it appears, superseded. The only one I am aware of is the altered attitude of the Tory party, and I presume its heightened biddings. It is right I should say that into any counter-bidding of any sort against Lord R. Churchill I for one cannot enter.

If this were a question of negotiation, I should have to say that in considering any project which might now be recommended by Mr Parnell I should have to take into view the question whether, two or three months hence, it might be extinguished like its predecessor, on account of altered circumstances.

But it is not a question of that kind, and therefore I have no difficulty in saying it would ill become me to discourage any declaration of his views for Ireland by a person of so much ability representing so large a body of opinion. I have always felt, and I believe I have publicly expressed, my regret that we were so much in the dark as to the views of the Home Rule or Nationalist party; and the limit I assign to the desirable and allowable is one which I have often made known in Parliament and elsewhere. I should look therefore to such a paper as you describe, and appear to tender, as one of very great public interest.[5]

Your injunctions as to privacy will be carefully observed by me. I embark on a short yachting expedition tomorrow and I hope to be at Hawarden within the next three weeks.

[1] Sir Thomas Brassey's yacht; the party included Mrs. and Mary Gladstone, Mrs. Bridge (wife of the admiral), Sir A. Clark, A. Morley, L. V. Harcourt, G. Leveson Gower. Lady Brassey's diary of the voyage is in 'Mr Gladstone in Norway', *C.R.*, xlviii. 480 (October 1885), L. V. Harcourt's in the Bodleian, Mary Gladstone's in *Mary Gladstone*.
[2] S. Tromholt, *Under the rays of the Aurora Borealis*, 2v. (1885).
[3] Hammond, 421.
[4] See 4 Aug. 85n.
[5] Parnell's paper, the 'proposed Constitution for Ireland', was not received, despite promptings, until early November; see to Mrs. O'Shea, 3 Nov. 85.

9. 10 S. Trin.

Prayers in cabin mg & aft. On my back but wind S.S.W. not violent: good progress. Read Life of J. Skinner[1]—Salmon's Introd. to N.T. Our hosts most kind. Sir T. B[rassey] appears quite in a new light: of consummate seaman as well as excellent man.

10. M.

Great progress but much motion. On my back, avoided wind sickness. We all but touched Ekassund [Egersund] about 9. After that stiff weather & very sharp movement. After four I got some sleep. This day I could not read: but meditated & reviewed. Alas. Many suffered: C.G. valiantly stood out. How the things spun about the Cabin.

11. Tu. [Stavanger]

With daylight, worked in towards Stavanger: a day of most welcome rest. Read Under Aurora: Murray's Handbook & Vocab.:[2] Norway Pilot: Howell's foregone conclusion.[3] 12–2½. Landed. Examined the ex-cathedral. Kindly received by the people. Visited our guide's House. Duchess of Montrose came on board.

12. Wed. [Hardanger Fiord]

We started for Hardanger Fiord. Two short bouts of rolling before entering the region. Read as yesterday, & Sir T. Brassey's 1882 Voyage.[4] We anchored at Liwick [Lervik]. Ashore we examined the Church: & tombstones all having prayer for the dead. Saw a house reputed 700 years old: large timber baulks, and central aperture in the roof, now closed with glass. Also visited a store & bakery. Bread here 50% dearer than with us?

13. Th.

A delightful journey up the Hardanger to Vick. Read Tromholt—Howells—Fortn. on Pasteur, & Paris Press.[5] Anchored at Vick: walked up the river: saw Mr Walters who rents it for £30.

14. Fr. [Odde]

Ashore before 4 A.M. as the anchor wd not hold. After a long fight gave in & we went to Odde.[6] Luncheon there & a drive of 13 m to the four falls through splendid scenery. The people know me by sight & testify great interest. Conversation with Sir T. Brassey. Finished Foregone conclusion—Read Tromholt (II)—Fortn. on Ld Peterborough.[7]

---

[1] See 16 Oct. 83.
[2] J. Murray, *Handbook for travellers in Norway*, with a vocabulary.
[3] W. D. Howells, *A foregone conclusion* (1875).
[4] Probably *sc.* 1883: Sir T. Brassey, *A voyage in the 'Sunbeam'* (1883).
[5] *F.R.*, xliv. 149, 178 (August 1885).
[6] At the southern end of Hardanger Fiord.
[7] *F.R.*, xliv. 203 (August 1885).

15. Sat.

Expedition by boat & foot to another great fall but too late & we had to be content with a grand walk. Finished Sophus Tromhot. Read Smith's Babylonia[1]—Fortn. Rev. on Ld Peterborough. Saw an interesting farm interior: & a strong close trunk made without nails. Weather dull.

16. 11 S. Trin.

Bp of Durham[2] celebrated H.C. at 8.30. Also an evening service at 7. 11–1. Attended the Norwegian service which gave much to observe. Fine rain. The women came in black, with the white caps. Sitting *almost* through the whole service. Luther's Hymn tune.[3] Vestment used only on celebrations: twice a year. Close attention especially from the women. Service here once in 3 weeks. Many tears were I believe observed, at a farewell sermon. We had luncheon at Hardanger Hotel. Good wine. The Bp [of Durham] & his Chaplains dined.

17. M.

Journey of $9\frac{1}{2}$ hours to the magnificent Voringfoss: the noblest waterfall I have seen: in which majesty & force are combined rarely with grace & a kind of tenderness. Walked 18 miles on very rough ground to my own astonishment. The Eidfjord lake also is sublime. Echo. Astonished at one Cariole horse. Read Edinb. Rev. on the 'Waters'[4]—Dulaure, Cultes[5]—Brassey's interesting Tract.[6] Sir A. Clark examined my throat.

18. Tu. [Bergen]

At Rosendal midday. Visited the [Kvindherred] Church & made notes. Saw the Baron:[7] intelligent & warm. Reached Bergen at nine, by moon. Conversation with Sir T.B. on plans. A little Homeric work! Saw the Consul.[8] Read Dulaure—Smith's Babylonia (finished)—The Iliad—Vocabulary &c. Went in a Norwegian boat to the ship. The man utterly refused money. This pleases me more than the approval of foreign Cabinets and such. NB. the early harvest in the Fiords. Nearly all is cut: & considered *late*.

19. Wed.

Saw the very interesting Museum. Shopping. Drove to Mr Jebsen's[9] & round the lake. A *feast* at the [Hotel] Norge. A crowd cheered our landing. Read Dulaure—G. Smith's Assyria. The soft air is against my throat. Sir A. Clark resumed the daily course of treatment.

[1] G. Smith, *Notes on . . . Assyria and Babylonia* (1872).
[2] On holiday nearby; Brassey, 487.
[3] 'Ein Feste Burg'.
[4] *E.R.*, clxii. 286 (July 1885).
[5] J. A. Dulaure, *Histoire abrégée des differents cultes*, 2v. (1825).
[6] Sir T. Brassey, 'The navy and recent ship-building policy' (1885).
[7] Baron Rosenkrone of Rosendal; see Brassey, 492.
[8] Herman D. Janson, British vice-consul.
[9] The former consul.

20. Th.

Read as yesterday. We drove to Mr Gaade's:[1] the environs lovely as is the place. Saw the curious & now very rare fabric of a church which he has transplanted. Party came on board. We went off in the evening. Large numbers know me and are most friendly.

21. Fr. [Songe Fiord]

Finished Smith's Assyria: read Dulaure: also I now daily do a little work upon the language. A long and splendid sail up the Sogne Fjord to Gudvangen:[2] arrived after dusk: the scene wonderful. We seemed to have dropped to the bottom of a gigantic well with magnificent outlines. Corn harvest advanced in the *higher* part: NB = hay, & much before the cherries.

22. Sat.

Finished Dulaure. Read Psychical Transactions.[3] Work on Vocabulary. Drive of 10 miles up to Stalheim: magnificent. Off in afternoon to Aureland wh is also very grand. Greeted by a gift from the Priest of fish fruit & flowers. All seem to know us. Wrote to Ld R. Grosvenor & the Priest.

To LORD R. GROSVENOR, chief whip, 22 August   Add MS 44316, f. 25.
1885.[4]

In the plenitude of my wisdom I came away without getting your proper address, and I have to write one rather at a venture. Neither can I tell you where to write to me but I expect to be at Lerwick on Tuesday week. You will know on receiving this whether you can write to me there.

I should like to be in possession of my memorandum[5] and I ought to have left a copy with you rather than the original.

This is a beautiful country and through Brassey's great kindness we have had a most happy time barring some bad weather on the passage to Stavanger. But as to the main purpose of my voyage, the recovery of throat and voice (while my general health is excellent & I have made an 18 miles walk) I cannot yet speak with any confidence. I should ask to be landed at Thurso, and then should go home by the East Coast but for the fear that it would not be possible to make private journey through Scotland.

Upon the whole I incline to think that the proper course for me to take will be to write a *lengthened* Address on the basis described (as far as it goes) in the Memorandum. I have reflected much & shall reflect more what to say about Ireland. Before closing[?] it I would have to know whether anything & what would come from your Lady correspondent. Perhaps you could in the meantime ask her what is likely.

[1] Local landowner; had restored medieval wooden church; see Brassey, 495.
[2] At the head of the Näröfjord, the innermost part of the Sognefjord.
[3] *Journal of the Society for Psychical Research*, ii. 449 (July 1885). On 26 June 1885, proposed by F. W. H. *Myers (1843–1901), fellow of Trinity, Cambridge), seconded by H. Sidgwick, president, Gladstone had been elected an hon. member, and thus entitled to receive the journal ('for private circulation to members only').
[4] Holograph.
[5] Probably the mem. for the talk with Hartington, 7 Aug. 85; Gladstone saw and wrote to Grosvenor that day.

I suppose it should be printed as a small pamphlet, and published *first* in the Edinburgh Liberal papers.
[P.S.] You can here stalk reindeer over a large tract for £11 and hire a salmon river for
£30.

23. *12 S. Trin.*

Norwegian service at 11. Mg prayer on board at 12. Examined Ch & Chyard.
Saw the Priest, very pleasing: and the Fretheim family. Wrote to Mr Fretheim.[1]
Worked on Norw. Collects. In afternoon went to the Lake. Read Life of Skin-
ner—Salmon's Introduction.

24. *M.* [*Lysterfiord*]

Pleasant day in the Lysterfjord,[2] a garden of Eden. Saw Urna's Church, see
Memm.[3] Anchored at Ese. Read Le Play—Reville's Hist. Religion. Worked on
Norwegian collects. Clark's treatment continued daily.

25. *Tu.*

A long day, & great northerly gale, through wild stony rock, almost no popula-
tion to Moldö, Skorpö & other grand outlines; sealions, guards of Norway (Sir
A.C.). A little taste of sea swell. Read Le Play—Reville—Acct of Niagara.
Worked on Norwegian.

26. *Wed.* [*Molde*]

Very rough morning on the outside. More population, less grandeur, no harvest.
Reached Molde[4] at 6: beautifully placed. Lunched at Aalesund. A woman threw
flowers over us: a man brought me my photograph & was delighted with my
writing on it. The people cheered our departure. Read Le Play—Mongredien on
the Distress.[5] Wrote draft of part of an Address.[6] Entertainment in saloon.[7]

27. *Th.*

We went to the Romsdaal Fiord & drove up the splendid valley: but a watery
day spoiled our work. Returned in evening to Molde. Entertainment in Saloon.
Read Le Play—Thursfield on Ireland.[8] Wrote abbozzo[9] of part of an address.

---

[1] Christian Fretheim, of the congregation, had presented an ancient bowl; Brassey, 498.
[2] The long, N.E. branch of the Sognefjord.
[3] Add MS 44769, f. 220.
[4] In Moldefjord, N.E. from Sognefjord.
[5] A. Mongredien, *Trade depression, recent and present* (1885).
[6] For the election; Add MS 44769, f. 234; published on 18 September, *T.T.*, 19 September
1885, 8a.
[7] Sentence added, perhaps intended for this day: 'Recollect the bold rounded rock mountain
which shoots into the sky: & the curious Bible of 1551 at Stalheim.'
[8] E. Thursfield, *England and Ireland* (1884).
[9] 'sketch'. See 26 Aug. 85.

28. *Fr.*

At Molde flags flying, hotels illuminated in evening: brass band came out & played to the ship. We drove, & went to old silver shops. Found an ash 11½ feet round: also larch 7½. In evg, wind went to North. Osborne[1] arrived about mid-day. Went on board: we all dined in evening. Much conversation with the Prince: told him the truth about Egypt. Back at 11 PM, dismissed with blue lights. Read Le Play finished III—Thursfield on Ireland. Wrote more of abbozzo. Much conversation with N. Consuls. Helen's birthday: God bless her.

29. *Sat.* [*On* Sunbeam]

Sir A.C. made his last application to my throat. We did not start till noon: amidst renewed manifestations of good will. Nothing could be more touching than my reception by (I may truly say) the people of Norway. Aalesund at 4 P.M. In half an hour we passed Godo on the right & were in open sea, smooth but with swell. Wrote to C.L. Wood: also on Homer & pol. Address. Read Le Play. A fair night after we turned to sailing.

30. *13 S. Trin.*

A comfortless day but still staved off sickness. Unable to read, but heard & followed the Litany with half open door. It should have been a great opportunity for reflection: and it did a little serve to teach me how cold I am & how far from God: how terrible is, at its acmé, the calling which I have now pursued for 53 years: last, & least, & lowest, among the sinful children of God.

31. *M.*

Made for the mainland instead of Lerwick: a better course & less motion. Kept my bed under shelter of Shetlands. Read Le Play & Skinner's Life. Opposite Wick in afternoon. Provost & others came off, sadly tossed about. Spent the night sailing coastwise. Conversation with Sir A. Clark medical & non-medical. Tel. to Fasque.

Tues. Sep. One. 1885. [*Fasque*]

Fog. Could not make Inverness in time for reply tel. & train. But by very happy chances we got away from Fort George by train, after a little farewell speech to the ship's company.[2] I might say much of our host & of the hospitality we have received. All along the rail the Scotch were even kinder than the Norwegians. At 4¾ we reached Laurencekirk & drove to Fasque[3] where we were affectionately received.[4] Walk with my brother & in the woods. Read Le Play—Skinner's Life. Wrote to P[ost] Master Lerwick—Lady G.

---

[1] i.e. the yacht of the Prince of Wales, on his way to kill Scandinavian elk; Magnus, *Edward VII*, 190.

[2] In Brassey, 502.

[3] His brother's house (formerly his father's) in the Mearns N. of Brechin (see 15 Aug. 31n.); his first stay there since 29 June 74.

[4] It was his br.'s golden wedding.

2. Wed.

Wrote to Sir A. Clark—Perth Stationmaster—Lord R. Grosvenor—Mr Hans Jacobsen (Bergen)[1]—Karl Siemens.[2] Arranging papers: reading Speeches &c. Heavily embarrassed by those on Ireland.[3] Saw Reporter of Scotsman.[4] Drive with the party. Read Le Play—Sinclair on Scottish Dialect.[5]

It is deeply interesting to me to be here. The house is still a home. I sleep in the room where my mother died, sit in the room where my Father died. Dearest Jessy sleeps under the chapel.[6] And my brother is in many ways an edifying sight.

To LORD R. GROSVENOR, chief whip, 2 September 1885.[7]   Add MS 44316, f. 27.

I wrote to you from Norway: our movements here have been quickened, we missed Lerwick for sea reasons, and I have written there to secure getting any letter of yours. On Monday we intend to go on to Hawarden.

I want your opinion particularly on the notion I have formed that I must write a sort of Pamphlet Address: say equal to 10 or twelve pages of good print. I might then postpone speaking (if it is to come) until the last moment. The topics are so numerous that it is impossible to go over them in a short Address so as to be of any use.

My brother is an excellent man & we are on the happiest footing, but on every ground of feeling I abstain while here from every sign however slight of political life.

You would have been surprised as well as pleased at our reception in Norway. It was most touching. And the Fiords are marvellous. But that North Sea. oh, oh, oh. You & all good seamen should go there as often as you can. Why not stalk reindeer like Ingram and others. You get a salmon river for £30, and a forest for one or two hundred. I took this little paper because the post goes so early. I shall hardly have time to read Hartington before it[8]—but I have read Parnell: a very remarkable & rather formidable speech, much what I expected. When do you leave Inchrorie & come back into the land of civilisation?

3. Th.

Wrote after much consideration to Ld Hartington: also to Granville—Sir J. Lacaita—C. Lacaita—Chester Station Master. Drive round by Fordoun and Drumtouchty, & the new Church. The workmen so hearty! Drive beautiful.

---

[1] The Norwegian pilot who assisted *The Sunbeam*; letter of thanks in *T.T.*, 18 September 1885, 8d.

[2] Karl H. von Siemens of Siemens Brothers Ltd.

[3] Parnell in Dublin, 1 September, *T.T.*, 2 September 1885, 6c; England must either give Ireland 'the complete right to rule ourselves' or 'govern us as a Crown Colony without any parliamentary representation whatever'; but the constitution required was 'that which is enjoyed by each and all of the larger colonies and that is practically what we are asking for'; see O'Day, *Parnell*, 86.

[4] *The Scotsman*, 3 September 1885, 4a: 'glancing at a report of the speech of Mr Parnell at Dublin on Tuesday, and observing the statement ... that Scotland had lost her nationality, Mr Gladstone remarked that Mr Parnell "is a very thoughtful man, and, as a rule, measured in his language, but he never said a sillier thing than that"'.

[5] See 9 Oct. 58.

[6] i.e. his daughter, whose body he brought to Fasque for burial in the family vault; see 9–12 Apr. 50.

[7] Holograph.

[8] Hartington at Waterfoot, *T.T.*, 31 August, 8a replying to Chamberlain and to Parnell's 'national independence' speech of 24 August.

Walk over Hunter's Hill: all changed. We have whist every evening. Read Le Play—Statist. account of Scotland[1]—Ann. Register 1800.[2]

To LORD HARTINGTON, M.P., 3 September   Chatsworth MSS 340. 1801. 1885.[3] '*Private*'.

I have returned to *terra firma* extremely well in general health, & with a better throat: in full expectation of having to consider anxious and doubtful matters, and now finding them rather more anxious and doubtful than I had anticipated.

As yet I am free to take a share or not in the coming political issues, and I must weigh many things before finally surrendering this freedom.

I have read with much admiration and concurrence your opening speech, but I own my regret that you have found or felt it necessary at this very early period to join issue in so pointed a manner with Parnell and his party. I speak thus freely, because, in the present state of things whatever either of us says bears upon the position of the other, and I have now to determine what to say, and what is the best manner of saying it.

Parnell's speech, which drew forth your remarks,[4] is as bad as bad can be; and his language admits of but one reply. Quite apart indeed from its demands upon England, his promises to all and sundry in Ireland are monstrous, and could only end in confusion to himself were his first purpose gained.

My reasons for regretting are not connected with any doubts as to the 'legislative independence' of Ireland. But it seems to me that—

1. It is the duty of the Government and not the Opposition to lead in this matter.

2. Premature or early declarations from us supply a new point of departure for R. Churchill and his party in their tricks.

3. The whole question of the position, which Ireland will assume after the general election, is so new, so difficult, and as yet, I think, so little understood, that it seems most important to reserve until the proper time all possible liberty of examining it.

4. It is not what Parnell says now, but what Ireland will say and do at the election, that forms the call upon us for definite declarations.

5. The whole hope of the Tories lies in the Irish party, without whom they do not consider themselves to have a chance of winning. They will not surrender the alliance without a struggle: and all words of ours, which help them by compromises to maintain it, are injurious to Imperial interests; which have already been so heavily damaged by their conduct as to Spencer and as to the Crimes Act.

6. Every object is, I think, gained for the present, by declaring substantively our views as to the unity of the Empire.

7. Parnell's language is even now doubtful and fluctuating, & the *Times* of August 26th was, I think, prudent in endeavouring to draw him out into further explanations.

8. I wish there were good hopes of effecting a disintegration in the new Parliament, like that of 1880. But the anti-Parnell section had then a leader; Shaw, in his latest utterance, declared that a great Irish question still stands for solution: the seceders will all receive a treatment such as not to encourage imitation; and the new attitude of the Tory party shifts the poles of the problem.

[1] See 26 Jan. 76.
[2] *Annual Register for the year 1800*, with extensive reporting of the union debs.
[3] Version in Holland, ii. 78. Hartington replied, 6 September, ibid., ii. 80, suggesting a 'meeting and discussion' to prevent irreconcilable differences.
[4] i.e. those reported on 31 August; see 2 Sept. 85n.

I cannot expect that you will see much in these ideas, but I thought it only fair to state them.

With regard to my own conduct, I hold to the intention I named before leaving England. The subject of Ireland has perplexed me much even on the North Sea. You may at any rate depend on my saying nothing without the fullest consideration I can give it.

We go to Hawarden on Monday. I direct to Devonshire House, not knowing your exact whereabouts.

4. Fr.

Wrote to Ld Rosebery?[1]—Ld Hartington—Sir T. Brassey—Mr E. Robertson—Mr Moore—Mr Rodgers—Mr Bell—Mr Milne. Worked on Address. Drive to Balbegno (old Hall), the Burn (stories of Sir J.G.) and river—back by Balfour. Read Le Play.

To LORD HARTINGTON, M.P., 4 September 1885.   Add MS 44148, f. 116.

With reference to my letter of yesterday I send you a text of an article from the Scotsman of yesterday. It has been defending yr. speech against the Times, & against Parnell, with admirable courage and ability. But you will notice the sentence I have scored[2] from a [sc the] newspaper quite satisfies me [sic].

5. Sat.

Wrote to Ld R. Grosvenor—Ld Hartington Tel.—Mr Ellerbeck—Mr A. Arnold. Worked on Address: a very difficult job. Drove to the Village for a variety of calls. Saw Mr Belcher—Mr Murray. Walk up the Garrol in afternoon. Read Arabian Nights.[3] Finished Le Play's remarkable book (except Vol. II.)

To LORD ROSEBERY, 5 September 1885. 'Private'.   N.L.S. 10023, f. 84.

A letter from Lacaita recently received is dated at Mentmore. From this it appears to me likely that you will be running northwards soon (with Lady Rosebery I trust restored to full health) and I want to know whether there is any chance of getting you to stop at Hawarden. I should much value the opportunity of seeing you, and in any case I want to know your mind about Ireland. I frankly own that I am a good deal embarrassed and perplexed by the speeches made de part et d'autre.

Just as I had got thus far I received a telegram from Hartington who will probably show you what I have written to him.

That madcap W. Blunt is reported as having spoken about Ireland with much tact and prudence.[4]

R. Grosvenor comes to Hawarden Tuesday: Lacaita with Godley Saturday.[5]

---

[1] Added in pencil; next day's letter.
[2] Appended: few politicians would refuse Ireland management of her own affairs if U.K. integrity safeguarded.
[3] *Arabian nights entertainments* (1785).
[4] Speech as tory candidate for Camberwell; Blunt noted of it: '. . . made my declaration about Ireland [on 2 September]. It is the first public declaration made, since Parnell's speech, in favour of Home Rule'; W. S. Blunt, *Gordon at Khartoum* (1911), 486.
[5] Rosebery replied on 8 September, Add MS 44288, f. 240, unable to come, but suggesting Hartington be invited, adding: 'Parnell's declarations have filled me with pleasure. It [sic] frees our

6. *14 S. Trin.*

Chapel mg & evg. Visited A. Moore & Mrs Jolly, Mrs Sherriffs. Read Lilly on the new [naturalism]—Ld Balfour on Scotch Church: very thin[1]—Salmon Intr. to New Testament—and the beautiful Biography of Mr Skinner.

7. *[Hawarden]*

Bade a reluctant farewell to Fasque and its inhabitants. 9-10$\frac{1}{2}$. Journey to Hawarden. Saw Clark at Perth. Saw Jas Anderson. Wrote to R. Grosvenor. Worked 'some' on Address. Read Reville on Religions. Found all well, thank God. And how happy would this return be, were I but able to obey the voice of Nature, and relieve my worn neck from the yoke of politics.

[The inside back cover contains, in pencil, at top:—]

Mrs Bolton, 6 Scarsdale Terrace.

---

hands to do what we think right without being misled by the will o' the wisp idea of satisfying the Irish party, while it renders impossible the unholy alliance with the other side.'

[1] *F.R.*, xliv, 240. 277 (August 1885).

[VOLUME XXXVII][1]

[The inside front cover has some erased writing in pencil, then, in ink:—]

Wherefore I abhor myself: and repent in dust and ashes.
Job. ch. [xlii] v. [6].

Private.

No 37

Sept. 8. 1885—June. 11. 87.

μηδὲ μαλθακὸς γένῃ
Eumenides 75.[2]

τί δρᾷς; ἀνίστω, μή σε νικάτω κόπος
Ibid. 133.[3]

Od XX. 18. τέτλαθι δὴ κραδίη.[4]

Hawarden Sept 1885.

8. Tu.

Made a *beginning* with the innumerable boxes, parcels, packets, from London & elsewhere. Wrote to Ld Hartington—Ld Dalhousie—Ld Rosebery—Keeper V[otes] Office—Mr Greig—Sir Thos G.—Mr Duck—Mrs Newton. R. Grosvenor came for the day. *Much* work on my draft Address: approved by him. Read 'Russia Europe & the E'.[5]

To LORD HARTINGTON, M.P., 8 September 1885.[6]   Chatsworth MSS 340. 1804.

I am of opinion with you that your views and declarations upon Ireland will carry with them the great mass of British opinion. It would be strange if, when you have thought it necessary to declare, the world in general should deem it necessary to hold back. I am not

---

[1] Lambeth MS 1451.
[2] 'Be not faint-hearted.'
[3] 'What are you doing? Stand up, do not be overcome with weariness.' Morley printed these fragments from Aeschylus, as one, at the head of his chapter on the Midlothian campaign of 1879, ii. 584.
[4] 'Endure now heart.'
[5] *Russia, Europe and the East. By a foreigner* (1885).
[6] Part in Holland, ii. 81. Copy sent to Granville, who told Hartington, 11 September, Chatsworth 340. 1806: 'there is force in his objections to a meeting'.

in favour of offering any measure, but strongly in favour of waiting. And if, as I expect or think likely, very serious embarrassment arises after the Dissolution in connection with demands purporting to come from the Irish nation, and if the way to deal with them is then found to have been in any way hampered by rapid announcements, the people who now applaud you will by a perfectly natural process turn round upon you and charge you with imprudence.

However, I am too sensible of the tremendous difficulties of the whole subject to be over confident in my own opinion. To choose among great evils and inconveniences is the only course open to us.

Now about a meeting. Have you considered 1. the notice it would attract. 2. the difficulty of choosing who should attend it. 3. the risk of its bringing matters to a hostile issue then and there—for we could not adjourn to another day as with a Cabinet. 4. The effect it would have in binding you and the party to such opinions as I might afterwards emit. (Also the delay.)

Upon the whole I consider that there is but one question for such a meeting to decide, namely, whether it is their united desire that I should take a share in the Election. And this, especially after what you have said in your letter, I am disposed to take for granted. If this be so, the only course is to let me, knowing as I do your position and as I am to know Chamberlain's, deliver my opinions in a personal way with such degree of weight as any one may think proper to give them. This will be more practicable because I have almost made up my mind that my Address, if it is to be in the sense of going on, must be rather in the nature of a Pamphlet. Of course it will be my duty and my effort to avoid all conflict with any declared Liberal opinion entitled to weight, especially with yours.

R. Grosvenor will be here to-day, or possibly tomorrow, and I will go over the whole thing with him.

As I cannot get at you before Friday, I may probably send this through Rosebery. I do not know whether I shall see him, but I wish him to know the whole case, especially with a view to Midlothian.

In conclusion, I earnestly hope that you and that our friends will give to the Irish case a really historical consideration. Depend upon it you cannot *simpliciter* fall back on the important debate of 1834. The general development since that time of popular principles, the prolonged experience of Norway (I might perhaps mention Finland), and the altogether new experience of Austro-Hungary, along with them the great power we have placed in the hands of the Irish people, require the reconsideration of the whole position. And in *one* point Parnell gives some ground of hope, for he seems to contemplate a constitution for Ireland *octroyé* by Parliament.

I have laboured very hard at the Irish portion of my (possible) Address.[1]

That rogue R. Churchill has it seems as I expected, left you in exclusive possession of the foreground of the fight.

P.S. Am I right in supposing that in Nov. 1883 we were reducing our force in Egypt to a Brigade? or to what other amount?

9. *Wed.*

Ch. 8½ A.M. Lumbago: but not disabling. R.G. came again. Finished MS & sent it by him to London to be put in type. Hard work enough. Wrote to Mr

---

[1] Hartington replied, 10 September, Add MS 44148, f. 132, wanting a meeting; 'you are the leader of the party': the meeting should 'ascertain ... whether ... the various sections of the party can acquiesce in the policy you propose to adopt'.

Chamberlain—Ld Granville—Sir W. Phillimore—Mr Macmillan—Lady Mar—Mr Hutton—Mr Brown—G. Elliot—& minutes. Read Russia &c.

To J. CHAMBERLAIN, M.P., 9 September 1885.   Chamberlain MSS 5/34/38.

I suppose we have all of us our difficulties & I am fighting with my own. The question for me is between cutting out, which I personally much desire, & which I am free to do, or on the other hand going through the Election, with a view to render to the party such service as I can in helping to maintain its unity, which I desire to see maintained for two very special reasons. 1. Only the Liberal party can (*if* it can) cope with the great Irish question which may arise three months hence. 2. Because of the demoralised & danger-ous condition of the Tory party, with R. Churchill in its bosom & to a great extent in its Leadership.

I have prepared with much labour & anxiety such an Address as I might issue if I ask for re-election. In this it is my duty, & my desire to avoid collision with either wing of the party. But I can & shall only do this if I believe it to be really desired by the representative men. Hartington has urged me to do it. I wish to know your view upon the point if you will kindly give it me.

I have seen R. Grosvenor, & am in communication with Rosebery. I write after having read your telling speech at Warrington[1] & where I differ should proceed as above described. I think it will be wise for me frankly to introduce your name & to explain our relations.

[P.S.] You will doubtless speak for Dilke.[2]

10. Th.

Forenoon in bed. Wrote to Rev. C.L. Hutchins[3]—Ld Rosebery—Mr A. Arnold. Read 'Russia' &c. (finished)—Handley on taking Orders[4]—M'Farlan on Nor-way.[5] Walk with Herbert.

To LORD ROSEBERY, 10 September 1885.   N.L.S. 10023, f. 90.

I send you copy of a letter I wrote to Granville yesterday.[6] But the question in it is answered, in the affirmative by one I have from him this morning. Please to return the copy.

What shall I say to Mr McLean?

R. Grosvenor took my MS to London yesterday and I expect to have the proof in two or three days.

It would be a great relief indeed, if with you I could feel pleasure at Parnell's recent declarations. I seem to be rather like the juror, who sat with eleven most obstinate men, that he could not convince of the truths he himself saw. R. Churchill's speeches show that

---

[1] On 8 September, an attack on the whigs and a dissociation from Parnell on home rule; see Gar-vin, ii. 63–4, 92.

[2] Chamberlain replied next day, Garvin, ii. 93, rejoicing that Gladstone contemplated continued leadership, and warning that common action would be impossible unless the Hartingtonians 'ad-vance considerably'.

[3] Charles L. Hutchins, episcopalian priest in Medford, Mass.; on revision of American prayer book; Hawn P.

[4] *N.C.*, xviii. 432 (September 1885).

[5] W. L. MacFarlan, *Behind the scenes in Norway* (1884).

[6] On the political situation, asking if he would like to see Gladstone's draft address, Ramm II, ii. 392.

there is no idea of breaking off the alliance, on which a certain number of Tory seats at the election will depend. It is no gain to me to be relieved from 'the will of the wisp idea of satisfying the Irish party' as I have never had that expectation, or acted with such a view. What I do think of is the Irish nation, and the fame, duty, & peace of my country. Some of you, to speak freely—and without this why speak at all—seem to me not to have taken any just measure of the probable position of a serious dispute with the Irish nation. Chamberlain says what are 4 millions against 32. The answer depends wholly on the case. The 28 of England would not find it so very easy to deal with the three of Scotland. But Chamberlain with much prudence has taken the sting out by saying he is ready freely to give every thing that is compatible with the unity of the Empire.

I deeply regret our having lost the opportunity offered by the plan of a Central Board, which you favoured. Even the difficulties of detail, in any wider plan, may prove enormous.

I should be most happy to see Hartington if he were to propose himself. To invite him, at the moment of preparing my Address, would place me in a difficulty for not inviting others. And against inviting a meeting I have already given what seem to me conclusive reasons.

I admit the strength of the ties which bind you at Mentmore. Yet it would certainly be most advantageous if about Monday (when R.G. will again be here) you could break them for a night. I am treading upon eggs at every step: and the shells are unusually brittle.[1]
[P.S.] A fast train from London lets down at 'Sandycroft', scarcely 1½ mile off, in the afternoon 10.30–3.45.

11. Fr.

Forenoon in bed (damp). Wrote to Ld Hartington—Mr Chamberlain—Watsons—Ld Rosebery—Mr Westell—Ld Granville—Mr Soulsby[2]—Sir D. Salomons—Mr Macfarlan. Walk with W.H.G. Read Le Play Vol. II—M'Farlan on Norway (finished)—Davies, Eumenides.[3] A spell of work on books. Saw Mr Hutton (not R.H.)[4]

To J. CHAMBERLAIN, M.P., 11 September 1885.   Chamberlain MSS 5/34/39.
'Secret'.

I. I think your letter[5] is written under a misapprehension as to my present posture & aim. It gives me the idea that you think I am endeavouring to frame a political programme or plan for a Liberal Government. It is not so. I believe it to be premature. And I am certain that for me it is at this moment impossible. All my purpose, and this I find hard enough to execute, is to learn two things.

(1) Whether I can shape a reasonable & moderate plan of what may be termed roundly essentials in domestic Government for the party, wherewith to go through the general election: leaving it open to others to add what they may think proper to these essentials.

Granville says, & I entirely agree with him, that what we have now to do with is the Dissolution. The experiences of the election will enlarge our knowledge. It will tell us absolutely whether the Tories are to go to the wall. And it will show us, from Ireland and

[1] Rosebery wired, crossing with this letter, proposing he come to Hawarden; Add MS 44288, f. 245. See 14 Sept. 85.
[2] William Jameson Soulsby, commissioner of lieutenancy, London.
[3] J. F. Davies, *The Eumenides of Aeschylus* (1885); see journal's fly-leaf at 1 Sept. 85.
[4] Not further identified; not in H.V.B.
[5] See 9 Sept. 85n.

elsewhere, more clearly than we see them now, the proper conditions of a Liberal Government.

With much consideration & labour I have, in substance, framed a long paper, with I think answers to these conditions, & in which I carefully avoid committing any other person in *any* degree beyond the minimum of four subjects, which I try to treat in a manner which no real Liberal would object to without tightly drawing the lines; not even on these do I speak except for myself. They are Procedure, Local Govt. (including liquor laws), Land, & Registration, i.e. supplemental provisions to the Reform Act.

(2). On the basis thus declared, I want to know secondly whether it is wished that I should go forward, or retire. This question I can only put to few in correspondence; I put it specifically to you Hartington & Granville. I have Granville's yes, founded I think on confidence.

II. I understand you (*vos*)[1] in your letter, & in your speech to lay down certain propositions which you think essential to a Liberal *Government*, & as to which you also think it essential that they should not now be shut out from any basis laid down for the Election. If my view is right, what you have said places no insurmountable barrier in my way.

III. I regret to have alarmed you most needlessly about the naming. It has no relation to any subject of differences; but it is in connection with defensive remarks on the general structure & working of the party, which I endeavour to justify.

What I have said will I hope clear the ground which I opened in my last letter.

IV. Should I not receive affirmative replies to my inquiry (2) it will perhaps remain for me to consider whether I can put forth my address, not abating any of its cautions but stating expressly that I speak for myself alone—or whether for me the end has come.[2]

[P.S.] I sorrowfully agree in your view of the present aspect of the Irish question: but on the whole I shed tears over the grave of the Central Board, & am extremely unsanguine as to a legislative settlement.

To LORD HARTINGTON, M.P., 11 September 1885.[3]   Chatsworth MSS 340. 1808.

My first impulse was to telegraph,[4] as I think you wish; but I found the *matter* of my reply ill suited to the wire—it is that we should be most happy to see you, but that my draft is gone to London to be put in type, so that you could not see the *corpus delicti* before Sunday or Monday: on Monday Grosvenor will be here: perhaps Rosebery.

I am unable to surmount the difficulties connected with my calling a meeting, which must be at the least an epitome of the late Cabinet. But do not let me in the least interfere with your liberty of action. I hope indeed that you are in communication at any rate with Granville, and any others who like him have an uniting faculty.

I entertain none of the suspicion of you, which you think possible, with regard to an 'unexpressed personal object'. I wish I could as easily dismiss the suspicion from your mind—which I own surprises me—as to my intention in asking you to inform yourself

[1] i.e. you, plural: Chamberlain and Dilke.
[2] Chamberlain replied next day, Garvin, ii. 94, encouraging (with Dilke) Gladstone's continuing leadership, anxious about his address omitting items, and seriously apprehensive about his treatment of land. Section xiii (on the party) of Gladstone's published 'Address' in fact named nobody.
[3] In Holland, ii. 86.
[4] See 8 Sept. 85n.

thoroughly on certain historical cases. I had no other purpose than that of promoting, what I think dangerously deficient in many quarters, an historical and therefore a comprehensive view of the Irish question.

Which of the following methods of proceeding seems to you preferable.

a. That my Address should be brought in draft under the view of the men who would form an epitome—so brought by you. I do not advise this on the whole.

b. That I should publish my Address, abating none of its cautions, but stating explicitly that it is mine, and binds nobody else. To this I am not averse, and indeed I have already inserted words in this direction, which might be widened.

c. Of course I might retire, and plead my 53 years:[1] but I am afraid that, with my sense of the obligations I owe to the party, I should be.obliged also to make some mention of the difficulties arising from divergences.

d. You may have some modes better than any of those to suggest.

I think that in the main your apprehensions arise from this that you and I are considering different things: you on what footing a new Liberal Government should hereafter be formed: I, on what footing, far more free and open, the Liberal party should now go to the Election. The former of these is, I think, premature, and, I am certain, far beyond my power. The latter I think to be within reasonable compass, and not to entail detriment at present to any one.

I had hoped that, before my leaving London, we were further advanced than now seems to be the case, on the basis of my rough memorandum of August 6th. To it, in my Address (with immense expansion) I have, I believe, strictly adhered: the main deviation is a discussion on gratuitous education, which is not in the Radical sense. What I say on Ireland is simply an expansion and adaptation of what I have already said often, namely, that Ireland may have all that is compatible with the unity of the Empire. When I said it would have sufficed for you to declare the unity of the Empire, I meant it would have sufficed for *your* purpose. But I have had to say much more than you on the Irish question, and could not now hold back from what I have frequently promised.

Your letter obviously sets you free with regard to me and my proceedings. I hope that what I have now written may do something in the way of enabling you to define your course.[2]

[P.S.] Nothing can be more unlikely according to *present* appearances than any effective or great legislative action for Ireland.

12.

Damp: again kept bed. Wrote to Sir W. Harcourt—Mr Rickards—F.B. Palmer[3]— Mr Appleby—W.R. Owen—Rev. Mr Arthur (Lpool)[4]—Bp Titcomb—Mr Godwin—Mr Adcock—and minutes. Work on books. Read Phythian's Norway[5]—Davies, Eumenides. Neuralgia came on in evg. Corrected proofs and amended: a difficult combination.

[1] In the Commons.
[2] Hartington replied, 12 September, Add MS 44148, f. 138, relieved at Gladstone's Irish views: he had anticipated 'some inclination in that direction [separation]'.
[3] Francis B. Palmer, s. of Rev. Sir W.*; sent his *Shareholders Companion* (5th ed. 1885).
[4] None found; possibly W. Macintosh Arthur, priest in Bury.
[5] J. C. Phythian, *Scenes of travel in Norway* (1877).

To Sir W. V. HARCOURT, M.P., 12 September 1885.   MS Harcourt dep. 9, f. 165.
'Most Private'.[1]

I returned home this week, and my first business was provisionally to throw my thoughts into order for a possible address to my constituents: necessarily a very long one, framed only for the Dissolution, and written of course with my best care to avoid treading on the toes of either the right or left wing.

I have communicated with Granville, who thinks me right in not attempting to make others responsible for the *terms* of this address—and with Hartington and Chamberlain. By both of them I am a good deal buffeted, perhaps the former even more than the latter. They are in states of mind such as, if they were put in contact, would lead to an explosion. Both I think are wrong in this that they write as if they were fixing the platform of a new Liberal Government, whereas I am solely endeavouring to help, or not to embarrass, Liberal candidates for the Election. The question of a Government may have its place later on, not now.

Having explained the general idea with which I propose to write, I asked H. & C. whether it was upon the whole their wish that I should go on or cut out. To this question I have not yet got a clear affirmative answer from either of them.

Chamberlain has his ulterior views, with which, so far as I understand them, I am not much in sympathy: Hartington seems to be in a jealous frame of mind, and has I think been at Kimbolton.[2]

I think the upshot will perhaps be this 1. That, by writing with the intents I have described, I should to any extent they may require limit the responsibility of my Address to myself personally, & let it go, like other people's Addresses, for what it is worth. 2. If after the Dissolution it is found to be inconvenient (I hope it won't) then *lavar d'incomodo*,[3] and cut out but 3. Hold myself ready to meet a present *emergency* if it proves to be desired and feasible.

You will not I think deem this very unreasonable.[4] Your son charmed us all on board the Sunbeam.
[P.S.] R. Grosv. & Rosebery came here on Monday.

13. 15 S. Trin.

Ch. mg & evg. C. cured my neuralgia in the night by quinine and chloroform. Saw Godley & H.J.G. on my draft—Mr R. H. Hutton. Wrote to Ld Hartington— Ld R. Grosvenor—Ld Salisbury. Read Bp Titcomb's Pastoral[5]—Reville, Prolegomena[6]—Landor on Popery[7]—Salmon on New Testament.[8]

To LORD HARTINGTON, M.P., 13 September 1885.[9]   Chatsworth MSS 340. 1810.

Your letter, for which accept my best thanks, does much for my difficulty on your side; as, if I understand it right, the protest which you register signifies that you are not willing

---

[1] Part in Gardiner, i. 539.
[2] i.e. with the Duchess of Manchester.
[3] 'Wash away the inconvenient.'
[4] Harcourt replied, 17 September, Add MS 44199, f. 246: 'nothing can save the Liberal Party, & the Liberal cause except your remaining at its head'.
[5] J. H. Titcomb, 'The Church of England in Northern and Central Europe' (1885).
[6] A. Réville, *Prolegomena of the history of religions*, intr. F. Max Müller (1884).
[7] W. S. Landor, *Popery: British and foreign* (1851).
[8] See 26 July 85.
[9] Holland, ii. 89.

to be bound to the *extent* to which I find myself in regard to Ireland, but that you do not on that account withdraw from the general opinion that under all the circumtances it is desirable that I should issue an Address, directed in my view to the Election, & so framed as by no means to imply that I hold the party ripe for action except upon the four subjects which I named to you in London & wrote down in my Memorandum.[1]

I shall be very glad, if you come on here tomorrow with R. Grosvenor, to give you every further explanation you may desire. Certainly as to Ireland I do not in principle go beyond what I have already said in public.

14. M.

Wet ∴ no church. I hope soon to be free again. Wrote to Mr Chamberlain—Ld Granville—Ld Derby—Herbert J. Gladstone. A stiff day on the proofs & amendments. Saw Ld R. Grosvenor—Ld Rosebery—E. Wickham on Davies—Mr Godley (who went off).[2] Read Phythian's Norway.

To J. CHAMBERLAIN, M.P., 14 September 1885.   Chamberlain MSS 5/34/40.
'*Secret*'.

Many thanks for your letter of the 12th,[3] which only reached me this morning. I do not think any matter of difficulty remains.
1. On consideration, as my naming you though in a defensive manner would be unusual, I have thought it on the whole better to treat of co-operation among the several sections of the party without naming names.
2. I have named free education along with H. of Lords & State Church, as subjects which I do not find in a state to be brought into the programme for the Dissolution that programme being a political minimum on which I assume that, with some freedom as to details, we are all agreed (in this I take Procedure, Local Govt., Land & Registration only). After so much has been said on Free or rather gratuitous Education, I could not be altogether silent, but I have expressly reserved my own final opinion on it, & treated it as a subject having *pros & cons*.
3. On Local Govt. I have named the great objects immediately in view & said further questions may arise as to the attributions & purposes.
4. On Land, according to your request, I send you what I propose. I have striven very hard to be perfectly fair as between you & Hartington, confining my affirmations to what I suppose the entire bulk of the party to be agreed on.
5. I also send my short bit on Registration, in order that, if it contain any phrase which should be altered, you or Dilke may kindly point it out.

I had neither space nor knowledge to warrant details. If you find anything *positively* wrong in it, kindly send a line tomorrow to my son Herbert, Lib. Registr. Office, 41 Parliament Street. Of course I am anxious now to get forward.[4]
[P.S.] In writing all the parts of the Address which directly touched your questions, I have borne carefully in mind the language of your recent speech as to the footing which you claimed for them.

---

[1] See 7 Aug. 85.
[2] i.e. leaving Gladstone without a secretary, save his family.
[3] See 11 Sept. 85n.
[4] Chamberlain replied, 20 September, Garvin, ii. 97, 'dishonoured' if he joined a govt. 'on the narrow basis . . . now presented' which ignored all his recent proposals.

To LORD DERBY, 14 September 1885.   Derby MSS.

I am afraid that, pleasant as it is to visit you at Knowsley, we must deny ourselves that gratification at present.[1] The five years of office involved with me a total abstinence from private affairs. The two months which have passed since working out of the communications on resignation have been devoted (with considerable benefit) to my throat and voice. My private and domestic affairs, though not on a large scale, yet after so long a fast demand some attention, and I must even beg off an engagement to go to the Ripons. This rupture would hardly permit of contracting any new ties. What my wife and I would earnestly ask to substitute would be that you and Lady Derby should persuade Lord Lyons to accompany you hither when he has run out his appointed time with you. Is this not very feasible?

Since and before I got to Hawarden, I have been much exercised in the preparation of an Address. With much consideration and some doubt, I concluded it to be my duty to do this (and to go through the Election), if I could so do it as to avoid irritating either of our wings, and more or less to help our candidates. Taking great pains to inform myself as to the sentiments of Hartington and Chamberlain, who may be considered to be our two poles, and using all the best means of care and inquiry that I could, I have now completed this serious task, and I hope to come out on Thursday.[2]

15. Tu.

Ch. 8½ A.M. Wrote to Herbert J.G.—Ld Kimberley—Messrs Watson—Mr Childers—Ld Spencer—Mr Carlyle—Sig. Meale[3]—and minutes. Worked on books & unpacking. Saw E. Wickham—Ld Rosebery—Mr Broadhurst—Sir J. Lacaita. Walk with Sir J.L. Read Phythian's Norway—Paul Hermes[4]—Le Play Vol II.— Canon Moore on Ch. of Ireland[5]—District RR Report of Meeting.

To LORD KIMBERLEY, 15 September 1885. *'Most Private'*.   Add MS 44228, f. 203.

With much difficulty I have brought myself to the conclusion that I ought to offer myself for re-election. I need not now attempt to state the considerations which have ruled me: the situation is complex, and they are not very simple.

I soon saw that my Address must under the circumstances approximate to the nature of a rather short Pamphlet. It was not easy to maintain its just title to the qualifying epithet. Its purpose is to do what good it can in the Election. It was written with a strenuous effort to avoid anything that could cause irritation or pain to our right wing or our left, & with this view I tried to know & measure as accurately as I could the views of the two men who most represent them respectively, Hartington & Chamberlain: who were also the two that had principally put themselves before the public. I used in fact what seemed the best securities for steering a straight course in the water full of currents.

---

[1] See Derby's invitation of 12 September, Add MS 44142, f. 144.

[2] Derby replied, 21 September, ibid., f. 145: 'Your address has produced exactly the effect which the best friends and warmest supporters of the late Cabinet could have wished', its timing also excellent: 'the party is united again, but it will not remain so 24 hours after you leave it. I am afraid there is for you no possible release from the cares of leadership.'

[3] G. Meale of Naples sent good wishes; Hawn P.

[4] Pen-name of W. R. Thayer, American author, but unlikely here; perhaps an ed. of *Hermes Trismegisti*, tr. (1885).

[5] Probably T. Moore, 'The case for establishment' (1885).

Granville to whom I referred on account of Foreign affairs, & of his detached position, has been pleased with the draft. I hope the Address will be published on Thursday. This is only a succinct account but I have been pretty hard pressed.[1]

To LORD SPENCER, 15 September 1885. '*Most private*'.   Althorp MSS K8.

I send you a copy of a letter which I have addressed to Kimberley & which touches matter that concerns you & all our colleagues. I have not been able to keep all informed as I could have wished.

Ireland has been in my own mind by far the greatest difficulty. I fear for a new Irish question open, after the Dissolution, like a chasm under our feet. Now that the Central Board scheme is extinct, I cannot pretend to say I see my way.

16. Wed.

Ch. 8½ A.M. Wrote to Lady S. Opdebeek—Herbert J.G. Tel. & 2 L.—Mr Trevelyan—Mr Hitchman. Corrected Revises. Wolverton came. Much conversation. Read Paul Hermes.

17. Th.

Ch. 8¼ AM. Wrote to Marquis of Lorne—Ld R. Grosvenor—Mrs Bolton—Sir C.W. Craufurd—Mrs Th.—Ld Rosebery—Mr W. Smith—Mr E. Robertson—Watsons—Rev. Gillespie[2]—Mr Raven[3]—Mr S. Lawley—Mr Adcock—Herbert J.G.—& minutes. Conversation with Wolverton: also with Lacaita. Read Phythian (finished)—O'Byrne[4] on Home Rule.[5] Worked hard on books.

To LORD R. GROSVENOR, chief whip, 17 September   Add MS 44316, f. 35.
1885.[6]

Had you on receiving the application from London recommended changing our decision about sending to Scotsman & D. Review in Priority [*sic*].[7] But I had nothing from you. Wolverton came here & we discussed the matter fully, and *adhered* as I think was right. The inclosed was sent me from Glasgow. I knew nothing of the writer & did nothing upon the very peremptory request. From what I hear, I fear you will not be able to prolong greatly your stay in Scotland.

All accounts that come in to me are very sanguine.

---

[1] Kimberley replied, dated 13 September but clearly later, Add MS 44228, f. 205, delighted at Gladstone's decision: 'no one but yourself could steer the party in an even course between our right and left wings, and the future of this country will depend upon the impulse given at the commencement of the new political era. To give that impulse will be the fitting crown of your political life. I see no reason why we should split up. . . .'

[2] Perhaps Charles George Knox Gillespie, anglican chaplain in Holland.

[3] Perhaps John James Raven, priest and headmaster of Yarmouth grammar school.

[4] Here to 22 Sept. in facsimile in Masterman, 320.

[5] Perhaps E. W. O'Brien, 'The radical programme for Ireland', *N.C.*, xviii. 362 (September 1885), an attack on county boards and national councils, or perhaps the speech in Dublin on 1 March by W. O'Brien which Gladstone recalled in 1890 as 'the crucial moment' of decision for home rule (see Loughlin, 36).

[6] Holograph; inclosure untraced.

[7] i.e. for publication of Gladstone's election address.

To LORD LORNE, 17 September 1885. '*Private*'.   Add MS 44492, f. 94.

I received this morning a copy of your Address, & as it has a correction in your own handwriting I think it may have come from yourself, & I thank you very much for it.

No one will complain of it as weak-kneed. Tomorrow I hope that a long Address, which has cost me much (but perhaps not enough) care & anxiety, will be in the Edinburgh papers & it will be sold in the streets of London in the afternoon as a penny tract. You will see from it that we are to a great extent in sympathy, though there are some points as to which I hold back in opinion & leaning, & other matter where I do not speak so freely, because you write to express your own sentiments, whereas the purpose of my paper is two sided, & seeks to hold our left & right wings in touch with one another for & through the election.

But if I take your Address as an advanced Address, an Address that runs more rapidly than my own old & stiffening limbs can move, I see nevertheless in such a paper many elements of advantage. In the old days of the Kirk, before the Disruption (you will remember the division of Church parties as it then stood) I recollect the description given (without any intention of antithesis) 'he is a violent Moderate'. This kind of violent moderation has been running, like a scurf[1] in an ill-farmed field, about and over the House of Lords. It is high time that the tones of a decided Liberalism should obtain a somewhat more free scope among Peers & Peers' sons. I have not the disposition of some Whig Lords to reaction on Conservative as much as on Liberal grounds. For more than two centuries our Liberal movements have been led by Liberal Lords and I hold this to have been not only an important but a vital point in our history, which, without it, would have been materially different from what it is. I keenly desire the continuance of this feature, & I state this frankly to you (as I would if I had the proper opportunity & title, even to the *highest*[2] of your connections) because though you are a Commoner, & I hope the Duke's prolonged life may long keep you one, I of course reckon you as eminently bound up in the Peerage.

[P.S.] I am very anxious to know in detail of your views about Ireland, in connection with your Canadian experience.[3]

18. *Fr.*

Ch. 8½ A.M. Wrote to Mr Cowan (Beeslach)—Sir Ch. Dilke—Rev. Dr. Rigg—Mr Weeder—Mr D. Davies. Worked much on books. Drive & walk with C. Read OByrne finished—Documents of 1782—Grattan Vol. V[4]—Le Play.

To Sir C. W. DILKE, M.P., 18 September 1885.   Add MS 43875, f. 270.

I thank you for your note[5]—and I was very glad to find that the Land Paragraph, as well as the earlier one on Registration, passed muster.

The subjects in immediate view ought to keep not me, but the party, employed & united for three or four years—alors comme alors.

But all may be traversed by a blast from Ireland.

I have no great expectations from Parnell for the autumn, but I am astonished at the

---

[1] 'a thin layer of turf' (O.E.D.).
[2] i.e. the Queen, Lorne's mother-in-law.
[3] As governor-general 1878–83; Lorne, 20 September, Add MS 44492, f. 102, sent extensive notes on 'Irish provincial government' but opposing a 'national parliament'.
[4] *Memoirs of... Henry Grattan* (1846); vol. v is on the union debs. and their aftermath.
[5] Of 16 September, Add MS 44149, f. 365, approving of the address.

rather virulent badness of what he has uttered with respect to Irish Government. How much worse it is, for example, than Healy's article.[1]

Let me congratulate you very cordially on your approaching marriage and offer my best wishes.[2] This I should have done some days earlier but for the heavy pressure of correspondence and otherwise which has been upon me since I came back.

19. Sat.

Ch. 8½ A.M. Wrote to Ed. D. Post Lpool—Ed. Scotsman—Ld Rosebery—Mr Ph. Campbell—and minutes. Drive & walk with C. Worked on Books. Read Pitt's Speeches on the Union[3]—Sheridan's do[4]—Father O'Malley on Home Rule[5]—Le Play.

I have long suspected the Union of 1800. There was a case for doing something: but this was like Pitt's Revolutionary war, a gigantic though excusable mistake.

20. 16 S. Trin.

Ch. mg & evg. Wrote to Mad. Novikoff—Lord Lyons. Read Bp Goodwin on Life—Fairbairn on Ch. Histories[6]—Reville Prolegomena—Bible Myths &c.—Pfleidrer Hibbert L.[7]

21. M. St Matt.

Church & Holy C. 8½ A.M. Wrote to Ed. Daily Reviews—Mr P. Maitland—Ld Ripon—Mr Holmes Ivory. Read my Will & Codicils:[8] almost all now inapplicable. I *must* go through with this matter. Also worked on books & papers. Read Le Play Const. d'Anglet.[9]—Eumenides Aesch. With regard to my Will I am really rather shocked to find the risk I have been running of having my dearest ones in much perplexity. But I have for long felt while in office that to give brain-force and time to my own affairs was *robbery*.

22. Tu.

Ch. 8½ A.M. Wrote to Mr Chamberlain—Ld Granville—Mr Cowan—Mr Geo. Harris—Mr J. Maine—Watson & Smith—and minutes. Prosecuted my examination of property & consideration of a Will. Worked on books & effects. Drive

---

[1] T. M. Healy, 'The advance towards home rule', *C.R.*, xlviii. 433 (September 1885).

[2] Dilke married Emilia Pattison in October, after having been secretly engaged since 1884; news of the Crawford divorce case and Dilke's involvement as co-respondent had broken *ca.* 20 July 1885.

[3] In vols. iii and iv of *The speeches of . . . William Pitt* (1806); and see 15 June 32.

[4] R. B. B. Sheridan, 'Speech in reply to Mr. Pitt's speech on the union with Ireland' (1799).

[5] T. O'Malley, *Home Rule on the basis of federalism* (1873); see 9 July 73.

[6] Both in *C.R.*, xlviii. 352, 439 (September 1885).

[7] O. Pfleiderer, *The Hibbert lectures 1885 . . . on the influence of the apostle Paul on the development of Christianity* (1885).

[8] For earlier wills and codicils, see 9 June 47, 21 Nov. 49, 26 Dec. 61, 2 Jan. 79. His operative will was signed on 26 November 1896.

[9] P. G. F. Le Play, *La constitution de l'Angleterre*, 2v. (1875).

with C. Walk with Mary & 'Maggie'. Read D'Arblay's Journal[1]—De Vesci on Ireland[2]—Le Play Réforme Sociale.

23. Wed.

Ch. 8¼ A.M. Wrote to Duke of Newcastle—Ld R. Grosvenor—Mr Freeman—Ld Rosebery—Messrs Barker—Ed. Daily Review (for S.L.)[3]—and minutes. Made progress in sketching a will. Worked on arranging books & photographs: it seems an interminable labour. Read Mad. D'Arblay—Stanhope's Life of Pitt[4]—Le Play Reforme Sociale.

To E. A. FREEMAN, 23 September 1885. '*Private*'.   Add MS 44548, f. 44.

Your letter[5] reached me yesterday. I am if possible even more anxious now than I was during the anti-Jingo struggle, for the liberties of the Balkan Peninsula. But the question now opened is for me a most difficult one; inasmuch as international law was a main instrument for the preservation of the ground already gained, & it would be very difficult for me to take any ground involving a disparagement to it, though I suppose no-one can say the Eastern Roumelians are offenders, any more than the Belgians were in 1830 when they broke the Treaty of Vienna.

Suppose that this affair be made a pretext for a movement of Austria upon Salonica: we shall have then all the fat in the fire, & who can answer for the immediate issue? For the present I must wait & ruminate till I can see my way: but I would advise anyone who takes a part to dwell on the importance of not widening by *any action from without* the circle of distribution, in case Turkey should take up arms. For Austria would mean I suppose in this case seventy millions of people.

Since the Treaty of Berlin the Sultan has utterly nullified all provisions & plans for reform, & it seems hardly possible that the Western corner can keep quiet, but it may be found that a revolt there would mean a savage civil war.

[P.S.] I am sorry that Parliament is not to have you, but I cannot wonder at your resolution.

To LORD R. GROSVENOR, chief whip, 23 September   Add MS 44316, f. 38.
1885.[6]

1. I have read de Vesci's Tract with great interest. It shows all his good and kindly feelings. But since he wrote the plan he criticises has vanished into air—and a yet wider scene has opened; in the which, if, as is probable, I am unable to do good, I will try at any rate not to do any harm.

2. I hope your stags, for which you express a yearning, are or soon will be down: you will then have I trust a noble and successful sport in killing Candidates when they are duplicate. This I am told is the case in from 30 to 40 Constituencies[7]—and it appears to be the most dangerous, perhaps the only dangerous, feature in our whole position.

---

[1] See 27 Dec. 43.
[2] Described next day to Grosvenor as a 'tract'; no copy found; none at Abbeyleix; perhaps a long letter?
[3] Not found published; an Edinburgh liberal daily.   [4] See 2 Apr. 61.
[5] Of 21 September, Add MS 44492, f. 109, asking for 'some sign from you' on the 'great blow struck for right and freedom' in S.E. Europe.
[6] Holograph; de Vesci had requested Grosvenor to forward his 'tract'; Add MS 44316, f. 36.
[7] Grosvenor reported this an exaggeration: 13 in London, all in hand, 14 outside London, 'only 2 or 3 of which are really serious', i.e. Camborne and Lincoln; ibid., f. 40.

3. I think the reception of the Address has been good. Chamberlain growls a little, I think without cause: Dilke not at all.

4. My eldest son's motive in dropping Parliament (after 20 years) will be the better care of his estate the recovery of which from a smash more than sufficient to kill has been to a certain extent checked by the double pressure of corn and coal distress, those being its two props. I think however he should not be considered wholly out of the case, if in connection with his name or otherwise, a good opportunity were to come up. I refer to his name, because even poor Harry has been *asked* to stand: whom a necessity sufficiently grievous to us in our old age drives back to India in the course of a few months.

5. This Revolution in Eastern Roumelia, though not in itself bad, opens a dangerous outlook.

24. Th.

Ch. 8¾ A.M. Damp &c. kept me at home in evg. Wrote to Ed. Daily News¹—Herr Orange² l. & B.P.—Mr Westell—Mr Maclean—Mr Billington—& minutes. Worked away on my books. Read Eumenides—Madame D'Arblay—Le Play Ref. Sociale. The Sidgwicks³ came: more acute than ever, & not less pleasant.

25. Fr.

Ch. 8½ A.M. Wrote to J. Watson & Smith—Mr P. Campbell Tel.—Mr Hitchman—Mr Wiggin MP.—Mr Swinburne⁴—Sir S. Scott & Co—Ed. Daily Review per S.L.—Ld Rosebery—& minutes. Worked further on books. And on materials of Will, & of investments. Read Mad. D'Arblay—Eumenides. Spent the late evening wholly in conversation with the Sidgwicks.

26. Sat.

Ch. 8½ A.M. Spent the morning in work on my books: a sure time-devouring affair. Wrote to Mr Chamberlain—Mr M'Coll—Mr Carlisle—Robertson & Nicholson—and minutes. Drive with C. Woodcraft with H. Read Eumenides—D'Arblay—Grattan 1783.⁵

To J. CHAMBERLAIN, M.P., 26 September 1885.⁶   Chamberlain MSS 5/34/42.

I felt well-pleased & easy after receiving your note of the 21st., but there is a point I should like to put to you with reference to your self-denying ordinance making the three points conditions of office.

Supposing Parnell to come back 80 to 90 strong, to keep them together, to bring forward a plan which shall contain in your opinion adequate securities for the Union of the

---

¹ Not found published.

² Unidentified.

³ Henry and Eleanor Sidgwick; she was A. J. Balfour's sister and Helen Gladstone's vice-president at Newnham, Cambridge.

⁴ If A. C. Swinburne, not in *The Swinburne letters*, ed. C. Y. Long; Swinburne was violently anti-Gladstonian. See 25 June 85.

⁵ On 28 October 1783, on the absence of a right to deny or betray Irish liberty: 'such a right would be, in fact, no right, but the licence of self-destruction'; *The speeches of... Henry Grattan* (1822), i. 180.

⁶ In Garvin, ii. 97; Gwyn, ii. 187.

Empire, & to press this plan under whatever name as having claims to precedence (claims which could hardly be denied even by opponents)—do you think no Government should be formed to promote such a plan unless the three points were glued on to it at the same time?

Do you not think you would do well to reserve allowance for a case like this.

I hope you will not think my suggestion—it is not a question—captious & a mantrap. It is meant in a very different sense.

A Liberal majority is assumed in it.

27. 17 S. Trin.

Ch 11 AM & 6½ PM. Wrote to Sir W. Farquhar—Watsons—Mr Howell—Ld Rosebery. Read Finlayson on Drummond[1]—Wood on Inspiration[2]—Stubbs, Mythe of Life[3]—W. Carlisle on Evil Spirits[4]—Reville.

28. M.

Ch. 8½ A.M. Wrote to Metropoln of Bulgaria[5]—Mr F. Hill—Mr Childers—Mr E. Howell[6]—Mr Dobson—and minutes. Finished the rough draft of my Will. Walk with C. Woodcraft with H. Worked on books. Sir A. Clark came, and examined throat. Finished Eumenides—read D'Arblay.

To H. C. E. CHILDERS, M.P., 28 September 1885.   Childers MS 5/171.
'*Private*'.[7]

I have a decided sympathy with the general scope & spirit of your proposed declaration about Ireland.[8]

If I offer any observations, they are meant to be simply in furtherance of your purpose.

1. I would disclaim giving any exhaustive list of Imperial subjects, & would not 'put my foot down' as to Revenue but would keep plenty of elbow room to keep all Customs & Excise which might probably be found necessary.

2. A general disclaimer of particulars as to the form of any local Legislature might suffice without giving the Irish expressly to know it should be decided mainly by their wish.

3. I think there is no doubt Ulster would be able to take care of itself in respect to Education, but a question arises, & forms I think the most difficult part of the whole subject whether some defensive provisions for the owners of land & property should not be considered.

4. It is evident you have given the subject much thought & my sympathy goes largely

---

[1] T. C. Finlayson, *Biological religion* (1885); critique of H. Drummond's *Natural law*.

[2] J. R. Wood, *Devotional readings* (1885).

[3] See 12 Jan. 81.

[4] See 23 Apr. 82.

[5] On the situation there; *T.T.*, 1 October 1885, 7f; Gladstone told Hill, on 24 September, Add MS 44492, f. 116: 'the truth is that I am much embarrassed by the events in Eastern Roumelia . . .'.

[6] Liverpool publisher.

[7] In Morley, iii. 235.

[8] Childers had formulated a plan for federal home rule; considering it impracticable as a whole, he proposed an address based on its Irish portion; he told Gladstone, 27 September, Add MS 44132, f. 183: 'provided Imperial matters are clearly reserved . . . an Irish Legislature and Executive might in my opinion have full authority for the rest'; such matters he then listed, including customs and excise revenue and perhaps 'some reservation as to education in Ulster'. For Childers' speech at Pontefract, see *T.T.*, 13 October 1885, 12a.

to your details as well as your principle. But considering the danger of placing confidence in the leaders of the National party at the present moment, & the decided disposition they have shown to raise their terms on any favourable indication, I would beg you to consider further whether you should *bind* yourself at present to any details or go beyond general indications. If you say in terms (& this I do not dissuade) that you are ready to consider the question whether they can have a Legislature for all questions not Imperial this will be a great step in advance; & any thing you may say beyond it I should like to see veiled in language not such as to commit you.

29. *Tu. St M. & all A.*

Ch 8½ AM. Wrote to Mr Wilfrid Blunt[1]—Editor D. Review—Ld Granville—Mr P. Maitland—Watsons—and minutes. Finished & signed my Will which is a relief. Read to C. the parts specially concerning her which she approved. Full examination by Sir A.C. and treatment of throat. He is well pleased. Woodcraft with Herbert. Worked on books. Read Mad. D'Arblay.

To P. W. CAMPBELL, Midlothian liberal agent,   Add MS 44548, f. 45.
29 September 1885.

Many thanks for your exact compliance with my suggestions about the title page of the address.[2]

I have yesterday & today seen Sir A. Clark who is very well satisfied with the condition of my throat, as improved & improving.

We have made the following sketch for the future

1. I wait to learn whether the Government adhere to their intention & engagement to dissolve at the earliest moment, i.e. say in all November.

2. When I know this, then measuring backwards say three weeks from the probable time, I would go up to London, see Sir A. Clark & Dr. Semon & get their final opinion how much I might undertake.

3. From the time of this inspection, I should be entirely at the command of the country, & if my 'three weeks' requires enlargement, you will please let me know.

4. But you may at once safely assume that I am good for two or three speeches not requiring *great* exertion of voice. I recollect addressing in 1879 or 80 the *City* Election Committee, I think, over a 1000 in a very convenient room. Sir A. Clark considers it important that after the first speech there should be an interval of some days before the second. You will I daresay keep Mr. Cowan duly informed as occasion may require of what passes between us.

Wed. 30.

Ch. 8½ A.M. Wrote to Duke of Argyll. Worked say 5 hours on books. Read Mad. D'Arblay—Bodley's Remains[3]—Le Play, Réforme Sociale. Dined at Mr Johnson's. Conversation with him on Agriculture and with Mr Gamon.

---

[1] Declining to be drawn into controversy over Egypt in 1882: 'I am reluctant to say what I think as to your conduct in Egypt'; *T.T.*, 2 October 1885, 4f (see also *T.T.*, 25 September 1885, 4f).

[2] i.e. title to be 'On the Liberal Party', with 'published by authority' on the title page; Add MS 44116, f. 25.

[3] Sir T. Bodley, *Reliquae Bodleianae: or some genuine remains of Sir Thomas Bodley* (1703).

To the DUKE OF ARGYLL, 30 September 1885.   Add MS 44548, f. 46.

I lose no time in answering your letter,[1] & will take first the subject which is uppermost in your mind.

I am very sensible of your kind & sympathetic tone, & of your indulgent verdict upon my address.

It was written with a view to the election & as a practical document, aiming at the union of all, it propounds for immediate action what all are supposed to be agreed on. This is necessarily somewhat favourable to the moderate section of the Liberal Party. You will feel that it would not have been quite fair to the advanced men to add some special reproof to them. And reproof if I had presumed upon it would have been two-sided.

Now as to your suggestion that I should say something in public to indicate that I am not too sanguine as to the future. If I am unable to go in this direction—& something I may do—it is not from want of sympathy with much that you say. But my first & great cause of anxiety is, believe me, the condition of the Tory party. As at present constituted, or at any rate moved, it is destitute of all the effective qualities of a respectable Conservatism. A respectable Conservatism in my view was that of Peel–Stanley–Graham Opposition & Government. There was in that party an enlightened spirit of progress in all administrative questions, a strong & determined anti-Jingo temper, & a firm adhesion to all elementary principles of Government. On this basis a Conservative Party is of the utmost value to the country. I never speak in public, you will find, of Sir R. Peel & his friends except in terms of respect. But what of the present Conservative Party ever speaks of them in such terms. I know of none. Lord Aberdeen is sometimes mentioned but only to be denounced. In none of these grand features I have indicated do they in the least correspond with the old Conservatism (which indeed Disraeli expressly renounced, & which I have heard G. Hamilton attack within the last 2 years). For their administrative spirit I point to the Beaconsfield finance. For their foreign policy, they have invented Jingoism, & at the same time by their conduct re Lord Spencer & the Irish Nationalists, they have thrown over, & they formed their government by means of throwing over, those principles of executive order & caution which have hitherto been common to all governments. Add to this that while in Opposition they lived upon stirring popular passion & excitement, of which the latest example was when Lord R. Churchill, who is the governing spirit, declared that he received our statement on the Afghan frontier as the shame & humiliation of his country.

Why do I mention all these things? They are very bad, but their badness is not the reason. I mention them 1. because out of such a Conservative party you will never get Conservative work, & specially 2. because these are the men who play directly into the hands of the extreme wing of Liberalism. To whatever point Churchill & the boasted Tory democracy drag the Conservatives, that very point supplies a *new point of departure* for what you would call the Chamberlain section.

This is a slight & very imperfect indication of very important & painful topics.

I was not & am not afraid of the natural democracy (an exceeding mild one) of the rural constituencies. But when 1. they have been well dosed with the factitious Tory democracy, 2. when that has had its natural fruit in a further large addition of alcohol from extreme men on our side, then it is a different affair.

There are other Chapters which I have not time to open. I deeply deplore the oblivion into which public economy has fallen: the prevailing disposition to make a luxury of panics, which multitudes seem to enjoy as they would a sensational novel or a highly

---

[1] In Argyll, ii. 395: hearsay suggests that Gladstone has changed his longheld view that franchise extension was no cause for alarm.

seasoned cookery: & the leaning of both parties to Socialism which I radically disapprove. I must lastly mention among my causes of dissatisfaction the conduct of the timid or re-actionary Whigs. They make it day by day more difficult to maintain that most valuable characteristic of our history which has always exhibited a good proportion of our great houses at the head of the Liberal movement.

If you have ever noted of late years a too sanguine & high-coloured anticipation of our future, I should like to be reminded of it. Many thanks for what you say of the Gleanings but I must not enter upon that & many other matters now. I wish there was a hope of see-ing you.

Thurs. Oct One 1885.

Ch. 8¼ A.M. Wrote to Professor Davies—Mr H.G. Martin—Mr Rogers—Editor Berwick Advertiser[1]—Mr Spens—Mr W.Y. Paul. Three more hours reduced my rooms & books to apparent order: but much detail remains. The Derby-Bedford party came & went. I had an hour's good conversation with Lord D.[2] Tea in the open air. Read Mad. D'Arblay—Powell on South Africa[3]—Newman agt Fairbairn.

2. Fr.

Ch. 8½ A.M. Wrote to Sir M.H. Beach[4]—E.W. Hamilton—Mr Budge—Mr Col-lingwood—Ld Spencer—Mr Gregory MP—M.F. Roberts—Rev. Mr Renham[5]—Mr F. Impey[6]—Miss E. King—Mr A.S. Murray—Mr Bell—Mr Carlisle BP.—and minutes. Worked, more quietly, on books. Read Mad. D'Arblay—Stansfield on Liberal Programmes.[7] A. Gordon came: conversation with him: G. Russell came.

3. Sat.

Ch. 8¼ A.M. Wrote a very long letter to WHG.[8] Wrote to Mrs King—Mr Hyde—Mr Douglas. Walks & conversation with A. Gordon to whom I told much. Worked mildly on books. Conversation with Herbert. Read Le Play.

4. 18 S. Trin.

Ch. mg (with H.C.) and evg. Wrote to Mr A. Reader. Read Réville (finished)—Life of B. Gilpin[9]—Hennell, Inquiry[10]—and [blank]. Saw Mr Russell—Mr MacColl.

---

[1] Denying charge of having championed slaveowners in the 1830s; *Berwick Advertiser*, 3 October, 3c.

[2] Derby noted: 'Gladstone discoursed for full half an hour, with scarcely any interruption from me. . . . I listened with some surprise, for though I knew that he favored the Irish claims, I was not prepared for what is in fact a declaration in favor of Home Rule'; *Derby*, 30-3.

[3] G. Baden-Powell, 'English money in South Africa', J. H. Newman, 'The development of religious error', *C.R.* xlviii. 457, 503 (October 1885).

[4] See 10 Oct. 85n.

[5] Nonconformist; not further identified.

[6] Perhaps Frederick Impey of Bayswater.

[7] *C.R.*, xlviii. 570 (October 1885).

[8] The history of the Hawarden estate from 1847; Morley, i. 340.

[9] See 16 Aug. 29.

[10] C. C. Hennell, *An inquiry concerning the origin of Christianity* (1838).

5. M.

Ch. 8½ A.M. Wrote to Mr Mundella—Ld Granville—Mr Wooller—O.B. Cole—T.O. Moore—The Queen—Mr Bourne—Mr Murray—Mr Campbell. Conversation with Herbert—Mr MacColl—Mr Russell—& much with Ld R. Grosvenor who was here 12–4½. Read M. Le Play.

6. Tu.

Ch. 8½ A.M. Wrote to Sir J. Millais—M. Laveleye—Ld Carrington—Mr Russell Smith—Mr W. Watt—Mr Darlington—Mr E. Howell—Mr Sugme [*sic*]—Mrs Robinson. The Brassey tribe came. Worked somewhat on books. Worked on answer to Dr Réville.[1] Read Mad. D'Arblay.

7. Wed.

Ch. 8½ AM. Wrote to . . . Tel.—Ld R. Grosvenor. Worked on Réville. Twelve to dinner. Mr Chamberlain came.[2] Walk & much conversation. Read Letters from Hell[3]—Cox on Aryan Mythology[4]—Culte de Priape.[5] What wide & sore disclosures!

8. Th.

Ch. 8½ A.M. Wrote to Ld Granville l.l.l.—Sir H. Ponsonby—D. of Westmr Tel.—V. Consul Jansen l. & B.P.—Mr Bryce MP—& minutes. Saw Sir Thos Brassey—Marquis Vitelleschi[6]—Mr Chamberlain—three hours of stiff conversation. Read Mad. D'Arblay—Letters from Hell.

To J. BRYCE, M.P., 8 October 1885.   Bryce MS 10, f. 50.

I thank you very much for your letter: and I am glad to hear a good account of Montenegro.[7]

If one looks to the original Montenegrins, the men of the Black Mountain proper, I take it that they are individually superior, not to Servians only, but to almost any troops in the world.

I have felt considerable anxiety about this movement in Eastern Roumelia. It is a thing good in itself, but then it opens all the questions of the Balkan Peninsula, and I am not sure that we are ready to close them. But I hope that, as the movement has occurred, it will be consummated pure, simple, and complete, and will be kept within its own border. If any thing is due to the Turk, let him have it in filthy lucre: which, in public as in private concerns, it is sometimes well worth while to pay, for the sake of avoiding a row.

I can never hope to see Montenegro: but I sometimes hope one or more of my sons may pay it a visit.

---

[1] Published as 'Dawn of creation and of worship', *N.C.*, xviii. 685 (November 1885) and *Later gleanings*, 1. See 19 July 85.
[2] For this and next day, see Chamberlain, *Political memoir*, 166–8.
[3] G. Macdonald, *Letters from hell* (1884); *Mary Gladstone*, 362, notes her recent meeting with him.
[4] G. W. Cox, *The mythology of the Aryan nations*, 2v. (1870).
[5] Part of the *Musée Secret*?; see 17 Oct. 85.   [6] See 3 July 75.
[7] Letter of 6 October, reporting his visit and reaction to the E. Roumelian revolution; Bryce MS 11, f. 86.

9. Fr.

Ch. 8½ AM. Wrote to Lady S. Opdebeck—Librairie du Bibliophile—Mr E. Howell—Bp of Chester—Ld R. Grosvenor—Rev. Dr. Rainy—Mr P. Campbell—Mr G. Watts—Mr Childers—Mr Rogers—Mr Merry—& minutes. Read & ruminated on Ireland, & wrote important stuff. Read Mad. D'Arblay—Gavan Duffy to Ld Carnarvon[1]—M'Caul on the Mosaic Record[2]—Higgins on do.[3]

To LORD R. GROSVENOR, chief whip, 9 October 1885.[4]   Add MS 44316, f. 44.

1. I could not at once reply to your telegram because I was expecting from hour to hour a telegram from Ponsonby bearing on the subject of it.
2. Thanks for your intelligence about time of Dissolution.[5] Do you expect that we shall hear more soon?
3. Can you kindly get rid of this letter for me (A)[6] and of the Workman's Tribute to which it relates?
4. The letter from Mr Rogers[7] is more serious. If you think the inclosed reply will do, please to send it on, and if not (for I am puzzled) then to advise me. If it goes on query whether a copy should be sent to him from your office with my kind regards.
5. Could you be so kind as to send me a copy of the Canada Union & Government Act 1840 ⟨(or close to that year)⟩ and Canada Government (Dominion) Act 1867?[8]
6. I had about 4 hours of conversation with Chamberlain and probably Granville may show you my reports.
7. I am rather inclined to reconsider a sentence of exclusion from a particular place which I mentioned to you—under the particular circumstances of the case as they now stand.[9] Bear in mind what I said to you as to the effect of leading a section upon the question of being head of the whole.
[P.S.] I have been working on Ireland: & have got a speech in me, if I dare speak it. Gavan Duffy's letter to Carnarvon[10] is worth reading.

10. Sat.

Ch. 8½ A.M. Wrote to Ld Granville l.l.l.—The Queen l.l.—W.H.G.—E. Hamilton—Editor of Times[11]—Chancellor of the Exchequer—Scotts—& minutes. A very stiff day of writing. Sir T. Salt came over about the Whitby[12] seat. WHG

---

[1] Sir C. G. Duffy, 'The price of peace in Ireland. A letter to ... the earl of Carnarvon' (1885); a conservative argument for an Irish parliament.
[2] A. McCaul, *Aids to faith* (?); see *Later gleanings*, 24.
[3] W. M. Higgins, *The mosaical and mineral geologies* (1832).
[4] Holograph.
[5] Expected at end of November, Add MS 44316, f. 42.
[6] Not found.
[7] Letter from F. Rogers, radical journalist, requesting Gladstone's adjudication between competing liberal candidates; Grosvenor thought Gladstone's draft (Add MS 44492, f. 160) insufficiently evasive; Add MS 44316, f. 46.
[8] Grosvenor sent both the Acts; Add MS 44316, f. 47.
[9] This may refer to a suggestion from Sir T. Salt that Gladstone, or one of his sons, should stand for Shipley; ibid., f. 48; after consideration, W. H. Gladstone declined to stand, needing to attend to the Hawarden estate and as 'they seem to require a more advanced man'; to Grosvenor, 15 October, ibid., f. 56.
[10] See this day.
[11] Enclosing his letters of 2 and 10 October to Hicks Beach on the Crimes Act; in *T.T.*, 13 October 1885, 8a.   [12] *Sic*; *sc.* Shipley?

412 THE GLADSTONE DIARIES

possible.[1] Read Mad. D'Arblay—Anecdotes de Bachaumont[2]—Cuvier Theory of the Earth.[3] Worked a little on Books.

11. 19 S. Trin.

Ch. mg & evg. Wrote to Sir H. Ponsonby—Bp of Chester—Mr F. Rogers—Mr Carlisle B.P.—Mr A. Reader—Mr M'Coll—Mr Knowles—and draft for Herbert JG to send to Labouchere. Worked on Réville reply. Read Letters from Hell— Whewell on Astronomy &c.[4]—Life of B. Gilpin—Hennell's Inquiry.

Supplied to Herbert [Gladstone] 0.11.85. Private.[5]   Hawarden MSS.

I can go so far as to give you my own impressions as to my Father's view, derived from observation & from conversations with him at times. I doubt whether he has as yet communicated *largely* on this matter with his late colleagues.

I feel sure that he has thought much before using the words of his Address relating to Ireland, and that he means to stand by them in both the main particulars. i.e. first to uphold the unity of the Empire and surrender or compromise nothing that is essential for it, secondly that there is no limit to the powers he would gladly see, compatibly with this condition, given to Ireland for the management of all affairs properly her own.

Farther he, as I think, in no way disapproves of the efforts of the nationalists to get the Tory party to take up their question; as, if this could be done, it might be the shortest way to a settlement. I have however heard him say that, unless they wish permanently to sink or swim with the Tories, they had better bring the matter to a very speedy upshot.

⟨Although he sometimes tries to think through things beforehand⟩ I doubt whether he would consider the gratuitous launching of a plan by him at the present stage to be the best way to forward it: & from his Address he seems to expect that Ireland may through her representatives speak plainly and publicly for herself.

I have heard him speak of the protection of the minority in a country so long torn by dissentions as a difficult point requiring careful consideration. I do not believe procedure would stand in his way as to this particular subject.

(Have you noticed J. Morley's declarations. I have been pleased with them.)

12. M.

Ch. 8½ A.M. Wrote to Lord R.G. l. & Tel.—Ld Granville—Mr Westell—Dean of Wells—Messrs Murray. Worked much on Réville reply. Somewhat on books. Saw Herbert on Ireland—W.H.G. on Shipley.[6] Read Mad. D'Arblay—Barrys 50 Years Concessions.[7]

[1] Despite considerable pressure, W. H. Gladstone did not stand in 1885; he had been M.P. for Whitby 1868–80. Gladstone may here have muddled 'Shipley' and 'Whitby'.
[2] L. Petit de Bachaumont, *Anecdotes piquantes* (1881).
[3] See 8 Aug. 50.
[4] W. Whewell, *Astronomy and general physics considered . . .* (1833).
[5] Gladstone's holograph; mostly incorporated in H. J. Gladstone to Labouchere, 12 October, Hammond, 416; Labby saw through the device and forwarded the contents to Healy and Chamberlain; see Thorold, 237.
[6] i.e. on the constituency.
[7] Second v. of R. Barry O'Brien; see 9 Oct. 83.

13. Tu.

Ch. 8½ A.M. Wrote to Mr R. Wilberforce—Ld Granville—Scotts—Mr A. G. Symonds—Sir R. Owen—Bp of Winchester—Mr Knowles—Mr Tilsley[1]—Mr R. Steele—Mr J.D. Christie—Mr Peterson—Rev. J. Cullen—& minutes. Worked on Réville MS & examined Humboldt, McCaul, Vestiges of Creation, & other books. Read Mad. D'Arblay—Oldcastle's Newman.[2] We worked on a large Oak by Break-neck Brow.

14. Wed.

Ch. 8½ A.M. Wrote to Duke of Newcastle—Lady S. Opdebeck—Mr Knowles— German Ambassador—and minutes. The Oak felled. Eaton party incl. Sir R. Morier,[3] and the A. Russells[4] came for the afternoon. Worked on AntiRéville. Read Oldcastle's Newman. Some of the letters are perfect gems of expression & feeling: a few one much regrets.

15. Th.

Ch. 8½ A.M. Wrote to Ld R. Grosvenor—O.B. Cole (BP)—Mr Gueshoff[5]—Mr T. Salt l.l.—Mr E. Howell—Mr Ph. Campbell—and minutes. Worked considerably on AntiRéville. Walk with Dalhousie. Bright[6] came & the R.L.s. Twelve to dinner. Read Mad. D'Arblay.

16. Fr.

Ch. 8½ A.M. Wrote to Mr Gueshoff Tel.—Mr Knowles. . . . Finished my Reply to Réville & dispatched it. Ten to dinner. Read Mad. D'Arblay—Wordsworth's Excursion.[7] Münster came to luncheon. Long talk, & walk, with him.

17 Sat.

Ch. 8½ A.M. Wrote to Mr G. Stanmer—Ld Rosebery—Mr Fairley—Mr Digby— Scotts—Agnes G.—Watsons—Mr Howell—& minutes. Read Poems of V.[8]— Richelieu & Mary of Medicis[9]—Musée Secret, & Introdn by M. Roux:[10] striking—Mad. D'Arblay. Worked on books. Woodcraft with Harry.

18. 20 S. Trin.

Ch mg & [blank.] Wrote to Dr Von Döllinger—Herbert J.G.—Mr J. Bennett—M. Tricoupé—Mr Campbell. Conversation with HJG on Ireland. Read Gilpin's Life—Letters from Hell—Poems of V.

---

[1] On disestablishment, *T.T.*, 16 October 1885, 7d.
[2] J. Oldcastle [W. Meynell], *Cardinal Newman* (1883).
[3] Passed over for the Vienna embassy by Gladstone and Granville in 1884.
[4] i.e. Lord A. Russell; see *Derby*, 34.
[5] Ivan Evstratiew Gueshoff, 1849–1924; Bulgarian politician, on a visit to U.K.; this letter, on Bulgarian union and deprecating Greek and Servian interference, in *T.T.*, 17 October 1885, 8b; see also Ramm II, ii. 411.   [6] Walling, *Diaries of Bright*, 531.   [7] For quotation; *Later gleanings*, 36.
[8] *Poems by V.* [i.e. Mrs Archer Clive] (latest ed., 1872).
[9] Perhaps C. B. Petitot, *Mémoires du Cardinal Richelieu* (1819).
[10] Perhaps pornography, untraced; or H. Roux's work on Herculaneum remnants (1840).

To H. J. GLADSTONE, M.P., 18 October 1885.   Hammond, 446.[1]

To return to the subject of our Irish conversations.

1. It is impossible to say whether a saving Liberal majority, if returned against a Coalition of Tories and Nationalists at the Election, could be kept *together* for a settlement of the Irish question—or to say what the effect of a split among them would be. This is a risk inseparable from the supposed Irish plan for the Election. The Irish ought to deal with the Tories and settle the matter with them before the Election. It is quite conceivable that, if this be not done, the Tories might then refuse or excuse from settling, and might be kept in by a Liberal secession of men, partly incorporated with the Irish, partly unwilling to concede to them.

I know for myself what in these cases I should *not* do, but it is too soon to speak for others.

2. What I have said seems to assume that a plan could be devised, which would meet the two fundamental conditions. This as yet is not known. But I think the greatest difficulty in the way of such a plan is the protection of the Landlords, not of a Protestant minority. However I make the *assumption*.

3. The dilemma, which you put to me about the House of Lords, is not difficult of solution. Subject to (2) the assumption is that the H. of Lords fairly backed by popular opinion, as at one time the Jingoes seemed to be, rejects a plan carried by a sheer Liberal majority. In such a case the Liberals plainly, not being sure of the country, must resign. It is infallibly certain that the incoming Tories must at once make the concession.

3. An Opposition made up of Liberals and Nationalists (always subject to (2)) might work: but a Liberal Government could not stand on that basis to procure a settlement. This I take to be fundamental. Nothing but a sheer and clear majority in Parlt could enable Liberals in Government to carry a plan. Personally I shake myself free of any other idea.

4. It is quite right to deal with the Tories. But they will avoid Aye or No and keep the thing dangling. If this is tolerated it is likely to spoil all hope of a settlement.

19. M.

Ch. 8½ A.M. Wrote to The Servian Minister[2]—Mr C. Flower (Tel)[3]—Sir A. Clark—M. de Laveleye—Mr T. Salt—Duke of Argyll—Mr J. Hoy—Sir F. Milner MP.[4]—Mr Shepherd—Mons. Gueshoff—Mr Parkhurst—Mr Grimwade—Mr Wilson—Mr Hammond—Sec. G. Trunk Co.—& minutes. Worked 'some' on books. Read Mad. D'Arblay—Monro Introdn to Iliad[5]—Ripon's Speech[6]—A.L. on Mayo[7]—Troubles of 1549 (Pocock).[8] Woodcraft with W. & H.J.G.

[1] No holograph or contemporary copy found.

[2] C. Mijatovich, who had replied to Gladstone's letter to Gueshoff (see 15 Oct. 85); in *T.T.*, 20, 21 October 1885, 8b, 10a.

[3] Cyril Flower, 1843-1907; liberal M.P. Brecknock 1880-5, Luton 1885-92, when cr. Lord Battersea.

[4] Sir Frederick George Milner, 1859-1931; 6th bart. 1880; tory M.P. York 1883-5, Bassetlaw 1890-1906. Contested York 1885.

[5] D. B. Monro, *Iliad Book I. With an essay on Homer's grammar and notes* (ed. of 1885).

[6] Probably that at Ripon, in *T.T.*, 17 October 1885, 6e.

[7] Untraced.

[8] N. Pocock, *Troubles connected with the Prayer Book of 1549* (1884).

20. Tu.

Ch. 8½ AM. Wrote to Sir H. Ponsonby—Watsons (Tel.)—Mr Hankey—Sir J. Lubbock—Mr Westell—Lady S. Opdebeck—& minutes. Read Mad. d'Arblay—
Troubles of 1549—The Radical Programme[1]—Owen on The Thames Valley
Man[2]—Hehn on Wandering of Animals.[3] Saw the Talbot children & said a word
to E. on his profession. Worked on books. Woodcraft as yesterday.

21. Wed.

Ch. 8½ AM. Wrote to Knight of Kerry[4]—Mr Knowles—Watsons—and minutes.
Saw E. Hamilton—who went—R. Grosvenor 12-2. Woodcraft. Tea with Mr
Trotter. Corrected proofs of my (ill-written) article. Read Poems of V (finished)
+.—Hehn's Wanderings—O.T. Revisers Preface—QR on Septuagint &c.[5]—
Madame D'Arblay. Woodcraft. Worked on letters. Tea at Mr Trotter's [sic].

22. Th.

Ch. 8½ A.M. Wrote to Ld Granville—Mr Campbell—Mr Knowles—Mr Hitchman—Messrs R. & N. Worked on books. Read Mad. D'Arblay—Liberation Soc.s
plan. (It is outrageous).[6] Ten to dinner: Harcourt,[7] Whitbread, Mayhew. Saw
Mayhew on Mines.[8]

23. Fr.

Ch. 8½ A.M. Wrote to Mr Knowles l. tel. & BP—Sec. of Bootle Club[9]—Sir R.
Owen—Mrs Th. Further examination & cautions inserted[10] by reason of Sir R.
Owen's very interesting statement. Worked a little on books. Saw Mr Whit-
bread jun.[11] Read Mad. D'Arblay (IV)—Müller Scientific Mythology[12]—Essay on
Swift.[13]

24. Sat.

Ch. 8½ A.M. Wrote to Ld R. Grosvenor—Ld Granville—Mr C. Parker—Lady
Cork—Mr Blagg—Bp of Peterboro—Mrs O'Shea—S. Lyttelton—Mr Wilkins—

---

[1] *The Radical Programme; with a preface by . . . Chamberlain* (1885); published in July, a collection of
articles in *F.R.*, from 1883.

[2] Sir R. Owen, *Antiquity of Man* (1884); on skeleton at Tilbury.

[3] V. Hehn, *The wanderings of plants and animals* (1885).

[4] See 18 Oct. 77.

[5] *Q.R.*, clxi. 281 (October 1885).

[6] One of Liberation Society's electoral pamphlet series; for its Welsh meeting, see *T.T.*, 21
October 1885, 10f.

[7] And L. V. Harcourt; see his diary entry quoted in *Derby*, 35.

[8] Horace Mayhew, b. 1845, of Broughton Hall, Hawarden; mining engineer; agent for the
Hawarden estate 1886–93; interested in Canadian development.

[9] Election business *re* Whitbread.

[10] In proofs of his article.

[11] Samuel Howard Whitbread, 1858–1944; sec. to sundry liberals in 1880s; contested Bootle 1885;
later a liberal M.P.; staying at Hawarden.

[12] Perhaps F. Max Müller, 'The lesson of "Jupiter"', *N.C.*, xviii. 626 (October 1885).

[13] *An essay on the life and character of Dr. Jonathan Swift* (1755).

Rev. R. Jenkins—Mr Jeans—Rev. H. Ottley—M. Foville[1]—Rev. R.H. Manley[2]—J. Jones[3]—Messrs Cassell—& minutes. Long conversation & walk with Bp of Chester on Palmer.[4] Walk with Ly E. Cavendish. Read Mad. D'Arblay—Wilkins on Homer[5]—The Iliad—with reference to dactylics—I. & XXIII.

To LORD R. GROSVENOR, chief whip, 24 October   Add MS 44316, f. 69.
1885.[6]

I inclose two letters from O'Sheas *he* and *she*, together with copy of my reply. The subject matter of the letters is very curious.[7] If I am to see the 'paper' the sooner I see it the better.
[P.S.] I address acc. to the Duchess's instructions.

To Mrs. O'SHEA, 24 October 1885.   Add MS 44269, f. 230.

I have received your letter with one from your husband of the same date.[8]
I rely on your kindness to convey my answer. The suggestions you have made lie wholly within the province of Lord Richard Grosvenor. I will at once forward them to him and may perhaps see him: in any case I will not fail to tell him what I think however he already knows, that I shall be very sorry if Captain O'Shea should fail to obtain a seat in the new Parliament. You will I am sure understand me in saying that if I were to go beyond this it would lead to much inconvenience and confusion of duties.
With regard to the paper you so kindly offer,[9] if it is intended for me I shall be happy to receive it. There is no chance of my leaving this place earlier than Wednesday morning.
[P.S.] For security's sake it would be better that the packet should reach me while here.

25. 21 S. Trin.

Ch. 11 A.M. and [blank.] Wrote to Mr Chamberlain—Mr P. Campbell—Mr Westell—E. Hamilton—Mrs Th.—Mr Knowles. Read Jones's Poems—Schmidt, Social effects of Xty[10]—Barrow 'Towards the Truth'.[11] Late at night I read the MS account of my dear Father's death: It enchained me.[12] Walk with M.G.

---

[1] Alfred de Foville, professor at l'Ecole des science politiques, Paris, had sent his *Etudes économiques et statistiques sur la propriété foncière: le Morcellement* (1885).
[2] Richard Henry Manley, rector of Stoke Climsland.
[3] John Jones of Winchester; later letter on the bible in Hawn P.
[4] i.e. on the proposed new ed. of Palmer's *Treatise*.
[5] G. Wilkins, *The growth of the Homeric poems* (1885).
[6] Holograph.
[7] See next letter.
[8] On O'Shea's candidacy in Co. Clare; Add MS 44269, ff. 73, 226. He eventually stood for Exchange, Liverpool; see 18 Nov. 85.
[9] Mrs. O'Shea: 'I have the paper I mentioned to you, respecting a Scheme, ready when you care to receive it'; this paper, sent on 30 October, is different from that of early 1885 on local govt. (see to Spencer, 27 June 85, to Mrs. O'Shea, 4 Aug. 85 and Hammond 419); this second paper, the 'proposed Constitution for Ireland' by Parnell is in O'Shea, ii. 18 (misdated as early 1884) and Hammond, 422. See 3 Nov. 85.
[10] C. G. A. Schmidt, *The social effects of early Christianity* (1885).
[11] J. C. Barrow, '*Towards the truth*' (1885).
[12] See 7, 9 Dec. 51 and *Autobiographica*, ii. 80.

To J. CHAMBERLAIN, M.P., 25 October 1885.   Chamberlain MSS 5/34/43.

I return the Free Education List with thanks. It is curious. But on the other side Rigg whom you thought rather 'small beer' has been followed by a weightier authority, Illingworth, who, if I understand him right 1. Is not opposed to you in principle 2. thinks (as I do) that the proposal involves a strong interference with the voluntary schools 3. Deems an attempt at such interference premature & inexpedient.

An instinct blindly impresses me with the likelihood that Ireland may shoulder aside everything else.

But I would beg you to revolve much in your mind the policy and duty, without me as well as with me, of keeping together the Liberal party till its list of agreed subjects is exhausted 'or thereby' (I am rubbing up my Scotch).[1]

[P.S.] Bright has been here—in excellent force & temper.

I had almost forgotten to thank you for my little bit of Socialism. I remember it well: & the old Duke of Newcastle (a high Tory, but a great gentleman) smelt a rat and asked me (1832) what I meant. I do not recollect my reply. Probably rather lame.

26. M.

Ch. 8¼ A.M. Wrote to Ld Granville—Mrs Heywood—W.H.G.—Mr Heneage—Sir A. Clark—Mr Curteis[2]—and minutes. Walk with F.L. Gower. Read Records St Martin's Liscn[3]—Foville, Le Morcellement[4]—Madame D'Arblay. Ten to dinner.

27. Tu.

Ch. 8½ AM. Wrote to Ld R. Grosvenor—Mr Darlington—Ld Southesk—S. Lyttelton—Mr Johnston—Mr Bosworth Smith—Chester Station Master—and minutes. Ld Rosebery came. Walks & much conversation.[5] Saw W.H.G. Ten to dinner. Read Foville—Madame D'Arblay.

To LORD SOUTHESK, 27 October 1885. '*Private*'.   Add MS 44548, f. 47.

Let me at the threshold & heartily thank you for the terms of personal kindness in which with evident sincerity you write to me.[6] If in my reply from trying to be concise I appear abrupt you will forgive me. I will not argue the case of compensation to the holders of long leases: for I have not the facts fresh in my memory: & either I was not aware or must have forgotten that any issue was raised, on that matter, with respect to the rights of property—and that the rights of property were boldly defended by the party

---

[1] This letter made Chamberlain 'uneasy'; he replied next day 'unable to see my way at all about Ireland', agreeing *re* Illingworth's resolution, and insisting on municipal acquisition of land; Garvin, ii. 114.

[2] A. M. Curteis, former fellow of Trinity, Oxford; a liberal, alarmed at disestablishment; Hawn P.

[3] *Sic*; untraced.

[4] See 24 Oct. 85.

[5] Rosebery's diary this day: 'Had walks with Mr G. before & after lunch. Much talk of Ireland. I told him plainly he could not decline to form Govt. "Am I" he exclaimed "to remain at this work till I drop into my grave?" Meanwhile his family has settled the question for him'; Dalmeny MSS.

[6] On 24 October, Add MS 44492, f. 230, 'announcing my withdrawal from the Liberal Party' especially because of retrospective nature of Agricultural Holdings Act, 'Anarchy . . . driving into the foundations of the Rights of property'; disestablishment; fear of 'the Socialistic government of no distant future'.

whom, perhaps, you propose to join. Apart from this omission, you will see from what I say how very far I am from being able to concede any of the points you urge.

1. Union with Radicals. Liberals & Radicals have been united ever since I heard of either: just as there have always been in the Tory party, by the side of temperate men (too often expelled in the course of time for their temperance) men of wild reactionary opinions.

2. Respect for property. I contend that this has been more scrupulously shown by our Governments than by the Tories. I conceive the treatment of Scotch Church Patrons on the abolition of Patronage to have been essentially confiscation. In disestablishing the Irish Church, we paid every patron the market value.

3. Socialism. Here I am much at one with you. I have always been opposed to it. It is now taking hold of both parties, in a way I much dislike; & unhappily Lord Salisbury is one of its leaders, with no Lord Hartington (see his speech at Darwen) to oppose him.

4. I will now put together all remaining matters. I am far from disguising their importance. And forgive me if I tell you with great freedom that the true check upon Radicalism (& modern Radicalism wants a check) is the continuance of men like Hartington, Derby & others in the Liberal party: & that nothing has done & is doing, so much for Radicalism as the secessions, avowed or virtual, from our attenuated body of Peers.

I say without fear of contradiction that we the Liberals of the late Government have done more for the House of Lords, within the last year, by saving it in its own despite from a conflict that would have destroyed it, than it had done for itself, or the Tories from it, during many a long year.

Every secession that takes place renders the repetition of any like service more & more difficult.

And now as to Disestablishment. Hopeless of obtaining a majority on the questions really before us, almost hopeless of gaining a sufficient number to be a majority when counting in their Parnellite allies, the Tories are endeavouring to divide the Liberal party by twisting into the foreground a question which is at the present absolutely impossible in England, & within what distance from impossibility in Scotland you yourself may possess means of judgment quite equal to mine.

But I now speak of the nearer future. In a more distant future when the questions which now supply Liberalism with a firm & safe basis of action are disposed of, other questions will arise, or questions already known like Disestablishment will assume a new & more practical aspect.

What will then, probably, happen? The Tory party, which was split in 1829, & more seriously in 1846, will not split as it is now constituted, as it showed on the grand occasion of last July. It has not principle & conviction sufficient to split it.

But I think differently of the Liberals: &, as far as one may venture on looking into the future, I am of opinion that it has a split in the distance. I do not enter on particulars—Socialism, House of Lords, Established Church—but I do not see how when opinions & projects now speculative become practical a split of the Liberal party is to be avoided.

Is not that the time when those who feel these matters to touch their conscience, should reserve to themselves the exercise of their judgment accordingly? And, if that *is* the time, does it not seem to follow that this *is not*?

P.S. I hope I do not take an unhandsome advantage in saying this one word more. If your change has reference to my withdrawal, might it not stand over to be considered when I withdraw?

28. *Wed. SS. Simon & Jude.*

Ch. 8½ A.M. Wrote to Lady Aberdeen—Mr D. Macgregor[1]—Mudies—Mr R. Williams—Westell—Rev. Mr Mackay—Stibbs—Mr G. Bellis—Mr E. Crowther—Rev. B. Wilberforce—and minutes. The Roseberys went. Saw Mr A. Morley. He went. Walk & long conversation with F.L.G. Worked on books. Saw SEG. Read Mad. D'Arblay—Shee's Alasco, Preface & play.[2]

29. *Th. [London]*

Ch. 8½ A.M. 11¼-3½ to Euston with Harry. Wrote to Watsons—Mr Knight—Mr Jamieson—Mr Wood—Mr Blagg—Rev. Mr Oliver[3]—Rev. Macdonald[4]—Central Press[5]—C.G. Shopping. Saw Sir A. Clark & Dr Semon: favourable report. Dined with Mr Knowles. Conversation with Mr Hurlbert on the state of France.[6] Saw Mrs Th.—Mad. Novikoff: but as she was not alone could not say what I wished about Russia. Read Senèque et St Paul[7]—Greville's Journal (1837).[8]

30. *Frid. [Hawarden]*

Wrote to Mr Westell—Lady Clark—Sir Thos. May—Ed. Fin. Reform Almanack[9]—and minutes. Worked in H. of C. Library on S. African papers. Busied about books. Saw Ld Kensington—Mr Murray—Ld Granville—H.J.G.—Mrs Th. 4.30-9.30 Home to Hn. Read Senèque et St Paul.

31. *Sat.*

Ch. 8½ A.M. Wrote to Mr Bosworth Smith l.l.[10]—Sir F. Herschell—Watsons—Mr Horsley RA—Mr Blagg—Mr P. Campbell—Ed. D. News[11]—Treasurer Middle Temple—and minutes. Read Ducane on Crime.[12] Granville came: conversation with him. Woodcraft with W.H.G.

---

[1] Donald MacGregor, proprietor of the Royal hotel, Edinburgh, offered a suite for Gladstone which he declined; Hawn P. The Gladstones stayed there in 1886; see 17 June 86.

[2] M. A. Shee, *Alasco: a tragedy in five acts* (1824).

[3] Perhaps Thomas Oliver, incumbent of St Martin's, Liverpool.

[4] Perhaps George *MacDonald, 1824-1905; novelist; once an Independent minister; see 7 Oct. 85n.

[5] Unable to answer correspondents individually; *T.T.*, 30 October 1885, 9f.

[6] William Henry Hurlbert, 1827-95; American journalist; wrote on France for Knowles in *F.R.*, in late 1880s.

[7] C. Aubertin, *Etude critique sur les rapports supposés entre Sénèque et St. Paul* (1857).

[8] The 2nd v. of the *Greville Memoirs*.

[9] *Financial Reform Almanack for 1886*, 54 misquoted Gladstone as an unqualified disestablishmentarian; corrections and apologies in *P.M.G.* and *D.N.*, 6 and 7 November; see Add MS 44493, ff. 57-61.

[10] Published as 'Letter to R. Bosworth Smith on disestablishment, 31 October 1885', in *T.T.*, 2 November 1885, 9c and Lathbury, i. 184.

[11] Unable to choose where two liberals stand in competition; *P.M.G.*, 3 November 1885, 7.

[12] E. F. Ducane, *The punishment and prevention of crime* (1881).

Nov 1. 22 S. Trin & All Saints

Wrote to Sec. Central Press 1. & Tel. 1.1.—Lord Southesk—Mr Knowles. Read Anderson on Glory of the Bible[1]—Martineau Autobiography[2]—Barry OBrien on Ireland[3]—B. Gilpin's Life. Walk & conversation with Ld G. especially as to the O'Shea communications.[4]

2. M.

Ch. 8¼ A.M. Wrote two drafts to Mrs O'Shea:[5] conversation with G. on this weighty matter. Also wrote to Pres. Coll. Surgeons (Ed.)[6]—Mr C.E. Mathews—Mr Barnett—Mr Elflone[7]—Mr H. Davey MP—Ld Brabourne—Messrs Mudie—Bp of Exeter—Mr Robinson—Sir Jas Watson—Mr R.W. Davey—Rev. Dr. Cairns—Mr T.W. Jones—Profr Ramsay—Dr. Mallich—Col. C.C. Long—Rev. A. Stewart—M. Gen. Anderson—Rev. B. Waller[8]—and minutes. Woodcraft with W. & H. Read Mad. D'Arblay—Dicey on Constitutional Law.[9] R. Grosvenor came in evg.

3. Tu.

Ch. 8½ AM. Much conversation with R.G. on the Chamberlain affair & on Parnell's paper. Supplied him with draft to Mrs OShea. Also Wrote to Ld R.G. (Chambn)—Principal Rainy—Mr E. Leon—Sir W.R. Gordon[10]—Mr T. Brett—Mr W. Ruggins—Mr Parry—Mr R. Machhardy—Mr D. Miles—Mr Fairgrieve—Mr E. Gunn—Sir J. Lubbock—Mr T. Sloan—Mr E.C. Mace.—eight B.P. packets (Art.)—and minutes. Woodcraft with W. & H. Read Foville—Madame D'Arblay.

To Mrs. O'SHEA, 3 November 1885. [Draft][11]   Add MS 44269, ff. 234-6.

[First draft]: I thank you for the interesting paper which you have sent me on the part of Mr Parnell.[12] ⟨As the development of an idea that plays its part in the national politics it cannot but[13] be useful. I think a good deal on the subject and it will help me in so thinking⟩.

[1] Robert Patrick Anderson, soldier, had sent an early version of his *Commentary on the first chapter of Genesis* (1889); Hawn P and next d.
[2] Harriet Martineau, *Autobiography*, 3v. (1877).
[3] R. Barry O'Brien, 'Irish wrongs and English remedies: a statement of facts': *N.C.*, xviii. 707 (November 1885): the article originally suggested by Gladstone, see to Knowles, 5 Aug. 85.
[4] Parnell's 'proposed Constitution for Ireland', just arrived; see 24 Oct. 85n.
[5] See next day.
[6] Business untraced; letter not in archive of Royal College of Surgeons, Edinburgh.
[7] C. Elflein, on the Huxley controversy; later asked for a post; Hawn P.
[8] C. B. Waller of Woodford; on Genesis; Hawn P.
[9] A. V. Dicey, *Lectures introductory to the study of the law of the constitution* (1885). Dicey's Austinian emphasis of parliamentary statutory precedence appealed to Gladstone in the home rule context; he discussed him in introducing the Govt. of Ireland bill on 8 April 1886; see R. A. Cosgrove, *The rule of law: A. V. Dicey* (1980), 135 and Introduction above, vol. X, section vii.
[10] None thus; perhaps Sir William Gordon, 1830-1906; 6th bart.; soldier.
[11] Undated holograph drafts, marked by Gladstone 'Dft No 1' and 'Dft No 2'; dated from diary text. In Hammond, 423.
[12] Parnell's 'proposed Constitution for Ireland'; see 24 Oct. 85n.
[13] Word added in pencil, not in Gladstone's hand.

You are already aware that I could not enter into any competition with others upon the question how much or how little can be done for Ireland in the way of self-government. Before giving my practical opinion I must be much better informed as to the facts & prospects on both sides the water and know with whom and in what capacity I am dealing.

Further I have seen it argued that Mr Parnell and his allies ought to seek a settlement of this question from the party now in office, and I am not at all inclined to dissent from this opinion, for I bear in mind the history of the years 1829, 1845, 1846 and 1867, as illustrating the respective capacity of the two parties to deal under certain circumstances with sharply controverted matters. In this view no question can arise for those connected with the Liberal party until the Ministers have given their reply upon a subject which they are well entitled to have submitted to them.

I am aware that important questions arise as to the dispositions of Liberal candidates and members to-be, and as to the effect the circumstances of the Election may have upon them. But these questions are not under my controul.

One observation only I will hazard on the form of the plan here presented. It would have been of advantage, if it had been as fully and as carefully developed as the former paper on the Central Board. I observe for interest [?*sc.* instance] that finance is only touched at a single point and that no provision is offered for the Irish share in the National Debt, in Naval Defence, or in Royal Charges. This is only by the way.

If the Government are asked, I shall be glad to know their reply so soon as it can legitimately become public property. What I think essential to any hope of a satisfactory issue is that any answers given on behalf of either party should be given on its own ground, and quite independently of the other party.

I return the paper herewith.

[Second draft][1]   I (Mr G wishes me to) thank you for the paper which you have sent me (him) ⟨on behalf of⟩ containing the views of Mr Parnell⟨. The⟩ on the subject of Irish Government. The important subject to which it relates could but be ⟨dealt with⟩ considered by the Government of the day but all information in regard to it is of great interest to me (him). I shall (he will) strictly observe your injunction as to secrecy and ⟨I may add that I⟩ intend(s) to take a very early opportunity in Midlothian of declaring my view of the present position ⟨held by⟩ of the Liberal & Conservative parties ⟨respectively at the present juncture will⟩ in relation to Mr Parnell and his friends, ⟨as well as to the question⟩ and to the policy they propose to pursue.
(Lord RG will I am sure do all he can to promote Captain O'Shea's views but his power ⟨of the⟩ at this advanced stage is limited & I wish the need could have been earlier known.)

To Principal R. RAINY, 3 November 1885.[2]   Add MS 44548, f. 48.

I have read your letter[3] with deep interest & with the attention it so well deserves.

But I must observe upon it that while it most naturally, & perhaps necessarily, takes a Scottish view of the question of Disestablishment, & deals only with influences operating on that side of the Border, yet the question of Parliamentary action is open to many other influences, which might gravely affect, or indeed reverse the result.

---

[1] Clearly this was the version, after excisions, sent to Mrs O'Shea, as it is docketed at the top by Gladstone: 'Lord RG will write this except as to the last para in his own person, & return me the original.'
[2] In P. C. Simpson, *The life of Principal Rainy*, ii. 33 (1909).
[3] Of 27 October, Add MS 44492, f. 238: 'Scottish party managers' strenuously suppressing attempts to formalise disestablishment demands in Scotland.

Every day I am pressed from quarters quite unsuspected, with alarms lest for want of strong declarations from me on that is to say *for* the English Church many Liberal seats should be lost.

I have always thought that in Scotland the course which equity dictates is also the one most favourable to the Disestablished Churches; that is, to treat the question as Scottish, & effectually to sever it from the case of England.

On this principle of severance I have acted during the present autumn, & shall continue so to act.

But the only practical mode of severance is leaving Scottish Disestablishment to the Scottish people.

Now, were I, or others in like position, to press disestablishment on the electoral bodies, might it not be said that this *is not* leaving it to the Scottish people.

And most certainly the effect in England, where the Church is much stronger, would be disastrous.

The truth is that the one case is the inverse of the other. In Scotland Disestablishment is I believe pressed largely as a test by the Liberals. In England Establishment is keenly pressed as a test by the Tories: & the request is coolly made that no Liberal shall vote for a candidate favourable to disestablishment.

This we entirely resist, but the resistance appears to be incompatible with a forward movement in Scotland.

This note will serve as I hope to explain in some degree my present position—we may perhaps have an opportunity of conversation shortly.

Do not forget the possibility that a question of Irish Government may come up with such force and magnitude as to assert its precedence over every thing else.

4. Wed.

Ch. 8¾ A.M. Wrote to Mr Bennett—Ed. Fin. Reform Almanack[1]—Mr Strangeways—Mr Murray—Cardinal Manning—Scotts—Lady Phillimore B.P.—Mrs Bernard Beere[2]—and minutes. Woodcraft with W. & H.—Tea at Miss Rigby's. Read Mad. D'Arblay—Dicey, Law of the Constitution—& Radical Programme.

5. Th.

Ch. 8½ A.M. Wrote to Lady F. Cavendish B.P.—Bp of Oxford—Bp of Durham—Lord Rosebery—Mr Childers—Sir W. Phillimore—Mr D. M'Gregor—Mr Macilwraish—Ld R. Grosvenor—Mr Macintosh—Mr MacColl BP—Mr Hitchman—Mr Lefevre—Mr Patten—Mr Westell—Rev. S.E.G.—and minutes. Worked on books. Woodcraft with W. & Harry. Read Mad. D'Arblay—Dicey on Law of Constitn.

6. Fr.

Ch. 8½ AM. Wrote to Cardinal Manning—Mr Chamberlain—Ld Brabourne—Ld R. Grosvenor—Mr Webster MP—Mr Buchanan MP[3]—and minutes. Read Mad.

[1] Further *Corrigendum* to its quotation from diarist on disestablishment, *Financial Reform Almanack for 1886*, 54, corrected in later eds.; see 30 Oct. 85 and n.

[2] Lived in York Terrace.

[3] Thomas Ryburn Buchanan, 1846–1909; liberal M.P. Edinburgh 1881–5, 1888–92, E. Aberdeenshire 1892–1900; briefly unionist in 1886.

D'Arblay—Foville Morcellement—Manning on the Election.[1] Saw S.E.G. Woodcraft with three sons.

To J. CHAMBERLAIN, M.P., 6 November 1885.   Chamberlain MSS 5/34/44.

The plot thickens as to Disestablishment, and I ask in the first place if you can send me
a letter of yours to Mr. Taylor Innes.

In the second place I should be glad of your tactical opinion.

We are in danger I think of getting into a false position. South of the Border the Tories
try to make it a test question, and we protest. If we do this, and rightly, how can we countenance making it a test question North of the Border?

No doubt we or some of us may have said that we separate the English & the Scotch
cases and will leave the Scotch case to Scotland. But, if in Scotland it is now made a test
question, *our* desire to separate the two will not prevent its being made a test question
against us in England.

I must carefully consider my ground, and must deal with the matter (I think) early next
week in Midlothian.

The English case is for me simple. Within is a note of my opinions.

Much harm has I think been done *among the best men* by the plan propounded in 'the
Radical programme'—which, between you & me, I conceive to be outrageously unjust.
[P.S.] Will Ireland be the first & overruling business? The chances of it increase.
P.S. I had nearly forgotten to add my hope that when you speak again you will work well
at some time the question of Fair Trade, and, if you think fit, ask Dilke also to turn his
great abilities that way. This touches bugbear No 2.—and I am asking the best qualified
men to look to it

[Enclosed note]:   The *principle* of disestablt. has not yet been accepted by the English
people. Until there has been that acceptance, unequivocal & decisive, it cannot properly
be entertained in Parlt. I cannot say whether that acceptance will ever come but I feel as
certain as of any thing future the question has no existence for this Parlt.

My opinion of 1865, Desiderata
            1. Then—attention
            2. Now—conviction—political victory—administrative execution
Method—Needless to speak of?
It cannot be that of 'the radical programme'

To LORD R. GROSVENOR, chief whip, 6 November   Add MS 44316, f. 97.
1885.

1. I return Chamberlain: but keep Mr Graham.[2] What can I do except keep my ground
throwing Chamberlainism into the far future, & taking care not to assume the colours
thereof? Also throwing the responsibility of it on Tory democracy.
2. I am preparing as well as I can to deal with Disestablishment—probably next Wednesday. (The PLAN in the Radical programme is I think outrageous, apart from the principle.)
3. Please let some one *tomorrow* refer back to Salisbury's article, written last winter in I

---

[1] H. E. Manning, 'How shall Catholics vote?', *Dublin Review*, xiv. 403 (October 1885); no party
recommended, emphasis on 'Christian education'.
[2] James Graham, liberal organiser in W. Scotland, reported, 4 November, 'Scotland . . . is working
itself into *a fury* against Mr Chamberlain and his propositions'; Add MS 44316, f. 89.

think the National Review in which he gave his estimate of the Tory strength under the new franchise.[1] This is what I want.[2]

7. Sat.

Ch. 8½ A.M. Wrote to Mr J. Bennett—Messrs Brown—Mr A. Murray—Mr N. Travers[3]—Sir J. Lambert l. & B.P.—Mr N. Mackey[4]—Mr T. Thornton—Messrs Watson—Rev. W. Balfour[5]—Mr Mitford—Sir T. Acland BP—Ld Rosebery—Sir W. Phillimore—Ld R. Grosvenor—& minutes. Made a beginning of a paper on Hermes, and read for it.[6] Read Mad D'A: finished IV. The couple are, both, *admirable*. Read Dicey. Worked on a sycamore with WHG.

To LORD ROSEBERY, 7 November 1885.   N.L.S. 10023, f. 110.

It was only a suggestion (rather a cool one, but elections destroy the sense of shame) not an opinion, about the dining. But I have perhaps misled you as to my purpose. I was not thinking about a step towards them but about reconciling them to a step the other way. I have indicated to Rainy that the leaders are in a false position if one side the Border they countenance proceedings which make Disestablishment a test while on the other side of it they dissuade & condemn. And the question is how far I am to go with public declarations in this sense for *Scotland. Can I or can I not go up to the point defined by Mr Stewart?*[7]

I think it best to say on Monday that I will treat disestablishment on Wednesday, as I should not like [to] touch it without such preparation as a survey on the spot may afford.

When we meet we may say a few words on the Irish question as treated at Belfast.

Please to consider the inclosed extract from D. News of 3d—Can we really believe that Bismarck is favourable *in principle* to a Danubian or Balkan Confederation?[8] If it be practicable it would be a magnificent thing for the peace of Europe. So I have always thought since I first heard of the idea: but I have never dared to mention it lest I should draw down hostility upon it. What would you think of letting H. Bismarck see this as a curious bit of newspaper talk, & laying the ground so as to make it easy for him to let out if so disposed. (See also D News correspondence of today).[9]

I understand you are prepared for our arriving man, wife, son, daughter. Of S. Lyttelton I know nothing but he is aware that with Harry I am independent.[10]

I write to Mr Thornton.[11]

---

[1] Salisbury's signed article, 'The value of redistribution: a note on electoral statistics', *National Review*, iv. 145 (October 1884). Gladstone quoted Salisbury's figures on 9 November (*Political speeches, 1885*, 43) to argue that the best the tories could achieve was a minority 'converted into a majority by the aid of the Nationalist vote for Ireland'.

[2] Letter incomplete; no subscription.   [3] Newenham Thomas Travers of Twickenham.

[4] Perhaps the London chemist.

[5] William Balfour, 1821-95; Edinburgh United Presbyterian minister and defender (against Rainy) of establishment.

[6] Part of the papers headed 'Lessons from Homer', marked 'cancelled' in 1886; Add MS 44699, f. 250.

[7] Rosebery's letter of 6 November, Add MS 44288, f. 265, observed: 'there is no imaginable force that can make disestablishment a part of the work of the next parliament, therefore it is not fair to make it a test question'.

[8] *D.N.*, 3 November 1885, 5c, report from an 'eminent Bulgarian's' tour of chancelleries.

[9] Letter from 'Still a Liberal' and correspondents' reports, *D.N.*, 7 November 1885, 5g.

[10] i.e. as to secretary.

[11] (Sir) Thomas Thornton, 1829-1903; Dundee solicitor and liberal agent.

8. 23 S. Trin.

Ch. 11 A.M. (read the Lessons) and 6½ P.M. Wrote to Mr Chamberlain—Mrs Th.—Ld R. Grosvenor—Mrs Birks BP—Elliot Stock[1]—Dr Kinns[2]—Rev. Dr Farsnit[3]—Mr Gliddon—Mr Bryce. Read Waller, Farsnit, & others on Genesis—Bernard Gilpin. SEG preached on the Election: extremely well. Conversation with him on Disestablishment.

To LORD R. GROSVENOR, chief whip, 8 November   Add MS 44316, f. 100.
1885.[4]

To save time, sending you a letter touching Sir W. Macarthur,[5] I send a reply also which please to send on *if it is entirely proper*, I not having enough of the circs. to form a judgment: if not, return or destroy it. He bothered me a great deal about Fiji, but 'public opinion' supported him.
2. I return De Vesci's letter which I have read with care and sympathy. He will have read Hartington's speech with disquiet. For my part I shall enter upon no particulars until *Ireland* has spoken.
3. We are off to Midlothian tomorrow morning. Several Addresses have come to me. Speaking more generally all the accounts brought by Herbert and others are good. I hope yours also. But in Scotland it may be probably necessary to deprecate making Disestablishment a test question, as we have done in England.
4. I am sorry to find that the very narrow and unjust plan of Disestablishment published in the Radical Programme was written by John Morley. It is I fancy the plan of the Liberation Society.

9. M. [Dalmeny]

Off at 8¼. Animated journey to Edinburgh. Delivered at four or five places conversation-speeches to the head or heads who with the reporter were within our carriage. At Edinb. spoke 40 m in Albert Hall [in Shandwick Place] to an audience of very manageable size & excellent temper.[6] Then to Dalmeny amid much enthusiasm. Tel. to Prince of Wales. Read L. Tollemache's Pattison[7]—Willis on the Land Laws.[8] Saw Mr Carmichael—Mr Craufurd.

10. Tu.

Wrote to Hartington, and minutes. Also Telegrams. Saw Ld Ripon (Ireland)—Ld Rosebery—Mr Crawfurd—Mr Menzies[9]—Mr Blake. Read Greville's Journal—Parnellism unmasked[10]—Stubbs on the Land.[11]

---

[1] London publisher.
[2] Samuel Kinns of New York; sent his *Moses and geology* (8th ed. 1885).
[3] Not traced, as is his work.
[4] Holograph.
[5] Letters untraced; Macarthur, the maveric liberal imperialist M.P., was defeated at Newington.
[6] On Ireland; *T.T.*, 10 November 1885, 7d.
[7] L. A. Tollemache, *Recollections of Pattison* (1885).
[8] Perhaps in E. C. Willis, *The law of bankruptcy* (1884).
[9] Probably Robert Stewart Menzies, 1856–89; liberal M.P. E. Perthshire 1885-9.
[10] *Parnellism unmasked. Its finance exposed. By an Irish Nationalist* (1885).
[11] C. W. Stubbs, *The land and its labourers* (2nd ed. 1885).

To LORD HARTINGTON, M.P., 10 November   Chatsworth MSS 340. 1827.
1885.[1]

I have not to excuse, but thank you for, your letter.[2]

Either directly or through Granville, you know all my mind down to a certain date. Latterly I have been considering my general line of action in Scotland. I do not think I have anything to say here which can create difficulty for you. The question in my mind rather is up to *what* point, in general politics, I ought to go in your sense.

I made a beginning yesterday in one of my conversation-speeches, so to call them, on the way; by laying it down that I was particularly bound to prevent if I could the domination of sectional opinion over the body and actions of the party.

I wish to say something about the modern Radicalism. But I must include this that, if it is rampant and ambitious the two most prominent causes of its forwardness have been

1. Tory democracy.

3. [*sic*] The gradual disintegration of the Liberal aristocracy.

On both these subjects my opinions are strong. I think the conduct of the Duke of Bedford and others has been as unjustifiable as it was foolish, especially after what *we* did to save the House of Lords from itself in the business of the franchise.

Nor can I deny that the question of the House of Lords, of the Church, or both, will probably split the Liberal Party. But let it split decently, honourably, and for cause. That it should split now would, so far as I see, be ludicrous.

I am sorry that Chamberlain raises and presses his notion about the compulsory powers for the Local authorities. I should have said, try freedom first. But when it is considered how such a scheme must be tied up with safeguards, and how powerful are the natural checks, I hardly see, and I am not sure that you see, in this proposal *stuff* enough to cause a breach.

I am no partisan in fine of Chamberlainism, but I think that some 'moderate Liberals' have done much to foster it; and that, if we are men of sense, the crisis will not be yet.

With regard to your withdrawal, and my taking office, a very few weeks will in all likelihood supply conditions of judgment, which we do not at this time possess. At present things look as if at first Ireland would dominate the situation.

So far I have been writing in great sympathy with you: but now I touch a point when our lines have not been the same.

You have, I think, courted the hostility of Parnell. Salisbury has carefully avoided doing this, and last night he simply confined himself to two conditions, which you and I both think vital, namely, the unity of the Empire, and an honourable regard to the position of the 'minority', *i.e.* the landlords. You will see in the newspapers what Parnell, *making* for himself an opportunity, is reported to have said about the elections in Ulster now at hand.

You have opened a vista, which appears to terminate in a possible concession to Ireland of full power to manage her own local affairs. But I own my leaning to the opinion that, if that consummation is in any way to be contemplated, action at a stroke will be more honourable, less unsafe, less uneasy, than the jolting process of a series of partial measures.

This is my opinion; but I have no intention, as at present advised, of signifying it. I have all along, in public declarations, avoided offering anything to the Nationalists beyond describing the limiting rule which must govern the question. It is for them to ask: and for

---

[1] In Holland, ii. 91; Morley, iii. 240.

[2] Of 8 November, Add MS 44148, f. 142: his party position 'every day more difficult'; his differences with Chamberlain overwhelming; the 'moderate men in the party' only retainable through Gladstone's 'taking a strong and decided line against the radicals'.

us, as I think, to leave the space so defined as open and unencumbered as possible. I am much struck by the increased breadth of Salisbury's declaration last night: he dropped the 'I do not see how'.[1]

We shall see how these great and difficult matters develop themselves. Meantime be assured that, with a good deal of misgiving as to the future, I shall do what little I can towards enabling all Liberals at present to hold together with credit and good conscience.

11. Wed.

Wrote.... Conversation with Rosebery on the Disestablishment scare. Much rumination, & made notes which in speaking I could not manage to see. Off to Edinb. at 2.30. Back at six. Spoke 70 min. in Free Kirk Hall: a difficult subject.[2] The present agitation does not strengthen in my mind the principle of Establishment. Read Greville—Stubbs.

12. Th.

Wrote to Mr Strickland—Mr Bissell[3]—Mr Casement—Mr G. Lefevre—Mr Simon—and minutes. Read Ann. Register 1819[4]—Greville's Journal—Lotze's Microcosmus.[5] Conversation with Lady Stepney about Alice.[6] Walk by the River Bank. Saw Ld R—Mr Carmichael.

13. Fr.

Wrote to Ld Balfour of Burl.—Sir J. Lubbock—Mr Ashton—Mr Hamilton—Ld Rosebery (Irel)—and minutes. Walk with a party. Conversation with Lady Stepney about Alice. Saw Rosebery on Ireland. Read Greville—Stubbs. Went to Edinb. for the Rosebery dinner. Made a short speech. He spoke with real power.[7]

To LORD ROSEBERY, 13 November 1885.[8]   N.L.S. 10023, f. 112.

You have called my attention[9] to the recent speech of Mr Parnell,[10] in which he expresses a desire that I should frame a plan for giving to Ireland, without prejudice to Imperial unity and interests, the management of her own affairs. The subject is so important that, though we are together, I will put on paper my view of this proposal.

For the moment I assume that such a plan can be framed. Indeed, if I had considered

[1] Salisbury at Mansion House, *D.N.*, 10 November 1885, 2h: within Imperial security, 'all that was possible' should be done.
[2] On disestablishment; *T.T.*, 12 November 1885, 6a. See Simpson, *Life of Rainy*, ii. 39 for an excellent description of Gladstone's handling of the meeting, a blow to Scottish disestablishment.
[3] J. Broad Bissell, liberal candidate in E. Bristol.
[4] *Annual Register* (1819); perhaps for its account of the deb. on Catholic emancipation.
[5] By R. H. Lotze, tr. in 2v. (1885).
[6] See 22 Nov. 77; identity of 'Alice' uncertain; possibly A. de Rothschild, Rosebery's relative; see 1 Aug. 85.
[7] Banquet to Rosebery from the Scottish liberal club; *T.T.*, 14 November 1885, 5e.
[8] In Morley, iii. 239.
[9] i.e. verbally.
[10] Of 10 November; O'Brien, *Parnell*, ii. 108.

this to be hopeless, I should have been guilty of great rashness in speaking of it as a contingency that should be kept in view at the present election.

I will first give reasons which I deem to be of great weight against my producing a scheme; reserving to the close one reason, which would be conclusive in the absence of every other reason.

1. It is not the province of the person leading the party in opposition to frame and produce before the public detailed schemes of such a class.

2. There are reasons of great weight which make it desirable that the party now in power should, if prepared to adopt the principle, and if supported by an adequate proportion of the coming House of Commons, undertake the construction and proposal of the measure.

3. The unfriendly relations between the party of Nationalists and the late Government in the expiring Parliament have of necessity left me, & those with whom I act, in great ignorance of the interior mind of the party, which has in Parliament systematically confined itself to very general declarations.

4. That the principle and basis of an admissible measure have been clearly declared by myself if not by others before the country; more clearly I think than was done in the case of the Irish Disestablishment; and that the particulars of such plans in all cases have been, and probably must be, left to the discretion of the Legislature, acting under the usual checks.

But my final and paramount reason is that the production at this time of a plan by me would not only be injurious, but would destroy all reasonable hope of its adoption.

Such a plan, proposed by the heads of the Liberal Party, is so certain to have the opposition of the Tories *en bloc*, that every computation must be founded on this anticipation.

This opposition, and the appeals with which it will be accompanied, will render the carrying of the measure difficult even by a united Liberal party, hopeless or most difficult should there be serious defection.

Mr Parnell is apprehensive of the opposition of the House of Lords. That idea weighs little with me. I have to think of something nearer, and more formidable.

The idea of constituting a Legislature for Ireland, whenever seriously and responsibly proposed, will cause a mighty heave in the body politic.

It will be as difficult to carry the Liberal party, and the two British nations, in favour of a Legislature for Ireland, as it was easy to carry them in the case of Irish Disestablishment.

I think that it may possibly be done; but only by the full use of a great leverage.

That leverage can only be found in the equitable and mature consideration of what is due to the fixed desire of a nation, clearly and constitutionally expressed. Their prepossessions will not be altogether favourable; and they cannot in this matter be bullied.

I have therefore endeavoured to lay the ground by stating largely the possibility, and the gravity, even the solemnity, of that demand.

I am convinced that this is the only path which can lead to success. With such a weapon we might go hopefully into action. But I well know, from a thousand indications, past and present, that a mere project of mine, launched into the air, would have no *momentum* which could carry it to its aim.

So, in my mind, stands the case.

[P.S.] The *first* essential, as I have said in public, is a sufficient and independent Liberal majority; the second is to keep it together. If these two can be had, there is no fear of the House of Lords. It would not dare: and if it did, would repent quickly, and probably in vain.

14. Sat.

Wrote on Ireland. Wrote to Mr M'Lachlan—Ld Selborne—Herbert J.G.—Mr Williams—Mr Pirie—Mr Anderson—& minutes. Saw The Lord Provost[1]—Ld Rosebery. Read Greville—Lotze—Ann. Reg. 1819.

Bases.[2]

Secret. No. 2.
1. Irish Chamber for Irish affairs.
2. Prorogatives of the Crown and Oath of Allegiance same as for Imperial Parliament.
3. Protection of minority and nominated members.
4. Equitable share of Imperial charges first charge on revenue of Ireland.
5. Schedule A. Imperial subjects reserved.
6. Schedule B. Imperial charges shared.
7. Except as to defence Imperial authority suspended in Ireland.
8. Irish representation in Imperial Houses to remain, for Imperial purposes only. Nov. 14. 85.

Secret. No. 1.   or, more briefly
                          ———

1. Irish Chamber for Irish affairs.
2. Irish representation to remain as now for Imperial affairs.
3. Equitable division of Imperial charges by fixed proportions.
4. Protection of minority.
5. Suspension of Imperial authority for all civil purposes whatsoever. Nov. 14. 85.

Sketch[3]

Secret. No. 3.
Establish an Irish Chamber to deal with all Irish, as distinct from Imperial questions.
To sit for [ ] years.
Subject to the same prerogatives of the Crown, as the Imperial Parliament.
Provisions for securing to minority a proportionate representation.
Provision for Imperial Charges to be made by appointing a due fixed proportion thereof to be the first charge on Irish Consolidated Fund.
Imperial charges to be set out in Schedule: Royalty, The Debt, Army & Navy, the chief.
One third of House to be named in Act: two thirds to be the present representation duplicated: except Dublin University to remain as now, Royal Univ. to have two members.
Nominated members to sit until Parliament otherwise provide, (vacancies to be filled by the Crown?)
Officers of State & civil functionaries in Ireland to cease to be subject to any British authority, except as herein provided, to be suspended in Ireland so long as the conditions of this Act are fulfilled.
Matters of defence remain under Imperial authority as now.
Crown property held for civil purposes to be at the disposal of the Chamber.
Irish representation in both Houses of the Imperial Parliament to remain as now, for Imperial subjects only.

[1] Alexander F. Mitchell.
[2] Holograph memoranda on one sheet, in this order; Add MS 56446, f. 157. In Jenkins, 307.
[3] Holograph, and secretary's copy, at Add MS 56446, f. 162ff. In Jenkins, 307.

If speech or vote be challenged question to be decided by the House or the Speaker thereof.

Schedule of subjects withdrawn as Imperial from the Irish Chamber.

Irish representatives to share in all questions of grievance & ministerial responsibility which touch the reserved subjects only.

Specify parts of Act alterable by Chamber, including particulars of representation, except such as secure proportionate representation of minority.

With regard to all civil establishments whatever it is presumed that Irish Officers of State will be under the sole control of the Chamber and advise the Crown for Irish purposes (as e.g. in Canada Canadian Officers of State).

A seat in the Imperial Parlt. not to disqualify for sitting in the Irish Chamber.

Seat in Irish Chamber not to disqualify for holding office in Great Britain.

Auxiliary forces to be charged on Ireland & only raised by authority of Chamber but when raised to be under controul of the Crown. Nov. 14. 85.

Several limitations like those on the State Governments in America ought to be inserted in any plan.[1]

To H. J. GLADSTONE, M.P., 14 November 1885.   Hawarden MSS.
'Secret'.[2]

There is much to be said in favour of your suggestion: but it is dangerous for me to give out anything, however obvious it may be, which could be carried to the Government that they might outbid it.

It is beyond all doubt that if 1. the sense of Ireland be adequately declared in a certain direction, and if 2. the Liberal party is placed by the Election in a position to take up the question, then there ought to be early communication with those who would be the organs of Irish desire.

You might state your opinion to this effect, and your opinion also that this is my opinion. But remember to do nothing that can indicate a desire on our part to draw them off from communicating with the Government if they are so inclined.

I conceive that the obvious bases of any admissible measure would be 1. Irish Chamber for Irish affairs. 2. Irish representation to remain as now in both Houses but only for Imperial affairs. 3. Equitable division of Imperial charges by fixed proportions. 4. Protection of Minority. 5. Suspension of Imperial authority for all civil purposes whatever.

I send you herewith for perusal & return a letter in which I have given the conclusive reasons against my acting on Mr Parnell's suggestion that I should produce a plan.

It was I think an error on his part to put forward the House of Lords. *If* ever they were to be in a position to act as he suggests, they would put forward his authority, and make much of it.

To LORD SELBORNE, 14 November 1885.   Selborne MS 1869, f. 75.

I have been engaged here, amongst other things, in resisting to the best of my ability, one & the same attempt made both North & South of the Border in opposite directions. The attempt is to govern all Liberal votes at the coming election according as the Candidate is for or against Disestablishment. The principle is the

---

[1] This sentence added by Gladstone on the copy.
[2] Copy; in Hammond, 447.

same, the application different: in Scotland the enemy of Disestablishment is to be proscribed, in England the friend.

In these circumstances, & working as I thought in the common cause, I was perplexed at finding you had subscribed the Grey declaration. It was however, I thought, subject to a possible doubt as to its degree of stringency. But today I read a letter of yours in the Times[1] which states that if you had a vote you would be slow to give (that is, I conceive, you would not give) it to a Disestablisher.

Do I read you wrongly? I hope so. But I also fear that many will read you as I do.

If I read you rightly, can we found a Liberal party on the ground of excluding from Parliament every Liberal who votes for Disestablishment? Can this be done by any one? And if by any one whose hands may be more free, can it be done by us, who have sat in Cabinet with Chamberlain & Dilke, not to mention any other Disestablisher. I am perplexed on the subject of your letter. I think it very likely the Liberal party will come to grief before many years are over, perhaps on this very question: still, we would not hang a man before the day appointed for execution of his sentence.[2]

15. 24 S. Trin.

$10\frac{1}{4}$-2. To St John's Edinb. (H.C.) Wrote to Lady Susan Opdebeck—Mr Sidebottom l.l.[3]—Mr Ackers[4]—Mr Seymour Kay—Mr Sharp—& minutes. Walk with Goschen.[5] Read Lotze—Robinson on Genesis—Stewart on do.[6]

16. M.

Wrote to Mr Mitchell—Mr Wigmore—Mr Jolly—Mr Christie BP—and minutes. Saw Mr Richardson—Ld Rosebery—Mr Campbell. Long walk in this fine park. Finished Greville Vol I—read Stubbs. Large party.

17. Tu.

Wrote to Mr Ackers MP—Mr Bruce Tel. Worked on papers for Speech. 1.40-6.15 to West Calder where I spoke $1\frac{1}{4}$ hour to a capital audience. HNG told Lt Greeleys experience.[7] Read Greville—Stubbs.

18. Wed.

Wrote to Bp Bromby[8]—Ld Hartington—Ed. Scotsman[9]—Mr Sidebottom—Mr S. Smith—Mr Powell—Mr D. Frew—Dean of Wells—Rev. Dr. Hutton—Lord R.

---

[1] Reprinted in Selborne II, ii. 182.

[2] Long reply, 17 November, ibid., ii. 183: Gladstone exaggerated Selborne's position; none the less, 'the national interest ought to be preferred'.

[3] Thomas Harrop Sidebottom, 1826-1908; tory M.P. Stalybridge 1874-80, 1885-1900; Add MS 44493, f. 70; *T.T.*, 21 November 1885, 7e.

[4] B. St.J. Ackers, unsuccessful tory candidate for S. Gloucs.; exchange of letters in *T.T.*, 20 November 1885, 4f.

[5] Goschen was returned as a liberal for E. Edinburgh.

[6] R. H. Lotze, *Microcosmus*, 2v. (1885); W. Robinson, 'The first chapter of the Bible' (1856); D. Stewart, *A concise Hebrew grammar* (1872), with a chapter on Genesis.

[7] Adolphus Washington Greely, U.S. arctic explorer staying at Dalmeny; see *Mary Gladstone*, 367.

[8] Charles Henry Bromby, 1814-1907; bp. of Tasmania.

[9] Charles Alfred Cooper, 1829-1916; liberal (unionist) editor of *The Scotsman* 1876-1906.

Grosvenor l.l. & Tel.—Mrs O'Shea Tel.—Mr Savage[1]—and minutes. Read Greville—Macneill on Irish Parlt.[2] Walk with Rosebery. Dinner party. Conversation with Dr Rainy.

To LORD R. GROSVENOR, chief whip, 18 November   Add MS 44316, f. 110.
1885.[3]

[First letter:]1. I send you herewith a telegram from Mrs O'Shea—my reply is noted on it.
2. Your estimates though reduced will do well enough.[4]
3. All pleased and sanguine here. Disestablishment scare nearly over.
4. Write & say whether you recommend any particular topic—my next speech is on Saturday.
5. It would be very convenient if you could inform me when you write of your probable *direction*.
[P.S.] Correspondence very heavy

[Second letter:] [The telegraph is the worst possible channel for correspondence on these delicate subjects, but][5] I have telegraphed to you to express my interest in Captain O'Shea's Election for the Exchange ward Liverpool. By his personal zeal and his prompt exertions he obtained for the Government in 1882 information as to Mr Parnell's desire and intention to respect the law, which entirely removed all title on the part of the Executive to detain him in confinement and he thereby in my judgment conferred a service on the country, which Englishmen and Irishmen ought alike to recognise. Both as a general supporter of Liberal policy, and on the special ground I have named, I shall have great pleasure in learning that he is widely accepted, and is likely to be triumphantly returned by the electors of the District.
[P.S.] I have written this in the evening for the morning mail: use it precisely as you think proper.[6]

To LORD HARTINGTON, M.P., 18 November 1885.[7]   Chatsworth MSS 340. 1833.

Many thanks for Powerscourt's letters,[8] which are noteworthy signs. I have shown the longer and more important one to Lady Spencer. Have you seen Dickson M.P.'s Liberal Programme for Ireland (now some months old)?[9] It is of use I think as recognising the greatness of the coming epoch or crisis, but of no value as to means of meeting

---

[1] Thomas J. Savage of Kingston-on-Thames; on the Huxley controversy; Hawn P.
[2] J. G. S. Macneill, *The Irish parliament; what it was and what it did* (1885).
[3] Holograph.
[4] Sent to Lyttelton on 17 November, Add MSS 44316, f. 107: England and Wales: 298 liberals, Scotland 57, Ireland 3 = 312, 'giving us 46 as a good working majority over all other sections—but remember that this is only guess-work'; agents confident, but some candidates less so.
[5] Gladstone's brackets; holograph.
[6] Grosvenor, as far as has been found, did not use Gladstone's encomium; O'Shea, though supported by Parnell as one of the exceptions allowed for by the Nationalist manifesto, was narrowly defeated; P. J. Waller, *Democracy and sectarianism* (1981), 59 and F. S. L. Lyons, *C. S. Parnell* (1977), ch. x.
[7] Version in Holland, ii. 94.
[8] One, of 10 November, on Catholic requirements for Irish education, Chatsworth MSS 340. 1830.
[9] T. A. Dickson, 'An Irish policy for a liberal government' (1885).

it. It represents the work of improvement in Ireland as a work only begun, and seems to claim for her the time of the coming Parliament, to the immense detriment, once more, of Great Britain. The difficulties of one decisive measure for Ireland are indeed formidable; but those of another long series of Parliamentary operations seem to be heart-breaking, though I should wish well to any one engaged in the arduous undertaking. As one example, the Education question never can be solved satisfactorily in London. Spencer's plan gave me no hope whatever. The whole question is so complex that I am not surprised at your or any one's shrinking from any particular solution of it, only thankful when any one seems able to cast upon it a ray of hope.

The main questions are, does Irish Nationalism contemplate a fair division of Imperial burdens, and will it agree to just provisions for the protection of the landlords. I do not think that on the other hand sufficient allowance has been made for the *enormous* advantage we derive from the change in the form of the Nationalist demand from Repeal of the Union (which would reinstate a Parliament having *original* authority) to the form of a Bill for a derivative Chamber acting under Imperial authority. The whole basis of the proceeding is hereby changed.

I do not quite see what protection the Protestants of Ulster want, apart from the Land of the four provinces.

Yesterday I had a good meeting at West Calder. I declined Parnell's request for a plan, put in a word for Spencer, and complimented Scottish Liberalism on its avoidance of extremes. I may say something more about Radicalism before you go.

I have no means of judging between you and others who are more sanguine as to the elections. Here there is a great revival of confidence. Hamilton writes very cheerfully. R. Grosvenor has reduced his expectations, but they are still sufficiently high.

I hope that R. Churchill has made proper amends to you.[1] If he has not, it shows a strong *brutal* element within him.

19. *Th.*

Wrote to M.G. .... and minutes. Read Greville—Swift Macneill—Dickson On Ireland?[2] Saw Mr Cooper. Walk with Lady Spencer.

To LORD SELBORNE, 19 November 1885.   Selborne MS 1869, f. 79.

I thank you for your explanation.[3] But I do not see in what material respect I have misinterpreted you. I admit that you allow exceptions. But I think that you lay down a general rule (in the Grey declaration I do not recollect any exceptions). As an hypothetical voter, you put the Church against party, & so putting it you would be slow to recognize the claim of a Disestablisher to your vote. This I understand as meaning that (unless in some exceptional case) you would refuse it.

As far as I know the attempt to use the Church as a 'test question' *in England* has been entirely from the side of the Tories and the Church.[4] In Scotland I have done my best to stop it, with great pain, natural enough, to the Disestablishers.

Doubtless the time may come when the choice will have to be made between the Church & the party, and when many will answer it as you do.

---

[1] Series of election taunts; see W. S. Churchill, *Lord Randolph Churchill*, i. 461ff. (1906).
[2] See to Hartington, previous day.
[3] See 14 Nov. 85n.
[4] Selborne's reply, 21 November, Selborne II, ii. 186: 'my belief ... is *directly the reverse*'.

20. Fr.

Wrote to Ed. Scotsman—Ed. D. News—Mr Ackers—and minutes. Read Greville—Stubbs—Swift Macneill (finished). Conversation with Rosebery: on his letter to Labouchere[1] & on Ireland. Walk with him. Saw Mr T.G. Law.

21. Sat.[2]

Wrote to Mr Bruce—and minutes. Read Greville (finished II)—Stubbs (finished). Worked on materials. 2-7. Expedition to Dalkeith. Spoke 1¼ h. to 3000: with better voice than heretofore. Tea at the Provost's afterwards.

22. Preadvent S.

St Mary's Cathedral in Edinb. with Holy Communion. Carriage business of this kind is very unsatisfactory. Conversation with Mr Goschen.[3] Read Life of Moffatt[4]—Flint on Establishment[5]—Stewart's Genesis—and Tracts.

23. M.

Tel—To Ld R. Grosvenor—10¾-4¾ To the Mercat Cross ceremonial, Address, speeches, Luncheon. The spectacle was very interesting.[6] Read Greville.

24. Tu.

Wrote to Scotts—Ld Selborne—Mr Bumpus[7]—Ld R. Grosvenor—and minutes. Read Greville—Mercat Cross Histories. Worked on papers. 2-5½ to Edinb. Spoke 1¼ h in music hall.[8] Voice not so free as on Saturday. Saw Gen. Elliot[9]—Ld Rosebery.

To LORD SELBORNE, 24 November 1885.   Selborne MS 1869, f. 83.

A hasty line to say this: we appear to have been using the phrase 'Test question' in entirely different senses.[10] As long as I can remember constituencies have differed in colour, and with reference to those differences their leaders have made choice of candidates. This is a totally different proceeding from the present attempt in England to

[1] Labouchere to Rosebery, 19 November, requested Gladstone (in the light of his negotiations with the Irish) to convince the Irish that, if the Lords threw out an Irish 'settlement' bill, he would demand a dissolution; Rosebery replied this day that Gladstone could not speak on such a hypothesis; N.L.S. 10041, ff. 10-16.

[2] National League's manifesto, denouncing the liberal party as 'perfidious, treacherous and incompetent' and calling on Irish voters to vote against it, published this day; T.T., 23 November, 11d (with Parnell's supporting speech).

[3] See to Harcourt, 1 May 86.

[4] J. S. Moffat, *The lives of Robert and Mary Moffat* (1885).

[5] Probably R. Flint, 'The duties of the people of Scotland to the Church of Scotland' (1882).

[6] Account in T.T., 24 November 1885, 12a; cf. 18 Mar. 85n. The cost to Gladstone for the restoration was £450, see Add MS 44493, f. 293.

[7] John Bumpus, London bookseller.

[8] 'the most powerful, passionate, and effective of the present campaign'; T.T., 25 November 1885, 12a.

[9] Alexander James Hardy Elliot; major-general commanding troops in Scotland 1885.

[10] See 19 Nov. 85.

induce every individual Elector to make the matter of the Church a test question for the purpose of his own vote.

I need not say it is a sore thing to me that you should have found yourself impelled by conscience to be the champion (subject to exception) of this sort of test question, after our long connection, and at a time when my chief duty and constant labour is to throw back and to discourage all professions of extreme opinions. But this is regret, not complaint, for I must not complain in any case of conscience, least of all would it be tolerable in a case like yours.

25. *Wed.*

Wrote to Mr M. Francis—Mr M'Corquodale[1]—Mr Druce[2]—Mr De Peryer—Mrs S. Douglas—Mr Willis—Mr N. Travers—Mr R. Lockhart[3]—Mr Liddle[4]—Mr J. Sinclair—Mr T. Blake[5]—Mr J.L. Fould[6]—Mr W. Paterson[7]—Rev. Mr Pickford—and divers telegrams for the Election. Conversation with Ld Rosebery—Mr Cooper—E. Hamilton. Read Greville—(Paterson's) Mercat Cross[8]—Duke of Gordons Narrative of 1689.[9]

26.

Wrote to Musurus Pacha—Mr Goschen—Mr Stibbs—Mrs Montgomery—Mr Monk—Mr Fairbairn—Mr Rhind[10]—Mr Russell—Mr Craigie—Mr Muirhead—Mr Christie—telegrams & minutes. Walk with Rosebery. A second day of indifferent Election news: only Scotland has done *well*. But the English boroughs are now ¾ over. After these, a change is likely. Read Greville's Journals.

To G. J. GOSCHEN, M.P., 26 November 1885.   Add MS 44161, f. 318.

It was my duty while the contest was pending to refrain strictly from the expression of opinion as between Liberal candidates. My reference to you in speech,[11] much resented, was scarcely a deviation from this rule, though probably I should not have made it had not there been remarks made in England which I thought unfair and which I made the subject of private remonstrance. Now that all is over, I write to express my great pleasure in your triumphant return as my old friend and Colleague.

[1] George McCorquodale, Knowles's printer.
[2] Albert Druce, chairman of Mile End Liberal and Radical Assoc.; need for arbitration to resolve split candidacy there; Add MS 44493, f. 115.
[3] Perhaps Robert Lockhart, jnr., of Powark Terrace, Edinburgh.
[4] Thomas Liddle, Edinburgh solicitor.
[5] Thomas Blake, 1825-1901; liberal M.P. Forest of Dean 1885-7.
[6] James L. Foulds, landowner in Corstophine.
[7] William Paterson, Edinburgh solicitor.
[8] The entry in D. Paterson, *Paterson's British Itinerary*, 2v. (1785).
[9] George, 1st duke of Gordon, 'An account of the besieging of . . . Edinburgh' (1689).
[10] Marble bust of Gladstone by John Rhind, d. 1892, exhibited at Royal Scottish Academy 1886, property of the Scottish Liberal Party. See next day.
[11] Reference on 24 November (*Political speeches, 1885*, 129) to liberal candidates opposed at last minute by 'gratuitous invaders', i.e. B. F. C. Costelloe who unsuccessfully opposed Goschen (hardly himself a local figure or an orthodox liberal (he stood as an independent liberal)) in E. Edinburgh.

I am glad also to have had an opportunity of free conversation with you on grave contingencies which may soon come into view.

The aspect of the Elections as far as they have gone, has not been favourable to the most recent forms of advanced Liberalism. But I am bound to say that in my opinion the relative prospect of Toryism in the English Boroughs has been due in the main to the two Bogies of the Church and Fair Trade, and chiefly the last, which is the worst and in every way despicable.

27. Frid.

Sat to Mr Rhind (as in D. St.). Sent a daring Telegram to Sir G.M. Grant.[1] Wrote to Countess Spencer—Ld R. Grosvenor—Mr Brown—Maj. Anstruther— Mr Mackay—Miss Mackenzie—Mr Hughes—Ed. Scotsman[2]—Mr Kettlewell— and telegrams. Drove with R. into Edinburgh to the Polling Places &c. Saw Mr Cowan—Ld Aberdeen—Mr Finlay—Mr Brodie—Mr Van Zant.[3] Finished Greville. Read Chamberlain's Speeches.[4]

To LORD R. GROSVENOR, chief whip, 27 November   Add MS 44316, f. 117.
1885.[5]   1. (Herewith) A from Dr [B. W.] Foster may be worth showing to your Brother & keeping in your Archives. From it you will infer in what sense I had written to him.
2. I shall not answer B unless you advise it.
3. Fair Trade + Parnell + Church + Chamberlain have damaged us a good deal in the Boroughs. I shall be anxious to know your estimate for the Counties. I place the *causae damni* in what I think their order of importance.
4. I have been doing all I can to cure some of the worst difficulties on this side of the Border. But how splendidly old Scotland votes! What *bottom* it shows.
5. We hope to be at Hawarden soon after midnight tomorrow.

28. Sat [Hawarden]

Greeted in the morning with the Midlothian Poll.
G. 76   D32   Majority 46.[6]
Still more moving is the general fidelity of Scotland. Wrote to Ld R. Grosvenor—Mr Ph. Campbell—Mr Patton—Mr Poulson—Rev. P. Beech—Mr Ivory—Mr Omond—Mr Cowan—Mr Strachey—and minutes. Busy morning. Off to Edinb. at 1.45. Speech at Rosebery Club Meeting. Ditto at great Corn Exchange Meeting (R. admirable at both). Then to the Station. Tumultuous

---

[1] Wire supporting Sir George Macpherson-Grant (1839–1907; 3rd bart.; liberal (unionist) M.P. Elgin 1879–86) as the sitting member against C. H. Anderson, independent liberal. Grant just held the seat, the tories second, Anderson third. Ironically, Anderson held the seat for the liberals in 1886 against the unionist Grant.
[2] On an error *re* railway finance; *Political speeches 1885*, 120.
[3] Ferdinand S. Zandt, d. 1892; American friend of Rosebery.
[4] *Speeches of . . . Joseph Chamberlain*, ed. H. W. Lucy (1885).
[5] Holograph. Grosvenor replied, 29 November, Add MS 44316, f. 118, that he returned Foster for the Hawarden archive (not found, but Gladstone's draft letter of support at Add MS 44493, f. 111), that 'B' (a letter from Coffey) was no longer relevant, and that 'I don't see my way to more than a majority over the Tories alone (*sine* Parnellites) of 20!'
[6] Actual result: Gladstone, 7879; C. Dalrymple, 3248; majority, 4631.

journey from 6.5 to 12.30 Hawarden, very rapid. Crowds at the stations: much more disciplined N. than S. of the Border. Some little speeches: chiefly to Reporters. Saw Sir H. James.

29. *Adv. S.*

Ch. 11 AM and H.C. 6½ PM. Wrote to Mr Ingram—Lord R. Grosvenor Tel. l.l.—Mr ... (for Courtenay)—and minutes. Read Blunt on 'R. Catholics'[1]— Latimer's Sermons[2]—Letters from Hell.[3]

30. *M. St Andrew.*

Ch. 8¼ A.M. Wrote Telegrams—to Derbysh. Staffordsh. Denbighsh. Orms- kirk—&c.[4] Also wrote to Père H. Loyson—Professor Leger[5]—Sig. Mazzola—Mr Grant Wilson[6]—Capt. Petrie[7]—Dean of Norwich—Messrs Bickers—St Louis Irishman—Ed. St Louis Republican[8]—Syndics Cambridge Press[9]—Miss N. Waite B.P.[10]—Mr Moss[11]—Mr Peck—Mr Stiller—Mr Wilson—Mr E. Stock—and minutes. Read Gower Papers (began).[12] Lord R. Grosvenor arrived. Attended his Buckley Meeting, & spoke 40 m from the Rostrum: great enthusiasm.[13]

Tues. Dec. One 1885.

Church 8½ A.M. Wrote Telegrams. Also to Ld Hartington—Mr W. Thom- son—Mr Ph. Campbell—Sir A. Cunliffe—Bp of St Andrews—Mr Routledge— Mr Ebsworth—Rev. N. Hall—Ld Rosebery l.l.—Mr Knowles—Mr W. Agnew—Mr Procktor—Mr M'Gregor—Miss Calder—and minutes. We went to poll in evg.[14] Long conversation with R. Grosvenor on men & things. Read the Gower Papers—19th Cent. Articles by Max Müller, and C. Flatten on Leopardi.[15] Also Healy in Nov. Contemp.[16]

---

[1] One of J. H. Blunt's many works on the reformation.
[2] Hugh Latimer, *Sermons*, probably ed. in 2v. (1788).
[3] See 7 Oct. 85.
[4] Supporting candidates.
[5] Very probably Louis Paul Marie Leger, 1843-1923; authority on Austria-Hungary; correspon- dence untraced, but an interesting contact at this moment. See E. Birke, *Frankreich und Ostmittel- europa* (1960), ch. x.
[6] George Grant Wilson of Claverton Street, Pimlico; business untraced.
[7] Probably Capt. Francis W. H. Petrie of S. Kensington (but an Edinburgh name).
[8] Replying to address of support from St Louis Irishmen, on 'systematic co-operation of Irish Nationalists and English Tories ... which has taken from us and won for Toryism between 20 and 30 seats'; *T.T.*, 1 December 1885, 12a.
[9] Not traced in C.U.P. archives; ordering a book?
[10] Nellie Waite of Cheltenham sent her autograph book for signing: 'I hope you will excuse me and not think me rude'; Hawn P.
[11] Samuel Moss, in support of O. Morgan; Add MS 44493, f. 157.
[12] O. Browning, ed., *The despatches of Earl Gower... 1790-1792* (1885).
[13] *T.T.*, 1 December 1885, 9b.   [14] Lord R. Grosvenor fairly easily returned for Flintshire.
[15] *N.C.*, xviii. 900, 978 (December 1885).
[16] T. M. Healy, 'Ulster and Ireland', *C.R.*, xlviii. 723 (November 1885); Ulster was declaring 'against the Union' electorally.

To LORD HARTINGTON, M.P., 1 December 1885.   Chatsworth MSS 340. 1839.

I need not say I rejoice in your election. The seat was certain: the majority is grand—and things now seem to be going pretty well.

But my main purpose is to say a word about Goschen. I rejoice in his election on many grounds. 1. He is a friend, a man of honour, a man of great ability. 2. I think he was not well used by two of our friends—and this I signified to one of them three or four weeks ago. 3. He will help you to maintain a balance of the party.

Have you by chance written to Bright? Would it not be well if you were to thank him for having laboured, though not from Goschen's exact point of view, to maintain that balance.

I have tried to be as good as my word, in severing myself from sections, and setting up the word Liberal without epithet, as my ensign.

One word more. Do you know anything of Forster? Would you like me to write him a letter of congratulation if I can concoct one?[1]

R. Grosvenor is here, & sanguine: though we cannot now hope to *beat* Tories + Nationalists. My four sons & I all go to vote for him today: we hope for a *very* large majority.

I had never fully heard Rosebery before. His power of speaking is great: his activity ceaseless: his influence grows more & more: his future full of interest.

To LORD ROSEBERY, 1 December 1885.   N.L.S. 10023, f. 121.

My 'three to me' looks well, had I only made the bet. We have now two successive days of increment. I shall be surprised if it stops here. The English are holding their ground, while our Scotch and Welsh Reserves come up. We cannot hope to pass Tories + Nationalists; but *possibly* we may be not far short of them.

R. Grosvenor is with us. My sons and I (Rector included) go to vote for him this afternoon together—except that Harry is unfortunately in another polling district. Last night I let out again at Buckley and bid a rapturous audience try to beat the Midlothian majority. They cheered, they roared, for Midlothian: which seems to be becoming what the Romans I think called '*centuria praerogativa*'?[2]

I feel as if some effusion with you would be a *necessity*; of course only
                    When the hurly burly's done[3]
I am delighted with the course which Salisbury seems to be taking in the Balkan Peninsula. Probably he is supported by the Queen, 1. for Battenburgian reasons 2. as against Russia, which she hates. What little I could do to help him, I have done, & will do. He has now got back to his original soundness, as I trust, in matters of the Balkans.

I am just going to write a strong letter for Ramsay.

We hope Lady Rosebery has not suffered from her activity, I ought to say her activities, during the election, and once more, now on paper, record our thanks to you and her for immeasurable kindness.

[P.S.] I am thinking whether I can get up a letter to Forster.

---

[1] Hartington replied, 3 December, Add MS 44148, f. 158, that he would, though the letter would not receive 'any very cordial response'.

[2] The *centuria* with the right to vote first, its decision being publicised before the rest of the voting; Cicero believed its influence on the final outcome was often decisive, an omen of the outcome (Pro Murena 38, pro Plancio 49, de divinatione 1. 103, 2. 83).

[3] *Macbeth*, I i. 3.

2. *Wed.*

Ch. 8½ A.M. Wrote to G.L. Gower now MP.[1]—Messrs Dimsdale[2]—Mr Bryce—
Mr E. Ashley—Sir T. May l.l.—Telegrams, & minutes. Saw Mr Humphreys.
Read Huxley on Réville[3]—& Ld Gower's Dispatches. Harry *so* useful!

To J. BRYCE, M.P., 2 December 1885. *'Private'.*   Bryce MS 10, f. 52.

By way of return for the last part of your interesting letter,[4] let me express the
hearty pleasure with which I see your place in a seat which rests on the firm rock of
Scottish Liberalism, nay on the firmest part of that rock, saving always my dear and
true Midlothian, namely the Aberdeen granite. Long may you hold it.

I follow with lively interest all you say of the Balkan Peninsula. Most thankful I am
to see Salisbury, as far as appears, acting well and worthily in that quarter, and heartily
will I do the little I can do to support him. King Milan has been and is the pest of
Servia. It is a question with me whether to give tongue against him. I would do it at
once were I sure it would not tend somewhat towards complicating the situation.

What a report you bring from Ulster! What a situation, were we in Government! A
fraction of a nation, represented nearly if not quite all through by Tories or by Parnellites, asks us to go to loggerheads, unsupported anywhere, with the nation, and to offer
it County Boards, each board of which would be a several instrument for boxing our
ears. That will not I. Perhaps had we had large and cordial Ulster support, it might
have abridged our freedom more than it would have enlarged our Votes.
[P.S.] Scotland, Scotland, Scotland!

Che sovra gli altri come aquila vola.[5]

3. *Th.*

Ch. 8½ A.M. Wrote to Mr Ph Campbell—Watsons—Earl Selborne—L. Stanley—Ld R. Grosvenor—Mr Cook MP—Dr. Webster B.P.—K. Larios[6]—Rev. Mr
Ward—Mr T. Brett—Rev. Mr Lloyd—Mr Jacks—Reeves & Turner—Mr D.
Gray—Rev. Paul Bush[7]—Mr O. Browning—Telegrams and minutes. Also
between 6 & 7 in consequence of communication from R.G. began & wrote
off an Address to Midlothian, with a view to stirring up supporters in general.
Finished Huxley. Read Gower Dispatches—Dicey Law of the Constitn.[8] Walk
with W. & HNG. Herbert gallantly went off to Denbighshire.[9]

---

[1] George Granville Leveson-Gower, 1858-1951; his private secretary 1880-5 (often referred to as
'Mr Leveson'); liberal M.P. N.W. Staffs. 1885-6, Stoke 1890-5.

[2] London bankers.

[3] T. H. Huxley in *N.C.*, xxviii. 849 (December 1885); on Réville and Gladstone.

[4] Of 1 December, from Dublin, Bryce MS 11, f. 92; on his visit to the Balkans with A. Evans,
and on the election in Ulster: 'the Parnellite vote is being generally given to the Tory candidates
as against Liberals. . . . All the Ulster Liberals whose opinion I have enquired are not only strenuous supporters of the Union, but opposed to any Central Council for Ireland . . . the furthest point
they are willing we should go is the establishment of County Boards.'

[5] Dante, *Inferno*, iv. 96: 'Which flies above the others like an eagle'. Bryce replied on 11 December, Bryce MS 11, f. 99, sending a memorandum on Ireland.

[6] Wrote from London on Greek affairs.

[7] Rector of Duloe; on the Irish church; exchange in *T.T.*, 10 December 1885, 12b.

[8] See 2 Nov. 85.

[9] Campaigning successfully for G. O. Morgan.

To the Electors of Midlothian, 3 December 1885. *The Scotsman*, 4 December 1885, 5a.

Gentlemen,—I now address to you, in writing, the final and fervent thanks which I endeavoured to speak on Saturday in the Corn Exchange of Edinburgh; and I do it under circumstances which show that in giving me 7879 votes against the 3248 recorded by my opponent, you were anticipating and expressing the verdict of the country on the Liberal and Tory claims respectively.

The Tory and disguised Tory journals of London have to-day awakened from their dream of victory to an extorted acknowledgment of wide and spreading disaster. They never, indeed, had much to rest on, but they had something. On Saturday the gross Liberal majority, as far as known, was only two. The returns were then in the main those of English boroughs, and they showed—Liberal seats, 108; Tory seats, 117. This Tory majority of nine, such as it was, could not have existed, even with the powerful aids it had derived from the commands of Mr Parnell, the panic of the Church, and the imposture of Fair-trade, had not folly been pushed in five constituencies having Liberal majorities to the point of handing over the seats to Tory minorities, by dividing the Liberal force under two candidates, instead of concentrating it for one. Thus, even at that point, the returns ought to have been—Liberals, 113; Tories, 112.

Since that time, as I told various audiences on Saturday, that it could hardly fail to be, not only have the Scottish and Welsh reserves begun to fall, together with the long-headed constituencies of Yorkshire and the North, but Tories have also found, to their surprise, that there is life in the rural labourer, and that he is manifesting that life by voting for those whose unwearying labour gave him the franchise, in despite of most persistent Tory opposition. Not the outworks of Toryism only, but the citadels have been carried, and Wilts, Dorset and Somerset, as well as Lincoln, Norfolk, and Suffolk, have rebelled on behalf of liberty and justice, and of that reasonable and manly progress which has done so much for the country during the last half-century, and will do so much for it while supported, as at this moment, by the nation during the next.

So the upshot thus far is, that the majority, which on Saturday was two, is now forty, and that, as it has increased from day to day, it may, and I believe will, increase yet more. Naturally enough, there is dismay among the Tories. They ask themselves how this can be stopped. They know that but for the imperative orders issued on their behalf by Mr Parnell and his friends, whom they were never tired of denouncing as disloyal men, the Liberal majority of forty would at this moment have been near a hundred.

But the Parnell alliance, the Church panic, the visionary promises of Fair-Trade have all spent their force in the towns. The counties evidently do not care for them. The farmers know that they do not owe one good law to the Tories. The working men know what they owe to the Tory party, who maintained the Corn Laws, stinted their food, kept down their wages, and resisted the enfranchisement of which they are now making such good use. Again, I ask, how can the Tories stop the contagion of liberty and justice which is running through the land, and touching successively all points of the compass? Will they publish some manifesto? What new alliance can they form? What new panic can they raise? Is the armoury empty at last? Is their invention quite exhausted? One thing Lord Salisbury cannot do. He cannot attempt a junction with those who are called Moderate Liberals, for he has very lately told us that two things only are real—Radicalism and Toryism, and that everything between them is a mockery, delusion, and snare. Will he, then, scare the country with some picture of a violent Liberalism? His efforts will be in vain. He cannot get rid of the testimony of a long experience. That experience has shown that it is the collective Liberalism, the general sense of Liberals, which has guided the counsels of the party from the days of the first Reform Bill until now, and so it will be still. The result is before the constituencies in the reforms of fifty years, and the last, not least, is the work of the county franchise. It is not the Church, nor the nobles, nor the landlords, nor the rich men, nor the idle and luxurious men, that have done the work of the last few days. It was said of Inkerman that it was emphatically the soldiers' battle. I say of this election in the counties that it is emphatically, and in a fuller sense than ever it was heretofore, the people's election.

You may say, gentlemen, that this letter is more an English one than a Scottish one. But the Union between the countries which we love is at this moment being more and more closely drawn by the manful deeds of the population of the English counties, and there is not one of the 7879 Mid-Lothian Liberals of Friday last that will not, for the consummation of their work, bid them heartily God-speed.

4. Fr.

Ch. 8½ AM. Wrote to Dr. Professor Reusch l. & BP—Ld Granville—Ld Spencer—D. of Argyll—Mr Knowles—Dean of Rochester l. & BP—Ed. Christian Million[1]—Ridgways—Ld Rosebery—and minutes. Woodcraft with W. & HNG. Read Gower Dispatches—Dougal Anglosaxon Alliance[2]—Liberal Evang. Clergyman on Disestablishment (excellent)[3]—Leeds on American Constitn.[4]

To LORD SPENCER, 4 December 1885.   Althorp MSS K8.

Many thanks for your letter.[5] I did not, as Lady Spencer will have told you feel justified in asking you, *because*, while I have Ireland on the brain, I do not feel sure that I have anything to say that is worth your hearing: but I am delighted that you should come; if of your own motion you do not grudge the trouble. We propose Wednesday. In a blind way, but progressively more & more, I feel that Ireland will be *the* big subject, as a matter to which the country, or the London public, so long remained insensible: and it is possible there may be very stiff resolutions to be taken. I look to the government, if they continue to be the Government, to assume the initiative; and, if it be adequate & safe, my mind is to support them heartily, as I have tried to do on the Afghan frontier and in the Balkans. But if not, and if good can be done I may be bound to take my turn at such a supreme moment.

My wife writes to Lady Spencer. I am delighted at your brother's health, & his return.

[P.S.] I wish Lady S. could have *heard* the Music Hall audience in Edinburgh when I mentioned your name.

5. Sat.

Wrote to Sir J. Carmichael[6]—Mad. Novikoff—Sir R. Owen[7]—Mr J. Wilson—Rev. Mr Savile—Mr E. Griffith—Sir D. Salomons—Mr Wilberforce—Mrs Th—

[1] In *Christian Million*, 10 December, 115: Knowles will not permit a cheap ed. for working men of 'Creation and worship'.

[2] J. R. Dougall, 'An Anglo-Saxon alliance', *C.R.*, xlviii. 693 (November 1885).

[3] Perhaps 'Church defence ... by the author of "The Banner"' (1885).

[4] J. W. Leeds, *A history of the United States of America* (1877).

[5] Of 2 December, on the elections, and ready to come to Hawarden; *Spencer*, ii. 80.

[6] On the election; *T.T.*, 8 December 1885, 10d.

[7] For his article on Huxley; see 6 Aug. 61.

and minutes. Read (Vol) Gower Dispatches—Beau Brummell (new Ed.)[1]—Milnes on Homer (1829).[2] Woodcraft with sons. Much conversation with Granville who came.

6. 2 S Adv.

Ch. 11 AM and H.C.—$3\frac{1}{4}$ P.M. for the Baptism of the dear little grandchild—$7\frac{1}{4}$ PM. for S.s excellent sermon. Further conversations with Granville: we are already in promising harmony. Read Row on Immortality[3]—3 excellent Sermons on Disestablishment. Consulted Portlock Lyell Buckland on Geology and Scripture.[4] Wrote to Ld R. Grosvenor—Ld Spencer—Mr Godley.

To LORD R. GROSVENOR, chief whip, 6 December   Add MS 44316, f. 138.
1885.[5]

It will now probably become most important to learn the actual relations of the Nationalists to the Govt. The Liberal party may waive the question of confidence on the Address if they are faced by two parties acting together which make up or exceed half the House. But if the Irish & the Govt. part company, how is it possible to allow some 250 men, against 420, or even against 330, to hold the Executive power & direct the Legislative business of the Session?

If it becomes requisite to be assured of the position of the Irish party, probably this could best be got at by some public explanation from me—but here is matter for reflection, & there is time. In any event, the principle that the Ministers must have the confidence of the House of Commons is now the root principle of our institutions (for every case except where an immediate appeal to the people is contemplated)—& this would therefore be the question of questions on the day of the Queen's Speech, *anterior* in order even to the question of Ireland.

7. M.

Ch. $8\frac{1}{2}$ A.M. Wrote to J. Dumaresq[6]—Sir T. Acland—Ld Rosebery Tel—Sir R. Owen—Ld Spencer Tel—Mr Stuart Gray—Duke of Argyll—Mr Dobson—Archdn Palmer l. & B.P—Ld W. Compton—Reeves & Turner—Mr J.W. Macdonald—and minutes. Read Gower Volume—Owen's Palaeontology[7]—Douglas on the Earth[8]—Burke. Woodcraft with sons.

To Archdeacon E. PALMER, 7 December 1885.   Bodley MS Eng. Lett. d. 433, f. 48.

In p. 22 of a paper which I send you by this post, I have referred to Evolution, i.e. moral and historical evolution as known to Christian letters. (I ought to have put in

---

[1] W. Jesse, *The life of George Brummell*, 2v. (revised ed. 1886); supplied opening quotation for his article, 8 Dec. 85.

[2] R. M. Milnes, 'The influence of Homer' (1829).

[3] C. A. Row, *Historical evidence of the resurrection* (1873).

[4] Used in his article; see 8 Dec. 85.

[5] Holograph copy, headed 'Extract. W.E.G. to Ld R.G./D.6.85'.

[6] Perhaps John Saumarez Dumaresq, 1873-1922; distant relative; later a rear-admiral.

[7] See 7 Dec. 61.

[8] Probably J. Douglas, *An introductory geography* (1867).

Butler.) In the Nineteenth Century for January [*sc.* December][1] Professor Huxley p. 854 reproaches me for not including among teachers of evolution (I do not know whether he means *physical* or *moral*, but I think physical) 'the founders of Greek philosophy to say nothing of Indian sages.' I need not trouble you on Indian sages. But I should be very much obliged if you could tell me whether as far as you know the founders of Greek philosophy have taught evolution in *either* of its forms, especially physical?

I asked Dean Scott, who says he knows nothing of it, but advised me to apply to you. I am sure you will forgive my appeal.

8. *Tu.*

Ch. 8½ A.M. Wrote to Dr Carpenter—Sir R. Green Price—Miss Poore—Mr Macgeagh—Mr Dougal—Mr P. Campbell—Macbean—A.R. Gladstone—Tel., and minutes. Wrote on Huxley's Article.[2] Read books for MS and Burke on American Taxation.[3] Woodcraft with WHG. Rosebery came, also Spencer: long and interesting conversations.[4]

9. *Wed.*

Ch. 8½ A.M. Wrote to Mr P. Campbell l.l.—Watson & Smith—Ld Granville—Rivingtons—Rev. Mr Holden—Mrs Bolton—Mr Best—Mr Knowles—Mr Godley—Mr E. Best—& Tel. Wrote partially on H.s article. Forenoon conversation with S. & R. Evg also with S.—R. went. Read Burke on America—Gower Vol. The Elgin Emissary's reports are *most* able. Walk with Spencer & drive.

To LORD GRANVILLE, 9 December 1885.   Add MS 56446, f. 168.

Pray shed around my, and our, heartiest and warmest congratulations on the much desired victory of E. Cavendish.

You have I think acted very prudently in not returning here. It would have been violently canvassed.

Your report is as favourable as could be expected.

I think my conversations with Rosebery and Spencer have also been satisfactory.

What I expect is a healthful slow fermentation in many minds, working towards the final product.

It is a case of between the devil and the deep sea.

But our position is a bed of roses compared with that of the Government.[5]

I have a remarkable letter from Lord Hampden. He recognises the fact that Ireland has come to the front and thinks the hands of the Government should be forced on this subject.

[1] See 2 Dec. 85.
[2] 'Proem to Genesis: a plea for a fair trial', *N.C.*, xix. 1 (January 1886); *Later gleanings*, 40; a reply to Huxley and Max Müller's defences of Réville.
[3] See 16 Jan. 38.
[4] Rosebery's diary this day, Dalmeny MSS: 'I advised Mr G to call meeting of party. This he always hates. His view is 1. If Tories can come to arrangement with Parnell & produce complete scheme, they shd be supported. 2. If not, no time shd be lost in opposing them. 3. A vote of want of confidence without reference to Ireland wd be the best form. 4. But if it must have reference to Ireland it shd be moved by Liberal leaders & not Parnell. He leans at present to proceeding by resolution.'
[5] Printed to here in Morley, iii. 261 and Ramm II, ii. 414.

Have you considered at all what distribution of offices in the event of a Liberal Government, should be made?

Rosebery has gone, Spencer goes, Wolverton & Acland come tomorrow.

10. Th.

Ch. 8½ A.M. Wrote to Duke of Argyll—Rev. Aubrey Moore[1]—Scotts—Ld R. Grosvenor—Dr Adsetts—Reeves & Turner—J. Ashman[2]—Durie & Co—Mr T. Watson—Mr T.T. Moore—Mr R. Watkin—& minutes. Spencer went: Wolverton & Sir T. Acland came. My sons & I cut two trees. Startling conversation of the deepest interest with C. on another.[3] Wrote on Huxley. Read Burke.

Toryism in other days had two legs to stand upon: a sound leg, and a lame leg. Its sound leg was Reverence: its lame leg was Class-interest. Reverence it has almost forgotten. It no longer leans upon that leg. It leans now upon its lame leg, the leg of Class interest, more and more: and to mend the matter, as it stumps along, it calls out progress.

Does Lady Herbert remember the *only* bitter and contemptuous thing, that Sidney Herbert ever said in Parliament? and what, and who, drew it from him?[4] WEG D.10.85.[5]

To LORD R. GROSVENOR, chief whip, 10 December 1885.   Add MS 44316, f. 144.

I inclose three letters bearing upon election matters, to which I cannot safely reply without receiving your advice.

Your telegrams have been most interesting: and the whole result now that we have in substance reached it is extraordinary.

What do you say to Dilke's speeches—D. News of today.[6] Is it merely the usual individualism and indiscretion of the advanced twins?—or is it a purposed indication that the Irish are in no case to expect their help in Parliament after having made so light of it in Ireland.

Pray come here whenever you see reason.

[P.S.] Your majority in this County did not fully come up to my ideas.[7]

11. Frid.

Ch. 8½ A.M. Wrote to Duke of Argyll—Sir H. Acland—Mr Campbell—Ld Rosebery Tel.—Mr Godley—Rivingtons—Mr Knowles—Monsig. Dillon[8]—Mr

[1] Aubrey Lackington Moore, 1848–90; tutor at Keble, Oxford; involved in Palmer republication plans (see 21 Mar. 81).

[2] John Ashman, Durham miner and liberal; sent verses on the election; Hawn P.

[3] 'Drew marriage' added in pencil; engagement of Mary Gladstone to Harry Drew.

[4] Probably Herbert's remark in 1846, prompted by Disraeli, that the agriculturalists were 'whining for help'; see Blake, 187. Involvement of Lady Herbert at this time, untraced.

[5] Add MS 44770, f. 4.

[6] See Dilke in *T.T.*, 10 December 1885, 8d: advanced liberals should support 'the present government in their local government proposals' in the next parliament.

[7] Grosvenor replied, 11 December, Add MS 44316, f. 146: 'you have rightly guessed the *two* reasons for Dilke's speech. I am told that both Chamberlain & Dilke will place every obstacle in the way of a Government (Liberal) being formed until *after* Dilke's trial is over in Feby. I never would have believed that there were 3000 Tories in Flintshire. . . .'

[8] Thomas Dillon of St. Mary's, Bayswater.

Rathbone—R. Lyttelton—Rev. Mr Lea[1]—Lady Aberdeen—Dr Charteris. Walk with Acland & conversation with Wolverton. With C. on dearest M.s matter. Wrote very little on Huxley. Hunted up & down in Phillips's manual for the Birds, and other matter. Read Burke on America.

To Dr. H. W. ACLAND, 11 December 1885.   Acland MS d. 68, f. 74.

Your brother who (I am glad to say) is here thinks you may help me in a difficulty which I will describe.

In a paper to which Huxley has replied I too hastily assumed there was a general acceptance of the fourfold succession of fishes, birds, beasts and men—in a rough general way—as rightly placed by the author of Genesis. Huxley substantially admits that fishes are first and man last but transfers my 2 and 3.

My classification is I think fully or rather substantially warranted by Owen's Table of Succession in his Palaeontology p. 5 1861[2] where he places Birds traced by footprint below the mammals and Reptiles, very low in his menzoic tables. I have been in correspondence with him and have asked him whether he adheres to his Table but have not yet got an answer. He has referred me to Phillips, republished by Ethridge and Seeley.[3] In their I. 464 I find a *reference* to the birds of the secondary rocks but in a delightful little diagram of the Seven Ages (II. 5) I find fish, reptiles, Mammals, Man, but no notice of birds whatsoever.

In fact I have been able to discover nothing as yet either to confirm Owen's Birds by footprints (beyond the I. 464) or to cancel it. If it be confirmed I do not see that it is wrong to place the succession, in a rough and general way, as I have placed it in my paper pp. 11, 12 sent by this post.

Can you help me to further knowledge either in Phillips or elsewhere.

P.S. I think I can deal with the question sufficiently if the Birds by footprints hold their ground. The account in Genesis need not I think be held bound to notice the Amphibia which precede these Footprint Birds.[4]

12. Sat.

Ch. 8½ A.M. & H.C. Wrote to Mr Jenkinson[5]—Sir Thos Acland—Mrs O'Shea—Hon. H. Elliot[6]—Mr Thos Lea—Ld Granville—Sir R. Owen—Mr Horner Tel.—Mr Hewett—Rev. Mr Mountfield[7]—and minutes. Worked on reply to Huxley. Much conversation with A.[8] & W.: also with W. before he went. Woodcraft with my sons. Read Dicey. Phillips's manual.

---

[1] Thomas Lea of Kidderminster, on difficulty of incorporating catholic voters; Hawn P.

[2] R. Owen, *Palaeontology, or a systematic summary of extinct animals and their geological relations* (2nd ed. 1861).

[3] J. Phillips, *Manual of geology*, ed. R. Ethridge and H. G. Seeley, 2v. (1885).

[4] Acland replied, 13 December, Add MS 44091, f. 141, on the 'cosmology of Genesis', not intended as a scientific record; future scientific developments will put Huxley out of date; proofs of Prestwich on geology sent.

[5] See 28 Nov. 82; as head of Irish C.I.D. had written supporting home rule; Gladstone circulated his letter; see Add MS 44493, f. 212 and Hammond, 435.

[6] Hugh F. H. Elliot, 1848–1932; liberal (unionist) M.P. N. Ayrshire 1885–92.

[7] Perhaps D. W. Mountfield, recently curate in Wavertree.

[8] For Acland's notes, see Appendix I.

Secret. 1. Irish question ought to be handled with delay

2. and if possible by Tories with aid of Nationalists

3. As they are half the House of Commons this would *warrant* the adoption of a waiting policy by the Liberals.

4. The basis ought to be a. perfect political equality of Ireland with England & Scotland b. Equitable, not illiberal, partition of Imperial charges c. Protection for the Irish minority d. management of Irish affairs, legislative & administrative, by Irish authority.

5. But *if* Tories & Nationalists part company, what then? WEG D.12.85.[1]

To Mrs. O'SHEA, 12 December 1885. '*Private &*   Add MS 44269, f. 241.
Confidential'.[2]

1. I am glad to hear that Mr Parnell is about to see 'Lord C' (Carnarvon as I read it). I have the strongest opinion that he ought if he can to arrange with the Government, for the plain reason that the Tories will fight hard against any plan proceeding from the Liberals: all or most of the Liberals will give fair play & even more to a plan proceeding from the Tories.

2. I am of opinion and all my public words and acts have shown & will show that as matter of public interest this subject is great, as matter of public honour is overwhelming, for all concerned in it.

3. No plan can go forth as mine or as approved by me for the plain reason that in my opinion no such plan can properly proceed from any *British* source but one, viz. the Government of the day. Rely upon it the issue will show that no resource can be dispensed with, & certainly not the *authority* which waits upon the Executive power.

4. If you ask me whether I think a plan based on the paper you sent me can be adopted, I must ask what *is* its basis? Is it

(a) to deal not merely with all Ireland but with Ireland as a whole

(b) to place Irishmen on a level of full political equality with Englishmen & Scotchmen

(c) to make a fair not illiberal partition of *Imperial* charges

(d) to make an equitable provision for protecting the minority

(e) to give Ireland by Statute legislative and administrative power over Irish as apart from Imperial affairs.[3]

13. 3 S. Adv.

Ch. 11 A.M. and 6½ P.M. Wrote to Duke of Argyll—Lady Aberdeen—Ld Rosebery—Ld Tennyson. Walk with Acland & much conversation. Saw Mr

[1] Holograph, Add MS 44770, f. 15; H. J. Gladstone's copy at Add MS 46044, f. 74.

[2] In Hammond, 451. Mrs O'Shea wrote on 10 December, Add MS 44269, f. 237, again asking Gladstone's reactions to the 'Scheme', whether it 'is at all possible' and informing him of a meeting between Parnell and Carnarvon 'in a day or two'.

[3] Mrs O'Shea replied, 15 December, ibid., f. 243: 'In reply to query A. also B.C.D. and E. I am authorised to reply in the affirmative', and enclosed a letter from Parnell to Mrs O'Shea, 14 December, copy at ibid., f. 247 and in O'Shea, *Parnell*, ii. 26, stating 'the rough sketch which I sent you some weeks back appeared then and still appears to me the smallest proposal which would be likely to find favour in Ireland, if brought forward by an English Minister, but it is not one which I could undertake to suggest publicly myself, though if it were enacted, I would work in Ireland to have it accepted bona fide as a final settlement, and I believe would prove to be one'.

MacColl.[1] Read Gilpin's Life finished—Maconochie on Disestabl[ishment][2]—Apology for Jarret[3]—Count Tolstoy's Xt's Xty.[4]

To LORD ROSEBERY, 13 December 1885.   N.L.S. 10023, f. 134.

1. I inclose copy of your letter.[5]

2. I did not mean to urge you to see L. but remembered you were that way inclined.

3. I am in sympathy with your letter. The only thing that strikes me as a little awkward for you if disclosed is your argument that P. would be compelled to apply to us.

4. But I believe you are quite right in thinking he has a time allowed him for legal action, and T. P. O. [Connor] quite wrong in saying *they* can afford to wait indefinitely: though I also believe they have a good deal of money.

5. I agree most strongly that I must remain obstinately silent as to my plans. My lines are these.

Question most urgent.

Can only be dealt with by the Government of the day

Most desirable it should be dealt with by this Govt.

P. should come to an understanding with them

I not being the government will not produce a plan.

If P. and the Government cannot agree, that opens a new situation.

6. New lines of correspondence open upon me, and reason is given me to believe that very important *permanent* officers believe Home Rule is necessary.[6]

7. Dilke's speech[7] is a pretty exhibition! On the whole I am minded to ignore it.

I do not mean to be sat upon by D. or by D & C, if other things call on me to act.

8. It is more than probable, should that new situation come, that your suggestion of a meeting will have to be acted on.

I think P. is at present busy with the Government.

[P.S.] I think it may be best to ignore Dilke (No 7)

14. M.[8]

Ch. 8½ AM. Wrote to Rivingtons—Mr Heneage—Lord Cork—Miss Saunders—Mr Campbell. Saw Mr MacColl—Sir Thos Acland—H.J.G.—Ly Brownlow & Ly Cowper, who came to luncheon & went about the Park. Worked on Reply to Huxley. Read Burke. Finished the very interesting Gower Volume.

15. Tu.

Went to the beautiful morning service at Eaton. Saw the Duke—the Duchess —Lady M. Alford: and A. Balfour to whom I said what he will probably repeat

---

[1] For this visit—he saw Salisbury late on 14 Dec.—see *MacColl*, 118ff. and *G.P.*, 313.

[2] Perhaps untraced pamphlet by James Maconechy, vicar of Paddington.

[3] Josephine E. Butler, *Apology for* [*Rebecca*] *Jarrett* (1885); the prostitute and agent in the 'maiden tribute' case.

[4] Count L. V. Tolstoy, *Christ's Christianity* (1885); his apologia.

[5] Of 12 December, Add MS 44288, f. 279, on a talk with Labouchere: 'He had a letter from Herbert which contained the bases on which Herbert believed you would be willing to legislate'; Rosebery 'personally averse to negociation with Parnell at this time'.

[6] i.e. Jenkinson, see 12 Dec. 85; Spencer told Gladstone on 22 December (*Spencer*, ii. 88) of Sir R. Hamilton's home rule mem. of 21 October 1885.   [7] See to Grosvenor, 10 Dec. 85.

[8] This day H. J. Gladstone went to London 'to give the party the essential information'; *After Thirty Years*, 311.

in London.[1] Wrote to Ld Hartington—D. of Westminster—Ed. Daily News[2]—Mr Childers. Worked on Reply to Huxley. Walked with H.N.G. Read Burke—Phillips on Succession of Life[3]—Kinns Mosaic Geology.[4]

To LORD HARTINGTON, M.P., 15 December 1885.   Chatsworth MSS 340. 1850.
'*Most Private*'.

I think you ought to see two direct communications which I have received, the first of them very unexpected, from Jenkinson:[5] & I should be very glad if you would send them on, under like seal of secrecy, to Granville, & ask him to forward them to Spencer on their way back to me. You will gather from the second the character of my reply.

So far as I can learn, Salisbury & Carnarvon are rather with Randolph,[6] but are afraid of their colleagues & their party.

It seems not doubtful that the urgency & bigness of the Irish question are opening to men's minds from day to day.

I am glad to learn that the Cabinet remain where they are though I hardly understand the plan of asking a vote of confidence. Are we to vote it in order that they *may* introduce a measure of Home Rule—or in order that they may *not*?

16. Wed

Ch. 8½ A.M. A day of anxious & very important correspondence. Wrote to Mr Mundella—Mrs OShea—Mr A. Balfour[7]—Mr Campbell—Mrs Bennett—Ld Hartington Tel.—Lady Phillimore.—Sir H. Acland—Mr Best—Mr E.Hamilton—& minutes. Matters of today required meditation. After dealing with the knottiest point, I resumed Huxley. We felled a good ash. Read Burke—Dicey. Suspended the Balfour letter. Saw S.E.G. on M[ary].

To Dr. H. W. ACLAND, 16 December 1885.   Acland MS d. 68, f. 70.

I thank you for your admirable letter—for the interesting Volume of Phillips, which I suppose is too old to bring into line—and for the very valuable proof of Prof. Prestwich. *May I quote it?* or at least *the talk with the long tongues of comparative life?* Judging from this and from the Seeley-Etheridge-Phillips, Huxley has not been very cautious in what he says of the juniority of man? But I shall take care not to put myself in opposition to him, especially if without a *buffer*. I should like to send you my proof. What I want is to make a Butlerian argument upon a general and probable correspondence.

All of us young and old were delighted with your Brother. Long may he flourish a true model of the English gentleman.[8]
[P.S.] We shall long for a further improvement at Keble.

---

[1] See 16, 20 Dec. 85.
[2] Perhaps information on movements; see *D.N.*, 16 December 1885, 5f.
[3] J. Phillips, *Life on earth* (1860).
[4] See 8 Nov. 85.
[5] Supporting home rule; see 12 Dec. 85n. Hartington sent them on, commenting that if these were the terms 'it is useless to think of stopping short of separation'; Add MS 44148, f. 164.
[6] Thought to be canvassing some sort of home rule.
[7] Suspended until 20 Dec. 85.
[8] Acland replied, 17 December, MS Acland d. 68, f. 70, having got Prestwich's permission to quote, and supply, references to Phillips.

To E. W. HAMILTON, 16 December 1885.   Add MS 48607A, f. 132.

Not sooner than 1881, not later than 1883, rather probably in 1882, Home Rule came up in the House of Commons and I spoke in the sense of wanting to know what it meant, & of enlarged freedom for Ireland—Plunkett took me sharply to task, and as his speeches were rare they would afford the best clue.[1] I want at the same time to get the pith of what he (or any other at the same time) said, and the words of what I said. Could you in any way help me in this.

If I remember right I was pulled up by the Queen and had to stand to my point.[2]

How the fermentation is going on.

To Mrs. O'SHEA, 16 December 1885.[3]   Add MS 44269, f. 249.

I have your letter of yesterday;[4] and as, with any views of the Irish question, I do not wish to be responsible for any loss of time that can properly be avoided, I reply at once. Any letters now passing between us are highly confidential, I would almost say sacred. At the same time, I shall not write a word without being prepared to stand by the consequence, should it at any time become public. Reading the able & comprehensive letter which you enclose *together* with your reply to my alphabetic inquiry, I remark as follows.

Communications *from* Mr Parnell & his friends I have always desired, & for years I have publicly expressed my inability to pronounce upon Home Rule until it was explained to me. In this matter great progress has now been made.

Communication *with* Mr Parnell by the proper persons, as the chosen organ of five sixths of the lawfully chosen Irish members has now become not only warrantable but (as I think) imperative. The question remains who are the proper persons.

They are in my view, long ago stated publicly, the Government of the day. First because only a Government can handle this matter. Secondly because a Tory Government with the aid it would receive from Liberals, might most certainly, safely and quickly settle it.

Mr Parnell's letter interprets with accuracy, & with moderation, my speeches in Scotland. It also states justly, as I think, the paramount claim of the question to immediate settlement—though I intend to avoid particulars, I will not scruple to say that in my judgment the point of *urgency* can hardly be overstated: that this matter lies in a region alone & beyond that of Parliamentary procedure, as well as that of party, personal, & sectional interests & difficulties: & that my acts & words have been, & will be, governed entirely by the consideration of what is best for the 'cause' by which I mean the settlement.

I do not know that my opinions on this great matter are unripe: but my position is very different from that of Mr Parnell. He acts on behalf of Ireland: I have to act [not?] for Ireland inclusively, but for the State. (Perhaps I should rather say *think*, or, *speak*). He has behind him a party of limited numbers for whom he is plenipotentiary fully authorised. I have a large party behind me, whose minds are only by degrees opening, from day to day I think, to the bigness & the bearings of the question, and among them there may be what the Scotch call 'division courses'.

I must consider my duties to the Government on the one side, to Ireland as represented by him on the other. With him, I can find no fault, if thinking it his duty to

---

[1] i.e. the deb. on Smyth's amndt. on 9 Feb. 82; summary sent by Hamilton on 18 December, Add MS 44191, f. 41.

[2] Exchange of letters in *L.Q.V.*, 2d series, iii. 259–62; copies sent by Hamilton, ibid.

[3] In Hammond, 451.

[4] See 12 Dec. 85n.

obtain the best terms he can, he tries to find out the terms one party will give, carry them to the other, & not decide upon them till he has compared so to speak the final terms of both.

Such a process could not be kept secret or disavowed. When before the world, it would damage a Tory proposal, it wd. ruin a Liberal proposal, if not as to the final issue yet as to all through which that final issue was to be reached [*sic*].

Supposing the time had come when the question had passed legitimately into the hands of the Liberals, I should apprehend failure chiefly from one of two causes. 1. If it could be said that the matter had been settled by negotiation with Mr Parnell before the Tories had given their reply. 2. If the state of Ireland as to peace, or as to contracts, were visibly worse than when Lord Spencer left it.

I should do an ill service to Mr Parnell were I at this moment so to speak or act as to minister to any disintegration of the forces behind me, or to increase in any way the tremendous difficulties we should have to encounter, were we, the Liberals, called upon to act.

I will now bring together the threads of my letter.

Holding that the Irish party ought at once to ascertain the intentions of Ministers, I ask myself in what can I give legitimate help for this purpose. I might make it known to the Government that if they will bring in an honourable & also an adequate measure, they shall have, with a fair reservation of opinion upon details, all the support I can give them. I should proceed in the same spirit as that in which I have already endeavoured to proceed with respect to Afghanistan & the Balkan Peninsula. Secondly, if I am asked to go beyond my public declarations, & to give my express concurrence to the basis of a plan, my present impression is that this could not be done safely except through some fresh public declaration. This, which would be no small matter, I might undertake carefully to weigh: but I must be first assured that the Government have had a fair opportunity given them.

There is much weighty matter in the latter portion of your inclosure[1] on which it would at this moment be premature to touch.

[P.S.] I am not in communn with Mr L. Your inclosures are returned but I have copies.[2]

17. Th.

Ch. 8½ A.M. Wrote to Ld Hartington—Duke of Argyll—Mr Knowles—Messrs Robn & N.—Ld R. Grosvenor—Telegrams to Press Assn., C. News & other quarters on the Irish rumours about me.[3] Worked much on MS. Woodcraft with Harry. Read Burke—Mark Rutherford[4]—Courtenay's Articles on I.[5]

---

[1] On proposed meeting with Carnarvon, now not 'for a week or two as I [Parnell] wish to know how the other side is disposed first'; Add MS 44269, f. 248.

[2] This P.S. added in holograph on secretary's copy. Mrs O'Shea replied next day, ibid., f. 254: 'I believe I am justified in saying that Mr Parnell feels that any communication with the present Government would be useless ... they cannot settle it.'

[3] i.e. 'the Hawarden Kite'; see Appendix I. Gladstone wired: 'The statement is not an accurate representation of my views, but is, I presume, a speculation upon them. It is not published with my knowledge or authority, nor is any other beyond my own public declarations'; *D.N.*, 18 December 1885, 3a. See also Jenkins, 263–5 and M. R. D. Foot, 'The Hawarden kite', *University of Leeds Review*, xxix. 79 (1986/7).

[4] W. H. White, *Mark Rutherford's deliverance* (1885).

[5] Sent by Courtenay; perhaps his two articles of 1880 in the *International*; see G. P. Gooch, *L. H. Courtney* (1920), 236–9.

To LORD HARTINGTON, M.P., 17 December 1885.[1]   Chatsworth MSS 340. 1853.

The whole stream of public excitement is now turned upon me, and I am pestered with incessant telegrams which there is no defence against but either suicide or Parnell's method of self-concealment.

The truth is I have more or less of opinions and ideas, but no intentions or negotiations.

In these ideas and opinions there is I think little that I have not conveyed in public declarations: in principle, nothing. I will try to lay them before you.

I consider that Ireland has now spoken; and that an effort ought to be made *by the Government* without delay to meet her demands for the management by an Irish legislative body of Irish as distinct from Imperial affairs.

Only a government can do it and a Tory Government can do it more easily and safely than any other.

There is first a postulate—that the state of Ireland shall be such as to warrant it.

The conditions of an admissible plan I think are

1. Union of the Empire and due supremacy of Parliament.

2. Protection for the minority—a difficult matter, on which I have talked much with Spencer, certain points however remaining to be considered.

3. Fair allocation of Imperial charges.

4. A statutory basis seems to me better and safer than the revival of Grattan's Parliament, but I wish to hear much more upon this; as the minds of men are still in so crude a state on the whole subject.

5. Neither as opinions nor as intentions have I to any one alive promulgated those ideas as decided on by me.

6. As to intentions, I am determined to have none at present—to leave space to the Government—I should wish to encourage them if I properly could—above all on no account to say or do anything which would enable the Nationalists to establish rival biddings between us.

If this storm of rumours continues to rage, it may be necessary for me to write some new letter to my constituents, but I am desirous to do nothing, simply leaving the field open for the Government, until time makes it necessary to decide.

Of our late colleagues I have had most communication with Granville, Spencer, Rosebery. Would you kindly send this on to Granville.

I think you will find it in conformity with my public declarations though some blanks are filled up. I have in truth thought it my duty without in the least committing myself or any one else to think through the subject as well as I could, being equally convinced of its urgency and its bigness.

If H. and N. are with you pray show them this letter, which is a very hasty one, for I am so battered with telegrams that I hardly know whether I stand on my head or my heels, and am sure to commit some *bêtise*.

With regard to the letter I sent you, my opinion is that there is a Parnell party and a separation or civil war party, and that the question which is to have the upper hand will have to be decided in a limited time.

My earnest recommendation to everybody is not to commit himself. Upon this rule, under whatever pressure, I shall act as long as I can. There shall be no private negotiation carried on by me but the time may come when I shall be obliged to speak publicly. Meantime I hope you will keep in free and full communication with old colleagues. Pray put questions if this letter seems ambiguous.

[P.S.] Pray remember I am at all times ready for personal communication here should you think it desirable.

[1] In Holland, ii. 99.

18. Fr.

Ch. 8½ A.M. Wrote to Mr Courteny l. & tel.—Mr Chamberlain—P. Campbell—
E. Hamilton—A.R. Waller—Mr Sheldon—Ld Granville—Mr Knowles—Mr
Stead—Mr Crossley—Mr O'Shea[1]—and minutes. Saw S.E.G. respecting Archd.
Denison. Saw HNG—HJG. Felled a tree with W.H.G. Finished MS & dis-
patched it to Mr Knowles.[2] Read Burke. What a magazine of wisdom he is,
on Ireland & America! Read Mark Rutherford.

To J. CHAMBERLAIN, M.P., 18 December 1885.   Chamberlain MSS 5/34/46.
'Secret'.[3]

I thank you very much for your references to me in your speech last night.
In this really serious crisis, we must all make efforts to work together; and I gladly
recognize your effort.
Moreover, reading as well as writing hastily, I think we are very much in accord.
Both reflection, and information, lead me to think that time is very precious, and
that the hour glass has begun to run for a ⟨final⟩ definitive issue.
But I am certainly and strongly of opinion that only a Government can act, that
especially *this* Government should act, and that we should now be helping and encouraging them to act, as far as we legitimately can.
In reply to a proposal of the Central News to send me an interviewer I have this
morning telegraphed to London—'From my public declarations at Edinburgh *with
respect to the Government*, you will easily see I have no communication to make.'
Be *very incredulous* as to any statements about my views & opinions. Rest assured I
have done & said *nothing* which in any way points to negotiation or separate action.
The time may come, but I hope it will not. At present I think most men, but I do not
include you, are in too great a hurry to make up their minds. Much may happen before
(say) January 12. The first thing of all is to know *what will the Govt. do*. I hope they have
been in communication with Parnellites, and I hope with Parnell.

To W. T. STEAD, editor of the *Pall Mall Gazette*,   Add MS 44303, f. 364.
18 December 1885.

If conscience and conviction shall bring the P.M.G. & myself upon the same lines at
a critical moment, I am very glad.[4] I look to the Government for action. If such action
requires negociation, I hope they will not shrink from it. As for myself I think it is my
duty, at the present moment, to eschew both; but to think, & think & think.
Except what I have publicly spoken and written, all ideas ascribed to me are in truth
other people's opinions of my opinions: as the colours of the rainbow are in us, not in
it.

[1] No copy found; the names of Stead, Crossley and O'Shea are written with a 'ditto' mark
under 'Mr Knowles'; but a link with the male O'Shea at this moment seems unlikely.
[2] See 8 Dec. 85.
[3] In Garvin, ii. 142; Chamberlain's reply next day, ibid., anticipated 'tremendous defeat' and
working class hostility on a dissolution on the question; see also Chamberlain, *Political memoir*,
170.
[4] Stead (from Holloway gaol) offered the *P.M.G.*'s support for home rule but opposed an imperial veto only used on the Irish ministry's advice as 'not home rule but separation'. See F.
Whyte, *W. T. Stead*, i. 222 (1925) and Add MS 44303, f. 361.

You are right in thinking I should disown the *veto* imputed to me.
[P.S.] Professor Dicey's recent work on the Law of the Constitution is important with respect to the question of the *Veto*. Mr Frederic[1] has kindly written to me. I do not like to multiply lines of communication. Please to thank him & say his article has my best attention.

19. Sat.

Ch. 8½ AM. Also 11½–2¾ went to Chester for the Dean's funeral.[2] Most solemn & seemly. Saw D. of Westr—Ld Tollemache—Canon Blomfield—and others— Mrs Jacobson. Wrote to Ld Hartington—Sir T. Acland—Mrs O'Shea—Mr Th. Rogers—Ld Spencer—Robn & Nichn—Watsons—Duke of Argyll—Dr Kinns— Press Assn & C. News tel. (important). Arranging letters, after the late pressure & confusion. Read Burke—finished III—Mark Rutherford.

If I should at any time have any plan or intention to announce on the question of Irish Government it will be done publicly on my responsibility and not by anonymous irresponsible declaration. Political friends assured that I remember my obligations to them may safely understand that I am bound to none of the ideas announced in my name. After saying this, I hold myself excused from replying in the present state of facts to any further inquiries, rumours, or allegations.[3]

To LORD HARTINGTON, M.P., 19 December 1885.   Chatsworth MSS 340. 1857.

I thank you for stating your difficulty; but I do not concur in the statement.[4] I think 1. that I have not made quite the statement you ascribe to me; 2. that you have yourself gone further in statement than I have.

I am not *aware* of having said except privately to you the Govt. ought to try to 'meet the Irish demand'. But more than a month ago I said in Edinburgh they ought to endeavour to settle the Irish question. I thought I was then expressing a general opinion: in your letter is the first adverse notice of it I have had. I certainly did & do think they ought after what has happened to make an attempt to settle the whole question of the future Government of Ireland. But I am not aware of having added since that time to any public committals.

Now you *if* I remember right have gone a great deal further, have expressed a readiness to reconstruct the administrative system in Ireland: & have indicated a gradual adoption of measures ending in Home Rule or something of the kind. Do not suppose I say this by way of blame.

My telegram on the Standard rumour was confined I think to answering the exact questions put to me. But finding the matter had grown big I framed this morning, of course before your letter, a much broader one stating, which is the fact, that I am not bound to any of the opinions imputed to me.

[1] Possibly Frederic Harrison, occasional contributor; proof of *P.M.G.* article is at Add MS 44303, 363.
[2] J. S. Howson.
[3] Holograph dated 19 December 1885, Add MS 44493, f. 240; released to press; *D̃.N.*, 21 December 1885, 6c.
[4] 'My chief difficulty is this;—how to reconcile the advice which you give that we should not commit ourselves, with the position which has been created by the rumours of which you complain'; it is now known you think 'an effort should be made by the Government to meet the Irish demand'; Add MS 44148, f. 177.

Now considering that I have thought people astonishingly blind to the approach of a gigantic question, & have thought it our absolute duty to try to prepare them for it, I think I have laboured hard to avoid committing anyone, & have succeeded as far as was practicable.

On the other hand it is certainly true that for at least *fourteen* years I have been proclaiming the doctrine that, subject to the unity of the Empire & needful supremacy of Parliament, the desires of Ireland for self-Government in local affairs, once well ascertained, should be favourably considered.

Moreover if you will turn to the debate for the Address in 1882 I think you will find (though I have not the speech before me *in extenso*) that you then expressed yourself in similar terms—a most important declaration.[1]

To Mrs. O'SHEA, 19 December 1885. '*Private and*   Add MS 44269, f. 256.
Confidential'.[2]

1. I accept absolutely the explanation as to the purpose for which Mr P. desires some development of the ideas I have often publicly expressed.
2. But refer to the two things, either of which I said would probably be fatal.
3. Let me too refer to facts public and patent. Up to this moment the Nationalists are the ostensible allies of the Government and opponents of the Liberals. By their means, the Government have gained and we have lost a majority in the towns. Under these circumstances as there is irritation to soothe, as well as prejudice to overcome, most of all there is novelty and strangeness to convert into familiar observation and reflection.
3. I think duty to the Govt. (as & while such), duty to my own party, and duty to the purpose in view, combine to require that I should hold my ground: should cherish the hope that the Govt. will act; and that Mr Parnell as the organ of what is now undeniably the Irish party should learn from them whether they will bring in a measure or proposition to deal with & settle the whole question of the future government of Ireland.
4. Again I write at once, for as my suggestion would take some little time, I am desirous to lose none that I can save. Should I on reflection at all incline to modify what I have said, I will write in a couple of days.
   [P.S.] I think I have not explained myself sufficiently under (2). My fear is that to open myself on this subject before the Govt. have answered or had full opportunity of answering, would probably be fatal to any attempt to carry with me the Liberal party. I *retain* your enclosure.

To LORD SPENCER, 19 December 1885.   Althorp MSS K8.

I am truly sorry you should be troubled on my account. I write in much haste, about to set out for the Dean of Chester's funeral.

The question to you I think impudent. Your answer is different from Granville's; *both* be assured I have not budged from the ground described by me in our conversations. Nothing less likely than that I should hereafter do so without your knowledge.

Irish question urgent, big, not to be paltered with.

Our duty to think about it,

---

[1] 'Securing for every part of the United Kingdom ... as much selfcontrol and management of their own affairs as can be conferred upon them' but opposed to an 'independent' parliament in Dublin; Hartington in *H* 266. 1056 (17 Feb. 1882).
[2] In Hammond, 454.

But to have no plan or instruction, as matters now stand.

Only the Government can deal with it.

I look to them. Parnell should do the same.

I might add to these scraps that I would gladly to the best of my power support them. While, as you know, thinking over the rudiments of a plan, I adhere to my public declaration at Edinburgh that I can supply none, and wait (how long may be a question) to hear what the Government have to say.

Amidst a tumult of communications, I may get confused, but I believe this will hold water.[1]

Two things more. 1. If you have Hansard, pray turn to the long debate on the Address in 1882, & read especially Plunkett, Gibson, Labouchere, Chaplin, HARTINGTON, & me.[2] 2. I presume [?] the difficult subject of protection for the minority—and incline to think an *interval* measure as to land purchase, by way of sample, might be made contemporaneous.[3]

20. *4 S. Adv.*

Ch 11 AM & 6½ P.M. S.s sermon nothing less than admirable. Wrote to Ld Hartington—Duke of Argyll—Mr Balfour MP—Sir H. Acland—& minutes. Read Mark Rutherford II—Count Tolstoy[4]—Asa Gray's remarkable Lectures[5] —Overton Church life.[6]

To A. J. BALFOUR, president of the local government   Add MS 49692, f. 7.
board, 20 December 1885. '*Private*'.[7]

On reflection I think that what I said to you in our conversation at Eaton[8] may have amounted to the conveyance of a hope that the Government would take a strong and early decision on the Irish question. For I spoke of the stir in men's minds, & of the urgency of the matter, to both of which every day's post brings me new testimony.

This being so, I wish, under the very peculiar circumstances of the case, to go a step further and say that I think it will be a public calamity if this great subject should fall into the lines of party conflict.

I feel sure the question can only be dealt with by a Government, & I desire specially on grounds of public policy that it should be dealt with by the *present* Government. If therefore they bring in a proposal for settling the whole question of the future Government of Ireland, my desire will be, reserving of course necessary freedom, to treat it in the same spirit in which I have endeavoured to proceed with respect to Afghanistan & with respect to the Balkan peninsula. You are at liberty if you think it desirable to mention this to Lord Salisbury. But for a great pressure on me, I should have sent this letter sooner. I am writing however for myself and without consultation.

---

[1] Press reports consequent on the 'kite'; Spencer had wired that no scheme of home rule had received his approval; *Spencer*, ii. 86.

[2] Thus far mostly in *Spencer*, ii. 87.

[3] See to Hamilton, 16 Dec. 85.

[4] See 13 Dec. 85.

[5] A. Gray, *Natural science and religion* (1880).

[6] J. H. Overton, *Life in the English church, 1660–1714* (1885).

[7] Printed in *After Thirty Years*, 396; Balfour replied equivocally on 22 December, unable as yet to consult Salisbury; ibid., 397. See 3 July 86.

[8] See 15 Dec. 85.

To LORD HARTINGTON, M.P., 20 December 1885.[1]   Chatsworth MSS 340. 1858.

I kept mine of yesterday back as there was no post.

On Tuesday I had a conversation with Balfour at Eaton which, in conformity with my public statements I think conveyed informally a hope that they would act. As the matter is so serious, and as its becoming a party question would be a great national calamity I have written to him to say without committing others that, if they can make a proposal for the purpose of settling definitively the question of Irish Government, I shall wish, with proper reserves, to treat it in the spirit in which I have treated Afghanistan and the Balkan peninsula.

I think the situation has been made *for* us by the election of 85 Irish members. Next to this, by the uncontradicted statements as to the opinions of several and those most important members of the Cabinet.

If Parnell gets a negative from them, and thereupon splits, the question of Confidence appears to rise.

We ought soon to be informed on what day they mean to proceed to business.

21. M. St Th.

Ch. 8½ A.M. Wrote to Mr Knowles—Mr Childers BP—Mr Rimblett—Mr Macknight—Sir W. Macarthur—C. Anderson—F.A. Channing—Ed. Berksh. Bell[2]—Mr Montaguire—Mr Croxden Powell—Lady Muir[3]—Mr Rathbone MP—Rev. Mr Pearson—Mr Simpson—Rev. Mr M. Brown—Mr Howland—W. North—Rev. Mr Bamber—Rev. Mr Thomas—J.B. Smith—Mr Davis—Mr Watson—Mr Rawson—Mr Dobbs—D. Lewis—H. West—Mr Purvis—& minutes. Corrected some proof. Lord R.G. came & went: Three hours conversation friendly but with difference. Read Dicey—Mark Rutherford.

22. Tu.

Ch. 8½ A.M. Wrote to Sir H. Acland l & BP—Mr B. Quaritch—Mrs O'Shea—Mr G. Prentice—Mr Knowles—Ld Granville—Mr Forster—Rev. D.T. Gladstone—Scotts—Duke of Argyll tel.—and minutes. Corrected my proofs, with a light heart, in consequence of favourable communications. Woodcraft with Willy. Sorted letters for an hour. Read Solomon's Mines[4]—Abp Walsh v. Lord Meath.[5]

To LORD GRANVILLE, 22 December 1885.   Add MS 56446, f. 196.

In the midst of these troubles I look to you as a great feud-composer, and your note just received is just what I should have hoped and expected.

Hartington has been I think in a state of morbid sensibility which will not let him rest, nor measure the position & the circumstances in which he stands.

He wrote to me on Saturday announcing that he was going up to see Goschen, but as I thought inviting a letter from me which I wrote and it was with no small surprise that I read him yesterday in the Times.

[1] In Holland, ii. 103.
[2] Published illustrated profiles; ceased publication soon after this letter.
[3] Probably the wife of Sir W. Muir, principal of Edinburgh university.
[4] H. Rider Haggard, *King Solomon's mines* (1885).
[5] W. J. Walsh, 'Reply to the Earl of Meath's attack upon the priests and people of the county of Wicklow' (1885).

However, I repeated yesterday to R. Grosvenor all that I have said to you about what seems to me the plain duty of the *party* in the event of a severance between Nationalists and Tories. Meantime I care not who knows my anxiety to prevent that severance, and for that reason among others to avoid all communications of ideas and intentions which could tend to bring it about.[1]

On this ground, I have taken lately into[?] consideration the only substantive step which I have made for a good while. Meeting A. Balfour accidentally at Eaton, I have written to him, for his Uncle's information, my desire (without committing others) to give the Government such aid as I properly can in the event of their preparing a proposal to deal with the whole subject of Irish Govt.

The report seems to have had strength, as well as credibility, that Ashbourne drew a plan: and, as they say, the plan lately published in the Dublin Express. R.G. tells me he is *all but* cut in Dublin; eyed askance. Carnarvon is said to be for inquiry.

[P.S.] I liked Spencer's answer (next to yours) to that impertinent Central News.[2]

To Mrs. O'SHEA, 22 December 1885. '*Private and*   Add MS 44269, f. 258.
confidential'.

I write again but it is in confirmation of what I have before written. The Nationalists are in the face of the world in practical alliance with the Tories. Any communication of views from me to them would be certainly regarded as the offer by me of a bribe to detach them from the Tories. It is therefore impossible. The first step for me is to know, & that the world should also know, whether that alliance continues or not. This involves the course of procedure, to which I have already pointed. One thing I may add. Some talk of a Committee. A fishing Committee I should regard as a subterfuge perhaps even as a fraud. But a Committee to which a responsible Govt. undertakes to submit a policy or plan, ought not perhaps at this stage to be excluded from consideration, so great are the possibilities of fearful miscarriage, so high the obligation to put a ban upon no idea that has an element of hope. If the Govt. had in view a method of this kind, I should myself be disposed at any rate to think if it could be made workable.

I will also add that I *have taken* steps to make known to them my personal disposition to give what aid I can should they take up the question.

23. *Wed.*

Ch. 8½ A.M. Wrote to Ld Hartington, & copy—Mr MacColl—Mr Balfour—Ld Spencer—W.L. Gladstone—P. Campbell—E. Hamilton—Duke of Argyll—Herr L. Reich[3]—G. Prentice—V. Scully[4]—E. Swift—J. Jones—W. Hilson[5]—Sir C. Duffy—J. Day—and minutes. Wrote Mema on Irish question. Read Solomon's Mines—Dicey Law of Constitn—Macdonnell on Home Rule.[6] Felled a Sp. Chestnut with W.

[1] Version to here in Morley iii. 268 and Ramm II, ii. 418; Morley thus omitted the section on the negotiation with Balfour.

[2] See Ramm II, ii. 416.

[3] Probably Lucian Reich of Karlsruhe, author.

[4] Thomas Vincent Scully of Hyde Park; probably s. of the M.P.

[5] William Hilson, autograph collector in Jedburgh.

[6] Perhaps R. M'Donnell, *Irish nationality in 1870*, 2nd ed. with notes on the 'Home rule movement' (1870).

I. *Separation*. It is much debated whether the Irish people are in favour of separation. I lean to the opinion that they are not. After all we must not presume them to be political madmen.

But their opinion on separation is not the main question. The main question is, what is the opinion of England and Scotland? That I do not suppose any one doubts. Nor will any one doubt their power to give effect to that opinion. In a question of separation, they would tow Ireland behind them, as a great ship tows a little boat. But Ireland will not ask them.

Ireland had a Parliament for centuries, under no restraint from *English* law. It was only restrained for one half century: and then in 1800 absorbed.

For myself I regard a proposal to separate Ireland exactly as if it were a proposal to separate Devonshire and Cornwall.

II. *Police*. It is forgotten by many, that the minimum now offered to Ireland is County Government on the British basis. This both involves and *maximises* the whole difficulty as to Police. The Police will be placed under the Municipalities and the Counties.

If a measure of Home Rule can be adjusted, the transference, of the County Police especially, could not take place at the first moment, for the two measures could not be contemporaneous.

Moreover, in the Parnell plan for a Central Board, there was included a provision for the separate representation of property in the County Boards. Such a provision might I conceive be put into a County Board Bill if it lay under the wing of a greater measure. But in a Be-all and end-all County Boards Bill it is very hard to see how it could find a place. (In any case the Police, now an army, would be broken up into forty or fifty bodies, under separate authorities.[)] These bodies would be little likely to surrender their power to a central authority in Dublin. A great (and I hope beneficial) change would be sure to take place in the character of the Police.

On our side we should I think be bound to provide that they should not suffer in their personal interests by this change. This would cost money; which ought to be regarded as among the necessary conditions of the settlement.

III. *The Landlords*. Ample scope is secured for the consideration of this question by the comprehensiveness of the phrase which I think has thus far been used: 'protection for the minority'.

The topic is vital, and it has many branches, actual or possible. 1. The Veto. 2. A nominated element, temporary or otherwise. 3. Reservation of Legislation on contracts, after the manner of the State Governments in the U.S. 4. Representation of minorities, in the Irish constituencies. 5. Separate representation of property in County Boards. And perhaps others; including 6. Land Purchase. I am aware of no mode in which this could be effected wholesale or so as to make the State a principal. But there might be a provisional continuance, possibly, of such effects as have been already made, & in the policy might be included a plan or prospect of larger dealings with & through the new local[1] Legislature.

There is however something most grave in the idea of bringing about a wholesale emigration of the resident proprietors and depriving society of those who should be its natural heads and leaders.   WEG Dec. 23. 85.[2]

---

[1] Could read 'loyal'.
[2] Holograph; Add MS 44312, f. 229; the 'offhand' comments sent to Spencer this day.

To A. J. BALFOUR, president of the local government   Add MS 49692, f. 11.
board, 23 December 1885. '*Private*'.[1]

I thank you for your note; and, taking its spirit into view, I think I ought to complete my former communication by assuring you that, while expressing a desire that the Government should act, I am not myself acting. Time is precious, and is of the essence of the case. But, wishing them to have a fair opportunity of taking their decision, I have felt that *so long* as I entertained the hope connected with that wish (and how long that will be of course I cannot say), I should entirely decline all communication of my own views beyond the circle of private confidence, and only allow to be freely known my great anxiety that the Government should decide and act in this great matter.

To E. W. HAMILTON, 23 December 1885.   Add MS 48607A, f. 133.

I am grateful though my silence may seem otherwise. I had not an idea of the trouble you would take about the 1882 Debate: but it is interesting and important.[2] I have almost a mind to write to Shaw and ask for the date of the speech in which he declared his Leadership and his view of Home Rule.[3] I then followed him in complimentary and encouraging terms.

A sad pity that his reputation is now tainted,[4] as it appears.

I am doing all I can to get the Government to the point, and this is *all* that I am doing. I adhere exactly to the answer I gave in Edinburgh to Mr Parnell, and look to them.

I do not doubt that they are seriously divided.

If they will not act, there may be consequences.

[P.S.] It may very possibly become right to act upon your idea as to publishing.[5] A happy Christmas to you.

To LORD HARTINGTON, M.P., 23 December 1885.[6]   Chatsworth MSS 340. 1869.

I think I had better pass by your published letter.[7] In this big business, which is likely to dwarf every other, my duty and desire are to look for points of agreement, actual or possible, and not of difference.

As to these, notwithstanding all that has occurred, I by no means despair.

IF the Government refuse to act, and split off from their Nationalist supporters, that will bring a grave responsibility upon the Liberals, anterior to and apart from the Irish question.

You will probably have seen R. Grosvenor, and both he, and Granville at Chatsworth, will probably have spoken to you on this matter.

---

[1] Printed in *After Thirty Years*, 397; Balfour acknowledged this letter on 28 December and wrote on 4 January that he had shown 'yr last letter' to Salisbury who expressed a sense of its 'courtesy and conciliating spirit' but felt 'it suggests a communication of the views of the government which at this stage would no doubt be at variance with usage'; ibid., 398. See 3 July 86.

[2] See 16 Dec. 85.

[3] See 14 Mar. 86.

[4] Bankrupted by the failure of the Munster bank.

[5] Hamilton, 19 December, Add MS 44191, f. 56, sent extracts of Gladstone's Aberdeen speech on Ireland, 26 September 1871, proposing an edition (never done) of 'your public declarations on the subject'.

[6] In Holland, ii. 104.

[7] On home rule; *P.M.G.*, 21 December 1885, 8.

To LORD SPENCER, 23 December 1885.   Althorp MSS K8.

I thank you for your very interesting inclosures, most of all for your letter.

The spirit in which you approach the great and difficult question of Irish Government is the only spirit which gives any hope of a tolerable issue. Absolute renunciation of prejudices, calm and searching reflection, abhorrence of all passion and exaggeration, a fair, not illiberal, estimate of humanity: these are among the indispensable conditions of progress in such a case. To which I will add for the moment great reserve.

I inclose some offhand comments on main points raised by your and by Hamilton's letters.[1]

I heartily wish we could exchange ideas and information orally from day to day.

One step in advance I have taken by two letters to Mr. A. Balfour, which I inclose, and which I hope and think you will approve. Please to return them.

The relations of the Government to the Nationalists ought to be cleared up between this time and the meeting. This only they can do.[2]

I also enclose a letter from MacColl to Herbert: no I find it is to me.[3] I had spoken freely to him: but was quite unaware that he was going to see Salisbury. I shall take care that he makes it clear that he had no authority, and carried no message, from me, and that his account was his opinion of my opinions and intentions.[4] The account of Salisbury himself is very interesting. A happy Christmas.

24. Th.

Ch. 8½ A.M. Wrote to Mr P. Campbell Tel.—Mrs O'Shea—Mr Whitaker—D. of Argyll—Paymr General—Messrs Watson—Mr G. Brook—Mr Jas Wilson—Mr MacCarthy—and minutes. We are now old & young a good Xmas party. Woodcraft with sons. Worked on books. Read Solomon's Mines—Dicey Law of the Constitn.

To Mrs. O'SHEA, 24 December 1885.[5] *'Private & confidential'*.   Add MS 44269, f. 266.

From the terms of your letter yesterday,[6] I think you wrote it with mine of the 22d before you. But it seems to me as if I had failed to make my position intelligible. Had I been in a majority, it, and my course, would have been different. I have made another effort in the memorandum within. Observe I do not know what the Govt. will do, or what the Irish party will do. These are the two essential factors. The time is short.

1. My wish & hope still are that Ministers should propose some adequate & honourable plan for settling the question of Irish Govt., and that the Nationalists should continue in amicable relations with them for that purpose. My desire would be to use every effort to promote such a plan. This course would be best for Irish & for Imperial interests. If it is adopted, I see my way.

2. I have no title to ask the Administration, whether they will adopt it. Mr Parnell has such a title. He has already made one arrangement with the Administration, on the basis

---

[1] Sir R. Hamilton's letter to Spencer favouring home rule without land purchase; see *Spencer*, ii. 88-9, Hammond, 435.

[2] Thus far in *Spencer*, ii. 89, with Spencer's letter of 22 December.

[3] MacColl's impression of Salisbury's Irish views; *MacColl*, 122.

[4] See MacColl to Salisbury, 24 December; *MacColl*, 124.

[5] In Hammond, 460.

[6] Add MS 44269, f. 260; the nationalist/tory alliance has been faithfully carried out but 'goes no further'.

of 'no coercion' exchanged against the Irish Vote, which has worked satisfactorily to both parties. There was an alliance, so to call it, during pleasure. This alliance has not been dissolved. In the eye & estimation, therefore, of the world, it *exists* for every practical purpose.
3. The slightest communication of plans or intentions from me to Mr Parnell would be ineffaceably stamped with the character of a bribe given to obtain the dissolution of the Alliance.
4. Foreseeing these embarrassments, I used every effort to obtain a clear majority at the Election: and failed.
5. I am therefore at present a man in chains. Will Ministers bring in a measure such as described? If 'Aye' I see my way. If No: that I presume puts an end to all relations of confidence between Nationalists & Tories. If that is done, I have then upon me, as is evident, the responsibilities of the *Leader of a Majority*. But what if neither Aye or No can be had— will the Nationalists then continue their support, & thus relieve me from responsibility, or withdraw their support, & thus change essentially my position.

Nothing but a public or published dissolution of a relation of amity publicly sealed could be of any avail.[1]

To LORD ROSEBERY, 24 December 1885. '*Secret*'.   N.L.S. 10023, f. 139.

I send a line to say how I wish we could meet daily. It is impossible to give you in writing any account of my very large and many-threaded correspondence.

The awkward circumstance is that Hartington has *again* 'been and done it'.

The following I think sum up the matter:—
1. I keep in large and satisfactory correspondence with Spencer.
2. I have expressed through Balfour my desire to support Ministers in a just and adequate measure. This is the *only* forward step I have made.
3. To all overtures I reply by entirely declining to make any communication of plans or intentions (except as above) in present circumstances, but trying as far as I can to bring about action of the Government.
4. Should Nationalists split from Tories and this be known to the world, it would change our position.
5. Read and get Cooper[2] to print the *first* article in the Dublin Express of last Saturday. Ashbourne's paper.
6. Monck, the best Irish opinion, is entirely for. So are (this is most secret) Hamilton, Under Secretary, and Jenkinson (with dark anticipations otherwise) head of Detective Police.
[P.S.] The *rent* is the great difficulty. I was shocked and grieved at the death of Sir George Harrison.[3] It would be an *excellent* thing if they would take Herschell for the vacancy.[4] I cannot understand Childers. His queer letter about Pontefract[5] looks to me as if he did not wish to come into Parliament.

[1] Mrs O'Shea replied on 29 December, enclosing a letter from Parnell to herself of 28th, Add MS 44269, f. 270, on absence of 'the slightest possibility of the Conservatives offering any settlement under present circumstances', but noting absence of liberal promises to the Irish: 'they have nothing to go upon except Mr Gladstone's statements in Midlothian'.
[2] Charles Cooper of *The Scotsman*.
[3] Just elected for S. Edinburgh; see 1 Jan. 86n.
[4] Rosebery preferred Childers to Herschell for his 'declared opinions on Home Rule'; Add MS 44288, f. 290.
[5] On his defeat there by a combination of Irish and soldiers; he was returned for S. Edinburgh *vice* Harrison; *Childers*, ii. 235-7.

25. Fr. Xmas Day.

Ch. 11 A.M. & H.C.—Evg 7. Wrote to Mr Battersby—Mr Knowles—Scotts. Read R. Moffat's Life[1]—Mark Rutherford (finished)—Cox on Job,[2] & text—and [blank.]

26. Sat. St Steph.

Ch. $8\frac{1}{2}$ A.M. Wrote to Mr Knowles tel. & l.—Ld Spencer l. & B.P.—Ld Gran-ville—Mr Scase BP—Mr Childers—Sir H. James MP.—and minutes. Wrote P.S. to Article.[3] Walk with C. Lyttelton. Wrote P.S. to my AntiHuxley Art. Read Dana on 'Reconciliation'[4]—Dicey on the Constitn—Solomon's Mines.

1. Government should act.
2. Nationalists should support them in acting.
3. I have done what I can to bring about (1). I am confident the Nationalists know my desire. They also publicly know there can be no plan from us in the present circs.
4. If (1) and (2) come about, we, who are half the House of Commons, may under the circs. be justified in waiting for the production of a plan.
5. This would be, in every sense, the best situation.
6. But if Ministers refuse to take up the question—or if from their not actually taking it up, or on any grounds, the Nationalists publicly dissolve their alliance with them, the Govt. then have a party of 250 in the face of 420; and in the face of 335 who were elected to oppose them.
7. The *basis* of our system is that the Ministry shall have the confidence of the H. of Com-mons. The exception is, when it is about to appeal to the people. The rule applies most strongly when an Election has just taken place. Witness 1835, 1841, 1859, and the *three* last Elections, after each of which the rule has been acted upon, silent inference standing instead of a vote.
8. The present circs. warrant I think an understanding, as above, between Ministers and the Nationalists: but not one between us & the Nationalists.
9. If from any cause the alliance of T. & N., which did exist, and presumably does exist, should be known to be dissolved, I do not see how it is possible for what would then be the Liberal majority to shrink from the duty appertaining to it as such, and to leave the business of Govt. to the 250 men whom it was elected to oppose.
10. This looks towards an Amendment to the Address praying H.M. to choose Ministers possessed of the confidence of the House of Commons.
11. Which under the circs. should I think have the sanction of a previous meeting of the party.
12. An attempt would probably be made to traverse this proceeding by drawing me on the Irish question.
13. It is impossible to justify the contention that, *as a condition previous* to asserting the right and duty of a Parliamentary majority, the party of the leaders should commit them-selves on a measure, about which they can form no final judgment, until by becoming the Govt. they can hold all the necessary communications.
14. But in all likelihood jealousy will be stronger than logic: and to obviate such jealousy, it might be right for me [to go] to the very farthest allowable point.

[1] See 22 Nov. 85.   [2] See 15 May 81.
[3] Published following Réville's reply to his article, *N.C.*, xix. 176 (January 1886).
[4] See also *Later gleanings*, 39.

15. The case supposed is, the motion made—carried—ministers resign—Queen sends for me.

Might I go so far as to say, at the first meeting, that, in the case supposed, I should only accept the trust if assured of the adequate, that is of the general support of the party to a plan of duly guarded Home Rule?

16. If that support were withheld it would be my duty to stand aside.

17. In that event, it would I conceive become the duty of that portion of the party, which was not prepared to support me in an effort to frame a plan of duly guarded Home Rule, to form a Government itself, if invited by the Queen to do so.

18. With me the Irish question would of course remain paramount: but, preferring a Liberal Government without an adequate Irish measure to a Tory Government similarly lacking, such a Liberal Government would be entitled to the best general support I could give it. W.E.G. Dec. 26. 85.[1]

To LORD GRANVILLE, 26 December 1885.   Add MS 56446, f. 202.
'*Secret*'.

I have put down on paper in a Memorandum, as well as I can, the possible forms of the question which may have to be decided at the opening of the Session. I went over the ground in conversation with you, & afterwards with R. Grosvenor: and I requested R. Grosvenor who was going to London to speak to Hartington in that sense. After his recent act of publication, I should not like to *challenge* him by sending him the written paper. Please however to send it on to Spencer who will send it back to me.[2]

I am not sure whether you yet know[3] that I have signified through A. Balfour, whom I met at Eaton, my desire to see the Govt. take up the Irish question & support them in it.

Happy Christmas time & New Year to you all.

27. *S. aft Xm.*

Ch 11 AM & [blank]. Wrote to Cardinal Manning—Rev. Dr. Reusch—Mr Knowles—Rev. A. Moore. Walk with E.W. Read Life of Bunyan[4]—Browne, Mosaic Cosmogony[5]—Overton's Church Life—Lea, Superstition and Force.[6]

28. *M. H. Innocents.*

Ch. 8½ A.M. and H.C. Wrote to Ld Spencer—Professor Dana[7]—Ld Granville—Master Foster—Rev. Mr Drew—Mr C.R. Hill. Irish conversation with H.J.G. Woodcraft with Willy. Saw Mary on the great coming event. Everything substantial stands well except age: and that is not *too* much awry. Read Priaulx Quaest. Mosaicae[8]—King's Solomon's Mines (finished)—Dicey on the Constn.

---

[1] Sent to Granville and Spencer this day marked '*Secret*'; Add MS 56446, f. 204; in Morley, iii. 270.
[2] Printed to here in Morley, iii. 268 and Ramm II, ii. 418.
[3] But see 22 Dec. 85.
[4] J. Brown, *John Bunyan, his life, times and work* (1885).
[5] E. H. Browne's note on Gen. i. 5; *Later gleanings*, 50.
[6] H. C. Lea, *Superstition and force* (1866).
[7] James Dwight Dana, 1813–95; professor of natural history and geology at Yale. See *Later gleanings*, 39 and *N.C.*, xix. 176 (January 1886).
[8] See 28 Feb. 58.

[1]Each constituency (except University) to choose a second representative. The double constituency to constitute the H. of Commons. Together with two members from the Royal University. Irish Peers in each House of Parlt. to be under the same rules as Irish ministers in H. of Commons. Great seal?

[2]1. Ireland to pay of the ascertained Imperial charges for Debt, Army & Navy, Royalty, Foreign & Colonial Establishments? up to the sum now fixed. Arrangements to last for 20 years & until the Imperial & local Parlt. shall jointly determine otherwise. Should it be reduced Ireland will share in the reduction. Should it be increased Ireland will not be called on for any further charge. In the event of war Irish Parlt. will regulate its own contributions.

Members from Ireland may speak & vote on any of the questions reserved in A. On other subjects their speech or vote may be challenged by any five members. If in the judgment of the Speaker the matter be one of Foreign, Indian or Colonial concern, he shall disallow the challenge.
If otherwise he shall disallow the capacity of the member to take part in the proceeding. Not to be liable to serve on any Committee except one relating (in the judgment of the Chair if called for) to one of the questions above referred to.

Schedule A.
Debt. Civil List & royal charges. Army (but not auxiliary forces). Navy. Collection of Revenue:
Shall be first charges on all Revenues in Ireland revised by or coming under the controul of Parliament. Shall not for 20 years exceed $\frac{1}{9}$ of the whole under each head. May at any time thereafter be readjusted on the basis of approximate population.

This courtship most honourable to the Liberal party. Reason glanced at Duffy 8.19.
Suppose a great proposal to settle Irish Govt *a*) from Tory Govt: Liberal support relied on: cite 1829, 1845, 1846, 1867; *b*) from Liberal Govt: Tory opposition relied on: and powerful.
Our position admirable. They acceding to Irish wish open to reproach i.e. Irish support their only hope.
We not open to reproach—We have done without it—and perhaps can again.
But *heartily hope Tory Govt will make some effective proposals, which we may support.*

Ireland: My previous declarations—Require no enlargement—Position of the two parties respecting.
Of the Conservative or Tory party. Opposed by Irish Popular p[arty?]: Wholly 1833–59—partially 1859–80. Supported by them 1880–5. 1880–5 outweighs 1833–80. Present attitude: of courtship. Why? evidently some special reason. More natural to court the stronger. *Why* court the weak?

Ireland. Present relation of 'Irish party' to Parlt. constitutes a national disgrace. Question shall Ireland be wholly governed in & from England is *after 85 years* of experiment one that should be diminished a) finally, b) soon. Great advantage of having Ireland represented authentically so as to deal in a binding manner.

[1] These mema., dated December 1885, at Add MS 56447, ff. 187–94.
[2] This sheet dated 'D. 28'.

To ask Her Majesty's Government whether they intend to introduce, at the outset of public business for the present Session, a measure to settle definitively a mode for the future government of Ireland?

To ask HMG what are the arrangements which they propose for entering upon the regular business of the Session? and, if these should involve an Adjournment after the swearing in of members then further to ask whether they intend to introduce at the outset of that business, a proposal for settling definitively the future government of Ireland.[1]

To LORD SPENCER, 28 December 1885. '*Secret*'.   Althorp MSS K8.

When you get the memorandum[2] I have sent to Granville you will find that it is confined to considering some alternatives and ways of procedure, and does not touch the difficulties inherent in the question of a separate government for Ireland.

This not because I think them disposed of but because they belong to another branch of the case before us.

I have no doubt they are both great and diversified; the chief one of all being that on which we concurred here pretty largely. In principle I think you and I are agreed; but I look at the question rather as one meeting us *in limine* than as arising in ulterior stages. I have not the smallest fear, for several reasons, of any attempt to employ the Police as a military force against us: what I feel apprehensive about is the preliminary question[:] shall we have a state of legality in Ireland to start from? If we can have this, I should feel pretty sanguine as to the future; but I know not that at the present moment we have any warrant for assuming it. By a state of legality, I mean a condition not substantially worse than that in which you left the country. Nor do I know how situated as we now are, it is possible to get at the facts, which until Parliament has met will remain at the command of the Government exclusively.[3]

29. Tu.

Ch. 8½ A.M. Wrote to Mr Chamberlain & copy—Messrs Robn & N.—Miss Goalen—Mr Mundella—Miss S. Bland[4]—Messrs Watson—Master Stanley—Rev. Mr M'Coll—Mr Hazzopulo—Mr Hutton—Prince of Wales—Rev. Mr Wainman—& minutes. Visit to Mr Wainman.[5] Family dinner of 14 at the Rectory: all so well done: Lucy, & Mr Drew, included. Servants' Ball at the Castle.

Postal deliveries & other arrivals were 700 & kept Harry with a band pretty hard at work. Immeasurable kindness almost overwhelmed us. I wrote a general letter of acknowledgment for the papers.

There was also the heavy and incessant weight of the Irish question, which offers daily phases more or less new.

It was a day for intense thankfulness but alas not for recollection and detachment. When will that day come? Until then, why string together the commonplaces & generalities of great things really unfelt. What is my true standing before God? How much has He shown me! yet this I have not learned.

---

[1] Date scrawled; Add MS 56447, f. 189.

[2] See 26 Dec. 85.

[3] Spencer replied next day, Add MS 44312, f. 242, agreeing as to tactics but pointing out danger of presuming liberal unity: 'opinion is running strongly against a bold Irish measure among leading men of our side'.

[4] Probably wedding arrangements.

[5] E. Wainham, minister (briefly) of the Methodist New Connexion chapel, Hawarden.

I hope there is in me a general desire to accept His will. I am certain that there is one keen & deep desire to be extricated from the life of contention in which a chain of incidents have for the last four years detained me against all my will. Then indeed I should reach an eminence from which I could look before & after. But I know truly that I am not worthy of this liberty with which Christ makes free His elect. In His own good time something I trust will for me too be mercifully devised.

Read Plowden, History of Ireland[1]—Mr Burke Vols VI & IX—Dicey Law of Constn (finished).

To J. CHAMBERLAIN, M.P., 29 December 1885.   Chamberlain MSS 5/34/47.

I thank you very much for your kind congratulations on the return of my birthday hackneyed as it is but attended with many bounties of Providence.

I am still awaiting in hope some clearing up of the relations between the Government & the Nationalists as a first necessary condition of our obtaining some daylight as to our position & duties.

My position remains quite unchanged: unless it be as to a further effort to make clear to the Govt. the desire I have publicly declared to support them, if possible, in this great Irish business.

The interval probably of a week between the choice of Speaker & the opening of business will allow I hope convenient time for early & even if needful for later stages of counsel.

30. Wed.

Ch. 8½ A.M. Wrote to Master of Balliol—Ld Granville—Sir Thos G.—Mr C. Villiers—Sir M. Beach—Ld R. Grosvenor—Ld Spencer—Mr Guinness Rogers—Dr Galloway[2]—Ld Huntly—Sir Henry James. Walk with W.H.G. Read Plowden Hist. Ireland—Rowcroft, Tales of a Colonist[3]—and 19th. [Century.][4]

To LORD R. GROSVENOR, chief whip, 30 December 1885.[5]   Add MS 44316, f. 154.

1. Speakership. I inclose a note from Beach, and beg you to forward mine to Villiers if you approve.[6] Sloane Street?
2. We ought soon to know the day for beginning regular public business? on the 12th I presume the hour is two o'clock?
3. I have written to James about Bradlaugh—and he seems to have that matter pretty well in hand.
4. The favourable letter about Ireland from Greville[7] has been followed by one from—Huntly!
5. The Nonconformists are very indignant with the 'Liberal' Church people—and no wonder.
6. Nothing new in the Irish question beyond (much study and) further efforts on my part

---

[1] F. Plowden, *An historical review of the state of Ireland*, 2v. (1803). See 18 Aug. 45.
[2] William Galloway, physician in Dundee; sent his *Dissertations on . . . Genesis* (1885).
[3] See 14 Feb. 46.
[4] i.e. his own article and Réville's reply; see 8, 26 Dec. 85.
[5] Holograph.
[6] Arrangements for seconding Peel's nomination.
[7] Add MS 44493, f. 248.

to make sure that the Govt. should really know my desire for their acting on it, in an adequate manner, & my desire to support them if possible.

Having now discharged myself of necessary matters of business let me thank you cordially for your kind words and add how much we hope that the journey to Bath will fully answer to your desires and expectations. Winter began with us yesterday. I suppose you will soon return to town if possible.

To LORD SPENCER, 30 December 1885. '*Secret*'.   Althorp MSS K8.

I send you once more my memorandum,[1] as I *think* you will find that your reference to it at the critical point does not correspond with its language. It proposes in (11) a consultation with the entire party in the H. of C. before the moving [of] any amendment.

And consultation with leaders, again, would of course come before that meeting of the party: the reference of this memorandum to you & to Granville being in truth the first informal step (or one of the first) towards such a consultation.

I assume then for the present that I need not argue the order of proceeding. But you raise a point of substance & a very formidable one.

I understand your idea to be that inasmuch as leaders of the party are likely to be divided on the subject of a bold Irish measure, & a divergence might be exhibited in a vote on the Address, it may be better to allow the Tory Government with 250 supporters in a House of 670 to assume the direction of the Session & continue the administration of Imperial affairs.

I do not undervalue the dangers of the other course. But let us look at this one. 1. It is an absolute novelty. 2. Is it not a novelty which strikes at the root of our Parliamentary Government? under which the first duty of a majority freshly elected, according to an uniform course of precedent, & a very clear principle, is to establish a Govt. which has its confidence. 3. Will this abdication of primary duty avert or materially postpone the (apprehended) disruption of the party? Who can guarantee us against an Irish or Independent amendment to the Address? The Govt. must in any case produce at once their Irish plan. What will have been gained by waiting for it?

The Irish will know three things. 1. That I am conditionally in favour of at least examining their demand. 2. That from the nature of the case I must hold this question paramount to every interest of party. 3. That a part, to speak within bounds, of the Liberal party will follow me in this respect.

Can it be supposed that in these circumstances they will long refrain, or possibly will refrain at all? With their knowledge of possibilities behind them, *dare* they long refrain?

An immense loss of dignity, in a great crisis of the Empire, would attend the forcing of our hands by the Irish or otherwise.

There is no necessity for an instant decision. My desire is thoroughly to shake up all the materials of the question. The present leaning of my mind is to consider the faults & dangers of abstention greater than those of a more decided course. Hence, in part, my great anxiety that the present Govt. should move.

Please send this on to Granville.

P.S. I asked R. Grosvenor to speak to Hartn. in the general sense of the Memm. But, since his separate action by the letter in the Times, I cannot safely go further at present.[2]

---

[1] See 26 Dec. 85.
[2] Partly printed in *Spencer*, ii. 95 and Morley, iii. 272.

31. Th.

Ch. 8½ A.M. Wrote to King of the Belgians—Sir W. Harcourt—Ld Granville—E. Hamilton—Mr J. Drew[1]—Ld Wolverton—Mrs O'Shea—Mr P. Campbell—Mr Knowles—Dr Winne.[2] The contents of Hamilton's letter recd. today I confess made me indignant for a while.[3] Gymnastics in the Schoolhouse: witnessed for ¾ hour. Read Plowden—Rowcroft—Three federation articles in 19th Cent.[4] Mr Wainman to luncheon.

A troubled anxious day, not more congenial to reflection than a tempest to a marriage. Go then old year with thy work undone: and O may the time come for doing it, and come quickly. Not even the first stage of true penitence, with recollection and detachment, have I yet attained. I sometimes hope I have the desire to be penitent. So be it.

Secret. I gather it to be on the whole the opinion of Mr. Parnell that, as matters now stand, and in the absence of any pledge from me as to the question of Irish Government, beyond my public declarations already known, he cannot look forward to an avowed severance of his friends as a party from the Administration, so as to throw upon the Liberal party the responsibilities of a Parliamentary majority; unless I am able to lay it down, as an understood rule of future Liberal policy, that, in the event of the accession of the party to power, there will not be proposed under any circumstances any measure of what is termed coercion for Ireland; understanding by that phrase any provisions reviving, or in the direction of, those of the Acts of 1881 & 1882.

No candid observer can be insensible to the gravity of the facts presented in Mr. O'Brien's tables (19th Century, Nov. & Jan.)[5] as to exceptional legislation; or to the great importance, in their bearing on this subject, of the course taken by the present Govt. on its accession, & of the declarations of several of its members.

In considering the point supposed to be before me, I take for my guide, as I have done during many months, my regard to the paramount importance of the Irish question, & my determination not to waste or compromise any resource which may eventually become available for its settlement.

My opinion, however, continues to be that any present negotiation with the Nationalists, or any state of things in Ireland, as to the public peace & as to contracts, materially worse than when Lord Spencer left it, would in all likelihood preclude any satisfactory handling of this great question by the Liberal party. So likewise, such a declaration with regard to special legislation, as is sketched above, would in my judgment have the same effect. Without referring to other grounds, it is on this ground inadmissible.

Should the ostensible alliance of the two parties continue, & should the debate on the Address pass off without a crisis, I take it for granted that both the expectations of parties, & the state of facts taken at large, will render necessary the production of the plans of the Government for Ireland at a very early date, & probably as the first important legislative business of the Session.　　　　　W.E.G. Dec. 31./85.[6]

[1] John, fa. of Harry Drew; of Powderham, Devon.
[2] J. M. Winn, London physician; corresponded on religion; Hawn P.
[3] Hamilton conveyed angry reactions to the 'kite'; see letter below and *Rosebery*, 176.
[4] H. Thring, 'The fallacy of "imperial federation"', R. Barry O'Brien, 'Federal union with Ireland'; D. Kay, 'Home rule in Austria-Hungary', *N.C.*, xix. 22–65 (January 1886).
[5] See 1 Nov. 85 and this day.
[6] Holograph and secretary's copy at Add MS 56446, ff. 221ff.

To LORD GRANVILLE, 31 December 1885. '*Secret*'.   Add MS 56446, f. 214.

1. I will write briefly to Harcourt.

2. The complications of the situation, due to the existence of *two* other parties with neither of which we can negotiate, and greatly aggravated by the premature action of Hartington and Dilke, make difficult even such questions as in a more natural state of things would have been easy; and in particular render[?] extremely difficult the question of the time & mode of communication with leading men of the party, a question in which I feel my own personal responsibility to be deeply involved.

3. I think however I shall have your assent in what I am now about to say. The desire of meeting together is really I think prompted by an apprehension that my mind is made up to make, or tends towards making, some decisive motion on the Address. Now I think it quite possible, and if I judge from the present moment even likely, that there may be no palpable split between Tories and Nationalists before the Address, and therefore that we shall not then be palpably and obviously saddled with the responsibilities of a majority. In this case I should readily fall in with what seems to be the prevailing disposition among leading men, and let the Address pass as far as I am concerned without any such motion: only waiting the *prompt* production of the Irish plans of the Govt., and reserving[?] a right to obtain from them satisfactory declarations on that head.

4. I have done nothing, and shall do nothing, of myself, except what I firmly believe that those whom I speak of not only ought to, but in principle would assent to and even desire. Should I meditate anything not in their sense, I will take care that they are not taken by surprise. I think you will deem it not unreasonable that beyond this, and inclusively as to time (but not in any case beyond the 12th), I should retain my liberty: acting under a responsibility perhaps the heaviest ever laid upon me, and one of which I feel that no other person can relieve me.

5. Spencer will probably forward to you today a letter from me, in no way at variance with this, but dealing in argument with the other alternative, namely that of our having, through an avowed secession of the Nationalists from the Tories, an undeniable Parliamentary majority. Would it be too much to ask you to send him this letter.

6. I shall be glad of your opinion on another question. With whom on coming to London, shall I hold the first, limited but collective, consultation? I incline to think thus: Granville, Spencer, Derby, Rosebery, Hartington, Harcourt, Chamberlain. Childers is not in Parlt. & may very possibly be absent in Edinburgh.

7. Labouchere's letter in the Times is very able.[1] I am struck, & under the circs. pleased, by Argyll's leaving open the question how far the American Constitution may help us for Ireland.

[P.S.] On the question of having Irish members in the Imp. Parlt. my mind is open.
6 PM.

P.S. Opened to thank you for yours just received. I am rather indignant at the Central News telegram & inclined to think there should be no intercourse with such people till they apologise.

To E. W. HAMILTON, 31 December 1885.   Add MS 48607A, f. 135.

Your letter is as always kind.[2] I cannot say I think the views it *conveys* reasonable. Especially on the part of Hartington: I forbear details.

---

[1] *T.T.*, 30 December, 5c, defending home rule, favourable to absence of Irish from Westminster.

[2] Of 30 December 1885, Add MS 44191, f. 59: Hartington and Harcourt 'somewhat sore at not having received any intimation of your wishes and intentions at the present critical juncture', specifically on the kite, H. J. Gladstone's correspondence with Parnellites, and Gladstone's talk with Balfour.

Some little time ago I asked Granville to communicate with Harcourt. Last night I heard from him that my request had been misunderstood. I wrote to Harcourt this morning.

I feel quite certain that Herbert has never pledged me to any opinions.[1] I do not disapprove of his giving, when he thinks it advisable and within bounds of discretion, what he thinks I think.

I refer your letter to him.

I have spoken & written to Balfour. 1. feeling certain it was in the sense of my late colleagues. 2. saying it was for myself individually 3. apprising those colleagues with whom I have principally communicated during the last two or three weeks.

After my contradictions in the newspapers, it is somewhat humiliating to be asked whether I have a plan formulated; but I have no plan.[2]

My work is almost beyond my power. It ought to include a careful historical study, the thing now least thought about: but today for example this business has kept me so busy that I have not even had time yet 7 PM to write an important letter on the arrangements required by my daughter's marriage.

It seems to me strange, if through the *indiscretion of others* there has been a story about a letter from me to the Queen, & a contradiction *from me* is expected without my being told it was desired.

I keep no copy of this note.

[P.S.] I hope *not* to have from Hartington the letter you describe.[3]

To Sir W. V. HARCOURT, 31 December 1885.   MS Harcourt dep. 9, f. 167.

I thank you very much for your kind letter to my wife and wish you all very heartily a happy New Year.

The Irish question must have lain heavy upon us all and it sometimes makes me feel as if I were ground into the dust. Its pressure is aggravated by the impossibility of maintaining communications at once confidential and secret. There will however I conceive be plenty of time in London between the Speakership & the Address (either 7 or 9 days I understand) for all practical purposes. Meantime my path has been pretty clear. The only real & responsible addition which I have made to my public declaration has been in a direction which I have felt confident my friends, i.e. those with whom I am in relations of confidence, would approve: namely by making efforts to make the Govt. understand *my* anxiety (not presuming to commit others) that they should handle the question and if possible to support them in it. Until we meet I shall continue to hold the same ground: very likely doing nothing at all of a substantive character; but in any case doing nothing, except what is agreeable to the general desire for quietude on the Address, without notice.

I hope that the nation will not behave in this Irish business as they did with regard to the American War; but it is quite on the cards.

The Speakership is settled. But what of the Chairmanship of Committees? Peel in 1835 proposed Bernal the old Liberal Chairman. But now there is none. I suppose there will be a fight.

My wife writes to tell you of the coming marriage of our *second* daughter. It is unadorned in the sense of worldly goods but it promises the most solid happiness.

---

[1] Gladstone's marginal note on Hamilton's letter: 'He [H. J. Gladstone] gave no revelations of any views as being mine.'

[2] Hamilton asked: 'What they want definitely to know is a) whether you have a plan formulated, & b) if so, what its main features are.'

[3] 'I think that Hartington will himself prefer a request for a meeting next week.'

1. [*January 1886*] *Frid. Circumcision.*

Ch. 8½ A.M. Wrote to Mr Broadhurst MP—Mr Cobb MP[1]—Ld Rosebery—Mr Spensley MP[2]—Scotts—Ld Castletown—Mr Slater—Rev. Dr Kinns—Mr Travers—Rev. L. Stokes[3]—Mr Ireland—Mr J. Nicolson—Mr Baillie. Woodcraft with W.H.G. Read Plowden—also Macaulay's Pitt—Stanhope's—Calmon's[4]—Rowcroft Tales of Colonies.

To LORD ROSEBERY, 1 January 1886.   N.L.S. 10023, f. 143.

I have this morning received the inclosed[5] and I lose no time in transmitting it hoping for answer by return. The questions generally are such as I can easily return: but does not the suggestion as to a Ballot seem worth considering? Was there any mistake or omission? A body of 3000 Rads can give trouble: while a ballot would I imagine dispose of them. I do not know who the writers are.

[P.S.] Nothing new in the way of a step on my part since you last heard: unless it be an attempt to insure that the Govt. should be aware of my hope they would take up the Irish question, and disposition to support them.

2. *Sat.*

Ch. 8½ AM. Wrote to Ld Hartington—Salvo di Pietra[6]—Mr Moncrieff—Mr Brewster—Rev. Mr Nicoll—M. Gennadios—Mr Linton[7]—Mr Eason—Mr Newman—Mr Waldie—Mr Barnett—Mrs Alder—& minutes. Also distributed my Articles, duly inscribed, by post, to Card. Manning, Dr Reusch, Sir R. Owen, T. Acland, H. Acland. Prof. Prestwich,[8] Duke of Argyll, Prof. Dana, Bp of Winchester, Rev. A. Moore. Party from Eaton. Walk with Miss B. Ponsonby:[9] conversation with Lady P. Read Plowden (much)—Tales of the Colonies—Reville's Reply to me.[10]

To LORD HARTINGTON, M.P., 2 January 1886.   Chatsworth MSS 340. 1883.
'*Secret*'.[11]

Unfortunately the subject of your letter[12] makes it impossible to reply by telegram, & I receive it on the evening when there is no post to London.

---

[1] Henry Peyton Cobb, 1835–1910; radical M.P. Rugby 1885–95.

[2] Howard Spensley, 1834–1902; in Australia, then liberal M.P. Finsbury 1885–6.

[3] Louis Stokes, curate of Buckland; ed. Thirlwall's *Letters* (1881).

[4] For Stanhope, see 2 Apr. 61; for M. A. Calmon, see 13 July 65.

[5] Not found; from Reekie (radical organiser in S. Edinburgh) on the vacancy there (filled by Childers) caused by Sir G. Harrison's death; see Rosebery's reply, 2 January, Add MS 44289, f. 1, also suggesting that Gladstone should not intervene, and that he call a meeting of 'your late colleagues'.

[6] Subprefect in Sicily; sent letter of respect; Hawn P.

[7] H. J. Linton of London, on Dickens; Hawn P.

[8] (Sir) Joseph Prestwich, 1812–96; geologist; kt. 1896.

[9] Barbara, Ponsonby's unm. sister.

[10] See 30 Dec. 85n.   [11] Holland, ii. 108.

[12] Of 1 January, Add MS 44148, ff. 190, 192; can Gladstone wire whether Hartington should come to London; will Gladstone 'early' make his 'views and intentions' known, first to leaders, then to the party?

I. On the 17th of December I communicated to you *all* the opinions I had formed on the Irish question; but on the 21st you published in the Times a re-affirmation of opposite opinions.

On the Irish question I have not a word to add to that letter. I am indeed doing what little the pressure of correspondence permits to prepare myself by study & reflection. My object was to facilitate study by you & others—I cannot say it was wholly gained. But I have done nothing & shall do nothing to convert those opinions into intentions, for I have not the material before me. I do not know whether my 'postulate' is satisfied. Nor do I know whether you are right in supposing there is a breach, by which I mean a breach to become public on the Address, between Tories & Nationalists. The imperfect information which I possess rather looks towards an opposite conclusion. So that I am totally unable to submit any proposal for consideration; & desirous of gaining whatever lights intervening time may possibly afford.

I admit that the incessant & incurable leakages of the late Cabinet supply me with an additional reason for circumspection.

But I have taken care by my letter of the 17th that you should know my opinions *en bloc*. You are quite welcome to show it if you think fit to those with whom you meet. But H. has I believe seen it, & the others if I mistake not know the substance.

II. But besides the question of legislation for Ireland, there is the question of Parliamentary procedure. For considering this, the time available in London will I think be ample—I have through R. Grosvenor put you in possession of my ideas; but they are floating ideas only. In mine of the 23rd I stated my view which you wrote down accurately in your letter, but have made inaccurate by a correction. There is no doubt that a very grave situation is upon us, a little sooner or a little later. All my desire & thought are how to render it less grave: for next to the demands of a question far higher than all or any party interests is my duty to labour for the consolidation of the party.

Should I see cause to anticipate the breach you expect (of course this might happen) I will at once let you know.

What (I find) Granville has written you may be found to be of weight.

Pray show this letter if you think fit to those on whose behalf you write.

I propose to be available in London about 4 p.m. on the 11th, at Lucy's, for any who wish to see me. We cannot get from the Whip the day of the Speech.

As to my 'postulate' (q.v.) I have doubts whether it can be dealt with by an Opposition. A meeting of the party is a serious matter but may be found requisite.

3. *S. aft. Circn.*

Ch. 11 A.M. & H.C. (S. preached admirably) and 6½ P.M. Wrote to Messrs Gray & Richie—Ld Granville—Sir W. Harcourt—Ld Rosebery—Mr M'Coll B.P. Read Prof. Driver's article on Mosaic Geology and other works thereon.[1]—Defoe's Church of Scotland.[2]

To Sir W. V. HARCOURT, M.P., 3 January 1886.[3]   MS Harcourt dep. 10, f. 1.

I thank you very much for your letter, and for all its kind thoughts and words.

I am a little apprehensive of any exposition of the 'causes of the present discontents'. For 1. You are not in possession of all the materials. I have had divers and serious

---

[1] S. R. Driver, 'The cosmology of Genesis', *The Expositor* (January 1886).
[2] D. Defoe, *An historical account of the bitter sufferings . . . of the episcopal church in Scotland* (1707).
[3] Dated '1885', but clearly 1886.

discontents myself: but have tried to keep them to myself. 2. It seems to me that all our best efforts are or should be pre-engaged upon the future. The question of Irish Government as it stands before us, & whichever way we lean, is I think the biggest of our time: & my own share of the responsibility is, in my own view, the largest I have ever had.[1]

To LORD ROSEBERY, 3 January 1886.[2] N.L.S. 10023, f. 146.

1. As to Edinburgh. I will certainly non-intervene: & say a word about you.
2. For your suggestion as to a meeting of 'my late colleagues'. Have you really considered all that is involved in my gathering together those 16 gentlemen? My mind is not yet clear though I have thought much of it, *whom* I should call when I make a call. A call must doubtless be made but there are many reasons against making it too soon one of which is that I have nothing more to say than is already known in full or in substance to all who so far as I know are busying themselves in this matter. All things considered I am sometimes inclined to doubt whether I may not have been too free in my communications to some rather than too reserved.[3]
[P.S.] I fear from your letter you will hardly join if I propose three cheers for auld *Reekie*.[4]

4. M.

Ch. 8¼ A.M. Wrote to Robn & Nichn—Watsons—Mr Gennings [*sic*][5]—Geo. Harris—Miss Tennant—Mr A. Peel. Gave the morning principally to reviewing my private money affairs: the first time for three years as I find on reference. Woodcraft with H. & H. Read Annual Register on Ireland 1782, 98, 99[6]—Tales of the Colonies.

5. Tu.

Ch. 8¼ A.M. Wrote to The Khedive of Egypt—Sir W. Harcourt—Mr A. Peel—Ld R. Grosvenor—Mr Balfour—Ld Granville—Sir T. Acland—Circular to Liberal Members—and minutes. Worked on books. Examined various Volumes of Poetry: with little fruit. Read Rowcroft—Plowden—Mrs Dall on Shakespeare.[7]

To A. J. BALFOUR, president of the local government board, Add MS 49692, f. 12.
5 January 1886. '*Most private*'.

I entirely agree with you[8] and Lord Salisbury on the subject of any communication of the intentions of Ministers respecting Ireland to me: if my note appeared to convey any suggestion to that effect, it was quite opposed to my intention.

---

[1] Harcourt replied, 4 January, Add MS 44200, f. 1: 'I did not mean to refer to *personal* or *party difficulties.*... The discontents I spoke [of] were the *Irish discontents.*'
[2] Dated '1885' by Gladstone, but clearly a slip.
[3] Rosebery replied, 7 January, Add MS 44289, f. 3, still urging a meeting.
[4] See 1 Jan. 86n., 'auld Reekie' also being the nick-name for Edinburgh.
[5] Perhaps the letter declining invitation to visit U.S.A.; *T.T.*, 7 January 1886, 9f.
[6] *Annual Register* (1782), ch. 8 on the Irish Commons, (1798) chs. 6–8 on the rebellion, (1799) ch. 14 on the Union.
[7] C. W. H. Dall, *What we really know about Shakespeare* (1886).
[8] See 23 Dec. 85n., 3 July 86.

To LORD R. GROSVENOR, chief whip, 5 January 1886.[1]   Add MS 44316, f. 158.

1. I inclose the circular according to your intimation.

2. I assume unless otherwise instructed that the House will meet at two on Tuesday.

3. Villiers in a nice letter begs off seconding Peel for the Chair. He has asked Acland (who moved Brand in 80), and if Acland declines will I think take Bright or Pease.

4. I propose to reach Euston at 3.30 on Monday: and I go to 21 Carlton H. Terrace where you would find me at four or thereabouts.

5. Next morning at 11 I propose to gather & consult some of the late Cabinet. It is not very easy to choose, and it would not do to summon all. Perhaps about six to begin with.

6. As far as *present* appearances go, I do not much expect any *avowed* severance between the Govt. and Parnell before the Address. This may postpone the necessity for any sharp decision.

7. I understand the P. and Princess of Wales are to be at Eaton 19th to 23d. I do not know whether they will be disposed to come over here. If they are I must try to get back again, possibly on the night of 21st.

6. *Wed. Epiph (C's birthday).*

Ch. 8½ A.M. and H.C.—most of us present. Wrote to Professor Prestwich—Mr Carlisle—Messrs Scrivener—Ed. Xtn Million[2]—Ed. Jewish World[3]—Dowager Ly Aberdeen BP—Mr Bidder—S. Harris—J. Hodges—Dr Wallich.[4] W., H., & H. with me: 2 trees felled. Worked on books. Read Tales of a Colonist—Mrs Dall on Shakespeare—Lenormant, Eleusinian Myst.[5]

7. *Th.*

Ch. 8½ A.M. Wrote to Ed. Daily News l.l.[6]—Royal Bank Edinb.—Ld R. Grosvenor l.l.—Mr Chamberlain—Ld Spencer—Rev. Mr Fleming—Mr Meehan—Mr Westell—E. Wood—Mr Bright—F. Moss[7]—Messrs Cassell—D. Milne—Scotts, and minutes. Drive with C. Read Rowcroft—Reusch on Galileo (C.R.)[8]—Dall on Shakespeare.

[1] Holograph. This letter crossed with Grosvenor's this day, Add MS 44316, f. 161: 'By the newspapers Parnell does not intend to move an amendment to the Queen's Speech, but to bring forward a definite motion later on. I hear that Randolph Churchill had a long and *not* satisfactory talk with Healy in Dublin.'

[2] Not found published; it carried an enthusiastic leader on his Genesis article, 7 January, 172.

[3] In *Jewish World*, 8 January, 5d: thanks for kind notices of his articles; 'while the several nations had their parts alloted to them, that alloted to the Hebrew race was by far the most important of them all'.

[4] George Charles Wallich, physician; earlier in correspondence, Add MS 44492, f. 263.

[5] See 5 Jan. 80.

[6] Complaining at *St. James Gazette*'s misconstruction of an 1835 speech; *D.N.*, 9 January 1886, 5h.

[7] On decline of London liberalism from 'number and power of the leisured', as distinct from the occupied', and absence of local govt.; *T.T.*, 9 January 1886, 10b.

[8] F. H. Reusch, 'Galileo and the Roman inquisition', *C.R.*, xxxviii. 665 (October 1880).

To LORD R. GROSVENOR, 7 January 1886, '*Secret*'.[1]   Add MS 44316, f. 165.

[First letter:] 1. Your intelligence seems to report two schemes rather irreconcileable one with the other (a) the Parnell intention, (b) the Randolph-Healy *Concordat*.

2. Both are in accord with my impression (not conviction) that there will be no ostensible breach between Tories & Nationalists on the day of the Address. Whether this be a public advantage or not, it will be at any rate a momentary relief & will afford time to cast about for more knowledge.

3. I should regard the withdrawal *en bloc* as by far the most formidable thing that can happen. It will be followed by an assembling in Dublin, which brings into view very violent alternatives. If Parnell is wise he will keep to the game he has been upon heretofore, viz. the ejecting of Governments. He must of course begin with the present one. Then a Liberal Government *not* prepared to deal with him. Or if there were a Liberal Government prepared to *try* dealing with him, their ejectment would soon be provided for by others.

4. I am not quite certain how long we ought to persist in the system of making no spontaneous communication to Parnell: this is matter for consideration.

5. I am also considering whether it will be possible (1) for me, (2) for others to take this ground, & hold it as a policy while possible: a. Only the Govt. can propose in this matter with a hope of public benefit. b. To make a proposal would require a knowledge of the state of Ireland which an Opposition does not possess. c. And would at once throw the question upon the lines of party. d. *Ergo* we will wait to hear what the Govt. have to say, & give it a dispassionate consideration. e. Not thereby meaning that should I be unable to support their plan I will bring forward another. f. And recommend the party to follow suit, keep its own counsel, turn over the subject from all points of view, & reserve its freedom of action until an occasion may arise when there may be a hope of acting usefully.

6. You may remember your proposing (here) & my not liking, that, if Parnell moved an amendment on the Address, we should walk out of the House. You may think I am now by another road drawing nearer to you.

7. We ought on no account, if it can be avoided, to *join issue* with Ministers on 'the Government of Ireland'. On this point I am very clear.

[Second letter:] 1. As at present advised I have no intention of giving a dinner on the night before the Address. It is an innovation, and I doubt i.e. am not sure if it has any consecutive sanction. I never gave such a dinner in Opposition: and *never* attended one, *except* at Hartington's. Moreover looking back on old Journals from the time of Peel, I find it was not given in the Lords so recently as 1867; for we had (Feb 4) then a meeting of both Houses from 9PM to 11PM. All this I have given you (& I could add) because it is curious. But these are not my conclusive reasons. One above all others governs me, and that you will perhaps guess. If not I will tell you on Monday. I talked the matter over with Granville when he was here.

2. I do not know whether you have heard the growl as to my possible difficulties in the matter of Secretariat when I get to London. Whether you have or not had this specimen of my amiable temper, I beg that *nothing* whatever be done at present. Let me get up there & see how deep the waters are & how I can buffet them.

[P.S.] Acland declines. I write to Bright. I suppose Hartington will come up for Tuesday.

[1] Holograph, with copy to Spencer, Add MS 56447, f. 5. See 5 Jan. 86n. and Grosvenor's undated note, Add MS 44316, f. 164 'that Parnell is going to move a definite resolution in favour of a separate Parlt. for Ireland, & when this is refused to withdraw with all his men en bloc', and that 'Churchill did, at a second interview, come to some arrangement with Healy, but what it was I know not'.

Would you ask him to come to 21 C.H. Terrace at 11.30 if convenient to him. I do not propose on that morning to go beyond Granville, Spencer, Hn., Harcourt, Chamberlain.

8. Fr.

Ch. 8½ A.M. Wrote to Messrs Watson & Smith—Alderman Redmond—Scotts—Mrs Caroline H. Dall[1]—Mr Drew sen—Mr Mundella—Mr Lyell[2]—Ld Granville—Mrs Ingram. Saw Herbert on the office of Whip, &c.[3]—Harry on the marriage arrangements: he is *most* valuable. Wrote mem. for Mr Drew accordingly. Read Mrs Dall (finished)—Tales of the Colonies—Cont. Rev. of N. 79 on W.E.G.[4]—Pearsall Smith's International Copyright.[5] Made additions to my Will-schedule.

9. Sat.

Ch. 8½ A.M. Wrote to Ld R. Grosvenor Tel.—Mr Pearsall Smith—Card. Manning—Mr Macmaster—Sir D. Lange—J. O'Brien—Jas Thomson—Mons Phardys[6]—Curate of Old Weston[7]—Ld Spencer—Ld Rosebery—Mrs O'Shea—G. Harris—C. Allan—Mr Meredith[8]—Mrs Holmes—and minutes. Finished Tales of the Colonies—Read Beaconsfield, Home Letters[9]—Burke & Laurence Corresp.[10] Worked on books & papers: preparations for journey, alack! Made many extracts from Burke—sometimes almost divine.[11]

To CARDINAL MANNING, 9 January 1886.[12]   Add MS 44250, f. 235.

Many thanks for your two interesting letters.[13] I do not think, nor do you appear to think, my main argument is in any way inconsistent with your general propositions and view as to the two planes. I thank you for the criticism on the passage in p. 19. My intention was to keep absolutely within the intention of Paul's declaration in Cor. XV. 24–7. But as you have perceived my words are too large and do not duly discriminate.

Having found my scientific backer for the first article had not been sufficiently vigilant, I have taken other measures for the second, and have little fear of any formidable attack from that quarter.

[P.S.] The Irish question grows bigger and bigger. I have expected it would do so. I consider it my main duty for the time to avoid rash ⟨and⟩ or premature announcements. It cannot be too much weighed and sifted, by all.

[1] Mrs. Caroline Wells Healey Dall, American writer and feminist. See 5 Jan. 86.
[2] (Sir) Leonard Lyell, 1850–1926; nephew of the geologist; liberal M.P. Orkney 1885–1900; cr. bart. 1894, baron 1914.
[3] Grosvenor's hostility to home rule made his continuance unlikely; A. Morley replaced him on 31 January; *G.P.*, 348.
[4] Reviews of *Gleanings*; see 31 Oct. 79.
[5] R. Pearsall Smith, 'International copyright by an American' (1886).
[6] N. B. Phardys, published on Greek politics in 1880s.
[7] D. F. W. Quale; business untraced.
[8] Robert Fitzgerald Meredith, rector of Halstook, corresponded on dormant baronies.
[9] *Home letters, written by the late Earl of Beaconsfield*, ed. R. Disraeli (1885).
[10] *The epistolatory correspondence of... Burke and Dr French Lawrence* (1827).
[11] Add MS 44471, ff. 4–19.
[12] Holograph.
[13] Of 6 and 7 January, Add MS 44250, f. 228, on Huxley: 'Holy Scripture is not a book of science', and critical of Gladstone's passage of p. 19 of his article: 'the word "scaffold" might imply that it is coextensive with Christianity ... I cannot treat Darwinism & evolution with as much courtesy as you do'.

To Mrs. O'SHEA, 9 January 1886.[1]   Add MS 56446, f. 84.

The proposal contained in your enclosure[2] is indeed a large & important one, & you cannot I think be unprepared for my reply to your suggestion that I should advise.

Advice from me would be negociation, & negociation by me in the present position of the case, would be fatal to any prospects of being useful which may, I am far from saying which does[,] lie before me.

I reply at once accordingly to your desire.

Your survey is of one portion of the field, mine of another.

I go to Town on Monday when I shall of course have opportunities of consultation as to my course of action. I do not expect it will lead me to retract or qualify anything which I have written, or said.

To LORD ROSEBERY, 9 January 1886.   N.L.S. 10023, f. 149.

I am obliged to go up on Monday and therefore to spin past you. Whether my calls in town will be close and constant after Wednesday I cannot yet tell; but it is probable. I think it not unlikely you may be coming up in the interval before the Address: in which case you would see my correspondence.

Present appearances are, *no* open breach between Parnell and the Govt. on the opening. If this be so I incline to the utmost possible reserve. There is a rumour that the Govt. may try to force in the Address a vote of confidence, which would seriously affect the situation.

10. *1 S. Epiph.*

Ch. 11 AM & 6½ PM. Wrote to Ld Hartington—Messrs. W. Ayre—Mrs Th.—Messrs. T. Andrews[3]—Mr Knowles—Hon. Mrs E. Talbot—and minutes. Pretty full family dinner. Read Elliot and Genesis and other tracts—Elam on Evolution[4]—Le Normant on the Fall.

11. *M. [London]*

Ch. 8½ A.M. Wrote to Mr Pimblett—Mayor of Lpool—Rev. Dr Hutton—Mr Crump[5]—Sir A. Clark—and minutes. 10.50–3.50 to London.[6] Saw Sir C. Dilke—Ld R. Grosvenor—Sir W. Harcourt—Ld Granville—Mr Godley—Mr Hamilton. Read Macaulay's Warren Hastings[7]—Beaconsfield's Home Letters.

---

[1] Copy in Mrs Gladstone's hand.

[2] Letter from Parnell of 6 January forwarded that day by Mrs O'Shea, Add MS 44269, f. 275; Parnell reported 'representations of the chief landlord associations in Ireland. It is thought that if this arrangement (compulsory purchase) were carried out, there would remain no large body of opinion amongst the landowning class against the concession of a full measure of autonomy to Ireland, as the Protestants, other than the owners of land, are not really opposed to such concession.'

[3] London carpenters.

[4] C. Elliott, *A vindication of the Mosaic authorship of the Pentateuch* (1884); see 23 Dec. 76.

[5] Arthur Crump sent his *Short inquiry into the formation of political opinion* (1885); not noticed as read.

[6] Staying with Lucy Cavendish in Carlton House Terrace.

[7] In his *Essays*.

12. Tu.

Wrote to Col. King—Acting Editor P.M.G.[1] H of C. 2-3½ for appointment of Speaker. 11.30-1¼. Granville, Spencer, Harcourt, Chamberlain on Ireland. Rather chaotic Nos. 3 & 4. Also saw Mrs Th. (tea)—Mr Mundella—Mr Bright[2]—Ld Hartington—Mr Knowles—Lord R.G. Read M.s Warren Hastings, the most *brilliant* perhaps of all his pieces—and Maine on Popular Govt.[3]

13. Wed.

Wrote to Mr Lefevre—& minutes. H of C. 2-3½. Took the Oath.[4] Saw Lord RG—Ld Kimberley—Mr Mundella—Mr Bright—Ld Derby—Ld Hartington—Mr Knowles. Read on Ireland all my available time of the day, including Sir J.F. Stephen's ferocious pamphlets.[5] Read Miss Pardoe on Louis XIII.[6]

14. Th.

Wrote to Ld Hartington—Messrs Merello[7]—Mr M.R. Martin[8]—Mr Rowe[9]—Rev. J.C. Jones—Mr Jas Watt—Mr Smithers—Mr Steele[10]—Rev. Mr. Cartman[11]—Ld Spencer—& minutes. Dined at Sir W. Harcourt's. Saw Ld R. Grosvenor—Ld Granville—Ld Ripon—Ld Hartington—Ld Rosebery—Lady Airlie—H.J.G. Read Pardoe Louis XIII. Shopping.

To LORD HARTINGTON, M.P., 14 January 1886.   Chatsworth MSS 340. 1905.

I have now read, for the first time I believe, the statement you gave me.[12] The first two & a half lines contain an absolute untruth which governs & colours the whole. The details are in many parts wholly unfounded & nearly all the rest are absurd caricature. We are all accustomed to have our ideas a good deal enlarged by interpreters but in this picture I find no real likeness to any conversation I have ever held with anybody.
[P.S.] I observe there is no reference to Herbert in this article.

To LORD SPENCER, 14 January 1886. '*Secret*'.   Althorp MSS K296.

I return 1. Selborne's very able but I think deplorable paper.[13] His hostility is I fear 'set' and I find he has actually declined Granville's invitation for the eve of the meeting. After

---

[1] (Sir) Edward Tyas *Cook (1857-1919, journalist and editor), on Gladstone's 100 best books, Add MS 44494, f. 26.

[2] Bright noted: 'not much talk with him.... He will speak in debate on the Address'; Walling, *Diaries of Bright*, 534.

[3] Sir H. J. S. Maine, *Popular government* (1885); sent by Tennyson, see 26 Apr. 86.

[4] As did Bradlaugh, Speaker Peel treating him, at the start of the new Parliament, as any other member; Arnstein, 310.

[5] Series of letters in *T.T.*, some reprinted; see L. Stephen, *Life of Sir James Fitzjames Stephen* (1895), 461.

[6] Early chs. of I. S. H. Pardoe, *Louis XIV and the court of France*, 3v. (1847).

[7] *Sic?*; perhaps the London sherry shippers.

[8] R. M. Martin of Brighton, on a cartoon; Hawn P.

[9] George Hunter Rowe, aged 16, for an autograph; Hawn P.   [10] Reading uncertain.

[11] John Cartman, vicar in Yorkshire; supporting home rule; Hawn P.

[12] Untraced article from 'the National Press stable' (see Hartington's quasi-apology, 15 January, Add MS 44148, f. 201).

[13] Of 28 December 1885, opposing home rule; in Selborne II, ii. 196.

his extravagant line on the Church question I was not unprepared for this. 2. Hamilton's[1] letter (I had understood you to refer to some other scheme). The idea he holds in common with Giffin [*sic*][2] of bringing the responsibility of an Irish Government to bear on the question of land-purchase is of great value. But it is not I think at all thoroughly worked out in his letter. *Who* is to place this responsibility on an Irish Parliament? His great object is to settle the Land question before any grant of Home Rule: that is before an Irish Parliament exists. Can any act but its own effectually saddle it with the engagement? Can the vote of the Imperial Parliament suffice to impose it? Even if concurred in by the bulk of the Nationalist party? This is a grave & difficult matter & lies at the root of the discussion. I do not altogether see my way.

I send you a letter from Lefevre which adopts conditionally Labouchere's basis, & enters into computations: some points in it are well stated.

Carnarvon's resignation of course means that he will not govern Ireland without some larger concession.[3] It is outrageous in the (new) Daily News to taunt him.[4]

15. Fr.

Wrote to E. Hamilton—Ed. D. Telegraph—Mr Rae[5]—Ld Granville—Mr A. Reid[6]—Mr Chamberln—& minutes. Dined with Mr Knowles: a lively evening. I am constantly pursuing my thoughts on Ireland, and noting particulars. Long conversation with Mr J. Morley.[7] Saw Ld R.G.—H.J.G.—Gen. . . .—Mr Lecky. Read Pardoe—Q.R. on Ch & State.[8] We went sorrowfully to see dear Harry off[9] at 8 P.M. May God have him evermore in His holy keeping.

16. Sat.

Wrote to Mr Digby[10]—Mayor of Belfast[11]—Mr Drew—Archdn Colley—& minutes. Saw Mr Trevelyan—Ld Granville—Sir C. Tennant. Dined with the A. Lytteltons. Read Q.R. on H. of Lords—also the Political Article[12]—and Pardoe, Louis XIV.

---

[1] i.e. Sir R. Hamilton of Dublin Castle.

[2] Full statement of Giffen's views in *The Statist*, 6 February 1886; see Loughlin, 85.

[3] Carnarvon's resignation was leaked in the *Standard* on 13 January, though he did not formally resign before the govt. fell.

[4] H. W. Lucy had just replaced F. H. Hill as editor of the *Daily News*.

[5] Robert R. Rae, on his work on '*pure* English'; Hawn P.

[6] Andrew Reid, political journalist; ed. many works on liberalism.

[7] Morley's diary this day: 'Called on Mr Gladstone at 11 at C.H. Terrace. Talked w. him for about 40 minutes. Told him abt. D[aily] N[ews] [whose leaders Morley was writing]: asked if there was likely to be a basis of co-opn. in the party: he sd. on the whole he felt t[ha]t there was: t[ha]t after talking w. his colleagues he thought practical union was not impossible. Sd. t[ha]t he had just read over his manifesto—& he sd. pers[onally][?] to me: he stuck to it. He had "expressed opinion, but not plans or intention." We must advance by stages: consider each stage as it arises: next stage is the Address. Told me his preferred course on Thursday. Sd. he felt the importance of not taking a false step wh. might produce repetition of G.3 & Ld. North. I thought, as I have often done before, t[ha]t he regards Parnell far too much as if he were like a serious & respons[ible] party leader of ord[in]ary[?] English style. That vitiates his idealism[?], I fear. Told me he much liked my two speeches [on home rule at Newcastle and Chelmsford].'

[8] *Q.R.*, clxii. 1 (January 1886).   [9] To India.

[10] William Digby, secretary of the National Liberal Club.

[11] Sir Edward James Harland, 1831–95; shipping magnate; cr. bart. 1885; lord mayor, Belfast 1885–7; Unionist M.P. N. Belfast 1889–95.   [12] *Q.R.*, clxii. 239 (January 1886).

To Sir E. J. HARLAND, lord mayor of Belfast,   Add MS 56447, f. 8.
16 January 1886.[1]

I have this day received from you by telegraph a request that I would receive today or tomorrow a deputation from Belfast, of which the object is not stated; but which is to see Lord Salisbury, & which on that account, & from rumours which have reached me, I presume to have reference to the condition of Ireland, and to measures proposed to be adopted in regard to it.

I am very desirous to be possessed of all information bearing upon this great subject, and no information could be more acceptable to me than such as could be imparted by the great community of Belfast.

But it is impossible for me to receive it, under the channel afforded by public deputations. Such a course on my part would exhibit me at a competition with Her Majesty's Government in a field of labour & responsibility which is at present exclusively their own, and would tend to accredit a statement alike mischievous and groundless which is now actively propagated from quarters and with motives that I shall not attempt to describe to the effect that I have signified an intention to make or adopt proposals with reference to Irish legislation.

It is for Her Majesty's Ministers, with the means of information they possess, to determine what they may think it their duty to propose. It is for me as an unofficial member of Parliament, to give to these plans a careful and dispassionate consideration: & to devise nothing and do nothing, which can throw obstacles in the way of their full and independent action.

[P.S.] I rely upon your kindness to make known this reply to Sir Thomas Maclure and to the body on whose behalf you write.

17. 2 S. Epiph.

St James's mg: St And. Wells St aft. Trail of boys & others there & back. Saw Ld Granville l.l.—Sir A. Clark—Ld Kenmare. Wrote to Mayor of Belfast—Mr Henri.[2] Read Life of Suckling[3]—Bp Gloucr. on Fundamental Doctrine(!)[4]—Wiseman on Religion & Science.[5]

18. M.

Wrote to Bailie Turnbull[6]—Ld Granville l.l.—Mr Childers—Mr H.W. Lee[7]—Mr Drew, sen.—and minutes. Saw Ld Hartington—Sir T. May—Ld R. Grosvenor l.l.—Mr Godley—Ld Kenmare—H.J.G.—Ld Granville. Read Pardoe's Louis XIV—Lynd on Home Rule[8]—... on Cemuda Zollverein.[9] Godley & Lyttelton dined.

---

[1] In D.N., 20 January 1886, 6e.

[2] T. Henri, oculist in Newgate Street, London; advised Gladstone on pince-nez fitted with '"Pure Periscopic" pebbles'; Hawn P.

[3] Perhaps A. J. Suckling, Selections from the works of Sir J. Suckling (1836); with his life.

[4] C. J. Ellicott, Are we to modify fundamental doctrine? (1885).

[5] N. P. S. Wiseman, Twelve lectures on the connection between science and revealed religion (1836).

[6] Robert Turnbull, chairman of S. Edinburgh Liberal Association, sent resolution opposing Childers' candidacy there; Hawn P.

[7] Harry Wilmot Lee, registrar of the Charterhouse, of which Gladstone was a governor.

[8] R. J. Lynd, 'The present crisis in Ireland' (1886).

[9] Not found.

19. Tu.

Wrote to Mr Chappell—Drybrough & Gibson[1]—W.H.G.—Mr Drisker?[2]—and minutes. Saw H.J.G.—Ld RG.—Ld R.G. *cum* Ld Spencer—Ld Granville. Half an hour with Mr Henri about my eyes. Read Pardoe—Arnold on Ireland.[3]

20. Wed.

Wrote to Mr F. Sikes[4]—Sir M.H. Beach—Ld Granville—The O'Donoghue—Sir J. Ramsden—Ld R. Grosvenor—& minutes. Saw H.J.G.—Ld R.G.—Ld Granville— Ld Rosebery—Mr Morley—Mr Bryce. Read Pardoe—Debates on Ireland 1782[5]— Butt's Speech 1874.[6] Conclave on the Speech 9-11 PM. & on Procedure.

21. Th.

Wrote to Mr Reeve—and minutes. 11-1. Conclave at Granville's on the Speech. Only Hartington stiff. Saw Ld Granville—Ld R.G.—Ld Rosebery—H.J.G. A morning of much oppression. H of C. $4\frac{1}{2}$-$8\frac{1}{2}$. Spoke on Address $1\frac{1}{4}$ hour. A great weight off my mind.[7] Read Life of Provost Hodgson[8]—Pardoe's Louis XIV finished Vol I.

Ireland. Present. Granville's. Jan. 21. 86. 11 AM.[9]

+ Granville	× Hartington
+ Kimberley	Harcourt
Derby	+? Trevelyan
+ Spencer	+ Chamberlain
(+) Rosebery	Dilke
Northbrook	W E.G.

22. Fr.

Wrote to Mr Rae—Macmillans—Ld Spencer—Ld Waveney[10]—Mr Horsman—Mr Pitkin—Mr G. New[11]—and minutes. Interesting dinner at 'The Club'. H of C. $4\frac{1}{2}$-$7\frac{1}{4}$ and 10-11.[12] Saw Ld Granville—Ld Spencer—Ld R.G.—Scotts—H.J.G.—Mr Chamberlain—Sir W. Harcourt. Dined with the Mays. Read Miss Pardoe, finished I.

[1] Photographers in Dalkeith; Hawn P.

[2] Not found.

[3] See 5 Apr. 82.

[4] Frederick Sikes, English law student in Cork, had written that 'with rare exceptions, the Home Rule feeling is all talk'; Hawn P.

[5] See 4 Jan. 86.

[6] On home rule, 30 June 1874, *H* 220. 700; see D. Thornley, *Isaac Butt* (1964), 230. Gladstone was then at Fasque for a funeral.

[7] Responsibility lay with the govt. to state clearly its Irish policy; he not required to go beyond his election address; *H* 302. 100.

[8] *Life and letters of W. B. Hodgson*, ed. J. M. D. Meiklejohn (1883).

[9] Add MS 44647, f. 2. Meaning of + unclear; n.b. Hartington's 'stiffness'.

[10] Acknowledging receipt of resolutions from Ulster liberals; *T.T.*, 1 February 1886, 6b.

[11] Geoffrey New, secretary of Evesham Liberal Association, sent a supporting resolution; Hawn P.

[12] Queen's speech; *H* 302. 193.

23. Sat.

Wrote to Ld de Vesci—Mr Homersham Cox—Mr Silkin—Bishop of Derry—M. Paulliat[1]—Ld Hartington—Chancr of Exr—& minutes. Saw H.J.G.—Lord R.G.—Ld Kimberley—Ld Rosebery—Mr Currie. $5\frac{3}{4}$-$7\frac{1}{4}$. Tea & long conversation with Lady L. & Lady B. I was delighted with the recovery especially. Dined at Mr Currie's. Read Pardoe.

24. 3 S. Epiph.

St James's mg and All Saints aftn. Wrote to Mrs O'Shea—Ld Spencer—Ld Granville. Read Brady's Elisabethan Church papers[2]—Bp of Derry's Sermons[3]—Suckling's Life—H. Cox, First Century of Xty.[4]

To Mrs. O'SHEA, 24 January 1886. '*Secret*'.[5]   Add MS 56446, f. 86.

I write to acknowledge your letter[6] which reached me yesterday afternoon. I hope to answer it more fully by Tuesday. I may however refer you to what I said in a long letter to you about communications from me to Mr. Parnell, before the Government had had its opportunity in full.[7] I must consider a little further how I stand now in reference to this point.

I may however say that it is difficult for me to determine my course about the motion of Mr. Jesse Collings,[8] until I learn, probably from the debate, how far it is a matter of interest to the newly enfranchised rural labourers and their representatives. For the present I will say no more.

25. M. St P.

Wrote to Rev. O. Shipley—Ld Hartington—Mr de Burgh[9]—Mr D. Campbell[10]—Mrs Blake—Lord Wolverton—and minutes. Visited Exhibition of Old Masters. Saw Mrs Bolton—Dr Semon—Sir W. Harcourt—H.J.G.—Ld Granville—Lord R.G.—Ld Kimberley—Mr Currie—Ld Hartington—Ld Wolverton. H of C. $4\frac{1}{2}$-8 and $10\frac{1}{2}$-11.[11] Dined at Mr Currie's. Resolved on supporting Jesse Collings.[12] An anxious day. Read Pardoe—to cool down my brain.

---

[1] Perhaps Louis Pauliat, historian of Madagascar.

[2] See 15 May 68.

[3] W. Alexander, *The great question* (1885).

[4] H. Cox, *The first century of Christianity* (1886).

[5] Copy by H. J. Gladstone.

[6] Of 23 January, Add MS 44269, f. 280: Parnell now willing to help in ousting the govt. if given 'a reasonable assurance' that Gladstone would be sent for and that he would form a ministry; but he would have 'to support the govt.' if change only meant a Hartington-Chamberlain ministry, which he has 'already been invited by Mr. C. to help in . . . but has declined to do so'. H. J. Gladstone's attached note reads: 'You will see that the enclosed . . . bears out exactly what I have heard from Labouchere about Parnell & Chamberlain.'

[7] See 16 Dec. 85.

[8] See 25, 26 Jan. 86.

[9] H. de Burgh of Dublin, on subscription for Thomas Mackevin; Hawn P.

[10] Greenock accountant and liberal, on A. D. Elliot's 'whippersnapper' speech; Hawn P.

[11] Spoke successfully against dividing on amndt. on Burma; absent from vote, carried by govt., on Barclay's amndt. on agricultural distress; *H* 302. 334.

[12] See next day.

26. Tu.

Wrote to Mrs O'Shea—Demarch of Athens Tel.[1]—Mr Bisset[2]—Mr Hirst[3]—Ld Provost of Glasgow. Saw H.J.G.—Lord R.G.—Lord Wolverton—Do *cum* Lord Granville—Mr West.

H of C. 4½-8¾ & 11-1¼. I spoke on J. Collings's motion[4] & we were driven by events to act at once. We beat the Government, I think wisely, by 329:250 so the crisis is come: better than on Thursday.[5] Dined at Mr West's.

To Mrs. O'SHEA, 26 January 1886. '*Secret*'.[6]   Add MS 56446, f. 88.

In further reference to your letter of the 23rd. I have now determined to speak & vote for the motion of Mr. Jesse Collings, and I refer you to a short speech which I mean to make on it. Any other matter touched in your letter you will probably consider to be disposed of by the series of my public declarations.

27. Wed.

Wrote to Ld Selborne—Duke of Argyll—Ld Hampden—Ld Spencer—Mr Inglis. Dined at the Speaker's. Drive with C. Saw H.J.G.—Mr Godley—Ld Granville— Sir H. James—Ld Hartington—Ld Spencer—Ld Wolverton—The Speaker—Lady M. Compton,[7] who is charming—U.S. Minister. I feel *now* a good deal exhausted after conversations such as I pass a good part of the day in holding. Read Pardoe. Whist at the Speaker's.

To the DUKE OF ARGYLL, 27 January 1886.   Add MS 56446, f. 21.

I need not & I cannot fully tell you with what deep solicitude we have followed the tidings of your home fears & cares. I dare not press you to say anything but with what joy we should learn that you are again at ease & that your treasure is opened to you.

When you are free to write, pray let me know the meaning of a passage in your long letter to the Times[8] which ranged from land to Home Rule—I understood you to say that something like the American arrangement of Central & Local Governments might be applicable either to the case of Ireland, or to the case of the United Kingdom more at large. Is this so? You certainly opened *a* door: & occupied as I am with a most grave situation I hope to learn what ray of light comes through it.

You said to me some time ago, 'what a team you have to drive.' The question may now be near, shall I be compelled to mount the box? There need be no fears connected with the division of last night. It was the safest we could have, & at the proper time when the question comes for consideration in connection with new local authority I feel very

---

[1] Hoping Greece will pause before confronting the Powers; *T.T.*, 27 January 1886, 10b.
[2] A. Bisset of Finchley sent essays; Hawn P.
[3] Alfred Hirst of Huddersfield had written on politics; Hawn P.
[4] Regretting no relief measures or allotment ('three acres and a cow') plans in Queen's speech; *H* 302. 443.
[5] When the item of the Address deploring Irish 'legislative disturbance' would be reached.
[6] Copy by H. J. Gladstone. See 24 Jan. 86n.
[7] Perhaps Lady Mabel Violet Isabel, da. of 4th marquis of Northampton.
[8] Of 26 December 1885, in *Argyll*, ii. 411.

confident it can be properly adjusted. Ireland is now the overwhelming question, and the quasi notice given by the Govt. last night sharpens the alternatives before us.

The Peers of the late Govt. are generally, I think in a very reasonable state of mind.[1]

To LORD SELBORNE, 27 January 1886.   Selborne MS 1869, f. 137.

The serious issue of last night's debate raises no immediate question on the subject debated of an unmanageable kind, but brings into view the possibility of an early call upon the Liberals to take office. Nor can I at once exclude myself from the contingencies opened by the present situation; or refrain inwardly from asking myself whether we can again hope for your cooperation.

It is very sad to think of the dissolution of our old political connection even as a possibility, and even though I am sure it would not be attended with any change in personal feelings. But I am sensible that while your letters bearing on a Church-test at the Election raised a shade of apprehension in my mind, what I have learned of your opinions about Ireland through Spencer[2] has much strengthened that apprehension, nor could I fail to note your absence from Granville's opening dinner, which I believe had been the subject of correspondence between you.[3] I wish I could hide it, fairly, from myself, but it looks to me as if—whatever you may contemplate as *positive* means of governing Ireland—you intended to shut yourself out from considering whether there are any practicable conditions which warrant & recommend the creation by Statute of an Irish legislative body for Irish affairs.

I am sure you will understand & excuse my expressing to you what weighs upon my mind.

28. Th.

Write to Sir H. Verney—Mr J.H. Hughes[4]—Mr Dunn—and minutes. H of C. $4\frac{1}{2}$.[5] Dined at Sir C. Forster's. Saw H.J.G.—Lord R.G. l.l.—Ld Wolverton—Ld Granville—Ld Spencer *cum* Ld Rosebery—M. Gennadios on Greece—M. de Stahl—M. Bylandt—Gen. Brackenbury—Mad. Novikoff—Mr Fowler—Ld Hartington.

29. Fr.

Wrote to Mrs O'Shea—Musurus Pacha—Mrs Th.—Mr G.F. Wright—& minutes. Saw H.J.G.—Ld RG l.l.—Ld Hampden—Mr A. Morley—Ld Wolverton l.l.—Mrs Th.—A. Lyttelton—Mr Hobhouse—Sir H. Ponsonby. Ten to dinner. Wrote a most stiff paper on a false alarm.[6] Read Burke on Ireland—Pardoe Louis XIV. At a quarter after midnight, in came Sir H. Ponsonby with verbal communication from H.M.[7] which I at once accepted.

---

[1] Argyll replied, 29 January, Add MS 44106, f. 89: his wife improved; the possibility of an American-style Supreme Court and written constitution not practicable; the Parnellite 'alliance' dangerous; the liberal governmental peers 'think far too much . . . of mere Party cohesion'.

[2] See to Spencer, 14 Jan. 86.

[3] See letters in Selborne MS 1869, f. 115.

[4] John H. Hughes, secretary of St. Peter's Willesden, on its affairs; Hawn P.

[5] House adjourned, Beach announcing the resignation; *H* 302. 532.

[6] Not found. Gladstone probably had wind of the Queen's overture this day to Goschen, which he quickly declined, refusing to go to Osborne; *L.Q.V.*, 3rd series, i. 26.

[7] The invitation to form an administration.

To Mrs. O'SHEA, 29 January 1886. '*Secret*'.   Add MS 56446, f. 90.

It has come round to me this morning that Mr. Parnell is apprehensive lest, in the event of my becoming Minister, I should continue the method of making my views known to him through my public declarations only.

I cannot wonder (if it be so) at his entertaining such an idea, still less at its causing him uneasiness.

I therefore write to say, in few but explicit words, that this idea & practice of mine has had reference to a time when I have been (& continue to be), a private member only; & when also I was deeply anxious on all accounts that the Tory Government should take up the question.

Full interchange of ideas with Ireland through her members, & with them through their leader, is in my opinion an indispensable condition of any examination of the subject which he has well called 'autonomy' undertaken by a responsible Minister.

My position I may add is at this moment what it was.[1]

30. Sat.

Wrote to Ld Granville–Ld Hartington–Sir H. James–Ld Selborne–Ld Sydney–Mr Chamberlain–Ld Granville–Sir F. Herschell–and telegrams &c. A very long laborious today from 9 A.M. to 8 with an hour's intermission: see recording Memorandum.[2] Quiet dinner. Ld Spencer in evg 11–12 on the sad question of the F.O.[3] Read Miss Pardoe.

I propose to examine whether it is or is not practicable to comply with the desire widely prevalent in Ireland, and testified by the return of 85 out of her 103 representatives, for the establishment, by Statute, of a Legislative body, to sit in Dublin, and to deal with Irish as distinguished from Imperial affairs; in such a manner, as would be just to each of the three Kingdoms, equitable with reference to every class of the people of Ireland, conducive to the social order and harmony of that country, and calculated to support and consolidate the unity of the Empire on the combined basis of Imperial authority and mutual attachment. W.E.G.[4]

To LORD HARTINGTON, M.P., 30 January 1886.   Chatsworth MSS 340. 1923.

I thank you very much for your letter.[5] I need not go into argument to the anterior and historic part: in the later portion you have I think adequately reproduced your opinion

---

[1] Mrs O'Shea replied next day that Parnell 'has *not* expressed *any* apprehension' as reported by Labouchere; in future Parnell thinks 'it would be most prudent' to communicate 'through myself or Lord R. Grosvenor as Mr Parnell has not a high opinion of Mr Labouchere's discretion'; Add MS 44269, f. 285.

[2] Mema. until 6 February in *Autobiographica*, iv. 73–8.

[3] Granville's failing powers meant he had to be persuaded to sit in cabinet but not as foreign secretary; Spencer's overture to Granville was initially unsuccessful; ibid., iv. 108ff.

[4] Sent to the Queen; printed in *L.Q.V.*, 3rd series, i. 37; R.A. Queen Victoria's journal, 3 February 1886: 'Received a letter from Mr Gladstone and his strange memorandum which I annex'; drafts in Add MS 44771, f. 43. On 2 February he backtracked, stressing his election address as the point of reference and this mem. as 'the outside possible result'; *L.Q.V.* ibid., 38. This mem. was read to those being invited to join the cabinet; Morley 'took it, behind all the words about future examination and so forth, to point pretty definitely to Home Rule in some shape or other'; *Recollections*, i. 213, an account apparently based on Morley's diary for 31 January 1886, but significantly longer than the entry there.

[5] Reasons for declining office; 30 January, Add MS 44148, f. 212.

that fair facilities should be given for the effort I am to make, & your reasons for that opinion again I thank you.

Do you think it will be well that I should send for Goschen after what you said this morning? or would you convey to him a kind message to explain why it is not done?[1]

To LORD SELBORNE, 30 January 1886, '*Secret*'.　　　　Selborne MS 1869, f. 151.

I thank you very much for the kind tone of your letter.[2]

I have now received the Queen's Commission. You will make allowance for me if I deal briefly with the points you raise, three I think in number.

1. The landlords. The settlement of the Tithe question under the Melbourne Govt. was compulsory, & in this respect is probably not applicable to the present case. But in some points it supplies useful instruction. On this question, if it stands alone as a difficulty I would ask you to come up at once & consult with Spencer who will I think be in town before the afternoon is far advanced.

2. On the presence of Irish members in the Imperial Parliament, my mind is entirely open. There are strong arguments both ways. But I think you will see that the new Cabinet must in considering this vast question have an absolutely free hand as to all the particular arrangements, and could not be tied in any point by a foregone conclusion.

3. You have also a passage referring to those who might have place & power in the Cabinet. I do not feel sure of the construction I ought to put upon the words. In the formation of the body views as to the Irish question must of necessity be the principal determining element. But my desire, & as far as depends on choice my intention is that it should be of the same breadth as the former Cabinet, & should be a genuine representation of the Liberal party.

Of my wishes I need not further speak: but after what I have said you will be able to judge whether you can adopt the view taken in this letter.

31. 4 S. Epiph.

St James's mg. All Saints aftn. Except Church, my day from one to eight was given to business—See record. Wrote to Ld Wolverton—The Queen—Sir W. Harcourt—Ld Granville. I got only fragmentary reading of the Life of the admirable Mr Suckling, and other books. At night came a painful & harassing incursion of letters, & my sleep for once gave way: yet for the soul it was profitable driving me to the hope that the strength of God might be made manifest in my weakness. I saw Spencer—Granville—Hamilton[3]—Herbert.

To Sir W. V. HARCOURT, M.P., 31 January 1886.　　　　MS Harcourt dep. 10, f. 8.

With regard to the assurances which you ask[4] I hoped I had satisfied you by my statement that I should do *nothing* to compromise in any way the freedom of the Cabinet as to action on the basis I propose without its assent. I have not in any way considered the

---

[1] Hartington thought Goschen would be pleased, but with no practical effect; ibid., f. 217.

[2] See 27 Jan. 86n.

[3] Hamilton acted as an executive secretary during the cabinet's formation; see *Autobiographica*, iv. 105ff.

[4] In this day's letter, Harcourt nervous of precommitment of cabinet, as Morley's appt. amounted to a declaration for Home Rule; Gardiner, i. 563, with this reply.

question of when & how as to communication with the Irish party but I shall do nothing to abridge what I have just stated.

It is for me in forming a Government to propose the terms on which I ask others to join with me: unquestionably they commit no one to the advocacy ⟨possibility?⟩ of a separate Parliament.

Nor can the appointment of John Morley have any such effect.

The terms of announcement of policy to the world cannot now be decided on: but as far as I understand your view & can now consider it I agree very much with you.

You remember our conversation on Monday about the difficulty of forming the Cabinet in the House of Commons. I told you today how much I should rely upon you for assistance *there*. My request to you is to take high office in the House of Commons. I understood you to accede to it. If I was wrong I much regret it.

[P.S.] With regard to appointments what I said was that I had dealt only with what were *special*: the most important are War, the Chancellorship, & the Admiralty, this last subject to a qualification. This I thought Hamilton had conveyed while I was occupied here.

To LORD WOLVERTON, 31 January 1886.   Add MS 56447, f. 28.

For the sake of the object in view I by no means exclude the consideration of a scheme such as you have sketched.[1] I should be glad if you were to see Spencer upon the principle of it. But it would surely be unwise of me, with the certainty of such work in the Irish matter, to charge myself also with any *laborious* department as that of finance properly handled always ought to be in a considerable degree.

Mond. Feb. One. 1886.

Wrote early to Granville—Tel. from Osborne. Off at 9.10 to Osborne. Two audiences 1½ hour in all: everything good in the main points. Large discourse upon Ireland in particular. Saw Sir H. Ponsonby—Lord Lorne.[2] Returned at 7¾. Saw Granville—do cum Spencer & Ld R. Grosvenor—Also E. Hamilton. Read Pardoe's Louis XIV. I kissed hands & am thereby Prime Minister for the third time. But as I trust for a brief tenure only. Slept well, D.G.

2. *Tu.*

Wrote to M. Gennadios—Ld Rosebery l.l.—Mrs Bolton—Sir C. Dilke—The Queen l. & Tel.—Mr Trevelyan—Mr Chamberlain—Mr Morley—and as in record. Read Pardoe. Attended dearest Mary's marriage at 11.30 & gave her away.[3] In the sight of God it is good; & man too has smiled upon it. Saw Ld R. Grosvenor—Sir H. Ponsonby—Prince of Wales—Mr Primrose—Lord Rosebery— in truth, interviews without end through most laborious day, of which a rough & hasty record will be found in my *scraps* on the formation of the Government.

---

[1] No letter found; apparently a suggestion that Gladstone again add the exchequer to the premiership.

[2] Victoria was anxious for his employment as under-sec. for colonies; Wales vetoed his joining the govt.; on 4 February Victoria vetoed his appt. as Irish viceroy; *L.Q.V.*, 3rd series, i. 39–44.

[3] Marriage of Mary Gladstone to Harry Drew.

To Sir C. W. DILKE, M.P., 2 February 1886. 1 P.M.   Add MS 44149, f. 367.

I write to you, on this first day of my going regularly to my arduous work, to express my profound regret that any circumstances of the moment should deprive me of the opportunity and the hope of enlisting on behalf of a new Government the great capacity which you have proved in a variety of spheres and forms for rendering good and great service to Crown and country.

You will well understand how absolutely recognition on my part of an external barrier is separate from any want of inward confidence, the last idea I should wish to convey.

Nor can I close without fervently expressing to you my desire that there may be reserved you a long and honourable career of public distinction.[1]

To J. MORLEY, M.P., 2 February 1886, '*Secret*'.   Add MS 44255, f. 57.

I thank you for your letter and the inclosure and I do not anticipate any difficulties of a serious nature from what you have said.[2] In the spirit and in the main I agree. It would be too much to say I have a design to propose an Irish Legislative body: for I do not sufficiently see my way as to what it would be reasonable to recommend to the Cabinet, the Queen and Parliament. But what I propose is an examination of the whole subject which would include as you state(?).[3] Of my leanings and desires you can judge for yourself.

On the removal, total or partial of the Irish members my mind is quite open: and I do not suppose you have a stereotyped opinion. About land, I think it has a logical priority, but that practicably it is one with the other great members of the Trilogy, social order and autonomy.

[P.S.] I need not add any further the necessity of absolute secrecy. Viewing the liberty you have kindly given me, I will turn over the subject in all its aspects; but I do not in saying this at all seek to qualify what I have said in the body of this note.

3. *Wed.*

Wrote to Sir L. Playfair—Mr Chamberlain—Mr O. Morgan—Mr C. Russell and a host more as in Memorandum. Conclave at Granville's most of the day. Incessant difficulties: *eppure si muove*.[4] Saw Mr Primrose[5]—Mr Trevelyan—HJG—Sir H. Ponsonby—Ld RG—Ld Wolverton—Mr Goschen—Sir J. Carmichael—G. Leveson—Mr C. Bannerman—Mr Mundella—Sir L. Playfair—Earl Morley—Ld Ripon—and the Prince of Wales at Marlborough House. Dined there, one of 40 odd. Saw Bp of Peterborough—Count Hatzfeldt—Lord Rothschild—Rustum Pacha.[6] Wrote draft

[1] In R. Jenkins, *Sir Charles Dilke* (1958), 232; Dilke replied, pleased and touched; Add MS 44149, f. 368.

[2] In reply to Gladstone's question whether 'I [Morley] had gone further than you on the Irish question', he this day sent extracts from his speech at Chelmsford, 'the high-water-mark of my Irish deliverances', i.e. '1st. The creation of a statutory legislative body. 2nd. Previous to the creation of the statutory body, some settlement of the Land question which would prevent the tenants from confiscating the property of the landlords'; Add MS 44255, f. 54.

[3] Copyist's query.

[4] 'yet it stirs'.

[5] Henry Primrose, nominated as head of the secretariat by Hamilton; *Autobiographica*, iv. 107.

[6] Rustum Pasha, 1810-95; of Italian origin; Turkish ambassador in London 1885-95; see 11 Jan. 67 and Ramm II, ii. 501.

of Address to Midlothian.[1] Read A. Arnold on Ireland[2]—Miss Pardoe: finished Vol. II.

4. Th.

Bowels disturbed in the night, from over pressure I think. Wrote to Mr Heneage—Playfair—Fowler—O. Morgan—C. Flower—Ld Wolverton. Saw Mr Primrose—Ld Kenmare—Ld R. Grosvenor—Ld Rosebery—Sir L. Playfair. A letter from the Queen today made me anxious: I called in Granville and replied.[3] Corrected & sent Address to my constituents. Conclave held here.

5. Frid.

For detailed proceedings see Mem. for the day. Wrote to Mr Marjoribanks—Mr Childers—Mr Chamberlain—Ld Aberdeen—Mr Collings—Ld Cork l.l.—Duchess of Roxburgh—Mr Morley—Mr Broadhurst—Mr Bryce—Ld W. Compton—Mr Davey—The Queen l.l. & tel.—Ld Hartington—Herbert G. Long conclave again. We are now getting nearly through. Saw Ld Granville—Ld Aberdeen—Mr Morley—Ld Cork—Mr Broadhurst—Lord R.G.—Mr Primrose—Mr A. Morley. Dined at Mr Currie's. Conclave at Granville's. Drive with C.

To LORD HARTINGTON, M.P., 5 February 1886.   Chatsworth MSS 340. 1933.
'*Private*'.

I have pleasure in assuring you that not only had I not made, but I had not heard of, that use of your letter of the 30th[4] which has led you to write again.

And it has been seen by so very few eyes, that I cannot help feeling sceptical as to the information from you.

But I accept the second letter like the first. There is nothing in it to which I feel tempted to take exception.

6. Sat. [*Mentmore*]

Wrote to Mr C. Bannerman—Mr Collings—Ld Monson—Ld Spencer Tel. & l.—Ld Ripon Tel.—The Queen l.l.—Mr Craig Sellar—Sir C. Reed—Ld Granville—Sir T. Brassey—Sir W. Harcourt. Saw Mr Primrose—Lord R.G.—Mr A. Morley—Ld Granville. Off at 3.15 to Mentmore.[5] Much thought on Ireland, I hope with profit. Read Village Conversations (admirable)[6]—OConnor Power on Ireland[7]—Miss Pardoe.

---

[1] Add MS 44771, f. 53.

[2] See 19 Jan. 86.

[3] Victoria required him to '*state explicitly what* his "examination" would lead to'; *L.Q.V.*, 3rd series, i. 42.

[4] Hartington wrote this day to say that use was being made of his letter of 30 January to present him as a supporter of Gladstone's Irish policy; Add MS 44148, f. 220.

[5] Rosebery's great house; see 19 Mar. 64.

[6] *Village conversations. No. 1-5* (1873-7).

[7] J. O'C. Power, *The Anglo-Irish quarrel, a plea for peace* (1886).

To Sir W. V. HARCOURT, chancellor of the   MS Harcourt dep. 10, f. 14.
exchequer, 6 February 1886.

I must not let the week absolutely close without emphatically thanking you for the indefatigable & effective help which you have rendered to me during its course in the difficult work now mostly accomplished.

It has been found that we shall not be ready to meet the House of Commons until Thursday week. You kindly undertook to consider what course we should take as to the mutilated Address. It will be well if we can follow the precedent of 1841.

Have you thought about the Rules of Procedure? There would be much advantage in proceeding upon the Draft prepared by the late Government. Had you in the conclave which examined it finally decided to recommend a Committee? If so why should we not take up this proposal and might we not with some hope of success move Hartington to take charge of the work?

I think of writing to Trevelyan to point out that now, before we touch Ireland, the more limited subject of the Crofters Bill might properly be dealt with & that we should with the Lord Advocate go to work upon it at once.

7. 5 S. Epiph.

Ch mg (with H.C.—most solemn thoughts for Ireland)—and evg. Long conversation with Ld R. on Foreign politics. Wrote to Rev. Mr Voysey—Ld Carlingford. . . . Read A. Guyot (finished)[1]—2ᵉ Lettre aux Positivistes Francaise[2]—Voysey's Sermon in reply.[3]

To LORD CARLINGFORD, 7 February 1886.   Carlingford MSS CP1/238.
'*Private & confidential*'.

Approaching the close of an arduous constructive work, I write a line to say how much I had wished to propose to you the assumption, in association with us, of an important charge, but for two circumstances which in combination offered an impediment I could not surmount. Firstly you were at a distance not permitting communication by post (quick as the post now is). Secondly, liberal as you have habitually been in your frame of mind towards Ireland, your conversation towards the close of the last session in a Cabinet on the subject left me without means of judging what would be your exact attitude amidst the immense difficulties of the present crisis, & it was too hazardous to attempt to clear up these difficulties by telegraphic messages *en clair*. The peculiarity of my work on this my third occasion of forming a Government has been the necessity of mixing in almost all cases political explanations with the choice & distribution of offices.

I thought this explanation due to you & I feel sure you will receive it in the sense in which it was intended. Still more sure do I feel that you will judge our intentions & the case with which I had to deal in that spirit, which alone can give any hope of a satisfactory issue to an understanding beset with an overpowering array of unfavourable chances.

I heard you were on the *Riviera*, for health: if so I trust all your expectations have been fully realised.[4]

[1] A. H. Guyot, *Creation, or the biblical cosmology* (1884).
[2] Not found.
[3] Perhaps C. Voysey's four sermons in reply to Gladstone's *C.R* articles (1876); see 10 Mar. 76.
[4] Letter sent to Mentone, only received by Carlingford on 19 February, when he replied that he 'should have felt it difficult on this occasion to accept an invitation to join the Government'; but if he could support its measures, he would; Add MS 44123, f. 252.

8. M.[1]

Wrote to The Queen—Mr Chamberlain—Sir W. Harcourt. And worked for some hours in drawing my ideas on Ireland into the form of a plan. Drove with Lady Rosebery to Ascott &c. Read Miss Pardoe—Arnold Forster on Ireland.[2] Thin & poor.

To J. CHAMBERLAIN, president of the local government   Chamberlain MSS 5/34/52.
board, 8 February 1886.

I have come down here for a few days, mainly to lessen the strain upon my voice, which has been going back. But the strain of last week is beginning to remit, and other subjects of thought to come on. Prominent among these is the subject of your ideas about Ireland. After coming up I expect to have work with Sir R. Hamilton & with Spencer. But by the end of the week, say on Saturday morning,[3] if you are then ready, I should like to have a good long exposition from you—in time for your conveniently going home, as I think you often do.

I have written to Collings about the Salary.[4] If I cannot convince you and him, I shall give in. Of course Harcourt is entitled to raise the point if he thinks fit. But you perhaps have communicated with him. As for me, in these matters, I am like Lot's wife, solitary and pickled on the plain of Sodom.

[P.S.] I hope all will go well elsewhere *today*.

To Sir W. V. HARCOURT, chancellor of the exchequer,   MS Harcourt dep. 10, f. 16.
8 February 1886. '*Secret*'.[5]

No fear. I have not the least intention of having a row about the £300.[6] I am awaiting a note from Jesse. If he holds out, I shall (without compromising your rights), at once give way to Chamberlain's will; not to his reasons which are null. I had also made up my mind to write to him today or tomorrow and invite a communication towards the end of the week. But people give me credit I think for working six times faster than I can work. There is an old & good saying 'put one foot before another'. Still there must always be one foot after another. My hands are full, and my pace I suppose is slow.

There is one Irish subject which I much wish to discuss with you when I come back & after your meditated excursion: say about Thursday or Friday.

I understand your mind is finally made up about your official house, except a room, in the negative. If so it will be much to the advantage of my staff that we should all resume our positions.[7] But if you decide or lean otherwise we can all do quite well in the First Lord's House.

[P.S.] On consideration I think, as you seemed to think, it is a question as between Wolmer & Grey for the Board of Trade. I will communicate with Mundella. Again, R.G. recommends others against both, specially C. Acland—and him I think the *best*.

---

[1] Trafalgar Square 'riots' this day.
[2] *N.C.*, xix. 215 (February 1886).
[3] See 13 Feb. 86.
[4] Gladstone proposed to reduce the salaries of the secretaries of trade and local govt. by £300; Garvin, ii. 176.
[5] Part in Gardiner, i. 568.
[6] Harcourt suggested Gladstone meet Chamberlain to smooth over the irritation of the reduction of Collings's salary; Add MS 44200, f. 27.
[7] i.e. Harcourt not using 11 Downing Street, thus leaving it for Gladstone's secretaries.

9. Tu.

Rheumatism very sharp in the night. Kept my bed & was much better. Wrote to M. Gennadios—Mr Rathbone—C. Acland—S. Morley—Mr Childers Tel.—Ld Rosebery—Ld Granville—Ld Dalhousie—Queen tel. Read Miss Pardoe—Sens de Couleur chez Homère[1]—Le Roi de Thessalie.[2]

10. Wed. [London]

Wrote to Ld Rosebery—Dowager Ly Sandhurst—Mr Childers—Mr P.W. Campbell—Mr Theobald—The Queen l.l.—and minutes. 3 to 4 hours of stiff work on my Irish MSS. Off at 2.15 to London. Saw Mr Primrose—Mr A. Morley—Ld R.G.—Ld Granville—and conclave on offices. Read Miss Pardoe. Dined with Lucy Cavendish. Saw Mr A. Lyttelton.

To H. C. E. CHILDERS, home secretary, 10 February 1886.   Add MS 44548, f. 51.
'*Secret*'.

One word on telegrams of the kind I sent you last night.[3]

Queen telegraphs, when a little excited, to different ministers on the same subject, without anything in the body of the message to show it (possibly Sir H. Ponsonby might correct this). My message was simply a form of saying the Queen had telegraphed to me.

Of course I suspend all judgment on this most deplorable business.

To LORD ROSEBERY, foreign secretary, 10 February 1886.   N.L.S. 10023, f. 157.

I have found the air here singularly good & healthful & I am ready to report officially to that effect if need be.

You have I think done very wisely in asking for a report on Wolff from Baring.[4]

The only objection I can devise to your telegram No. 63 is that all our acts in foreign matters are viewed with a somewhat illnatured jealousy, which will discover that in disclaiming 'material' departure you already contemplated some departure from the policy of Lord Salisbury. But this will in any case easily come straight in a fuller instrument.

With regard to Greece I think it will be politic soon to mention the matter to the Cabinet as there may be a disposition in some to take up the case for Greece with rather a high hand. I hope this will not be so.

[P.S.] I want to say a word to you about Bryce—& about George Leveson Gower.[5]

11. Th.

Wrote to Ld Wolverton—Ld Granville—Ld Kilcoursie—Turkish Ambassador—Mr Mellor MP—The Queen—Scotts—and minutes. Saw Mr Primrose—Ld RG—Mr A. Morley—Mr Childers—Sir W. Harcourt—Mr Acland—Ld Wolverton—Mr Hamilton—Ld Spencer—Ld Granville—Do *cum* Sir R. Hamilton[6]—The Turkish Ambassador—Ld Rosebery—Musurus Pacha—Ld Aberdeen—Ly Aberdeen. Twelve to dinner. Read Miss Pardoe.

---

[1] Not found. [2] A. Ecilaw, *Le roi de Thessalie* (1886).
[3] Not found; presumably the Trafalgar Square disturbances.
[4] Wolff's mission to Egypt; Cromer, ii. 372.
[5] Suggested, with Brand, by Rosebery on 4 February for the Address; Add MS 44289, f. 12.
[6] Gladstone was using Sir R. G. C. Hamilton's mem. of 1885, written for Carnarvon, effectively advocating 'an extensive Home Rule scheme'; E.H.D., 11 February 1886.

12. Fr.

Wrote to The Queen—Sir W. Harcourt l.l.—Lord de Vesci l.l.—Mr Mitford—Turkish Ambassador—Mr S. Mitchell—Harry N.G.—Ld Granville—& minutes. Saw Ld Kilcoursie—M. Stahl[1]—Mr Primrose—Mr Godley—Duke of St Albans—Mad. Stahl—Ld Granville—Ld Rosebery. Dined at Mr Tennant's. Read Miss Pardoe Louis XIV.

To H. N. GLADSTONE, 12 February 1886.[2]   Hawarden MSS.

I write you a few hurried lines for today's mail.

We are glad to have had your good accounts of your passage & to imagine you now safely housed.

You see the old date[3] has reappeared at the head of my letter. The work last week was extremely hard from the mixture of political discussions on the Irish question, by way of preliminary condition, with the ordinary distribution of offices which while it lasts is of itself difficult enough. I do not think there is any one in the history of this country except the late Lord Derby & myself who has ever had three times over the business of forming a Government.

Upon the whole I am well satisfied with its composition. It is not a bit more radical than the Government of last June: perhaps a little less. And we have got some good young hands, which pleases me very much.

Yet short as the Salisbury Government has been, it would not at all surprise me if this were to be shorter still, such are the difficulties that bristle round the Irish question. But the great thing is to be right: and as far as matters have yet advanced I see no reason to be apprehensive in this capital respect. I have framed a plan for the land and for the finance of what must be a very large transaction. It is necessary to see our way a little in these at the outset, for, unless these portions of any thing we attempt are sound and well constructed, we cannot hope to succeed. On the other hand if we fail—as I believe the late Ministers would have failed even to pass their plan of repressive legislation, the consequences will be deplorable in every way. There seems to be no doubt that some, and notably Lord R. Churchill, fully reckoned on my failing to form a Government.

Herbert seems to like his installation in his new office.[4] Harcourt as Chancellor of the Exchequer is fighting manfully to get down the Estimates a little. I have tried to make the Greeks reasonable, and the Sultan has written to thank me.

I must not conclude this note without thanking you again, dearest Harry, for the capital assistance you gave me as Private Secretary. I could have or wish for nothing better.

Our marriage at St Margaret's last week was beautiful. The presents are over 300—and the influx not yet over. Sixteen packages sent from London to Hawarden.

To Sir W. V. HARCOURT, chancellor of the   MS Harcourt dep. 10, ff. 21–3.
exchequer, 12 February 1886. '*Private*'.

[First letter:]   The inclosed letter is intended for you to use if you think proper in your communications with the fighting Departments;[5] and I hope you may perhaps be enabled to simplify any discussions in the Cabinet.

---

[1] M. de Staal, the Russian ambassador, and his wife.

[2] Part in Morley, iii. 296.

[3] *Sc.* place, i.e. Downing Street?   [4] Financial sec. for war.

[5] Harcourt this day sent comments on the admiralty and war office estimates: 'they are not promising especially Ripon's'; Add MS 44200, f. 40.

[Second letter:]   I have carefully considered, in a general way, the subject of our great Estimates and I will set briefly before you the result, as I know that there are *primâ facie* reasons which might tend towards inducing the heads of the two Departments to place them at a high figure.

I have considered the Irish question most on that side, on which I felt myself most competent to approach it, namely the side of land and finance. It is plain to me that if we are to cherish a rational hope of dealing effectively with the huge mass of the Irish question, we must found ourselves on an operation as to land, calculated on a scale which will exceed that of *any* former transaction of this country: even of those before the close of the great war.

I am the last to desire any unnecessary extension of demands on our financial strength. But I am morally certain that it is only by exerting *to the uttermost* our financial strength (not mainly by expenditure but as credit) on behalf of Ireland, that we can hope to sustain the burden of an adequate Land measure; while, without an adequate Land measure, we cannot either establish social order, or face the question of Irish Government.

There is before us the possibility, even the likelihood of a vast issue of Consols to those now holders of land. A portion of these will be sellers, added to the ordinary supply of sellers. A large addition to sellers without a corresponding strength to buy, would seriously depreciate the public Stocks, depress our credit, and engender discontent among those ⟨to⟩ whom, it would be said, we had paid off in the form of an unavailable security. It is the Government alone which, by keeping up its purchasing power, can maintain the balance of the market. One main & indispensable basis of that power is surplus of income over charge; and this, as the country would ill endure additional taxation for the purpose, involves moderation of expenditure.

To sum up. Irish emergency at the present moment dominates and overshadows every other emergency. The considerations which led to an increase of Naval charge last year, and which then threatened a coming increase of military charge, appear, in the present condition of affairs, to be void of that urgency, which evidently belongs to the Irish case.

I therefore hope that these augmentations will be either wholly waived, or at the least very greatly modified, at least for the season of the Irish crisis.

I may add one other fact, not immaterial. I cannot doubt that in the event of our passing a great Irish measure, the Constabulary, or the main part of it, will speedily become a formal or virtual part of the occupying force of Ireland, and will thus release a number of regiments now detained there.

The case appears to be one altogether exceptional, in which purely professional reluctance ought not to be allowed to weigh.[1]

To LORD DE VESCI, 12 February 1886.   De Vesci MSS DD/DRU 5/1.

You were kind enough to send me a short time ago some interesting facts in relation to rents on a number of estates in Ireland.

At that time the late Ministers were in office, and I thought it most desirable to leave the whole field of Irish legislation open to them. I therefore, while welcoming all information I might receive, deemed it best to do nothing which might seem to be done in competition with them, and to avoid all such discussion upon particulars as it is frequently requisite to hold with the classes & persons best informed at times when subjects of great importance are under examination by a Government. I mean such subjects as with respect to Ireland I have recently indicated in an address to my constituents soliciting re-election—(I annex extracts for convenience of reference).

I desire now to invite free communication of views from the various classes & sections

---

[1] Harcourt sent this with his mem. to Ripon and Campbell-Bannerman; Add MS 44200, f. 46.

most likely to supply full and authentic knowledge of the wants & wishes of the Irish people, I mean of all classes of the Irish people, whether belonging to a majority or a minority, and whether they may be connected with the land, with industry, or with property in general.

It would not be in my power to gather this knowledge by receiving large deputations for oral discussion, to which I am not at present equal: but I should highly value all indications, especially if they go to the heart of the questions before us, which would aid my colleagues and myself in the difficult task of determining how we may best, at this important juncture discharge our duties to Ireland and to the Empire.[1]

EXTRACTS

'There were three great Irish questions demanding our care: social order, the settlement of the land question, and a widely prevalent desire for self-government, extending beyond what is felt in Great Britain as to local affairs, but necessarily subject in all respects to the law of imperial unity.'

'It will be among the very first duties of the new Govt. to use its official opportunities for forming such an estimate as only a Ministry can form of the social state of Ireland, especially with regard to crime, to the fulfilment of contracts, to the pressure of low prices upon agriculture, & to personal liberty of action.'

13. Sat.

Wrote to the Queen—Sir W. Harcourt—. . . Drive with C. Saw Mr Primrose—Mr A. Morley—Mr Chamberlain[2]—Lady Holker—and minutes. Began putting things a little in order. Drive with C. Saw . . . Lucy dined. Wrote on Ireland (Irish authority). Read Miss Pardoe, finished III—Dr Jekyll & Mr Hyde.[3]

To H. C. E. CHILDERS, home secretary, 13 February 1886.[4]   Add MS 44132, f. 209.

Is not the word 'Committee' open to some exception. I think the Gentn. whom you have wisely chosen can be no more than at most associates or assessors? Perhaps this is too late.[5]

To Sir W. V. HARCOURT, chancellor of the exchequer, 13 February 1886.   MS Harcourt dep. 10, f. 25.

1. I think a foundation has been laid for good. Should you not consult with Kimberley as to this increase in the Indian Army? And with Ripon, who was very sceptical about it? I think C. Bannerman ought to give particulars as to the actual meaning *on economic grounds* of proceeding rapidly with Coaling Stations abroad.

2. Have you asked Hartington or *sounded* him as to undertaking the question of Procedure in continuation of what he had already done.

---

[1] Sent with a note requesting permission to publish; the letter was widely published; De Vesci's reply, 13 February (De Vesci MSS DD DRU 5/1) also widely published, gave the view of the Irish Loyal and Patriotic Union, that though Home Rule had been the 'nominal issue' of the Irish elections, land had been the real issue; a satisfactory land settlement would kill the demand for self-government; *T.T.*, 16 February, 6c, 17 February, 6d. See 19 Feb. 86.

[2] Who urged priority of Irish land, then education and local govt.; he then wrote his 'Land Purchase' mem.; *Political memoir*, 189ff.

[3] By R. L. Stevenson, just published.

[4] Written on Childers' letter mentioning a 'Committee' including Wolseley and Ritchie 'on the conduct of the Police', i.e. in the Trafalgar Square affair.

[5] Childers docketed the letter: 'we could not think of a better word'.

To LORD SPENCER, lord president, 13 February 1886.   Althorp MSS K296.

I return your admirable letter.[1] For my own part I subscribe to every word, unless it be the phrase 'bought out' which may be interpreted too broadly. Will you not show it to some of our colleagues: particularly Granville & Morley. I feel tempted to wish the Queen could see it, but I fear it would be premature.

Will you arrange with Morley to have the most salient facts as to the social state of Ireland ready for notice in the Cabinet on Monday—when (or soon) we ought I suppose to place formally on record what is in fact the presumed basis of our Administration—that we do not think special criminal legislation to be the proper mode of meeting the present wants and evils of Ireland.

You will know better than any one what heads to present, but I would include: a monthly summary of crime ending with the fragment of February; the boycotting figures; the increase of boycotting or tendency to increase before your resignation; the facts of Land Purchase; the facts of eviction; any facts bearing on the payment of rents (NB there has not been any No 2 to Vesci's No 1).

My own belief is that the menacing announcement of the Salisbury government as to coercive legislation would have ended in a miserable Parliamentary breakdown after infinite exasperation.

14. 6 S. Epiph.

Chapel Royal mg (striking sermon from the Subdean)[2] and [blank.] Wrote to Duke of Leinster[3]—Ld Selborne—Atty General—Ld Granville. Saw Ld Spencer—Sir A. Clark. Read Life of Vaux & Catechism[4]—Suckling's Life(+)—Brady.[5]

To Sir W. V. HARCOURT, chancellor of the   MS Harcourt dep. 10, f. 27.
exchequer, 14 February 1886.

It is for you to settle the day of taking the Estimates in Cabinet, in concert with W.O. & Admty—I hope tomorrow. The paper you have circulated will I am sure impress the Cabinet very much. I can understand no reason, as yet, for increase in Army E. In the case of ships there may be some amount of difficulty from contracts already given.

To LORD SELBORNE, 14 February 1886. '*Private*'.   Add MS 44548, f. 53.

I have received your letter with the same sense of pain under which it was written.[6]
Would that I could suggest an answer to your argument in the confession of Mrs. Crawford, or detect a flaw in it. I cannot.

---

[1] Spencer sent his letter to Lansdowne; Add MS 44313, f. 31 and *Spencer*, ii. 107: 'No Land Purchase for example will be permitted to work unless some real form of Home Rule is given. . . . The Landlords must be bought out.'

[2] Edgar Sheppard, 1845–1921; sub-dean of Chapel Royal 1884–1921.

[3] In fact the duchess; offer of mistress of the robes, declined; duchess of Bedford agreed to act without official appointment; Add MS 44494, f. 251.

[4] L. Vaux, *A catechism on Christian doctrine* (1885 reprint of 1583 ed.).

[5] See 24 Jan. 86.

[6] On a conversation on 1 February on the Dilke case; the verdict 'a grave scandal to the law. . . . The petition ought, for *all purposes*, to have been treated (in Scotch phrase), as "non-proven" and therefore dismissed'; 14 February, Add MS 44298, f. 205.

15. M.

Wrote to Sir W. Harcourt—Mr Whitbread—The Queen—Ld Granville—Lady Holker—Ld de Vesci Tel.—& minutes. Cabinet 2.30-5.45. Good. Saw Mr Primrose—Ld R.G.—Mr A. Morley—Mr J. Morley—Ld Chancellor—Mr Mundella. Dined at Grillions: much conversation & chaff with the Duke of Bedford. Read Dr Jekyll & Mr Hyde.

Cabinet. Mond. Feb. 15. 1886. 2.30 PM.[1]
1. Proceedings on Address. 1) To omit all after the word tenure on the ground that we cannot recommend[?][2] 2) Set up Committee of Supply at the earliest moment.
2. Estimates.[3] General sense of Cabinet that the 30m̅ of last year should be (the limit)[4]
3. Procedure: as soon as possible. Propose committee. Chair. Ask S. Whitbread or Goschen.
3a. Joint Committee on India. Propose in Lords? K. to ask Hartington to take the Chair—Chanr. Chamb. & Harcourt. Also Bannerman.
4. Crofters. Trevelyan to give notice of Bill for Monday.
0   5. Greece & the Balkans.
0   6. State of facts as to Order in Ireland.
7. Burmah. 1. Announced in Queen's Speech. 2. Notice for Monday (Dufferin's request to see who is to give notice)
Privy Seal.
Scotch Universities and Welsh Intermediate Educn.?: give notice.
Railway Rates Bill: notice to be given.[5]
O. Morgan's [Burial] Bill—Childers to inquire.[6]
Burmah: 1. Not to recede[?] from the Queen's formal announcement.[7] No anticipation of prolonged deficit. 3. No good native ruler. (4. French Treaties with Burmah)

To S. WHITBREAD, M.P., 15 February 1886. *'Private'.*   Add MS 44548, f. 54.

The Cabinet have decided that they ought to ask the House of Commons to refer the question of procedure to a Committee—such as was contemplated in the conferences held before the resignation of the late Government.

May I hope that you will consent to be proposed as Chairman of the Committee? No other arrangement could be so satisfactory to Parliament & the country.[8]

[P.S.] I believe you were the proposer of the plan of reference which we entirely accept.

---

[1] Add MS 44647, f. 3.
[2] i.e. the Conservatives' Address; closing paras. to be waived in 'the spirit of the precedent set by Sir Robert Peel in 1841'; CAB 41/20/5. See 18 Feb. 86n.
[3] Jottings for these at Add MS 44647, f. 19.
[4] '(the limit)' added later; see to Harcourt, 20 Feb. 86.
[5] The highly contentious Railway and Canal Traffic bill; see W. H. G. Armytage, *A. J. Mundella* (1951), 241ff.
[6] Childers was the second sponsor of Morgan's Burial Grounds Bill (Bill withdrawn in June).
[7] i.e. in earlier Queen's Speech, marked in Gladstone's copy, Add MS 44647, f. 10: 'the permanent incorporation of the Kingdom of Ava with my Empire'.
[8] Whitbread accepted; Add MS 44494, f. 277.

16. Tu.

Wrote to Lady Cardwell—Duchess of Leinster—The Queen—Sir H. Ponsonby. Twelve to dinner: a few in evg. Saw Mr P[rimrose][1]—Mr A.M.—Ld R. Grosvenor— Ld Rosebery—Ld Kimberley—Sir W. Harcourt—Ld & Lady Aberdeen. Read Orleans Memoirs.[2]

Cabinet. Tues. F. 16. 86. Noon.[3]
1. Burmah. Kimberley for recognising the annexation. Ripon ditto against his original opinion. Accepted. (Morley suggested Mingoon.)[4] Notify to Foreign Powers.
2. Greece. Rosebery described the position as to Greek fleet. Accepted. Chamberlain dissenting but also Morley—acquiesced.
3. Egypt. The Wolff scheme: & Wolseley's opinion of our responsibility to act [ask for?] the papers & Baring's opinion.
4. Privy Seal. To be held by First Lord. Cabinet think present precedence shd be maintained even for Commoner.
5. Chamberlain mentioned he has evidence of a cheque of Ld Salisbury's for £25 to Peters (accomplice[?] of Kelly).[5]

To Sir W. V. HARCOURT, chancellor of the   MS Harcourt dep. 10, f. 47.
exchequer, 16 February 1886.

Will you not let these papers[6] be *seen*, at any rate by a few, before the Cabinet, for instance, Ripon, Bannerman, Granville, Childers (as ex C. of E.). I agree with you that under the circs of today 1. There can be no new taxes. 2. We cannot both arrest the Sinking Fund and have the deficits unprovided for. 3. I hope Ripon will be able to meet his building contracts by retrenchment in other directions.

To Sir H. PONSONBY, the Queen's secretary,   Add MS 44548, f. 54.
16 February 1886.

With reference to the unemployed, I have communicated with the Home Secretary & the President of the Local Government Board, and I send you copy of the Memorandum which Mr. Childers sends me on behalf of both.

There is a very good case I believe for the appeal of the Lord Mayor to voluntary aid: but it is to be borne in mind that the bulk of the working classes are (comparatively) not ill but well off, through the cheapness of commodities, especially provisions: to make the State minister to the poor of London at the expence of the nation would be dangerous in principle: and the machinery which puts public works in action is slow & cumbrous, while the established local authorities are armed by the existing law with simple [*sc.* ample?] means of finding work for the unemployed.[7]

---

[1] Not Parnell, whom Gladstone was avoiding seeing; Morley, iii. 304.
[2] W. C. Taylor, *Memoirs of the House of Orleans*, 3v. (1849).
[3] Add MS 44647, f. 20.
[4] One of the various princes considered as a possible ruler; ibid., f. 9.
[5] Conservative *agents provocateurs*; Chamberlain was attempting to link the tories with the London riots on 8 February; *G.P.*, 375.
[6] Three papers on the estimates, sent on 14 February; Add MS 44200, f. 55.
[7] The upshot was Chamberlain's famous circular of 15 March encouraging local authorities to cooperate with poor law boards for temporary public works; see J. Harris, *Unemployment and politics* (1972), 75ff.

17. Wed.

Wrote to the Queen—Mr Whitbread—& minutes. Council at Windsor & audience.[1] Saw Mr P.—Mr A.M.—Ld R. Grosvenor—Sir H. Ponsonby—Ld Granville—Ld Spencer—Lord E. Clinton. On return, conclave at Granville's on return $4\frac{1}{2}$-6, on procedure tomorrow. Read Roi de Thessalie—Memoirs House of Orleans.

To Sir W. V. HARCOURT, chancellor of the   MS Harcourt dep. 10, f. 49.
exchequer, 17 February 1886.

Here is a rough sketch as my contribution.

As to principle.[2] The Address is based upon a Speech which we did not advise. And acknowledges with thanks, (in the latter part) intentions we do not adopt. We have no power to advise any *other* Speech. Therefore 1. We accept ⟨it⟩ the Address down to the point, to which it has been accepted by the House. 2. We propose to let the rest drop.

As to precedent. In 1841 and 1859, the House amended the Address against the Government & the Govt. resigned. So far the cases are parallel. But in those years the outgoing Government before actual resignation disposed of the Address and presented the answer. ⟨This⟩ It has not been done now. This however stands good. The House has *never debated any Address or part of an Address except such as has been moved in accord with or on the part of the responsible Govt.*[3]

18. Th.

Wrote to Sir W. Harcourt—Ld Granville—Sir H. Ponsonby—Mr Parker MP—The Queen l.l.—Ld Ailesbury—and minutes. H of C. $4\frac{1}{2}$-$8\frac{3}{4}$. Had to speak a good deal. Maintained obstinately my silence on Repeal & Home Rule.[4] Content. Saw Mr P.—Mr A.M.—Ld Hartington 11–$12\frac{1}{4}$—Ld R. Grosvenor—Sir J. Lubbock—Ld Granville—Mr Hamilton *cum* Sir R. Welby $2\frac{1}{4}$-$3\frac{1}{4}$ on Finance for Ireland. Dined at Lucy's. Read Le Roi de Thessalie.

I have had a satisfactory talk with Hartington. 1. He advises that *before* the orders of the day I should indicate the course of business & give hope of our making some intimation respecting Ireland within a reasonable time. 2. He is willing to be useful in obtaining *Landlord* information about Irish Landlord. 3. Shrinking from the Chair for India, as perhaps an affair of two Sessions, he is more willing to entertain the question of the Chair on Procedure.

R. Grosvenor concurs as to 1.—I think of complying. WEG Feb. 18/86.[5]

To Sir H. PONSONBY, the Queen's Secretary,   Add MS 45724, f. 187.
18 February 1886.

I send you a letter which Broadhurst our Under Home Secretary, an *excellent* man, and an ex-Labourer, has written to Rosebery. I think Her Majesty would kindly permit him to take

[1] Gave the Queen a mem. on Irish land and 'Local self-government or autonomy', in *L.Q.V.*, 3rd series, i. 61 (Gladstone's docket on his copy, Add MS 44771, f. 74, shows he gave it her this day, *pace* Buckle's note).

[2] The rest, a separate undated mem. in Gladstone's hand.

[3] Harcourt on 16 February on balance discouraged early contact with the opposition on the Address; Add MS 44200, f. 59.

[4] Statement on the govt.'s policy and amndts. to the Speech; *H* 302. 581.

[5] Holograph, Add MS 56446, f. 43; circulated; Harcourt's note: 'I agree—a good in itself—& still more so as advised by Hartington. W.V.H.'; Chamberlain's note: 'I agree. J.C.'

a little time before getting his Court Dress, so that he may grow more accustomed to what is for him a *very* novel situation.[1]

19. Fr.

Wrote to Mr Courtney—Ld Rosebery—Ld de Vesci—The Queen—Chancr of Exr—and minutes. H of C. 4½–8½.[2] Saw Mr P.—Mr A.M.—Mr Hamilton *cum* Sir R.W.—Lord Aberdeen—Ly Rosebery—Chancr of Exr. Luncheon at 15 G. Square. Read Lady Cork's Vol.[3]—Le Roi de Thessalie—Memoirs of House of Orleans.

To Sir W. V. HARCOURT, chancellor of the   MS Harcourt dep. 10, f. 59.
exchequer, 19 February 1886.

Beyond all doubt the Cabinet have decided that the Naval & Military estimates taken together are not to exceed sensibly the charge of last year as it was reported to us in Cabinet. Moreover I feel quite certain that I have myself in regular course reported this decision to Her Majesty. I will send this note to my private secretary who will verify my statement by referring to my letter to the Queen in his custody. Moreover it was referred to the heads of the two Departments together with you & Childers to consider and decide, not whether this should be done, but *how* it could best be done.

I have used the phrase 'sensibly' and of this term I am not sure but of the meaning quite sure. It is elastic to a moderate extent—it might be construed to admit only *tens* of thousands, it might be more largely taken to admit hundreds of thousands but if the latter then undoubtedly *very very* few of them.

[P.S.] Please to take this for the present as standing on memory only. I think Childers will confirm.[4]

To LORD DE VESCI, 19 February 1886. '*Private*'.   De Vesci MSS DD/DRU 5/1.

You have, as you were entitled to do, laid before the world your general argument against compliance with the demands or wishes of the majority of Irish members, but my suggestion to you embraced other matters.[5]

We have to look for substantive remedial measures as the best means of dealing with the social state of Ireland; and prominent among these is, (so far as I am aware) in the mind of Irish Landlords the idea that there should be devised a plan of a large, a very large nature, allowing of extensive expropriation under proper & effective conditions.

Am I wrong in believing that this subject has been considered not only by individuals, but by associations of landlords? If it be so & if there were a disposition to make known to me, I do not say general & broad arguments, but ideas tending to a settlement, I should think it an advantage in the practical consideration of a subject so interesting at the present juncture to us all. It may be that you are in personal communication with the leaders of such bodies, & if you think good can be done by directing their attention to the invitation contained in my published letter, pray proceed accordingly.[6]

[1] Broadhurst was excused; Add MS 45724, f. 188.   [2] Questions; *H* 302. 713.
[3] Countess of Cork, *Memoirs and thoughts* (1886), with a poem by Canning.
[4] Harcourt's note with this letter reads: '*Mr Gladstone's letter*. This letter written on afternoon of 19 Feb. . . . my letter of resignation was sent subsequently that evening.'
[5] See 12 Feb. 86.
[6] De Vesci replied, 21 February, Add MS 44495, f. 19, unaware of any scheme formulated and asking permission to circulate Gladstone's letter (given 23 February); on 22 March he sent part 1 of the Irish Loyal and Patriotic Union's 'Social order in Ireland under the National League' (1886), and on 6 April, part 2; ibid., ff. 50, 177.

20. Sat.

Wrote to Mr T.G. Law—Chancr of Exchr—W.H.G. l.l.—Ld Spencer—Ld Kimberley—The Queen—Mr Childers—R.C. Abp of Dublin—and minutes. Read Le Roi de Thessalie—Beaconsfield's Letters II.[1] Worked on Land Scheme.[2] Dined at Mr Curries. NB. Interviews omitted.

To H. C. E. CHILDERS, home secretary, 20 February   Add MS 44548, f. 55.
1886.[3]   Since Harcourt wrote the inclosed letters, I have told him in writing that the matter has been decided by the Cabinet, & that it was referred to you to carry the decision into effect.

I rely on you with your great knowledge of the Departments to suggest the means of retrenching particular votes better than any other man.

If you & Harcourt frame your scheme, I hope the others will accede—the thing having been decided.

Harcourt I understand has a margin, something within 500 m[ille]. Ripon has I should think the preferable claim on this or on a good part of it.

To Sir W. V. HARCOURT, chancellor of the   MS Harcourt dep. 10, f. 61.
exchequer, 20 February 1886.

[First letter:]   My note of the Cabinet of Monday[4] is 'General sense of Cabinet that 30 millions of last Session should be'

The sentence owing to some casual interruption is not finished but the meaning is perfectly plain—Probably I should have added 'the limit' or 'the basis'[5]

[Second letter:]   The mode of operation I think is that Childers, with his knowledge of particulars should cut down the Estimates & then you two jointly propose this as the fulfilment of the commission intrusted to the four. I wrote to C. in this sense today.[6]

To LORD SPENCER, Lord President, 20 February 1886.   Althorp MSS K296.
'Secret'.

I have put down my ideas on Ireland in different Chapters: I now send to you the first of these, on Land, & shall be glad to have a conversation with you on it before I do anything else.

Unless you think it is sufficiently advanced now for me to send it on to some of our colleagues most interested in the subject.

I have considered the finance of the question a good deal with Welby & Hamilton. It does not look bad.[7]

[1] See 9 Jan. 86.
[2] Mema. on Irish land, printed for cabinet, of 21 and 23 February, Add MS 44632, f. 69 and below, Appendix II.
[3] Copy to Harcourt, MS Harcourt dep. 215, f. 29; Childers replied on 21 February with a sharp attack on Harcourt's competence, see to Harcourt, 22 Feb. 86n. and Add MS 44132, f. 212.
[4] See 15 Feb. 86.
[5] Harcourt's letter this day described 'the absolute *non possumus*' of Ripon and Campbell-Bannerman; Add MS 44200, f. 65.
[6] Harcourt replied this day that this 'will not answer'; Gladstone must oversee the settlement personally; MS Harcourt dep. 10, f. 67.
[7] Spencer thought comment best done verbally; Add MS 44313, f. 35.

To Archbishop W. J. WALSH, 20 February 1886.   Add MS 56447, f. 43.

I have the honour to acknowledge Your Grace's communication to me[1] on the 17th of the views entertained as pending questions with respect to Ireland by yourself & your Episcopal Body and I request Your Grace to accept my sincere thanks for this communication.

21. Sexa S.

Chapel Royal mg and evg. Wrote on Irish Land. Read G. Spencer's Life[2]—Bp of Derry's Sermons[3]—Vaux Catechism—Irish Church papers (Elis.)[4]

22. M.

Wrote to Lady Cork—Dr Kurschmächer[5]—Sir W. Harcourt—the Queen l.l.—& minutes. H of C. $4\frac{1}{2}$-$8\frac{1}{2}$ & 9-$11\frac{1}{2}$. A good deal of speaking.[6] Cabinet 2-$4\frac{1}{4}$. Saw Mr P.—Mr A.M.—Chr of Exr—Mr Childers—Ld Rosebery. Read Lady Cork—Le Roi de Thessalie.

Cabinet. Mond. Feb. 22. 86. 2 PM.[7]
1. Wolff mission. Can we take the Vote today? Yes. Waiting information, we do not interfere.[8]
2. Greece. Rosebery gave information. Proposes to instruct for a blocade in the sense of the Italian instructions.
3. Servo Bulgarian agreement. Porte gives up claim of mainly mutual assistance in deference to our objections.
   Proposals of the 3 Empires. 'Prince of Bulgaria' to be nominated Govr. of Eastern Roumelia. Against as to organic statute.
4. Compensation for law riot. a. resist payment? b. Police Fund to pay? c. Committee? Adopt (b).
5. Crofter's Bill considered.
Resumé on Thurs. 2 PM.

[Harcourt:][9] Am I to show enclosed to Ripon & C. Bannerman?
[Gladstone:] My idea is as follows—that you should say to the two Colleagues: 'I propose to meet Childers & consider with him what plans we can propose to you for giving effect to decision of Cabinet about A. & N. Estimates—We wish to have your A. B. & C. D. to inform us and facilitate our labour—I am sure you will allow this'. WEG F.22.
[Harcourt:] *This is what we have already fully done*. Unless we go further than this & if we are not to have your authoritative intervention I do not see that we shall do any thing except to waste more time.
[Gladstone :] I do not understand it—Let us settle in conversation[?] with Childers.

---

[1] Not found.
[2] P. Devine, *Life of Fr. Ignatius of St Paul* [*i.e. G. Spencer*] (1866).
[3] See 24 Jan. 86.
[4] See 24 Jan. 86.
[5] On his book on Homer; Add MS 44548, f. 57.
[6] Proposing select cttee. on procedure; *H* 302. 921.
[7] Add MS 44647, f. 22.
[8] Row about expenses, see 1 Mar. 86.
[9] Harcourt MS dep. 10, f. 69.

To Sir W. V. HARCOURT, chancellor of the   MS Harcourt dep. 10, f. 80.
exchequer, 22 February 1886. '*Immed*'.

I am most willing to see C. Bannerman and Ripon: but pray remember I have no authority above or beyond that of the Cabinet. In one point I think you are hardly aware of the duties of your own position as Chancr. of the Exchequer. It is beyond all doubt one of the duties of his great office to enter upon *particulars* with his colleagues of War and Admiralty.[1] Again & again I have done this as C. of E., with Somerset and Cardwell for example. The difference in your case is that you have the advantage of an *expert* at your back who agrees with you & will work for your end.

When once I know you will use your efforts in this sense, I will put all the pressure I can upon the two colleagues. But obviously if each Minister refuses to look *beyond* the exigencies of his own department under the commission of the Cabinet, the rival claims cannot meet.

[P.S.] Pray understand that I shall work entirely with you, & that I consider the matter to be *res judicator*. But I can only work under rule. When we meet, tell me if Morley went beyond the mark in any way on Friday.

23. *Tu.*

Wrote to Ld De Vesci—The Queen—Sir A. Hobhouse—& minutes. H of C. 4½–8½. Spoke on Irish Taxation.[2] Saw Mr P.—HJG—Mr A.M.—Ld Spencer 3–4½ on Irish Land. 11–1¼. To Cardwell's Funeral at Highgate Cemetery. Read Le Roi de Thessalie (finished)—Memoirs House of Orleans.

24. *Wed.*

Wrote to Ld Spencer—Sir H. Ponsonby—and minutes. Dined at Ld Rosebery's. H. of C. 2–4. (Tenants in town).[3] Wrote on the Irish Authority. Saw Mr P—Mr A.M.—Sir R.W. *cum* Mr H.—Ld Granville—M. Stahl—Ld Rosebery—Mad. D'Aubigny. Read Mem. H of Orleans—N.A. Rev. on Amn Landlordism.[4]

To LORD SPENCER, Lord President, 24 February 1886.   Althorp MSS K296.
'*Secret*'.

Please to send on to Granville, when you have read them, my Notes on the subject of an 'Irish Authority'.[5] He has thought about it: and will appreciate the difficulties on the two main points when they arise. As one reflects more & more the argument for simplifying is more & more apt to prevail.

I inclose a postscript which tends in this direction.[6]

25. *Th.*

Wrote to The Queen l.l.—Sir H. Ponsonby—Scotts—Mr Chamberlain—Watsons—and minutes. Eight to dinner. H of C. 4½–8 & 10½–12.[7] Cabinet 2–3½. Saw Mr P.—

---

[1] Gladstone thus echoed Childers' charge (Childers to Gladstone, 21 February 1886, 'Secret', MS Harcourt dep. 215, f. 25) that Harcourt was 'abdicating the functions' of the chancellor in not dealing in details.

[2] As 'a subject that does not bear being handled by demonstrative evidence'; *H* 302. 1070.

[3] Private member's bill on Irish town houses withdrawn; *H* 302. 1151.

[4] T. P. Gill in *N.A.R.*, cxlii (January 1886).

[5] Notes probably written this day, Add MS 44771, ff. 185–96.   [6] Not found.

[7] Trevelyan introduced the Crofters Bill; *H* 302. 1304.

Mr A.M.—Chancr of Exr l.l.—Scotts—Ld Kimberley—Att. General—Mr Childers—Ld Chancr cum Att. Gen. Read N.A. Rev. on Canada[1]—Memoirs H. of Orleans.

Cabinet. Thurs. Feb. 25. 1886. 2 PM.[2]
1. Crofters Bill. Compulsory leases of hill pastures only to landlord's own existing tenants.
2. Women's Suffrage. Open question: members of Cabinet generally agt.
3. Wolff Mission. *When?* No further postponement. reserve judgment on merits.
4. Estimates—fixed. Harcourt announced result increase 1ₘ̃ more or less. Accepted.

To J. CHAMBERLAIN, president of the local government   Add MS 44548, f. 58.
board, 25 February 1886. '*Secret*'.

May I print your paper on Irish Land with a view to 'circulation' in the Cabinet?[3]

26. Fr.

Wrote to The Queen l.l.—Mr Childers—& minutes. Walk to a bookseller's: a long tail all the way back. Saw Mr P.—Mr A.M.—Duke of Grafton—Mr Hamilton. Conclave on Irish Land. H of C. 5-8½.[4] Read La Cité Chinoise[5]—Memoirs H. of Orleans.

27. Sat.

Wrote to The Queen—Sir H. Ponsonby—Ld R. Gower—Att. General and minutes. Dined at L.C.s. Saw Cray [R]. Saw Mr P.—Mr A.M.—Sir H. Ponsonby—Mr Godley—A. Lyttelton—Mr Hamilton. Read Mem. H. of Orleans—Cité Chinoise—19th Century on Ireland.[6]

To Sir H. PONSONBY, the Queen's Secretary,   Add MS 44548, f. 58.
27 February 1886.

After consideration I have not reported to the Queen a question put yesterday in the House of Commons to the Attorney General by a self-confident youth (Mr. Baumann)[7] concerning supposed hissing when the Queen's name was given in due course at a dinner celebrated in honour of the Representatives of Labour in the new House.

I acted thus because as a *Parliamentary* incident it was altogether momentary & trivial.

In itself it appears to have been grossly & ludicrously exaggerated by the Morning Post. In the more considerable journals the report did not mention it.

No hissing was heard by the Attorney General or by Lord Hobhouse the Chairman. It has

[1] Symposium on Canada, including Lorne; *N.A.R.*, cxlii. 36 (January 1886).
[2] Add MS 44647, f. 26.
[3] Answer by Chamberlain on the bottom: 'Certainly if you wish it.' Paper printed, dated 15 February, CAB 37/18/22: land purchase, central board, county councils ('framed hastily' according to Garvin, ii. 183). See 13 Feb. 86n.
[4] Stuart's motion for ratepayers' direct control of London police; *H* 302. 1395.
[5] By G. E. Simon (1885).
[6] R. Giffen, 'The economic value of Ireland to Great Britain'; also four articles on home rule; *N.C.*, xix. 329 (March 1886).
[7] See *H* 302. 1387; Russell, in reply, reviewed the press reporting. Arthur Anthony Baumann, 1856–1936; tory M.P. Camberwell 1885–92.

on inquiry however been found that, in a portion of the room, there was some hissing; though not enough to be heard in other parts of it. The occurrence of it is a most disagreeable fact though the extent was small. The monstrous magnifying of it is a great offence.

28. Sexa S.

Ch. Royal mg & aft. Saw Ld Spencer—Prof. Stuart. Read Bp of Derry's Sermons—Brady on English Orders—Huxley: Evolution & Theology: (rather thin & pretentious)[1]—Life of Hodgson[2]—Spencer's Memoirs.[3]

Monday, March 1. 1886.

Wrote to Mr Childers—Ld Spencer—and minutes. H of C. $4\frac{3}{4}$–9. Spoke on Wolff and Egypt.[4] Worked on Ireland.[5] Saw Mr P.—Mr A.M.—Duke of Grafton—Att. General—Ld Spencer—Mr Bryce. Read Mem. H of Orleans—La Cité Chinoise—Courtney on Ireland (proof).[6]

2. Tu.

Wrote to The Queen l.l.—Mr Childers. . . . H of C. $4\frac{3}{4}$–$8\frac{1}{2}$ and $9\frac{1}{2}$–11.[7] Read Mem. H of Orleans. Saw Mr P.—Mr A.M.—Sir W. Harcourt—Mr Morley—Mr Childers—Mr Fowler.

3. Wed.

Wrote to The Queen—The Maharajah[8]—Mr Fowler—and minutes. Three hours of stiff conclave on the plan for Irish Land. Saw Mr P.—Mr A.M.—Mr Hamilton—The Speaker—Att. General—Mr Childers—Sir C. Reed. Dined with the Speaker. Read Mem. H. of Orleans—Irish tracts.

4. Th.

Wrote to Mr Morley—Ld Kimberley—Mr Lefevre—Cherif Pacha—The Queen—and minutes. H of C. $5\frac{1}{4}$–$8\frac{1}{4}$ and 10–1. Spoke on Ireland. Div. 360:204.[9] Saw Mr P.—Mr A.M.—Sir H. Ponsonby—Mr Walker Solr—Mr Stuart MP. Read Mem. H of Orleans. Attended the Drawingroom: observed the variations of H.M.s *accueils*.

5. Fr.

Wrote to Ld Granville—Ld Onslow—Att. General—The Queen—& minutes. Conclave on Irish Land 2–$3\frac{1}{2}$. Progress made. Saw Mr P.—Mr A.M.—Mr Childers.

[1] T. H. Huxley, 'The evolution of theology', *F.R.*, xix. 346 (March 1886).
[2] See 21 Jan. 86.   [3] See 21 Feb. 86.
[4] Backhandedly defending Wolff's expenses; *H* 302. 1579.
[5] Revising mema. of 21, 23 February, with further mema. of 2 and 10 March; Add MS 44632, ff. 149–165.
[6] Presumably of L. H. Courtney, 'Ireland', *C.R.*, xlix. 457 (April 1886); no correspondence found.
[7] Questions; misc. business; *H* 302. 1767.
[8] i.e. Dhuleep Singh.
[9] On Holmes' motion to withhold Irish supply until govt. policy on 'social order' known; *H* 302. 1937.

Audience of H.M. at 3.30. Very gracious: but avoided serious subjects. Dined at Sir C. Forster's. Saw Wallace: Cray [R]. H. of C. $4\frac{3}{4}$–$7\frac{3}{4}$. Spoke on the Peerage: voted in *only* 202:166.[1] Read Mem. H of Orleans.

Ireland. There is no truth whatever in the statement annexed.[2] It is hardly necessary to say this: but it gives me an opportunity of stating the exact point which we have reached.

I hope we shall first consider the question of Irish Land.

I have circulated a paper on this subject by Mr Chamberlain.

Another paper has been prepared and on Wednesday was placed in the hands of Sir Henry Thring to consider the method of shaping it into a Bill. I hope it may be ready for the Cabinet to consider next week.

When this is in form I hope to set about shaping proposals financial, political, and administrative, with relation to the future Government of Ireland. WEG Mch 5, 1886.[3]

6. Sat

Wrote to Sir T. Acland—and minutes. Read T. Cooke, House of Orleans. Saw Mr P.—Mr A.M.—Lord R.G. Yesterday & today Mr Weigall[4] painted me at luncheon. Saw Sir R.W. & Mr H. on Irish Finance. Conclave on Irish question 11–1½. (Gr., Sp., Sir W.H., J.M.). Drive with C: walk: saw Wallace: dined at Spencer House (Sheriffs). Saw Ld Spencer—Ld Ripon—Ld Rosebery.

7. Quinqua S.

Prayers alone. Kept to my bed with cold. Read Memoir of G. Spencer—Bp of Derry. Saw Sir J. Carmichael.[5]

8. M.

Wrote to the Queen—& minutes. Saw Sir A. Clark—Ld Granville l.l.—Mr P.—Ld Rosebery l.l.—Mr A.M.—Mr Mundella—Mr Chamberlain. Not able to attend Cabinet.[6] Read House of Orleans.

9. Tu.

Wrote to Ld Granville—Mr Childers—& minutes. Saw Mr P.—Mr A.M.—Abp of Canterbury—Mr Hamilton (Irish finance). Read 'We Two' (began)[7]—H of Orleans finished Vol. II. Saw Sir A. Clark. Good progress but the cold weather makes him strict.

---

[1] Opposed Labouchere's resolution that heredity incompatible with representative govt.; *H* 303. 44.

[2] Press cutting: Gladstone about to submit to the Cabinet a draft plan for 'Home Rule, pure and simple'.

[3] Add MS 44772, f. 208.

[4] Henry Weigall, 1829–1925; photograph of this poor portrait in N.P.G., original's whereabouts unknown.

[5] Primrose's assistant as secretary.

[6] For proceedings, see *G.P.*, 381.

[7] Edna Lyall [A. Bayly], *We two* (1885).

To H. C. E. CHILDERS, home secretary, 9 March 1886.   Add MS 44548, f. 60.

I cannot help hoping that you will, as Mundella has agreed to do, support Harcourt tonight in meeting with a negative Dillwyn's Resolution about the Welsh Church. We have in the Cabinet at least three known Disestablishers, Chamberlain, Morley & Trevelyan, & I cannot press them further than to abstain. These men of younger standing do not appreciate the force of the argument against countenance given by Cabinet Ministers to abstract Resolutions. But I think & hope you do, & it is upon that ground that I express the hope that you will be inclined to vote with Harcourt, not because I could possibly ask you to pledge yourself in principle to the maintenance of an Established Church in Wales. This I should think Harcourt would carefully avoid.

It is very desirable to avoid multiplying causes of the Queen's mistrust at this particular moment. As the day is near at hand when we shall want all our strength to be used in that quarter for the great purpose of the present juncture.[1]

10. Ash Wed.

Wrote to Ld Rosebery—and minutes. Read Memoirs H. of O. III—Salmon on Irish Disestablisht.[2] Saw Mr P.—Mr A.M.—Sir A. Clark—Sir H. Thring—Ld Spencer. Two hours of stiff work recasting the Land paper with Sir H.T.[3] Also went through the Finance with E. Hamilton.

It was sad to miss Church today. But I saw Sir A. Clark who would not let me stir. I had my life to review. All of it outside what is called public life shows even in my own eyes as so utterly destitute of nobleness: yet any movement of penitence in me is utterly weak & effete. Whatever energies I possess are drawn off by the inexorable demands of my political vocation.

O, tis a burden Cromwell tis a burden Too heavy for a soul that hopes for heaven.[4]

To LORD ROSEBERY, foreign secretary, 10 March 1886.   Add MS 44548, f. 60.

It occurs to me that the draft about Suez Canal is rather more cold & less friendly in its effect than it probably was in your intention—& that you might soften your plan of postponement by some general expressions of desire to be in harmony with the Government of France on the subject of the Suez Canal.

As to Epirus there was no pledge of any kind as I consider to treat the arrangement as final but neither was there any indication that we regarded it as provisional so that Turkey might have ground for complaint if we referred it without fresh cause. I never understand what pretext the Greeks can have for saying we got them less than the *Treaty of Berlin* intended.

11. Th.

Wrote to Mr Goschen—Mr Trevelyan—Mr Fowler—The Queen—WHG—and minutes. Read Mem. H of O.—'We Two'. Saw Sir A. Clark—Mr P.—Mr A.M.—Ld

---

[1] Childers replied this day that though regarding establishment as a question of expediency rather than principle, he was 'very reluctant to vote directly against the motion'; Add MS 44132, f. 220. Childers and Harcourt voted with Dillwyn against Grey's amndt.; votes on Dillwyn's motion (defeated 152:251) not recorded individually; *H* 303. 366.

[2] G. Salmon, 'Thoughts on the present crisis of the Church of Ireland' (1870).

[3] See 1 Mar. 86n.

[4] *Henry VIII*, iii. 2; several times quoted; see 24 July 80 fly leaf.

Rosebery—Sir H. Thring—Mr Hamilton. Work & interviews on Irish Land & Finance.[1]

12. Fr.

Wrote to Mr Fowler—The Queen—& minutes. Saw Mr P.—Mr A.M.—Sir T. Brassey—Mr Bright—Sir W. Harcourt—W.H.G?—Ld S. *cum* Mr M. on Irish Land. Nine to dinner. Read Mem. H of O.—We Two.

Lord Spencer; Mr Morley: I should like to see you this afternoon on some points preliminary to Cabinet tomorrow 1. As to confining Bill to first option 2. as to communication with Nationalists 3. as to a Cabinet Committee on Irish Govt.—urge or no. Choose your own hour—3.30 or 5.30 or any other would suit me. W.E.G. Mch 12.[2]

To G. O. TREVELYAN, Scottish secretary, 12 March 1886.   Add MS 44548, f. 60.

(1) My first impression is that the Government are not called upon to interfere as a Government about Mr. Finlay's Bill, & that you should be quite free to take your own course about it.[3] I find considerable difficulty in understanding its legal scope & effect. I do not remember accurately all that was said in my speech of 1874[4] but I have never seen cause to recede from any part of it.

2. I feel the force of what you say about the Crofters' Bill,[5] & it seems a case to make hay while the sun shines. Please to tell me when we meet what time you & the Lord Advocate think it will take in Committee. I certainly think that when we are *through* with the *essential* Finance of the (financial) year we ought to look for an opportunity of letting you go forward.

13. Sat.

Wrote to Mr Fowler—The Queen l.l.—and minutes. Read H of O—We Two. Cabinet 2–5½. Worked on Irish Land. Saw Mr P.—Mr A.M.—Mr Hamilton *cum* Sir R. Welby—Ld Granville *cum* Ld Spencer—Sir A. Clark: who sternly forbade my dining with the French Ambassador. Read We Two—House of Orleans.

Cabinet. Sat. Mch. 13. 86. 2 PM[6]
1. Goschen's question[7]—answer to be affirmative but Commission to be without indic[atio]n of foregone conclusion—& to include [1844] Bank Act.
2. Channel Tunnel. Continue our previous tunnel.
3. Irish Land. WEG explained paper & views.[8]
   Chamberlain criticised & opened subject of Home Rule. Kimberley & others ditto.
   WEG stated his view that there be an Irish authority one & legislative.
   Spencer Morley Granville Bannerman Rosebery Ripon Childers all in tone favourable.
   Chancellor leant to severing.[9]

---

[1] Mem. on finance of land purchase; Add MS 44632, f. 187.
[2] Add MS 44647, f. 33.
[3] Trevelyan, 11 March, Add MS 44335, f. 197, asked permission to oppose Finlay's bill on the Scottish church.   [4] On Scottish church patronage, 6 July 74.
[5] Important 'that the Bill should pass promptly'; ibid.
[6] Add MS 44647, f. 35. Note at top reads: 'N.B. Cabinet Mch. 8. 2½ PM. I was absent.'
[7] On 22 March on R.C. on trade depression; *H* 203. 1491.
[8] See Appendix II.
[9] Reading uncertain; perhaps 'reserving'; probably Harcourt, see *G.P.*, 383.

W.E.G. commended for consideration before next Cabinet
1. years purchase & 84-5 rental as base.
2. How far to press duality.

Are we bound in honour or policy to do more than give to the landlords of Ireland fair optional terms of withdrawal from their position? Why should we not do this &, having done this, leave the Irish Land question to Ireland herself?[1]

14. 1 S. Lent.

Chapel Royal mg & evg. Wrote to Mr Shaw—Rev. Mr Jenkins[2]—and [blank.] Read M.H. Hierarchy—Case of the Church & Wales—and divers Tracts.

Cancelled.[3] In consequence of the closeness of the connection between the two subjects of Irish Land and Irish Government, which the Cabinet have justly felt, I think the best arrangement will be, *in lieu* of meeting on Tuesday, that I should press forward the drawing into a Bill of the first option, with such developments for the creation of a small proprietary as I mentioned yesterday; and that, while this is being done, I should endeavour to set into better shape materials which I have prepared on the subject of Irish Government, so that my colleagues would have the whole matter in view at once & would decide the first question with all the light derived from the second. The House of Commons would in the meantime deal with necessary Finance, & with the Crofters' Bill. W.E.G. Mch. 14. 86.

[Circulated version:] On consideration, instead of summoning the Cabinet for Tuesday, I think I shall do better to press forward the drawing into a Bill of the First Option (Irish Land), with provisions for a Sinking Fund and for creating a small proprietary of the kind I mentioned yesterday. For this purpose I will summon the draftsmen tomorrow. While they are at work I will endeavour to get my materials on Irish Government a little into shape so as to throw any light in my power upon the subject; but, while conceiving it possible that a Land measure might be adapted to more forms than one of Irish Government (& while holding open the question as to some part of the North,) I cannot see my own way to any satisfactory measure except it be one which shall constitute a Statutory Legislative Chamber in Dublin. In the House of Commons, I expect that necessary Finance, & the Crofters Bill, will occupy the next two or three weeks. W.E.G. Mch. 14. 86.[4]

To W. SHAW,[5] 14 March 1886.   Add MS 44548, f. 61.

I am very anxious to refer to a speech of which I have a lively recollection but which I have been unable to trace in Hansard. In it you introduced yourself as the leader, chosen at the time, of the Home Rule party, &, in a most loyal tone, you asserted your constitutional position. I was greatly struck with it at the time, & I expressed my appreciation of it immediately or soon afterwards in the debate. Could you favour me with the exact date? I am sure you

---

[1] Undated holograph; Add MS 44647, f. 37.

[2] R. C. Jenkins had sent his tract on the church in Wales; Add MS 44548, f. 61.

[3] Add MS 44647, f. 40; sent to Spencer and Granville who advised against circulation as it would 'place before him [Chamberlain] our whole plan, which if he is bent on retiring would not be altogether prudent'; ibid., f. 38.

[4] Add MS 44647, f. 41; marked 'Circulated Mch. 15'.

[5] i.e. the former home rule leader, now a bankrupt; see 17 July 80.

will forgive my troubling you. I must add the expression of my regret that we are deprived of your able assistance in Parliament.[1]

15. M.

Wrote to Att. General—Ld Granville—Ld Rosebery—Mr Fowler—The Queen l.l.—Mr Goschen—Mr Trevelyan—Mr Chamberlain—& minutes. Saw Mr P.—Mr A.M.—Conclave (Thring, Jenkins,[2] Sir R. W[elby] & E. H[amilton]) Irish Land at 2.30. Very stiff—Sir T. May—Ld Rosebery—Called on French Ambassador & converstion. Saw Sir W. Harcourt—Mr B. Currie—Mr Bryce. At night came two counter resignations![3] I got Granville & Spencer into council, & wrote to T. & C. my letters *ad interim*. Dined at Mr B. Currie's. Read Cooke Taylor, H. of Orleans.

To J. CHAMBERLAIN, president of the local government   Chamberlain MSS 5/34/53.
board, 15 March 1886.[4]

I have received your letter: shall I own that as a matter of time it takes me by surprise.

I admit the breadth of the grounds of objection which you lay, but they relate to ideas in my mind. Free in the fullest sense to reject my plans, you have kindly given me your promise to examine them in common with the Cabinet. Of what I may propose on Irish Government you know little but shreds and patches: even the paper on land is not definitive. But can you as a member of a Cabinet think of resigning in consequence of my ideas, otherwise than as of a possibility which may become a duty but which at this moment would surely be premature.

It has been absolutely beyond my power, though I have worked as hard as my age permits, to fashion a *plan* of Irish Government. I need not say that bricks and rafters which are prepared for a house are not themselves a house.

All I ask of you at this moment is that you will allow me the needed minimum of time to make ready my proposals for the Cabinet, I might even ask until the Cabinet has decided on them, but of this at present I say nothing.

I thank you much for the kind tone in which you write.

To LORD ROSEBERY, foreign secretary, 15 March 1886.   Add MS 44548, f. 61.

I have seen Waddington. He spoke about the Suez Canal & thought any differences between us were narrow. I said something which indicated that they probably turned upon the amount of *ingérence* to be exercised by the Commission. He gave me to understand it was not unlikely some conciliatory proposition would be made.

[P.S.] He is very anxious to see the Newfoundland affair *closed*.

---

[1] Shaw was unable to give a date (see 19 Mar. 86n. for reply). His speech on 27 February 1880 supported 'constitutional, rational, intelligent agitation' rather than fighting as the right and effective course for home rulers to 'achieve their ends'; Gladstone followed him, welcoming his approach; *H* 250. 1580, 1587.

[2] Sir Henry Jenkyns, 1838–99; Thring's assistant and, shortly, successor as parliamentary draftsman.

[3] i.e. Trevelyan and Chamberlain.

[4] Rendering in Chamberlain, *Political memoir*, 197, with Chamberlain's two letters of this day on resignation spelling out objections to what he understood as Gladstone's proposals, and his reply agreeing to hold over resignation.

To G. O. TREVELYAN, Scottish secretary, 15 March   Add MS 44335, f. 201.
1886. '*Secret*'.

When I received your letter I had just been considering the *day* when we might go forward, I hope not after the 25th, with a full command of time, on the Crofters Bill—and your reply today did not prepare me for what has arrived.[1]

I feel that you have written in great kindness, and that you have stated grounds of difference from my views and leanings which if I persist and you persist may, when my proposals are definitive, and when they become realities through acceptance by the Cabinet, warrant your resignation which I shall under any circumstances much deplore.

But I am confident you will feel that the time has not come for such a step. The Government was formed to examine a certain subject and the proposals that might be made on it with the full liberty of each member to reject them. But they are not as to Irish Government before you in any shape, nor even as to land are they before you in a shape representing my own developed conclusions.

The fact that you have seen in them what, *if* adhered to by me and by the Cabinet, will separate us, can be no reason, surely, for your resigning before a proposal is definitively made at least—I might say before a decision is taken. I have seen many and many a resignation, but never one based upon the intentions, nay the immature intentions of the Prime Minister, and in a pure anticipation of what may happen. I therefore hope I may regard the consideration of your letter as adjourned, but of course leaving to you its revival if you find the time and the course shall have come.[2]

16. Tu.

Wrote to Ld Hartington—Ld Spencer—The Queen—and minutes. Eight to dinner. Saw Mr P.—Mr A.M.—Ld Granville—Mr Stansfield [*sic*]—Mr E. Russell. Worked on Ireland. H of C. $4\frac{1}{4}$-$5\frac{1}{2}$ and 7-8.[3] Finished Cooke Taylors House of Orleans.

To J. CHAMBERLAIN, M.P., 16 March 1886.[4]   Chamberlain MSS 5/34/54.

What you are willing to give on ground of my convenience, I readily accept on the grounds mentioned in my note of last night: and I will take care that you have *notice* before the discussion is resumed in the Cabinet. Both subjects are so tough and difficult, and my distractions are so many and heavy, that I cannot be ready for some little time to present them for practical purposes.

There are points of your statement on which I think you would find that your objections did not apply, but I cannot hopefully say this of the whole.

To LORD HARTINGTON, M.P., 16 March 1886.   Chatsworth MSS 340. 1948.
'*Secret*'.

Many thanks for the letters on Irish Land which you have been good enough to send me.[5]

---

[1] Add MS 44335, f. 199: 'I am sorry to say that the experience of Saturday's Cabinet proved to me that I am not justified in continuing to be a member of the Government'; Gladstone's statements at it on land purchase, British-Irish financial relations, and 'a separate Irish Parliament . . . will lead . . . the Cabinet in a direction quite opposite to that which I can follow'.

[2] Trevelyan agreed this day, ibid., f. 203, to 'consider my letter as adjourned'.

[3] Questions; misc. business; *H* 303. 979.   [4] Rendering in Chamberlain, *Political memoir*, 198.

[5] Report from W. Currey, Hartington's Irish agent, on landlords' views: 20 years purchase of judicial rent and compulsory purchase; Loughlin, 87-8.

I think that if we give a certain number of years' purchase it will *be* higher than it will appear. Because it seems necessary to take as the basis the nett rental of 1884-5 & because in that year Irish rentals generally had not undergone the same amount of adjustment to agricultural prospects & prices as those of England & Scotland.

To take any later years would stimulate, I apprehend, an anti-rent agitation.

17. Wed.

Wrote to Ld Spencer—Mr Lynch[1]—and minutes. H. of C. 12½-1¾.[2] Ireland plans: a stiff day till 6.30. Saw Mr P.—Mr A.M.—Sol. Gen. Scotl.—Mr C. Flower—Herbert J.G.—Ld Granville—Ld Spencer *cum* Mr Vernon[3]—Mr S. Rendell—Mr Richard. Dined at Mr S. Rendells, to meet the Welsh members. Read 'We Two'.

18. Th.

Wrote to Mr Childers—Ld Spencer—Mr Anderson—Mrs O'Shea—Lady Hothfield—Lady Susan O.—and minutes. Saw Mr P.—Mr A.M.—Ld Kimberley—Count Karolyi—Sir W. Harcourt. Saw Ricardo [R.] Dined at Ld Hothfield's: much conversation with Duchess of Edinb. and with Lord H. 5½-7¼. Conclave at H. of C. on Ireland. Ld S., Ld G. J.M. Read State of Ireland 1731.[4] H of C. 5-7¾.[5]

Mch. 18. 86.[6] Ask Harcourt if possible to find out *absolutely* Chamberlain's intentions.

Consider whether to submit *next* to Cabinet the plan of Irish Govt. All incline to *Aye*.

After papers on Irish Govt. have been read to consider time & mode of communicating their way.

To H. C. E. CHILDERS, home secretary, 18 March 1886.   Add MS 44548, f. 62.
'*Secret*'.

Yesterday I got into shape the financial position of a possible Irish measure & I now send it you for examination. It exhibits the machinery on which I propose that we should depend not only for giving security to the British tax payer, but for giving confidence to the Creditors of Great Britain.

The mere balance of figures you have already in a rough way & I will not ask you to enter upon them now. They are prepared in concert with the Treasury & are I think as trustworthy as they can be made.

Even if Land Purchase entailed no liability Finance would still be one of the gravest parts of the whole subject & further the balance would be the wrong way. Of this Labouchere & Co (see Daily News) apparently have no idea.

No one has yet seen this paper.[7]

---

[1] Note of thanks to Stanislaus J. Lynch, Irish land commissioner, for help in London on Irish land; Add MS 44548, f. 62.

[2] Finlay's Church of Scotland Bill; *H* 303. 1057.

[3] John E. Vernon, another Irish land commissioner, helping in London.

[4] *An inquiry into some of the causes of the ill situation of the affairs of Ireland* (1731).

[5] Estimates; *H* 303. 1184.

[6] Notes of meeting with Granville, Spencer and Morley, Add MS 44647, f. 45.

[7] Childers replied this day that in general the 'proposed machinery would work well', except that customs should be imperially controlled and the provisions for war were inadequate; Add MS 44132, f. 226.

To LORD SPENCER, Lord President, 18 March 1886.   Althorp MSS K296.

I would suggest your asking Kimberley to join you today, if you think fit.

I hope you will be able to put into shape the remaining points of the Land Plan.[1]

The second option would I think perhaps be inconvenient to start with—but it might be put in while the measure was advancing, if found desirable. The question of precedence between the two plans seems to be one of policy. But to *unship* the Landlords I take to be in point of honour impossible.

19. Fr.

Wrote to Sir H. Thring—Ld Spencer—The Queen—Watsons—Ld Granville—Mr Bright—Mr Brown jun.—Mr Childers—The Queen—and minutes. Dined at Sir C. Forster's. Walk. Saw Baker [R]. Saw Mr P.—Mr A.M.—Mr Childers—H.J.G. H of C. $4\frac{3}{4}$–$8\frac{1}{4}$. Spoke on Richard's Res.—Irish intentions—& otherwise. Also $10\frac{1}{4}$–$11\frac{1}{4}$.[2] Read We Two.—Pacification Européenne.[3] Worked on Irish Papers for the Queen.

To John BRIGHT, M.P., 19 March 1886.   Add MS 43385, f. 342.

I think it may interest you to read this letter of Shaw's.[4] Please to return it. I should much like to see you for a few minutes in my room at the House of Commons either today or Monday after questions are over.

To H. C. E. CHILDERS, home secretary, 19 March 1886.   Add MS 44548, f. 63.
'*Secret*'.

Would it not suffice if there were a provision that neither country should impose any differential duty against the other.

I see two objections which appear very strong to the method you have sketched. 1. It would place Imperial Officers in contact everywhere with Irish Taxpayers. 2. If we are to tax Ireland for purposes of war, it would require the presence of the Irish members in Parliament at Westminster.[5]

20. Sat.

Wrote to Ld Hampden—Ld Granville—Mr Trevelyan—Sir W. Harcourt—& minutes.[6] Finished my Mem. for the Queen: & showed it without indication to Bright.[7] Saw Mr P.—Sir W. Harcourt—Mr A.M.—Mr Morley—Mr Bright: long &

---

[1] Extensive comments with notes by Harcourt sent next day; Add MS 44313, f. 50.

[2] Stonewalled when questioned on Irish time-table; spoke on crown duties; opposed Richard's motion on parlt. control of foreign and military policy; *H* 303. 1371, 1382, 1400.

[3] Untraced.

[4] W. Shaw to Gladstone, 17 March, Add MS 44495, f. 276; on his speech: 'I think I stated that the immense majority of those who sought Home Rule were strongly opposed to separation. . . . I still hold the same opinion. . . .' See 14 Mar. 86.

[5] The Irish Govt. Bill included an additional contribution from Ireland in wartime, despite absence of Irish M.P.s from Westminster.

[6] First draft on 'Irish Government' finished this day; Add MS 44632, f. 189 and Appendix II.

[7] Huge mem., reviewing Irish history, sent to the Queen dated 23 March; part in *L.Q.V.*, 3rd series, i. 85.

weighty[1]—Ld Ribblesdale—Mrs Th. who told me very interesting things about C. Villiers—Sp. Lyttelton on his back. Dined with the A. Lytteltons. Saw Jul [R]. Read We Two.

Lord Granville, Lord Spencer, Mr Morley, Sir W. Harcourt: I have been considering whether it would be wise to limit the possible operation of the Land Transfer Act to 60m̃ instead of 120m̃ 1. There would be less risk of its shocking the moneyed world, and acting on the Funds. 2. There seems to be something not quite rational in putting out the mention of vast sums in an Act when one cannot be *certain* of any operation at all, the whole being tentative. 3. It would of course be open to Parliament hereafter to enlarge the sum, if the Act worked well and freely. 4. If there be a disposition to cooperate, this ought to attract doubters. If there be not, it would be less easy to break on Land about 60 millions, after proposing forty. W.E.G. Mch. 20. 86.[2]

Lord Spencer seems to suppose the measure is now complete. It is not so. It only embraces ¾ of the rented lands. In taking ⅔ [*sic*] I should reserve the liberty of Parliament. If it worked well with this supply for 2 or 3 years, more wd. then be added. I presume that the great tactical advantages are hardly questioned. W.E.G. Mch. 20[3]

To Sir W. V. HARCOURT, chancellor of the   MS Harcourt dep. 10, f. 93.
exchequer, 20 March 1886.

It would be quite worth while for me to see Chamberlain to offer to cut down 120–60m̃.[4] This I should be glad to do. It is not possible to work a Cabinet on the basis of universal discussion without purpose. At any rate aet. 77.

21. 2 S. Lent.

Ch. Royal mg & aft. Made an addition to my Memorandum. Saw Sir J. Carmichael—Sir A. Clark (aureoniophone[?])—Ld Blantyre—Lady Granville. Saw Mrs Cray, 4 m. off—hopeful case [R]. Read R.C. Hierarchy[5]—Townsend, Schoolmen[6]—We Two.

22. M.

Wrote to Ld Granville tel.—Mary Drew—Mr Morley—Dowager Lady Sandhurst—The Queen—and minutes. Read We Two. Saw Mr P.—Ld Hampden—Mr A.M.—Ld Rosebery—Mr Trevelyan, little use—Sir W. Harcourt—Mr Childers—

---

[1] Bright thought the 1881 Land Act definitive, home rule a surrender, and the protestants neglected; Walling, *Diaries of Bright*, 536 and *G.P.*, 387.

[2] Add MS 44647, f. 46; Granville's attached note agreed.

[3] Add MS 44647, f. 48; Spencer's attached note stated that ¾ was 'practically the whole question'; Morley's note agreed to the reduction.

[4] Meeting suggested this day by Harcourt; Add MS 44200, f. 96.

[5] Untraced.

[6] See 27 Aug. 82.

Ld Rosebery—Ld Kimberley. Conclave on Irish affairs & the situation.[1] H. of C. 4¾-8. Spoke rather vehemently on the Volunteer motion: but deliberately.[2] Dined at Grillions: conversation with Ld Wemyss.

Mch 22. 5¼ PM at H of C. Ld G., Ld S., J.M.:[3] The Queen: Postpone communication till she leaves.[4] Land: meet tomorrow at 5.30. Trevelyan: WEG reported. Chamberlain: advised to hold no further communication with him before *the* Cabinet. WEG's plan: then to propose *one* Home Rule Resolution—that it is expedient &c. This was much approved. Ulster: schemes projected & talked over.

To J. MORLEY, Irish secretary, 22 March 1886. '*Secret*'.   Add MS 44255, f. 65.

On the points of communication *westward*, I conceive that we stand thus
1. Individually, I am perfectly ready to give to Ireland the right to impose protective duties on British goods. Had I to consider Irish prejudices, I should deem this the safest way of eventually & thoroughly getting rid of them. But the main thing is to pass our measures. In this view we have to weigh British prejudices, & the 567 (or 566) members in a position to back them. Upon the whole would not the wisest plan be a reciprocal arrangement to the effect that either country, raising the Customs Duty on the produce of the other, shall impose a corresponding duty of Excise. It *might* be considered unnecessary to bind them with regard to goods merely imported from Great Britain e.g. tobacco, if they think fit to try growing it. In the Irish interest, we ought to press our views as much as possible with respect to this point.
2. On the point of a Delegation from Ireland. To me this appears very rational. Would not the proper course be to refer in an opening speech to this subject as one hardly ripe perhaps to be entertained at present but open in principle for consideration hereafter if it should be found desirable, & capable of being disposed of without any risk or prejudice to the body of the arrangements now proposed to be made. I have asked that you may see an interesting dispatch just come from Sweden in relation to the arrangements there for the Foreign Affairs of that United Kingdom. They have not arrived at a final adjustment, but I would call attention to the fact that executive communications have hitherto sufficed & are deemed likely to suffice. *Might not these be at any rate our first resort in the case of Ireland*? Please to consider this.
3. As to proportionate representation in the way of duality. I think *one third* for the proprietary element was Mr. Parnell's first idea. Surely it cannot be thought that a constituency of £25 occupiers would return a homogeneous body of Tories; & I should have thought ⅕ an excessive estimate of the anti Nationalists on the other side, to be chosen by the popular electorate. In the States General of France, the popular bench was only *equal* to the two others: & yet I suppose you would say France was less united, certainly less organised, than Ireland, until menaces of foreign intervention & mistrust of the Court consolidated the revolutionary elements.

---

[1] Morley's diary this day: 'After quest[io]ns—in Mr. G.'s room. Granville & Spencer also. Mr. G. just had interview w. G. T[revelyan]—hopeless: will not consent to give Irish authority control of law and order. . . . Harcourt came in to say we were going to be beaten on proposal to increase grant to volunteers. Mr. G. went out to make a speech of remonstrance—came back in about quarter of an hour—but in such a state of irritat[io]n & excitement we cd. not make much of our business.'
[2] Vehement opposition to Vincent's motion to increase grant on Volunteers, as the Commons' duty was to decrease, not increase, national expenditure; *H* 303. 1520.
[3] Add MS 44647, f. 50.
[4] Buckingham Palace for Windsor.

If you find this point hard to work, could you not ask for some harmonising suggestions from the other side?

I am glad the critical heads seem to be few.

23. Tu.

Wrote to The Queen l.l.—and minutes. Saw Mr P.—Mr Knowles—Mr Whitbread—Mr A.M.—Mr Wiggin MP.[1] Visited Christie's. Saw 3 X. Worked on Ireland. Drive with C. & walk. Read We Two. H of C. $4\frac{3}{4}$-8.[2] Conclave on Irish difficulties $5\frac{1}{2}$-$7\frac{3}{4}$.[3]

Conclave. Mch. 23. 86. H of C. $5\frac{1}{2}$: Granville, Spencer, Morley, Harcourt.[4]
1. As to unshipping Land. No[:] stand or fall on *either* & *both*.
2. Land—particulars—stand over.
3. Disposal of offices: Whitbread, Illingworth, Dalhousie, Stansfield [*sic*], Bright, Fowler. Conversation.
4. Agreed to take ⟨Land⟩ Irish Govt. first.
5. To announce this week in very general terms.
6. The Cabinet on Friday to propose as within.
That it is expedient to ask Parliament to establish by Statute, under carefully framed provisions, a Legislative Body in Dublin ⟨for the management of Irish as distinguished from Imperial affairs⟩.[5]

1. The position of the Landlord in Ireland has been directly associated with State Policy all along. Since the State began to draw towards the people, his position has become more isolated, hostile, and weak. He continues to be at once the great opponent of popular privilege, and the salient point of friction with the people in the relations of rural life. It is doubtful whether the Irish Chamber could be trusted to treat him fairly.

It is hardly doubtful that he would persuade powerful parties and interests in this country that it would not treat him fairly. This seems to[6] be a *debt of honour* due to him.
2. Land purchase is objected to on account of financial complications. But the worst of the financial complications exist already, & Land purchase *will relieve them*.

They are then two. A. in respect of Imperial contributions, Ireland must reimburse us to the extent of say 4m̃ for Imperial contributions. How is this sum to be secured?

[1] Henry Wiggin, 1824–1905; liberal (unionist) M.P. E. Staffs. 1880–5, Handsworth 1885–92; railway director.
[2] Questions; local taxation; *H* 303. 1643.
[3] Morley's diary this day: 'After questions, consultat[io]n in Mr. G.'s room: Spencer, Granville, Harc[our]t: order of proceeding altered: H.R. to come first: S. very uneasy. Proceedings vis a vis the Q[ueen] decided. H. pressed for Cabinet this week. G. vy. unwilling. But must be done. Cd. the Q. authorise C. and T. to explain [i.e. in the Commons] without G.'s advice? No. The proper plan wd. be for *him* to write to H.M. to ask whether she wd. allow them to explain. H.thought otherwise: G. vy. confid[en]t. Vy. vehement on the 'childish lawlessness' of resigning merely because disclosure had b[ee]n made at last Cabinet of 'an idea in the mind of P.M.' Hence warmly repudiated notion that they were for his convenience.
Requested us to go to my room to consider filling of offices. We discussed the business—found it less easily done than said. . . . Mr. G. joined us: irritable, fidgety: strong for J. B[right] & W[hitbread]—but none of us sanguine. . . .'
[4] Add MS 44647, f. 51.
[5] Ibid., f. 53. See cabinet of 26 Mar. 86.
[6] Reading of preceding 3 words uncertain.

Only by a drastic *controul*: to which Ireland will much more readily submit, if we combine with this large exaction an operation beneficial to her. Without Land Purchase, it is hardly possible to make both ends meet in Irish Finance. With it, provided it operates pretty fairly, we can give her a clear surplus. B. We have already 14ⓜ due from Ireland for British Loans. And an increasing portion of it is due directly from the Occupier to the Treasury. Of this most dangerous system a good scheme of Land Option will enable us wholly to get rid.

3. Under the contemplated machinery of a Receiver Generalship backed by a Court & the Court backed by the whole public force in Ireland, the money is absolutely safe.

4. A fair option of escape from a false position, tendered once for all to the Landlords of Ireland, might very greatly ease the passing of the entire political settlement. WEG Mch 23/86.[1]

The French offer or suggestion of an offer seems to me a fair one, and I do not see what claims we have to Rapa or what right the Colonies have to cause our making a claim. I may however not be fully informed. W.E.G. Mch. 23. 86.[2]

24. *Wed.* [*Combe Wood*]

Wrote to Sir M. Beach—Ld Spencer—Ld Rosebery—Sir G. Philipps—Mr A. Morley. N.P. Gallery meeting 2.30. Saw Mr P.—Sir H. Thring—Mr A.M.—Mr Heneage—Sir H. Ponsonby—Ld Wolverton. Drove to Combe in evg. Audience of H.M. at 3: no indication of a seeming storm. Tea at Kensington Palace with Lorne & Princess L[ouise]. Read Life of E. Darwin[3]—finished We Two.

To LORD SPENCER, Lord President, 24 March 1886.   Althorp MSS K296.

If tomorrow at 2 will do for considering the points of the Land Scheme, will you summon those, who you may think should attend, to come here at that time.

I have seen Thring who can come. Harcourt will I think be engaged, and has no appetite for it.

25. *Th. Annunciation* [*London*]

Wrote to Ld Spencer—Sir W. Harcourt—Ld Granville—and minutes. The bowels were attacked in the night. Back at D. Street at 11 AM and went to bed. Saw Mr P.—Sir A. Clark—Mr A.M.—Ld Rosebery—Mr Whitbread. Read Life of E. Darwin—Froude English in Ireland III.[4] Came round well.

To Sir W. V. HARCOURT, chancellor of the   MS Harcourt dep. Adds 10.
exchequer, 25 March 1886.

I am unfortunately obliged to take to my bed today. I think I have good hopes of being forthcoming tomorrow. Will you kindly state for me in H of C. that on Thursday April 8 I propose to bring forward the subject of Irish policy.

[1] Add MS 44772, f. 155.
[2] Holograph in MS Harcourt dep. 10, f. 101.
[3] By J. Dowson (1861).
[4] J. A. Froude, *The English in Ireland in the eighteenth century*; see 25 Nov. 72 (new ed. 1881). Gladstone extensively quoted this work when introducing the Land Bill (*H* 304. 1782), Froude being an effective witness, as Gladstone's Irish policy was his 'especial aversion' (*D.N.B.*).

To LORD SPENCER, Lord President, 25 March 1886.   Althorp MSS K296.

I am sorry to report myself obliged to take to my bed today.

You will judge whether to postpone the meeting of this afternoon (until Saturday the same hour?) or whether to meet, & communicate with me by reference.

As regards the letter received from you yesterday,[1] I think the difficulties connected with the order of the Bills are yet in the distance. What in my mem. I put down as decided by us all on Tuesday only embraced the introduction: though the other stages may be presumed to follow. If the landlords *refuse* our Land plan, then they liberate us, as it seems to me. If they accept it, I have no doubt of being strong enough to carry it.

26. Fr.

Wrote to Ld Rosebery l.l.—The Queen l.l.—and minutes. H of C. $4\frac{3}{4}$-8.[2] Saw Mr P.—Sir W. Harcourt—Mr A.M.—Ld Dalhousie—Ld Spencer *cum* Ld Granville l.l.—Mr Stansfeld. Cabinet 2-3$\frac{1}{2}$. C. and T. split from us. I went to work immediately to supply their places.[3] Read E. Darwin—English in Ireland.

Cabinet. Friday. Mch. 26. 86. 2 PM[4]

1. India Committee. Persevere. *Nem. con.*
2. Words proposed as for Irish Govt. as within.[5]

Trevelyan objected on the ground of law & order—wd. delegate particular powers: allocate money—& cut down 103 Irish numbers to one half.

Chamberlain objects to removal of Irish members—& to controul over revenues—& to any thing but [   ][6] powers—& to giving over judges & magistrates.

Trevelyan thinks his plan wd. have to be imposed: not work eventually.

Chamberlain—you must frankly admit the legislative capacity of the body does not exclude 'Parliament'—wd give police—not the higher judges.[7]

27. Sat.

Wrote to The Queen l.l.—Ld Elgin—Ld Granville—Mr Trevelyan—Mr Chamberlain—Ld Spencer—& minutes. Read Froude's History. Dined at Ld Tweedmouth's. Saw Mr P.—Mr A.M.—E. Hamilton (Irish finance)—2-4$\frac{1}{4}$ Conclave on Irish Land—Ld Dalhousie, accepts—Mr Stansfeld, accepts—4$\frac{1}{2}$. Conclave on the Situation.[8] Saw Ld Rosebery—Ld Tweedmouth—Ld Wolverton.

[1] Arguing for priority for land purchase, see *Spencer*, ii. 110.

[2] Questions; estimates; *H* 304. 37.

[3] Stansfeld at the L.G.B., Dalhousie at the Scottish office.   [4] Add MS 44647, f. 56.

[5] Resolution agreed at conclave on 23 March; Chamberlain's questions then extracted further details.

[6] Word illegible; sense suggests 'delegated' (see Chamberlain, *Political memoir*, 199), but that not written.

[7] Chamberlain noted that on Gladstone's reply to his questions 'Trevelyan and myself again tendered our resignations and left the room'; *Political memoir*, 199.

[8] Morley's diary this day: 'At 2 to Downing St. to settle land bill w. Thring etc. Afr. Mr. G. told us what the Q. had written about the resignatns. When I was summoned back, found Mr. G. in something very like an altercat[ion] with Ld. S. as to what had taken place on 23rd. Very painful indeed. S. very plaintive: G. vehement & masterful beyond belief.'

To J. CHAMBERLAIN, M.P., 27 March 1886.   Chamberlain MSS 5/34/55.

Your resignation has now been accepted by the Queen and I lose no time in apprising you that the fact of its having been tendered and accepted may now be freely mentioned.[1]

In regard to this transaction, I have yielded to the inevitable, with profound regret, and a sense of public mischief which I trust we shall all of us do what in us lies to mitigate.

Your great powers could ill be dispensed with even in easy times. I shall rejoice, during what remains to me of life, to see them turned to the honour and advantage of the country.

To LORD SPENCER, Lord President, 27 March 1886.   Althorp MSS K296.

Not comprehending the cause of your uneasiness,[2] which I would gladly relieve, I am driven to guess, & it occurs to me you may think my idea is to carry Irish Government through the Commons before doing anything on Land. But I have no such idea: & I am inclined to think we should take the 2nd R. of Land before Committee on Irish Government. I see no reason to doubt that before I.G. can pass we shall pretty well know whether Land is likely to pass.

At present I do not share your apprehensions even as to the disposition of the Irish party about Land. But be this as it may I entirely agree that (barring the case of refusal by the Landlords) we are bound to strive equally for the passing of the two measures.

[P.S.] J. Morley who knows D[alhousie] most intimately says he has no doubt of his capacity.

To G. O. TREVELYAN, M.P., 27 March 1886. *'Private'*.   Add MS 44335, f. 205.

The Queen accepts your resignation and you are free to announce it as you please. I witness the snapping of this tie with unfeigned, and with unmixed regret. My heartiest good wishes wait upon your future career. I only grieve to think that I have lost all power to give effect to them.

28. 3 S.L.

Chapel Royal mg & evg. Saw Ld Spencer. Read R.C. Hierarchy—Strickland's Life of Lady Jane Grey: How heavenly![3]—Hist. St Mary Woolnoth &c.[4]—Indian Religion.

M. 29.

Wrote to Mr Heneage—The Queen l.l.—and minutes. Cabinet 2-4¼. Saw Mr P.—Mr Childers—Mr A.M.—Ld Kimberley—Mr Morley—Ld Spencer—Sir T.E. May—The Speaker. H. of C. 4¾-8¼.[5] Read Froude's History. The burden on mind & nerve becomes exceeding heavy: heavier than I ever felt it. May God sustain his poor failing & unworthy instrument. Saw M'Lachlan: *recidive* [R].

---

[1] A dispute ensued as to what else could be mentioned, Gladstone objecting to the reading of cabinet correspondence; see Chamberlain, *Political memoir*, 199ff., 4, 11, 15 Apr. 86.

[2] Spencer's 'uneasiness' untraced.

[3] In A. and E. Strickland, *Lives of the Tudor princesses* (1868).

[4] J. M. S. Brooke and A. W. C. Hadden, *The transcript of the register* [*of St. Mary Woolnoth*] (1886).

[5] Statement on business; Crofters Bill cttee; *H* 304. 109.

Cabinet. Monday Mch. 29. 2 PM.[1]
1. New appointments. Apology.[2]
2. Announcement of Bill for I.G.
                          of Land
                          In what terms?
3. See Paper of Mem. on Irish Govt. Bill.

Mem. 1 & 2. Choose between the two different systems.
1. We retain power of Customs & of Excise on Customable Articles & thus pay ourselves out of Irish receipt the Irish Imperial Contribution, handing over the balance.
2. Ireland takes all power of Customs & Excise (except protective), all revenues from their Receiver General, who credits as with the Imperial Contribution & passes over the balance.

Mem. 2. Revenue &c.
Plan 1 introduces a smaller amount of charge as to ordinary revenue—prevents the possibility of embarrassment to the trade between the two countries, which is now a wasting trade. But who is to collect the Land rents on purchased Estates all over the country? If Imperial officers, a great department of legal action continues in English hands, & a direct contact with a multitude of tenants. If Irish, how will the public creditor be satified with the security for our Consols?
Plan 2 1. avoid a great abridgment of the power of the Irish Legislative body. 2. also avoids placing (virtually) *direct* taxation in one body, *indirect* in another. 3. Our great object is to make the whole internal operation of law Irish. But Plan 1 brings Imperial functionaries into contact at very numerous points with the Irish taxpayer. 4. Under Plan 1 the interest of the Irish Legislature in promoting collection of revenue will perhaps be less palpable. 5. Retaining any power of ordinary taxation necessitates retaining Irish members at Westminster.[3]

Chief points for Cabinet. Mch 29 & Ap 1.[4]
✓   1. Right to lay protective duties.
✓   2. Composition of Legislative Body.
✓   3. Reservation as to Ulster. Yes.
✓   4. Reservation as to a voice for Ireland upon exterior relations: [5]Irish members to be removed from both Houses at once.
✓   5. Proportion of contribution *per capita*, & on revenue.
✓   6. The Judges.
✓   7. Use of the word Parliament. No.
      8. Subjects excluded.
      9. Transition[?] of the civil govt. Unless and until Parliament shall with consent of the Irish Legislature make other provision. See letter to H.M. Ap. 2. 86.

75 members to be elected by a constituency of £20 occupiers to sit for a prescribed term or terms not exceeding in any case ten years subject to the provisions of the Ballot Act.

---

[1] Add MS 44647, f. 58.
[2] For leaks of the appts.; *G.P.*, 392.
[3] Add MS 44647, ff. 59–61; docketed 'send copy to Mr Morley before 8 o'clock Mch. 29 86'. Note of members of cttee. on 'Finance of Irish Govt. Scheme: Kimberley, ⟨Chancellor⟩, Spencer, Morley, Harcourt, W.E.G.', ibid., f. 62.
[4] Add MS 44647, f. 67.
[5] Rest of item added in Rosebery's hand.

H.M. may by Order in Council not less than one month before the meeting of the L B fix the areas and all other particulars in relation to such election.

All Elections to the Irish Legisl. Body shall be subject to the provisions of the Acts relating to Bribery and Corruption & to Election Expenses.[1]

30. Tu.

Wrote to The Queen—Rev. Mr Liddell—Mr Morley—and minutes. Saw Mr P.— Mr Childers—Mr A.M.—Mr Morley—Att. General—Sir W. Harcourt. Further study with W. & H. on the Irish Finance. Saw Ld Ripon. H of C. 5-7$\frac{3}{4}$ & 10$\frac{1}{2}$-12$\frac{1}{4}$.[2] Read Froude Vol III. Drive with C. & walk: *short* visit to Christie's.

31. Wed.

Wrote to The Queen—Ld Rosebery—W.H.G.—and minutes.[3] Saw Mr P.—Mr J. Morley—Mr A.M.—Sir E. Grey—Sir R.W. *cum* Mr E.H.—Mr Hastings[4]—Mr Montagu[5]—and other MPs.—Ld Spencer. Cabinet Comm. 2-4$\frac{1}{2}$.[6] 13 to dinner. Read Froude. Drive with C. & walk.

Committee of Cabinet. March 31. 86.[7]

Basis of future contribution to Imperial Expenditure $\frac{1}{14}$. Amount

Basis of future contribution to Imperial Expenditure $\frac{1}{14}$. Amount	3475m
Present contribution to Imp. Exped.	[2]210
Gain	1265
less $\frac{1}{2}$ Constab[ulary] charge	565

No duty of Customs shall be imposed without imposing a corresponding duty (of Excise) upon the same article.

Present *real* contribution of Irish Exchequer to Imperial Charge	2,210
$\frac{1}{14}$ Future contribution in cash (to be paid out of a revenue of which 1400m belongs to us)[8]	3,475

Thurs. Ap. One 1886.

Wrote to Mr Gourley MP—Mr Childers—The Queen—Sir J. Cowell—and minutes. Dined with Mr Knowles. H of C. 4$\frac{3}{4}$-8.[9] Worked on Irish question. Saw

[1] Undated holograph; Add MS 44647, f. 70.

[2] Spoke last, but did not vote, on Scottish disestablishment, paired with Broadhurst; *H* 304. 341; *T.T.*, 3 April 1886, 11f.

[3] Further versions of printed mema. on Irish govt. and finance dated this day; Add MS 44632, ff. 197-8.

[4] George Woodyatt Hastings, 1825-1917; liberal (unionist) M.P. E. Worcs. 1880-92.

[5] (Sir) Samuel Montagu, 1832-1911; banker; liberal M.P. Whitechapel 1885-1900; cr. bart. 1894.

[6] Morley's diary this day: 'Commee. of Cabinet 2-4.15: finance considered. Harcourt very paradoxical—ridiculed the whole thing. Kimberley, a terrible chatterer—one wonders how a man can have lived so long in affairs, with such wordy fashions[?]. Interview at H. of C. with *P*. Extremely dismayed[?]. See Mem. [not found]. Dined at home with H. Fowler: then went to Speaker's Levee. Saw Mr. G. and told him of my interview w. P. "Very well; then we throw up the sponge: we won't, we can't, we ought not." Sd. we had better bring it before next day's Cabinet.'

[7] Add MS 44674, f. 63.

[8] Reduced to $\frac{1}{15}$ on 6 Apr. 86.

[9] i.e. the latter part of the cabinet was held in his room at the Commons; *G.P.*, 395.

Mr P.—Mr A.M. Cabinet 2-4$\frac{1}{4}$ & 5$\frac{1}{4}$-8. I was sorely tried by H.[1] Angry with myself for not bearing it better. I ought to have been thankful for it all the time. Saw Cray & another [R]. Read Froude—& the three Irish articles in 19th Cent.[2]

Cabinet. Thurs. Ap. 1. 1886. 2 PM.[3]

1. Bulgaria: R[osebery] stated Powers would probably meet, invited by Porte, to sign agreement irrespective of the Prince.
2. Proposal to summon Greece to disarm—& failing this, to apply pressure. Harcourt objects—acquiesces.
3. Irish Finance Committee: report: Standard $\frac{1}{14}$ & stick to it. Prohibitions of Irish Legislature to lay differential or protective duties &c.: referred for settlement. Neither country to lay new duties on articles the producer or manufacturer of the other. Composition of the Legislative body considered.
'Parliament': No.[4]
The Judges, & others.
Excluded subjects considered.

To E. G. GOURLEY, M.P., 1 April 1886.   Add MS 44548, f. 66.

I thank you very much for the suggestion contained in your note.[5] The subject of a meeting of the party has been much before my thoughts—I am disposed to think that circumstances may render it highly beneficial. But the time of holding it, supposing it to be held, requires careful consideration. Such meetings do not bear early repetition, & I must therefore be cautious not to throw away an opportunity. It would be disadvantageous to state the propositions without the reasons; & to act in total ignorance of the views of opponents. My present impression is that the period before the introduction of the Bill would not be so suitable, as a somewhat later stage might perhaps prove to be.

2. Fr.

Wrote to Mr Gourley—The Queen 11111—Sir H. Thring—and minutes. Finished Froude. Worked much on Ireland. H of C. 4$\frac{1}{2}$-7$\frac{3}{4}$.[6] Dined at Rosebery's. Saw Mr P.—Mr A.M.—Mr Morley—Ld Rosebery—Conclave on Ireland 2-4.[7]

---

[1] Spencer worked to prevent Harcourt's resignation; *G.P.*, 396.

[2] By Ebrington, Barry O'Brien, W. E. H. Lecky; *N.C.*, xix. 606 (April 1886).

[3] Add MS 44647, f. 66. See also the list at 29 Mar. 86 and cttee. of 31 Mar. 86.

[4] 'Although the word Parliament is applied by Statute to the Legislative Houses of Canada (perhaps to distinguish them from the Provincial bodies) it ought not to be applied in the Statute to the Irish Legislative Body'; CAB 41/20/13 and *G.P.*, 396. Extent of cabinet modifications to Gladstone's printed paper of 31 March seen by corrections marked on it at Add MS 44632, f. 194.

[5] Not found.

[6] Questions; misc. business; *H* 304. 607; reported to have paired with Broadhurst (favourable) in votes on Scottish disestablishment; *T.T.*, 3 April 1886, 11f.

[7] Summons to Granville, Spencer, Kimberley, and Morley to discuss 'present state of the arrangements' and whether 'there are any further points of difficulty' requiring cabinet discussion; Add MS 44647, f. 77. Childers also present; *G.P.*, 397.

To Sir H. THRING, parliamentary draftsman, 2 April 1886.   Add MS 44548, f. 66.

I send you a copy of the memorandum on Irish Government amended in manuscript according to the decisions of the Cabinet. It may be taken as a guide.[1]

3. Sat. [Combe Wood]

Wrote to Mr Morley l.l.l.—Scotts—Ld Hume[2]—and minutes. Saw Mr P.—Mr A.M.—Mr Bright.[3] Long sederunt with W. & H. on the Irish figures. Worked on Irish papers. Off to Combe at 4. Saw Wolverton & Mr Blackwood. Read Holyoak Tracts[4]—Duchesse d'Orleans, Letters[5]—Bennet, Oxford Movement.[6]

To J. MORLEY, Irish secretary,   Add MS 44548, f. 66; Add MS 44255, f. 68.
3 April 1886.

[First letter:]   I think you might do well to tell Parnell that in our view his claim to stand at $\frac{1}{20}$ is a *shadow*.

It turns on the 1400 m[ille], which, or *thereabouts*, unquestionably belongs to us, but goes into the Irish Exchequer.

We propose to *leave it there*. He will find this 1400 m. is *more* than the difference between (even) $\frac{1}{14}$ or $\frac{1}{20}$.

But I shall probably have to ask the Cabinet to lower the $\frac{1}{14}$ to $\frac{1}{15}$, & leave to Ireland the whole constabulary charge. This is the result of another & close examination of corrected figures with Welby & Hamilton of which I am to have the exact results on Monday in I trust a final form.

[Second letter:]   I begged you in a former note to make an easing explanation westwards about the fraction. I write now to say I think it would be well for you to lay out the two methods of proceeding as to Customs Duties & Excise on customable articles: and to learn whether the choice between them may be treated as an open question without incapacitating them from supporting us.

The one method being, to retain the taxing power to this extent in the Imperial Parliament, and retain also at Westminster say $\frac{1}{15}$ or 40 Irish members—the plan which Childers strongly prefers. The other the plan which we have put in the Bill.

The Cabinet might like to know what degree of liberty they have on this subject. I have no doubt of the superiority of the plan we have selected: but it is a question whether we ought to wreck the whole plan for it. I think it would be possible in the opening statement to treat the choice between the two plans as open provided you find that Ireland would so regard it.

I am however by no means sure that the Cabinet will assent to the retention of Irish members on any terms.

[1] On 8 April, Add MS 44332, f. 139, Thring proposed putting all Irish land questions in the Land Purchase Bill, and consequently adding a clause to the Home Rule Bill 'saving the Land Purchase Act to be passed during the present session'; docketed by Gladstone 'Mr M. If this would suffice I see no objection'; Morley agreed.
[2] *Sic*; C. A. D. Home, 1834–1918; 12th earl of Home; on the *Douglas Book* sent by W. Fraser; Add MS 44496, f. 148.
[3] Bright found him 'weary and not so brisk and eager'; Walling, *Diaries of Bright*, 539.
[4] G. J. Holyoake, *Deliberate liberalism* (1886).
[5] Ed. W. C. Taylor (1849).
[6] W. J. E. Bennett, *Some results of the Tractarian movement of 1833* (1867).

4. 4 S. Lent.

Ch mg & H.C. Service in House at 2.15. Wrote to Ld Chancellor—Mr Chamberlain—Mr Trevelyan—Sir J. Carmichael Tel.—Mr Primrose. Saw Mr Morley—Ld Spencer cum Ld Granville: (long & fruitful)—Sir A. Clark. Read R.C. Record—Reusch, Bible & Nature[1]—Catholic Politics (Bp V.)[2]

To J. CHAMBERLAIN, M.P., 4 April 1886.[3]   Chamberlain MSS 5/34/57.

The Queen has at once given permission & you will be at liberty as soon as you think fit after my statement on Thursday to explain in public what were the differences of opinion on the question of Irish Government which in your judgment rendered it obligatory upon you to resign your office.

To LORD HERSCHELL, lord chancellor, 4 April 1886.   Add MS 44548, f. 66.

Spencer came down here today & has explained to me in detail some difficulties you had felt, & suggestions you had been good enough to make, on the Irish Government Bill. We conversed upon them pretty fully, aided by Granville & experienced no difficulties except such as I think may well be got rid of. He expects to see you tomorrow & I hope will be able to give you considerable satisfaction. He is quite invaluable.

I am afraid that I can give, practically, no attention to questions of drafting, between this time & Thursday. I shall be quite willing to accept (what I may call) the Mundella Clause, if you are satisfied with it. We have a common object. I rather sympathise with your feeling that Ireland will get very good pecuniary terms. But we shall be well paid in being relieved from the constantly growing charge of the Irish Civil Service, & in the remission of a large part of the very heavy claim upon our money.[4]

5. M. [London]

Wrote to Ld Spencer—Mr J. Collings—The Queen—and minutes. Four hours at Combe on the matter for my speech: $1\frac{1}{2}$ with W. & H. on the figures: $1\frac{1}{2}$ with Morley and Parnell on the root of the matter, rather too late for me, $10\frac{1}{2}$–12.[5] Saw Ld Spencer—Mr P.—Mr A.M.—Mr Morley—Lady May. Dined at Sir T. May's. H of C. 5–8.[6] A hard day.

---

[1] F. H. Reusch, *Nature and the bible*, 2v. (1886); see also 14 Dec. 84.

[2] H. A. Vaughan, 'The true basis of Catholic politics' (1883).

[3] In Chamberlain, *Political memoir*, 200; a similar letter was sent to Trevelyan.

[4] See Herschell's letter of 5 Apr., Add MS 44496, f. 171: Gladstone's proposal 'does not fulfil the requirements laid down', especially in its financial arrangements.

[5] Parnell gave up control of customs and direct and continuous representation at Westminster, demanding in exchange reduction in Irish financial contribution; Morley, iii. 305-7, *G.P.*, 400. Morley's diary this day: 'P. came to my room 8.30: at 9.30 sent in note to Mr. G. who was dining at May's—asking him to come at 10.30. Went on talking w. P. and working at notes of Bill. When the time came, found Mr. G. in his room. . . . Told him how things stood. He asked me to open points of discussn. Then we went in. He shook hands w. P., and sat between P. & me—P. on the sofa where poor old Forster had laid his weary head many a night—he died today. We sat and got to work: P. very close, tenacious, & clever. Terms of finance the real issue. After an hour & half Mr. G. began to fail: "I fear I must go: I cannot sit late as I used to do". It was now 12, so I pressed him out of the room and followed him for a moment into his own. "Very clever", was his remark on P. The pt. is that they are to have more cash in return for surrender of customs & abandonmt. of rep[resentatio]n at W[estminster].'

[6] Crofters bill; *H* 304. 761.

To J. COLLINGS, 5 April, 1886.   Add MS 44548, f. 67.

I receive your letter of resignation[1] with much regret, but I fear with no option left me. I therefore reluctantly accept, & I am truly sorry to find there can be a state of things in which persons who have not only not offended but have, by themselves & their agents 'taken all reasonable means' to avoid offence, can nonetheless be exposed by a judicial sentence to so severe a penalty.

To LORD HERSCHELL, lord chancellor, 5 April 1886.   Add MS 44548, f. 67.

Thanking you for your letter & referring to mine of last night I am only now aware of the nature of your financial difficulty: & I say at once that, although the lenient provision as to diminution in charges for Defence seemed to me in itself equitable, yet looking at the measure as a whole, I would far rather withdraw the clause than allow it to be a difficulty in your way.

To meet the case of the Civil Service, I am inquiring what is the maximum rule of compensation ever allowed on abolition of office. I think Her Majesty might be empowered to give this maximum amount, if *she shall think fit*, to persons dismissed by the new Irish Government.

6. Tu.

Wrote to The Queen l.l.—Sir H. Thring—and minutes. Worked on Irish question.[2] Cabinet 12-2¼. Saw Mr P.—Ld Dalhousie—Sir A. Clark—Mr A.M.—Sir A. Clark—Mr Morley—Mr Agnew—Ld Spencer. Nine to dinner. Today Harcourt was worse than ever in Cabinet. He really had nothing to propose, only ranting complaints, most inexplicable. Read [blank.]

Cabinet. Tues. Ap. 6. 1886. Noon.[3]
1. Proportion of Irish contribution $\frac{14}{15}$[4]
2. W.E.G.'s plan A   Ap. 6[5]—approved (H objecting vehemently) (Pencil addition favoured by Ld Chancr.
3. Second Order to be by Election with property qualification for members as in late English law.
4. Prohibit establishment of religion.
5. Drafting. Spencer, Morley, Ld Chancellor.
6. (Communications with the Irish to proceed as heretofore).

7. Wed.

Wrote to Ld Hartington—Mr Chamberlain—and minutes. Worked hard upon this vast Irish subject. Saw Mr P.—Ld Hartington—Sir A. Clark (third inhalation)

---

[1] Unseated on petition, thus resigning as secretary of the local government board; Add MS 44496, f. 169.

[2] 'It was not until this morning that the important change, involving the retention in Imperial hands of the Customs and Excise, was effected.... Mr G. announced that Parnell, being convinced that he had no chance of getting the power to set up Protection, was willing to give up the customs and Excise duties, and to give them up without any direct representation of Ireland at Westminster, provided he could secure somewhat more favourable financial terms, that is, rather a larger balance to the good'; E.H.D., 6 April 1886.   [3] Add MS 44647, f. 78.

[4] i.e. a reduction of the Irish contribution; see 5, 6 Apr. 86 and *G.P.*, 401.

[5] No separate document found.

—Mr A.M. l.l.—Mr Hamilton—Mr Morley *cum* Ld Spencer—also Ld Spencer, late. Read Dr Craig's (catchpenny) book.[1] Dined at Ld Breadalbane's. Delightful music: Mad. Neillson, Col. Stephens, Miss Wemyss.[2]

To LORD HARTINGTON, M.P., 7 April 1886.   Chatsworth MSS 340. 1964.

I shall be happy to see you at three.[3] But I am, at the first blush, inclined to urge that, while my speech may afford plenty of grounds of *resistance* to those who are prepared to refuse consideration of any plan founded on our basis, there cannot really be an useful *discussion* of the plan until the Bill is before you?

If Chamberlain speaks, how can Trevelyan be shut out? How can the Nationalists, or the Orangemen, if they find in the speech reasons for giving at once some opinion on the principle, be overridden by a majority?

I am not aware of any analogous proceeding. The nearest perhaps is the case of a Budget. But then, while the discussion of detail is reserved, the first step is habitually allowed to be taken.

Again in this case what is to become of the Budget on Monday, & above all of the Land which surely should be introduced before Easter?

I own myself much disinclined.

8. *Th.*

The message came to me this morning: 'Hold thou up my goings in thy paths: that my footsteps slip not.'[4]

Wrote to Sir W. Harcourt—and minutes.

Settled finally my figures with Welby & Hamilton—other points with Spencer & Morley. Reflected much. Took a short drive.

H of C. $4\frac{1}{2}$-$8\frac{1}{4}$.[5] Extraordinary scenes outside the House & in. My speech, which I sometimes have thought could never end, lasted nearly $3\frac{1}{2}$ hours. Voice & strength & freedom were granted to me in a degree beyond what I could have hoped. But many a prayer had gone up for me & not I believe in vain. Came home, & went early to bed: of course much tired. My legs felt as after a great amount of muscular motion, not with the weariness of standing.

Read Chevalier d'Eon.[6]

To Sir W. V. HARCOURT, chancellor of the   MS Harcourt dep. 10, f. 103.
exchequer, 8 April 1886.

Many thanks for your opening intimation as to the Budget. I am glad to find that matters are, relatively, so satisfactory.[7] And to think that you are now earning the reward of a gallant fight on the Estimates in the infancy of our chequered, perhaps brief, certainly not uninteresting, ministerial existence.

[P.S.] I too have a Budget tonight; but it is one out of eight! sections of my subject.

---

[1] Perhaps E. T. Craig, *The Irish land and labour question* (1882); an unorthodox cooperativist.
[2] Musical entertainment at Harcourt House; E.H.D., 7 April 1886.
[3] Requested by Hartington, 6 April, Add MS 44148, f. 224.   [4] Psalm xvii. 5.
[5] Moving motion for leave to introduce the Government of Ireland Bill; *H* 304. 1036, Bassett, *Speeches*, 601.
[6] *Les loisirs du Chevalier d'Eon*, 13v. (1774), including a stay in England by the transvestite.
[7] Harcourt on 7 April sent 'the very simple proposals of the Budget'; Add MS 44200, f. 104.

9. Fr.

Wrote to Mr Heneage—Ld Kimberley—The Queen l.l.l.l—and minutes. H. of C.
5–8½ and 9¾–1¼.[1] Read Chev. D'Eon. Attended the obituary service for Forster at
the Abbey 11½–1. Saw colleagues & others before it: all most kind. Cabinet 2–4.
Conclave on vacancies which thicken.[2] Saw Mr P.—Mr A.M.

Cabinet. Frid. April 9. 86. 2 PM.[3]
1. Order of business. On Monday—for Irish Govt. Budget when? 1. Tues. 2. Thurs. Easter
holidays. Monday to 2d Monday after [Easter]. Land—Thurs. 15 or Mond. 19.
2. Budget. See Mem. within.[4] Accepted.
3. Kenrick's motion. Govt. supports [Sir R.] Cross's amendment.[5] But endeavour to get
Tuesday.

Conversation with A. Morley: Heneage's office, who retires.[6] In order of choice: 1. Vivian,
Sir H., 2. U. Shuttleworth, to be followed by Illingworth, 3. Sir Jos. Pease.

To E. HENEAGE, chancellor of the duchy, 9 April 1886.   Add MS 44548, f. 67.

I confess to the retention of my opinion that it will be a Parliamentary error if you
retire upon the announcement of a scheme for which at present you have no responsibility, & with regard to which you cannot tell what will happen before the Bill can be read
a second time a month or five weeks hence.[7]

But as I gave you my reasons with great fulness some time back, & they have not satisfied your mind, I have reluctantly concluded to accept your decision as final: & I will convey your resignation to the Queen today. Upon your learning that she accepts it—of
course not before—you will be at liberty to speak of it.

To LORD KIMBERLEY, Indian secretary, 9 April 1886.   Add MS 44548, f. 68.

The times move on fast & I am obliged to march rapidly with them. Heneage goes—I
propose to take Shuttleworth from you. Taking counsel as I have been able with Granville, Spencer, Harcourt & A. Morley, I think Illingworth is the best man we can take to
represent your Department in the House of Commons, & I rely on your kind assent. The
fact is that every question is now practically swallowed up in the Irish question, & Parliament will do little or no serious business till it is settled.[8]
[P.S.] I hope you will get this early tomorrow morning.

10. Sat.

Wrote to Ld Granville l.l.—Mr Morley—Ld Morley—Mr Stafford Howard—Mr
Borlase—King of the Belgians—Mr Cowan—Scotts—Bp of Winchr—Sir W.

[1] Statement on business; tangled with Chamberlain on land purchase and the resignation letters;
H 304. 1179, 1186.
[2] Resignation of Cork as master of the horse, Heneage as chancellor of the duchy.
[3] Add MS 44647, f. 79.
[4] Gladstone's jottings, and mem. by Hamilton at ibid., ff. 80–1.
[5] Motion proposing free education not moved; see CAB 41/20/15.
[6] Resigning as chancellor of the duchy, succeeded by Kay-Shuttleworth.
[7] See this day's letter, resigning; Add MS 44496, f. 196.
[8] Kimberley regretted losing Shuttleworth but accepted Illingworth; Add MS 44228, f. 242.

Harcourt. Saw Mr P.—Ld Morley—Mr A.M. l.l.—Ld Granville—Ld Wolverton—
Att. General—Ld Rosebery—Ld Dalhousie—& Scotts. Drive with C. Attended
the Lyceum for Faust:[1] most remarkable as to both performance and mise en
scène. Read Chev. D'Eon.

Ld Spencer, Mr Morley: What are the points in the Land Bill requiring reference to the
Cabinet? 1. The scale of years' purchase. 2. Shall State or occupier be Landlord, or shall
we leave it open. Any others?

You will find me here at three if further conversation is required. In any case, I have my
brief yet to get. If we require the Cabinet to meet on these points, should it be Monday or
Wednesday? W.E.G. Ap. 10. 86.[2]

To Sir W. V. HARCOURT, chancellor of the   MS Harcourt dep. 10, f. 106.
exchequer, 10 April 1886.

I am delighted with the idea of your speaking[3]—which I feared Budget on the Brain
might stop: and the mine you propose to work is one that can hardly be worked too
much. Measures will be taken for bringing in independent support.

To LORD MORLEY, commissioner of works, 10 April   Add MS 44548, f. 68.
1886. '*Secret*'.

I received with much pain the letter[4] you have addressed to me. I entirely admit your
freedom but cannot admit that the true date of it has arrived.

For a member of the House of Lords: I believe the constitutional course is to exercise
his judgment when the measure comes before him. To act before there is even a veto of
the House of Commons is in my view, & as far as the experience of my life has taught me,
a double departure from it.

I trust that on this point of view you will not force me to register my protest. You will
find me here at ½ past 2 if you can conveniently call.

To J. COWAN, chairman of the Midlothian liberal   ·   Add MS 44548, f. 68.
association, 10 April 1886.

I am very grateful for the matter of your telegram,[5] & for your kindness in sending it. It
is of a piece with all good conduct. I assure you that if this great subject should bring me
among my constituents I shall look them in the face with a good conscience, with a convinced understanding, & with a sense that they are not, so far as I am concerned, taken by
surprise.

11. 5 S.L.

Chapel Royal mg and aftn. Got a walk afterwards. Wrote to Sir H. Ponsonby
Tel.—Ld Granville—The Queen l.l.—Mr Irving—Mr Chamberlain. Saw Sir J.

---

[1] With Irving, Ellen Terry, and Fanny Stirling in W. G. Wills' version. See next day.

[2] Add MS 44647, f. 83.

[3] Harcourt proposed to follow Churchill (Add MS 44200, f. 112) and did so, at a little distance; *H*
304. 1439.

[4] 9 April, Add MS 44496, f. 200, resigning, which he insisted on, despite this appeal.

[5] Not found.

Carmichael—Ld Spencer. Read Longfellow's Life[1]—Christie's remarkable Poem[2]—R.C. Records—Reusch, Bible & Nature (Transl.)—Adam, Religious World.[3]

To J. CHAMBERLAIN, M.P., 11 April 1886.   Chamberlain MSS 5/34/59.

I am much concerned to hear that you propose to revert tomorrow to the subject of your personal explanation. At the same time I have no right or power to limit you otherwise than in the matter touched on Friday.[4]

No one I think has questioned, certainly I have not, the good faith of your belief that you had my assent & the Queen's permission to enter for the purpose of personal explanation on the subject of Land Purchase not yet before Parliament.

I am most desirous to avoid anything like personal controversy between us, which I do not think would be edifying to the world. But I cannot subscribe to all the recitals in your letter.

The least I can do, if the matter be farther agitated, will be (publicly) to postpone explaining upon your explanation until the Land question is opened when I should have to make a statement which I think conclusive upon the whole matter.

To Henry IRVING, 11 April 1886.   Add MS 44548, f. 69.

I must write a line to thank you for the performance of last night: especially for your own share in it, the most remarkable part of a remarkable whole.

Arriving early, we heard the apology for Miss Terry's cold. But for this I could not have found there was anything for which to apologise. And really I thought Mrs. Stirling's performance the very best I have ever seen of hers.

I do not know how much time has been given to preparing the mise en scène: but had it been ten years I suppose it could not have been done better.

12. M.

Wrote to Ld Rosebery—Sir U.K. Shuttleworth—Arthur L.—Sir W. Harcourt—Ld Cork—Mr Chamberlain—The Queen l.l.—and minutes. Saw Mr P.—Mr A.M.—Canon MacColl—Ld Granville—Sir W. Harcourt. Eight to dinner.[5] H of C. $4\frac{3}{4}$–8 and $9\frac{1}{2}$–12.[6] 2–4 Conclave revising the Bill.[7] Read Chev. D'Eon—Bowen Harrow Songs.[8]

To Sir W. V. HARCOURT, chancellor of the   MS Harcourt dep. Adds 10.
exchequer, 12 April 1886.

Carmichael will submit a suggestion about the debate for your approval. He will tell you my arrangement with the Att. General last Friday. If you greatly prefer proceeding today, he would probably give way: but I rather scruple interference against his will as it *might* be very inconvenient to him. I think however he would have every right disposition in the matter.

---

[1] S. Longfellow, *Life of H. W. Longfellow*, 2v. (1886).

[2] A. J. Christie, *The end of man* (1886).

[3] R. Adam, *The religious world displayed*, 3v. (1809).

[4] Restrictions on using Gladstone's letters publicly, making it 'an explanation of my conduct not yours'; Chamberlain MSS 5/34/58 and *Political memoir*, 204.

[5] See *G.P.*, 403.   [6] Questions; Govt. of Ireland Bill; *H* 304. 1313.

[7] Final version of the bill; Add MS 44633, f. 4.   [8] By E. E. Bowen (1886).

13. Tu.

Wrote to Ld Granville—Mayor of Lpool—Mr Childers—Mr Jones Parry—The Queen l.l.—& minutes. Dined with the Wests. Saw Mr P.—Ld Granville—Mr A.M.—Mr Morley. Drive with C. Worked on Irish Qun. Read D'Eon. H. of C. 4¾–8 & 10–1½.[1] I spoke 1¼ hour from midnight, and was 'astonied' as Holy Scripture says[2] at the strength given me in voice & tongue, after a day in which I felt to the uttermost the sum of weakness isolation & dependence.

14. Wed.

Wrote to Ld Methuen—Mayor of Boston—Sir H. Ponsonby—The Queen—and minutes. Cabinet 2–4½. Dined with the Hayters. Worked on Ireland. Read D'Eon—Froude Vol. II. Saw Mr P.—Ld Rosebery—Mr A.M.—Ld Spencer—Mr H. Cosham[3]—Ly Spencer—Saw two. s[ister]s [R].

Cabinet. Wed. Ap. 14. 2 PM.[4]
1. Conversation on preparing Local Govt. Bill and Registration Bill—first of the two.
2. Irish Land Scheme. 1. The sum to be inserted in the Bill. 1 year, 10₥; 1 year 20₥; 1 year 20₥. 2. (In Bill) Scheduled Districts—(Congested)—when Irish authority may become proprietor. 3. As a rule occupiers to become owners; unless tenants object, being under £4. 4. Scale of years—20 years normal. Comm[issio]n may raise to 22 or lower. No minimum.
3. Harcourt: raised the question of the presence of the Irish members. Considered it vital, & to be recognised as vital by all. He was the sole objector to my language of last night. Hoped we would not survive till this change was made.[5]
3 [*sic*] *Eastern Question.* Summons & visit [by the Allied fleet] to Piraeus—to be followed in case of refusal by a blockade after the Scheldt precedent of 1832.
4. Burials Bill previously Harcourt's to be brought in by O. Morgan—with slight alterations.
5. Irish Arms Act expires June 1.

To LORD METHUEN, lord in waiting, 14 April 1886.   Add MS 44548, f. 71.
'*Private*'.

I thank you very much for your kind letter.[6]

Under no circumstances should I have looked upon any letter of resignation from you as other than an act of what you believed to be duty.

I am glad that all proceedings are to stand over, for (do I use too great freedom in saying it) I have felt resignations *in the middle of my speech* to be highly premature.

My speech is still unfinished, the policy of the Government will in no sense be before

---

¹ Govt. of Ireland Bill then given 1° R; *H* 304. 1534.

² Ezra, ix. 3.

³ Handel Cossham, 1824–90; liberal M.P. E. Bristol 1885–90.

⁴ Add MS 44647, f. 85. Holograph note reads: 'Granville—only two resignations *in this Cabinet* today, happily both withdrawn'; ibid., f. 89.

⁵ Morley's diary this day: 'Cabinet 2–4.30. Preceded by a curious scene of violence agst. Mr. G. made by Harct. to S. and me. Repetition in Cabt.—not much less direct. Mr. G. said he held exactly my opinions abt. exclus[io]n of Irish members—namely that no feasible alternative cd. be invented.'

⁶ Resigning in due course, with apologies for form and season; 13 April, Add MS 44496, f. 245.

the world until after Friday on the production of the Bill. I said last Thursday that nothing but physical impossibility prevented me from presenting together two measures, which are *for us* at least indispensable.

All this I represented to [Lord] Morley, but in vain. He set the ball rolling. At my age, being on the eve of political extinction, I view with the deepest concern the rapid disintegration of the Liberal Party among the Peers. Few causes, so far as I can see, will more effectually contribute to the advance of democracy, or will more seriously endanger the continuance of that moderate & stable character which has hitherto marked the course of British legislation.

I am therefore relieved & gratified (over & above the kind words you use) when a Peer of your stamp calls in time as his counsellor, on a matter of far reaching consequence, & one on which he cannot (as I think) have any political responsibility for a considerable period.

15. Th.

Wrote to Mr Childers—Govr of Minnesota[1]—Mr Ridler—Mrs Th.—Mr Chamberlain—The Queen—& minutes. Worked hard on Irish Land. Conclave on Scheme $12\frac{1}{2}$-$2\frac{3}{4}$. Drive with C. Dined at Sir T. May's. H of C. $4\frac{3}{4}$-8 & $10\frac{1}{4}$-$12\frac{1}{4}$.[2] Saw Mr P.—The Speaker—Mr A.M.—Sir T.E. May.

To J. CHAMBERLAIN, M.P., 15 April 1886.[3]   Chamberlain MSS 5/34/61.

You may I think now consider yourself quite at liberty to refer to any matter in the Cabinet with reference to the Land Bill.

I intend to state the fact of the amount stated in the first sketch, and of its subsequent reduction. I think that your & Trevelyan's objection first turned my mind to the more rigid examination which showed me that, though I cannot answer [for][4] the future if the plan works well and largely, it would have been *wrong* to ask for the sum I first named. I have no objection to state this if you desire it. I should like to take the course which may on the whole be most conciliatory, & least likely to aggravate any breach in the party.

16. Fr.

Wrote to The Queen. . . . Saw Mr P.—Mr A.M.—Mr Morley—Ld Spencer—Sir R. Welby *cum* Mr Hamilton. Worked hard on Irish Land. Drive with C. Finished D'Eon. H. of C. $4\frac{1}{2}$-8 and after dinner. Proposed vote of thanks to Sir T. May. And introduced Irish Land Bill in a speech of two hours or more.[5] Again I had to be thankful for much support. Sleep disturbed.

17. Sat. [*Hawarden*]

Wrote to Sir G. Dasent—Ld Mountbretton[6]—Mrs O'Shea—Sir H. Ponsonby—Ly Sydney—Mr Calcraft—The Queen l.l.—and minutes. Read Lady S.s Tract[7]—QR

---

[1] Untraced message of support.
[2] Speaker announced May's retirement; Harcourt's budget; *H* 304. 1631, 1637.
[3] In Chamberlain, *Political memoir*, 206.
[4] Reading on holograph uncertain; this is the copyist's rendering at Add MS 44548, f. 71.
[5] *H* 304. 1774, 1778; *Speeches on the Irish question*, 73, with text of bill.
[6] *Sc.* Monk Bretton.
[7] Religious tract sent by Lady Sandhurst; Add MS 44548, f. 72.

on Xtn Brothers.[1] 12–1¼. Conclave on succession to Sir T. May. A 2d on Farrer vacancy.[2] Saw Mr P. l.l.l.—Mr A. Morley l.l.l.—Mr Mundella—Mr Godley—Ld Rosebery. Off to Hn 3.30–9.30. Conversation with dear Stephy.

To LORD SYDNEY, lord steward, 17 April 1886.   Add MS 44548, f. 71.

Cannot you persuade Suffield to make common stock with the other Household Lords.[3]

There would have been something almost ludicrous in the daily sputtering of these resignations had not *some* Peers had the good sense to wait a little: I might almost say the sense of proprieties which surely required them to hear the whole plan—never known until last night—before abandoning an administration which has their general confidence. I rely on your kindly doing what you can.

We go to Hawarden this afternoon.

18. *Palm S.*

Holy Communion 8 A.M.—Ch. 11 AM & 6½ PM. Wrote to Dowager Ly Sandhurst—Sir T.E. May—Mr Primrose l.l. Read Curteis' Devotions[4]—Cheynell on Chillingworth[5]—Q.R. on Bp Lightfoot's Ignatius & Polycarp[6]—and Tracts.

To Sir T. E. MAY, 18 April 1886.   May MSS.

Your resignation being now, unfortunately for us, complete, I bethink me of the recommendation which I have signified my readiness to make.

It appeared to me that, in the natural order, the next step will be to settle the future provision to which you are entitled. This I presume will be done at once. And when it is done I should with your permission have much pleasure in submitting your name for a Peerage.

Whatever happens let it be borne in mind that this has not been asked but tendered.[7]

19. *M.*

Ch. 8½ A.M. Wrote to Mr Russell MP—Mr Morley l.l.—Ld Spencer—Speaker of Quebec Assembly[8]—Primrose & Carmichael Tel. l.l.l.—Mr C. Peel—Mr Palgrave—Buda Pesth Academy[9]—and minutes. Read Salambo[10]—Scotts History of the Union[11]—Burton on Do[12]—Joyce Acts of the Church.[13] Drive, & walk with C. Worked on books.

---

[1] *Q.R.*, clxii. 325 (April 1886).

[2] May succeeded by R. Palgrave (C. L. Peel declining), Farrer by H. G. Calcraft. Gladstone unsuccessfully pressed for Sir H. Maine *vice* May (see to Tennyson, 26 Apr. 86).

[3] Sydney wrote this day, Add MS 44318, f. 508, on his attempts to prevent Suffield resigning as master of the buckhounds.

[4] G. H. Curteis, *Spiritual progress* (1855).

[5] F. Cheynell, *Chillingworth: novissima* (1644).

[6] *Q.R.*, clxii. 467 (April 1886).

[7] May replied next day accepting; Add MS 44154, f. 194.

[8] Thanks for a resolution of support; Add MS 44548, f. 73.

[9] Not found; more support?   [10] G. Flaubert, *Salammbô* (1862).

[11] Probably W. Scott, *History of Scotland*, 2v. (1830).

[12] In J. H. Burton, *History of Scotland*, 7v. (1867–70).

[13] J. W. Joyce, *Acts of the church, 1531–1885* (1886).

To J. MORLEY, Irish secretary, 19 April 1886.   Add MS 44548, f. 73.

[First letter:]   I have written the enclosed letter on the case of the Receiver General, to be employed by you, if you find cause, according to need & precedence.

[Second letter:]   I suppose that my statement about the Receiver General may make at the moment a sore place with the Irish Members. But I am confident that on reflection they will see that the whole thing hangs together & that we have acted strictly in the real interests of the plan.

It is not the localised men or the egotists or the concealed foes, but, if I am right, many of the best friends to us, & to the measures, who are staggered by the proposal of this great advance. It *is* a very serious matter to add largely to the figure of the National Debt, although we have a justifying cause for it. It is an extraordinary proceeding, & it requires suitable accompaniments.

I imagine there is no parallel in history for pecuniary relations such as we are about to establish between Great Britain & Ireland.

See what a big affair it is.

I will not speak of the Imperial contributions for *service*—were that alone in question, the necessity for a special provision might not have been so palpable.

In regard to machinery, we must proceed on the assumption of the maximum to which the change may come; for plainly we cannot alter it in the middle of the process. There is—

1. A sum of I think 13m already outstanding, lent by the Exchequer to Ireland.
2. Then 40m of the National Debt.
3. Then 50m to be authorized under the Bill of last Friday.
4. And *possibly*, 2 or 3 years hence, another 50m may be required.

Here is a total of over 150m on which we must found our provisions: an enormous amount. But the amount is not so much to the point as the principle. We go so far outside the limits of finance & attempt to reconstruct fundamentally the paramount industry of Ireland. For a time, seventy or 60%, in round numbers, of the gross revenues & (public) rents of Ireland may be due to us.

Viewed roughly, this is one of those cases, the analogue of which in private life would commonly lead to the constitution of a trust, in the interest of the proprietor, because by such means his debts are cheapened through security, & his living surplus is insured.

Further, although as matter of policy I am obliged to thrust the Receiver General into an almost offensive prominence, yet in practice, when the system is at work, he will offend nobody & never be heard of. Who in England, except at the centre, even knows of the existence of the Paymaster General or the Auditor & Comptroller General? He will be a personage invisible & mute.

To sum up, he is necessary

1. To help the passing of a measure quite out of the common way
2. As a just accompaniment to an inordinate liability on our part
3. To disarm, as far as possible, the hostility of the British monied class
4. And the jealous, fastidious, susceptibilities of the public creditor, so as to help us in the great & important work of keeping the Funds at or near their present rate
5. In the special interest of Ireland which cannot build up a credit of her own, while these great liabilities are upon her, without the firm groundwork, as to her engagements with us, which this proposal in particular is intended to supply. Ireland, as towards us, must be Caesar's wife.

But I have still another topic. Need the arrangement be perpetual? Here I touch upon a subject, which I have not thought it prudent thus far to open publicly. If the Irish are thrifty, & if they proceed on the only true economical principle of helping the nation, through the Exchequer, & not the classes, these financial prospects, peace continuing, are in my opinion (sic.)[1]

I do hope they will go vigorously to work in the constitution of their local police. In this question, oddly enough, it is we who are endeavouring to promote self-government in Ireland. We are seeking to maintain a controul not over the police of Ireland but over the particular body called constabulary, with the aim of contracting it as quickly as possible. If they aid us in this, they ought within no great number of years to save nearly half of their million.

Putting together all the elements of gain, they will have 1. A surplus to start with, 2. A revenue from the Land Sale & Purchase plan if it works, 3. great economies on the constabulary, 4. Economies on the Judiciary, & on law expenditure which is now scandalous, 5. Economies on the Post Office expenditure which is I fear in gross excess. Should all or the chief part of these come up well they will be very rich, & the best use they can make of their wealth will be to devote a liberal portion of it to quickening the action of the sinking funds by enlarging their account, & thus bringing about a contraction of the sphere of the Receiver General, & perhaps his eventual extinction (if they do not get too fond of him).[2]

To E. R. RUSSELL, M.P., editor of *Liverpool Daily Post*,   Add MS 44548, f. 72.
19 April 1886. '*Secret*'.

Reading the London letter in the Liverpool Post of today,[3] I write you this note, in sympathy with that communication, to assure you very emphatically that in the affair of the Chamberlain resignation I have, for the sake of the Liberal party & the Irish Bills, carried the principle of reticence to the utmost possible extent. Were it otherwise, Mr. Morley would have some strange things to tell. The most interesting point of all for the world would be to obtain a knowledge what was Mr. Chamberlain's own plan for dealing with Irish Land. He complained that the schemes have been framed by me, not in the Cabinet (about which he knows little): but within one week after the formation of the Government I sent for him expressly in order to learn in full his views on Irish Land. And I did learn them, but will not describe them. I told him in a note last week that I had done & should do every thing I could to avoid a public controversy with him, as I did not think it would be 'edifying'. But he has tried me rather hard.[4]
[P.S.] When I have spoken of my reliance on the people, I have of course meant it.

To LORD SPENCER, lord president, 19 April 1886.   Add MS 44548, f. 73.

I think there are two sufficient answers to the objections you mention[5] & you have given them both.

1. When there are in a given measure provisions involving good faith Parliament will always estimate them liberally—its general practice is to go beyond the mark rather than fall short of it.

[1] Copyist's 'sic'.
[2] Morley replied next day that the raising of this question had been a party point, not the consequence of the Receiver's own misgivings; Add MS 44255, f. 46.
[3] On Gladstone's 'most marked manner' in suggesting a *rapprochement* with Chamberlain; it also reported 'a very strong tendency' in two Birmingham districts for Gladstone rather than Chamberlain; *Liverpool Daily Post*, 19 April 1886, 5g.
[4] Russell's reply, 21 April, Add MS 44496, f. 297, thanked Gladstone for 'so great a proof of your confidence at this trying moment'.
[5] To limitation on advance for buying Irish estates; *Spencer*, i. 114.

2. If the Irish authority does not fulfil its pecuniary obligations, the whole thing goes to the ground.

To which I add—

1. It is beyond doubt that if we had asked the outside sum for the Landlords, they would have got nothing at all.

2. Can anyone suppose that if I am wrong in this—if Parliament would have been willing to enact an issue of 20฿ per annum for each of six years—& if in the 2nd or 3rd years it had been found that the repayments were not made—Parliament would still suffer the issues of 20฿ to be made all the same for years 4, 5 & 6?

There is a vigour of interpretation which these things will hardly bear. I advise anyone to read the history of the West India case in 1833 & 1832.

20. Tu.

Ch. 8½ A.M. Wrote to Lady S. Opdebeck—Sir H. Ponsonby l.l.—The Queen—Ld Granville—Mr Morley—Mr A. Morley—Rev. Mr Greig—Duke of Argyll—Ld Sydney—Mr Primrose tel.—and minutes. Saw [blank.] Drive, & walk with S. Read 'Pausanias'[1]—Burton Hist. Scotl.—O'Connor, Hist. of Irish.[2]

To the DUKE OF ARGYLL, 20 April 1886.   Add MS 44548, f. 75.

I thank you for your letter:[3] I still hope you will eat your dinner with me on the Queen's birthday (if I am *in*), & encourage some like-minded men to keep you in countenance.

My memory like yours 'goes slipping back upon the golden days' which can never die away.

I think I should say two things, & two only. 1. I have not as yet spoken, & may not, speak, at all freely. And 2. I have never been engaged in so conservative a work, as now against you Separatists. Yes I add 3. Repent of what you wrote to me about Mr. Burke,[4] who, on Ireland & America, is an immortal monument of civil wisdom.

[P.S.] Pray consider not only your next step, but your *next but one*.

To A. MORLEY, chief whip, 20 April 1886.   Add MS 44548, f. 74.

I inclose to you a copy of what I have written to [J.] Morley.[5]

With men like most of my colleagues it is safe to go to an extreme of possible concession. But my experience in Chamberlain's case is that such concession is treated mainly as an acknowledgement of his superior greatness & wisdom, & as a fresh point of departure accordingly.

It is the *people*, & in the main the people only, to whom we have to look.

[P.S.] I take this thing upon myself; but my adoption of C.'s terms would at once split the Cabinet.

---

[1] *Pausanias' description of Greece*, tr. A. R. Shilleto, 2v. (new ed. 1886); see also 11 Aug. 63.

[2] See 15 Jan. 83.

[3] Of 19 April, Add MS 44106, f. 85; Gladstone's intellect becoming 'a "Universal Solvent" . . . a purely Destructive Force'.

[4] On 25 December 1885, Add MS 44106, f. 79: 'I am sorry you are studying Burke. Your 'Perfervidum Ingenium Scoti" does not need being touched with a live coal from [a] hot Irish Altar!'; no 'parallelism or even analogy' should be drawn between 1886 and George III and the colonies.

[5] A. Morley, 19 April, Add MS 44253, f. 5, on need 'by all legitimate means' to secure Chamberlain's support; could Gladstone write to him?

To J. MORLEY, Irish secretary, 20 April 1886.   Add MS 44548, f. 74.

I have your letter with one from A. Morley & another from Herbert from C[hamber-lain] to L[abouchere]—which please to send back to me.

I cannot write Kootooing letters to Chamberlain & I doubt as to their effect. He views his speech as a great effort at conciliation. I could only reply by a 'note of admiration'.

Practically the matter stands thus. 1. The controul over Imperial taxation *is* reserved. 2. On the presence of Irish members I refer to what I said on Mr. Whitbread's speech. 3. Decency, principle, & policy alike forbid me to enter into private arrangements about alterations of the Bill in Committee. My proceedings in this matter must be public pro-ceedings. And my public proceedings must be governed by a view of all the considera-tions on the case.

[P.S.] I observe you have seen the two letters, so I do not send them.

21. Wed.

Ch. 8½ A.M. Wrote to Sir J. Carmichael—The Queen—Lady M. Alford—Mr Coram—Mr Morley—Mr Roche—& minutes. Worked on books. Examined some sites. Read Burton Hist. Scotl.—O'Neill Daunt's Lectures[1]—Pausanias—Strickland, Tudor Princesses—Editha Coplestone.[2]

To Sir J. M. CARMICHAEL, 21 April 1886.   Bodley MS Don. a 9, f. 99.

I am not afraid of Primrose's absence,[3] however much I value his presence. All your working, as far as my experience has yet given me light, has been to my entire satisfac-tion.

Please to inquire at the Foreign Office about the mode of voting in the Things or Par-liaments of the three Scandinavian countries, where there are four orders. Do they vote separately or conjointly, and on what occasions, and do they *sit* separately or together.

To J. MORLEY, Irish secretary, 21 April 1886.   Add MS 44548, f. 75.

Thanks for what you tell me about Parnell.[4] He is a man of much insight.

You see how strongly the tide is running on the admission of Irish members. This has reference, I think, not so much to the anomaly about taxation, as to the needless fears[?] about the unity of the Empire. I have no doubt that like a wise man you will watch events, & keep your own counsel.

On the question itself, so far as principle is concerned, I have been all along in a state of sublime impartiality, in the inner sanctuary of my own mind.

And I now believe, that, if we had proposed to retain them, we should have been run in upon not less fiercely from the other side.

I cannot see my way to a working plan, nor, as yet, even conceive of an expedient, unless upon the Whitbread basis.

Was there ever more egregious folly than that of the Separatist Liberals in taking all the difficulties & responsibilities upon themselves & allowing the Tories to remain virtu-ally & generally uncommitted.

---

[1] W. J. O'N. Daunt, *Essays on Ireland* (1886).

[2] 'Connie', *Edith Coppleston* (1886).

[3] Carmichael, nervous of his inexperience, reported Primrose absent for a week's holiday; Add MS 44496, f. 277.

[4] No letter found.

I will not move an inch in the direction of Chamberlain without consultation. Perhaps not much with it. He has in him, with other notable gifts, a good deal of repulsive power.

I look anxiously for any signs of yielding from the Landlords with such a bait before them. But I have seen none. This may however have to do with the reticence of the Tories.

22. Th.

Ch. 8½ AM & H.C. Wrote to Sir H. Ponsonby—Sir R. Welby—Sir A. Gordon—Sir J. Carmichael—Ld Rosebery (on partial concert)—& minutes. Woodcraft with Herbert & conversation. Read Pausanias—Strickland Tudor Pr.—Editha Cople-stone—and—

To LORD ROSEBERY, foreign secretary, 22 April 1886.   N.L.S. 10023, f. 174.

One word, meant to be helpful, for a contingency which may arise though I hope it will not.

The concert of the Six is a great thing, & any defection from it a serious blow. But a concert short of unanimity is not always to be despised. England France & Russia wielded (somewhat awkwardly) the moral authority of Europe at Navarino in 1827. Palmerston had it, with at least immediate success, in 1840, against France: the alliance in the Crimean War was a relic of an European concert, & not a mere combination of two powers. Finally, when in 1880, we concocted the plan of sending a ship or ships to Smyrna, & had received the refusals of three Powers, we were meditating a concert of the other trio at the moment when the Sultan, having heard of the project but not of the refusals, gave way.

Of course I cannot say how far these precedents would apply to the Greek case.[1]

I have always meant to say to you, but have perhaps forgotten it, that I have no idea in what way the Greeks can found a claim of right on the Treaty of Berlin.

To Sir R. E. WELBY, secretary to the treasury, 22 April 1886.   Add MS 44548, f. 76.

You are perfectly right.[2] I have said it, & shall repeat from time to time. By far the finest thing would be if Chamberlain could be invited & induced to bring into view *his* plan of Land Purchase, which I have got in print.[3] That would be a treat.

23. G. Friday.

Ch. at 10.30 and (part of Hours) 1¾-3¼. Wrote to Ld Spencer—Sir J. Carmichael—& minutes. Read Bazeley's Life[4] (what a lesson to a wretch like me)—Three Essays in Symp. on Immortality[5]—Harrison's Charge[6]—Carlon, England's Sin.[7]

---

[1] Rosebery replied on 25 April, Add MS 44289, f. 29, that the 'note will be presented by *all* the Powers', and on 27 April, ibid., f. 30: 'Greece has yielded most ungraciously'.
[2] Welby, 21 April, Add MS 44338: 'I am surprised to find how few people are really aware how the late Govt. committed this country to 1. the expropriation of the Irish landlord 2 . . . rent collection in Ireland without intermediary.'   [3] See 25 Feb. 86.
[4] E. L. Hicks, *Henry Bazely; the Oxford evangelist* (1886).
[5] *Immorality. A clerical symposium* (1885).
[6] B. Harrison, 'The continuity of the Church . . .' (1886).
[7] C. B. Carlon, 'England's sin. Honour sold, truth betrayed' (1884).

To Sir J. M. CARMICHAEL, 23 April 1886.   Bodley MS Don. a. 9, f. 102.

I admit with regret that the point taken in your letter[1] cannot, so far as I know, be satis-factorily disposed of. The provision, to which objection is made, is no child of mine. It is the offspring of the Report of the Lords' Committee, the most dangerous socialistic docu-ment of modern times, for it was sure to find at once a powerful class ready to propagate the mischief.

It became the basis of the Land Purchase Act of last year. It is now being objected to us that we are doing less for the tenant than the Tory Act did. And it is true. We have a little qualified and restrained the mischief. Supposing that instead of our Bill we had extended the Act of 1885 to 50₥ instead of 5₥, a man of Lord M[onteagle]'s intelligence will at once see the case would have stood worse.

But so far as there is a rival policy to ours in the matter of Land Purchase, it is the extension of the Act of 1885.

24. Easter Eve.

Ch. 8½ A.M. and 7 P.M. In the forenoon came the deeply touching death of Laura Lyttelton: who had so intense a life! Rest & peace be hers—consolation & profit her excellent husband's.[2] Wrote to Lady S. Opdebeck—Sir G. Prevost—M. de Laveleye—Col. Donegan[3]—Lady Stapleton—Rev. Dr Dale—Mr Mac-kiver—Rev. Dr Parker—Mr Buchanan—Sir J. Carmichael tel.—Archdn Harrison—Canon Eliot—& minutes.

To H. C. E. CHILDERS, home secretary, 24 April 1886.   Bodley MS Don, a 9, f. 97.

I think the Cabinet must be consulted on the question of Chapters and Cathedrals.

I should incline to advise asking the Archbishop of Canterbury as head of the Bishops and of the Commission (I think) whether either were prepared to advise a course to be taken under the present circumstances. We might suggest some heads for consideration, as contributory not inclusive.

In regard to these heads I should generally be prepared to proceed on your lines but I think a) the Surplus Fund ought not to be diminished unless all calls have been met: b) I do not think the care of the Fabrics can well be taken by the Commission: but I should like to see the Fabric monies put effectually beyond the reach of the Chapters for any but Fabric purposes.[4]

To the editor of the *Daily Chronicle*, 24 April 1886.[5]   Add MS 44548, f. 76.

It is not my custom, for obvious reasons, to comment on statements made in hostile metropolitan newspapers. But, having a sincere respect for the Daily Chronicle, I would call your attention to an allegation in a leading article of today that I have heretofore taught that Home Rule would be 'a source of Imperial danger'.

I will not challenge you for the proof of this assertion, which I believe to be made in good faith, but entirely in error.

---

[1] Not found; that of this day, Add MS 44497, f. 16, on Danish Parliament (see 21 Apr. 86), clearly not relevant. For the Lords' committee, see *PP* 1882, xi. 1.

[2] i.e. Alfred Lyttelton; see 21 May 85.

[3] Lt. col. James Henry Francis Donegan of the Royal Munster Fusiliers; Add MS 44496, f. 285.

[4] Childers docketed: 'Will you, or shall I, mention this at the next Cabinet? . . .' But see 4 May 86.

[5] In *Daily Chronicle*, 26 April, 5d; its leader found the 'Irish scheme . . . neither just, expedient or practicable'. The liberal *Chronicle* took a strong (though later diminishing) unionist line on Ireland.

So far as I am aware of my own teaching, it contains no such doctrine, but in general calls for explanations of the meaning of Home Rule, in order to clear up the question whether it would or would not be a source of Imperial danger.

We have now learned the demand of Ireland from the mouth of $\frac{5}{6}$ of her constitutionally chosen representatives; & it shows that Home Rule means the establishment of a Legislative body in Ireland for the management of only Irish affairs.

Such Home Rule is, in the language of my Address of last September, a source not of danger but of strength—the danger, if any, lies in refusing it.

Probably the writer has had in his mind the scheme of No Rent, which I denounced in strong terms in 1881: terms which, were there occasion, I should use again.

You will I am sure do justice on this subject, I do not say to me, but to the great public interests which are involved.

To Rev. R. W. DALE, 24 April 1886. '*Private*'.   Add MS 44548, f. 77.

I must write you one line to thank you for the masterly manner in which at Birmingham you have confronted a most difficult situation.

It is only by a temper like yours, conjoined with ability (which in such a case cannot of itself suffice whatever its amount) that the Irish question can be satisfactorily dealt with.

I have wholly abstained, & if possible I shall wholly abstain, from criticizing Mr. Chamberlain's own plans of stopping evictions, advances to landlords for their rents, Federation, & Land Purchase.[1]

25. *Easter Day.*

Church 8 A.M. (H.C.) 11 A.M., $6\frac{1}{2}$ P.M. Wrote to the Earl of Aberdeen—Dowager Ly Sandhurst—The Speaker—& minutes. Read Christie's End of Man[2]—Bazely's Life (finished) Noble.—Sympos. on Immortality.

26. *E. Monday.*

Ch. $8\frac{1}{2}$ A.M. and H.C. How I need it. Wrote to Lord Tennyson—Mr A. Morley—Sir H. Bruce[3]—Mr Knollys—Ld Rosebery—Mr Macmillan—& minutes. Large, well-behaved, enthusiastic, & disquieting crowds from the E. today—as on Saturday. Read G. Duffy's Article[4]—Mill on Repr. Government[5]—Pausanias—'Love too is Vanity'.[6]

To A. MORLEY, chief whip, 26 April 1886.   Add MS 44548, f. 79.

Would there be any practical inconvenience in my postponing my return until tomorrow week? I had not thought of it, but my wife has been obliged unexpectedly to make an engagement for Monday, & I [do] not want to break company with her if my absence is *perfectly* innocent. But if there is any sort of cause for my return pray let me know as she could come up later with Herbert.

[1] Dale replied, 26 April, Add MS 44497, f. 41, with 'hearty thanks for your generous letter', and argued for retaining Irish MPs at Westminster.
[2] See 11 Apr. 86.
[3] Sir Henry Hervey Bruce, 1820-1907; Ulsterman; formerly tory M.P.; on land purchase; Add MS 44548, f. 79.
[4] C. G. Duffy, 'Mr Gladstone's Irish constitution', *C.R.*, xl. 609 (May 1886).
[5] See 16 Apr. 61.
[6] Not found.

I am well satisfied with such intelligence as reaches me. As usual at Easter large parties (2000 & upwards) come over here from Yorkshire. They are certainly in a state of higher enthusiasm than ever.

You will judge what I think of Chamberlain's line. The less I say the better. I am afraid it is *in* him, & that he cannot help it.[1]

Is there to be a meeting in Edinburgh for Goschen & (?).[2] If there is, I am half inclined to send down a letter.

To LORD TENNYSON, 26 April 1886.   Add MS 44548, f. 79.

I did not think lightly of your kindness in sending me Maine's book[3] (I have since tried in vain to make him Clerk of the House of Commons) & I valued also the admonition conveyed in the fine passage which accompanied it. It set me on a fresh act of self-examination, & under such extraordinary responsibilities these acts cannot be too many or too strict.

According to the laws of human nature it is difficult to suppose that at seventy six, with senses gradually closing in, and memory for all things recent failing fast, I can have thrown myself into the midst of these tempestuous billows; without these two things, first a clear conviction, & secondly a strong sense of personal call.

For 42 at least out of the 54 years of my public life, Ireland has had a rather dominant influence over it. Which is those of my opponents that has had occasion to study it as resolutely & for the same time?

My work & purpose in this matter are I can assure you in the highest sense Conservative: as adversaries, if unhappily they succeed, will too soon learn to their cost & to that of the country.

I feel a strong assurance that the subject of *In Memoriam* would have been with us, & I cannot surrender hope of the author.

But I have another purpose in writing which is to offer to you & your wife our deep sympathy in your present anxiety about your son Lionel. May it please God to raise him up for you in health & strength, & in all events to commend to you effectually His holy will. It is a great trial. Youth is on his side, & we cannot but look to it with hope.

27. Tu.

Ch. 8½ A.M. Wrote to Ld Halifax—Sir J. Carmichael l. & tel.—Alfred Lyttelton—and minutes. Drive. Woodcraft with W. Conversation with Canon M'Coll. Read Lecky's Hist.[4]—Pausanias finished I.—Ann. Register—Love too is Vanity—Tudor Princesses.[5] The Rector, ever ready for self-sacrifice in things small & great, went off to Laura's funeral.

To Sir J. M. CARMICHAEL, 27 April 1886.   Bodley MS Don. a. 9, f. 104.

I think the V. Stuart investigations very useful.[6] By all means let him write. I do not see why the printing should not be paid out of Special Service if necessary. I think however

---

[1] Morley wrote on 3 May, Add MS 44253, f. 7, that if Chamberlain and those who 'take his view of that question vote against us, we shall be in a decided minority'; but opinion for the bill is growing.

[2] *Sic* in copy.   [3] See 12 Jan. 86.

[4] See 17 Apr. 78.   [5] See 28 Mar. 86.

[6] Calculations by H. W. Villiers-Stuart on Irish food prices and pauperism, to show that Irish land is good security to taxpayers for advance necessary under the purchase scheme: small farms better than large; Add MS 44496, f. 132.

there should be some other, more vulgar and simple, indications of price than the zigzags, which require something of a practised eye and mind to use them. Extremes for decades might be stated in recitals.

Tell Mr. V. S. with my best compliments that I can recollect the best oaks in the Three Kingdoms (those of Aberdeenshire and the Mearns) at 13/- certainly per quarter, but I am pretty confident at 12/- and still lower. About 1849-50.

To LORD HALIFAX, 27 April 1886.   Add MS 44548, f. 80.

I have much pleasure in proposing to you that you should become an Ecclesiastical Commissioner, for I feel sure you will discharge the office extremely well. It is wholly outside politics. Lord Brownlow took it from my hands.

At the same time I cherish a lively hope that you will not eventually find yourself outside our politics. Our work is I am sure conservative & restorative, not only because as Mr. Chamberlain sees it withdraws a great amount of factitious support from Radicalism in Parliament, but also because it gives solidity to the Empire. If you are moved by the authority of Lord Selborne, I must tell you that after my communications with him at the close of January his recent utterances have caused me very great surprise. But this is a matter fitter for conversation than for hurried writing.

28. Wed.

Ch. 8½ A.M. Wrote to Mr Villiers Stuart—Sir H. Ponsonby—Mrs Th.—Mrs O. Morgan tel.—Ld Rosebery—Rev. Mr Jenkins—Mr Labouchere Tel.—and minutes. Read Pausanias—Lecky's Hist—Moll's England & Wales[1]—Tudor Princesses—Love & Vanity—Mahon on Ireland.[2]

To LORD ROSEBERY, foreign secretary, 28 April 1886.   N.L.S. 10032, f. 176.
'Secret'.

I congratulate you from my heart on the issue of the Greek affair announced in your letter.[3]

I do not remember an instance of such an achievement carried through in the *first quarter* of a Foreign Secretaryship. And it is one to which your personal action has beyond doubt largely contributed. It is a great act, and a good omen.

I am far from thinking Greece has by her conduct established any claim on us (so far as my present information goes). On the other hand my impression is that it has not been an affair of the people (or the king), but got up by the Government: as it was in Servia, where that *roitelet*[4] Milan has been a mischief-maker from the first, & will be to the end.

I am glad that M of Bulgaria, who began ill, has now come out well.

Your idea about Kirk pleases me.[5] I suppose you think Bismarck has on the whole

---

[1] H. Moll, *New description of England and Wales* (1724).

[2] In P. H. Stanhope, Lord Mahon, *Correspondence between William Pitt . . . and the Lord Lieutenant of Ireland 1781-1787* (1842).

[3] See 22 Apr. 86n.

[4] 'kinglet'.

[5] Rosebery favoured the Sultan of Zanzibar ceding 'part of his territory to Germany in exchange for a guarantee of the rest from France, Germany and ourselves' and suggested sending for Kirk: 'this would please the Germans and be in some respects convenient to us, as we could leave a good man there'; 27 April 1886, Add MS 44289, f. 30. Sir John *Kirk, 1832-1922, British consul and political agent at Zanzibar. For the Anglo-German Agreement of Oct. 1886, see *Africa and the Victorians*, 197.

behaved well about the Greek business. If so I certainly would pursue an accommodating course when at all practicable in other matters.

It is also very desirable, while we have this big Irish business on hand, that no other important issue of a disturbing character should be raised.

Many tactical lessons are to be learned from Peel's conduct, and I recollect that in 1846, with the repeal of the Corn Law in view, he went very great lengths indeed, perhaps even too great, in order to avoid side issues.

Quite apart from our concern in it, the aspect of the Irish controversy is the most curiously interesting I have ever known. Nothing has struck me more than the Hartington meeting, when he could not have a vote of confidence from his own constituency. More and more this becomes a battle between the nation and the classes. Never were we so weak in the classes as we are now. (How I am to rig out a Queen's birthday dinner, I can hardly conceive+.) On the other hand, the action of what seems to be the nation has been most remarkable.

I am afraid the Speakership would hardly bear the weight of your proposal. It is difficult to know *quid ferre recusent, quid valeant humeri*.[1] I have thought and worked a good deal on the principle of it; but making use of H.M. in Council as organ.[2] I agree very much however with Whitbread (*there* is something like a Whig) that there should be an interval before the question is definitively raised.

One should keep the mind in as elastic a state as possible, to look at every suggestion from a constructive point of view. I take for instance the inclosed as giving food for thought. (Please to return it.) On the division now approaching, & on the precise numbers, very much will depend. I doubt the possibility of now forecasting what will have to be done after it. I am inclined at present to view a very small majority as nearly equivalent to a minority.

[P.S.] I have been thinking whether in connection with this Edinburgh meeting I might fire off a letter to Mr Cowan or the Constituency. How does this strike you.[3]

+ I shall have to send into the highways & hedges.

29. Th.

Ch. 8½ A.M. Wrote to Lady S. Opdebeck—Messrs Walker—D. of Argyll—Rev. Dr Dale—M. de Solomé[4]—and minutes. Duchess of Westminster & Miss Wemyss here. Photographed by [blank.] Read Tudor Princesses—Roden Noel Essays on Poetry[5]—Pausanias—Love is vanity—Russie-Pologne.[6]

To Rev. R. W. DALE, 29 April 1886.   Add MS 44548, f. 81.

I thank you for setting out so clearly several of the points touching the presence or the absence of the Irish members from Parliament at Westminster.[7]

As the subject has never been out of my head for 48 hours together during the last six months, I will make bold to say that the number of points touched by it, & their conflict

---

[1] Horace, *Ars Poetica*, 39–40; 'what your shoulders refuse, and what they have the strength, to bear'.

[2] Rosebery, 27 April, Add MS 44289, f. 30, suggested the Speaker be empowered to invite Irish assembly to depute 103 members on particular days for imperial subjects at Westminster ('I suppose it will not hold water . . .').

[3] See 30 Apr. 86.

[4] On a sketch of Robertson Gladstone; Add MS 44548, f. 81.

[5] By R. B. W. Noel (1886).

[6] Many pamphlets on this.

[7] See 24 Apr. 86n.

one with another, is such that nothing can place it fully before the world except a comprehensive & dispassionate debate upon it. The determining condition will I think be found to be the temper in which men approach the question. It has buffeted me sorely. The case of the Veto is different. It cannot be solved by any theory, but has been solved practically by a Colonial policy now nearly half a century old which combines the judicious use of it with the free action of responsible Government.

30. Fr.

Ch. 8½ A.M. Wrote to Mr Primrose l. & tel. l.l.l.—Mr Campbell tel.—Ld Granville—Abp of Cashel—Mr F. Hill—Mr A. Morley tel.—and minutes. Worked much on a letter projected to Midlothian.[1] Walked with the Rector & explained as well as I could my ideas about building. Read Pausanias—Tudor Princesses—Love is Vanity—Stead in the Contemp. Rev.[2]

Sat May One SS. Phil. & J.

Ch. 8¼ A.M. Worked on & finished letter to Electors. Wrote to Mr Labouchere tel.—Mr Primrose Tel. for Rosebery—Reform Club Lancr tel.—Mr Campbell tel.—Mr Cowan—Sir W. Harcourt—Lady Aberdeen—The Queen—Mr Knowles—& minutes. Finished & sent off my public letter to constituents of Midlothian.

To Sir W. V. HARCOURT, chancellor of the   MS Harcourt dep. 10, f. 107.
exchequer, 1 May 1886.

My communications from Midlothian have been important and you see that it has been chosen as a head quarters of adverse operations. They with other circumstances have led me to address a letter to my constituents, which you will probably see in the papers of Monday or Tuesday. The latter part of it touches the question what is the meaning of the second reading. In writing it, I have thought much of you: and but for you I should have gone further; as I see it said (but have not yet read him) that Morley has done.

You and I are not so far off as I *think* you suppose. But you ride the higher horse, and I go at an amble. I adhere to my eulogy on Whitbread. But I am not bold enough to say that his speech is capable of any meaning or application ⟨which⟩ such as would satisfy the high flyers for the admission of Irish members, more of whom seem to me to have considered the enormous difficulties in their way, and a *portion* of whom are probably working the topic as the most available instrument for destroying the Bill. In a matter so difficult, I do not think any one can form absolute conclusions till he comes very near the sticking point. I am sure you will look at the matter in a wise and kindly spirit.

[P.S.] Poor Goschen says 5 months ago he was thinking only of the authorised programme. Now 5½ months ago Rosebery asked him to Dalmeny. I walked him out & opened to him every thing. He did not say one word of acceptance *or objection*: & went on as adherent.[3]

---

[1] On home rule, in *Speeches on the Irish question*, 171, Edinburgh *Daily Review*, 3 May 1886 and *T.T.*, 4 May 1886, 5d.
[2] W. T. Stead, 'Government by journalism', *C.R.*, xl. 653 (May 1886).
[3] See 22 Nov. 85.

2. 1 S.E.

Ch 11 AM with H.C. and 6½ P.M. Wrote to Mons. A. Danton[1]—Mr Primrose for Lord R. tel. l.l.—Sir T.D. Acland—Mr Stansfeld—and minutes. Read Luccock Introd[2]—White on Immortality[3]—Wemyss Reid on Forster[4]—Dawson on Genesis & Layman on Ath Creed.[5]

3. M.

Ch. 8½ A.M. Wrote to Mr Thorne tel. l.—Ld Spencer—Miss Swanwick—Scotts—Sir H. Ponsonby—Mr Primrose Tel. 1 for Ld R.—l. and minutes. Arranged with Barker for some new bookcases. Conversation H[erbert] who goes to Leeds. Read Pausanias finished II.—A Modern Daedalus.[6] Backgammon with S.E.G.

4. Tu. [London]

Ch. 8½ A.M. Last night somewhat disturbed. Lying awake I felt my nothingness and inward desolation. Surely this is an admirable form and force of discipline. D.G. also for the rest (though a saddened rest) of our vacation. Wrote minutes & completed preparations for journey. Finished A Modern Daedalus—read Thoughts on the present Discontents[7]—Arthur's wild pamphlet.[8] 10¾–4. Hn to D. St. Much enthusiasm. House & Cabinet 4½–8. Wrote to The Queen l.l.—Mr Gray—and minutes. Saw Mr P.—Ld Granville—Ld Kimberley—Mr Morley.

Cabinet. Tues. May 4. 1886. 5 PM.[9]
1. Conversation at large on the question of excluding Irish members. In reduced numbers? For taxation only? All against retention unlimited in numbers & subjects.
2. Party meeting—does not seem practicable.[10]
3. Rosebery: recital as to Greece.

5. Wed.

Wrote to Sir T.E. May—Sir H. Ponsonby—Ld Clifton—Mr J. Morley—Ld Rosebery—Prince of Wales—Ld Granville—D. of Argyll—& minutes. Migrated to the large room: needlessly redecorated, not by us. Wrote Mem. on the Situation. Saw Mr P.—Herbert J.G.—Mr A.M.—Mr Morley—Scotts—Lady Derby. Wrote Mem. on the 'situation' for Cabinet. Read Burke, Thoughts—Gunning's Reminiscences.[11]

[1] Thanking him for a work; Add MS 44548, f. 82.

[2] H. M. Luccock, ed., J. R. Woodford, *The great commission* (1886).

[3] E. White, *Life in Christ* (1846); immortality the privilege of the regenerate.

[4] *F.R.*, xlv. 593 (May 1886); forwarded to Spencer for its comments on Forster's resignation, 'absolutely without foundation'; Add MS 44548, f. 83.

[5] *Thoughts on the Athanasian creed. By a layman* (1886).

[6] T. Greer, *A modern Daedalus* (1885).

[7] By Burke (1770); see 26 Mar. 45.

[8] Probably Arthur T. Lyttelton, 'Dogmatic religion' in *Lectures on church doctrine* (1886).

[9] Add MS 44647, f. 93.

[10] See 27 May 86.

[11] H. Gunning, *Reminiscences of the University*, 2v. (1854); on Cambridge.

Memorandum on Bill for Irish Government *2nd Reading Division*

2 R OF IRISH GOVERNMENT BILL.

In anticipation of the Cabinet on Friday, I will endeavour in this Memorandum to bring before my colleagues the exact state of the case, as it stands before us, with respect to the exclusion of Irish Members from the Imperial Parliament, and the condition of Ireland as to Imperial affairs.

I. *Under the Bill as it stands.*

1. The whole Irish representation in both Houses is to be recalled, if any alteration is to be made in the Statute itself on which there has not been a previous agreement between the two Legislatures.

2. The Imperial contribution being fixed, and based upon peace charges, Great Britain can only obtain aid from Ireland towards a war expenditure by the free action of the Irish Legislative Body upon a Message from the Crown, which aid of course might be withheld.

3. It is impossible to restrain the right of free speech on any subject Imperial or other, or to refuse it to the Body while allowing it to the members. The Addresses of the Legislative Body, if founded in reason, would on excluded subjects have no power, but they might have a great deal of influence.

Such is the provision already made, and, whether from imperfect comprehension or not, deemed insufficient.

II. The question then arises, what more can we rightly and safely do, in order to secure against risk the second reading of the Bill?

(1) and first let me exclude what I think the Cabinet believe we cannot safely do. We cannot agree to the simple retention of the Irish Representation in the two Houses as it stands under the Act of Union?

Nor, I assume, can we agree to its retention with the condition of reduced numbers?

(I observe in passing on the question of reduced numbers that it would involve a new legislative machinery to provide for the choice of them: while the 103 and the 28 would be those entitled under the Act of Union.)

(2) Mr Stansfeld has suggested[1] that perhaps the case might be met by a simple form of Federation, with division of subjects, for Scotland and Wales as well as Ireland. Whether or not this method might have been originally entertained I will not say: but at the present stage it would involve the withdrawal of the Bill, and to this I do not see my way. I mention the point however in case others should think we can work in this direction?

I will confine myself to suggesting changes which though undoubtedly important would not alter the principle of the Bill, nor extensively modify its framework.

1. The first point to be considered is the force of the argument against taxation without representation. Volenti non fit injuria; and we have the consent of the Irish members.

But it is a very large interpretation of their mandate, if we take this consent as binding Ireland to bear all changes of Excise and Customs Duty which may be enacted at Westminster during a long and not absolutely limited future.

When the exclusion of Irish members was originally proposed by me, there was to be no Parliamentary taxation of Ireland.

We imported Parliamentary taxation of Ireland into the plan, in order to gain the great object of fiscal unity.

I for one must plead guilty to having at the moment partially lost sight of the bearing of this change on the exclusion of Irish members. Both on principle, and as matter of policy, I am prepared to agree that the Irish representation (even if need be in both Houses) shall revive, so as to give the Irish members a *right* of attending at Westminster on any question of *altering* taxation for Ireland. (It would be needful to exclude the unusual

---

[1] Letter of 4 May, in J. L. and L. B. Hammond, *James Stansfeld* (1932), 282.

renewal of the Tea Duty and to have some special enactment for Bills simply of reduction or repeal.)

There would be some inconvenience in this, as there might be intrigues with the Irish to overthrow a Ministry through its Budget.

But we know the worst of this inconvenience now. Since the Act of Union, I think that only two Ministries (one of them already in a minority) have been overthrown, i.e. driven out, on Budgets. These cases were in 1852 and 1885. The Ministry of the day would have full opportunity of forecasting consequences in determining on its finance.

At the worst, whereas it has to deal now with Irish members who have no other legislative avocation, it would then have to deal with Irish members whose place of ordinary duty, and of preference, would be in Dublin.

I commend this proposal to careful consideration: especially if it is likely to have considerable influence on the coming division; which is of the most vital moment.

2. But undoubtedly it would not satisfy the whole craving that exists.

Can anything more be done? Taxation being so far disposed of, there remain, in threefold division

    (a) The Crown, and Defence.

    (b) Foreign and Colonial relations.

    (c) subjects reserved on practical grounds such as Patents, Copyright and so forth.

On (a) I do not see how to modify the Bill with any sort of advantage.

On (b) the 'sentiment' presses for a change. But how could Irish members, unless always here, be enabled to participate in dealing with a class of subjects which are mainly in the hands of private members, (at least I should say in the proportion of twenty occasions against one) and perfectly uncertain as to the time and method of handling? (For instance: Irish members would have had to be 'notified' for the motion of Sir J. Pease last night, on which the House was *counted* out.)

Two suggestions however have been made which might conceivably cover both (b) and (c).

The first is that provision might be made in the Act for regular communication between the British and Irish Executives on the (b) and (c) subjects. Foreign policy is thus managed as between Sweden and Norway; but their system is even now not quite determined, and it is founded on discussion in the presence of the Sovereign. I do not as yet see that much could be made of this. Time and convenience would bring about these communications spontaneously. Nor would the plan do much to meet the 'sentiment' now operative.

Another perhaps less unhopeful suggestion has been made from an unofficial source. It is that a Standing Committee or Delegation might be appointed, to meet from time to time during the (London) Session; to be composed (1) from and by both Houses here, and (2) from and by the two Orders of the Irish Legislative Body, in some reasonable proportion such as *perhaps* one third; to have power to report and make recommendations upon any of the subjects reserved in the Statute (except the Crown and Defence?) On the class of matters reserved, which are embraced in (c), I can conceive that such a Committee might be very useful. As to Foreign and Colonial questions, it might afford some safety-valve, if any be needed. But further: I am inclined to think it might go some considerable way towards meeting the *sentiment* which craves for symbols of Imperial Unity, while it would have no dangerous connection, under any ordinary circumstances, with the great and delicate question of the responsibility, and the stability, of Ministries here.

In conclusion; I conceive that whatever we adopt, or whatever we open as admissible, at this juncture, will hardly leave room for much farther change, except in details.

                                          W.E.G., May 5, 1886.

P.S. Very early in the day, I suggested that Irish members might be allowed to appear on particular subjects, if the Irish Legislative Body should ask it *pro hac vice* by Address to the Crown. There would however be difficulty I fear in framing a proposal on this basis and while in principle it is not inadmissible (as I think) the plan of a Committee or Delegation appears to me easier and better.[1]

6. *Th.*

Wrote to Mr Morley—Duke of Leinster—Ld Kenmare—Govr of Tennessee—The Queen—Mayor of Montreal[2]—Ld Spencer—Mayor of Pittsburg—& minutes. Saw Mr P.—Herbert J.G.—Mr A.M. l.l.l.—Ld Granville l.l.—Mr Illingworth—Sir W. Harcourt—Sir T. Acland—Mr Whitbread—Mr Morley. Read Gunning—& Burke's Thoughts.

7. *Fr.*

Wrote to D. of Argyll—Ld Rosebery—Ld Spencer—Sir H. Ponsonby—The Queen l.l.l.—& minutes. H of C. 4½-7¼.[3] Ly Phillimore & Alice dined. Saw Mr P[rimrose]—Herbert J.G.—Mr A.M.—Mr Henri—Mr Childers. Worked on Ireland. Read Gunning.

Secret. To see Mr Parnell[4] *2 o.c. May 7. 86.*[5]
1. Threefold modification. a) Tax call; b) Joint commission; c) Presence by Address.
2. Among alternatives open to consideration after 2nd R[eading] (but choice must depend on character of debate & of division): a) Resignation; b) Dissolution; c) Take Committee on Bill in Autumn Sittings.[6]

To LORD ROSEBERY, foreign secretary, 7 May 1886.   N.L.S. 10023, f. 180.

I am sorry to have made your hair stand on end, & I think you have used the word protest in some haste, as it usually follows rather than begins discussions, but I am comforted in thinking that there is no necessity probably for raising any disputable point.[7] The idea of a joint Commission may be reasonably entertained without stereotyping at the first moment the precise limit at all points of its office.

In all the twists & turns of this difficult subject, I have been working not to give effect to cherished predilections but to bring & keep people together & find the shortest & safest way to a great end. And great help in this I have had & shall have from you.

I hope you will get back from Windsor as soon as you can. Though Chamberlainism is rather in the dust, Hartingtonism is on its high horse, & I am sorry to say that though things are said to be moving in the right direction, & I have much faith in the country, the Parliamentary outlook is at this moment very far indeed from being clear.

[P.S.] You will do a very good stroke of work if you can get me Prince Edward (*alias* Albert Victor) for the 29th.

---

[1] Add MS 44772, f. 95 and Hammond, 506. Circulated next day, see Add MS 44548, f. 84.
[2] Thanks for Resolutions of support; Add MS 44497, f. 1.   [3] Questions; *H* 305. 528.
[4] Parnell probably did not come; see to Mrs. O'Shea next day.
[5] Add MS 44647, f. 94; note, ibid., f. 95, reads: 'I am coming over to see you soon—when shall I find you—it is rather urgent—(not on these notes principally. W.E.G. my. 7. 86.' 'I will go to you soon, by the Duke of York's steps, so as to be sure not to miss you [Granville].'
[6] i.e. if 2°R passed.
[7] Rosebery, unable to attend Cabinet, wrote on 6 May, Add MS 44289, f. 38, 'to protest as regards the Delegation on foreign and colonial questions'.

8. Sat. [Combe Wood]

Wrote to Ld Rosebery—The Queen—Mrs O'Shea—and minutes. Cabinet 2½–4½. Saw Mr P.—Herbert J.G.—Mr A.M. l.l.l.—Mr Stansfeld—Sir J.C.—Ld Granville— Ld Chancr—Ld Wolverton—Mr Lawson—Ld Ashburnham—Lady Maidstone— Mr M'Coll. Read Gunning. Dined at Mr Barkers: & drove to Coombe Wood afterwards.

Cabinet. Sat. May 8. 1886. 2.30 P.M.[1]
Considered the situation—& WEG's general course[?] of observations for Monday on changes in the Bill marked A[2] was generally approved.
Chancellor *not* to see Chamberlain.[3]

To J. MORLEY, Irish secretary, 8 May 1886.   Add MS 44548, f. 85.

I am sure you will not stereotype any idea *against* modifications: a variety of modes of action in the debate are open to us. I agree with you[4] that the animus of Chamberlain's letter is such as makes it hopeless to frame a measure of conciliation *for him*. His interrogation is not I think (though he blunders in expression) so bad: & I am inclined to agree with you about Dale's suggestion as raw material. He is a good fellow.
I have sent a message to Eltham.

To Mrs. O'SHEA, 8 May 1886. '*Urgent*'.[6]   Add MS 44269, f. 300.

Morley is most anxious to see Mr. Parnell—is anything known at Eltham of his whereabout? This is really urgent. Morley has failed to trace him here. I inclose a form of Government Telegram on which please to write & dispatch at once your reply.

9. S.E.2.

Ch mg. Home service aftn. Saw Ld Granville. Wrote to the Queen—Mr A. Morley. Read Martyrdom of Isaac[7]—Bibliotheca Sacra, U.S.[8] a most creditable publication—Becker on the Authorship of the Imitation.[9]

To A. MORLEY, chief whip, 9 May 1886.   Add MS 44548, f. 86.

[First letter:]   (1) Granville has been here this afternoon & unfortunately had gone shortly before your note[?] arrived. (2) The L[abouchere] Memorandum* in your No. 2 is

---

[1] Add MS 44647, f. 96.
[2] Not found.
[3] See *G.P.*, 415.
[4] See Morley's letter this day, Add MS 44255, f. 84: Chamberlain's public letter makes any 'compromising' expedients useless: 'they will only give an impression of weakness on our part, without conciliating the little section who work with Chamberlain'; Morley sent R. W. Dale's 'suggestion'.
[5] Note written at 5.20 p.m., Add MS 44255, f. 86: 'My friend [i.e. Parnell] is much more stiff against the retention even than he was before.... He thinks we shall win the second reading....'
[6] Holograph, with envelope; wire this day replying: Parnell will call at the Irish Office; Add MS 44269, f. 302.
[7] Not found.
[8] *Bibliotheca Sacra and theological review*, published in New York.
[9] V. Becker, *L'auteur de l'Imitation* (1882).

the best thing I have seen. I have written to you on it. My note should not I think actually go out of your hands except it be to the Chancellor who may I think regard the present position as sufficiently promising to warrant an interview with L. (3) Please let these notes be given to Primrose for copying when convenient—also L.'s No. 2.

[Second letter:] *Secret.*   Your two notes & the inclosures have just come into my hands together. After reading them I think I need not notice the first particularly, but only the second.

In its enclosure* are 3.

Point one. Taxation. I am instructed, from yesterday, to promise this shall be done if agreeable to the House.

Point 2. I have authority to speak of this with favour.

Point 3. To the principle of this I am favourable & I have no reason to believe the Cabinet are hostile. I am not so certain, as with respect to the two former, that a practical proposal can be easily put into shape. But I may refer to the subject in no adverse spirit.

*Inclosures [*from Labouchere*] referred to above.*

1. That the Govt. will assent to the principle of full representation upon all questions of taxation.

2. That some means will be found by which the Irish opinions on questions excluded from the Dublin Parlt. shall be conveyed to the Imperial Parlt., such as a joint committee representing England, Scotland & Ireland.

3. That the Irish Parlt. has the right by address to claim representation upon any question of Imperial policy.

Such modifications as are needed to give full effect to above will be made in Bill.[1]

10. M. [London]

Wrote to Mr Trevelyan—D. of Argyll—The Queen—and minutes. Returned to D. St. 1.45 P.M. Worked on Irish question for the Debate. H of C. $4\frac{1}{2}$-9 and $10\frac{1}{2}$-$11\frac{1}{2}$. Spoke $1\frac{3}{4}$ hours.[2] The reception decidedly inferior to that of the Introduction. Saw Mr P.—Herbert J.G.—Mr A.M. l.l.l. Read Gunning. Saw Graham [R].

11. Tu.

Wrote to Sig. di Marzo[3]—Ld Granville Tel—Ld Spencer—Mayor of Lpool—Ld Aberdeen—Mr Morley—The Queen—and minutes. Saw Mr Deverell & Mr Richards on the S. O[pdebeck] & Newcastle affairs. Saw Mr P.—Herbert J.G.—

---

[1] Labouchere's statement of Chamberlain's terms; he told Chamberlain this day 'the "cave in" is complete', though there was difficulty about wording the third point; Chamberlain replied, 'you are being bamboozled by the old Parliamentary hand'; Thorold, 308-9. See 11 May 86.

[2] Beginning the deb. on 2°R; *H* 305. 574.

[3] Gualberto di Marzo of Florence; Hawn P.

Mr A.M. l.l.l.—Mr Whitbread—Sir W. Harcourt & Mr Childers—Lord Chancel-
lor & Mr Morley[1]—Mr Broadhurst. H of C. $3\frac{3}{4}$-$6\frac{1}{4}$, 7-$8\frac{1}{4}$, $9\frac{3}{4}$-$11\frac{1}{2}$.[2] Prospects much
clouded for 2 R. Read Gunning finished Vol I.—Leaf, Introd. to Iliad[3]—Lang-
ridge, verses.[4] Dined with Lucy.

House of Commons.

(Each House to be dealt with separately) Irish Members (103) shall be invited by Mr
Speaker to attend.

1. When the Govt. makes a proposal for the alteration or repeal of any tax now levied in
   Ireland by the authority of Parliament, or for the imposition of any new tax. (This
   might be framed to include the regular annual renewal).
2. When on the proposal of any member of Parliament the House of Commons shall
   have once voted for a Bill to repeal or reduce a tax; and (in order to give sufficient
   notice) after such first vote, an interval of not less than one week shall be allowed
   before a second vote is taken.
3. When the Joint Commission appointed by this Act shall have reported that in its judgment a change in the law touching any of the reserved subjects, on which it is statut-
   ably authorized to report, is expedient, and any proposal shall be submitted to the
   House in conformity with such report.
4. When the Irish Legislative Body shall have signified by Address to the Crown its
   desire to promote an alteration in the Law [or in any treaty with a Foreign Power?] on
   any of the reserved subjects.
5. When the Irish Legislative Body shall have signified by Address to the Crown, Her
   Majesty assenting thereto, its desire either to initiate or to share in any proceedings in
   Parliament on any of the reserved subjects.

   Alternative for 4 and 5: Another plan, simpler and perhaps safer, would be to omit
   No 4 altogether, and leave its matter to be covered, as it would be covered, by No 5.
   WEG May 11. 1886.[5]

12. Wed.

Wrote to Mr A. Morley—Mr C. Bannerman—Mr Morley—Mr Illingworth—Mr
Bright—Sir W. Harcourt—The Queen Tel. Assembly of Massachusetts, N.
Scotia, and Dr Duckworth[6]—Mr Kennet Barrington.[7]—& minutes. Dinner party.
Saw Mr P.—Herbert J.G.—Mr A.M.—Mr Morley—Mr A.M. *cum* Mr Morley.[8]
Luncheon at 15 G.S.

[1] Morley's diary this day: 'Mema. from Mr. G. for further compromise. Took it to Ld. Chancellor—and then we went together to Mr. G.'s room: I criticised it. Qy. whether Herschell shd. see J.C.:
while we were talking, letter came from C., saying he thought no good cd. come of interview: it came
to that. Mr. G. begged me to communicate with A. Morley, (principally, I think, to get a talk alone
with H.) On the bench, aft., he sd. he had shown his Mem. to two anti-exclusionists, Har[court] and
Childers, and also to two exclusionists, Hers[chel]l & me. & *none* of us seemed in love [?line] with it.'
[2] Misc. business; *H* 305. 722. Govt. of Ireland Bill not debated this day.
[3] W. Leaf, *The Iliad* (1886).
[4] Probably F. Langbridge, *Love knots and bridal bands, poems, rhymes* (1883).
[5] Marked 'Draft. Secret'; Add MS 44772, f. 108. See to A. Morley, 9 May 86.
[6] (Sir) Dyce Duckworth, 1840-1928; physician; kt. 1886; see Add MS 44490, f. 201.
[7] Offered knighthood to (Sir) (Vincent Hunter) Kennett Barrington, 1844-1903, of the Red Cross.
[8] Morley's diary this day: 'At 3 wt. over to Mr. G.—talked for a half-hour. Back to H. of C.: all very
glum at report that J.C. had had a good meeting of his [illegible]. Exchanged friendly word w.
R. Churchill. Long talks w. Arnold Morley. P came to my room: does not much like postponement,

To John BRIGHT, M.P., 12 May 1886.   Add MS 43385, f. 346.

I have not troubled you for a long time, & I do not know whether, or in what sense if at all, your mind has worked since our last meeting. But I am now about to express a very strong hope that you may come up to town tomorrow & even to make that hope a request, so far as I may.

The great interests now at stake warrant my doing this. For it is not a request touching directly support for the Bill. It is founded on the fact that men of weight, & men of character, of the Liberal party but in very different attitudes with respect to the present debate, are working upon lines which would give you as I believe the opportunity of doing what they think a great public service (I do not speak of my own concurrence) in a simple manner, & without doing any violence to your own opinions & tendencies so far as I am aware of them.

These are the grounds which I trust justify my hope & request.[1]

To H. CAMPBELL-BANNERMAN, war secretary,   Add MS 41215, f. 13.
12 May 1886.

It may be right to summon the Cabinet tomorrow to give you your mandate or make you sure of it. If it is done would 12 or 2 suit you best? I corrected yesterday the proof of so much of my speech as referred to the question of Irish members, & hope to send it you in an accurate form. Meanwhile I send you a copy of a letter I have just addressed to [J.] Morley. The method has only just occurred to me.[2] If the stage had been an earlier one, the suggestion might, I am inclined to think, have been recommended. Please consider it carefully.[3]

To Sir W. V. HARCOURT, chancellor of the   MS Harcourt dep. 10, f. 110.
exchequer, 12 May 1886.

You & I were both rather in the yielding mood yesterday about the proposal to take Friday. But A. Morley is very desirous it should not be done. And J. Morley is really anxious to get the 2d reading of his Arms Bill for which after the Order for Supply Friday would almost certainly afford an opportunity. Please to consider whether on this ground we cannot stand to our guns, of course promising Monday.

There is much matter in ferment today as you will probably have gathered from reports. The question of postponement is assuming rather a new shape. I reckon on a cool computation of times that we could not get the Bill out of the House ⟨before⟩ by the first of August.

To A. MORLEY, chief whip, 12 May 1886. '*Private*'.   Add MS 44548, f. 87.

I sent you the letter to Illingworth.[4]

And also a copy, which I think might be sent to Whitbread. Should you not bring them

---

but sees the difficulty. W[en]t back to Mr. G. w. A. Morley: told him the story. Postponement aft. 2nd. reading practically settled for the momt. Not at all happy about it.'

[1] Bright agreed to reverse his plans and come, though 'not in favour of Home Rule' and regretting the absence of a broad base of support for the bill, finding himself 'forced in a direction contrary to my wishes'; letter of 13 May, Add MS 44113, f. 224.

[2] Though this was in fact his original solution; see 14 Nov. 85.

[3] No reply found.

[4] Dated this day, replying positively to Illingworth's suggestion of a party meeting; Add MS 44497, ff. 201–4.

into communication? Herbert would I am sure readily be an auxiliary to you for this purpose if wanted. I cannot commit the Cabinet, & I feel its powers of original action now to be somewhat limited. But I feel very sure my colleagues would not raise difficulties, with such an object in view, as to any mode of operation which they deemed honourable & practicable.

Pray observe what I have said as to the support needed to make any suggestion available. Our friends might tomorrow reserve their fire, & leave the Debate, after Campbell Bannerman, mainly to the Irish.

[P.S.] I may be out $1\frac{1}{2}$–$3\frac{1}{2}$.

To J. MORLEY, Irish secretary, 12 May 1886. '*Secret*'.   Add MS 44255, f. 88.

Perhaps unavoidably from the circumstances of the case the Government is being placed through extraneous importunity in an inferior position by being required to perform the work of the Committee before the 2nd reading of the Irish Bill. Our promise to consider with open mind any suggestion on the subject of recalling the Irish members is put down, even by some of our own party, as equal to zero. I believe what we have promised & said is quite enough to go to the country on. But the policy of getting the second reading if possible remains as clear as ever—& one should never weary of desiring any honourable means.

1. Whitbread has in hand the idea of postponing the Committee to the autumn, & of having this strongly & from many quarters urged upon us in debate provided a sufficient strength can in this way be secured.

2. Subject to the same condition, further reflection suggests to me a proposal growing out of what I yesterday sketched, to which it would be difficult for Chamberlain to object (as it seems to me). It is this—that the Irish members might come back, upon Address, for handling any reserved subject named therein, & the House of Commons if it shall think fit may direct Mr. Speaker to summon them accordingly. With an analogous provision for the House of Lords.

Neither this nor any other expedient can now, as far as I see, be put out tentatively. But if there were a justifying prospect of support, I should be sorry to lose the 2nd reading for want of willingness to accept such a provision. I think the security practically complete.

I should be glad to see you about this as soon as may be convenient. Meantime I will send a copy to C. Bannerman.

13. *Th.*

Wrote to The Queen l.l.—Mrs O'Shea—and minutes. Saw Mr P.—Herbert J.G.[1]— Mr A.M. H of C. $4\frac{3}{4}$–$8\frac{3}{4}$, 10–$12\frac{1}{4}$.[2] Read Gunning—Armstrong's Poems.[3]

14.

Wrote to Mr Whitbread—Mr Morley—Mr R.H. Hutton—Mr Bright—Ld Hampden—The Queen l.l.—Sir W. Phillimore—and minutes. Conversation with Lucy. Drive with C.—Walk. Saw Mr P.—Herbert J.G.—Mr A.M.—Mr Whitbread l.l.— Sir H. Ponsonby—Scotts—Mrs Baker—Mr Harrison. Read Gunning.

---

[1] Two MS pages blank here.
[2] Govt. of Ireland; *H* 305. 912.
[3] G. F. Armstrong, *Stories of Wicklow* (1886); verses.

To John BRIGHT, M.P., 14 May 1886.   Add MS 43385, f. 352.

1. I am concerned to find that the demand[s] on your patience & patriotism were so untimely; & I am, in the same proportion, sensible of, & thankful for the self-sacrificing effort you have made.

2. I should not have ventured to press you in obedience to a desire of my own, or, a desire of any ordinary man.

But I look upon Whitbread,[1] relatively to the present circumstances, as not an ordinary man. I think he will probably communicate with you, on the very question you have started, that of time.

3. You have no doubt asked yourself the question, how is all this to end? Can it end in any way but one?

4. The offences of Nationalists have been great: the worst of them, I frankly say, was committed against *you*, by Sexton, in a well known speech. *He* has given you a splendid opportunity; & I am confident you will turn it to account.

5. Are you not struck with the warm emotion, & strong conviction, of the great British race throughout the world: that race which already tops 100 millions, & which increases by several millions every year.

We shall I hope meet soon.

To LORD HAMPDEN, 14 May 1886.   Add MS 44548, f. 89.

There is much fermentation going on now, friendly as well as hostile; & it is not beyond hope that it may take effect in some mode of composing the present difficulties such as you would not disapprove.

There is no doubt, I think, that a majority of the House is friendly to the 'principle' of the Bill: & the immediate aim is to turn this fact to the proper account.

I say a majority, even after deducting some who say they are & are not.

I am delighted with the prospect of seeing you on the 29th.

To J. MORLEY, Irish secretary, 14 May 1886.   Add MS 44548, f. 89.

I think that considering the various rumours, proposals, & embryonic notions of proposals, which are now floating as notes in the air, & the possibility that some one of them may take form, it would be very desirable that you should see Parnell & learn further his mind upon them.

A preliminary fact is that if we had a fair majority (2 R) at our back we could not send the Bill to the Lords by the 1st of August.

Can there be truth in the statement by the Postmaster General that Hartingtondom, let alone Chamberlaindom, is ready to vote a Resolution in favour of Home Rule on the withdrawal of the Bill?

If so, whether an admirable proposal or not, it is a great event.

But I think it obvious that if such a thing were named to me I ought to reply by asking *to see the Resolution for which they* (& who?) *are ready to vote*.

Our obligations are to the cause—the Irish—the party—& nothing & no-one else.[2]

For Mr. M[orley]. In connection with the points so well put by Mr. P[arnell] there are some to be weighed, as far as they go, in the other scale.

---

[1] Gladstone sent Bright's reply to Whitbread, commenting 'there is *perhaps* a little daylight to be seen in what he says about time'; Add MS 44548, f. 88.
[2] No reply found.

1. The best electioneering authorities are of opinion that a delay before a Dissolution would be advantageous to the Irish policy. 2. If a certain number—were it so low as seven or ten—of votes could be gained by a ready accession or the idea of delay, there would be, in all likelihood, a nett addition, or nearly so, to the number of supporters of the policy in the next Parliament. 3. Refusal of such an offer would greatly damage at the Election those who had refused it in the estimation of a Liberal Constituency. 4. Even were the 2R carried by a moderate majority, the Bill could not be carried through within the period of an ordinary Session. 5. It is fair to ask on the other side—would it not be open to the Government, deferred on the second reading, to begin a *new Session* in October & then reintroduce it, if this were thought more politic than immediate Dissolution?[1]

To Mrs. O'SHEA, 14 May 1886.   Add MS 44548, f. 88.

I have received your telegram.[2] I think you will find that under the three rules laid down by the Government on Monday there is no need for fear. But if there is any apprehension on this subject, a word at any time to my colleague Mr. Morley will suffice to bring about an opportunity for all needful explanations. I must say the Irish have spoken admirably well in the opening of this debate. All I hear from them makes me wish that they shall bear a considerable & large part in it. Their words will find their way to the hearts of the nations on this side the Channel.

15. Sat. [Combe Wood]

Wrote to Ld Ripon—Sir Jos. Pease—and minutes. Dined at Coombe Hill. Worked on arranging papers. Saw Mr P.—Herbert J.G.—Mr A.M. l.l.—Ld Granville—Ld—Mons. Reinach[3]—Ld Wolverton *cum* Mr West. Read Gunning—and Castelvetro Introdn.[4]

To Sir J. W. PEASE, M.P., 15 May 1886.   Add MS 44497, f. 231.

Your kind letter[5] opens a subject indeed grievous[?]; for the battle is sharp & will I fear be sharper.

Whatever might be the consequence of the withdrawal of the Bills upon the present Govt., that is a very secondary question, & I would at once recommend it to my colleagues, if I believed that with more time we could as you think frame a measure which would unite to us the dissentient portion of the Liberal party.

I am aware of no hope that we could compass such an end: & I must observe that the whole force of the dissentient party *has not yet availed to tender to us a single suggestion in a practicable shape*.

But we have tendered such suggestions as have occurred to us, & as, at the date of tendering, we could see our way to executing. How have they been received?

---

[1] Initialled and dated 14 May 1886; Add MS 44255, f. 90. Morley's diary this day: '... At 10.30 interview with Mr. G. in his room: showed me a paper w. 5 poss. expedients, including even withdrawal of Bill and holding on: rather distressing to see the desperate sort of tenacity with wh. he clings to his place.'

[2] Need for govt. commitment to 'firm adherence to your principles of the intense faith'; Add MS 44269, f. 303.

[3] See 4 Nov. 76.

[4] L. Castelvetro, probably *Sposizione . . . a xxix canti dell'Inferno Dantesco* (1886 ed.).

[5] Of 14 May, Add MS 44497, f. 223: no 2°Rs without 'yet unknown, and difficult to conceive, alterations . . . in the Irish measures': why not withdraw the Bills and prepare new measures in the autumn?

Was it not easy to say, these suggestions are insufficient, but they indicate your position towards us, let us see what more we can do by painstaking consideration.

While nothing has been advanced in aid, our propositions have been received with silence & indifference, in some cases perhaps with contempt.

Meantime the body of the nation, so far as we can judge, has hailed our imperfect efforts with enthusiasm, & so has the great British race throughout the world.

I accept with grief all your prophecies of mischief: &, like the roll in Jeremiah, I could add to them many more words.[1]

To LORD RIPON, first lord of the admiralty, 15 May 1886.   Add MS 43515, f. 42.

I am waiting for a state of things which *may* (but it is uncertain) give me something to refer to the Cabinet, with a view of acting on the Division.

In the event of a miscarriage of the Bill, I am for a stout course. Pray mention this to any colleague if occasion offer. Of course any absolute decision[?] can only be reached when we have the exact circs. before us.

16. 3 S.E. [London]

Chapel Royal mg & evg. Wrote to E. Hamilton—Sir Thos Acland. Read Bp of Gloucester on Feu Lamented Truth:[2] a work greatly below its mark—Mivart, Contemp. Evolution[3]—Salisbury's Speech!![4] Dined with the Northbournes: a great pleasure. Conversation with Ld Northbourne—Ld Dalhousie—A. Morley.

17. M.

Wrote to Mary Drew—D. of Argyll—D. of St Albans—The Queen—and minutes. Wrote Mem of conversation with Sir H.P. H of C. $4\frac{1}{2}$-$8\frac{1}{2}$ and $9\frac{1}{4}$-$11\frac{1}{2}$.[5] Read Gunning. Saw Mr P.—Mr Whitbread—Mr A.M.—Sir H. Ponsonby.

Sir H. Ponsonby called on me today to inquire on the part of H.M., whether I could give her any light as to what was likely to follow the division on the 2d Reading of the Irish Government Bill.

I said that there was so much matter seething and simmering, and so much of uncertainty whether it would come to anything, that I could say but little, though it was probable in two or three days I might be able to form something more like a forecast.

The balance of chances in the present circumstances was against the Bill, but modes of proceeding had been suggested, and appeared to be desired, by a fringe of the opponents, and by a fringe of our supporters, which might if adopted carry the Bill through the second reading.

One suggestion, which had been made by a friend, and to which a certain number of intending opponents had given their adhesion, was that the Bill, after being read a second time should be postponed until the autumn or a new Bill then brought in.[6] This idea was still in agitation.

---

[1] Pease replied, 20 May, Add MS 44497, f. 246, urging proceeding by Resolution; 2°R would fail, as would a subsequent election.

[2] Probably C. J. Ellicott's 'diocesan progress', but none found for 1886.

[3] See 14 May 76.

[4] 'Separation and nothing else is the question upon which you have to decide'; 'you would not confide free representative institutions to the Hottentots, for instance'; *T.T.*, 17 May 1886, 6.

[5] Govt. of Ireland Bill; *H* 305. 1165.

[6] See 15 May 86.

Sir H.P. might acquaint H.M. that viewing the contents of the Bill we had arrived at the conclusion that, if fair allowance be made for adequate discussion, it would not be possible to carry the measure within the ordinary limits of the session, as it could not go to the House of Lords until the month of August was running.

I told him that in my judgment a reasonable adjustment of the question respecting the attendance of the Irish members in Parliament might be arrived at so as to maintain the common concern of the countries in imperial matters but I gave this as my own opinion only and said it was clearly impossible for the Government, when the suggestions it had already made were met by malcontents with a cold and unfriendly reception, to put out new suggestions with loss of dignity and, presuming the same temper to exist, no hope of profit.

Sir H.P. said as from himself there seemed to be good sense in an idea expressed by Lord Penzance that if the union were really preserved the difficulty would be removed.

I said it became a question of terms and their interpretation. I conceived that the Union is maintained in essence by the Bill as it stands, but our duty was to consider anxiously even the unfounded jealousies of persons favourable to our real aims; we had therefore sought to exhibit this Union more fully by the amendments we had proffered, and it would be our duty to act further in that sense if the way could be opened without prejudice to the aim of the Bill.

I did not explain to him what I had referred to as a reasonable adjustment.

He said—and to say this was not improbably a main part of his purpose in calling on me—that I might have heard statements to the effect that the Queen would refuse us the power of dissolution should we advise it. There was not a word of truth in them: she had said nothing of the kind.

I answered that I had not heard such statements beyond this that Lord R. Churchill confidently expected H.M. would take that course—I could well conceive that H.M. had not found occasion to say anything on the subject but I should have given no credence to such statements had I heard them.

The advice to be given might depend on other circs. than the Aye or No of the division, for instance the smallness of the majority might affect it. It was of course the duty of the Govt. while making every allowable effort to conciliate yet upon failure of such efforts to be firm in perseverance.

I referred to the extraordinary speech of Lord Salisbury on Saturday,[1] but this was antecedently to the main conversation.[2]

18. Tu.

Kept bed for a time. Wrote to Ld Rosebery—The Queen—& minutes. Read Gunning (finished)—Craik Romance of the Peerage[3]—Le Rêve de Paddy.[4] H of C. 4½-9. Saw Mr P.—Mr J. Morley—Mr A.M.—Mr Morley *cum* Mr Parnell: who is very noteworthy in conversation.[5]

[1] See 16 May 86.
[2] Holograph dated 17 May 1886; Add MS 44772, f. 111; marked 'Secret'. In Autobiographica, iv. 79.
[3] G. L. Craik, The romance of the peerage, 4v. (1848-50); family history.
[4] H. S. Thomas, Le rêve de Paddy et le cauchemar de John Bull (1886).
[5] Morley's diary this day: 'Talk w. Mr. G. as to draft of proposed resolutn.: Chambn. had had a very conciliatory talk w. Herbert G. night before: but I don't believe a word of it all the same. Arranged for interv[iew] w. P. At 7 he & Mr. G. met in my room: lasted an hour & more. P. strong for stand[in]g to our guns & not withdrawing. Might agree to postpone committee until autumn sitting. Mr. G. had not been well all day—and P. told me afterwds. that he had not realised how old Mr. G. was: the light came full strength[?] on his face from the large window, but his eye was undimmed.

Circulate.[1] There is *no truth* in any rumour now in circulation that the Queen has expressed her intention to refuse a Dissolution should it be advised by Her Ministers.

These rumours are probably of one family with those put about in the end of January that the Queen would not accept any Government except one pledged to the 'Repeal' Paragraph of the Speech.

The inclosed mem.[2] records a conversation between Herbert & Chamberlain after the House last night, held at C's request.

19. *Wed.*

Wrote to Mr Downing—Duke of Argyll—Att. General—Mr A. Morley—Mr Morley—Mr Heneage—and minutes. Read Ld Clare's Speech[3]—Liberal Promises.[4] Saw Mr P.—Herbert J.G.—Mr A.M.—Mr Hamilton—Mr Schnadhorst[5] *cum* Mr A. Morley—Mr Whitbread cum do—Mr Morley—Ld W. Compton—Sir H. Vivian—Sir J. Caird.

Circulate: Nothing has yet come up for the Cabinet to consider. I have seen Whitbread today. He is astonished at Hartington's speech with respect to a Resolution; as quite inconsistent with language held to him.

The speech at Bradford has, like the speech of Salisbury, caused dismay among the more moderate Secessionists. Meanwhile we have ascertained that the Irish view with extreme aversion any alternative beyond the postponement of the Committee on the Bill to Autumn sittings.

I told Whitbread that if there was a possible idea of a Resolution, Hartington's speech had nearly killed it.

Whitbread did not think men could now be worked upon by the prospect of postponement after 2 R; but apparently was unaware that there had been a real reaction in that direction, whether a sufficient one or not.

Schnadhorst would like the Dissolution postponed. But not if postponement were to be purchased by showing the white feather. It could only be desirable he thinks if following a clear affirmation of the principle of the Bill by a good majority. WEG May 19. 86[6]

To A. MORLEY, chief whip, 19 May 1886.   Add MS 44548, f. 90.

Events appear now to have made a Resolution unavailable(?)[7]

1. Hartington has stated with great force (in an ultra speech)[8] the arguments against it: & I think it plain it could only be adopted as a practical solution by consent.

"Most satisfactory man", was Mr. G.'s exclamat[ion] when P. left us. P. came to me again at 12: had seen some of his men: all agreed that withdrawal in any shape or form wd. be very bad: urged me to impress this on Mr. G.'

  [1] Holograph dated 18 May, Add MS 44647, f. 97.
  [2] Add MS 46110, f. 102; see *G.P.*, 423; proposal for liberal reunion on premise that a resolution in principle would be substituted for the bill.
  [3] J. Fitzgibbon, Lord Clare, 'Speech in the House of Lords of Ireland ... to concur in such measures as may best tend to unite the two kingdoms' (1800).
  [4] Untraced.
  [5] Hamilton came in to hear Schnadhorst answering to 'Dissolution or no Dissolution?': 'he had no doubt that an immediate appeal ... was preferable to any appearance of "showing the white feather"', a view appealing to Gladstone; E.H.D., 19 May 1886.
  [6] Add MS 44772, f. 130.   [7] Copyist's query.
  [8] At the liberal unionist meeting on 14 May; *G.P.*, 421.

2. He has also shown up Chamberlain's intention to maintain a general inter-meddling power at Westminster for Irish affairs: in a word to degrade the Irish body below the level of a municipality.

3. From the Irish quarter there have been sounds which appear to show dissent from such a course. They dissented much from Labouchere's proposal last night to withdraw the Bill after the 2nd Reading, or postpone it. It would be far from difficult probably to deal with, & get over, this dissent, especially if we did no more than postpone to the autumn. But their arguments against abstract Resolutions (which might be taken *verbatim* from my speeches on many questions) would be most awkward.

I think you should at once call Whitbread's attention to 1 & 2.

20 Th.

Wrote to Ld Wolverton—The Queen—& minutes. H. of C. 4½–6, 7–8¾, 10½–12½. Spoke on the Seditious Speeches.[1] Drive with C. Saw Mr P.—Sir H. Ponsonby—Mr A.M.—Ld Stalbridge—Abp of Dublin[2] & Chaplain (RC)—G.L. Gower. Read Craik, Peerage.

21. Fr.

Wrote to Ld Granville—Sir Jos. Pease—Ld de Vesci—Ld R. Churchill[3]—The Queen—& minutes. Dined with Mr Hutton. Saw Mr P.—Herbert J.G.—Mr A.M.—Mr Morley—Mr Morley *cum* the ODonoghue—Mr Hutton—Mr Illingworth & others. H of C. 4½–7¾ & 10½–12.[4] Read Craik.

To Sir J. W. PEASE, M.P., 21 May 1886. Add MS 44497, f. 258.

I do not change my estimate of the spirit & intent with which you write but I am afraid your letter does not advance matters.[5]

The substitution of a Resolution for a Bill is *prima facie* a distinct condemnation of the Bill set aside. No case of it, in a primary question, has occurred to my knowledge, except that of the India Bill in 1858. This case illustrates my position. The Bill had been laughed & mocked out of court. But it did not suit the purpose of the majority to replace Lord Palmerston, whom it had just turned out. Tories, John Russell, Manchester men, Peelites, were all agreed in this, and the Palmerston party saw they had no option. So Resolutions were adopted *by consent* (and immediately followed by another Bill).

A Government cannot afford to degrade itself by the confession of errors it has not committed. If its Bill is essentially bad, & it does not see this, it is not fit to frame a good one, & some one else shd. undertake the task. If its Bill is essentially good, but defective in some particulars of importance, the place for amending them is in the Comtee: & the fundamental rules of the House, which are a wise expression of principles, give you the 2nd R. to meet this very case; & then, if the particulars shd. not be adequately mended, they give you the 3rd. R. on wh. to reject the Bill.

I will not say Aye or No to the question whether a Resolution *by consent* as in 1858, i.e.

---

[1] i.e. Churchill's statements on Ulster; *H* 305. 1564. Churchill, absent, replied vigorously by letter, Gladstone resting his case on Churchill's 'Ulster will fight; Ulster will be right' letter to Young of 7 May; letters in *T.T.*, 24 May 1886, 4c.

[2] William Walsh, 1841–1921; archbishop of Dublin 1885; supported home rule as a minimum.

[3] See 20 May 86n.

[4] Govt. of Ireland Bill; *H* 305. 1667.

[5] See 15 May 86n.

supported at least by the United Liberals & the Nationalists (418 agst 252 Tories) wd have been admissible. It is not before me. Lord Hartington, to speak of no one else, has killed it.

As regards the country, you will excuse me if (without pretending anything like certainty) I in contemplating my *fourteenth* Dissolution—if that is to be the issue—am more confident than I should be.

If we are for the principle, what more than the principle is asserted by a 2°R.

I observe that among those who recommend a Resoln. (after we have turned tail upon the Bill) some do *not* mean to give an effective autonomy. Would a Resoln. comprehending them be an *honest* Resoln.?

As to the coming in of the Tories, that wd. be the certain & early triumph of the policy. As to the mischiefs hanging over the Liberal party, wh. wd be grave public mischiefs, we are at one.

22. Sat.

Wrote to Ld Rosebery—Messrs Robn & N.—Sir F. Milbank—Mr Chamberlain—& minutes. Dined at the Russian Embassy. Mad. & Madlle. both noteworthy. Great kindness & courtesy. Walk & drive. Gave S. Dora[1] to Mrs Baker [R]. Saw Mr P.—Ld Derby—Mr A.M.—Ld Kimberley—Mrs Harcourt [*sic*]. Read Craik—Rêve de Paddy.

23. 4 S.E.

Chapel Royal mg & evg. Saw Mr P.—Ld Spencer. Minutes on my engagement for tomorrow. Read Havigal, The King[2]—Wiseman's Lectures on H. Eucharist[3]—B. Rabutin on Me. de Sevigné[4]—Mivart Contemp. Evolution.

To LORD HARTINGTON, M.P., 23 May 1886.   Add MS 44148, f. 234.

I have been endeavouring to place myself in a condition to answer the appeals made to me on Friday about the length of the debate, by making inquiries in various sections of the House.

While thus engaged I read in the Observer a statement imputed to you that pressure is in course of being exercised on your friends by party associations 'for which purposes the debate is to be indefinitely prolonged'.

I feel obliged to ask whether these words (or the sentiments conveyed by them) are correctly imputed to you? I hope not, for you will see how they bear upon any attempt of mine to discharge the duty which you among others have placed upon me.[5]

24. M.

Wrote to Sir D. Currie—The Queen Tel. & l.—Mr Bonham Carter—Mr Hutton—Mr Washington Moon[6]—Sir H. Ponsonby. Lady & Miss Phillimore dined. 12¼-1.

[1] i.e. the *Life* of Dora Pattison (see 15 Feb. 80).
[2] F. R. Havergal, *Coming to the King* (1886).
[3] N. P. S. Wiseman, *Lectures on the Real Presence* (1836).
[4] R. de Rabutin, Count de Bussy, *Lettres de Mme de Sévigné* (1726).
[5] Holograph; perhaps not sent; no copy in Chatsworth MSS.
[6] George Washington Moon (1823-1909, critic and theologian) had sent his *The revisers' English* (1881).

Prelim. funeral service at St Margaret's for Ld Farnborough. Saw Mr P.—Ld Hampden—Mr A.M. l.l.l.—Herbert J.G.—Attorney General. Read Craik—W. Moon on Revision English.

To R. H. HUTTON, editor of *The Spectator*, 24 May 1886.　　　　Add MS 44548, f. 92.

I cannot let such a note[1] pass without acknowledgement. There is indeed much pain: but there is the comfort that belief in sincerity & integrity carries us through all in a case like yours: which is to me, let me add, simply a mystery, for it would be absurd to say you were warped by the spirit of class.

But you ask me a question about the 'Unionists'. I can only answer under protests: for while we are both Unionists in intention, you are in act as much a Disunionist according to my opinion, as I can be according to yours.

I *do* think that the common ruck of your 'Unionists' from Dukes downwards are warped by the spirit of class, but that few comparatively are aware of it, & few consequently compromise their integrity. So, among the opponents of Peel in 1846, there were some of the best men I ever knew. And the average were men worthy of respect.

Am I warped by the spirit of anti-class? Perhaps—I cannot tell. My dislike of the class feeling gets slowly more & more accentuated: & my case is particularly hard & irksome, because I am a thoroughgoing inequalitarian.

For the fountainhead of my feelings & opinions in the matter I go back to the Gospels.

Have you asked yourself why in many cases—say in Greece & in Bosnia—the upper class was renegade, the mass remained Christian?

25. *Tu.*

Wrote to Lord Acton—The Queen l.l.l.—and minutes. Cabinet 12–1.20. To Windsor 1.20–5.15. Audience of the Queen 45 m.: all pleasant. Saw Sir H. Ponsonby—Mr P.—Sir W. Harcourt—Mr A.M.—Mr S. Buxton.[2] H of C. $5\frac{1}{2}$–8 and $10\frac{1}{2}$–1.[3] Dined at Lady Stepney's. Read Craik.

Cabinet. Tues. May 25. 1886. Noon.[4]
Shall there be a meeting. Yes—Thurs. W.E.G.'s line of observation. NB to notice supremacy as well as the points in Mem.[5]
Arms Bill on Thursday.

Secret.[6] Pledged against: 8 Chamberlain, 66 Hartington & others: 74. 47 hopeful in various degrees, but largely. Upward progress since Lord Salisbury's speech. e.g. Powell Williams.

---

[1] Of 22 May, Add MS 44215, f. 332: pleasure at their meeting, regret at their conflict over Ireland.
[2] Sydney Charles *Buxton, 1853–1934; liberal M.P. Peterborough 1883–5, Poplar 1886–1914; colonial under-sec. 1892–5; in later liberal cabinets. Wrote widely on politics, his *Finance and politics*, 2v. (1888) probably already in preparation.
[3] Govt. of Ireland Bill; *H* 306. 41.
[4] Add MS 44647, f. 102.
[5] Jottings for speech at party meeting at ibid., f. 103.
[6] Undated holograph; Add MS 44647, f. 106.

Retention.[1] Contention is, that Ireland ought still to retain through her representatives a title to be heard in Parliament on Imperial = all reserved matters. *Principle* already regarded with favour. No *plan* offered by objectors. Omission of Clause 24;[2] cannot agree: a) goes beyond the objective view; b) settles nothing. We have examined further—I think[?], principle being sound, that the application of it can be arranged in a practical shape on this basis that the proposed retention or participation shall be subject to the discretion not of individuals but of the respective Houses.

26. Wed.

Wrote to Mr Mundella—Dr Cameron MP—Capt. Verney MP.—Sir T. Brassey— and minutes. Drive with C. Battersea Park—the road a beautiful solitude. Saw Beker [R]—Mr P.—Count Karolyi—Mr A.M.—Countess K.—Lady Sydney. Dined with Austrian Ambassador. Dalhousie party afterwards. Read Craik. Prepared materials for a statement of importance & of extreme delicacy tomorrow.

Circulate urgent. Irish Govt. Bill. Question of time.
Our view at the Cabinet yesterday was that I should apprise the meeting tomorrow that, on account of dates, there could be no effectual progress with the Bill within the limits of the ordinary Session, & that we should therefore propose to take no further steps at present, but that we looked forward to proceeding with the Bill, or the subject, in the early autumn.

I am however distinctly informed that the effect on the division will be much more favourable if I am able to inform them that our proposal will be to introduce in the early autumn a new bill with the necessary amendments or perhaps *better to introduce the Bill afresh with the necessary amendments*.

Accordingly, I am very desirous (being in much doubt whether this is not on all grounds the *best* form of proceeding) to be at liberty to announce accordingly tomorrow.[3] I agree K[imberley]
I fear that such an announcement will be taken to mean that we are going to bring in a new bill on different lines—and that, if we are not, then when the time comes, our last state will be worse than the first. But if Mr Gladstone believes that this announcement is the only way of getting the second reading, I agree. J. M[orley]
I agree with what Mr Morley has written but I am content to leave the matter to Mr Gladstone. H[erschell]
'To introduce the Bill afresh with the necessary amendments' commends itself I think A. J. M[undella]
I believe that the phrase last quoted is the best: and I think it ought to be distinct & unmistakeable. H. C. B[annerman]

27. Th.

Wrote to Sir W. Dunbar—Sir H. Ponsonby—The Queen—& minutes. Saw Mr P.—Sir H. Ponsonby—Mr A.M. 111—Mr Stansfeld—Mr Parnell *cum* Mr Morley[4]—Mr P. alone—A. Lyttelton—Lady Farnborough. Dined with A. Lyttelton.

[1] Undated holograph; Add MS 44647, f. 107.   [2] Clause ending Irish representation.
[3] Holograph dated 26 May 1886; Add MS 44772, f. 118.
[4] Morley's diary this day: 'Previous to meetg. w[en]t to Mr. G. to tell him the contents of letter from P.—deprecating strongly withdrawal of bill in any form. Found Mr. G. studying his notes: he was rather disconcerted. 'That is a nice morsel you have brought me', he sd. I urged him to leave

Drive with C. Meeting at F.O. 12–1¾. Spoke near an hour.[1] It went off extremely well. Read Craik—Oldcastle's Manning.[2]

To Sir H. PONSONBY, the Queen's secretary, 27 May   Add MS 44548, f. 93.
1886.

In the Attorney General's most able speech[3] (for such it was generally acknowledged to be) the passage about wealth & intellect attracted least of my attention & admiration. It did not stir up passion between the two sides of the House, from which I think the Debate has on the whole been very free, though I sometimes see the account of a violent speech outside, & I do not include the Orangemen who are chartered liberties & not I think ill natured men. But what I felt was that while the case of wealth is undeniable, & that power terribly against us, to allow that intellect is against us seems too like allowing that reason is against us, which would indeed leave us singularly in the lurch.

Mr. Burke said with great truth that the only ultimate titles to govern were in wisdom & virtue. I do not think this can be much mended.

Her Majesty pays me a most kind & graceful compliment but such light as I have is fast burning out. I constantly feel in listening to speakers in the House of Commons how they are doing what I cannot do.

To Lord Rosebery I will certainly report Her Majesty's gracious mention of him.

[P.S.] I am much pleased to see the journey northwards has thus far been so prosperous.

28. Fr.

Wrote to Mr A. Neeld[4]—Surveyor, Chester—The Queen l.l.—Sir W. Harcourt—Mr Blackw.—Dr Sieveking—Mr Wh. Cooper[5]—The Speaker—& minutes. Drive with C. Saw Mr P.—Mr A.M. 111. Read Craik finished I—Ld Cloncurry on Ireland.[6] H. of C. 4¾–8¼ and 9¾–12¼.[7]

To Sir W. V. HARCOURT, chancellor of the   MS Harcourt dep. 10, f. 112.
exchequer, 28 May 1886.

I agree to your proposed draft on the silver question.[8] It leads me, however, in the interest possibly of both India & England, to revert to the question of the present relation

form of postponement of bill an open questn. He wished me to go downstairs & see Arnold M[orley]: he took the opposite view to mine—as was natural. Meeting went off well enough—but I don't believe in these tactics. . . . At 7 P. came to my room, & I went for Mr. G.[—]discussed situation. P. talked of not voting for 2R. Then, I sd., 'I'll resign, for then all will be up: we shall lose strongest of our arg[uments], viz. that you accept.'

  [1] *T.T.*, 28 May 1886, 10a: if the bill given 2°R, it would be withdrawn, reintroduced in an autumn session with clauses on Irish representation at Westminster reconstructed; see also Add MS 44772, 118 and *G.P.*, 426.

  [2] J. Oldcastle [i.e. W. Meynell], *The Cardinal Archbishop of Westminster* (1886).

  [3] Russell's speech on 25 May, *H* 306. 66, about which the Queen complained: wealth and intellect had counselled Louis XVI and George III to refuse timely concessions.

  [4] Perhaps Aubrey Dallas Neeld of Clewer, Windsor.

  [5] Knighthoods for Edward Henry Sieveking, 1816-1904, physician, and William White Cooper 1816-1 June 1886, surgeon.

  [6] *Personal recollections . . . of Valentine Lord Cloncurry* (1849); Anglesea's 'the only attempt at an impartial rule in Ireland'. See 3 June 86. Notes at Add MS 44770, f. 69.

  [7] Reply to Beach on meaning of his speech on 27 May: only 'restructuring' would be on Irish M.P.s at Westminster; the 2°R a vote for a Bill, not an abstract principle; *H* 306. 321.

  [8] Opposing bimetallism; Add MS 44200, f. 127.

of the military establishments & accounts. One hears that India grumbles at the present system as costly to her. I believe it to be very costly indeed to us and to make India the real regulator of our Army Estimates. I should be very glad if there could be a Committee of Cabinet to consider this subject where I believe there may be room for a drastic reform.

[P.S.] Would it not be well to insert in your draft, without laying very extensive stress upon it, a notice of the fact that the question of silver is now before the Commission.

29. Sat

Wrote to Ld Granville—Sir W. Harcourt—Mr Bryce—Sir H. Ponsonby—and minutes. Company for review in A.M. Saw Mr P.—Mr A.M.—Ld Tweeddale— Miss Tennant & the family—Ld Derby. Birthday dinner to forty one of whom more half may have been antiIrish. I said a word to most of those in H. of C. The young Prince most kind. Read Ld Cloncurry. Much tired.

To Sir W. V. HARCOURT, chancellor of the   MS Harcourt dep. 10, f. 114.
exchequer, 29 May 1886.

Please to look at Albert Grey's question to me on Monday No 34[1] and to consult if you think fit, with the Chancellor or the Attorney General as to the answer I should give. Be it observed, however, that I made, so far as my memory goes, no declaration at all about any particular application of the Secret Service money (Times report supports me). A. Morley will hold himself at your command. Doubtless you will consider whether the present system *can* be maintained, and, if it be clear that it cannot, whether a short shrift would not be best.

There is one thing which I feel to be rather connected, though indirectly, with this subject. I think it extremely hard on the constituents of labouring men to be obliged *after bearing the charge of an election* to support them in actual Parliamentary service, while *pensions* are provided for ex-holders of salaried (lay) offices—are taken by men belonging to *families* of immense wealth—or in cases where a man accepts an Earldom & having thereby ⟨making⟩ *made* his means insufficient, thereupon takes a pension. After having administered these pensions for 10 or 11 years, I think them thoroughly unsatisfactory: and on grounds both of principle & policy I wish them abolished, & should be disposed to encourage now my idea of a movement for the purpose. Of course without touching actual holders.[2]

30. 5 S.E.

Chapel Royal mg & evg. Saw Ld Granville—Sir J. Carmichael—Ld Spencer. Read Struggles for Life[3]—Wright Exegetical Studies (Jonah)[4]—Moriarty's R.C. Book[5]—Eadie's Lect. on the Bible.[6]

[1] Question not reached.
[2] Harcourt replied on 30 May that payment of members was bound to 'come up in connection with this matter'; Add MS 44200, f. 129.
[3] *Struggles for life; or the autobiography of a dissenting minister* (1854).
[4] C. H. H. Wright, *Biblical essays on Job and Jonah* (1886).
[5] Perhaps J. J. Moriarty, *All for love; or, from the manger to the cross* (1883).
[6] Perhaps J. Eadie, *Lectures on the Bible to the young* (1848).

31. M.

Wrote to Sir C. Tennant—Mr Dickson—Ld Hampden—Gov. Louisiana[1]—Mr Morley—The Queen—& minutes. Read Ld Cloncurry—(N.C.) Godkin on Ireland[2]—Fortnightly X & XI.[3] Dined at Sir C. Forsters. Saw Mr P.—Sir W. Harcourt—Mr A.M. 111—Sir R. Peel—Mr Moulton.[4] H of C. $4\frac{3}{4}$-8 and $10\frac{1}{2}$-$12\frac{3}{4}$.[5] Great dismay in our camp on the report of Chamberlain's meeting.[6]

Tues. Jun. 1. 1886.

Wrote to Prince Albert Victor—Mrs Cooper[7]—The Queen—& minutes. Nine to dinner. Conversation with Sir A. Clark & Lucy on my continuance in work. Saw Mr P.—Ld Rosebery—Mr A.M. 11—Herbert J.G.—J. Morley. Drive with C. H of C. $4\frac{3}{4}$-$8\frac{1}{4}$ & $10\frac{1}{2}$-$1\frac{1}{4}$.[8] Read Ld Cloncurry—Burton's Hist. Scotland.[9]

2. Wed.

Wrote to Mary Drew—E. Hamilton—& minutes. Fourteen(?) to dinner. Drive with C. Saw Mr P.—Sir H. Ponsonby—Mr A.M.—Mr Illingworth—Ld Rosebery. Read Ld Cloncurry—& the long debates on the Canada Cut of 1791.[10]

To E. W. HAMILTON, 2 June 1886.   Add MS 44548, f. 95.

I like to see your arguments, always so clearly stated; but I do not on this occasion agree with them.[11]

Seven times in my recollection has a Government distinctly referred its case to the people: in five of them, it was in consequence of an adverse vote of the House of Commons—once in 1866 it did not, but resigned, I was a party to this. Our reason was the apathetic state of the people at that date, which does not now apply. But I have always felt great doubt whether we were not wrong. It requires very strong & definite reasons indeed to break away from such a course of precedent.

This is only one argument out of many. Another touches myself, but this only goes to the point that my next resignation must be more than a resignation of office. The hour that has next to strike for me is not the first but the last upon the dial.

[1] No letter found.

[2] E. L. Godkin, 'American home rule', *N.C.*, xix. 793 (June 1886).

[3] i.e. articles 10 and 11, on coming election and Ireland, in *F.R.*, xlv. 861, 869 (June 1886).

[4] (Sir) John Fletcher Moulton, 1844-1921; lawyer and liberal M.P. Clapham 1885-6, Hackney 1894-5; later a judge. Spoke for the bill on 4 June.

[5] Questions; Govt. of Ireland Bill; *H* 306. 505.

[6] Chamberlain read out parts of Bright's letter stating he would vote against the bill; votes taken at the meeting supported voting against 2°R rather than abstaining; *G.P.*, 428-9.

[7] D. of her husband; see 28 May 86n.

[8] Questions; Govt. of Ireland Bill; *H* 306. 672.

[9] See 19 Apr. 86; quoted on 22 June to show Scottish union not the product of bribery; *Speeches on the Irish question*, 246.

[10] Division into Upper and Lower Canada; discussed in his speech on 7 June; *Annual Register* (1791), ch. vi.

[11] Hamilton's letter this day arguing against dissolution as 'playing into Chamberlain's hands'; Add MS 44191, f. 76.

3. Th. Ascension Day.

Chapel Royal (& H.C.) 11 A.M. Westminster Abbey at $2\frac{3}{4}$–$4\frac{1}{2}$ for a singularly beautiful musical service. Wrote to Mr Morley—The Queen—& minutes. H of C. $4\frac{3}{4}$–$8\frac{3}{4}$ & $10\frac{1}{4}$–1.[1] Saw Mr P.—Mr A.M.—Mr Moulton. Read Ld Cloncurry's slovenly but yet important book.

To J. MORLEY, Irish secretary, 3 June 1886.　　　　　　Add MS 44548, f. 95.

I entirely agree with you that we cannot budge.

But I think T. P. [O'Connor] gives a perfectly just & undeniable exposition of what has been said.[2]

The five conditions to draw the lines within & not beyond, which it is our duty, as I conceive, to consider any amendments which may suggest themselves, or may be suggested, to us, either in the proposed interval of time, or in Committee on a re-introduced Bill. I shall be here at two but this note conveys all that occurs to me.

4. Fr.

Wrote to Dean of Westmr—Dr Bridge—Mr Osborne Morgan—Mr Moulton[3]— Sir Jos Pease—The Queen Tel.—Mr Bryce—Mr Trevelyan—& minutes. Worked on Irish Question. Drive with C. Saw Mr P.—Sir J.C.—Mr A.M. 111—Herbert J.G.—Sir J. Pease—A. West. Read Ld Cloncurry—Ld Macaulay 1833 Repeal.[4] Dined with the Wests. H of C. $4\frac{3}{4}$–$7\frac{3}{4}$ & $10\frac{1}{2}$–$12\frac{1}{4}$.[5]

To H. C. E. CHILDERS, home secretary, 4 June 1886.　　　　Add MS 44548, f. 96.

My wife has expressed better than I could our feelings on the sad & heavy disposition with which it has pleased God to visit you.[6] I can only express the hope that He may also supply you with every consolation.

I write now to say that we shall in any case I think require to have a Cabinet on Tuesday immediately after the division.

The *odds* are still I imagine in favour of the rejection of the Bill. In that case our *main* subject of discussion will of course be a Dissolution or a resignation—though it is just possible there may be other alternatives. I wish to present this weighty matter to you in case you should not be able to attend. You will I am sure forgive me if I have done what was needless.

5. Sat. [Dollis Hill]

Wrote to Mr A. White[7]—Mr K. Barrington—Mr Quilter MP[8]—Mayor of Weymouth—Sir U. Shuttleworth—& minutes. Dined at Ld Dalhousie's. To Dollis Hill afterwards. Saw Mr P.—Sir D. Currie—Mr A.M.—Mr Parker—and other

---

[1] Announced end of 2°R deb. for 7 June; *H* 306. 846.

[2] Specific allusion unclear; T. P. O'Connor (*Memoirs of an old parliamentarian*, ii. 36 (1929)) emphasised the unfairness of treating the 2°R deb. as if it were the cttee.

[3] Clarifying his statement at the Foreign Office meeting; *T.T.*, 5 June 1886, 12c.

[4] T. B. Macaulay, 'Speech . . . on the repeal of the Union with Ireland, 6 February 1833'.

[5] Questions; *H* 306. 1015.

[6] Death of his son, Francis.

[7] Possibly Arnold White, 1848–1925; journalist and liberal imperialist.

[8] (Sir) William Cuthbert Quilter. 1841–1911; liberal (unionist) M.P. Sudbury 1885–1906.

Scots members at Lord Dalhousie's. Read Ld Cloncurry—Sir Jonah Barrington—Lefevre & Fitzmaurice on Foreign cases of Home Rule.[1]

6. S. aft. Asc.

Willesden Church mg (with H.C.) and evg. Strong manifestation of popular favour outside (1 P.M.). Read Wiseman's Lectures[2]—Wright's Exeget Studies.[3] Saw Sir R. Hamilton—Ld Spencer—Ld Rosebery—Mr Marjoribanks.

7. M. [London]

Wrote to Mary D.—The Queen—& minutes. Worked on Irish question & speech through the forenoon at Dollis in quiet. Saw Mr P.—Mr Morley—Mr A. Morley—Mr Childers (in divin).[4] Read Ld Cloncurry—Swift on the Test.[5]

H of C. $4\frac{3}{4}$–$8\frac{1}{2}$ and $9\frac{3}{4}$–$2\frac{1}{4}$. We were heavily beaten on the 2d Reading, by 341 to 311.[6] A scene of some excitement followed the declaration of the numbers: one or two Irishmen[7] lost their balance. Upon the whole we have more ground to be satisfied with the progress made, than to be disappointed at the failure. But it is a serious mischief. Spoke very long: my poor voice came in a wonderful manner.

To LORD WOLVERTON, 7 June 1886. '*Secret*'. Add MS 44548, f. 96.

We may, probably enough, have to consider tomorrow morning the contingency of Dissolution. What would you incline to advise?[8] I take it for granted that it would be after winding up—say in the first days of July.

8. Tu.

Wrote to Mr Ridler—The Queen Tel. l.l. & letter—Lady S. Opdebeeck—Ld Granville—Mr J. Cowan—Prince Albert Victor (Edward)—Prince Geo. of Wales—Ld Advocate—& minutes. Read Pennant on the Horse[9]—Cooke on the Union[10]—Swift's Tracts. Saw Mr P.—Ld Rosebery—Mr Childers—Mr A.M.—Mr

---

[1] G. S. Lefevre, 'Home Rule: precedents' and E. G. Petty-Fitzmaurice, 'Home Rule: in Austria', *N.C.*, xix. 424, 443 (March 1886).

[2] See 23 May 86.

[3] See 30 May 86.

[4] i.e. in the division lobby.

[5] J. Swift, 'Letter concerning the Sacramental Test' (1708) in his *Works*, viii. 367; notes at Add MS 44770, f. 131.

[6] Spoke concluding the debate: 'one of those golden moments of our history ... which rarely return, or, if they return, return at long intervals, and under circumstances which no man can forecast.... Ireland stands at your bar expectant, hopeful, almost suppliant ... she asks a blessed oblivion of the past ...' *H* 306. 1235, *Speeches on the Irish question*, 141. After the division, he moved the adjournment until 10 June.

[7] Healy and O'Connor; *H* 306. 1245.

[8] Wolverton advised that 'If Dissolution is a necessity, it shd ... be *at once*': pre-harvest better than a winter campaign and the register fresher, unless we wait till January; '"Resignation" seems to me only giving the Tories the dissolution'; 7 June, Add MS 44349, f. 204.

[9] T. Pennant, *History of quadrupeds*, 2v. (1781).

[10] E. Cooke, *Arguments for and against an Union ... considered* (1798); notes in Add MS 44770, f. 99.

Flower—Ld Wolverton—Mr Marjoribanks. Ten to dinner. Saw Burdett, & another [R].

Cabinet. Tues. June 8. 1886. ⟨*Noon*⟩ *altered to 2 PM.*[1]
1. Resign or dissolve. Dissolve *nem con.*
2. Business of Supply.
3. Bills.

1. To dissolve Parlt. is the quickest way to the solution of a question in which all delay is a grievous evil.
2. We have submitted a great subject to a Parlt. chosen when it was (we admit) very partially before the country. Viewing its nature, the country has a strong claim to elect a Parliament upon it.
3. We are a young Parliament unencumbered with other controversies & able to present a very simple issue to the nation, which is a great advantage.
4. We have had as Ministers far greater authority for propelling this question than we could have had, or could now have, as an Opposition. Had we been in Opposition last night, I doubt whether we could have voted two hundred strong. We should lose all or much of this force by resigning.
5. It is almost a rule that a Ministry defeated under circumstances like ours, upon a vote of confidence, or a great policy, appeals to the country. I am aware of *no instance to the contrary.*
6. We have been constantly challenged to a Dissolution with reasons for the challenge, and not to take it up would be a proof of faintheartedness and a sign of mistrust and weakness.
7. While the opposite strength is in organisation, ours is in enthusiasm, and enthusiasm is especially apt to be chilled & flattened by such signs and proofs.
8. I can say with confidence that, whatever be the *strength* of our friends, their enthusiasm at the present juncture exceeds that of any former occasion. In serving us as a Government, it is centralised & brought to a head. If we were out of Government we should be I fear little more than the most numerous section of the Liberal Party.
9. It is also I apprehend of great consequence that in Ireland, with a view to holding in the people, we should maintain the visible continuity of our action, and not let the flag go down.
10. All speculations, founded on the difficulties in which successors would find themselves, are too subtle & refined for the country to understand; & practically power has never been given up, within my knowledge, on the grounds of such speculations.
11. I am sensible of the dismay embarrassment & losses in the Liberal camp should we dissolve when business is wound up, but it seems to me that a prolongation of fighting among ourselves indoors would probably aggravate rather than lessen these difficulties outside.
12. My conclusion is: a Dissolution is formidable but resignation would mean, for the present juncture, abandonment of *the cause.*   WEG. June 8. 86.[2]

---

[1] Add MS 44647, f. 113; marginal note reads: 'C. Bannerman, Rosebery: Balmoral.' Note in another hand, ibid., f. 117, describes view of Schnadhorst as unhesitatingly 'preferring *dissolution* ... the earlier the better ... it is impossible to form a confident judgment as to the result. Believes it probable that a majority would be returned in favour of the issue decided last night.' For Rosebery's doubts, see *G.P.*, 433. Morley noted in his diary: 'Mr. G. gave reasons ... for the course that was adopted. Nobody whispered dissent, tho' at least 3 of us had b[ee]n against it before'.

[2] Add MS 44647, f. 121; written in pencil, presumably notes for this day's Cabinet, the 'reasons' noted by Morley; (copy at Add MS 44772, f. 139).

To J. COWAN, president of the Midlothian liberal   Add MS 44548, f. 97.
association, 8 June 1886. '*Secret*'.

I think it right to give you the earliest intimation of the likelihood of a very early dissolution, say within 4 weeks of the present date. Please however to keep this in the strictest secrecy until you hear further. You will perhaps reflect on any steps which it may become proper soon to take, & communicate in strict confidence with Mr. Campbell.

Of course, & especially after the dilapidation which has taken place among local leaders, I shall look to paying my own expenses.[1] It may also be requisite for me to make my appearance on the ground at a very early date? Hoping for good accounts in due time of your health.

9. Wed.

Wrote to Mr Cohen MP—Sir W. Harcourt—Watson's—Mr P.W. Campbell—Count Corti—Mr Hallewell—and minutes. Saw Mr P.—W.H.G.—Mr A.M.—Ld Rosebery—Lord Kimberley—Mr Knowles. Open Cabinet 12-2 to settle course of proceedings.[2] Dined with Sir H. Thompson: a very agreeable party. Read Ld Cloncurry—Penruddock on the Union.[3] Saw M'Lachlan, Mills [R].

To P. W. CAMPBELL, Midlothian liberal agent,   Add MS 44548, f. 97.
9 June 1886. '*Secret*'.

Tomorrow it will be my duty to announce in the House of Commons that before the end of the month this seven-months Parliament will be dissolved. I wrote to Mr. Cowan yesterday with a less specific intimation, but I find he is in Fife & this may delay his communicating with you. Our friends in Scotland generally have been anxious for early action. Lord Rosebery goes down to Balmoral tonight. I think he will probably pass Monday in Edinburgh & will be ready to communicate with me.

Though naturally shrinking from new labours I am disposed to think 1. that I should issue at once a short but pointed address to the Constituency & 2. that it may be desirable for me to run down very soon for one or two speeches by way of early blasts of the horn for the coming battle. On this I shall await advice when the necessary considerations have been given.

Necessary occasion for my *constant* presence in the House of Commons will I think probably soon have passed away.

[P.S.] I may find an opportunity perhaps this time of getting under Mr. Macgregor's[4] roof.

10. Th.

Wrote to Lady Russell—Mr Drummond—The Queen—and minutes. Saw Mr P.—Ld Dalhousie—Mr A.M.—Mr Parker M.P.—Sir T. Brassey—do *cum* Mr Fowler. H of C. 4¾-6¼ & 9-10¾.[5] Worked on rudiments of Address. Read Ld Cloncurry finished—Macmillan on the Grattan Parliament.[6]

---

[1] Hitherto, Gladstone's election expenses had been paid for him.
[2] This phrase *sic*; clearly describes previous day's proceedings; entries for 8 and 9 June probably written together and a slip made.
[3] Not found.
[4] See 28 Oct. 85, 17 June 86.
[5] Announced dissolution by the end of June, and procedure for winding up business; *H* 306. 1304.
[6] J. Dowd in *Macmillan's Magazine*, liv. 139 (June 1886).

11. Fr.

Wrote to Messrs Watson—Ld Spencer—Mr M'Carthy[1]—Mr Anderson[2]—The Queen—Ld Granville—A. Gladstone—Mr P.W. Campbell. H of C. 4½-6½ & 9-10.[3] Worked again on rudiments of an Address. Saw Mr P.—Ld Emly—Sir J.C.—Ly Farnborough—Mr A. Morley—Mr [E.]R. Russell M.P. Read Müller, 'Goethe and Carlyle'[4]—Cox on the Church.[5]

12. Sat. [Holmbury]

Wrote to Ld Spencer—Mr Primrose—Mr Westell—Messrs Murray—and minutes. Off to Holmbury 10.30: arr. 1 P.M. Worked till six on my Address which required much care.[6] Read Beaconsfield's Letters:[7] much matter in the papers. Saw A. West—F. Leveson—Sir G. Dasent. Whist in evg.

To LORD SPENCER, lord president, 12 June 1886.[8]   Althorp MSS K296.

The whole position as to Irish Land Purchase has now been rendered most cloudy and equivocal[9]

1. by the conduct of the Irish Landlords
2. by the action of Hartington & others who keenly wish for the Bill but have thrown dirt upon it with a view to damaging Home Rule.

Yet I think with you we ought *not* to recede from any of our positions, and not to go beyond mild intimations that time and circumstances must of course act upon this question as upon all others.

The bulk of the Home Rule subject swollen by stiff contest will make the method of *pari passu* handling (I think) impossible.

I hope there need be no new difficulty on this matter now, which is really in the shade. I have great confidence in the real strength of the argument for it.[10]

13. S.

Church at 11 A.M. (with H.C.) and evg. Wrote to Mr Primrose Tel.—Ld Rosebery Tel.—Scotts—Sir Kenneth Mackenzie—Dr Simon[11]—and minutes. Read Wright's Exeget. Studies—Wiseman's Lectures finished.

---

[1] Thanking him for verses on Ireland, printed in *Gladstone or Salisbury*, ed. A. Reid (1886), 1.

[2] C. H. Anderson; letter of support for his candidacy for Elgin boroughs; Add MS 44498, f. 9.

[3] Supply; *H* 306. 1498.

[4] *C.R.*, xlix. 772 (June 1886).

[5] See 24 Jan. 86.

[6] In *Speeches on the Irish question*, 179 and *T.T.*, 14 June 1886, 9f; drafts at Add MS 44772, ff. 144-62.

[7] See 9 Jan. 86.

[8] *Spencer*, ii. 120.

[9] Spencer, 11 June, Add MS 44313, f. 75; the land bill unpopular, but Gladstone could have carried it.

[10] Spencer replied this day on folly of landlords in not seeing necessity for home rule, and need to maintain land as part of the home rule policy; *Spencer*, ii. 121.

[11] J. Simon, physician; on a cheque involving a rescue case; Add MS 44548, f. 99.

To Sir K. A. MUIR MACKENZIE, 13 June 1886.   Add MS 44548, f. 99.

I understand that it is clearly known you would, if you became a candidate for the Inverness Burghs, carry the seat.

Will you think it a very great liberty if at such a crisis I venture to echo the wish & hope of Lord Granville that you may be disposed to give us the advantage of your presence in Parliament.

It is most important that the country should speak on this occasion clearly & unequivocally; & it is hardly less important that men of the best stamp should be returned.

Only the election can test relative numbers of friends & foes. What I can say from personal experience is that never in my life have I witnessed such enthusiasm. This is a great comfort to one who believes we are engaged in setting wrong right, & in making short work of what we feel will be a long controversy.[1]

14. M.

Wrote to Ld Spencer—Mr Primrose Tel. l.l.l.l.—and minutes. Read Louise de la Kerouaille[2]—Beaconsfield's Letters. Tried to persuade my host[3] to come forward for Parliament. Conversation with Ld Acton. Tea party at 5. The place never so beautiful.

To LORD SPENCER, lord president, 14 June 1886.[4]   Althorp MSS K296.

I am not sure from yours received today[5] whether I quite understand your view of my last letter on land purchase.

There can be no harm I think in making any amount of argument in favour of our plan and its principle.

But as to the relation of the two subjects I think it would be a mistake either to recede from or to restate what we formerly said.

To restate at this date would be a new measure.

We ought I think to keep in our hands a perfectly [sic] liberty of rejudging the case when the proper time comes, in the measure which honour and policy may recommend. But let us, I should say, keep to the old point of departure, nothing having occurred which would justify a new one, & to say we stand in ⟨April⟩ June in all points precisely as we did in April would be a new one.

I do not find fault with the landlords or say they have refused our offer. We shall probably be far better able to judge some time after the elections; all I would say is let us not prejudge but let the matter stand without adding or subtracting. Restarting with a new date would be adding.

15. Tu.

Wrote to Mr A. Morley—Sir T. Acland—Mr Campbell—Mr Primrose—Ld Granville—Watsons—Messrs Miles—Mrs Drew—Mr J. Morley—Mr Williamson—Mr Taylor Innes—The Queen—and minutes. Wrote rudiments of a Speech. Drive

---

[1] No reply found; draft of further letter of 19 June at Add MS 44498, f. 35. Mackenzie did not contest the seat; see 23 June 86.

[2] H. Forneron, *Louise de Kerouaille, duchesse de Portsmouth* (1886).

[3] E. F. Leveson-Gower, Granville's br.; retired as liberal M.P. 1885; see 3 Apr. 62.

[4] *Spencer*, ii. 122.

[5] Ibid., ii. 121.

walk & conversation Ld Acton—Mr Lowell. Read Forneron, Louise de Kerouaille—Beaconsfield Letters.

To Sir T. D. ACLAND, 15 June 1886.   Bodley MS Eng. lett. d. 89, f. 58.

Your address[1] is I think a just and clear exposition of views most loyally maintained. It
will be a sad grief and shock if *you* are not upheld in them.

I am not ready to say *peccavi* about Class, and to say the truth I do not quite understand
your objection. But if I refer to the question again it will probably be with more fulness
and less risk of misapprehension.

16. Wed. [London]

Wrote to A. Morley—Ld Selborne—The Queen l.l.—Prince of Wales—M. Drew—
Ld Rosebery—& minutes. Saw Mr P.—W.H.G.—Mr Th. Hay—Mr A. Carnegie[2]—
Mr A.M. l.l.—Ld Granville—Ch. of Exr *cum* Mr Childers—Ld Rosebery *cum*
these and alone—Scotts—Mrs Th.—Mr Bryce—H.J.G. Left Holmbury 9½ A.M.
Shopping. Read Beaconsfield's Letters finished—Louise de Kerouaille.

17. Th. [Royal Hotel, Edinburgh]

Wrote to Rev. Dr. Hutton—Ld Granville—Mr Caine[3]—Mr Primrose l. & tel.—
Messrs Watson—Miss L. Clark—and minutes. Off at 10.5. Edinb. 8.50. Royal
Hotel. Wonderful demonstrations all along the road. Many little speeches:
could not be helped. Saw Mr Primrose—Mr Cowan—Mr Campbell—Mr
Brown(?)—& others. Read M. Napier's letters[4]—Sir J. Davis on Ireland.[5]

18. Fr.

Wrote to Mr Primrose Tel.—Mr Macfie—Mr Parker MP—The Queen—Mr
Cottrill[6]—Lord Emly—Helen G (tel.)—and minutes. Saw W.H.G.—Mr Camp-
bell—Mr Cowan—Mr Childers—Rev. Mr. . . . (Presbn)—W. H. James—Mr Cot-
terill. Beautiful drive in afternoon. Spoke at a crowded meeting in evg: 1½ hour.[7]
Again God gave me a voice according to the need. Worked much on Ireland.
Read Davis—Molloy's Charles II[8]—Midl. Speeches & old Essay.

19. Sat.

Wrote to Helen G.—Mr Primrose Tel. l.l.—Mr A. Morley Tel.—Ld Spencer—Sir
K. M'Kenzie—and minutes. Worked on Irish question. Saw W.H.G.—Mr

---

[1] Sent on 13 June, with the note: 'Pray don't anger moderate men by any more remarks on Class';
Bodley MS Eng. lett. d. 82, f. 91. Acland was defeated in Somerset, Wellington. See 28 June 86n.
[2] Forwarding letter from A. Morley unsuccessfully asking Carnegie to stand at the election; Add
MS 44548, f. 101.
[3] Exchange in *T.T.*, 21 June 1886, 6c.
[4] See 13 Sept. 80.
[5] Sir J. Davis, *A poem on the immortality of the soul . . . historical relations concerning Ireland* (1733).
[6] C. C. Cotterill of Fettes College, proposed this day's vote of thanks.
[7] *Speeches on the Irish question*, 187.
[8] J. F. Molloy, *Royalty refused, or London under Charles II*, 2v. (1885).

Childers—Mr Campbell—Mr Cowan. Read Molloy's Charles II—Guinness Rogers's Tract[1]—Moore's Visions.[2] Drove out to Beeslaw[3] to dine. Mr Cowan is excellent. Walk on the way back: then a crush which was trying & might have been dangerous.[4]

20. Trin. S.

St John's (& H.C.)[5] at 11 A.M. Lines of people all the way to hotel. Beautiful order kept. Cathedral in evg. Carried, by desire of police. Wrote to The Queen tel.—Mr Bannister Fletcher[6]—Mr H. Fowler—Mr Caine[7]—and minutes. Saw Mr Ivory—Mr Campbell—W.H.G. Read The Coptic Liturgy—Wrights Exegetical Studies.

21. M.

Wrote to Mr Primrose—Mr Husted—Ld Rosebery—and minutes. Worked much on Irish Question. Music Hall Meeting at 3. Again spoke $1\frac{1}{2}$ hour, voice coming in a marvellous way by necessity & command.[8] Visited the Exhibition. Then drove round Arthur's seat.[9] Saw Lady Aberdeen—WHG—Mr Cowan—Mr Campbell—Mr Ivory and others.[10] Workman's deputation at $7\frac{3}{4}$: very striking. Dined at Mr B. Primrose's—good company. Read Molloy's Charles II.

To LORD ROSEBERY, foreign secretary, 21 June 1886.   N.L.S. 10023, f. 185.

I forward a letter from Ivory[11] about the Scotsman as good as possible in respect to Ivory, as bad as possible in respect to Cowper [sc. Cooper] who has joined the ranks or rather the clique of the impostors, who say they are for Home Rule & save their consciences by putting a non-natural sense upon the words. The feeling here is truly wonderful, especially when the detestable state of the press is considered.[12]

22. Tu. [Hawarden]

Wrote to Watson's—The Queen—& minutes. Worked on Irish question. Saw Mr D. Macgregor,[13] our *host* in truth—Mr Campbell—Mr Ivory—Mr Cowan—Sir C.

---

[1] J. G. Rogers, *The Ulster problem* (1886).   [2] Untraced.
[3] *sc.* Beeslack; Cowan's house at Milton Bridge.
[4] A tram had to be diverted to get him back to the hotel through the crowds; *T.T.* 21 June 1886, 7c.   [5] Episcopalian church at the West End.
[6] Successfully encouraging Bannister Fletcher, 1833-99, to stand again for Chippenham (but he lost); Add MS 44548, f. 102.
[7] Further exchange, *T.T.*, 22 June 1886, 10f.
[8] *Speeches on the Irish question*, 211.
[9] The hill beside Holyrood Palace, E. of the old town in Edinburgh.
[10] Including on the platform Richard Burdon *Haldane, 1856-1928; lawyer, philosopher, and liberal M.P. E. Lothian 1885-1911; later in liberal and labour cabinets; and William Jacks, 1841-1907; liberal M.P. Leith burghs 1885-6, Stirling 1892-5; voted against home rule 1886 but repented. See 10 July 86.
[11] Not found, though returned by Rosebery.
[12] Rosebery replied, 22 June, Add MS 44289, f. 43: 'Cooper . . . is in the full irritation of a man who has got into an inextricably false position. . . . I hope the Edinburgh Evening News is helpful. It is enormously read by the working classes.'
[13] Proprietor of the Royal hotel.

Tennant—Mr Mackiver—& others. Off to Glasgow at 12¾. Meeting at 3. Spoke 1 h. 20 m.[1] Off 5.50: reached Hawarden 12.30 or 40. Some speeches by the way: others I declined. Entertained splendidly by Sir C. Tennant. The whole a scene of triumph. God help us His poor creatures. Read Molloy finished Vol I—Wilkinson on Ireland.[2]

23. *Wed.*

Wrote to Helen G.—Mr Prince Manch Tel.—D. of Westminster—Dr Foster[3]—Sir K. Mackenzie—A. Morley—Prince of Wales—Sir R. Peel—W.L. Gladstone Tel.— Lady F. Cavendish—other telegrams, incl. Tel. to Carlisle—& minutes. Found a chaos in my room: on wh I set to work. Saw Mr Lee & Mr Mather—W.H.G. Walk with C. Read The Wanderer[4]—Irish Tracts of 1841.

To A. MORLEY, chief whip, 23 June 1886.   Add MS 44548, f. 102.

1. I agree about Chester. Perhaps I may write Dr. Foster a letter.[5]

2. I will speak at *no more* places. Others must be set to work.

Besides the 5 big speeches, I have already made short but real speeches at Galashiels, Hawick, Carlisle 2, Skipton, Edinburgh working men, Carnforth, & I think one or two more. I do not think the man holding my office ought to be the universal agitator. (I may say in confidence that the Queen has already been expostulating.)

3. My Scotch tour has exceeded any of the former, & has not been attended with any one unsatisfactory circumstance.

4. What are, in a word, your present anticipations—in what direction do they move—& what does Schnadhorst say?

It must be after all rather blind work.[6]

[P.S.] I mentioned with warm commendation the name of F. Leveson Gower in Glasgow, where *two* candidates are wanting: the one against Mitchell being, if good, with almost a *certainty*.

To Sir R. PEEL, 23 June 1886.[7]   Add MS 44548, f. 103.

I cannot but highly appreciate the sacrifice you have made, in obedience alike to conscience, & to wise & patriotic duty, by quitting your seat at Blackburn, with which family recollections were so closely connected.

I learn that you are about to contest the Boroughs of the County of Inverness, a County to which my mother's family belonged, & in which on that account, being myself half a Highlander, I have always felt a special interest.

---

[1] Beginning with Chalmers on Ireland, 1818; *Speeches on the Irish question*, 238.

[2] H. S. Wilkinson, *Eve of Home Rule. Impressions of Ireland* (1886).

[3] Support for him against Westminster's influence in Chester; *T.T.*, 26 June 1886, 11f. See 14 July 86n. (Sir) (Balthazar) Walter Foster, 1840–1913; physician; liberal M.P. Chester 1885–6; Ilkeston 1887–1910; Chairman N.L.F. 1886–90; minor office 1892–5; kt. in resignation honours 1886.

[4] *The Wanderer; or female difficulties. By the author of Evelina* [i.e. Mad. d'Arblay], 5v. (1814).

[5] See this day.

[6] No reply found.

[7] In *D.N.*, 28 June 1886, 3h and elsewhere. Peel was the only tory to abstain on the home rule division; he unsuccessfully contested Inverness burghs against the liberal unionist R. B. Finlay. He thanked Gladstone for this letter which he thought 'will probably ensure my success'; Add MS 44498, f. 64.

You are to be opposed by Mr. Finlay, a lawyer of great & successful ability; & one of the keenest & most vehement adversaries to the policy which you & I think to be recommended by broad principles of justice & by clear dictates of expediency.

Mr. Finlay argued in Parliament that, because Scotland is satisfied with her incorporating union, therefore Ireland ought to be satisfied with her Union, & will be satisfied if only you try her long enough.

He says this in the teeth of the fact that Ireland becomes from year to year more determined to obtain constitutionally the management of her own affairs, & that our attempts to coerce her which before 1832 might be called intermittent, have now become for half a century incessant.

To meet our British views, Ireland has abated her claims, & they have been supported by 313 members on a division. What rational man can suppose that Ireland will ever abandon them?

Disgust Ireland; keep your Parliament paralysed; & your legislation in arrear; shock the sense of the civilised world, as our relations with Ireland have ever shocked it; & as to social order in Ireland, why let it shift for itself, or else we can try the old method of coercion! Such seem to me to be the nostrums of Mr. Finlay. He calls & thinks himself a Liberal Unionist but this is Toryism of the worst type, the Toryism which breaks up Empires, the Toryism of George III & Lord North, not the Toryism which will ever stand associated with the name of Robert Peel.

I feel confident that reflection will bring round to a better mind so clever a man as Mr. Finlay, if the Electors of the Inverness Burghs will by returning you provide him with an interval of repose. If these Electors, or any of them, think me entitled to give an opinion on a matter touching Inverness, you are quite at liberty, should you think fit to make known to them this letter which is intended to convey my hearty desire for your success.

24. Th.

Ch. 8½ A.M. Wrote to Mr Mitford—Mr Primrose Tel. l.l.l.—Sir W.B. Gurdon Tel.—Mr Fox (re Gaskell) Tel.[1]—Lady Phillimore—The Queen—Duke of Westminster Tel. & l.—Mr Young—Lady F. Cavendish—The Queen—& minutes. Read La Morte[2]—Ld Ebury's silly pamphlet.[3] Worked on Ireland. The place so lovely. Conversation with Willy, whom we do not try to force.[4]

25. Fr.

Wrote to The Queen—Mr Primrose Tel.—Electoral Comm. I. of W. Tel.—Brooks, W. Dulwich Tel.[5]—Ld Chancellor—Major Gen. Robertson—Ld Rosebery—Ld Spencer—Watson & Smith—Scotts—Mr Emery (Fakenham) Tel.[6]—Tel. to. . . . Off to Manchester at 1. Great meeting in Free Trade Hall: strain unwise. Five miles through the streets: a wonderful spectacle half the way. Spoke 1 h. 20 m.[7] Entertained at Mr Agnew's dinner party. Saw W.H.G.—Mr Taylor—& at Manchester numbers. Read La Morte (Feuillet)—Molloy's Charles II.

[1] G. C. M. Gaskell, unopposed liberal in Morley.
[2] O. Feuillet, *La Morte* (1886).
[3] R. Grosvenor, Lord Ebury, 'The laity and church reform' (1886).
[4] Who declined to stand for election, see 3 July 86.
[5] No liberal candidate was found for Dulwich.
[6] *Sic*; no candidate or constituency of these names.
[7] *Speeches on the Irish question*, 259.

26. Sat. [Courthey]

Wrote to The Queen—Lord St Cyres[1]—Mr Primrose L. & tel. l.l.l.—Mr A. Morley Tel.—Mr Bright Tel.—Bacup Tel.—Northallerton Tel—and minutes. Saw Deputation from Sheffield. Deputation from Salford & made a speech.[2] Off at 2.30. processional drive to Town Hall, visited the Mayor, then to station, & reached Courthey[3] before 5. Unabated enthusiasm. Finished La Morte (Feuillet). Read Molloy Charles II. Our nephews most kind and hospitable, & very attractive.

27. 1 S. Trin.

Childwall Ch mg & aft. Excellent choir & a wonderful voice. Wrote to A. Morley—Mr Hutton—Mr Primrose Tel.—Mr Lawson Tait Tel.[4]—Mr S. Lyttelton Tel. Delightful hymn singing (WEG of course mute) in evg. Saw Mr Melly—Mr Holt. Read Somerville 7 Churches[5]—Teaching of the Apostles.[6]

To A. MORLEY, chief whip, 27 June 1886.   Add MS 44548, f. 105.

1. At every point of my movements I have found the display of enthusiasm far beyond all former measure. I left the people of Manchester in excellent heart & hope, but with doubts as to Agnew.

2. I inclose a letter from Holmes Ivory, very interesting, entirely trustworthy. The substance of it ought without his name but with verifying assurances, to go, as it strikes me, to the press. There is a good evening workman's paper in Edinburgh. You can not give too much attention to the case of Goschen. If it be better, Mr. Ivory would I think do this in Edinburgh.

3. Pray consider the following. I see it stated in the Pall Mall Gazette most of the uncontested seats are against us.[7] This & London & the Home Counties & the backwardness of Ireland, may cast the balance the wrong way at the outset; & an ill impression may produce (?)[8] Would it not be well to republish a little daily table of the last Election in November and December in four columns. 1. Liberal. 2. Conservative. 3. Majority. 4. Nationalists.

4. As to my going to London (a) I have twice had my chest rather seriously strained, & I have at this moment a sense of internal fatigue within it which is quite new to me from the effects of a bad arrangement in the hall at Manchester. Should anything like it be repeated at Liverpool tomorrow I shall not be fit physically to speak for a week if then. (b) Mentally I have never undergone such an uninterrupted strain as since January 30 of this year. In forming & reforming of the Government, the work of framing the Bills, & *studying the subject* (which none of the opponents would do) have left me almost stunned—& I have the autumn in prospect with, perhaps, most of the work to do over again if we succeed. (c) The Queen wrote to me in Edinburgh rather objecting to my electioneering beyond my own constituency. I defended myself but in doing it *gave her Glasgow & South Lancashire* as the limit. (d) I must also say that I have rather strained the

---

[1] Congratulating him on tenure as deputy chairman of B.I.R.; Add MS 44548, f. 104.
[2] *Speeches on the Irish question*, 280.
[3] Home of his nephews (sons of his br. Robertson), near Liverpool.
[4] Unsuccessful liberal candidate for Bordesley, Birmingham.
[5] A. N. Somerville, *The churches in Asia* (1885).
[6] C. Taylor, *Teaching of the twelve Apostles* (1886).
[7] *P.M.G.* published daily lists of seats uncontested by liberals.
[8] Secretary's query.

proprieties in laws [*sic*] of my office, & cannot do it more. (e) As to peers see my telegram of today. The objection is to me unintelligible: the example of Derby conclusive.

I really think a week at Hawarden is something like a necessity for me: & I think I shall hardly have 2 hours without some urgent telegram. I must try to write two careful letters to Lawson Tait & Buxton.

28. M. [*Hawarden*]

Wrote to Mrs Jacobson—Lord Granville Tel—Mr Summers—Mr Hutton—Mr Primrose tel.—Mr T.P. O'Connor—Ld Rosebery—Sir Geo. Errington—M. Daunt—and minutes. Worked up the Irish Question once more and spent 2.30–7.15 on my last function, 7 or 8 miles of processional uproar, and a speech of 1 h. 40 min. to 5000 or 6000 people in Hengler's Circus.[1] Few buildings give so noble a presentation of an audience. Saw Sir T. Brassey, Mr Holt, Mr Kennedy, Mr Ward Beecher,[2] and others. Once more my voice held out in a marvellous manner. 'I went in bitterness, in the heat of my spirit: but the hand of the Lord was strong upon me'.[3] Hawarden before Post time. Read Molloy's Charles II.

29. Tu. St Peter.

Ch. 8½ AM. Wrote to Mr Theodore Fry[4] Tel.—Mr Meiklejohn[5] Tel.—Gen. Sir A. Clarke Tel.—Mr Primrose l. & Tel. l.l.—Lady Granville Tel.—Mr Macdonnell[6]—Mr Tait Lawson(?)[7]—Mr Sydney Buxton[8]—Sir A. Clark—Ld Elgin—Sir W. Phillimore—and minutes. Saw Depn. from W.hampton. Drive with C. A very hard day of grave letters & messages to write. Read Sir J. Davis on Ireland[9]—Molloy's Charles II.

30. Wed.

Ch. 8½ A.M. Wrote to Mr Pocock Tel.—Mr Whiteley Tel.—Mr Verney Tel.—Mr Bickersteth Tel.—Mr G. Russell Tel.—Mr Primrose l. and Tel l.l.l.—Mr Hubbard—Mr Balfour[10]—P.M.G. Tel.—Ed. D. News—Bp of Salford L. & tel.—Ld Granville Tel.—A. Morley tel. and l.—Mr Th. Fry Tel.—and minutes.[11] Final conversation with Willy. He could only have been forced, and this I will never do.[12] Read Davis (finished)—ONeill Daunt 86y Irish Hist.[13]—Molloy's Charles II (finished).

---

[1] *Speeches on the Irish question*, 283: comments on 'the classes'; see above, vol. X, Introduction, section II.

[2] Rev. Henry Ward Beecher, 1813–87; American anti-slavery journalist and clergyman; br. of H. B. Stowe.　　　　　　　　　　　　　　　　　　　　　　　　　[3] Ezekiel, iii. 14.

[4] (Sir) Theodore Fry, 1836–1912; manufacturer and liberal M.P. Darlington 1880–95; cr. bart. 1894.

[5] John Meiklejohn, d. 1902; professor of education, Edinburgh; liberal candidate Glasgow, Tradeston, 1886; *T.T.*, 30 June 1886, 10f.

[6] G. P. Macdonnell, on the elections; *P.M.G.*, 6 July 1886, 10.

[7] See 27 June 86; *T.T.*, 2 July 1886, 10f, 6 July 1886, 5f.

[8] Letter to the metropolitan constituencies; *T.T.*, 1 July 1886, 7c and *Speeches on the Irish question*, 357.　　　　　　　　　　　　　　　　　　　　　　　[9] See 17 June 86.

[10] In *T.T.*, 1 July 1886, 7c, *re* quotation from Randolph Churchill.

[11] This and next day's telegrams in *T.T.*, 3 July 1886, 8d.　　　　　[12] See 24 June 86.

[13] W. J. O'Neill Daunt, *Eighty-five years of Irish history*, 2v. (1886); see to Kimberley, 7 July 86.

To A. MORLEY, chief whip, 30 June 1886.   Add Ms 44548, f. 106.

You have not written to me about the Land Purchase Act so perhaps there is no real urgency.[1]

I have said I think as much as I could to ease the situation.

But why does not the Daily News (for example), instead of printing appeals to me for declarations which it would be indecent to make, point out to electors that all they have to do is to *return members who sympathise with them in objecting to Land Purchase*, or to the Land Purchase Bill. Let them have no delicacy about us in that matter—we have no title to bind them. They may be sure that, Home Rule or no Home Rule, the Tories when they come in will give them plenty of Land Purchase. (Personally I think that the war to the knife which Hartington & his party, Derby included, have made on the Land Purchase Bill of itself materially modifies our situation in regard to it.)

Thurs. Jul One. 1886.

Ch. 8½ A.M. Wrote to Dowager Lady Phillimore—Messrs Watson—Mr Barlow—Messrs Schee—Mr G.O. Morgan—Mr A. Morley tel. l.l.—Mr Borlase tel.—Mr Primrose tel. l.l.l. & L.—Mr Ankers tel.—Ipswich party tel.—Mr Hall Tel.—Mr Adcock—Messrs Pease & Cockwood Tel.—Grantham Tel.—Mr Hall (Bolton) Tel.—C.G.—Holmes Ivory l. & Tel. l.l.—& minutes. Saw Depn from Wrexham—Mr Johnson. Helen came: a capital worker. Conversation with her on Holloway Coll.[2] Read O'Neill Daunt—The Wanderer[3]—G.A. Denison & other pamphlets.

To J. E. BARLOW,[4] 1 July 1886.   Add MS 44498, f. 91.

In reply to your question about the East Denbighshire Election I observe that there are before the Electors 1. Mr Osborne Morgan, 2. his opponents, 3. the Irish people.

1. As to Mr Osborne Morgan I shall say nothing, for you know him as well as I do, to be your upright, able, tried, & trusted friend.

2. As to your opponents, you ought to know them also pretty well by this time. It is not the first time, nor the tenth, that they have raised the cry of alarm & ruin. All their lives they have been at it. And when? Always when those great & good measures have been proposed, which have made the age illustrious: Reform of Parliament, abolition of the Corn Laws, abolition of Slavery, abolition of religion tests, abolition of Church Rates, abolition of the Irish Church [Establishment], freedom of Burials, defence of the rights of tenants, & many more. *Which* of them did these men give you? *Which* of them did they not oppose and cry down as destructive to the Constitution, the throne, religion, property, and all the rest? If the men of Wales are tired of getting so many good measures, they may return Tories. But [if] they want more, do not let them vote for those who have resisted and abused all they ever got.

3. There are lastly the Irish nation. For it is the nation, represented in Parliament by more than five to one of their members sitting for towns & counties. People say they are never content. Nor would you be content, if you had been opposed as they have been, above all if after having had a Parliament of your own for five hundred years and more and had then had it taken away by a mixture of violence and corruption at the Union

---

[1] Morley replied, 1 July, Add MS 44253, f. 15, that he had written to Lucy, ed. of the *Daily News*, about land purchase, and that Gladstone's statement 'would have given satisfaction'.

[2] See n. below.   [3] See 23 June 86.

[4] (Sir) John Emmott Barlow, 1857–1932; unsuccessful liberal candidate Denbigh district 1886; M.P. Frome 1892–5, 1896–1918.

which disgraces the name of England and is no where to be found in its history. This Parliament they have ever striven to get back. They now ask not for repealing the Union, but only for giving them a subordinate legislature, as we have done with immense advantage in the Colonies, to manage, not Welsh or Scotch or English or Imperial, but their own affairs. Give it them because it is just. Give it promptly and graciously, not waiting as the Duke of Wellington waited with Roman Catholic Emancipation, to yield under terror of civil war.

Let Wales on this great occasion be worthy of itself.[1]

To Mrs. GLADSTONE, 1 July 1886.   Hawarden MSS.

Another very hard [day] today—but then, when the work is off, this place is refreshment.

I should think that by this time I must have communicated separately with forty or fifty places.

At the same time we seem here & there to be wofully behind with Candidates—I never understood the policy of making the Dissolution so very early: but I did not set up my own opinion.

I must say they overdo it about the City—what is the difference between my letter & a speech except for the 2000 or 3000 who might hear it.

Who is your Lady S?

If Breadalbanes are in town would you like to invite them & Rosebery's, & Mad. Albani & Gye, & EWH, + Spencer to dine any day next week after Monday—*or* Neilson vice Albani.

I am glad you slept well—so did I. I took up a good supply of strawberries.

Helen came all right, will be rarely [? *sc* really] useful, intensely sensible about Holloway College, as to which Queen has I think been rather hasty.[2] Ever your afft   WEG

2. Fr.

Ch. 8½ A.M. Wrote to The Queen—Mr A. Morley Tel (for Costelloe)—Mr Primrose Tel. l.l.l.l.l.—Mr Darbishire Tel.—Mr Nisbett Tel.—Sir J. Gorst Tel.[3]—Mr Hutton—Mr Reid Tel.—Mr Holmes Ivory Tel.—Herbert J.G. Tel.—R. Wyllie Tel.—C.G.—Mr Beal Tel.—Mr Soper Tel.—Mr Bright l.l. (letters).

Elected for Midlothian: and for Leith, at 12 hours notice![4] Now begins the great struggle. Govern it O Most High. In the flesh I desire defeat & ease: but this is base & to be put down.

Read 'The Wanderer'—Shamrock's Two Unions,[5] poor—Fortnightly, 3 articles on Ireland 'l'uno peggior del altro'.[6]—and even some Pausanias! Worked a little on books.

[1] Published locally; Morgan held E. Denbighshire by 26 votes, 'unexpectedly' (Morgan, *Wales in British politics*, 73).

[2] The Queen opened Holloway college the previous day; Helen Gladstone eventually declined an invitation to be its head.

[3] Defending Spencer; *T.T.*, 5 July 1886, 4c.

[4] See A. B. Cooke, 'Gladstone's election for the Leith district of burghs, July 1886', *Scottish Historical Review* (1970), Bassett, 247 and 10 July 86. He was unopposed in both seats. He told Ivory, Add MS 44498, f. 106: 'the idea occurred to me between six and seven last evening when I first learned the facts', i.e. supposed unionism of Jacks, the liberal candidate (see letters below). R. C. Munro-Ferguson held the seat for the liberals in August against Jacks and others.

[5] Untraced.   [6] *F.R.*, xlvi. 98ff. (July 1886).

To John BRIGHT, M.P., 2 July 1886.[1]   Add MS 44113, f. 229; Add MS 43385, f. 355.

[First letter:]   Your unexpected accusations have given me more pain than anything, or all things, that have happened during this controversy.[2] I am compelled to remonstrate against them. But I desire to adhere to every word I said in Scotland of you and of my intentions concerning you.

[Second letter:]   I am sorry to be compelled again to address you.

1. In your speech you charge me with having successfully concealed my thoughts last November.

You ought to have known that this is not the fact. For in reply to others, from whom this gross charge was more to be expected than from you, I pointed out last week that on the 9th of November in Edinburgh I told my constituents that if the Irish Elections went as was expected, the magnitude of the subject they would bring forward would throw all others into the shade and that it 'went down to the very roots and foundations of our whole civil and political constitution'. (Midlothian speeches 1885 p. 44.)

Do you now adhere to your accusation?

2. You say I have described a conspiracy now existing in Ireland as marching through rapine to the break up of the United Kingdom.

This also is contrary to the fact.

In 1881 there was in my opinion such a conspiracy against the payment of rent and the union of the countries, and I so described it. In my opinion, there is no such conspiracy now, nor any thing in the least degree resembling it. You put into my mouth words which coming from me would be an absolute falsehood.

3. You charge me with a want of frankness because I have not pledged the Government to some defined line of action with regard to the Land Purchase Bill. A charge of this kind is, between old colleagues and old friends, to say the least unusual. Evidently you have not read the Bill or my speech on its introduction, and you have never been concerned in the practical work of legislation on difficult and complicated subjects. ⟨But it might have occurred to you, as you have been in the Cabinet⟩ The foundation of your charge is that, on one of the most difficult & most complicated of all subjects, I do not, in the midst of overwhelming work, formulate ⟨a new plan⟩ at once a new course or method of action, without consulting the colleagues to whom I am so much bound, and from whom I receive much invaluable aid. It might I think have occurred to you, as you have been in the Cabinet, that such a course on my part would have been indecent and disloyal, and that I should greatly prefer to bear all the charges and suspicions which you are now unexpectedly the man to fasten upon me.

4. You state you are convinced it is my intention to thrust the Land Purchase Bill upon the House of Commons. If I am a man capable of such an intention, I wonder you ever took office with ⟨a man⟩ one so ignorant of the spirit of the Constitution, and so arbitrary in his character. Though this appears to be your opinion of me, I do not think it is the opinion held by my countrymen in general. You quote not a word in support of your charge. It is absolutely untrue. Every candidate friendly or unfriendly will form his own view and take his own course on the subject. We must consider to the best of our power all the facts before us. But I certainly will not forego my right to make some effort to amend the dangerous and mischievous Land Purchase Law passed last year for Ireland, if such effort should promise to meet approval.

[1] Both this day's letters in *D.T.*, 5 July 1886, 5g.

[2] Wrangle about Bright's claim that 'a year ago all Liberals held his [Ryland's] opinions on the Irish question'; see Gladstone's wire of 26 June, requesting a source; Add MS 44113, f. 228, *T.T.*, 26 June 1886, 9f, 28 June 1886, 6c.

I have done what I could to keep out of controversy with you, and while driven to remonstrance against your charges I advisedly abstain from all notice of your statements, criticisms, and arguments.[1]

To R. H. HUTTON, editor of *The Spectator*, 2 July 1886.   Add MS 44548, f. 106.

Rely upon it I can never quarrel with you or with Bright.[2] What vexes me is when differences disclose baseness which sometimes happens.

For opponents generally I have four prescriptions. 1. Study the abominable, the almost incredible history of the Union. (How many of them have done it? Mr. Lecky?) 2. Soak & drench yourselves with the writings of Mr. Burke on Ireland, especially on the Grattan Parliament: most of all with his writings on the American War. 3. Look a little at the effects of Home Rule (a) in Europe (b) in the colonies (No man can confute my quotation from Duffy's Article on Canada). 4. Consider a little what is representation & what does it mean.

This fourth I venture to prescribe for you. Long have I seen that few men, few Liberals, believe in liberty: but you I think are one. Fewer still seem to me to believe in representation, to have sounded the depths of this probably the greatest discovery of human, say of Christian civilisation; or to have measured its power. And here, to speak frankly, I fear you are *not* one. I am not dealing with the Irish party, I am dealing with the Irish nation. The party is simply the go-between. Unless indeed this *is* a nation having a double dose of original sin. And this is really at the bottom of most of the adverse argument.
[P.S.] N.B. M.P. for Midlothian and *Leith* at 12 hours notice.

3. *Sat.*

Ch. 8½ A.M. Wrote to Mr Primrose L.l.l. & tel. l.l.l.—Mr Campbell Tel.—Holmes Ivory l. & Tel.—Rev. Mackenzie Tel.—Mr J. H. Bridges[3]—W.H.G.—Mr Balfour—C.G.—Chief Constable Ward—Mr T. Hall—Ld Wodehouse[4]—Mr J. Williams (Holywell) tel & l.—Mr Barrow Haslingden Tel—Mr O. Williams (for Stepney)—Ld Granville—and minutes. Read Bridges & Harrison on Ireland, each excellent[5]—Pausanias—The Wanderer. C.G. returned. Helen excellent as Priv. Sec. Indeed I have tried almost all my children, & never with a failure.

To A. J. BALFOUR, M.P., 3 July 1886.   Add MS 49692, f. 13.

I am very glad not to have to add to my many controversies a controversy with you. The publication of my words quite satisfies me.[6]

I believe you have asked why I did not propose a plan on the meeting of Parliament. The answer is that such a proceeding would have been entirely contrary to my views of public duty declared in my speech at Edinburgh. I am not aware that there was any statement any where that I intended to cut in anticipation of the Government. If there was it was entirely & absolutely false.

---

[1] Bright's reply is in *T.T.*, 6 July 1886, 8a.
[2] Hutton's letter, 1 July, Add MS 44215, f. 334: pain on contemplating their differences on Ireland.
[3] John Henry Bridges, 1832–1906; physician and positivist; see this day's letter.
[4] Letter of support; *P.M.G.*, 6 July 1886, 10.
[5] Frederic Harrison, 'Mr. Gladstone!—or anarchy!' (1886).
[6] *D.T.*, 28 June 1886, 5e printed a report by the London correspondent of the *New York Sun* on the Eaton meeting of 15 Dec. 85 and the ensuing letters; the Gladstone–Balfour exchanges between 20 December 1885 and 5 January 1886 were printed in full in *D.T.*, 5 July 1886, 5e, *T.T.*, 5 July 1886, 10a.

To J. H. BRIDGES, 3 July 1886.   Add MS 44548, f. 108.

I must snatch a moment to thank you for your admirable letters on 'the Home Rule question 18 years ago'.[1] Not adopting absolutely every opinion which is set forth in them, I never the less feel that though born before their time, they were a wise & noble anticipation. They exhibit the genuine & almost necessary result of the application of that historic study to the Irish case, which the anti-Irish of the present day, Tory, Whig, & Radical, seem alike to deprecate with an instinctive consciousness that it is fatal to their cause. I should be glad with your permission to consider what could be done towards bringing them into wide circulation at the present juncture.

To Mrs. GLADSTONE, 3 July 1886.[2]   Hawarden MSS.

1. Inclosed is a most interesting letter from Willy,[3] with my reply[4] which please to pass on.
2. Undoubtedly I have much advantage in the beginnings & endings of the day here & I hope, considering what is before me, you will not think me unreasonable in staying until Tuesday.
3. The Leith proposal was mine, & was worked out on the spot with immense prudence by Campbell, Ivory and Cowan.
4. Today's returns i.e. those in today's papers are relatively bad but they are not *complete* as they ought to be—not including the uncontested seats as to changes. For instance the gain of Leith does not appear. But I think the chances now are slightly against us, i.e. the Tories *with* Seceders are not unlikely a little to outnumber the Government *with* the Nationalists. This sets me a ruminating much on what is to happen. I am afraid that without a majority it is far from unlikely that we may be kept in office until the October Session. Ever your afft   WEG

To T. HALL,[5] 3 July 1886.   Add MS 44548, f. 107.

The proceedings at Leith filled me with delight. The stratagem attempted was beyond example, & its defeat was all the more signal as a public benefit.

From no personal exertion, however excessive, would I have shrunk in order to contribute to such a result: and I trust that for the honour of Leith, & for the general advantage, the facts will become widely known.[6]

Leith will now have time to consider her position, & probably ample opportunity for a wise & honourable choice.

I have been compelled to decline on all sides very strong calls for *personal* visits & addresses, & you will I am sure see that only the very peculiar circumstances, now happily disposed of, would have justified an exception.

---

[1] J. H. Bridges had sent his *The Home Rule question eighteen years ago* (1886); Hawn P. See to Bryce, 8 July 86.

[2] Part in Bassett, 248.

[3] W.H. to W. E. Gladstone, 2 July, Hawn P: 'It was a bitter moment to me to stand out against your appeal the other day . . . whenever I came to consider the matter I found that there remained in my mind the fixed opinion that Home Rule was not the thing Ireland required & was not necessary for clearing the honour of England.'

[4] No longer extant.

[5] Thomas Hall, paint manufacturer, involved in Gladstone's candidature in Leith; Cooke, art. cit., 187.

[6] Explanation by W. Jacks, liberal turned quasi-unionist (less so than Gladstone supposed), is in *T.T.*, 5 July 1886, 7f.

4. 2 S. Trin.

Ch. 11 A.M. with H.C. & 6½ PM. Wrote to Mr Rowley Hill—Mr Naughton—Ld Rosebery—Wms & Norgate—C.R. Smith—Mr H. Manton[1]—Sir J. Gorst—Mr Primrose—Ld Spencer—and minutes. Read Traite de Paillardise[2]—Life of R. Moffat[3]—Morgenröthe[4]—Religion of Amorzulus.[5] The storm is upon us. Some disturbance but much peace. Evening at the Rectory.

To LORD ROSEBERY, foreign secretary, 4 July 1886.   N.L.S. 10023, f. 193.

Your news[6] is certainly bad, & as regards the faith-keeping disposition of Russia, extremely bad. And evidently the step you have taken was the proper one, nor, upon reading the marked parts of the protocols, can I see that you said too much of it to Staal, while I am extremely glad you told him that it concerned all the signatory Powers.

It is a noteworthy fact, if you are right in supposing it to be a fact that Russia has squared the Powers. On the occasion of the fleets article Austria was by no means squared, & held I think language which implied that if we chose to resent the breach of Treaty she would march abreast of us, but we should I think have found her a wretched ally in such a case.

As the breach of faith is evident, there remains the question how far in international law, by precedent or otherwise, is an act of this kind equivalent to a breach of one of the articles of the Treaty to which the Protocols belong.

I understand the doctrine that this is a slap at us, in so far as we have, with what I think incredible & inexcusable folly, allowed ourselves to be the catspaw of the other Powers in relation to the Black Sea & the Straits. On the merits of the case, I cannot conceive anything more absurd. If there is anywhere a strong interest in opposing Russia's free use of the Straits, it is an interest of Austria, or of Turkey, or of the Free States of the Danube.

I am not greatly shocked at the language of Salisbury in the Protocols about the Straits which we hold *in terrorem* against Russia. I cannot think that very modern article of the law of Europe which determines their present conditions is in principle tenable, or will last, although the mode of altering it is a serious affair.

In about a week we shall I suppose be determining what course we shall take in view of a manageable, or more probably unmanageable, Parliament. On the many inlooks & outlooks of that subject my mind is I think pretty open: certainly nearer to you than it was after June 7.

I had lots to say on your letter but it has been impracticable. We shall I think stay here, at any rate, for a good part of the week.

[P.S.] *Since* writing I have read Morier's telegram. No doubt you will do all you can to expedite the settlement of the Afghan Frontier *or* show the *malice prepense* of Russia in putting it off.

To LORD SPENCER, lord president, 4 July 1886.[7]   Althorp MSS K296.

I write one hasty line to thank you for your very interesting letter[8] & to express my fear, from the turn things are at present taking, that you will hardly make out your little holi-

---

[1] Henry Manton of Birmingham; on Bright; Add MS 44548, f. 109.   [2] Untraced.
[3] See 22 Nov. 85.   [4] Perhaps *Die Morgenröthe der Weisheit und der Baum des Lebens* (1862).
[5] Word scrawled; untraced.
[6] Of 3 July, Add MS 44289, f. 49: 'bad news. The Russian government has announced that it means that Batoum shall at once cease to be a free port'.   [7] *Spencer*, ii. 127.
[8] Of 1 July from France, Add MS 44313, f. 85; enthusiasm for Gladstone's speeches; possibility of a home rule victory at the polls.

day in peace, as probably in about a week the Cabinet will have to meet & determine upon its course.

If there is to be an anti-Irish Government, the sooner it begins the sooner it will end. Every body is dancing on the dead body of the Land Bill.

Whoever of us may suffer in this business your record at any rate is clear.

5. M.

Ch. 8½ A.M. Wrote to Ld Carnarvon[1]—Mr Primrose Tel l.l.l.l.l.l.—Ed. P.M. Gazette Tel. l.l.—Mr Ballard Tel.—(Duckham) Tel.—Mr Hunter Tel.—(Barrow) Tel.—Mr Lough (Cornwall) Tel.—Mr Bailey (Warwicksh.) Tel.—Mrs Stead—Sir A. Hayter—Messrs Henderson St Andrews Tel.—Press Assn tel.—Mr Evans Tel.—Mr Buchanan (Drumb.) Tel.—Sir T. Brassey—Mr A. Arnold—and minutes. Read Chambers on Scotch Gypsies[2]—O'Neill Daunt (finished I)—Pausanias. Dined at Rectory. That dear Stephy was suffering but made little of it.

6. Tu.

Ch. 8½ A.M. Wrote to Sir T. Brassey Tel.—Mr Primrose l. & tel. l.l.l.l.l.—Maitland (for Errington) Tel.—Evans (re Courtney) Tel—Owen (for S. Rendell) Tel.—Mr Ivory & Mr Campbell Tel.[3]—Dr Foster Tel.—Mr Stewart Tel.—Mrs Stume—Hon Mr Glyn—Herbert J.G.—Ld Granville—and minutes. Drive with C. Read The Wanderer—Dicey on I. in 19th Cent.[4]—Pausanias. Worked a little on library. The Elections perturb me somewhat: but One ever sitteth above.

To P. C. GLYN, 6 July 1886.   Bodley MS Don. a. 9, f. 99.

Considering the spirit exhibited in Dorsetshire at the last election, and the high qualifications which you as well as others possess, in the character of Candidates, to so consistent a degree, I cannot but feel sanguine in the hope that with the other rural counties she will on this great occasion give her voice on behalf of the course of peace, justice and a genuine instead of a forced union with Ireland, and will thus help to set Parliament free for the legislation on behalf of Great Britain for which the masses of the people, and the rural population most of all, are looking with so much anxiety.

I need not assure you and your comrades how warmly I desire your success.[5]

7. Wed.

Ch. 8½ A.M. Wrote to Mr Buxton Tel.—Mr Primrose Tel l.l.—Ch. O. Williams Tel.—Ed. S.W. Daily News Tel.[6]—Ld Rosebery l. & tel.—Mr Dick (Doonholm Ayr) tel.—Mr Pearce (Govan) Tel.—Mr Rube (Glasg) Tel.—Sir H. James—Bp Bromby—Ld Kimberley—Mr P. Stanhope—Mr Barry O-Brien—and minutes. Dinner at the Rectory & backgammon with S. Read Pausanias—B. O'Brien's Tract[7]—ONeill Daunt on Ireland.

[1] Dispute on home rule; *T.T.*, 6 July 1886, 5f., with other telegrams of this day, draft copies of which are in Add MS 44498, ff. 131ff.
[2] W. Chambers, *Exploits and anecdotes of the Scottish gypsies* (1886).
[3] This and other telegrams this day in *T.T.*, 7 July 1886, 9f.
[4] E. Dicey in *N.C.*, xx. 1 (July 1886).   [5] Glyn lost his seat.
[6] This and other telegrams in *T.T.*, 8 July 1886, 6d.
[7] R. B. O'Brien, *Articles on Ireland 1886* (1886).

To Sir H. JAMES, attorney general, 7 July 1886.		James MS M45. 202.

To Dilke, as an old colleague, I am very desirous to do at any rate not less than justice & in this day of his difficulty aggravated by defeat I should be much obliged to you if you would kindly let me know whether he has, or rather whether he has not now done all that lay in his powers to procure an opportunity of bringing his case into the light, & further whether, although his application I believe has not been granted, he has some chance remaining of gaining his object. Apart from the Irish business he is a great Parliamentary loss & it is impossible not to feel for him. This presses especially upon me, because it has fallen to my lot, of necessity, to pass him by on certain occasions.
[P.S.] We have a puzzling time before us; & you, perhaps, one still more puzzling.[1]

To LORD KIMBERLEY, Indian secretary, 7 July 1886.		Add MS 44548, f. 110.

In O'Neill Daunt's History of 86 years Volume II—p. 170[2] a just compliment is paid to you as Viceroy of Ireland by an old & implacable Repealer more given to censure than to praise.
The book is not very well done. It blames with justice the anti-rent conspiracy & traces to it some of the anti-Nationalism now possessing the landlord class.
It is pretty clear now that the adverse majority of 30 is likely to be increased & cannot be done away. We shall have to consider next week what may be a very nice & is certainly a very important question, namely whether or not to resign at once. We cannot too much talk & think it over among ourselves before the Cabinet which will have to decide.

To R. Barry O'BRIEN, 7 July 1886.		Add MS 44548, f. 111.

I thank you for your admirable tract.
In my opinion one of the main subjects for consideration at this time by the friends of self Government in Ireland should be the means & mode of supplying the people of Great Britain with the historical information, in which their 'titled' & 'educated' leaders are so woefully deficient.
You have already done much & may do more.
One word only on p. 6. Were the United Irishmen rebels from the beginning (or separatists)? I had thought they only became such subsequently to the great epoch of Lord Fitzwilliam.[3]

To J. E. THOROLD ROGERS, 7 July 1886.		Add MS 44548, f. 111.

It was with much more than a common concern that I learned your defeat.[4]
Since your entrance into Parliament you have contributed much, & never so powerfully as on the occasion of our greatest need, namely in the late debates, towards strengthening that historical element in the House of Commons, which on one side does not super abound, & on the other side appears to be absolutely nil.
Pray consider whether you could write in a rather popular form an account of the Irish Union not bringing it to bear by application to the controversy of today, but on the other hand not scrupling to call a spade a spade, & setting out in their true colours the abomin-

[1] James thanked Gladstone for his 'kind feeling towards Dilke' who, he thought, had done all he could, though unsuccessfully; 9 July, James MS M45. 203. See 24 July 86.

[2] See 30 June 86. Kimberley was viceroy 1864–6.

[3] O'Brien replied next day with references to vol. ii of his *Fifty years of concessions*; Add MS 44498, f. 164.

[4] In Southwark; Rogers wrote, 6 July, Add MS 44498, f. 149: 'Bright has inflicted an irreparable injury on the party.'

able means, & the [blank] conspiracy, used to bring it about. I believe in both the causes of defeat you state. Bright himself is in a state of crass ignorance on the whole subject, & is I am afraid too old to learn: but the electorate & even the journalists may take it in by degrees. Or is there any other aspect of the subject which you incline as a man of letters to deal with. Pray consider the matter & let me hear. I think I could find a little money to prevent risk of loss by publishing a bit of history.

I shall not forget your closing paragraph but you know that my opportunities are rare & the pressure on me great.

8. *Th.*

Ch. 8½ A.M. A little tumult in my mind distracted me: but the Psalms were beyond belief edifying. Wrote to Sir Thos Acland—Mr Primrose tel. l.l.l.l. and L.—Mr Holmes Ivory Tel.—Herald Holywell tel.—Ld Carnarvon—Mr Summers MP. tel. l.l.—Mr Campbell—The Queen—Mr C. Bannerman—Mr Mackae [*sic*] tel. l.l.—Sir Thos Acland—W.H.G.—Sir W. Harcourt—Mr Bryce—and minutes.

Afternoon. The defeat is a smash. I accept the will of God for my poor country or the English part of it. To me personally it is a great relief: including in this cessation of my painful relations with the Queen, who will have a like feeling. Read The Wanderer—Pausanias—ONeill Daunt. Dined at the Rectory: backgammon with S.

To J. BRYCE, M.P., 8 July 1886. '*Private*'.   Bryce MS 10, f. 64.

I am afraid your engagements at the F.O. are likely to wind up with speed and I wish you would take in hand the manipulation of the Irish subject, or the superintendence of that manipulation, in the aspects which belong 1. (& mainly) to history. 2. to an outlook beyond these shores.

Could not you, Thorold Rogers, Barry O Brien, (possibly Lefevre), and such like men meet to consider this, & what expence would be incurred, that we might examine the means of meeting it. J. Morley would I think help to advise.

The whole iniquities of the Union, and the subsequent English history which is shameful though less profoundly and unmixedly shameful, must be laid bare & become common property.

The people do not *know* the case.

Remember that Corn Law Repeal was neither (generally) cared about nor understood till Cobden illuminated it with his admirable intellect, Bright putting in the passion.

Part of the work at any rate must be done through the press.

[P.S.] Mr Bridges[1] writes from the Brambles Wimbledon that we have his full authority to do what we please in bringing his letters into circulation. I have already written to Th. Rogers as to *himself*. MacColl might possibly be made available. At any rate he is very clever & very honest.[2]

---

[1] See 3 July 86.

[2] Bryce promised in reply on 10 July, Bryce MS 11, f. 143, to organise publicity: 'the people have not yet come to understand the facts of the question and the principles flowing therefrom . . . when they have been made to comprehend the facts, they will not shrink from the practical conclusions'. The volume was published as J. Bryce, ed., *Hand-Book of Home Rule: being articles on the Irish question by various writers* (1887), including Gladstone on 'Lessons of Irish history in the eighteenth century'.

To W. H. GLADSTONE, 8 July 1886.   Hawarden MSS.

I hope you are both enjoying Penmaenmawr: the little people still more.

I think you have in hand the editing of my five principal Election speeches? There is no hurry: but my idea is that they should be published in a thin volume together with the five Parliamentary speeches already printed, and the Addresses to Midlothian. The whole business is historical, and will come up again in the future, probably at no distant day. Perhaps you would put three or four lines before your part of the work as editor to let it appear that they have not been verbally revised by me.[1] The country and Scotch reporting are very good, far better than the Parliamentary.

We shall perhaps remain here as late as Wednesday.

The defeat is a smash. I rejoice however in Scotland and Wales. I rejoice to have had a share in doing what has been done. I grieve that England will seemingly not learn the lesson written in the book of fate until she has to learn it with more or less of pain and shame. Ever your afft. WEG.

To Sir W. V. HARCOURT, chancellor of the   MS Harcourt dep. 10, f. 119.
exchequer, 8 July 1886.

I had just written these words when your letter[2] arrived. There is no truth in the rumour about a Cabinet on Tuesday or Wednesday. I think Monday week may be more likely. I am most anxious for full deliberation, & think we ought to leave a Cabinet until we have had a good deal of opportunity among ourselves sporadically to consider the case, which is of great importance, and in my view of great nicety and difficulty.

One important argument in favour of following the three precedents for an immediate resignation wholly disappears in this case. It would not I think expedite public business within the walls of Parliament as it is almost an understanding that work will be postponed until October.

On the main issue of wait or not wait my mind is quite open.

I do not feel sure that I understand the reasons for your desire that we should force the Seceders to put us out. You may think as I do that the majority of them would not do it on a direct vote of censure but would do it on an Irish amendment. Is it for the interest of the country or of the party that the new Parliament should begin by voluntarily committing itself against Home Rule?

There would be some difficulty in our advising a Speech. In 1841 the Whigs in a minority of 80 ... 90 boldly made their Speech against the Corn Law. It would not be satisfactory to advise a Speech without colour. There are more points, but we must reserve all.

Your telegram from Derby gave me great pleasure: & it is most gallant of you to undertake the speaking tour, but to fight a losing cause well is the only or best test of manhood.

9. Fr.

Ch. 8½ A.M. Wrote to Mr M. Napier Tel.[3]—Mr Primrose tel.—Mr Hilson (Jedburgh) tel.—Ld Granville L.l.l.—Mr J. Morley—Dr Foster—Mr Kitson—& minutes. Worked on books. Read Pausanias—Goldwin Smith's Pitt No II[4]—O'Neil Daunt (finished). Dined at Rectory. Backgammon. How suitable the Psalms of all these days. Need, & solace.

[1] *Speeches on the Irish question* follows this pattern; the preface by P. W. C[ampbell] states the 'whole has been revised on Mr. Gladstone's behalf'.   [2] Not found.
[3] On request of Margot Tennant, Add MS 44498, f. 166.
[4] In Goldwin Smith, *Three English statesmen* (1867), i.e. Pym, Cromwell, Pitt; see 6 Aug. 67.

To J. KITSON, 9 July 1886.   Add MS 44548, f. 113.

To suffer in a good cause is a thing so honourable & noble, that I will not offer to con-
dole with you,[1] but I am truly sorry that after so much of the most intelligent & patriotic
exertion you should [not] form one of our Parliamentary band.

We have Scotland, Wales, Ireland, Yorkshire & I hope the North: & we have with us the
civilized world. From this movement it is probable that our cause will visibly move upwards.
It has indeed enormously moved upwards within the last 12 months. Its final triumph is certain. The only question is how much there will there be of unhappiness for Ireland, of difficulty & delay, of pain & shame for England before the consummation will be reached.

But I earnestly hope that you may yet be enabled by a successful scrutiny to take your
place among us. In any case I am sure it will be felt that your high character has been
raised even higher by your conduct during the present struggle.

To J. MORLEY, Irish secretary, 9 July 1886.   Add MS 56445, f. 195.

We have both I apprehend been too busy to give visible signs that we are conscious of
one another's existence. But I now cordially congratulate you on your signal performances, & on the victory so well deserved.

Scotland & Wales are splendid. Poor Hodge,[2] another of our allies, I fear may lose
heart.

The more complete our smash now, the more bitter will be the humiliation England, &
England alone of the four, will have to go through.

Every body will be puzzled, no one happy. *We* shall have to consider a most nice question between meeting Parlt. & resigning at once. We must try to sift that matter among
ourselves as much as possible before we meet in Cabinet to take a final decision. By Wed.
next the outlook will be, though very desolate, tolerably clear in a general way, though I
do not suppose the case will be ripe for the Cabinet before Monday week.

We alone can decide, but I think we ought to know what others with a legitimate
intent, have to say: & one of my objects in writing is to ask you to ascertain from Parnell
what he has to suggest.

Are we to go at once: are we to meet Parlt.: if we meet Parlt. what tone is the speech to
adopt: & are we in that case to contemplate as a possibility remaining till Oct.

If this last be within the compass of probability I am inclined as regards the next ulterior step to say the best mode of proceeding *then* wd. be by Resolution.[3]

10 Sat.

Ch. 8½ AM. Wrote to Mr Summers tel.—Chairman Hawick tel.—Mr A. Morley L.
l.l. & tel. l.l.—Mr Henderson Anstruther tel.—Mr Primrose L. & tel. l.l.—Ld
Rosebery l.l.l.—Mr M. Napier—Mr Marjoribanks—G. Leveson Gower (alas
defeated)—Mr S.H. Whitbread—and minutes. Worked on books. Dined at Rectory & backg. Read A. Dicey on Home Rule[4]—The Wanderer—Pausanias—
Castlereagh Corresp.[5]

[1] Defeated in Leeds Central by 13 votes; elected for Colne Valley 1892.
[2] i.e. English peasantry.
[3] Morley's reply, 11 July, Add MS 44255, f. 99, stated he hoped to see Parnell that day; no account
found; on 19 July, ibid., f. 101, Morley reported: 'Parnell, of course, is anxious for us to hold on to the
last moment' as he would need to 'take up a new and difficult line'.
[4] Probably A. V. Dicey, 'The Home Rule movement', *The Nation*, xlii. 444 (June 1886); not *England's case* (see 10 Nov. 86).
[5] R. Stewart, Lord Castlereagh, *Memoir and correspondence*, 12v. (1848–53).

The smash. In the main the work of the faint-hearted or weak kneed Liberals like Mr Goschen. But its result will be far otherwise. (The factious increase of Conservative strength will not counterbalance what follows.)

1. The Radicals among them will, in order to regain their place in the ranks, be more Radical than ever.

2. The Nationalists will in their present position be a powerful radical contingent.

3. England overrides Wales & Scotland. This will bring forward Scotch & Welsh questions on national grounds.[1]

To G. G. LEVESON-GOWER, whip, 10 July 1886.[2]   Add MS 44548, f. 114.

I am sadly and most sorely grieved at your defeat. But you suffer in a noble cause. It will be some consolation to you to observe how, even at the moment, the whole civilised world is with us. You have, I hope, long, long years before you, & I do not think that many of them, though probably some, will have passed before you receive your vindication. I advise you to take resolutely to the study of Irish history. I have done in that way the little that I could: & am amazed at the deadness of vulgar opinion to the blackguardism and baseness (no words are strong enough) which befoul the whole history of the Union.

It is an open question in my mind whether, if this folly lasts, the thing may not in the end contribute to Repeal, which I should greatly regret. Time will be the great instructor. And, in truth, when we consider all things, much has been done in a very limited time. I am so glad you have had your share in it.

To E. MARJORIBANKS, M.P., 10 July 1886.   Add MS 44548, f. 114.

In forwarding these papers about Leith[3] I supply a brief statement from memory of my own share in the affair.

1. On Thursday July 1 I received in the middle hours a telegram (from a Mr. Hall I think but his letter is in Downing Street) containing a statement that the Provost could not stand. I knew nothing then of Jacks' defection & could not understand the message.

2. Between 5 & 6 p.m. by the 2nd post a letter from the same gentleman explained the case. It at once occurred to me that my acting in the matter might be useful. I wrote a letter to Holmes Ivory, & an account of what I was doing to London: also a telegram to Ivory to tell him a letter was on the way. In this letter I said that if on consultation it was found practicable I might be nominated, & I would if necessary go down & speak.

3. I was not yet aware that the nomination stood for the next day. But I very soon learned this & I telegraphed to Ivory say about 7 p.m. my offer to stand. The rest remains with Ivory who with Cowan & Campbell seems to have done right.

4. I considered Jacks to have distinctly pledged himself to us by attending on my platform[4] & by the language of support which I understood that he had used.

5. As far as I am concerned I have no wish for privacy, but I do not as yet see that Jacks has any claim for any disclaimer from us as to what others said or did.

I leave the matter *wholly* in your hands.[5]

---

[1] Holograph dated 10 July; Add MS 44772, f. 173.

[2] Version in *P.M.G.*, 17 July 1886, 7.

[3] See also 2–3 July 86.

[4] On 21 June; *Speeches on the Irish question*, 211.

[5] Marjoribanks replied, 12 July, Add MS 44332, f. 163, that 'Jacks has been abominably shifty but I am inclined to think that his recent action was due to a desire to keep away a Unionist'; letter for Jacks's agent enclosed for approval.

To LORD ROSEBERY, foreign secretary, 10 July 1886.   N.L.S. 10023, f. 197.

The work of the F.O. makes it hardly fair to say a word to you on anything else, nor will I now attempt to answer the letter which lies unanswered. Nor do I ask any reply from you, but only beg you to turn over, & over, & over, in your mind the grave & nice question we shall have to decide after about a week in consequence of the smash of themselves & us which our friends the seceders have effected.

My mind goes back to your idea at the beginning of June, when I think you leaned towards resignation. I have always been disposed to hold that no Government has a right to advise Dissolution, unless it sincerely & rationally believes that it has a fair chance of approval. The Tory party has never had a majority on any one of its own *four* dissolutions (1852, 1859, 1868, 1880). Our experts, however, while admitting the difficulties of the case, were all of opinion that we should at the least sensibly mend our position. Could we have seen the real state of things in this respect, I think I should have been with you a month ago (think of its being only a month ago!). In such a matter I always follow the experts, as the more probable opinion; having none of my own.

We have now to 'take stock' of the situation & very carefully, & consider whether we shall turn out at once, or meet Parliament—and if the latter, then what sort of speech we shall advise, & for what sort of issue we shall 'ride'. My paramount anxiety is that we shall thoroughly sift, i.e. *expiscate* the question.

I propose to come up in the middle of the week. By Saturday or probably Monday we may be ready for a Cabinet.[1]

11. 3 S. Trin.

Ch. 11 AM and 6½ P.M. Wrote to Mr Holmes Ivory—Mr Primrose—Ld Rosebery tel.—Ld Granville—Rev. Dr Allon—Ed. 19th Cent.—Mr Knowles—Ed. Manch. Guardian[2]—Mr Moulton—Mr Childers—Mr A. Arnold—and minutes. Read Q.R. on Missions—Do on Eastern Sacred Books[3]—Biological Religion[4]—The Salvation Army.[5] Dined at the Rectory.

12. M.

Ch. 8½ A.M. Wrote to Mr Primrose tel. l.l.—Ld Rosebery Tel.—Mr A. West—Ld Granville—Mr J. Lang—Mr C. Bannerman—and minutes. Wrote Mem. on duty of Cabinet & future policy. Worked on books. Walk with S.E.G. & conversation with him on meditated Nucleus-Building.[6] Read Mr G. Smith on Canada[7]— Castlereagh Correspondence—Pausanias V—The Wanderer. Rectory dinner. Conversation with Johnson. Backgammon.

'*Secret*'.[8] My ideas are immature & uninformed, but at the present stage, & apart from what touches myself personally, I incline to think as follows

---

[1] Rosebery replied, 12 July, Add MS 44289, f. 55: 'my mind is conclusively in favour of resignation'.

[2] *Manchester Guardian*, 14 July, 5f, printed various letters from Gladstone supporting candidates.

[3] *Q.R.*, clxiii. 116, 180 (July 1886).   [4] See 27 Sept. 86.

[5] Perhaps *All about the Salvation Army* (1884).

[6] Start of plans for the separate library at Hawarden (eventually St Deiniol's Library).

[7] Goldwin Smith in *N.C.*, xx. 14 (July 1886).

[8] Add MS 56445, f. 197.

1. That we should wait until the elections are closed, or all but closed, & should then tender our resignations on the broad ground that the Irish question is primarily a question of social order & that we have a sufficient reason to believe the new Parliament wd. at the present moment decline to adopt the measures which in (our) judgment the state of that question requires.
2. Various secondary measures contribute to support this main proposition.

    a. It is best for Ireland that the party strongest in the new Parliament, & alone likely to command a majority at the outset, should be at once confronted with its responsibilities.

    b. We are bound to consider, in its proper place, what will most tend to reunite the Liberal party. It is in opposition, & not in Govt., that the Liberal party tends to draw together.

    c. A particular reason gives especial force to this consideration at the present time, namely that many of the seceders have (or at least they had) one important point in common with us, they refused to contemplate coercion as the proper means to be adopted for governing Ireland.

    d. Could we hope to remodel our measures, this might be ground for an endeavour to make up a majority through a union of Liberals, Seceders & Nationalists. I, however, though I might suggest some amendments do not at all see my way to remodelling the Bill, or presenting a new Bill.

    e. Our perhaps too eager recognition of the claims of Irish landlords has been most unscrupulously used against us. The hopes with which our offer was declared to be made, have been totally disappointed. It is impossible I think to maintain without any change that relation between the two Bills which in April we declared to be established for that juncture. Yet it wd. be most difficult, if we remained in Govt. to advise a speech from the throne, to know how to deal with the subject, from which we could not escape in debate. Out of Govt., we have a fresh start, & every man is free to deal with each part of the subject on its merits. This is what individually I shd. desire to do.

    f. It also seems important to consider that if we remain an amendment to the speech will be moved & carried of such a nature as to commit the new Parlt. at once against what is called Home Rule. If we resign, then, as the Tories wd. be much more prudent in Govt. than in opposition, & as the main prize wd. be already in hand, they might avoid any strong declarations in their speech from the throne. Further, if they made one, the House wd. not, in the common course be committed to it by the Address. Further still, & especially if the Address were drawn (as in 1833) to commit the House, an excellent opportunity might be afforded for an amendment directed against coercion. Thus there is on one side almost a certainty that the new House wd. place a yoke upon its own neck: on the other a likelihood that this might be avoided; & also a chance of making some ground against coercive legislation.
3. With regard to a general line of action in Parlt., this presents itself to me as an outline.

    a. On the Irish question to support, not court, any reasonable declaration of [*sc* which] the Irish Parlt. party may find necessary for making good their ground against the party of force. To resist coercion, as the alternative, & bad alternative of Home Rule. To maintain the authority of the Chair, & the police of the House. And finally b. Apart from the Irish question to support freely, & promote, Liberal measures generally; with some favour for Scotland & Wales, & for such measures as might best mark the old dividing lines of party, now much obscured by the Secession.

    Of these it wd. not be difficult to point out examples. One of them I think would certainly be that, which in my address of last Sept. was described by the imperfect phrase of Registration, but which involves quickening, simplifying, & enlarging all the operations connected with the franchise. W.E.G. July 12. 1886.

1. Will agencies of Liberal reunion ever begin to work, while the Irish question is to the front, unless either a. We obtain a decided predominance—now impossible—or b. we are out of office.
2. If the Tories come in, which is the more probable alternative, those agencies will at once begin to operate with effect.
3. If we meet Parliament in August, the Liberal Seceders will probably not venture to put us out by an amendment to the Queen's Speech? (the Address would of course be framed so as not to commit them)—and in that case we should have to remain in office until October and then produce our proposals. As to these, and particularly as to Land Purchase, should we not be much more disembarrassed after the breaking up of the present Ministry?
4. It is with accession to office that the difficulties of an anti-Irish Government will begin. Is it not a necessity as matters now stand that they should have an opportunity given them to try their hand? If they fail to form a Government our position will at once be very greatly strengthened. If they succeed they will have to face a task which will be found in a certain time too much for them. But may we not say the sooner they begin the sooner they will end their work whether by retirement or more probably by carrying the measure? and what is to be desired is that the *end* should come as soon as possible.[1]

To A. E. WEST, 12 July 1886. '*Very private*'.   Add MS 44548, f. 116.

On the formation of the Salisbury Government last year I thought the arrangement as to the First Lordship of the Treasury highly objectionable on various grounds. But it was not forced on the consideration of the House, as it would be if it were renewed, on the next consideration of an estimate, or as it might be by any one.

Some of the objections are palpable on the surface. But there is one which cannot be fully appreciated except by persons who have had a large experience either of my office or of the Foreign Office. When the Foreign Minister is Head, 1) the Government must in this country be a Government of Departments, and 2) there is no one either to assist or at all check the Foreign Minister.

As matter of fairness I should be glad if *a propos des bottes*, & as matter of history, you could convey the state of my mind.[2]

[P.S.] One does not see why Iddesleigh might not take F.O.[3] especially as S's health is not strong.

13. Tu.

Ch. 8½ A.M. Wrote to Macrae (Dingwall) Tel—Dr Foster l.l.—Ld Rosebery Tel.—Dr Parker—Mr Mundella—Mr Campbell—Mr Primrose L. & tel. l.—Mr Marjoribanks MP—Mr Labouchere MP—& minutes. Read Pausanias Finished V.—Castlereagh Correspondence III—The Wanderer. Dined at Rectory. Backgammon.

[1] Undated holograph; Gladstone's later note reads 'Fragment about Jul. 1. 86', but clearly later than then.
[2] West replied, 14 July, Add MS 44342, f. 84, that he had communicated 'the substance of your letter' to Iddesleigh through his son (i.e. Gladstone's god-son).
[3] He did, to the Queen's regret; see *L.Q.V.*, 3rd series, i. 166-7.

To H. LABOUCHERE, M.P., 13 July 1886.   Add MS 44548, f. 116.

I thank you for your interesting letter.[1] Tomorrow I come up to town, with nice matters for consideration in immediate view, but with no doubt or hesitation in my mind as to the principles on which to proceed. No step will be taken either by the Cabinet or by myself personally without much consideration.

I need hardly assure you that nothing will induce me to entertain for a moment the Home Rule of the Pall Mall Gazette.[2]

My personal powers of action are limited & must grow more & more so, but the claim of Ireland & of the rest of the country in connection with it, is strong & must not be lightly dismissed.

To E. MARJORIBANKS, M.P., 13 July 1886.   Add MS 44548, f. 117.

Many thanks for looking into the Jacks affair.[3] Two remarks occur to me.

1. I spontaneously offered myself for nomination—would it then be correct to say more than that as against Edinburgh the Leith people did it all.

2. Is the latter part of your letter quite safe in dealing with a shifty fellow like Jacks? I should have thought it safer to say that if his desire & intention be to support us, he will readily find the means of expressing them & then there could be further correspondence. You however know your men & are probably a better judge than I am.

To A. J. MUNDELLA, president of the board of trade,   Add MS 44548, f. 117.
13 July 1886. '*Private*'.

I thank you very much for your kind letter.[4] I share all your sanguine anticipations, & I am considering whether I should make an [effort?] to counteract discouragement by an Address [*sic*].

I think that the constitutional & the political arguments lean, so far as I can yet see, in favour of immediate resignation rather than meeting Parliament with our small though crack army of 200 men. I am however above all things desirous that we should act upon full discussion & consideration.

I go to town tomorrow, have asked you to a Cabinet dinner on Saturday & I think of Monday for the Cabinet.

14. Wed. [London]

Ch. 8½ AM. Wrote to Duke of Westminster[5]—Chester Postmaster tel—Mr Primrose tel.—Mr Ivory tel.—and minutes. Finished Wanderer Vol III.—read G. Smith Pym, Cromwell—Morley on Voltaire.[6] 3½-8¾. To D. St. To my great concern, & despite of all precautions, a great concourse at Euston, and a smaller one in D. St.

---

[1] Not found.

[2] Gladstone should stay in office, making up a majority on the basis of 'Hartingtonian Home Rule'; *P.M.G.*, 8, 13 July 1886.

[3] See 2, 3, 10 July 86.

[4] Of 12 July, Add MS 44258, f. 241; general opinion is 'we ought not to resign'; Thring 'with tears in his eyes' advocates 'face the new House and die fighting'; this a general view.

[5] Complaining at his electioneering, 'a fresh blow at the aristocracy', *T.T.*, 16 July 1886, 6e.

[6] J. Morley, *Voltaire* (1872, new ed. 1886); see 16 Jan. 72.

15. Th.

Wrote to Ld Wolverton—Att. General—Mrs O'Shea—Sir J. Lambert—Mr C. Bannerman—and minutes. Saw Mr P[rimrose]—H.J.G. long conversation—Mr A. Morley—Ld Kimberley—Ld Granville—Sir L. Playfair—Lady Derby *cum* Lady Airlie &c.—5 o'clock Tea. Dined at Lucy's. Read Canning on Ireland[1]—Lady Bellairs on Transvaal.[2]

To LORD WOLVERTON, 15 July 1886.   Add Ms 44548, f. 117.

I can venture to convey to you as a friend what I should not like to go to you either in a formal, or in a less direct, manner. It is simply this. *Assuming* for argument's sake that the Cabinet shall decide upon immediate resignation, would it be at all agreeable to you that I should place your name before the Queen for a Viscountcy? If yes, I should have a cordial pleasure in doing it.[3]

Well, we shall have much to say when we meet.

16. Fr.

Wrote to E. W. Hamilton & copy—J. Watson & Smith—Mr Bradlaugh—H.N.G.—and minutes. Read Canning on Ireland—Goldwin Smiths Three Statesmen. Saw Mr Primrose—H.J.G.—Mr Childers—Ld Elgin[4]—Mr Holmes Ivory—Mr Morley. Long conversation with Count Münster—Sir C. Tennant. Dined at Sir C. Tennant's. Worked on books.

To E. W. HAMILTON, 16 July 1886. '*Private*'.[5]   Lambeth MS 2760, f. 195.

I thank you for your letter[6] and I have thought it over in connection with the great issues now depending.

As I fear there *does* exist in the world the baseness you describe, I believe on the whole that what you say is true and wise, and I give you my promise accordingly.

[1] Perhaps G. Canning, 'Speech on Lord Morpeth's motion for a committee on the state of Ireland' (1812).   [2] See 8 May 85.

[3] Wolverton declined: it would 'be misinterpreted': he welcomed 'serving under you once more' to complete 'the great work for Ireland'; 16 July, Add MS 44349, f. 214.

[4] Victor Alexander *Bruce, 1849-1917; 9th Earl of Elgin 1863; Household office and Commissioner of Works 1886; Indian viceroy 1894-8; colonial secretary 1905-8. Chairman of Scottish liberal assoc. during 1886 election.

[5] Gladstone's copy.

[6] Hamilton was told by MacColl that MacColl 'had heard through Stead that there was a conspiracy on foot to blacken Mr. G.'s private character' by setting spies on him to test the truth of stories about his nocturnal activities; MacColl believed these stories had a 'baneful effect' in the London constituencies and had even 'been instilled like poison into H.M.'s mind' (E.H.D., 14 July 1886). Hamilton therefore wrote this day, Lambeth MS 2760, f. 192, warning Gladstone, not mentioning MacColl or Stead by name, that he had information about 'a conspiracy on foot to blacken your private character', telling him of the impending spies and of the use of these 'calumnies . . . by canvassers in the metropolitan constituencies' and of 'friends and admirers . . . not knowing what to believe and how to account for what they hear; while explanations are difficult to make; and if made are disbelieved. I need not enlarge upon the extreme risk to which actuated by high motives you have subjected yourself; and I will only beg you to consider how greatly that risk is enhanced when the spirit of malice and hatred is so rampant as it is at the present moment. I will only add that your traducers have in their pay a certain woman prepared to support their calumnies . . .'; Hamilton did not mention the Queen.

There are two cases which I should have liked not to stop altogether; one of them particularly where the person concerned had desires to get away and join friends in Australia. But it may be possible to do something in this consistently with what I have written.

To H. N. GLADSTONE, 16 July 1886.   Hawarden MSS.

Another turn of the wheel has placed us on the underside; but the turning has not ended, only begun. We, the promoters of Home Rule, continue in the certitude of our belief that the measure will & must pass. But I cannot find on the part of the opponents any corresponding certitude that it will not. They are waiting upon Providence, or upon what people take to be synonymous, the chapter of accidents: living from hand to mouth, united in objecting to *what we* propose, and united in nothing else.

As to what is immediately before us, I may roughly take the four sections of the House thus C. 320, L. 190, N 86, thus leaving *74* for *DL*. Every body, or almost every body sees that we must go, the only question being whether we are to disappear say in ten days or in a month. What is to follow? Of a new Government the Tories must supply both the front bench and the rank and file—Hartington probably would not join them, and if he did I doubt if he would carry twenty out of his seventy four with him: nor would there be any one to supply him with substantial aid for I doubt whether James, the only considerable henchman remaining to him after the defeat of Goschen, Trevelyan, and Brand, would on any consideration go into the Tory camp. Probably H. can do more for them outside than he could do inside, but it is not yet at all known whether he has any disposition to sustain them except upon Irish policy. The general outlook is of an uncertain, weary, changeful time, until a settlement of the Irish question is reached; and that settlement can only be real by Home Rule, or partial and temporary by some strong coercion, which it will be difficult perhaps impossible to pass, and quite impossible to maintain for any length of time.

As to myself personally the element of old age, incurable as it is, renders all these matters extremely perplexing. What I think possible is that, if such an arrangement be cordially accepted by my friends & colleagues, I should obtain a dispensation from ordinary and habitual attendance in Parliament but should not lay down the leadership so as to force them to choose another leader, and should take an active part when occasion seemed to require it, especially on the Irish question. The proper policy for the Liberals, put out of the Government[,] will be to promote freely and actively Liberal legislation generally in cooperation with the Dissentients, so as to allow the party to re-form itself.

Remembering what you were to be [*sc.* me?] during the election of last winter I have felt much for your embarrassment & perplexity in your remoteness at this moment and I wish I could convey this to you more quickly than by the post, but on the other hand I have said more than I would have said were you at hand, adding as I now do that I think the Cabinet will next Tuesday decide on an immediate resignation. God bless you. Your afft Father W E Gladstone.

17. Sat.

Wrote to The Queen—Mr Holmes Ivory—Mr Bryce—and minutes. Drive with C. Twelve to breakfast: an interesting party. Saw (specially) Rev. Dr Allon—Mr Knowles—Mr MacColl—Mr Bryce—Dr Parker—Mr A. Morley—Lord Acton—Ld Wolverton—Mr Primrose—Sir J.C.—Sir W. Harcourt—Ld Rosebery—and others. Cabinet dinner (*minus* Granville[1]). Fin. G. Smith's Lectures—read Shelley on Ireland.[2]

---

[1] Who was ill.   [2] P. B. Shelley, 'An address to the Irish people' (1812).

To J. BRYCE, M.P., 17 July 1886.   Bryce MS 10, f. 66.

I subjoin a very rough sketch of the outlines of our great subject—which may, or may not, be of use to you in trying to map out the work.[1] I think that any *money*[2] shd. be exclusively for history ending with 1800.

I. *History*.

1. History—before Ld. Fitzgerald (whom we ought to treat as epochmaking).
2. History 1795–1800: the concentration of horrors.
3. History—the conduct of England towards Ireland, at various[?] points good and bad, 1800–1886.

II. *Political argument*.

1. The great Plunkett argument of *ultra vires*. Never satisfactorily disposed of.
2. The argument from the unquestioned independence *de jure* & *de facto*, of 100 years back. What has become of this independence? It could only be lost by conquest or gift. It has been lost by *neither*.
3. The title of Ireland to speak through her 85 members: she has now spoken twice, formally, in the first year of her emancipation.
4. Authorities of the time in the Union.

III.

1. The manner in which the difficulties connected with the Repeal of the Union have been got rid of, by the spontaneous reduction of the Irish demand to Home Rule.
2. The historical evidence that the alleged authorities of the intermediate period were a. agt. premature disturbance of a great settlement, b. agt. Repeal, the creation of an independent Legislature not against Home Rule.
3. The fear that in the case of prolonged resistance the effect may be as in former cases the extension of the demand, & the re-substitution of Repeal for Home Rule.

IV.

1. The argument from foreign experience, negative and positive.
2. From our colonial experience.
3. From the present state of European, American, & Colonial opinion.

V.

1. The question *how is the Queen's govt. to be carried on* in Ireland? *War* we could cope with. But social order, public confidence, *can we* reestablish?
2. The intermediate phase—soap bubbles.
3. Coercion. Can a Bill be carried? Can it, if at all, be carried without expelling the Nationalist representation? How if, on being expelled, the 85 meet in Dublin & claim to be constitutionally the Irish Govt.?
4. For how long will a. the Liberal party, b. the public sentiment endure the method of Crown Colony?
5. What will be the capacity of the British Parlt. for its general purposes, during the time while these questions are being worked out to their solution?[3]

---

[1] See 8 July 86.
[2] See 26 July 86.
[3] Ibid.

18. *4 S. Trin.*

Chapel Royal mg & evg. Saw Sir W. Phillimore.[1] Read Green's Life of Coltman[2]—Souvenirs de Léonard[3]—Becker's Auteur de l'Imitation[4]—Martineau on Expansion! of the Church.[5] Drive with C.

19. *M.*

Wrote to Mr Leake MP—Ld Granville—Mr Westell—Lady Farnborough—Mr Holden—Sir H. Ponsonby Tel.—& minutes. Packed & sent off my two *hampers* of Books. Dined at Lansdowne House. Saw H.J.G.—Mr P.—Ld Spencer—Sir J.C.— Mr Hamilton—Mr Agnew—Ld Rosebery. Read Burke's Correspondence.[6] Luncheon at Mrs Th.s.

20. *Tu.*

Wrote to Watsons—The Queen l. & tel.[7]—Sir Thos Acland—Ld Rosebery—Mr Quaritch—Ld Braye—and minutes. Read Burke's Correspondence. Cabinet 2–3. See minute. 3–4½. Conclave on list of honours. Went with Mrs Th. to see the cottage at Hampstead.[8] Curious lessons of wealth: redeemed however or qualified by much liberality on Mrs T.s part. Dined with the Bass's who have made Chesterfield House a kind of gem. Then we went to Grosvenor House, where it was needful to show. The Duke [of Westminster] in perfect humour & extremely courteous.[9]

Cabinet. Tues. Jul. 20. 86. 2 P.M.[10]
1. W.E.G. asked shall Cabinet resign now or meet Parlt. & be put out on the amt. respecting Ireland wh may be expected as a matter of course.
   Various considerations stated but unanimous *aye*. Leave given me to state to the Queen that we had reviewed the whole case & many considerations wh for the most part tended in the same direction, but that specially present to our minds were
   1) the consideration of social order[11]
   2) desire to give successors as much time as possible.
2. W.E.G. (after first speaking to Sir W.H. & Mr C.) announced that if it were deemed advisable by the Cabinet, he, though he could not undertake ordinary as habitual

---

[1] Representing the Queen's Proctor (i.e. effectively representing Dilke) in the Crawford/Dilke case which opened on 16 July. See 21, 23 July 86.
[2] Might read Cottman; even so, untraced.
[3] J. Léonard, *Souvenirs de Léonard* (n.d.).
[4] See 9 May 86.
[5] J. Martineau in *C.R.*, 1. 6 (July 1886).
[6] No separate complete letters then available; Burke's *Works* ed. Fitzwilliam and Bourke, 8v. (1852) included extensive correspondence; *Letters, speeches and tracts on Irish affairs*, ed. M. Arnold (1881); see 8 Nov. 81.
[7] Offering the resignation of the cabinet; *L.Q.V.*, 3rd series, i. 162. Salisbury kissed hands on 25 July.
[8] Woodbine Cottage, West End Lane, Hampstead, rented by Mrs Thistlethwayte and subsequently used by her more than 15 Grosvenor Square.
[9] See 14 July 86n.
[10] Add MS 44647, f. 119.
[11] In Ireland; see *L.Q.V.* 3rd series, i. 162.

attendance in Parlt. was willing to retain the responsibility of leadership, & to place himself at the disposal of his friends to appear & take a part when they might call upon him: & of course to have special heed to the calls of the Irish question.[1]

3. Some conversation on the future. Desire to promote the general cooperation with the Dissentients on Liberal grounds—& decision to maintain the character & do the work of *the* Opposition.

4. Rosebery explained that the Afghan Commission had reached the impossible point—a record of this to be left for successors.

To Sir T. D. ACLAND, 20 July 1886.   Bodley MS Eng. lett d. 89, f. 60.

Your note of the 16th gratified me much. You may I think, when you have leisure, like to read what I said on the subject of class, in a passionless discussion with Lowe—Articles V and VI of the little Volume herewith which pray keep.[2]

It was indeed a brave and a kind of yours [*sic*] to go and fight for Walter Phillimore.[3]

21. Wed.

Wrote to The Queen l.l.l.—Mr Nimmo[4]—and minutes. Read the deplorable report of yesterday on the Crawford case: & conversation with C.[5] Saw Mr P.— Mr A.M.—Mr G. Russell—Ly Stepney. Read Lucas's Life[6]—Burke's Correspondence. Dined with Mr G. Russell: Marlb. House afterwards, but I retired from the door not having the proper dress. Saw Mr Davis & the Blenheim Pictures.[7]

22. Th.

Wrote to Mrs Stume—Ld Granville—Sir C. Forster—J. Watson & Smith—J. Westell—Mr Knollys—and minutes. Saw Mr P.—Mr A.M.—Major Isaac[8]—Mr Hibbert—Mr A. Young—Ld Chancr—Conversation with Helen on Holloway. Dined at Sir A. Hayter's. Conversation with Mrs Oppenheim[9]—Lady Hayter[10]—Ly Herschell. Read The Anti-Union[11]—(Frantic) Hist. Rebellion of 1641[12]—Burke Correspondence—Life of Lucas. Saw Ly Granville to convey offer of a step in the peerage.[13]

23. Fr.

Wrote to The Queen—Col. Tomlinson—Ld Rosebery—Mr Westell—and minutes. Saw Mr P.—Ld Spencer—Ld Rosebery—Mr Hamilton—Sir A. West.

[1] 'all applauded', Rosebery noted; *G.P.*, 441.
[2] i.e. *Gleanings*, i.
[3] Beaten in St. George's, Hanover Square.
[4] J. C. Nimmo (distant relative?) on the Gladstones and Leith; Add MS 44548, f. 118.
[5] Mrs Crawford's evidence: 'we all three were in one bed'; *T.T.*, 21 July 1886, 12.
[6] E. Lucas, *The life of Frederick Lucas, M.P.*, 2v. (1886).
[7] See 7 May, 21 June 84.
[8] Lewis Henry Isaacs, 1830–1908; major and tory M.P. 1885–92.
[9] Society hostess and friend of E. W. Hamilton.
[10] Henrietta, wife of Sir A. Hayter and niece of A. J. B. Hope.
[11] *The Anti-Union*, 27 December 1798; notes in Add MS 44770, f. 131.
[12] E. B[orlase], *History of the execrable Irish rebellion* (1680).
[13] A marquisate; declined.

Twelve to dinner. Read Anti-Union—Burke's Correspondence—Chapter of Autobiography.[1] Worked on books. The terrible cant of the Dilke verdict sadly & deeply marks this day.[2]

24. Sat.

Wrote to Ld Chancellor l.l.—Rev. Mr Dunkerly—Dr Mitchell—Rev. Mr Hargreaves—Sir Thos G.—The Queen l.l.—Rev. S.E.G.—and minutes. Saw Mr P.— Mr A.M.—Lady Rosebery. Further with Helen on the Holloway case of wh she seems to have made a very solid examination.[3] Read Leonard's Mem.—Burke's Correspondence—Anti-Union (finished). Dined with Mr Knowles. Mrs Russell (U.S.) lectured on Genesis.[4]

To LORD HERSCHELL, lord chancellor, 24 July 1886.   Add MS 44548, f. 119.
'*Private*'.

[First letter:]   Some appear to suppose that, in addition to the too copious matter for reflection which the verdict of yesterday in the Crawford case supplies, we have upon us the duty of considering whether the name of Sir C. Dilke should be struck off the list of the Privy Council.

Of course I look to you for advice in such a matter, if there be occasion to advise.

Looking at the deplorable case ignorantly & from without, I had leant to the supposition that a more formidable question might arise, that of false swearing, with which we have no concern, & that until this question should be raised or put aside the minor subject could hardly come into view. For I presume that the perjury or no perjury involves the whole merits of the case.

You will I daresay kindly set me right if there be need. The mere horror of the subject is enough to bewilder any misunderstanding.

[Second letter:]   1. Am I to understand from your letter[5] that you think the sad case of Dilke has now reached a point at which the Ministry, if in a normal position itself ought to prevent, & now to advise the removal of his name from the list of the Privy Council. 2. If this be the true position, then I own there appears to me to be some equity, in facing the case ourselves instead of leaving it to be dealt with by political opponents? 3. But, on the other side of the case, if a prosecution for perjury, or any further proceeding at law, is contemplated or possible, might not the removal of his name be premature, as tending in a measure to prejudge the case? 4. Would you think it well to communicate with the Attorney General who has also been his Counsel? 5. If the right conclusion be that his name should go off, & likewise that the time has come, then ought not he himself to request it? Might not the Attorney General or James put this in motion? In his letter to Chelsea, he accepts the verdict, as far as public life goes; & the Privy Councillorship clearly appertains to public life? 6. I am afraid that *if* we come to advise when moved by

[1] See 17 Sept., 26 Oct. 68; the prototype for 'The Irish question' (see 26 July 86).
[2] Verdict this day against setting aside the decree *nisi*, i.e. implying that Dilke had committed adultery with Mrs Crawford.
[3] See 1 July 86n.
[4] Not further identified.
[5] Herschell's letter this day, Add MS 44498, f. 278, thought a prosecution for perjury 'unlikely'; if H.M. sought advice, then advice would have to be that he should resign: but this might be 'more fitly' left to our successors. See 28 July 86.

an inquiry from the Queen, there might be in it something like a confession, by implication, of remissness.

These are the points which occur to me.

25. 5 S. Trin. & St J.

Our 47th marriage anniversary: & T.G.s 82 birthday. Laziness kept me from writing to C.[1] I do nothing beyond reading by free will. Chapel Royal mg & evg. Saw Ld Sydney. Wrote to Ld Granville—The Queen—S.E.G. Read Life of Lucas—Wiseman's Lectures[2]—Laird on Genesis+[3]—Nippold's Rothe.[4]

26. M.

Wrote to The Queen—Messrs Murray—Mr Westell—Sir A. Gordon—Ld Granville—Sir H. James—J. Watson & Smith—W.H.G.—Mr Bryce—Mr J. Cowan—Maj. Carmichael Smith.[5] Saw Mr P.—Sir J.C.—Sir C. Foster—Mr A.M. Worked on packing books &c. Read Deane's Hist. Ireland[6]—Life of Lucas. Wrote Mem. on Ireland.[7] Drive with C.

To J. BRYCE, M.P., 26 July 1886. 'Private'.   Bryce MS 10, f. 70.

The time has come for deciding whether or not to apply any portion of the Special Service Fund at my disposal to the elucidation of Irish History. I should be glad to know what you think on the subject & perhaps you would speak to Arnold Morley. I think that if it is done the money should be given in aid of purely historical investigation, and that it had better be limited to what precedes the year 1800. The sum might I think be min. £250 and max. £350 and I would ask you to take charge of it. If you think it can quite well be dispensed with we might perhaps let this idea fall to the ground.[8]

27. Tu.

Wrote to J. Morley—Rev. S.E.G.—Miss Marsh—Ld Elgin—and minutes. Drive with C. & walk. Saw Mr P.—Mr A.M.—Mr J. Morley—Sir H. James—Mr Waddington—Ld Ripon—Ld Chancellor. I sent for James to converse respecting Dilke: & heard from him depressing intelligence as to the intentions of the new Government. Dined at Ld Ripon's. Read Hist. of Ireland—Life of Lucas.

---

[1] Who wrote a charming note, in Magnus, 362.

[2] See 23 May 86.

[3] By John Laird, Scottish minister; but no copy found.

[4] F. Nippold, *Richard Rothe*, 2v. (1873-4).

[5] Thanking Maj. Carmichael Smyth for his pamphlets on the trans-Canada railway; Add MS 44548, f. 121.

[6] C. P. Deane, *A short history of Ireland* (1886).

[7] Start of 'The Irish Question. I. History of an idea. II. Lessons of the election' (1886, dated 19 August with postscript dated 22 August). The penny ed. has an 'Addendum' dated 13 October. See 13 Oct. 86.

[8] Bryce replied this day, Bryce MS 11, f. 145, that he had formed a group of 'seven or eight persons likely to give useful counsel', and that he and A. Morley agreed that the secret service money might be legitimately employed in such publicity. On 2 August, Bryce MS 11, f. 148, Bryce sent a plan for several volumes of essays by various writers, eventually published as the *Handbook* (see 8 July 86n.).

To Miss C. MARSH, 27 July 1886.   Add MS 44548, f. 121.

I thank you much for your note;[1] & though I greatly deplore the issue, & the ideas of the Prayer in question, yet, from the moment when I heard it was your composition, I knew perfectly well that it was written in entire good faith, & had no relation to political controversy in the ordinary sense.

I cannot but think that, in bringing the subject of Irish intolerance before the Almighty Father, we ought to have some regard to the fact that, down to the present day, as between the two religions, the offence has been in the proportion of perhaps an hundred to one on the Protestant side, & the suffering by it on the Roman side.

At the present hour, I am pained to express my belief that there is far more of intolerance in action from so-called Protestants against Roman Catholics, than from Roman Catholics against Protestants.

It is a great satisfaction to agree with you, as I feel confident that I must do, in the conviction that of Prayer we cannot possibly have too much in this great matter, &, for my own part, I heartily desire that, unless the policy I am proposing be for the honour of God & the good of His creatures, it may be trampled under foot & broken into dust.

28. Wed.

Wrote to Ld Granville—Sir H. James—The Queen l.l.—and minutes. Dined with the Miss Monks. 2–4. Quasi-Cabinet at Lord Granville's. All approved of my standing out as to the Honours which the Queen fights. She has different measures, I fear, for different parties. Saw Mr P.—Mr A.M.—M. Waddington—Ld Granville—Ld Kenmare(?). Packing of papers & preparations for clearing out. Read Life of Lucas.

Meeting at Ld Granville's. Jul. 28. 86. 2 PM.[2]
Honours. W.E.G. advised to defend the three cases refused by H.M.[3]
Dilke. No action to be taken. NB he refuses to apply.[4]
Continuous proceeding with *Supply in order to* postpone any decl. of Irish policy till 1887. To be disapproved: but the question of opposing to be reserved.

29. Th.

Wrote to Mr Griffiths—Sir H. James—Dr Foster—Sir H. Ponsonby—Mr Weston—Sir W. Harcourt—Sir T. Brassey—Sir M.A. Bass—Sir H. Thring—Mr Hamilton—Mr Palmer—Mr J. Kitson—Mr J. Cowan—Serj. Simon—Ld Granville—Mr H. Jenkyns—and minutes. Read Life of Lucas (finished I)—began Kidnapped.[5] Saw Mr P.—Mr A.M.—Sir H. Thring—Mr F.L. Gower—Ld Rosebery.

To Sir H. JAMES, attorney general, 29 July 1886.   James MS M45. 217.
'*Private*'.

I considered the case of Dilke[6] quoad P[rivy] C[ouncil] very fully yesterday with nearly the whole of my outgoing colleagues; and we agreed ⟨after full consideration⟩ that we

[1] Not found; for the evangelical Catherine Marsh, see 5 Jan. 68.   [2] Add MS 44647, f. 132.
[3] A baronetcy and two knighthoods refused; Guedalla, *Q*, ii. 421, *G.P.*, 453.
[4] i.e. Dilke refuses voluntarily to apply to resign his Privy Councillorship.
[5] By R. L. Stevenson, just published.
[6] On 28 July, Gladstone asked James for any further points about the Dilke case; James MS M45. 215.

could not act *in invitum*, & had no option but to let the question stand over, unless in case of a request from him, which would alter the situation. I have made this opinion to the Queen: & I think it leaves me no more to say.

30. Fr.

Wrote draft of letter to A. Morley.[1] Saw Mr P.—Sir H. Ponsonby[2]—Duchess of Roxburghe (respecting D. of Newcastle).

For closing audience I write a Mem.[3] Every change leaves a gap: but this gap is one which I cannot personally & selfishly wish to be filled.

Read through Kidnapped: a book to be recommended.

31. Sat. [Combe Wood]

Wrote to Messrs Robertson & N.—Mr Murray—Mrs Currie—& minutes. Began with framing a paragraph for P.M.G. on Mr Lucy's outrageous declaration in the D.N.[4] Went to finish my rapid survey of the R. Academy: the most barren annual Exhibition I have known. Attended Miss Vyner's[5] marriage, & the breakfast after it. Short P.P.C.[6] visit to Mrs Th: I told her how glad I should be if I could be able to feel that I had been of the smallest use to her in any particular. Finished packing & clearing out: & went to Wolverton's at Coombe at 5.30. Conversation with him & with Granville. Read Burke's Corresp. III—began 'Merciful or Merciless'.[7]

6 S. Trin. Aug One. 1886.

Attack of neuralgia in the night. Got quinine in evg. Ch at 12.30 for H.C.—Aftn service in the House. Saw Sir W. Harcourt—Mr A. Morley. Wrote to Messrs Watson—Ld Salisbury—H.W. Primrose. Read 'Mort Edifiante' &c.—Merciful or Merciless—French Protestants in English Homes.[8]

To LORD SALISBURY, 1 August 1886.   Add MS 44548, f. 124.

I send herewith a copy of a letter addressed by me a few days ago to the Queen respecting the sad case of Dilke in connection with the retention of his name on the list of the Privy Council—Her Majesty is aware of my placing this letter in your hands.

If there be any point connected with your becoming First Lord of the Treasury on which you may have occasion to desire information from me, I shall be happy to wait upon you for the purpose.

Otherwise, I beg you not to take the trouble to acknowledge this note.[9]

---

[1] See 3 Aug. 86.   [2] See Magnus, 363.

[3] Dated 2 August, in *After Thirty Years*, 339. Victoria found him 'pale and nervous'; *L.Q.V.*, 3rd series, i. 168.

[4] *P.M.G.* this evening, 8a, denied para. in *D.N.* (ed. H. W. Lucy) that Gladstone especially welcomed Churchill's appt. as leader of the Commons.

[5] Mary Evelyn, da. of his friend Mrs Vyner, m. Lord A. F. Compton, 2nd s. of Lord Northampton, later a unionist M.P.

[6] 'Pour prendre congé'; to take leave: note left on visiting cards.

[7] S. E. O'Dell, *Merciful or merciless* (1886); a novel.

[8] S. W. Kershaw, *Protestants from France in their English home* (1885).

[9] Salisbury replied, 2 August, Add MS 44499, f. 1, that he agreed that, the case being *sub judice*, no advice be tendered 'for the present at all events'. Dilke remained a Privy Councillor.

2. M.

Found the Quinine doing its duty. Wrote to the Queen—and minutes. Drive with C. Visited the field of entertainment to 300 Telegraph Boys. Wrote short minute of conversation with H.M. Read Merciful or Merciless—Burke's Correspondence III.—Life of Lucas—French Protestants in Engl. Homes (finished).

To Sir W. V. HARCOURT, M.P., 2 August 1886.   MS Harcourt dep. 10, f. 121.

I have reflected on your report of Chamberlain's conversation.[1] And I remember that, during the worst of all his proceedings after resignation, he was always declaring his anxiety for an accommodation. The test of all such declarations must be in his acts, and the coming election at Birmingham supplies such a test. You appeared to regard his conduct in this election at Birmingham (it must be remembered what he did in the same district ⟨before⟩ on the last occasion) as quite uncertain, and yet to attach some value to his general words; which I am inclined to regard as worn out by frequent use.

At any rate I see clearly the defining lines of my own position. I am in Parliament to contribute if I can to the settlement of the Irish question, & in no case to impede it. Any settlement that Ireland accepts I should be very loath to impede. I even ask myself whether it might be possible for the new people to frame some initial plea for Federation and begin by dealing with the Irish part of it. This mode if feasible would correspond with one at least of Chamberlain's many declarations.

Next to the Irish question I desire to do everything for the reunion of the party, though with doubts whether this can be effected until Ireland is out of the way, and therefore with a disposition to mislike *primâ facie* whatever may seem like a plot to gain time & unity to prolong our present embarrassments. As in the case of Ireland, so in the matter of reunion, I am above all things determined not to be personally an obstacle in the way of what is good.

3. Tues.

Wrote to Mr Primrose l.l.—Sir W. Harcourt—Ld Hartington, & draft do.—Corr. & sent letter to A. Morley[2]—also minutes. Saw Ld Wolverton—Ld Granville—Ld Acton. Drove with C. to White House. Read Lucas II—Merciful or Merciless.

To LORD HARTINGTON, M.P., 3 August 1886.[3]   Chatsworth MSS 340. 2034.

I fully appreciate the feeling which has prompted your letter,[4] & I admit the reality of the difficulties you describe. It is also clear, I think, that, so far as title to places on the front opposition Bench is concerned, your right to them is identical with ours. Nor can I for a moment regard some insignificant newspaper statements or suggestions as fit to be taken into the account by either of us in dealing with this far from easy matter.

I am afraid, however, that I cannot materially contribute to relieve you from embarrassment. The choice of a seat is more or less the choice of a symbol; and I have no such acquaintance with your political views & intentions, as could alone enable me to judge what materials I have before me for making an answer to your enquiry.

[1] See Gardiner, ii. 3. The Chamberlainites did not contest Matthews' by-election in E. Birmingham.
[2] On inability to reply to all letters etc. sent him; *T.T.*, 5 August 1886, 6c.
[3] In Holland, ii. 175.
[4] Of 3 August, Add MS 44148, f. 235, on who should sit where in the Commons; until 1892 the liberals and the liberal-unionists sat together on the opposition front and back benches.

For my own part, I earnestly desire, subject to the paramount exigencies of the Irish question, to promote in every way the reunion of the Liberal party: a desire, in which I earnestly trust that you participate. And I certainly could not directly or indirectly dissuade you from any step which you may be inclined to take, and which may appear to you to have a tendency in any measure to promote that end. Beyond this general but decided declaration my state of information does not at this moment enable me to go.

4. Wed.

Wrote to Mr Knowles—Mr Primrose l.l.—Scotts—and minutes. Saw Mr Godley—Ld Wolverton. Wrote some fragments. Read Life of Lucas—Merciful or Merciless—Sturge's 'Wanted a Leader'—Dicey on Ireland (19th C.).[1] Under quinine pain is gone: there is still a salutary check on eating.

5. Th.

Went to London for the choice of a Speaker & seconded the motion, with a hint about the Irish.[2] Saw The Speaker—Sir W. Harcourt—H.J.G.—Ld Acton—Mr Primrose—Ld Rosebery—Mr Agnew. Dined at Ld Acton's, & back to Coombe. Read Lucas—ODell—Burke.

6. Fr.

Worked on Irish MS. Wrote to. . . . Read Odell—Burke. Drive with C.

7. Sat.

Wrote to W.H.G.—Sir W. Harcourt. Worked on M.S. Read Burke Corr.—Finished. Merciful or Merciless. Read Celibate Worthies.[3] Saw Ld W[olverton]. Uproarious Beggar my N.[4] in evg.

To Sir W. V. HARCOURT, M.P., 7 August 1886. MS Harcourt dep. 10, f. 123.

I have had a note from Morley on his conversation with you. Would you mind being at the House on Monday at a quarter to two? Not later: earlier if you think necessary. But my purpose would not require much time: and I desire to get sworn, and be out of the House *before* 2.30 in order to keep an engagement in the country. Silence will mean *yes*.

8. 7 S. Trin.

Ch mg & house Ch aft. Wrote to Mrs Stume—and minutes. Saw Sir J. Carmichael—Sir R. Welby—Ld W. *cum* H.J.G. Read Synesius[5]—Charlotte Elis. Derry[6]—Angus's Butler.[7]

---

[1] J. Sturgis, 'Wanted: a leader' and E. Dicey, 'The unionists' campaign', *N.C.*, xx. 183, 294 (August 1886).

[2] Need for 'justice to a small party'; *H* 308. 8.

[3] J. Copner, *Celibate worthies* (1885).

[4] 'Neighbour'; the card game.

[5] Perhaps S. H. Boyd, *Select poems of Synesius and Gregory Nazianzen* (1814).

[6] C. E. Tonna, *Derry, a tale* (1886 ed.).

[7] J. Angus, *An analysis of Butler's Analogy* (1882).

9. M. [*Wanborough*][1]

Wrote to The Speaker—Mr A. Morley—Sir D. Currie l. & Tel. Saw Sir W. Harcourt—Mr J. Morley l.l.—H.J.G.—Ld Wolverton. Read Burke's Corresp.—Celibate Worthies. Went to London at noon, to be sworn in & for other business. Then joined C. at Norbiton, & drove to Wanborough, Sir A. West's house dated 1527. Welby came. Whist in evg.

10. Tu.

Wrote to Mrs Paterson—Warden of Bradfield—Mr Carlisle—Mr Knowles—Duke of Argyll. Read Burke's Corresp. III—Partridge on Ireland[2]—The Revolt of Flanders[3]—Duke of Argyll's Speech.[4] Drove to Countess Visconti's to hear Grossmith:[5] very entertaining but less than on the stage. Saw Callingham.[6] Whist in evg. Worked on Irish MS.

11. Wed.

Wrote to Sir W. Harcourt. Worked on Irish MS. Drove to Busbridge & the Heidenhall view: all most beautiful. Whist in evg. Read Burke—Partridge—Memoirs of Nollekens.[7]

To Sir W. V. HARCOURT, M.P., 11 August 1886.   MS Harcourt dep. 10, f. 125.

I shall be most happy to dine with you on Tuesday. On Friday we go to 21 Carlton H. Terrace. I have not yet fixed any hour for arriving but if you wish to make any appointment I can keep it. As regards your table Arnold Morley was the only person who had occurred to me—I understood you had intended Whitbread and Illingworth.

Acton has invited me to go with him to Munich and Tegernsee on Monday week—if I can pluck up my courage I am inclined to do this, should there be no serious issue pending.

I interpret Randolph's excuse to the Lord Mayor as meaning that he does not intend to appear in the character of second fiddle to Lord Salisbury or to any body any where. Morley promised a visit here today, but he has not appeared.

12. Th.

Wrote to Col. Nolan. Saw J. Morley—A. Morley. Worked on MS. Read Burke—Nollekens—Dillon on Irish Finance[8]—Hancock on do.[9] Whist in evg. Tree planting & just touched the axe. Another lovely drive.

[1] By Guildford; for the visit, see West, *Recollections*, ii. 309.
[2] J. A. Partridge, *The making of the Irish nation: and the first-fruits of federation* (1886).
[3] [E. Robinson], *The revolt of Flanders* (1848); verse drama.
[4] No report found of a recent speech.
[5] George *Grossmith, 1847–1912; author of *The diary of a nobody*; created many of Gilbert and Sullivan's 'patter' roles; well-known for private cabarets.
[6] The bailiff; West, *Recollections*, ii. 310.
[7] J. T. Smith, *Nollekens and his times*, 2v. (1828).
[8] No separate title found; perhaps one of Dillon's articles in *United Ireland* on the Govt. of Ireland Bill; see F. S. L. Lyons, *John Dillon* (1968), 79.
[9] W. N. Hancock, *Local government and taxation in Ireland* (1875).

13. Fr. [London]

Wrote to Miss Thomson—Ld Spencer—Mr Morley—W.H.G. Worked on MS. Read Burke finished III—Nollekens Memoirs—Scottish Review.[1] 3½-7. Drive to Esher & rail to London. Saw Sir W. Harcourt—C. Lyttelton & Sp. Lyttelton. Tired, without reason?

14. Sat

Wrote to Sir A. Woods—Sir H. Ponsonby—E. Lynchner—J. Robinson—Mr Gillman[2]—Mr Rawlins—Miss Molesworth—A. Gardner—Mr Roundell—J. Ross—Mr Gellatly[3]—Mr Elton.[4] Much time spent in putting to order. Worked on MS. Read Adolphus Vol VI[5]—Conder's Ireland(!!)[6]

15. 8 S. Trin.

Church piecemeal in mg (All Saints & St Philip's)—Guards evg. Saw Mr Mac-Coll—Lord Acton, who dined: Wrote to Garter [sic] & copied it out. Read Sympneumata[7]—Scottish Rev. 'A Mesmerist'[8]—Synesias (finished).

16. M.

Wrote to W.H.G.—Mr T.B. Potter MP—E.W. Hamilton—Mr A. Morley—W.H.G.—Mr Courtier. Worked on MS. flogging myself up to the mark. Read Adolphus Hist. VII—Thiers Rev. Francaise.[9] Saw Mr MacColl—Mr Cooke.[10]

17. Tu.

Wrote to Ld R. Gower—Rev. Mr Benham—Mr Whitbread—Ld Hartington. Worked again on MS. Saw Ld Granville—Mr A. Morley—Ld Acton—Sir W. Harcourt—Mr J. Morley. Read Thiers Hist Rev. Dined at Sir W. Harcourt's. Restated my position as to the Leadership: & touched on the situation for the 19th.

To LORD HARTINGTON, M.P., 17 August 1886.   Add MS 44148, f. 241.

Having had occasion to refer to a speech made by you at Sheffield on the 29th of June I find the Times reports you to have said that when you were Secretary for Ireland (1) you did not receive from the Government much assistance in carrying forward a Bill for County Government in Ireland. (2) You were perhaps *more a Home Ruler than I was*; for you prepared a measure to dispatch local business in Ireland through the system of

---

[1] 'Home rule for Scotland', *Scottish Review*, viii. 1 (July 1886).
[2] Harry Gillman, U.S. consul in Jerusalem; on hymn translation; Hawn P.
[3] William Gellatly, Dundee merchant and home ruler; Hawn P.
[4] Probably Charles Isaac Elton, 1839-1900; Q.C. and tory M.P. 1884-5, 1886-92.
[5] J. Adolphus, *The history of England, from the accession to the decease of George III*, 7v. (1840-5).
[6] A. Conder, *The discontent of Ireland* (1886); concessions made in Gladstone's land acts 'led to the present state of discord and anarchy'.
[7] Untraced religious work (read on Sundays).
[8] Turgeniev's short story in *Scottish Review*, viii. 61 (July 1886).
[9] See 13 Mar. 43.
[10] Of Murray's, publishing the pamphlet. See 13 Feb. 75.

provisional orders, but you were not able to obtain the attention of your colleagues in the measure.[1]

On the first of these points, I believe that, at a time when the Government was greatly weakened, we failed to carry many measures & among them a County Government bill for Ireland. But as you complain of a want of support from the Government for that measure, I would ask you whether or where you prepared for that support and failed to obtain it? and whether you believe that the measure might have been carried but for the want of support which you sought and failed to obtain.

As regards the second, my memory has no trace of your measure and I am therefore led to ask you whether and when you brought it before the Cabinet, or before myself?[2]

18. Wed.

Wrote to Mr Dankin—Mr Campbell—Mrs Bolton. Saw Mr A. Morley—Mr Cooke—Mr Primrose—Sir J. Carmichael—Mr Cooke—Ld Acton—Ld Thring. Read Thiers Rev. Française. Entertained by Ld Acton at the Quadrant: we took a purely flying view of the Exhibition. The spectacle was on the whole very interesting. Drive with C.

19. Th.

Wrote to C.T. Gladstone—Mr Taylor Innes—Rev. N. Hall—Mr Bunting—Rev. Mr Hales—Ld Hartington—Mr J. Norton—Ld Aberdeen—Murray—Mr Noble. 11–12¼. Meeting at Lord Granville's on the Speech. 4½–8½. H. of C. Spoke on the Speech. Astonished at the announcements by the Govt, both as to time & matter.[3] Six to dinner. Drive with C. Worked on proofs. Read Thiers.

20. Fr.

Wrote to Mad. Novikoff—Town Clerk of Cork—Mr Carlisle—Mr Waters—Rev. S.E.G.—and. . . . H of C. 4¾–7¾.[4] Drive with C. Worked much on proofs. Saw Sir W. Harcourt—Mr Morley—H.J.G.—Ld Spencer *cum* Ld Kimberley—Sir W.H. *cum* Mr Morley—Mr Cooke. Read Mabelan on H.R.[5]

21. Sat. [*Coopers, Chislehurst*]

Wrote to Mr Pritchard—C. Ryan—Messrs Murray—Neate (B.P.)—Mr F.J. Thomas—W.H.G.—Mr J. Ireland—Mrs Th.—Mr A. Wilson—& minutes. 3.50 To Coopers.[6] Saw Mr Cooke—HJG—Mr A. Morley—Sir J. Lacaita—Sir J. Carmichael. Drive at Coopers. Saw the Sydneys. Made a short speech in the evening. Corr. Revises & wrote P.S. for pamphlet. Read Mabelan—Thiers Hist. Rev. Franc.

[1] *T.T.*, 29 June 1886, 5f.

[2] Materials—no longer extant—sent by Hartington, 21 August, Add MS 44148, f. 245.

[3] *H* 308. 83, 103: he complained at absence of substance in the Speech.

[4] *H* 308. 170.

[5] David Mabelan had sent his *Home rule and Imperial unity. An argument for the Gladstone-Morley scheme* (1886).

[6] House near Chislehurst of Charles Morley, 1847-1917; br. of A.; liberal M.P. 1895-1906. See *D.N.*, 23 August 1886, 4e, 5g.

22. 9 S. Trin.

Parish Ch mg & evg. Saw Mr Murray (Rev).[1] Wrote to Messrs Murray. Read
Sympneumata—La Ch. C. Romana e la Ch. GrecoRussa[2]—Catm of Oriental
Ch.[3]

23. M. [London]

Wrote to Sir T. Acland—Ld Hartington—Sir A. Woods—Mr Mabelan. Reached
London at 11. H of C. 4½-8.[4] Consultation on the Debate. Saw Scotts—Mr
Cooke—H.J.G.—Ld Acton. Read Thiers Hist.—Sympneumata finished—Grat-
tan's Address on Retirement[5]—Mabelan on H.R. (finished).

To Sir T. D. ACLAND, 23 August 1886.   Bodley Ms Eng. lett. d. 89, f. 62.

I am going to bring out a pamphlet which will meet one or two of the chief points in
your letter.[6]

I am sanguine, that is I entertain no doubt as to the upshot. But I dare not predict any
thing intermediate. Nor dare I say whether the grant will be widened, perhaps unduly
widened, as the consequence of delay.

The strange proposals of the Government complicate the question and may postpone
the issue: or may hasten it.

Nationality supplies the greatest strength, I think, to the Irish demand: *because* 1. It *was*
self-governed (1782-1800). 2. The selfGovernment was stolen from it—by fraud and
force. 3. It has never in any way condoned the crime. *Nullum tempus occuruit populo.*

24. Tu.

Wrote to Ld Kimberley—Sir C. Forster—Press Assocn—Watsons—Central
News. H of C. 4½-7¾. Spoke 50 m.[7] Shopping: arrangements for departure. Saw
Mr Bryce—H.J.G.—Mr T.P. O'Connor—Sir C. Russell—Sir C. Tennant. Dined at
Sir C. Forster's. Read Thiers, finished Vol I.

25. Wed. [Travelling]

Wrote to Mr Thomas. Saw H.J.G.—Ld Granville—Mr Morley—Mr A. Morley—
Sir J. Carmichael—Miss Irby. Off at 11. Good passage 85 min. Dined at Brussels
& walked in the Garden. Cultivation & crops appeared to me better than on the
English side. We travelled all night. Cologne 5.30 A.M. Read Inferno I.II—
Hervé, Crise Irlandaise[8]—The Undiscovered Country.[9]

26. Th. [Frankfurt]

Wrote to C.G. To Frankfort at 11¼. We are now in great heat. Saw British Consul—Ld Wolverton. Entertained to dinner in the Palmgarten by Madame

[1] F. H. Murray, rector of Chislehurst; see 19 Nov. 73.   [2] Not found.
[3] Perhaps *Catéchisme détaillé de l'église catholique Orthodoxe d'Orient* (1851).
[4] Queen's Speech; *H* 308. 295.
[5] H. Grattan, 'Address to his fellow citizens' (1797).
[6] Untraced. See 26 July 86.
[7] Irish land; in dispute with the Speaker; *H* 308. 413.
[8] E. Hervé, *La crise Irlandaise* (1885).
[9] By W. D. Howells, 2v. (1882).

Oppenheimer[1] who has built almost a palace. Drove in the town, saw the Cathedral: the electric Railway at work. Off at ten.

27. Fr. [Tegernsee]

Reached Munich about 8. Hospitably met by the brothers in law.[2] We got an hour in the Pinakothek, interesting though of the second class. 11–2. To Tegernsee.[3] Much conversation with Dr Döllinger. Read yesterday and today Dante Inferno—The undiscovered country—Hervé, Crise Irlandaise.[4]

28. Sat.

Wrote to C.G. Helen's birthday: may all blessings crown her. It is already shown to be a most valuable life. Conversation as yesterday. Walk with the party. Read Dante Inf.—Hervé Crise Irlandaise—Undiscovered Land (finished).

29. 10 S. Trin.

H. & I. had the morning prayers. Wrote to W.H.G. Walk. Read Dante—Lupton's St John Damasc.[5]—Revue Theologique on Assumption of Moses[6]—Versions of Scripture.

30. M.

Wrote to Herbert G. Saw Baron Mohrashar[7]—Madame Adlerberg[8]—Dr Döllinger: who gratified me much by his view of my pamphlet. Read Dante—Hervé Crise Irlandaise—Lupton's St John Dam.

31. Tu.

Wrote to Mr Cooke. Photographed wholesale. Saw Lehnbach who shames me by promising a picture.[9] Read Malmento[10]—Monro on Hom. Birthplace[11]—Hist. Rev. on Greville Papers[12] (a misplaced[)]—Dante—St John. Damasc. Conversations daily with Acton & 'the Professor'.

Wed. Sept. One. 1886.

Read Dante—Augier Les Effrontés[13]—Malmonti's Venezia—Acton on German Historians.[14] Walk with A. & Dr D. Heat strong & steady, not immoderate.

---

[1] Wife of Charles Oppenheimer, British consul in Frankfurt.   [2] i.e. Acton and Arco-Valley.
[3] Döllinger's house in Bavaria; see 17 Sept. 79.   [4] See 25 Aug. 86.
[5] By J. H. Lupton (1882).   [6] Untraced.
[7] Sic; probably a mis-spelling; unidentified.
[8] Probably a relative of Count N. Adlerberg of the Russian embassy.
[9] Double portrait of Gladstone and Döllinger, dated September 1886, in Städtische Galerie in Lenbachhaus, Munich.
[10] P. G. Molmenti, La Dogaressa di Venezia (1884).
[11] D. B. Monro's article in E.H.R., i (1886); notes in Add MS 44772, f. 189.
[12] Anon. 'Notes' in E.H.R., i. 105 (1886).
[13] G. V. E. Augier, Les Effrontés. Comédie en cinq actes (1861).
[14] The first article in the first E.H.R., i. 7 (January 1886).

2. Th.

Read Augier—Lupton's St John Damasc.—Dante—Augier Effrontés—Malmonti. Walk with A. & the Professor. The Königsmark with guests in party dined.

3. Fr.

Wrote to Mr Morley—Herr Krüger—C.G. Walk with Ld A. & Dr D. Read Dante (& am making a little *conspectus*)—Daniel Rochat[1]—St John Damascus (finished)—Malmonti's Venice.

4. Sat.

Walk with Dr D. & a good conversation on the Olympian system. Also with F. Gower, who arrived with a party. Read Didon on Marriage[2]—Guyau in Rev. des 2 Mondes[3]—Dante—Sardou, Daniel Rochat—Malmonti. 11 at dinner.

5. 11 S. Trin.

Helen read the prayers as last S. Wrote to Lucy Cavendish—Messrs Murray—C.G. Conversation with F. Leveson [Gower]—Ld Acton. Read Dante—Rev. des 2 Mondes on Voltaire & Rousseau (Brunetière)[4]—Brown's Venerable Bede[5]—Didon on Marriage—Langen's St John of Damascus.[6]

6. M.

Wrote to Sir W. Harcourt—Messrs Murray. Read Dante—De Noiresterres on Voltaire[7]—Malmonti—Augier Fils du Giboyer.[8] Walk with Dr D. and Lord A. It is wonderful to hear them pour forth their learning in two great streams.

To Sir W. V. HARCOURT, M.P., 6 September 1886.[9]　　　MS Harcourt dep. 10, f. 127.
'*Secret*'.

I am extremely vexed at the report in Friday's Times of the Speakers encounter with you.[10] You seem to have behaved with perfect dignity but I think he committed the gravest error I can remember ever to have been committed in the Chair. The great difficulties of his office are not to be dissembled, & doubtless he was vexed at the very great prolongation of the debates on the Address. But the Government have made themselves responsible for the course the discussions have taken, by the unprecedented step of declaring their meditated policy on the occasion. What could be more legitimate than when Randolph's speech was directly relevant to the amendment—, and where it contained a direct reference to the Orange men of 1798 as a model, you should discuss their

[1] By V. Sardou (1880); another comedy.
[2] H. L. Didon, *Indissolubilité et divorce* (1880).
[3] On evolution; *Revue des Deux Mondes*, lxxvii (September 1886).
[4] *Revue des Deux Mondes*, lxxvii (July 1886).
[5] G. F. Browne, *The venerable Bede* (1879).
[6] J. Langen, *Johannes von Damaskus* (1879).
[7] G. Le Brisoys Desnoiresterres, *Iconographie Voltairienne* (1879).
[8] Another comedy by G. V. E. Augier (1861).
[9] Not sent until next day.
[10] Speaker prevented Harcourt from discussing Orangemen's history *re* the Belfast riots; *T.T.*, 3 September 1886, 5e.

conduct: & this even if he had been an ordinary member, much more then when you were canvassing the conduct of a Minister. You have not suffered but the reverse: it is Peel who has suffered, for evidently a shock has been given by the proceeding and it will be difficult to get rid of the consequences. I am very sorry for it inasmuch as he is a man of excellent qualities and had done very well in a most difficult post. I was not however, from observation in the last Parliament without fears of him in the Irish business, & it was on this account that in seconding him I adopted a method which I thought might help to place him on his guard in Irish matters.

Your speech seemed to me admirable, and indeed I am very well satisfied with all that has met my eye. I find some reference made to words of yours on the Land question (which however I have not seen) as if they varied somewhat from the supposed opinions of others among us, but I daresay it is all straight.

My absence I think has been useful. Not to vote on these amendments would have been inconvenient in my case, and to vote on them would have been more inconvenient. It has been most wise not to collide with the Dissentient Liberals (whom I cannot call Unionists), but the position taken by H. & C. & apparently agreed to by the followers is such that matters cannot last long after the real meeting of Parliament without further developments in one sense or another. Only one pure lie has been invented about me, as far as I know, since I came away; that about going to Ireland. I leave such things to Randolph and Iddesleigh. And one stupid error of a pressman about Prince Alexander. He grossly misunderstood what I said.

The prospects in the Balkan [*sic*] are bad. I have heard a curious & ⟨apparently⟩ I am assured true account of the Empress's hatred of Alexander. It is said to be that his father was the pander between Alexander II & his mistress, & gave the Battenbergs residence for the purpose: the present Czar siding strongly with his mother. This of course does not justify.

7. *Tu.*

Wrote to Sir W. Harcourt and Messrs Cook. Expn to Schiersee. Drive, & walk back: mostly with Dr D. We conversed on comparison between Hebrews & Homeric Greeks: & other subjects. Read Dante—Desnoiresterres on V.—Augier (finished).

To Sir W. V. HARCOURT, M.P., 7 September 1886.   MS Harcourt dep. 10, f. 130.
'*Private*'.

I did not send off the accompanying letter yesterday as I felt I had a (lady's) post script to add.

On considering Parnell's three proposals[1]—leaseholders, revision of judicial rents, stay of ejectment on depositing 75 per cent—I do not see my way as to any of them. The third is the pinching point but (as I read it) it seems like a permission to the Irish people to deduct 75 per Cent from their rents. At the same time I feel, more and more, that the *appointment of a Commission to inquire into rents is in itself an admission that there is a* prima facie *case for reduction in certain cases*: and that *to allow eviction, in such cases, during the examination of the matter, is totally indefensible*.

Consequently have not the Government, by undertaking to inquire into rents, brought upon themselves a necessity for some enactment, to stay evictions where inability to pay by reason of fall in prices in sufficiently established? Does not this next lead to the propo-

---

[1] Parnell's land bill, whose rejection was followed by the Plan of Campaign; O'Brien, *Parnell*, ii. 160, 169ff.

sition that there ought *now* to be, with a view to such cases, some enactment, on the lines, mainly, of our compensation for Disturbance Bill of 1880?

I do not recollect all the conditions laid down in that short Bill, which the House, if I remember right, passed before any inquiry into rents had been determined on. They were very severe, but proof of inability, & of a reasonable disposition to pay, were main ones; and I am not at the moment able to see why there might not, & whether there should not, be such an enactment now.

Now for practical questions. 1. Ought not Morley, ⟨with⟩ whom I beg you to see as soon as convenient in this matter, to communicate with Parnell respecting his intended Bill? 2. It seems likely that as regards this third point of eviction they might agree (if my underlined proposition is admitted). 3. Is it not a question whether, EVEN if Parnell did not agree to frame his Bill accordingly, we ought not to vote *for a second reading*, with a view to amending it in this sense? 4. Should matters reach such a point I am of course ready to come back, & think I ought to do it. 5. I do not however suppose the question could well come to issue before (say) Monday week?

8. *Wed.*

Wrote to Sir W. Harcourt—Herbert G.—C.G.—and [blank.] Read Dante—Von Strauss, Essays[1]—Le Monde où on s'Ennuye[2]—and [blank.]

9. *Th.*

Wrote to Mr Drummond—Br Consul. Wrote on Olympian Relig.[3] Read Dante—Von Strauss, Essays—Legge, Chinese Religions[4]—Dumas, Ami des Femmes[5]—Scherer, Homeric Question!![6]—Voltaire et Rousseau.

10. *Fr.*

Wrote to Sir W. Harcourt—l. and tel. Received the Parnell Bill[7] in MS. I am best out of the way. Drive with Ld A & Dr D. Conversation with him. Read Dante (finished Inferno)—Von Strauss Essays—Voltaire et Rousseau. Packed & settled for departure. Farewell conversation with Dr Döllinger in evg. He was most kind & affectionate.

To Sir W. V. HARCOURT, M.P., 10 September 1886.   MS Harcourt dep. 10, f. 132.

'*Private*'.

(With reference to my letter of Tuesday and telegram of today) I received this morning through Prof. Stuart in MS. the clauses of Parnell's Bill; and I find that the clause for staying proceedings on ejectment is founded not on the fact that the Crown has appointed a commission of inquiry, but on the enactment he proposes for a general reopening of judicial rents. This is a totally different basis from what I had contemplated. I am of course in

[1] V. F. von Strauss und Torney, *Essays zur allgemeinen Religions wissenschaft* (1879).
[2] Comedy by E. Pailleron (1881).
[3] Recommencement of work on this; various articles in 1887.
[4] J. Legge, *The religions of China* (1880).
[5] By A. Dumas, *fils* (1864).
[6] Perhaps comments on Homer and German literature in W. Scherer, ed. F. Max Müller, *A history of German literature*, 2v. (1886).
[7] See 20 Sept. 86.

a special position with reference to the Land Act of 1881 and I have never committed myself to reopening of any of its provisions. The question is a different one for Parnell who never accepted it as a settlement, and who is perfectly free. Our independent friends generally are free also. No one is so bound as I am. I do not know what you or Morley may be disposed to do. But I think myself best out of the way on the discussion of such a Bill as Parnell's. For I do not wish to cut across his path, unless on some great question of ⟨policy⟩ principle. He is perfectly justified in availing himself of the admission made by the Government in respect of rents; an admission which we have always avoided, and of which they will I think find the consequences to be very formidable. Adhering in principle to the policy of our Bills, I do not wish to be charged with this new and very formidable subject. As we have an Irish policy which enabled us to pass it by, I think that any of us may claim to stand upon that policy, and need not, unless he thinks proper, enter upon the adjustment of another policy, that of our opponents, different from ours at every point, and strangely called by Hicks Beach a sober one.

My idea of an enactment would have been to the effect that whereas H.M. had been pleased to issue a Commission of Inquiry into judicial rents *therefore* provision should be made for staying proceedings on ejectment in respect of such rents, where unpaid through an inability to pay proved to the satisfaction of the Court.

Will you cause my thanks to be given to Professor Stuart, and say to him, or through him to Parnell, as much as you think needful & proper to be said. I shall think no more of intervening, unless I can do it on the principle, described in my letter of the 7th. We go to St Martin tomorrow. Please let Morley see this.

[P.S.] I am well satisfied thus far with the Govt. about Bulgaria.

11. Sat. [St. Martin]

4 A.M.–9 P.M. Journey to Munich (where we staid five hours) Simbach and St Martin.[1] We were received with singular kindness. At M., long sitting to Lehnbach, & visited the National Museum. Read assiduously Victor Hugo's Histoire d'un Crime.[2] Charming band at & after supper.

12. 11 S. Trin.

H. read our prayers. Wrote to Messrs Murray—Messrs Cook (for tickets)—C.G. Read (very curious) Walsh's Four Letters[3]—Loiseleur, Molière[4]—Nouv. Contr.— Venerable Bede—Progrès Indefini, Thornissen.[5] Walk in evg with the party.

13. M.

Wrote to Cooks Tel.—Sir W. Harcourt l. and Tel.—Went to the Premonstratensian Monastery. Found the *Prelat* very courteous & his German audible even to me. Read Histoire d'un Crime (finished I)—La Mare au Diable.[6] Walk with Acton: conversation on Father Walsh.

---

[1] The castle of Count Arco-Valley, Acton's br. in law, in Upper Austria, 8 miles from Ried; see 17 Sept. 79.

[2] Hugo's savage polemic on the *coup d'état* of 1852; published 1877.

[3] Peter Walsh, *Four letters on several subjects to persons of quality*, n.d.; notes in Add MS 44792, f. 137; no copy found; Walsh was an Irish franciscan staying with Acton.

[4] J. Loiseleur, *Les points obscurs de la vie de Molière* (1877).

[5] J. J. Thornissen, *Quelques considérations sur la théorie du progrès indefini* (1860).

[6] By Georges Sand (1846).

To Sir W. V. HARCOURT, M.P., 13 September 1886.   MS Harcourt dep. 10, f. 134.

Your letter & Morley's letters of the 10th[1] reached me this morning, your telegram yesterday: many thanks for all. I observe, that the Bill has been altered and I quite agree that there seems to be a case for supporting the second reading, though I propose entirely to avoid any committal to reopen the Land question except as the consequence of the appointment of a Commission.

Now as to time, about which you are naturally anxious. Observing that the terms of the Bill were not settled before post on Saturday I feel great doubts whether it can be circulated so soon as tomorrow and I do not think it possible for the Govt. to force the second reading on Thursday or even on Friday. It will be a new Bill and not the Bill, mainly, which P. had announced in moving the introduction. The Govt. are masters of the situation simply so far as regards setting aside Supply—when Supply is over Parnell becomes master and can choose his day when the Appropriation Bill is going through its stages. It would surprise me less, all circs. considered, if the day were after Monday, than if before it. However, a telegram on Wednesday might in case of need bring me to London on Friday morning. It would be a long story on paper but there is reason for my staying here until Friday unless some positive reason forbids—I will explain when we meet.

I hope the Speaker will by future care efface the memory of his sad blunder in your case. A second such case would make his position untenable. Any crisis in the Chair would be lamentable & that not only on account of his own high character and good conduct. Any successor would take the Chair under most difficult circumstances, and its authority would be shaken. A liberty of occasional mistake is needful for most men, and not least for the Speaker, though in his case it is most inconvenient. Will you kindly let Morley see this. I telegraphed to you this morning 'come for 20th letter follows'.

14. Tu.

We drove to see the new Prison. Much conversation with Ld Acton. Finished La Mare au Diable. The Appx. as curious as the tale is charming. Read Thornissen—and L'Ancienne France.[2]

15. Wed. [Gmunden]

Wrote to M. Thomson—H. Seymour—C.G.—Wms & Norgate—Mr Green. Read Daudet's Letters[3]—L'Ancienne France—Life of Lytton Vol. I.[4] Off at 1.30 to Gmunden by broken rail journey. Hotel Bellevue.[5] Evening wild. The lake very beautiful: its banks the resort of Count Chambord & other great folks.

16. Th. [St. Martin]

To Ischl by steam & rail: to Halstatt Lake by road. Day indifferent but the scenery too beautiful to be spoiled. Hotel Kaiserin Elis. good: under the Mayor. Examined shop windows. Back to St Martin by Rail. Met Lady Lothian & Lady Brownlow at I. Read Lytton—Hist. d'un Jeune Homme Pauvre[6]—and Sapho.

---

[1] Harcourt's letter of 7 September on Parnell's bill; Add MS 44200, f. 162.
[2] *L'Ancienne France; l'industrie et de l'art decoratif* (1887 1st traced ed.).
[3] A. Daudet, *Lettres de mon moulin* (1869).
[4] E. R. B., Lord Lytton, *The life . . . of Edward Bulwer, Lord Lytton* (1885).
[5] First class hotel, on Traunsee.
[6] O. Feuillet, *Le roman d'un jeune homme pauvre* (1858).

17. Friday [Pulsau]

Wrote to Bp Strossmayer—& M. Dorfuisth[1] in French: also to Mr A. Morley. Read Hist. d'un J.H. Pauvre. Packing & preparations. Walk in the woods. Olympian conversation with Acton. Farewell to this most kind house. Off at 8.30 PM to and by Pulsau.

18. Sat. [Travelling]

Journey continued without intermission by Mainz (change) Cöln (change & reregistry) Brussels, to Calais. Read Cooke's Third Voyage, ill-edited by Mr Haweis.[2]

19. 13 S. Trin. [London]

Ch. St James's mg with H.C.—St And. Wells St aft. Wrote to C.G. l. & tel.—Wms & Norgate—Mr T. Hall[3]—Mr Greensmith—Mr Vernon—Mr W. Rathbone—Mr Tegeman. Saw Sir W. Harcourt—Mr Marjoribanks—Ld Granville—Ld C. Bruce—Mr Richmond. Read Life of Liszt[4]—Young on Genesis[5]—Chautaugua movement.[6] Worked off some of the chaotic mass which awaited me.

20. M.

Wrote to J. Bettany—Pres. Geneva League[7]—C.G.—Ed. Torquay Times[8]— Euston Station Master—Sir G. Grey—Ed. D. News. Dined at Sir W. Harcourt's. Saw Sir J. Lacaita—Mr Murray—A. Morley—J. Morley—Conclave at Granville's— Mr Childers. H. of C. $4\frac{1}{4}$-$7\frac{1}{2}$ and $9\frac{3}{4}$-$12\frac{1}{2}$. Spoke at some length on the Parnell Bill.[9]

21. Tu.

Wrote to Lord Acton—Messrs Longbourne[10]—C.G.—Mr D. Campbell—E. Yates—Mr Emmanuel—T. Dix—Mr Fitzgerald—J. Murray—and Mr J.M. Jones.[11] Dined with Mrs Peel. Saw Sir J. Carmichael—Ld Wolverton—Mr Duff—Mr A. Morley—Scotts—Ld Hartington (to whom I told my mind). H of C. $4\frac{1}{2}$-8 and 10-$2\frac{1}{2}$. Voted in 202:297: an important *preliminary* division.[12] Read [blank.]

---

[1] Not further identified.

[2] *The third and last voyage of Captain Cook*, ed. H. R. Haweis (1886).

[3] Accepting hon. presidency of Leith Liberal Club; *T.T.*, 23 September 1886, 10c.

[4] Perhaps that by L. Nohl (1882).

[5] B. C. Young, *Modern discoveries of science anticipated by the Bible* (1886).

[6] *The Chautauqua literary and scientific circle* (1885).

[7] Business untraced. Charles Lemonnier of the International League of Peace and Liberty, based in Geneva; see F. H. Hinsley, *Power and the pursuit of peace* (1963), 120, 122.

[8] Thanking it for its historical articles on Ireland, *Torquay Times*, 24 September 1886, 5a.

[9] Parnell's Tenant Relief Bill (copy at Add MS 44633, f. 142); *H* 309. 1044.

[10] London solicitors; business untraced.

[11] To J. Morgan Jones, expecting a 'new development in the political life of Wales', but reluctant to take part at this stage; *T.T.*, 28 September 1886, 8d.

[12] For Parnell's bill; *H* 309. 1247.

To Sir W. V. HARCOURT, M.P., 21 September 1886.   MS Harcourt dep. 10, f. 136.

Overleaf is what I said on Tuesday the 24th. [August]. Hartington says he never read that part of my speech—but only what related to Parnell's amendment. Use it or not precisely as you think proper, as it *may suit or not* the general tenour. I have no wish in the matter.

22. Wed. [Hawarden]

Wrote to Agnes—Town Clerk of Limerick—Mr Heap[1]—Mr Armstrong—Mr Kelly—Mr D.C. Thomson—Robn & Nichn. 1¼-7. to Hawarden: all going well there thank God. Saw E. Hamilton—Sir J. Carmichael—Mr A. Morley—Herbert J.G. Read Memoirs of Baron Trenck[2]—Hist. d'un Jeune H. Pauvre. And made a beginning with the chaos here.

23. Th.

Ch. 8¼ A.M. and Harvest Home Service Evg. Wrote to The Queen—Mr Bowden—Mr Salkeld—Mr Thomas—Mr Greene—Mr Drewe—T. Clerk Waterford—Dr Swartnout[3]—Manchr Examr Tel. 1. Heavy work unpacking many hundreds of volumes. Drive with C. Read (finished) Feuillet's Jeune Homme Pauvre. Saw Mr Linklater.

24. Fr.

Ch. 8½ A.M. Wrote to Rev. Mr Dunkerley—Ld Brabazon—Mr Ayres—Mr Thorndike Rice—Mr Fryer. Worked much on books. Visited the new Coal Pit with Herbert. Read Scotch Modesty displays[4]—Le Flaix on Irish question[5]—Fermory on Wolfe Tone[6]—Mitchells Hist. Ireland.[7] Examined with S.E.G. the candidatures for St Thomas Toxteth.[8]

25. Sat.

Ch. 8¼ A.M. Wrote to Central News Tel.—Town Clerk Limerick—[J.]B. Pond (London) Tel.—Mr P. Kelly—Mr F. Hastings—Mr J. Westell—Mr H. Hart[9]—Mr Dawson Rogers[10]—Mr A. Gardner—Mrs Wickham. Worked on papers & books: expanding upstairs. Saw Dr Doby[11] who reports favourably though the

---

[1] C. Heap sent his work on existence; Hawn P.

[2] *Memoirs of Frederick Baron Trenck* (tr. 1878).

[3] Reading uncertain; perhaps Swartoret.

[4] *Sic*; untraced.

[5] E. Fournier de Flaix, *L'indépendance politique et agraire de l'Irlande* (1886).

[6] P. R. Fermoy [i.e. R. Johnson], *A commentary on the memoirs of T. Wolfe Tone* (1828).

[7] J. Mitchel, *The history of Ireland*, 2v. (1869); Ulster protestant, but an Irish nationalist.

[8] On S. E. Gladstone's advice, Gladstone replaced Dunkerley, promoted to a rectory (see 12 Jan. 82), by John Stephenson, previously an S.P.G. missionary in India.

[9] Horace Hart of the Oxford University Press (compiler of Hart's *Rules* (1883)) had sent copy of Gladstone's Class List in 1831; Add MS 44499, f. 51.

[10] Edmund Dawson Rogers (1823–1910, liberal and manager of National Press Agency) had requested permission to print 200,000 copies of *The Irish question*; Hawn P. He asked for 'some new features' to encourage sales: see 13 Oct. 86.

[11] M. M. Dobie of Chester, see 11 Apr. 82; attended Mary Drew during her dangerous illness.

temperature is higher than could be wished and I now at length fully know that an extreme danger is being followed by an anxious recovery. Read Fermoy on Tone—Etruria Capta—The invisible Empire.[1]

26. 14 S. Trin.

Ch. 11 A.M. and 6½ P.M. Wrote to Duke of Buccleuch—Abbot of Reichersberg[2]—Mr Hazzopulo—Mr J. Martin—Ed. Court Journal. Dear Mary a *thought* better. Read Sermon on Chancy—Vie et ouvrages de B. Pascal[3]—Rhymed French Evangile.[4]

27. M.

Wrote to T. Clerk Waterford[5]—Ld Houghton—Mr Martineau—Mr Digby—Mr Heywood. Walk with Mr Dunkerley & conversation on Lpool & St Thomas matters. Also consultation in evg with Mr D & SEG on the appointment. Read Mitchell's Hist Ireland—Pompadour Memoirs[6]—Mary Frampton Journal[7]—and began my work (or resumed it) on the Realien of Homer. Worked on books & papers.

28. Tu.

Ch. 8½ A.M. Wrote to Mrs Benstead—Vicar of Wookey[8]—Rev. Mr Gore—Town Clerk of Cork—Mr Green—Chairman of B.I.R.—Mr Hawksford—Mr Gill MP.[9]—Messrs Wallis—Mr B. Young. Further conversation with Mr D. an admirable man. Once more I took the axe & we began on a very large Sp. chestnut. Read Laird on the Proem[10]—Mitchell's Hist. Ireland—Pompadour's Memoirs—Irish Tourist of 1775.[11]

29. Wed St Mich.

Ch. 8½ A.M. with H.C. Wrote to Rev. Mr Williamson—A. Macdougall[12]—Mr P. Still[13]—Ed. Blackwood[14]—Mr B. Dobell—Mayor of Clonmel. Saw Dear Mary: with less mark of illness than I had anticipated. Dr Griffith[15] cheers us. Wood-

---

[1] Neither traced.
[2] German monastery; correspondence untraced.
[3] One of the many eds. of Pascal.
[4] Untraced.
[5] Various letters to Irish municipal officials, arranging their visit of 4 Oct. 86.
[6] J. Beaujoint, *The secret memoirs of Mme. la Marquise de Pompadour* (1886).
[7] *The journal of Mary Frampton*, ed. H. G. Mundy (1885).
[8] T. T. Holmes.
[9] Henry Joseph Gill, 1836-?; Dublin publisher; home rule M.P. Westmeath 1880-3, Limerick 1885-8.
[10] J. Laird, again no copy found (see 25 July 86).
[11] A. Young, *Tour in Ireland with general observations . . . 1776-79*, 2v. (1780); see 30 Sept. 86.
[12] Of the Scottish N.L.F., thanking him for its manifesto and supporting its inquiry into Scottish home rule; *T.T.*, 2 October 1886, 7d.
[13] Percy Still of Inchbrook, had written on Schiller; Add MS 44499, f. 61.
[14] On Brabourne's article; *T.T.*, 7 October 1886, 11e.
[15] Perhaps Griffith Griffith, physician from Pwlheli.

craft with WHG. Read Mitchell's Hist. Ireland—Brabourne on Ireland[1]—G. Smith on the Election (exceeding heavy)[2]—The Wanderer.[3]

30. Th.

Ch. 8½ A.M. Wrote to Sir H. Ponsonby—Mrs Newcomb—Ld Acton—Mr Harny (BP)—Watsons—Rev. Temple (BP)—K. Bowden—Messrs Courlander—Mr Russell—Surgeon Curran[4]—Mr Whitting—Lawrence (Dublin) Tel.—Burnley Liberals (Tel.)—Walsall (Dora) meeting (Tel.)—Herbert J.G. Worked on books & papers. Worked on Homer Realien. Read Pompadour Memoirs—Tour in Ireland (finished)—Hayward's Letters. Saw Mr Mayhew. Conversation with Herbert (*inter alia*) on the strange American proposal.[5] Woodcraft with W. & H.

Frid. Oct. 1. 1886.

Ch. 8¼ A.M. Wrote to Mr Carlisle l. & B.P.—Col. Morrison—Mr J. Morris—Mr Hyndeman[6]—Mr A. Goddard—Mr Farrington—Mr Brophy—Mrs Bolton B.P.—Major Pond—Miss Tennant. Worked again on books & papers: and was kept at home by constant rain. Worked on Homer. Read Ruskin's Praeterita[7]—Life of Baron Trenck.

2. Sat.

Ch. 8¼ A.M. Wrote to Town Clerk of Cork—J. Watson & Smith—Mr Clode—Mr Fraser Gluck[8] B.P.—Ld Spencer—Mr Paterson—Mr Hogarth—Mr Hopps. Worked on books. Worked on Homer. A little woodcraft. Read The Wanderer—Tyler on Olymp. Theology.[9] Sir A. Clark came in evg: it will still he says be a work of time.

3. 15 S. Trin.

Ch 11 AM & H.C.—and evg. Conversation with Sir A.C. Wrote to Mr Siemens—Mrs Martin—Rev. Mr Wells—Mr Sherlock. Read Wells on Xtn & nonXtn[10]—Cartwright's Diary[11]—and [blank.]

4. M.

Ch. 8¼ A.M. Wrote to Rev. J. Stephenson—Mr R. Williams—Mr C. Tyler—Mr Bunting—Mr C. Field—Edr Blackwood Tel.—Mr W. White—City Press & P.A.

[1] Lord Brabourne, 'Facts and fictions in Irish history', *Blackwood's*, cxl. 419 (October 1886).
[2] In *N.C.*, xx. 305 (September 1886).   [3] See 23 June 86.
[4] Perhaps John James Curran, surgeon in Cork.   [5] See 2 Oct. 86.
[6] H. M. Hyndman (see 12 Mar. 80) sent congratulations 'for pressing on the appointment' of the cttee. on Indian administration; Hawn P.
[7] See 21 June 85.
[8] James Fraser Gluck, curator, Buffalo library, U.S.A., had asked for one of Gladstone's literary MSS; Add MS 44498, f. 220; he sent that of 'Russia and England' (see 14 Feb. 80).
[9] W. S. Tyler, *The theology of the Greek poets* (1867).
[10] J. Wells, *Christ and the heroes of heathendom* (1886).
[11] *The diary of Thomas Cartwright, bishop of Chester* (1843).

Tel. $10\frac{1}{2}$–12. Putting together my materials. 12–2. The function came off, I spoke on the situation $1\frac{1}{4}$ to $1\frac{1}{2}$ hour.[1] 2–$4\frac{1}{4}$. The luncheon (with one toast): then the grounds, the old Castle, coffee, & off. The party (40 to 50) behaved extremely well in all ways. I was however thoroughly tired set up by an hour or two in my armchair. Read The Wanderer—Letters on Ireland.[2]

5.

Ch. $8\frac{1}{2}$ A.M. Wrote to Miss Tennant BP.—Watsons—Mrs Th.—Rev. J.C. Boyce[3]—Visc. Anson—Rev. H. Burton—Rev. Mr Fagan[4]—Messrs Robn & Nichn—Mr Morris. We brought down the unusually tough old Sp. Chesnut. Dear Mary better. May it continue. Saw Mr Ottley. Finished Letters ('Notes') on Ireland. Read Fagan's Art.—and Bachaumont's Anecdotes.[5] What a world!

6. Wed.

Ch. $8\frac{1}{2}$ A.M. Wrote to Courlanders B.P.—Mr Murray—Mr H. Dobell[6]—Mrs Bolton—Mr Bromby—Mr Dawson Rogers—Mr Lecky. Got my first tolerably clear forenoon on Homer. A little work on books. Read Ruskin's Praeterita—M. Wollstonecraft on French Rev.[7]—and the Wanderer.

7. Th.

Ch. $8\frac{1}{2}$ A.M. Wrote to Rev. Mr Blakiston—Mr Cameron—H.N.G.—Mr P.M. Egan—Mrs Jupson—Mr G. Milnes—Mr Hewitson—Mr J. Lawson—Bp of Chester. Worked on Homer. Wrote on Ireland. Read Dr Zerffi on Ireland[8]—Walpole's Hist. Vol. V.[9]—The Wanderer—Ruskin's Praeterita. H. went. Constance[10] came.

8. Fr.

Ch. $8\frac{1}{2}$ A.M. Wrote to Rev. Mr Dunkerley—Ld Granville—Helen G.—Mr Dawson Rogers—Mr J. Allen—Mr S. Walpole—Mr H. Lee—Mrs Bishop—Mr Tilston—Messrs Gillig[11]—Mr H. Room—Hon. Mr Canning—Mr Green—Editors Life of Christison.[12] Worked on Homer (Il. B. VI). Read Life of Christison—Ruskin's Praeterita—finished The Wanderer. Kibbling the big tree with H. Conversation with Dr Doby on Mary's case: it gave much comfort.

[1] *T.T.*, 5 October 1886, 10a.
[2] Perhaps 'Letters from Ireland 1886' in *T.T.*, reprinted 1887.
[3] Nonconformist clergyman.
[4] Perhaps George H. F. Fagan, vicar of Exwick 1885–9.
[5] See 10 Oct. 85.
[6] Henry Dobrell, London solicitor.
[7] M. Wollstonecraft, later Godwin, *An historical and moral view of the origin and progress of the French Revolution*, i (1794).
[8] G. G. Zerffi, 'The Irish question in history' (1886).
[9] S. Walpole, *A history of England from the conclusion of the Great War*, 5v. (1878–86).
[10] J. N. Gladstone's daughter.
[11] C. A. Gillig of Gillig's United States Exchange Co.
[12] *The Life of Sir R. Christison, edited by his sons*, 2v. (1885–6).

9. Sat.

Ch. 8½ A.M. Wrote to Mr Chr. Walley—Mr A. Macleod—Ld Thring—Mr Campion—Mr Carlyle[1]—Mr Whitaker—Mr Brunner[2]—Garter King at Arms—Sir A. Clark Tel. Worked on Homer. Walk with Sir W. Phillimore. Saw Mary: no change to mark. Read Ruskin's Praeterita—M. Wollstonecraft French Rev.

10. 16 S. Trin.

Kept my bed all day for cold. C. read prayers with & for me. Read Bp Cartwright's Diary—Eccl. Documents (Camden)[3]—Obiter Dicta (Via Media)[4]—Von Strauss, Essays. Saw Sir W. Phillimore. Some conversation respecting his Father.

11. M.

Rose between 3 & 4. Wrote Notes on the Palmerston incident of Dec. 1853.[5] Wrote Mr Macmillan—Dr Dillon—Dr Collingwood—Mr Tilston—Dr Sutherland—Mr Lawless[6]—Mrs Bishop. Came down in afternoon rather imprudently to work my correspondence. Read Von Strauss Essays—Wollstonecraft Fr. Rev.—Obiter Dicta.

To A. MacMILLAN, publisher, 11 October 1886.   Add MS 55243, f. 31.

Kindly send, by goods train, to Miss H. Gladstone, Newnham College, Cambridge, 12 Primers of Homer & 8 Homeric Synchronism. I do wish you would get rid of that heavy stock of Synchronism at any price—my royalty going down in proportion.[7] Your account has just reached me, for which thanks.

I am preparing the materials of more Homeric work, but I can hardly say that anything is yet upon the stocks. Olympian Religion is what, with time, I hope to handle fully.

12. Tu.

Bed strictly kept all day: discipline efficient. Read Wollstonecraft—Obiter Dicta (finished).

There is a disposition to grudge as wasted these days. But they afford great opportunities of review. Especially as to politics and my politics are now summed up in the word Ireland, for probing inwardly the intention, to see whether all is truly given over to the Divine will. Conversation with Herbert on his business.

---

[1] Sc. Carlisle; notes on his ed. of Hayward, 10 October, at Add MS 44772, f. 190.

[2] (Sir) John Tomlinson Brunner, 1842-1919; chemical manufacturer; liberal M.P. Northwich 1885-6, 1887-1910; cr. bart. 1895.

[3] Probably N. Pocock, 'Troubles connected with the Prayer Book of 1549', *Camden Society*, 2nd series, xxxvii (1885).

[4] A. Birrell, 'The Via Media' in *Obiter Dicta* (1884).

[5] For Carlisle's ed. of Hayward; Palmerston's resignation (withdrawn) on reform; see 16 Dec. 53ff., Morley, i. 490 and Add MS 44499, f. 82.

[6] Richard Lawless of Kildare had appealed for home rule; Hawn P.

[7] Letter docketed by Macmillan's: 'stock of Homeric Synchronism at July 1, 1886 1329 (1000 being in quires). Sales last year 5 copies.' Gladstone had already suggested a discount on 22 August 1879; Add MS 55243, f. 29. Macmillan replied, 14 October, Add MS 44246, f. 142, gloomy about 'the sale of Homeric Synchronism even at a reduced price doing much'.

13. Wed.

Rose at noon: the cough now subdued. Worked on Addendum for the republication at 1d of my Irish Tract.[1] Wrote to Mr Dawson Rogers—J. Grant—Mrs Bolton—Rev. Mr Jones—Rev. Mr Manley—Rev. Mr Blakiston—Mr Croxden Powell—Mr Richardson—Mr Carlisle—Mr Whitaker—Messrs Hodges—Mr Baird—Mr Shelvey. Read Prof. Barlow's Lecture[2]—M. Wollstonecraft. The Leveson Gowers came.

14. Th.

Unjustly forbidden by C. to go to Church. Wrote to Messrs Watson—Mr Hindley—Mr Caldwell—Messrs Robn & Nicholson—Bp of Liverpool—Rev. Mr Stephenson—Mr Mitchell—Mr Salkeld. Wrote on the Zeus Legend of Il. I & worked on Homer. Read Wollstonecraft—Imbert (M. Antoinette &c.)[3]—Ruskin, Praeterita.

15. Fr.

Church at length resumed. $8\frac{1}{2}$ AM. Wrote to Lady Gladstone—Dean of Wells—Mrs Bolton—Mr Gardner—Mr A. Reid—Mr Dawson Rogers—Mr G. Holt. Worked all the morning on the Olympian sedition. Also on the Realien. Walk with F. Leveson. Conversation on Sir F. Doyle & his book.[4] Read Praeterita—Wollstonecraft (finished). Eight to dinner. Whist.

16. Sat.

Ch. $8\frac{1}{2}$ A.M. Wrote to E.W. Hamilton—Sir A. Gordon—Rev. C. Barnes—Mr R. Monro—Mr D. Tringle—Mr J.E. Wright—Mr Jas Davidson[5]—Mr A.M. Weir.[6] Worked on Homer. Finished Praeterita Vol I. Read Healy on Ireland.[7] Sir A. Clark came: reported well on the whole D.G: in a most lucid & masterly manner.

Today I burned a number of old letters, kept apart, which might in parts have suggested doubt & uneasiness: two of the writers were Mrs Dale and Mrs Davidson:[8] cases of great interest, in qualities as well as attractions certainly belonging to the flower of their sex. I am concerned to have lost sight of them.

---

[1] See 26 July, 25 Sept. 86; the 'addendum' also in *T.T.*, 20 October 1886, 9f.

[2] J. W. Barlow, 'The history of Ireland during the period of parliamentary independence' (1875).

[3] Reading uncertain; perhaps 1st v. of A. L. Imbert de St.-Amand, *Les femmes de Versailles*, 4v. (1885–95).

[4] Sir F. H. Doyle, *Reminiscences and opinions* (1886), with much material on Gladstone's youth, and bad-tempered comments on his liberalism.

[5] Of Greenock; Add MS 44497, f. 192.

[6] Alexander McC. Weir of Nottingham; home ruler b. in Ulster; Hawn P.

[7] T. M. Healy, *A word for Ireland* (1886).

[8] For Mrs Dale, *née* Summerhayes, the courtesan whose portrait Gladstone commissioned, see above, v. lx, 30 July 59 and Matthew, *Gladstone*, 156; Mrs Davidson may be the married name of Miss Cowper, ibid.

17th. 17 S. Trin.

Ch mg & evg. Wrote to Mr D. Fortune[1]–Ld Rosebery–Mr Judges–Mr Farrier. Read Q.R. on N.T. Critm & on Amn Poetry[2]–Origen contr. Celsum[3]–Ratcliffe, Chapter of Nature[4]–Collins, Treatise on do.[5]

18 St Luke. M.

Ch. 8¼ A.M. and H.C. Wrote to Dear Agnes on her birthday. Worked on Homer. Also to Dr Ratcliffe–Mr Rathbone MP–Mrs Th.–Gen. Robertson–Mr Coates–Rev. Mr Rambaud[6]–C. Hindley–Mr Wentworth. Woodcraft with W.H.G. Tea at Milly Glynne's. Read L. Morris Gyeia[7]–Healy on Ireland– Lefevre on Religions.[8]

19. Tu.

Ch. 8¼ A.M. Wrote to Mr E. Hamilton–Mr Carlisle–Dr Furnivall–Mrs Bolton–Messrs Stonehaven–Mr Bithel–Ld Rosebery–Mr Stephenson. Sent to Mrs B.[9] my remarks on a letter of a most singular character sent for perusal. Worked on Homer. Read Grand Trunk Report–Proceedings of Psychical Society[10]–Lefevre on Religions–Morris's Gyeia (finished).

20. Wed.

Ch. 8½ A.M. Wrote to Town Clerk of Cork–Mr Vickers–Mr Hesselby–Mr L. Morris–Mr A. Reader–Mr E.J. Seaton–Mr S. Hay–Dr Madden–R. Cameron– Mr Gillies–Mr Summers MP–Mr Rossiter–Mr J.S. Campbell–Acting Editor PMG.[11] Saw Mary yesterday & today. Dined at the Rectory. Backgammon. Woodcraft with W. & H. Worked on Homer. Read Healy on Ireland (finished)– O'Connells Memoirs.[12]

21. Th.

Ch. 8¼ A.M. Wrote to Mr G.T. Stephenson–Rev. Lawrence–Rev. J.T. Parr– Rev. J. Young–T. Hall[13]–Mr Whitaker–J. Grant. Woodcraft with W. & H. Worked on books & made up gift packets. Worked on Homer. Read O'Connell–and . . . on Cant.[14]

[1] Of the St Rollox Liberal Association, on home rule; *T.T.*, 19 October 1886, 9f.
[2] *Q.R.*, clxiii. 363, 460 (October 1886). [3] *Origen contra Celsum*, ed. G. Selwyn (1860).
[4] C. B. Radcliffe, *A new chapter in the story of nature* (1886).
[5] H. Collins, *Nature as exhibiting the works and goodness of God* (1886).
[6] Probably Edmund Francis Rambaut, episcopalian priest in Dublin.
[7] L. Morris, *Gyeia; a tragedy* (1886).
[8] A. P. E. Lefèvre, *Essais de critique générale. Religions et mythologies comparées* (1871).
[9] Mrs Bolton; see 4 Apr. 82.
[10] *Journal of the Society for Psychical Research*, ii. 408 (October 1886); see 22 Aug. 85n.
[11] Edward Tyas *Cook, probably its para. on his Etonian sculling; *P.M.G.*, 21 October 1886, 7.
[12] D. O'Connell, *A memoir on Ireland native and Saxon. Vol. i: 1172–1660* (1843, only vol. published); see today's comment to unknown correspondent of Cork, in *T.T.*, 22 October 1886, 7f. See to Bryce, 28 Oct. 86.
[13] Greetings to new Leith Liberal Club, *T.T.*, 23 October 1886, 6c.
[14] *The world of Cant* (1881).

22. Fr.

Ch. 8½ A.M. Wrote to Mr E. Hamilton—Mr C. Lacaita—Mr Shirreff—Rev. Mr Fowler—Mr Dickson—Rev. Mr Ashcroft—Mr Hipsley—Mr Bithell. Woodcraft with sons. Worked on Homer. A beginning appeared today of real relief for Mary; confirmed by the days following. Read O'Connells Memoirs and [blank.]

23. Sat.

Ch. 8½ A.M. Wrote to Wms & Norgate. Read O'Connell's Memoir. Worked on Homer. Went out in aft. to cut alders: badly stung in the eyelid by a wasp. This stopped all work: & gave great pain for a while. Saw Burlingham.

24. 18 S. Trin.

Saw the two Doctors. No Church or air allowed. Dictated letter to Acton. Wrote without seeing, to Mrs B. C. read the Prayers in evg.

25. M.

Ch. 8½ A.M. Wrote to Rev. Mr Stevenson (sending Presentation)[1]—Mr Fisher—Mr Evans—Mr Phillips—Mr Laver—Sir R. Rawlinson—Mr Kensit[2]—Mr Denneby. Walk with Helen. Worked on books. Worked on Homer. Read Wadd on Corpulence[3]—OConnell's Memoir—One shall be our Leader.[4]

26. Tu.

Ch. 8½ A.M. Wrote to Mr W. Diss? BP—Mr Edwards B.P.—Mr Gill MP—Mr Taunton—Mr C.S. Perks—Rev. Mr. White—Mr Stikle—Made Book Pacel Leith Club—do St Oswald's Coll.[5] Woodcraft with sons. Worked on Homer. Read O'Connell's Memoir (finished)—Higgins on Bacon Shakespeare[6]—and Hipsley's Undine.[7]

27. Wed.

Ch. 8½ A.M. Wrote to Rev. Mr Thornhill—Sir W. Harcourt—Mr Morley—Mr C.H. Higgins—Mr Westell—Messrs Murray. Worked on Homer. Woodcraft with WHG. Tea with Mary who thank God has made a visible stage upwards. Read Peruvian Letters[8]—Seward's Collectanea (Ireland).[9] Saw Mr Smith MP. Whist in evg.

---

[1] To St. Thomas, Toxteth; see 24 Sept. 86.
[2] John Kensit; on Vaticanism; Hawn P.
[3] W. Wadd, *Cursory remarks on corpulence* (1816).
[4] Not found.
[5] St. Oswald's College, Ellesmere.
[6] Lectures sent by C. H. Higgins of Birkenhead (Hawn P.); no published copy found.
[7] By W. Hipsley (1886).
[8] Perhaps R. Roberts, *The Peruvian letters*, 2v. (1774).
[9] W. W. Seward, *Collectanea Hibernica*, 3v. (1812).

To Sir W. V. HARCOURT, M.P., 27 October 1886.   MS Harcourt dep. 10, f. 138.

Possibly you know that we have been long in a state of anxiety lest our daughter Mary's illness should again assume a character of acute danger. But within the last few days thank God there has been a favourable movement such that we now look cheerfully forward though the journey must be a long one before she recovers health. Her condition permits me to say that we shall be most happy to see you (*vos*, in dual or plural,[1] as the case may be) on your way to Leeds, if as I hope you are patriotically going there to pound Randolph. The Granville's are going to Knowsley and will I hope then come here: I have also written to Morley.

Here I have waiting you my Irish speeches in a Volume—which I did not know how to send touring after you, for Dodd[2] does not give me your address in the *New Forest*: presuming no doubt that as a public enemy while there you dwell in some cave.

[P.S.] My eye, fairly bunged up by a wasp, is now open again. 3 P.M. The doctors have just been & make an excellent report. I think you know the stations to which we send— Broughton Hall & Sandicroft. Chester 7 miles.

28. SS. Simon & J.

Ch 8½ A.M. This morning the blessing was given to Stephy of a little boy born:[3] & all well. Wrote to Sir J. Lambert—Mr A. Acland MP—Miss Clare—Mr Barry O'Brien—Mr Hennessy—Messrs Ludlow. Worked on Homer. Read Higgins, 2d Lecture[4]—Brabourne in Blackwood.[5] Whist in evg. Woodcraft.

29. Fr.

Ch. 8½ A.M. Wrote to Messrs Longbourne—Mr Oldham—U.S. Minister—Mr Crombie (& BP)[6]—Mr Acrell BP—Mr Fermor—Mr Quin—Mr Gill MP—Mr Westell—Mr Tripp—Dr Higgins—Mr F. Lyons. Woodcraft with my sons. Worked on Homer. Read Mackay on Tennyson[7]—Brabourne (Vol) on Home Rule[8]—The World of Cant.[9] Whist in evg.

30. Sat.

Ch. 8½ A.M. Wrote to Editor of Blackwood[10]—Archbp Walsh—Mr D. Fortune— Rev. Woodward—Mr R. Saunders—J. Heaton MP[11]—Mr D.E. Davies—Irish Pupils Holywell. Worked on Homer. We began the work of cutting the torn beech (N.) Read The World of Cant—Hipsley's Undine—Canning on the Union.[12] Granville came: conversation with him.

---

[1] i.e. Harcourt and his son.

[2] *Dodd's Parliamentary Companion*.

[3] Albert Charles Gladstone, d. 1967; soldier and bachelor; 5th bart. 1945; assisted in publication of the early volumes of these diaries.

[4] See 26 Oct. 86.   [5] See 29 Sept. 86.

[6] Perhaps John William Crombie, 1858–1908; Aberdonian author and liberal M.P. Kincardineshire from 1892.

[7] C. MacKay, 'Locksley Hall', *Notes and Queries* (9 Oct. 1875); see 15 Dec. 86.

[8] E. H. K. Hugessen, Lord Brabourne, *Facts and fictions in Irish history; a reply to Mr Gladstone* (1886).

[9] See 21 Oct. 86.

[10] More on Brabourne (see 29 Sept. 86), *T.T.*, 4 November 1886, 10c.

[11] John Henniker Heaton, 1848–1914; tory M.P. Canterbury 1885–90.

[12] See 15 July 86.

To Archbishop W. J. WALSH, 30 October 1886.   Add MS 44499, f. 120.

Circumstances of which a part have been noticed in the newspapers, have prevented my thanking your Grace for your communications without an unseemly delay,[1] which however I am sure you will excuse.

I am very sensible of the weight attaching to what your Grace has said, as well as of the importance of the topics themselves.

I will only touch & that briefly, on the key question, that of Home Rule. Constant meditation, as I may call it, has not led me to contemplate as legitimate or desirable a contraction of the scale on which the Home Rule Bill was framed.

Indeed as I stated to the Deputations here, I incline to think that the pecuniary arrangements to be proposed ought to be considered on a wider historical basis than was possible in the time which was so grudgingly given us for framing the measure. I do not know what would be the result, but it might be favourable in a pecuniary sense, to Ireland.

But looking to the strange position of affairs I think questions may arise more complex & formidable than any that I foresee in the extent of the Bill. What I am most afraid of is an endeavour to shuffle off the question on the pretext of procedure—of Land Purchase or some other plea, equally plausible and equally unsound. If I am right as to the direction which my fears are taking this question cannot be too maturely weighed.

There is another subject which is delicate but which I do not so much dread. It seems possible that offers may be made, which could not be accepted as final, but which might be tolerated as intermediate if they contained substantial & considerable good. On this point of some nicety, I think it likely that Irish opinion would weigh very much with (what I call) the Liberal party.

31. 19 S. Trin.

Ch 11 A.M. and 6½ P.M. Wrote to Messrs Ludlow—Mr E.A. Arnold—Mr Holmes—Sir R. Hamilton—Mrs Bolton—Mr Primrose—Mr Parker MP. Conversation with G. and walk. Read Origen—World of Cant—Shirreffs on Religious Certainty.[2]

Ph[ilosophy]. I suppose the principal factors, which make up our being, to be the reason, the affections, and the imagination. I now do not speak of the passions which are disturbers more than organs of our higher existence. Nor do I enter on the question whether the understanding, and the fancy ought, both or either of them, to be treated as separate faculties, or as partial and imperfectly developed forms of the reason and imagination respectively.

But of these three great organs I would observe that they are to be regarded not merely as each working outwards, but in the relation to one another, the participation I would say one of another which is inseparable from and preliminary too [*sic*] such working outwards.

The business for instance of the imagination is to project truth in forms of beauty: having for a righthand instrument figures of resemblance, and for an effective handmaid melody of language. But neither of these supply it with the materials on which it is to work. These it must derive from our percipient faculty. But this office belongs to the reason: and the character of its perceptions is largely influenced by the affections. Upon the entire domain thus opened it is the prerogative of the imagination to work. If the

[1] Cuttings of an interview sent on 18 October; Add MS 44499, f. 97.

[2] Untraced article or sermon, probably sent by J. M. Shirreffs, Scottish minister (see 14 Nov. 86).

reason is not exact and clear the products of imagination will be confused and cloudy. If the affections be stunted, if the heart be dry and sunken, the imagination may have a progeny but it will not embrace or command human sympathies. Neither will it lead men to good, for the affection towards good I have here included among the family of affections, instead of severing it, and dubbing with the name of conscience—a most useful and indispensable name in practical discussions—the joint product, in a given subject matter of the reason and the affection towards good.

Each of these great faculties forms in fact a portion of the field on which and from which the others operate. O.31.86.[1]

Mon. Nov. One 86 All Saints.

Ch 8½ as usual. Holy Commn in dear Mary's room at 9¼. Wrote to Ld Wolverton—Mrs Bolton BP.—J.H. Quin—Rev. D. M'Gregor[2]—H. Marshall—Rev. J. Bullock[3]—Mr Burdett Smith. Conversation with Granville: & walk. Harcourt & Morley came. 2 h in evg with them on Ireland. Worked on Homer. Read World of Cant—Lambert Jones on Romanism.[4]

2. Tu.

Ch 8½ A.M. Wrote to Rev. Dr Nevin—Mr Bullen—Messrs Barker—Mr Oldham—Mr J.L. Jones—Mr C. Cox—Mrs A. Shaw—Editor of Blackwood—Mr Braithwaite—Mr J. Bate—Mr C. Dawson—Mr Chas Ford. Forenoon mainly with Sir W.H. & Mr M. Worked on the great beech.[5] Worked on Homer. Read Neaera[6]—Bullen, Elisabethan Lyrics[7]—Shorthouse Sir Perceval.[8]

3. Wed.

Ch. 8½ A.M. Wrote to Mr Childers—A. Reader—H.W. Lee—J. A. Cowen—A. Morley—W.J. Smith—J.A. Robson—W. Smethurst. Worked on Homer: finished the Iliad, say 35th or 30th time? & every time richer and more glorious than before. Read Shorthouse, finished. Looked [up] some of my very ancient verses. I cannot make up my mind whether they have merit or not.

4. Th.

Ch. 8½ A.M. Wrote to Ld Granville—Mr Macmillan—Herr Fleischer—Mr Croxden Powell—Mr Burnett—Mr S.D. Neill—Lt Govr N.W. Terr. Canada[9]—Mr Cameron—Scotts—Mr Turner—P.C. Wells—C.T. Dawson—Mr Sleeth. Began the Odyssey. Read Ld Carnarvon (with misgivings)[10]—Repeal Essays[11]—Undine

---

[1] Add MS 44772, f. 194.

[2] Donald Macgregor of Edinburgh; Hawn P.

[3] John Bullock, headmaster of St. Oswald's (see 26 Oct. 86).

[4] Sent by J. Lambert Jones; no copy found.

[5] Harcourt noted: 'the G.O.M. took odd chops at a big tree which will take about as long felling as the Union'; Gardiner, ii. 11.

[6] J. W. Graham, *Neaera. A tale of ancient Rome*, 2v. (1886); see to Macmillan, 4 Nov. 86.

[7] A. H. Bullen, *Carols and poems* (1886).   [8] By J. H. Shorthouse (1886).

[9] Edgar Dewdney; correspondence untraced.

[10] Carnarvon's translation of the Odyssey, just published; see to Macmillan, this day.

[11] Perhaps F. Fairplay, pseud., *Repeal of the Union* (1831); comparison with Holland/Belgium.

(finished). Tea with Mary. Much improvement: more yet remains behind. Worked on the big tree.

To A. MACMILLAN, publisher, 4 November 1886.   Add MS 55243, f. 33.

I saw with much pleasure that Lord Carnarvon had become a Translator of the Odyssey and thought it did him much honour. I now thank you very much for the Book, which arrived this morning; and I shall have the opportunity of profiting by his labours as I had to begin the poem today—for about the 25th time, as I guess.

The fact is that I give all such time as I can to the study of the text with a view to my work on the Olympian religion, which I am not without hope of working into shape during the approaching winter.

Let me also thank you for Neaera, which I have just begun, and find every inducement to go through with.

But I was interrupted in order to read Mr Shorthouse's book. I find it a beautiful tale, of a tone nobly high, and indicating in some respects as compared with John Inglesant social growth and a more practical hand. I hope it will have a wide circulation. Ld Rosebery liked it very much. So does my daughter Mrs Drew, who is still an invalid but now thank God able to read.

If you keep the Concordance to the *Odyssey* (Oxford), would you kindly send me one & put it on my account. (I cannot quite forgive the Delegates for putting the Hymns into it. They might as well have put Quintus Calaber.)[1]

5. *Fr.*

Ch. 8½ A.M. Wrote to Ld Wolverton[2]—F. Rowlands—Mr Russell MP—H. Whitten—Mr Stibbs—Mr Morton—G. Brown. Worked on Homer. I must now if ever buckle to with my work on Olympian Religion. The great beech was brought down: a noble sight. Circuit of it, on the floor, at cut 20 f. 8 in. Read Prison Despotism.[3] A day of dissipation! Friends to luncheon, tea at Mary Rigby's, dinner with W.H.G., & whist.

6. *Sat.*

Ch. 8½ A.M. Wrote to Prof. Dr Pierson[4]—Mr Bennett—Mr Andrews—Capt. Norman[5]—Mr Weeks—Maj. Gen. Robertson[6]—Mr Swift Macneill.[7] Kibbling the great tree. Spent the evening in an endeavour to examine & arrange a little my Homeric and other papers. My memory is unhappily too weak to deal with my materials. Read Prison Despotism—Repeal Essays.

---

[1] Better known as Quintus Smyraneus, 4th century A.D. poet; wrote a continuation to the *Iliad*. Macmillan, who acted as O.U.P.'s publisher, ignored this sally in his reply, 26 November, Add MS 44256, f. 143, which asked permission to publish Gladstone's view of *Neaera*.

[2] Probably the undated letter on liberal reunion, *T.T.*, 10 November 1886, 10d.

[3] Not found under this title; clearly a substantial work; possibly E. F. Du Cane, *Punishment and the prevention of crime* (1885).

[4] Perhaps Arthur Tappan Pierson, American episcopalian author.

[5] Charles Boswell Norman, soldier; wrote on Armenia; see Add MS 44499, f. 247.

[6] Major-general Henry Larkins Robertson.

[7] John Gordon Swift *MacNeill, 1849–1926; Christ Church, Oxford; barrister, author and home rule M.P. 1887–1918.

7. 20 S. Trin.

Ch. 11 A.M. (H.C.) and [blank.] Wrote to Bulgarian Deputies[1]—Ed. Daily News—Dean of Wells—Messrs Watson—Mr Bowron—Mr Primrose—Mr Murray. Read Collins on Nature[2]—Psychosis on Our Philosophers[3]—Mr Williamson on Tithe[4]—Memoir of Dr Johnson[5]—The Truthseeker.[6]

8. M.

Ch. 8½ A.M. Wrote to Mr Williamson MP—Mr E. Russell—Mrs E. Williams—Mr A. Morley—Mr W.H. Proctor—Mr T. Hall—Miss Rowe. Rearranged my Homeric Department of books. Worked on Homer. Read Memoir of Rev. Dr Johnson—Prison Despotism—Hale on Language.[7] Kibbling—single-handed.

9. Tu.

Ch. 8½ A.M. Wrote to Maj. Gen. Robertson—Mr Childers—Mr Pogdon—Mr Bennett—Mr Coulter—J.A. Robson—Mr Suter—Rev. T. Long—Mr Marlow—Scotts—Mr Westell—Mr Mackay—Acct. Gen. Bank of E.—Messrs Hargrave—Mr Montgomery[8]—Consul Gillman. Worked on Homer. Agnes came. Herbert went. We shall miss him. But it is a good errand.[9] Read Prison Despotism—Scenes in Commons[10]—Montgomery on Burke[11]—Hale on Language finished.

10. Wed.

Ch. 8½ A.M. as usual, and 3¾ PM for the Baptism of little Albert. Wrote to Mr A. Anderson—Mr Taylor Innes[12]—Mr Stanley Little—Mrs Prinsep—D. Stewart—Rev. H.P. Stokes[13]—Miss Truitt BP—H. Leech—H. Hale—L.T. Jones. Walk with W.H.G. Worked on Homer. Read Dicey on Home Rule[14]—Prison Despotism (finished)—Tracts.

11. Th.

Ch. 8½ A.M. Wrote to Rev. Mr Carter—Mr Horatio Hale—Rev. Mr Mayow—Mr Weissmann—Mr Taylor Innes—H. Walters—Mr Gladstone Turner—Moderator

[1] In *D.N.* and *T.T.*, 10 November 1886, 10d.   [2] See 17 Oct. 86.

[3] 'Psychosis', *Our modern philosophers* (1884).

[4] Stephen Williamson (1827-1903, liberal M.P. St. Andrews 1880-5 (defeated after a tie), Kilmarnock 1886-95) had sent his *Relations between church and state and the tithing system* (1886).

[5] Perhaps [W. Shaw], *Memoirs of the life and writings of Samuel Johnson* (1785).

[6] The periodical ed. J. P. Hopps (see 11 July 74).

[7] Horatio Hale, of Buffalo, U.S.A., had sent his 'The origin of languages' (1886); Add MS 44499, f. 153.

[8] Hugh de Fellenberg Montgomery, b. 1844; Christ Church, Oxford; landlord in Fermanagh; this and later letters on Burke and Ireland in *T.T.*, 8 December 1886, 7f; see also *T.T.*, 16 June 1886, 7c.

[9] Family business and travel in India.

[10] D. Anderson, *Scenes in the Commons* (1884).

[11] H. de F. Montgomery, *Gladstone and Burke* (1886).

[12] On liberal reunion, *T.T.*, 12 September 1886, 7d.

[13] Henry Paine Stokes, vicar of St. James, Wolverhampton.

[14] A. V. Dicey, *England's case against Home Rule* (1886); see 12 Nov. 86.

of High Constables—H. Quilter[1]—R. Dunlop—J. Fenton—A. Bunting—H.H. Jones—Thos Lee. Worked on Apollo. Read Errata—Country Conversations[2] (aloud to Mary)—Neaera.

12. Fr.

Ch. 8½ A.M. Wrote to Archbishop Walsh—Prof. Dicey—Mr Murray—Rt Hon. J. Morley—Messrs Cocks—Jos Brown—Messrs Sutton—Rev. S.E.G. Discussed with dear S. the proper form of his proposed letter on gift out of Tithe. Second reading to Mary out of Village Conversations. That excellent Constance G. went off. Worked on Homer. Woodcraft with WHG. Read also Neaera.

To PROFESSOR A. V. DICEY, 12 November 1886.   Add MS 44499, f. 162.

I have to acknowledge with my best thanks the receipt of your volume on Home Rule; and of the letter relating to it, evidently yours, though accidentally unsigned.[3]

It was with pleasure that I had seen the announcement of this work on Mr Murray's list—I said to myself 'we are now sure of a work which will supply logic, knowledge, perspicuity and perfect integrity of aim, to a cause which in my opinion *has*, if I except the last, been singularly wanting in them: and will be a valuable auxiliary to us all in correcting or consolidating judgment.

During 48 hours since the work arrived, I have not read a great deal of it. This is really a tribute to its importance, for the reading it is a real study, and a new study, offering itself, has serious competitors to put aside.

However, what I have read shows me that my anticipations were in the main right; and I again thank you for doing (as I trust) a much needed act, raising namely the level of our controversy.

The case between us stands somewhat better than you modestly suppose. There is some, there is even much of the book which meets with my agreement; and my hearty agreement.

No doubt there is also much, to which I cannot yield assent. I will briefly notice three points. 1. I doubt (so far as I have read) whether you have at all embraced the nature of our, or my, contention as regards the historical argument. I was sensible, from the first, of the disadvantages inseparable from its introduction. Accordingly I think you would find that, acting in all things on the remote hope of an early accommodation, I scarcely touched it in the early stages. *Now*, we must go forward with it: we cannot dispense with any of our resources, and the historical argument has the most important judicial bearings on our arguments as to the Act of Union.

2. Next, as to the knowledge of the historical facts. I have worked on them to the best of my ability, and harder I think than any other politician: but I am far from having fully mastered them. Forgive me for saying that some things in your work, and especially what you say of 1641,[4] leads me to doubt whether you have accomplished this comprehensive study; even, for example, whether you have read O'Connell's Memoir upon Ireland,[5] consisting principally of citations, which ought I think to be regarded as among the first elements of necessary knowledge of this subject.

---

[1] Harry Quilter, 1851–1907; artist and author; had sent his *Sententiae artis* (1886).
[2] See, probably, 6 Feb. 86.
[3] Brief note by an amanuensis; Add MS 44499, f. 145.
[4] Probably the passage on p. 9 on need to avoid 'the poisonous venom of historical recrimination'.
[5] D. O'Connell, *A memoir on Ireland, native and Saxon*; see 20 Oct. 86.

3. I think you are quite in error, a very secondary error, I admit, when you dwell on what is termed my appeal to the masses. I have laid down no abstract or general proposition: if I have, it is perhaps the one contradictory of what you impute to me. Generally, I have done no more than repeat and apply what I argued out more fully in a very dispassionate controversy with Mr Lowe (as he then was). I take the liberty of sending you, through Mr Murray, the little volume which contains (on my side) the discussion. You will find my proposition stated in p. 198.[1] It is on the popular judgment—whatever be the mental factors—by which the judgment is reached. It is limited to the last 50 years. You reply to me in part from the 18th century (on which there is much to say) it allows 'a possible exception or two'. Now let me consider your instances. (a) R.C. Emancipation. This is my chief 'possible exception' (b) The criminal code. *Whose work was it?* The work of the classes. *Who were its Reformers?* Men, proscribed by the classes as a whole, recommended the changes: a Liberal Government proposed and carried them, (I speak of the last half century) a Govt, having at least $\frac{3}{4}$ of the classes against it. Who were the disapprovers? To a great extent the Judges!! My belief is, & my recollection so far as it goes, that the people were strongly favourable. (c) The Poor Law. I agree in your estimate of this Reform. The Times was its great opponent; to which Peel in 1835 rendered his thanks for its powerful general support. I remember it well. To speak the truth, I consider that neither the classes nor the masses had much to do with it. It was a reform enormously advantageous to the pecuniary interest of the classes. It would have been rather strange had they opposed it. But here again it was conceived and carried by a Govt. then denounced almost more than any other by the classes as revolutionary. Credit is due to that Government: especially to that incomparable man, Lord Althorp; and to the enlightened Commissioners; and also without doubt to the wise conduct of Peel & the Duke. But the motive force which carried the Bill was (in my judgment) the residue of the great wave of the Reform Act: as undoubtedly the Land Act of 1870 was carried by the residue of the wave which had carried the Irish Church Act.

(d) Shall I confess that I am a little surprised at your reference to the Wars? True, the people have often been wrong in favouring them. But where is there perhaps even a single case in which the classes have not been very much more, & more obstinately, wrong?

I have been too long upon this subject. It is a great one. My limited proposition is still, I know, both broad and pregnant. It is a very mournful, as well as very instructive conclusion. It is, at any rate, one formed by a man who, in intercourse, contact, and conflict with practical human nature in all its orders and degrees, has enjoyed opportunities to an extent allowed to few in any period of history, and who, if wrong, is egregiously and very culpably wrong.

I write freely to you, as one who will comprehend at once such reserves as are naturally inherent in propositions of this kind: and one, let me add, whose writings, so far as they are known to me, tend to attract not only high appreciation, but confidence and esteem.[2]

13. Sat.

Ch. 8½ A.M. Wrote to Mr Lushington (Guy's)[3]—Mrs Townsend—Mr Martin—Mr Iglehart—Mr Roach Smith—Mr Turnbull—Reeves & Turner—Mrs Dickinson.

---

[1] *Gleanings* i. See above, vol. X, Introduction, section II.

[2] Dicey replied by amanuensis, 17 November, Add MS 44499, f. 162, that he would look at O'Connell, though doubting its value, and that Gladstone's letter had not 'shaken my opinion of the value of the appeal to popular judgment'.

[3] See 25 Feb. 78n.

Woodcraft with W. Read Country Conv. to Mary—Neaera—Mahaffy Social Life of the Greeks.[1]

14. 21 S. Trin.

Ch 11 A.M. (H. Drew preached extremely well) (Read the Lessons) & 6½ P.M. Wrote to Mr Fitzpatrick—Mr Shirreffs—Sec. Treasury—Mr J. Lawson—Bp of Ripon—Ld C. Campbell—Mr A. Reid. Read Pearsons Sunday Lecture[2]—Bp Dowden's Congress Sermon[3]—both very polemical but ever from opposite sides—Bindley, Council of Chalcedon[4]—Hime on Unbelief.[5] Worked with Stephy on his Tithe Letter, & the Tithe Fund.

15. M.

Ch. 8½ A.M. Wrote to Mr Swift Macneill—Mr Bindley—J. Seddon—Dr Hime—F. Allen—F. Edwards—A.M. Howell—R. Radford—W. Hyde. Woodcraft with W.H.G. Tea with the Mayhews & conversation with him. Worked on Homer. Read Renouf, Hibbert Lectures[6]—Brugsch, History[7]—Neaera—Mahaffy. Finished reading Country Conversations to Mary.

16. Tu.

Ch. 8½ A.M. Wrote to Sir W. Harcourt—Mr Weatherly—Mad. Novikoff—Ly F. Cavendish—Dr Weissmann B.P.—Rev. J. Bownes—T. Hall—J. Kensit—A. Radford—T. Winden. Woodcraft with W.H.G. Sat (a kind of sitting) to Mr Holland of Hull.[8] Worked on Homer. Read Buchholz Realien—Mahaffy, Social Life—Neaera finished Vol. I.—Redmond on 1798.[9]

To Sir W. V. HARCOURT, M.P., 16 November 1886.   MS Harcourt dep. 10, f. 140.

1. I send you 1) a curious letter from Colin Campbell[10] on account of his correspondence with H.O.—H.O refused access to the Records, & said this had been done by *successive Secretaries of State*.[11] Do you know anything of this? How can the concealment be warranted? or maintained?
2. Also 2) a letter 'absolutely private' on which I can say nothing—I do not know whether you are in the same predicament.[12]

---

[1] J. P. Mahaffy, *Social life in Greece* (1874).
[2] J. A. Pearson, 'The observance of Sunday in England' (1867).
[3] J. Dowden, 'Religion in relation to the social and political life of England' (1886).
[4] T. H. Brindley, *Definitio Fidei apud Concilium Chalcedonense* (1887).
[5] By M. C. Hime (1885).
[6] P. le P. Renouf, *Lectures on the origin . . . of religion* (1879); on Egypt; see 16 Nov. 84.
[7] See 3 Jan. 79.
[8] Almost certainly a photographer.
[9] John Edward *Redmond (1856–1918; Commons clerk 1880; home rule M.P. Wexford 1881–91, Waterford 1891–1918; Parnellite leader from 1891) had sent his *The truth about '98* (1886).
[10] Argyll's son (see 10 Oct. 78), involved in a sensational divorce.
[11] Harcourt replied, 17 November, Add MS 44200, f. 180, that he had controlled access to the P.R.O.
[12] Not found; Harcourt also 'ignorant of its meaning'; ibid.

3. John Morley will probably come here Nov. 27–9. It would not be fair to ask you. I hope for Ripon soon, but do not know his day. I remain of opinion that the support of the postponement by DLs would render all notion of identity a pretence. But qu. is it not to be assumed as nearly matter of course that Parnell will oppose it, and free us into the field even if reluctant? On the other hand I wish we could learn how the Irish would view an intermediate measure good in itself though insufficient. My inclination would be to regard it with favour: but I should be disposed to give weight to the Irish view.

4. Randolph, by taking up the Liberal Programme, has, as was to be expected, caused a *superfetation* of Radical ideas on our side. I do not know how you view this. I will not break with the 200 or the radical section of them if I can help it. But I am rather too old to put on a brand new suit of clothes.

A wonderful season. Happy & thankful to report that my daughter now makes rapid progress. There is however a long hill to mount.

[P.S.] I think an Austro-Anglian war against Russia a very unsatisfactory business. Nothing but European action could repress her if she means mischief. But I think Salisbury is blustering.

17. *Wed.*

Ch. 8½ A.M. Wrote to Sec. Sc. Geogr. Soc.—Sec. Liberal Club Co—Mr de Montgomery—Mr Marchmont—Mr Kennedy—A.S. Davis—Ld Dufferin—J. Morley—Mr Haes.[1] Woodcraft with W.H.G. Worked on Homer. Read Picton's Lecture[2]—Archd. Denison on Schools &c.[3]—Neaera finished Vol I. The Tomkinsons[4] came: 13 to dinner. Conversation with Lavinia.

18. *Th.*

Ch. 8½ A.M. Wrote to Editor of 'Young Man'[5]—Mr Stibbs—Oliver & Boyd[6]—Mr Primrose—Mr Quayle—Messrs Murray—do for Lawson—do for Seddon—Mad. Du Guet[7]—Mr H. Gray—Mr Redmond M.P.—Ed. Worcestershire Chron.[8]—Lady F. Cavendish. Woodcraft with W. Worked on Homer. Read Odyssey—Neaera—and [blank.]

19. *Fr.*

Ch. 8½ A.M. Wrote to Mr Illingworth l.l.[9]—Ed. Daily News—Lord Thring—Warden Talbot—Dr H. Hime[10]—Mr Campbell—Mr Thompson. Read Odyssey—

---

[1] Perhaps Thomas Hayes, in correspondence 1886; Hawn P.

[2] J. A. Picton, *The conflict of oligarchy and democracy. Six lectures* (1885).

[3] G. A. Denison, *The schools of Christendom. The decay of Greek and Latin. The science of flogging* (1886).

[4] James and Emily Tomkinson of Willington Hall, Cheshire; liberals.

[5] No copy found.

[6] See 2 Nov. 65.

[7] Spiritualist at 38 N. Audley Street, London, sent 'autographs' from the other world; Hawn P.

[8] On E. V. Schuster's sermon on the reformation, *Worcestershire Chronicle*, 27 November, 3d.

[9] Thanking Alfred Illingworth (1827–1907, liberal M.P. Bradford 1880–95) for Bradford's resolution of confidence; Add MS 44499, f. 181; *D.N.*, 22 November 1886, 5e.

[10] Maurice Charles Hime of Foyle College, Londonderry had sent his 'Morality' (8th ed. 1884); for young men.

Neaera (Vol. II.)—Webb's Reply (rather late?).[1] Worked on books. Woodcraft agt the offensive Elders. Worked on Homer. Read Homer—Neaera. Lucy Cavendish came.

20. Sat.

Ch. 8¼ A.M. Wrote to Sec. Bank of England—Messrs Blackwood—Messrs Tennant—Ed.Young Man[2]—Mr Marlow—Mr Bowden—Mr Downing—Mr Griffith—Mr Beecher—Mr Douglas. Worked on Homer. Woodcraft with WHG. Read Odyssey—Neaera—Hoare on Ireland. Introdn.[3]

21. Preadv. Sunday.

Ch 11 A.M. and 6.30 P.M. Wrote to . . . Rev Mr Halsey—Mrs Th. Read Halsey on Disestabl.—Lambert, The Church's cause[4]—Davies Bps & their Religion[5]—Dawson Points of Contact[6]—Hime on Morality[7]—Rowell, Sense of Pain.[8]

22. M.

Ch. 8¼ A.M. Wrote to Mr Montgomery—Mr Brodie[9]—Mr Lunn B.P.—Mr Samuel B.P.—Mr Radford (Messrs Murray)—Mr Macmillan—Mr Stibbs B.P.—Mr Rawson—Mr Whitehead. Read Neaera finished—Sheridan on Parliaments[10]—Hoare's Ireland 1806. Read Odyssey. Worked on Homer. Woodcraft with W.H.G.

23. Tu.

Ch. 8¼ A.M. Wrote to Mrs Weatherly—Ld Granville—Sir B. Foster—General Brown[11]—The Queen Tel.—Press Assocn. Tel.—Mr Burnes—Mr Spackman[12]—Mr Davies—Mr C. Nosotti[13]—Mr Share—Mr Newbold—Rev. S.E.G. Read World of Cant—Hoare's Tour in Ireland—and [blank.] Worked on Homer. Conversation with Mary on her birthday: now so hopeful and bright.

24. Wed.

Ch. 8¼ A.M. Wrote to Mr Mundella—Mr Wilson Shaw—Daily News Tel l.l.—Mr A. M'Dougall—Mr Robertson—Rev. Mr Schuster[14]—Messrs Kelly B.P.—Mr

[1] A. Webb, *The opinions of some protestants regarding their Irish catholic fellow-countrymen* (1886).
[2] See 18 Nov. 86.
[3] R. C. Hoare, *Journal of a tour in Ireland* (1807).
[4] F. Lambert, 'The Church's cause' (1886).
[5] M. Davies, *The bishops and their religion* (1886).
[6] J. W. Dawson, *Points of contact between revelation and natural science* (1885).
[7] See 19 Nov. 86n.
[8] G. A. Rowell, *An essay on the beneficient distribution of the sense of pain* (1857).
[9] To W. R. Brodie of Edinburgh, on liberal reunion; *T.T.*, 25 November 1886, 6b.
[10] T. Sheridan, 'A discourse on the rise and power of parliaments' (1677).
[11] Henry Ralph Browne, retired Indian general living in Flintshire.
[12] Belfast hatter; Hawn P.
[13] Upholsterer in Oxford Street.
[14] See 18 Nov. 86n.

Davey—S. Ramsey—Mr Deans—Mr Dowson—Mr Wilkin. Woodcraft with WHG. Read Odyssey—Hoare's Ireland—World of Cant (finished)[1]—L. Say (anon) French Finance.[2]

25. Th.

Ch. 8½ A.M. Wrote to Rev. T. Roberts—E. Hamilton—Ed. Daily Post—Mrs Cockle—Messrs Cox—Mr Knowles—Mrs Th.—Mr Clough Tel.[3]—Mr F. Dean— Ld Rosebery. Worked on Homer. Read Odyssey—Trenck's Memoirs[4]—Hoare Tour in Ireland. Woodcraft with W.H.G. Two very pleasing Lancs. men came to see us.[5]

26. Fr.

Ch. 8½ A.M. Wrote to Sec. for Scotland[6]—Sir H. Ponsonby—Rev. Dr Parker—Mr Collins—C. Martyn—C. Stevenson—W. Sinclair—D. Kavanagh—J. Deans—Mr Hudson—Mr Hope Hume—F. Darrant. Worked on Homer. Read Odyssey—finished Baron Trenck—Hoare's Tour in Ireland. Felled a sycamore with WHG.

27. Sat.

Ch. 8½ A.M. Wrote to Mr C. Bannerman—Ld Granville—Mr Cyrus Field—Mr Macmillan—Rivingtons—M. Jackson—Mr Clare. Woodcraft with W.H.G. Collected the 'signs of Phoenicianism' (or 'notes').[7] Read Odyssey—Hoare on Ireland (finished)—Jackson on America.[8]

28. Adv. S.

Ch 11 AM and H.C. 6½ P.M. Wrote to Sec. Nat Lib. Club Co—Rev. Dr Parker l.l.[9]—Mr J. Murray. Read Vaughan's Poems, how fragrant[10]—Liturgy of St Chrysostom—Xtn Confession from a Modern Point of View.[11] Walk with Ripon & Morley, & much conversation. They are two excellent men: but their visit made a bad Sunday.

29. M.

Ch. 8½ A.M. Wrote to Lord Aberdeen—J.J. Foster—G.J. Russell—V. Scully— Messrs Turnbull—Mr Bryce—J. Morley—F.B.O. Cole—W. Hall. Walk & conversation with Morley. A little woodcraft in aftn. Read Odyssey—Mr Donald-

[1] See 21 Oct. 86.
[2] Not found.
[3] Perhaps Walter Owen Clough, 1846-1922; accountant; liberal M.P. Portsmouth 1892-1900.
[4] See 22 Sept. 86.
[5] But did not sign the Visitors' Book.
[6] A. J. Balfour; business untraced.
[7] For his Homeric file.
[8] H. M. Jackson, *Glimpses of three coasts* (1886).
[9] On nonconformist support; *T.T.*, 30 November 1886, 8c.
[10] H. Vaughan, *Poems* (1884 ed.).
[11] Untraced tract.

son's Address [1]—Mr Phelan's do.[2]—Limburg-Brower, Civilisation des Grecs (began).[3]

30. Tu.

Ch. 8½ A.M. Wrote to Ed. Southport Guardian—Mr J. Morley—J. Evans and Messrs Murray—War Secretary[4]—B. Currie—J.W.F. Rogers[5]—A. Dewholme—Newsman—J. Bryce—J. Simson. Worked on Homer. Woodcraft with W. Read Odyssey—Limburg Brouwer—Jackson's America.

To J. BRYCE, M.P., 30 November 1886.   Bryce MS 10, f. 73.

I am not surprised to hear that you have had difficulties[6] but much gratified to find that your skill and persistence have surmounted them. There are various volunteers in the field. Only yesterday I learned from Morley that Childers is writing on the Fitzwilliam case, with good access to documents. His work ought to be important. Morley and Thring have been in communication on Dicey's book, the most considerable & grave argument by far that has appeared on that side, but not one to abash us. I think his foundation, viz. the decision on Irish Govt. according to English wants, very assailable.

I have not as yet seen any facts to lead me to suppose the H.R. movement in Scotland likely to take any dangerous shape, but perhaps you no [*sic*] more. We I think have solid ground under our feet in declining to admit as a postulate that there is to be equal treatment throughout for the three countries. I feel every confidence that Scotland will make up her mind quietly & cautiously, whatever Blackie may do, & that England will not fight against a deliberate demand from beyond the Tweed. For her to prescribe Home Rule & two Parliaments for England would be too absurd. I do not suppose any very extensive change to be necessary. But the Union has certainly had a good deal of credit to which it had little or no claim: and I am doubtful whether Private Legislation can be disposed of by a non-representative Body. I speak only of the little I have seen. You may know more.

Wed. Decr. One. 1886.

Church 8½ A.M. Wrote to Sir U. Shuttleworth—Mad. Dognon—Mr N. Payne—Bp of London—Miss Billing—Mr H. Williams—Mr A. Mure—Mr Croxden Powell—Rev. Mr Stephenson—Supt Goods LNW Chester. Visited the Potters with Lucy. Read Odyssey—Hayman, Preface to V. III[7]—Limburg Brouwer—Jackson on U.S.

2. Th.

Ch. 8½ A.M. Wrote to Mr P.W. Campbell—Mrs Bolton—Rev. Mr Bourne—Lady Gladstone—Ld Selborne—Mr Carteret—Mr A.M. Rose—Princ. Librarian

[1] Possibly one of Sir J. Donaldson's addresses to St. Andrews' students; published collected 1887.
[2] J. Phelan, 'The Democratic position on the tariff' (1886).
[3] See 9 Nov. 74.
[4] W. H. Smith; timetable for supply; Add MS 44300, ff. 288, 292.
[5] Of London; sent his *Grammar and logic* (1883); Hawn P.
[6] Bryce wrote on 8 October from Italy, Bryce MS 11, f. 152, that despite difficulties from J. Morley, the collection of essays (see 8, 17, 26 July 86) was proceeding.
[7] Hayman's *Odyssey*; see 25 Jan. 73.

Museum—Mr Hayes. Walk with party. Read Odyssey—Hayman's Introduction—Limburg Brouwer—Jackson's America. Dined at the Rectory. Lucy read us Langridge's Ballads.[1] Backg with SEG. interrupted by another of Mary's 'drawbacks' not we trust really formidable.

3. Fr.

Ch. 8½ A.M. Wrote to Rev. Mr Page Roberts[2]—Rev. T. Roberts—Mr M'Ghee—W. Stead—A. Ogden—Rev. T. Davies—Miss Ryan—Reeves & Turner—M. Villars (Journal des Débats)[3]—W.H. Hoyt[4] and others. Walk with S.E.G. & calls. Read Odyssey—Limburg Brouwer—Jackson's America (finished)—(Through Dark to Light, 3D)[5]—Xantippè, & Poems.[6]

4. Sat.

Church 8½ A.M. & H.C. Wrote to Mr Williamson MP—A.E. Evans—R.A. Brown[7]—G. Davenport (BP)—Mr Ellis Lever[8]—J. Searle. Worked on Homer. Read 'Our Country'[9]—Limburg Brouwer Vol. 2. Twelve to dinner. Long conversation with C. Parker on Sir R. Peel.[10]

5. 2 S. Adv.

Ch. 11 AM 6½ PM. Wrote to Rev. H.G. Dickson—Mr Grange—W. Price—H.C. Burdett—A. Macdonalt. Read Dixon's Sermon[11]—Selborne on Ch. Establishment[12]—Thiele, Compendium der Religionsgeschichte—Page Roberts, Sermons: &c.

6. M.

Ch. 8½ A.M. Wrote to Reeves & Turner—Mr Knowles—Miss Irby—V. Oger[13]—D.T. Davies—T.S. Buyers—T. Evans. Worked on Homer. Felled a tree with W.H.G. Read Odyssey—Our Country—Mr Baring Gould's Mehala.[14]

[1] See 11 May 86.
[2] W. Page Roberts had sent his *Liberalism in religion* (1886); Hawn P.
[3] Probably a comment (not found published) on its report on Dillon and the Plan of Campaign in 'Lettres d'Irelande', *Journal des Débats*, 1 December 1886.
[4] William H. Hoyt, of Stamford, Conn., U.S.A. and others sent an axe, 'the pioneer implement of our civilization'; Hawn P.
[5] *Through dark to light* (3rd ed. 1886?).
[6] Perhaps [F. Sandvoss], *Kalypso, von Xanthippus* (1886).
[7] Thanking R. Ainslie Brown, Edinburgh liberal, for resolution of support; *T.T.*, 7 December 1886, 6e.
[8] Opposing the London coal tax; *T.T.*, 8 December 1886, 5e.
[9] *'Our country'; an essay* (1855).
[10] 1st vol. of C. S. Parker's *Peel* published 1891; its preface thanks diarist 'for assistance given in several conversations' as well as for loan of letters and use of his books on Peel at Hawarden.
[11] Perhaps J. Dixon, 'The pain of the present' (1859).
[12] R. Palmer, Lord Selborne, *A defence of the Church of England against disestablishment. With a letter to ... Gladstone* (1886).
[13] Victor Oger, translator; see Add MS 44259, f. 349.
[14] S. Baring Gould, *Mehalah: a story of the salt marshes*, 2v. (1884).

7. Tu.

Ch. 8½ A.M. Wrote to Sir J.A. Picton—T.A. White BP—Mrs Reid[1]—Mr Tagart—Mr Brading—Treasurer Edinb. Coll. Phys.—H. Burdett BP—Mr Morgan Jones—H.R. Gordon. Woodcraft with W.H.G. Worked on Poseidon.[2] Read Mehalah—Limburg Brouwer. Ten to dinner. Mr Stephenson[3] came; we were all greatly pleased with him. Woodcraft with WHG.

8. Wed.

Ch. 8½ A.M: 7½ P.M. Storm. But Mr S. and I walked in it. Much conversation. Wrote to Canon Monahan[4]—Ld Granville—Ed. Glasg Mail[5]—Messrs Sutton—Mr Whitehead—Rev. J. Ffoulkes[6]—Messrs Jacobs & Davis—J. Tagart—Mr Morley—Mr Lloyd B.P.—Mr Digby—J. Tavener—W. Tucker—C.W. Poole. Read Mehala: a remarkable book: and [blank.] Worked on Homer.

To J. MORLEY, M.P., 8 December 1886.[7]   Add MS 44255, f. 139.

I have received your very clear statement,[8] and I reply in much haste for the post—making the same request as yours for a return.[9]

1. I am glad to find the Dillon speech[10] is likely to be neutralised, I hope effectively. It was really very bad. I am glad you write to him.

2. As to the campaign in Ireland I do not at present feel the force of Hartington's appeal to me to speak out. I do not recollect that he ever spoke out about Churchill, of whom he is now the enthusiastic follower.

3. But all I say and do must be kept apart from the slightest countenance direct or indirect to illegality. We too suffer under the power of the landlords, but we cannot accept this as a method of breaking it.

4. I am glad you opened the question of intermediate measures. Did he clearly understand the idea? Namely not that we were to disown our aim or disguise our sentiments, but only that we were to abstain from open and violent warfare against some measure *ex hypothesi* good in itself. Any such measure, I apprehend, must increase the means at the

---

[1] Thanking Mrs. H. G. Reid of Aston Hall Women's Assoc. for support; *P.M.G.*, 2 October 1886, 7.

[2] Developed out of Homeric writings at this time, published as 'The greater gods of Olympus: I. Poseidon', *N.C.*, xxi. 460 (March 1887).

[3] See 24 Sept. 86n.

[4] James Hunter Monahan, canon and treasurer of Christ Church, Dublin, had sent his book; see 12 Dec. 86.

[5] Denying he supports Irish rent strikes; *T.T.*, 11 December 1886, 9d.

[6] Nonconformist clergyman.

[7] Copy in Morley's hand; part in Morley, iii. 371.

[8] Of 7 December, Add MS 44255, f. 134, of 'an interview . . . with my friend [i.e. Parnell] . . . the fixed point in his tactics is to maintain the alliance with the English liberals', Morley pointing out in that context the 'mischief' of speeches such as Dillon's; Morley also raised the need for 'a provisional acquiescence to intermediate projects of self-govt., good in themselves, tho' not in his view adequate'.

[9] Morley replied next day, ibid., f. 141: 'P. very clearly understood the idea as to an intermediate proposal'; on 12 December, ibid., f. 143, Morley reported 'a long talk' with Parnell: 'the meetings will be stopped, and the whole movement calmed as much as possible'; he could not support measures producing 'a pseudo-legislative' system, but 'he would assent to a scheme for county boards'.

[10] On 5 December, suggesting retribution on the police etc. after home rule; see F. S. L. Lyons, *John Dillon* (1968), 86–7.

disposal of the Irish people for pressing Home Rule, if continuing disposed to do so. I can hardly think P. would take an extreme view of this. It is, however, a matter for much deliberation.

5. Upon the whole, I suppose, he sees he cannot have countenance from us in the plan of campaign. The question is how wise[?] is disavowal. I have contradicted a Tory figment in Glasgow that I had approved.

9. Th.

Ch. 8½ A.M. Wrote to Sig. Tumbini l. & B.P.[1]—Ld Ripon—Mr Knowles—Mr Halton—Mr Bedding—Mr Horwill—A. Elliot—Mr Barry O Brien—Mr Minchin—R. Hamilton. Worked on Poseidon. Woodcraft with W.H.G. Read Limburg Brouwer—Mehala—The Hayward Letters.[2]

To LORD RIPON, 9 December 1886. '*Secret*'.[3]   Add MS 43515, f. 45.

You are very gallant in taking so large a share of work. I agree with you that the Unionists are rather savage; Chamberlain contemptuous as usual towards us, and Hartington rather too like 'a bull in a china shop.' Still I would not, as long as it can be avoided, do anything to stereotype the breach. I send you (please to return it) copy of a letter which I have written to Granville; to whom I point out the *modus vivendi* as I view it. I was struck by the fewness of Dissentient M.P.s at this imposing assemblage; and, though I feel disposed to waive criticism upon the leaders, I do think that we may fairly appeal to the general body (many of whom are not at all tied to the Leaders,) on either or both these grounds. 1. the *modus vivendi*. 2. The duty of resisting any attempt at coercion, if it is proposed without liberal political legislation for Ireland, as now seems too likely.

Probably this latter may be the best form, for us, of the issue to be raised at the meeting of Parliament. We may also, I think, very fairly criticise the Government whose boasted triumph has brought about a disastrously altered state of things in Ireland: combination against rents, prohibition of public meetings, proceedings against members of Parliament, and generally a new shock to public confidence. I yesterday heard from Morley: and from him I gather that Dillon will do something towards explaining or withdrawing his most improper speech at Castlerea.

Were I speaking at this time, I should certainly not accept Hartington's obliging invitation; but should say that neither threats of vengeance nor violence of language, nor illegal combination, nor resistance to law, could have any countenance from us: differing in this essential matter from R. Churchill, of whom Hartington is now chief supporter.

And this is compatible with all liberty of speech as regards the Government, who have brought about this state of things, and who when they thought there would be tranquility in Ireland, put it forward as a reason why there need be no legislation in satisfaction of her wants and desires.

If you think fit to cite me in what I have here said about law and order in Ireland, I am more than content.

[P.S.] If you fall in with Spencer please to show him these.

[1] B. Tumbini of Portici, Naples, had sent a work; Hawn P.
[2] See 28 Jan. 85n.
[3] Ripon has asked his advice, for a speech, about 'the "Unionist" meetings'; Add MS 43515, f. 43 and Add MS 44287, f. 58.

10. Fr.

Ch. 8½ A.M. Wrote to Mr C. Bannerman—Canon MacColl—M.S. OBrien—R. Askey—Rev. Mr Jones—G.M. Towle—T. Turnerelli—Messrs Murray—Messrs Macmillan—Rev. Mr Tucker—Mr Beveridge[1]—Scottish Leaders[2]—Press Assocn Tel. The Aberdeens paid us a visit of 3 hours on their way. I gave him my private correspondence on Ireland to read. Felled an oak with W.H.G. Conversation with him on Hn affairs. Worked on Poseidon. Read Mehalah—Ly Aberdeen on the Jubilee[3]—Limburg Brouwer—Towle's Hist. of Ireland.[4]

To H. CAMPBELL-BANNERMAN, M.P.,   Add MS 41215, f. 27.
10 December 1886. '*Secret*'.

Pray make no apology for writing to me on matters of public interest.[5] It is not correspondence such as yours, or as that of other friends, which forms for me some degree of difficulty & a burden.

1. Hartington seems to be very far from careful in his references, & you have spotted a gross error. The Government have, as you observe, promised a measure providing for some kind of local government in Ireland, & the Dissentient leaders have made very large declarations in this respect. Six months or near it have been taken for consideration. What I contend is that Ministers will be bound to produce their measure when Parliament has met, & above all that the Dissentients are bound to make them produce it, which undoubtedly they have power to do. If they do not use this power, what becomes of their claim to be the true representatives of the Liberal party.

2. From what I hear, it is not unlikely that Dillon will do something to retract or explain his speech. It is one which, treated on its merits, *deserves* censure.

3. I incline to think however that our best method of proceeding is to disavow gently but firmly all countenance in whatever shape to threats, violent language, conspiracy against contracts, or disorder. If you think proper to make such disavowal you are quite welcome to cite me as concurring. I have already said the same thing to our excellent colleague, Ripon.

4. I see no objection whatever to the allowances you propose to make for the Irish people, & I should dwell strongly on two things: (1) Ministers themselves reopened the question of rents, signified that in some cases they *could not* be paid, appointed a Commission to inquire in what cases, & then left the law to take its course by evictions in the meantime. (2) The deplorable change in the state of Ireland since the cup of hope was dashed away from the lips of the people. Stoppage of public meetings: proceedings against members of Parliament: abandonment (Salisbury's speech) of the pledge to introduce one Irish liberal measure: rumours of proximate coercion: in short all that could be done to throw back Irish opinion into an attitude of hostility to laws coming from London.

P.S. I have now read Trevelyan's speech. I think it might, at least in comparison with some others, deserve a civil word. He says he is strongly for financial, industrial, educational autonomy in Ireland. Might we not say that if a proposal of that kind were made it would at least be one indication of goodwill & that goodwill is a thing of great value.

---

[1] James Beveridge, Glasgow liberal; Hawn P.
[2] i.e. the new liberal *Scottish Leader* (see 31 Dec. 86).
[3] Untraced article.
[4] G. M. Towle had sent his *Young people's history of Ireland* (1886).
[5] Letter of 8 December, Add MS 44117, f. 71, on planning a speech: was Hartington right in saying you urged the govt. to produce 'their Home Rule scheme' without delay?

11. Sat.

Ch. 8½ A.M. and the Holy Sacrament. Wrote to Hon. Sir C. Trevelyan—Mr Mundella—Lord E. Clinton—Mrs Duffy (N.Z.)[1]—Messrs Wilson—Mr Norbury—Mr Andrews—Mr Selkirk—Rev. Mr Kemp. Worked on Poseidon. Woodcraft in aftn. Read Mehalah—Tennyson's *new* Locksley Hall & old[2]—Limburg Brouwer —and [blank.]

12. 3 S. Adv.

Ch 11 AM 6½ P.M. Wrote to Mr Mostyn Williams—Ld Granville—Ld Spencer—Mr Dowdham—Mrs Th. (& Mem)—Mr Knowles—Mr Craik.[3] Read Monahan on Ardagh Diocese[4]—Ker on the Psalms[5]—Selborne on Disestablt—Bp of Derry's Poems.[6] C. laid up.

13. M.

Ch. 8½ A.M. C. rallied beautifully. Wrote to Mr Macfarlane—Bp of Derry—Mrs Bolton—Mr Morley MP—Mr Skifny—Prof. Stuart MP—Mr M'Closkey—Lord Spencer Tel. Worked well on Poseidon. Read Mahalah—Our Country. Mr Mundella came, on his way to Rhyl. After dinner he gave us a very interesting family & personal history. Much conversation on Ireland.[7] Woodcraft.

14. Tu.

Ch. 8½ A.M. Wrote to Mr W.H. Morrison—Mr Clayton—Mr Knowles—Mr Th. Hall—A. Ireland—J. Carchart[?]—G. Kemp—Mr Garrett *cum* Mr Herbert. Sent off Poseidon: (with a little blank in him.). Mr M. went in aftn. Further conversation with him. Read Molyneux: (& Preface of 1770) on Ireland[8]—Mehalah (finished)—Waifs & Strays.[9]

15. Wed.

Ch. 8½ A.M. Wrote to Rev. D.T. Gladstone—Mr Knowles—Mr Cooks—J.R. Jones—J. Collins—T.J. Brown—A.E. Brown—G. Herbert—M.J. Lund—E. Roberts—Mr Wilding—Mr Drummond—Mad. Novikoff BP—J. Courtenay—Messrs Murray (2)—Press Assocn (Tel.)—C. Collingwood—G.J. Campbell—T. Grimwood—Messrs Gibb & Bruce. Read Tour in Wales (Hn)[10]—Hayward's

[1] Marie Duffy of Auckland sent 'a slight testimony' from New Zealand 'lady admirers'; Hawn P.
[2] Tennyson, *Locksley Hall; sixty years after* (1886); see 15 Dec. 86.
[3] Perhaps (Sir) Henry *Craik, 1846-1927; sec. of Scottish education dept. 1885-1904.
[4] J. Monahan, *Records . . . of Ardagh and Clonmacnoise* (1886).   [5] By J. Ker (1886).
[6] W. Alexander, *St Augustine's holiday and other poems* (1886).
[7] Mundella's letter of 10 December defended diarist's view of Burke; he spoke Gladstonianly to the Welsh N.L.F. on 14 December; *T.T.*, 14, 15 December 1886, 10b, 7d.
[8] W. Molyneux, *The case of Ireland's being bound by Acts of Parliament in England, stated* (1770 ed.)
[9] *Waifs and strays; archaeological notes* (1886).
[10] Perhaps *Tourist's guide in Wales* (1886).

Letters—Our Country. Reperused the Two Locksley Halls—& made a slight attempt at a beginning.[1] Sent off completion of Poseidon.[2]

16. Th.

Ch. 8½ A.M. Wrote to Mr Marjoribanks MP—A. Morley—J.R. Beavis—M. Macleod—Mr Simmonds—Mr Savory—Rev. Mr Thomas—Mr Westell—Murrays—Mrs Bennett—J.W. Berra—Treasurer of Guy's Hosp.—D. Wright. Read Hayward's Letters—Molyneux on Ireland—Our Country (finished). Worked on papers: & meditated for the projected paper, without immediate result.

17. Fr.

Ch. 8½ A.M. Wrote to W. Thompson—Ld Tennyson—Wms & Norgate—Rev. Page Hopps—W. Clowes—R. Giffen—H. Lawton—J. Nimmo—W. Benison—A. Philip—Manager LNW at Chester. Worked on Tennyson paper wheels driving heavily. Read Molyneux on Ireland—Leopardi, new Vol.[3]—Hayward's Letters. Woodcraft with W.H.G. Worked on papers. Worked on MS.

18. Sat.

Ch. 8½ AM with H.C. Wrote to Chancr of Exchequer—Sir W. Phillimore—Sir W. Harcourt—The P.M. General—Ed. Daily News—Messrs Murray (2)—Ed. British Weekly—Mrs Oliver—Mr Smalley—C.D. Jones—H.E. Moore—J.W. Berra—G. Hunter—Mr Herbert—Mr Burgoyne. Worked on MS. for 19th Century. Read Hayward's Letters—and [blank.] Worked on M.S. Sir A. & Lady Clark came. Swept 80 yards of path!

To LORD R. CHURCHILL, leader of the House and chancellor   Churchill MSS 2220. of the exchequer, 18 December 1886. '*Confidential*'.

I have to thank you for your courtesy in appraising me at this early date of the particulars in which the Government propose to amend the procedure of the House of Commons, and of their intention to give precedence to the subject.[4]

In the last stages of this important matter, that of the present year, I had but a minor concern, and I will therefore at once communicate with Sir W. Harcourt who represented principally the late Administration on the Committee. The matter will remain strictly confidential and will not go beyond those of my late colleagues who were especially concerned. In the meantime I do not trouble you with any observations but I thank you for your obliging readiness to consider any suggestion which I may tender to you.

To Sir W. V. HARCOURT, M.P., 18 December 1886.   MS Harcourt dep. 10, f. 142.

I inclose 1. A letter from Randolph. 2. His inclosure. 3. my reply. Please to consider these & hold on them such communications as you think fit with those of our late col-

---

[1] See 11 Dec. 86 and, for Tennyson's 'Locksley Hall', first published in *Poems* (1842), 15 Oct. 42; Gladstone's refutation of Tennyson's pessimism in *Locksley Hall: sixty years after* was published as '"Locksley Hall" and the Jubilee', *N.C.*, xxi. 1 (January 1887).

[2] See 7 Dec. 86.

[3] G. Leopardi, *Le poesie* (new ed. 1886).

[4] Information sent by Churchill on 17 December, Add MS 44499, f. 244.

leagues who were specially concerned. I do not feel myself master of the subject in its present bearings, and I shall on general grounds be much disposed to fall in with whatever may be your advised conclusions. But it seems to me that the weight laid on the Speaker is overgreat? and that the proposal to shut out all amendments on the Address is inadmissible and indeed astonishing.[1]

[P.S.] I hope Spencer sent you for perusal, from me, a dozen or so of letters on Irish matters—in *two* I.R. bands.

19. 4 S. Adv.

Ch 11 A.M. and 6½ P.M. Wrote to Sir B. Foster l.l.—Rev. J.G. Rogers—Rev. R.R. Suffield—Mayor of Crewe—Mr Colpitts Robinson[2]—S. Norton—J. Tildesley. Read Ker's Sermons[3]—Bp Courtenay on Future State[4]—Bp Alexander's Poems. Stiff frost and snow.

20. M.

Ch. 8¼ A.M. Wrote to Mayor of Recanati[5]—Mr Summers MP—Rev. D. Mackenzie—Lord Selborne—Messrs Philipp & Co.—Mr Morley—T. Scheyer—A. M'Kenzie. Worked better on the Tennyson M.S. A little woodcraft with W.H.G. Read Hayward letters—Dupanloup & Peyraud on Ireland.[6]

21. Tu.

Ch. 8¼ A.M. Wrote to Madlle Bles (paid)[7]—Mr Knowles—E.W. Hamilton—W. Forbes—Mr Russell MP—Mr Clements—Mrs Bolton BP—Mr Downes—Mr Cosford BP—Mr Clancy—Dr Forshaw. Worked on MS. & sent off first moiety. Read Haywards Letters.—G. Russell's (strange) article in Murray's Review.[8] Woodcraft with WHG. Discussed the Locksley Hall with Mary.

22. Wed.

Ch. 8¼ A.M. The frost went away. Wrote to W.L. Gladstone—Mad. Merlot[9]—Duke of Argyll—Mr Giffen—Mr Jackson—Rev. T. Morgan—Messrs O'Shea[10]—Mr Cooper—Mr Jos Heath—Mr Latter[11]—West Derby Union Chaplain. Worked on the MS. Read Hayward letters—Penna on Voice production[12]—and other Tracts. Walk with C. The Wickham party came.

[1] Long mem. by Harcourt on Churchill's proposals for procedure at Add MS 44200, f. 186.
[2] *Sic*; unidentified.   [3] J. Ker, *Sermons* (2nd ed. 1886).
[4] R. Courtenay, *The future states* (1843).   [5] Correspondence untraced.
[6] A. Perraud, *Études sur l'Irlande* (1862), with a letter by Dupanloup.
[7] Rescue work?
[8] G. W. E. Russell, 'The uses of adversity', *Murray's Magazine*, i. 18 (January 1887); Gladstone's 'enormous authority' was really a source of weakness as whatever he wished was 'blindly adopted', especially *re* Ireland; Gladstone's letter to Russell this day, denying Parnell had visited Hawarden (asserted by Russell), is in *T.T.*, 23 December 1886, 5f.
[9] Rescue work?
[10] *Sic*; no obvious firm; perhaps the two O'Sheas, Captain and Mrs.
[11] Reading uncertain; see, perhaps, 10 Oct. 83.
[12] F. Penna, *Production of voice* (1886).

23.

Ch. 8½ A.M. Wrote to Manager Press Assn—Ld Granville—Mr Knowles—Aldn Clements—HNG (BP.)—Mr Stuart Rendell—Mr Morley—Mr Penna—Mr Wylde[1]—Mr O'Byrne. News of the Churchill resignation came before ten.[2] It will have I think varied & far-reaching consequences. Worked hard on the Locksley Hall MS and sent it off to press. Took my walk at 7.20 P.M. Read Hurrish.[3]

24. Xm. Eve.

Ch. 8½ A.M. Wrote to Sir W. Harcourt—Dr Beveridge B.P.—Mr E. M'Clure—Mr Martineau—Rev. Woodward—Mr R. Brown jun.—Mr Knowles—Luke Hemer—Mr Edwards—Mr Brodrick—Mr Tartaglione. A merry little scene with the five Wickham children, a blooming group, & good. Saw Edwards on the sad incident of yesterday,[4] to which he gives a less gloomy colour. Spent the forenoon in reading and digesting the news in multifarious forms. I reckon it good in the main. Corrected my Poseidon in proof. Woodcraft with W.H.G. Read Hurrish.

To Sir W. V. HARCOURT, M.P., 24 December 1886.   MS Harcourt dep. 10, f. 152.

I suppose we shall agree that, amidst all this devilry, your clôture and my devolution, & all the rest of it, may for the moment sleep quietly in my drawer. When Johnnie [Russell] upset the coach in 1834, Shiel said to me with impish glee 'the devil's in the wind'. Seven devils are in it now. Yet not very malign spirits.

1. There is a chance for a longer recess—if a Coalition is formed, this I take to be certain.
2. The question is raised whether after all R. Churchill has a conscience. This is a good, for it is really material to the country that he should have.
3. Even the poor shrunken decrepit form that was once in my young days stalwart, the form of public Economy[,] may have some life breathed into it. In this matter I have every inclination to become a joint in Randolph's tail.
4. It seems to me that come what may there is in this affair some essential *progress* in the Irish controversy. Chamberlain's speech is perhaps a sign of the times.[5] I do not well see how Hartington can avoid joining: he must go forward or backward. Of course if he comes in it must be with friends.

But on the whole 'my bosom's lord sits lightly on his throne['.] My battledore heartily (if that implement has a heart) returns your 'happy Christmas' and New Year. Our Christmas thank God is happier than our Autumn—My daughter has made much progress & though she has not yet got down stairs we have every hope of her proper restoration.

---

[1] Replying to comments by P. Wylde of Bollington on Bright and Ireland: Gladstone will 'remain silent . . . I do not mean, if I can help it, to write one word which can possibly give him pain'; *Leeds Weekly Express*, 1 January 1887, 5d.

[2] Announced in this day's *Times*, 9f.

[3] E. Lawless, *Hurrish. A study*, 2v. (1886).

[4] A servant's drunkenness; Hawn P.

[5] For Chamberlain's overture of 23 December, see *T.T.*, 24 December 1886, 4e, M. Hurst, *Joseph Chamberlain and liberal reunion* (1967), 107ff., and Chamberlain, *Political memoir*, 233ff.

25. Xm Day.

Ch 8 AM (H.C.) 11 A.M. and 7 PM. Wrote to Duke of Argyll B.P.—Mr Lucy[?] B.P.—Mr Morley MP. l.l.—Mr A. Morley MP—Mr Mundella—Mr Childers—Mr Holt—A. Merritos—Sir B. Foster. The utmost turmoil. My letter opening ended 1¼ PM. But it is a day of special blessings. Mary was carried downstairs for the first time. Read Guinness on the Week[1]—Bp of Carlisle on do— ... on future Recognition[2]—C. Collingwood on the Bible[3]—Life of Mrs Rudd.[4]

To J. MORLEY, M.P., 25 December 1886. '*Secret*'.[5]   Add MS 44255, f. 154.

Between Christmas services, a flood of cards & congratulations for the season and many interesting letters, I am drowned in work having just at 1¼ PM ascertained what my letters *are*. So forgive me if, first thanking you very much for yours,[6] I deal with some points rather abruptly.

1. Churchill has committed an outrage as against the Queen, & also the Prime Minister, in the method of resigning & making known his resignation. This of course they will work against him.

2. He is also wrong in supposing that the Finance Minister has any ruling authority on the great Estimates of Defence. If he had, he would be the master of the country. But although he has no right to demand the concurrence of his colleagues in his view of the Estimates, he has a rather special right, because these do so much towards determining Budget & Taxation, to indicate his own view by resignation. I have repeatedly fought estimates to the extremity with an intention of resigning *in case*. But to send in a resignation makes it impossible for his colleagues, as men of honour, to recede.

3. I think one of his best points is that he had made before taking office recent & formal declarations on behalf of economy, of which his colleagues must be taken to have been cognisant, & Salisbury in particular. He may plead that he could not reduce these all at once to zero.

4. Cannot something be done, without reference to the holes that may be picked, to give him through D. News or our country press some support as a champion of economy. This talk about the Continental war I for one regard as pure nonsense when aimed at magnifying our Estimates.

5. With regard to Hartington. What he will do I know not, & our wishes could have no weight with him. But it may be worth while considering whether it would be right, or not, to work in the direction of yes or no through the Daily News or the Provincial Press. The position is one of such difficulty for H, that I am very sorry for him; though it never was more true that he who makes his own bed in a certain way must lie on it. Chamberlain's speech hits him very hard in case of acceptance. I take it for granted that he will not accept to sit among thirteen Tories but will have to demand an entry in force i.e. with three or four friends. To accept upon that footing would I think be the logical consequence of all he has said & done since April. In logic he ought to go forward, *or* as Chamberlain has done, backward. The Queen will I have no doubt be brought to bear upon

---

[1] H. G. Guinness, *The week and its origin* (1886), rejoinder to bp. of Carlisle in *C.R.*
[2] *C.R.*, 1. 524 (October 1886).
[3] C. Collingwood, *The bible and the age* (1886).
[4] Perhaps *Authentic anecdotes of the life... of Mrs M. Rudd*, 2v. (1776).
[5] Part in Morley, iii. 364.
[6] Of 24 December, Add MS 44255, f. 152: Chamberlain's speech 'only second in importance to the resignation' of Churchill; it has a 'very different' tone: perhaps the time has come 'for sounding him informally'.

him, & the nine tenths of his Order. If the Irish question rules all others, all he has to consider is whether he (properly flanked) can serve his view of the Irish question. But with
this logic we have nothing to do. The question for us also is (I think) what is best for our
view of the Irish question. I am tempted to wish that he should accept; it would clear the
ground. But I do not yet see my way with certainty.

6. With regard to Chamberlain. From what has already passed between us you know that,
apart from the new situation, & from his declaration, I was very desirous that everything
honourable should be done to conciliate and soothe. Unquestionably his speech is a new
fact of great weight. He is again a Liberal *quand même*; & will not on all points (as good old
Joe Hume used to say) swear black is white for the sake of his views on Ireland. He ought
not to waste this new fact, but take careful account of it. On the other hand I think he will
see that the moment for taking account of it has not come. Clearly the first thing is to see
who are the Government. When we see this, we shall also know something of its colour &
intentions. I do not think Randolph can go back. He would go back at a heavy discount. If
he wants to minimise, the only way I see is that he should isolate his vote on the Estimates, form no *clique* & proclaim strong support in Irish matters & general policy. Thus
he might have a round about road of return. The invitation to Goschen in the Standard
of yesterday is rather a question of Bright's pills for an earthquake & is absurd in other
respects. In *many* things Goschen is more Liberal than Hartington & he would carry with
him next to nobody.

7. On the whole I rejoice to think that, come what may, this affair will really effect
progress in the Irish question.

8. I am much inclined to recommend that as several of *us* are now in & about London,
you & they should meet daily at some convenient place to compare notes. I have letters
today from Childers, Mundella, Arnold Morley: and this sort of stir may draw one or two.

9. Birthdays & other things are buzzing about me, but as to any declaration of a critical
kind I will hold my hand.

[P.S.] A Happy Xmas to you. It will be happier than that of the Ministers. I assume you
will see J.C. ere long.

26. S. aft Xm.

Ch. 11 A.M. and 7 P.M. Wrote to Ld Spencer—Col. Donegan—Mr Daley—Mr
Knowles—Mr R. Brett—Mr Kenning—Mr Darlington. Read Bp Courtenay[1]—
Collingwood on the Bible—Reign & character of Charles II.[2]

27. M. St John.

Ch. 8½ A.M. Wrote to Sir W. Harcourt—Mr Knowles—Lady Clark BP—Mr R.
Brown jun.—Mrs Birks BP.—Rev. Dr Moore[3]—Mr J. Archer—Mayor of Chester—
Mr Gibson & others—Mr Hutchinson. Wrote draft of l. for Chester.[4] Corrected
proofs for 19th C. Felled an oak with WHG. Read Hayward's Letters—Hurrish.

[1] See 19 Dec. 86.

[2] C. Barker, *Character and anecdotes of Charles II* (1853).

[3] Edward Moore, d. 1916; principal of St. Edmund Hall, Oxford, 1864–1913.

[4] Perhaps a message for the meeting on 30 December for Foster (see 23 June 86); see *D.N.*,
31 December 1886, 3e.

To Sir W. V. HARCOURT, M.P., 27 December 1886.   MS Harcourt dep. 10, f. 168.
'*Secret*'.

I quite agree with you, though my perceptions are slower than yours, that the speech of Chamberlain is an important event of which due account must be taken. I even think it ought to lead to a *modus vivendi* in the Liberal party. I have however two reservations to make. First I think it my own duty to make no binding declarations till I know who are the Government and what general forecast of its course can be reasonably formed. Secondly that the importance of Chamberlain's speech lies more in the temper it shows, and the change from his own position of extreme hostility, than in the plan which with characteristic facility and rapidity he has laid down. I do not think the *modus vivendi* lies in the preliminary framing of a Land Bill, and the proclaimed postponement to it by us of what we declared to be our mode of dealing with the question of social order in Ireland, (which he ought to have seen was beginning with the impossible,) but rather in ascertaining whether, if Home Rule cannot be had at once, there can be had a measure worth Ireland's taking in the province of Local Government, with the assent of 1. the Liberals, 2. The Nationalists, 3. The Dissentient Liberals, either the whole or a section of them.

When Morley was last here he told me of a sort of overture he had had from Chamberlain, and I did all I could to encourage him in turning it to account; and spoke emphatically of my own position as meant by me to be in no case an obstacle to national and public good. He was then looking forward to seeing Chamberlain, and is now I think confirmed in this intention, which, on account of their old friendship, and their affinity as Radicals, seemed to me most appropriate.

Not that I deprecate Chamberlain's being seen by any one else and should you see him I hope there is nothing in this letter which will obstruct your conversation with him.

I am going to pay him a harmless compliment in an article growing out of the new Locksley Hall in the January Nineteenth Century.[1] I ought to have mentioned my opinion that Chamberlain, though his power of opposing and damaging especially in debate is great, has no large following to offer us, nor one of which the quality would make up for defect in quantity.[2] On the whole thus far varied and also ambiguous as are the contingencies opened the present proceedings can hardly tend to other than good.

A most happy New Year then to you all. In the enjoyment of 'the season', we certainly have the pull over Ministers.

28. *Tu.*

Ch. 8½ A.M. Wrote to Mr Gibson to Down Tel. Reported D. Post Tel. Saw WHG.—E. Wickham. Wrote to E.W. Hamilton—W. Primrose—Mr Richards—Mr Porteous—J.E. Elsam—Mr Arden—Dr Maurice Hime—Mr Knowles—Ld Ripon—Mr Morley—Mr Bryce—Mr Deeley. Walk with E. Wickham. Wrote on Zeus. Read Hurrish—Hayward's Letters.

[1] Progress in local govt., where Chamberlain 'is the most brilliant and famous name'; *N.C.*, xxi. 11 (January 1887).

[2] Harcourt's extracts from this letter were read to Chamberlain; MS Harcourt dep. 10, f. 172 and Chamberlain, *Political memoir*, 238.

To J. BRYCE, M.P., 28 December 1886.   Bryce MS 10, f. 75.

I have been obliged to postpone until today my answer to your interesting letter.[1] Christmas and the week following are the absolute reverse of holiday time for me: I seem to be in intercourse with all Humanity *Tutta quanta.*

I think your plan is a very good one and I have only two remarks to make.

1. Though I think you are quite right not to begin *ab ovo*, I should be glad if in a few preliminary lines there could be a reference to O'Connell's really important work[2] which consists mainly of *quotations* and disposes of the whole case down to the Restoration.

2. Either in your Volume, or in some form there ought to be a Tabulated Statement of the Voting on the Act of Union. There is in Grattan a statement drawing the line between the representative and non-representative portions of the House of Commons. Those who voted in 1799 & 1800 should be divided between these. And it should be shown what, in the way of money, title, promotion, office & the like, befel those who supported the measure. This is done *partially* in Mitchell.[3] The last division is unimportant, when the men had not to go back to their constituents. If this cannot be done in your volume, I imagine it might be done in the Irish Parliament Street Press.

Notwithstanding your fears, I cannot think the Scotch will largely bite at such a bait as a cut and dried plan of Home Rule. My correspondence, which is large, in no way leads me to expect it. Argyll is going to publish an historical book on Scotland since the Union, of course intended to act on the Irish case. Scotland since the Union is one thing: Scotland by and through the Union is another. I give no judgment, however.

What a political Saturnalia we have got. It is hard to foresee the upshot. But I think that whatever the form progress will be marked on the Irish question: even if Randolph were to patch it up & go back again 'reburnished' in Disraeli's phrase.

29. Wed.

Ch. 8½ A.M. & H.C. in Mary's room immediately afterwards. Wrote to Duke of Westminster—Editors of Newspapers[4]—Sir W. Harcourt—Mr Labouchere—Ld Mayor Dublin—Ld Fitzgerald—T.P. O'Connor—Mr Gilbert Smith[5]—Mr Griffiths—F. Knollys—Mr Bryce MP—Mr Vickery—A.M. Murray—F. Piper.

This day in its outer experience recalls the Scotch usage which would say 'terrible pleasant'. Despite of Home Rule, & the ruin of Telgr. wires by snow, my letters & postal arrivals today even much exceeded those of last year. Even my share of the reading was very heavy. Arranged with Press Association Reporter for public thanks. The day was gone before it seemed to have begun, all amidst stir and festivity. The estimate was 900 arrivals.

O for a birthday of recollection! It is long since I have had one. There is so much to say on the soul's history: but *bracing* is necessary to say it, as it is for reading Dante. It has been a year of shock and strain. I think a year of *some* progress: but of greater absorption in interests which though profoundly human are quite off the line of an old man's direct preparation for passing the River of Death. I have not had a chance given me of escaping from this whirl-

---

[1] Bryce wrote on 22 December, Bryce MS 11, f. 158, on plans for the Irish volume (see 8, 17, 26 July 86) and on the dangers of the Scottish home rule movement.

[2] See 20 Oct. 86.

[3] See 24 Sept. 86.

[4] Letters of thanks for birthday greetings.

[5] Of Chester; sent a work; Hawn P.

pool, for I cannot abandon a cause which is so evidently that of my fellowmen *and* in which a particular part seems to be assigned to me. Therefore am I not disturbed 'Though the hills be carried into the midst of the sea'.[1]

To Sir W. V. HARCOURT, M.P., 29 December 1886.   MS Harcourt dep. 10, f. 180.

I am very glad you are in London.[2] And it is just as well that I should not be there: as the proceedings are in their nature tentative. Viewing the chances of the weather I can hardly wish you a journey hither: but, should you find occasion to come, you will be most welcome.

It occurred to me on reading Chamberlain that we had not sufficiently allowed for the dual nature of the question before him: 1. what is fit to be done, 2. who is to do it. On whole [*sic*] I expect it will be found that the first question practically as well as logically is who are to be the Government.

I am in the pleasant troubles of a birthday: on which Chester reinforces the local P.O. with one extra clerk and we send up a Donkey cart to bring down the first delivery. It is well that my family is tolerably populous, or the business of opening could hardly be managed. I inclose for your perusal a birthday letter from Illingworth which has a tail about Chamberlain. No other independent MP. has written yet to me on that subject.

I am afraid Chamberlain falls into a mistake, the commonest of all mistakes in the Liberal party: namely the supposition that where the power to do harm is great there is a commensurate power to do good. Whereas the useful power is often not a tenth part of the evil one.

I am afraid I cannot stiffly contend for my hasty presumption about Randolph's conscience.

[P.S.] I cannot help sending you the inclosed caricature, now quite out of date: relying on your *honour* to return it.

To H. LABOUCHERE, M.P., 29 December 1886. '*Private*'.   Add MS 44499, f. 304.

Taking as my objective point not my return to office, which I have so often taken & left, but the attainment of Home Rule for Ireland, I assure you that I shall think many times before saying or doing anything which I believe to be likely either to frustrate or retard it.

I look upon the events of last week as in favour of the cause, whatever special form the issues may ultimately take,—Modes & particulars of action can hardly be considered until we know who are to be the Government.

I construe Mr Chamberlain's attitude & language thus. 'I prefer to you the Government with Churchill—I prefer you to the Government without Churchill: but conditionally'. This is a step on his part, which at the proper time I would not overstate nor understate; but I do not know that the proper time has yet arrived.

It is, according to my observation, a besetting sin of the Liberal party, to measure, each for himself, the power of doing good by the power of doing mischief: whereas, I think, the average politician (which Mr C. is not) can do ten times as much mischief as he can with equal effort do good. Especially is this true of evil & good in the House of Commons.

I do not wish the forward step which Mr C. has taken on his own responsibility to be thrown away, but I think very great caution, & very great regard to others, is to be observed, especially by me, at the present moment. The tendency of the late exciting events is to stir men's minds from their moorings: & we must be on our guard.

Thank you very much for writing.[3]

---

[1] The Prayer Book's rendering of Psalm xlvi. 2.
[2] Harcourt on 28 December, Add MS 44200, f. 209, reported on Chamberlain's '"Eirenikon" which appears to me of the greatest importance'.   [3] Labouchere's letter untraced.

30. Th.

Ch. 8¼ A.M. Wrote to R. Brown jun.—Wms & Norgate—Sir W. Harcourt—Ld Granville—C. Andrews—Messrs Murray (2)—P.W. Campbell—Ld Stalbridge—Mr Marjoribanks—Herbert J.G.—Mr Mackiver—Mr Carlisle—Mr Morley MP—A. Fryer—Rev. A. Lees—T.W. Brown—Mr Huxtable. Saw Sir B.W. Foster. Got out at 4 PM for a short walk. Read Hurrish—Hayward.

To Sir W. V. HARCOURT, M.P., 30 December 1886.   MS Harcourt dep. 10, f. 190.

Undoubtedly if I live to another birthday I shall go mad. Make allowance for this in reading the present letter.

1. The general effect of the *winwan* or hurlyburly that whistles and whirrs round about us is to incline me to a great tranquillity in my inner self. I think our position is broader as well as more solid than that of others, & that we may soon have opportunities of making it broader still.

2. I shall receive with great interest the accounts that may come of any conversation that Chamberlain may hold with you, with Morley or with any other of our friends.[1] To see Randolph is I suppose a main object of his journey to London. His interview with Hartington may not be altogether without awkwardness.

3. One of the things that make me feel the necessity of caution is the very inadequate sense he seems to have of the inherent difficulties of legislation on the great matters before us.

4. I rely upon Dr. Dale's character and friendly disposition as firmly, as I warmly admire his ability.[2] His therefore exhibits, I fear, the real difficulties of the case. He does not seem to have asked him[self] how the great wars of the last Century were carried on, when Ireland contributed nothing (instead of a very large sum) except of her own free will, when the population was nearly ⅓ of the whole population of the British Isles and when her proportion of their wealth was far greater than now, and yet no imperial difficulty arose in consequence. It is my respect for Dr Dale which makes me rather sad in reading him. It would require a man more ingenious than I am to frame a Home Rule Bill on his lines.

5. But I agree with you that the crisis is in the nature of a healthy development. Good will surely come out of it.

6. The inclosed from my Agent gives not one of Chamberlain's best utterances; it was evidently before the resignation. *We* stand midway in his estimation between the Govt. + Churchill and the Govt. − Churchill.

[1] Chamberlain saw Harcourt this and next day, setting up an 'amicable but informal Committee' for discussion of points of difference; Chamberlain, *Political memoir*, 237ff.

[2] See Harcourt to R. W. Dale, 29 December, MS Harcourt dep. 215, f. 133, on the quarrel with Chamberlain, and letter from Dale forwarded to Gladstone, ibid., f. 125, worried by his mistaken assumption that the Government of Ireland bill exempted Ireland from war taxation (it expressly provided for this) and requesting 'a Home Rule Bill which retained England, Scotland, Wales & Ireland in one Imperial Parliament, *with all that this involves*'; Dale thought Gladstone's ascendancy, unrivalled since Pitt, reflected an allegiance to him but not to home rule.

31. Fr.

Ch. 8½ A.M. Wrote to Ed. Scottish Leader 2[1]—Messrs Murray—G.J. Campbell—Ed. Daily News—Ed. Leeds Express[2]—Mr Bancroft—Ed Xtn Leader—Ld Methuen—Mr Morley—W.H. Flower—Mr Knowles—Messrs Wesley[3]—Mr Sunmill. [4]And other work which now I cannot remember (Jan. 31.87.). But the tumult was such as to show me sadly how distant I still am from the accomplishment of my great hope of a time for the beating down of strongholds, for recollection & detachment. Fiat voluntas tua.

[1] Congratulations and good wishes for the launching of the new Edinburgh liberal daily, founded to fill the gap caused by the Unionism of almost all the Scottish liberal papers; Gladstone added comments on the Churchill resignation: difficult 'to withhold at least a degree of provisional sympathy from a resignation which is variously referred to a desire for public economy; for a liberal and sympathising policy towards Ireland; and for a judicious abstention from intervention on insufficient grounds in Continental quarrels . . .'; letter sent to *D.N.*, see *D.N.*, 3 January 1887, 5e.

[2] Forwarding his letter to Wylde (see 23 Dec. 86n.) and his *Scottish Leader* letter, the latter in *Leeds Evening Express*, 3 January 1887, 3e.

[3] William Wesley, bookseller off the Strand.

[4] Space left; rest of entry added on 31 January 1887.

APPENDIX I
Glimpses of Gladstone

A

Rosebery's account of conversations with Gladstone

1 August 1882[1]   I had dinner with Mr Gladstone last night and after dinner he drew me aside on a sofa & we had a talk of at best an hour. I spoke with brutal frankness as I usually do to him because I think that nobody else tells him what they think at all.

He first spoke of the situation at home, of the Arrears bill & the position created by the Lords. They mean to take the amendments in the Commons to give a pause for the country to speak & the peers to reflect. If the peers insist, they prorogue: and in that case he thought of visiting Midlothian.

Thence he moved to the general situation—Egypt which they hope to neutralise and which he hopes may not be a long business. Ireland which he considers daily improving. Procedure which should not take long & where the important point is the construction of grand committees for local business. Then the way would be clear for his retirement. He was no longer fit for constructive legislation. He could not do this year what he did last. I said 'then who is?' He said 'Plenty, we have plenty of good men.'

This led him to speak of the reconstruction of his cabinet. Of course the accumulation of offices in a few hands in the cabinet pointed to a pause before reconstruction. I said that I could only regard that pause in the light of a slight upon those outside the cabinet, that there having been successively three vacancies in the cabinet which were not filled up could only give the impression that there were none fit to fill them: that this was intensified by his taking in Carlingford last year to fill a vacancy whom the year before he considered unfit to sit in his cabinet: that since then he had applied to three different individuals Derby Goschen & Whitbread to enter his government & on their refusal had simply dropped reconstruction. I said that I had no personal feeling in the matter whatever he might think, and that to no human being in the world but him would I say this. He interrupted eagerly to assure me of his certainty of my having no personal feeling.

He then replied, and I think very weakly. I interrupted occasionally & we kept up a sort of running fire of small arms with good & indeed affectionate manners on both side & perfect good temper.

He said Carlingford owing to the loss of his wife could not well be taken into the cabinet when it was formed. I said the loss of his wife did not prevent his being offered the Embassy to Constantinople & the Viceroyalty of Ireland, both situations where a wife was required which was not the case. He denied that he had been offered these posts (but I proved before he left the room that he had.)

[1] N.L.S. 10176, f. 53.

He said he was necessary to carry the Land Bill through the H of L: that the position of the Govt. was that of an army guarding five miles & a half of wall, where half a mile was attacked & all the force had to be concentrated there. I replied that it was not a good policy to leave the five miles entirely abandoned as Scotland had been. He said Scotland had had a cabinet minister but that he had left. I said that did not make the position of Scotland any better. I instanced the hardship to a country of having no cabinet ministers from the Electric Lighting bill which Chamberlain got placed first on a Scottish Saturday & deliberately took up five hours of time. We then went into a general argument about Scottish legislation in which he said that this session she would have got more than England. 'Yes' I said 'but this is all we have to shew for three sessions and tomorrow we shall have our first minute of government time since this Parliament met in 1880.'

Then back to the cabinet: the three offers were made purely with a view to his Chancellorship of the Exchequer being given up. 'What' I said 'Derby?' 'Yes' he said almost fiercely 'Derby too.'

Then a discussion followed as to the relative merits of Derby & Goschen. I thought Goschen the more valuable man of the two. He said he thought my 'usually accurate judgement of men was at fault'. We argued this point some little time. I also told him that I thought Whitbread absolutely unknown outside the House of Commons. 'Possibly' he said 'but very valuable in.' 'Of that' I replied 'I can be no judge.'

5 January 1883.[1] After breakfast [at Hawarden] Mr G. put on a little Inverness cape & a straw hat & invited me to walk round & round the square garden. Talked much of his health, excellent except in one point that the night's sleep, 8 hours or so, which is what keeps his brain & nervous energy going, he cannot depend on. Much discourse on this. He generally has neuralgia at the end of a Session & pays for his work in that way. Then he spoke of his troubles. 'The Queen alone' he said fiercely 'is enough to kill any man.' I could not help laughing at his manner—but he said 'this is no laughing matter though it may sound so' & proceeded with all their mutual troubles—Derby, Dilke, the Archbishop, the Duchess of Roxburghe & the robes. In the midst of this he saw that the dog had been making a hole in the flowerbed & became fierce at once, pursuing him, & throwing the stick he had been shaking at him, in doing which he dropped his hat: he then picked up hat & stick & resumed discourse. He soon tired however.

B
Sir T. D. Acland's notes of conversations with Gladstone, 1885

14 July [*1885*]. '*Dinner Party 1885*'[2] WEG had a long talk with Goschen about Ireland Goschen objecting to the National Council (Fortnightly)[3] because

[1] Rosebery's diary, Dalmeny House.

[2] Bodley MS Eng. lett. d. 82, f. 60, the heading and date noted on the accompanying envelope.

[3] [T. H. S. Escott and G. Fottrell], 'The Radical programme: (No. 7): local government and Ireland', *F.R.*, xliv. 1 (July 1885).

elective, & therefore not to be trusted with executive functions, & likely to act as delegates of the proletariat against property.

Gladstone took a diffe[rent] view specially pointing to the effect of 80 Nationalists in Parlt. & the difficulty of governing Ireland but I will not attempt to write what he said.

He spoke with difficulty as to his voice.

But after Goschen he beckoned me to sit on the sofa by him—& said the Lib party wd. break up—he should have no more to do with leading still less with combinations of moderate Lib's & conservs. The only thing that could call him out wd. be the need of settling some great ansr[?] to the Council question.

He promised to give me all the light he could.

before dinner he said he could subscribe to all I had written to him about *social* or Socialist legislation but he feared the Tories wd. go far & try to outbid the Lib's in that[.]

he said to speak of what is more immediate C. was moderate!!

I think the convn. after dinner threw light on this.

Saturday Dec. 12 [1885] *'Notes of a conversation at Hawarden'*[1]   A long discussion on H.R.

1. The two points alone reserved were the defence of the Island army & navy.
2. Some protection to the Land Owners (& the minority?)

I asked how ab. Police—Only ansd. by general[itie]s. If London were selfgovd. wd it be content with Metrop. Police in Home Secy—Any self gov. body must manage it's police—the I. pol. very highly paid.—is an army only not brigaded &c.

I asked how could we ensure our share of the revenue—something was said about an imperial pay master or agent holding the funds—spirits &c. The main point seemed to be deference to Irish Customs ideas habits. E.G. some of the best Landlords condemned for managing on English principles—refcs made to an Act of 1815 preamble about inability to collect rent.

I asked how far support cd. be relied on—one answer was that the question had not been raised in the election ∴ MPs were free—no fear of rank & file— N.C.O's—Comd O[fficers] more doubtful.

One great point seems to be need for not delaying.

The main principle is the constitutional voice of the representatives.

I asked how we know that they represent truly—not only result of intimidation. Ansr. Can't go behind the constitutional voice of the voters.

As to the tactics. I understand the idea to be first find out whether the conservs. & Parnell are acting together—whether either have a definite plan. If not then we sd bring out a plan.—I think first endeavouring to find out whether it will be accepted.

Notes after visit to WEG/85[2]   As I understand what is now in view it is.

1. That Home Rule must be dealt with promptly.
2. That it must be dealt by a responsible Govt.

[1] Bodley MS Eng. lett. d. 82, f. 101; partly printed in Jenkins, 262.
[2] This and the following version are at Bodley MS Eng. lett. d. 82, ff. 103–5.

3. Thirdly that the acceptance of any plan by Parnell & his followers is a condition of success.

On a matter of party Tactics my opinion is worthless[;] on No. 3. See below.

As regards the policy itself[:] That it involves entire control of Irish affairs both in Legislation and Administration subject only to two reservations

A. Control of the Army & Navy. B. some protection to Land owners (& I presume to the Loyal Minority)

Copy. Decr. 20 [1885]

As I understand what is now in contemplation, it is

1. That Home Rule must be dealt with promptly.
2. That it must be dealt by a responsible Government.
3. That the acceptance of any plan by Parnell & his followers is a condition of success.

(so far as Tactics)

4. (as to Policy) That any plan worthy of consideration involves the entire control of Irish affairs both legislative and administrative, by an Irish Parliament or Legislative assembly of some kind subject only to two reservations[:] A. Control of Army & Navy. B. Some protection to the Land owners and the Minority

I understand that some Veto is under considn.

as to Tactics (1) & (2) I do not say anything. I am no judge. But on No. 3 I confess that I feel the greatest repugnance to acknowledge ⟨that⟩ such a man as Parnell such men as his and 85 ⟨men who are his⟩ nominees raised up in bitter hostility to the Liberal leaders as the ultimate judges of what is to be held consistent with 'justice & wisdom'. Having regard to the various interests which they have crushed in this Election.

I am aware that any ideas of going behind the constitutional voice of the present Irish MPs is brushed aside as out of the question—I do not presume to argue the point but I am not satisfied.

There are several matters which I do not understand but which seem to be important. Whether there are to [be] Ministers of the Crown separately appointed for Ireland—I don't understand the meaning or working of constitutional Govt. except through a united Cabinet responsible to the Imperial Legislature. I don't understand how the execution of the Law is to be provided for as to appointment of Judges, Magistrates & ⟨Police⟩ control of the Police.

C

Lord Derby's diary: Gladstone's visits to Knowsley, 1881 and 1883[1]

26 October 1881   Great precautions were & are taken against any attempt on the Premier's life: police day & night, all round the house, & others along the road from Edgehill.

---

[1] From Lord Derby's diary in the Liverpool Record Office, reproduced by kind permission of the Earl of Derby.

27 October 1881   After breakfast we took our guests into the libraries, where much talk, the Premier discoursing on every possible subject with infinite volubility, & in a manner more genial & pleasant than his normal demeanour would lead one to expect. There followed a walk, which it was arranged I should propose to Gladstone, in case he wished to discuss any public affair seriously: but Mrs Gladstone volunteering to join us, the walk was short, & there was no discussion.

After luncheon came a deputation from L[iver]pool, of 12 or 14 persons, followed by a train of reporters. They presented an address to the Premier, which he acknowledged, & then proceeded to deliver a speech on the state of Ireland which occupied more than half an hour. The audience being small, he spoke in a low voice, & turned his back on the reporters, so that they had trouble to follow him. His language was more sanguine than I could have used, or could agree in: but I suppose a minister is bound to be optimistic in his views. He spoke of the Land League as a body whose object was rapine, denied that they represented any considerable section of the Irish people, affirmed that their influence was due wholly to terror, & seemed confident that they would be speedily put down. Apart from his under-stating the danger of the position, which I think he does, his language was likely to please all except extreme partisans, being firm & uncompromising as to the necessity of maintaining order. I observed that he spoke from full notes, occupying several pages of M.S. but he did not refer to them much.

28 October 1881   It was settled that I should walk alone with the Premier.... Mr G talked freely of politics during his walk, but with no special significance. He praised very highly the young men of the party who would form the Cabinet of the future: especially Dilke & Trevelyan. He was not uneasy, he said, as to the feeling of the English people: they were quiet & contented: I interposed that there seemed in England no feeling against the rich, such as one saw on the Continent. No, he said, there was none: the fault of the English lay in the opposite direction, in the excessive deference paid to wealth. He said little of Ireland, spoke bitterly of Parnell but to my surprise passed a high compliment on Healy, whom most people think the worse of the two. (But Healy has praised the Land Act).

He did not think there were more than 10 or 12 really disaffected Irishmen in the House. He believed the Irish people as a body to be loyal (I did not dispute, but could not agree). But he said he foresaw trouble in the future—there would be great noise & talk in parliament, & but little done: he was not sorry to be nearly out of it all. As to foreign affairs he was anxious. He thought the war of revenge between France & Prussia must come: he would not be comforted when I observed that the same threats had been used after Waterloo. He was deeply disappointed as to Italy, which he had expected to be the most conservative power in Europe, owing to the boundaries of Italy being for the most part fixed by nature; but on the contrary, they were a disturbing element, anxious for military glory, & for the possession of territories beyond sea, which could be of no use to them.

He talked of the treaty with France now pending, but in a tone of greater indifference than he showed on any other subject—observing that he had great doubts as to the policy of commercial treaties, but if we failed to make one with France, the political effect would be bad—it might make a coldness between the [two countries].

He confirmed something that I said as to the unceasing exertions of Bismarck in various ways to make mischief between England & France—saying that he (B.) had caused it to be signified to him (Gladstone) while in opposition, at the time of the Constantinople Conference, that he ought to press for the seizure of Egypt. At the same time Bismarck was telling the French that we meant to seize the country, & stirring them up to resist the attempt. (This is exactly what he did in regard to all the proceedings of the Conference, which he was determined from the first should fail).

Gladstone's curious interest in the eastern christian broke out in his treatment of a document which he had received, being a complaint from certain Bosnians of ill usage by Austria. As it came from unknown persons, & stated no facts, except in the vaguest terms, I should not have thought it of much importance—nor do I see how our government could interfere in the matter—but he recurred to it again & again, with an earnestness which to me seemed disproportionate to the cause. He talked a great deal (but not to me) about the Hungarian bishop, Strossmayer, about whom I am told he was enthusiastic, but I don't know on what grounds.

We had some conversation about the land & tenant-right, but on that his ideas were as he saw himself unfixed. He seemed to favour the notion of establishing in England something like the Ulster custom, allowing the tenant to sell his interest. He did not seem much moved by the plea that in that case the tenant would be selling, not merely the value of his improvements, but the right to appoint his successor, which is not his but the landlord's. He was more impressed by the argument that in case of such sale the incoming tenant would be entitled to demand that his rent should not be unduly raised—and that a land court would be necessary to decide what rents should be. He had evidently no plan, but it was equally evident that the bent of his mind was to give everything to the tenant that could be given without too manifest injustice. On one point he was clear. He did not believe in a peasant proprietary for England, & said so distinctly. He thought that whether desirable or not in itself, it was impossible for the actual economical state of the country. The small holder would always be bought out.

29 October 1881   During the whole of Gladstone's stay, some 12 or 15 policemen surrounded the house, watching it day & night. He received one threatening letter while here, & according to Mrs G. no day passes that does not bring one or more. The Home Office are uneasy and insist on precautions: not I suppose fearing a conspiracy against his life, so much as the possible act of some half crazy fanatic, excited by the reading of Fenian newspapers. . . . Much talk & comparing of notes as to the Premier. The general impression seems to be, & certainly it is that left on my mind, that he is more agreable [*sic*], more light & easy in conversation, than would be expected from his manner in public: no subject comes amiss to him, he is ready to discourse on any, great or small, &

that with the same copiousness & abundance of detail which characterises his speaking. He has no humour, rarely jokes, & his jokes are poor when he makes them. There is something odd in the intense earnestness with which he takes up every topic: I heard him yesterday deliver a sort of lecture on the various different ways of mending roads, suggested by some remark about the L[iver]pool streets. He described several different processes minutely, & as if he had been getting up the subject for an examination.... Since the days of old Lord Brougham, I have heard nothing like his restless & eager volubility: he never ceases to talk, & to talk well. Nobody would have thought that he had cares on his mind, or work to do. His face is very haggard, his eye wild: a lady who saw much of him said 'He has the eye of a madman.' And it is certain that in his way of thinking & conversing there is much that suggests eccentricity. M. was much struck with his singular power of becoming enthusiastic in his admiration of what he likes or appreciates: talking before her & Lady Reay of a woman (one Miss Pattison)[1] who had taken up the life of a hospital nurse, he said it made him proud of human nature that such characters could be found—or words to that effect. He spoke much of Cobden, of whom a biography has just appeared:[2] thought his intellect over-rated, his views more narrow and mistaken than his admirers would readily allow, but praised in vehement terms what he called the nobleness of his moral nature.... He talked of Carlyle, to whom he would not allow the title of a thinker, but considered him a great poet who preferred to write in the form of prose. He gave some reminiscences of the past. Thought the history of England might have been different if Sir R. Peel had come in as he ought in 1839: at that time he was not specially pledged to protection, & might have adopted freetrade without incurring the reproach of inconsistency, or quarrelling with his party. He did not think Sir Robert Peel had ever seriously considered the matter, till forced to do so by the exigencies of office—nor had he, Gladstone. His opinions were therefore rather developed than changed.

There was much other talk, but I have noted only a few points that especially struck me.

8 October 1883   About 6 the Premier came, with Mrs & Miss Gladstone, also Miss Hope. He was in good spirits, & talked abundantly. He dwelt on the increasing liability (as he thinks it to be) of the English people to panics & terror without cause: instancing the Channel Tunnel, & the continued talk about our being undefended. He thought there was no feeling of the kind before the date of the Crimean war, & mentioned that the D. of Wellington used in the time of Sir R. Peel's government, to write alarmist letters on the subject of defences, of which no notice was ever taken.

He talked very eagerly about some calculation which he has seen as to the increase of the English-speaking race (English & American):[3] which according

---

[1] Dora Pattison; see 15 Feb. 80.

[2] i.e. Morley's *Life of Cobden*; see 24 Oct. 81.

[3] In F. B. Zincke, *The plough and the dollar, or the Englishry of a century hence* (1883); see 6 May 83. Zincke calculated that, at present rates of increase, population by 1980 would be (in millions): U.S.A. 800, Canada 64, Australia 48, South Africa 16, United Kingdom 70; the total world population of

to this reckoning was to number 600 million a hundred years hence: I said something as to the extreme uncertainty of such speculations on the remote future, the impossibility of foreseeing all the conditions, & so forth: which he took well, but did not seem to agree in. He volunteered to speak freely about Ireland & Irish politics: believes that the time of outrages is over, & that the movement will now be, as he put it, confined within the limits of legality. I tried to induce him (being alone) to give his real views as to the prospects of Home Rule: he went readily into the question, but perhaps by my own fault, I could not follow him: he talked about the prejudice & timidity of the English mind where Ireland was concerned, said that he would never agree to anything that would destroy the supremacy of the imperial parliament: but did not seem absolutely to reject the notion of a subordinate Irish parliament: but as to this he was very vague, & I think did not wish to be otherwise. He did not think the Parnellites strong enough ever to cause real danger or do serious mischief: they would be, he said, like vermin about a man's person, troublesome & disagreeable, able to give annoyance, but not to interfere with his action. Before he gave any public answer to a demand for Home Rule, he wanted to ask what it meant, & require to have a definite proposal before him. This was the clearest utterance that I could obtain from him, & certainly it is to the point. He referred to Forster in a very disparaging tone, having evidently not forgiven him: & praised Trevelyan warmly.

9 October 1883 . . . Talk with the Premier about Trevelyan, whom Ld Spencer wishes to put into the Cabinet, but he (Mr G) does not wish it: partly alleging general objections, such as the danger of giving offence to other candidates, partly dwelling on the extreme distaste which the Queen, as he says, expresses to Trevelyan personally. Talk of a Speaker: he discusses claimants for the place: likes Dodson well: but thinks there is an objection to transferring any man direct from the Cabinet to the Chair: prefers Hibbert, who he says is popular in the House, & he seems to think that the objection to a cabinet minister does not equally apply to a minor official.

Talk of the Queen, he finds her wholly altered: thinks she is now more reactionary (his own word) than any politician living.

Talk of the order of measures—he is decidedly in favour of dealing with the County Franchise alone next year, & adding, if possible, the county government bill: redistribution of seats to be dealt with in the next session, but in the same parliament. He says this is Bright's view, & he believes it to be right.

At dinner, he & Rathbone discussed the growth of American fortunes of late years: agreeing that in the States 50 years ago it was rare to find a man who owned £100,000: whereas now millionaires in the English sense are common. They both agreed that the American system of protection was the chief if not the sole cause of this change. I could not see it so, but did not dispute the point.

'Englishry' (English-speaking persons) being 1 billion, with the U.S.A. the dominant political and economic unit; this last view fitted Gladstone's (see above, ix. xlii). See also to H. Tennyson, 27 Dec. 83.

10 October 1883 . . . I left him [Gladstone] in the library with Latter,[1] & rejoining them, I found Mr G explaining to the librarian the various styles of bookbinding in Paris & London, with the names of the leading binders & the merits of each. One would think that he had made bookbinding a special study.

We did not talk much English politics, but something set him off on the subject of Servia, as to whose internal politics he discoursed at length, but I have forgotten what he said.

He talked of Northcote, said he had every quality of a leader except backbone: did not see who could take his place if he were disabled or deposed: Hicks Beach was the best, of the other oppositionists, if only he could keep his temper, which he was apt to lose: Cross he thought greatly fallen off & repeated the old story as to his seldom being quite sober late at night (Q. whether true? I doubt): thought Smith a good man of business, but quite incapable of leading, & not much liked in the House.

Talk of French affairs: he traced the financial difficulties of France mainly to the system, which he describes as having been founded by Napoleon 3rd (but I think it is of older date) of bribing the constituencies by large outlays of public money. Yet he thought that however heavy the taxation might become, France would remain solvent. He praised the wonderful frugality & skill in all kinds of work, of the people: & thought their wealth increased more rapidly than that of any other European country.

11 October 1883 . . . Went early with a large party to see the works of the Mersey tunnel, about which the Premier was anxious. We left at 10, got there at 11, went under the river nearly to the end of the boring, the way being muddy, with some dripping from above; there was not much to see, but what there was was well seen by the electric light. Spending about an hour there (note, Mr G made a short speech to us in the tunnel, being asked, as I suppose, to do so by the directors) we drove to the Walker Art Gallery . . . drove home through a crowd, whose cheering & shouting seemed to give Mr G keen pleasure—more than one would have thought a man would feel, who has been so much used to it. All the way to L[iver]pool & back, & during the sightseeing, he continued to talk in his most animated style: I have heard nothing like it since Macaulay. The matter was nothing extraordinary, except for the vast variety of subjects over which he ranged: but the manner, words & voice gave an interest to even ordinary remarks on ordinary topics. . . . I heard the Premier after dinner discussing with Rendell the exact position of French students in science & art, & comparing their system with ours. He seemed to know all about it & to think the foreign method superior to ours, but I could not make out in what respects.

12 October 1883 Talk with the Premier in his room, & later, out of doors: he began by saying that he wished to discuss some pending questions with me: but after the first five minutes he seemed to forget them & wandered off into a general dissertation on politics, interesting in parts, less so in others, but curious as begining out of nothing in particular, & leading up to no conclusion. For the

---

[1] The librarian.

first time, a suspicion crossed my mind that there is something beyond what is quite healthy in this perpetual flow of words—a beginning perhaps of old age. He dwelt on very varied subjects—on the Prince Consort, Stockman, & the mischievous influence which those two had exercised on English affairs—on the cost of the Indian army, & that which it involved to the English army also—on the necessity of economy, to which we were pledged by a resolution of the H. of C.—I asked where he thought savings could be made? he said in the judicial departments especially, the salaries of the judges were too high, & they had many well-paid officials about them with little to do—in education also which was managed on a wasteful system—and above all, in grants in aid for local purposes, which he denounced as calculated to encourage needless expenditure, & educate the people in habits of profusion. He seems to think a great deal may be done in the way of reduction in these matters. He praised Childers as having been an admirable administrator, but feared ill health had weakened his power of work. He reverted often to the government of Sir R. Peel, as that in which administrative matters were better looked after than ever before or since.

He left us at 3 for Hawarden: at the last moment there was a scramble & bustle about missing or forgotten luggage, & in the end he went off with a greatcoat of mine, his own being lost. I imagine his & Mrs Gladstone's domestic arrangements to be incoherent. He talked much, I forget on whose inducement, about the Newcastle family: said, his friend, the Duke who was minister, had an extraordinary power of self-delusion: & one of his fancies was that he was ruined: he having in fact a good & even large income though his estate was a good deal encumbered. He thought the present Duke in danger of being led into bad company, his mother having gone into disreputable society & ended by turning Catholic. Wishes us to be acquainted with him: but as he described the youth as being a cripple of little natural ability & with a strong turn to devotion, I do not feel disposed to cultivate the acquaintance.

In Mr G's conversations, he referred several times to the Queen & always in a tone of regret, not unmixed with bitterness. He told me that he now regretted the fusion of the English & Indian armies in 1860, & thought it a mistake. I heard this with pleasure, having been one of a very small minority who objected to the amalgamation at the time.

D

Herbert Gladstone's diary: his conversation with his father, 4 August 1885, and his account of the 'Hawarden Kite'[1]

Aug 4. 85   Last night till 5 in the House waiting for the 2 R. of Infants Bill. Went over this evening with Helen[,] A Godly [*sic*] & G. Russell to Dollis Hill to dine with parents. After dinner had a long talk with Father in the garden. He is much exercised over the future. He will not lead quâ Liberal v Conservative—he will not lead a section or division of the party. But he is ready to come forward to fight the General election if matters shape favourably in two directions.

[1] H. J. Gladstone's diary, Hawn P.

1. The Irish party must formulate a practical scheme of Local Govt. for I. including a central board or Nat. Council calculated to work efficiently & which the Liberal party might agree to accept. They must undertake to cooperate in this scheme in its passage through Parlt. & in its actual working in Ireland. 2. The Liberal party must be practically united in their Irish policy.

Apart from I. the difficulties are not so great. He wd put in the forefront as battle lines

1. Reform of Procedure 2. Free land 3. Local Gt. in counties including Local Option 4. London Gt. Behind these come the Reform of the H. of L. & Disestablishment, on which the public mind is not yet made up.

But Ireland remains the gt. difficulty. Parnell having at the beginning of the year sent in a scheme of Local Gt. wh. he was ready to accept has now virtually withdrawn from it; declares he wants something upon the lines I indicated at Leeds; & now when pressed to say whether his scheme must be regarded as a dead letter does not reply. Father still believes in Parnell & holds that his letter from Kilmainham, his offer to withdraw from public life after the Phoenix murders, his vote on the $\frac{2}{3}$ cloture, & his general moderation in the House entitles him to some confidence in his intentions & courage. I do not take this view & told Father that I had heard from Labouchere that Healey [sic] thinks Parnell is now playing a wholly personal & selfish game—that he is vindictive & will never forgive his imprisonment, that he is afraid of the responsibility wh. a settlement of the administrative & Local Gt. questions wd throw upon him; & that he is therefore against coming to terms. He is for waiting upon events & looking to the Tories at least as much as to the Ls. As the feeling so far as I can learn among Parnell's own colleagues is for a settlement, the line he has taken in avoiding an understanding wh. separates him from them, bears out Healy's view of him. At the same time he is so strong that an open split now is not possible, though it may come before long. Davitt is the enemy of Parnell, & may when he gets his opportunity bid against him in Ireland. The fact then appears to be that Parnell's party does not know its mind. No wonder for its members are so different. There is O'Brien a fanatical separatist backed by some of the younger men, & feared by all. There is Arthur O'Connor an Ultramontane Protectionist Tory who detests the Liberals. There are 'Federalists' often more enthusiastic & honourable but [of an] impractical kind like T. D. Sullivan & Molloy—Bigoted anti England men like Biggar & O'Kelly—& lastly able & dangerous men like Healy, T. P. O'Connor & Sexton who wd gladly welcome a settlement on a fair basis especially one wh. gave openings to men of their party. The question is what do these men want, & what will they evolve? Do they wish things to remain unsettled & to wait upon events? Or will they agree upon a thoroughgoing measure of self Govt. which the Liberals under their old leader can give them? With this question our conversation ended. Will the Irish take local Gt. with a Central Bd. from Mr G. or agree upon some practical scheme which does not threaten or impair the Unity of the Kingdom.

Dec ⟨*13*⟩ *14 Monday*   I take up the pen again. Parnell did not prove practical through the mediumship of the O.S. As the elections drew near his lieutenants were anxious for a settlement but as my correspondence with Labouchere shows P. himself was inaccessible & appeared to wish to vote against us. He made a bid to WEG wh. was declined in Midlothian i.e. to formulate a scheme—& then threw the whole weight of his party against us at the polls. At least 25 seats went to the Tories through the Irish vote. At Leeds I put the I[rish] Q[uestion] in the forefront & warned my people that it wd. have priority next Session by force of circs—& I stood & was elected as a Home Ruler. Father's views have always been favourable to a large measure of Local Gt. in I. In 82¹ he virtually admitted the principle. When the Tories in July threw over Ld. Spencer for Parnell, I said to him Dont you think that we must now go forward & give Parnell what he wants? that it is useless to give him what he doesn't want i.e. a County Govt. Bill, or what he doesn't care for i.e. a Central Bd & that if we concede anything we must give them a Parliament. He said I think, we must. His views of late are expressed in his letters to me & in mine to Labouchere.²

Now the whole position is on the boil. Last week a letter was published in the Times from me to Mr Frank Miles in favour of a Parlmt.³ Next day the London papers commented on this—the D. News had a H.R. article called by the P.M.G. a tip from Hn.⁴ & the whole question came to the front.

This evening a letter from Wemyss Reid on the tactics of the Radical leaders esp. Dilke determined me to go to London to meet R. & talk over the question with friends. Went up by 5.25 & called on Bryce at 11 p.m. in Bryanston Sq. Found him full of the question, anxious to go ahead but perplexed by difficulties praecipue Land & police. Very loyal & thinks party will follow.

Dec 15   Long talks with Labouchere at the N[ational] L[iberal] C[lub], & with Reid at the Reform. Enlarging upon long letters I had written to both of them. R. tells me that Morley entirely disagrees with Dilke & approves altogether of the view of the situation presented in my letter to R. R. promises to influence all the provincial papers to wh. he has access in the right direction. It is a triumph to have got over the L[eeds] M[ercury] & it will give us valuable help.

Labouchere gives curious accounts of R. C[hurchill] vide his letters. R.C. apparently is a veritable sieve for letting out Cabinet secrets & makes no secret of the fact that he wished to bargain with Parnell & that some of his colleagues favoured a very big measure of reform for Ireland wh. was rejected by Ld. S. Spoke also to E. Ponsonby, Digby, Kitson, Rogers, O. C. Power. Dined with EWH, & Henry James, Algy West & Ld Wolverton joining us eventually at Brooks'. Very pleasant. Ld W. quite a Radical, & H.J. telling us amusing stories about Randolph.

---

¹ Speech on the Address, 9 Feb. 82.

² See to H. J. Gladstone, 18 Oct., 14 Nov. 85.

³ Letter to Frank Miles, an artist at Kelsterton, Flintshire, unexpectedly sent by Miles and printed in *T.T.*, 12 December 1885, 6d: 'Nothing could induce me to countenance separation; but if five-sixths of the Irish people wish to have a Parliament in Dublin, for the management of their own local affairs, I say, in the name of justice and wisdom, let them have it.'

⁴ See *D.N.*, 12 December 1885, first leader, home rule in tone ('we are brought face to face with the question of Home Rule in Ireland, and we cannot doubt that it has already engaged the attention of Liberal statesmen'), and encouraging an all-party settlement; *P.M.G.*, 'A "Straight Tip"—from Hawarden', 12 December 1885, 1a.

Dec 16   Long talk with Dawson Rogers at the Nat. Press Agency Office in Whitefriars St., & with one of his Editors Mr Austin. Gave them the situation. In afternoon with H.N.G. to see the Baroness von Daunop[?] at Baron Reuter's house & stayed so long that I missed my train & went back to Hn. by Irish Mail.

Dec 17   Fat all in the fire. Standard publishes 'Authentic plan' of Mr G.,[1] & the evening papers & telegraph agencies go wild in the afternoon. Hn. flooded with telegrams & all the world is agog. What a coil. How very odd it is that people refuse to see their house is ablaze till the fire engines come to put it out. Every man of sense saw what was coming in I. this election, & what wd. have to follow. The inevitable is on us that is all. So far as I can see the leakage has been considerable. L. must have let out a good deal, R. a certain amount with discretion, & the N[ational] P[ress] A[ssociation] has sent the whole lot out. This is what it says, & it is an accurate report of my 'private' interview.[2] Father quite compos.

Dec 18   To Wigan with H.N.G. & had most interesting day going over Iron Works, Coal Mine & to the Mill with Mayhew.
· Excitement over I.Q. continues. Leeds Mercury, Scotsman, Dundee Adv., L'pool D. Post & Mercury, Manchester Gn., Western Evening News, write well. This is mostly due to Reid. Father pleased.

Herbert Gladstone's account to Lady Frederick Cavendish of the events of November–December 1885, written on 31 December 1885[3]

I wish to tell you my view of the 'Revelations' and the part which I had consciously or unconsciously in connection with them. The main cause of the explosion was the tension of the public mind; for if you analyse the proposals you will find that there is little in them which cannot be taken (a) from the speech on the Address in 82[4] (b) from the Manifesto (c) from the Nov. speeches. Given the wish to create a sensation and a convenient opportunity for such creation, a little padding and much *a priori* argument pretty nearly account for all that appeared. But there was something more I admit. You know that the results of the Irish elections produced a great impression on all who have resolutely shut their eyes upon the inevitable until it came. A great many people who for years have urged and urged upon their constituencies and friends the necessity for immediate administrative reforms of the Irish Government, in

[1] *The Standard*, 17 December 1885; this report stated that a proportion of the members of an Irish legislature would be Crown nominees.

[2] In Hammond, 449, and *P.M.G.*, 17 December 1885, 8a, in a report headed 'HOME RULE. Mr. Gladstone's scheme. Details of the proposed Bill. Lord Spencer won over'; the *P.M.G.*'s summary stated that Irish representation would continue at Westminster for Imperial purposes; its leader began: 'Mr. Gladstone has once more, and that under the most trying circumstances, vindicated his right to be regarded as the only leader of the English people . . . the great statesman . . . has decided to declare in favour of a thorough and satisfactory measure of Home Rule for Ireland. . . . A "grand old man" indeed.'

[3] Headed 'Confidential'; Add MS 56445, f. 144: a typed copy, marked by J. Morley 'Copy. Original returned to Herbert G. 23/7/1902.' Holograph at Add MS 46046, f. 56. Lady Frederick Cavendish showed the letter to Hartington (Jenkins, 263n.).

[4] 9 Feb. 82.

order to break the shock of the bald demand by a large and wholly unappeased Parnellite contingent for Home Rule, believe prompt and conciliatory action in the direction of an Irish Parliament to be the only method for preserving peace and the *best* method for securing fair terms for the Minority in Ireland. They have not been idle. As the idea of Home Rule is comparatively new, that is when it verges on the practical, to most Liberals, and repugnant and even odious to a large number, you have the general conditions which go to create a phase of great political excitement.

I now go more into details but I preface them with a statement of my own personal position.

The Irish question is the one question on which I feel very deeply and with reference to which I can sacrifice my opinions to nobody. As soon as I was on my feet at Leeds I determined in justice to myself to assert my right to free opinion and with some limitations, free action. Where I felt specially bound to be careful was on questions of foreign policy and on the practical politics of the day when we were in office. Further it was my duty to be absolutely loyal to the responsible Ministers. But being convinced that with reference to Ireland, one fundamental error vitiated noble attempts to redress grievances, and that this error lay at the bottom of the great but yet limited acts of justice which were expected to settle everything, I resolved to do the little I could towards making this error good.

I have therefore acted and spoken freely on my own responsibility for five years; when convenient the Tories have endeavoured to associate my Father with my views, but I have spoken my mind so persistently that if our own political friends choose to consider whenever I say or do anything in connection with Irish matters that I am made use of by my Father for his own purposes and ends they overlook my right to full political liberty governed only by my own sense of responsibility, and they do him cruel injustice. My rights matter nothing except to myself and I can look after them. But injustice to him is a crime in my eyes. He always has had faith in his colleagues—may he not expect the same from them? And now I come at last to facts and events, which, however, you may understand better by what I have written. Now bear in mind the general strained condition of the public mind on the top of which so to speak these events occurred.

On Friday Dec. 11th [*sc.* Saturday 12th] (I give dates from memory but with all essential accuracy) appeared the D. News article which came to me as a great surprise. The P.M.G. had an article upon it, 'A tip from Hawarden'. This was absolutely untrue for no attempt had been made directly or indirectly to inspire it so far as I know.

About that time appeared Dilke's extraordinary speech at Chelsea, and public attention was caught by what was thought to be the genus of a split in the party.

Now as it happened I wrote a casual letter, without any idea of its being published, earlier in the week to an artist staying near here. He wrote to ask if he might publish it and I consented as it only contained what I am known to have said before. I expected to see it in the Chester Chronicle but it appeared prominently in the Times,[1] was commented upon by the London papers and gave colour to the P.M.G. and its 'tip from Hawarden'.

---

[1] See notes to H. J. Gladstone's diary, above, for this and other newspaper references.

On Monday the 14th I got a letter from Wemyss Reid (Editor of Leeds Mercury) to the effect that there was a regular plot on foot among a section of the party to shelve the Irish Question, to keep the Tories in office, and to prevent under *any* circumstances my Father from forming a Government. This tallied with information which had reached me from other quarters and I resolved without consulting my Father to go up to London and find out how matters really stood.

I had also got letters from various people who were utterly at sea owing to prevalent rumours, amongst others from the Manager of the Nat. Press Agency whom I know. He complained, (and his Organisation includes I believe 170 newspapers), that the whole party was drifting to loggerheads and that no one knew what to believe.

On Tuesday I had a talk with Reid at the Reform Club. I had written to him on Monday at length on the subject of the Irish elections as bearing on the question of the Irish Government, and our talk referred chiefly to that sectional 'plot' to which I have alluded and into which I will not go. I will only say that the conspiracy failed. The following were the three propositions on which I dwelt, and on which I knew I might dwell, as most essential to the present policy of my Father and I believe of the whole party

1. That the Government should deal with the I.Q. and that a fair and thorough proposal from them would receive Liberal support.

2. That until he was formally called upon to assume responsibility nothing would extort a scheme or plan from my Father.

3. No negotiations with the Irish party—and no communications with a view to the arrangement of a plan unless and until the Liberals are placed by the action of Parnell or Salisbury in a position publicly and formally to take the question up in Parliament.

I talked over the possibilities of a settlement with Reid and on some points expressed my opinions of what I believed were my Father's opinions. But as my Father has frequently said to me 'I have opinions—they are nothing more—I refuse to be pledged to them—I am only bound to my public declarations'—I have invariably on paper and in conversation guarded myself against committing him to anything, and I have never authorised or encouraged anyone to ascribe to him views which he has not enunciated in public, still less proposals for a definite policy. I know that he has communicated *in full* all his ideas of what the policy of the party should be now and contingently, to his colleagues. I have undoubtedly expressed on several points my opinion of his opinions—always giving it as nothing more—and if it has appeared to some from newspaper statements that there has been any action direct or indirect to pull strings behind the backs of his colleagues or to deal unfairly by them, I say that the whole blame must rest on my shoulders, if there be reason for blame.

On Wednesday morning (16th) I saw Dawson Rogers of the Nat. Press Agency. I went to see him entirely in consequence of his letter to me. His Agency supplies leading articles for country newspapers—and my talk with him—(it was supposed to be confidential)—was to guide him and his editors and to prevent them from being absolutely at sea. Remember that the public mind was already excited.

I spoke to D.R. and his chief editor—I read from no paper, I gave no paper, and not a single note of what I said was taken. They asked questions and I answered them. Naturally in a conversation of this kind I repeatedly gave my own opinion—I had nothing else to give except on such clear points of policy as I have specified above.

I came back here the same day. Next morning we heard by telegraph of the Standard 'revelation'. Its publication was due to a gross breach of confidence in some quarter. Reid dined with Mudford on the Wednesday, and has positively assured me (1) that he told M. nothing (2) that M. told him he had got Mr. G.'s proposals in writing. Further, R. told me that he had urged M. not to publish them as Mr. G's proposals, because he felt sure that Mr. G. would declare them unauthorized and incorrect. I have no information as to who supplied the St[andard] with this.

The Standard was followed by the P.M.G., and here I must say that the N.P. Agency went far beyond anything I had authorised or intended, for they jumbled up into one Authoritative Statement much of what I had said—distinct beliefs, possible opinions, contingent policy without stating the contingencies, qualified ideas without the qualifications, and they headed most sentences with *Mr. G.* thinks, holds, and so forth. For instance the probable course of Lord Hartington and Mr Goschen was stated as if this came from my Father. What happened was this. I pointed out my Father's position and views *before* the Irish elections, and to the inevitable effect upon them of Parnell's overwhelming victory. But I pointed out that this effect was limited as is obvious from his Address speech in 82.

Then the question naturally came up, What will the leaders of the Moderate Liberals do? I gave *my* opinion which I need not re-state, but I repudiate all responsibility for the shape in which it appeared. I spoke to D. Rogers as I had spoken to Reid, but I had no idea that an unauthorized account of a confidential talk with me was to be immediately sent as a bald statement to the papers. My object was rather a negative one—to give ideas for leading articles and to prevent friendly newspapers from falling into a trap.

You may say I was to blame for not being more careful—justly perhaps. One lives and learns and I shall be in future more on my guard. The N.P.A. wished to show that it had information—hence its telegraphed paragraph—and the P.M.G. getting the paragraph as usual wished to create a sensation, and put above it half-inch head letters. The Magazine then exploded. I enumerate the various events which led up to it.

1. 86 Parnellites returned—Surprise speculation some excitement.

2. My letter to Frank Miles in Times. Excitement worked up by London newspapers on the ground of Mr G's 'conversion' to H. Rule.

3. D. News article.

4. P.M.G.'s 'Tip from Hawarden.'

5. Dilke's speeches, followed by R. Chamberlain [*sic*] and others. Tories see a chance of getting Radical help and of a Liberal split. *They* set to work, as also does the Times and especially its Dublin correspondent—a red-hot Orange Tory. Excitement grows, now chiefly worked up by Tories for party purposes.

6. Standard 'Revelation.' }
7. P.M.G. with N.P. Agency's news } The shell which fired the powder

With all these matters my Father had no more connection than the man in the moon, and until each event occurred he knew (excluding No. 1) no more of it than the man in the street.

So far as I am concerned, while I am sorry for the form and manner in which some things appeared, in regard to my general action I have nothing to conceal and no apology to make. If I had not acted we should have got into hopeless confusion. It may be true that influential men are now all at variance on the question. On the other hand the Liberal Press is for the most part working smoothly and well on certain given lines. Not to mention advanced papers like the Liverpool Mercury and Daily Post, the Birmingham Post, Manchester Guardian and Western Morning News, such bitterly anti-Irish papers· as the Leeds Mercury and Scotsman are now writing moderately but firmly for reform based 1) on the constitutionally expressed wishes of the Irish people 2) on limitations securing the interests of the Empire and of the Irish minority.

A shock has been given to the public—but it is in my opinion better that the British public should be aroused to danger and to the facing of difficult and even perilous responsibility by a cold shower bath, rather than by the customary method of disorder and crime.

I have betrayed no confidences. I have not intrigued against anybody for myself or for any one else—though I have done something to stop the intrigues of others. Where I have made mistakes, it has been in over-rating the discretion of men whose direct interest it may have been to be indiscreet.

Those who do not share my Irish views may disapprove of what I have done; but I am not in office and[,] subject to my duty to my Father and *his* duty to his late colleagues, I have the right to act freely in advancing the policy which I believe to be just, wise and *now* essential. I conclude this long letter as I began, by saying that all this coil [*sic*] might have been made before. In my address at Leeds, and in several speeches, I declared myself a Home Ruler, and was elected as such by over 6,000 Yorkshiremen. The world might have known then what I thought and have made exactly the same reference [*sc.* inference] then as it has done now that my Father shared my views and wished to catch the Irish vote.

The explosion as I have shown was due to an unforeseen and curious combination of incidents and to the energetic efforts of the Tories to work the Anti Irish cry[?], 30 of them having been safely returned by Irish votes, against the Liberals, rather than to the formation or publication of any fresh views by my Father.

May the end of this great question be good; I can only pray that your great loss may tend more and more to bring ultimate peace to Ireland.

APPENDIX II

Gladstone's papers for the Cabinet on the Irish Settlement, 1886

Secret.   1.—*Irish Land.* [*23 February 1886*][1]

1. ACT to come into operation when Parliament shall have passed an Act defining the words 'Irish authority.' 1*a*. If more than one body shall be charged by Parliament with the functions hereinafter described, the singular shall cover the plural.

2. Act to come into operation on passing of said Act, and to continue in operation until the 31st March, 1889, and thereafter in regard to all engagements theretofore contracted.

3. Not more than (*twenty*) millions of Consols may be issued under Act in any one year, and not more than (*one hundred and twenty*) millions of Consols in all.

4. Such Consols to be issued on application of Irish authority, certified by Receiver-General of public revenues in Ireland (*whose appointment provided for in the Act defining Irish authority*).

5. They are to correspond in all respects, including the payment of interest, with the Consols now existing.

6. They shall be issued at par.

7. If and when, under the limitations of this Act, Consols cannot be issued to a vendor forthwith, scrip may be issued in lieu thereof, bearing interest [*at 3l. 5s. per centum*] until the issue shall be made in Consols.

8. Applications under this Act can only be received when made in respect of the whole number of agricultural and cottage holdings, comprised in any one estate belonging to one proprietor in Ireland, and being in the occupation, not of the proprietor or his servants, but of tenants.[2]

9. All applications for purchase under Act shall be registered, and shall rank according to priority.

10. But on obtaining registry security shall be given to the extent of one year's rent, which shall be forfeited to Her Majesty upon default to fulfil the engagement, unless Land Court shall, at instance of party, certify that such default was not due to the party liable, but was unavoidable.

11. The amounts of rent payable by occupiers, where, under this Act, Consols shall have been issued and paid over by the Irish authority, shall be fixed by the said authority; and when received shall form part of the public revenues of Ireland. And until so fixed, the amount of rent payable by law at the time of the transfer shall continue payable.

12. Net rental shall be rental less charges payable by law.

13. The landlord, or the Irish authority, in No. I and No. II, and in the case of No. II the tenants, may make application to the Land Court to the effect that, on account of circumstances especially affecting any particular estate for which

[1] Initialled and dated 23 February 1886; printed for cabinet 25 February; Add MS 44632, f. 69.
[2] Printed marginal note: 'Exclude holdings ordinarily rented and now on offer for rent.'

notice has been given, the relative value of the annual rental is not properly represented by the number of years' purchase herein set forth; and the Court may, on examining the matter, add [   ] years to, or deduct [   ][1] years from, the said number. This margin will not be sufficient to meet all the inequalities in Ireland. But we are offering an option which parties will not accept where it would not operate in their favour.

The Irish authority may require, and if need be compel, Corporations to sell on the terms of this Act.

(I.)

Irish *Landlord* may require Irish authority to purchase from him any estate or estates as above defined, and to pay for it or them in Consols at par.[2] The basis shall be the amount of net rental certified by Land Court to have been the amount due for the year ending   November, 1885, or thereafter agreed to by landlord and tenants. Subject, as in the Tithe Act of 1838, to a deduction of 25 per cent.[3] Subject, also, to an addition to capital sum of any arrears of rent, from and after that date, which he is also certified to have duly endeavoured and to have been unable to collect. The amount receivable shall be (*twenty*) years purchase of the sum thus ascertained for agricultural holdings, and (*sixteen*)[4] years purchase for cottage holdings. If it shall in any case be certified that the incumbrances on any such estate amounted, in November 1885, to a sum greater than the sum determined as above, then the landlord may require to be bought out upon receiving such greater sum.[5] Landlord empowered to claim to be bought out under this Act shall be the person beneficially entitled at the time of the introduction of this Act, or his heirs, or the person to whom at that date he may be under covenant to transfer his interest. No other person taking any estate as incumbrancer or by purchase to be so empowered.

(II.)

When all the Tenants of any estate in Ireland, or a number of the Tenants, not less than four-fifths of the whole in number and value, such number being willing and able to pay the charge on account of the whole, shall make application without the consent of the landlord for the purchase of their holdings, they may require Irish authority as before to purchase in Consols at par, subject to conditions hereinafter stated. The basis of the purchase in this case shall be the amount of net rental ascertained as before for the year ending November 1885, together with arrears as above, subject to a deduction of 10 per cent[6] only. But the number of years purchase to be paid shall be fixed as under No. I. In this class of purchases by expropriation, the purchasers shall be entitled to require the Irish authority to issue to them in aid an amount of Consols equal to the net

[1] Ibid.: 'Not exceeding two years.'

[2] Ibid.: 'Three modes of proceeding under Act: one for *Landlord*, one for *Tenants*, one for *Landlord and Tenants jointly*.'

[3] Ibid.: 'Lord Spencer doubts whether this will leave a sufficient inducement to the landlord to purchase. See my separate Memorandum A.'

[4] Ibid.: 'Too much probably.'

[5] Ibid.: 'Lord Spencer doubts on this point.'

[6] Ibid.: 'Or $12\frac{1}{2}$ per cent.'

rental minus 25 per cent., and the residue shall, unless provided by the tenants, be provided in such manner as may be directed by the Irish authority.

(III.)

The landlord and tenants acting jointly may proceed upon the conditions of 'The Land Purchase Act, 1885', subject to the following modifications:— (1.) The Irish authority shall stand as towards the parties in lieu of the Lords of the Treasury. (2.) Issues to be in Consols in lieu of cash. (3.) Irish authority shall be entitled to receive in addition to the annual payments a charge intended to cover costs of collection. (4.) Instalments to be so adjusted as to close the transaction in thirty years.[1]

February 23, 1886.   W. E. G.[2]

Memorandum (A).[3]

Sir R. Welby and Mr. Hamilton suggest that in the plan of optional expropriation $17\frac{1}{2}$ years should be substituted for 15 on the full rental, $22\frac{1}{2}$ for 20 on the reduced rental. They do not give reasons for passing by the precedent of the Tithe Commutation, which had the sanction alike of the Liberal and the Conservative parties. At first sight, the deduction under the Tithe Act appears to justify, *à fortiori*, a like deduction in the expropriation of the lands; for 1. That was compulsory: this is optional. 2. That gave the tithe-owner one good but inconvertible security in lieu of another: here the security is not only good but convertible, and we must reckon on its being largely converted in order to obtain a higher rate of interest on the capital. We have in our own hands to a great extent the means of purchasing so largely as to sustain the price.

True, we want to induce the landlords to sell; but we have also to induce the Irish nation to buy, *moyennant*, an enormous use of British credit, which alone can supply the means of bringing the two parties together. True, the plan speaks of net rental; but that simply means gross rental, less public burdens.

---

[1] An amended version, dated 10 March 1886, printed for cabinet on 11 March, Add MS 44632, f. 163, adds:

'[I am doubtful whether to complicate the Act by keeping alive this method of procedure.] If it shall be thought proper to secure by direct enactment to the tenants of the particular estate, or to the Irish tenants generally, a positive benefit from the land transactions, I suggest the following:— Not less than one-half of the difference between the annual sum due to the Imperial Exchequer upon any estate purchased, and the net sum receivable as rent from such estate shall be applied to the benefit of the tenants thereof, or of Irish tenants at large, in such manner as shall seem best to the Irish Authority.

'Finally, of possible methods of dealing with the Irish Land question, four at once present themselves, associated respectively with the initative of—1. The Landlord. 2. The Tenant. 3. The two in combination. 4. The State, acting by compulsory law.

'Of these the three first are comprised in the foregoing outline. Among the many points which demand consideration, none better deserves it than the following question. Inasmuch as the great object of the measure is not to dispose of the entire subject of Irish land, but to afford to the Irish landlord refuge and defence from a possible mode of government in Ireland which he regards as fatal to him, should we, or should we not, do well to rest satisfied with legislating upon the first of the four enumerated bases by which the case of the landlord is met?'

[2] There are further MS amendments on another copy at Add MS 44632, f. 166, which includes changing 'Irish Authority' to 'Legislative Body'.

[3] Add MS 44632, f. 73.

Effective deductions from net rental are— 1. Management. 2. Law charges (including cost of managing incumbrances). 3. Bad debts.

In many cases, these cost more than 25 per cent. In others they may cost less; but we must act in the rough; and we do not compel the landlord to sell. Further—1. The landlord will, as a rule, escape from his incumbrancers, who commonly obtain 4½ or 5 per cent. 2. He obtains a security immediately convertible and *without cost*. 3. Above all, what are the rents which form the basis of the transaction? The rents of Ireland generally for 1884–85 have not undergone the reduction so general in England and Scotland. Deductions made for the particular occasion would not count: we take the rent due.

We cannot consider the judicial rents as representing reduced rents. The judicial rent is simply a fair rent. It was known that there was over-renting in Ireland. The Act of 1881 sought to reduce the over-rents to the standard already recognized as fair by the practice of their neighbours.

The owner of an estate of 2,000*l.* a-year, who pockets 1,500*l.*, will receive 30,000*l.* (subject to increase or decrease by the Lands Court), yielding only 900*l.* a-year. But apart from State purchase, he could not have kept his rents, in present circumstances, up to 1,500*l.* Let us suppose he would on the average have had to reduce them to 1,200*l.* He can sell his 30,000*l.* in Consols, and, investing it with unexceptionable security, obtain his 1,200*l.*, or, at 5 per cent., with tolerable security, 1,500*l.*

I cannot at present think there is a case for the proposed increase.

February 21, 1886.   W. E. G.

Secret. Draft.   *Irish Government* [*20 March 1886*][1]

I. *Legislative Body*. Her Majesty may by Proclamation appoint a Legislative ⟨Chamber or Parliament⟩ Body to be assembled in Dublin as soon as conveniently may be after the ⟨1st⟩ 31st day of ⟨April⟩ March 1887, for the treatment of Irish affairs.
2. The said Legislative Body or Parliament shall be subject in like manner with the two Houses of the Imperial Parliament to all the prerogatives of the Crown.
3. But its duration shall not extent beyond [*four?*] five years. [I assume that in proposing one Legislative Body for Ireland, the question ⟨would⟩ will be left open for consideration during the progress of the Bill, whether any particular portion of Ireland might may be excepted ⟨and might continue as now. I find it difficult to see how an *effective* scheme of land purchase could be made applicable to any such excepted portion.⟩ altogether or may be placed under any exceptional provisions.]
4. Her Majesty may place under the authority of the Irish Legislative Body for the purposes of ⟨Irish⟩ civil government and administration, any buildings or lands belonging to the Crown in Ireland.

II. *Extent of Legislative Power*. 1. It shall be lawful for the Queen, by and with the advice of the Irish Legislative Body or Parliament, to make laws for the peace,

[1] Add MS 44632, f. 189. Marked by Gladstone 'amended'; his MS amendments are incorporated above; excised passages are marked ⟨ ⟩. A revised version of 31 March, ibid., f. 194, was presented to Cabinet, 1 April 86.

order, and good government* of Ireland in relation to all matters not coming within the titles hereby defined: that is to say:—(i.) The provisions of this Act, and of the Land Purchase Act of the present Session, except in so far as they are expressly declared in the bodies thereof respectively to be alterable. (ii.) Contracts made before the passing of this Act under the Land Acts of 1870 and 1881. (iii.) Matters touching the Crown or its Prerogatives, Succession, and Regency. (iv.) Matters touching Army, Navy, Defence, and Establishments thereto belonging. (v.) Foreign and Colonial relations. (vi.) Trade and Navigation[?], except as to duties, allowances, and prohibitions, which are within the jurisdiction of the Irish Legislature; but so only that no differential duty of customs shall be levied in Ireland, and no duty of customs without a corresponding duty on the same article of domestic production.[1] (vii.) The Articles marked A:[2] & patents dated before the Act.

2. Also such of the following subjects as may be agreed upon by the British and Irish Governments, unless when presented to the Irish Legislative Body an Address be presented to Her Majesty praying that they may not be excluded: the Postal Service, and services associated with it; Census; Quarantine; Patents.

3. Money may be voted for volunteers or any form of auxiliary force; but the formation, organization, discipline, and action of such forces shall appertain exclusively to the Commander of Her Majesty's forces in Ireland.

4. If question shall arise whether any provision of any Irish Act be *ultra vires*, it shall be decided by the Judicial Committee of the Privy Council, one or more Lords of the Irish Privy Council, learned in the Law, sitting thereon.

5. Nothing herein contained shall extend to prevent the passing of any Bill touching civil offices in Ireland and the mode of appointment thereto.

III.—*Executive Power*.[3] 1. It is hereby declared that the Executive Power in Ireland is, and shall continue to be, vested in Her Majesty.

2. Every civil appointment in Ireland shall continue as it is now until altered by Statute,—in cases where it rests upon Statute,—or by Her Majesty upon Address from the Legislative Body of Ireland.

3. Civil Officers in Ireland, appointed before the passing of this Act, shall hold their offices under the same conditions in all respects as at present [but their salaries, while legally payable, shall be charged upon the Consolidated Fund of Ireland?].

4. All Judges of the Superior Courts of Ireland shall continue, as now, to hold

---

* The words preceding are *mutatis mutandis* from 'The British North America Act, 1867,' section 91. [Gladstone's note.]

[1] The printed version incorporating the amendments has, next to this passage, in type: '[As to the excepted matters I entertain no doubt]'; and in the secretary's hand: 'The adjustment of this topic has been referred to Ld. Kimberley Mr Mundella & Sir H. Thring with a view 1. of leaving the Irish Body free as to purposes of revenue 2. of restraining it as to duties protective, differential, or affecting the trade between the two Islands in agricultural produce or manufactures to be specified.'

[2] Coinage and legal tenure; copyright; Beacons, buoys and lighthouses; weights and measures; naturalization and aliens.

[3] Next to this section is printed: '[See Canada (B.N. America) Act, sec. 9.]'.

office during good behaviour, and shall only be removable upon Address from each of the two Orders of the Legislative Body; and their salaries shall be charged upon the Consolidated Fund of Ireland.

5. The Irish Authority mentioned in 'The Land Purchase Act, 1886,' shall be such Officer or Officers of the Executive Government in Ireland as ⟨by Advice and consent of⟩ upon Address from the Legislative Body Her Majesty shall ⟨in any Act for the purpose⟩ by Order in Council appoint.

IV. *Composition of the Legislative Body.* 1. I assume for the present:—(i.) That some provision is needed for stability beyond what would be afforded by a homogeneous popular body elected on the basis of the present Parliamentary constituency. (ii.) That the Representative Peers (twenty-eight) will not retain for life under the Act their seats in the House of Lords; that it is not desirable simply to dismiss them; that it is desirable to do anything that may tend to attach them to Ireland; and that they ought to have at least the option of being included in the Irish Legislative Body. (iii.) That the principal provision for duality of orders within the Legislative Body might be nomination, or election by a constituency with a high franchise, or both combined. That of these the chief weight should be given to election. (iv.) That the composition of the Legislative Body may with propriety be fixed for a term of years, and thereafter made subject to its own discretion in most, or even in all respects; not however so as to interfere with the ⟨statutory⟩ rights of individuals under this Act.

2. Next I point out that we may have:—(i.) Two Orders in two separate Houses. (ii.) Two Orders constituting one House without distinction of powers; a simple aggregation of individuals. (iii.) Two Orders, sitting and deliberating in one House, but with a power of voting separately as if they were two Houses, on the demand of a majority of either Order. It is suggested that the vote of one Order on any vote of the majority of the Body shall only be available until a Dissolution shall have taken place.

3. So much for the disposition of the materials: now for the materials themselves. I suggest:—(A.) A First Order. (i.) The twenty-eight Peers to have the option of sitting in the Irish Legislative Body for life. The places of those not accepting at the outset, and of those who die, to be filled as in (ii). [Form to be provided for accepting at any date before day which may be appointed for meeting of the Legislative Body.] (ii.) Seventy-five persons to be chosen by a constituency occupying at a value of 20*l.* or 25*l.* and upwards, probably from larger areas than the present, or they might be chosen from the most populous of the present Parliamentary districts, the others waiting for vacancies to elect representatives. As these ought not to disappear all at once (their *raison d'être* being the prevention of sudden change), might they not be chosen in third parts (as nearly as may be) for five, ten, and fifteen years respectively? and all subsequent elections to be for ten years. These two would constitute the First Order, which, after a time, would become homogeneous.

4. (B.) A Second Order. (i.) Unless and until Parliament shall, with consent of the Irish Legislature, make other provision, the 103 persons now representing Ireland in the Imperial Parliament shall cease to be Members thereof,

and all elections made in Ireland[1] after March 31, 1887, to supply their places, shall be elections to the Irish Legislative Body only, and the 103 persons above named shall be Members of the Legislative Body in Ireland, if they accept seats therein.

[Form to be provided as above.]

If they do not accept, new elections to be holden to supply the vacancies.

(ii.) 101 other persons to be chosen by the present Parliamentary constituencies for counties and boroughs, to be Members of the Legislative Body.[2]

(iii.) The Legislative Body may, notwithstanding anything in this Act contained, pass a Bill enabling the Royal University of Ireland to return two Representatives, if it shall think fit.

(iv.) Upon any dissolution of the Legislative Body, two Members to be chosen by each county and each town division.

(v.) If either Member now representing Dublin University fail to accept a seat in the Legislative Body, a representative to be chosen in his place by the constituency of the said University.

[3]5. The Legislative Body will thus consist of—

First Order	...	...	...	103
Second Order	...	...	...	206
		Persons	...	309

nearly the number of the old Irish House of Commons.

6. These particulars have been set out to raise the points for consideration.

7. Of the three modes of combining the Orders, on the whole I prefer the third. Either of the two others might, I fear, provoke strong opposition: one from the Radical side as ruling affirmatively the question of a second Chamber, or one from the Tory side as ruling it in the negative.

March 20, 1886.   W. E. G.

SECRET. DRAFT.   IRELAND. Finance [31 March 1886][4]

1. The Exchequer of Great Britain and Ireland respectively shall be credited with all present duties actually paid into it, although the articles charged may cross the Channel for consumption.[5]

2. All receipts into the Irish Exchequer shall constitute the Consolidated Fund of Ireland.

3. There shall be appointed by the Lords Commissioners of the Treasury a

[1] The cabinet of 1 April 1886 altered this to 'for the Counties & Towns of Ireland & for Dublin University'.

[2] Cabinet of 1 April 1886 added: 'with the same manner as the members for Ireland are now chosen'.

[3] Cabinet of 1 April 1886 deleted the remaining clauses, replacing them with: '5. Until the Irish Legislature shall otherwise provide, all elections to the Irish Legislative Body shall be subject to the provisions of the Acts relating to Secret Voting, to Bribery & Corruption, & to Election Expenses.'

[4] 'Print No. 2', Add MS 44632, f. 197; earlier version, much amended, dated 20 March 1886, is at ibid., f. 192.

[5] Gladstone's marginal note: '1. This the arrangement intended, but it is not to be inserted in the Bill.'

Receiver-General of all public revenues in Ireland, and a Deputy, or Deputies, to act under him in any county or counties of Ireland. The Receiver-General and his Deputies shall be paid out of the British Exchequer.

4. To him shall be paid by every Receiver or Collector of public revenues or other public monies all and every sum received by them.

5. He shall thereout pay over monthly or oftener, in priority—

(i.) All sums legally due to the Imperial Exchequer in respect of Loans, Advances, or Consols issued to the Irish Government, with the Sinking Fund thereon.

(ii.) All sums due from Ireland in respect of contributions to Imperial expenditure.

(iii.) All Consolidated Fund charges imposed by this Act to the persons entitled.

(iv.) One moiety of the charge of the Irish Constabulary to the proper offices and shall pay over the whole balance of his receipts to the Consolidated Fund of Ireland, to be used as the Irish Legislature may direct.

6. In respect of contributions to Imperial expenditure, there shall be charged upon the Consolidated Fund of Ireland the following sums:—

	£
(1.) In respect of the Irish share of the National Debt ..	1,570,000
(2.) In respect of the ordinary charge of Army and Navy ..	1,785,000
(3.) In respect of Civil Charges	120,000
Total.	3,475,000[1]

7. The said charges shall continue for a period of [*thirty*] years from the 1st April, 1887, and thereafter until Parliament, with consent of the Irish Legislature, shall otherwise determine.

8. During the operation of the Act there shall be no increase of any of the sums payable by Ireland in respect of its Imperial contribution.

9. In the event of the reduction of the charges (2) and (3) in any financial year, one-fourteenth part of that reduction shall be carried to the credit of the Irish Exchequer.

10. In the event of a declaration of war, upon message from the Crown, sums may be voted in aid, and provision of Ways and Means for the raising of such sums may be made. Also Her Majesty may, under the Great Seal of England, give authority for the voting of money in relation to other subjects hereinbefore excepted from the powers of Irish legislation.

11. No tax or charge upon the people may be voted except upon the proposal of the Crown.

12. All sums now charged upon the Consolidated Fund of Great Britain and Ireland for the payment of Judges or other public officers in Ireland shall, while legally payable, continue to be charged upon the Consolidated Fund of Ireland.

13. An audit may be appointed similar to that of the Auditor-General in London for the control of the proceedings of the Receiver-General.

---

[1] Marginal printed note reads: '(N.B. The basis of the Imperial charges is Ireland, $\frac{1}{14}$; England and Scotland, $\frac{13}{14}$.)' This was the proportion changed to $\frac{1}{15}$ by the compromise of early April (see 1–6 Apr. 86). In the version of 20 March 1886 this proportion was given as $\frac{1}{13}$, changed in pencil to $\frac{1}{14}$.

14. And he may be sued for malversation in any of the Superior Courts of Ireland.

15. The Receiver-General shall not be empowered to appoint the local Receivers and Collectors of public moneys, but shall have the same authority to ascertain and direct their proceedings, so far as respects the moneys they have received, as is possessed by the Board of Inland Revenue in England with regard to persons collecting revenue, and shall have a like power of dismissal.

16. He shall also be entitled to sue them in the Court of Exchequer for malversation in respect to moneys received by them, and in respect to those only.

17. But the prosecution of persons for non-payment of taxes or other moneys due, and the control and government of local Receivers and Collectors in regard to the collection of such moneys shall rest with the Government of Ireland only.

18. The Chief Baron, and one or more of the Judges of the Court of Exchequer, shall only be appointed by the Irish Government, subject to the consent of the Lord High Chancellor of England.

19. The Court of Exchequer may sit for pleas of Revenue in Dublin or elsewhere, and shall have power to call, if it shall think fit, upon the Heads of the public force in Ireland for the execution of its judgments.

March 31, 1886.   W. E. G.

APPENDIX III

Gladstone's pamphlets and articles written in 1881–1886

This list, which does not include political speeches reprinted as pamphlets or letters published in daily newspapers, is in the order of appearance in the diary. The date gives the reference to the footnote describing the work in full; the note is usually placed at the day on which the start of planning or writing is noticed by Gladstone.

'Senti, senti, anima mia', *N.C.* (September 1883)	23 July 82
'Aggression on Egypt' (21 July 77) republished with preface	12 June 84
Preface by Gladstone to *The catechism of John Hamilton*	27 Sept. 84
'Dawn of creation and of worship', *N.C.* (November 1885)	6 Oct. 85
'Proem to Genesis: a plea for a fair trial', *N.C.* (January 1886)	8 Dec. 85
'Postscript' to Réville, *N.C.* (January 1886)	26 Dec. 85
'The Irish Question. I. History of an Idea. II. Lessons of the Election' (1886)	26 July 86
'The greater Gods of Olympos. I. Poseidon', *N.C.* (March 1887)	7 Dec. 86
'"Locksley Hall" and the Jubilee', *N.C.* (January 1887)	15 Dec. 86

APPENDIX IV

Map of the Sudan

(reproduced by kind permission of Professor Adrian Preston)

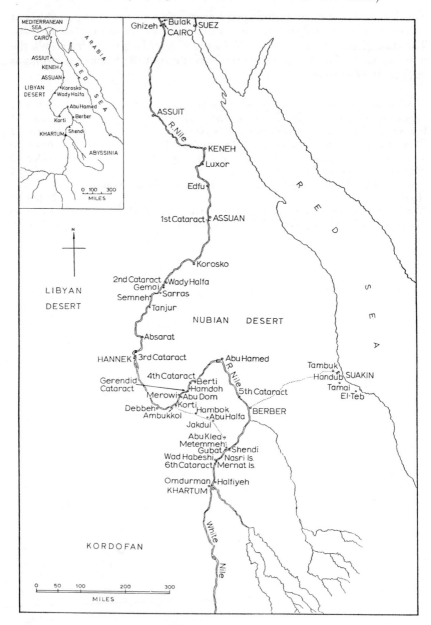

WHERE WAS HE?
July 1883–1886

The following list shows where the diarist was each night; he continued at each place named until he moved to the next one. Names of the owners or occupiers of great houses have been given in brackets on the first mention of the house.

2 July 1883	London	22 January	London
7 July	Berkhampstead (Lady S. Spencer)	1 February	Osborne House
		2 February	London
9 July	London	19 March	Coombe Warren, Kingston (Currie)
11 July	Windsor Castle		
12 July	London	31 March	London
14 July	Dollis Hill (Aberdeen)	2 April	Coombe Warren
16 July	London	7 April	London
29 July	Dollis Hill	8 April	The Durdans (Rosebery)
30 July	London		
4 August	Osborne House (The Queen)	15 April	Holmbury
		21 April	London
6 August	London	27 May	Hawarden
25 August	Hawarden	9 June	London
8 September	On the 'Pembroke Castle' (Currie)	14 June	The Deanery, Windsor
		16 June	London
13 September	Off Kirkwall, Orkney	21 June	Combe Wood, Kingston (Wolverton)
15 September	Off Norway		
16 September	Copenhagen	23 June	London
18 September	At sea	28 June	Combe Hurst, Kingston (Mrs. Vyner)
21 September	London		
22 September	Hawarden	30 June	London
8 October	Knowsley Hall (Derby)	5 July	Dollis Hill
12 October	Hawarden	7 July	London
24 October	London	12 July	Combe Wood, Kingston
27 October	Hawarden	14 July	London
8 November	London	19 July	Wellington College, Wokingham
17 November	Stratton Park (Northbrook)		
		21 July	London
20 November	London	26 July	Eton College
24 November	Windsor Castle	28 July	London
26 November	Keble College, Oxford (E. S. Talbot)	12 August	Hawarden
		27 August	Dalmeny (Rosebery)
30 November	London	3 September	Invercauld House, Braemar
4 December	Hawarden		
17 December	Soughton Hall (J. S. Bankes)	8 September	Balmoral
		10 September	Mar Lodge
18 December	Hawarden	15 September	Haddo House
5 January 1884	Hawarden	17 September	Brechin Castle, Brechin

20 September	Glamis Castle
22 September	St Martin's, Perthshire (Sir A. Clark)
24 September	Dalmeny
26 September	Hawarden
6 October	London
9 October	Hawarden
21 October	London
1 November	Cliveden
3 November	London
8 November	Durdans
10 November	London
22 November	Seacox Heath, Hawkhurst (Goschen)
24 November	London
25 November	Windsor Castle
26 November	London
6 December	Hawarden
1 January 1885	London
3 January	Hawarden
20 January	London
22 January	Hawarden
28 January	Norris Green (J. P. Heywood)
30 January	Holker Hall (Devonshire)
5 February	London
16 February	Hawarden
11 March	Windsor Castle
12 March	London
28 March	Durdans
30 March	Lion Mansions, Brighton
4 April	Holmbury (Leveson-Gower)
9 April	London
19 May	Windsor Castle
20 May	London
22 May	Hawarden
4 June	London
13 June	Coombe Hurst
15 June	London
20 June	Dollis Hill
22 June	London
27 June	Dollis Hill
3 July	Keble College, Oxford
6 July	London
11 July	Combe Wood, Kingston
13 July	London
18 July	Combe Wood, Kingston
20 July	London
21 July	Dollis Hill

25 July	London
27 July	Dollis Hill
30 July	London
1 August	Waddesdon (Rothschild)
3 August	Dollis Hill
7 August	London
8 August	Voyage to Norway on 'Sunbeam' (Brassey)
1 September	Fasque
7 September	Hawarden
29 October	London
30 October	Hawarden
9 November	Dalmeny
28 November	Hawarden
11 January 1886	London
6 February	Mentmore (Rosebery)
10 February	London
24 March	Combe Wood
25 March	London
3 April	Combe Wood
5 April	London
17 April	Hawarden
4 May	London
8 May	Combe Wood
10 May	London
15 May	Combe Wood
16 May	London
5 June	Dollis Hill
7 June	London
12 June	Holmbury
16 June	London
17 June	Royal Hotel, Edinburgh
22 June	Hawarden
26 June	Courthey
28 June	Hawarden
14 July	London
31 July	Combe Wood
9 August	Wanborough (West)
13 August	London
21 August	Coopers, Chislehurst (C. Morley)
23 August	London
25 August	Travelling
26 August	Frankfurt
27 August	Tegernsee
11 September	St. Martin
15 September	Gmunden
16 September	St Martin
17 September	Pulsau
18 September	Travelling
19 September	London
22 September	Hawarden

LIST OF LETTERS BY CORRESPONDENT, PUBLISHED IN VOLUME XI

A note on the editing of these letters will be found with the equivalent list in Volume VII.

Acland, C. T. D., *M.P.*
29 May 1885
Acland, *Dr.* H. W.
29 October 1883
11 December 1885
16 December 1885
Acland, Sir T. D., *M.P.*
13 November 1884
15 June 1886
20 July 1886
23 August 1886
Acton, J. E. E. D., 1st Baron Acton
3 February 1884
31 August 1884
27 January 1885
11 February 1885
Adderley, C. B., 1st Baron Norton
24 October 1884
Argyll, Duke of, see Campbell
Arnold, Matthew
8 August 1883

Balfour, A. J., *M.P.*
20 December 1885
23 December 1885
5 January 1886
3 July 1886
Bannerman, H. Campbell-, *M.P.*
30 May 1885
12 May 1886
10 December 1886
Baring, T. G., 1st Earl of Northbrook
15 December 1883
24 January 1884
10 February 1884
11 February 1884
12 February 1884
4 March 1884
24 April 1884
28 May 1884
2 June 1884
4 June 1884

4 August 1884
12 August 1884
14 August 1884
12 November 1884
14 November 1884
20 November 1884
19 December 1884
24 December 1884
6 January 1885
Barlow, J. E.
1 July 1886
Belfast, Mayor of,
16 January 1886
Bencke, A. H.
11 October 1883
Benson, Archbishop E. W.
11 January 1884
20 April 1884
12 May 1884
2 July 1884
9 July 1884
9 January 1885
Blackwood, Messrs., *publishers*
31 December 1884
Brand, H. B. W., *M.P.*, 1st Viscount Hampden
3 December 1883
3 January 1884
24 January 1884
11 April 1884
14 May 1886
Bridges, J. H.
3 July 1886
Bright, John, *M.P.*
23 May 1884
25 November 1884
1 June 1885
19 March 1886
12 May 1886
14 May 1886
2 July 1886

15 December 1885
17 December 1885
19 December 1885
20 December 1885
23 December 1885
2 January 1886
14 January 1886
30 January 1886
5 February 1886
16 March 1886
7 April 1886
23 May 1886
3 August 1886
17 August 1886
Cecil, R. A. Gascoyne-, 3rd Marquis of
    Salisbury
27 November 1884
1 December 1884
5 December 1884
19 June 1885
1 August 1886
Chamberlain, J., *M.P.*
2 July 1883
2 August 1883
10 August 1883
3 December 1883
6 December 1883
19 December 1883
22 December 1883
26 July 1884
6 October 1884
8 October 1884
28 October 1884
31 October 1884
31 January 1885
5 February 1885
25 February 1885
6 May 1885
20 May 1885
22 May 1885
1 August 1885
9 September 1885
11 September 1885
14 September 1885
26 September 1885
25 October 1885
6 November 1885
18 December 1885
29 December 1885
8 February 1886
25 February 1886
15 March 1886

16 March 1886
27 March 1886
4 April 1886
11 April 1886
15 April 1886
Childers, H. C. E., *M.P.*
5 July 1883
18 August 1883
10 September 1883
12 September 1883
15 September 1883
25 September 1883
7 November 1883
14 January 1884
19 January 1884
21 January 1884
25 January 1884
8 March 1884
20 March 1884
28 April 1884
30 May 1884
6 June 1884
8 June 1884
16 June 1884
23 September 1884
2 October 1884
3 October 1884
8 November 1884
16 December 1884
21 December 1884
31 December 1884
9 January 1885
29 January 1885
2 February 1885
16 February 1885
5 April 1885
7 May 1885
14 May 1885
20 May 1885
31 May 1885
23 July 1885
25 July 1885
28 September 1885
10 February 1886
13 February 1886
20 February 1886
9 March 1886
18 March 1886
19 March 1886
24 April 1886
4 June 1886

Lingen, Sir R. R. W.
  27 January 1885
  30 January 1885
Lorne, Lord, see Campbell

MacColl, Rev. M.
  30 January 1884
  2 July 1884
  13 July 1884
Mackenzie, Sir K. A. Muir
  13 June 1886
Macmillan, A., *publisher*
  11 October 1886
  4 November 1886
Malet, Sir E. B.
  18 November 1884
Manning, Cardinal H. E.
  21 February 1884
  9 January 1886
Marjoribanks, E., *M.P.*
  10 July 1886
  13 July 1886
Marsh, Miss C.
  27 July 1886
May, Sir T. Erskine
  18 April 1886
Methuen, F. H. P., 2nd Baron Methuen
  14 April 1886
Midlothian, electors of
  3 December 1885
Millais, J. E., *artist*
  24 June 1885
Morley, A., *M.P.*
  20 April 1886
  26 April 1886
  9 May 1886
  12 May 1886
  19 May 1886
  23 June 1886
  27 June 1886
  30 June 1886
Morley, J., *M.P.*
  25 October 1883
  2 February 1886
  22 March 1886
  3 April 1886
  19 April 1886
  20 April 1886
  21 April 1886
  8 May 1886
  12 May 1886
  14 May 1886

  3 June 1886
  9 July 1886
  8 December 1886
  25 December 1886
Morley, Lord, see Parker
Mundella, A. J., *M.P.*
  13 July 1886

New Zealand, Speakers of Legislative Houses of
  26 October 1883
Northbrook, Lord, see Baring
Northcote, Sir S. H., *M.P.*, 1st Earl of Iddesleigh
  11 December 1883
  14 November 1884
  29 November 1884
  12 June 1885
  15 June 1885
  25 June 1885
Novikov, Madame O.
  8 August 1883
  1 July 1885
  16 November 886

O'Brien, R. Barry, *author*
  4 October 1883
  7 July 1886
Ornsby, R., *author*
  24 November 1883
O'Shea, Mrs.
  4 August 1885
  8 August 1885
  24 October 1885
  3 November 1885
  12 December 1885
  16 December 1885
  19 December 1885
  22 December 1885
  24 December 1885
  9 January 1886
  24 January 1886
  26 January 1886
  29 January 1886
  8 May 1886
  14 May 1886

Palmer, Archdeacon E.
  7 December 1885
Palmer, Rev. Sir W.
  21 November 1883

DRAMATIS PERSONAE, 1881–1886

An index to the whole work will appear in the concluding volume, together with a bibliography of Gladstone's reading as recorded in the diary. Meanwhile readers may be helped by this list of persons mentioned; most of the references refer to the first occasion of mention in the diary. A plain date indicates a first mention in the diary text, usually with a footnote at that date if the person has been identified; a date with 'n' (e.g. 27 Oct. 82n) indicates a mention in a footnote to a person or event noticed by the diarist on that day.

This list covers the years 1881–1886 and must be read together with the lists at the end of volumes two, four, six, eight and nine. People mentioned in those lists are not repeated here. Readers who wish to identify a person mentioned in the diary, but who is not in this list below, should refer to the five previous lists. The exceptions are names that occur in the first nine volumes but are more fully identified by a footnote in these volumes; these are marked † following their date, in the list below. A few cross-references from this list are to names in previous lists. Names mentioned on the fly leaf of an MS volume of the diary are marked (f.l.) with the nearest date. To increase the list's usefulness as a guide to identification, priests have their initials prefixed by *Rev.*, *Bp.* etc., and some other occupations have been briefly indicated.

People with double-barrelled, or particuled, surnames appear under the last part of the name, except that names in M' and Mc are under Mac, Irish names in O' are under O, and D'Houne, De Coverley, De Burgh, and De Marzo, are under D.

Rulers and royal dukes are given under their regal or Christian names. Other peers, and married women, are listed under their surname, with cross-references from their titles and maiden names.

Aberdeen, *Lady*, *see* Gordon
Ackers, B. St. J., 15 Nov. 85
Acland, *Sir* W. A. Dyke, *2nd Bart.*, 29 Oct. 83
Acrell, *Mr.*, 29 Oct. 86
Addis, *Rev.* W. E., 28 Jan. 84
Adlerberg, *Madame*, 30 Aug. 86
Adsetts, *Dr.*, 10 Dec. 85
Ahmed Khandeel, 26 June 83
Albani, *Dame* E., *singer*, 14 Sept. 84
Alden, E. W., 4 July 85
Alexander *of Bulgaria*, *Prince*, 26 May 81
Alexis, *Grand Duke*, 9 Mar. 81
Amos, *Mrs.*, 31 Mar. 82
Amos, *rescue*, 24 Aug. 83
Anderson, C. H., 27 Nov. 85n
Anderson, *Miss* M., 8 Nov. 84
Anderson, *Maj. gen.* R. P., 1 Nov. 85n
André, *Prof.*, 4 Oct. 83
Andrews, C., 30 Dec. 86
Andrews, *Messrs* T., 10 Jan. 86
Ankers, *Mr.*, 1 July 86
Aplin, *Mr.*, 23 May 83

Archer, J., 27 Dec. 86
Archer, T., 26 Dec. 81
Argyropulos, *Mr.*, 23 Oct. 83
Armitage, *Mrs.*, *rescue*, 5 Dec. 84
Arthur, *Rev.* W., 19 Nov. 81
Arthur, *Rev.* W. M., 12 Sept. 85 (?)
Ashburnham, B., *4th Earl of Ashburnham*, 14 Apr. 83n
Ashburnham Collection, 12 Mar. 83
Ashman, J., 10 Dec. 85
Askey, R., 10 Dec. 86
Asquith, E. A. M. *née* Tennant, 28 Feb. 81 (?)
Avery & Sons, *Messrs.*, 8 Jan. 84
Aylmer, J. E. Freke-, 3 Nov. 82
Ayre, *Messrs* W., 10 Jan. 86

Baggally, *Capt.*, 28 May 84n
Baker, *Mrs.*, *rescue*, 22 May 86
Balfour, A., 14 Aug. 84 (?)
Balfour, *Rev.* W., 7 Nov. 85
Bankes, J. S., 7 Apr. 82
Banton, W., 23 Feb. 81 (?)

Callingham, *Mr.*, 10 Aug. 86
Cameron, *Mr.*, 16 Dec. 84
Campbell, D., 25 Jan. 86
Campbell, *Miss* E. A., 4 Apr. 84
Campbell, G. J., 31 Dec. 86
Campello, *Count* E. Di, 17 Sept. 81
Candall, *Mr.*, 12 July 83
Cantacuzene, *Prince* G., 19 June 83
Capper, *Mr.*, 10 June 85
Carbutt, E. H., 26 July 83
Cardon, R., 19 May 83
Carey, J., 20 Feb. 83n
Carlisle, H. E., 28 Jan. 85
Carlyle, *Mr.*, 15 Sept. 85
Carnegie, A., 31 July 82
Carnegie, J., *9th Earl of Southesk*, 17 Sept. 84
Carpenter, *Bp.* W. Boyd, 18 Mar. 81
Carrington, A., 9 Sept. 82
Cartman, *Rev.* J., 14 June 86
Cartwright, *Sir* (W.) C., 19 June 82
Cary, *Miss*, 2 Jan. 81
Casement, *Mr.*, 12 Nov. 85
Cavan, *Earl of, see* Lambart
Cave, A. T. T. Verney-, *5th Baron Braye*, 28 May 83
Cavendish, *Miss* A., 24 Apr. 83n
Cavendish, H. F., *Lady Chesham*, 1 Mar. 84
Cecil, J. E. H. Gascoigne-, *Lord Cranborne, 4th Marquis of Salisbury*, 29 Nov. 83
Cetewayo, *King of the Zulus*, 29 Aug. 81
Chadwick, D., 14 Dec. 81
Challemel-Lacour, P.-A., 27 Feb. 83
Chant, *Mr.*, 20 Sept. 81
Chappel, *Rev.* W. P., 25 Dec. 84
Charteris, *Dr.*, 11 Dec. 85
Chérif Pasha, 3 Jan. 84
Chermside, (*Sir*) H. C., 29 Mar. 84
Chesham, *Lady, see* Cavendish
Chester Chronicle, reporter of, 30 Sept. 84
Chittenden, G. R., 15 June 81
Christian IX *of Denmark*, 17 Sept. 83
Christian, *'Little'*, 27 Mar. 85
Christie, J. D., 13 Oct. 85
Church Association, 30 May 82
Clarke, *Sir* A., 5 July 83
Clemenceau, *President* G., 8 Feb. 83
Clements, *Alderman*, 23 Dec. 86
Clifden, *Lady, see* Ellis
Clifford, *Sir* R. C. Spencer, *3rd Bart.*, 9 Aug. 83

Clifton, *Mrs.*, *rescue*, 4 Dec. 83
Clinton, *Lady* E., *see* Pamphilji
Clinton, H. P. A. D., *7th Duke of Newcastle*, 19 Dec. 83
Clough, W. O., 25 Nov. 86 (?)
Coatcott, *Dr.*, 5 Aug. 83
Cobb, H. P., 1 Jan. 86
Cockle, *Mrs.*, 25 Nov. 86
Coelögon, *Col.* de, 25 Jan. 84n
Cole, F. B. O., 29 Nov. 86
Colley, *Ven.*, 16 Jan. 86
Collings, J., 9 June 81
Collingwood, C., 15 Dec. 86
Colthurst, *Col.* D. La T., 20 Jan. 81
Compton, *Lord* A. F., 31 July 86n
Compton, *Lady* M., *née* Vyner, 31 July 86
Compton, *Lady* M. V. I., 27 Jan. 86
Cook, *Sir* E. T., 12 Jan. 86n
Cooper, C. A., 18 Nov. 85
Cooper, W. W., 28 May 86
Coquelin, *Mons.*, 1 June 83
Corbet, W. J., 22 July 84
Corrie, D., 7 July 81
Corry, *Mrs. or Miss*, 24 Apr. 83
Cossham, H., 14 Apr. 86†
Costelloe, B. F. C., 26 Sept. 83 (?)
Cotes, C. C., 9 Aug. 84
Cotterill, C. C., 18 June 86
Courlander, *Messrs.*, 30 Sept. 86
Cowell, *Miss* L., 24 Apr. 83n
Craig, H. V. Gibson-, 14 Sept. 84
Craig, W. Y., 5 Feb. 81
Craik, *Sir* H., *1st Bart.*, 12 Dec. 86 (?)
Cranborne, *Lord, see* Cecil
Crawford, *Mrs.* E., 8 Feb. 83
Crawford, *Mrs.* F., 11 Nov. 82 (?)
Cray, *rescue*, 27 Feb. 86
Crombie, J. W., 29 Oct. 86 (?)
Cross, J. W., 5 Feb. 83
Crossley, *Mr.*, 18 Dec. 85
Crowther, E., 28 Oct. 85
Crump, A., 11 Jan. 86
Cullen, *Rev.* J., 13 Oct. 85
Cullinan, W. F., 22 Apr. 81
Cundall, J. H., 6 July 81 (?)
Curran, *Surgeon* J. J., 30 Sept. 86 (?)
Currey, W., 16 Mar. 86n
Currie, B. W., 19 Mar. 84
Curteis, A. M., 26 Oct. 85
Curzon, F. N., 24 June 82
Cuyler, *Rev. Dr.* T. L., 1 Aug. 85

Flower, C., *1st Baron Battersea*, 19 Oct. 85
Flower, W. H., 31 Dec. 86
Ford, E. O., 15 May 82
Forewood, *Mr.*, 7 June 83
Forsey, C. B., 1 June 85
Forshaw, *Dr.*, 21 Dec. 86
Forster, *Miss* F. Arnold-, 4 Apr. 81n
Forster, H. O. Arnold-, 12 Apr. 82n
Fort, R. *jnr.*, 2 Nov. 82
Fortune, D., 17 Oct. 86
Forwood, A. B., 12 Dec. 82n
Foster, *Sir* (B.) W., 23 June 86
Foster, J. J., 29 Nov. 86
Foulds, J. L., 25 Nov. 85
Foville, A. De, 24 Oct. 85
Fox, *Mr.*, 24 June 86
Francesco, F., 13 July 81
Freiheit, Die, 26 Mar. 81
Frenchly, D., 20 Jan. 82
Frith, W. P., 21 Nov. 81
Fry, *Sir* E., 4 Apr. 83
Fry, J. S., 1 June 85n
Fry, *Sir* T., *1st Bart.*, 29 June 86
Fryer, A., 30 Dec. 86

Gaade, *Mr.*, 20 Aug. 85
Galley, E., 16 Aug. 81
Galloway, *Lady, see* Stewart
Galloway, *Dr.* W., 30 Dec. 85
Gamon, *Mr.*, 30 Sept. 85
Garfield, *President* J. A., 21 July 81n
Garfield, *Mrs.* L., 21 July 81
Garth, *Miss* E., 23 Apr. 84
Gascoigne, *Mrs.*, *rescue*, 21 July 83
Gaskell, G. C. M., 24 June 86
Geddis, J. W. J., 16 Sept. 84
Gellatly, W., 14 Aug. 86
Gibb & Bruce, *Messrs.*, 15 Dec. 86
Giblin, W. R., 9 Sept. 84
Giers, N. K., 15 Jan. 81
Gill, H. J., 28 Sept. 86
Gillespie, *Rev.* C. G. K., 17 Sept. 85
Gillig, C. A., 8 Oct. 86
Gillman, H., 14 Aug. 86
Ginsburg, C. D., 15 July 83
Giovanni, M. Di, 1 June 83†
Giulani, *Prof.*, 20 Dec. 82
Givan, J., 10 Sept. 81
Gladstone, *Sir* A. C., *5th Bart.*, 28 Oct. 86
Gladstone, A. C., *née* Wilson, 20 Dec. 84
Gladstone, C. G., 27 May 83
Gladstone, E. C., 5 Jan. 82

Gladstone, H. W., 2 Sept. 82
Gladstone, S. S. 21 Apr. 81
Gladstone, W. G. C., 14 July 85
Gluck, J. F., 2 Oct. 86
Goddard, A., 1 Oct. 86
Godwin, M., *née* Wollstonecraft, 28 Nov. 83
Goldsmid, *Lady* J., 26 Oct. 82
Gordon, H. R., 7 Dec. 86
Gordon, I. M., *Lady Aberdeen*, 17 Dec. 83n
Gordon, *Sir* W., *6th Bart.*, 3 Nov. 85 (?)
Gore, *Bp.* C., 11 Jan. 85
Gould, L. E., 17 Feb. 81
Gowan, F. B., 21 July 82
Gower, G. G. Leveson-, 2 Dec. 85
Gower, *Lady* V. A. Leveson-, 8 Apr; 85
Graham, *rescue*, 16 Feb. 81
Grant, *Sir* G. Macpherson-, 27 Nov. 85
Gray, E. A. Stuart-, *15th Earl of Moray*, 24 Sept. 84n
Gray, E. D., 17 Aug. 82
Gray, H., 18 Nov. 86
Gray, *Sir* Walter, 4 July 85
Greely, *Lt.* A. W., 17 Nov. 85
Green, *Rev.* S. F., 6 Sept. 81
Green, *Sir* W. Kirby, 1 Jan. 81
Greene, J. B., 19 Oct. 83
Grévy, *President*, F-P-J., 27 Feb. 83
Grey, *Sir* E., *3rd Bart., 1st Viscount Grey of Fallodon*, 4 June 85
Griffith, *Dr.*, G., 29 Sept. 86
Grimes, C. C., 23 Sept. 83
Grimwade, S., 19 Oct. 85 (?)
Grimwood, T., 15 Dec. 86
Grossmith, G., 10 Aug. 86
Grosvenor, S. M., *Lady Grosvenor, see* Wyndham
Grosvenor, C. S. T., *née* Stuart Wortley, 25 June 81
Grosvenor, N. de l'A., 25 June 81
Grosvenor, *Miss* V. C., 28 Oct. 83
Gueshoff, I. E., 15 Oct. 85
Gunn, E., 3 Nov. 85

Haldane, R. B., 21 June 86n
Hale, *Mr.*, 9 Oct. 83
Hale, H., 8 Nov. 86n
Halkett, *Mrs.*, 21 Feb. 82
Hall, S. C., 18 Jan. 85
Hall, T., 3 July 86
Halsey, *Rev. Mr.*, 21 Nov. 86
Hamilton, *Sir* R. G. C., 8 May 82